Thirteenth Edition

Principles of Information Systems

Ralph M. Stair
Professor Emeritus, Florida State University

George W. Reynolds
Instructor, Strayer University

CENGAGE
Learning®

Australia • Brazil • Mexico • Singapore • United Kingdom • United States

Principles of Information Systems, Thirteenth Edition
Ralph M. Stair & George W. Reynolds

Vice President, General Manager, Science, Technology and Math: Balraj Kalsi

Senior Product Director: Kathleen McMahon

Senior Product Team Manager: Joe Sabatino

Product Team Manager: Kristin McNary

Associate Product Manager: Kate Mason

Senior Director, Development: Julia Caballero

Content Development Manager: Leigh Hefferon

Associate Content Developer: Jonathan Gross

Senior Content Developer: Michelle Ruelos Cannistraci

Art and Cover Direction, Production Management, and Composition: Lumina Datamatics, Inc.

Intellectual Property Analyst: Brittani Morgan

Project Manager: Kathy Kucharek

Manufacturing Planner: Ron Montgomery

Cover Image(s): everything possible/ Shutterstock.com

Library of Congress Control Number: 2016941569

ISBN: 978-1-305-97177-6

Cengage Learning
20 Channel Center Street
Boston, MA 02210
USA

Cengage Learning is a leading provider of customized learning solutions with employees residing in nearly 40 different countries and sales in more than 125 countries around the world. Find your local representative at **www.cengage.com**

Cengage Learning products are represented in Canada by Nelson Education, Ltd.

To learn more about Cengage Learning Solutions, visit **www.cengage.com**

Purchase any of our products at your local college store or at our preferred online store **www.cengagebrain.com**

Unless otherwise noted all items © Cengage Learning®

Printed at Quad/Graphics, USA, 11-16

For Lila and Leslie
—RMS

To my grandchildren: Michael, Jacob, Jared, Fievel,
Aubrey, Elijah, Abrielle, Sofia, Elliot, Serena, and Kendall
—GWR

Brief Contents

Contents

PART 2   Information Technology Concepts   83

3   Hardware and Mobile Devices   84

4   Software and Mobile Applications   136

PART 3   Business Information Systems   295

7   Electronic and Mobile Commerce   296

PART 4   Planning, Acquiring, and Building Systems   455

11   Strategic Planning and Project Management   456

12   System Acquisition and Development   502

PART 5   Information Systems in Business and Society   559

13   Cybercrime and Information System Security   560

14   Ethical, Legal, and Social Issues of Information Systems   598

Preface

As organizations and entrepreneurs continue to operate in an increasingly competitive and global marketplace, workers in all business areas including accounting, customer service, distribution, finance, human resources, information systems, logistics, marketing, manufacturing, research and development, and sales must be well prepared to make the significant contributions required for success. Regardless of your future role, even if you are an entrepreneur, you need to understand what information systems can and cannot do and be able to use them to help you achieve personal and organizational goals. You will be expected to discover opportunities to use information systems and to participate in the design and implementation of solutions to business problems employing information systems. To be successful, you must be able to view information systems from the perspective of business and organizational needs. For your solutions to be accepted, you must recognize and address their impact on coworkers, customers, suppliers, and other key business partners. For these reasons, a course in information systems is essential for students in today's high-tech world.

Principles of Information Systems, Thirteenth Edition, continues the tradition and approach of previous editions. Our primary objective is to provide the best information systems text and accompanying materials for the first information systems course required for all business students. We want you to learn to use information systems to ensure your personal success in your current or future role and to improve the success of your organization. Through surveys, questionnaires, focus groups, and feedback that we have received from current and past adopters, as well as others who teach in the field, we have been able to develop the highest-quality set of teaching materials available to help you achieve these goals.

Principles of Information Systems, Thirteenth Edition, stands proudly at the beginning of the IS curriculum and remains unchallenged in its position as the only IS principles text offering basic IS concepts that every business student must learn to be successful. Instructors of the introductory course faced a dilemma. On one hand, experience in business organizations allows students to grasp the complexities underlying important IS concepts. For this reason, many schools delayed presenting these concepts until students completed a large portion of their core business requirements. On the other hand, delaying the presentation of IS concepts until students have matured within the business curriculum often forces the one or two required introductory IS courses to focus only on personal computing software tools and, at best, merely to introduce computer concepts.

This text has been written specifically for the introductory course in the IS curriculum. *Principles of Information Systems, Thirteenth Edition*, addresses the appropriate computer and IS concepts while also providing a strong managerial emphasis on meeting business and organizational needs.

Approach of This Text

Principles of Information Systems, Thirteenth Edition, offers the traditional coverage of computer concepts, but places the material within the context of meeting business and organizational needs. Placing information systems concepts within this context and taking a management perspective has always set this text apart from other computer texts, thus making it appealing not only to MIS majors but also to students from other fields of study. The text is not overly technical, but rather deals with the role that information systems play in an organization and the key principles a manager or technology specialist needs to grasp to be successful. The principles of IS are brought together and presented in a way that is understandable, relevant, and interesting. In addition, the text offers an overview of the entire IS discipline, while giving students a solid foundation for further study in more advanced IS courses such as programming, systems analysis and design, project management, database management, data communications, Web site design and development, information system security, big data and analytics, electronic and mobile commerce, and informatics. As such, it serves the needs of both general business managers and those who aspire to become IS professionals.

The overall vision, framework, and pedagogy that made the previous editions so popular have been retained in the Thirteenth Edition, offering a number of benefits to students and instructors. While the fundamental vision of this market-leading text remains unchanged, the Thirteenth Edition more clearly highlights established principles and draws on new ones that have emerged as a result of business, organizational, technological, and societal changes.

IS Principles First, Where They Belong

Exposing students to basic IS principles is an advantage even for those students who take no IS courses beyond the introductory IS course. Since most functional areas of the business rely on information systems, an understanding of IS principles helps students in their other course work. In addition, introducing students to the principles of information systems helps future business managers and entrepreneurs employ information systems successfully and avoid mishaps that often result in unfortunate consequences. Furthermore, presenting IS concepts at the introductory level creates interest among students who may later choose information systems as their field of concentration.

Author Team

Ralph Stair and George Reynolds have decades of academic and industrial experience. Ralph Stair brings years of writing, teaching, and academic experience to this text. He wrote numerous books and a large number of articles while at Florida State University. George Reynolds brings a wealth of information systems and business experience to the project, with more than 30 years of experience working in government, institutional, and commercial IS organizations. He has written numerous IS texts and has taught the introductory IS course at the University of Cincinnati, Mount St. Joseph University, and Strayer University. The Stair and Reynolds team presents a solid conceptual foundation and practical IS experience to students.

Goals of This Text

Because *Principles of Information Systems, Thirteenth Edition*, is written for business majors, we believe that it is important not only to present a realistic perspective on IS in business but also to provide students with the skills they can use to be effective business leaders in their organizations. To that end, *Principles of Information Systems, Thirteenth Edition*, has three main goals:

1. To provide a set of core IS principles that prepare students to function more efficiently and effectively as workers, managers, decision makers, and organizational leaders
2. To provide insights into the challenging and changing role of the IS professional so that students can better appreciate the role of this key individual
3. To show the value of the IS discipline as an attractive field of specialization so that students can evaluate this as a potential career path

IS Principles

Principles of Information Systems, Thirteenth Edition, although comprehensive, cannot cover every aspect of the rapidly changing IS discipline. The authors, having recognized this, provide students with an essential core of guiding IS principles to use as they strive to use IS systems in their academic and work environment. Think of principles as basic truths or rules that remain constant regardless of the situation. As such, they provide strong guidance for tough decision making. A set of IS principles is highlighted at the beginning of each chapter. The use of these principles to solve real-world problems is driven home from the opening examples of cutting edge applications to the dozens of real-world examples of organizations applying these principles interspersed throughout each chapter to the interesting and diverse end-of-chapter material. The ultimate goal of *Principles of Information Systems, Thirteenth Edition*, is to develop effective, thinking, action-oriented students by instilling them with principles to help guide their decision making and actions.

Survey of the IS Discipline

Principles of Information Systems, Thirteenth Edition, not only offers the traditional coverage of computer concepts but also provides a broad framework to impart students with a solid grounding in the business uses of technology, the challenges of successful implementation, the necessity for gaining broad adoption of information systems, and the potential ethical and societal issues that may arise. In addition to serving general business students, this book offers an overview of the entire IS discipline and solidly prepares future IS professionals for advanced IS courses and careers in the rapidly changing IS discipline.

Changing Role of the IS Professional

As business and the IS discipline have changed, so too has the role of the IS professional. Once considered a technical specialist, today the IS professional operates as an internal consultant to all functional areas of the organization, being knowledgeable about their needs and competent in bringing the power of information systems to bear throughout the entire organization. The IS professional must view issues through a global perspective that encompasses the entire enterprise and the broader industry and business environment in which it operates.

The scope of responsibilities of an IS professional today is not confined to just his or her organization but encompasses the entire ecosystem of employees, contractors, suppliers, customers, competitors, regulatory agencies, and other entities, no matter where they are located. This broad scope of responsibilities creates a new challenge: how to help an organization survive in our highly interconnected, highly competitive global environment. In accepting that challenge, the IS professional plays a pivotal role in shaping the business itself and ensuring its success. To survive, businesses must strive for the highest level of customer satisfaction and loyalty through innovative products and services, competitive prices, and ever-improving product and service quality. The IS professional assumes a critical role in determining the organization's approach to both overall cost and quality performance and therefore plays an important role in the ongoing growth of the organization. This new duality in the role of the IS worker—a professional who exercises a specialist's skills with a generalist's perspective—is reflected throughout *Principles of Information Systems, Thirteenth Edition*.

IS as a Field of Study

Computer science and business were ranked #1 and #4, respectively, in the 2016 Princeton Review list of top 10 college majors based on research covering job prospects, alumni salaries, and popularity. A 2016 U.S. News & World Report study placed computer systems analyst, software developer, and Web developer as three of the top 20 best jobs for 2016 based on hiring demand, median salary, employment rate, future job prospects, stress level, and work–life balance. The U.S. Bureau of Labor Statistics identified software developers, computer systems analysts, and computer support specialists as among the fastest growing occupations for the period 2012 and 2022. Clearly, the long-term job prospects for skilled and business-savvy information systems professionals is good. Employment of such workers is expected to grow faster than the average for all occupations through the year 2022. Upon graduation, IS graduates at many schools are among the highest paid of all business graduates.

A career in IS can be exciting, challenging, and rewarding! Today, perhaps more than ever before, the IS professional must be able to align IS and organizational goals and to ensure that IS investments are justified from a business perspective. The need to draw bright and interested students into the IS discipline is part of our ongoing responsibility. Throughout this text, the many challenges and opportunities available to IS professionals are highlighted and emphasized.

Changes in the Thirteenth Edition

A number of exciting changes have been made to the text based on user feedback on how to align the text even more closely with changing IS needs and capabilities of organizations. Here is a summary of those changes:

- **Did You Know?** Each chapter begins with two or three examples of cutting edge applications illustrating the concepts covered in the chapter.
- **Critical Thinking Exercises.** Each exercise features a scenario followed by two review and two critical thinking questions. Placed at the end of each major section of each chapter, these exercises test the student's grasp of the material just read. Students must analyze a real-life scenario and synthesize the information provided to develop a recommendation of what needs to be done. The exercises can also be used to stimulate class discussion or as additional "mini cases" that may be assigned as individual or team exercises.

- **Updated case studies.** Two end-of-chapter case studies for each chapter provide a wealth of practical information for students and instructors. Each case explores a chapter concept or problem that a real-world organization has faced. The cases can be assigned as individual or team homework exercises or serve as the basis for class discussion.
- **Updated summary linked to objectives.** Each chapter includes a detailed summary, with each section of the summary updated as needed and tied to an associated information system principle.
- **Updated end-of-the chapter questions and exercises.** More than half of the extensive end-of-chapter exercises (Self-Assessment Test, Review Questions, Discussion Questions, Problem-Solving Exercises, Team Activities, Web Exercises, and Career Exercises) are new.
- **New chapters covering the latest IS developments.** New chapters include Database Systems and Big Data, Business Intelligence and Analytics, Strategic Planning and Project Management, System Acquisition and Development, and Cybercrime and Information System Security. These chapters cover important topics such as data governance, Hadoop, NoSQL databases, Cross-Industry Process for Data Mining, various business analytics techniques, self-service analytics, SWOT analysis, the nine project management knowledge areas, project steering team, agile development, DevOps, extreme programming, Pareto principle, advanced persistent threat, cyberterrorism, next-generation firewall, risk assessment, and zero-day attack.
- **Extensive changes and updates in each chapter.** The remaining chapters in the text have all been extensively updated to provide the latest information available on a wide range of IS-related topics including hundreds of new and current examples of organizations and individuals illustrating the principles presented in the text. In addition, a strong effort was made to update the art work and figures with over 50 new figures and images.

Online Solutions

MindTap™

MindTap for Stair/Reynolds *Principles of Information Systems, Thirteenth Edition*, is a truly innovative reading experience with assignments that guide students to analyze, apply, and improve thinking! Relevant readings, multimedia, and activities are designed to move students up the levels of learning, from basic knowledge and comprehension to application, analysis, synthesis, and evaluation. Embedded within the eReader, ConceptClips focus on the challenge of understanding complicated IS terminology and concepts. Student-tested and approved, the videos are quick, entertaining, and memorable visual and auditory representations of challenging topics. Also embedded within the MindTap eReader, animated figures and graphs provide a visual and at times interactive and auditory enhancement to previously static text examples.

MindTap allows instructors to measure skills and outcomes with ease. Personalized teaching becomes yours through a Learning Path built with key student objectives and the ability to control what students see and when they see it. Analytics and reports provide a snapshot of class progress, time in course, engagement, and completion rates.

ConceptClips

ConceptClip videos help students learn and comprehend intro-level information systems terminology by introducing new terms in a friendly and memorable way. Sixteen new concept clips have been created for a total of 44 concept clips.

Adaptive Test Prep

This application allows students to take sample tests designed specifically to mimic the test bank question instructors use to build real exams. Over 750 questions are included.

Student Resources

Accessible through CengageBrain.com, the student companion Web site contains the following study tools (and more!) to enhance one's learning experience:

PowerPoint Slides

Direct access is offered to the book's PowerPoint presentations that cover the key points of each chapter.

Classic Cases

A frequent request from adopters is that they'd like a broader selection of cases to choose from. To meet this need, a set of over 50 cases from the text are included here. These are the author's choices of the "best cases" from these editions and span a broad range of profit, nonprofit, small, medium, and large organizations in a broad range of industries.

Instructor Resources

Instructor Companion Site

As always, we are committed to providing the best teaching resource packages available in this market. All instructor materials can be found on the password-protected Web site at *http://login.cengage.com*. Here you will find the following resources:

- **Instructor's Manual** The comprehensive manual provides valuable chapter overviews; highlights key principles and critical concepts; offers sample syllabi, learning objectives, and discussion topics; and features possible essay topics, further readings, cases, and solutions to all of the end-of-chapter questions and problems, as well as suggestions for conducting the team activities. Additional end-of-chapter questions are also included.
- **Sample Syllabus** A sample syllabus for both a quarter and semester-length course is provided with sample course outlines to make planning your course that much easier.
- **PowerPoint Presentations** A set of impressive Microsoft PowerPoint slides is available for each chapter. These slides are included to serve as a teaching aid for classroom presentation, to make available to students on the network for chapter review, or to be printed for classroom distribution. The goal of the presentations is to help students focus on the main topics of each chapter, take better notes, and prepare for examinations. Instructors can add their own slides for additional topics they introduce to the class.
- **Figure Files** Figure files allow instructors to create their own presentations using figures taken directly from the text.

Test Bank and Cengage Learning Testing Powered by Cognero

Cognero is a full-featured, online-assessment system that allows instructors to manage test bank content, quickly create multiple test versions, deliver tests in several forms including from an LMS, and create test banks anywhere with Internet access!

To access Cognero, log into your Cengage Learning SSO account at http:// login.cengage.com. Add this title to the bookshelf. Once the title is properly added to the bookshelf, a link to access Cognero will appear alongside the link to the instructor companion site. Technical questions, guides, and tutorials are hosted on Cengage Learning Technical Support Web site—http:// support.cengage.com.

ACKNOWLEDGMENTS

Creation of a text of this scope takes a strong team effort. We would like to thank all of our fellow teammates at Course Technology for their dedication and hard work. We would like to thank Joe Sabatino, our Product Director, for his overall leadership and guidance on this effort. Special thanks to Jonathan Gross and Michelle Ruelos Cannistraci, our Content Developers who shepherded the text through the production process and kept us on track. We are grateful for the excellent work by Michelle Ruelos Cannistraci in managing the creation of the many supplements to accompany the text. Our appreciation also goes to Arul Joseph Raj, Joseph Malcolm, Brittani Morgan, Jennifer Ziegler, Aruna Sekar, Kathy Kucharek, and Mathangi Anantharaman.

We would also like to thank Kristen Maxwell of Evil Cyborg Productions for creating the ConceptClips videos that so humorously bring many key terms found in the text to life.

We would especially like to thank Mary Pat Schaffer for her outstanding work in editing the text and keeping track of the many revisions and changes. She also did an outstanding job in writing many of the end-of-chapter cases and creating initial drafts of four of the chapters.

Our Commitment

We are committed to listening to our adopters and readers in order to develop creative solutions to meet their needs. The field of IS continually evolves, and we strongly encourage your participation in helping us provide the freshest, most relevant information possible.

We welcome your input and feedback. If you have any questions or comments regarding *Principles of Information Systems, Thirteenth Edition*, please contact us through your local representative.

PART 1

Information Systems in Perspective

Chapter 1
An Introduction to Information Systems

Chapter 2
Information Systems in Organizations

CHAPTER 1

An Introduction to Information Systems

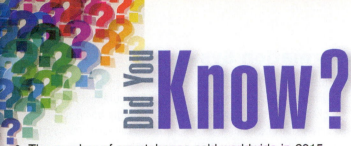

Did You Know?

- The number of smartphones sold worldwide in 2015 exceeded 1.4 billion—over twice the combined sales of desktop, laptop, and tablet computers. The smartphone is increasingly becoming the device of choice for accessing the Internet and corporate databases.

- Although the success rate has improved over time with improved methods, training, and tools, 94 percent of very large software projects fail or are challenged. For example, Federal officials badly managed the development of a Web site to sell health insurance under the Affordable Care Act, costing taxpayers hundreds of millions of dollars in cost overruns.

- Financial losses from cybercrime and the cost of hardware, software, and various countermeasures implemented to fight cybercrime are estimated to be as high as $400 billion annually worldwide. A data breach at Target exposed personal information about 110 million customers, led the CEO to resign, and cost the company an estimated $148 million.

Principles

- The value of information is directly linked to how it helps decision makers achieve the organization's goals.

- Information systems are composed of fundamental components that must be carefully assembled and integrated to work well together.

- Managers have an essential role to play in the successful implementation and use of information systems—that role changes depending on which type of IS system is being implemented.

- An organization's infrastructure technology forms the foundation upon which its systems and applications are built.

- Organizations employ a variety of information systems to improve the way they conduct business and make fact-based decisions.

- Many challenges and potential benefits are associated with harnessing the rapid growth of data within organizations.

- Strategic planning and project management are keys to ensuring that the organization is working effectively on the right projects.

- Information systems must be applied thoughtfully and carefully so that society, organizations, and individuals around the globe can reap their enormous benefits.

Learning Objectives

- Distinguish data from information and knowledge, and describe the characteristics of quality data.

- Identify the fundamental components of an information system and describe their function.

- Identify the three fundamental information system types and explain what organizational complements must be in place to ensure successful implementation and use of the system.

- Identify and briefly describe the role of each component of an organization's technology infrastructure.

- Identify the basic types of business information systems, including who uses them, how they are used, and what kinds of benefits they deliver.

- Describe how organizations are using business intelligence and business analytics to capitalize on the vast amount of data becoming available.

- Discuss why it is critical for business objectives and IS activities to be well aligned through system planning, development, and acquisition.

- Identify several major IT security threats as well as some of the legal, social, and ethical issues associated with information systems.

Why Learn about Information Systems?

We live in an information economy. Information itself has real value, and in order to stay competitive, organizations require a steady flow of information about their business partners, competitors, customers, employees, markets, and suppliers. Information systems are increasingly being used to gather, store, digest, analyze, and make sense out of all this information. Indeed, information systems are even embedded in and control many of the products we use on a daily basis. Using information systems, individuals communicate instantaneously with one another; consumers make purchases online using mobile devices; project members dispersed globally and across multiple organizations collaborate effectively; financial institutions manage billions of dollars in assets around the world; and manufacturers partner with suppliers and customers to track inventory, order supplies, and distribute goods faster than ever before.

Information systems will continue to change businesses and the way we live. Indeed, many corporate leaders are using technology to rework every aspect of their organization from product and service creation through production, delivery, and customer service. To prepare to participate in and lead these innovations, you must be familiar with fundamental information concepts. Regardless of your college major or chosen career, knowledge of information systems is indispensable in helping you land your first job. The ability to recognize and capitalize on information system opportunities can make you an even more valuable member of your organization and will ultimately help advance your career.

As you read this chapter, consider the following:

- How are organizations using information systems to accomplish their objectives and meet ever-changing business needs?
- What role might you have in identifying the need for, acquiring, or using such systems?

This chapter presents an overview of the material covered in the text. The chapter is divided into five major sections corresponding to the five sections of the text. The chapters included in each section of the text are highlighted as a subsection and briefly summarized. The essential material will receive fuller treatment in subsequent chapters.

Part 1: Information Systems in Perspective

We begin by examining the topics covered in "Part 1: Information Systems in Perspective," which includes an "An Introduction to Information Systems" and a discussion of "Information Systems in Organizations."

An Introduction to Information Systems

Information is a central concept of this book. The term is used in the title of the book, in this section, and in every chapter. To be an effective manager in any area of business, you need to understand that information is one of an organization's most valuable resources. Information is not the same thing as data, and knowledge is different from both data and information. These concepts will now be explained.

Data, Information, and Knowledge

data: Raw facts such as an employee number or total hours worked in a week.

information: A collection of data organized and processed so that it has additional value beyond the value of the individual facts.

Data consists of raw facts, such as an employee number, total hours worked in a week, an inventory part number, or the number of units produced on a production line. As shown in Table 1.1, several types of data can represent these facts. Information is a collection of data organized and processed so that it has additional value beyond the value of the individual facts. For example, a sales manager may want individual sales data summarized so it shows the total sales for the month. Providing information to customers can also

TABLE 1.1 Types of data

Data	Represented By
Alphanumeric data	Numbers, letters, and other characters
Audio data	Sounds, noises, or tones
Image data	Graphic images and pictures
Video data	Moving images or pictures

help companies increase revenues and profits. For example, social shopping Web site Kaboodle brings shoppers and sellers together electronically so they can share information and make recommendations while shopping online. The free exchange of information stimulates sales and helps ensure shoppers find better values.

Another way to appreciate the difference between data and information is to think of data as the individual items in a grocery list—crackers, bread, soup, cereal, coffee, dishwashing soap, and so on. The grocery list becomes much more valuable if the items in the list are arranged in order by the aisle in which they are found in the store—bread and cereal in aisle 1, crackers and soup in aisle 2, and so on. Data and information work the same way. Rules and relationships can be set up to organize data so it becomes useful, valuable information.

The value of the information created depends on the relationships defined among existing data. For instance, you could add specific identifiers to the items in the list to ensure that the shopper brings home the correct item—whole wheat bread and Kashi cereal in aisle 1, saltine crackers and chicken noodle soup in aisle 2, and so on. By doing so, you create a more useful grocery list.

Turning data into information is a **process**, or a set of logically related tasks performed to achieve a defined outcome. The process of defining relationships among data to create useful information requires **knowledge**, which is the awareness and understanding of a set of information and the ways in which that information can be made useful to support a specific task or reach a decision. In other words, information is essentially data made more useful through the application of knowledge. For instance, there are many brands and varieties of most items on a typical grocery list. To shop effectively, the grocery shopper needs to have an understanding of the needs and desires of those being shopped for so that he knows to purchase one can of Campbell's (not the store brand!) low-sodium chicken noodle soup for the family member who is diabetic along with two cans of Campbell's regular chicken noodle soup for everyone else.

In some cases, people organize or process data mentally or manually. In other cases, they use a computer. This transformation process is shown in Figure 1.1.

The Value of Information

The value of information is directly linked to how it helps decision makers achieve their organization's goals. Valuable information can help people perform tasks more efficiently and effectively. Many businesses assume that reports are based on correct, quality information, but, unfortunately, that is not always true. For example, Experian (a global information services firm that provides credit services, marketing services, decision analytics, and consumer services) estimates that on average, 22 percent of an organization's customer contact data is wrong.[1] Companies can easily waste over $100 per inaccurate customer contact data record on things like direct-mail marketing sent to wrong addresses and the inability to properly track leads. For an

process: A set of logically related tasks performed to achieve a defined outcome.

knowledge: The awareness and understanding of a set of information and the ways that information can be made useful to support a specific task or reach a decision.

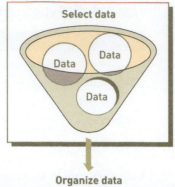

Select data

Organize data

Data (1,1)	Data (1,2)	Data (1,3)
Data (2,1)	Data (2,2)	Data (2,3)
Data (3,1)	Data (3,2)	Data (3,3)
Data (n,1)	Data (n,2)	Data (n,3)

Manipulate data

| Total 1 | Total 2 | Total 3 |

FIGURE 1.1

Process of transforming data into information

Transforming data into information starts by selecting data, then organizing it, and finally manipulating the data.

organization with 100,000 customers and a 22 percent error rate, that projects to a loss of $2.2 million.[2]

Characteristics of Quality Information

Fundamental to the quality of a decision is the quality of the information used to reach that decision. Any organization that stresses the use of advanced information systems and sophisticated data analysis before information quality is doomed to make many wrong decisions. Table 1.2 lists the characteristics that determine the quality of information. The importance of each of these characteristics varies depending on the situation and the kind of decision you are trying to make. For example, with market intelligence data, some inaccuracy and incompleteness is acceptable, but timeliness is essential. Market intelligence data may alert you that a competitor is about to make a major price cut. The exact details and timing of the price cut may not be as important as being warned far enough in advance to plan how to react. On the other hand, accuracy and completeness are critical for data used in accounting for the management of company assets, such as cash, inventory, and equipment.

What Is an Information System?

Another central concept of this book is that of an information system. People and organizations use information systems every day. An **information system (IS)** is a set of interrelated components that collect, process, store, and disseminate data and information; an information system provides a feedback mechanism to monitor and control its operation to make sure it continues to meet its goals and objectives. The feedback mechanism is critical to helping organizations achieve their goals, such as increasing profits or improving customer service.

A **computer-based information system (CBIS)** is a single set of hardware, software, databases, networks, people, and procedures that are configured to collect, manipulate, store, and process data into information. Increasingly, companies are incorporating computer-based information systems

information system (IS): A set of interrelated components that collect, process, store, and disseminate data and information; an information system provides a feedback mechanism to monitor and control its operation to make sure it continues to meet its goals and objectives.

computer-based information system (CBIS): A single set of hardware, software, databases, networks, people, and procedures that are configured to collect, manipulate, store, and process data into information.

TABLE 1.2 Characteristics of quality information

Characteristic	Definition
Accessible	Information should be easily accessible by authorized users so they can obtain it in the right format and at the right time to meet their needs.
Accurate	Accurate information is error free. In some cases, inaccurate information is generated because inaccurate data is fed into the transformation process. This is commonly called garbage in, garbage out.
Complete	Complete information contains all the important facts. For example, an investment report that does not include all important costs is not complete.
Economical	Information should also be relatively economical to produce. Decision makers must always balance the value of information with the cost of producing it.
Flexible	Flexible information can be used for a variety of purposes. For example, information on how much inventory is on hand for a particular part can be used by a sales representative in closing a sale, by a production manager to determine whether more inventory is needed, and by a financial executive to determine the amount of money the company has invested in inventory.
Relevant	Relevant information is important to the decision maker. Information showing that lumber prices might drop is probably not relevant to a computer chip manufacturer.
Reliable	Reliable information can be trusted by users. In many cases, the reliability of the information depends on the reliability of the data-collection method. In other instances, reliability depends on the source of the information. A rumor from an unknown source that oil prices might go up may not be reliable.
Secure	Information should be secure from access by unauthorized users.
Simple	Information should be simple, not complex. Sophisticated and detailed information might not be needed. In fact, too much information can cause information overload, whereby a decision maker has too much information and is unable to determine what is really important.
Timely	Timely information is delivered when it is needed. Knowing last week's weather conditions will not help when trying to decide what coat to wear today.
Verifiable	Information should be verifiable. This means that you can check it to make sure it is correct, perhaps by checking many sources for the same information.

into their products and services. Investment companies offer their customers a wide range of powerful investment tools, including access to extensive online research. Automobiles are available with advanced navigation systems that not only guide you to your destination but also incorporate information regarding the latest weather and traffic conditions to help you avoid congestion and traffic delays. Watches, digital cameras, mobile phones, music players, and other devices rely on CBIS to bring their users the latest and greatest features.

The components of a CBIS are illustrated in Figure 1.2. An organization's **technology infrastructure** includes all the hardware, software, databases, networks, people, and procedures that are configured to collect, manipulate,

technology infrastructure: All the hardware, software, databases, networks, people, and procedures that are configured to collect, manipulate, store, and process data into information.

Dukes/Shutterstock.com
Noolwlee/Shutterstock.com
Andresr/Shutterstock.com
Sashkin/Shutterstock.com
Dusit/Shutterstock.com
NasonovVasiliy/Shutterstock.com

Software   **Networks**   **People**

Hardware   **Procedures**   **Hardware**

FIGURE 1.2

Components of a computer-based information system

Hardware, software, networks, people, and procedures are part of a business's technology infrastructure.

store, and process data into information. The technology infrastructure is a set of shared IS resources that form the foundation of each computer-based information system.

People make the difference between success and failure in all organizations. Jim Collins, in his book, *Good to Great*, said, "Those who build great companies understand that the ultimate throttle on growth for any great company is not markets, or technology, or competition, or products. It is one thing above all others: the ability to get and keep enough of the right people."[3] Thus, it comes as no surprise that people are the most important element in computer-based information systems.

Good systems can enable people to produce extraordinary results. They can also boost job satisfaction and worker productivity.[4] Information systems personnel include all the people who manage, run, program, and maintain the system, including the chief information officer (CIO), who leads the IS organization. End users are people who work directly with information systems to get results. They include financial executives, marketing representatives, and manufacturing line operators.

procedure: A set of steps that need to be followed to achieve a specific end result, such as enter a customer order, pay a supplier invoice, or request a current inventory report.

A **procedure** defines the steps to follow to achieve a specific end result, such as enter a customer order, pay a supplier invoice, or request a current inventory report. Good procedures describe how to achieve the desired end result, who does what and when, and what to do in the event something goes wrong. When people are well trained and follow effective procedures, they can get work done faster, cut costs, make better use of resources, and more easily adapt to change. When procedures are well documented, they can greatly reduce training costs and shorten the learning curve.

Using a CBIS involves setting and following many procedures, including those for the operation, maintenance, and security of the system. For example, some procedures describe how to gain access to the system through the use of some log-on procedure and a password. Others describe who can access facts in the database or what to do if a disaster, such as a fire, earthquake, or hurricane, renders the CBIS unusable. Good procedures can help companies take advantage of new opportunities and avoid lengthy business disruptions in the event of natural disasters. Poorly developed and inadequately implemented procedures, however, can cause people to waste their time on useless rules or result in inadequate responses to disasters.

Information Systems in Organizations

Most organizations have a number of different information systems. When considering the role of business managers in working with IS, it is useful to divide information systems into three types: personal IS, group IS, and enterprise IS.

personal IS: An information system that improves the productivity of individual users in performing stand-alone tasks.

Personal IS includes information systems that improve the productivity of individual users in performing stand-alone tasks. Examples include personal productivity software, such as word-processing, presentation, and spreadsheet software.

In today's fast-moving, global work environment, success depends on our ability to communicate and collaborate with others, including colleagues, clients, and customers. **Group IS** includes information systems that improve communications and support collaboration among members of a workgroup. Examples include Web conferencing software, wikis, and electronic corporate directories.

group IS: An information system that improves communications and support collaboration among members of a workgroup.

enterprise IS: An information system that an organization uses to define structured interactions among its own employees and/or with external customers, suppliers, government agencies, and other business partners.

Enterprise IS includes information systems that organizations use to define structured interactions among their own employees and/or with external customers, suppliers, government agencies, and other business partners. Successful implementation of these systems often requires the radical redesign of fundamental work processes and the automation of new processes. Target processes may include purely internal activities within the organization (such as payroll) or those that support activities with external customers and suppliers (order processing and purchasing). Three examples of enterprise IT are transaction processing, enterprise, and interorganizational systems.

organizational complement: A key component that must be in place to ensure successful implementation and use of an information system.

For each type of IS, certain key **organizational complements** must be in place to ensure successful implementation and use of the system. These complements include:

- **Well-trained workers.** Employees must be well trained and understand the need for the new system, what their role is in using or operating the system, and how to get the results they need from the system.
- **System support.** Trained and experienced users who can show others how to gain value from the system and overcome start-up problems.
- **Better teamwork.** Employees must understand and be motivated to work together to achieve the anticipated benefits of the system.
- **Redesigned processes.** New systems often require radical redesign of existing work processes as well as the automation of new processes.
- **New decision rights.** Employees must understand and accept their new roles and responsibilities including who is responsible for making what decisions. Roles and responsibilities often change with introduction of a new system.

Managers have an essential role to play in the successful implementation and use of information systems. That role changes depending on which type of IS system is being implemented, as shown in Table 1.3, which also highlights other characteristics and provides examples of each type.

TABLE **1.3** Examples and characteristics of each type of information system

	Personal IS	Group IS	Enterprise IS
Examples	Personal productivity software, decision-support system	Email, instant messaging, project management software	Transaction processing systems, enterprise systems, interorganizational systems
Benefits	Improved productivity	Increased collaboration	Increased standardization and ability to monitor work
Organizational complements (including well-trained workers, better teamwork, redesigned processes, and new decision rights)	• Does not bring complements with it • Partial benefits can be achieved without all complements being in place	• At least some complements must be in place when IS "goes live" • Allows users to implement and modify complements over time	• Full complements must be in place when IS "goes live"
Manager's role	• Ensure that employees understand and connect to the change • Encourage use • Challenge workers to find new uses	• Demonstrate how technology can be used • Set norms for participation	• Identify and put into place the full set of organizational complements prior to adoption • Intervene forcefully and continually to ensure adoption

Critical Thinking Exercise

Kroger's QueVision System Improves Customer Service

Kroger has annual sales in excess of $100 billion and operates stores across the United States under various names, including Kroger's, Ralph's, and Harris Teeter. In surveys, Kroger's customers have consistently rated waiting at the checkout lane as the worst part of the grocery shopping experience. In response, Kroger developed its QueVision computer-based information system, which relies on real-time data feeds from point-of-sale systems as well as infrared sensors over store doors and cash registers to count customers entering the store and standing at checkout lanes. The system also uses historical point-of-sale records to forecast the number of shoppers that can be expected and, therefore, the number of cashiers that will be needed. All this was done to achieve the goal of ensuring that customers never have more than one person ahead of them in the checkout lane. The system provides feedback by displaying customer checkout time on a screen that both employees and customers can see—delivering a visible measure of how well the whole system is working. The system is now deployed at over 2,300 stores in 31 states and has cut the average time a customer must wait to begin checkout from four minutes to 30 seconds.[5]

You are a new store manager at a Kroger store where the QueVision system has been deployed for two years. Unfortunately, since you took charge of this store two weeks ago, you have received numerous complaints about the system from store cashiers and baggers. These employees are requesting that you either turn off the screen that displays customer checkout time or add more cashiers and baggers to each shift to reduce checkout times, which are currently averaging over six minutes.

Review Questions

1. Would you classify the QueVision system as a personal, group, or enterprise system?
2. Four key organizational complements must be in place to ensure successful implementation and use of a new system. Which two of these components seem to be missing at your store?

Critical Thinking Questions

1. Employees are requesting that you turn off the screen that displays customer checkout time or add more cashiers and baggers to each shift to reduce wait times. What action would you take to address the concerns of the cashiers and baggers?

   a. Turn off the QueVision system now.
   b. Add more cashiers and baggers to each shift as soon as possible.
   c. Observe the checkout process and performance of cashiers and baggers for a few days before taking action.
   d. Tell the cashiers and baggers their performance is unacceptable and to "step it up."

2. Provide a brief rationale for your recommended course of action.

Part 2: Information Technology Concepts

Next, we look at the topics covered in "Part 2: Information Technology Concepts," including "Hardware and Mobile Devices," "Software and Mobile Applications," "Database Systems and Big Data," and "Networks and Cloud Computing." This discussion will help you understand basic concepts and prepare you for more in-depth coverage in the individual chapters.

Hardware and Mobile Devices

hardware: Computer equipment used to perform input, processing, storage, and output activities.

Hardware consists of computer equipment used to perform input, processing, storage, and output activities. The trend in the computer industry is to produce smaller, faster, and more mobile hardware, such as smartphones, laptops, and tablet computers. In addition, hardware manufacturers and entrepreneurs are hard at work developing innovative new hardware devices, such as the following:

- Advanced keyboards that turn individual keys on a keyboard into trackpad-covered buttons where certain dual-purpose keys could be depressed to multiple levels to complete different tasks; the spacebar, for example, can serve its usual purpose. But add capacitive touch and it becomes a cursor; press a little harder to generate a mouse click. (Capacitive touch relies on the electrical properties of the human body to detect when and where on a display the user touches. Because of this, capacitive displays can be controlled with very light touches of a finger.)
- Laptops and displays that connect wirelessly, thus eliminating the need for expensive HDMI or DisplayPort display cables
- Computing devices with embedded 3D cameras, which will be able to recognize objects and even measure distances between things
- Keyboards that enable users to log in to Web sites via fingerprint authentication so they won't have to remember dozens of passwords for different sites
- Very-high resolution display devices that will show content in incredible detail and dramatically improve the viewing experience (think clarity and resolution way beyond 1080p HD)
- Computerized event data recorders (EDRs) that, like an airplane's black box, record vehicle speed, possible engine problems, driver performance, and more

While desktop, laptop, and tablet computers continue to be used in a variety of settings, smartphones have become the primary device used by people around the world to communicate, go online, and access and share information. In 2013, the number of smartphone users first exceeded the number of personal computer users, and the gap keeps growing, with the number of smartphones sold worldwide far exceeding the combined sale of desktops, laptops, and tablets as shown in Figure 1.3. This rapid growth has been spurred by the improving affordability and capability of smartphones, the increasing speed and coverage of wireless networks, longer battery life, and the availability of hundreds of thousands of smartphone applications and games. For many people in developing countries, a smartphone is their first computer and their only Internet-connected device. For those in developed countries, it is common for individuals who do have a computer to also have a smartphone. It is projected that roughly one-third of the world's population will own a smartphone by 2018.[6]

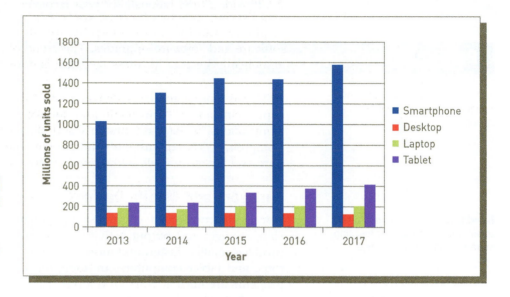

FIGURE 1.3

Millions of computing devices sold worldwide[7]

The number of smartphones sold worldwide far exceeds the combined number of desktop, laptop, and tablet computers.

Software and Mobile Applications

software: The computer programs that govern the operation of a particular computing device, be it desktop, laptop, tablet, smartphone, or some other device.

Software consists of the computer programs that govern the operation of a particular computing device, be it desktop computer, laptop, tablet, smartphone, or some other device. There are two types of software: system software and application software. System software—such as Google's Android or Apple's iOS—oversees basic computer operations such as start-up, controls access to system resources, and manages memory and files. Application software, such as Microsoft Office, allows you to accomplish specific tasks, including editing text documents, creating graphs, and playing games. Both system software and application software are needed for all types of computers, from small handheld devices to large supercomputers. In choosing application software, you must choose software that will work with the operating system installed on your computing device.

As of June 2015, 1.6 million applications were available for devices that run under the Android operating system and roughly the same (1.5 million) available for download from Apple's App Store.[8,9] The number of apps for each operating system is increasing by roughly 25,000 to 50,000 per month.

Business application software can be categorized by whether it is intended to be used by an individual, a small business, or a large multinational enterprise. For example, Quicken has long been a favorite accounting application for individuals who need money management and budgeting tools to help them watch their spending, increase their savings, and avoid late fees with alerts on upcoming payment due dates. QuickBooks, an accounting application popular with small businesses, enables users to create invoices, track sales and expenses, process credit card payments, run payroll, and generate financial, tax, and sales reports. SAP ERP Financials is an accounting application used by many large, multinational organizations to manage the complexities of global accounting and reporting requirements. SAP's software records all financial transactions in a comprehensive general ledger; supports sophisticated reporting requirements; provides management accounting tools for orders, projects, cost centers, and profit centers; enables the speedy and accurate closing of the firm's books; and helps manage risk and compliance across accounting and finance.

An important trend in the design of business application software is the attempt to imitate the look, feel, and intuitive ease of use associated with consumer apps that can be downloaded from the Google Play Store and the Apple App Store. Indeed, usability and user-interface design are key factors in delivering apps that business users will actually use. In some organizations, employees can log on to enterprise app stores to acquire the latest company software and software upgrades. This trend of consumer technology practices influencing the way business software is designed and delivered is called the **consumerization of IT**.

CDW is a leading provider of integrated information solutions to corporate customers in small, medium, and large private and public organizations in the United States and Canada. The firm has established its App Marketplace Web site (*http://appmarketplace.cdw.com*) where customers' employees can identify leading enterprise mobile app solutions. The Web site is easy to navigate with apps organized by industry and app functions. The apps there have already been vetted by CDW to perform effectively and reliably. In addition, for those needing custom mobile apps, the Web site identifies mobile app partners who have a proven track record of building, deploying, and updating top enterprise applications.

Database Systems and Big Data

A **database** is an organized collection of facts and information, typically consisting of two or more related data files. An organization's database can contain facts and information on customers, employees, inventory, sales, online purchases, and much more. A database is essential to the operation of a computer-based information system.

As anyone who works in marketing or sales knows, one of the biggest challenges that any business faces is the ability to generate new leads in an effort to locate customers. As businesses have looked for ways to meet this challenge, numerous vendors have seized the opportunity by offering access to databases of potential clients in various industries, as shown in Table 1.4.

consumerization of IT: The trend of consumer technology practices influencing the way business software is designed and delivered.

database: An organized collection of facts and information, typically consisting of two or more related data files.

TABLE 1.4 Sample of marketing databases used to generate sales leads

Industry	Database Vendor	Number of Records (Thousands)
Auto dealers	Oddity Software	110
Barber shops	Usable Databases	53
Dry cleaning/laundry	Oddity Software	42
Gas stations with convenience stores	CHD	56
Healthcare providers and decision makers	SK & A	2,100
Music retail outlets	Almighty Music Marketing	10
Nursing and retirement homes	MCH	34
Pet shops and pet supply stores	Oddity Software	15

data warehouse: A database that stores large amounts of historical data in a form that readily supports analysis and management decision making.

extract-transform-load (ETL): The process by which raw data is extracted from various sources, transformed into a format to support the analysis to be performed, and loaded into the data warehouse.

A **data warehouse** is a database that stores large amounts of historical data in a form that readily supports analysis and management decision making. In a process called the **extract-transform-load (ETL)** process, raw data is extracted from various sources, transformed into a format that will support the analysis to be performed, and then loaded into the data warehouse. Data warehouses frequently hold a huge amount of data; they often contain five years or more of data. Many organizations employ data warehouses to hold the data they need to make key business decisions:

- Walmart operates separate data warehouses for Walmart and Sam's Club. Through these data warehouses, the company allows suppliers access to almost any data they could possibly need to determine which of their products are selling, how fast, and even whether they should redesign their packaging to fit more product on store shelves.[10]
- Harrah's (part of the Caesar's Entertainment casino empire) uses a data warehouse to determine how much money particular gamblers are willing to lose in a day before they will decide not to come back the next day.[11]
- Continental Airlines uses a data warehouse to help it determine who its most valuable customers are and to find ways to keep them satisfied—for example, by proactively making alternative travel arrangements for them if their flights get delayed.[12]
- Macy's uses a terabyte-sized data warehouse to target improvements in four key areas of its e-commerce business: measuring the profitability and effectiveness of banner advertising, analyzing customer interactions and paths through its Web site, improving fulfillment capabilities, and correlating online sales with store sales to cross-sell and upsell customers across its distribution channels.[13]

The digital universe (the collection of all data that exists) is doubling in size every two years as shown in Figure 1.4.[14] Organizations are challenged by this rapid growth and at the same time scrambling to take advantage of the opportunities provided by this data. **Big data** is a term used to describe data collections that are so enormous (think petabytes or larger) and complex (from sensor data to social media data) that traditional data management software, hardware, and analysis processes are incapable of dealing with them. To gain a perspective on the quantity of data some organizations are struggling to manage, consider that the amount of data traveling over mobile networks alone is expected to exceed 10 exabytes per month by 2016.[15] Table 1.5 defines the units of measure for data.

big data: A term used to describe data collections that are so enormous (think petabytes or larger) and complex (from sensor data to social media data) that traditional data management software, hardware, and analysis processes are incapable of dealing with them.

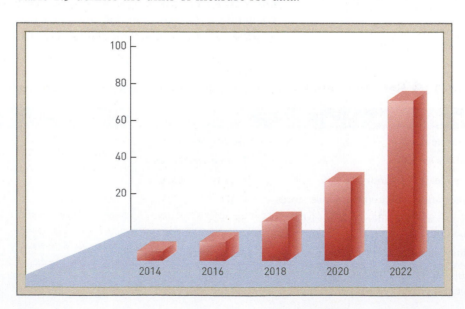

FIGURE **1.4**

The size of the digital universe (zettabytes) doubles every two years

The amount of digital data is expected to double every two years.

TABLE 1.5 Units of measure for data

Unit of Measure	Size	Equivalent To
Byte	1 byte	One alphanumeric character
Kilobyte	1,000 bytes	The text of a joke or very short story
Megabyte	1,000 kilobytes	800 pages of text
Gigabyte	1,000 megabytes	7 minutes of HD-TV
Terabyte	1,000 gigabytes	The Hubble Space Telescope collected more than 45 terabytes of data in its first 20 years of observations
Petabyte	1,000 terabytes	50 years' worth of DVD-quality video
Exabyte	1,000 petabytes	44 billion 25 gigabytes Blu-ray discs
Zettabyte	1,000 exabytes	The amount of text created by every man, woman, and child on earth tweeting continuously for 100 years
Yottabyte	1,000 zettabytes	One thousand times the grains of sand on all of Earth's beaches

To avoid being paralyzed by information overload, organizations and indeed society itself must find a way to deal with this oncoming tsunami of data. This challenge has several aspects, including how to choose which subset of data to keep, where and how to store the data, how to find the nuggets of useful data that are relevant to the decision making at hand, and how to derive real value from the relevant data.

Ideally, the many challenges associated with big data will be conquered, and more data will lead to more accurate, insightful analyses and better decision making, which in turn, will result in deliberate actions and improved business results. For that to happen, society will need to address the many issues associated with big data, including concerns over invasions of privacy and the potential for overly intrusive monitoring of individuals by governments and organizations.

Networks and Cloud Computing

network: A group or system of connected computers and equipment—in a room, building, campus, city, across the country, or around the world—that enables electronic communication.

Networks connect computers and equipment in a room, building, campus, city, across the country, or around the world to enable electronic communication. Wireless transmission networks enable the use of mobile devices, such as smartphones and tablets. Telecommunication companies are now working on fifth-generation wireless communications that will enable transmission speeds 10 times faster than currently available on wireless networks—with greater coverage area and lower battery consumption—possibly as soon as the year 2020. Such technology will be needed to support the increased demand for faster transfer of data and video.

Internet: The world's largest computer network, consisting of thousands of interconnected networks, all freely exchanging information.

The **Internet** is the world's largest computer network, consisting of thousands of interconnected networks, all freely exchanging information. People use the Internet to research information, buy and sell products and services, email and instant message one another, participate in social networks (e.g., Facebook and LinkedIn), make travel arrangements, complete banking transactions, make investments, download music and videos, read books, and watch movies among other activities.

public cloud computing: A means of providing computing services wherein a service provider organization owns and manages the hardware, software, networking, and storage devices, with cloud user organizations (called tenants) accessing slices of shared resources via the Internet.

With **public cloud computing**, a service provider organization owns and manages the hardware, software, networking, and storage devices, with cloud user organizations (called tenants) accessing slices of shared resources via the Internet. The service provider can deliver increasing amounts of computing, network, and storage capacity on demand and without requiring any capital investment on the part of the cloud users. Thus, public cloud computing is a great solution for organizations whose computing needs vary greatly depending on changes in demand. Amazon, Cisco Systems, IBM, Microsoft, Rackspace, Verizon Communications Inc., and VMWare are among the largest cloud computing service providers. These firms typically offer a monthly or annual subscription service model; they may also provide training, support, and data integration services.[16] Online content provider Netflix uses the Amazon Web Services (AWS) cloud computing service to provide global delivery of some 10 billion hours of content per month. AWS enables Netflix users anywhere in the world to stream TV shows and movies to computers and mobile devices.[17]

World Wide Web (WWW): A network of links on the Internet to files containing text, graphics, video, and sound.

The **World Wide Web (WWW)**, better known simply as "the Web," is a network of links on the Internet to files containing text, graphics, video, and sound. Information about the documents and access to them are controlled and provided by tens of thousands of specialized computers called Web servers. The Web is one of many services available over the Internet, and it provides access to millions of files. New Internet technologies and increased Internet communications and collaboration are collectively called Web 2.0.

intranet: A network that enables communication, collaboration, search functions, and information sharing between the members of an organization's team using a Web browser.

The technology used to create the Internet is also being applied within organizations to create **intranets**, which enable communication, collaboration, search functions, and information sharing between the members of an organization's team using a Web browser. For example, the Swiss Medical Group, based in Buenos Aires, Argentina, is a network of professionals, clinics, and laboratories that provide healthcare services and postgraduate medical education programs. It employs an intranet to provide its 9,000 employees with communication tools, company and industry news from various sources, announcements regarding new assignments for employees, tutorials, an online phone directory, videos, and document management services.[18]

extranet: A network based on Web technologies that allows selected outsiders, such as business partners and customers, to access authorized resources of a company's intranet.

An **extranet** is a network based on Web technologies that allows selected outsiders, such as business partners and customers, to access authorized resources of a company's intranet. Many people use extranets every day without realizing it—to order products from their suppliers, track shipped goods, or access customer assistance from other companies. Federal Express (FedEx) was one of the first large companies to empower customers to serve themselves at their convenience through the use of a corporate extranet. A fundamental FedEx belief is that the information it provides customers about its services is more important than the services themselves. Customers can access the FedEx extranet to obtain a full range of shipping, billing, and tracking services. See Figure 1.5.

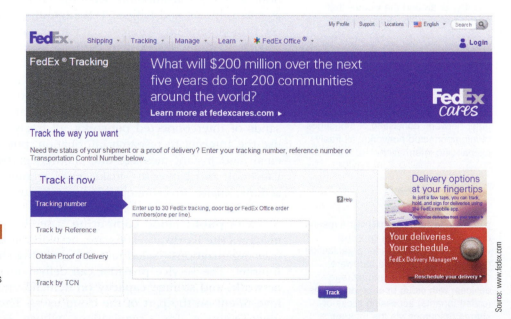

FIGURE 1.5

Extranets

When you sign in to the FedEx site (*www.fedex.com*) to check the status of a package, you are using an extranet.

Source: www.fedex.com

Internet of Things (IoT): A network of physical objects or "things" embedded with sensors, processors, software, and network connectivity capability to enable them to exchange data with the manufacturer of the device, device operators, and other connected devices.

The **Internet of Things (IoT)** is a network of physical objects or "things" embedded with sensors, processors, software, and network connectivity capability to enable them to exchange data with the manufacturer of the device, device operators, and other connected devices. In theory, the IoT would enable us to connect almost any device with an on/off switch to a network—automobiles, appliances, components of an aircraft engine, heart monitor implants, packing labels, ingestible pills, wearable devices, and even highway sensors that can warn of traffic and hazardous road conditions. Each thing is uniquely identifiable and capable of interoperating with other "things" within the existing IoT infrastructure, often by connecting to a central hub. The IoT also includes cloud services, which enable the collection and analysis of data so people can process the data and take appropriate action via mobile apps.

Until recently, the IoT has been most closely associated with machine-to-machine communications, such as that employed in the manufacturing, gas, oil, and power industries. For example, in oil and gas drilling operations, remote sensors can measure important parameters such as pressure, flow rates, temperatures, and fuel levels in on-site equipment. These variables are transmitted to a computer that automatically adjusts the operation of the equipment to optimize hydrocarbon production, improve operational safety, and protect the environment.

Internet of Everything: A network that encompasses not only machine-to-machine but also people-to-people and people-to-machine connections.

The **Internet of Everything (IoE)** encompasses not only machine-to-machine but also people-to-people and people-to-machine connections. It is estimated that the total number of devices supported by the IoE could reach 50 billion by the end of 2020[19] See Figure 1.6. This rapid growth is being fueled by the increasing availability of network access, the creation of more inexpensive smart devices with sensors and network capabilities built into them, the rapid growth in smartphone penetration, and the creativity and innovation of people who are able to see and capitalize on the almost unlimited opportunities.[20]

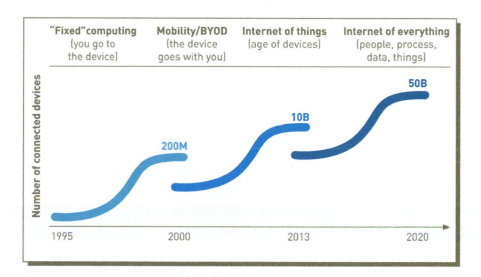

FIGURE 1.6

Growth of the Internet of Everything (IoE)

The Internet of Everything will connect tens of billions of devices.

General Electric (GE) is making a major strategic investment in the Internet of Things by offering its Predix Cloud service for industrial data and analytics. Predix will enable GE customers to connect sensors placed on industrial machinery such as jet engines, wind turbines, and locomotives to remote computing centers "in the cloud," where the data from the sensors can be processed and analyzed to determine settings for optimal operating efficiencies and to schedule preventative maintenance to avoid unexpected failures.[21]

Critical
Thinking
Exercise

NARCOMS Database to Aid MS Victims

Multiple sclerosis (MS) causes a disruption in the transmission of nerve signals between the brain, spinal cord, and the rest of the body. Disrupted nerve signals cause the symptoms of MS, which can vary from one person to another, but often include difficulty walking, dizziness, fatigue, involuntary muscle spasms, pain, stiffness, tremors, vision problems, and weakness.

The North American Registry for Care and Research in Multiple Sclerosis (NARCOMS) is a database created to capture the real-life experiences of people living with MS. The database contains information about each patient's symptoms and their severity over time, medications taken, and courses of treatment. Physicians, scientists, and pharmaceutical companies can use this data to better understand MS by tracking patients' disease course, comparing results of alternative courses of treatment, measuring the effectiveness of medications, and identifying useful indicators of the severity of the disease.[22]

Anyone with a diagnosis of MS can participate in NARCOMS and contribute to its research studies. Participants are asked to fill out an initial enrollment questionnaire and then complete surveys twice a year. Although roughly 400,000 people in the United States have been diagnosed with MS, fewer than 40,000 have elected to participate. More participants are needed in order for the database to be fully representative of people living with MS.[23]

Review Questions

1. Identify the fundamental hardware components that are likely included in the NARCOMS system.
2. Assume that a record for each participant in the NARCOMS database contains between 200 and 500 bytes of data. What is the maximum size of the database in gigabytes for the total 100,000 target number of participants? Would NARCOMS qualify as a big data project?

Critical Thinking Questions

You are a member of a highly successful advertising agency whose CEO suffers from MS. She has asked you to develop a proposal for the National Multiple Sclerosis Society to increase the number of participants in NARCRMS to 100,000 people within 12 months. There will be no charge to the society for this work, but the CEO has set a budget of $2 million. She has asked your full-time effort for the next year to lead this effort to success.

1. Identify three strong reasons why some MS victims might elect to participate in NARCOMS while most do not.
2. Outline a course of action that you think would successfully increase the number of NARCOMS participants by 60,000 over the next 12 months.

Part 3: Business Information Systems

Information systems are used in all functional areas of business organizations, as summarized here:

- **Accounting and finance.** Information systems are used to forecast revenues and expenses, determine the best sources and uses of funds, manage cash and other financial resources, analyze investments, and perform audits to make sure that the organization is financially sound and that all financial reports and documents are accurate.
- **Customer service.** Information systems are used to capture data about customers and their interactions with the company to better understand their needs and issues and enable superior customer service.

- **Human resources.** Information systems help human resource staff screen job applicants, administer performance tests to employees, monitor employee productivity, and generate required government reports.
- **Manufacturing.** Information systems are used to process customer orders, develop production schedules, control inventory levels, and monitor product quality.
- **Research and development.** Information systems help R&D staff design products, gather input from customers that leads to new ideas and improvements, and enable the sharing of information with a worldwide community of researchers.
- **Sales and marketing.** Information systems help sales and marketing personnel develop new goods and services (product analysis), determine the best advertising and sales approaches (promotion analysis), and set optimal product prices to get the highest total revenues (price analysis).

Information systems are also used in nearly every industry, as the following examples show:

- **Agriculture.** Farmers attach a yield monitor and a global positioning unit to their combines to determine how much grain should be harvested in each field. This data is entered in a system that produces a color-coded map that predicts the expected yield. From this, farmers can determine where they should add soil additives or fertilizer, for example, to increase the yield.
- **Finance.** Banks use information systems to help make sound decisions regarding loans, invest wisely, and provide online services, such as bill payment and account transfers for account holders.
- **Health care.** Healthcare organizations use information systems to diagnose illnesses, plan medical treatment, track patient records, and bill patients See Figure 1.7. Health insurance companies and health maintenance organizations (HMOs) use Web technology to access patients' insurance eligibility information, pay medical claims, and analyze data to manage costs.

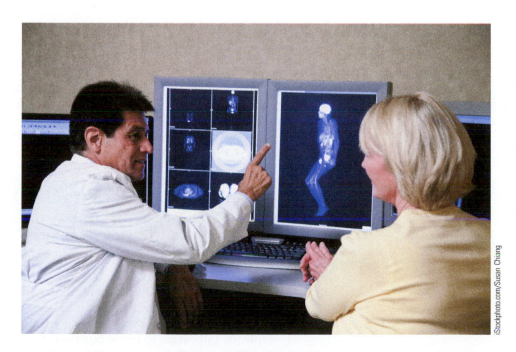

FIGURE 1.7

Information systems in health care

Healthcare organizations use information systems to diagnose illnesses, plan medical treatment, track patient records, and bill patients.

- **Mining.** Companies use global positioning systems to identify and evaluate promising areas for mineral exploration, model mine construction, and display geochemical and hydrological data. Mining companies also

use information systems to gather the necessary data when applying for mining permits, to assess the environmental impacts of a proposed mine, and to design mine closure and reclamation plans.
- **Professional services.** Accounting, tax preparation, and investment firms use information systems to improve the speed and quality of the services they provide to customers.
- **Retail.** Companies use information systems to help market products and services, manage inventory levels, control the supply chain, and forecast demand, as well as take orders directly from customers over the Web.

This part will discuss "Electronic and Mobile Commerce," "Enterprise Systems," "Business Intelligence and Analytics," and "Knowledge Management and Specialized Information Systems."

Electronic and Mobile Commerce

E-commerce involves the exchange of money for goods and services over electronic networks, and it encompasses many of an organization's outward-facing processes—such as sales, marketing, order taking, delivery, procurement of goods and services, and customer service—that touch customers, suppliers, and other business partners (Figure 1.8).

e-commerce: Involves the exchange of money for goods and services over electronic networks and encompasses many of an organization's outward-facing processes—such as sales, marketing, order taking, delivery, procurement of goods and services, and customer service—that touch customers, suppliers, and other business partners.

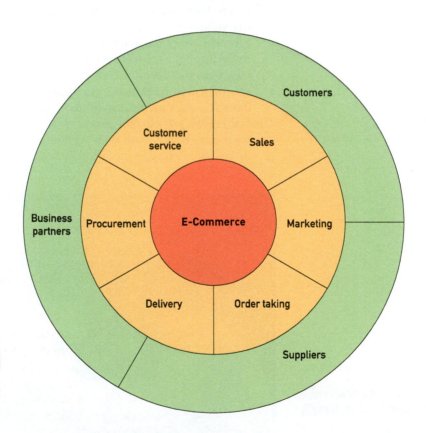

FIGURE 1.8

The scope of e-commerce
E-commerce covers a wide range of business activities.

E-commerce enables organizations and individuals to build new revenue streams, to create and enhance relationships with customers and business partners, and to improve operating efficiencies (see Table 1.6). E-commerce is critically important to many businesses.

Greyston Bakery is a $12 million company with 130 employees that makes brownies and cookies for wholesale and retail distribution. Sales to its largest client Ben & Jerry's generates more than half its revenues. The business was started in the mid-1980s as a means to provide employment for the

TABLE 1.6 Benefits of e-commerce

Benefit	How Achieved
Build new revenue streams	• Reach a broader geographic dispersion of consumers
Create and enhance relationships with customers and business partners	• Increase customer engagement • Improve loyalty of customers who initially buy offline • Increase opportunity to build loyalty through multiple channels
Improve operating efficiencies	• Lower customer acquisition cost • Lower operating costs per sale • Reduce the expense of supporting and servicing existing customers

poor and homeless in Yonkers, New York. To meet this goal, Greyston follows an open-hiring policy, taking people directly off the street without background or reference checks. The highly successful bakery has expanded its operation to include sales from its Web site, further boosting its revenues and enabling it to hire more workers.[24]

Mobile commerce (m-commerce) is the buying and selling of goods and/or services using a mobile device, such as a tablet, smartphone, or other portable device. Mobile commerce can be used to support all forms of e-commerce—business-to-business (B2B), business-to-consumer (B2C), consumer-to-consumer (C2C), and government-to-citizen (G2C).

Electronic business (e-business) goes beyond e-commerce by using information systems and networks to perform business-related tasks and functions, such as:

- Gathering product demand forecasts directly from the distributors of your product in order to aggregate them and develop a master production schedule (rather than internally generating a forecast based on historical data, with no input from your distributors)
- Sharing product data (e.g., design specifications and bills of material) electronically with suppliers and contract manufacturers as your products evolve through research and development, product design, prototyping, process design, and manufacturing

Enterprise Systems

Computers have been used to perform common business applications since the 1950s. These early systems were designed to reduce costs by automating routine, labor-intensive business transactions. A **transaction** is any business-related exchange such as a payment to an employee, a sale to a customer, or a payment to a supplier. A **transaction processing system (TPS)** is an organized collection of people, procedures, software, databases, and devices used to process and record business transactions.

One of the first business systems to be computerized was the payroll system. The primary inputs for a payroll TPS are the number of employee hours worked during the week and the pay rate. The primary output consists of paychecks. Early payroll systems produced employee paychecks and related reports required by state and federal agencies, such as the Internal Revenue Service (IRS). The cost of these early systems was more than offset by the reduction in the number of people required to complete payroll processing. Other high-volume, repetitive processes, such as order processing, customer billing, and inventory control, were soon computerized as well.

mobile commerce (m-commerce): The buying and selling of goods and/or services using a mobile device, such as a tablet, smartphone, or other portable device.

electronic business (e-business): The use of information systems and networks to perform business-related tasks and functions beyond those performed for e-commerce.

transaction: Any business-related exchange such as a payment to an employee, a sale to a customer, or a payment to a supplier.

transaction processing system (TPS): An organized collection of people, procedures, software, databases, and devices used to process and record business transactions.

A **management information system (MIS)** is an organized collection of people, procedures, software, databases, and devices that provides routine information to managers and decision makers. MISs were first developed in the 1960s and were typically used to produce managerial reports. In many cases, these early reports were produced periodically—daily, weekly, monthly, or yearly. Because of their value to managers, MISs proliferated throughout the management ranks. Manufacturing, marketing, production, finance, and other functional areas of an organization were often supported by their own TPS and MIS. An MIS typically provides standard reports generated using data from a TPS. See Figure 1.9.

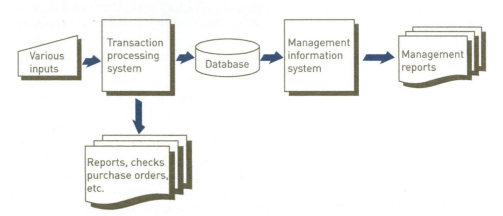

The TPS receives input from various sources, which it then edits and processes to create various outputs and to update a database of valid transactions. This database can be accessed by an MIS to create various reports, including periodic reports, exception reports, summary reports, drill-down reports, and on-demand reports.

Information systems that process business transactions (e.g., sales, shipments, payments) have evolved over the years and offer important solutions for organizations of all sizes. Traditional transaction processing systems (TPSs) and management information systems (MIS) are still being used today, but increasingly, companies are turning to enterprise resource planning systems.

An isolated information system that is not easily capable of exchanging information with other information systems is called an **information silo**. The "silo mentality" is a way of thinking that occurs when groups of people do not share information, goals, tools, priorities, and processes with other departments. Such thinking degrades operations, reduces employee productivity, and can lead to the overall failure of a company or its products and services. Unfortunately, this sort of silo mentality was the basis for the design of many TPS and MIS systems.

In recent years, more organizations have begun implementing **enterprise resource planning (ERP) systems** that support their routine business processes, maintain records about those processes, and provide extensive reporting and data analysis capabilities. These systems employ a database of key operational and planning data that can be shared by all employees across all organizational units and, when appropriate, with customers and suppliers—eliminating the problems of missing and inconsistent information caused by multiple transaction processing systems that support only one business function or one department in an organization. ERP systems have expanded in scope so that they now provide support for business analytics and e-business. Although ERPs were initially thought to be cost effective only for very large companies, these systems have since been implemented by many small and midsized companies.

Every industry has its own unique business practices. In order to address these differences, ERP software vendors offer specially tailored software modules designed to meet the needs of specific industries, such as consumer-packaged-goods manufacturing, higher education, utilities, banking, oil and gas, retail, and the public sector. Most ERP software packages are designed so that an organization does not have to implement the entire package at once. Companies can pick and choose which software modules to install based on their business needs. Many organizations choose to implement some modules but delay implementing others until the necessary resources are available. Table 1.7 and Figure 1.10 illustrate and explain the primary components of an ERP system, and Figure 1.11 offers a look at the user interface for SAP ERP, a popular ERP software.

TABLE 1.7 Primary components of an ERP system for a manufacturing organization

Module	Business Functions Addressed
Supply chain management	Manages all activities involved in sourcing and procuring raw materials, converting raw materials to finished product, warehousing, and delivering finished product to customers
Customer relationship management	Automates and integrates the sales, marketing, and customer service functions to capture and store customer and prospect contact information, account data, and sales opportunities in one central location
Product lifecycle management	Manages product information throughout the entire life cycle of a product from ideation, design and manufacture, through service and remaining product disposal—across all departments, contractors, and suppliers
Maintenance, repair, and operations	Automates and supports activities involved with the planning and scheduling of maintenance and repairs for any sort of mechanical, plumbing, or electrical device, along with the tracking of inventory and ordering of necessary parts and supplies
Accounting	Tracks the flow of data related to all the cash flows that affect an organization; manages functions related to setting up and maintaining the general ledger, accounts payable, accounts receivable, and payroll
Human resource management	Supports activities related to previous, current, and potential employees of the organization; provides tools for workforce analysis and planning, hiring, training, job and task assignment, performance evaluation, salary administration, managing employee benefits, retirement, and outplacement

The primary reasons for implementing an enterprise system include easing adoption of improved work processes (best practices), increasing access to timely data for decision making, and eliminating obsolete transaction processing systems and associated infrastructure. When implemented effectively, ERP systems can deliver the following benefits:

- Provide a global view of operational and planning data, enabling companies to identify issues and opportunities and to address them proactively
- Lower the cost of doing business through the elimination of redundant processes and systems
- Ensure compliance with various financial and manufacturing standards
- Automate core business operations—such as lead-to-cash, order-to-fulfillment, and procure-to-pay processes—using industry best practices
- Improve customer service by providing one source for billing and relationship tracking

Source: www.sap.com

FIGURE 1.10

ERP components

An ERP system consists of many components that provide shared access to a database of business information.

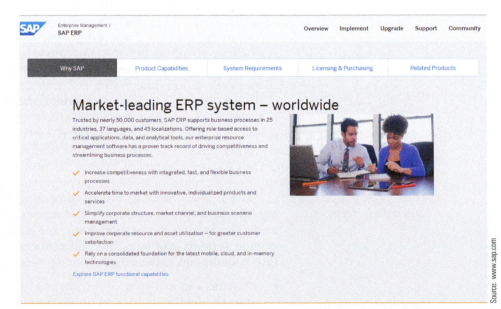

FIGURE 1.11

Enterprise resource planning (ERP) software

SAP AG, a German software company, is one of the leading suppliers of ERP software. The company employs more than 50,000 people in more than 130 countries.

- Reduce time to market by sharing evolving product data across all contractors and suppliers involved in the concept design, detail design, and production of new products

Many ERP vendors are making their software products and services available in the cloud. This approach can provide additional benefits, including:

- Safe access to data in the cloud from virtually anywhere, on any device
- Reduced infrastructure, hardware, and IS management costs
- Increased flexibility to scale infrastructure up or down as business needs dictate
- Opportunities to redirect IS resources away from managing infrastructure to working on strategic projects
- The ability to get up and running in days instead of months

Business Intelligence and Analytics

Things, individuals, and organizations generate massive amounts of data as a by-product of their activities. In addition, many individuals and organizations seek out third-party data providers, such as market research firms, government agencies, and social network operators, in an attempt to satisfy their unquenchable thirst for more and more data. To be of any value, all this data must be stored, analyzed, and reported.

Just as different music and movie stars have been popular over the years, different terms have been used to describe the technology and processes used to support management reporting and decision making. Over time, decision support systems, executive information systems, online analytical processing, business intelligence, and business analytics have gained in capabilities and expanded in scope to add new functionality but all have had the goal of deriving the most value out of the data available.

business intelligence (BI): A wide range of applications, practices, and technologies for the extraction, transformation, integration, visualization, analysis, interpretation, and presentation of data to support improved decision making.

Business intelligence (BI) includes a wide range of applications, practices, and technologies for the extraction, transformation, integration, visualization, analysis, interpretation, and presentation of data to support improved decision making.

business analytics: The extensive use of data and quantitative analysis to support fact-based decision making within organizations.

Business analytics can be simply defined as the extensive use of data and quantitative analysis to support fact-based decision making within organizations. It can be used to gain a better understanding of current business performance, reveal new business patterns and relationships, explain why certain results occurred, optimize current operations, and forecast future business results. Business analytics includes software components for accessing, transforming, storing, analyzing, modeling, and tracking information, as well as components for communicating the results of all that analysis.

data scientist: A person who understands the business and the business analytics technology, while also recognizing the limitations of their data, tools, and techniques; a data scientist puts all of this together to deliver real improvements in decision making with an organization.

A number of components must be in place for an organization to get real value from its business analytics efforts. Most importantly, an organization needs creative **data scientists**—people who understand the business and the business analytics technology, while also recognizing the limitations of their data, tools, and techniques. A data scientist puts all of this together to deliver real improvements in decision making within an organization. To ensure the success of a business analytics program, the management team within an organization must have a strong commitment to data-driven decision making. Organizations that can put the necessary components in place can act quickly to make superior decisions in uncertain and changing environments to gain a strong competitive advantage.

Knowledge Management and Specialized Information Systems

knowledge management system (KMS): An organized collection of people, procedures, software, databases, and devices that stores and retrieves knowledge, improves collaboration, locates knowledge sources, captures and uses knowledge, or in some other way enhances the knowledge management process.

A **knowledge management system (KMS)** is an organized collection of people, procedures, software, databases, and devices that stores and retrieves knowledge, improves collaboration, locates knowledge sources, captures and uses knowledge, or in some other way enhances the knowledge management process. Consulting firms often use a KMS to capture and provide the collective knowledge of its consultants to one another. This makes each consultant much more valuable and avoids "re-inventing the wheel" to solve similar problems for different clients.

The workforce at NASA is aging, and it is essential for the organization's future success that critical knowledge not be lost as workers retire. Rather, their specialized knowledge must be captured and retained for future use. NASA employs knowledge management to document and integrate lessons learned from decades of missions to effectively manage the risk involved in future space exploration and human space flight.[25]

Specialized information systems include a wide range of artificial intelligence systems (robotics, vision systems, natural language processing and voice recognition systems, learning systems, and expert systems) that can simulate human intelligence processes. Multimedia systems, virtual reality systems, assistive technology systems, and systems based on game theory are additional types of specialized information systems.

Critical Thinking Exercise

Business Analytics for Gaming Firm

Penn National Gaming, through its subsidiaries, owns and operates more than 25 horseracing and casino gaming facilities throughout the United States and in Canada. It is the operator of the popular Hollywood Casinos around the country plus the M Resort Spa Casino and Tropicana Las Vegas. In aggregate, its operations include some 33,000 gaming machines, 800 table games, 4,500 hotel rooms, and 10 million square feet of property.[26] Millions of patrons visit Penn National Gaming facilities each year.

The firm is considering developing a large database to capture the data generated at each property. This will be augmented with data about each patron—their demographics, purchases, gambling preferences and habits, and the services they request as a guest. The data will be used by the firm's management to make quick, well-informed decisions to maximize Penn National Gaming's income while packing more entertainment value into each patron's visit. The data will also be used to develop targeted direct mail campaigns, customize offers for specific customer segments, and adapt programs for individual casinos.

Review Questions

1. Collecting and analyzing all this data will draw Penn National Gaming in to the realm of big data and business analytics. How would you define the term business analytics?
2. Penn National Gaming will also need to recruit new kinds of human resources including data scientists. What do data scientists do?

Critical Thinking Questions

1. Identify three data sources that might be tapped to obtain the desired data about its patrons.
2. What sort of data privacy issues might be associated with the establishment of its patron database?

Part 4: Planning, Acquiring, and Building Systems

project: A temporary endeavor undertaken to create a unique product, service, or result.

A **project** is a temporary endeavor undertaken to create a unique product, service, or result. A project attempts to achieve specific business objectives and is subject to certain constraints, such as total cost and completion date. Projects are the way that much of an organization's work gets done. For example, a consumer goods company executes a project to launch a new product, an operations manager leads a project to outsource part of a firm's operations to a contract manufacturer, a hospital executes a project to load an app onto physicians' smartphones that enables them to access patient data anywhere. At any point in time, an organization may have dozens of ongoing projects, including multiple information system-related projects. However, since every organization has a limit to its available resources, it is essential that projects are directed at supporting key business objectives and goals, as outlined in the firm's strategic plan. This part will cover the topics of "Strategic Planning and Project Management" and "System Acquisition and Development."

Strategic Planning and Project Management

Ever since the dawn of the computer age, various surveys of business and IT executives have stressed the need to use strategic planning to improve alignment between the needs of the business and the activities of the information systems organization. In this context, alignment means that the IS organization and its resources are focused on efforts that support the key objectives defined in the strategic plan of the business. This implies that IS and business managers have a shared vision of where the organization is headed and agree on its key strategies. This shared vision will guide the IS organization in hiring the right people with the correct skills and competencies, choosing the right technologies and vendors to explore and develop, installing the right systems, and focusing on those projects that are needed to move the organization closer to its vision and meeting its mission.

In an organization where the IS and business managers have a shared vision, the impact of the IS staff on the rest of the organization will be extremely positive, and the IS group will be viewed as a well-respected business partner. An IT organization not aligned with the key objectives of the business will find it difficult to even gain management support for its proposed efforts. Much of its work will fail to hit the mark and it will not be well received by the rest of the organization.

The Standish Group has been tracking the success rate of projects for over 20 years. Although the success rate has improved over time due to improved methods, training, and tools, 94 percent of very large (multimillion dollar efforts) software projects still fail or are challenged (i.e., are late, over budget, or lack required features) as shown in Figure 1.12.[27]

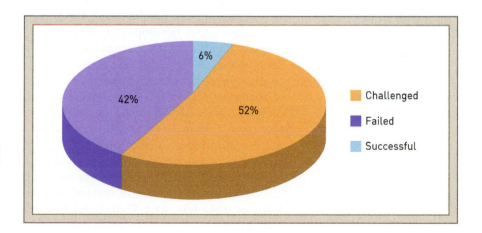

FIGURE **1.12**
Resolution of very large software projects 2003–2012
Over 90 percent of large software projects are challenged or fail.

No matter what the industry and no matter whether the organization is a for-profit company or a nonprofit organization—large or small, multinational or local—good project management is a positive force that enables an organization to get results from its efforts. At any point in time, an organization may have dozens or even hundreds of active projects aimed at accomplishing a wide range of results. Over the next few years, it is expected that many organizations will focus on projects that apply analytics to large amounts of business data, take advantage of cloud computing, and create more mobile applications for their customers and employees.

System Acquisition and Development

System acquisition is the process used to obtain the information system resources needed to provide the services necessary to meet a specific set of needs. Those needs may be very broad and encompass many users, such as in the acquisition of a new enterprise resource planning system. Or they may be very narrow in scope, affecting just a single user, such as in the acquisition of personal computer software to enable an individual to prepare a federal tax return. There are two fundamental strategies for system acquisition: buy off-the-shelf software or build a custom application.

Buying existing software developed by a software manufacturer enables an organization to test drive and evaluate it before making a major commitment to purchase it and install it. Once purchased, the existing software can be installed with minimal disruption so that user needs can be quickly met and the organization can begin reaping the benefits from the information system. Buyers of the software do not actually own the software, nor can they access it to make changes or improvements; they are simply licensed to use the software on a computer. With no access to the underlying source code, user organizations must pay maintenance and support costs to the manufacturer or to a third party authorized to fix bugs or add new functionality. For some organizations, these costs can become excessive. As a result, many organizations are turning to **open source software**, which is software distributed for free, with access permitted to the source code so that it can be studied, changed, and improved by software professionals at the various user organizations—with no maintenance charges. Indeed, the amount and quality of support for open source software is dependent on whether or not there are people, resources, and interest among the user community to develop updates and fix bugs.

The activity of building information systems to meet users' needs is called **system development**. Systems development projects can range from small to very large and are conducted in fields as diverse as nuclear science research and video game development. If an organization elects to build a system, it can use its own employees (perhaps augmented with contractors) to develop the system, or it can hire an outside company to manage and/or perform all of the system development work. The latter approach allows an organization to focus on what it does best, by delegating software development to companies that have world-class development capabilities. This can be important since the system development efforts for even relatively small projects can require months, with large projects requiring years of effort. Unfortunately, as already pointed out, in spite of everyone's best efforts, a significant number of large system development projects are likely to fail.

By choosing a software service provider, users can gain access to needed software remotely, as a Web-based service via the cloud. Pricing is based on a monthly or per user fee and typically results in lower costs than a licensed application. Because the software is hosted remotely, users do not need to purchase and install additional hardware to provide increased capacity. Furthermore, the service provider handles necessary software maintenance and upgrades.

Table 1.8 summarizes the three basic alternatives for obtaining software to meet users' needs.

system acquisition: The process used to obtain the information system resources needed to provide the services necessary to meet a specific set of needs.

open source software: Software that is distributed for free, with access permitted to the source code so that it can be studied, changed, and improved by software professionals at the various user organizations—with no maintenance charges.

system development: The activity of building information systems to meet users' needs.

TABLE 1.8 Alternatives for meeting users' information system needs

Strategy	Pros	Cons
Buy off-the-shelf software	+ A software solution can be acquired and deployed relatively quickly. + An organization can "test drive" software before acquiring it.	− Unmodified, the software may not be a good match to an organization's needs. − Maintenance and support costs can become excessive.
Build custom application	+ Customized software is more likely to be a good match to an organization's needs. + A custom application provides the potential to achieve competitive advantage.	− The cost to build a system can be quite high compared to the cost of purchasing of off-the-shelf software. − Customizing software can mean it will be months or even years before the software solution is ready to deploy.
Choose a software service provider	+ Users do not need to purchase and install additional hardware or software. + The service provider handles necessary hardware and software maintenance and upgrades.	− Complex pricing arrangements and hidden costs may reduce expected cost savings. − Performance issues may cause wide variations in performance over time.

Critical Thinking Exercise

Strategic Plan Review

You are a member of the finance organization of a midsized manufacturer, with two years of experience with the firm. Your manager serves as a liaison between the finance group and the IS organization for budget review. The IS organization has just completed its annual strategic planning and budgeting process. Their plans, which include a $25 million budget (a 6 percent increase over last year), were forwarded to your manager for review. Your manager shared the IS strategic plan and budget with you a week ago and scheduled a meeting today to get your input and perspective.

Review Questions

1. What do you think are the hallmarks of a good strategic plan?
2. Would you expect to see more funds allocated to system development or to buying existing software and using software service providers? Why?

Critical Thinking Questions

1. Your manager shocks you when she announces that she has recommended you for promotion and that one of your new responsibilities would be to serve as the new finance liaison with the IS organization. She asks, "What do you feel needs to be done to help prepare you for this new responsibility?"
2. Finally, she asks, "What steps would you take and what resources would you use to review the current IS strategic plan and budget?"

Part 5: Information Systems in Business and Society

Information systems have been developed to meet the needs of all types of organizations and people. The speed and widespread use of information systems, however, opens users to a variety of threats from unethical people. Computer criminals and terrorists, for example, have used the Internet to steal millions of dollars and promote terrorism and violence. Computer-related attacks can come from individuals, groups, companies, and even countries; however, some studies have shown that most of corporate security attacks come from people inside the company.

This part will cover "Cybercrime and Information System Security" and the "Ethical, Legal, and Social Issues of Information Systems."

Cybercrime and Information System Security

Information systems provide a highly profitable venue for cybercriminals, who take advantage of the opportunity to reach millions of potential victims. **Cybercriminals** are motivated by the potential for monetary gain; they hack into computer systems to steal, often by transferring money from one account to another or by stealing and reselling credit card numbers, personal identities, and financial account information. Financial losses related to cybercrime—including the cost of the hardware, software, and various countermeasures implemented to fight cybercrime—are estimated to be as high as $400 billion annually worldwide.[28] Figure 1.13 shows some commonly occurring cybercrime incidents.

cybercriminal: A computer hacker who is motivated by the potential for monetary gain; cybercriminals hack into computer systems to steal, often by transferring money from one account to another or by stealing and reselling credit card numbers, personal identities, and financial account information.

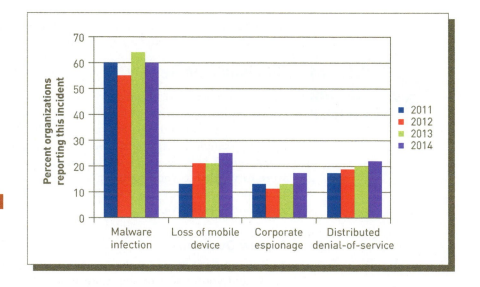

FIGURE **1.13**

Commonly occurring cybercrime incidences

Cybercrime is a serious issue for organizations.

cyberterrorism: The intimidation of a government or a civilian population by using information technology to disable critical national infrastructure (e.g., energy, transportation, financial, law enforcement, emergency response) to achieve political, religious, or ideological goals.

Cyberterrorism is an increasing concern for organizations and countries around the globe. **Cyberterrorism** is the intimidation of a government or a civilian population by using information technology to disable critical national infrastructure (e.g., energy, transportation, financial, law enforcement, emergency response) to achieve political, religious, or ideological goals. Cyberterrorists try on a daily basis to gain unauthorized access to a number of important and sensitive sites, such as the computer systems of foreign intelligence agencies and government ministries as well as private companies around the world. In particular, companies in the oil and gas industry are seen as high-value targets. Some cyberterrorists are interested in taking control over the flow of oil and natural gas in computer-controlled refineries and the movement of oil through pipelines. This could result in devastating consequences—with oil and gas being cut off from freezing populations in the dead of winter or skyrocketing prices at the gasoline pumps.

With organizations relying on information systems to accomplish their mission and remain in operation, the security of information systems and their data is of utmost importance. Organizations must safeguard their systems and confidential company data, including private customer and employee information, against malicious acts of theft and disruption. However, the need for computer security must be balanced against other business needs. Business managers, IS professionals, and IS users all face a number of complex trade-offs regarding IS security, such as the following:

- How much effort and money should be spent to safeguard against computer crime? (In other words, how safe is safe enough?)
- What should be done if recommended computer security safeguards make conducting business more difficult for customers and employees, resulting in lost sales and increased costs?
- If a firm becomes a victim of a computer crime, should it pursue prosecution of the criminals at all costs, maintain a low profile to avoid the negative publicity, inform affected customers, or take some other action?

A strong security program begins by assessing threats to the organization's computers and network, identifying actions that address the most serious vulnerabilities, and educating end users about the risks involved and the actions they must take to prevent a security incident. An organization's IS security group must lead the effort to prevent security breaches by implementing security policies and procedures, as well as effectively employing available hardware and software tools. However, no security system is perfect, so systems and procedures must be monitored to detect a possible intrusion. If an intrusion occurs, there must be a clear reaction plan that addresses notification, evidence protection, activity log maintenance, containment, eradication, and recovery.

Ethical, Legal, and Social Issues of Information Systems

The use of information systems raises a number of ethical, legal, and social issues, including job losses caused by increasingly sophisticated, humanlike systems, invasion of privacy through various data collection programs, freedom of expression versus censorship, and the issues caused by unequal access to computer technology and the Internet.

ethics: A set of beliefs about right and wrong behavior. Ethical behavior conforms to generally accepted social norms—many of which are almost universally accepted.

Many organizations and professional associations have developed codes of ethics to help guide their members in making difficult decisions, including those connected to the use of information systems. **Ethics** is a set of beliefs about right and wrong behavior. Ethical behavior conforms to generally accepted social norms—many of which are almost universally accepted. In many situations, the decision on what course of action to take is further complicated because it involves significant value conflicts among the various stakeholders as to what is the fairest option to pursue. Such a decision represents an ethical dilemma, and all parties involved can benefit when ethical considerations are introduced into the decision-making process.

The use of information about people (employees, customers, business partners, etc.) requires balancing the needs of those who want to use the information against the rights and desires of the people whose information may be used. On the one hand, information about people is gathered, stored, analyzed, and reported because organizations can use it to make better decisions (see Figure 1.14). Some of these decisions can affect people's lives profoundly—whether or not to extend credit to a new customer, to hire one job candidate versus another, or to offer a scholarship or not. In addition, increased competitiveness in the global marketplace has intensified the need to understand consumers' purchasing habits and financial condition. Companies use information they gather about people to target marketing efforts to consumers who are most likely to buy their products and services. Organizations also need basic information about existing customers in order to serve them better. It is hard to imagine an organization having a relationship with its customers without having data about them. Thus, many organizations implement customer relationship management (CRM) systems that collect and store key data from every interaction they have with a customer.

On the other hand, many people object to the data collection policies of government and other organizations because they believe such policies strip people

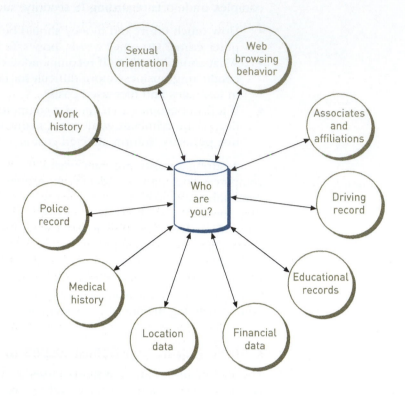

FIGURE **1.14**

Much information is being gathered about people
Personal privacy is difficult to safeguard.

Internet censorship: The control or suppression of the publishing or accessing of information on the Internet.

digital divide: The gulf between those who do and those who don't have access to modern information and communications technology such as smartphones, personal computers, and the Internet.

net neutrality: The principle that Internet service providers (ISPs) should be required to treat all Internet traffic running over their wired and wireless broadband networks the same— without favoring content from some sources and/or blocking or slowing (also known as throttling) content from others.

of the power to control their own personal information. In addition, many people are concerned not only about the potential abuse that control of such data may bring but also about the potential for data breaches, resulting in disclosure of personal data. A combination of approaches—new laws, technical solutions, and privacy policies—is required to effectively balance the needs of all sides.

Internet censorship is the control or suppression of the publishing or accessing of information on the Internet. Censorship can take many forms— such as limiting access to certain Web sites, allowing access to only some content or modified content at certain Web sites, rejecting the use of certain key words in search engine searches, tracking and monitoring the Internet activities of individuals, and harassing or even jailing individuals for their Internet use. For those fortunate enough to live in a nonauthoritarian country, it may be difficult to even imagine that Internet censorship goes on. Yet many authoritarian regimes rely on a mix of sophisticated technology and old-fashioned intimidation to ensure that dissent and the flow of free information online is repressed.

The **digital divide** is a term used to describe the gulf between those who do and those who don't have access to modern information and communications technology such as smartphones, personal computers, and the Internet. Roughly 40 percent of the world's population or around 3 billion people have an Internet connection, but the worldwide distribution of Internet users varies greatly from region to region.

Net neutrality is the principle that Internet service providers (ISPs) should be required to treat all Internet traffic running over their wired and wireless broadband networks the same—without favoring content from some sources and/or blocking or slowing (also known as throttling) content from others. The debate over net neutrality raises questions about how best to keep the Internet open and impartial, while still offering ISPs sufficient incentive to expand their networks to serve more customers and to support new services.

The rapid growth of the Internet of Things is being fueled by the increasing availability of network access, the creation of more inexpensive smart devices with sensors and network capabilities built into them, the rapid growth in smartphone penetration, and the creativity and innovation of people who are able to see and capitalize on the almost unlimited opportunities.[29] Clearly the growth of the IoT will present major issues around Internet access.

Critical Thinking Exercise

Robo-Advice for Millennials

Your investment firm has been working hard to develop a robo-adviser service that uses computer algorithms to provide financial planning for its millennial clients. There is widespread consensus across the investment community that millennials raised in an environment of video games and social networks are looking for just this kind of investment robo-advice service.

You are a member of a field test unit for the robo-advice service. Your team of 12 people has trained some 250 people (in the 25 to 35 target age range) in the basics of investing and how to take best advantage of the robo-advice service. The trial results have been discouraging. Many of the trial clients ignored the robo-advice completely and simply turned into hyperactive traders, executing multiple trades per week. Alarmingly, even those who followed the robo-advice did not fare well, losing an average of 5 percent on their investments even though the market (as measured by the S&P 500) increased nearly 4 percent during the six-month trial period.

Review Questions

1. What other fields besides investing might benefit from the use of a robo-advice system?
2. What sort of legal, ethical, and social issues are raised when creating a robo-advice type of system? Do the builders of such a robo-advice system owe a special duty or responsibility to its users?

Critical Thinking Questions

The members of the field trial team are gathered to discuss their findings and develop conclusions in advance of a meeting next week with the firm's senior management team. Just 10 minutes into the meeting, it is clear that none of the field trial team members feels confident that the new service is offering sound advice. However, some members of the trial team argue that the roll-out of the service should commence as planned; they maintain that problems can be identified and fixed as more users come on board and the firm gains more experience working with investors and the robo-advice system. Their rationale is based at least in part on self-survival—to recommend against roll-out is probably a career-ending move, as the firm has already invested so much in the program, which it has already begun promoting to customers. Others members of the team argue that the product is simply not ready for large-scale use. They argue that the current system should be scrapped and the firm should forget about the idea of a robo-advice service.

1. Are there other alternative strategies for the robo-advice service that make sense? Which approach would you recommend and why?
2. How might you present your approach to senior management in such a way that it has a good chance of being accepted—and that the risk to your future employment is minimized?

Summary

Principle:

The value of information is directly linked to how it helps decision makers achieve the organization's goals.

Data consists of raw facts; information is a collection of data organized and processed so that it has additional value beyond the value of the individual facts. The value of information created depends on the relationships defined among existing data. Turning data into information is a process performed to achieve a defined outcome. This process requires knowledge, which is the awareness and understanding of a set of information and the ways in which that information can be made useful to support a specific task or reach a decision.

Information has many different characteristics. It can be accessible, accurate, complete, economical to produce, flexible, relevant, reliable, secure, simple to understand, timely, and verifiable. The importance of each of these characteristics varies depending on the situation and the kind of decision you are trying to make. The value of information is directly linked to how it helps people achieve their organizations' goals.

Principle:

Information systems are composed of fundamental components that must be carefully assembled and integrated to work well together.

An information system (IS) is a set of interrelated components that collect, process, store, and disseminate data and information; an information system provides a feedback mechanism to monitor and control its operation to make sure it continues to meet its goals and objectives.

A computer-based information system (CBIS) is a single set of hardware, software, databases, networks, people, and procedures that are configured to collect, manipulate, store, and process data into information.

An organization's technology infrastructure includes all the hardware, software, databases, networks, people, and procedures that are configured to collect, manipulate, store, and process data into information.

Principle:

Managers have an essential role to play in the successful implementation and use of information systems—that role changes depending on which type of IS system is being implemented.

When considering the role of business managers in working with IS, it is useful to divide information systems into three types: personal IS, group IS, and enterprise IS.

For each type of IS, certain key organizational complements must be in place to ensure successful implementation and use of the system. These complements include well-trained workers, better teamwork, redesigned processes, and new decision rights.

Principle:

An organization's infrastructure technology forms the foundation upon which its systems and applications are built.

Hardware consists of computer equipment used to perform input, processing, storage, and output activities.

Smartphones have become the primary device used by people around the world to communicate, go online, and access and share information.

Software consists of computer programs that govern the operation of a particular computing device, be it desktop, laptop, tablet, smartphone, or some other device.

The trend of consumer technology practices influencing the way business software is designed and delivered is called the consumerization of IT.

A database is an organized collection of facts and information, typically consisting of two or more related files.

A data warehouse is a database that stores large amounts of historical data in a form that readily supports analysis and decision making. An extract-transform-load process is used to prepare the data for the data warehouse.

Big data is a term used to describe collections of data that are so large and complex that traditional database management software, hardware, and analysis processes are incapable of dealing with them.

Networks connect computers and equipment in a room, building, campus, city, across the country, or around the world to enable electronic communications.

With public cloud computing, a service organization owns and manages the hardware, software, networking, and storage devices, with cloud user organizations (called tenants) accessing slices of shared resources via the Internet.

The Internet of Things (IoT) is a network of physical objects or things embedded with sensors, processors, software, and network connectivity capability to enable them to exchange data with the manufacturer of the device, device operators, and other connected devices.

The Internet of Everything (IoE) encompasses not only machine-to-machine but also people-to-people and people-to machine connections. It is estimated that the total number of devices connected to the Internet of Everything could exceed 50 billion by the end of 2020.

Principle:

Organizations employ a variety of information systems to improve the way they conduct business and make fact-based decisions.

E-commerce involves the exchange of money for goods and services over electronic networks, and it encompasses many of an organization's outward-facing processes. Electronic business goes beyond e-commerce by using information systems and networks to perform business-related tasks and functions.

A transaction processing system (TPS) is an information system used to process and record business transactions.

A management information system (MIS) is an information system that provides routine information to managers and decision makers.

Many organizations are replacing their transaction processing systems and management information systems with enterprise resource planning (ERP) systems that support their routine business processes, maintain records about those processes, and provide extensive reporting and even data analysis capabilities. At the core of a modern enterprise resource planning system is the capability to support e-business and business analytics.

Business analytics is the extensive use of data and quantitative analysis to support fact-based decision making within organizations.

Data scientists are people who understand the business and the business analytics technology, while also recognizing the limitations of their data, tools, and techniques. A data scientist puts all of this together to deliver real improvements in decision making. To ensure the success of a business analytics program, the management team within an organization must have a strong commitment to data-driven decision making. Organizations that can put the necessary components in place can act quickly to make superior decisions in uncertain and changing environments to gain a strong competitive advantage.

A knowledge management system is an information system that stores and retrieves knowledge, improves collaboration, locates knowledge sources, captures and uses knowledge, or in some other way enhances the knowledge management process.

Principle:

Strategic planning and project management are keys to ensuring that the organization is working effectively on the right projects.

Strategic planning is a means to improve alignment between the business and the information systems organization so that the IS organization and its resources are focused on efforts that support the key objectives that are important to the organization. This implies that IS and business managers have a shared vision of where the organization is headed and agree on its key strategies. This shared vision will guide the IS organization in hiring the right people with the correct skills and competencies, choosing the right technologies and vendors to explore and develop, installing the right systems, and focusing on those projects that are needed to move the organization closer to its vision and meeting its mission.

System acquisition is the process used to obtain information system resources needed to provide the services necessary to meet a specific set of needs.

The three basic alternatives for obtaining software to meet users' needs are: buy off-the-shelf software, build a custom application, or choose a software service provider.

Principle:

Information systems must be applied thoughtfully and carefully so that society, organizations, and individuals around the globe can reap their enormous benefits.

Cybercriminals are motivated by the potential for monetary gain. The financial losses from cybercrime—including the cost of the hardware, software, and various countermeasures implemented to fight cybercrime—are estimated to be as high as $400 billion annually worldwide. Cyberterrorism is also an increasing concern for organizations and countries around the globe.

A strong security program begins by assessing threats to the organization's computers and network, identifying actions that address the most serious vulnerabilities, and educating end users about the risks involved and the actions they must take to prevent a security incident.

Information systems play a fundamental and ever-expanding role in society, business, and industry. But their use also raises a number of serious ethical, legal, and social issues, including job losses caused by increasingly sophisticated, humanlike systems; invasion of privacy through various data collection programs; freedom of expression versus censorship; and the issues caused by unequal access to computer technology and the Internet.

Many organizations and professional associations have developed codes of ethics to help guide their members in making difficult decisions.

Key Terms

big data

business analytics

business intelligence (BI)

computer-based information system (CBIS)

consumerization of IT

cybercriminal

cyberterrorism

data

data scientist

data warehouse

database

digital divide

e-commerce

electronic business (e-business)

enterprise IS

enterprise resource planning (ERP) system

ethics

extract-transform-load (ETL)

extranet

group IS

hardware

information

information silo

information system (IS)

Internet

Internet censorship

Internet of Everything (IoE)

Internet of Things (IoT)

intranet

knowledge

knowledge management system (KMS)

management information system (MIS)

mobile commerce (m-commerce)

net neutrality

networks

open source software

organizational complements

personal IS

procedure

process

project

public cloud computing

software

system acquisition

system development

technology infrastructure

transaction

transaction processing system (TPS)

World Wide Web (WWW)

Chapter 1: Self-Assessment Test

The value of information is directly linked to how it helps decision makers achieve the organization's goals.

1. _____ is a collection of raw facts organized and processed so that it has additional value beyond the value of the individual facts.
   a. Data
   b. Information
   c. Knowledge
   d. Expertise

2. Turning data into information is a _____, or a set of logically related tasks performed to achieve a defined outcome.

3. Two quality characteristics that are critical for data used in accounting for the management of company assets, such as cash, inventory, and equipment are _____.
   a. flexibility and accuracy
   b. security and relevancy
   c. accuracy and completeness
   d. relevancy and economical

Information systems are composed of fundamental components that must be carefully assembled and integrated to work well together.

4. Technology infrastructure includes all the hardware, software, _____, networks, people, and procedures that are configured to collect, manipulate, store, and process data into information.

5. According to Jim Collins in his book *Good to Great*, those who build great companies understand that the ultimate throttle on growth for any great company is not markets, or technology, or competition, or products; rather, it is one thing above all others: _____.
   a. great customers
   b. great systems
   c. great leadership
   d. great people

Managers have an essential role to play in the successful implementation and use of information systems—the role changes depending on which type of IS system is being implemented.

6. When considering the role of business managers in working with IS, it is useful to divide information systems into these three types: _____.
   a. enterprise IS, group IS, and personal IS
   b. small and simple, medium and multifaceted, and large and complex
   c. operational, tactical, and strategic
   d. management support, operational, and enterprise systems

7. Which of the following is not a key organizational complement that must be in place to ensure successful implementation and use of the system?
   a. well-trained workers
   b. better teamwork
   c. the latest technology
   d. new decision rights

An organization's technology infrastructure forms the foundation upon which its systems and applications are built.

8. _____ are the primary device type used by people around the world to communicate, go online, and access and share information.
   a. Personal computers
   b. Laptops
   c. Smartphones
   d. Tablets

9. The trend of consumer technology practices influencing the way business software is designed and delivered is called the _____.

10. _____ is a computing environment in which a service provider organization owns and manages the hardware, software, networking, and storage devices, with cloud user organizations (called tenants) accessing slices of shared resources via the Internet.

Organizations employ a variety of information systems to improve the way they conduct business and make fact-based decisions.

11. _____ involves the exchange of money for goods and services over electronic networks, and it encompasses many of an organization's outward-facing processes—such as sales, marketing, order taking, delivery, procurement of goods and services, and customer service—that touch customers, suppliers, and other business partners.

12. A _____ is an organized collection of people, procedures, software, databases, and devices that provides routine information to managers and decision makers.
    a. transaction processing system (TPS)
    b. management information system (MIS)
    c. enterprise resource planning (ERP) system
    d. supply chain management system

13. Over time, decision support systems, executive information systems, online analytical processing, business intelligence, and business analytics have gained in capabilities and expanded in scope to add new functionality, but they have all had the goal of _____.
    a. processing business transactions as rapidly and accurately as possible
    b. deriving the most value out of the data available
    c. providing routine information to managers
    d. enabling the sharing of information across organizations units

14. An organized collection of people, procedures, software, databases, and devices that stores and retrieves knowledge, improves collaboration, locates knowledge sources, and captures and uses knowledge is called a _____.

Strategic planning and project management are keys to ensuring that the organization is working effectively on the right projects.

15. An IT organization not aligned with the key objectives of the business will _____.
    a. be recognized as a technology leader in its industry
    b. find it difficult to even gain management support for its proposed efforts
    c. be positioned to deliver a series of breakthrough projects
    d. be viewed as a partner with the business

16. The two fundamental strategies for system acquisition are: _____.
    a. customize an existing package and acquire open source software
    b. use a standard software package or customize software
    c. build software in-house or contract for software
    d. buy off-the-shelf software or build a custom application

Information systems must be applied thoughtfully and carefully so that society, organizations, and individuals around the globe can reap their enormous benefits.

17. Which of the following statements about computer security is not true?
    a. Cyberterrorism is an increasing concern for organizations and countries around the globe.
    b. Information systems provide a new and highly profitable venue for cybercriminals.
    c. The need for computer security must be balanced against other business needs.
    d. Educating end users about the risks involved and the actions they must take to prevent a security incident is a not key part of any security program.

18. _____ is a term used to describe the gulf between those who do and those who don't have access to modern information and communications technology such as smartphones, personal computers, and the Internet.

Chapter 1: Self-Assessment Test Answers

1. b
2. process
3. c
4. databases
5. d
6. a
7. c
8. c
9. consumerization of IT
10. Cloud computing
11. E-commerce
12. b
13. b
14. knowledge management system
15. b
16. d
17. d
18. Digital divide

Review Questions

1. How is data different from information? How is information different from knowledge?
2. Identify and briefly define six characteristics that describe the quality of data.
3. What is an information system? What is the role of feedback in a system?
4. Identify the six basic components of any computer-based information system.
5. What is meant by an organization's technology infrastructure?
6. When considering the role of business managers in working with IS, it is useful to divide information systems into three types. Name and briefly describe those three types.
7. Identify and briefly describe the four key organizational complements that must be in place to ensure successful implementation and use of an information system.
8. Define the term "software." What are the two primary types of software? How are they different?
9. What is meant by the phrase consumerization of IT?
10. What is the extract-transform-load process?
11. Define the term "big data."
12. What is cloud computing?
13. What is an extranet and how is one used?
14. How is the Internet of Everything different from the Internet of Things?
15. How would you distinguish between e-commerce and e-business?
16. Briefly describe the differences among transaction processing systems, management information systems, and enterprise resource planning systems.
17. What is meant by the term "business analytics"? What other terms have been used for business analytics systems?
18. What is knowledge management? How might it be used?
19. What are the components of a shared vision on which the business and IS organization must agree?
20. Identify an advantage and a potential disadvantage of using open source software.
21. What is the difference between a cybercriminal and a cyberterrorist?
22. Identify three specific social issues associated with the use of information systems.

Discussion Questions

1. What do you hope to learn from this course that will make it worthwhile for you? Do you think a basic understanding of information systems is important to you? Why or why not?
2. Describe how you might use information systems in a career area of interest to you.
3. How might completing this course help you in some of the courses you will take during your academic career?
4. It has been estimated that the amount of digital data is doubling every two years. Discuss some technological and social implications and issues associated with this rapid growth of data.
5. What are some of the social implications of the use of smartphones by an increasing percentage of the world's population?
6. Which of your school's information systems is the worst or most difficult for you to deal with? Describe an ideal system that would replace this one. What role might students play in defining and building this replacement system?
7. Discuss why it is critical for information systems to be linked to the business objectives of an organization.
8. For an industry of your choice, describe how a CBIS could be used to reduce costs or increase profits.
9. An organization has struggled for over three years in an attempt to implement and use an ERP system. It has finally decided to scrap this system, at great cost, and convert to a new ERP system from a different vendor. Identify and discuss actions management should take to ensure the success of the new system.
10. Identify specific benefits of the cloud computing model. Can you identify any potential risks associated with using this approach?
11. Describe three exciting new applications that are becoming feasible as a result of the growth of the Internet of Everything.
12. Do research to identify a company that has gone beyond e-commerce to use information systems and networks to achieve an e-business environment to perform business-related tasks and functions. Briefly describe the scope of the company's e-business functions.
13. Identify a specific company that could benefit from the use of big data and business analytics. What sort of data is required? How might this data be used in decision making?
14. What are the cornerstones to an organization's security program?

Problem-Solving Exercises

1. Prepare a data disk and a backup disk (using USB flash drives) for the problem-solving exercises and other computer-based assignments you will complete in this class. Create one folder for each chapter in the textbook (you will need 14 folders total). As you complete the problem-solving exercises and other work for each computer, save your assignments in the appropriate chapter folder. Designate one disk as your working copy and the other as your backup.

2. Create a table that lists 10 or more possible career areas—including estimated annual salaries and brief job descriptions. Rate how much you think you would like each potential career area on a scale from 1 ("don't like") to 10 ("like the most"). Sort the careers from high to low rating and print the results. Sort the table according to annual salaries, from high to low, and then print the resulting table. Sort the table from the most liked to least liked, and then print the results.

3. Use presentation software to create a set of three slides that identifies the top three things you hope to learn from this course and why each is important to you. If requested, share your findings with the instructor and/or class.

Team Activities

1. Before you can do a team activity, you need a team. As a class member, you might create your own team, or your instructor might assign members to groups. After your group has been formed, meet and introduce yourselves to each other. Find out the first name and contact information for each member. Find out one interesting fact about each member of your team as well. Brainstorm a name for your team. Put the information on each team member into a database and print enough copies for each team member and your instructor.

2. With the other members of your group, use word-processing or group collaboration software to write a summary of the members of your team, the courses each team member has taken, a summary of employment, and the expected graduation date of each team member. Send the report to your instructor via email.

3. With your team, use an Internet search engine or skim through several business periodicals (*Bloomberg Businessweek*, *Computerworld*, *Forbes*, *InformationWeek*, *PC World*, *Wall Street Journal*, *Wired*, etc.) to find recent articles that describe potential social or ethical issues related to the use of the Internet of Things. Use word-processing software to write a one-page report summarizing your findings. Identify one or two issues that you think are most significant.

Web Exercises

1. Throughout this book, you will see how the Internet provides a vast amount of information to individuals and organizations, and you will examine the important role the Web plays. Most large universities and organizations have an address on the Internet (a Web site or home page). The address of the Web site for this publisher is *www.cengage.com*. You can gain access to the Internet through a browser, such as Internet Explorer or Firefox. Using an Internet browser, go to the Web site for this publisher. What did you find? Try to obtain information about this book. You might be asked to develop a report or send an email message to your instructor about what you found.

2. Do research on the Web to find information on Internet censorship. Identify those countries with the strongest degree of Internet censorship, and state specific reasons why those countries are so poorly rated.

3. Go to the Web site for the U.S. Bureau of Labor Statistics, and find information about the occupations with the greatest projected job growth in terms of the number of people who will be needed. Use a graphics program to illustrate the growth of the 10 fastest growing occupations. Write a brief summary of your findings.

Career Exercises

1. In the Career Exercises section found at the end of every chapter, you will explore how material in the chapter can help you excel in your college major or chosen career. Identify 10 job characteristics that are important to you in selecting your career (e.g., involves travel to foreign countries, requires working in a project team). Place these characteristics in rank order based on their relative importance to you.

2. Research two or three possible careers that interest you. Create a report describing the job opportunities, job responsibilities, job characteristics, and possible starting salaries for each career area.

Case Studies

Case One

Connecting Patient Monitoring Devices to EHRs

An electronic health record (EHR) is a computer-readable record of health-related information on an individual. The compiled data in an EHR can include information about patient demographics, medical history, family history, immunization records, laboratory data, ongoing health problems, progress notes, medications, vital signs, and radiology reports. Ideally, EHRs incorporate data from all healthcare facilities a patient uses, making the data easily accessible to healthcare professionals.

EHRs hold out the promise of improving health care and reducing costs, but for now, many hospitals are struggling to automate the capture of raw data from the various patient monitoring devices—such as vital sign monitors, ventilators, and electrocardiogram machines—and pass the data directly into each patient's EHR. This task is made more difficult because different devices and/or vendors often use different standards for communicating over the network. As a result, specialized software is required to receive the data and translate it into a form suitable for updating the EHR. Until communications standards are implemented across the healthcare industry, each new piece of monitoring equipment that outputs a nonstandard signal requires a new interface with the EHR. So if a promising new vital sign monitoring device is developed, some hospitals looking to use the device may be required to create a new software middleware layer to connect the new device to the EHR. Connecting monitoring devices and EHRs is expected to become a major business growth area over the next decade.

Many software vendors and device manufacturers are moving quickly to capitalize on the opportunities involved with automating the many clinical-support activities that involve monitoring devices. The Center for Medical Interoperability has enlisted many of the nation's largest healthcare systems as part of its effort to strongly encourage device vendors to adopt communications standards that will ease the problems with interoperability. The Food and Drug Administration is working to encourage the development of interoperable devices by defining some 25 device standards. Solving the interoperability problem will require an agreement on standards through the cooperation of multiple stakeholders.

Critical Thinking Questions:

1. What benefits can be achieved through the successful implementation of EHRs? What additional benefits will be gained by feeding data directly from patient monitoring devices directly into EHRs?
2. Can you identify any legal, ethical or social concerns with the use EHRs? What additional concerns arise from connecting patient monitoring devices to the IoT?
3. What actions need to be taken by EHR software vendors, patient monitoring device vendors, government agencies, and hospital administrators to enable patient monitoring devices to be safely and reliably connected to EHRs?

SOURCES: Atherton, Jim, "Development of the Electronic Health Record," *AMA Journal of Ethics*, March 2011, *http://journalofethics.ama-assn.org/2011/03/mhst1-1103.html*; Tahir, Dennis, "Getting the Data Stream Flowing: Hospitals Want Monitoring Devices and EHRs to Communicate," *Modern Healthcare*, May 9, 2015, *www.modernhealthcare.com/article/20150509/MAGAZINE/305099980*.

Case Two

BMW: Automaker Competes on the Digital Front

One of the biggest trends driving competition in the auto industry in recent years is the race to offer new and better "connected-car" technologies—including those that enhance safety, monitor maintenance requirements, provide Internet connectivity, and offer seamless integration with smartphones and wearable devices. A 2015 study of the worldwide auto industry projected that customer spending on connected-car technologies will exceed €40 billion ($42 billion) in 2016; that number is expected to more than triple to €122 billion ($129 billion) by 2021. Tech-savvy consumers increasingly expect their cars to serve as extensions of their personal technology, and one company working hard to exceed those expectations is German automaker Bayerische Motoren Werke AG—or BMW, as it is more commonly known.

BMW was founded in 1916 as a manufacturer of aircraft engines, but the company soon branched out into other areas. Today, the BMW Group manufactures motorcycles in addition to its three premium car brands (BMW, MINI, and Rolls-Royce), and it is now represented in over 140 countries—including 30 production locations in 14 countries. With close to 2 million cars sold in 2014, BMW is one of the world's most-recognized luxury car brands, with a reputation for consistently delivering high-quality cars built on a foundation of advanced mechanical engineering. To maintain its edge, BMW is now expanding its focus to find ways to improve its cars through cutting-edge technological innovations.

According to Dieter May, BMW's digital business models senior vice president, "Our competitor is not Audi, Jaguar Land Rover or Mercedes, but the space of consumer electronics players." As May sees it, one of the biggest questions facing BMW—and other auto makers—in the coming years is "How do we take the connected home, personal digital assistants, and advanced sensor technology, and connect all these trends?"

BMW has responded to this question by building an extensive array of new technologies into its latest models. Through BMW's iDrive information and entertainment system, drivers can access ConnectedDrive, a portal offering a wide range of location-based services, including concierge services, real-time traffic information, and access to more than 12.6 million searchable "points of interest," ranging from gas stations to restaurants to tourist attractions. Another ConnectedDrive feature, the Head-Up Display, projects important driving information—such as current speed and warnings from the car's night vision system—on the windshield, allowing the driver to keep his or her eyes on the road. The Speed Limit Info feature uses a car-mounted camera along with data from the navigation system to keep drivers informed of current speed limits, including those in effect due to road construction and weather conditions. ConnectedDrive, which can be controlled from the driver's smartphone, also offers mobile office features, such as the ability to dictate and send messages, and a ConnectedDrive Store, where users can purchase apps and services directly through the iDrive interface. And at the high end of BMW's model line, the 7 Series full-size sedan, BMW's flagship vehicle, is the first model to accept gesture-control commands for the iDrive display as well as a completely automated self-park feature that can be operated when the driver is outside the vehicle.

BMW is also working to ensure that the car-buying experience is keeping up with customers' expectations by encouraging its dealerships to create more digital showrooms, with flat screen displays and virtual demonstrations to appeal to the many customers who are accustomed to the online shopping experience. In addition, BMW is adding "product geniuses"—like those found in Apple's retail stores—to its showrooms. The specialists have no responsibility to sell; their job is simply to spend whatever time is necessary to explain and demonstrate each car's various technological features to potential BMW customers.

To continue to develop the complex technological innovations it needs to maintain its edge over competitors,

BMW has explored possible partnerships with technology companies such as Apple. Currently, however, the auto maker is focused on building up its in-house expertise and speeding up its internal software development cycles. In 2014, BMW spent over €4.5 billion ($4.75 billion) on research and development, and it spent, on average, more than €6,000 ($6,370) per car on connected-car technology. BMW is making it clear to potential customers and competitors alike that is committed to competing and winning on the digital front.

Critical Thinking Questions:

1. Other than selling more cars, what potential benefits do connected-car technologies offer auto makers such as BMW in terms of enhancing long-term customer relationships?
2. What responsibilities does BMW have to its customers regarding the data it captures via the various connected car technologies that it builds into its cars?
3. Of the primary components of an ERP system that were identified in this chapter, which modules are likely to be of highest importance to BMW if it continues to focus on in-house development of new technological features and services rather than partnering with an established personal technology company, such as Google or Apple? Would those tools need to change if BMW establishes a long-term partnership with a technology company?

SOURCES: Muller, Joann, "5 Big Trends Driving The Auto Industry in 2015," *Forbes*, January 19, 2015, *www.forbes.com/sites/joannmuller /2015/01/05/5-big-trends-driving-the-auto-industry-in-2015*; Vierecki, Richard, Ahlemann, Dietmar, Koster, Alex, and Jursch, Sebastian, "Connected Car Study 2015: Racing Ahead with Autonomous Cars and Digital Innovation," Strategy&, September 15, 2015, *www.strategyand. pwc.com/global/home/what-we-think/reports-white-papers/article-dis play/connected-car-2015-study*; "Annual Report 2014," BMW Group, *www.bmwgroup.com/e/0_0_www_bmwgroup_com/investor_relations /finanzberichte/geschaeftsberichte/2014/_pdf/12507_GB_2014_en_Fi nanzbericht_Online.pdf*, accessed November 23, 2015; Murphy, Margi, "BMW Internalizes IT to Claw Back Customer Data," *ComputerworldUK*, June 24, 2015, *www.computerworlduk.com/news/data/bmw-our-compe titor-is-not-audi-jaguar-land-rover-or-mercedes-but-consumer-electro nics-players-3616944*; Green, Chloe, "Rise of the Intelligent Car," *InformationAge*, July 7, 2015, *www.information-age.com/industry/soft ware/123459790/rise-intelligent-car-how-digital-technologies-are-creat ing-third-wave-car-makers*; "BMW ConnectedDrive," BMW USA, *www .bmwusa.com/standard/content/innovations/bmwconnecteddrive/con necteddrive.aspx#home*, accessed November 28, 2015; "7 Series," BMW USA, *www.bmwusa.com/bmw/7series*, accessed November 28, 2015; Taylor, Edward and Love, Julia, "Tim Cook Visited BMW in Germany to Learn How to Build an Electric Car," *Business Insider*, July 31, 2015, *www.businessinsider.com/r-apple-bmw-in-courtship-with-an-eye-on -car-collaboration-2015-7*; "BMW Tosses Salesmen for 'Geniuses'," *The Wall Street Journal*, February 19, 2014, *www.wsj.com/articles /SB10001424052702304450904579364833799765354*.

Notes

1. Haselkorn, Erin, "To Be a Marketing Master Mind, You Need Quality Data," Experian Marketing Services, April 15, 2014, *www.experian.com/blogs/marketing-forward/2014/04/15/to-be-a-marketing-mastermind-you-need-quality-data*.
2. Shah, Jay, "Calculate the Cost of Bad Data Using This Easy Equation," Informed Logix, April 2, 2015, *www.infogix.com/calculate-cost-bad-data-easy-equation*.
3. Collins, Jim, *Good to Great: Why Some Companies Make the Leap and Others Don't*, New York: Harper Business, 2001.
4. Carroll, Ron, "People Are the Most Important System Component," Box Theory, *www.boxtheorygold.com/blog/bid/12164/People-Are-the-Most-Important-System-Component*, accessed June 10, 2015.
5. Laurianne McLaughlin, "Kroger Solves Top Customer Issue: Long Lines," *InformationWeek*, April 2, 2014, *www.informationweek.com/strategic-cio/executive-insights-and-innovation/kroger-solves-top-customer-issue-long-lines/d/d-id/1141541*.
6. "2 Billion Consumers Worldwide to Get Smart(phones) by 2015," eMarketer, December 11, 2014, *www.emarketer.com/Article/2-Billion-Consumers-Worldwide-Smart phones-by-2016/1011694*.
7. "Global Smartphone Shipments Forecast from 2010 to 2019 (in million units)," The Statistics Portal, *www.statista.com/statistics/263441/global-smartphone-shipments-forecast*, accessed June 11, 2015 and "Forecast for Global Shipments of Tablets, Laptops and Desktop PCs from 2010 to 2019 (in million units)," Statistica, *www.statista.com/statistics/272595/global-shipments-forecast-for-tablets-laptops-and-desktop-pcs*, accessed June 10, 2015.
8. "Number of Android Applications," App Brain Stats, June 11, 2015, *www.appbrain.com/stats/number-of-android-apps*.
9. "Number of Apps Available in Leading App Stores as of May 2015," The Statistics Portal, *www.statista.com/statistics/276623/number-of-apps-available-in-leading-app-stores*, accessed June 12, 2015.
10. Harris, Derrick, "Why Apple, eBay, and Walmart Have Some of the Biggest Data Warehouses You've Ever Seen," GIGAOM, March 27, 2013, *https://gigaom.com/2013/03/27/why-apple-ebay-and-walmart-have-some-of-the-biggest-data-warehouses-youve-ever-seen*.
11. Ibid.
12. Ibid.
13. Vowler, Julia, "US Data Warehousing to Make the Most of Web Data," *ComputerWeekly.com*, *www.computerweekly.com/feature/US-data-warehousing-to-make-the-most-of-Web-data*, accessed January 19, 2014.
14. Williams, David, "EMC: World's Data Doubling Every Two Years...," IT Brief, April 15, 2014, *http://itbrief.co.nz/story/emc-worlds-data-doubling-every-two-years*.
15. "Big Data: A New World of Opportunities," NESSI, December 2012, *www.nessi-europe.com/Files/Private/NESSI_WhitePaper_BigData.pdf*.
16. "Cloud Computing Options," *PC Today*, June 2014.
17. "AWS Case Study: Netflix," Amazon Web Services, *https://aws.amazon.com/solutions/case-studies/netflix/?pg=main-customer-success-page*, accessed September 26, 2015.
18. "Implementation of Intranets," Innovaction Research Group, *www.innovactiongroup.com/Corporate-Intra nets*, accessed June 16, 2015.
19. "Internet of Things: FTC Staff Report and a New Publication for Businesses," Federal Trade Commission, January 2015, *www.ftc.gov/system/files/documents/reports/federal-trade-commission-staff-report-november-2013-workshop-entitled-internet-things-privacy/150127iotrpt.pdf*.
20. Bradley, Joseph, Barbier, Joel, and Handler, Doug, "Embracing the Internet of Everything to Capture Your Share of $14.4 Trillion," Cisco White Paper, *www.cisco.com/web/about/ac79/docs/innov/IoE_Economy.pdf*.
21. Kuehner-Hebert, Katie, "GE to Launch 'Internet of Things' Service," *CFO*, August 5, 2015, *http://ww2.cfo.com/the-cloud/2015/08/ge-launch-internet-things-service*.
22. "NARCOMS MS Research Effort Seeks Participants: MS Registry Enables Researchers to Find Solutions for People with MS," National Multiple Sclerosis Society, March 16, 2015, *www.nationalmssociety.org/About-the-Society/News/NARCOMS-MS-Research-Effort-Seeks-Participants-MS-R*.
23. Schwartz, C.E., Bode, R.K., and Vollmer, T, "The Symptom Inventory Disability-Specific Shorts Forms for MS: Reliability and Factorial Structure," *Archives of Physical Medicine and Rehabilitation*. March 21, 2012, *www.ncbi.nlm.nih.gov/pubmed/22446293*.
24. Buchanan, Leigh, "The New York Bakery That Hires Everyone, No Questions Asked," *Inc.*, September 21, 2015, *www.inc.com/leigh-buchanan/greyston-bakery-hires-everyone-no-questions-asked.html*.
25. Luttrell, Anne, "NASA's PMO: Building and Sustaining a Learning Organization," Project Management Institute, *www.pmi.org/Learning/articles/nasa.aspx*, accessed June 26, 2015.
26. "About | Penn National Gaming," *www.pngaming.com/About*, accessed November 4, 2015.
27. "Big, Bang Boom," *Huffington Post*, *http://big.assets.huffingtonpost.com/BigBangBoom.pdf*, accessed May 30, 2015.
28. Durbin, Steve, "Cyber Crime: Battling a Growth Industry," The Connected Business, September 5, 2014, *www.ft.com/cms/s/2/34cb2b04-34cf-11e4-ba5d-00144feabdc0.html#axzz3atmza4RA*.
29. Morgan, Jacob, "A Simple Explanation of 'The Internet of Things'," *Forbes*, May 13, 2014, *www.forbes.com/sites/jacobmorgan/2014/05/13/simple-explanation-internet-things-that-anyone-can-understand*.

Information Systems in Organizations

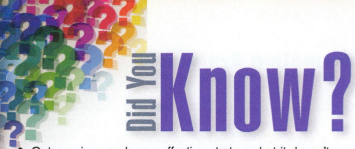

Did You Know?

- Outsourcing can be an effective strategy, but it doesn't always work. Boeing made a strategic decision to outsource development of the 787 Dreamliner aircraft with a goal of reducing costs and cutting development time by two years. However, complications led to a temporary worldwide grounding of the aircraft a little more than a year after its launch, denting the plane's public reputation.

- Successful companies such as General Electric have developed strategies for addressing the "soft side of implementing change." These strategies are designed to help employees embrace change and the new way of working and can mean the difference between success and failure of change efforts.

- Technology is one of the fastest-growing areas in the U.S. economy, and information systems professionals such as software developers, computer systems analysts, computer support specialists, and data scientists are in high demand.

Principles

- Organizations are open systems that affect and are affected by their surrounding environment.

- Positive change is a key ingredient for any successful organization.

- Information systems must be implemented in such a manner that they are accepted and work well within the context of an organization and support its fundamental business goals and strategies.

- The information system worker functions at the intersection of business and technology and designs, builds, and implements solutions that allow organizations to effectively leverage information technology systems.

Learning Objectives

- Sketch a general model of an organization showing how information systems support and work within the automated portions of an organizational process.

- Define the term value chain and identify several examples within a typical manufacturing or service organization.

- Define the term innovation and identify two types.

- Define reengineering and continuous improvement and explain how they are different.

- Discuss the pros and cons of outsourcing, offshoring, and downsizing.

- Define the term "the soft side of implementing change," and explain why it is a critical factor in the successful adoption of any major change.

- Identify and briefly describe four change models that can be used to increase the likelihood of successfully introducing a new information system into an organization.

- Define the types of roles, functions, and careers available in the field of information systems.

Why Learn about Information Systems in Organizations?

After graduating, a management major might be hired by a transportation company and be assigned to an information system project designed to improve employee productivity. A marketing major might use a software application to analyze customer needs in different areas of the country for a national retailer. An accounting major might work for a consulting firm using an information system to audit a client company's financial records. A real estate major might work in a virtual team with clients, builders, and a legal team whose members are located around the world. A biochemist might conduct research for a drug company and use a computer model to evaluate the potential of a new cancer treatment. An entrepreneur might use information systems to advertise and sell products and bill customers.

Although your job might be different from those in the above examples, throughout your career, you will almost certainly use information systems to help you and your organization become more efficient, effective, productive, and competitive. However, the implementation of new information systems has a major impact on an organization, affecting people's roles and responsibilities, their day-to-day routines and processes for accomplishing work, who they interact with, what skills and knowledge they need, and how they are rewarded and compensated. The resulting changes can be highly disruptive and agonizing to work through, and as a result, the introduction of a new system often faces considerable resistance. As a manager in an organization undergoing such change, you must anticipate resistance and work actively to mitigate it. Failure to rise to this challenge can lead to the failure of a promising information system project.

This chapter provides the information and tools you need to better understand people's resistance to change and management's role in overcoming this resistance.

As you read this chapter, consider the following:

- Why is there a natural resistance to the implementation of new information systems?
- What must leaders do to prepare their organization for the changes that accompany the successful adoption of a new information system?

Information systems (IS) continue to have a major impact on the role of workers and on how organizations as a whole function. While information systems were once used primarily to automate manual processes, today they are transforming the nature of work itself and, in many cases, the nature of the products and services offered. Organizational leaders have an essential role in preparing the organization to not just accept but to embrace the changes necessary for success. In this chapter and throughout the book, you will explore the benefits and issues associated with the use of information systems in today's organizations around the globe.

Organizations and Information Systems

organization: A group of people that is structured and managed to meet its mission or set of group goals.

An **organization** is a group of people that is structured and managed to meet its mission or set of group goals. "Structured" means that there are defined relationships between members of the organization and their various activities, and that processes are defined that assign roles, responsibilities, and authority to complete the various activities. In many cases, the processes are automated using well-defined information systems. Organizations are considered to be open systems, meaning that they affect and are affected by their surrounding environment. See Figure 2.1.

Providing value to a stakeholder—customer, supplier, partner, shareholder, or employee—is the primary goal of any organization. The value chain, first described by Michael Porter in a classic 1985 *Harvard Business Review* article titled "How Information Gives You Competitive Advantage,"

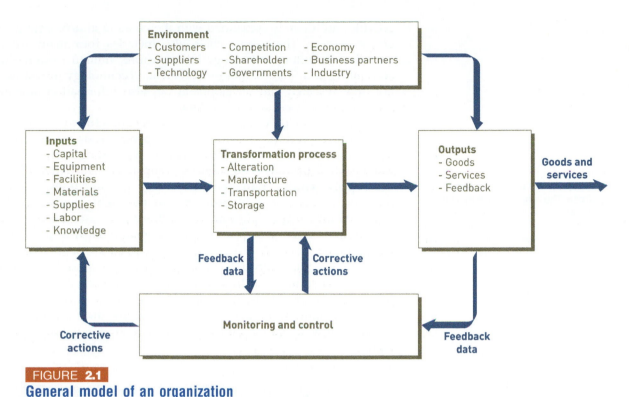

FIGURE 2.1

General model of an organization

Information systems support and work within the automated portions of an organizational process.

value chain: A series (chain) of activities that an organization performs to transform inputs into outputs in such a way that the value of the input is increased.

supply chain: A key value chain whose primary activities include inbound logistics, operations, outbound logistics, marketing and sales, and service.

reveals how organizations can add value to their products and services. The **value chain** is a series (chain) of activities that an organization performs to transform inputs into outputs in such a way that the value of the input is increased. An organization may have many value chains, and different organizations in different industries will have different value chains. As an example of a simple value chain, the gift wrapping department of an upscale retail store takes packages from customers, covers them with appropriate, decorative wrapping paper, and gives the package back to the customer, thus increasing the customer's (and the recipient's) perceived value of the gift.

In a manufacturing organization, the **supply chain** is a key value chain whose primary activities include inbound logistics, operations, outbound logistics, marketing and sales, and service. See Figure 2.2. These primary

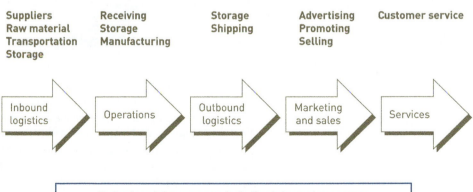

FIGURE 2.2

Supply chain

The primary and support activities of the manufacturing supply chain are concerned with creating or delivering a product or service.

activities are directly concerned with the creation and/or delivery of the product or service. The supply chain also includes four main areas of support activities, including technology infrastructure, human resource management, accounting and finance, and procurement. (Technology infrastructure includes not only research and development but also information systems hardware, software, databases, and networks.)

The concept of value chain is also meaningful to companies that don't manufacture products, including tax preparers, restaurants, book publishers, legal firms, and other service providers. By adding a significant amount of value to their products and services, companies ensure their success.

Supply chain management (SCM) encompasses all the activities required to get the right product into the right consumer's hands in the right quantity at the right time and at the right cost—from the identification of suppliers and the acquisition of raw materials through manufacture and customer delivery. The organizations that compose the supply chain are "linked" together through both physical flows and information flows. Physical flows involve the transformation, movement, and storage of supplies and raw materials. Information flows allow participants in the supply chain to communicate their plans, coordinate their work, and manage the efficient flow of goods and material up and down the supply chain. See Figure 2.3.

supply chain management (SCM): The management of all the activities required to get the right product into the right consumer's hands in the right quantity at the right time and at the right cost—from the identification of suppliers and the acquisition of raw materials through manufacture and customer delivery.

Nataliya Hora/Shutterstock.com

FIGURE 2.3

Ford Motor Company assembly line

Ford Motor Company's use of information systems is a critical support activity of its supply chain. The company gives suppliers access to its inventory system so that the suppliers can monitor the database and automatically send another shipment of parts, such as engine parts or bumpers, eliminating the need for purchase orders. This procedure speeds delivery and assembly time and lowers Ford's inventory-carrying costs.

Organizations are constantly fine-tuning and adjusting their supply chain. For example, many companies are increasing their use of free shipping to customers in hopes of increasing sales and profits. Amazon is experimenting with AmazonFresh, a Web site that offers fast, free delivery of groceries on orders over $35 and other products in the Los Angeles and Seattle areas. Customers can place an order by 10 am and have it by dinner; orders placed by 10 pm will be delivered by breakfast time. The e-commerce giant is also experimenting with a new drive-up store concept that will allow consumers to order grocery items online and then schedule a pickup at a dedicated facility. Many organizations are also outsourcing much of their outbound distribution activities, including the storage and shipping of finished products to customers and the return of items from customers. Amazon, DHL, FedEx, Rakuten, Shipwire, UPS, and other companies are highly skilled and efficient at performing these functions.

What role do information systems play in supply chain management activities and other organizational activities? A traditional view of information systems holds that organizations use them to control and monitor processes and to ensure effectiveness and efficiency. In this view, information systems are external to the supply chain management process and serve to monitor or control it.

A more contemporary view, however, holds that information systems are often so intimately involved that they are *part of* the process itself. From this perspective, the information system plays an integral role in the process, whether providing input, aiding product transformation, or producing output. Zara and Coles are two examples of organizations that have incorporated information systems into the supply chain and made them integral parts of this process.

Zara is a Spanish clothing and accessories retailer with headquarters in Arteixo, Spain, and 2,000 stores spread across 88 countries.[1] Its founder, Amancio Ortega, had humble origins, but today is the third richest man in the world. Consumer clothing trends are constantly changing, creating a highly competitive environment in which companies compete not only on price but also on their ability to deliver products that are new and stimulating to their customers. To meet this challenge, Zara has developed an extremely responsive supply chain that enables it to go from design stage to sales floor in a maximum of three weeks rather than the six-month industry average. Zara can deliver new products twice a week to its stores around the world. Mobile computers and point-of-sales systems are used to capture and review data from stores on an hourly basis to spot new trends as early as possible. This data includes sales and inventory data and anecdotal information gleaned by sales assistants as they chat with customers and as the sales assistants gather unsold items that customers tried on, but left in fitting rooms. All this data is sent to Zara's headquarters where it is carefully analyzed by design teams who decide what new designs will be prototyped and produced in small quantities to see what sells. In addition, inventory optimization models help the company determine the quantities and sizes of existing items that should be delivered to each store. Zara's outstanding supply chain (which includes information systems as an integral component) has led to improved customer satisfaction, decreased risks of overstocking the wrong items, reduced total costs, and increased sales.[2]

Coles is the second largest supermarket chain in Australia. The company employs advanced analytics to improve consumer demand forecasts, and it uses sophisticated customer-loyalty analysis tools to deepen its understanding of customer buying patterns so it can plan effective marketing programs. Coles uses a supplier portal that supports effective working relationships between the chain and its more than 3,000 suppliers, providing better coordination and communications, which, in turn, help the company reduce costs and achieve consistent delivery times along the supply chain. The portal also provides suppliers with information they can use to assess their performance and identify opportunities of improvement. Coles works closely with suppliers to take effective measures toward continuous improvement, including frank discussions about opportunities for improvement.[3] All these actions have gone a long way toward reducing the number 1 complaint from Coles' customers—item stockouts. They have also paved the way for improved inventory management and better supplier relationships.[4]

Virtual Teams and Collaborative Work

virtual team: A group of individuals whose members are distributed geographically, but who collaborate and complete work through the use of information systems.

A **virtual team** is a group of individuals whose members are distributed geographically, but who collaborate and complete work through the use of information systems. The virtual team may be composed of individuals from a single organization or from multiple organizations. The team can consist of just two people up to hundreds of team members. One benefit of virtual teams is that they enable organizations to enlist the best people in different geographical regions to solve important organizational problems. Another benefit is that they provide the ability to staff a team with people who have a range of experience and knowledge that stems from a variety of professional experiences and cultural backgrounds.

Often, it is difficult for members of a large virtual organization to meet at a time that is convenient for everyone on the team due to the time zone differences in their various geographic locations. Thus, members of a virtual team may seldom meet face to face. However, quick communication exchanges among members can be key to project success. Thus, virtual team members may need to continually monitor their email, instant messages, and team Web site and be prepared to participate in an audio or video teleconference on short notice. See Figure 2.4. Virtual team members must be prepared to do work anywhere, anytime. As a result, members of a virtual team may feel that their work day never ends.

VGstockstudio/Shutterstock.com

FIGURE 2.4

Group videoconference

A virtual organizational structure allows collaborative work in which managers and employees can effectively work in groups, even those composed of members from around the world.

Communications are greatly improved when participants can see one another and pick up facial expressions and body language. Thus, even with sophisticated information system tools, virtual teams still benefit from occasional face-to-face meetings. This is particularly true at the beginning of new projects when the team is just forming and defining goals, roles, and expectations on how its members will work together. Virtual organization members must also be sensitive to the different cultures and practices of the various team members to avoid misunderstandings that can destroy team chemistry. It helps if virtual team members take the time to get to know one another by sharing experiences and personal background information.

International advertising, marketing, and public relations firm Ogilvy & Mather maintains offices in 161 cities all over the world and employs some 15,000 workers. The firm promotes the brands of its multinational clients by combining local market know-how with a worldwide network of resources to build powerful campaigns that address local market needs while also reinforcing global brand identity. The firm relies on multiple virtual teams across the organization to implement this strategy.[5]

Critical Thinking Exercise

Reducing New Product Stockouts at Coles

You have been employed in the supply chain management organization of Coles for the past two years. You are very excited when you are asked to join a team being formed to address serious inventory management problems often associated with the introduction of new products. Too often, customers who make a trip to Coles to purchase a highly advertised new product are disappointed to find the store is out of stock of that particular item. Such stockouts result in lost sales for both Coles and the product supplier and the potential loss of customers as shoppers look elsewhere to find the new product. The resulting loss of customer goodwill can have a long-term effect on sales. Solving this problem will require a balancing act; the company needs to carry sufficient inventory of new products to meet customer demand while avoiding excessive inventory levels that increase costs.

The team you have joined consists of nine people representing the finance, marketing, and supply chain management organizations at both Coles and two of Coles' largest suppliers. The team is charged with looking at a wide range of solutions, including improved analytics and forecasting systems, customer-loyalty analysis tools to provide insights into customer buying patterns, and improved distribution methods to cut costs and delivery times.

Review Questions

1. Identify some of the advantages of running a virtual team such as this. What are some of the keys to success when working with a virtual team?
2. What sort of complications might be expected when forming a multiorganizational virtual team?

Critical Thinking Questions

1. The leader of the team has asked that each member share a brief personal background paragraph that outlines the individual's knowledge and experience relevant to solving this problem. Create a paragraph for a team member who is a well-qualified, but relatively inexperienced representative of the Coles supply chain management organization.
2. What actions would you recommend to minimize potential start-up issues for this virtual team?

Change in the Organization

Your organization's current products, services, and ways of accomplishing work are doomed to obsolescence. Fail to change and your competition will take away your customers and your profits. Positive change is a key ingredient for any successful organization. This section will discuss important topics related to change, including innovation, reengineering, continuous improvement, outsourcing, offshoring, and downsizing.

Innovation

innovation: The application of new ideas to the products, processes, and activities of a firm, leading to increased value.

Innovation is the application of new ideas to the products, processes, and activities of a firm, leading to increased value. Innovation is the catalyst for the growth and success of any organization. It can build and sustain profits, create new challenges for the competition, and provide added value for customers. Innovation and change are absolutely required in today's highly competitive global environment; without both, the organization is at risk of losing its competiveness and becoming obsolete. The following is a list of just a few of today's most innovative products:

- Tile is an innovative new product that helps solve a universal problem that we all encounter—occasionally misplacing everyday items and wasting time trying to find them. Tile is a smartphone app combined with small devices (tiles) that consumers can stick on their keys, TV remote controls, purses, and wallets. A proximity sensor plays a musical sound through the smartphone app when you come within 100 feet of the tile, so you can walk around to see if the missing item is hiding nearby.
- Healthcare technology company iHealth has introduced several different sensors that can measure and report on a wide array of biometric data, including steps taken, distance covered, and calories burned; sleep efficiency; blood pressure; glucose level; and blood oxygen saturation level and pulse rate.
- Butterfleye offers a new, economical home security product that employs a megapixel camera smart enough to recognize you, members of your family, and even your pets. If a stranger is caught inside your home within view of the camera, Butterfleye uses your home Wi-Fi system to alert you via an app.
- NeuroMetrix created Quell, an FDA-approved device that stimulates the brain to block pain receptors for patients with chronic conditions. The device is worn around the calf and calibrated to the user's body to ensure that it delivers the exact amount of relief needed. Quell performs functions similar to existing devices that today must be surgically implanted at much higher cost.

Various authors and researchers have identified different ways of classifying innovation. A simple classification developed by Clayton Christensen, a leading researcher in this field, is to think of two types of innovation— sustaining and disruptive.[6]

Sustaining innovation results in enhancements to existing products, services, and ways of operating. Such innovations are important because they enable an organization to continually increase profits, lower costs, and gain market share. Procter and Gamble has invested hundreds of millions of dollars into making sustaining innovations to its leading laundry detergent, Tide, which was first introduced in 1946. The innovations include: the reformulation of Tide so it works as well in cold water as it does in hot water; the creation of concentrated Tide, which reduces packaging and distribution costs; and the addition of scent, which makes clothes smell fresher. These innovations have allowed Tide to remain one of the leading detergents for several decades, with around $5 billion in worldwide annual sales.[7] The brand currently holds a 38 percent share of the North American laundry soap business.[8]

A disruptive innovation is one that initially provides a lower level of performance than the marketplace has grown to accept. Over time, however, the disruptive innovation is improved to provide new performance characteristics, becoming more attractive to users in a new market. As it continues to improve and begins to provide a higher level of performance, it eventually displaces the former product or way of doing things. The cell phone is a good example of a disruptive innovation. The first commercial handheld cell phone was invented in 1973. It weighed 2.5 pounds, had a battery life of less than 30 minutes, cost more than $3,000, and had extremely poor sound quality.[9] Compare that with today's ubiquitous cell phones that have one-tenth the weight, one-fifteenth the cost, and 25 times longer battery life; smartphones can not only place calls but also serve as a camera, a video recorder, and a handheld computer that can run applications and access the Internet.

Reengineering and Continuous Improvement

reengineering (process redesign/business process reengineering, BPR): The radical redesign of business processes, organizational structures, information systems, and values of the organization to achieve a breakthrough in business results.

To stay competitive, organizations must occasionally make fundamental changes in the way they do business. In other words, they must innovate and change the activities, tasks, or processes they use to achieve their goals. **Reengineering**, also called **process redesign** and **business process reengineering (BPR)**, involves the radical redesign of business processes, organizational structures, information systems, and values of the organization to achieve a breakthrough in business results. See Figure 2.5. Successful reengineering can reduce delivery time, increase product and service quality, enhance customer satisfaction, and increase revenues and profitability.

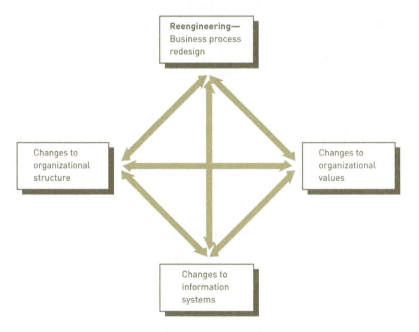

FIGURE 2.5

Reengineering

Reengineering involves the radical redesign of business processes, organizational structure, information systems, and the values of an organization to achieve a break-through in business results.

General Electric employs a strategy it calls GE Advantage to reengineer business processes to increase its speed to market, improve the quality of its products and services, reduce costs, and achieve competitive advantage. This strategy has been applied to its new product introduction process to reduce the time it takes to bring a new product to market (in some cases by more than 50 percent), improve the quality of its designs, and lower development costs.

continuous improvement: Constantly seeking ways to improve business processes and add value to products and services.

In contrast to reengineering, the idea of **continuous improvement** (often referred to by the Japanese word "Kaizen") is a form of innovation that constantly seeks ways to improve business processes and add value to products and services. This continual change will increase customer satisfaction and loyalty and ensure long-term profitability. Manufacturing companies make continual product changes and improvements. Service organizations regularly find ways to provide faster and more effective assistance to customers. By doing so, organizations increase customer loyalty, minimize the chance of customer dissatisfaction, and diminish the opportunity for competitive inroads.

Boeing has a long tradition and culture supportive of continuous improvement, which has yielded many positive results. For example, the time to assemble its popular long-range, wide-body, twin-engine 777 jet airliner has been reduced almost in half through the implementation of many small improvements—from 71 days in 1998 to just 37 days today.[10] Table 2.1 compares the strategies of business process reengineering and continuous improvement.

TABLE 2.1 Comparing business process reengineering with continuous improvement

Business Process Reengineering	Continuous Improvement
Strong action taken to solve serious problem	Routine action taken to make minor improvements
Top-down change driven by senior executives	Bottom-up change driven by workers
Broad in scope; cuts across departments	Narrow in scope; focuses on tasks in a given area
Goal is to achieve a major breakthrough	Goal is continuous, gradual improvements
Often led by resources from outside the company	Usually led by workers close to the business
Information systems are integral to the solution	Information systems provide data to guide the improvement team

Outsourcing, Offshoring, and Downsizing

A significant portion of expenses for most organizations goes toward hiring, training, and compensating employees. Naturally, organizations try to control costs by determining the number of employees they need to maintain high-quality goods and services without being overstaffed. Strategies to contain these personnel costs include outsourcing, offshoring, and downsizing.

outsourcing: A long-term business arrangement in which a company contracts for services with an outside organization that has expertise in providing a specific function.

Outsourcing is a long-term business arrangement in which a company contracts for services with an outside organization that has expertise in providing a specific function. Organizations often outsource a process so they can focus more closely on their core business—and target their limited resources to meet strategic goals. Typically, the outsourcing firm has expertise and other resources that enable it to perform the service better, faster, and/or more cheaply. As a result, many companies now outsource jobs such as call center services, payroll activities, information system operations, computer support services, and security services.

offshore outsourcing (offshoring): An outsourcing arrangement where the organization providing the service is located in a country different from the firm obtaining the services.

Offshore outsourcing (also called **offshoring**) is an outsourcing arrangement in which the organization providing the service is located in a country different from the firm obtaining the services. Offshoring of tasks that require significant customer interaction has led to problems due to culture and language differences for some companies. As a result, many companies are reevaluating their decision to offshore their call center and customer support services, as well as the outsourcing of other activities.

Deutsche Bank has extended an offshore outsourcing agreement with Accenture to provide its procurement and accounts payable services. The original contract was signed in 2004 and was set to expire in 2016. Through its agreement with Accenture, Deutsche Bank was looking to reduce operational costs, improve spending control, and simplify its sourcing and procurement services.

The arrangement has worked well, and the two organizations recently signed a new contract to extend the initial agreement through the end of 2021.[11]

Citizens Bank of Rhode Island signed a five-year agreement with IBM to outsource its information systems services, with the goal of increasing efficiencies, lowering costs, and improving service. The bank's information systems employees are training replacements who work for IBM in India, where the average salary of IBM workers is about $17,000.[12] It is estimated that some 250 to 350 current employees and existing contractors will lose their jobs at Citizen Bank as a result of the offshore outsourcing move.[13]

Companies considering outsourcing need to take into account many factors. A growing number of organizations are finding that outsourcing does not necessarily lead to reduced costs. One of the primary reasons for cost increases is poorly written contracts that allow the service provider to tack on unexpected charges. Other potential drawbacks of outsourcing include loss of control and flexibility, the potential for data breaches of information stored on the service provider's computer hardware, overlooked opportunities to strengthen core competencies of the firm's own employees, and low employee morale. In addition, organizations often find that it takes years of ongoing effort and a large up-front investment to develop a good working relationship with an outsourcing firm. Finding a reputable outsourcing partner can be especially difficult for a small or midsized firm that lacks experience in identifying and vetting contractors.

Outsourcing part or all of a business process introduces significant risks that the service provider will introduce quality problems into the supply chain. For example, Boeing made a strategic decision to partially outsource development of the 787 Dreamliner aircraft, with a goal of reducing costs by $4 billion and cutting development time by two years. However, the development effort spiraled out of control—the project was ultimately billions of dollars over budget and three years behind schedule. And outsourcing complications led to severe quality challenges, including problems with the aircraft's lithium ion batteries, which resulted in a worldwide temporary grounding of the aircraft a little more than a year after its launch.[14]

downsizing: Reducing the number of employees to cut costs.

Downsizing, a term frequently associated with outsourcing, involves reducing the number of employees to cut costs. The euphemistic term "right-sizing" is sometimes also used. When downsizing, companies usually look to downsize across the entire company, rather than picking a specific business process to downsize. Downsizing clearly reduces total payroll costs, although the quality of products and services and employee morale can suffer. Shortly after Heinz merged with Kraft in March 2015, the food and beverage company announced that it would downsize its 46,000 employees in the United States and Canada by 2,500 people to save $1.5 billion in annual costs.[15]

Critical Thinking Exercise

Outsourcing Accounting Functions

You have been employed for two years in the accounting department of a midsized multinational consumer products company. Your performance has been outstanding, and it is clear that management feels you have great potential with the firm. However, you are quite surprised when your manager calls you into her office to tell you that you have been chosen to lead an effort to identify an outsourcing partner for the payroll, accounts payable, and accounts receivable functions. She assures you that there will be an excellent assignment for you after the outsourcing is successfully completed and all is functioning well in one to two years.

Review Questions

1. What benefits might your organization gain from outsourcing basic accounting functions?
2. Identify at least three major organizational challenges associated with transitioning these functions to an outsourcing firm.

Critical Thinking Questions

1. What concerns do you have about taking on responsibility for outsourcing these business functions?
2. What questions about this assignment would you like to have addressed?

Organizational Culture and Change

culture: A set of major understandings and assumptions shared by a group, such as within an ethnic group or a country.

organizational culture: The major understandings and assumptions for a business, corporation, or other organization.

organizational change: How for-profit and nonprofit organizations plan for, implement, and handle change.

soft side of implementing change: The work designed to help employees embrace a new information system and way of working.

Culture is a set of major understandings and assumptions shared by a group, such as within an ethnic group or a country. **Organizational culture** consists of the major understandings and assumptions for an organization. The understandings, which can include common beliefs, values, and approaches to decision making, are often not stated or documented as goals or formal policies. For example, salaried employees might be expected to check their email and instant messages around the clock and be highly responsive to all such messages.

Mark Twain said, "It's not the progress I mind, it's the change I don't like." **Organizational change** deals with how organizations successfully plan for, implement, and handle change. Change can be caused by internal factors, such as those initiated by employees at all levels, or by external factors, such as those wrought by competitors, stockholders, federal and state laws, community regulations, natural disasters, and general economic conditions.

Implementing change, such as a new information system introduces conflict, confusion, and disruption. People must stop doing things the way they are accustomed to and begin doing them differently. Successful implementation of change only happens when people accept the need for change and believe that the change will improve their productivity and enable them to better meet their customers' needs. The so-called **soft side of implementing change** involves work designed to help employees embrace a new information system and way of working. This effort represents the biggest challenge to successful change implementation; yet, it is often overlooked or downplayed, resulting in project failure. Indeed, both the Standish Group and Gartner, two highly respected organizations that track project implementations globally, believe that a significant contributor to project failures is overlooking the need to address employee adoption and resistance jointly.[16] Another resource claims that 30 to 70 percent of large information systems projects fail, at least in part, due to a failure to prepare the business users for the actual change to come.[17]

The California Department of Consumer Affairs is made up of more than 40 entities (including multiple boards, bureaus, committees, and one commission) that regulate and license professional and vocational occupations that serve the people of California. Each year, the department processes over 350,000 applications for professional licensure along with some 1.2 million license renewals. The BreEZe project was initiated in 2009 to streamline the way the department does its business and interacts with its license applicants and consumers.[18] The resulting information system was intended to eliminate many paper-based processes and speed up the entire licensing process. Unfortunately, the project team failed to adequately involve the business users in the definition of the system requirements and instead made many erroneous decisions about how the system should work. The initial cost estimate for the system was $28 million; however, as of early 2015, project costs exceeded $37 million and less than half the licensing and regulatory boards were using the system. It is estimated that it will cost a total of $96 million to complete the project. Much of the delay and overspending could have been avoided had the project team work better with the business users to understand their needs.[19]

change management model: A description of the phases an individual or organization goes through in making a change and principles for successful implementation of change.

The dynamics of how change is implemented can be viewed in terms of a change management model. A **change management model** describes the phases an individual or organization goes through in making a change and provides principles for successful implementation of change. A number of models for dealing with the soft side of implementing change will now be introduced.

Lewin's Change Model

Lewin's change model: A three-stage approach for implementing change that involves unfreezing, moving, and refreezing.

Kurt Lewin and Edgar Schein proposed a three-stage approach for change called **Lewin's change model**. See Figure 2.6. The first stage, unfreezing, is ceasing old habits and creating a climate that is receptive to change. Moving, the second stage, involves learning new work methods, behaviors, and systems. The final stage, refreezing, involves reinforcing changes to make the new process second nature, accepted, and part of the job.

Unfreezing Preparing for change	**Moving** Making the change	**Refreezing** Institutionalizing
Key Tasks	**Key Tasks**	**Key Tasks**
Communicate what, why, when, who, how	Motivate individuals involved or affected	Monitor progress against success criteria
Draw on others, and seek input, ideas	Coach, train, lead, encourage, manage	Establish processes, systems to institutionalize change
Define objectives, success criteria, resources, schedule, budget	Provide appropriate resources	Establish controls to ensure change is occurring
Finalize work plans	Provide on-going feedback	Recognize and reward individuals for exhibiting new behavior
Assign leaders and implementation teams		Provide feedback, motivation, additional training to individuals not exhibiting new behavior

FIGURE **2.6**
Lewin's change model
Change involves three stages: unfreezing (preparing for change), moving (making the change), and refreezing (institutionalizing the change).

Lewin's Force Field Analysis

force field analysis: An approach to identifying both the driving (positive) and restraining (negative) forces that influence whether change can occur.

driving forces: The beliefs, expectations, and cultural norms that tend to encourage a change and give it momentum.

restraining forces: Forces that make it difficult to accept a change or to work to implement a change.

A frequently encountered stumbling block to the successful implementation of change, including the implementation of a new system, is negative user reaction. People affected by the change may fear that their positions may be eliminated or their work altered in a way they do not like. Or they may see the introduction of a new information system as a threat to their power and influence. Such fears can lead to resentment, lack of cooperation, or outright resistance. Any of these reactions can doom a change project, no matter how carefully the rest of the project is planned.

Lewin extended his change model theory to include **force field analysis**, which identifies both the driving (positive) and restraining (negative) forces that influence whether change can occur. The **driving forces** are beliefs, expectations, and cultural norms that tend to encourage a change and give it momentum. **Restraining forces** are those that make it difficult to accept a change or to work to implement a change. For a change to occur, the strength of the driving forces must exceed the strength of the restraining forces.[20]

This can be done in one of two ways: first, by creating new driving forces or making existing driving forces stronger and, second, by eliminating or weakening existing restraining forces.[20]

Figure 2.7 is an example of a force-field analysis of a group of workers after they first learn that a new information system is to be installed. The feelings shown on the left side are restraining forces against the change. The feelings shown on the right side are driving forces that support the change. The length of the arrow represents the relative strength of that feeling. In this example, fear of loss of job is the strongest restraining force.

FIGURE 2.7

Lewin's force field analysis before addressing concerns

Many strong restraining forces will make it difficult to implement this change.

Negative feelings must be reduced or eliminated in order for a new system to gain acceptance. The fear of losing one's job can be eliminated by making it clear that the individual will remain employed by the company. The fear of major changes in one's job can be reduced by allowing the individual to participate in developing one's own new job description. If this is not possible, the person should be thoroughly informed of the new job requirements and provided any necessary training. The positive impact of the change should be stressed.

It is not enough to reduce or neutralize negative feelings. Positive feelings must also be created to truly motivate the individual. Managers must take the time to explain the many tangible and intangible benefits for the organization as well as for the individual. For instance, in many information system efforts, the new system may lead to job enrichment by enabling the individual to take on more responsibility or to work in a new and more interesting way.

Figure 2.8 is an example of a force field analysis of workers after managers have effectively prepared them to accept the system. At this point, the workers should recognize several things: (1) their role is essential to the success of the system, and they are making an important contribution to the organization, (2) the development of new skills and knowledge will enhance their career growth, and (3) each individual has an important responsibility to perform within the project to secure the potential benefits for both the individual and the organization.

FIGURE **2.8**

Lewin's force field analysis after addressing concerns

Restraining forces have been weakened and driving forces strengthened so there is a much likelihood of successfully implementing this change.

Leavitt's diamond: An organizational change model that proposes that every organizational system is made up of four main components—people, tasks, structure, and technology—that all interact; any change in one of these elements will necessitate a change in the other three elements.

Leavitt's Diamond

Leavitt's diamond is another organizational change model that is extremely helpful in successfully implementing change. **Leavitt's diamond** proposes that every organizational system is made up of four main components—people, tasks, structure, and technology—that all interact; any change in one of these elements will necessitate a change in the other three elements. Thus, to successfully implement a new information system, appropriate changes must be made to the people, structure, and tasks affected by the new system. See Figure 2.9.

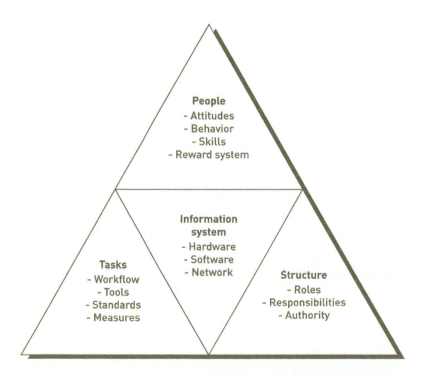

FIGURE **2.9**

Leavitt's diamond

Any change in technology, people, task, or structure will necessitate a change in the other three components.

People are the key to the successful implementation of any change. They must be convinced to adopt a positive attitude about the change and be willing to exhibit new behaviors consistent with the change. This is likely to require a change in the reward system to recognize those who exhibit the desired new behaviors. Thorough training in any required new skills is also needed.

The organization structure must be modified with appropriate changes in roles, responsibilities, and lines of authority. Along with these changes are required changes in communication patterns, relationships, and coordination among those affected by the change.

The tasks required to complete the work and the flow of work between tasks also need to be changed. For each task, standards on how the work is to be performed and measures for the quality of completion need to be established. New tools may be required to perform the tasks.

As a result, the major challenges to successful implementation of an information system are often more behavioral issues than technical. Successful introduction of an information system into an organization requires a mix of both good organizational change skills and technical skills. Strong, effective leadership is required to overcome the behavioral resistance to change and achieve a smooth and successful system introduction.

organizational learning: The adaptations and adjustments made within an organization based on experience and ideas over time.

Organizational learning is closely related to organizational change. All organizations adapt to new conditions or alter their practices over time—some better than others. Collectively, these adaptations and adjustments based on experience and ideas are called **organizational learning**. Hourly workers, support staff, managers, and executives learn better ways of fulfilling their role and then incorporate them into their day-to-day activities. In some cases, the adjustments can require a radical redesign of business processes (reengineering). In other cases, adjustments can be more incremental (continuous improvement). Both adjustments reflect an organization's strategy, the long-term plan of action for achieving its goals.

User Satisfaction and Technology Acceptance

technology acceptance model (TAM): A model that specifies the factors that can lead to better attitudes about an information system, along with higher acceptance and usage of it.

Reengineering and continuous improvement efforts (including implementation of new information systems) must be adopted and used to achieve the defined business objectives by targeted users. The **technology acceptance model (TAM)** specifies the factors that can lead to better attitudes about the use of a new information system, along with its higher acceptance and usage. See Figure 2.10. In this model, "perceived usefulness" is defined as the degree to which individuals believe that use of the system will improve their performance. The "perceived ease of use" is the degree to which individuals believe that the system will be easy to learn and use. Both the perceived usefulness and ease of use can be strongly influenced by the expressed opinions of

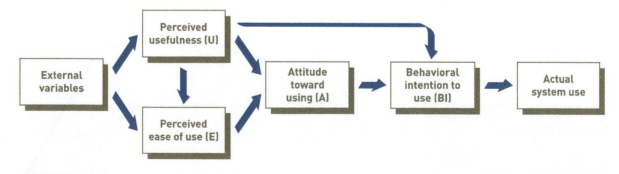

FIGURE **2.10**

Technology acceptance model

Perceived usefulness (U) and perceived ease of use (E) strongly influence whether someone will use an information system. Management can improve that perception by demonstrating that others have used the system effectively and by providing user training and support.

others who have used the system and the degree to which the organization supports use of the system (e.g., providing incentives and offering training and coaching from key users). Perceived usefulness and ease of use in turn influence an individual's attitude toward the system, which affect their behavioral intention to use the system.[21]

Avon Products is an international manufacturer and direct seller of beauty, household, and personal care products. Avon products are sold through six million independent and mostly part-time sales representatives worldwide who sell direct to family, friends, and personal contacts.[22] In 2013, Avon piloted a new sales system in Canada. The system was intended to streamline the ordering process through the use of iPads, which would allow the sales rep to display products to customers and then check inventory and place orders online. It was estimated that the project would generate some $40 million per year in cost savings and increased sales. Unfortunately, the system was poorly designed and did not meet the sales rep's expectations in terms of ease of use. Sales reps were often unable to log in to the system, and when they did get logged in, the system frequently would not accept orders, save orders correctly, or reserve inventory based on the orders placed. The system was neither useful nor easy to use. As a result, one Avon executive sales manager estimates that as many as 16,000 Canadian sales reps quit in large part out of frustration with the new system. The pilot was such a disaster that Avon wrote off the project at a cost of nearly $125 million.[23]

Diffusion of Innovation Theory

diffusion of innovation theory: A theory developed by E.M. Rogers to explain how a new idea or product gains acceptance and diffuses (or spreads) through a specific population or subset of an organization.

The **diffusion of innovation theory** was developed by E.M. Rogers to explain how a new idea or product gains acceptance and diffuses (or spreads) through a specific population or subset of an organization. A key point of this theory is that adoption of any innovation does not happen all at once for all members of the targeted population; rather, it is a drawn-out process, with some people quicker to adopt the innovation than others. See Figure 2.11. Rogers defined five categories of adopters, shown in Table 2.2, each with different attitudes toward innovation. When promoting an innovation to a target

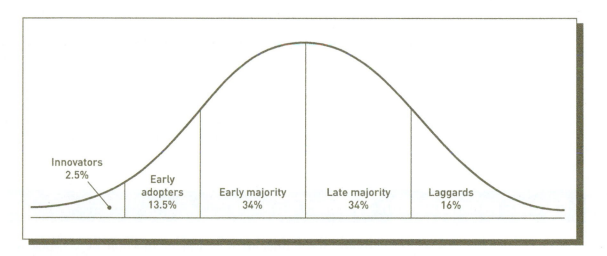

FIGURE **2.11**

Innovation diffusion

Adoption of any innovation does not happen all at once for all members of the targeted population; rather, it is a drawn-out process, with some people quicker to adopt the innovation than others.

Source: Everett Rogers, *Diffusion of Innovations.*

TABLE 2.2 Five categories of innovation adopters

Adopter Category	Characteristics	Strategy to Use
Innovator	Risk takers; always the first to try new products and ideas	Simply provide them with access to the new system and get out of their way
Early adopter	Opinion leaders whom others listen to and follow; aware of the need for change	Provide them assistance getting started
Early majority	Listen to and follow the opinion leaders	Provide them with evidence of the system's effectiveness and success stories
Late majority	Skeptical of change and new ideas	Provide them data on how many others have tried this and have used it successfully
Laggards	Very conservative and highly skeptical of change	Have their peers demonstrate how this change has helped them and bring pressure to bear from other adopters

population, it is important to understand the characteristics of the target population that will help or hinder adoption of the innovation and then to apply the appropriate strategy. This theory can be useful in planning the roll-out of a new information system.

Critical Thinking Exercise

Change Management for ERP System Project

You are a member of the human resources organization of a midsized manufacturing company that is implementing a new enterprise resource planning system that will have a major impact on the way some 50 members of the company perform their jobs. In addition, many other employees will need to be retrained on how to obtain the management reports and perform the data analysis they need for decision making.

Review Questions

1. How could Lewin's force field analysis be applied to this project?
2. How might the diffusion of innovation theory be applied to this project?

Critical Thinking Questions

1. You have been asked by the human resources department manager to assess the project plans to prepare the business users for the major changes to come. How might you proceed to make this assessment in a manner that will build rapport and trust with the project manager?
2. Imagine that your assessment shows that no plans have been developed to prepare the business users for the major changes to come other than training them a few weeks before the system is to be implemented. What suggestions would you make?

Careers in Information Systems

Today, most organizations cannot function or compete effectively without computer-based information systems. Indeed, organizations often attribute their productivity improvement, superior customer service, or competitive advantage in the marketplace to their information systems. The information system worker functions at the intersection of business and technology and designs and builds the solutions that allow organizations to effectively leverage information technology.

Successful information system workers must enjoy working in a fast-paced, dynamic environment where the underlying technology changes all the time. They must be comfortable with meeting deadlines and solving unexpected challenges. They need good communication skills and often serve as translators between business needs and technology-based solutions. Successful information systems workers must have solid analytical and decision-making skills and be able to translate ill-defined business problems and opportunities into effective technology-based solutions. They must develop effective team and leadership skills and be adept at implementing organizational change. Last, but not least, they need to be prepared to engage in life-long learning in a rapidly changing field.

Specific technical skills that some experts believe are important for IS workers to possess include the following, all of which are discussed in various chapters throughout this book:

- Capability to analyze large amounts of structured and unstructured data
- Ability to design and build applications for mobile devices
- Traditional programming and application development skills
- Technical support expertise
- Project management skills
- Knowledge of networking and cloud computing
- Ability to audit systems and implement necessary security measures
- Web design and development skills
- Knowledge of data center operations

Technology is one of the fastest-growing areas of the U.S. economy, and information systems professionals are in high demand. The U.S. Bureau of Labor Statistics (BLS) forecasts an increase of 1.2 million new computing jobs in the time period 2012 to 2022, as shown in Table 2.3. This is an average of 124,000 new jobs per year.

TABLE 2.3 BLS projections of computer-related jobs, 2012 to 2022

National Employment Matrix Title	Number		Change	Job Openings due to Growth and Replacements
	2012	2022		
Computer and math occupations (all numbers in thousands)				
Computer and information research scientists	26.7	30.8	4.1	8.3
Computer systems analysts	520.6	648.4	127.8	209.6
Information security analysts	75.1	102.5	27.4	39.2
Computer programmers	343.7	372.1	28.4	118.1
Software developers, applications	613.0	752.9	139.9	218.5
Software developers, system software	405.0	487.8	82.8	134.7
Web developers	141.4	169.9	28.5	50.7
Database administrators	118.7	136.6	17.9	40.3
Network and computer systems administrators	366.4	409.4	43.0	100.5
Computer network architects	143.4	164.3	20.9	43.5
Computer support specialists	722.3	845.3	123.0	236.5
Computer occupations, all other	205.8	213.6	7.8	40.2
Total	**3,682.1**	**4,333.6**	**651.5**	**1,240.1**
Yearly average				**124.0**

Source: "Employment by Detailed Occupation 2012–2022," Bureau of Labor Statistics, *www.bls.gov/emp/ep_table_102.htm,* accessed August 13, 2015.

While a career in information systems can be challenging, exciting, and rewarding, there are also some drawbacks to such a career. As reliance on technology increases, organizations have increasing expectations of their information system workers—so much so that many workers feel constant pressure to increase productivity, take on new tasks, and work more than 40 hours per week. A high degree of stress can accompany the responsibility to fix major systems or network problems that are impacting a large number of users. One must often interact with end users or customers who are frustrated and not in the best of moods.

Figure 2.12 identifies the occupations that the BLS predicts will be the fastest-growing IS positions from 2012 to 2022 along with the median salary for those positions in 2015 (half the people employed in this position make more than this amount; half make less).

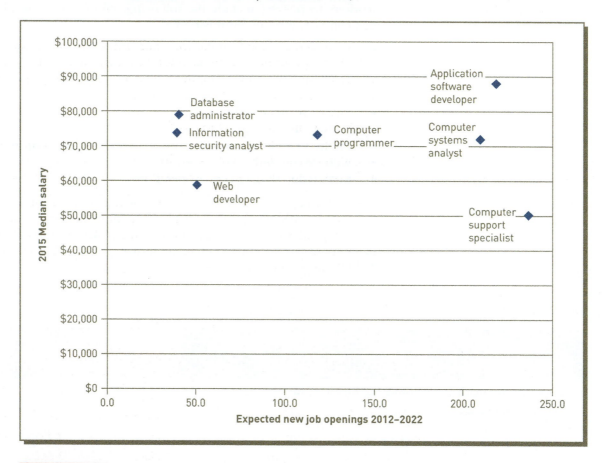

Occupational outlook for selected information systems positions

This chart shows the IS positions that BLS predicts will be among the fastest growing in the near future, along with the median salary for those positions in 2015.

Numerous schools have degree programs with titles such as business information systems, computer engineering, computer science, and management information systems. Figure 2.13 shows an estimate of the annual number of degrees awarded in computer science, computer engineering, and information (including information systems, information science, information technology, and informatics) in the United States and Canada. It appears that there will be a shortfall of about 33,900 workers per year.

Opportunities in information systems are also available to people from foreign countries. The U.S. L-1 and H-1B visa programs seek to allow skilled employees from foreign lands into the United States. Opportunities in these programs, however, are limited and are usually in high demand. The L-1 visa

FIGURE **2.13**

Supply versus demand for IS workers

The total number of IS-related job openings is expected to average about 124,000 per year between 2012 and 2022, while the number of IS-related graduates is expected to average about 88,100 per year—for a shortfall of 35,900 workers.

Source: "Computer Science Job Statistics", Exploring Computer Science, *www .exploringcs.org/resources/cs-statistics*, accessed August 19, 2015.

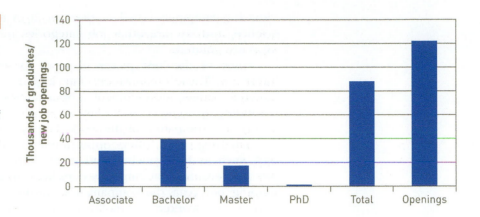

program is often used for intracompany transfers for multinational companies. The H-1B program can be used for new employees. The United States distributes its annual 85,000 allotment of visas via a lottery system wherein small tech companies submitting a single H-1B visa application must compete against large organizations that submit thousands of applications to increase their odds of winning the lottery.[24]

As part of the application process to obtain H-1B approval from the Labor Department, an employer is required to attest that the H-1B workers will not adversely affect the working conditions of workers similarly employed. However, in some cases, it appears that companies are hiring lower-paid H-1B workers to replace existing employees. For instance, in 2015, about 400 information system workers at Southern California Edison were fired and their work was shifted to H-1B contractors from Tata and Infosys. Another 100 or so information system workers at Northeast Utilities in Connecticut also lost their jobs to H-1B contractors.[25]

Proponents of the H-1B program believe that it is invaluable to the U.S. economy and its competitiveness. Table 2.4 shows the top 15 users of H-1B

TABLE **2.4** Top H-1B visa employers in 2013 to 2014

Rank	Company	Headquarters	Visas Granted		
			2013	2014	Total
1	Tata	India	6,258	7,149	13,407
2	Cognizant	United States	5,186	5,228	10,414
3	Infosys	India	6,298	4,022	10,320
4	Wipro	India	2,644	3,246	5,890
5	Accenture	Ireland	3,346	2,376	5,722
6	Tech Mahindra	India	1,589	1,850	3,439
7	IBM	United States	1,624	1,513	3,137
8	HCL	India	1,766	927	2,693
9	Larsen & Toubro	India	1,580	1,001	2,581
10	Syntel	United States	1,041	1,149	2,190
11	IGATE Technologies	United States	1,157	927	2,084
12	Microsoft	United States	1,048	712	1,760
13	Amazon	United States	881	811	1,692
14	Google	United States	753	696	1,449
15	CapGemini	France	500	699	1,199

Source: Thibodeau, Patrick and Machlis, Sharon, "Despite H-1B Lottery, Offshore Firms Dominate Visa Use," *Computerworld*, July 30, 2015; Machlis, Sharon and Thibodeau, Patrick, "Offshore Firms Took 50% of H-1B Visas in 2013," *Computerworld*, April 1, 2014.

visas for computer-related workers in 2013 to 2014. Engineering, medicine, science, and law are other job categories in which large numbers of H-1B visas are granted.

Some of the best places to work as an IS professional are listed in Table 2.5. These organizations rate high for a variety of reasons, including benefits, career development opportunities, diversity, company facilities (including, in some cases, an employee gym or swimming pool), training programs, and the nature of the work. For example, Sharp HealthCare, based in the San Diego area, offers opportunities to work with cutting-edge technology, such as telemedicine, and many formal and informal training classes. Avanade ensures that employees are kept up-to-date by requiring 80 hours of training per year; the company also provides a $2,000 annual allowance to improve its workers' work–life balance. Serv1Tech offers employees up to $5,000 per year for tuition or certification, and it makes an annual $5,000 contribution to each employee's 401(k) fund.[26]

TABLE 2.5 Best places to work as an IS professional

Rank	Small (<1,000 Employees)	Medium (1,001 to 4,999 Employees)	Large (> 5,000 Employees)
1	Noah Consulting	Credit Acceptance	Quicken Loans
2	Sev1Tech	Lafayette General Health	USAA
3	Commonwealth Financial Network	Avanade	Erickson Living
4	Secure-24	Autodesk	Sharp HealthCare
5	Connectria	Nicklaus Children's Hospital	Prudential Financial
6	Axxess	Financial Industry Regulatory Authority	LinkedIn
7	GlobalScape	CHG Health Services	Owens Corning
8	Bounce Exchange	NuStar Energy	DHL Express
9	Liquidnet	Akamai	University of Notre Dame
10	National Rural Electric Cooperative Association	Halifax Health	Genentech

Source: "2015 100 Best Places to Work in IT," *Computerworld*, July 2015.

Roles, Functions, and Careers in IS

IS offers many exciting and rewarding careers. Professionals with careers in information systems can work in an IS department or outside a traditional IS department as Web developers, computer programmers, systems analysts, computer operators, and in many other positions. Opportunities for IS professionals also exist in the public sector. In addition to technical skills, IS professionals need skills in written and verbal communication, an understanding of organizations and the way they operate, and the ability to work with people and in groups. At the end of every chapter in this book, you will find career exercises that will help you explore careers in IS and career areas that interest you.

Most medium to large organizations manage information system resources through an IS department. In smaller businesses, one or more people might manage information resources, with support from outsourced services. (Recall that outsourcing is also popular with many organizations.) As shown in Figure 2.14, the typical IS organization is divided into three main functions: operations, development, and support.

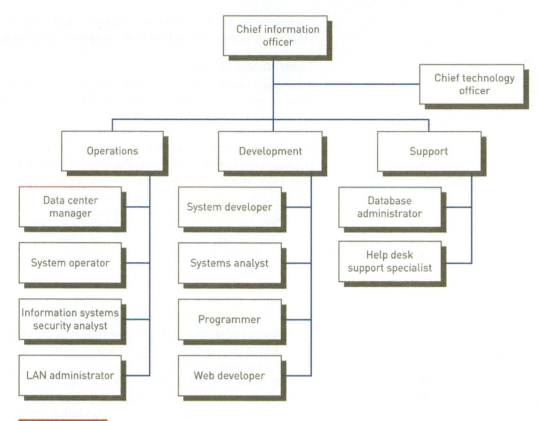

Three primary functions of the information systems organization
Each of these functions—operations, development, and support—encompasses several different IS roles.

Typical IS Titles and Functions

The organizational chart shown in Figure 2.14 is a simplified model of an IS department in a typical medium-sized or large organization. The following sections provide a brief description of these roles. Smaller firms often combine the roles shown in Figure 2.14 into fewer formal positions.

Chief Information Officer

The role of the chief information officer (CIO) is to employ an IS department's equipment and personnel to help the organization attain its goals. CIOs also understand the importance of finance, accounting, and return on investment. They can help companies avoid damaging ethical challenges by monitoring how their firms are complying with a large number of laws and regulations. A good CIO is typically a visionary who provides leadership and direction to the IS department to help an organization achieve its goals. CIOs need technical, business, and personal skills.

Senior IS Managers

A large organization may have several people employed in senior IS managerial levels with job titles such as vice president of information systems, manager of information systems, and chief technology officer (CTO). A central role of all these people is to communicate with other areas of the organization to determine changing business needs. Managers outside the IS organization may be part of an advisory or steering committee that helps the CIO and other IS managers make decisions about the use of information systems. Together, they can best decide what information systems will support corporate goals. The CTO, for example, typically works under a CIO and specializes in networks and related equipment and technology.

Operations Roles

The operations group is responsible for the day-to-day running of IS hardware to process the organization's information systems workload. It must also do capacity planning to expand and upgrade equipment to meet changing business needs. The operations group is constantly looking for ways to reduce the overall cost and increase the reliability of the organization's computing. This group is also responsible for protecting the company's IS systems and data from unauthorized access. Professionals in the operations group include those in the following positions:

- **Data center manager.** Data center managers are responsible for the maintenance and operation of the organization's computing facilities that may house a variety of hardware devices—mainframe and or supercomputers, large numbers of servers, storage devices, and networking equipment. Data center managers supervise other operations workers to accomplish the day-to-day work needed to support business operations as well as complete software and hardware upgrades. They also plan for capacity changes and develop business contingency plans in the event of a business disruption due to a fire, power outage, or natural disaster.
- **System operator.** System operators run and maintain IS equipment. They are responsible for efficiently starting, stopping, and correctly operating mainframe systems, networks, tape drives, disk devices, printers, and so on. Other operations include scheduling, maintaining hardware, and preparing input and output.
- **Information systems security analyst.** IS security analysts are responsible for maintaining the security and integrity of their organizations' systems and data. They analyze the security measures of the organization and identify and implement changes to make improvement. Security analysts are responsible for developing and delivering training on proper security measures. They also are responsible for creating action plans in the event of a security breach.
- **LAN administrator.** Local area network (LAN) administrators set up and manage network hardware, software, and security processes. They manage the addition of new users, software, and devices to the network. They also isolate and fix operations problems.

Development Roles

The development group is responsible for implementing the new information systems required to support the organization's existing and future business needs. Importantly, they must also modify existing information systems as the needs of the organization evolve and change. They are constantly on the watch for new ways to use information systems to improve the competitiveness of the firm. Professionals in the development group include those in the following positions:

- **Software developer.** These individuals are involved in writing the software that customers and employees use. This includes testing and debugging the software as well as maintaining and upgrading software after it is released for operation. Software developers frequently collaborate with management, clients, and others to build a software product from scratch, according to a customer's specifications, or to modify existing software to meet new business needs.
- **Systems analyst.** Systems analysts frequently consult with management and users, and they convey system requirements to software developers

and network architects. They also assist in choosing and configuring hardware and software, matching technology to users' needs, monitoring and testing the system in operation, and troubleshooting problems after implementation.

- **Programmer.** Programmers convert a program design developed by a systems analyst or software developer into one of many computer languages. To do this, they must write, debug, and test the program to ensure that it will operate in a way that it will meet the users' needs.
- **Web developers.** These professionals design and maintain Web sites, including site layout and function, to meet the client's requirements. The creative side of the job includes creating a user-friendly design, ensuring easy navigation, organizing content, and integrating graphics and audio (Figure 2.15). The more technical responsibilities include monitoring Web site performance and capacity.

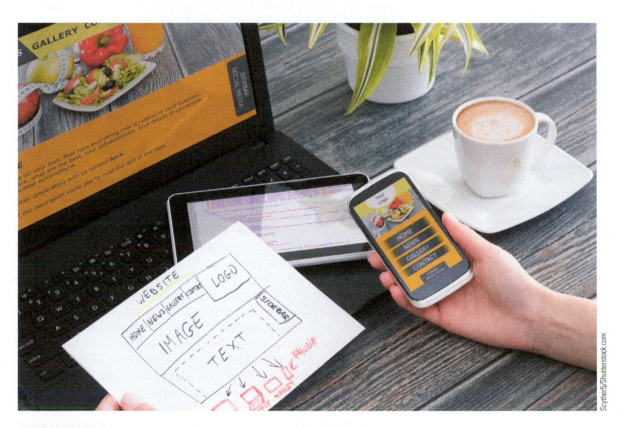

FIGURE 2.15

Web developers

Web developers create and maintain company Web sites.

Support

The support group provides customer service for the employees, customers, and business partners who rely on the firm's information systems and service to accomplish their work. The support group responds to queries from these constituents and attempts to be proactive in eliminating problems before they occur. They often develop and provide training to users to enable them to better use information systems services and equipment. Professionals in the support group include those in the following positions:

- **Database administrator.** Database administrators (DBAs) design and set up databases to meet an organization's needs. DBAs ensure that the databases operate efficiently, and they perform fine-tuning, upgrading, and testing modifications as needed. They are also responsible for implementing security measures to safeguard the company's most sensitive data.

- **System support specialist.** These skilled specialists respond to telephone calls, electronic mail, and other inquiries from computer users regarding hardware, software, networking, or other IS-related problems or needs. System support specialists diagnose the problem through dialogue with the user, research solutions, and implement a plan to resolve the problem or refer the issue to specialized IS staff. Many organizations set up "drop-in" centers, where users can come to meet face-to-face with the help desk specialists to get help.

IS-Related Roles outside the IS Organization

In addition to IS workers placed within the IS organization, some companies have people who take on IS-related roles but reside outside the IS organization. For example, data scientists, can be found in the marketing, sales, and supply chain management departments of large organizations. Data scientists are responsible for understanding the business analytics technology as well as the business, and then putting all of that together to deliver improvements in decision making.

Based on a recent survey of 165 organizations representing over $45 billion in information technology spending in Europe and the United States, only about 60 percent of all information technology outlays are controlled by the information systems department. This means other business units are responsible for 40 percent of the total information technology costs within an organization.[27] **Shadow IT** is a term used to describe the information systems and solutions built and deployed by departments other than the information systems department. In many cases, the information systems department may not even be aware of these efforts.

At one time, shadow IT was limited to employee or departmental purchases of nonstandard computing devices and off-the-shelf software from office supply stores. However, the scope of shadow IT spending has greatly expanded, largely due to cloud computing and the availability of enterprise software, file-sharing apps, and collaboration tools as a service. Cloud service providers can deliver increasing amounts of computing, network, and storage capacity on demand and without requiring any capital investment on the part of the cloud users. These cloud providers typically offer a monthly or annual subscription service model; they may also provide training, support, and data integration services. All of this makes it easier for department managers to skirt formal procedures associated with the purchase of large capital expense items—including scrutiny by the information system department.

Shadow IT enables business managers to quickly create highly innovative solutions to real business problems and to test out these solutions. Such systems may serve as prototypes that evolve into future approved IT solutions. However, shadow IT solutions frequently employ nonapproved vendors, software, or hardware and may not meet the IS department standards for control, documentation, security, support, and reliability. This raises security risks and issues in regard to compliance with essential government and industry standards, such as Basel III (international standards for the banking industry), FISMA (Federal Information Security Management Act of 2002), GAAP (Generally Accepted Accounting Principles), HIPAA (Health Insurance Portability and Accountability Act), IFRS (International Financial Reporting Standards), and Sarbanes-Oxley Act (accounting regulations for publicly traded companies).

Issues often arise when a shadow IT solution "breaks" and questions are raised about who is responsible for fixing it and supporting the end users. The IS department may not have developed it, or not even been aware of it, but business users expect their help in "fixing" it. Table 2.6 presents a summary of the pros and cons associated with shadow IT.

shadow IT: The information systems and solutions built and deployed by departments other than the information systems department. In many cases, the information systems department may not even be aware of these efforts.

TABLE 2.6 Pros and cons of shadow IT efforts

Pros	Cons
Enables the business to test quick solutions to business needs without delays brought on by involvement of information systems.	The systems and processes developed may lack necessary levels of security required to meet compliance standards.
Can create an innovative, synergistic partnership between the information systems department and other business units.	Can create tension between the CIO who has responsibility for technology within the organization and business managers who want more of a role in the information system decisions.
Provides the opportunity to evaluate and test many more information system initiatives.	Individual departments may buy services, software, and hardware that the company could get a better deal through central purchasing.
	May be wasteful and duplicate work already being done by the IS organization.
	Issues can arise over responsibility to fix "nonapproved" solutions.

The information systems department may become more comfortable with shadow IT if it sees the IS department's role as maximizing the effective use of technology in the company rather than controlling the use of technology. Also shadow IT provides another source of funds to tackle high-priority projects.

Certification

certification: A process for testing skills and knowledge; successful completion of a certification exam results in a statement by the certifying authority that confirms an individual is capable of performing particular tasks.

Often, the people-filling IS roles have completed some form of certification. **Certification** is a process for testing skills and knowledge; successful completion of a certification exam results in an endorsement by the certifying authority that an individual is capable of performing particular tasks or jobs. Certification frequently involves specific, vendor-provided, or vendor-endorsed coursework. Popular certification programs include Microsoft Certified Systems Engineer (MCSE), Certified Information Systems Security Professional (CISSP), Oracle Certified Professional, and Cisco Certified Security Professional (CCSP). Getting certified from a software, database, or network company may open the door to new career possibilities or result in an increase in pay. According to a recent survey, 65 percent of employers use IT certifications to differentiate between equally qualified candidates, while 72 percent of employers require some form of IT certification as a requirement for certain job roles. In some organizations, earning certain certifications can result in a pay increase or eligibility for a new role. The following is a list of some of the more in demand certifications.[28]

- Citrix Certified Enterprise Engineer
- Comp TIA Security+
- GIAC Certified Windows System Administrator
- Certified Computer Examiner
- AWS Certified SysOps Administrator-Associate (Cloud)
- EC-Council Certified Security Analyst
- Mongo DB Certified DBA
- Microsoft Certified Solution Developer: Applications Lifecycle Management
- Cisco Certified Design Associate

Other IS Careers

In addition to working for an IS department in an organization, IS personnel can work for large consulting firms, such as Accenture, IBM, and Hewlett-Packard. Some consulting jobs entail frequent travel because consultants are assigned to work on various projects, wherever the client is. Such jobs require excellent project management and people skills in addition to IS technical skills. Related career opportunities include computer training, computer and computer-equipment sales, and computer equipment repair and maintenance.

Other IS career opportunities include being employed by technology companies, such as Oracle, IBM, HP, Microsoft, Google, and Dell. Such a career enables an individual to work on the cutting edge of technology, which can be challenging and exciting.

As some computer companies cut their services to customers, new companies are being formed to fill the need. With names such as Speak with a Geek and Geek Squad, these companies are helping people and organizations with computer-related problems that computer vendors are no longer solving.

Some people decide to start their own IS businesses rather than continue to work for someone else. One such entrepreneur, Lavanya Purushothaman, started ATS Solutions, a UK-based company that offers software development services and consulting to a wide range of industries and business areas. Small business owners like Purushothaman often prefer to be their own boss, with the freedom to think innovatively and take on new challenges.[29] Other people become IS entrepreneurs or freelancers, working from home writing programs, working on IS projects with larger businesses, or developing new applications for the iPhone or similar devices. Some Internet sites, such as *www.freelancer.com*, post projects online and offer information and advice for people working on their own. Many freelancers work for small- to medium-sized enterprises in the U.S. market. People doing freelance or consulting work must be creative in pursuing new business, while also protecting themselves financially. Freelancers and consultants must aggressively market their talents, and to ensure they are paid, should insist that some or all of their fees for a given project are put into an escrow account.

Working in Teams

Most IS careers involve working in project teams that can consist of many of the positions and roles discussed earlier. Thus, it is always good for IS professionals to have good communication skills and the ability to work with other people. Many colleges and universities have courses in information systems and related areas that require students to work in project teams. At the end of every chapter in this book are team activities that require teamwork to complete a project. You may be required to complete one or more of these team-oriented assignments.

Finding a Job in IS

Traditional approaches to finding a job in the information systems area include attending on-campus visits from recruiters and getting referrals from professors, friends, and family members. People who have quit jobs or been laid off often use informal networks of colleagues or business acquaintances from their previous jobs to help find new jobs.

Many colleges and universities have excellent programs to help students develop résumés and conduct job interviews. Developing an online résumé can be critical to finding a good job. Many companies only accept résumés online and screen job candidates using software to search for key words and skills. Consequently, mentioning the right key words and skills in your resume can mean the difference between getting and not getting a job interview. Some corporate recruiters, however, are starting to actively search for employees rather than sifting through thousands of online résumés or posting jobs on their Web sites. Instead, these corporate recruiters do their own Internet searches and check with professional job sites such as *www.branchout.com*, *www.indeed.com*, *www.linkedin.com*, and *www.ziprecruiter.com* to name just a few. Other companies hire college students to help them market products and services to other students. In addition to being paid, students can get invaluable career experience. In some cases, it can help them get jobs after graduation.

Students who use the Internet to access other nontraditional sources to find IS jobs have more opportunities to land a job. Many Web sites, such as Monster, Career Builders, Indeed, Simply Hired, Snagged a Job, TheLadders, LinkedIn, and ComputerJobs, post job opportunities for information system careers as well as more traditional careers. Most large companies list job opportunities on their corporate Web sites. These sites allow prospective job hunters to browse job opportunities and get information on job location, salary, and benefits. In addition, some sites allow job hunters to post their résumés. Many people use social networking sites such as Facebook to help get job leads. Corporate recruiters also use the Internet and social network sites to gather information on current job candidates or to locate new job candidates.

Many professional organizations and online user groups can be helpful in finding a job, staying current once employed, and seeking new career opportunities. These groups include the Association for Computer Machinery (ACM: *www.acm.org*), the Association of Information Technology Professionals (AITP: *www.aitp.org*), Apple User Groups (*www.apple.com/usergroups*), and Linux user groups based in various countries around the world.

Many companies use Twitter to advertise job openings in industries such as advertising and public relations, consulting, consumer products, and education, among others. Many organizations in the information systems industry, including Google (@googlejobs), Intel (@jobsatIntel), Microsoft (@Microsoft_-Jobs), and Yahoo (@EngRecruiter), also use Twitter to advertise job openings.

Students should review and edit what is posted about them on social media sites, as employers often search the Internet to get information about potential employees before they make hiring decisions. Over 90 percent of respondents to a recent survey either use or plan to use some form of social media—such as Facebook, LinkedIn, or Twitter—in their recruiting.[30]

Critical Thinking Exercise

Product Supply Turns to Shadow IT

You are a section manager in the product supply department of a midsized manufacturing firm. The department manager has called a meeting of all section managers to outline his plan to contract with a cloud service provider to provide sales forecasting and inventory management software and services. The goal is to reduce the number of out-of-stock occurrences while maintaining a minimum level of finished product inventory. The cloud service provider requires detailed order, shipment, and promotion data for the past three years in addition to ongoing current data. Members of the product supply department will be able to access the software to develop sales forecasts and make better manufacturing and inventory decisions.

Review Questions

1. What are the arguments for and against shadow IT?
2. What are the possible motivations for your manager to recommend the use of shadow IT?

Critical Thinking Questions

1. What potential issues could arise from this proposed project?
2. The department manager has just completed his discussion and is asking for comments and questions. What would you say?

Summary

Principle:

Organizations are open systems that affect and are affected by their surrounding environment.

An organization is a group of people that is structured and managed to meet its mission or set of group goals. Organizations affect and are affected by their environment.

The value chain is a series of activities that an organization performs to transform inputs into outputs in such a way that the value of the input is increased.

The supply chain is a key value chain whose primary activities include inbound logistics, operations, outbound logistics, marketing and sales, and service. Supply chain management encompasses all the activities required to get the right product into the right consumer's hands in the right quantity at the right time and at the right cost.

Information systems have transformed the nature of work and the shape of organizations themselves. They are often so intimately involved in the activities of the value chain that they are a part of the process itself.

A virtual team is a group of individuals whose members are distributed geographically, but who collaborate and complete work through the use of information systems.

Principle:

Positive change is a key ingredient for any successful organization.

Innovation is the application of new ideas to the products, processes, and activities of a firm, leading to increased value. Innovation is the catalyst for the growth and success of any organization. Innovation may be classified as sustaining or disruptive.

Business process reengineering is a form of innovation that involves the radical redesign of business processes, organizational structures, information systems, and values of the organization to achieve a breakthrough in results. Continuous improvement is a form of innovation that continually improves business processes to add value to products and services.

Outsourcing is a long-term business arrangement in which a company contracts for services with an outside organization that has expertise in providing a specific function. Offshore outsourcing is an outsourcing arrangement in which the organization providing the service is located in a country different from the firm obtaining the services. Downsizing involves reducing the number of employees to cut costs. All these staffing alternatives are an attempt to reduce costs or improve services. Each approach has its own associated ethical issues and risks.

Principle:

Information systems must be implemented in such a manner that they are accepted and work well within the context of an organization and support its fundamental business goals and strategies.

Organizational culture consists of the major understandings and assumptions for a business, a corporation, or an organization. According to the concept of organizational learning, organizations adapt to new conditions or alter practices over time.

Organizational change deals with how organizations successfully plan for, implement, and handle change. The ability to introduce change effectively is critical to the success of any information system project.

Several change models can be used to increase the likelihood of successfully introducing a new information system into an organization.

Lewin's three-stage organization change model divides the change implementation process into three stages: unfreezing, moving, and refreezing. The model also identifies key tasks that need to be performed during each stage.

Lewin's force field analysis is an approach to identifying the driving (positive) and restraining (negative) forces that influence whether change can occur.

Leavitt's diamond proposes that every organizational system is made up of four main components—people, tasks, structure, and technology—that all interact. To successfully implement a new information system, appropriate changes must be made to the people, structure, and tasks affected by the new system.

The user satisfaction and technology acceptance model specifies the factors that can lead to better attitudes about the use of a new information system, along with higher acceptance and use of it.

The diffusion of innovation theory explains how a new idea or product gains acceptance and diffuses through a specific population or subset of an organization. A key point of this theory is that adoption of any innovation does not happen all at once for all people; rather, it is a drawn-out process, with some people quicker to adopt the innovation than others. The theory groups adopters into five categories and recommends a different adoption strategy for each category.

Principle:

The information system worker functions at the intersection of business and technology and designs, builds, and implements solutions that allow organizations to effectively leverage information technology systems.

Successful information system workers need to have a variety of personal characteristics and skills, including the ability to work well under pressure, good communication skills, solid analytical and decision-making skills, effective team and leadership skills, and adeptness at implementing organizational change.

Technology is one of the fastest-growing areas of the U.S. economy, which has a strong demand for information system workers.

Opportunities in information systems are available to people from foreign countries under the H-1B and L-1 visa programs.

The IS organization has three primary functions: operations, development, and support.

Typical operations roles include data center manager, system operator, information system security analyst, and LAN administrator.

Typical development roles include software developer, systems analyst, programmer, and Web developer.

Typical support roles include database administrator and system support specialist.

Only about 60 percent of all information technology outlays are controlled by the information systems department. Shadow IT is a term used to describe the information systems and solutions built and deployed by departments other than the information systems department. In many cases, the information systems department may not even be aware of these efforts.

Certification is a process for testing skills and knowledge; successful completion of a certification exam results in an endorsement by the certifying authority that an individual is capable of performing particular tasks or jobs. Certification frequently involves specific, vendor-provided, or vendor-endorsed coursework.

Besides working for an IS department in an organization, IS personnel can work for a large consulting firm or a hardware or software manufacturer. Developing or selling products for a hardware or software vendor is another IS career opportunity.

Key Terms

business process reengineering (BPR)

certification

change management model

continuous improvement

culture

diffusion of innovation theory

downsizing

driving forces

force field analysis

innovation

Leavitt's diamond

Lewin's change model

offshore outsourcing

offshoring

organization

organizational change

organizational culture

organizational learning

outsourcing

process redesign

reengineering

restraining forces

shadow IT

soft side of implementing change

supply chain

supply chain management (SCM)

technology acceptance model (TAM)

value chain

virtual team

Chapter 2: Self-Assessment Test

Organizations are open systems that affect and are affected by their surrounding environment.

1. Organizations are considered to be _____ systems, meaning that can affect and are affected by their surrounding environment.

2. The _____ is a series of activities that an organization performs to transform inputs into outputs in such a way that the value of the input is increased.
   a. supply chain
   b. inbound logistics
   c. value chain
   d. manufacturing

3. _____ encompasses all the activities required to get the right product into the right customer's hands in the right quantity at the right time and at the right cost.

4. Which of the following is not a true statement regarding the use of virtual teams?
   a. Virtual teams enable the organization to enlist the best people in different geographical regions to solve important organizational problems.
   b. The use of virtual teams provides the ability to staff a team with people who have a wide range of experience and knowledge that stems from a variety of professional experiences and cultural backgrounds.
   c. It is usually easy and convenient for all members of a virtual team to meet at the same time and physical location.
   d. Members of a virtual team may feel that their work day never ends.

Positive change is a key ingredient for any successful organization.

5. Continuous enhancement of an existing product is an example of _____ innovation.

6. A long-term business arrangement in which a company contracts for services with an outside organization located in another country to provide a specific business function is called _____.
   a. business process reengineering
   b. outsourcing
   c. downsizing
   d. offshore outsourcing

7. _____ of large information system projects fail, at least in part, due to a failure to prepare business users for the actual change to come.
   a. Less than 15 percent
   b. Over 80 percent
   c. About 48 percent
   d. Between 30 and 70 percent

Information systems must be implemented in such a manner that they are accepted and work well within the context of an organization and support its fundamental business goals and strategies.

8. The three stages of Lewin's change model include (1) ceasing old habits and creating a climate that is receptive to change; (2) learning new work methods, behaviors, and systems; and (3) _____.
   a. reinforcing changes to make the new process second nature, accepted, and part of the job

b. fine-tuning existing work processes and systems so they become more streamlined and efficient

c. replacing existing users that refuse to accept the change

d. rewarding those responsible for the change

9. The _____ change model is helpful in identifying and addressing negative feelings that make it difficult for users to accept the move to a new information system.
   a. Leavitt's diamond
   b. Lewin's force field analysis
   c. Diffusion of innovation theory
   d. Lewin's change model

The information system worker functions at the intersection of business and technology and designs, builds, and implements solutions that allow organizations to effectively leverage information technology systems.

10. The Bureau of Labor Statistics forecasts an increase of _____ new computing jobs in the time period 2012 to 2022.
    a. .12 million
    b. .5 million
    c. 1.0 million
    d. 1.2 million

11. The typical information systems organization is typically divided into three functions, including support, development, and _____.

12. _____ is a process for testing skills and knowledge; successful completion of a certification exam results in an endorsement by the certifying authority that an individual is capable of performing particular tasks or jobs.

Chapter 2: Self-Assessment Test Answers

1. open
2. c
3. Supply chain management
4. c
5. sustaining
6. d
7. d
8. d
9. b
10. d
11. operations
12. Certification

Review Questions

1. What is the difference between a value chain and a supply chain?
2. What activities are encompassed by supply chain management?
3. What are some of the characteristics of a virtual team?
4. Identify and briefly describe the differences between the two types of innovation discussed in the chapter.
5. Briefly define the term "business process reengineering."
6. What is meant by continuous improvement?
7. What is outsourcing? How is it different from offshoring?
8. What is meant by the term "the soft side of implementing change"?
9. What do the terms "organizational culture" and "organizational learning" mean?
10. Sketch and briefly describe Leavitt's diamond.
11. List and describe three popular job-finding Web sites.
12. Describe the role of a CIO within an organization.
13. What is meant by the term "shadow IT"?

Discussion Questions

1. Discuss a value chain of which you are a part. What is the purpose of the value chain? What is your role? How do you interact with other members of the value chain? How is the effectiveness of the value chain measured?
2. Discuss a virtual team of which you are a member. What is the role of the team? How were the members of the team chosen, and what unique skills and experiences does each member bring to the team? How does the team communicate and share information?

3. What things might managers in an organization do that could unintentionally discourage innovation by their employees? How can innovation be encouraged?

4. Identify and briefly discuss the similarities and differences between outsourcing and downsizing. How might an enlightened management team deal with the negative impacts of either downsizing or outsourcing?

5. Identify several aspects of the culture shared by members of a group to which you belong. Are there any aspects of this culture that you think are negative and detract from what the group is trying to accomplish?

6. Your manager has asked for your input on ideas for how to improve the likelihood of successful adoption of a major new information system that will be used by members of the company's finance department. What suggestions would you offer?

7. You have been asked to assess the success of a recently implemented system that has been deployed across the entire supply chain of a large organization. How might you go about trying to measure the technology diffusion of this system? How else might you assess the success of this system?

8. Describe the advantages and disadvantages of using the Internet to search for a job.

9. Assume you are a member of a committee responsible for replacing your organization's retiring CIO. What characteristics would you want in a new CIO? How would you go about identifying qualified candidates?

10. Identify several personal characteristics needed to be successful in an information system career. Which of these characteristics do you think you possess?

Problem-Solving Exercises

1. Figure 2.15 presents the occupational outlook (median salary and number of job openings) for selected information systems positions. Obtain data from the U.S. Bureau of Labor Statistics and use a spreadsheet program to create a similar figure for five occupations of your choice.

2. Use graphics software to develop a force field analysis of the restraining forces and driving forces that would impact your decision to change majors or to seek a new job.

3. Do research to learn more about GE's Change Acceleration Management process. Prepare a slide presentation that summarizes the key steps in the process and outlines the advantages of this process.

Team Activities

1. With your team, interview a manager in a successful organization about that organization's culture. Try to identify both positive and negative aspects of that culture. Discuss whether the manager employs any organizational change model when introducing a major change.

2. Develop a set of interview questions and outline a process that you and your team might follow to assess the degree of user satisfaction and technology acceptance of a major new system.

3. Do research to learn about the use of focus groups to gain insight into how people view a new product or idea. With your team, design a set of focus group questions that could be used to assess a work groups feelings about a new information system to be implemented.

Web Exercises

1. Do research online to identify the number of new H-1B visas granted this year by job category—administrative specializations, education, engineering, information systems, law, medicine and health, math and physical science, and other.

2. Identify the three top-ranked places to work as an IS professional. What makes these places so attractive? Are these features and benefits of importance to you?

3. Do research on the Web to learn about how recruiters use social network data to help screen job applicants. Does what you learn raise any concerns about how you could be viewed?

Career Exercises

1. Do research on an entrepreneur that you admire. Write a brief description of how the individual was able to start a business. What challenges had to be overcome? Did the individual encounter failure before becoming a success?
2. For you, what would be the most positive aspects of a career in information systems? What would be the least positive aspects of such a career?
3. Use presentation software (e.g., Microsoft PowerPoint) to prepare a brief slide presentation that describes your idea job in terms of role, responsibilities, interaction with others, degree of decision-making authority, and other characteristics important to you.

Case Studies

Case One

Railroads Struggle to Implement Positive Train Control

Positive train control (PTC) is a complex system designed to prevent the human errors that cause roughly 40 percent of train accidents, including train-to-train collisions, derailments caused by excess speed, train movement through track switches left in the wrong position, and unauthorized incursion into work zones. PTC uses wireless communications to relay visual and audible data to train crew members regarding when the train needs to be slowed or stopped. This guidance is based on several factors, including the train's location and speed, as determined by GPS, track geometry, the status and position of approaching switches, and speed limits at approaching curves, crossings, and other speed-restriction areas. PTC communicates with the train's onboard computer, which audibly warns the engineer and displays the train's safe-braking distance, based on conditions at that time. Should the engineer fail to respond appropriately, the onboard computer will activate the brakes and safely slow or stop the train.

The National Transportation Safety Board (NTSB) has investigated 145 "PTC-preventable" railroad accidents that occurred since 1969. The NTSB estimates that some 300 deaths and over 6,700 injuries could have been prevented had PTC systems been in place. Congress mandated in the Rail Safety Improvement Act of 2008 that railroads implement PTC systems on rail lines that (1) carry more than 5 million tons annually, (2) carry poisonous or toxic materials, or (3) carry commuter rail passenger service. The act specified a deadline of December 31, 2015, for implementation of PTC.

Metrolink is a commuter rail system serving southern California and the greater Los Angeles area. A 2008 Metrolink accident that killed 25 and injured 100 is often cited as the event that drove Congress to pass the Rail Safety Improvement Act. In that accident, a Metrolink commuter train collided head-on with a Union Pacific train because the Metrolink engineer, who had been texting, failed to stop for a red signal.

An executive of the Association of American Railroads estimates that PTC has been installed on 8,200 miles out of the 60,000 miles where PTC technology is mandated. He also believes that, for a number of reasons, the railroads cannot complete the installation of PTC until the end of 2018 and that it will take an additional two years to test that all the system components work together correctly.

The Federal Railroad Administration (FRA) estimates the cost of the PTC system to be $52,000 per mile of track—for a total of more than $3 billion for the 60,000 miles of track to be covered. Meanwhile, the railroads estimate the total cost will be more than $9 billion and claim they have spent $5.2 billion on this effort already.

One complicating factor relates to the fact that PTC systems require access to a wireless frequency in order to operate. The Federal Communications Commission regulates the use of radio frequencies and grants exclusive access or licenses to certain frequencies. This ensures that operators don't interfere with one another by broadcasting signals over the same frequency. Demand for access to frequencies in the wireless broadband spectrum has soared due to the rapid growth in use of cell phones, smartphones, and mobile computing devices. The railroads must acquire a license to operate their wireless PTC system at a certain frequency, but another company may already own the rights to that frequency band in a certain area. In some cases, railroads have struggled for years to buy the rights to airwaves to operate their PTC equipment.

Tracks on which multiple carriers operate present a higher risk of collisions. The continued smooth, uninterrupted operations of each PTC system as the train crosses tracks operated by different rail carriers is critical even when that carrier's PTC system is built on hardware, software, and track switches from an entirely different set of vendors.

Critical Thinking Questions

1. Develop a force field analysis that approximates the strength of the driving and restraining forces for PTC.
2. The high cost of implementing changes to infrastructure always raises questions about priorities. Should investments in infrastructure be made to address high-impact, low-probability events (such as human-error-caused accidents) or should investments be

focused on low-impact, high-probability events (such as the need for ongoing cleaning and maintenance of train stations and installing air conditioning)? Make an argument in favor of accelerating deployment of PTC giving three strong reasons supporting this decision. Now take the other side and present a strong argument against PTC deployment and offering an alternative solution.

3. Do research to determine the current status of PTC deployment. Summarize your findings in a couple of paragraphs.

SOURCES: "An Introduction to Positive Train Control," *metrolinktrains.com/agency/page/title/ptc*, accessed October 3, 2015; "Report to Congress on the Status of Positive Train Control Implementation," U.S. Department of Transportation Federal Railroad Administration, August 7, 2015, *www.fra.dot.gov/eLib/details/L16962*; Shear, Michael D. and Mouawad, Jad, "Amtrak Says Shortfalls and Rules Delayed Its Safety System," *New York Times*, May 14, 2015, *nytimes.com/2015/05/15/us/amtrak-says-it-was-just-months-away-from-installing-safety-system.html?_r=0*; "Investigating the Philadelphia Amtrak Train Derailment," *New York Times*, May 12, 2015, *nytimes.com/interactive/2015/05/13/us/investigating-the-philadelphia-amtrak-train-crash.html*; "About Us," *www.metrolinktrains.com/agency/page/title/member_agencies*, accessed October 3, 2015.

Case Two

Nordstrom's Innovation Efforts Recognize the Importance of the Soft Side of Implementing Change

Based in Seattle, Washington, Nordstrom Inc. is an upscale department store chain that operates more than 300 stores across the United States and Canada. The company got its start in 1901 as a small shoe store in downtown Seattle, and it has since grown into a well-regarded fashion specialty chain with net sales of more than $13.1 billion in 2014. Nordstrom has built a loyal customer following through its quality products and its almost legendary customer service. The company prides itself on its culture, which supports and empowers employees, and for the last decade, the company has consistently been named one of Fortune magazine's "100 Best Companies to Work For."

In keeping with its commitment to quality, Nordstrom has invested heavily in innovation throughout its organization—by embracing omnichannel retailing strategies that allow customers to make purchases in the store, online, and via mobile devices, and through its approach to developing and supporting the variety of information systems that fuel the company's growth.

For instance, Nordstrom looked for innovative solutions to help it revamp its approach to developing mobile apps after a detailed analysis of internal processes determined that its typical development cycle for updating customer mobile apps was 22 to 28 weeks—far too long to keep the company competitive in the rapidly changing mobile marketplace. The project was successful (cutting development cycles down to 30 days or less) because the company took the time to thoroughly map all of the processes—and then shared that detail with employees and other stakeholders. Through that process it became clear to everyone involved how much

change was needed in order for the company to stay competitive on the digital front. In addition, having every step mapped out showed each individual team how it needed to change.

According to Courtney Kissler, Nordstrom's vice president of e-commerce and store technologies, the process analysis work that Nordstrom performed at the start of the project provided the data that helped build momentum for change within the organization. Kissler's advice to other teams looking to make such a transformation is, "Make the conversation as much about data as possible and not about emotion. A lot of the skeptics come around once they see [the data]."

In another effort to strengthen its innovation practices, the retailer recently made changes to its "Innovation Lab," which it established in 2010 to focus on jumpstarting technology projects. Over time, the company came to realize that those efforts needed to be better integrated into the business groups in order to spur collaboration between the technology innovators and other Nordstrom employees—and encourage acceptance of new initiatives. Therefore, the company moved most of its technologists out of its central lab and into the different business groups so they could work more closely with end users, especially those who work directly with customers. This approach "works better because we have a broader intake of new ideas from both business and technology teams," according to Nordstrom CIO Dan Little.

These changes in the way Nordstrom is innovating and providing the information systems that support its core business mean that Nordstrom employees—both on the technical and the business side—need to learn new ways of working with technology and the development process. However, the changes also mean that new innovations have a higher chance of adoption and acceptance because end users are more connected to the innovation process.

Keeping an organization as large as Nordstrom competitive and innovative requires all employees to embrace change. And for Nordstrom, its focus on the soft side of implementing change is paying off. Nordstrom has been able to build on its organizational culture to encourage innovation and acceptance of change. As Sam Hogenson, vice president of technology at Nordstrom, puts it, "If you don't pay attention to culture, everything is really hard to do. But if you do, everything else works."

Critical Thinking Questions

1. How might Nordstrom's decision to move many of its technology innovators out of its central Innovation Lab and into the business groups allow the retailer to better focus on the soft side of implementing change?
2. What resistance from the business units might have inhibited the movement of technology innovators into business groups? What strategies or actions could management have taken to reduce this resistance?
3. Nordstrom's Vice President of E-Commerce and Store Technologies, Courtney Kissler, is a strong proponent of innovating through continuous improvement. How do you think Nordstrom's organizational culture and

its focus on the soft side of implementing change could enhance its continuous improvement initiatives?

SOURCES: "Nordstrom Company History," Nordstrom, Inc., *http://shop .nordstrom.com/c/company-history?origin=leftnav*, accessed December 6, 2015; "The World's Biggest Public Companies: #864 Nordstrom," Forbes, May 2015, *www.forbes.com/companies/nordstrom*; "100 Best Companies to Work For: 2015," *Fortune, http://fortune.com/best-compa nies*, accessed December 7, 2015; Murphy, Chris, "Nordstrom VP: Take Emotion Out of Agile Transformation," *InformationWeek*, May 4, 2015,

www.informationweek.com/strategic-cio/digital-business/nordstrom-vp-take-emotion-out-of-agile-transformation/a/d-id/1320242; "DOES14 - Courtney Kissler - Nordstrom - Transforming to a Culture of Continuous Improvement," DevOps Enterprise Summit 2014, October 29, 2014, *www.youtube.com/watch?v=0ZAcsrZBSlo*; Nash, Kim S., "Nordstrom's Innovation Revamp Leads to E-commerce Texting App," *Wall Street Journal (CIO Journal blog)*, May 28, 2015, *http://blogs.wsj.com/cio/2015 /05/28/nordstroms-innovation-revamp-leads-to-e-commerce-texting -app*; Reed, J. Paul, "DevOps in Practice: Nordstrom," *O'Reilly, www .oreilly.com/ideas/devops-in-practice/page/2/nordstrom*.

Notes

1. "Zara," Inditex, *www.inditex.com/brands/zara*, accessed July 28, 2015.
2. Ruddick, Graham, "How Zara Became the World's Biggest Fashion Retailer," *Telegraph*, October 20, 2014, *www.telegraph.co.uk/finance/newsbysector/retailand consumer/11172562/How-Inditex-became-the-worlds -biggest-fashion-retailer.html*.
3. "Coles Supplier Portal," Coles, *www.supplierportal.coles .com.au/csp/wps/portal/web/Home*, accessed July 28, 2015.
4. Braue, David, "Coles Supply-Chain Revamp Means Stockouts Are Down (Down, Down,)" *ZDNet*, August 15, 2013, *www.zdnet.com/coles-supply-chain-revamp -means-stockouts-are-down-down-down-7000019419*.
5. "Ogilvy & Mather Worldwide," Ogilvy & Mather Worldwide, *www.wpp.com/wpp/companies/ogilvy-mather -worldwide*, accessed July 28, 2015.
6. Christensen, Clayton, "Disruptive Innovation," Clayton Christensen, *www.claytonchristensen.com/key-concepts*, accessed July 29, 2015.
7. "P&G," *ad brands.net, www.adbrands.net/us/pg_us .htm*, accessed August 18, 2015.
8. "P&G Boosts Prices to Offset Cheaper Tide," Cincinnati Business Enquirer, February 11, 2014, *www.bizjournals .com/cincinnati/morning_call/2014/02/pg-boosts-prices -to-offset-cheaper-tide.html*.
9. Buck, Stephanie, "Cell-ebration! 40 Years of Cellphone History," *Mashable*, April 3, 2013, *http://mashable.com /2013/04/03/anniversary-of-cellphone*.
10. Phillips, Abagail, "Continuous Innovation at Boeing Leads to Success in a Highly Competitive Industry," *Lean*, October 24, 2014, *www.manufacturingglobal. com/lean/199/Continuous-innovation-at-Boeing-leads -to-success-in-a-highly-competitive-industry*.
11. Jain, Rahul, "Deutsche Bank Extends Accenture BPO Procurement Contract," *The Outsource Blog*, July 3, 2015, *www.theoutsourceblog.com/2015/07/detusche -bank-extends-accenture-bpo-procurement-contract*.
12. Thibodeau, Patrick, "In a Symbolic Shift, IBM's India Workforce Likely Exceeds U.S.," *Computerworld*, November 29, 2012, *www.computerworld.com/article /2493565/it-careers/in-a-symbolic-shift--ibm-s-india -workforce-likely-exceeds-u-s-.html*.
13. Thibodeau, Patrick, "As It Sets IT Layoffs, Citizens Bank Shifts Work to India by Web," *Computerworld*, August 13, 2015, *www.computerworld.com/article/2970435 /it-outsourcing/as-it-sets-it-layoffs-citizens-bank-shifts -work-to-india-via-web.html*.
14. Denning, Steve, "What Went Wrong at Boeing?," *Forbes*, January 21, 2013, *www.forbes.com/sites/stevedenning /2013/01/21/what-went-wrong-at-boeing*.
15. "Kraft Heinz Announces Job Cuts in U.S. and Canada," *Reuters*, August 12, 2015, *www.nytimes.com/2015/08 /13/business/kraft-heinz-announces-job-cuts-in-us-and -canada.html?ref=topics&_r=0*.
16. Hornstein, Henry, "The Need to Integrate Project Management and Organizational Change," *Ivey Business Journal*, March/April 2012, *http://iveybusinessjournal .com/publication/the-need-to-integrate-project-manag ement-and-organizational-change*.
17. Zhu, Pearl, "Five 'Super Pitfalls' Why Large IT Projects Fail, *Future CIO*, May 2014, *http://futureofcio.blogspot .com/2013/03/five-super-pitfalls-why-large-it.html*.
18. "California Department of Consumer Affairs' BreEZe System," California State Auditor, *www.auditor.ca.gov /reports/summary/2014-116*, accessed August 11, 2015.
19. Ortiz, Jon, "$96 Million California IT Project Late, Flawed, Busting Budget," *State Worker*, February 12, 2015, *www.sacbee.com/news/politics-government/the -state-worker/article9918857.html*.
20. Kaminski, June, "Theory Applied to Informatics—Lewin's Change Theory," *Canadian Journal of Nursing*, Winter 2011, *http://cjni.net/journal/?p=1210*.
21. Davis, F. D., "Perceived Usefulness, Perceived Ease of Use, and User Acceptance of Information Technology," *MIS Quarterly*, Volume 13, Issue 3, pp. 319–339.
22. "Investor Relations," Avon, *http://investor.avoncom pany.com/CorporateProfile.aspx?iid=3009091*, accessed August 12, 2015.
23. "Avon Products," *Why Projects Fail Blog*, January 21, 2014, *http://calleam.com/WTPF/?p=6248*.
24. Thibodeau, Patrick and Machlis, Sharon, "Despite H-1B Lottery, Offshore Firms Dominate Visa Use," *Computerworld*, July 30, 2015, *www.computerworld.com/article /2954612/it-outsourcing/despite-h-1b-lottery-offshore -firms-dominate-visa-use.html*.
25. Thibodeau, Patrick, "Southern California Edison IT Workers 'Beyond Furious' over H-1B Replacements," *Computerworld*, February 14, 2015, *www.computer-world.com/article/2879083/southern-california-edison-it-workers-beyond-furious-over-h-1b-replacements.html*.
26. "2015 100 Best Places to Work in IT," *Computerworld*, July 2015.
27. Groenfeldt, Tom, "40 Percent of IT Spending Is outside CIO Control," *Forbes*, December 2, 2013, *www.forbes*

.com/sites/tomgroenfeldt/2013/12/02/40-percent-of-it-spending-is-outside-cio-control/2.

28. Hein, Rich, "IT Certification Hot List 2015: 10 That Deliver Higher Pay," *CIO*, March 3, 2015, *www.cio.com/article/2891552/careers-staffing/it-certification-hot-list-2015-10-that-deliver-higher-pay.html*.

29. "Starting an Information Technology Business," *Female Entrepreneur Association*, August 28, 2014, *femaleentrepreneurassociation.com/2014/08/starting-an-information-technology-business*.

30. Smith, Darrell, "Job Front: Social Media Expected to Play Bigger Role in Hiring," *Sacramento Bee*, February 4, 2013, *www.sacbee.com/2013/02/04/5162867/job-front-social-media-expected.html*.

Macrovector/Shutterstock.com

PART 2

Information Technology Concepts

Hardware and Mobile Devices

Did You Know?

- The Large Hadron Collider (LHC)—built to gain a better understanding of what our universe is made of and how it began—captures about 3 gigabytes of data per second. One gigabyte can store seven minutes of HD-TV. The mission of the LHC Computing Grid is to store and analyze all this data using 132,922 physical processors, 300 petabytes of online disk storage, and 230 petabytes of magnetic tape storage. For perspective, one gigabyte can store seven minutes of HD-TV while one petabyte is equivalent to 13.3 years of HD-TV.

- Current technology allows chip manufacturers to create chips with features that measure as small as 14 nanometers (nm) across. For perspective, a molecule of water is around 0.5 nm across. Not only are chips getting smaller, but they are getting faster and require less energy. These improved chips will be in your computing devices, smartphones, and wearable computers making them more powerful and useful.

- Biomedical engineers are exploring a process called bioprinting, which uses 3D printers to create living tissue capable of naturally integrating into the body. This will eventually enable the construction of fully functional human organs.

Principles

- The computer hardware industry is rapidly changing and highly competitive, creating an environment ripe for technological breakthroughs.

- Computer hardware must be carefully selected to meet the evolving needs of the organization and its supporting information systems.

- The computer hardware industry and users are implementing green computing designs and products.

Learning Objectives

- Identify and briefly describe the functions of the primary components of a computer.

- Give an example of recent innovations in computer processor chips, memory devices, and input/output devices.

- Identify the characteristics of various classes of single-user and multiuser computer systems, and discuss the usage of each class of system.

- Identify some of the challenges and trade-offs that must be considered in implementing a data center.

- Define the term "green computing" and identify the primary goals of this program.

Why Learn about Hardware and Mobile Devices?

Organizations invest in computer hardware to improve worker productivity, increase revenue, reduce costs, provide better customer service, speed up time to market, and facilitate collaboration among employees. Organizations that don't make wise hardware investments are often stuck with outdated equipment that is unreliable and that cannot take advantage of the latest software advances. Such obsolete hardware can serve as an anchor to progress and can place an organization at a competitive disadvantage. Managers, no matter what their career field and educational background, are expected to help define the business needs that hardware must support. In addition, managers must be able to ask relevant questions and evaluate options when considering hardware investments for their areas of the business. This need is especially true in small organizations, which might not employ information system specialists. Managers in marketing, sales, and human resources often help IS specialists assess opportunities to apply computer hardware and evaluate the options and features specified for the hardware. Managers in finance and accounting must keep an eye on the bottom line—guarding against overspending—yet be willing to invest in computer hardware when and where business conditions warrant it.

As you read this chapter, consider the following:

- What major competitive advantages can organizations gain from the effective use of computer hardware and mobile devices?
- What impact do the increasing capabilities and decreasing costs of hardware over time have on how organizations are using information system hardware?

This chapter focuses on the hardware components of a computer-based information system (CBIS). Recall that hardware refers to the physical components of a computer that perform the input, processing, output, and storage activities of the computer. When making hardware-purchasing decisions, the overriding consideration of a business should be how hardware can support the objectives of the information system (IS) and the goals of the organization.

Anatomy of a Computer

Computer system hardware components include devices that perform input, processing, data storage, and output, as shown in Figure 3.1. These include the processor, memory, and input/output devices, all of which are discussed in this section.

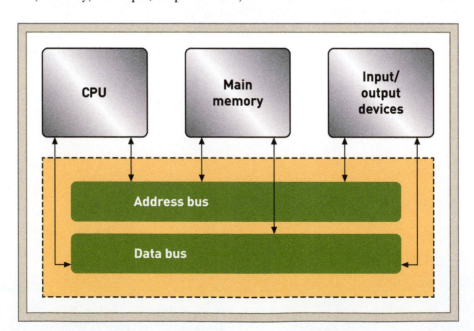

FIGURE **3.1**

Basic anatomy of a computer

Computer hardware components include the processor (CPU), memory, address and data bus, and input/output devices.

Processor

The **central processing unit (CPU)** or simply processor is the part of a computer that sequences and executes instructions. **Memory** provides the processor with a working storage area to hold program instructions and data. It rapidly provides data and instructions to the processor. **Input/output devices** provide data and instructions to the computer and receive results from it. Data and instructions are routed to and from the various components over the **bus**, a set of electronic circuits.

The components of the computer work together to complete the instructions (e.g., add, multiply, divide, subtract, compare) of a computer program to accomplish the goals of the user (e.g., send/receive email, develop a profit forecast, pay an invoice). Completing an instruction involves two phases (instruction and execution), which are broken down into the following four steps (see Figure 3.2):

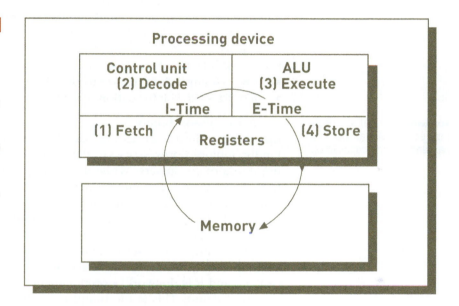

- **Instruction phase:**

  - **Fetch instruction.** The computer reads the next program instruction to be executed—along with any necessary data—into the processor.
  - **Decode instruction.** The instruction is decoded and passed to the appropriate processor execution unit.

- **Execution phase:**

  - **Execute instruction.** The computer executes the instruction by making an arithmetic computation, logical comparison, bit shift, or vector operation.
  - **Store results.** The results are stored in temporary storage locations called registers or in memory.

Each processor produces a series of electronic pulses at a predetermined rate, called the **clock speed**, which governs the speed at which these steps are completed. Clock speed is measured in **gigahertz (GHz)**, which is a unit of frequency that is equal to one billion cycles per second. Many of today's personal computers operate in the 1 to 4 GHz range. The higher the clock speed, the shorter the interval between pulses and the faster instructions can be completed.

Unfortunately, the faster the clock speed of the processor, the more heat the processor generates. This heat must be dissipated to avoid corrupting the

---

central processing unit (CPU): The part of a computer that sequences and executes instructions.

memory: A component of the computer that provides the processor with a working storage area to hold program instructions and data.

input/output device: A computer component that provides data and instructions to the computer and receives results from it.

bus: A set of electronic circuits used to route data and instructions to and from the various components of a computer.

FIGURE 3.2

Execution of an instruction

(1) In the instruction phase, a program's instructions and any necessary data are read into the processor. (2) The instruction is then decoded by the control unit of the CPU so that the central processor can understand what to do. (3) In the execution phase, the arithmetic and logic unit (ALU) component of the CPU does what it is instructed to do, making either an arithmetic computation or a logical comparison. (4) The results are then stored in the registers or in memory. The instruction and execution phases together make up one machine cycle.

---

clock speed: A series of electronic pulses produced at a predetermined rate that affects machine cycle time.

gigahertz (GHz): A unit of frequency that is equal to one billion cycles per second; a measure of clock speed.

data and instructions the computer is trying to process. Thus, processors that run at higher temperatures need bigger heat sinks (a device or substance for absorbing excessive heat), fans, and other components to eliminate the excess heat. This increases the size and weight of the computing device.

Processor Families

This section will introduce the concept of instruction set architecture and processor family and briefly discuss three of the most commonly used processor families.

The **instruction set architecture (ISA)** of a computer defines the basic set of commands (opcodes) that the processor can execute. Examples of opcodes include:

- ADD—Add two numbers together.
- COMPARE—Compare numbers.
- IN—Input information from a device (e.g., keyboard).
- JUMP—Jump to designated memory address.
- JUMP IF—Conditional statement that jumps to a designated memory address.
- LOAD—Load information from memory to the processor.
- OUT—Output information to device (e.g., monitor).
- STORE—Store information to memory.

A **processor family** is a set of processors from the same manufacturer that have similar features and capabilities. However within each processor family, multiple processors are developed to meet the many diverse computing needs of consumers. While the general ISA and feature set within a given family are identical, certain model specific variations occur. Different processors can use almost the same instruction set while still having very different internal design. For example, both the Intel Pentium and AMD Athlon processors use nearly the same instruction set.

x86 family. Intel, AMD, and VIA Technologies are the largest manufacturers of x86 processors. Servers based on the x86 processor dominate data centers, and it is the world's predominant personal computer CPU processor.

Intel Atom. This is the brand name for a line of ultra-low-voltage CPUs from Intel that is designed to generate less heat than the x86 chip. As a result, it requires less power and fewer additional components to dissipate the excees heat. As a result, the Intel Atom is used mostly in lightweight portable computers and mobile Internet devices.

ARM. These processors are used in computers that run Android, iOS, and other operating systems found in mobile devices such as laptops and smartphones. ARM is a designer of computer processors; it licenses its designs to chip manufacturers to build. ARM created a design for a family of processors based on Reduced Instruction Set Processing (RISC). RISC processors execute a small set of simplified instructions more quickly than complex instruction set computers based on the x86 processor. Because RISC processors require less power and generate less heat than standard x86 processors, ARM processors do not require big heat sinks and fans to remove excess heat. This results in smaller, lighter, more energy-efficient computing devices with longer battery life—ideal for use in smartphones and tablets.

The toughest challenge in designing a processor for a smartphone or tablet is balancing performance and power consumption. Many processor designs rely on a multiple-core configuration ARM calls big.LITTLE that includes high clock speed along with powerful cores, and slower, more energy-efficient cores. The powerful cores are used when high performance is required, such as for gaming computers. The more energy-efficient cores are used for less taxing tasks, such as Web browsing and email. This approach provides sufficient computing power to get the job done, but

instruction set architecture (ISA): A basic set of commands (opcodes) that the processor can execute.

processor family: A set of processors from the same manufacturer that have similar features and capabilities.

reduces heating problems and, consequentially, the drain on the battery to run a cooling fan. Mobile devices from Samsung and Qualcomm employ the big.LITTLE design.

Multiprocessing

multiprocessing: The simultaneous execution of two or more instructions at the same time.

coprocessor: The part of the computer that speeds processing by executing specific types of instructions while the CPU works on another processing activity.

multicore processor: A microprocessor that has two or more independent processing units, called cores, which are capable of sequencing and executing instructions.

Multiprocessing involves the simultaneous execution of two or more instructions at the same time. One form of multiprocessing uses coprocessors. A **coprocessor** speeds processing by executing specific types of instructions while the CPU works on another processing activity. Coprocessors can be internal or external to the CPU and can have different clock speeds than the CPU. Each type of coprocessor performs a specific function. For example, a math coprocessor chip speeds mathematical calculations, while a graphics coprocessor chip decreases the time it takes to manipulate graphics.

A **multicore processor** has two or more independent processing units, called cores, which are capable of sequencing and executing instructions. The multiple cores can run multiple instructions at the same time, thereby increasing the amount of processing that can be completed in a given amount of time.

Parallel Computing

parallel computing: The simultaneous execution of the same task on multiple processors to obtain results faster.

massively parallel processing system: A system that speeds processing by linking hundreds or thousands of processors to operate at the same time, or in parallel, with each processor having its own bus, memory, disks, copy of the operating system, and applications.

Parallel computing is the simultaneous execution of the same task on multiple processors to obtain results more quickly. Systems with thousands of such processors are known as **massively parallel processing systems**, a form of multiprocessing that speeds processing by linking hundreds or even thousands of processors to operate at the same time, or in parallel, with each processor having its own bus, memory, disks, copy of the operating system, and applications. The processors might communicate with one another to coordinate when executing a computer program, or they might run independently of one another under the direction of another processor that distributes the work to the various processors and collects their results.

The most frequent uses for parallel computing include modeling, simulation, and analyzing large amounts of data. For example, parallel computing is used in medicine to develop new imaging systems that complete ultrasound scans in less time and with greater accuracy, enabling doctors to provide better, more timely diagnoses to patients. Instead of building physical models of new products, engineers can create virtual models and use parallel computing to test how the products work and then change design elements and materials as needed.

The Lawrence Livermore National Laboratory in California is home to the Sequoia supercomputer, an impressive example of a massively parallel processing system. Sequoia is consistently ranked as one of the fastest computers in the world, with over 1.5 million processing cores that allow it to process over 17 quadrillion computations per second.[1] Although utilized primarily for nuclear weapons simulation, Sequoia was recently used by a group of researchers to model mantle convection (the process within the Earth's interior that is responsible for the movement of the Earth's tectonic plates and the earthquakes, volcanoes, and tsunamis that sometimes accompany those movements). The model could only be simulated on such a powerful computer and is a step toward developing a better understanding and prediction of natural disasters.[2]

grid computing: The use of a collection of computers, often owned by multiple individuals or organizations, that work in a coordinated manner to solve a common problem.

Grid computing is the use of a collection of computers, often owned by multiple individuals or organizations, that work in a coordinated manner to solve a common problem. Grid computing is a low-cost approach to parallel computing. The grid can include dozens, hundreds, or even thousands of computers that run collectively to solve extremely large processing problems. Key to the success of grid computing is a central server that acts as the grid leader and traffic monitor. This controlling server divides the computing task into subtasks and assigns the work to computers on the grid that have (at least temporarily) surplus processing power. The central server also monitors the processing, and if a member of the grid fails to complete a subtask, the server restarts or reassigns the task. When all the subtasks are completed, the controlling server combines the results and advances to the next task until the whole job is completed.

The Large Hadron Collider (LHC) was built to study the behavior of fundamental particles to gain a better understanding of what our universe is made of and how it began. The LHC hurls protons and other particles at each other at nearly the speed of light and then records what happens when they smash together. LHC detectors record particle collisions with 100 million read-out channels taking 14 million pictures per second. This translates to about 3 gigabytes of data per second or about 25 petabytes (25 million gigabytes) of data per year. The Worldwide LHC Computing Grid (WLCG) project is a global collaboration of more than 170 computing centers in 42 countries, linking up national and international grid infrastructures. Its mission is to store and analyze all this data on the LHC Computing Grid, which consists of 132,922 physical CPUs, 300 petabytes of online disk storage, and 230 petabytes of magnetic tape storage.[3]

Manufacturing Processors

integrated circuit (IC): A set of electronic circuits on one small piece of semiconductor material, normally silicon.

semiconductor fabrication plant: A factory where integrated circuits are manufactured; also called a fab or a foundry.

An **integrated circuit (IC)**—or chip—is a set of electronic circuits on one small piece of semiconductor material, normally silicon. ICs can be made extremely small with up to several billion electronic components packed into an area the size of a fingernail. Processors and memory chips are examples of integrated circuits. A **semiconductor fabrication plant** (also called a fab or foundry) is a factory where integrated circuits are manufactured. Extreme ultraviolet lithography (EUVL) is a highly complex process used in manufacturing computer chips with feature sizes that are extremely small—measured in nanometers (nm) or billionths of a meter. EUVL involves directing a laser beam at xeon gas to heat it up and eject electrons to etch the tiny components of the chip. The entire process must occur in a vacuum. Current technology allows chip manufacturers to create chips with features that measure as small as 14 nm across. For perspective, a molecule of water is about 0.5 nm across. Table 3.1 lists some of the Intel processors and their characteristics.

TABLE 3.1 Some members of the Intel family of processors

Chip	Family	Product Name	MaxClock Speed (GHz)	Number of Cores	Lithography (Nanometers)
x86	Xeon	E7-2850	2.0	10	32
x86	Core i7	Extreme Edition 980x	3.3	6	32
x86	Core i5	6600	3.9	4	14
x86	Pentium	4 G4400T	2.9	2	14
Atom	x7	Z8700	2.4	4	14
Atom	x5	Z8500	2.2	4	14

Intel, Samsung, and STMicroelectronics design and manufacture their chips in their own fab plants. Some organizations operate a semiconductor fab for the purpose of fabricating the designs of other companies. Such organizations are known as foundry companies. Qualcomm, Nvidia, and AMD are examples of fabless manufacturers; they outsource their manufacturing to foundry companies who fabricate the design.

Fabs are extremely expensive to set up and require many expensive devices to function. Intel is investing $6 billion to upgrade its fab plant in Kiryat Gat,Israel, and will hire 1,000 workers in addition to the 2,500 who already work there. It is believed that the plant will shift to making chips employing new 10-nanometer technology, which experts expect to arrive in 2016.[4,5]

Memory

main memory: The component of a computer that provides the CPU with a working storage area for program instructions and data.

Main memory provides the CPU with a working storage area for program instructions and data. The chief function of memory is to rapidly provide data and instructions to the CPU. In order for their systems to run efficiently, organizations must invest in a sufficient amount of main memory. Organizations also need large amounts of secondary storage to hold the huge quantities of data that cannot fit within the limits of main memory.

byte (B): Eight bits that together represent a single character of data.

Like the CPU, memory devices contain thousands of circuits imprinted on silicon chips. Each circuit is either conducting electrical current (on) or not conducting current (off). Data is stored in memory as a combination of on or off circuit states. Usually, 8 bits are used to represent a character, such as the letter *A*. Eight bits together form a **byte (B)**. In most cases, storage capacity is measured in bytes, with 1 byte equivalent to one character of data. The contents of the Library of Congress, with over 126 million items and 530 miles of bookshelves, would require about 20 petabytes of digital storage. It is estimated that all the words ever spoken by humans represented in text form would equal about 5 exabytes of information.[6] Table 3.2 lists units for measuring computer storage.

TABLE 3.2 Computer storage units

Name	Abbreviation	Number of Bytes
Byte	B	1
Kilobyte	KB	1,000
Megabyte	MB	$1,000^2$
Gigabyte	GB	$1,000^3$
Terabyte	TB	$1,000^4$
Petabyte	PB	$1,000^5$
Exabyte	EB	$1,000^6$
Zettabyte	ZB	$1,000^7$
Yottabyte	YB	$1,000^8$

Types of Memory

random access memory (RAM): A form of memory in which instructions or data can be temporarily stored.

Computer memory can take several forms. Instructions or data can be temporarily stored in and read from **random access memory (RAM)**. As currently designed, RAM chips are volatile storage devices, meaning they lose their contents if the current is turned off or disrupted, which can be caused by a power surge, a brownout, or electrical noise generated by lightning or nearby machines. RAM chips are mounted directly on the computer's main circuit board or in other chips mounted on peripheral cards that plug into the main circuit board. These RAM chips consist of millions of switches that are sensitive to changes in electric current.

RAM comes in many varieties: Static random access memory (SRAM) is byte-addressable storage used for high-speed registers and caches; dynamic random access memory (DRAM) is byte-addressable storage used for the main memory in a computer; and double data rate synchronous dynamic random access memory (DDR SDRAM) is an improved form of DRAM that effectively doubles the rate at which data can be moved in and out of main memory. DDR has been superseded by second-, third-, and fourth-generation DDR called DDR2, DDR3, and DDR4, respectively. DDR3 requires 1.5 volts of electrical power to operate, while DDR4 needs just 1.2 volts. DDR4 also supports a deep power-down mode, which allows the host device to go into standby without needing to refresh its memory—reducing standby power consumption by up to 50 percent. Thus, DDR4 reduces the energy required to run portable devices and servers. This means longer battery life for portable computer users and lower electric bills for organizations that operate servers farms.[7]

cache memory: A type of high-speed memory that a processor can access more rapidly than main memory.

Although microprocessor speed has roughly doubled every 24 months over the past several decades, memory performance has not kept pace. In effect, memory has become the principal bottleneck to system performance. **Cache memory** is a type of high-speed memory that a processor can access more rapidly than main memory to help ease this bottleneck. See Figure 3.3. Frequently used data is stored in easily accessible cache memory instead of slower memory, such as RAM. Because cache memory holds less data, the CPU can access the desired data and instructions more quickly than when selecting from the larger set in primary storage. Thus, the CPU can execute instructions faster, improving the overall performance of the computer system. Cache memory is available in three forms. The level 1 (L1) cache is on the CPU chip. The level 2 (L2) cache memory can be accessed by the CPU over a high-speed dedicated interface. The latest processors go a step further, placing the L2 cache directly on the CPU chip itself and providing high-speed support for a tertiary level 3 (L3) external cache. See Figure 3.4.

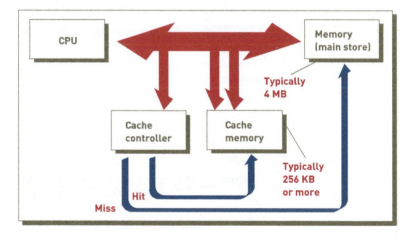

FIGURE 3.3

Cache memory

Processors can access this type of high-speed memory faster than main memory. Located on or near the CPU chip, cache memory works with main memory. A cache controller determines how often the data is used, transfers frequently used data to cache memory, and then deletes the data when it goes out of use.

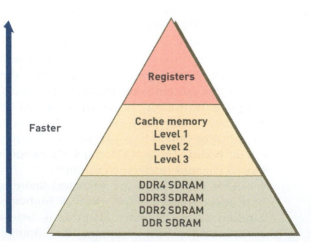

FIGURE 3.4

Relative speed of various types of storage

The closer memory is to the CPU, the faster the CPU can access it.

read-only memory (ROM): A nonvolatile form of memory.

Read-only memory (ROM), another type of memory, is nonvolatile, meaning that its contents are not lost if the power is turned off or interrupted. ROM provides permanent storage for data and instructions that do not change, such as programs and data from the computer manufacturer, including the instructions that tell the computer how to start up when power is turned on. ROM memory also comes in a couple varieties. Programmable read-only memory (PROM) is used to hold data and instructions that can never be changed. Electrically erasable programmable read-only memory (EEPROM) is user-modifiable read-only memory that can be erased and reprogrammed repeatedly through the application of higher-than-normal electrical voltage. EEPROM requires data to be written or erased 1 byte at a time.

Secondary Data Storage Devices

Storing data safely and effectively is critical to an organization's success. Driven by many factors—such as needing to retain more data longer to meet government regulatory concerns, storing new forms of digital data such as audio and video, and keeping systems running under the onslaught of increasing volumes of email—the world's information is more than doubling every two years. Nearly 6 zettabytes (6×10^{21} bytes) of information was created and stored in 2013 alone.[8] It is mainly unstructured digital content such as video, audio, and image objects that is fueling this growth. IBM, which is investing heavily in technologies (such as Watson, its cognitive computer system) that can help organizations manage all that unstructured data, estimates that more than 80 percent of the 2.5 billion gigabytes of data created every day comes in the form of unstructured data.[9]

secondary storage: A device that stores large amounts of data, instructions, and information more permanently than allowed with main memory.

For most organizations, the best overall data storage solution is likely a combination of different secondary storage options that can store large amounts of data, instructions, and information more permanently than allowed with main memory. Compared with memory, secondary storage offers the advantages of nonvolatility, greater capacity, and greater economy. On a cost-per-megabyte basis, secondary storage is considerably less expensive than primary memory. See Table 3.3. The selection of secondary storage media and devices requires understanding their primary characteristics: access method, capacity, and portability.

TABLE 3.3 Cost comparison for various forms of storage

Data Storage Type	Cost per GB			
	2009	2011	2013	2015
8 GB flash drive	$2.50	$2.48	$1.25	$.69
25 GB rewritable Blu-ray disc	$.44	$.11	$.30	$.30
72 GB DAT 72 data cartridge	$.21	$.24	$.26	$.21
50 4.7 GB DVD+R disks	$.09	$.31	$.07	$.08
500 GB portable hard drive	$.23	$.15	$.12	$.12
1 TB desktop external hard drive	$.12	$.09	$.10	$.10

Source: Office Depot, *www.officedepot.com*, December 2009, October 2011, October 2013, and October 2015.

As with other computer system components, the access methods, storage capacities, and portability required of secondary storage media are determined by the business requirements that must be met. An objective of a credit card company might be to rapidly retrieve stored customer data to approve consumer purchases. In this case, a fast access method is critical. In other cases, such as equipping the Coca-Cola field salesforce with smartphones, portability and ruggedness might be major considerations in selecting and using secondary storage media and devices.

In addition to cost, capacity, portability, and ruggedness, organizations must address security issues so that only authorized people are allowed access to sensitive data and critical programs. Because the data and programs kept on secondary storage devices are so critical to most organizations, all of these issues merit careful consideration.

Secondary data storage is not directly accessible by the CPU. Instead, computers usually use input/output channels to access secondary storage and then transfer the desired data to intermediate areas in primary storage. The most common forms of secondary storage devices are magnetic, optical, and solid state.

Magnetic Secondary Storage Devices

magnetic tape: A type of sequential secondary storage medium, now used primarily for storing backups of critical organizational data in the event of a disaster.

Magnetic storage uses tape or disk devices covered with a thin magnetic coating that enables data to be stored as magnetic particles. **Magnetic tape** is a type of secondary storage medium, which is frequently used for storing backups of critical organizational data in the event of a disaster. Examples of tape storage devices include cassettes and cartridges measuring a few millimeters in diameter, requiring very little storage space. Magnetic tape has been used as storage media since the time of the earliest computers, such as the 1951 Univac computer.[10] Continuing advancements have kept magnetic tape as a viable storage medium. For example, IBM and FUJIFILM Corporation of Japan recently achieved a recording density of 123 billion bits per square inch on low-cost magnetic tape. While still in development, this innovation represents the equivalent of a 220-terabyte tape cartridge (enough to hold the text of approximately 220 million books) that could fit into the palm of your hand.[11]

The High-End Computing Capability (HECC) Project at NASA offers scientists and engineers access to supercomputing systems services that are backed up by a 132-petabyte tape storage system.[12] Many such supercomputers, including those deployed at the National Center for Atmospheric Research, use robotic tape backup systems. See Figure 3.5.

hard disk drive (HDD): A direct access storage device used to store and retrieve data from rapidly rotating disks coated with magnetic material.

A **hard disk drive (HDD)** is a direct access storage device used to store and retrieve data from rapidly rotating disks coated with magnetic material.

Courtesy of Deutsches Klimarechenzentrum GmbH

FIGURE 3.5

Robotic tape backup system

The National Center for Atmospheric Research uses a robotic tape backup system to back up a fleet of supercomputers that solve the world's most computationally intensive climate-modeling problems.

A hard disk represents bits of data with small magnetized areas and uses a read/write head to go directly to the desired piece of data. Because direct access allows fast data retrieval, this type of storage is used by organizations that need to respond quickly to customer requests, such as airlines and credit card firms. For example, information on the credit history of a customer or the seat availability on a particular flight would likely be stored on a direct-access hard disk drive so that a customer-service representative or manager could obtain that data in seconds. Hard disk drives vary widely in capacity and portability.

Putting an organization's data online involves a serious business risk—the loss of critical data can put a corporation out of business. The concern is that the most critical mechanical components inside a HDD storage device—the disk drives, the fans, and read/write heads—can fail. Thus, organizations now require that their data storage devices be fault tolerant, that is, they can continue with little or no loss of performance if one or more key components fail. In response, disk manufacturers are continually developing new technologies that will improve the performance and reliability of their hard disk drives. For example, Western Digital's HGST subsidiary recently released the world's first 10-terabyte helium-filled hard drive—the Ultrastar He10 HDD. By using helium, HGST is able to decrease friction within its HDDs, allowing them to spin more reliably and consume less power than conventional designs. And according to HGST, the Ultrastar He10 has a mean-time-between-failure rating of 2.5 million hours, giving it the highest reliability rating of any HDD on the market.[13,14]

redundant array of independent/inexpensive disks (RAID): A method of storing data that generates extra bits of data from existing data, allowing the system to create a "reconstruction map" so that if a hard drive fails, the system can rebuild lost data.

A **redundant array of independent/inexpensive disks (RAID)** is a method of storing data that generates extra bits of data from existing data, allowing the system to create a "reconstruction map" so that if a hard drive fails, it can rebuild lost data. With this approach, data can be split and stored on different physical disk drives, using a technique called striping that evenly distributes the data. RAID technology has been applied to storage systems to improve system performance and reliability.

RAID can be implemented in several ways. RAID 1 subsystems duplicate data on the hard drives. This process, called "disk mirroring," provides an exact copy that protects users fully in the event of data loss. However, to keep complete duplicates of current backups, organizations need to double the amount of their storage capacity. Other RAID methods are less expensive because they duplicate only part of the data, allowing storage managers to minimize the amount of extra disk space they must purchase to protect data.

The National Foreign Language Center (NFLC) at the University of Maryland is a research institute dedicated to improving the nation's ability to understand and communicate with people around the world. The staff at the NFLC are involved in a variety of projects that develop and disseminate language information to policy makers across the United States. These projects generate large amounts of data that the institute had been storing on a Windows-based Dell server. However, with data accumulating at a rate of 150 to 200 gigabytes per month, the NFLC needed to implement a new storage solution. The NFLC opted for a RAID storage solution, which gave the institute enough storage space to offload thousands of large audio and video files, freeing up space on its Dell server. The RAID storage option offered the NFLC the ability to dramatically increase its capacity at a relatively low price per terabyte of storage.[15,16]

virtual tape: A storage device for less frequently needed data. With virtual tape systems, data appears to be stored entirely on tape cartridges, although some parts of it might actually be located on faster hard disks.

Virtual tape is a storage technology suitable for less frequently needed data. With virtual tape systems, data appears to be stored entirely on tape cartridges, although some parts might actually be located on faster hard disks. The software associated with a virtual tape system is sometimes called a virtual tape server. Virtual tape can be used with a sophisticated storage-management system that moves data to slower but less costly forms of storage media as people use the data less often. Virtual tape technology can decrease data access time, lower the total cost of ownership, and reduce the amount of floor space consumed by tape operations.

Optical Secondary Storage Devices

optical storage device: A form of data storage that uses lasers to read and write data.

An **optical storage device** uses special lasers to read and write data. The lasers record data by physically burning pits in the disc. Data is directly accessed from the disc by an optical disc device, which operates much like a compact disc player. This optical disc device uses a low-power laser that measures the difference in reflected light caused by a pit (or lack thereof) on the disc.

compact disc read-only memory (CD-ROM): A common form of optical disc on which data cannot be modified once it has been recorded.

A common optical storage device is the **compact disc read-only memory (CD-ROM)**, with a storage capacity of 740 megabytes of data. After data is recorded on a CD-ROM, it cannot be modified—the disc is "read-only." A CD burner, the informal name for a CD recorder, is a device that can record data to a compact disc. CD-recordable (CD-R) and CD-rewritable (CD-RW) are the two most common types of drives that can write CDs, either once (in the case of CD-R) or repeatedly (in the case of CD-RW). CD-rewritable (CD-RW) technology allows PC users to back up data on CDs.

digital video disc (DVD): A form of optical disc storage that looks like a CD but that can store more data and access it more quickly.

A **digital video disc (DVD)** looks like a CD, but it can store about 135 minutes of digital video or several gigabytes of data. At a data transfer rate of 1.352 megabytes per second, the access speed of a DVD drive is also faster than that of the typical CD-ROM drive. Software, video games, and movies are often stored and distributed on DVDs. See Figure 3.6.

Plus69/Shutterstock.com

FIGURE 3.6

Digital video discs and player
DVDs look like CDs but have a greater storage capacity and can transfer data at a faster rate.

DVDs have replaced recordable and rewritable CD discs (CD-R and CD-RW) as the preferred physical media for sharing movies and photos. Whereas a CD can hold about 740 megabytes of data, a single-sided DVD can hold 4.7 gigabytes, with double-sided DVDs having a capacity of 9.4 gigabytes. Several types of recorders and discs are currently in use. Recordings can be made on record-once discs (DVD-R and DVD+R) or on rewritable discs (DVD-RW, DVD+RW, and DVD-RAM). Not all types of rewritable DVDs are compatible with other types.

The Blu-ray high-definition video disc format based on blue laser technology stores at least three times as much data as a DVD. The primary use for this technology is in home entertainment equipment to store high-definition video, although this format can also store computer data. A dual-layer Blu-ray disc can store 50 gigabytes of data.[17]

DVD and Blu-ray discs are commonly used to store data; however, the discs can become unreliable over time as they are exposed to light, humidity, and chemical changes inside the disc itself. As a result, the data stored on such discs can become unreadable over time. Thus, disc manufacturers are focused on developing longer-lasting DVD and Blu-ray technology.

Scientists are experimenting with an even more advanced storage technologies, including the use of DNA molecules to store vast amounts of data for long periods of time. DNA molecules consist of four chemicals connected end-to-end, similar to the sequences of ones and zeroes that computers use to represent data. One gram of DNA is capable of holding 455 exabytes (one exabyte is equivalent to a billion gigabytes).[18] In addition, data could be stored in DNA for thousands of years. By comparison, today's most powerful desktop hard drives hold around 6 terabytes of data and might last 50 years.[19] At this time, the cost of synthesizing DNA to store data and the cost of decoding the data stored in DNA are prohibitively expensive, unless the data needs to be archived for at least 600 years. It will likely be a decade or more before the technology evolves to the point where DNA data storage is practical.[20]

Solid State Secondary Storage Devices

Solid state storage device (SSD): A storage device that stores data in memory chips rather than on hard disk drives or optical media.

A **solid state storage device (SSD)** stores data in memory chips rather than on hard disk drives or optical media. These memory chips require less power and provide much faster data access than magnetic data storage devices. In addition, SSDs have no moving parts, so they are less fragile than hard disk drives. All these factors make the SSD a preferred choice over hard disk drives for portable computers.

A universal serial bus (USB) flash drive is one example of a commonly used SSD. USB flash drives are external to the computer and are removable and rewritable. Most weigh less than an ounce and can provide a wide range of storage capacity. Samsung has developed a 15.36-terabyte solid state storage device based on 48-layer 3D chip technology.[21] This technology allows for vertical stacking of flash cells, thus requiring less space to store data. It also improves performance and requires less power.

Enterprise Storage Options

Businesses need to store the large amounts of data created throughout an organization. Such large-scale secondary storage is called enterprise storage and comes in four forms: attached storage, network-attached storage (NAS), storage area networks (SANs), and cloud computing storage.

Attached Storage

Attached storage methods include all the options just discussed—tape, hard disk drives (including RAID devices), virtual tape systems, optical devices, and solid state secondary storage devices—which are connected directly to a single computer. Attached storage methods, though simple and cost effective for single users and small groups, do not allow systems to share storage, and they make it difficult to back up data.

Because of the limitations of attached storage, firms are turning to network-attached storage (NAS) and storage area networks (SANs). These alternatives enable an organization to share data storage resources among a much larger number of computers and users, resulting in improved storage efficiency and greater cost effectiveness. In addition, they simplify data backup and reduce the risk of downtime. Nearly one-third of system downtime is a direct result of data storage failures, so eliminating storage problems as a cause of downtime is a major advantage.

Network-Attached Storage

network-attached storage (NAS): A hard disk drive storage device that is set up with its own network address and provides file-based storage services to other devices on the network.

Network-attached storage (NAS) is a hard disk drive storage device that is set up with its own network address and provides file-based storage services to other devices on the network. NAS includes software to manage storage access and file management, relieving the users' computers of those tasks. The result is that both application software and files can be served faster because they are not competing for the same processor resources. Computer users can share and access the same information, even if they are using different types of computers. Common applications for NAS include consolidated storage, Internet and e-commerce applications, and digital media.

CD-adapco is the world's largest independent provider of computational fluid dynamics (CFD) software and services. The company's products are used for complex engineering simulations by over 3,000 different organizations around the world. CD-adapco has deployed more than one petabyte of Panasas ActiveStor storage, an advanced NAS solution designed for technical computing environments. ActiveStor is a scalable, hybrid NAS platform that utilizes high-capacity hard drives and solid state drives in the same system.[22,23]

Storage Area Networks

A **storage area network (SAN)** is a high-speed, special-purpose network that integrates different types of data storage devices (e.g., hard disk drives, magnetic tape, solid state secondary storage devices) into a single storage system and connects that to computing resources across an entire organization. See Figure 3.7. SANs can provide important capabilities such as disk mirroring, data backup and restore, data archiving, data migration from one storage device to another, and the sharing of data among computing devices connected to the network.

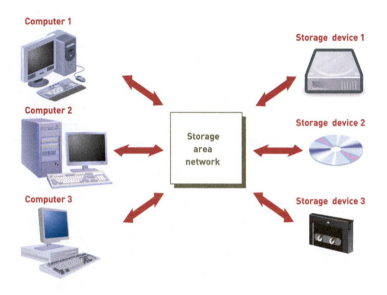

FIGURE 3.7
Storage area network
A SAN provides high-speed connections among data storage devices and computers over a network.

Using a SAN, an organization can centralize the people, policies, procedures, and practices for managing storage, and a data storage manager can apply the data consistently across an enterprise. This centralization eliminates inconsistent treatment of data by different system administrators and users, providing efficient and cost-effective data storage practices.

When the city of Riverside, California, created its "Riverside 2.0" strategic plan, it set goals related to cybersecurity, disaster preparedness, and government transparency. To meet those goals, the city needed to upgrade its data centers to a more flexible and scalable platform. As part of the project, the city migrated 500 terabytes of data to a new storage infrastructure that offered enterprise SAN performance—with almost double the previous storage capacity—to support its extensive array of e-government services as well as mission-critical applications, such as those related to public safety and utilities.[24]

A fundamental difference between NAS and SAN is that NAS uses file input/output, which defines data as complete containers of information, while SAN deals with block input/output, which is based on subsets of data smaller than a file. SAN manufacturers include EMC, Hitachi Data Systems Corporation, NetApp, Xiotech, and IBM.

As organizations set up large-scale SAN systems, they use more computers and network connections than in a NAS environment, and consequently, the

policy-based storage management: The automation of storage using previously defined policies.

network can become difficult to manage. In response, software tools designed to automate storage using previously defined policies are finding a place in the enterprise. Known as **policy-based storage management**, the software products from industry leaders such as Veritas Software Corporation, Legato Systems, EMC, and IBM automatically allocate storage space to users, balance the loads on servers and disks, and reroute network traffic when systems go down—all based on policies set up by system administrators.

The trend in secondary storage is toward higher capacity, increased portability, and automated storage management. Organizations should select a type of storage based on their needs and resources. In general, storing large amounts of data and information and providing users with quick access make an organization more efficient.

Storage as a Service

storage as a service: A data storage model where a data storage service provider rents space to individuals and organizations.

Storage as a service is a data storage model in which a data storage service provider rents space to people and organizations. Users access their rented data storage via the Internet. Such a service enables the users to store and back up their data without requiring a major investment to create and maintain their own data storage infrastructure. Businesses can also choose pay-per-use services, where they rent space on massive storage devices housed either at a service provider (such as Hewlett-Packard or IBM) or on the customer's premises, paying only for the amount of storage they use. This approach makes sense for many organizations, especially those with wildly fluctuating storage needs, such as those involved in the testing of new drugs or in developing software.

Increasingly, individuals and organizations expect to be able to access data, documents, databases, presentations, and spreadsheets from anywhere, with any sort of Internet-enabled device, such as a smartphone, tablet, or laptop. In response to this need, numerous cloud-based storage services have emerged, including Amazon's Elastic Compute Cloud, Apple iCloud, Dropbox, Google Drive, Microsoft SkyDrive, and Mozy. These services provide data storage at a rate of $2 or less per gigabyte a year.

Amazon's Simple Storage Service (Amazon S3) allows subscribers to upload, store, and download data. Amazon S3 stores subscriber data as objects within resources it calls "buckets." Subscribers can store as many objects as they want within a bucket and can write to, read, and delete objects in their bucket. Subscribers can choose to label their data private or make it publicly accessible. Subscribers can also elect to encrypt data prior to storage, and they can control who can create, delete, and retrieve objects in their buckets. Subscriber data is stored on redundant servers across multiple data centers to provide data redundancy and protect against accidental loss of data or natural disasters.

Social media start-up, Pinterest, operates a photo-sharing Web site where users create personalized boards with visual bookmarks—called pins—that link back to the sites they came from. Individuals and businesses use Pinterest to discover and save creative ideas—or to be discovered by the site's more than 100 million active users. The company describes itself as a visual bookmarking tool, but, perhaps more important, it also considers itself to be the world's first and biggest discovery engine. And with more than 50 billion pins created since it launched in 2010, Pinterest is a data-driven company.[25] The site's infrastructure growth is fueled by its user growth, and from the beginning, Pinterest has used Amazon Web Services, including the Amazon S3 data storage service, where it now stores over 8 billion objects and more than 10 petabytes of data. Pinterest logs approximately 14 terabytes of data each day, and the Amazon S3 service offers the company the scale and flexibility it requires to operate a large and rapidly growing consumer Internet service.[26–28]

Input and Output Devices

Input and output devices are the gateways to the computer system—you use them to provide data and instructions to the computer and receive results from it. Input and output devices are part of a computer's user interface, which includes other hardware devices and software that allow you to interact with a computer system.

As with other computer system components, an organization should keep its business goals in mind when selecting input and output devices. For example, many restaurant chains use handheld input devices or computerized terminals that let food servers enter orders and transfer them to the kitchen efficiently and accurately. These systems have also cut costs by helping restaurants track inventory and market to customers.

In general, businesses want input devices that let them accurately and rapidly enter data into a computer system, and they want output devices that let them produce timely results. Some organizations have very specific needs for input and output, requiring devices that perform specific functions. The more specialized the application, the more specialized the associated system input and output devices.

Getting data into a computer—input—often requires transferring human-readable data, such as a sales order, into a computer system. "Human-readable data" means data that people can read and understand. The temperature registered on a thermometer is an example of human-readable data. An example of machine-readable data is the universal bar code on many grocery and retail items that indicates the stock-keeping identification number for that item. To the human eye, the universal bar code is unintelligible and looks like a series of vertical bars of varying thicknesses. Some data, such as magnetic ink on bank checks, can be read by people and machines. Usually, people begin the input process by organizing human-readable data and transforming it into machine-readable data. Every keystroke on a keyboard, for example, turns a letter symbol of a human language into a digital code that the machine can manipulate.

Data Entry and Input

data entry: Converting human-readable data into a machine-readable form.

data input: Transferring machine-readable data into the system.

Getting data into the computer system is a two-stage process. First, the human-readable data is converted into a machine-readable form through **data entry**. The second stage involves transferring the machine-readable data into the system. This is **data input**.

Today, many companies use online data entry and input: They communicate and transfer data to computer devices directly connected to the computer system. Online data entry and input place data into the computer system in a matter of seconds. Organizations in many industries require the instantaneous updating offered by this approach. For example, when ticket agents for a concert venue enter a request for tickets, they can use online data entry and input to record the request as soon as it is made. Ticket agents at other terminals can then access this data to make a seating check before they process another request.

Source Data Automation

source data automation: Capturing and editing data where it is initially created and in a form that can be directly entered into a computer, thus ensuring accuracy and timeliness.

Regardless of how data gets into the computer, it should be captured and edited at its source. **Source data automation** involves capturing and editing data where it is originally created and in a form that can be directly entered into a computer, thus ensuring accuracy and timeliness. For example, using source data automation, salespeople enter sales orders into the computer at the time and place they take the orders. Any errors can be detected and corrected immediately. If an item is temporarily out of stock, the salesperson can discuss options with the customer. Prior to source data automation, orders were written on paper and entered into the computer later (usually by a clerk, not by the person who took the order). Often the handwritten information wasn't legible or, worse yet, order forms were lost. If problems occurred during data entry, the clerk had to contact the salesperson or the customer to "recapture" the data needed for order entry, leading to further delays and customer dissatisfaction.

Data entry and input devices come in many forms. They range from special-purpose devices that capture specific types of data to more general-purpose input devices. Some of the special-purpose data entry and input devices are discussed later in this chapter. First, we focus on devices used to enter and input general types of data, including text, audio, images, and video for personal computers.

Common Personal Computer Input Devices

A keyboard and a computer mouse are common devices used for entry and input of data, such as characters, text, and basic commands. Some companies manufacture keyboards that are more comfortable, more easily adjusted, and faster to use than standard keyboards. These ergonomic keyboards, such as the split keyboard, are designed to help users avoid wrist and hand injuries caused by hours of typing. Other keyboards include touch pads, which let you enter sketches on the touch pad while still using keys to enter text. See Figure 3.8. A mouse is used to point to and click symbols, icons, menus, and commands on the screen. The computer takes a number of actions in response, such as entering data into the computer system. Wireless mice and keyboards help keep a physical desktop free from clutter.

iStockphoto.com/Fotostorm

FIGURE 3.8

Drawing pad and integrated keyboard

A drawing pad and integrated keyboard can replace a traditional keyboard and mouse for input.

speech-recognition technology : Input devices that recognize human speech.

Speech-Recognition Technology

Using **speech-recognition technology**, a computer can interpret human speech as an alternative means of providing data or instructions. The most basic systems are designed to support a limited conversation on a fixed topic. For example, your insurance provider may employ a speech-recognition system to support calls to its billing department. The scope of the conversation is very limited, and the caller is guided to make one of a few possible and very distinct responses. For example, a typical prompt is "Do you wish to inquire about your monthly bill or make a payment?" More advanced systems can recognize continuous speech and convert it to text such as in closed-caption live TV broadcasts, sometimes with amusing results when key words are not properly converted to text.

Nurses at the Hudson Valley Heart Center in Poughkeepsie, New York, now use speech-recognition technology to record all of their patient history and progress notes, physical exam results, and discharge summaries. The software, which makes use of natural language-processing technology, automatically updates the hospital's electronic health record (EHR) system when a nurse adds new information for a patient. The hospital expects the new system to cut down on the amount of time nurses spend on documentation (currently estimated at 19 percent of their day, nationally).[29]

Motion-Sensing Input Devices

The major video game makers Microsoft, Nintendo, and Sony all have game controllers based on motion-sensing input devices. Kinect is a motion-sensing input device that enables the user to control the Microsoft Xbox as well as computers running the Windows operating system. The sensor is a horizontal bar positioned above or below the video display. It includes a Webcam-style device that interprets the user's hand gestures as instructions to quickly swipe through home screens and apps. The Wii Remote is the primary controller for Nintendo's Wii console. It can sense motion in all three dimensions and has an optical sensor that enables it to determine where the Wii Remote is pointing. This allows the user to interact with and manipulate items on the video screen via gestures and pointing. PlayStation Move is the motion-sensing game controller from Sony Computer Entertainment. It employs a handheld motion controller wand with sensors that detect its motion and a Webcam to track its position. These manufacturers hope that their motion-sensing input devices will broaden their user base beyond the typical gamer and increase their market share. However, such input devices may also prove useful in the operation of business information systems.

Scanning Devices

Scanning devices capture image and character data. A page scanner is like a copy machine. You either insert a page into the scanner or place it face down on the glass plate of the scanner and then scan it. With a handheld scanner, you manually move or roll the scanning device over the image you want to scan. Both page and handheld scanners can convert monochrome or color pictures, forms, text, and other images into machine-readable digits. Considering that U.S. enterprises generate an estimated 1 billion pieces of paper daily, many companies are looking to scanning devices to help them manage their documents and reduce the high cost of using and processing paper.

The NeatReceipt filing system is a compact, portable scanner and associated software that enable the user to scan business cards and convert them into digital contacts. NeatReceipt can also scan receipts to convert them into records of vendors and amounts that can be used for tax preparation.[30]

Optical Data Readers

Individuals and organizations can also use a special scanning device called an optical data reader to scan documents. The two categories of optical data readers are optical mark recognition (OMR) and optical character recognition (OCR). OMR readers are used for tasks such as grading tests and scanning forms. With this technology, pencils are used to fill in bubbles or check boxes on OMR paper, which is also called a "mark sense form." OMR systems are used in standardized tests, including the SAT and GMAT tests, and to record votes in elections.

In contrast, most OCR readers use reflected light to recognize and scan various machine-generated characters. With special software, OCR readers can also convert handwritten or typed documents into digital data. After data is entered, it can be shared, modified, and distributed over computer networks to hundreds or thousands of people. Previously, the use of OCR technology required a special scanner device that creates an image of the characters to be converted. Expensive OCR software was then required to convert that image into text. However, it is now possible to complete this process using the camera in an Android smartphone or tablet. Once the image is stored on the camera or tablet, you use the Google Drive app for Android to copy the image to Google Drive, where Google's software and servers will do the OCR conversion at no cost.

Magnetic Ink Character Recognition (MICR) Devices

In the 1950s, the banking industry was becoming swamped with paper checks, loan applications, bank statements, and so on. The result was the development of magnetic ink character recognition (MICR), a system for reading banking data quickly. With MICR, data is placed on the bottom of a check or other form using a special magnetic ink. Using a special character set, data printed with this ink is readable by both people and computers. See Figure 3.9.

magnetic stripe card: A type of card that stores a limited amount of data by modifying the magnetism of tiny iron-based particles contained in a band on the card.

Magnetic Stripe Cards

A **magnetic stripe card** stores a limited amount of data by modifying the magnetism of tiny iron-based particles contained in a band on the card. The magnetic stripe is read by physically swiping the card at a terminal. For this reason, such cards are called contact cards. Magnetic stripes are commonly used in credit cards, transportation tickets, and driver's licenses.

Magnetic stripe technology is still in wide use in the U.S. credit card industry. The data encoded on the magnetic stripe on the back of the card is read by swiping the card past a magnetic reading head. To protect the consumer, businesses in the United States have invested in extensive computer networks for verifying and processing this data. Software at the point-of-sale (POS) terminal automatically dials a stored telephone number to call an acquirer, an organization that collects credit-authentication requests from merchants and provides the merchants with a payment guarantee. When the acquirer company receives the credit-card authentication request, it checks the transaction for validity by reading the card number, expiration date, and credit card limit recorded on the magnetic stripe. If everything checks out, the authorization is granted. Should it later be discovered that the credit card was stolen or bogus, the merchant and the bank that partnered with the merchant are liable for the loss. The merchant loses the value of any goods or services sold plus the transaction fee associated with processing the sale. If the bank that issued the card does not have a charge-back right then, the bank bears the loss and the merchant is covered for the cost of the goods and services.

Unfortunately, the magnetic stripe is not a secure place for sensitive consumer information. The magnetic stripes on traditional credit and debit cards store contain unchanging data. Whoever accesses that data gains the sensitive card and cardholder information necessary to make purchases. The data on the stripe can be lifted from an existing card and copied onto a new card and used to make fraudulent purchases. Almost half of the world's credit card fraud now happens in the United States—even though only a quarter of all credit card transactions happen here.[31]

An employee of an Apple store in Queens, New York, was arrested and charged with using fraudulent credit cards to buy almost $1 million worth of

Apple gift cards. The man sold each $2,000 Apple gift card to a third party for $200. When he was arrested, the alleged fraudster was in possession of more than 50 American Express and Visa gift, debit, and prepaid credit cards with re-encoded magnetic stripes.[32]

Chip Cards

Credit cards with only magnetic stripes are finally being phased out in the United States. After October 1, 2015, a liability shift occurred—merchants who accept payments made via a chip card's magnetic stripe can continue to do so, however, they must accept responsibility for any fraudulent purchases. This provides a strong incentive for merchants to move to new payment terminals that accept the chip card.

Credit cards with chips employ the EMV (Europay, Mastercard, Visa) global standard for enabling chip cards to work at point-of-sale systems and automated teller machines. Unlike with magnetic stripe cards, every time an EMV card is used for payment, the card chip creates a unique transaction code that can never be used again. If a hacker somehow steals the chip information from one specific point of sale, typical card duplication will not work because the stolen transaction number created in that instance is not usable again and the card would just get denied.

Smart Cards

smart card: A credit card embedded with a computer chip that contains key consumer and account data; smart card users must either enter their PIN (chip-and-PIN) or sign (chip-and-sign) for each transaction to be approved.

Most European countries use smart card technology. **Smart cards** are embedded with computer chips containing key consumer and account data. Smart card users must either enter their PIN (chip-and-PIN) or sign (chip-and-sign) for each transaction to be approved. The smart cards require different terminals from those used for magnetic stripe cards. All the information needed for authorization is contained in the chip or is captured at the point-of-sale. With smart cards, merchants do not need to send data over networks to obtain authorization.[33]

Contactless Payment Cards

contactless payment card: A card with an embedded chip that only needs to be held close to a terminal to transfer its data; no PIN number needs to be entered.

Contactless payment cards contain an embedded chip and antenna that enables the consumer to simply hold the card close to a terminal to transfer the data necessary to make a payment. Typically, no signature or PIN entry is required for purchases less than $25, making transactions speedier than payments made by conventional credit or debit card or even cash. Contactless payment cards are ideal in situations where the consumer must make a fast payment, such as when boarding a form of mass transportation; however, some observers are concerned that it is relatively easy to scan details from contactless cards. During 2014, in the United Kingdom, where this form of payment is very popular, some 58 million contactless cards were used to make 15.8 billion transactions totaling £802 billion ($1.23 trillion), for an average transaction of £50.75 ($78.16).[34] American Express ExpressPay, ExonMobile SpeedPass, MasterCard PayPass, and Visa PayWave are contactless payment cards used in the United States.

Point-of-Sale Devices

point-of-sale (POS) device: A device used to enter data into a computer system.

Point-of-sale (POS) devices are devices used to capture data. They are frequently used in retail operations to enter sales information into computer systems. The POS device computes the total charges, including tax. In medical settings, POS devices are often used for remote monitoring in hospitals, clinics, laboratories, doctors' offices, and patients' homes. With network-enabled POS equipment, medical professionals can instantly get an update on the patient's condition from anywhere at any time via a network or the Internet. POS devices use various types of input and output devices, such as keyboards, bar-code readers, scanning devices, printers, and screens.

Much of the money that businesses spend on computer technology involves POS devices.

Many restaurants, bars, and retail shops are switching from traditional cash registers and costly credit card terminals to simpler devices that plug into smartphones and tablets. For example, a device called the Square Stand includes a built-in card reader that connects to an iPad and a hub device that connects to accessories, including a cash drawer, receipt printer, and scanner. With this device, a small retailer can have a cash register that keeps track of inventory and provides instant sales analysis for the cost of an iPad and $450 for the Square Stand, printer, and cash drawer, plus a per-transaction fee of 2.75 percent. PayPal and Groupon also offer similar devices.[35]

Automated Teller Machine (ATM) Devices

The automated teller machine (ATM), another type of special-purpose input/output device, is a terminal that bank customers use to perform transactions with their bank accounts. Other types of companies also use various ATM devices, sometimes called kiosks, to support their business processes. Some can dispense tickets, such as for airlines, concerts, and soccer games. Some colleges use them to produce transcripts.

Bar-Code Scanners

A bar-code scanner employs a laser scanner to read a bar-coded label and pass the data to a computer. The bar-code reader may be stationary or hand-held to support a wide variety of uses. This form of input is used widely in store checkouts and warehouse inventory control. Bar codes are also used in hospitals, where a nurse scans a patient's wristband and then a bar code on the medication about to be administered to prevent medication errors.

Several companies have created applications that convert a cell phone camera into a bar-code reader. You can scan a bar code from a print ad, packaging, or label to launch Web sites and buy items with a few clicks.

Radio Frequency Identification (RFID) Devices

radio frequency identification (RFID): A technology that employs a microchip with an antenna to broadcast its unique identifier and location to receivers.

Radio frequency identification (RFID) is a technology that employs a microchip with an antenna to broadcast its unique identifier and location to receivers. The purpose of an RFID system is to transmit data by a mobile device, called a tag (see Figure 3.10), which is read by an RFID reader and processed according to the needs of a computer program. One popular application of RFID is to place microchips on retail items and install in-store readers that track the inventory on the shelves to determine when shelves should be restocked. The RFID tag chip includes a special form of EPROM memory that holds data about the item to which the tag is attached. A radio frequency

FIGURE 3.10

RFID tag

An RFID tag is small compared with current bar-code labels used to identify items.

signal can update this memory as the status of the item changes. The data transmitted by the tag might provide identification, location information, or details about the product tagged, such as date of manufacture, retail price, color, or date of purchase.

Target Corporation is slowly rolling out RFID technology in its stores, starting with key vendors in high-priority categories, such as women's and kids' apparel and home décor. The retailer will use RFID smart labels attached to price tags in an effort that is expected to help the company improve inventory accuracy throughout its supply chain and better fulfill orders placed on its Web site for store pickup.[36,37] In a separate, small-scale RFID-enabled trial, Target utilized RFID-tag lanyards in its pop-up holiday store in New York City during the 2015 holiday shopping season. Visitors to the temporary store were given lanyards outfitted with RFID tags, which they could scan next to any product they wished to purchase. Shoppers then checked out using a digital shopping cart and received their product at the front of the shop. Although this trial was extremely limited (involving just 16 different products), it allowed Target to begin testing the concept of cartless shopping, which the retailer sees as a way to generate new sales and compete with online shopping sites.[38]

Pen Input Devices

By touching the screen with a pen input device, you can activate a command or cause the computer to perform a task, enter handwritten notes, and draw objects and figures. Pen input requires special software and hardware. Handwriting recognition software, for example, converts onscreen handwriting into text. Many tablet computers can transform handwriting into typed text and store the "digital ink" just the way a person writes it. People can use a pen to write and send email, add comments to documents, mark up presentations, and even hand draw charts in a document. The data can then be moved, highlighted, searched, and converted into text. If perfected, this interface is likely to become widely used. Pen input is especially attractive to people who are uncomfortable using a keyboard. The success of pen input depends on how accurately and at what cost handwriting can be read and translated into digital form.

Touch Screens

Advances in screen technology allow display screens to function as input as well as output devices. By touching certain parts of a touch-sensitive screen, you can start a program or trigger other types of action. Touch screens can remove the need for a keyboard, which conserves space and increases portability. Touch screens are frequently used at gas stations to allow customers to select grades of gas and request a receipt; on photocopy machines for selecting options; at fast-food restaurants for entering customer choices; at information centers for finding facts about local eating and drinking establishments; and at amusement parks to provide directions to patrons. They also are used in kiosks at airports and department stores. Touch screens are also being used for gathering votes in elections.

As touch screens get smaller, the user's fingers begin to block the information on the display. Nanotouch technology is being explored as a means of overcoming this problem. With this technology, users control the touch screen from its backside so that fingers do not block the display. As the user's finger moves on the back of the display, a tiny graphical finger is projected onto the touch screen. Such displays are useful for mobile audio players that are about the size of a coin.

Application developers are busy trying to find ways to take advantage of Apple's 3D Touch feature, which the company introduced in the fall of 2015 with its iPhone 6s smartphone. 3D Touch uses a pressure-sensitive touch screen that measures how forcefully you press down on the screen. The new feature adds "peek" and "pop" gestures to the tap, swipe, and pinch gestures with which most smartphone users are familiar. 3D Touch is designed to bring a new dimension of functionality to the iPhone, allowing users to both see and feel what a press can do.[39] OpenTable, an online restaurant-reservation and review service, has included 3D Touch features in the latest version of its iPhone apps. Users can 3D Touch the app's icon to quickly view favorited restaurants and upcoming reservations. Within the app, users can "peek" at a restaurant's details by pressing lightly on the name of the restaurant in a list of search results. Swiping up offers the ability to instantly see available reservation times, and pressing harder on a restaurant name "pops" a user to the restaurant's full profile.[40]

Output Devices

Computer systems provide output to decision makers at all levels of an organization so they can solve a business problem or capitalize on a competitive opportunity. In addition, output from one computer system can provide input into another computer system. The desired form of this output might be visual, audio, or even digital. Whatever the output's content or form, output devices are designed to provide the right information to the right person in the right format at the right time.

Display Screens

The display screen is a device used to show the output from the computer. Today a variety of flat-panel display screens are far lighter and thinner than the traditional cathode-ray tubes (CRTs) associated with early computers. Table 3.4 compares types of flat-panel display screens.

TABLE 3.4 Various types of flat-panel displays

Type	Description	Noteworthy Feature
Liquid crystal display (LCD)	Uses several layers of charged liquid crystals placed between clear plates that are lit from behind by a fluorescent light to create light and images	The viewing angle tends to be worse than that of plasma displays
Light-emitting diode (LED)	An LCD display that uses light-emitting diodes (LEDs) as backlight on the screen rather than a fluorescent lamp	Provides better contrast and lower energy consumption than LCDs
Organic light-emitting diode (OLED)	Functions by exciting organic compounds with electric current to produce bright, sharp images	Does not employ a backlight, which enables improved contrast and lower power consumption than LCD and LED LCD displays
Plasma	Uses electricity to excite gas atoms to light up appropriate phosphors on the screen to emit light and color	Performs well in dark conditions but not as well in well-lit rooms

With today's wide selection of display screens, price and overall quality can vary tremendously. The quality of a screen image is largely determined by the number of horizontal and vertical pixels used to create it. The images shown on your display device are composed of a million or more pixels. Resolution is the total number of pixels contained in the display; the more pixels, the clearer and sharper the image. A common resolution is 2,040 horizontal pixels × 1,536 vertical pixels. The size of the display monitor also affects the quality of the viewing. The same pixel resolution on a small screen is sharper than on a larger screen, where the same number of pixels is spread out over a larger area.

computer graphics card: A component of a computer that takes binary data from the CPU and translates it into an image you see on your display device.

graphics processing unit (GPU): A powerful processing chip that renders images on the screen display.

The **computer graphics card** takes binary data from the CPU and translates it into an image you see on your display device. It is the computer graphics card that controls the quality of the image and determines how many display devices can be attached to the computer. The computer graphics card holds the **graphics processing unit (GPU)**, a powerful processing chip that renders images on the display screen. After the computer graphics card takes binary data from the CPU, the GPU decides what to do with each pixel on the screen to create the image. As the GPU creates images, it uses RAM on the graphics card (called video RAM or VRAM) to store data about each pixel, including its color and location on the screen. One measure of a video card's performance is how many complete images the card can display per second, which is called the frame rate. The human eye can process roughly 25 frames per second; however, many video games require a frame rate of at least 60 frames per second to provide a good user experience.[41]

Because many users leave their computers on for hours at a time, power usage is an important factor when deciding which type of display to purchase. Although power usage varies from model to model, OLED displays are the most energy efficient, with LCD monitors generally consuming between 35 and 50 percent less power than plasma screens.

Aspect ratio and screen size describe the size of the display screen. Aspect ratio is the ratio of the width of the display to its height. The aspect ratio of width to height of 4:3 or 5:4 is good for people who use their computer to view or create Web pages or documents. Widescreen displays typically have an aspect ratio of 16:10 or 16:9 to allow improved viewing of movies and video games.

Companies are competing on the innovation frontier to create thinner, lighter, flexible, and more durable display devices for computers, cell phones, and other mobile devices. LG Display, a leading manufacturer of LCD and OLED displays, recently unveiled prototypes for a 55-inch double-sided OLED display that is just 5.3 mm thick, as well as a flexible 1-mm thick "wallpaper" OLED display that can be attached to the wall using a magnetic mat. The company also has working prototypes for a transparent display and one that can be rolled up like a newspaper. According to LG, its innovative OLED displays are flexible enough to curve around corners and are almost impossible to break.[42,43] Many of these displays are still in development as LG works through the complex manufacturing processes involved. In the meantime, the company is investing over $8 billion to build a new display panel manufacturing facility that is expected to be up and running in 2018.[44]

Printers and Plotters

One of the most useful and common forms of output is called hard copy, which is simply paper output from a printer. The two main types of printers are laser printers and inkjet printers, and they are available with different speeds, features, and capabilities. Some can be set up to accommodate paper forms, such as blank check forms and invoice forms. Newer printers allow businesses to create full-color, customized, and individualized printed output using standard paper and data input. Ticket-receipt printers, such as those used in restaurants, ATMs, and point-of-sale systems are in wide-scale use.

The speed of a printer is typically measured by the number of pages printed per minute (ppm). Similar to a display screen, the quality, or resolution, of a printer's output depends on the number of dots printed per inch (dpi). A 600-dpi printer prints more clearly than a 300-dpi printer. A recurring cost of using a printer is the inkjet or laser cartridge that must be replaced periodically—every few thousand pages for laser printers and every 500 to 900 pages for inkjet printers.

Inkjet printers that can print 10 to 40 ppm for black-and-white output and 5 to 20 ppm for color output are available for less than $175. With an initial cost much less than color laser printers, inkjet printers can print vivid hues and can produce high-quality banners, graphics, greeting cards, letters, text, and photo prints.

Laser printers are generally faster than inkjet printers and can handle a heavier print load volume. A monochrome laser printer can print 25 to 45 ppm and cost anywhere from $200 to $700. Color laser printers can print color pages at a rate of 10 to 35 ppm and are available in a wide range of prices—from $350 to more than $3,500 for a high-quality color laser printer.

A number of manufacturers offer multiple-function printers that can copy, print (in color or black and white), fax, and scan. Such multifunctional devices are often used when people need to do a relatively low volume of copying, printing, faxing, and scanning. Typical prices for multifunction printers range from $100 to $400, depending on features and capabilities. Because these devices take the place of more than one piece of equipment, they are less expensive to acquire and maintain than a stand-alone fax plus a stand-alone printer, copier, and so on. Also, eliminating equipment that was once located on a countertop or desktop clears a workspace for other work-related activities. As a result, such devices are popular in homes and small office settings.

Mobile print solutions enable users to wirelessly send documents, email messages and attachments, presentations, and even boarding passes from any smartphone, tablet, or laptop to any mobile-enabled printer in the world. For example, PrinterOn Enterprise enables any print requests from any mobile or fixed device to be routed to any of over 10,000 printers worldwide that are configured with the PrinterOn Enterprise service. Mobile users who use the service only need to access a directory of PrinterOn printers and locations and then send an email with the attachment to be printed to the email address of the printer. American Airlines Admiral Club, Delta Sky Club, Embassy Suites, and DoubleTree by Hilton have installed PrinterOn printers at many of their locations.[45]

Plotters are a type of hard-copy output device used for general design work. Businesses typically use plotters to generate paper or acetate blueprints, schematics, and drawings of buildings or new products. Standard plot widths are 24 inches and 36 inches, and the length can be whatever meets the need—from a few inches to many feet.

3D Printers

3D printers have created a major breakthrough in how many items will be "manufactured." See Figure 3.11. 3D printing technology takes a three-dimensional model of an object stored on a computer and sends it to a 3D printer to create the object using strands of a plastic filament or synthetic powder. The filament comes in spools of various colors and is fed through a heated extruder that moves in several directions to place super thin layers on top of each other. The stacks are then bonded together, often using ultraviolet light, to create a 3D object. 3D printers come with a wide range of capabilities in terms of how fast they can build objects and how large of an object they can build. 3D printers for home use typically run $1,000 and up, while commercial 3D printers can cost tens of thousands of dollars.[46]

3D printing is commonly used by aerospace firms, auto manufacturers, and other design-intensive companies. It is especially valuable during the conceptual stage of engineering design when the exact dimensions and material strength of the prototype are not critical. Some architectural design firms are using 3D printers to create full color models of their projects to show clients. Cincinnati Children's Hospital uses 3D printing to create models of patients' hearts so that physicians can plan their surgery.[47]

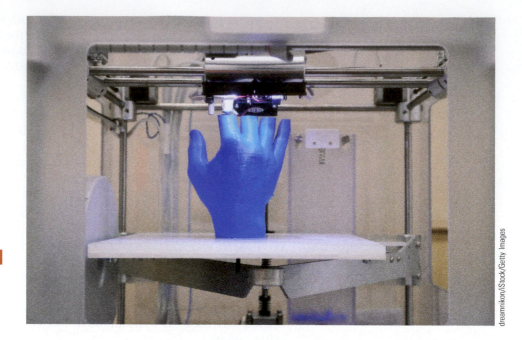

dreamnikon/iStock/Getty Images

FIGURE 3.11

3D printer

3D print technology is making it possible to print objects ranging from everyday objects to houses.

bioprinting: The use of 3D printers to build human parts and organs from actual human cells.

The automotive, electronics, and toy industries are early adopters of using 3D printing to improve upon traditional manufacturing processes. Ford Motor Company used 3D printing to design the new engine cover of its next-generation Mustang. Following traditional methods, an engineer would first create a computer model and then wait for about four months for a prototype to be produced, at a cost of $500,000. Using 3D printing, Ford can print the prototype in just four days at a cost of only $3,000.[48] A drag racing enthusiast created a remote control dragster capable of going 202 mph using 3D printing.[49]

3D printing can cut costs and reduce the waste and carbon footprint associated with traditional manufacturing. With 3D printing, production and assembly can be local, with no need to ship products thousands of miles to their destination. Only the raw materials needed to create the object—be it carbon fiber, metal powder, plastic filament, or some other substance—are used. Product parts can be replaced using parts manufactured with 3D printing so the entire product doesn't have to be disposed of and replaced each time it malfunctions.[50]

Biomedical engineers are exploring a process called **bioprinting**, which uses 3D printers to build human parts and organs from actual human cells. For example, bioprinting is being used to create custom breast implants and grafts for cancer patients using the recipient's own fat and skin cells.[51] Regenerative medicine pioneer Organovo is able to build blood vessels and cardiac tissue via a 3D printer that dispenses cells instead of ink. The firm plans to begin selling 3D printed liver tissue.[52]

Digital Audio Players

digital audio player: A device that can store, organize, and play digital music files.

MP3: A standard format for compressing a sound sequence into a small file.

A **digital audio player** is a device that can store, organize, and play digital music files. **MP3** (MPEG-1 Audio Layer-3) is a popular format for compressing a sound sequence into a very small file while preserving the original level of sound quality when it is played. By compressing the sound file, it requires less time to download the file and less storage space on a hard drive.

You can use many different music devices smaller than a deck of cards to download music from the Internet and other sources. These devices have no moving parts and can store hours of music. Apple first moved into the digital music market with its iPod MP3 player in 2001. In 2003, it launched its iTunes Music Store, where users can find music online, preview it, and download it in a way that is safe, legal, and affordable. Other MP3 manufacturers include Dell, Sony, Samsung, Iomega, Creative, and Motorola, whose Rokr product was the first iTunes-compatible phone. Today, you can use your smartphone to view YouTube videos, buy music online, check email, and more.

E-Book Readers

e-book: The digital media equivalent of a conventional printed book.

The digital media equivalent of a conventional printed book is called an **e-book** (short for electronic book). The Project Gutenberg Online Book Catalog offers over 50,000 free e-books and a total of over 100,000 e-books available. E-books can be downloaded from many sites, including the Project Gutenberg site (*www.gutenberg.org*), onto personal computers or dedicated hardware devices known as e-book readers. The devices cost anywhere from around $60 to $350, and users typically pay between $10 and $20 to download electronic versions of the best-selling books. E-book readers usually have the capacity to store thousands of books. The most current Amazon.com Kindle, Kobo Aura, Barnes & Noble Nook e-readers have e-paper displays that look like printed pages. A typical e-reader weighs less than three-quarters of a pound, is around one-half inch thick, and comes with a display screen ranging from 5 to 8 inches in size. Thus, these readers are more compact than most paperbacks and can be easily held in one hand. More recent versions of e-book readers display content in 16 million colors and high resolution. On many e-readers, the size of the text can be magnified for readers with poor vision.

Critical Thinking Exercise

Choosing Your Next Computer

You are looking for the latest and greatest portable computer to replace your five-year old laptop. You will use this computer for both work and personal computing tasks—everything from creating documents, spreadsheets, and presentations to surfing the Web and editing videos of your friends and family. You want a computer that is powerful, lightweight, and comes with a long battery life.

Review Questions

1. Should you purchase a computer with an x86 processor, an Intel Atom processor, or an ARM processor? What are the pros and cons of each type of processor? Will you want a multicore processor? Why or why not?
2. What sort of main memory and cache memory should you seek?

Critical Thinking Questions

1. What sort of secondary storage devices would most economically meet your needs?
2. Which input and output devices would be most useful to you?

Computer System Types

In general, computers can be classified as either special purpose or general purpose. Special-purpose computers are used for limited applications, for example, by military, government, and scientific research groups such as the CIA and NASA. Other applications include specialized processors found in appliances, cars, and other products. For example, automobile repair shops connect special-purpose computers to your car's engine to identify specific performance problems. As another example, IBM is developing a new generation of computer chips to develop so-called cognitive computers that are designed to mimic the way the human brain works. Rather than being programmed as today's computers are, cognitive computers, such as IBM's Watson computer, are able to learn through experiences and outcomes and mimic human learning patterns.

General-purpose computers are used for a variety of applications, including the business applications discussed in this text. General-purpose computer systems can be divided into two major groups: systems used by one user at a time and systems used by multiple concurrent users. Table 3.5 shows the general ranges of capabilities for various types of computer systems.

TABLE 3.5 Types of computer systems

Single-user computer systems can be divided into two groups: portable computers and nonportable computers.

	Single-User Computers			
	Portable Computers			
Factor	**Smartphone**	**Laptop**	**Notebook/Ultrabook**	**Tablet**
Cost	$150–$1,000	$300–$3,000	$300–$800	$75–$1,500
Weight (pounds)	<0.5	<6	<3	<2
Screen size (inches)	2–5.5	<20	<12	<13
Typical use	Combines a cell phone with a hand-held computer; run apps and text messaging services; access network and the Internet wirelessly	Run worker productivity software, access the Internet, play games, listen to music, and watch videos	Smaller version of a laptop, with sufficient processing power to run nearly every business application	Capture data at the point of contact, read email, access the Internet, read e-books, view photos, play games, listen to music, and watch videos
	Nonportable Computers			
Factor	**Thin Client**	**Desktop**	**Nettop**	**Workstation**
Cost	$200–$500	$500–$3,000	$150–$350	$1,500–$9,500
Weight (pounds)	<3	20–30	<5	<20–35
Typical use	Enter data and access applications via the Internet; can be portable or nonportable	Run worker productivity software, access the Internet, play games, listen to music, and watch videos	Small, limited capacity desktop computer; performs basic tasks such as Internet surfing, accessing Web-based applications, document processing, and audio/video playback[	Powerful desktop capable of performing engineering, computer aided design, and software development functions

Multiple-user computer systems include servers, mainframes, and supercomputers.

	Multiple-User Computers		
Factor	**Server**	**Mainframe**	**Supercomputer**
Cost	>$500	>$75,000	>$250,000
Weight (pounds)	>25	>100	≥100
Typical use	Execute network and Internet applications	Execute computing tasks for large organizations and provide massive data storage	Run scientific applications; perform intensive number crunching

Portable Computers

portable computer: A computer small enough to carry easily.

Many computer manufacturers offer a variety of **portable computers**, those that are small enough to carry easily. Portable computers include wearable computers, smartphones, laptops, notebooks, ultrabooks, and tablets.

Wearable Computers

wearable computer: An electronic device capable of storing and processing data that is incorporated into a person's clothing or personal accessories.

A **wearable computer** is an electronic device capable of storing and processing data that is incorporated into a person's clothing or personal accessories. Companies like Apple, FitBit, Google, Huawei, LG, Pebble, Samsung, Sony, TomTom, Xiaomi, and others offer health-tracking wrist bands or smart watches that can capture a wide range of data, including distance covered, elevation climbed, pace, calories burned, continuous heart rate, and quality of sleep. Most can also display call and text notifications and enable one to control songs from a mobile playlist. These products cost anywhere from $75 to $750.

Around one-half to two-thirds of U.S. employers with 15 or more workers have implemented some sort of employee wellness program. One-half of fitness band sales in the United States are to organizations that pass these devices along to its employees, often at no charge. Iron Mountain, the records and data management firm, awards employees points for completing various health- and wellness-related "challenges" that can later be converted into cash. One challenge requires employees to connect a wearable device to a computer portal and walk one million steps in a year.[53]

Chinese researchers have developed an e-skin that is just a few atoms thick so it can press close to the skin. The e-skin contains all the sensors needed to track and broadcast the wearer's blood pressure, pulse, and other vital measurements. The developers are hoping the material can be used to provide instant health assessment and real-time patient diagnoses.[54]

The Mi.Mu is a high-tech glove designed to ease the creation of music using computers and other technology through gestures, enabling musicians to avoid cumbersome dials and computer screens. When wearing the gloves, an upward movement of the hand raises the pitch, extending an index finger adds some reverb, and snapping your palm shut silences everything.[55] Google is partnering with Levi Strauss & Co to make conductive yarn that can be woven into garments to enable touch and gesture interactivity that would allow wearers to do things like press their sleeve to turn a light on or activate their smartphone to make a call.[56]

Smartphones

While features and capabilities vary from model to model and manufacturer to manufacturer, with most smartphones you can place calls, download and run apps (e.g., games, a contact list manager, and personal and business finance managers), send and receive text messages and email, view documents and files, take and send photos and videos, get driving directions via GPS, browse Web sites, and create a playlist of digital tunes. Smartphones employ a combination chipset called a "system on a chip," which includes processor cores, RAM and ROM memory, interface controllers and voltage regulators, as shown in Figure 3.12. With system on a chip, all the critical components of the smartphone are located in a relatively small area, making the device faster and more energy efficient and reducing assembly costs.

Mobile Computers

laptop: A personal computer designed for use by mobile users, being small and light enough to sit comfortably on a user's lap.

A **laptop** is a personal computer designed for use by mobile users, being small and light enough to sit comfortably on a user's lap. Laptops use a variety of flat-panel technologies to produce lightweight and thin display screens with good resolution. In terms of computing power, laptops can match most

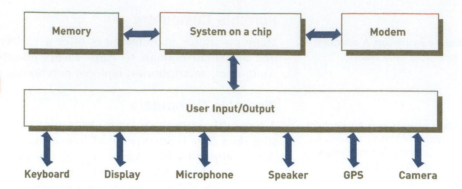

FIGURE 3.12

Anatomy of a smartphone
Smartphones employ a combination chipset called a "system on a chip," which includes processor cores, RAM and ROM memory, interface controllers, and voltage regulators.

tablet: A portable, lightweight computer with no keyboard that allows you to roam the office, home, or factory floor carrying the device like a clipboard.

desktop computers as they come with powerful CPUs as well as large-capacity primary memory and disk storage. This type of computer is highly popular among students and mobile workers who carry their laptops on trips and to meetings and classes. Most personal computer users now prefer a laptop over a desktop because of its portability, lower energy usage, and smaller space requirements.

Numerous portable computers are smaller than the typical laptop and have various names, including notebook and the even smaller ultrabook. The newest notebook computers come with a natural user interface, including both voice-control integration and touch screens; high-quality display screens; always-on, always-connected capabilities; all-day battery life; and processing power sufficient to run most business applications and games.

Tablet are portable, lightweight computers that can come with or without a keyboard and allow you to roam the office, home, or factory floor, carrying the device like a clipboard. You can enter text with a writing stylus directly on the screen, thanks to built-in handwriting-recognition software. Other input methods include an onscreen keyboard and speech recognition. Tablets that support input only via a writing stylus are called slate computers. The convertible tablet PC comes with a swivel screen and can be used as a traditional notebook or as a pen-based tablet PC. Most new tablets come with a front-facing camera for videoconferencing and a second camera for snapshot photos and video. Tablets are especially popular with students and gamers. They are also frequently used in the healthcare, retail, insurance, and manufacturing industries because of their versatility.

The Apple iPad is a tablet capable of running the same software that runs on the Apple iPhone and iPod touch devices, giving it a library of well over a million applications. It also runs software developed specifically for the iPad. The device supports Internet access over both wireless and cellular networks, and it includes an onscreen keypad, although a physical keyboard can also be attached. Apple offers a variety of iPad models, ranging from the iPad mini, which weighs 0.73 pounds and has a 7.9-inch screen, up to the iPad Pro, which weighs 1.5 pounds and has a 12.9-inch screen.

A number of computer companies offer tablets to compete with Apple's iPad, including the Amazon Fire, the Inspiron and Venue by Dell, the Nexus and Pixel from Google, the Tab 2 and Yoga from Lenovo, the Surface Pro from Microsoft, the Shield from Nvidia, the Tablet S and Xperia from Sony, the Encore and Excite by Toshiba, the Galaxy Tab and Galaxy Note from Samsung (see Figure 3.13), and the low-cost (less than $75) Aakash and Ubislate from the India-based company Quad.

Thin Clients, Desktops, and Workstations

Nonportable single-user computers include thin client computers, desktop computers, nettop, and workstations.

iStockphoto.com/Mixmike

Tablet
The Samsung Galaxy Note 10.1 Android tablet has a large touch screen and a quad-core processor.

thin client: A low-cost, centrally managed computer with no internal or external attached drives for data storage.

A **thin client** is a low-cost, centrally managed computer with no internal or external attached drives for data storage. These computers have limited capabilities and perform only essential applications, so they remain "thin" in terms of the client applications they include. As stripped-down computers, they do not have the storage capacity or computing power of typical desktop computers, nor do they need it for the role they play. With no hard disk, they never pick up viruses or suffer a hard disk crash. Unlike personal computers, thin clients download data and software from a network when needed, making support, distribution, and updating of software applications much easier and less expensive. Thin clients work well in a cloud-computing environment to enable users to access the computing and data resources available within the cloud. The Chromebook, which runs the Chrome OS operating system, is a highly portable device, is widely used in many schools, and is an example of a thin client.

As patient records within the healthcare industry have gone increasingly digital, many healthcare providers have struggled to find new ways to ensure that their staff have ready access to a patient's pertinent records. Chapters Health System, which provides post-acute, palliative, and hospice care for patients across west-central Florida, decided to upgrade to thin client technology in the form of Samsung Chromebooks for its staff of 140 caregivers, who frequently make rounds to hospitals, nursing homes, assisted living facilities, and private home. For Chapters Health, the Chromebooks offer affordable, lightweight, and secure access to clinical data—along with a nine-hour battery life.[57]

desktop computer: A nonportable computer that fits on a desktop and provides sufficient computing power, memory, and storage for most business computing tasks.

Desktop computers are single-user computer systems that are highly versatile. Named for their size, desktop computers can provide sufficient computing power, memory, and storage for most business computing tasks.

The Apple iMac is a family of Macintosh desktop computers first introduced in 1998 in which all the components (including the CPU and the disk drives) fit behind the display screen. Intel's Core i7 High-end Desktop Processor family of computers has eight cores, 20 megabytes of cache memory, and supports DDR4 memory. The CPU operates at a base clock frequency of 3.0GHz making it a popular choice for gamers.

nettop: A very small, inexpensive desktop computer typically used for Internet access, email, accessing Web-based applications, document processing, and audio/video playback.

A **nettop** computer is a very small, inexpensive desktop computer typically used for Internet access, email, accessing Web-based applications, document processing, and audio/video playback. A key feature of nettop computers is that they require perhaps one-tenth the amount of power to operate as a typical desktop computer.

workstations: A more powerful personal computer used for mathematical computing, computer-assisted design, and other high-end processing but still small enough to fit on a desktop.

Workstations are more powerful than personal computers but still small enough to fit on a desktop. They are used to support engineering and technical users who perform heavy mathematical computing, computer-assisted design (CAD), video editing, and other applications requiring a high-end processor. Such users need very powerful CPUs, large amounts of main memory, and extremely high-resolution graphic displays. Workstations are typically more expensive than the average desktop computer. Some computer manufacturers are now providing laptop versions of their powerful desktop workstations. The Mac Pro is a series of workstation and server computers based on the high performance Intel Xeon processor.

Larson & Darby Group is an architectural, engineering, interiors, and technology design firm that uses powerful HP Z workstations to run Autodesk AutoCAD and related software. Larson & Darby needs high-performance computing to meet the challenging demands of creating 3D models and then rendering those models to put design options in front of clients. If the computer hardware runs slowly, then designers must wait for drawings to regenerate when changes are made and this eats into design time. Reliability is also critical. Rendering can take hours on many projects and a hardware failure can mean losing a full day's worth of work.[58]

Servers, Mainframes, and Supercomputers

Servers, mainframes, and supercomputers are designed to support workgroups from a small department of two or three workers to large organizations with tens of thousands of employees and millions of customers.

server: A computer employed by many users to perform a specific task, such as running network or Internet applications.

A **server** is a computer employed by many users to perform a specific task, such as running network or Internet applications. While almost any computer can run server operating system and server applications, a server computer usually has special features that make it more suitable for operating in a multiuser environment. These features include greater memory and storage capacities, faster and more efficient communications abilities, and reliable backup capabilities. A Web server is one specifically designed to handle Internet traffic and communications. An enterprise server stores and provides access to programs that meet the needs of an entire organization. A file server stores and coordinates program and data files. Server systems consist of multiuser computers, including supercomputers, mainframes, and other servers.

scalability: The ability to increase the processing capability of a computer system so that it can handle more users, more data, or more transactions in a given period.

Servers offer great **scalability**, the ability to increase the processing capability of a computer system so that it can handle more users, more data, or more transactions in a given period. Scalability is achieved by adding more, or more powerful, processors. Scaling up adds more powerful processors, and scaling out adds many processors to increase the total data-processing capacity. Most new servers include onboard diagnostic capabilities that enable

mainframe computer: A large, powerful computer often shared by hundreds of concurrent users connected to the machine over a network.

supercomputers: The most powerful computer systems with the fastest processing speeds.

the server to alert the IS operations group to potential problems, a capability that used to be only available for high-end, mainframe computers.

A **mainframe computer** is a large, powerful computer shared by dozens or even hundreds of concurrent users connected to the machine over a network. Mainframe computers have been the workhorses of corporate computing for more than 50 years. They can support thousands of users simultaneously and can handle all of the core functions of a corporation. Mainframe computers provide the data-processing power and data-storage capacity that enables banks and brokerage firms to deliver new mobile services, credit card companies to detect identity theft, and government agencies to better serve citizens. Examples of companies using mainframe technology include ADP, which processes payroll for millions of employees at over 610,000 client companies; Mastercard, which manages 2 billion accounts and tracks $4.1 trillion of spending in 150 different currencies in 210 countries around the world; and UPS, which tracks the route of 18 million packages and documents each day in 200 countries and territories.[59–61]

IBM spent $1 billion and five years designing its new z13 mainframe system, which is capable of processing 2.5 billion transactions per day. Pricing for the z13 depends on configuration, but versions of the previous model ran as high as $1 million.[62]

Radixx International operates the computerized reservation systems for 40 small and midsize airlines with 90,000 directly connected travel agents. The reservation systems were running on a collection of 400 servers; however, Radixx recently switched to running on IBM mainframes, reducing its total cost of ownership by about 50 percent.[63]

Supercomputers are the most powerful computers with the fastest processing speed and highest performance. They are special-purpose machines designed for applications that require extensive and rapid computational capabilities. Originally, supercomputers were used primarily by government agencies to perform the high-speed number crunching needed in weather forecasting, earthquake simulations, climate modeling, nuclear research, study of the origin of matter and the universe, and weapons development and testing. They are now used more broadly for commercial purposes in the life sciences and the manufacture of drugs and new materials. For example, Procter & Gamble uses supercomputers in the research and development of many of its leading commercial brands, such as Tide and Pampers, to help develop detergent with more soapsuds and improve the quality of its diapers. And supercomputers are also used to help establish the safety ratings for vehicles sold in the United States. The ratings are based on sophisticated computer simulations, during which supercomputers crunch equations involving many different variables. These computer-generated simulations are combined with data taken from actual crash tests and analyzed to determine safety ratings that many consumers use as one factor in determining which car to buy.

Most new supercomputers are based on an architecture that employs graphics processing unit (GPU) chips in addition to traditional central processing unit (CPU) chips to perform high-speed processing. The speed of supercomputers is measured in floating point operations per second (FLOPS). Table 3.6 lists supercomputer processing speeds.

TABLE 3.6 Supercomputer processing speeds

Speed	Meaning
GigaFLOPS	1×10^9 FLOPS
TeraFLOPS	1×10^{12} FLOPS
PetaFLOPS	1×10^{15} FLOPS
ExaFLOPS	1×10^{18} FLOPS

The fastest supercomputer in the world as of November 2015 is the Tianhe-2 built by the National University of Defense Technology located in Hunan Province, China. It was built at an estimated cost of about $3 billion and is expected to be used for simulations, analysis, and government security applications.[64]

Table 3.7 lists the five most powerful supercomputers in use as of July 2015.

TABLE 3.7 Five most powerful operational supercomputers (July 2015)

Rank	Name	Manufacturer	Research Center	Location	Number of Cores	Speed (Petaflops)
1	Tianhe-2	NUDT	National University of Defense Technology (NUDT)	China	3.1 million	33.9
2	Titan	Cray	Oak Ridge National Laboratory	United States	0.56 million	17.6
3	Sequoia	IBM	Lawrence Livermore National Laboratory	United States	1.5 million	17.2
4	K	Fujitsu	Riken Advanced Institute for Computational Science	Japan	0.75 million	10.5
5	Mira	IBM	Argonne National Laboratory	United States	0.8 million	8.6

Source: Lendino, Jamie, "China's Tianhe-2 Still the Fastest Supercomputer in the World, but the US Is Catching Up," *Extreme Tech*, July 13, 2015, *www.extreme tech.com/extreme/209704-chinas-tianhe-2-still-the-fastest-supercomputer-in-the-world-but-the-us-is-catching-up*.

Critical Thinking Exercise

Upgrading an Organization's Computers

Your organization earns $50 million in annual sales, has 500 employees, and plans to acquire 250 new portable computers this year along with another 250 next year. The goal is to issue every employee a company-owned computer, which they can use at work and at home. The computers will be loaded with antivirus software and productivity software to meet each employee's business needs. Your organization has decided it will purchase the computers from the same manufacturer to obtain a quantity purchase discount. To the extent possible, the goal is to have the same hardware and software for everyone to simplify the troubleshooting and support of the computers. The chief financial officer has asked you to lead a project team to define users' computer hardware needs and recommend the most cost-effective solution for meeting those needs.

Review Questions

1. Which classes of portable computers could meet the needs of your organization?
2. What are the pros and cons of each class of portable computer?

Critical Thinking Questions

1. Who else (role, department) and how many people would you select to be a member of the team? How would your team go about defining users' needs?
2. Do you think that only one manufacturer and model of portable computer will meet everyone's needs, or should you define multiple portable computers based on the needs of various classes of end user?

Server Farms, Data Centers, and Green Computing

This section will cover three topics that provide a good overview of what the computer industry and various organizations are doing to meet their computing needs in a more efficient and environmentally friendly manner.

Server Farms

server farm: A facility that houses a large number of servers in the same room, where access to the machines can be controlled and authorized support personnel can more easily manage and maintain the servers.

Often, an organization will house a large number of servers in the same room, where access to the machines can be controlled and authorized support personnel can more easily manage and maintain the servers. Such a facility is called a **server farm**. Apple, Google, Microsoft, the U.S. government, and many other organizations have built billion-dollar server farms in small rural communities where both land and electricity are cheap.

Server manufacturers are competing heavily to reduce the power required to operate their servers and are making "performance per watt" a key part of their product differentiation strategy. Low power usage is a critical factor for organizations that run server farms made up of hundreds or even thousands of servers. Typical servers draw up to 220 watts, although new servers based on Intel's Atom microprocessor draw 8 or fewer watts. The annual power savings from such low-energy usage servers can amount to tens of thousands of dollars for operators of a large server farm. Server farm operators are also looking for low-cost, clean, renewable energy sources. For example, Apple runs a server farm in Maiden, North Carolina, on 167 million kilowatt hours of power generated from a 100-acre solar energy facility. This is enough power to operate 17,600 homes for a year.[65]

virtual server: A method of logically dividing the resources of a single physical server to create multiple logical servers, each acting as its own dedicated machine.

A **virtual server** is an approach to improving hardware utilization by logically dividing the resources of a single physical server to create multiple logical servers, each acting as its own dedicated machine, as shown in Figure 3.14. The server on which one or more virtual machines is running is called the host server. Each virtual server is called a guest server or a virtual machine, and it includes its own operating system to manage the user interface and control how the virtual machine uses the host server's hardware. The use of virtual servers is growing rapidly, with at least 70 percent of x86 server workloads virtualized.[66] In a typical data center deployment of several hundred servers, companies using virtualization can build 12 virtual machines for every actual server, with a resulting savings in capital and operating expenses (including energy costs) of millions of dollars per year. The hypervisor is a virtual server program that controls the host processor and resources,

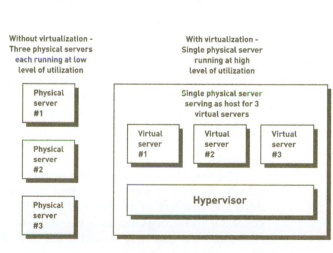

FIGURE 3.14
Virtual server
Virtualization is an approach to improving hardware utilization by logically dividing the resources of a single physical server to create multiple logical servers.

allocates the necessary resources to each virtual system, and ensures that they do not disrupt each other.

Cognizant, an IT, consulting, and business process outsourcing company based in New Jersey, is making use of virtual servers in some of its 100 development and delivery centers worldwide. At one point, the company had almost 7,000 physical servers, which became unstainable in terms of cost and management time. To address this problem, Cognizant utilized virtual server technology to reduce its number of physical servers by 90 percent. It now runs 8,000 virtual servers, representing 85 percent of its server capacity.[67]

container: A way for software developers and hardware managers to package applications and software components into a well-defined, compact envelope that can be used to more easily manage it, including moving it across various hosts.

Software developers and hardware managers can package applications and software components into **containers** that give whatever is inside a well-defined, compact envelope that can be used to more easily manage it, including moving it across various hosts. While virtual machines divide the host server into multiple operating systems, all containers use the operating system of their host server. This means containers require less memory to run and are faster to deploy than virtual machines.

Bank of America, Goldman Sachs, and the International Securities Exchange are just some of the organizations within the banking and financial services industries that have been exploring the possibility of using container software (such as CoreOS and Docker), partly in response to demands from their own developers who are looking for more efficient ways to deploy their applications. Like other organizations, banks and other financial institutions like the simplicity that containers offer; however, some institutions are still only using containers for in-house applications and for development due to security and regulatory compliance concerns. Recently, Goldman Sachs became one of the first financial institutions to launch some applications into production using containers in the public cloud.[68,69]

blade server: A server that houses many individual computer motherboards that include one or more processors, computer memory, computer storage, and computer network connections.

A **blade server** houses many computer motherboards that include one or more processors, computer memory, computer storage, and computer network connections. These all share a common power supply and air-cooling source within a single chassis. By placing many blades into a single chassis, and then mounting multiple chassis in a single rack, the blade server is more powerful but less expensive than traditional systems based on mainframes or server farms of individual computers. In addition, the blade server approach requires much less physical space than traditional server farms.

Data Center

data center: A climate-and-access-controlled building or a set of buildings that houses the computer hardware that delivers an organization's data and information services.

A **data center** is a climate-and-access-controlled building or a set of buildings that houses the computer hardware that delivers an organization's data and information services.

The rapid growth in the demand for additional computing capacity is causing an explosion in the growth of new and existing data centers. Rackspace is a major cloud-computing service provider that manages over 112,000 servers supporting its more than 300,000 cloud and hosting customers.[70] Apple, Facebook, AT&T, Rackspace, and IT services company Wipro are among firms that have spent hundreds of millions in a single year on new data centers. Google spends on the order of $4 billion a year on building data centers in an attempt to keep up with the burgeoning demand of its existing and new customers.[71] Apple is spending $2 billion to build one data center in Mesa, Arizona, to serve as a command center for its global networks.[72]

The need for additional data storage capacity is another factor driving the growth in data centers. According to one study, somewhere between one-third and one-half of all data centers will run out of space in the next several years. Of those organizations needing more database capacity, about 40 percent indicated that they would build new data centers, about 30 percent said they would lease additional space, and the rest indicated that they would investigate other options, including the use of cloud computing.

A further driving force behind the increased spending on new data centers is that some organizations are consolidating their data centers from many locations down to just a few locations. The goal of consolidation is to lower ongoing operating costs—less spending on utilities, property taxes, and labor. General Motors consolidated 23 data center locations into just two, reducing both its operating costs and energy usage.[73] The General Accounting Office reports that the federal government saved $2 billion between 2011 and 2014 from its data center consolidation efforts.[74]

Traditional data centers consist of warehouse-size buildings filled with row upon row of server racks and powerful air conditioning systems designed to remove dust and humidity from the air and offset the heat generated by the processors. Such data centers can use as much energy as a small city and run up a power bill of millions of dollars per year. Indeed, energy costs can amount to 25 percent of the total cost of operating a data center, with hardware expenses and labor costs the other 75 percent.

Businesses and technology vendors are working to develop data centers that run more efficiently and require less energy for processing and cooling. For example, Red Cloud, an Australian Web site hosting company, implemented a range of modular data center solutions from Cannon Technologies to increase its number of data centers by 11, thus adding 1 million square feet of available space. The module pods can be assembled in just a few days using only basic hand tools.[75] Google, Dell, Hewlett-Packard, Microsoft, and others have adopted similar modular data center approach. See Figure 3.15.

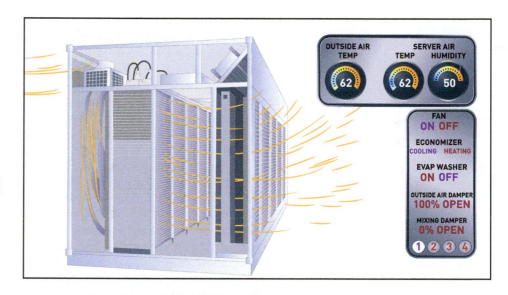

FIGURE 3.15

Modular data center

Microsoft employs a state-of-the-art modular data center.

Source: www.datacenterknowledge.com/archives/2013/01/31/microsofts-1-billion-roofless-data-center/

About half the energy usage of a traditional data center goes to operate its computers. The other half goes to cooling the computers, removing dust and humidity from the air, and lighting the facility, along with other systems that sustain the data center. Such a data center has a power usage effectiveness (PUE) of 2.0. (PUE = total power consumed/power required to run the computers). The ideal goal is a PUE of 1.0, which would indicate that all the power goes to running the computers. Google has been able to build data centers that operate with a PUE of 1.14.[76]

In a further attempt to lower ongoing operating costs, many organizations are locating their data centers in areas with milder climates and lower energy rates and land costs. For organizations in the United States, this translates to rural locations in the south and the northwest. Apple's $1 billion data center, Google's $600 million data center, and Facebook's $450 million data center are all located in rural North Carolina.[77]

The ability to absorb the impact of a disaster (e.g., hurricane, earthquake, terrorism attack, or war) and quickly restore services is a critical concern when it comes to the planning for new data centers. As a result, data centers of large information systems service organizations are often distributed among multiple locations in different areas of the country or even different countries to ensure continuous operations in the event of a disaster. If one data center in such an arrangement is affected by a disaster, its work load could be redirected to one or more of the distributed data centers not affected. IBM offers an extreme example of distributed data centers. Since 2009, IBM has opened nine data centers in Brazil, Mexico, Costa Rica, Chile, Colombia, Peru, and Uruguay to ensure around-the-clock services to its Latin American customers. Globally, IBM has more than 400 widely distributed data centers to meet the needs of its customers.[78] In addition to the distribution strategy, most data centers have implemented some form of backup generator or uninterruptible power supply in the event that the local power provider fails.

Green Computing

Electronic devices such as computer hardware and smartphones contain hundreds or even thousands of components. The components, in turn, are composed of many different materials, including some that are known to be potentially harmful to humans and the environment, such as beryllium, cadmium, lead, mercury, brominated flame retardants (BFRs), selenium, and polyvinyl chloride.[79] Electronics manufacturing employees and suppliers at all steps along the supply chain and manufacturing process are at risk of unhealthy exposure to these raw materials. Users of these products can also be exposed to these materials when using poorly designed or improperly manufactured devices. Care must also be taken when recycling or destroying these devices to avoid contaminating the environment.

green computing: A program concerned with the efficient and environmentally responsible design, manufacture, operation, and disposal of IS-related products.

Green computing is concerned with the efficient and environmentally responsible design, manufacture, operation, and disposal of IS-related products, including all types of computing devices (from smartphones to supercomputers), printers, printer materials such as cartridges and toner, and storage devices. Many business organizations recognize that going green is in their best interests in terms of public relations, safety of employees, and the community at large. They also recognize that green computing presents an opportunity to substantially reduce total costs over the life cycle of their IS equipment. Green computing has three goals: reduce the use of hazardous material, allow companies to lower their power-related costs, and enable the safe disposal or recycling of computers and computer-related equipment.

It is estimated that 51.9 million computers, 35.8 million monitors, and 33.6 million hard copy devices (printers, faxes, etc.)—representing a total of 1.3 million tons of waste—were disposed of in the United States in 2010 alone.[80] Because it is impossible for manufacturers to ensure safe recycling or disposal, the best practice would be for them to eliminate the use of toxic substances, particularly since recycling of used computers, monitors, and printers has raised concerns about toxicity and carcinogenicity of some of the substances. However, until manufacturers stop using these toxic substances, safe disposal and reclamation operations must be carried out carefully to avoid exposure in recycling operations and leaching of materials, such as heavy metals, from landfills and incinerator ashes. In many cases, recycling companies export large quantities of used electronics to companies in undeveloped countries. Unfortunately, many of these countries do not have strong environmental laws, and they sometimes fail to recognize the potential dangers of dealing with hazardous materials. In their defense, these countries point out that the United States and other first-world countries were allowed to develop robust economies and rise up out of poverty without the restrictions of strict environmental policies.

Electronic Product Environmental Assessment Tool (EPEAT) is a system that enables purchasers of electronic products to evaluate, compare, and select products based on a set of environmental criteria. EPEAT was first implemented in 2006 with Computer and Displays (IEEE 1680.1 standard) and has now expanded to Imaging Equipment, under the IEEE 1680.2 standard from January 2013. Products are ranked in EPEAT according to three tiers of environmental performance: bronze, silver, and gold. See Table 3.8.[81] Individual purchasers as well as corporate purchasers of computers, printers, scanners, and multifunction devices can use the EPEAT Web site (*www.epeat.net*) to screen manufacturers and models based on environmental attributes.[82]

Electronic Product Environmental Assessment Tool (EPEAT): A system that enables purchasers to evaluate, compare, and select electronic products based on a set of environmental criteria.

TABLE **3.8** EPEAT product tiers for computers

Tier	Number of Required Criteria That Must Be Met	Number of Optional Criteria That Must Be Met
Bronze	All 23	None
Silver	All 23	At least 50%
Gold	All 23	At least 75%

Some electronics manufacturers have developed programs to assist their customers in disposing of old equipment. For example, Dell offers a free worldwide recycling program for consumers. It also provides no-charge recycling of any brand of used computer or printer with the purchase of a new Dell computer or printer. This equipment is recycled in an environmentally responsible manner, using Dell's stringent and global recycling guidelines.[83] HP, which offers a similar program, has recovered 2.8 billion pounds of products since 1987.[84]

Computer manufacturers such as Apple, Dell, and Hewlett-Packard have long competed on the basis of price and performance. As the difference among the manufacturers in these two arenas narrows, support for green computing is emerging as a new business strategy for these companies to distinguish themselves from the competition. Apple claims to have the "greenest lineup of notebooks" and is making progress at removing toxic chemicals from its manufacturing process. Dell is focused on becoming "the greenest technology company on Earth." Hewlett-Packard often highlights its long tradition of environmentalism and is improving its packaging to reduce the use of materials. It is also urging computer users around the world to shut down their computers at the end of the day to save energy and reduce carbon emissions.

Critical Thinking Exercise

Moving to Green Computing

Your organization is a leader in the development of renewable energy sources based on enhanced geothermal systems and is viewed as a champion in the fight to reduce carbon emissions. The organization employs over 25,000 people worldwide and operates three global data centers, one each in the United States, Europe, and Southeast Asia. The CEO has asked all her C level executives for input on a proposed strategy to become a leader in green computing.

Review Questions

1. In what ways is a move toward green computing consistent with your organization's mission of developing renewable energy sources?
2. One green computing proposal is to consolidate the three data centers into one. Discuss the pros and cons of this approach.

Critical Thinking Questions

1. Identify two additional tactics the organization might take to accelerate its move toward green computing?
2. Identify the pros and cons or any issues associated with your proposed tactics.

Summary

Principle:

The computer hardware industry is rapidly changing and highly competitive, creating an environment ripe for technological breakthroughs.

Computer hardware should be selected to meet specific user and business requirements. These requirements can evolve and change over time.

The central processing unit, memory, input/output devices, and the bus cooperate to execute program instructions following a fetch, decode, execute, and store process.

Computer system processing speed is affected by clock speed, which is measured in gigahertz (GHz). As the clock speed of the CPU increases, more heat is generated, which can corrupt the data and instructions the computer is trying to process. Bigger heat sinks, fans, and other components are required to eliminate the excess heat. Chip designers and manufacturers are exploring various means to avoid heat problems in their new designs.

The Intel x86, Intel Atom, and ARM processors are each based on a different instruction set and are designed with different goals in mind.

A multicore processor is one that combines two or more independent processors into a single computer so that the independent processors can share the workload.

Parallel computing is the simultaneous execution of the same task on multiple processors to obtain results more quickly. Massively parallel processing involves linking many processors to work together to solve complex problems.

Grid computing is the use of a collection of computers, often owned by multiple individuals or organizations, that work in a coordinated manner to solve a common problem.

An integrated circuit—such as a processor or memory chip—is a set of electronic circuits on one small chip of semiconductor material. A fab or foundry is a factory where integrated circuits are manufactured. Fabless manufacturers outsource their manufacturing to foundry companies who fabricate the design.

Main memory provides the CPU with working storage for program instructions and data. The chief function of memory is to rapidly provide data and instructions to the CPU. Memory storage capacity is measured in bytes.

Random access memory or RAM is volatile; loss of power to the computer erases its contents. RAM comes in many different varieties, including dynamic RAM or DRAM (dynamic random access memory) and DDR SDRAM (double data rate synchronous dynamic random access memory). DDR has been superseded by DDR2, DDR3, and DDR4.

Cache memory is a type of high-speed memory that CPUs can access more rapidly than RAM.

Read-only memory (ROM) is nonvolatile and contains permanent program instructions for execution by the CPU. Other nonvolatile memory types include programmable read-only memory (PROM), erasable programmable read-only memory (EPROM), electrically erasable PROM (EEPROM), and flash memory.

Computer systems can store larger amounts of data and instructions in secondary storage, which is less volatile and has greater capacity than memory. The primary characteristics of secondary storage media and devices include access method, capacity, portability, and cost. Common forms of secondary storage include magnetic storage devices such as tape, hard disk drives, and virtual tape; optical storage devices such as CD-ROMs and digital video discs (DVDs); and solid state storage devices (SSDs) such as flash drives.

Redundant array of independent/inexpensive disks (RAID) is a method of storing data that generates extra bits of data from existing data, allowing the system to more easily recover data in the event of a hardware failure.

Network-attached storage (NAS) and storage area networks (SAN) are alternative forms of data storage that enable an organization to share data storage resources among a much larger number of computers and users for improved storage efficiency and greater cost effectiveness.

Storage as a service is a data storage model in which a data storage service provider rents space to people and organizations.

Input and output devices allow users to provide data and instructions to the computer for processing and allow subsequent storage and output. These devices are part of a user interface through which human beings interact with computer systems.

Data is placed in a computer system in a two-stage process: Data entry converts human-readable data into machine-readable form; data input then transfers machine-readable data into the system. Common input devices include a keyboard, a mouse, speech-recognition technology, motion-sensing input devices, scanning devices, optical data readers, magnetic ink character recognition (MICR) devices, magnetic stripe cards, chip cards, smart cards, contactless payment cards, point-of-sale (POS) devices, automated teller machines (ATMs), bar-code scanners, radio frequency identification (RFID) devices, pen input devices, and touch-sensitive screens.

There are numerous flat-panel display screens, including liquid crystal display (LCD), light-emitting diode (LED), organic light-emitting diode (OLED), and plasma devices. Display screen quality is determined by the computer graphics card, aspect ratio, size, color, and resolution. Other output devices include printers, plotters, digital audio players, and e-book readers.

3D printing has created a major breakthrough in how many items will be manufactured. Biomedical engineers are exploring a process called bioprinting, which uses 3D printers to build human parts and organs from actual human cells.

Principle:

Computer hardware must be carefully selected to meet the evolving needs of the organization and its supporting information systems.

Computer systems are generally divided into two categories: single user and multiple users.

Single-user systems include portable computers, such as wearable computers, smartphones, laptops, notebooks, and tablets.

Nonportable single-user systems include thin client, desktop, nettop, and workstation computers. Some thin clients (e.g., the Chromebook) are designed to be highly portable.

Multiuser systems include servers, blade servers, mainframes, and supercomputers.

Scalability is the ability to increase the processing capability of a computer system so that it can handle more users, more data, or more transactions in a given period.

A mainframe computer is a large, powerful computer shared by dozens or even hundreds of concurrent users connected to the machine over a network.

Supercomputers are the most powerful computers with the fastest processing speed and highest performance.

Principle:

The computer hardware industry and users are implementing green computing designs and products.

A server farm houses a large number of servers in the same room, where access to the machines can be controlled and authorized support personnel can more easily manage and maintain the servers.

A virtual server is an approach to improving hardware utilization by logically dividing the resources of a single physical server to create multiple logical servers, each acting as its own dedicated machine.

A data center is a climate-and-access-controlled building or a set of buildings that houses the computer hardware that delivers an organization's data and information services. The rapid growth in data centers is stimulated by the increased demand for additional computing and data storage capacity and by the trend toward consolidating from many data centers down to a few.

Organizations and technology vendors are trying a number of strategies to lower the ongoing cost of data center operations.

The ability to absorb the impact of a disaster and quickly restore services is a critical concern when it comes to planning for new data centers.

Green computing is concerned with the efficient and environmentally responsible design, manufacture, operation, and disposal of IT-related products.

Many business organizations recognize that going green can reduce costs and is in their best interests in terms of public relations, safety of employees, and the community at large.

Three specific goals of green computing are to reduce the use of hazardous material, lower power-related costs, and enable the safe disposal and/or recycling of IT products.

The Electronic Product Environmental Assessment Tool can be used by purchasers of electronic products to evaluate, compare, and select products based on a set of environmental criteria.

Key Terms

bioprinting

blade server

bus

byte (B)

cache memory

central processing unit (CPU)

clock speed

compact disc read-only memory (CD-ROM)

computer graphics card

contactless payment card

container

coprocessor

data center

data entry

data input

desktop computer

digital audio player

digital video disc (DVD)

e-book

Electronic Product Environmental Assessment Tool (EPEAT)

gigahertz (GHz)

graphics processing unit (GPU)

green computing

grid computing

hard disk drive (HDD)

instruction set architecture (ISA)

input/output device

integrated circuit (IC)

laptop

magnetic stripe card

magnetic tape

main memory

mainframe computer

massively parallel processing system

memory

MP3

multicore processor

multiprocessing

nettop

network-attached storage (NAS)

optical storage device

parallel computing

point-of-sale (POS) device

policy-based storage management

portable computer

processor family

radio frequency identification (RFID)

random access memory (RAM)

read-only memory (ROM)

redundant array of independent/inexpensive
   disks (RAID)

scalability

secondary storage

semiconductor fabrication plant

server

server farm

smart card

solid state storage device (SSD)

source data automation

speech-recognition technology

storage area network (SAN)

storage as a service

supercomputer

tablet

thin client

virtual server

virtual tape

wearable computer

workstation

Chapter 3: Self-Assessment Test

The computer hardware industry is rapidly changing and highly competitive, creating an environment ripe for technological breakthroughs.

1. The _____ is the part of the computer that sequences and executes instructions.
   a. CPU
   b. memory
   c. bus
   d. input/output devices
2. Clock speed is measured in GHz or _____.
   a. millions of instructions per second
   b. millions of cycles per second
   c. billions of cycles per second
   d. millions of floating point instructions per second
3. A key advantage of ARM processors over the traditional x86 complex instruction set processors is that _____.
   a. ARM processors do not generate as much heat
   b. ARM processors are more powerful
   c. ARM processors are larger
   d. ARM processors have a faster clock speed

4. The use of a collection of computers, often owned by multiple individuals or organizations, to work in a coordinated manner to solve a common problem is called _____.
   a. parallel computing
   b. massively parallel processing
   c. multicore processing
   d. grid computing
5. _____ is a highly complex process used in manufacturing computer chips with feature sizes that are extremely small.
6. L1 is the fastest type of cache memory built into a computer, faster even than DDR4 SDRAM memory. True or False?
7. The optical storage device capable of storing the most data is the _____.
   a. DVD
   b. Blu-ray disc
   c. CD-ROM
   d. double-sided DVD
8. A high-speed, special-purpose network that integrates different types of data storage devices into a single storage system and connects them to

computing resources across an entire organization is called a(n) _____.
a. network-attached storage
b. storage area network
c. storage as a service
d. enterprise data storage solution

9. _____ involves capturing and editing data where it is originally created and in a form that can be directly entered into a computer to ensure accuracy and timeliness.

10. After October 1, 2015, merchants who accept payments made via a chip card's magnetic stripe can continue to do so; however, they must accept responsibility for any fraudulent purchases. True or False?

11. _____ is a process that uses 3D printers to build human body parts and organs from actual human cells.

Computer hardware must be carefully selected to meet the evolving needs of the organization and its supporting information systems.

12. A combination chipset called a _____ includes processor cores, RAM and ROM memory, interface controllers, and voltage regulators.

13. A _____ is a low-cost, centrally managed computer with no internal or external attached drives for data storage.
a. tablet
b. thin client

c. nettop computer
d. workstation

14. Servers offer great _____, the ability to increase the processing capability of a computer system so it can handle more users, more data, or more transactions in a given period.

The computer industry and users are implementing green computer designs and products.

15. _____ is an approach to improving hardware utilization by logically dividing the resources of a single physical server to create multiple logical servers each with its own dedicated machine.
a. Server farm
b. Multiprocessing
c. Virtual server
d. Hypervisor

16. Which of the following is not a goal of green computing?
a. Enable the safe disposal or recycling of computers and computer-related equipment.
b. Allow companies to lower their power-related costs.
c. Reduce the use of hazardous material.
d. Reduce the cutting down of trees and other foliage.

17. Green computing is about saving the environment; there are no real business benefits associated with this program. True or False?

Chapter 3: Self-Assessment Test Answers

1. a
2. c
3. a
4. d
5. Extreme ultraviolet lithography or EUVL
6. True
7. b
8. b
9. Source data automation

10. True
11. Bioprinting
12. system on a chip
13. b
14. scalability
15. c
16. d
17. False

Review Questions

1. Identify four fundamental components of every computer.
2. What is the purpose of the computer bus?
3. How does clock speed govern the execution of instructions by a computer?
4. What is the x86 instruction set?

5. What is a multicore processor?
6. What is the difference between a foundry company and a fabless manufacturer?
7. How does the role of main memory differ from the role of secondary storage?
8. Which is the largest amount of memory—a gigabyte, petabyte, or terabyte?

9. Identify and briefly discuss the fundamental characteristic that distinguishes RAM from ROM memory.
10. What is cache memory and how is it used?
11. What is a solid state storage device?
12. What is RFID technology? Identify three practical uses for this technology.
13. When speaking of computers, what is meant by scalability?
14. How is a blade server different from a regular server?
15. Identify and briefly describe the various classes of single-user, portable computers.
16. Identify three reasons for increased spending on data centers.
17. Define the term "green computing," and state its primary goals.
18. What is the EPEAT? How is it used?

Discussion Questions

1. Discuss the role a business manager should take in helping determine the computer hardware to be used by the organization.
2. Identify the similarities and differences between massively parallel processing systems and grid computing.
3. Briefly describe the concept of multiprocessing. How does parallel processing differ from multiprocessing?
4. Discuss some of the technical and nontechnical issues that might come up in trying to establish a large grid computing project such as the Large Hadron Collider.
5. What is 3D printing? Discuss what you think the future is for 3D printing.
6. What is a multicore processor? What advantages does it offer users over a single-core processor? Are there any potential disadvantages?
7. Outline how the Electronic Product Environment Assessment Tool (EPEAT) can be used for rating computers.
8. Identify and briefly discuss the advantages and disadvantages of solid state secondary storage devices compared with magnetic secondary storage devices.
9. Briefly discuss the advantages and disadvantages of attached storage, network-attached storage, and storage area networks in meeting enterprise data storage challenges.
10. If cost were not an issue, describe the characteristics of your ideal computer. What would you use it for? Would you choose a tablet, laptop, desktop, or workstation computer? Why?
11. Briefly explain the differences between the magnetic stripe card, chip card, and the smart card. Which do you believe is safest for the consumer? Why?
12. Fully discuss why some organizations are consolidating many data centers into a few. Are there any potential drawbacks to this strategy?
13. Discuss potential issues that can arise if an organization is not careful in selecting a reputable service organization to recycle or dispose of its IS equipment.

Problem-Solving Exercises

1. Do research to find the total worldwide sales for hard disk drives and solid state storage devices over a five-year or more period. Try to get figures for the number of units sold as well as total storage capacity in some unit, such as gigabytes. Use graphing software to develop a chart showing these sales figures. Write a few paragraphs stating your conclusions about the future of the hard disk drive market versus solid state storage.
2. Develop a spreadsheet that compares the features, initial purchase price, and a two-year estimate of operating costs (paper, cartridges, and toner) for three different color laser printers. Assume that you will print 50 color pages and 100 black-and-white pages each month. Now do the same comparison for three inkjet printers. Write a brief memo on which of the six printers you would choose and why. Develop a second spreadsheet for the same printers, but this time assume that you will print 250 color pages and 500 black-and-white pages per month. Now which of the printers would you buy and why?
3. Use word-processing software to document what your needs are as a computer user and your justification for selecting either a desktop or some form of a portable computer. Find a Web site that allows you to order and customize a computer and select those options that will best meet your needs in a cost-effective manner. Assume that you have a budget of $850. Enter the computer specifications you selected along with the associated costs from the Web site into an Excel spreadsheet. Insert that spreadsheet into the document defining your needs.

Team Activities

1. Have you and your team do research on the Web to identify three large grid computing projects of interest to the team. Visit the home page for each of these projects to learn more about the goals of the project, results to date, and what is required if you wish to volunteer to help this project. Choose one of the projects, and volunteer to have your computer added to the grid. Write a brief paper summarizing why your team chose this particular grid computing project, what was required for your computer to join the grid, and how being a member of the grid affected your use of your computer.

2. With one or two of your classmates, visit three different retail stores or Web sites in search of your ideal smart watch. Document the costs, features, advantages, and disadvantages of three different watches using a spreadsheet program. Analyze your data, and write a recommendation on which one you would buy. Be sure to clearly explain your decision.

3. With the members of your team, visit a data center or server farm, perhaps at your university or a nearby computer services firm. (Be sure to obtain permission from the appropriate company resources prior to your visit). As you tour the facility, draw a simple diagram showing the locations of various pieces of hardware equipment. Label each piece of equipment. Document what has been done in terms of access control, power backup, surge protection, and HVAC. Discuss use of virtualization and containers at the site.

Web Exercises

1. Do research on the Web to find a description of Moore's Law. What are the implications of this law? Are there any practical limitations to Moore's Law?

2. Do research on the Web to learn more about bioprinting—both current and potential future applications.

3. Do research on the Web to learn more about Apple's decision to withdraw from the EPEAT program and why it later reversed that decision. Write a one-page report summarizing your findings.

Career Exercises

1. A friend of yours texted you that he is considering changing his major to computer engineering. He wants to meet with you and get your input on this move. Do some research to find out just what is a computer engineer and what do they do. What are the career prospects, and what sort of education and experience is required to become a computer engineer?

2. How might supercomputers be employed in your current or future career field?

3. Examine the possibility of a career in computer hardware sales. Which area of sales do you believe holds the brightest prospects for young college graduates—servers, mainframe computers, supercomputers, or high-volume storage devices? Why? What would be some of the advantages and disadvantages of a career in computer hardware sales?

Case Studies

Case One

ARM

The Acorn Computer Group developed the world's first commercial Reduced Instruction Set Computer (RISC) processor in the 1980s. The simpler commands employed in RISC computers enables the computer to operate faster, use less power, and take up less space—major advances over the early complex instruction set computer systems (CISC), which tried to pack as many actions into each command as possible. ARM was founded in 1990 as a spin-off of Acorn

Computer and Apple after the two companies began collaborating on the ARM processor for the Newton computer system—Apple's ill-fated attempt at a handheld computer.

The ARM business model involves the design and license of intellectual property rather than the manufacture and sales of actual semiconductor chips. ARM licenses the rights to build chips based on its design to the world's leading semiconductor and systems companies. These companies pay ARM a license fee for the original design along with a royalty on every chip or wafer produced. ARM has signed over 1,100 licenses with more than 300 companies. Some companies elect to license the ARM instruction set to design their own processors. See Table 3.9.

TABLE 3.9 Partial list of ARM licensees

Companies That License the ARM Chip Design to Incorporate It into Their Own System on a Chip	Companies That License The ARM Instruction Set to Design Their Own Processor
ApliedMicro	Apple
Broadcom	Broadcom
HiSilico	Intel
Rockchip	Marvell Technology Group
Samsung	Microsoft
STMMicroelectronics	Nvidia
	Qualcomm

Over 60 billion ARM chips have been shipped since the company was founded. Chips based on ARM designs are found in 99 percent of the world's smartphones and tablets. In addition, processors based on designs licensed from ARM are used in all sorts of computing devices, including microcontrollers in embedded systems such as antilock braking systems (ABS) systems for autos, smartTVs, and smartwatches. The number of ARM-designed chips sold is estimated to be 25 times that of Intel-designed chips.

Personal computer vendors upgrade their products every 12 to 18 months. The smartphone industry is demanding an upgrade every six months to a year. ARM is constantly striving to keep pace with these demands. The Cortex-A57 is a processor design by ARM that was announced in October 2012 and appeared in handsets two years later. The Cortex-A72, its successor, was announced in February 2015 and began to appear in mobile devices by the end of 2015.The Cortex A72 processor represents a 50 times increase in processing power compared with smartphone chips used just five years ago. Development of the Cortex A-72 continues the trend of smartphones getting more and more powerful and becoming our primary computing device, replacing the personal computer for many uses.

Meanwhile, Intel is now shipping chips code-named Sofia for inexpensive smartphones. These chips were made in conjunction with the Chinese company Rockchip, which has experience in turning around processor designs in a matter of months. Intel will soon begin to ship a high-end Atom chip called Broxton, which has a modular design that allows Intel to modify the chip and deliver updates at a faster pace. Broxton supports Intel's strategy of delivering products that can be easily customized—similar to the chip designs of ARM.

China assembles most of the world's smartphones and computers, but currently must import most of the technology that underlies them. Chinese authorities hope to gain a bigger role in the microchip industry and have made ownership of semiconductor intellectual property a priority. The issue of protecting intellectual property rights is a major concern for ARM and its customers entering or doing business and China.

Critical Thinking Questions

1. What are some of the challenges and opportunities facing the processor chip industry in general and ARM in particular?
2. Some chip industry observers and financial analysts believe that because of its licensing business model, ARM missed an opportunity to capture billions of dollars in sales of microprocessor chips it could have manufacturered. Compare sales, profits, and stock prices over a three-year period for ARM to two of its customers who do have fab plants and manufacture their own chips such as Samsung Electronics and Intel or AMD, a competitor. Do you believe that the ARM licensing rather than manufacturing business model has hurt the firm? Why or why not?
3. Do research to learn more about how China came to be the lead assembler of the world's smartphones and computers. What are some of the pros and cons of outsoucring this work to China?

SOURCES: "Company Profile," *www.arm.com/about/company-profile/*, accessed July 15, 2015; Vance, Ashlee, "ARM Designs One of the World's Most-Used Products. So Where's the Money?," Bloomberg Business, February 4, 2014, *http://www.bloomberg.com/bw/articles/2014-02-04/arm-chips-are-the-most-used-consumer-product-dot-where-s-the-money*; Hackman, Mark, "ARM Launches Cortex A-72 Platform, Powering Flagship Smartphones in 2016," PC World, February 3, 2015, *www.pcworld.com/article/2879037/arm-launches-cortex-a-72-platform-powering-flagship-smartphones-in-2016.html*; Hamblen, Matt, "The Rise of China's Smartphone Makers," Computerworld, December 30, 2014, *www.computerworld.com/article/2859707/the-rise-of-chinas-smartphone-makers.html* and "Intel Plans to Increase CPU Performance with New Atom Chips," Alvareztg Technology Group, *www.alvareztg.com/intel-plans-to-increase-cpu-performance-with-new-atom-chips.html/*, accessed July 16, 2015,

Case Two

Vivobarefoot Upgrades Technology Infrastructure
Vivobarefoot is an innovative shoe company that recently undertook a major review of its technology infrastructure to determine what changes needed to be made to support and accelerate the company's already rapid growth. Vivobarefoot's success is connected to the growing popularity of barefoot or "miminalist" running. In fact, the company lays claim to the first minimalist shoe, originally produced in 2004, offering an ultrathin, puncture-resistant sole that provides "maximum sensory feedback and maximum protection."

The specialist shoe company is headquartered in the United Kingdom, but also has a team based in China, where all of its manufacturing takes place. Vivobarefoot sells it shoes online, through a variety of partnerships around the world, and in its store in Covent Garden, a popular shopping district in London. According to founder Galahad Clark, the company went from selling 30,000 pairs of shoes per month to over 300,000 per month—over the course of just five years.

As with many companies that experience rapid growth, over the years, Vivobarefoot had acquired a hodgepodge of hardware and software that was no longer meeting its needs. According to Damian Peat, global operations director for the company, "We were working with some pretty archaic systems. We had three servers in our basement all running Windows Server 2003 and backed up to tape, and I would worry a lot about the chance of something not working." Vivobarefoot employees were also using multiple versions of Microsoft Office, and staff in China were forced to use personal Gmail accounts because they could not reliably access the company's Microsoft Exchange email server in London.

Managing the variety of hardware and software systems was becoming time consuming and costly. And, like thousands of other companies, Vivobarefoot was also faced with the reality that it would soon be forced to migrate away from Windows Server 2003, as Microsoft was ending its support of the outdated server operating system. According to Peat, "Upcoming end of support for Windows Server 2003 gave us concerns around security patching and mounting management costs, and we already had significant risk around data security. ...My priority became to get everything onto one safe, reliable platform as soon as possible."

After a review of available technologies, Vivobarefoot chose to replace Windows Server 2003 with Windows Server 2012 R2 and Hyper-V hypervisor software, giving the company both physical and virtual server capabilities, including the capacity the company needs to host file servers and business-critical applications, such as accounting software and stock management systems. The company also migrated to Office 365 in both its London and China offices. Office 365 had particular appeal for the company because, as a global cloud service, it is easily accessible in China, where staff are now more easily able to communicate—using Vivobarefoot email addresses rather than Gmail accounts. Vivobarefoot staff are also making use of Microsoft's OneDrive for Business, where they can store, share, and sync files. According to Peat, with these cloud-based upgrades, the company "can ensure everyone can see the same documents and access them whenever they need, which is really beneficial." As part of a phased process, the company is also moving many employees to Windows 8.1 laptops and Surface Pro tablets.

As part of its efforts to streamline its IT infrastructure at all levels, Vivobarefoot has also moved away from tape backups to a remote hosted backup service, and the upgraded server technology means that many other system management tasks have been simplified, as well. Data security has been improved, and IT staff have gained the ability to manage the company's servers remotely. While Vivobarefoot still has work to do to migrate all of its technology to the same platform, the company's efforts have gone a long way toward providing the company with an updated and more rational arrangement of hardware, software, and cloud computing.

Critical Thinking Questions

1. What are some of the competitive advantages Vivobarefoot gained through its infrastructure update?
2. One ongoing concern for Vivobarefoot is the quality and speed of the Internet service available to its office in central London. Given that, do you think it made sense for the company to move more of its IT services to the cloud? Go online and do some research about Microsoft's Office 365 product. What options does it offer for working offline if Internet service is not available? Does that change your opinion about Vivobarefoot's shift to the cloud?
3. Estimates for the number of computers still running Windows Server 2003 range from hundreds of thousands to several million—even though Microsoft has stopped supporting the product. What are the risks for companies that continue to use software or hardware technology after a vendor ends support for it?

SOURCES: "Frequently Asked Questions," Vivobarefoot, *www.vivobare foot.com/us/customer-services/frequently-asked-questions#FAQST1*, accessed December 11, 2015; Ho, Geoff, "Shoe Manufacturer Vivobarefoot to Step It Up to Fund Expansion Plans," *Express*, May 3, 2015, *www .express.co.uk/finance/city/574639/Shoe-manufacturer-Vivobarefoot -raise-money-fund-expansion-plans*; Worth, Dan, "Windows Server 2003 Migration Helps Shoe Seller Vivobarefoot Put One Foot in the Cloud," *V3.co.uk*, April 17, 2015, *www.v3.co.uk/v3-uk/news/2404420 /windows-server-2003-migration-helps-shoe-seller-vivobarefoot-put-one -foot-in-the-cloud*; "Pioneering Footwear Brand Unites Teams for Secure, Remote Working," Microsoft, *www.microsoft.com/en-gb/smb/customer -success-stories/vivobarefoot-unites-global-teams*, accessed December 11, 2015; Curtis, Joe, "How Vivobarefoot Escaped Windows Server 2003 in IT Upgrade," *IT Pro*, July 8, 2015, *www.itpro.co.uk/server/24948/how -vivobarefoot-escaped-windows-server-2003-in-it-upgrade*.

Notes

1. "Top 10 Sites for November 2015," Top500 Project Committee, *www.top500.org/lists/2015/11*, accessed December 11, 2015.
2. "Courant's Stadler and Colleagues Win 2015 Bell Prize," New York University, November 25, 2015, *www.nyu .edu/about/news-publications/news/2015/11/24/cour ants-stadler-and-colleagues-win-2015-bell-prize-.html*.
3. Mearian, Lucas, "CERN's Data Soars to 530M Gigabytes," *Computerworld*, August 14, 2015, *www.computerworld .com/article/2960642/cloud-storage/cerns-data-stores -soar-to-530m-gigabytes.html*.
4. "Israel Approves Intel's $6 Billion Investment in Chip Plant," *Reuters*, September 22, 2014, *www.reuters.com /article/2014/09/22/us-israel-intel-plant-idUSKCN0HH1 F720140922*.
5. Clark, Don, "IBM Reports Advances in Shrinking Future Chips, *Wall Street Journal*, July 9, 2015, *www.wsj.com /articles/ibm-reports-advances-in-shrinking-future- chips-1436414814*.
6. Seubert, Curtis, "How Many Bytes Is an Exabyte," eHow, *www.ehow.com/about_6370860_many-bytes-exabyte_ .html*, accessed August 8, 2013.

7. Patrizio, Andy, "All about DDR4, the Next-Gen Memory Coming Soon for PCs and Mobile Devices," *PC World*, June 24, 2014, *www.pcworld.com/article/2365823/next -gen-memory-is-coming-fast-here-s-what-you-need-to -know-about-ddr4.html*.

8. Malle, Jean-Pierre, "Big Data: Farewell to Cartesian Thinking?" *Paris Tech Review*, March 15, 2013, *www.paristechreview.com/2013/03/15/big-data-carte sian-thinking*.

9. "Media Alert: New IBM Cloud Service Enables Developers to Create Apps That Tap into Vast Amounts of Unstructured Data," IBM, December 7, 2015, *www-03.ibm.com/press/us/en/pressrelease/48257.wss*.

10. Mims, Christopher, "And the Longest Running Digital Storage Medium Is …," *MIT Technology Review*, July 13, 2011,*www.technologyreview.com/view/424669/and-the -longest-running-digital-storage-medium-is*.

11. "IBM Research Sets New Record for Tape Storage," IBM, April 9, 2015, *www-03.ibm.com/press/us/en/pressrelease/ 46554.wss*.

12. "High-End Computing Capability: Archival Storage System," NASA, *www.nas.nasa.gov/hecc/resources/storage _systems.html*, accessed December 11, 2015.

13. "HGST Ultrastar HDD Is a 10TB Helium Monster, Aims to Cope with Data Overload," *TechRadar*, December 1, 2015, *www.techradar.com/us/news/computing-compo nents/storage/hgst-ultrastar-hdd-is-a-10tb-helium-mon ster-aims-to-cope-with-data-overload-1310236*.

14. "Western Digital Welcomes Big Data with 10 TB Helium HDDs," *Infostor*, December 2, 2015, *www.infostor.com /storage-management/western-digital-welcomes-big -data-with-10-tb-helium-hdds.html*.

15. "Welcome to the NFLC," National Foreign Language Center, *www.nflc.umd.edu*, accessed December 12, 2015.

16. "Research Institute at the University of Maryland Offloads Large Library of Files to RAID Storage," *RADirect*, *www.rad-direct.com/Success_Story_NFLC.htm*, accessed December 12, 2015.

17. Inglis, Blair, "Sony Working on Blue-Ray Successor—Are PS4 Discs Soon to Be Outdated?" *The Six Axis*, July 30, 2013, *www.thesixthaxis.com/2013/07/30/sony-working -on-blu-ray-successor-are-ps4-discs-soon-to-be-out dated*.

18. Shadbolt, Peter, "The Eternity Drive: Why DNA Could Be the Future of Data Storage," *CNN*, February 25, 2015, *www.cnn.com/2015/02/25/tech/make-create-innovate- fossil-dna-data-storage*.

19. MacDonald, Glenn, "DNA Data Storage Lasts Thousands of Years," *Discovery*, August 7, 2015, *http://news.discov ery.com/tech/biotechnology/dna-data-storage-lasts-thou sands-of-years-150817.htm*.

20. Keith, Jonathan, "DNA Data Storage: 100 Million Hours of HD Video in Every Cup," Phys.Org, January 25, 2013, *http://phys.org/news/2013-01-dna-storage-million -hours-bd.html*.

21. Mearian, Lucas, "Samsung Unveils 15 TB SSD Based on Densest Flash Memory," *Computerworld*, August 17, 2015, *www.computerworld.com/article/2971482/cloud -security/samsung-unveils-15tb-ssd-based-on-densest -flash-memory.html*.

22. "About," CD-adapco, *www.cd-adapco.com/about#*, accessed December 12, 2015.

23. "Panasas ActiveStor Storage Speeds Modeling Computation at CD-adapco," Panasas, November 17, 2015, *www.panasas.com/news/press-releases/panasas -activestor-storage-speeds-modeling-computation-cd -adapco*.

24. "City of Riverside: Building the Connected Community of the Future," NetApp, December 2, 2015, *www.netapp. com/us/media/cs-city-of-riverside.pdf*.

25. Patel, Raj, "Discover Pinterest: Cloud Engineering," Pinterest, November 20, 2015, *https://engineering.pinterest. com/blog/discover-pinterest-cloud-engineering*.

26. Murphy, Margi, "Pinterest Nails down More Users after Building Apache HBase Analytics Tool," *TechWorld*, April 16, 2015, *www.techworld.com/news/big-data/pin terests-pinalytics-using-hadoop-get-grips-with-its-data -3608139*.

27. Shahangian, Mohammad "Powering Big Data at Pinterest," Pinterest, July 24, 2014, *https://engineering.pinter est.com/blog/powering-big-data-pinterest*.

28. "AWS Case Study: Pinterest," Amazon Web Services, *https://aws.amazon.com/solutions/case-studies/pinterest*, accessed December 13, 2015.

29. Conn, Joseph, "Nurses Turn to Speech-Recognition Software to Speed Documentation," *Modern Healthcare*, December 12, 2015, *www.modernhealthcare.com/arti cle/20151212/MAGAZINE/312129980*.

30. "Overview," Neat, *www.neat.com*, accessed October 16, 2015.

31. "Everything You Need to Know about the Switch to Chip Cards," *https://squareup.com/townsquare/emv*, accessed October 16, 2015.

32. Vaas, Lisa, "The $1 Million Apple iTunes Gift Card Scam," *Naked Security*, October 23, 2015, *https://naked security.sophos.com/2015/10/23/the-1m-apple-itunes- gift-card-scam*.

33. "US Credit Cards with Smart Chip Technology, The Points Guy, May 30, 2013, *http://thepointsguy.com/2013 /05/us-credit-cards-with-smart-chips*.

34. "Summary Figures (2014)," UK Cards Association, *www .theukcardsassociation.org.uk/2014-facts-figures/sum mary_figures_2014.asp*, accessed October 17, 2015.

35. "Square Helps More Sellers Grow Their Business Faster," Square, *https://squareup.com/?pcrid=3330880435& pdv=c&pkw=square+stand&pm=true&pmt=e*, accessed October 17, 2015.

36. Gagliordi, Natalie, "Target Will Roll Out RFID Price Tags to Improve Inventory Management," *ZDNet*, May 19, 2015, *www.zdnet.com/article/target-will-roll-out-rfid -price-tags-to-improve-inventory-management*.

37. Swedberg, Claire, Target Announces Nationwide RFID Rollout," *RFID Journal*, May 20, 2015, *www.rfidjournal. com/articles/view?13060*.

38. Schuman, Evan, "Target Prepping Stores with 'No Shopping Cart, No Bag'," *Computerworld*, *www.computer world.com/article/3013962/retail-it/target-prepping -stores-with-no-shopping-cart-no-bag.html*.

39. "3D Touch," Apple, *www.apple.com/iphone-6s/3d-touch*, accessed December 13, 2015,

40. Andrzejewski, Alexa, "OpenTable for iOS 9: The Shortest Path between You + Dining," OpenTable, December 25, 2015, *http://blog.opentable.com/2015/opentable-for-ios- 9-the-shortest-path-between-you-dining*.

41. Tyson, Jeff, Wilson, Terry V., "How Graphics Cards Work, How Stuff Works," *http://computer.howstuff works.com/graphics-card.html*, accessed October 17, 2015.

42. "LG Unveils Its New Flexible, Paper-Thin TV," *Science Alert*, August 11, 2015, *www.sciencealert.com/lg-unveils-its-new-flexible-paper-thin-tv*.

43. Hill, Simon, "LG Display Talks Flexible, Transparent, Double-Sided OLEDs in IFA Keynote," *Digital Trends*, September 4, 2015, *www.digitaltrends.com/home-the ater/lg-display-envisions-a-future-of-flexible-wafer-thin -oled-displays*.

44. Seppala, Timothy J., "LG's Spending Billions to Make More OLED Things," Engadget, November 26, 2015, *www.engadget.com/2015/11/26/lg-oled-manufacturing-plant*.

45. "PrinterOn", PrinterOn, *www.printeron.com/images /docs/PrinterOnAirportPrintingSolutions.pdf*, accessed August 19, 2013.

46. Saker, Anne, "Printing a 3D Heart to Save a Heart," *Cincinnati.com*, February 22, 2015, *www.cincinnati .com/story/news/2015/02/21/printing-heart-save-heart /23825279/*.

47. Ibid.

48. "3D Printing in the Automotive Industry," *FunTech*, January 7, 2015, *http://blog.funtech.com/2015/01/3d-print ing-in-automotive-industry.html*.

49. Sher, Davide, "World's Fastest RC Car 3D Printed on Ultimaker 2 Extended," October 12, 2015, *http://3dprin tingindustry.com/2015/10/12/worlds-fastest-rc-car-3d -printed-on-ultimaker-2-extended/*.

50. Gilpin, Lyndsey, "10 Industries 3D Printing Will Disrupt or Decimate," *Republic*, February 25, 2014, *www.techre public.com/article/10-industries-3d-printing-will-dis rupt-or-decimate*.

51. Benvin, Rich, "Biotech Startup Uses 3D Bioprinting to Create Custom Breast Implants and Grafts," *Bioprinting World*, July 27, 2015, *http://bioprintingworld.com/bio tech-startup-uses-3d-bioprinting-to-create-custom-breast-implants-and-grafts*.

52. Benvin, Rich, "3D Organ Bioprinting—Who Wants to Live Forever?," *Bioprinting World*, March 24, 2015, *http://bioprintingworld.com/3d-organ-bioprinting-who -wants-to-live-forever*.

53. Hamblen, Matt, "Wearables and Company Wellness Programs Go Hand-in-Hand," *Computerworld*, June 18, 2015, *www.computerworld.com/article/2937333/wear ables/wearables-and-company-wellness-programs-go-hand-in-hand.html*.

54. Fogarty, Kevin, "Card-Sized Diagnostics, e-Skin Are Future of Wearable Medicine," *Computerworld*, May 13, 2015, *www.computerworld.com/article/2922118/health care-it/health-sensing-e-skin-card-sized-diagnostics-are-future-of-wearable-medicine.html*.

55. Broder, Kevin, MD, "Glove from Imogen Heap Will Change the Way You Make Music," *Wearable Devices*, June 24, 2014, *www.wearabledevices.com/2014/06/24/ glove-from-imogen-heap*.

56. Arthur, Rachel, "Google and Levi's Want to Put Computers in Your Clothing," *Forbes*, June 16, 2015, *www.for bes.com/sites/rachelarthur/2015/06/16/google-and-levis-want-to-put-computers-in-your-clothing*.

57. "Chromebooks in Healthcare: Good for Patients and for Bottom Lines," Samsung, December 7, 2015, *https:// insights.samsung.com/2015/12/07/chromebooks-in -healthcare-good-for-patients-and-for-bottom-lines-2/*.

58. "Case Study: Larson & Darby Group," HP, *www8.hp.com/us/en/pdf/larson-darby-group-hi-res_tcm_245_1814936.pdf*, accessed November 2, 2015.

59. "About ADP," ADP, *www.adp.com/who-we-are.aspx*, accessed October 18, 2015.

60. "About Mastercard," Mastercard, *www.mastercard.us /en-us/about-mastercard/what-we-do/payment-proces sing.html*, accessed October 18, 2015.

61. "About UPS," UPS, *www.ups.com/content/us/en/about /index.html?WT.svl=SubNav*, accessed October 18, 2015.

62. Dignan, Larry, "IBM Rolls Out Z13, Repositions Mainframe for Mobile Transactions," *ZD Net*, January 13, 2015, *www.zdnet.com/article/ibm-rolls-out-z13-reposi tions-mainframe-for-mobile-transactions*.

63. Green, Timothy, "Here's Why IBM Is Still Building Mainframes," *The Motley Fool*, accessed October 18, 2015, *www.fool.com/investing/general/2015/01/24 /heres-why-ibm-is-still-building-mainframes.aspx*.

64. Chen, Stephen, "World's Fastest Computer, Tianhe-2, Might Get Very Little Use," *South China Morning Post*, June 20, 2013, *www.scmp.com/news/china/article /1264529/worlds-fastest-computer-tianhe-2-might-get-very-little-use*.

65. "A Rare Look inside Apple's Maiden, North Carolina Data Center [Video]," *iClarified*, posted April 25, 2014, *www .iclarified.com/40226/a-rare-look-inside-apples-maiden-north-carolina-data-center-video*.

66. "Guide to Virtualization Hypervisors," *Network Computing*, February 9, 2015, *www.networkcomputing.com /data-centers/guide-to-virtualization-hypervisors/d/d-id/ 1318945*.

67. "VMWare Case Study: Cognizant," VMWare, October 27, 2015, *www.vmware.com/files/pdf/customers/vmware -cognizant-15q1-cs-en.pdf?src=WWW_customers_vm ware-cognizant-15q1-cs-en.pdf*.

68. Crosman, Penny, "Why Tech-Savvy Banks Are Gung Ho about 'Container' Software," *American Banker*, December 3, 2015, *www.americanbanker.com/news/bank-tech nology/why-tech-savvy-banks-are-gung-ho-about-con tainer-software-1078145-1.html*.

69. Ovide, Shira, "Software Firms Scramble to Jump into Containers," *Wall Street Journal*, November 4, 2015, *www.wsj.com/articles/software-firms-scramble-to-jump -into-containers-1415149692*.

70. Morgan, Timothy Prickett, "Inside the Rackspace Open-Power Megaserver," *The Platform*, March 23, 2015, *www.theplatform.net/2015/03/23/inside-the-rackspace -openpower-megaserver*.

71. Arthur, Charles, "Technology Firms to Spend $150bn on Building New Data Centres," *Guardian*, August 23, 2013, *www.theguardian.com/business/2013/aug/23/ spending-on-data-centres-reaches-150-billion-dollars*.

72. Colt, Sam, "Apple is Building a $2 Billion Data Center in Arizona," *Business Insider*, February 2, 2015, *www.busi nessinsider.com/apple-is-building-a-2-billion-data-cen ter-in-arizona-2015-2*.

73. "GM's Latest Michigan Data Center Gets LEED Gold," *Data Center Dynamics*, September 13, 2013, *www.data*

centerdynamics.com/focus/archive/2013/09/gms-latest
-michigan-data-center-gets-leed-gold.

74. Boyd, Aaron, "Data Center Consolidation Biggest
Money Saver among IT Reforms," *Federal Times*, September 15, 2015, *www.federaltimes.com/story/govern
ment/it/data-center/2015/09/15/data-center-biggest
-saver/72325764*.

75. "Modular Data Center Expansion Planned for Red
Cloud," Wired Real Estate Group, *http://wiredre.com
/modular-data-center-expansion-planned-for-red-cloud*,
accessed October 18, 2015.

76. Babcock, Charles, "5 Data Center Trends for 2013,"
InformationWeek, January 2, 2013, *www.information
week.com/hardware/data-centers/5-data-center-trends-
for-2013/240145349?printer_friendly=this-page*.

77. Thibodeau, P., "Rural N.C. Becomes Popular IT Location," *Computerworld*, June 20, 2011, p. 2.

78. "IBM Opens New Cloud Data Center in Peru to Meet
Demand for Big Data Analytics," IBM, August 22, 2013,
www-03.ibm.com/press/us/en/pressrelease/41809.wss.

79. Wells, Brad, "What Truly Makes a Computer 'Green'?"
OnEarth (blog), September 8, 2008, *www.onearth.org
/node/658*.

80. "Electronics Waste Management in the United States
through 2009," U.S. EPA, May 2011, EPA 530-R-11-002
*www.epa.gov/wastes/conserve/materials/ecycling/docs
/fullbaselinereport2011.pdf*.

81. "EPEAT Environmental *Criteria*," EPEAT, *www.epeat.
net/resources/criteria*, accessed August 19, 2013.

82. "Electronic Environmental Assessment Tool," EPEAT,
www.zerowaste.org/epeat_devel/faq.htm, accessed October 18, 2015.

83. "Asset Resale and Recycling," Dell, *www.dell.com/learn
/us/en/uscorp1/services/asset-resale-and-recycling?
c=us&l=en&s=corp&cs=uscorp1*, accessed October 18,
2015.

84. "Product Return and Recycling," *www8.hp.com/us/en
/hp-information/environment/product-recycling.html#.
ViOsZo2FP4g*, accessed October 18, 2015.

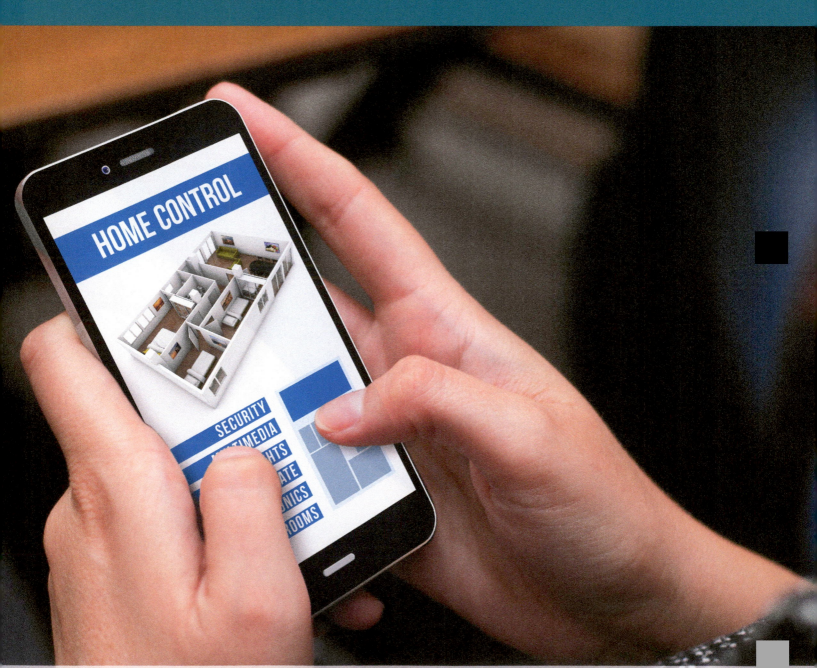

Did You Know?

- Know how you're constantly updating and upgrading programs on your computer and devices? You can thank IBM for that. They birthed the software industry in 1969 when they decided to charge customers separately for software and services. Although business computers had been in use since the mid-1950s, hardware manufacturers had bundled software with their hardware without charging for it.

- If you move to the Microsoft Windows 10 operating system, you will no longer have to upgrade to a new operating system every few years. Instead, Microsoft will be providing continual, incremental updates and improvements, rolled out automatically, perhaps as often as monthly for individual consumers. Windows 10 is here to stay!

- As of July 2015, Apple's App Store had over 1.5 million apps available for iOS device users, and Android users could choose from over 1.6 million mobile apps on Google's Play Store.

Principles

- Software is valuable in helping individuals, workgroups, and entire enterprises achieve their goals.

- The operating system is called the "soul of the computer" because it controls how you enter data into your computer, perform meaningful work, and display results.

- Organizations typically use off-the-shelf application software to meet common business needs and proprietary application software to meet unique business needs and provide a competitive advantage.

- The software industry continues to undergo constant change; computer users need to be aware of recent trends and issues in the software industry to be effective in their business and personal life.

Learning Objectives

- Identify and briefly describe the functions of two basic kinds of software.

- Define the term "sphere of influence," and describe how it can be used to classify software.

- Define the basic functions performed by the operating system.

- Identify current operating systems that are used for personal, workgroup, and enterprise computing.

- Discuss the role of the operating system in embedded systems.

- Discuss how application software can support personal, workgroup, and enterprise business objectives.

- Identify three basic approaches to developing application software and discuss the pros and cons of each.

- Identify programming languages commonly in use today.

- Identify several key software issues and trends that have an impact on organizations and individuals.

Why Learn about Software and Mobile Applications?

Software is indispensable for any computer system and the people using it. In this chapter, you will learn about system software—which includes operating systems, utilities, and middleware—and application software. The operating system is sometimes called the "soul of the computer," and without it, you would be unable to enter data into your computer, perform meaningful work, or display results. You use application software to help you accomplish tasks that enable you to accomplish tasks efficiently and effectively. Sales representatives use software on their smartphones and tablet computers to enter sales orders and help their customers get what they want. Stock and bond traders use software to make split-second decisions involving millions of dollars. Scientists use software to analyze the threat of climate change. Regardless of your job, you will likely use software to help you advance in your career and earn higher wages. You can also use software to help you prepare your personal income taxes, keep a budget, and stay in contact with friends and family online. Software can truly advance your career and enrich your life. We begin with an overview of software.

As you read this chapter, consider the following:

- How is application software tied to or limited by advances in hardware and operating systems?
- How can organizations ensure that their employees use appropriate software to support their work tasks and meet the goals of the enterprise?

An Overview of Software

system software: Software that includes operating systems, utilities, and middleware that coordinate the activities and functions of the hardware and other programs throughout the computer system.

application software: Programs that help users solve particular computing problems.

Software consists of computer programs that control the workings of computer hardware. Software can be divided into two types: systems software and application software. **System software** includes operating systems, utilities, and middleware that coordinate the activities and functions of the hardware and other programs throughout the computer system. **Application software** consists of programs that help users solve particular computing problems. Examples include a spreadsheet program or a program that captures and displays data that enables monitoring of a manufacturing process.

The effective use of software can have a profound impact on individuals and organizations. It can make the difference between profits and losses and between financial health and bankruptcy. As Figure 4.1 shows, companies recognize this impact; globally, spending on software now exceeds other IT

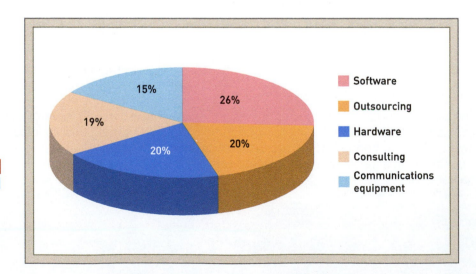

FIGURE 4.1
Software expenditures exceed spending on hardware
Since the 1950s, businesses have substantially increased their expenditures on software compared with hardware.

Pie chart legend:
- Software — 26%
- Outsourcing — 20%
- Hardware — 20%
- Consulting — 19%
- Communications equipment — 15%

expenditures, including spending on computer hardware. This is far different from when computers first were available; software was given away and customers paid only for the hardware.[1] Indeed, the software industry was born in 1969 when IBM decided to unbundle—and charge customers separately for—its software and services. Although business computers had been in use since the mid-1950s, hardware manufacturers had previously bundled software with their hardware without charging separately for it.

Software Sphere of Influence

Every organization relies on the contributions of individuals and groups across the enterprise to achieve its business objectives. One useful way of classifying the many potential uses of information systems is to identify the scope of the problems and opportunities that the software addresses. This scope is called the **sphere of influence**. For most companies, the spheres of influence are personal, workgroup, and enterprise. Table 4.1 shows how various kinds of software support these three spheres.

sphere of influence: The scope of the problems and opportunities that the software addresses.

TABLE **4.1** Software supporting individuals, workgroups, and enterprises

Software Type	Personal	Workgroup	Enterprise
Systems software	Smartphone, tablet, personal computer, and workstation operating systems	Network operating systems	Server and mainframe operating systems
Application software	Word-processing, spreadsheet, database, and graphics programs	Email, group-scheduling, shared-work, and collaboration applications	General-ledger, order-entry, payroll, and human-resources applications

personal sphere of influence: The sphere of influence that serves the needs of an individual user.

personal productivity software: Software that enables users to improve their personal effectiveness, increasing the amount of work and quality of work they can do.

workgroup: Two or more people who work together to achieve a common goal.

workgroup sphere of influence: The sphere of influence that helps workgroup members attain their common goals.

enterprise sphere of influence: The sphere of influence that serves the needs of an organization in its interactions with its environment.

Information systems that operate within the **personal sphere of influence** serve the needs of individual users. These information systems help users improve their personal effectiveness, increasing the amount and quality of work they can do. Such software is often called **personal productivity software**. For example, VIP Organizer is personal productivity software designed to help users develop to do lists, categorize tasks, keep notes and records in a single database, report on performance, and set deadlines and priorities.[2]

When two or more people work together to achieve a common goal, they form a **workgroup**. Workgroups include large, formal, permanent organizational entities, such as sections or departments, as well as temporary groups formed to complete a specific project. An information system in the **workgroup sphere of influence** helps workgroup members attain their common goals. Microsoft Outlook is an example of an application in the workgroup sphere of influence; see Figure 4.2. IBM Notes, another application in the workgroup sphere of influence, provides collaboration features such as team calendars, email, to-do lists, contact management, discussion forums, file sharing, microblogging, instant messaging, blogs, and user directories.[3] JGC Corporation is an engineering construction company with operations in more than 70 different countries. Many of its projects cost over $15 billion, last for 10 years or more, and involve hundreds of partner companies. JGC employs Lotus Notes to coordinate the work of project teams and relay information about project status, changes in work plans, and other critical information.[4]

Information systems that operate within the **enterprise sphere of influence** support an organization in its interactions with its environment, including customers, suppliers, shareholders, competitors, special-interest groups, the financial community, and government agencies. The enterprise sphere of influence for a company might include business partners such as suppliers that provide raw materials, retail companies that store and sell a company's

Microsoft product screenshots used with permission from Microsoft Corporation

FIGURE 4.2

Microsoft Outlook

Outlook is an application that workgroups can use to schedule meetings and coordinate activities.

products, and shipping companies that transport raw materials to the plant and finished goods to retail outlets. Many organizations use SAP enterprise resource planning software to capture customer orders, manage inventory, plan and ship customer orders, bill customers, and manage accounts payable and accounts receivable.

Critical Thinking Exercise

Establishing a Corporate App Store

You are a new hire in the finance organization of a large retail firm. You are amazed to see the number of different software applications (apps) employed by your coworkers, who use them for everything from maintaining personal calendars to calculating the rate of return on projects to forecasting sales and financial data. It seems that everyone has a favorite app for doing each of these tasks. For example, in the few weeks you have been here, you identified over half a dozen different apps that are being used to calculate the rate of return on projects and investments. Your coworkers download these apps from the Internet or build them using spreadsheet software. You previously worked as an intern at another large retailer that had established a corporate app store, which employees accessed to download corporate-approved apps that had been vetted and recommended for use for specific tasks. You wonder if such an approach should be implemented at your current employer.

Review Questions

1. Give an example of two tasks that an employee in the finance organization of this retail firm might perform that would have an impact restricted to their own personal sphere of influence.
2. Identify two tasks that an employee might perform that would have an impact on the workgroup and two that would have an impact on the enterprise sphere of influence.

Critical Thinking Questions

1. What risks are associated with letting employees use their favorite app to perform various tasks? Are these risks associated with tasks in the personal, workgroup, or enterprise sphere of influence?

2. Can you identify some advantages and disadvantages of establishing a corporate app store?

We will now discuss systems software including operating systems, utilities, and middleware.

Systems Software

The primary role of system software is to control the operations of computer hardware. System software also supports the problem-solving capabilities of application programs. System software can be divided into three types: operating systems, utility programs, and middleware.

Operating Systems

operating system (OS): A set of computer programs that controls the computer hardware and acts as an interface to application software.

An **operating system (OS)** is a set of programs that controls a computer's hardware and acts as an interface with application software; see Figure 4.3. An operating system can control one or more computers, or it can allow multiple users to interact with one computer. The various combinations of OSs, computers, and users include the following:

- **Single computer with a single user.** This system is commonly used in personal computers, tablets, and smartphones that support one user at a time. Examples of OSs for this setup include Microsoft Windows, Mac OS X, and Google Android.
- **Single computer with multiple simultaneous users.** This type of system is used in larger server or mainframe computers that support hundreds or thousands of people, all using the computer at the same time. Examples of OSs that support this kind of system include UNIX, z/OS, and HP-UX.
- **Multiple computers with multiple users.** This type of system is used in computer networks, including home networks with several computers attached as well as large computer networks with hundreds of computers attached, supporting many users, who may be located around the world. Network server OSs include Red Hat Enterprise Linux Server, Windows Server, and Mac OS X Server.
- **Special-purpose computers.** This type of system is typical of a number of computers with specialized functions, such as those that control

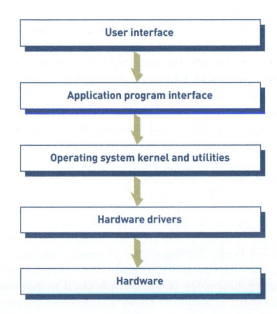

User interface

Application program interface

Operating system kernel and utilities

Hardware drivers

Hardware

FIGURE **4.3**
Role of operating systems
The role of the operating system is to act as an interface between application software and hardware.

sophisticated military aircraft, digital cameras, or home appliances. Examples of OSs designed for these purposes include Windows Embedded, Symbian, and some distributions of Linux.

The OS, which plays a central role in the functioning of a computer system, is usually stored on a hard drive in general-purpose computers and in solid state memory on mobile computers such as tablets and smartphones. After you start, or boot up, a computer system, the kernel of the OS is loaded into primary storage and remains there for as long as the computer is powered on. The **kernel**, as its name suggests, is the heart of the OS and controls its most critical processes. The kernel ties all of the OS components together and regulates other programs.

kernel: The heart of the operating system that controls the most critical processes of the OS.

Other portions of the OS are transferred to memory as the system needs them. OS developers are continually working to shorten the time required to boot devices after they are shut down and to wake devices from sleep mode.

You can also boot a computer from a CD, a DVD, or even a USB flash drive. A storage device that contains some or all of the OS is often called a rescue disk because you can use it to start the computer if you have problems with the primary hard disk.

Functions Performed by the Operating System

The programs that make up the OS perform a variety of activities, including the following:

- Control common computer hardware functions
- Provide a user interface and manage input/output management
- Provide a degree of hardware independence
- Manage system memory
- Manage processing tasks
- Provide networking capability
- Control access to system resources
- Manage files

Common Hardware Functions   The OS enables applications to perform a variety of hardware-related tasks, such as the following:

- Get input from the keyboard or another input device
- Retrieve data from disks
- Store data on disks
- Display information on a monitor or printer

Each of these tasks requires a detailed set of instructions. The OS converts a basic request into instructions that the hardware can process. In effect, the OS acts as an intermediary between the application and the hardware. The OS uses special software (called hardware drivers) provided by device manufacturers to communicate with and control a device. Hardware drivers are typically downloaded from the device manufacturer's Web site or read from an installation DVD and installed when the hardware is first connected to the computer system.

User Interface and Input/Output Management   One of the most important functions of any OS is providing a **user interface**, which allows people to access and interact with the computer system. The first user interfaces for mainframe and personal computer systems were command based. A **command-based user interface** requires you to give text commands to the computer to perform basic activities. For example, the command ERASE 00TAXRTN would cause the computer to erase a file named 00TAXRTN. RENAME and COPY are other examples of commands used to rename files and copy files from one location to another. Today's systems engineers and administrators often use a

user interface: The element of the operating system that allows people to access and interact with the computer system.

command-based user interface: A user interface that requires you to give text commands to the computer to perform basic activities.

command-based user interface to control the low-level functioning of computer systems. Most modern OSs (including those with graphical user interfaces, such as Windows) provide a way to interact with the system through a command line. See Figure 4.4.

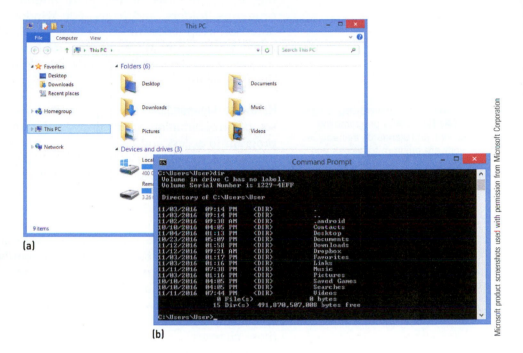

(a)

(b)

FIGURE **4.4**

Command-based and graphical user interfaces

A Windows file system viewed with a GUI (a) and from the command prompt (b).

graphical user interface (GUI):
An interface that displays pictures (icons) and menus that people use to send commands to the computer system.

A **graphical user interface (GUI)** displays pictures (called icons) and menus that people use to send commands to the computer system. GUIs are more intuitive to use than command-based interfaces because they try to anticipate the user's needs and they provide easy-to-recognize options. Microsoft Windows is one popular operating system with a GUI. As the name suggests, Windows is based on the use of a window, or a portion of the display screen dedicated to a specific application. The screen can display several windows at once.

Although GUIs have traditionally been accessed using a keyboard and mouse, more recent technologies allow people to use touch screens and spoken commands. Today's mobile devices and some PCs, for example, use a touch user interface—also called a natural user interface (NUI) or multitouch interface.

Speech recognition is also available with some operating systems. Microsoft and other operating system manufacturers have developed voice-command computer control software. Microsoft employs a special programming language called Speech Application Program Interface (SAPI) to associate your voice commands with specific actions performed by the computer. Apple's OpenEars makes it simple for you to add speech recognition and text to speech to your iPhone, iPad, or iPod. Siri, the personal assistant that acts as an app on the Apple iOS operating system, uses a natural language user interface to answer questions. Adacel is a company that develops advanced simulation and control systems for aviation and defense. It is working on a voice-activated control system to operate the display system on aircrafts.

Some operating systems provide sight interfaces that enable a computer to perform different commands or operations depending on where a person is looking on the screen. Some companies are also experimenting with sensors attached to the human brain (brain interfaces) that can detect brain waves and control a computer as a result. Sight and brain interfaces can be very helpful to disabled individuals.

Operating system developers must be extremely careful in making changes to their user interface. The Windows 8 touch interface represented a major change from its traditional mouse-driven point-and-click user interface. Initial user reaction was lukewarm at best, with many users complaining about the loss of the Start button to display a pop-up menu of programs, folders, and icons. For Windows 10 (there is no Windows 9), Microsoft responded to consumers' feedback by bringing back the traditional Start screen. Microsoft also tried to appease users accustomed to the tile-based interface of Windows 8 by adding a few tiles to the right side of the Start menu.

Hardware Independence An **application programming interface (API)** is a set of programming instructions and standards that enable one software program to access and use the services of another software program. An API provides a software-to-software interface, not a user interface. The API also provides software developers tools that allow them to build application software without needing to understand the inner workings of the OS and hardware. Software applications are designed to run on a particular OS by using the operating system's application program interface.

> **application programming interface (API):** A set of programming instructions and standards that enables one software program to access and use the services of another software program.

APIs also provide a degree of hardware independence so that the underlying hardware can change without necessarily requiring a rewrite of the software applications. **Hardware independence** refers to the ability of a software program to run on any platform, without concern for the specific underlying hardware. When new hardware technologies are introduced, the operating system, not the application software, is required to adjust to enable use of those changes.

> **hardware independence:** The ability of a software program to run on any platform, without concern for the specific underlying hardware.

A software manufacturing company or service provider will often release its API to the public so that other software developers can design products that employ its service. For example, Amazon.com released its API to other Web site developers so they could use it to access Amazon's product information; thus, allowing third-party Web sites to post direct links to Amazon products with updated prices and a "buy now" option.[5]

Memory Management The OS also controls how memory is accessed, maximizing the use of available memory and storage to provide optimum efficiency. The memory-management feature of many OSs allows the computer to execute program instructions effectively and to speed processing. One way to increase the performance of an old computer is to upgrade to a newer OS and increase the amount of memory.

Most OSs support virtual memory, which allocates space on the hard disk to supplement the immediate, functional memory capacity of RAM. Virtual memory works by swapping programs or parts of programs between memory and one or more disk devices—a concept called paging. This procedure reduces CPU idle time and increases the number of jobs that can run in a given time span.

Processing Tasks Operating systems use the following five basic approaches to task management to increase the amount of processing that can be accomplished in a given amount of time:

- **Multiuser.** Allows two or more users to run programs at the same time on the same computer. Some operating systems permit hundreds or even thousands of concurrent users. The ability of the computer to handle an increasing number of concurrent users smoothly is called scalability.
- **Multiprocessing.** Supports running a program on more than one CPU.
- **Multitasking.** Allows more than one program to run concurrently.

- **Multithreading.** Allows different threads of a single program to run concurrently. A thread is a set of instructions within an application that is independent of other threads. For example, in a spreadsheet program, the thread to open the workbook is separate from the thread to sum a column of figures.
- **Real time.** Responds to input instantly. To do this, the operating system task scheduler can stop any task at any point in its execution if it determines that another higher priority task needs to run immediately. Real-time operating systems are used to control the operation of jet engines, the deployment of air bags, and the operation of antilock braking systems—among other uses.

Not all operating systems employ all these approaches to task management. For example, the general-purpose operating systems with which we are most familiar (e.g., Windows, Mac OS, and Linux) cannot support real-time processing.

Networking Capability   Most operating systems include networking capabilities so that computers can join together in a network to send and receive data and share computing resources. Operating systems for larger server computers are designed specifically for computer networking environments.

Access to System Resources and Security   Because computers often handle sensitive data that can be accessed over networks, the OS needs to provide a high level of security against unauthorized access to the users' data and programs. Typically, the OS establishes a logon procedure that requires users to enter an identification code, such as a user name, and a password. Operating systems may also control what system resources a user may access. When a user successfully logs on to the system, the OS permits access to only the portions of the system for which the user has been authorized access. The OS records who is using the system and for how long, and it reports any attempted breaches of security.

File Management   The OS manages files to ensure that files in secondary storage are available when needed and that they are protected from access by unauthorized users. Many computers support multiple users who store files on centrally located disks or tape drives. The OS keeps track of where each file is stored and who is cleared to access them.

Current Operating Systems

Today's operating systems incorporate sophisticated features and impressive graphic effects. Table 4.2 classifies a few current operating systems by sphere of influence.

TABLE 4.2 Operating systems by sphere of influence

Personal	Workgroup	Enterprise
Microsoft Windows	Microsoft Windows Server	Microsoft Windows Server
Mac OS X, iOS	Mac OS X Server	
Linux	Linux	Linux
Google Android, Chrome OS	UNIX	UNIX
HP webOS	IBM i and z/OS	IBM i and z/OS
	HP-UX	HP-UX

From time to time, software manufacturers drop support for older operating systems—meaning that although computers and software running under these operating system will continue to run, the operating system manufacturer will no longer provide security fixes and updates. Without such patches, the users' computers are more susceptible to being infected by viruses and other malware. For example, Google announced that in 2016 it would be ending its support for its Chrome browser on Windows XP and Vista as well as on Mac OS X 10.6, 10.7, and 10.8. Google chose to drop support for these operating systems because they are no longer actively supported by Microsoft and Apple, respectively.[6]

Discontinuance of support is a strong reason to upgrade to new software. However, many organizations take the approach that "if it ain't broke, don't fix it." In their view, other projects take priority over updating software that is still functioning. However, this approach can lead to interruptions in key systems. For example, on November 7, 2015, planes were grounded for several hours at Paris' busy Orly airport when a computer that links air traffic control systems with France's main weather bureau stopped working. The computer was running on Windows 3.1, a 23-year-old operating system dropped from support by Microsoft over a decade ago.[7]

Personal Computing Operating Systems

This section summarizes information about several operating systems that are found on personal computers, portable computers, and mobile devices.

Microsoft PC Operating Systems In 1980, executives from IBM approached Microsoft's Bill Gates regarding the creation of an operating system for IBM's first personal computer. That operating system, which was ultimately called Microsoft Disk Operating System (MS-DOS), was based on Microsoft's purchase of the Quick and Dirty Operating System (QDOS) written by Tim Paterson of Seattle Computer Products. Microsoft bought the rights to QDOS for $50,000. QDOS, in turn, was based on Gary Kildall's Control Program for Microcomputers (CP/M). As part of its agreement with Microsoft, IBM allowed Microsoft to retain the rights to MS-DOS and to market MS-DOS separately from the IBM personal computer. The rest is history, with Gates and Microsoft earning a fortune from the licensing of MS-DOS and its descendants.[8] MS-DOS, which had a command-based interface that was difficult to learn and use, eventually gave way to the more user-friendly Windows operating system, which opened the PC market to everyday users. See Figure 4.5.

FIGURE 4.5

Microsoft Windows 10

Windows 10 brings back the familiar Start menu, replaces the Explorer browser with the Edge browser, and provides the Cortana personal assistant.

With its launch of Windows 10, Microsoft announced that it is moving away from its usual practice of releasing major new versions of its Windows operating system every few years (see Table 4.3 for an overview of the current and previous versions of Windows). Instead, the company will be

TABLE 4.3 Summary of Microsoft Windows operating systems

Year	Version	Highlights
1985	Windows 1.0	Ran as a graphical, 16-bit multitasking shell on top of an existing MS-DOS installation, providing an environment that could run graphical programs designed for Windows as well as existing MS-DOS software
1987	Windows 2.0	Introduced more sophisticated keyboard shortcuts as well as the ability to minimize and maximize Windows
1988	Windows 2.03	Allowed application Windows to overlap each other
1990	Windows 3.0	Introduced a multitasking capability with a protected/enhanced mode, which allowed Windows applications to use more memory; first widely successful version of Windows
1992	Windows 3.1	Introduced improved system stability and expanded support for multimedia, TrueType fonts, and workgroup networking
1995	Windows 95	Introduced numerous important features and functions, such as the taskbar, the Start button, and a new approach to user navigation; moved from a 16-bit architecture to a 32-bit architecture
1998	Windows 98	Introduced many features, such as the Quick Launch toolbar, the Active Desktop, single-click launching, Back and Forward navigation buttons, favorites, and the address bar in Windows Explorer, and image thumbnails; heavily criticized operating system, with major compatibility issues
1999	Windows 98 Second Edition	Included fixes for many Windows 98 problems and replaced Internet Explorer 4.0 with Internet Explorer 5.0; improved audio, modem, and USB support
2000	Windows 2000	An operating system for use on both client and server computers; marketed as the most secure Windows version ever, but it became the target of a number of high-profile virus attacks, such as Code Red and Nimda
2000	Windows ME	Rated Microsoft's worst OS by many industry observers; exhibited stability and compatibility issues; included Internet Explorer 5.5, Windows Media Player 7, and Windows Movie Maker software, which provided basic video editing functions that were designed to be easy for consumers to use
2001	Windows XP	Offered a major advance from the MS-DOS–based versions of Windows in terms of security, stability, and efficiency; introduced a significantly redesigned graphical user interface
2007	Windows Vista	Focused primarily on improving security; offered an updated graphical user interface and visual style dubbed "Aero" and a new search component called Windows Search; provided redesigned networking, audio, print, and display subsystems, as well as new multimedia capabilities, including Windows DVD Maker
2009	Windows 7	Provided an incremental upgrade to the operating system; intended to address Windows Vista's performance issues, while maintaining hardware and software compatibility; provided support for touch displays and 64-bit processors
2012	Windows 8	Introduced major changes to the operating system's platform and user interface to improve user experience on tablets; included a touch-optimized Windows shell, a Start screen that displays programs and dynamically updated content on a grid of tiles, the ability to sync apps and settings between devices, and the Windows Store for downloading and purchasing new software
2013	Windows 8.1	Included an improved Start screen, additional bundled apps, tighter OneDrive integration, Internet Explorer 11, a Bing-powered unified search system, and restoration of a visible Start button on the taskbar
2015	Windows 10	Brought back the familiar Start menu and desktop; introduced the Edge browser and the Cortana assistant, which responds to natural language and can perform a variety of organizational tasks for the end user, including setting reminders, scheduling calendar events, calculating math problems, and converting measurements and money

providing ongoing, incremental upgrades and improvements, rolled out automatically, perhaps as often as monthly for individual consumers. Organizations, whose information systems professionals desire minimal change in order to ensure reliable operations of corporate applications, may elect to opt out of such frequent updates. Microsoft hopes that the automatic, rapid update cycle will force users to stay current and discontinue use of older operating systems. One benefit of this approach is that it will allow Microsoft to gradually shift some of its resources away from updating and maintaining earlier versions of Windows. Ideally, those resources will instead be refocused on efforts to improve Windows 10. Microsoft also plans to make Windows 10 a common platform with a single app store for any machine—smartphone, laptop, desktop, xBox game station, etc. (with variations to allow for differing screen sizes and uses).[9]

Apple Computer Operating Systems   In July 2001, Mac OS X was released as an entirely new operating system for the Mac. Based on the UNIX operating system, Mac OS X included a new user interface with luminous and semitransparent elements, such as buttons, scroll bars, and windows along with fluid animation to enhance the user's experience.

Since its first release, Apple has upgraded OS X multiple times, as shown in Table 4.4. The first eight versions of the OS were named after big cats, the latest are named after places in California. OS X 10.11 El Capitan is Apple's latest operating system. See Figure 4.6. It offers enhanced security features as well as the ability to launch the iBooks app, and books you've already downloaded to your iPad, iPhone, or iPod Touch will appear in your library. Directions, bookmarks, and recent searches are automatically passed on to all your iOS devices, and you can now use natural language when using the Spotlight search feature (e.g., "spreadsheet I worked on yesterday"). The new Split View feature automatically positions two app windows side by side in full screen so you can work with both apps at the same time. Power-saving technology enables you to browse longer, and upgraded graphics-rendering technology has improved overall system performance compared to previous versions.[10]

Because Mac OS X runs on Intel processors, Mac users can set up their computers to run both Windows and Mac OS X and select the platform they want to work with when they boot their computers. Such an arrangement is called dual booting. While Macs can dual boot into Windows, the opposite is

TABLE 4.4 Summary of recent Mac operating systems

OS X Version	Name	Date Released
10.0	Cheetah	2001
10.1	Puma	2001
10.2	Jaguar	2002
10.3	Panther	2003
10.4	Tiger	2005
10.5	Leopard	2007
10.6	Snow Leopard	2009
10.7	Lion	2011
10.8	Mountain Lion	2012
10.9	Mavericks	2013
10.10	Yosemite	2014
10.11	El Capitan	2015

© Apple, Inc

FIGURE 4.6

Mac OS X El Capitan

El Capitan incorporates many features of Apple's mobile devices into its desktop operating system.

Source: Apple, Inc.

not true. OS X cannot be run on any machine other than an Apple device. However, Windows PCs can dual boot with Linux and other OSs.

Linux Linux is an OS developed in 1991 by Linus Torvalds as a student in Finland. The OS is distributed under the GNU General Public License, and its source code is freely available to everyone. It is, therefore, called an open-source operating system.

Individuals and organizations can use the open-source Linux code to create their own distribution (flavor) of Linux. A distribution consists of the Linux kernel (the core of the operating system)—which controls the hardware, manages files, separates processes, and performs other basic functions—along with other software. This other software defines the terminal interface and available commands, produces the graphical user interface, and provides other useful utility programs. A Linux distributor takes all the code for these programs and combines it into a single operating system that can be installed on a computer. The distributor may also add finishing touches that determine how the desktop looks like, what color schemes and character sets are displayed, and what browser and other optional software are included with the operating system. Typically, the distribution is "optimized" to perform in a particular environment, such as for a desktop computer, server, or TV cable box controller.

More than 100 distributions of Linux have been created.[11] Many distributions are available as free downloads. Three of the most widely used distributions come from software companies Red Hat, SUSE, and Canonical. Although the Linux kernel is free software, both Red Hat and SUSE produce retail versions of the operating system that earn them revenues through distribution and service of the software. openSUSE is the distribution sponsored by SUSE. See Figure 4.7.

Red Hat, an open-source software developer based in Raleigh, North Carolina, offers a range of Linux-based solutions. Its Red Hat Enterprise Linux distribution, first released in 2000, is an enterprise-grade operating system that can be deployed on desktops as well as servers.[12] Cerner Corporation is a Kansas-based provider of healthcare IT solutions whose software solutions are in use in over 18,000 healthcare facilities around the world.[13] When Cerner was looking to standardize the hosting environment for its flagship Cerner Millennium application suite, it chose to implement the Red Hat Enterprise Linux operating system. Millennium applications provide healthcare providers real-time access to a variety of data, including patient

FIGURE 4.7

openSUSE operating system

openSUSE is a distribution of Linux available as a free download.

information, diagnoses, lab results, and medication lists. When deciding on an operating system for its hosting environment for high-priority applications, an important consideration for Cerner was the fact that over 70 percent of its Millennium customers opt to host their applications using Cerner's hosting services. It was a priority for Cerner and its customers that the company implement a dependable and scalable solution. With its implementation of Red Hat's Linux distribution, Cerner found that it gained performance improvements and a lower total cost of ownership in addition to a more stable and scalable system.[14]

Google: Android and Chrome Over the years, Google has extended its reach beyond its popular search engine (Google) to offer application software (Google Docs), email services (Gmail), a mobile operating system (Android), Web browser (Chrome), and, more recently, a PC operating system—Chrome OS. The various releases of the Android operating system have been given tasty names such as Gingerbread, Jelly Bean, and Ice Cream Sandwich. Android has surpassed 1 billion users across all devices—with 80 percent of mobile phones worldwide operating on Android.[15]

Chrome OS is a Linux-based operating system for notebooks and desktop PCs primarily used to access Web-based information and services such as email, Web browsing, social networks, and Google online applications. The OS is designed to run on inexpensive low-power computers. Chrome OS for personal computers is designed to start fast and provide quick access to applications through the Internet. An open-source version of Chrome OS, named Chromium OS, was made available at the end of 2009. Because it is open-source software, developers can customize the source code to run on different platforms, incorporating unique features.

Workgroup Operating Systems

To keep pace with user demands, business technology must be able to support an environment in which network usage, data storage requirements, and data-processing speeds are increasing at a dramatic rate. Powerful and sophisticated operating systems are needed to run the servers that meet these business needs for workgroups.

Windows Server Microsoft designed Windows Server to perform a host of tasks that are vital for Web sites and corporate Web applications. For example, Microsoft Windows Server can be used to coordinate and manage large data centers. Windows Server delivers benefits such as a powerful Web server management system, virtualization tools that allow various operating systems to run on a single server, advanced security features, and robust administrative support. Windows Server 2016 provides further enhancements for containerization—with individual containers having their own Windows Server kernel that is not shared with the host machine. This ensures that users can run jobs without worrying that workloads running on one container will reach outside their bounds and interfere with either the host machine or other applications running on it. Windows Home Server allows individuals to connect multiple PCs, storage devices, printers, and other devices into a home network. Windows Home Servers provides a convenient way for home users to store and manage photos, video, music, and other digital content. It also provides backup and data recovery functions.

UNIX   UNIX is a powerful OS originally developed by AT&T for minicomputers—the predecessors of servers, which were larger than PCs and smaller than mainframes. UNIX can be used on many computer system types and platforms, including workstations, servers, and mainframe computers. UNIX also makes it easy to move programs and data among computers or to connect mainframes and workstations to share resources. There are many variants of UNIX, including HP-UX from Hewlett-Packard, AIX from IBM, and Solaris from Oracle. The UNIX platform (a computer capable of running the UNIX operating system plus the operating system itself) is considered a high-cost platform compared to Linux and Windows Server.

The Solaris operating system is a UNIX-based operating system originally developed by Sun Microsystems. Oracle, known primarily as a database management software firm, acquired Sun in 2010. Sun products included server hardware, the Solaris operating system, and the Java programming language. Oracle now offers so-called general-purpose engineered systems that include a combination of Oracle and Sun software running on powerful Sun servers, dubbed SPARC.[16] Office Depot is one of the largest retail office supply companies in the world, with some 1,400 stores in the United States, Europe, and the Middle East. The company upgraded the information system infrastructure used to run its ERP application to SPARC servers and the Solaris operating system to gain a 20 percent increase in performance.[17]

Red Hat Linux   Red Hat Software offers Red Hat Enterprise Linux Server, an operating system that is very efficient at serving Web pages and can manage a cluster of several servers. Distributions such as Red Hat have proven Linux to be a very stable and efficient OS. Red Hat Enterprise Virtualization (RHEV) software provides virtualization capabilities for servers and desktop computers to enable the hardware to run more than one operating system. See Figure 4.8.

Casio is a multinational electronics manufacturing company headquartered in Japan. Its products include calculators, mobile phones, cameras, musical instruments, and watches. Casio migrated to RHEV, and its virtual servers now use only 60 percent of the resources used by physical servers. The firm has also been able to ensure that in the event of a server failure, other servers will have the capacity to pick up the load without a serious effect on the entire system.[18]

Mac OS X Server   The Mac OS X Server is the first modern server OS from Apple Computer, and it is based on the UNIX OS. Designed for OS X and iOS, OS X Server makes it easy to collaborate, develop software, host Web sites and wikis, configure Mac and iOS devices, and remotely access a network. Smartphone users running iOS can now open, edit, and save documents on OS X Server.

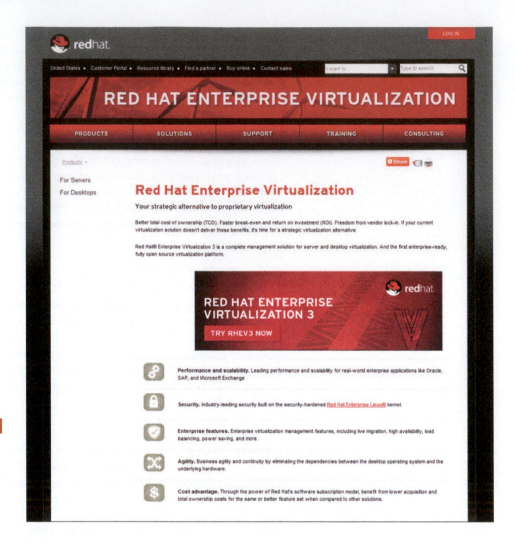

Red Hat Linux

Red Hat Enterprise Virtualization (RHEV) software provides virtualization capabilities for servers and desktop computers.

Source: *www.redhat.com*

Enterprise Operating Systems

Mainframe computers, often referred to as "Big Iron," provide the computing and storage capacity required for massive data-processing environments, and they provide systems that can support many users while delivering high performance and excellent system availability, strong security, and scalability. A wide range of application software has been developed to run in the mainframe environment, making it possible to purchase software to address almost any business problem. Examples of mainframe OSs include z/OS from IBM, HP-UX from Hewlett-Packard, and Linux. The z/OS is IBM's first 64-bit enterprise OS and is capable of handling very heavy workloads, including serving thousands of concurrent users and running an organization's critical applications. (The z stands for zero downtime.)

Mobile Operating Systems

Smartphones now employ full-fledged personal computer operating systems such as the Google Android, Apple iOS, and Microsoft Windows Phone that determine the functionality of your phone and the applications that you can run. These operating systems have software development kits that allow developers to design thousands of apps providing a myriad of mobile services.

Table 4.5 lists the top four mobile operating systems for smartphones and tablets based on worldwide market share as of the second quarter (2Q) of 2015. Table 4.6 lists the top tablet operating systems based on sales in 1Q 2015.

TABLE **4.5** Comparison of smartphone operating systems

Smartphone Operating System	Worldwide Market Share of Sales during 2Q 2015	Estimated Total Number of Applications	Estimated Rate of Increase in Number of New Applications
Google Android	82.8%	1,824,500 (Nov 2015)	980/day
Apple iPhone OS (iOS)	13.9%	1,500,000 (July 2015)	667/day
Microsoft Windows Mobile (to be replaced by Windows 10 Mobile)	2.6%	300,000 (June 2014)	550/day
Blackberry OS	0.3%	Not available	Not available

Sources: "Smartphone OS Market Share, 2015 Q2," International Data Corporation, August 2015, *www.idc.com/prodserv/smartphone-os-market-share.jsp*; Costello, Sam, "How Many Apps Are in the App Store?," *About Tech*, September 15, 2015, *http://ipod.about.com/od/iphonesoftwareterms/qt/apps-in-app-store.htm*; Whitney, Lance, "Windows Phone Store Hits More than 300,000 Apps," CNET, August 8, 2015, *www.cnet.com/news/windows-phone-store-hits-more-than-300000-apps.*

TABLE **4.6** Worldwide market share of tablet computer operating systems

Table Computer Operating System	Worldwide Market Share
Android	67%
iOS	28%
Windows	5%

Source: Shah, Agam, "Windows Forecast to Gradually Grab Tablet Market Share From iOS and Android," PCWorld, March 12, 2015, *www.pcworld.com/article/2896196/windows-forecast-to-gradually-grab-tablet-market-share-from-ios-and-android.html.*

Embedded Operating Systems

embedded system: A computer system (including some sort of processor) that is implanted in and dedicated to the control of another device.

An **embedded system** is a computer system (including some sort of processor) that is implanted in and dedicated to the control of another device. Embedded systems control many devices in common use today, including TV cable boxes, smartphones, digital watches, digital cameras, MP3 players, calculators, microwave ovens, washing machines, and traffic lights. The typical car contains many embedded systems, including those that control antilock brakes, air bag deployment, fuel injection, active suspension devices, transmission control, and cruise control. A global positioning system (GPS) device uses an embedded system to help people find their way around town or more remote areas. See Figure 4.9.

FIGURE **4.9**

GPS devices use embedded operating systems

A GPS device uses an embedded system to acquire information from satellites, display your current location on a map, and direct you to your destination.

Some embedded systems include specialized operating systems. For example, Palm, an early smartphone manufacturer, developed its well-regarded Palm webOS operating system to run its Pre and Pixi smartphones. Although webOS was considered innovative, Palm's smartphones were a market failure, and in 2010, HP bought the company along with webOS, hoping to use it to develop its mobile platform. HP's efforts were also unsuccessful, and in early 2013, LG bought all the assets associated with webOS from HP. LG now uses the specialized software in its smart TVs to enable users to watch streaming movies and television shows and YouTube videos, connect to social networks, play games, get news, and download apps.[19]

Some of the more popular OSs for embedded systems are described in the following section.

Windows Embedded Windows Embedded is a family of Microsoft operating systems included with or embedded into small computer devices. For example, Windows Embedded Compact includes several versions that provide computing power for TV set-top boxes, automated industrial machines, media players, medical devices, digital cameras, PDAs, GPS receivers, ATMs, gaming devices, and business devices such as cash registers. Microsoft Windows Embedded Automotive helps manufacturers provide drivers with everything they need to stay in touch with others, be entertained, and be informed. Drivers can also monitor vehicle performance, screen for maintenance issues, and allow remote tracking of the car's location. Speech recognition, touch interface, and hands-free technologies enable drivers to stay focused on the road and in control of their surroundings. The Ford Sync system uses an in-dashboard display, an industrial-strength operating system owned by BlackBerry called QNX, and wireless networking technologies to link automotive systems with smartphones and portable media players. See Figure 4.10.

FIGURE 4.10

Ford Sync 3 user interface
The Ford Sync 3 system allows drivers to wirelessly connect smartphones and media devices to automotive systems.

Source: McCracken, Henry, "Why Ford Dumping Microsoft's Automotive Software Was Inevitable—And Probably Long Overdue," Fast Company, *http://www.fast company.com/3039760/why-ford-dumping -microsofts-automotive-software-was -inevitable-and-probably-long-overdue.*

Syndicat Mixte Autolib' is an electric car-sharing program implemented by the city of Paris and surrounding municipalities. The goals of the program are to relieve traffic congestion, reduce noise and air pollution, and provide people with flexible transit options. Various components of the Windows Embedded operating system provide connectivity between the in-car system, rental kiosks, charging stations, and a central control system. Syndicat Mixte Autolib' has reduced carbon dioxide emissions by 1.5 metric tons annually and replaced 25,000 privately owned gas vehicles. Autolib' subscribers enjoy additional benefits including GPS navigation and free parking.[20]

Proprietary Linux-Based Systems Because embedded systems are usually designed for a specific purpose in a specific device, they are usually proprietary or custom-created and owned by the manufacturer. Sony's Wii, for example, uses a custom-designed OS based on the Linux kernel. Linux is a popular choice for embedded systems because it is free and highly configurable. It has been used in many embedded systems, including e-book readers, ATMs, smartphones, networking devices, and media players.

Utility Programs

utility program: A program that helps to perform maintenance or correct problems with a computer system.

Utility programs perform a variety of tasks typically related to system maintenance or problem correction. For example, there are utility programs designed to merge and sort sets of data, keep track of computer jobs being run, compress data files before they are stored or transmitted over a network (thus saving space and time), and perform other important tasks.

Just as your car engine runs best if it has regular tune-ups, computers also need regular maintenance to ensure optimal performance. Over time, your computer's performance can start to diminish as system errors occur, files clutter your hard drive, and security vulnerabilities materialize. Sysinternals Suite is a collection of Windows utilities that can be downloaded for free from the Microsoft Technet Web site. These utilities can be used to boost the performance of a slow PC, repair errors in the registry and on a hard drive, remove unnecessary files, improve system security and privacy, and optimize sluggish system processes as shown in Figure 4.11.[21]

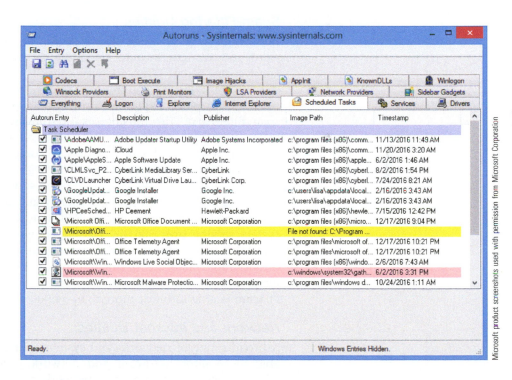

FIGURE 4.11

Sysinternals Suite
Sysinternals Suite is a collection of utilities for troubleshooting and maintaining a Windows system.

Although many PC utility programs come installed on computers, you can also purchase utility programs separately. The following sections examine some common types of utilities.

Hardware Utilities

Hardware utilities can be used to check the status of all parts of the PC, including hard disks, memory, modems, speakers, and printers. Disk utilities check the hard disk's boot sector, file allocation tables, and directories and analyze them to ensure that the hard disk is not damaged. Disk utilities can also optimize the placement of files on a crowded disk. Hardware manufacturers often provide utilities that can be used for their specific devices. Other companies such as Symantec, which produces Norton Utilities, offer hardware utilities that can be used to repair, maintain, and optimize a range of system types.

Security Utilities

Computer viruses and malware from the Internet and other sources can be a nuisance and worse—sometimes completely disabling a computer. Antivirus and anti-malware utilities can be used to constantly monitor and protect a computer. If a virus or other malware is found, it can often be removed. Firewall software is another important security utility for protecting a computer system. Firewall software filters incoming and outgoing packets, making sure that neither hackers nor their tools are attacking the system. Symantec, McAfee, and Microsoft are the most popular providers of security software.

File-Compression Utilities

File-compression programs can reduce the amount of disk space required to store a file or reduce the time it takes to transfer a file over the Internet. Both Windows and Mac operating systems let you compress or decompress files and folders. A Zip file has a .zip extension, and its contents can be easily unzipped to the original size. MP3 (Motion Pictures Experts Group-Layer 3) is a popular file-compression format used to store, transfer, and play music and audio files, such as podcasts—audio programs that can be downloaded from the Internet.

Spam-Filtering Utilities

Receiving unwanted email (spam) can be a frustrating waste of time. Email software and services include spam-filtering utilities to assist users with these annoyances. Email filters identify spam by learning what the user considers spam and routing it to a junk mail folder. In addition, many security utilities—such as Symantec's Norton Security and Kaspersky's Internet Security—include spam-filtering utilities. Businesses often invest in additional software to ensure better protection for enterprise-level email systems where spam containing viruses is a serious threat. A variety of companies, including Cisco, Barracuda Networks, and Google, offer spam-filtering software that can intercept dangerous spam as it enters the corporate email system.

Being able to block spam efficiently and accurately is a priority for organizations such as the Long Island Rail Road Company (LIRR), a commuter rail system serving over 300,000 passengers weekly in southeastern New York.[22] The LIRR uses enterprise-level messaging security software from GWAVA to protect more than 2,000 email accounts. Using GWAVA's software, which is integrated into the LIRR's overall communication infrastructure, the railroad's IT team is able to block more than 34,000 spam emails each month.[23]

Network and Internet Utilities

A broad range of network- and systems-management utility software is available to monitor hardware and network performance and trigger an alert when a server is crashing or a network problem occurs. IBM's Tivoli Netcool Network Management, Hewlett-Packard's Automated Network Management Suite, and Paessler's PRTG Network Monitor can be used to solve computer-network problems and help save money. As shown in Figure 4.12, PRTG Network Monitor creates a sensor for each network device and then monitors the device to make sure it is connected and working properly. If a device encounters a problem, the network manager is alerted via email or text message.

The University of Kentucky community includes more than 26,000 students and almost 11,000 employees on its campus in Lexington.[24] The university's computing infrastructure is made up of multiple local area networks (LANs)

FIGURE **4.12**
PRTG Network Monitor
PRTG Network Monitor and other network utility software can help you to keep track of network components, traffic flows, and network performance.

Source: *www.paessler.com/prtg*

that connect to the school's wide area network (WAN). One of those LANs includes over 1,000 desktop computers, 50 switches, 6 servers, and 2 routers. The university's network administrators use AdRem's NetCrunch network monitoring software to ensure uninterrupted service on the network, which serves 17 different on-campus labs. NetCrunch allows the school's IT personnel to monitor the network and track connectivity problems with minimum human attention, by providing early warnings regarding failures in device, server, and desktop performance. In particular, the utility has helped the network team cut down on connectivity problems related to port settings at switches and routers, thus improving network performance for the students and faculty who rely on it for a variety of learning, teaching, and research activities.[25]

Server and Mainframe Utilities

Some utilities enhance the performance of servers and mainframe computers. Blue Cross and Blue Shield of Kansas provides medical, dental, and life insurance coverage to 800,000 customers. As part of its service, it offers online access to health information stored in an IBM DB2 database running on an IBM z/OS mainframe. The company employs IBM mainframe utility programs to manage this operation effectively. The IBM z/OS Data Facility System Managed Storage utility applies the appropriate retention policies to data stored on direct access storage devices, and the IBM Tivoli Workload Scheduler is used to preform automated job scheduling to ensure critical jobs are completed on time.[26]

The main enabling technology for cloud computing is software that allows the creation of virtual servers, which separate a physical computing device into one or more "virtual" servers, each of which can be easily used and managed to perform computing tasks (see Figure 4.13). A server administrator uses software to divide one physical server into perhaps as many as a dozen virtual machines—with each virtual machine capable of processing a set of data for users from a given organization. In a typical cloud computing data center

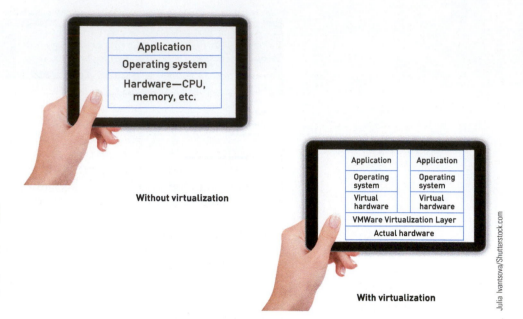

Without virtualization

With virtualization

Julia Ivantsova/Shutterstock.com

FIGURE **4.13**

Virtualization

Virtual servers that separate a physical computing device into one or more "virtual" servers, each of which can be easily used and managed to perform computing tasks.

deployment of several hundred servers, companies using virtual servers can save millions of dollars in capital and operating expenses (including energy costs) per year by dramatically reducing the number of actual physical servers in use.

Other Utilities

Utility programs are available for almost every conceivable task or function. Managing the vast array of operating systems for smartphones and mobile devices, for example, has been difficult for many companies. Many organizations unwisely allow employees to connect to corporate databases using smartphones and mobile devices with little or no guidance. Utility programs called mobile device management (MDM) software can help a company manage security, enforce corporate strategies, and control downloads and content streaming from corporate databases into smartphones and mobile devices. Columbia Sportswear Company uses VMWare's AirWatch MDM package to deliver mobile applications and manage hundreds of mobile devices in its retail stores and distribution centers. AirWatch allows the retailer's IT staff to manage the mobile devices from a central location, ensuring secure and consistent deployment of mobile devices and applications, including those used for tracking sales and monitoring staff scheduling.[27]

In addition, a number of companies, such as CNET, offer utilities that can be downloaded for most popular operating systems. CNET offers hundreds of utilities for Windows operating systems, including defraggers (fixes the problem of fragmentation, which occurs when data is broken up into discontinuous pieces that waste space on your hard drive), system cleaners (cleans tracks on your hard drive, deletes temporary files, and cleans your registry), uninstallers (safely removes unwanted software), and replacements for Notepad and Task Manager.

Middleware

middleware: Software that allows various systems to communicate and exchange data.

enterprise application integration (EAI): The systematic tying together of disparate applications so that they can communicate.

Middleware is software that provides messaging services that allow different applications to communicate and exchange data. This systematic tying together of disparate applications, often through the use of middleware, is known as **enterprise application integration (EAI)**. It is implemented to address situations in which a company acquires different types of information systems—often through mergers, acquisitions, or expansion—that need

service-oriented architecture (SOA): A software design approach based on the use of discrete pieces of software (modules) to provide specific functions as services to other applications.

to share data and interact. Middleware can also serve as an interface between the Internet and private corporate systems. For example, it can be used to transfer a request for information from a corporate customer on the company Web site to a traditional database on a mainframe computer and to return the results of that information request to the customer on the Internet.

The use of middleware to connect disparate systems has evolved into an approach for developing software and systems called SOA. **Service-oriented architecture (SOA)** is a software design approach based on the use of discrete pieces of software (modules) to provide specific functions (such as displaying a customer's bill statement) as services to other applications. Each module is built in such a way that ensures that the service it provides can exchange information with any other service without human interaction and without the need to make changes to the underlying program itself. In this manner, multiple modules can be combined to provide the complete functionality of a large, complex software application. Systems developed with SOA are highly flexible, as they allow for the addition of new modules that provide new services required to meet the needs of the business as they evolve and change over time.

SOA itself has evolved over time. One potential downside to SOA is that it can lead to expensive and challenging implementations of individual services that are too complex. In response, some organizations have shifted their SOA approach—starting with microservices at the department level, rather than at the enterprise level, and building from there. Microservices are designed to quickly solve tactical problems by doing one thing very well, and they offer organizations the opportunity to implement SOA using simplified components.[28]

Netflix, which describes itself as the world's leading Internet television network, has 70 million members in 60 countries watching more than 100 million hours of streaming TV shows and movies each day.[29] Recently, the company shifted its development approach to a microservices architecture approach, with many small engineering teams responsible for the development of hundreds of microservices that work together to stream content to customers. Each microservice represents a single-product feature that can be updated independently. This architecture, along with Netflix's continuous delivery approach to development, means that microservices can be upgraded and debugged on their own schedules, improving performance and reliability for the company's millions of customers.[30,31]

 **Critical Thinking Exercise**

Migration to New Operating System

The information systems support organization of your firm is keen to migrate all employees from whatever operating system they have now (mostly Windows 8) to Microsoft Windows 10. Making such a change can be a big deal for employees and can require them to get comfortable with a new user interface and ways of accomplishing their work.

Review Questions

1. What are some of the advantages of such a move?
2. What are some potential issues that could arise from this change?

Critical Thinking Questions

1. What are some of the negative forces that will cause employees to resist this change?
2. What are some creative things the IS team could do to overcome these resistance forces?

Application Software

The primary function of application software is to apply the power of a computer system to enable people, workgroups, and entire enterprises to solve problems and perform specific tasks. Millions of software applications have been created to perform a variety of functions on a wide range of operating systems and device types. The following are some of the dozens of categories of applications:

Business	Genealogy	Personal information manager
Communications	Language	Photography
Computer-aided design	Legal	Science
Desktop publishing	Library	Simulation
Educational	Multimedia	Video
Entertainment	Music	Video games

In almost any category of software, you will find many options from which to choose. For example, Microsoft Edge, Mozilla Firefox, Google Chrome, Apple Safari, and Opera are all Web browsers that enable users to surf the Web. The availability of many software options enables users to select the software that best meets the needs of the individual, workgroup, or enterprise. For example, Procter & Gamble Company (P&G), a large, multinational organization, chose the SAP Enterprise Resource Planning software with its vast array of options, features, and functionality to meet its complex global accounting needs. However, a small, neighborhood bakery might decide that Intuit's QuickBooks, an accounting software package designed for small businesses, meets its simple accounting needs.

In most cases, application software resides on the computer's hard disk before it is brought into the computer's memory and then run. Application software can also be stored on CDs, DVDs, and USB flash drives. An increasing amount of application software is available on the Web. Sometimes referred to as a **rich Internet application (RIA)**, a Web-delivered application combines hardware resources of the Web server and the PC to deliver valuable software services through a browser interface. Before a person, a group, or an enterprise decides on the best approach for acquiring application software, they should carefully analyze computing goals, needs, and budget.

rich Internet application (RIA): A Web-delivered application combines hardware resources of the Web server and the PC to deliver valuable software services through a Web browser interface.

Overview of Application Software

Proprietary software and off-the-shelf software are two important types of application software. **Proprietary software** is one-of-a-kind software designed for a specific application and owned by the company, organization, or person that uses it. Proprietary software can give a company a competitive advantage by providing services or solving problems in a unique manner—better than methods used by a competitor. **Off-the-shelf software** is produced by software vendors to address needs that are common across businesses, organizations, or individuals. For example, Amazon.com uses the same off-the-shelf payroll software as many businesses, but on its Web site, the company uses custom-designed proprietary software, which allows visitors to more easily find items to purchase. The relative advantages and disadvantages of proprietary software and off-the-shelf software are summarized in Table 4.7.

proprietary software: One-of-a-kind software designed for a specific application and owned by the company, organization, or person that uses it.

off-the-shelf software: Software produced by software vendors to address needs that are common across businesses, organizations, or individuals.

TABLE **4.7** Comparison of proprietary and off-the-shelf software

Proprietary Software		Off-the-Shelf Software	
Advantages	Disadvantages	Advantages	Disadvantages
You can get exactly what you need in terms of features, reports, and so on.	It can take a long time and a significant amount of resources to develop required features.	The initial cost is lower because the software firm can spread the development costs across many customers.	An organization might have to pay for features that it does not require and never uses.
Being involved in the development offers more control over the results.	In-house system development staff may be hard-pressed to provide the required level of ongoing support and maintenance because of pressure to move on to other new projects.	The software is likely to meet the basic business needs. Users have the opportunity to more fully analyze existing features and the performance of the package before purchasing.	The software might lack important features, thus requiring future modification or customization, which can be very expensive, and because users will eventually be required to adopt future releases of the software, the customization work might need to be repeated.
You can more easily modify the software and add features that you might need to counteract an initiative by competitors or to meet new supplier or customer demands.	The features and performance of the delivered software may fail to meet evolving business and end user needs.	The software is likely to be of high quality because many customer firms have tested the software and helped identify its bugs.	The software might not match current work processes and data standards.

Many companies use off-the-shelf software to support business processes. Key questions for selecting off-the-shelf software include the following:

- Will the software run on the OS and hardware you have selected?
- Does the software meet the essential business requirements that have been defined?
- Is the software manufacturer financially solvent and reliable?
- Does the total cost of purchasing, installing, and maintaining the software compare favorably to the expected business benefits?

Founded in 1955, H&R Block is the world's largest tax services provider, with 80,000 employees in 12,000 offices across the United States. In 2014, more than 24 million tax returns were prepared by H&R Block tax professionals and by clients using the company's digital tax solutions.[32] H&R Block places a priority on providing accurate and easily accessible information about the company—as well as tax preparation information and tips—through its online newsroom. When the tax preparer was building the newsroom for its corporate Web site, it opted to use an off-the-shelf software package called PressPage. By using a proven, off-the-shelf option, H&R Block was able to quickly deploy an online newsroom that included all of the features it needed, while taking advantage of PressPage's best practice expertise. The result was a user-friendly newsroom that complements the company's "brand journalism" approach to public relations.[33]

As mentioned in Chapter 1, workers in many organizations operate in a cloud-computing environment in which software, data storage, and other services are provided by the Internet ("the cloud"); the services are run on another organization's computer hardware, and both software and data are easily accessed. Examples of public cloud service providers, which make their services available to the general public, include Amazon Elastic Compute Cloud (EC2), IBM's Blue Cloud, Sun Cloud, Google Cloud Platform, Rackspace's Managed

Cloud, and Windows Azure Services Platform. Public cloud users can realize a considerable cost savings because the very high initial hardware, application, and bandwidth costs are paid for by the service provider and passed along to users as a relatively small monthly fee or per-use fee. Furthermore, companies can easily scale up or down the amount of services used, depending on user demand for services. Cloud computing also provides the benefit of being able to easily collaborate with others by sharing documents on the Internet.

Cloud services are often given popular acronyms such as SaaS (software as a service), PaaS (platform as a service), IaaS (infrastructure as a service), and HaaS (hardware as a service). **Software as a service (SaaS)** allows organizations to subscribe to Web-delivered application software. In most cases, the company pays a monthly service charge or a per-use fee. Many business activities are supported by SaaS. SaaS vendors include Oracle, SAP, NetSuite, Salesforce, and Google. Each year, The Container Store sells over $200 million worth of storage and organization products through its 70 retail stores.[34] The retail chain has grown rapidly, and it is committed to maintaining satisfaction for its 4,000 employees—a goal that was becoming more difficult to achieve given the limited resources of the company's IT, benefits, and payroll departments. In order to free up some of those internal resources, The Container Store migrated its payroll and benefit processes to UltiPro HCM, a SaaS provided by Ultimate Software. The SaaS solution helped the company streamline its payroll and benefits administration while increasing employee satisfaction by providing them real-time, online access to up-to-date salary and benefits information.[35]

Tableau software allows users to import databases or spreadsheet data to create powerful visualizations that provide useful information. Figure 4.14 shows a Tableau visualization that tracks the unemployment rate across the country over time. Orange indicates an unemployment rate exceeding the national average, whereas blue indicates rates below the national average.

Software as a Service (SaaS): A service that allows businesses to subscribe to Web-delivered application software.

Employment Horizon Chart

FIGURE 4.14

Tableau software

Tableau is available in desktop and cloud versions and helps users visualize data, such as how the unemployment rate changes over a 20-year period.

© Tableau Software

Amazon is considered one of the leading public cloud service providers because of the variety of services that it provides through its Amazon Web Services (AWS) platform. Amazon delivers one of the most reliable public cloud platforms available, and it is also rapidly adding new services, including tools for software developers and services to support version control and collaboration.[36] Airbnb is an online marketplace that connects travelers and property owners who are looking to rent out their properties to vacationers. Airbnb supports its business using cloud-based Web site, storage, and database-hosting services from Amazon Web Services. The company chose AWS because it offered the reliability and flexibility Airbnb requires to continue to grow its business—at a relatively low cost and with no minimum usage commitments.[37]

Google's Chromebook line of personal computers is an example of a consumer-focused implementation of the SaaS model. Built by Samsung and Acer, Chromebooks include only an Internet browser—with all software applications accessed through an Internet connection. Rather than installing, storing, and running software on the Chromebook, users access software that is stored on and delivered from a Web server. Typically the data generated by the software is also stored on the Web server.

While SaaS and cloud computing offer many benefits, these software delivery models also involve some risks. For example, sensitive information could be compromised by unauthorized access by employees or computer hackers. In addition, the company providing the hosting services might not keep its computers and network up and running as consistently as necessary, or a disaster could disable the host's data center, temporarily putting an organization out of business. Some companies also find it is difficult to integrate the SaaS approach with some of its existing software.

Personal Application Software

Hundreds of thousands personal software applications are available to meet the needs of individuals at school, home, and work—with new applications released on a daily basis. New computer software under development, along with existing GPS technology, for example, will enable people to see 3D views of where they are, along with directions and 3D maps to where they would like to go. The features of some popular types of personal application software are summarized in Table 4.8. In addition to these general-purpose programs, thousands of other personal computer applications perform specialized tasks that help users prepare their taxes, get in shape, lose weight, get medical advice, write wills and other legal documents, repair their computers, fix their cars, write music, and edit pictures and videos. This type of software, often called user software or personal productivity software, includes the general-purpose tools and programs that support individual needs.

The following sections discuss some of the most popular types of personal application software currently available.

Word Processing

Word-processing applications are installed on most PCs today. These applications come with a vast array of features, including those for checking spelling, creating tables, inserting formulas, and creating graphics. See Figure 4.15. Much of the work required to create this book involved the use of the popular word-processing software, Microsoft Word.

A team of people can use a word-processing program to collaborate on a project. The authors and editors who developed this book, for example, used the Track Changes and Review features of Microsoft Word to track and make changes to chapter files. With these features, you can add comments or make revisions to a document that a coworker can review and either accept or reject. Some cloud-based word-processing applications, such as Google Docs, allow multiple authors to collaborate in real time.

Spreadsheet Analysis

Many individuals and organizations use spreadsheet applications that offer powerful tools for manipulating and analyzing numbers and alphanumeric data. Common spreadsheet features include statistical analysis tools, built-in formulas, chart- and graphics-creation tools, and limited database

TABLE 4.8 Examples of personal application software

Type of Software	Use	Example
Word processing	Create, edit, and print text documents	Apache OpenOffice Writer Apple Pages Corel Write Google Docs Microsoft Word WordPerfect
Spreadsheet	Perform statistical, financial, logical, database, graphics, and date and time calculations using a wide range of built-in functions	Apache OpenOffice Calc Apple Numbers Google Sheets IBM Lotus 1-2-3 Microsoft Excel
Database	Store, manipulate, and retrieve data	Apache OpenOffice Base Microsoft Access IBM Lotus Approach
Graphics	Develop graphs, illustrations, drawings, and presentations	Adobe FreeHand Adobe Illustrator Apache OpenOffice Impress Microsoft PowerPoint
Personal information management	Helps people, groups, and organizations store useful information, such as a list of tasks to complete or a set of names and addresses	Google Calendar Microsoft Calendar Microsoft Outlook One Note
Project management	Plan, schedule, allocate, and control people and resources (money, time, and technology) needed to complete a project according to schedule	Microsoft Project Scitor Project Scheduler
Financial management	Track income and expenses and create reports to create and monitor budgets (some programs also have investment portfolio management features)	GnuCash Intuit Mint Intuit Quicken Moneydance You Need a Budget (YNAB)
Desktop publishing (DTP)	Use with personal computers and high-resolution printers to create high-quality printed output, including text and graphics; various styles of pages can be laid out; art and text files from other programs can also be integrated into published pages	Adobe InDesign Apple Pages Corel Ventura Publisher Microsoft Publisher QuarkXpress

capabilities. See Figure 4.16. Business functions include those that calculate depreciation, present value, internal rate of return, and the monthly payment on a loan. Optimization is another powerful feature of many spreadsheet programs that allows the spreadsheet to maximize or minimize a quantity subject to certain constraints. For example, a small furniture manufacturer that produces chairs and tables might want to maximize its profits. The constraints could be a limited supply of lumber, a limited number of workers who can assemble the chairs and tables, or a limited amount of available hardware fasteners. Using an optimization feature, such as Solver in Microsoft Excel, the spreadsheet can determine the number of chairs and tables that should be produced—given the labor and material constraints—to maximize profits.

While the built-in formulas available in many spreadsheet applications are powerful tools, they are not foolproof, as can be seen in the example of Carmen Reinhart and Kenneth Rogoff's famous 2010 study "Growth in a

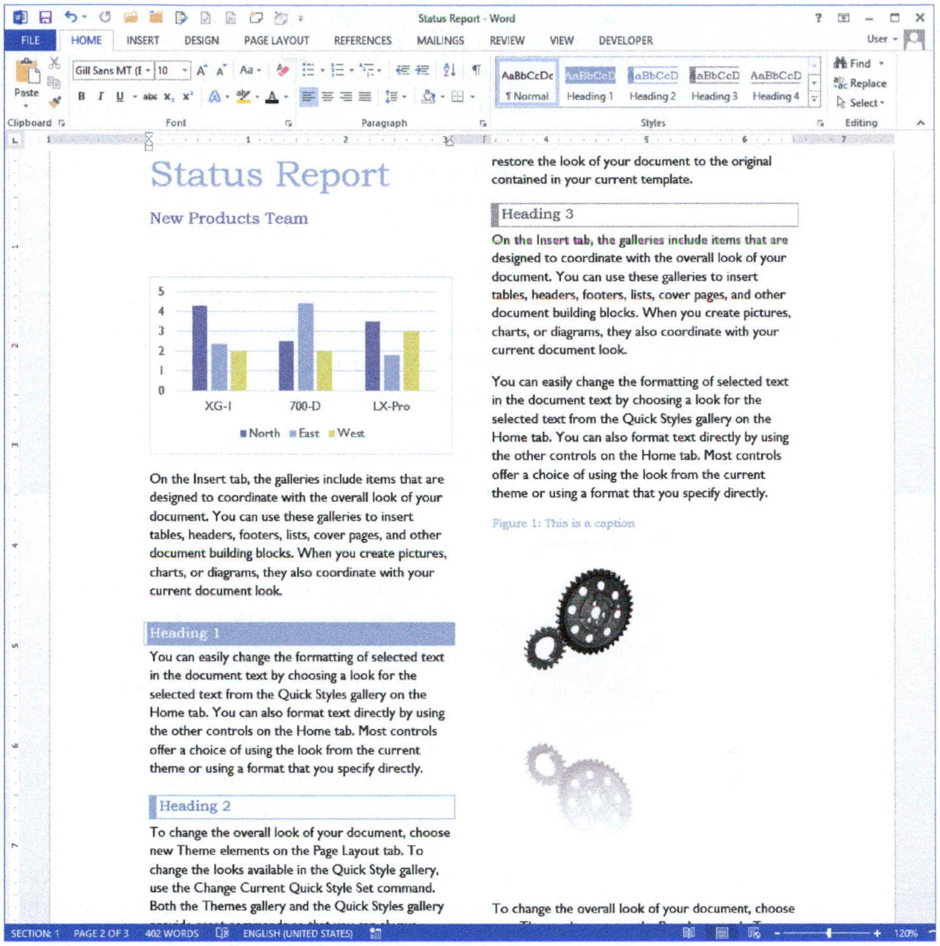

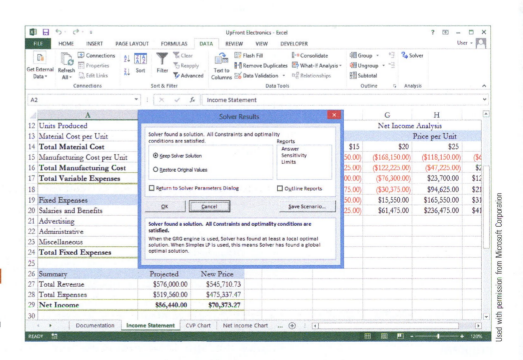

FIGURE **4.15**

Word-processing program

Word-processing applications, such as Microsoft Word, can be used to write letters, professional documents, work reports, and term papers.

FIGURE **4.16**

Spreadsheet program

Consider using a spreadsheet program, such as Microsoft Excel, when calculations are required.

Time of Debt," which concluded that a country's economic growth is reduced when its public debt level reaches 90 percent of GDP. In recent years, this finding has been used as a justification to push countries to reduce their deficits. However, a more recent study by Thomas Herndon, Michael Ash, and Robert Pollin uncovered that the original study has three major flaws. First, it excluded three occurrences of high-debt, high-growth nations. Second, it made some questionable assumptions about weighting different historical episodes. Third, it had an error in Excel spreadsheet formulas that excluded Belgium from their analysis. Correcting for these problem leads to an entirely different conclusion—"The average real GDP growth rate for countries carrying a public debt-to-GDP ratio of over 90 percent is actually 2.2 percent, not −0.1 percent as published in Reinhart and Rogoff."[38]

Database Applications

Database applications are ideal for storing, organizing, and retrieving data. These applications are particularly useful when you need to manipulate a large amount of data and produce reports and documents. Database manipulations include merging, editing, and sorting data, and database applications can be used in a variety of ways. You could use a database application to keep track of a CD collection, the items in your apartment, tax records, and expenses. A student club could use a database to store names, addresses, phone numbers, and dues paid. In business, a database application could be used to help process sales orders, control inventory, order new supplies, send letters to customers, and pay employees. Database management systems can be used to track orders, products, and customers; analyze weather data to make forecasts; and summarize medical research results. A database can also be a front end to another application. For example, you can use a database application to enter and store income tax information and then export the stored results to other applications, such as a spreadsheet or tax-preparation application.

Presentation Graphics Program

It is often said that a picture is worth a thousand words. With today's available graphics programs, it is easy to develop attractive graphs, illustrations, and drawings that help communicate important information. See Figure 4.17. The

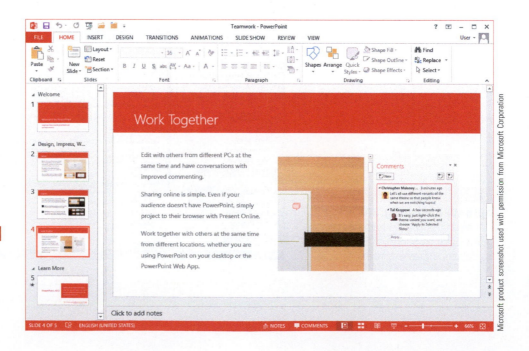

FIGURE 4.17

Presentation graphics program

Presentation graphics programs, such as Microsoft PowerPoint, can help you make a presentation for school or work.

category of presentation graphics applications includes programs that can be used to perform a variety of tasks, including creating advertising brochures, event announcements, and full-color presentations; some presentation graphics programs can also be used to organize and edit photographic images. And if you need to make a presentation at school or work, you can use a special type of graphics program called a presentation application—such as Microsoft PowerPoint—to develop slides and then display them while you are speaking. Because of their popularity, many colleges and departments require students to become proficient at using presentation graphics programs.

Many graphics and presentation programs, including Microsoft PowerPoint, consist of a series of slides. Each slide can be displayed on a computer screen, printed as a handout, or (more commonly) projected onto a large viewing screen for audiences. In PowerPoint, you can select a template designed for a specific type of presentation, such as recommending a strategy for managers, communicating news to a salesforce, giving a training presentation, or facilitating a brainstorming session. PowerPoint includes powerful built-in features that let you create a presentation step-by-step, including applying color and attractive formatting. You can also design a custom presentation using the many types of charts, drawings, and formatting available. Most presentation graphics programs also provide access to online clip art, such as drawings and photos of people meeting, medical equipment, telecommunications equipment, entertainment, and much more.

Personal Information Managers

Personal information management (PIM) software helps people, groups, and organizations store useful information, such as a list of tasks to complete or a set of names and addresses. PIM software usually provides an appointment calendar, an address book or contacts list, and a place to take notes. In addition, information in a PIM can typically be linked. For example, you can link an appointment with a sales manager in the calendar to information on the sales manager in the address book. When you click the appointment in the calendar, a window opens displaying information on the sales manager from the address book. Microsoft Outlook is an example of very popular PIM software. Increasingly, PIM software is moving online, where it can be accessed from any Internet-connected device. See Figure 4.18.

FIGURE 4.18

Personal information management software

Evernote lets you take notes, sync files across devices, save Web pages, and share your ideas with friends and colleagues. It runs on computers and on smartphones.

Evernote

Some PIMs allow you to schedule and coordinate group meetings. If a computer or handheld device is connected to a network, you can upload the PIM data and coordinate it with the calendar and schedule of others who are using the same PIM software on the network. You can also use some PIMs to coordinate emails inviting others to meetings. As users receive their invitations, they click a link or button to be automatically added to the guest list.

Software Suites and Integrated Software Packages

software suite: A collection of programs packaged together and sold in a bundle.

A **software suite** is a collection of programs packaged together and sold in a bundle. A software suite might include a word processor, a spreadsheet program, a database management system, a graphics program, communications and note-taking tools, and organizers. Some suites support the development of Web pages, and some offer a speech-recognition feature—so that applications in the suite can accept voice commands and record dictation. Software suites offer many advantages. The software programs within a suite have been designed to work similarly so that after you learn the basics for one application, the other applications are easy to learn and use. Buying software in a bundled suite is cost effective; the programs usually sell for a fraction of what they would cost individually.

Table 4.9 lists several popular general-purpose software suites for personal computer users. Microsoft Office has the largest market share. Most of these software suites include a spreadsheet program, a word processor, a database program, and graphics presentation software. All can exchange documents, data, and diagrams. In other words, you can create a spreadsheet and then cut and paste that spreadsheet into a document created using the word-processing application.

TABLE 4.9 Major components of leading software suites

Personal Productivity Function	Microsoft Office	Corel WordPerfect Office	Apache OpenOffice	Apple iWork	Google Apps
Word processing	Word	WordPerfect	Writer	Pages	Docs
Spreadsheet	Excel	Quattro Pro	Calc	Numbers	Spreadsheet
Presentation graphics	PowerPoint	Presentations	Impress and Draw	Keynote	Presentation
Database	Access		Base		

Some companies offer Web-based productivity software suites that do not require the installation of any software on your device—only a Web browser. Google, Thinkfree, and Zoho offer free online word processors, spreadsheet programs, presentation applications, and other software that can be accessed via the Internet.

After observing this trend, Microsoft responded with an online version of its popular Office applications. Microsoft Office 365 is available in a range of configurations designed for home or office use, for a monthly subscription fee. See Figure 4.19. Depending on the plan purchased, subscribers can access Microsoft Office applications such as Word, Outlook, Excel, Exchange for messaging, SharePoint for collaboration, and Skype for Business for conferencing. These cloud-based applications cost on the order of $10 per user per month depending on the features used. Microsoft offers plans for individuals, small businesses, enterprises, and education institutions. For example, any institution worldwide that licenses Office 365 ProPlus or Office Professional Plus for staff and faculty can provide access to Office 365 ProPlus for students at no

FIGURE 4.19

Web-based application suite
Microsoft Office 365 is a Web-based application suite that offers basic software suite features over the Internet using cloud computing.

additional cost. The online versions of Word, Excel, PowerPoint, and OneNote are tightly integrated with Microsoft's desktop Office suite for easy sharing of documents among computers and collaborators.

The H.J. Heinz Company, now part of Kraft Heinz Company, sells baby food, frozen entrees, ketchup, mustard, sauces, and other products in more than 200 countries. The firm wanted to help employees spend less time traveling and make it easier for them to share best practices, solve business problems, and come up with new ideas, regardless of their geographical locations. This led Heinz to adopt Microsoft Office 365 for its more than 20,000 employees who will use Exchange Online for email and calendaring, Sync for Business for conferencing and instant messaging, and Yammer (an enterprise social network) to share ideas and collaborate on projects. Heinz is also making the Office desktop suite available to its employees through Office 365 ProPlus.[39]

Other Personal Application Software

In addition to the software already discussed, many other interesting and powerful application software tools are available for personal and business use. In some cases, the features and capabilities of these applications more than justify the cost of an entire computer system. TurboTax, for example, is a popular tax-preparation program that annually saves millions of people many hours and even dollars in preparing their taxes. With just a quick online search, you can find software for creating Web sites, composing music, and editing photos and videos. Many people use educational and reference software and software for entertainment, games, and leisure activities. Game-playing software is popular and can be very profitable for companies that develop games and various game accessories, including virtual avatars such as colorful animals, fish, and people. Some organizations have launched programs designed to promote physical activity by incorporating the use of active video games (e.g., Wii Boxing and DanceDance Revolution) into broader physical education programs. Retirement communities also use video games to keep seniors physically active.[40] Engineers, architects, and designers often use computer-assisted design (CAD) software to design and develop buildings, electrical systems, plumbing systems, and more. Autosketch, CorelCAD, and AutoCad are examples of CAD software. Other programs perform a wide array of statistical tests. Colleges and universities often have a number of courses in statistics that use this type of application software. Two popular statistical analytics applications in the social sciences are SPSS and SAS.

Mobile Application Software

The number of applications (apps) for smartphones and other mobile devices has exploded in recent years. Besides the proprietary apps that come with these devices, hundreds of thousands of mobile apps have been developed by third parties. As of July 2015, Apple's App Store had over 1.5 million apps available for iOS device users, and Android users could choose from over 1.6 million mobile apps on Google's Play Store.[41] Microsoft and other software companies are also investing in mobile applications for devices that run on their software. For example, SceneTap, an application for iPhones and Android devices, can determine the number of people at participating bars, pubs, or similar establishments and the ratio of males to females. The application uses video cameras and facial-recognition software to identify males and females. SocialCamera, an application for Android phones, allows people to take a picture of someone and then search their Facebook friends for a match. However, many people consider facial-recognition software a potential invasion to privacy.

Table 4.10 lists a few mobile application categories. Many apps are free, whereas others range in price from 99 cents to hundreds of dollars.

TABLE 4.10 Categories of mobile applications

Category	Description
Books and reference	Access e-books, subscribe to journals, or look up information on the Merriam-Webster or Wikipedia Web sites
Business and finance	Track expenses, trade stocks, and access corporate information systems
Entertainment	Access all forms of entertainment, including movies, television programs, music videos, and information about local night life
Games	Play a variety of games, from 2D games such as Pacman and Tetris to 3D games such as Need for Speed, Call of Duty, and Minecraft
Health and fitness	Track workout and fitness progress, calculate calories, and even monitor your speed and progress from your wirelessly connected Nike shoes
Lifestyle	Find good restaurants, make a dinner reservation, select wine for a meal, and more
Music	Find, listen to, and create music
News and weather	Access major news and weather providers, including Reuters, AP, the *New York Times*, and the Weather Channel
Photography	Organize, edit, view, and share photos taken on your phone's camera
Productivity and utilities	Create grocery lists, practice PowerPoint presentations, work on spreadsheets, synchronize with PC files, and more
Social networking	Connect with others via major social networks, including Facebook, Twitter, and Instagram
Sports	Keep up with your favorite team or track your own golf scores
Travel and navigation	Use the GPS in your smartphone to get turn-by-turn directions, find interesting places to visit, access travel itineraries, and more

workgroup application software: Software that supports teamwork, whether team members are in the same location or dispersed around the world.

Workgroup Application Software

Workgroup application software is designed to support teamwork, whether team members are in the same location or dispersed around the world. This support can be accomplished with software known as groupware, which helps groups of people work together effectively. Microsoft Exchange Server, for example, has groupware and email features. Also called collaborative software, workgroup software allows a team to work together remotely, sharing ideas and work via connected computer systems.

Examples of workgroup software include group-scheduling software, electronic mail, and other software that enables people to share ideas. IBM Notes and Domino are examples of workgroup software from IBM. See Figure 4.20. (Notes runs on the end user's computing device, while Domino runs on a server and supports the end user.) Web-based software is ideal for group use. Because documents are stored on an Internet server, anyone with an Internet connection can access them easily. Google provides workgroup options in its online applications, which allow users to share documents, spreadsheets, presentations, calendars, and notes with other specified users or everyone on the Web. This sharing makes it convenient for several people to contribute to a document without concern for software compatibility or storage. Google also provides a tool for creating Web-based forms and surveys. When invited parties fill out the form, the data is stored in a Google spreadsheet.

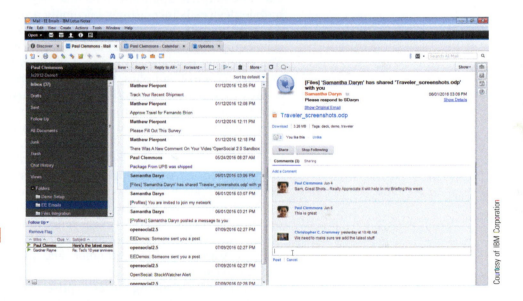

FIGURE 4.20

IBM Notes Social Edition

IBM Notes Social Edition is a workgroup software.

Clark Realty Capital (CRC) is a national real estate firm with nine offices across the United States. Its agents are constantly on the move, and in the past, they had difficulty staying connected to the latest version of important documents. This created problems because the firm's agents are constantly working to close deals on tight deadlines, which requires the ability to frequently and quickly update documents related to a transaction. The firm began sharing files via Google Drive to provide employees real-time access to the current version of each document, thus eliminating the need for email attachments and managing multiple versions of a file. Employees use Google Apps to create, access, and update these documents.[42]

Enterprise Application Software

Software that benefits an entire organization—enterprise application software—can be developed specifically for the business or purchased off the shelf. There are many categories of enterprise software, including the following:

Accounts payable	Invoicing
Accounts receivable	Manufacturing control
Airline industry operations	Order entry
Automatic teller systems	Payroll
Cash-flow analysis	Receiving
Check processing	Restaurant management
Credit and charge card administration	Retail operations
Distribution control	Sales ordering
Fixed asset accounting	Savings and time deposits
General ledger	Shipping
Human resource management	Stock and bond management
Inventory control	Tax planning and preparation

The total cost, ease of installation, ease of management, and the ability to integrate the software with other enterprise applications are the major considerations of organizations when selecting enterprise software. The ability to extend enterprise applications so that they can run on smartphones and other mobile devices is increasingly becoming a priority for many organizations.

Advantage Sign & Graphic Solutions, based in Grand Rapids, Michigan, sells equipment and supplies to businesses in the sign and graphics industry. The company operates 10 regional facilities that allow it to provide next-day delivery of most supplies to customers around the country.[43] In order to improve its profitability and attract more customers, the company implemented several NetSuite enterprise applications, including NetSuite ERP, CRM+, E-commerce, and Advanced Shipping. With the NetSuite software, Advantage was able to launch a new e-commerce site, reduce order-processing time by 65 percent, and decrease its on-hand inventory by 15 percent. Implementing an integrated set of enterprise applications simplified the company's operations and helped it better connect with customers.[44]

Enterprise software also helps managers and workers stay connected. At one time, managers and workers relied on email to stay in touch with each other, but business collaboration and enterprise social networking tools—such as Asana, blueKiwi, Yammer, and Jive—are replacing traditional email and text messaging.

Worldwide spending on enterprise software was estimated to be about $310 billion in 2015.[45] Most software spending goes to application software, as shown in Figure 4.21.[46]

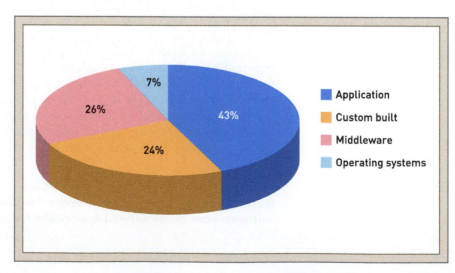

FIGURE 4.21

Spending by type of software
Of all software types, businesses spend the most on application software.

Application Software for Transaction Processing, Business Analytics, and Competitive Advantage

Specialized application software for learning enhancement and management, business analytics, information, decision support, and competitive advantage is available in every industry. For example, many schools and colleges use Blackboard or other learning management software to organize class materials and grades. Genetic researchers, as another example, are using software to visualize and analyze the human genome. Music executives use business analytics software to help them pick the next hit song.

Pima County Regional Wastewater Reclamation Department (RWRD) manages and maintains the Arizona county's sanitary sewer system, which serves 1 million people and treats 60 million gallons of wastewater each day.[47] The department recently implemented Wonderware's IntelaTrac mobile workforce and decision support software. The software, which is integrated with the automated SCADA (supervisory control and data acquisition) system that runs the sewer system, provides plant personnel with a range of reporting and analytics tools that have helped them to improve efficiency and reduce costs in RWRD's two wastewater treatment plants and seven regional sub-facilities. RWRD has been able to reduce energy consumption by 10 percent and double its plant capacity, while operating with the same number of people.[48]

But how are all these systems actually developed and built? The answer is through the use of programming languages, some of which are discussed in the next section.

Programming Languages

programming languages: Sets of keywords, commands, symbols, and rules for constructing statements by which humans can communicate instructions to a computer.

Both system and application software are written in coding schemes called programming languages. The primary function of a programming language is to provide instructions to the computer system so that it can perform a processing activity. Information systems professionals work with different **programming languages**, which are sets of keywords, commands, symbols, and rules for constructing statements that people can use to communicate instructions to a computer. Programming involves translating what a user wants to accomplish into a code that the computer can understand and execute. Program code is the set of instructions that signal the CPU to perform circuit-switching operations. In the simplest coding schemes, a line of code typically contains a single instruction such as, "Retrieve the data in memory address X." The instruction is then decoded during the instruction phase of the machine cycle.

syntax: A set of rules associated with a programming language.

Like writing a report or a paper in English, writing a computer program in a programming language requires the programmer to follow a set of rules. Each programming language uses symbols, keywords, and commands that have special meanings and usage. Each language also has its own set of rules, called the **syntax** of the language. The language syntax dictates how the symbols, keywords, and commands should be combined into statements capable of conveying meaningful instructions to the CPU. Rules such as "statements must terminate with a semicolon," and "variable names must begin with a letter," are examples of a language's syntax. A variable is a quantity that can take on different values. Program variable names such as SALES, PAYRATE, and TOTAL follow the sample rule shown above because they start with a letter, whereas variables such as %INTEREST, $TOTAL, and #POUNDS do not.

compiler: A special software program that converts the programmer's source code into the machine-language instructions, which consist of binary digits.

With higher-level programming languages, each statement in the language translates into several instructions in machine language. A special software program called a **compiler** translates the programmer's source code into the machine-language instructions, which consist of binary digits, as shown in Figure 4.22. A compiler creates a two-stage process for program execution. First, the compiler translates the program into a machine language; second, the CPU executes that program. Another programming approach is to use an interpreter, which is a language translator that carries out the operations called for by the source code. An interpreter does not produce a complete machine-language program. After the statement executes, the machine-language statement is discarded, the process continues for the next statement, and so on.

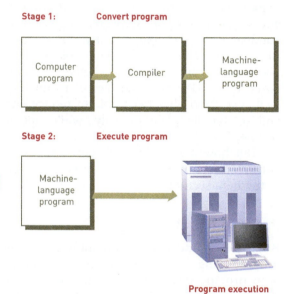

Stage 1: **Convert program**

Computer program → Compiler → Machine-language program

Stage 2: **Execute program**

Machine-language program →

Program execution

FIGURE 4.22

How a compiler works

A compiler translates a complete program into a complete set of binary instructions (Stage 1). After this is done, the CPU can execute the converted program in its entirety (Stage 2).

The majority of software used today is created using an integrated development environment. An integrated development environment (IDE) combines all the tools required for software engineering into one package. For example, the popular IDE Microsoft Visual Studio includes an editor that supports several visual programming interfaces and languages (visual programming uses a graphical or "visual" interface combined with text-based commands), a compiler and an interpreter, programming automation tools, a debugger (a tool for finding errors in the code), and other tools that provide convenience to the developer.

Software development kits (SDKs) often serve the purpose of an IDE for a particular platform. For example, software developers for Google's Android smartphone platform use the Java programming language along with the Android Studio with built-in Android Developer Tools to streamline their Android app development. They can also use special code libraries provided by Google for Android functionality, and they test out their applications in an Android Emulator.[49] See Figure 4.23.

IDEs and SDKs have made software development easier than ever. Many novice coders, including some who might have never considered developing software, are publishing applications for popular platforms such as Facebook and the iPhone.

Table 4.11 lists some of the most commonly used programming languages.

FIGURE 4.23

Emulator for Android smartphones

To develop for the Android, you use an SDK with a mobile device emulator so you can prototype, develop, and test Android applications without having to transfer them to a physical device.

TABLE 4.11 Commonly used programming languages for new software development

Language	Description
COBOL	An English language-like programming language designed for business use, COBOL has been in use since 1959. Billions of lines of COBOL code are still in use in systems around the world, including credit card systems, ATMs, retail/POS systems, banking and payroll systems, healthcare systems, government systems, reservation systems, and traffic signal systems. Due to its declining popularity and the retirement of experienced COBOL programmers, COBOL programs are gradually being migrated to new platforms, rewritten in modern languages, or replaced with software packages.
C	Developed in the early 1970s, C is the base for other popular languages, such as C#, Java, JavaScript, and Python. C is mostly used for implementing operating systems and embedded applications. Because it provides the foundation for many other languages, it is advisable to learn C (and C++) before moving onto other languages.
C ++	Originally designed to enhance the C language, C++ is used to develop systems software, application software, high-performance server and client applications, and video games.
Java	Java is a programming language developed by Sun Microsystems in the 1990s, and it is still widely used in the development of enterprise software, Web-based content, and games. Java is also used for mobile apps that run on the Android operating system.
JavaScript	A scripting language developed by Netscape, JavaScript derives much of its syntax from C. JavaScript can be used across multiple Web browsers and is considered essential for developing interactive or animated Web functions. It is also used in game development and for writing desktop applications.
PHP (Hypertext Preprocessor)	A popular programming language for Web developers, PHP is used to create dynamic Web sites and to develop apps. PHP is used in more than 200 million Web sites, including WordPress, Digg, and Facebook.
Python	Python is another scripting language used to develop Web sites and mobile apps. Python is considered a fairly easy language for beginners to learn due to its readability and compact syntax, and it is used in Web apps for Google, Instagram, NASA, Pinterest, and Yahoo!
Ruby	Ruby is a scripting language designed to be simple and easy to use for developing Web sites and mobile apps. It powers the Ruby on Rails (or Rails) framework, which is used on Scribd, GitHub, Groupon, and Shopify.
SQL	A language for accessing data in relational database management systems, SQL is most commonly used for its "Query" function, which searches relational databases. SQL was standardized in the 1980s by the American National Standards Institute (ANSI) and the International Organization for Standardization (ISO).

Critical Thinking Exercise

Walmart's VMI System

Walmart employs a special kind of enterprise system called an interorganizational information system it calls vendor-managed inventory (VMI) to improve product flow and lower its store inventories. Under this program, suppliers are responsible for managing the inventory of their products in Walmart's warehouses. Suppliers are granted access to a Walmart database that contains item-level sales and inventory data for their products only, which help the vendors develop product demand projections using a collaborative planning, forecasting, replenishment process. Each link in the supply chain is interconnected using information technology that includes a central database, store-level-point-of-sale systems, and a satellite network for fast and reliable communications.

Review Questions

1. Do you think that the VMI software is off-the-shelf or proprietary software? Why?
2. Should Walmart allow the suppliers to take a major role in defining and customizing the features and capabilities of this system or should they insist on a "one size fits all" approach?

Critical Thinking Questions

1. What special issues and considerations are likely to arise in the operation and support of an interorganizational system?
2. Given the business criticality of this system, would it make sense for Walmart to consider moving this system into a public cloud environment? What would be the advantages and disadvantage of such a move?

Software Issues and Trends

Because software is such an important part of today's computer systems, issues such as software bugs, copyrights and licensing, freeware and open-source software, upgrades, and global software support are receiving increased attention. These topics are covered in the following sections.

Software Bugs

A software bug is a defect in a computer program that keeps it from performing as its users expect it to perform. While some bugs are subtle—allowing errors to creep into your work undetected—other bugs are very obvious, causing programs to terminate unexpectedly. For example, not all goes smoothly when users upgrade to a new operating system. Applications that used to run without a problem under the old operating system may begin to experience difficulty. Users of Microsoft's Office for MAC 2016 who upgraded to Apple's El Capitan OS initially experienced application crashes for Outlook, Excel, PowerPoint, and Word. Although the bugs were eventually fixed, many users spent weeks dealing with the crashes.[50]

Most computer and software vendors say that as long as people design and program hardware and software, bugs are inevitable. The following list summarizes tips for reducing the impact of software bugs:

- Register all software so that you receive bug alerts, fixes, and patches.
- Check the manual or read-me files for solutions to known problems.
- Access the support area of the manufacturer's Web site for patches.
- Install the latest software updates.
- Before reporting a bug, make sure that you can recreate the circumstances under which it occurs.
- After you can recreate the bug, call the manufacturer's tech support line.

- Consider waiting before buying the latest release of software to give the vendor a chance to discover and remove bugs. Many schools and businesses don't purchase software until the first major revision with patches is released.

Copyrights and Licenses

Most companies aggressively guard and protect the source code of their software from competitors as well as customers. As a result, most software products are protected by law using copyright or licensing provisions. Those provisions can vary, however. In some cases, users are given unlimited use of software on one or two computers. This stipulation is typical for applications developed for personal computers. In other cases, users pay based on usage: If you use the software more, you pay more. This approach is becoming popular, with software placed on networks or larger computers. Most of these protections prevent you from copying software and giving it to others. Some software now requires that you *register* or *activate* it before it can be fully used. This requirement is another way software companies prevent illegal distribution of their products.

In a recent survey of 50 companies with more than 10,000 employees, 10 percent of the respondents indicated that their firm had been fined, assessed additional fees, or required to purchase backdated maintenance as a result of license compliance issues uncovered in a software audit. The costs ranged from less than $100,000 to more than $1 million.[51]

When people purchase software, they don't actually own the software, but rather they are licensed to use the software on a computer. This is called a **single-user license**. A single-user license permits you to install the software on one or more computers, used by one person. A single-user license does not allow you to copy and share the software with others. Table 4.12 describes different types of software licenses.[52] Licenses that accommodate multiple users are usually provided at a discounted price.

single-user license: A software license that permits you to install the software on one or more computers, used by one person.

Freeware and Open-Source Software

Some software developers are not concerned about profiting from their intellectual property, which has given rise to alternative copyrights and licensing agreements. Freeware is software that is made available to the public for free. Software developers might give away their product for several reasons. Some want to build customer interest and name recognition. Others simply don't need the money and want to make a valuable donation to society. Still others, such as those associated with the Free Software Foundation (*www.fsf.org*), believe that all software should be free. Freeware is placed in the public domain where anyone can use the software free of charge. (All creative works that reach the end of their term of copyright revert to the public domain.) Table 4.13 shows some examples of freeware.

Freeware differs slightly from free software. Freeware simply implies that the software is distributed for free. The term "free software" was coined by Richard Stallman and the Free Software Foundation, and it implies that the software is not only freeware, but also open source. Open-source software is distributed, typically for free, with the source code also available so that it can be studied, changed, and improved by its users. Over time, open-source software evolves in response to the combined contributions of its users. The Code For America (CFA) organization, for example, used open-source software to develop a map-based app for the city of Boston that allows individuals, small businesses, and community organizations to volunteer to shovel out specific hydrants that might be completely covered with snow in the winter. After creating the app for Boston, CFA made its efforts available for free

TABLE **4.12** Software licenses

License	Subtype	Description
Single-user license	General	This type of license allows the program to be installed and used on one CPU that is not accessed by other users over a network. The software can be used only on a single computer, and other users cannot access or run the software while connected to your computer.
	Perpetual license	A perpetual license allows the customer to install and use the software indefinitely. Technical support is included for a limited term, usually 90 days.
	Subscription license	A subscription license allows the user to use the software for a specified time period. This license usually includes technical support and access to upgrades and patches released during the term of the subscription. At the end of the term, the user has several options: (1) renew the subscription, (2) purchase a perpetual license at a discounted cost, or (3) remove the software from the computer.
	Freeware license	This license type is offered as freeware by the author and does not require paying any fee for use.
	Shareware license	This is a license to use software for a limited trial period. If you want to continue to use the software after the trial period, you must pay a shareware fee.
Individual/multi-user licenses	Volume licenses	A volume license allows the licensee to install the software on a certain number of computers. The licensee has to satisfy a minimum purchase requirement to receive a reduced price. When purchasing the licenses, the licensee usually receives one copy of the media and documentation, with the option of purchasing more.
	Site/enterprise	This license provides access to software at a single location. Typically, these licenses are individually negotiated with the publisher and vary widely in their provisions.
Network/multi-user licenses	Per server (network)	A per server license type requires that you have a single copy of the software residing on a file server. With per server licensing, a specified number of client access licenses (CALs) are associated with a particular server. The number of devices that can legally access that server simultaneously is limited to the number of CALs purchased for that particular server.
	Per seat (machine)	A per machine/seat license requires that you purchase a license for each client computer and/or device that needs to access the software. This license type is typically used in conjunction with a network license.
	Per processor	Under the per processor model, you acquire a processor license for each processor in the server on which the software is running. A processor license usually includes access for an unlimited number of users to connect. You do not need to purchase additional server licenses, CALs, or Internet connector licenses.

Source: "Software License Types," Tulane University, *http://tulane.edu/tsweb/software/software-license-types.cfm*, accessed November 28, 2015.

TABLE **4.13** Examples of freeware

Software	Description
Adobe Reader	Software for viewing Adobe PDF documents
AVG Anti-Virus	Antivirus security software
IrfanView	Photo-editing software
Pidgin	Instant messaging software
Thunderbird	Email, news, and chat software
WinPatrol	Anti-malware software

TABLE **4.14** Examples of open-source software

Software	Category
Drupal	Web publishing
Gimp	Photo editing
Grisbi	Personal accounting
Linux	Operating system
Mozilla Firefox	Internet browser
MySQL	Database software
Apache OpenOffice	Application software
ProjectLibre Open Project	Project management

to other cities and municipalities. Table 4.14 provides examples of popular open-source software applications.

Open-source software is not completely devoid of restrictions. Much of the popular free software in use today is protected by the GNU General Public License (GPL). The GPL grants you the right to do the following:

- Run the program for any purpose
- Study how the program works and adapt it to your needs
- Redistribute copies so you can help others
- Improve the program and release improvements to the public

Software under the GPL is typically protected by a "copyleft" (a play on the word "copyright"), which requires that any copies of the work retain the same license. A copyleft work cannot be owned by any one person, and no one is allowed to profit from its distribution. The Free Software Directory (*http://directory.fsf.org*) lists over 5,000 software titles of application software, systems software, and programming tools (e.g., compilers).

Why would an organization run its business using software that's free? Can something that's given away over the Internet be stable, reliable, or sufficiently supported to place at the core of a company's day-to-day operations? The answer is surprising—many believe that open-source software is often *more* reliable and secure than commercial software. How can this be? First, because a program's source code is readily available, users can fix any problems they discover. A fix is often available within hours of a problem's discovery. Second, because the source code for a program is accessible to thousands of people, the chances of a bug being discovered and fixed before it does any damage are much greater than with traditional software packages.

However, using open-source software does have some disadvantages. Although open-source systems can be obtained for next to nothing, the up-front costs are only a small piece of the total cost of ownership that accrues over the years that the system is in place. Some claim that open-source systems contain many hidden costs, particularly in terms for user support and debugging. Licensed software comes with guarantees and support services, whereas open-source software does not. Still, many businesses appreciate the additional freedom that open-source software provides. The question of software support is typically the biggest stumbling block to the acceptance of open-source software at the corporate level. Getting support for traditional software packages is easy—you call a company's toll-free support number or access its Web site. But how do you get help if an open-source package doesn't work as expected? Because the open-source community lives on the Internet, you look there for help. Through the use of Internet discussion areas, you can communicate with others who use the same software, and you might even reach someone who helped develop it. Ideally, users of popular open-source packages can get correct answers to their technical questions within a few hours of asking for help on the appropriate Internet forum. Another approach is to contact one of the many companies emerging to support and service such software—for example, Red Hat for Linux and Sendmail, Inc., for Sendmail. These companies offer high-quality, for-pay technical assistance.

Burton Snowboards was founded in 1977 by Jake Burton, who sold his first snowboards out of his Vermont barn. Since then, The Burton Corporation has become one of the world's leading manufacturers of snowboarding equipment and apparel.[53] As part of an upgrade of the company's existing SAP and Oracle applications, Burton decided to migrate its operating platform to SUSE Linux Enterprise Server, an open-source solution. SUSE, which is certified by both SAP and Oracle, offered the company a highly dependable and flexible platform for its business-critical systems. With SUSE, Burton is able to quickly make its own updates to adapt to changing business needs, but it also has access to ongoing support, including technical information and expert advice available through the SUSE Web site—all with the lower software cost that an open-source solution offers.[54]

Software Upgrades

Software companies revise their programs periodically. Software upgrades, which are an important source of increased revenue for software manufacturers, vary widely in the benefits that they provide, and what some people call a benefit, others might call a drawback. Deciding whether to upgrade to a new version of software can be a challenge for corporations and people with a large investment in software. Some users choose not to immediately download the most current software version or upgrade unless it includes significant improvements or capabilities. Developing an upgrading strategy is important for many businesses. American Express, for example, has standardized its software upgrade process around the world to make installing updated software faster and more efficient. The standardized process also helps the company make sure that updated software is more stable, with fewer errors and problems.

Global Software Support

Large global companies have little trouble persuading vendors to sell them software licenses for even the most far-flung outposts of their company. But can those same vendors provide adequate support for their software customers in all locations? Supporting local operations is one of the biggest challenges IS teams face when putting together standardized companywide systems. Slower technology growth markets, such as Eastern Europe and Latin America, might not have any official vendor presence. Instead, large vendors such as Sybase, IBM, and Hewlett-Packard typically contract with local providers to support their software in such regions.

One approach that has been gaining acceptance in North America is to outsource global support to one or more third-party distributors. The user company still negotiates its license with the software vendor directly, but it then hands the global support contract to a third-party supplier. The supplier acts as a middleman between the software vendor and user, often providing distribution, support, and invoicing.

In today's computer systems, software is an increasingly critical component. Whatever approach people and organizations take to acquire software, everyone must be aware of the current trends in the industry. Informed users are wise consumers.

Critical Thinking Exercise

Organization Weighs Use of Open Source Software

You began operating a small general electric contracting company two years ago. Originally, it was just you and your cousin, but it has grown to five licensed electricians, plus one office manager who takes calls from customers, schedules the work, and orders parts and supplies. Your company handles a wide range of work, including installing new circuit breaker panels, rewiring existing electrical systems for renovations and additions, and installing residential light fixtures, security lighting systems, swimming pool lighting, and ceiling fans. Business has really taken off, and your current manual systems and procedures can no longer keep pace. The office manager has been exploring several options and has identified three different software packages designed for small contractors. Each one of the packages includes software designed for managing parts and supplies inventory, scheduling jobs, and invoicing customers. Two of the software packages are from large, well-known companies, and each has an initial licensing cost of roughly $550 plus $100 per year for software support. The other software package is open-source software, with no initial cost and no support cost. The office manager is unsure how to proceed.

Review Questions

1. What is the primary difference between purchasing licensed software from a software manufacturer and using open-source software?
2. What are the pros and cons of using open-source software?

Critical Thinking Questions

1. What risks and start-up issues are associated with the use of any new software that is designed to replace manual procedures?
2. What actions can be taken to reduce these risks?

Summary

Principle:

Software is valuable in helping individuals, workgroups, and entire enterprises achieve their goals.

Software consists of programs that control the workings of the computer hardware. Software can be divided into two types: systems software, which consists of operating systems, utilities, and middleware, and application software, which consists of programs that help users solve particular computing problems.

One useful way of classifying the many potential uses of information systems is to identify the scope of problems and opportunities addressed by a particular organization or its sphere of influence. For most companies, the spheres of influence are personal, workgroup, and enterprise.

Principle:

The operating system is called the "soul of the computer" because it controls how you enter data into your computer, perform meaningful work, and display results.

An operating system is a set of programs that controls a computer's hardware and acts as an interface with application software.

There are various combinations of operating systems and computers, and users, including single computer with a single user, single computer with multiple simultaneous users, multiple computers with multiple users, and special-purpose computers.

The kernel is the heart of the operating system and controls its most critical processes.

The operating system performs a myriad of functions including controlling common hardware functions, providing a user interface and input/output management, providing a degree of hardware independence, managing system memory, managing processing tasks, providing networking capability, controlling access to system resources, and managing files.

Operating systems use multitasking, multiprocessing, and multithreading to increase the amount of processing that can be accomplished in a given amount of time. With multitasking, users can run more than one application at a time. Multiprocessing supports running a program on more than one CPU. Multithreading allows different threads of a single program to run concurrently.

The ability of a computer to handle an increasing number of concurrent users smoothly is called scalability, a feature critical for systems expected to handle a large number of users.

Software applications access and use the OS and other software applications by requesting services through a defined application programming interface (API). Programmers can use APIs to create application software without having to understand the inner workings of the operating system. APIs also provide a degree of hardware independence so that the underlying hardware can change without necessarily requiring a rewrite of the software applications.

Over the years, many OSs have been developed for the individual sphere of influence including Microsoft Windows, the Mac OS X, Linux, and Google Android and Chrome.

Microsoft Windows Server, UNIX, Red Hat Linux, Mac OS X Server, and HP-UX are operating systems used for workgroups.

IBM z/os, HP-UX, and Linux are operating systems used in the enterprise sphere of influence.

Smartphones now employ full-fledged personal computer operating systems such as the Google Android, Apple iOS, and Microsoft Windows Phone.

An embedded system is a computer system (including some sort of processor) that is implanted in and dedicated to the control of another device.

Mac iOS, Windows Embedded, Symbian, Android, and variations of Linux have been developed to support mobile communications and consumer appliances.

Utility programs can perform many useful tasks, typically related to system resource maintenance and management, and often come installed on computers along with the OS. This type of software is used to merge and sort sets of data, keep track of computer jobs being run, compress files of data, protect against harmful computer viruses, monitor hardware and network performance, and perform dozens of other important tasks.

Virtualization software simulates a computer's hardware architecture in software so that computer systems can run operating systems and software designed for other architectures, or run several operating systems simultaneously on one system.

Middleware is software that allows different systems to communicate and transfer data back and forth.

Principle:

Organizations typically use off-the-shelf application software to meet common business needs and proprietary application software to meet unique business needs and provide a competitive advantage.

Proprietary software is one-of-a-kind software designed for a specific application and owned by the company, organization, or person that uses it.

Off-the-shelf-software is produced by software vendors to address needs that are common across businesses, organizations, or individuals.

The software as a service (SaaS) model and recent Web-development technologies have led to a new paradigm in computing called cloud computing. "Cloud computing" refers to the use of computing resources, including software and data storage, on the Internet (the cloud), rather than on local computers. Instead of installing, storing, and running software on your own computer, with cloud computing, you access software stored on and delivered from a Web server.

Personal application software includes general-purpose programs that enable users to improve their personal effectiveness, increasing the quality and amount of work that can be done. Word-processing, spreadsheet analysis, database, presentation graphics, and personal information management applications are examples of this type of software. Sometimes these applications are bundled together and sold in what is called a software suite.

Apple's App Store has over 1.5 million apps available for iOS device users, and Android users can choose from over 1.6 million mobile apps on Google's Play Store.

Software that helps groups work together is often called workgroup application software. The category of software includes group-scheduling software, electronic mail, and other software that enables people to share ideas.

Software that benefits an entire organization—enterprise application software—can be developed specifically for the business or purchased off the shelf. There are many categories of enterprise software that support common business activities, such as accounts receivable, accounts payable, inventory control, and other management activities.

All software applications are written in coding schemes called programming languages, which are sets of keywords, commands, symbols, and rules for constructing statements to provide instructions to a computer to perform some processing activity.

Today, many software applications are being written or maintained using the following programming languages: COBOL, C, C++, Java, Java Script, PHP, Python, Ruby, and SQL.

Integrated development environments (IDEs) and software development kits (SDKs) have simplified and streamlined the coding process and have made it easier for more people to develop software.

Principle:

The software industry continues to undergo constant change; computer users need to be aware of recent trends and issues in the software industry to be effective in their business and personal life.

Software bugs, software copyrights and licensing, freeware and open-source software, software upgrades, and global software support are all important software issues and trends.

A software bug is a defect in a computer program that keeps it from performing in the manner intended. Software bugs are common, even in key pieces of business software.

Most companies aggressively guard and protect the source code of their software from competitors as well as customers. As a result, most software products are protected by law using copyright or licensing provisions

Freeware is software that is made available to the public for free. Open-source software is freeware that also has its source code available so that others may modify it. Open-source software development and maintenance is a collaborative process, with developers around the world using the

Internet to download the software, communicate about it, and submit new versions of it.

Software upgrades are an important source of increased revenue for software manufacturers and can provide useful new functionality and improved quality for software users.

Global software support is an important consideration for large global companies putting together standardized companywide systems. A common solution is to outsource global support to one or more third-party software distributors.

Key Terms

application programming interface (API)

application software

command-based user interface

compiler

embedded system

enterprise application integration (EAI)

enterprise sphere of influence

graphical user interface (GUI)

hardware independence

kernel

middleware

off-the-shelf software

operating system (OS)

personal productivity software

personal sphere of influence

programming language

proprietary software

rich Internet application (RIA)

service-oriented architecture (SOA)

single-user license

software as a service (SaaS)

software suite

sphere of influence

syntax

system software

user interface

utility program

workgroup

workgroup application software

workgroup sphere of influence

Chapter 4: Self-Assessment Test

Software is valuable in helping individuals, workgroups, and entire enterprises achieve their goals.

1. The two main categories of software are _____.
   a. enterprise and workgroup
   b. operating system and application
   c. application and system
   d. utilities and operating system
2. Application software that enables users to develop a spreadsheet for tracking their exercise and eating habits is software for the workgroup sphere of influence. True or False?

The operating system is called the "soul of the computer" because it controls how you enter data into your computer, perform meaningful work, and display results.

3. The heart of the operating system that controls its most critical processes is called the _____.

4. Software applications use the OS by requesting services through a(n) _____.
   a. integrated development environment
   b. application program interface
   c. utility program
   d. software development kit
5. _____ is an operating system that can run in all three spheres of influence.
   a. IBM z/os
   b. Windows 10
   c. MAC iOS
   d. Linux
6. A(n) _____ server simulates a computer's hardware architecture in software so that a single server can run operating systems and software designed for other architectures, or run several operating systems simultaneously on one system.

Organizations typically use off-the-shelf application software to meet common business needs

and proprietary application software to meet unique business needs and provide a competitive advantage.

7. _____ software is one-of-a-kind software designed for a specific application and owned by the company, organization, or person that uses it.
8. _____ computing refers to the use of computing resources, including software and data storage, on the Internet, rather than on local computers.
9. Software that enables users to improve their personal effectiveness, increasing the amount of work they can do and its quality, is called _____.
   a. workgroup software
   b. enterprise software
   c. utility software
   d. personal application software
10. Each programming language has its own set of rules, called the _____ of the language.

The software industry continues to undergo constant change; computer users need to be aware of recent trends and issues in the software industry to be effective in their business and personal life.

11. _____ is software that makes its source code available so that others may modify it.
    a. Freeware
    b. Off-the-shelf software
    c. Open-source software
    d. Software in the public domain
12. Software _____ are an important source of increased revenue for software manufacturers and can provide useful new functionality and improved quality for software users.
    a. bugs
    b. upgrades
    c. open source licenses
    d. third-party distributors

Chapter 4: Self-Assessment Test Answers

1. c
2. False
3. kernel
4. b
5. d
6. virtual

7. Proprietary
8. Cloud
9. d
10. syntax
11. c
12. b

Review Questions

1. Identify and briefly discuss the three spheres of influence used to identify the scope of problems and opportunities that software addresses.
2. What is the role of the computer operating system? Identify several activities performed by this key piece of software.
3. What is an application programming interface (API)? What purpose does it serve?
4. What is the kernel of the operating system?
5. Identify and briefly discuss five types of operating system user interfaces.
6. Identify and briefly describe the five basic approaches to task management employed in operating systems.
7. What role does a Linux distributor play?

8. The Mac OS X supports dual booting. What is this, and what benefits does it provide?
9. What is an embedded system? Give three examples of such a system.
10. Distinguish between proprietary software and off-the-shelf software.
11. What is middleware?
12. What is software as a service (SaaS)?
13. What is cloud computing? What are some pros and cons of cloud computing?
14. What is open-source software? What are the benefits and drawbacks for a business that uses open-source software?
15. Briefly discuss the advantages and disadvantages of frequent software upgrades.
16. What is the difference between freeware and open-source software?

Discussion Questions

1. How does Microsoft envision the future for Windows 10? Do you support this vision? Why or why not?

2. Assume that you must take a computer-programming language course next semester. How would you decide which language would be best for you to study? Do you think that a professional programmer needs to know more than one programming language? Why or why not?

3. Assume you are going to buy a personal computer. What operating system features are important to you? What operating system would you select and why?

4. You have been asked to develop a user interface for a person with limited sight—someone without the ability to recognize letters or shapes on a computer screen. Describe the user interface you would recommend.

5. You are using a new release of an application software package. You think that you have discovered a bug. Outline the approach that you would take to confirm that it is indeed a bug. What actions would you take if it truly were a bug?

6. What are some of the advantages and disadvantages of employing software as a service (SaaS)? What precautions might you take to minimize the risk of using one?

7. If you were the IS manager for a large manufacturing company, what concerns might you have about your organization using open-source software? What advantages might there be for use of such software?

8. Identify four types of frequently used software licenses. Which approach does the best job of ensuring a steady, predictable stream of revenue from customers? Which approach is best for a small company with only a few dozen employees?

9. How have software development kits (SDKs) influenced software development?

10. How can virtualization save an organization money?

Problem-Solving Exercises

1. Do research to compare the costs and features as well as the pros and cons of using Microsoft Office versus Office 365. Summarize your results using a spreadsheet. Which choice is the best solution for you? Why? Using presentation software, outline your thought process and key points in three or four slides.

2. Use graphics software to develop a chart showing the worldwide market share of smartphone operating systems for Apple iPhone OS and Google Android over the past five quarters. Now do the same for just the U.S. market share. What conclusions do you draw from these charts?

3. Do research to identify the embedded operating systems used in BMW, Chevrolet, Chrysler, Ford, Honda, Mercedes Benz, Nissan, and Toyota automobiles. Create a spreadsheet that displays the embedded system and make of automobile along with the auto manufacturer's name for system.

Team Activities

1. You and your team must make a recommendation to the director of information systems on which is the best cloud computing service for your school—from the perspective of the student. Do research on any three of the following, and then decide which service to recommend: Amazon Elastic Compute Cloud (EC2), IBM's Blue Cloud, Sun Cloud, Google AppEngine, and Windows Azure Services Platform. What factors influenced your recommendation?

2. You and your team members should learn how to use a computer operating system with which you are unfamiliar. Explore how to launch applications, minimize and maximize windows, close applications, save and view files on the system, and change system settings, such as how quickly a screen is turned off when not in use. Assess ease of learning and ease of use for the operating system. Team members should collaborate on a report, using the track changes features of Word or the collaborative features of Google Docs to summarize the team's findings and opinions about three personal computer operating systems.

3. "Spreadsheets, even after careful development, contain errors in 1 percent or more of all formula cells," according to Ray Panko, a professor of IT management at the University of Hawaii and an authority on bad spreadsheet practices. This means that in large spreadsheets there could be dozens of undetected errors.[55] Imagine that you and your team have been hired as consultants to a large organization. Outline several measures that the organization should take to ensure the accuracy of key spreadsheets that are used to make key business decisions.

Web Exercises

1. The Google Android operating system has over an 80 percent share of the worldwide smartphone operating system market. Do research to find out if industry observers are concerned that that such a strong position by one company may stifle competition and innovation. Write a few paragraphs summarizing your findings.
2. Do research on the Web to learn which programming language skills are currently most in demand in the job market. Write a brief report discussing the sources of information you used and summarizing your findings.
3. Use the Internet to search for information on real-time operating systems. Identify the key differences between real-time and non-real-time operating systems. Identify three situations in which real-time operating systems are needed.

Career Exercises

1. Think of your ideal job. Would it help you to learn a programming language to be effective in this position? Why or why not?
2. Identify three specific smartphone applications that would be of significant help to you in your current or next job. (You can include applications that already exist as well as ones that you wish existed.) Describe specific features of each application and how you would use them.
3. Think of your ideal job. Identify two existing software applications for each sphere of influence that you would likely use in this career.

Case Studies

Case One

Société de transport de Montréal (STM) Implements Innovative Mobile App

Montreal, in the Canadian province of Quebec, is considered one of the world's most livable cities. The city, whose official language is French, is the culture capital of Canada with opera, museums of history and fine art, a symphony orchestra, cathedrals, many fine restaurants, and international jazz and comedy festivals. The Société de transport de Montréal (STM) is the bus and metro public transit system serving roughly 1.4 million daily passengers in the greater Montreal area. STM riders can use a rechargeable smart fare card—called Opus—on which riders can add and maintain a balance to cover their transit fares.

STM tracks use of the Opus card to capture passenger riding history. This data has revealed an alarming problem—STM is losing about 13 percent of its riders through attrition each year. Analysis shows that this attrition can be attributed to a variety of causes, including deaths and moves out of the city. STM also determined that some amount of attrition is due to university students who, upon graduation, quit riding the STM and purchase or lease an auto to commute to their job.

After a year of looking at options, STM decided to launch a six-month pilot loyalty project to combat this problem. The scope of the project, which is limited to about 20,000 current riders, will test if the proposed solution works, identify full implementation costs, and identify any potential barriers to success as well as unintended consequences of the program. Results from the pilot will be used to modify the initial solution and/or rollout plan. The pilot project must meet certain predefined success criteria in order to support a recommendation for a full rollout.

The foundation of the loyalty program is a mobile app called STM Merci, which presents riders with exclusive, personalized offers based on their user profiles, travel habits, and level of ridership: top-tier, mid-tier, and first-tier. For a particular offer, for example, tickets to the Opera de Montreal, 100 top-tier riders might receive an offer for free tickets, while 100 mid-tier riders are offered 50 percent off tickets and 100 first-tier riders are offered 20 percent off tickets. STM hopes to recruit a large number of event and commercial partners willing to participate in the program in return for the strong geomarketing opportunities created from having riders view an offer on their mobile phones, often when they are literally feet from the promoted commercial location.

The STM Merci app can also communicate useful information to riders in real time. For example, it can let riders know that by taking a slightly later car from their usual station on a given day, they would have a much better chance of getting a seat. Or it could point out when they were spending more on single fares than the cost of a monthly pass (about $77 per month).

The app is carefully designed to allow riders to select how they want to interact with the STM Merci system. Riders who enter their Opus card number into the STM Merci app will receive more targeted and relevant offers based on the data in their profile. For example, riders whose profile indicates an interest in painting might receive an offer for a discount admission to Montreal Museum of Fine Art. Sushi lovers might get an offer for a free appetizer at a restaurant within a stop or two of their current location.

The data needed to support the STM Merci app is split into two separate databases to protect riders' right to privacy. Data deemed critical to running the STM operation—such as a rider's email address and ticket purchase history—are stored in one database under the rider's first name. This data is used to notify riders about delays, closures, and other mission-critical issues. Noncritical rider profile data, including food preferences, hobbies, and interests, is stored in a second database under the rider's last name. No marketer can access the two databases and merge them to send messages to an individual rider. This separation of databases satisfies Quebec's strict privacy laws, which prohibit collecting rider data beyond what is deemed critical for the organization.

Critical Thinking Questions

1. Identify four success criteria for the STM Merci pilot project that address retention of riders, cost/benefits, recruitment of STM Merci partners, and usability of the application. The criteria should specific, quantifiable, and time constrained to occur within a certain time period.
2. Do you believe that the database design will safeguard the privacy of STM riders? Why or why not? If not, what further changes are needed?
3. How might STM Merci pilot project members identify additional capabilities or features that could be added to the STM Merci app to encourage increased ridership?

SOURCES: Murphy, Ken, "Société de transport de Montréal (STM) Aims to Boost Ridership by 40% With a Mobile App," *SAP Insider*, January 1, 2014, *http://sapinsider.wispubs.com/Assets/Case-Studies/2014.Jauuary /STM*; "About the STM," Société de transport de Montréal, *www.stm.info /en/about/financial_and_corporate_information/about-stm*, accessed November 14, 2015.

Case Two

FIMC Launches Mobile App to Provide Enhanced Roadside Assistance Services

In any given year, more than 40 million people in the United States require some form of roadside assistance—whether it's to get a battery restarted, a flat tire changed, or a car towed to a local repair shop. No one wants to be stuck on the side of the road, so many consumers choose to purchase a roadside assistance plan that gives them access to help in the event of an emergency. Consumers have choice when it comes to purchasing a plan, with options available from automotive aftermarket retailers and service providers, employee groups, insurance and financial institutions, and trade associations.

Since 1974, Financial Insurance Management Corporation (FIMC), headquartered in Sarasota, Florida, has been developing, marketing, and implementing outsourced, membership-based roadside assistance programs for customers such as AAMCO Transmissions, Citibank, Precision Tune Auto Care, and Wells Fargo. Through its customized programs, which also offer health, home, and travel services and discounts, the company provides roadside assistance benefits to more than 2 million members in the United States, Puerto Rico, and Canada.

When an emergency happens—even if it's just a set of keys locked in a car—customers need and expect prompt service. And while FIMC prided itself on the high-quality customer service it provided via its call center and Web site, offering customers access to services via a mobile app was a logical next step. A primary goal for the company was developing an app that would deliver increased value to members by making it easier for them to access their benefits and take advantage of current promotions.

After researching alternatives, FIMC opted to go with a mobile solution developed by PointSource, a local software development firm, using IBM's MobileFirst platform. To ensure that the app was firmly grounded in the company's business objectives, FIMC and PointSource staff spent time translating the business requirements into a mobile strategy that fit within FIMC's time and budget constraints. Once the groundwork was completed, PointSource was able to build a prototype of the FIMC mobile app in less than four weeks— deploying the final application just three months after the project started.

An important project requirement for FIMC was that the app be integrated with the company's back-end systems, which hold membership data and benefits information. FIMC also needed an app that would be accessible by all of its members—no matter what type of mobile device they used. Rather than create multiple apps, PointSource developed a single, hybrid application that can run on both Android and Apple iOS devices. The app's intuitive interface provides members with one-touch roadside assistance, personalized discounts and promotions, claim submission tools, and deductible-management features. The mobile app's tools have improved the quality of the company's communications with its members. And, because members who have easy access to their benefits are more likely to renew their memberships, the app has helped FIMC increase its renewal rates. Using the app, customers can quickly renew their membership from any location, ensuring continuous service.

Working with PointSource, FIMC plans on launching a new version of its mobile app every month. The PointSource development team uses cloud-based development services that allow it to create work items to share with FIMC on an ongoing basis. This allows FIMC to remain involved with the development process and helps PointSource stay in touch with FIMC's priorities and changing business needs.

Critical Thinking Questions

1. How important do you think it is for FIMC and other companies offering roadside assistance services to provide customers with access to services via a mobile app? Do you think a mobile app will provide FIMC with a competitive advantage, or is mobile access something that most customers have come to expect?

2. A recent survey by IBM of 585 mobile application developers and managers found that only one-third of mobile development projects successfully met project criteria in terms of budget, schedule, and project objectives. Given that, what are some of the potential risks for companies, such as FIMC, that develop and deploy a mobile app on such a tight schedule?

3. When developing the FIMC app, PointSource used an IBM tool called Rational Test Workbench, which allowed developers to find and fix many software bugs before the app was released. Do research on the Web to find out more about this tool and how it might help developers cut down on the number of software bugs.

SOURCES: "What We Do," FIMC, *www.fimc.com/What-We-Do*, accessed January 12, 2016; "The American Traveler Motor Club & Home Benefits, Inc.," FIMC, *www.fimc.com/atmc*, accessed January 12, 2016; "IBM MobileFirst PointSource FIMC," IBM, *www-01.ibm.com /common/ssi/cgi-bin/ssialias?infotype=SA&subtype=ST&htmlfid=SW V14013USEN*, accessed January 12, 2016; IBM MobileFirst," IBM, *www .ibm.com/mobilefirst/us/en/*, accessed January 13, 2016; "About Us," PointSource, *www.pointsource.com/aboutus*, accessed January 13, 2016; "Rational Test Workbench," IBM, *www-03.ibm.com/software /products/en/rtw*, accessed January 12, 2016; "Star Qualities: What is Takes for Mobile Development Projects to Succeed", IBM, *www-01.ibm. com/common/ssi/cgi-bin/ssialias?subtype=XB&infotype=PM&htmlfid= BIE12345USEN&attachment=BIE12345USEN.PDF*, accessed January 13, 2016.

Notes

1. Devery, Quinn, "2012 Breakdown of Global IT Services, Software, and Hardware," August 8, 2013, *www.para net.com/blog/bid/151090/2012-Breakdown-of-Global-IT-Services-Software-and-Hardware-Spending*.

2. "Personal Productivity Software: VIP Organizer Is the Best Personal Productivity Software," VIP Quality Software, *www.vip-qualitysoft.com/products/organizer/per sonal_productivity_software*, accessed November 16, 2015.

3. "IBM Notes and Domino 9 Social Edition," IBM, *www-03.ibm.com/software/products/en/ibmnotes*, accessed November 16, 2015.

4. "IBM Case Study: JGC Corporation," IBM, *www-01.ibm.com/common/ssi/cgi-bin/ssialias?subty pe=AB&infotype=PM&appname=SWGE_LO_LE_U SEN&htmlfid=LOC14428USEN&attachment=LOC14428U SEN.PDF*, accessed November 16, 2015.

5. Roos, Dave, "How to Leverage an API for Conferencing," *How Stuff Works*, *http://money.howstuffworks.com/busi ness-communications/how-to-leverage-an-api-for-confer encing1.htm*, accessed November 17, 2015.

6. Olenick, Doug, "Google Drops Chrome Support for Older Microsoft and Apple Operating System," *SC Mag azine*, November 12, 2015, *www.scmagazine.com/goo gle-drops-chrome-support-for-older-microsoft-and-apple-operating-system/article/453592*.

7. Whittaker, Zack, "A 23-Year-Old Windows 3.1 System Failure Crashed Paris Airport," *ZD Net*, November 16, 2015, *www.zdnet.com/article/a-23-year-old-windows-3-1-system-failure-crashed-paris-airport*.

8. Bellis, Mary, "Putting Microsoft on the Map," *About.com*, *http://inventors.about.com/od/computersoftware/a/Put ting-Microsoft-On-The-Map.htm*, accessed November 17, 2015.

9. Rash, Wayne, "Microsoft Says Windows 10 Will Be the Last OS Upgrade You'll Ever Need," *eWeek*, January 21, 2015, *www.eweek.com/pc-hardware/microsoft-says-win dows-10-will-be-the-last-os-upgrade-youll-ever-need.html*.

10. "OS X El Capitan Available as a Free Update Tomorrow," Apple, September 29, 2015, *www.apple.com/pr/library /2015/09/29OS-X-El-Capitan-Available-as-a-Free-Update-Tomorrow.html*.

11. "Linux Definition," The Linux Information Project, *linfo.org/linuxdef.html*, accessed November 20, 2015.

12. "About Red Hat," Red Hat, *www.redhat.com/en*, accessed January 2, 2016.

13. Cerner to Present at JP Morgan Healthcare Conference," Cerner Corporation, *www.cerner.com/about/Investor _Relations*, accessed January 2, 2016.

14. "Cerner Boosts Performance and Stability," Red Hat, *www.redhat.com/en/success-stories/cerner*, accessed January 2, 2016.

15. Taves, Max and Richard Nieva, "Google I/O by the Numbers: 1B Android Users, 900M on Gmail," *CNET*, May 28, 2015, *www.cnet.com/news/google-io-by-the-numbers-1b-android-users-900m-on-gmail*.

16. Furrier, John and Dave Vellante, "Analysis: Is Sun Better Off after Acquiring Sun?," *Forbes*, July 9, 2013, *www .forbes.com/sites/siliconangle/2013/07/09/analysis-is-oracle-better-off-after-sun-acquisition*.

17. "How Office Depot Optimizes ERP by 20% With SPARC and Solaris," Oracle, *https://blogs.oracle.com/hardware /entry/how_office_depot_optimizes_erp*, accessed November 23, 2015.

18. "Casio Strengthens Its Core IT Infrastructure with Red Hat Enterprise Virtualization," Red Hat, *www.redhat .com/en/files/resources/en-rhev-casio-strengthens-its-core-it-infrastructure-9296587.pdf*, accessed November 23, 2015.

19. Carter, Jamie, "4 Best Smart TVs in the World 2015," *TechRadar*, January 14, 2015, *www.techradar.com /news/television/6-best-smart-tv-platforms-in-the-world-today-1120795*.

20. "Syndicat Mixte Autolib'," Microsoft, *www.microsoft. com/windowsembedded/en-us/customer-stories-details. aspx?id=34*, accessed November 24, 2015.

21. "Using Sysinternals Tools Like a Pro," How-To Geek School, *www.howtogeek.com/school/sysinternals-pro/les son1*, accessed November 24, 2015.

22. "Long Island Rail Road—General Information," Metropolitan Transportation Authority, *http://web.mta.info /lirr/about/GeneralInformation*, accessed January 7, 2016.

23. "The Long Island Rail Road Stays on Track with GWAVA Messaging Security," GWAVA, *www.gwava.com/success-stories/staying-on-track-success-story*, accessed January 7, 2016.

24. "About the University of Kentucky," University of Kentucky, *www.uky.edu/Admission/content/about-univer sity-kentucky*, accessed January 8, 2016.

25. "University of Kentucky," AdRem Software, *www.adrem soft.com/netcrunch/ss/?page=kentucky*, accessed January 8, 2016.

26. "BCBSKS Cuts Mainframe Software Costs with IBM," IBM, May 31, 2013, *www-01.ibm.com/software/success /cssdb.nsf/CS/STRD-988E7F*.

27. VMWare, "Enhancing the Retail Employee Experience—Columbia Sportswear Company," YouTube, October 7, 2015, *www.youtube.com/watch?v=aQbTBBHaryY& index=3&list=PL0Znya5COr_f2j0T8VTwgZPir0365csf1*.

28. Bloomberg, Jason, "Service-Oriented Architecture: Enabler of the Digital World," *Forbes*, February 9, 2015, *www.forbes.com/sites/jasonbloomberg/2015/02/09/ser vice-oriented-architecture-enabler-of-the-digital-world*.

29. "About Netflix," Netflix, *https://media.netflix.com/en*, accessed January 9, 2016.

30. Mauro, Tony, "Adopting Microservices at Netflix: Lessons for Architectural Design," NGINX (blog), February 19, 2015, *www.nginx.com/blog/microservices-at-netflix-architectural-best-practices*.

31. Mauro, Tony, "Adopting Microservices at Netflix: Lessons for Team and Process Design," NGINX (blog), March 10, 2016, *www.nginx.com/blog/adopting-microservices-at-netflix-lessons-for-team-and-process-design*.

32. "About Us," H&R Block, *http://newsroom.hrblock.com /about-us*, accessed January 8, 2016.

33. "Should You Custom-Build an Online Newsroom? Or Buy One Off the Shelf?," PressPage, December 10, 2015, *http://news.presspage.com/should-you-custom-build-an-online-newsroom-or-buy-one-off-the-shelf*.

34. "The Container Store Group, Inc., Announces Fourth Quarter and Full Fiscal Year 2014 Financial Results," The Container Store, April 27, 2015, *http://investor.contain erstore.com/press-releases/press-release-details /2015/The-Container-Store-GroupInc-Announces-Fourth-Quarter-and-Full-Fiscal-Year-2014-Financial-Results/default.aspx*.

35. "The Container Store," Ultimate Software, *www.ultimate software.com/UltiPro-Case-Study-The-Container-Store*, accessed January 8, 2016.

36. "Amazon Web Services Tops List of Most Reliable Public Clouds," Gigaom, January 7, 2015, *https://gigaom.com /2015/01/07/amazon-web-services-tops-list-of-most-reli able-public-clouds*.

37. "Airbnb Case Study," Amazon, *https://aws.amazon.com /solutions/case-studies/airbnb/?pg=main-customer-suc cess-page*, accessed January 8, 2016.

38. Plumer, Brad, "Is the Evidence for Austerity Based on an Excel Spreadsheet Error?," *Washington Post*, April 16, 2013, *www.washingtonpost.com/blogs/wonkblog/wp /2013/04/16/is-the-best-evidence-for-austerity-based-on-an-excel-spreadsheet-error*.

39. "Heinz—Global Food Leader Savors New Ideas and Cuts Costs with Office 365," *https://blogs.office.com/2014/05 /08/heinz-cuts-costs-with-office-365*, accessed November 25, 2015.

40. "Games: Improving Health," Entertainment Software Association, *www.theesa.com/games-improv ing-what-matters/health.asp*, accessed October 25, 2013.

41. "Number of Apps Available in Leading App Stores as of July 2015," *Statista*, *www.statista.com/statistics/276623 /number-of-apps-available-in-leading-app-stores*, accessed November 16, 2015.

42. "Clark Realty Capital Goes Google," Dito, *www.ditoweb .com/resources/case-studies/clark-realty-capital-goes -google*, accessed November 25, 2015.

43. "About Advantage Sign and Graphic Solutions," Advantage Sign and Graphic Solutions, *www.advantagesgs .com/About-Advantage-Sign-and-Graphic-Solutions*, accessed January 10, 2016.

44. "Advantage Sign and Graphic Solutions," NetSuite, *www. netsuite.com/portal/customer-testimonials/advantage-sign-supply-wholesale-distribution.shtml*, accessed January 10, 2016.

45. "Gartner Says Worldwide IT Spending to Decline 5.5 Percent in 2015," Gartner, June 30, 2015, *www.gartner .com/newsroom/id/3084817*.

46. Lunden, Ingrid, "Forrester: $2.1 Trillion Will Go into IT Spend in 2013; Apps and the U.S. Lead the Charge," *TechCrunch*, July 15, 2013, *http://techcrunch.com/2013 /07/15/forrester-2-1-trillion-will-go-into-it-spend-in-2013-apps-and-the-u-s-lead-the-charge*.

47. "Wastewater Reclamation," Pima County, *http://webcms. pima.gov/government/wastewaterreclamation*, accessed January 11, 2016.

48. "Pima County," Schneider Electric Software, *http://soft ware.schneider-electric.com/about-us/success-stories /pima-county-implements-situational-awareness-strat egy-to-improve-operational-effi-ciency-of-wastewater-facilities*, accessed January 10, 2016.

49. "Android Studio," Android, *http://developer.android.com/sdk/index.html*, accessed November 28, 2015.

50. Keizer, Greg, "Microsoft Gets an Earful as Office for MAC 2016 Users Amp IRE over Crashes," *Computerworld*, October 8, 2015, *www.computerworld.com/article/2990427/mac-os-x/microsoft-gets-an-earful-as-office-for-mac-2016-users-amp-ire-over-crashes.html*.

51. "CIO Quick Pulse: Putting Software Licenses to Work," Aspera, *www.aspera.com/en/resources/white-papers/cio-quickpulse*, accessed November 28, 2015.

52. "Software Licenses Types," Tulane University Technology Services, *http://tulane.edu/tsweb/software/software-license-types.cfm*, accessed November 3, 2013.

53. "History," Burton Snowboards, *www.burton.com/default/history*, accessed January 11, 2016.

54. "Customer Success: The Burton Corporation," *www.suse.com/success/stories/burton.html*, accessed January 11, 2016.

55. Olshan, Jeremy, "88% of Spreadsheets Have Errors," *MarketWatch*, April 20, 2013, *www.marketwatch.com/story/88-of-spreadsheets-have-errors-2013-04-17*.

Did You Know?

- The amount of data in the digital universe is expected to increase to 44 zettabytes (44 trillion gigabytes) by 2020. This is 60 times the amount of all the grains of sand on all the beaches on Earth. The majority of data generated between now and 2020 will not be produced by humans, but rather by machines as they talk to each other over data networks.

- Most major U.S. wireless service providers have implemented a stolen-phone database to report and track stolen phones. So if your smartphone or tablet goes missing, report it to your carrier. If someone else tries to use it, he or she will be denied service on the carrier's network.

- You know those banner and tile ads that pop up on your browser screen (usually for products and services you've recently viewed)? Criteo, one of many digital advertising organizations, automates the recommendation of ads up to 30 billion times each day, with each recommendation requiring a calculation involving some 100 variables.

Principles

- The database approach to data management has become broadly accepted.

- Data modeling is a key aspect of organizing data and information.

- A well-designed and well-managed database is an extremely valuable tool in supporting decision making.

- We have entered an era where organizations are grappling with a tremendous growth in the amount of data available and struggling to understand how to manage and make use of it.

- A number of available tools and technologies allow organizations to take advantage of the opportunities offered by big data.

Learning Objectives

- Identify and briefly describe the members of the hierarchy of data.
- Identify the advantages of the database approach to data management.
- Identify the key factors that must be considered when designing a database.
- Identify the various types of data models and explain how they are useful in planning a database.
- Describe the relational database model and its fundamental characteristics.
- Define the role of the database schema, data definition language, and data manipulation language.
- Discuss the role of a database administrator and data administrator.
- Identify the common functions performed by all database management systems.
- Define the term big data and identify its basic characteristics.
- Explain why big data represents both a challenge and an opportunity.
- Define the term data management and state its overall goal.
- Define the terms data warehouse, data mart, and data lakes and explain how they are different.
- Outline the extract, transform, load process.
- Explain how a NoSQL database is different from an SQL database.
- Discuss the whole Hadoop computing environment and its various components.
- Define the term in-memory database and explain its advantages in processing big data.

Why Learn about Database Systems and Big Data?

Organizations and individuals capture prodigious amounts of data from a myriad of sources every day. Where does all this data come from, where does it go, how is it safeguarded, and how can you use it to your advantage? In this chapter, you will learn about tools and processes that enable users to manage all this data so that it can be used to uncover new insights and make effective decisions. For example, if you become a marketing manager, you can access a vast store of data related to the Web-surfing habits, past purchases, and even social media activity of existing and potential customers. You can use this information to create highly effective marketing programs that generate consumer interest and increased sales. If you become a biologist, you may use big data to study the regulation of genes and the evolution of genomes in an attempt to understand how the genetic makeup of different cancers influences outcomes for cancer patients. If you become a human resources manager, you will be able to use data to analyze the impact of raises and changes in employee-benefit packages on employee retention and long-term costs. Regardless of your field of study in school and your future career, using database systems and big data will likely be a critical part of your job. As you read this chapter, you will see how you can use databases and big data to extract and analyze valuable information to help you succeed. This chapter starts by introducing basic concepts related to databases and data management systems. Later, the topic of big data will be discussed along with several tools and technologies used to store and analyze big data.

As you read this chapter, consider the following:

- Why is it important that the development and adoption of data management, data modeling, and business information systems be a cross-functional effort involving more than the IS organization?
- How can organizations manage their data so that it is a secure and effective resource?

database: A well-designed, organized, and carefully managed collection of data.

A **database** is a well-designed, organized, and carefully managed collection of data. Like other components of an information system, a database should help an organization achieve its goals. A database can contribute to organizational success by providing managers and decision makers with timely, accurate, and relevant information built on data. Databases also help companies analyze information to reduce costs, increase profits, add new customers, track past business activities, and open new market opportunities.

database management system (DBMS): A group of programs used to access and manage a database as well as provide an interface between the database and its users and other application programs.

A **database management system (DBMS)** consists of a group of programs used to access and manage a database as well as provide an interface between the database and its users and other application programs. A DBMS provides a single point of management and control over data resources, which can be critical to maintaining the integrity and security of the data. A database, a DBMS, and the application programs that use the data make up a database environment.

Databases and database management systems are becoming even more important to organizations as they deal with rapidly increasing amounts of information. Most organizations have many databases; however, without good data management, it is nearly impossible for anyone to find the right and related information for accurate and business-critical decision making.

Data Fundamentals

Without data and the ability to process it, an organization cannot successfully complete its business activities. It cannot pay employees, send out bills, order new inventory, or produce information to assist managers in decision making. Recall that data consists of raw facts, such as employee numbers and sales figures. For data to be transformed into useful information, it must first be organized in a meaningful way.

Hierarchy of Data

Data is generally organized in a hierarchy that begins with the smallest piece of data used by computers (a bit), progressing up through the hierarchy to a database. A **bit** is a binary digit (i.e., 0 or 1) that represents a circuit that is either on or off. Bits can be organized into units called bytes. A byte is typically eight bits. Each byte represents a **character**, which is the basic building block of most information. A character can be an uppercase letter (A, B, C, ..., Z), a lowercase letter (a, b, c, ..., z), a numeric digit (0, 1, 2, ..., 9), or a special symbol (., !, +, −, /, etc.).

Characters are put together to form a field. A **field** is typically a name, a number, or a combination of characters that describes an aspect of a business object (such as an employee, a location, or a plant) or activity (such as a sale). In addition to being entered into a database, fields can be computed from other fields. Computed fields include the total, average, maximum, and minimum value. A collection of data fields all related to one object, activity, or individual is called a **record**. By combining descriptions of the characteristics of an object, activity, or individual, a record can provide a complete description of it. For instance, an employee record is a collection of fields about one employee. One field includes the employee's name, another field contains the address, and still others the phone number, pay rate, earnings made to date, and so forth. A collection of related records is a **file**—for example, an employee file is a collection of all company employee records. Likewise, an inventory file is a collection of all inventory records for a particular company or organization.

At the highest level of the data hierarchy is a database, a collection of integrated and related files. Together, bits, characters, fields, records, files, and databases form the **hierarchy of data**. See Figure 5.1. Characters are combined to make a field, fields are combined to make a record, records are combined to make a file, and files are combined to make a database. A database houses not only all these levels of data but also the relationships among them.

bit: A binary digit (i.e., 0 or 1) that represents a circuit that is either on or off.

character: A basic building block of most information, consisting of uppercase letters, lowercase letters, numeric digits, or special symbols.

field: Typically a name, a number, or a combination of characters that describes an aspect of a business object or activity.

record: A collection of data fields all related to one object, activity, or individual.

file: A collection of related records.

hierarchy of data: Bits, characters, fields, records, files, and databases.

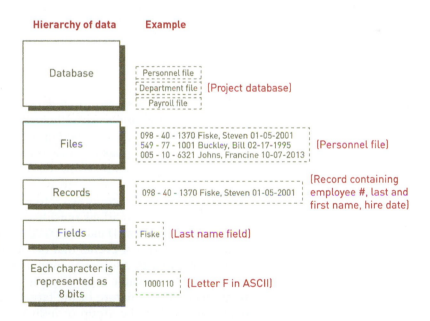

Hierarchy of data	Example
Database	Personnel file / Department file / Payroll file (Project database)
Files	098 - 40 - 1370 Fiske, Steven 01-05-2001 / 549 - 77 - 1001 Buckley, Bill 02-17-1995 / 005 - 10 - 6321 Johns, Francine 10-07-2013 (Personnel file)
Records	098 - 40 - 1370 Fiske, Steven 01-05-2001 (Record containing employee #, last and first name, hire date)
Fields	Fiske (Last name field)
Each character is represented as 8 bits	1000110 (Letter F in ASCII)

FIGURE 5.1

Hierarchy of data

Together, bits, characters, fields, records, files, and databases form the hierarchy of data.

Data Entities, Attributes, and Keys

Entities, attributes, and keys are important database concepts. An **entity** is a person, place, or thing (object) for which data is collected, stored, and maintained. Examples of entities include employees, products, and customers. Most organizations organize and store data as entities.

entity: A person, place, or thing for which data is collected, stored, and maintained.

attribute: A characteristic of an entity.

data item: The specific value of an attribute.

An **attribute** is a characteristic of an entity. For example, employee number, last name, first name, hire date, and department number are attributes for an employee. See Figure 5.2. The inventory number, description, number of units on hand, and location of the inventory item in the warehouse are attributes for items in inventory. Customer number, name, address, phone number, credit rating, and contact person are attributes for customers. Attributes are usually selected to reflect the relevant characteristics of entities such as employees or customers. The specific value of an attribute, called a **data item**, can be found in the fields of the record describing an entity. A data key is a field within a record that is used to identify the record.

Employee #	Last name	First name	Hire date	Dept. number
005-10-6321	Johns	Francine	10-07-2013	257
549-77-1001	Buckley	Bill	02-17-1995	632
098-40-1370	Fiske	Steven	01-05-2001	598

ENTITIES (records)

KEY FIELD

ATTRIBUTES (fields)

FIGURE 5.2
Keys and attributes
The key field is the employee number. The attributes include last name, first name, hire date, and department number.

Many organizations create databases of attributes and enter data items to store data needed to run their day-to-day operations. For instance, database technology is an important weapon in the fight against crime and terrorism, as discussed in the following examples:

- The Offshore Leaks Database contains the names of some 100,000 secretive offshore companies, trusts, and funds created in locations around the world. Although creating offshore accounts is legal in most countries, offshore accounts are also established to enable individuals and organizations to evade paying the taxes they would otherwise owe. The database has been used by law enforcement and tax officials to identify potential tax evaders.[1]
- Major U.S. wireless service providers have implemented a stolen-phone database to report and track stolen 3G and 4G/LTE phones. The providers use the database to check whether a consumer's device was reported lost or stolen. If a device has been reported lost or stolen, it will be denied service on the carrier's network. Once the device is returned to the rightful owner, it may be reactivated. The next step will be to tie foreign service providers and countries into the database to diminish the export of stolen devices to markets outside the United States.[2]
- The Global Terrorism Database (GTD) is a database including data on over 140,000 terrorist events that occurred around the world from 1970 through 2014 (with additional annual updates). For each terrorist event, information is available regarding the date and location of the event, the weapons used, the nature of the target, the number of casualties, and, when identifiable, the group or individual responsible.[3]
- Pawnshops are required by law to report their transactions to law enforcement by providing a description of each item pawned or sold along with any identifying numbers, such as a serial number. LEADS Online is a nationwide online database system that can be used to fulfill this reporting responsibility and enable law enforcement officers to track merchandise that is sold or pawned in shops throughout the nation. For

example, if law enforcement has a serial number for a stolen computer, they can enter this into LEADS Online and determine if it has been sold or pawned, when and where the theft or transaction occurred and, in the case of an item that was pawned, who made the transaction.[4]

As discussed earlier, a collection of fields about a specific object is a record. A **primary key** is a field or set of fields that uniquely identifies the record. No other record can have the same primary key. For an employee record, such as the one shown in Figure 5.2, the employee number is an example of a primary key. The primary key is used to distinguish records so that they can be accessed, organized, and manipulated. Primary keys ensure that each record in a file is unique. For example, eBay assigns an "Item number" as its primary key for items to make sure that bids are associated with the correct item. See Figure 5.3.

primary key: A field or set of fields that uniquely identifies the record.

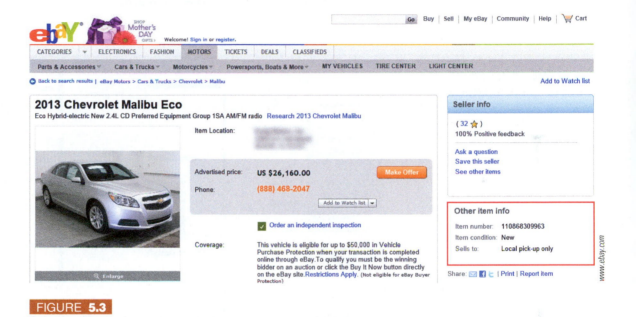

FIGURE 5.3
Primary key
eBay assigns an Item number as a primary key to keep track of each item in its database.

In some situations, locating a particular record that meets a specific set of criteria might be easier and faster using a combination of secondary keys rather than the primary key. For example, a customer might call a mail-order company to place an order for clothes. The order clerk can easily access the customer's mailing and billing information by entering the primary key—usually a customer number—but if the customer does not know the correct primary key, a secondary key such as last name can be used. In this case, the order clerk enters the last name, such as Adams. If several customers have a last name of Adams, the clerk can check other fields, such as address and first name, to find the correct customer record. After locating the correct record, the order can be completed and the clothing items shipped to the customer.

The Database Approach

At one time, information systems referenced specific files containing relevant data. For example, a payroll system would use a payroll file. Each distinct operational system used data files dedicated to that system.

Today, most organizations use the **database approach to data management**, where multiple information systems share a pool of related data.

database approach to data management: An approach to data management where multiple information systems share a pool of related data.

A database offers the ability to share data and information resources. Federal databases, for example, often include the results of DNA tests as an attribute for convicted criminals. The information can be shared with law enforcement officials around the country. Often, distinct yet related databases are linked to provide enterprise-wide databases. For example, many Walgreens stores include in-store medical clinics for customers. Walgreens uses an electronic health records database that stores the information of all patients across all stores. The database provides information about customers' interactions with the clinics and pharmacies.

To use the database approach to data management, additional software— a database management system (DBMS)—is required. As previously discussed, a DBMS consists of a group of programs that can be used as an interface between a database and the user of the database. Typically, this software acts as a buffer between the application programs and the database itself. Figure 5.4 illustrates the database approach.

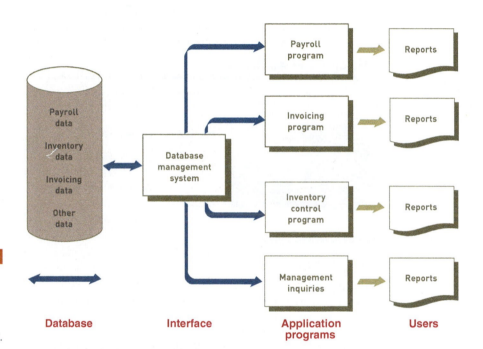

FIGURE 5.4

Database approach to data management

In a database approach to data management, multiple information systems share a pool of related data.

Critical Thinking Exercise

Vehicle Theft Database

You are a participant in an information systems project to design a vehicle theft database for a state law enforcement agency. The database will provide information about stolen vehicles (e.g., autos, golf carts, SUVs, and trucks), with details about the vehicle theft as well as the stolen vehicle itself. These details will be useful to law enforcement officers investigating the vehicle theft.

Review Questions

1. Identify 10 data attributes you would capture for each vehicle theft incident. How many bytes should you allow for each attribute?
2. Which attribute would you designate as the primary key?

Critical Thinking Questions

1. Should the database include data about the status of the theft investigation? If so, what sort of data needs to be included?
2. Can you foresee any problems with keeping the data current? Explain.

Data Modeling and Database Characteristics

Because today's businesses must keep track of and analyze so much data, they must keep the data well organized so that it can be used effectively. A database should be designed to store all data relevant to the business and to provide quick access and easy modification. Moreover, it must reflect the business processes of the organization. When building a database, an organization must carefully consider the following questions:

- **Content.** What data should be collected and at what cost?
- **Access.** What data should be provided to which users and when?
- **Logical structure.** How should data be arranged so that it makes sense to a given user?
- **Physical organization.** Where should data be physically located?
- **Archiving.** How long must this data be stored?
- **Security.** How can this data be protected from unauthorized access?

Data Modeling

When organizing a database, key considerations include determining what data to collect, what the source of the data will be, who will have access to it, how one might want to use it, and how to monitor database performance in terms of response time, availability, and other factors. AppDynamics offers its i-nexus cloud-based business execution solution to clients for use in defining the actions and plans needed to achieve business goals. The service runs on 30 Java virtual machines and eight database servers that are constantly supervised using database performance monitoring software. Use of the software has reduced the mean time to repair system problems and improved the performance and responsiveness for all its clients.[5]

One of the tools database designers use to show the logical relationships among data is a data model. A **data model** is a diagram of entities and their relationships. Data modeling usually involves developing an understanding of a specific business problem and then analyzing the data and information needed to deliver a solution. When done at the level of the entire organization, this procedure is called enterprise data modeling. Enterprise data modeling is an approach that starts by investigating the general data and information needs of the organization at the strategic level and then moves on to examine more specific data and information needs for the functional areas and departments within the organization. An **enterprise data model** involves analyzing the data and information needs of an entire organization and provides a roadmap for building database and information systems by creating a single definition and format for data that can ensure compatibility and the ability to exchange and integrate data among systems. See Figure 5.5.

data model: A diagram of data entities and their relationships.

enterprise data model: A data model that provides a roadmap for building database and information systems by creating a single definition and format for data that can ensure data compatibility and the ability to exchange and integrate data among systems.

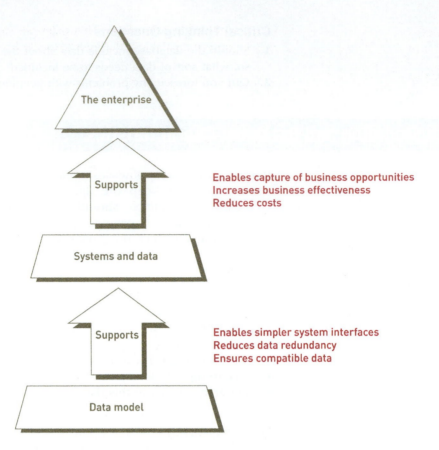

FIGURE **5.5**
Enterprise data model
The enterprise data model provides a roadmap for building database and information systems.

The IBM Healthcare Provider Data Model is an enterprise data model that can be adopted by a healthcare provider organization to organize and integrate clinical, research, operational, and financial data.[6] At one time, the University of North Carolina Health Care System had a smorgasbord of information system hardware and software that made it difficult to integrate data from its existing legacy systems. The organization used the IBM Healthcare Provider Data Model to guide its efforts to simplify its information system environment and improve the integration of its data. As a result, it was able to eliminate its dependency on outdated technologies, build an environment that supports efficient data management, and integrate data from its legacy systems to create a source of data to support future analytics requirements.[7]

Various models have been developed to help managers and database designers analyze data and information needs. One such data model is an **entity-relationship (ER) diagram**, which uses basic graphical symbols to show the organization of and relationships between data. In most cases, boxes in ER diagrams indicate data items or entities contained in data tables, and lines show relationships between entities. In other words, ER diagrams show data items in tables (entities) and the ways they are related.

ER diagrams help ensure that the relationships among the data entities in a database are correctly structured so that any application programs developed are consistent with business operations and user needs. In addition, ER diagrams can serve as reference documents after a database is in use. If changes are made to the database, ER diagrams help design them. Figure 5.6 shows an ER diagram for an order database. In this database design, one salesperson serves many customers. This is an example of a one-to-many relationship, as indicated by the one-to-many symbol (the "crow's-foot") shown in Figure 5.6. The ER diagram also shows that each customer can place one-to-many orders, that each order includes one-to-many line items, and that many line items can specify the same product

entity-relationship (ER) diagram: A data model that uses basic graphical symbols to show the organization of and relationships between data.

(a many-to-one relationship). This database can also have one-to-one relationships. For example, one order generates one invoice.

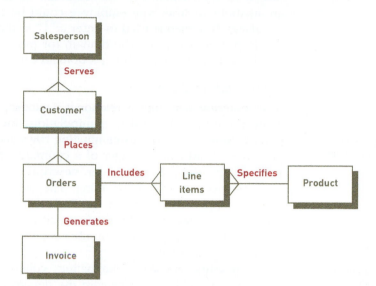

FIGURE 5.6

Entity-relationship (ER) diagram for a customer order database

Development of ER diagrams helps ensure that the logical structure of application programs is consistent with the data relationships in the database.

Relational Database Model

relational database model:
A simple but highly useful way to organize data into collections of two-dimensional tables called relations.

The **relational database model** is a simple but highly useful way to organize data into collections of two-dimensional tables called relations. Each row in the table represents an entity, and each column represents an attribute of that entity. See Figure 5.7.

Data Table 1: Project Table

Project	Description	Dept. number
155	Payroll	257
498	Widgets	632
226	Sales manual	598

Data Table 2: Department Table

Dept.	Dept. name	Manager SSN
257	Accounting	005-10-6321
632	Manufacturing	549-77-1001
598	Marketing	098-40-1370

FIGURE 5.7

Relational database model

In the relational model, data is placed in two-dimensional tables, or relations. As long as they share at least one common attribute, these relations can be linked to provide output useful information. In this example, all three tables include the Dept. number attribute.

Data Table 3: Manager Table

SSN	Last name	First name	Hire date	Dept. number
005-10-6321	Johns	Francine	10-07-2013	257
549-77-1001	Buckley	Bill	02-17-1995	632
098-40-1370	Fiske	Steven	01-05-2001	598

domain: The range of allowable values for a data attribute.

Each attribute can be constrained to a range of allowable values called its **domain**. The domain for a particular attribute indicates what values can be placed in each column of the relational table. For instance, the domain for an attribute such as type employee could be limited to either H (hourly) or S (salary). If someone tried to enter a "1" in the type employee field, the data would not be accepted. The domain for pay rate would not include negative numbers. In this way, defining a domain can increase data accuracy.

Manipulating Data

After entering data into a relational database, users can make inquiries and analyze the data. Basic data manipulations include selecting, projecting, and joining. **Selecting** involves eliminating rows according to certain criteria. Suppose the department manager of a company wants to use an employee table that contains the project number, description, and department number for all projects a company is performing. The department manager might want to find the department number for Project 226, a sales manual project. Using selection, the manager can eliminate all rows except the one for Project 226 and see that the department number for the department completing the sales manual project is 598.

selecting: Manipulating data to eliminate rows according to certain criteria.

projecting: Manipulating data to eliminate columns in a table.

Projecting involves eliminating columns in a table. For example, a department table might contain the department number, department name, and Social Security number (SSN) of the manager in charge of the project. A sales manager might want to create a new table that contains only the department number and the Social Security number of the manager in charge of the sales manual project. The sales manager can use projection to eliminate the department name column and create a new table containing only the department number and Social Security number.

joining: Manipulating data to combine two or more tables.

Joining involves combining two or more tables. For example, you can combine the project table and the department table to create a new table with the project number, project description, department number, department name, and Social Security number for the manager in charge of the project.

linking: The ability to combine two or more tables through common data attributes to form a new table with only the unique data attributes.

As long as the tables share at least one common data attribute, the tables in a relational database can be linked to provide useful information and reports. **Linking**, the ability to combine two or more tables through common data attributes to form a new table with only the unique data attributes, is one of the keys to the flexibility and power of relational databases. Suppose the president of a company wants to find out the name of the manager of the sales manual project as well as the length of time the manager has been with the company. Assume that the company has Manager, Department, and Project tables as shown in Figure 5.7. These tables are related as depicted in Figure 5.8.

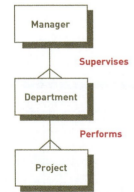

FIGURE 5.8

Simplified ER diagram
This diagram shows the relationship among the Manager, Department, and Project tables.

Note the crow's-foot by the Project table. This symbol indicates that a department can have many projects. The manager would make the inquiry to the database, perhaps via a personal computer. The DBMS would start with the project description and search the Project table to find out the project's department number. It would then use the department number to search the Department table for the manager's Social Security number. The department number is also in the Department table and is the common element that links the Project table to the Department table. The DBMS uses the manager's Social Security number to search the Manager table for the manager's hire date. The manager's Social Security number is the common element between the Department table and the Manager table. The final result is that the manager's name and hire date are presented to the president as a response to the inquiry. See Figure 5.9.

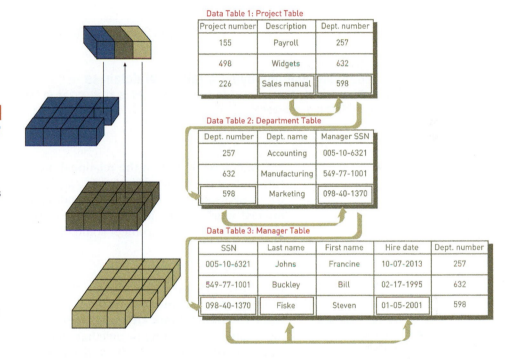

FIGURE 5.9

Linking data tables to answer an inquiry

To find the name and hire date of the manager working on the sales manual project, the president needs three tables: Project, Department, and Manager. The project description (Sales manual) leads to the department number (598) in the Project table, which leads to the manager's Social Security number (098-40-1370) in the Department table, which leads to the manager's last name (Fiske) and hire date (01-05-2001) in the Manager table.

Data Table 1: Project Table

Project number	Description	Dept. number
155	Payroll	257
498	Widgets	632
226	Sales manual	598

Data Table 2: Department Table

Dept. number	Dept. name	Manager SSN
257	Accounting	005-10-6321
632	Manufacturing	549-77-1001
598	Marketing	098-40-1370

Data Table 3: Manager Table

SSN	Last name	First name	Hire date	Dept. number
005-10-6321	Johns	Francine	10-07-2013	257
549-77-1001	Buckley	Bill	02-17-1995	632
098-40-1370	Fiske	Steven	01-05-2001	598

One of the primary advantages of a relational database is that it allows tables to be linked, as shown in Figure 5.9. This linkage reduces data redundancy and allows data to be organized more logically. The ability to link to the manager's Social Security number stored once in the Manager table eliminates the need to store it multiple times in the Project table.

The relational database model is widely used. It is easier to control, more flexible, and more intuitive than other approaches because it organizes data in tables. As shown in Figure 5.10, a relational database management system, such as Microsoft Access, can be used to store data in rows and columns. In this figure, hyperlink tools available on the ribbon/toolbar can be used to create, edit, and manipulate the database. The ability to link relational tables also allows users to relate data in new ways without having to redefine complex relationships. Because of the advantages of the relational model, many companies use it for large corporate databases, such as those for marketing and accounting.

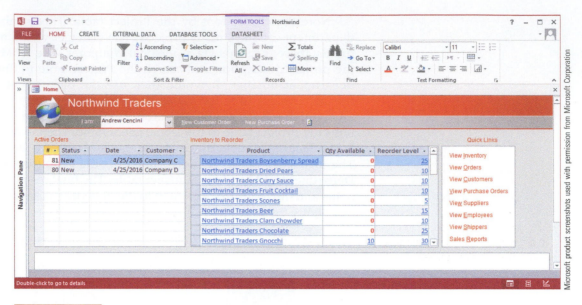

FIGURE **5.10**

Building and modifying a relational database

Relational databases provide many tools, tips, and shortcuts to simplify the process of creating and modifying a database.

Databases based on the relational model include Oracle, IBM DB2, Microsoft SQL Server, Microsoft Access, MySQL, Sybase, and others. The relational database model has been an outstanding success and is dominant in the commercial world today, although many organizations are beginning to use new nonrelational models to meet some of their business needs.

Data Cleansing

Data cleansing (data cleaning or data scrubbing): The process of detecting and then correcting or deleting incomplete, incorrect, inaccurate, or irrelevant records that reside in a database.

Data used in decision making must be accurate, complete, economical, flexible, reliable, relevant, simple, timely, verifiable, accessible, and secure. **Data cleansing (data cleaning or data scrubbing)** is the process of detecting and then correcting or deleting incomplete, incorrect, inaccurate, or irrelevant records that reside in a database. The goal of data cleansing is to improve the quality of the data used in decision making. The "bad data" may have been caused by user data-entry errors or by data corruption during data transmission or storage. Data cleansing is different from data validation, which involves the identification of "bad data" and its rejection at the time of data entry.

One data cleansing solution is to identify and correct data by cross-checking it against a validated data set. For example, street number, street name, city, state, and zip code entries in an organization's database may be cross-checked against the United States Postal Zip Code database. Data cleansing may also involve standardization of data, such as the conversion of various possible abbreviations (St., St, st., st) to one standard name (Street).

Data enhancement augments the data in a database by adding related information—such as using the zip code information for a given record to append the county code or census tract code.

The cost of performing data cleansing can be quite high. It is prohibitively expensive to eliminate all "bad data" to achieve 100 percent database accuracy, as shown in Figure 5.11.

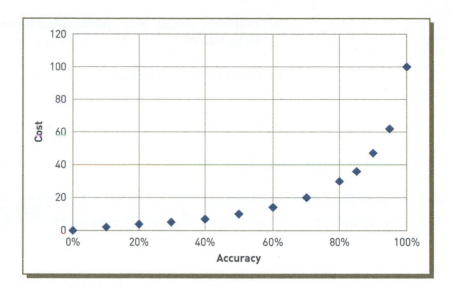

Tradeoff of cost versus accuracy

The cost of performing data cleansing to achieve 100 percent database accuracy can be prohibitively expensive.

Banco Popular is the largest bank in Puerto Rico. Some 3,000 bank employees in 200 branches use a customer database to obtain a complete view of 5.7 million personal and business accounts. The bank uses a data cleansing process to eliminate duplicate records and build an accurate and complete record of each customer, reflecting all of their various accounts (checking, savings, auto loan, credit card, etc.) with the bank. Part of this process includes identifying how many account holders live at the same address to eliminate duplicate mailings to the same household, thus saving over $840,000 in mailing expenses each year.[8]

Critical Thinking Exercise

Cleansing Weather Data

The process of weather forecasting begins with the collection of as much data as possible about the current state of the atmosphere. Weather data (barometric pressure, humidity, temperature, and wind direction and speed) is collected from a variety of sources, including aircraft, automatic weather stations, weather balloons, buoys, radar, satellites, ships, and trained observers. Due to the variety of data types taken from multiple data sources, weather data is captured in a variety of data formats, primarily Binary Universal Form for the Representation of meteorological data (BUFR) and Institute of Electrical and Electronics Engineers (IEEE) binary. These observations are then converted to a standard format and placed into a gridded 3D model space called the Global Data Assimilation System (GDAS). Once this process is complete, the gridded GDAS output data can be used to start the Global Forecast System (GFS) model.

For purposes of this exercise, imagine that the accuracy of the weather forecasts has been slipping. In your role as project manager at the National Center for Environmental Information (NCEI), you have been assigned to lead a project reviewing the processing of the initial data and placing it into the GDAS.

Review Questions

1. NCEI is responsible for hosting and providing access to one of the most significant archives on Earth, with comprehensive oceanic, atmospheric, and geophysical data. Good database design would suggest that an enterprise data model exists for the NCEI. Why?

2. Define the domain of acceptable values for barometric pressure, humidity, and temperature.

Critical Thinking Questions

1. What issues could cause the raw weather data received to be incomplete or inaccurate?
2. How might incomplete or inaccurate data be identified and corrected or deleted from the forecasting process? Are there risks in such data cleansing?

Relational Database Management Systems (DBMSs)

Creating and implementing the right database system ensures that the database will support both business activities and goals. But how do we actually create, implement, use, and update a database? The answer is found in the database management system (DBMS). As discussed earlier, a DBMS is a group of programs used as an interface between a database and application programs or between a database and the user. Database management systems come in a wide variety of types and capabilities, ranging from small inexpensive software packages to sophisticated systems costing hundreds of thousands of dollars.

SQL Databases

SQL: A special-purpose programming language for accessing and manipulating data stored in a relational database.

SQL is a special-purpose programming language for accessing and manipulating data stored in a relational database. SQL was originally defined by Donald D. Chamberlin and Raymond Boyce of the IBM Research Center and described in their paper "SEQUEL: A Structured English Query Language," published in 1974. Their work was based on the relational database model described by Edgar F. Codd in his groundbreaking paper from 1970, "A Relational Model of Data for Large Shared Data Banks."

ACID properties: Properties (atomicity, consistency, isolation, durability) that guarantee relational database transactions are processed reliably and ensure the integrity of data in the database.

SQL databases conform to **ACID properties** (atomicity, consistency, isolation, durability), defined by Jim Gray soon after Codd's work was published. These properties guarantee database transactions are processed reliably and ensure the integrity of data in the database. Basically, these principles mean that data is broken down to atomic values—that is, values that have no component parts—such as employee_ID, last_name, first_name, address_line_1, address_line_2, and city. The data in these atomic values remains consistent across the database. The data is isolated from other transactions until the current transaction is finished, and it is durable in the sense that the data should never be lost.[9]

SQL databases rely upon concurrency control by locking database records to ensure that other transactions do not modify the database until the first transaction succeeds or fails. As a result, 100 percent ACID-compliant SQL databases can suffer from slow performance.

In 1986, the American National Standards Institute (ANSI) adopted SQL as the standard query language for relational databases. Since ANSI's acceptance of SQL, interest in making SQL an integral part of relational databases on both mainframe and personal computers has increased. SQL has many built-in functions, such as average (AVG), the largest value (MAX), and the smallest value (MIN). Table 5.1 contains examples of SQL commands.

TABLE 5.1 Examples of SQL commands

SQL Command	Description
SELECT ClientName, Debt FROM Client WHERE Debt > 1000	This query displays clients (ClientName) and the amount they owe the company (Debt) from a database table called Client; the query would only display clients who owe the company more than $1,000 (WHERE Debt > 1000).
SELECT ClientName, ClientNum, OrderNum FROM Client, Order WHERE Client.ClientNum=Order.ClientNum	This command is an example of a join command that combines data from two tables: the Client table and the Order table (FROM Client, Order). The command creates a new table with the client name, client number, and order number (SELECT ClientName, ClientNum, OrderNum). Both tables include the client number, which allows them to be joined. This ability is indicated in the WHERE clause, which states that the client number in the Client table is the same as (equal to) the client number in the Order table (WHERE Client.ClientNum=Order.ClientNum).
GRANT INSERT ON Client to Guthrie	This command is an example of a security command. It allows Bob Guthrie to insert new values or rows into the Client table.

SQL allows programmers to learn one powerful query language and use it on systems ranging from PCs to the largest mainframe computers. See Figure 5.12. Programmers and database users also find SQL valuable because SQL statements can be embedded into many programming languages, such as the widely used C++ and Java. Because SQL uses standardized and simplified procedures for retrieving, storing, and manipulating data, many programmers find it easy to understand and use—hence, its popularity.

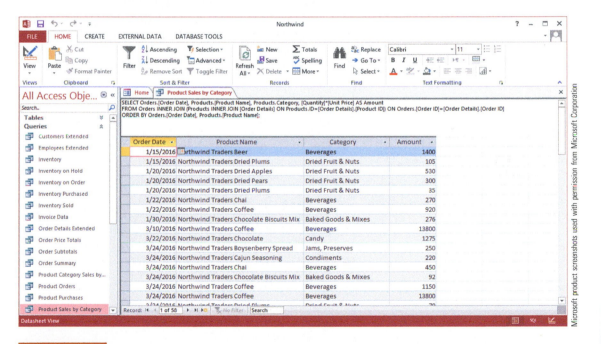

Microsoft product screenshots used with permission from Microsoft Corporation

FIGURE 5.12

Structured Query Language (SQL)

SQL has become an integral part of most relational databases, as shown by this example from Microsoft Access 2013.

Database Activities

Databases are used to provide a user view of the database, to add and modify data, to store and retrieve data, and to manipulate the data and generate reports. Each of these activities is discussed in greater detail in the following sections.

Providing a User View

Because the DBMS is responsible for providing access to a database, one of the first steps in installing and using a large relational database involves "telling" the DBMS the logical and physical structure of the data and the relationships among the data for each user. This description is called a schema (as in a schematic diagram). In a relational database, the schema defines the tables, the fields in each table, and the relationships between fields and tables. Large database systems, such as Oracle, typically use schemas to define the tables and other database features associated with a person or user. The DBMS can reference a schema to find where to access the requested data in relation to another piece of data.

schema: A description that defines the logical and physical structure of the database by identifying the tables, the fields in each table, and the relationships between fields and tables.

Creating and Modifying the Database

Schemas are entered into the DBMS (usually by database personnel) via a data definition language. A data definition language (DDL) is a collection of instructions and commands used to define and describe data and relationships in a specific database. A DDL allows the database's creator to describe the data and relationships that are to be contained in the schema. In general, a DDL describes logical access paths and logical records in the database. Figure 5.13 shows a simplified example of a DDL used to develop a general schema. The use of the letter *X* in Figure 5.13 reveals where specific information concerning the database should be entered. File description, area description, record description, and set description are terms the DDL defines and uses in this example. Other terms and commands can also be used, depending on the DBMS employed.

data definition language (DDL): A collection of instructions and commands used to define and describe data and relationships in a specific database.

```
SCHEMA DESCRIPTION
SCHEMA NAME IS XXXX
AUTHOR       XXXX
DATE         XXXX
FILE DESCRIPTION
      FILE NAME IS XXXX
        ASSIGN XXXX
      FILE NAME IS XXXX
        ASSIGN XXXX
AREA DESCRIPTION
      AREA NAME IS XXXX
RECORD DESCRIPTION
      RECORD NAME IS XXXX
      RECORD ID IS XXXX
      LOCATION MODE IS XXXX
      WITHIN XXXX AREA FROM XXXX THRU XXXX
SET DESCRIPTION
      SET NAME IS XXXX
      ORDER IS XXXX
      MODE IS XXXX
      MEMBER IS XXXX
      .
      .
      .
```

FIGURE **5.13**

Data definition language (DDL)

A data definition language (DDL) is used to define a schema.

data dictionary: A detailed description of all the data used in the database.

Another important step in creating a database is to establish a **data dictionary**, a detailed description of all data used in the database. Among other things, the data dictionary contains the following information for each data item:

- Name of the data item
- Aliases or other names that may be used to describe the item
- Range of values that can be used
- Type of data (such as alphanumeric or numeric)
- Amount of storage needed for the item
- Notation of the person responsible for updating it and the various users who can access it
- List of reports that use the data item

A data dictionary can also include a description of data flows, information about the way records are organized, and the data-processing requirements. Figure 5.14 shows a typical data dictionary entry.

FIGURE 5.14

Data dictionary entry

A data dictionary provides a detailed description of all data used in the database.

```
                    NORTHWESTERN MANUFACTURING

    PREPARED BY:            D. BORDWELL
    DATE:                   04 AUGUST 2016
    APPROVED BY:            J. EDWARDS
    DATE:                   13 OCTOBER 2016
    VERSION:                3.1
    PAGE:                   1 OF 1

    DATA ELEMENT NAME:      PARTNO
    DESCRIPTION:            INVENTORY PART NUMBER
    OTHER NAMES:            PTNO
    VALUE RANGE:            100 TO 5000
    DATA TYPE:              NUMERIC
    POSITIONS:              4 POSITIONS OR COLUMNS
```

Following the example in Figure 5.14, the information in a data dictionary for the part number of an inventory item can include the following information:

- Name of the person who made the data dictionary entry (D. Bordwell)
- Date the entry was made (August 4, 2016)
- Name of the person who approved the entry (J. Edwards)
- Approval date (October 13, 2016)
- Version number (3.1)
- Number of pages used for the entry (1)
- Data element name is Part name (PARTNO)
- A description of the element
- Other names that might be used (PTNO)
- Range of values (part numbers can range from 100 to 5000)
- Type of data (numeric)
- Storage required (four positions are required for the part number)

A data dictionary is a valuable tool for maintaining an efficient database that stores reliable information with no redundancy, and it simplifies the process of modifying the database when necessary. Data dictionaries also help computer and system programmers who require a detailed description of data elements stored in a database to create the code to access the data.

Adherence to the standards defined in the data dictionary also makes it easy to share data among various organizations. For example, the U.S. Department of Energy (DOE) developed a data dictionary of terms to provide a standardized approach for the evaluation of energy data. The Building Energy Data Exchange Specification (BEDES) provides a common language of key data elements, including data formats, valid ranges, and definitions that are designed to improve communications between contractors, software vendors, finance companies, utilities, and Public Utility Commissions. Adherence to these data standards allows information to be easily shared and aggregated without the need for extensive data scrubbing and translation. All stakeholders can use this standard set of data to answer key questions related to the energy savings and usage.[10]

Storing and Retrieving Data

One function of a DBMS is to be an interface between an application program and the database. When an application program needs data, it requests the data through the DBMS. Suppose that to calculate the total price of a new car, a pricing program needs price data on the engine option—for example, six cylinders instead of the standard four cylinders. The application program requests this data from the DBMS. In doing so, the application program follows a logical access path (LAP). Next, the DBMS, working with various system programs, accesses a storage device, such as a disk drive or solid state storage device (SSD), where the data is stored. When the DBMS goes to this storage device to retrieve the data, it follows a path to the physical location—physical access path—where the price of this option is stored. In the pricing example, the DBMS might go to a disk drive to retrieve the price data for six-cylinder engines. This relationship is shown in Figure 5.15.

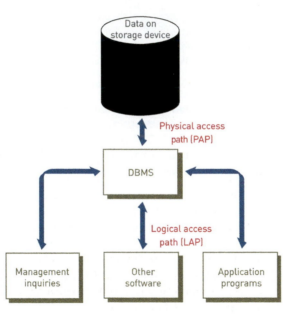

FIGURE 5.15

Logical and physical access paths

When an application requests data from the DBMS, it follows a logical access path to the data. When the DBMS retrieves the data, it follows a path to the physical access path to the data.

This same process is used if a user wants to get information from the database. First, the user requests the data from the DBMS. For example, a user might give a command, such as LIST ALL OPTIONS FOR WHICH PRICE IS GREATER THAN $200. This is the logical access path. Then, the DBMS might go to the options price section of a disk to get the information for the user. This is the physical access path.

Two or more people or programs attempting to access the same record at the same time can cause a problem. For example, an inventory control program might attempt to reduce the inventory level for a product by 10 units because 10 units were just shipped to a customer. At the same time, a purchasing program might attempt to increase the inventory level for the same product by 200 units because inventory was just received. Without proper database control, one of the inventory updates might be incorrect, resulting in an inaccurate inventory level for the product. **Concurrency control** can be used to avoid this potential problem. One approach is to lock out all other

concurrency control: A method of dealing with a situation in which two or more users or applications need to access the same record at the same time.

application programs from access to a record if the record is being updated or used by another program.

Manipulating Data and Generating Reports

After a DBMS has been installed, employees, managers, and other authorized users can use it to review reports and obtain important information. Using a DBMS, a company can manage this requirement. Some databases use Query by Example (QBE), which is a visual approach to developing database queries or requests. With QBE, you can perform queries and other database tasks by opening windows and clicking the data or features you want—similar to the way you work with Windows and other GUI (graphical user interface) operating systems and applications. See Figure 5.16.

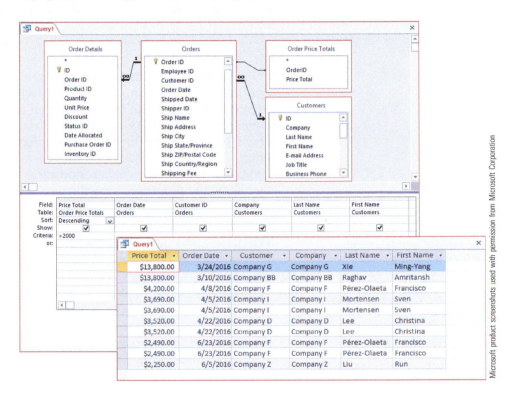

FIGURE 5.16

Query by Example

Some databases use Query by Example (QBE) to generate reports and information.

In other cases, database commands can be used in a programming language. For example, C++ commands can be used in simple programs that will access or manipulate certain pieces of data in the database. Here's another example of a DBMS query:

SELECT * FROM EMPLOYEE WHERE JOB_CLASSIFICATION="C2."

The asterisk (*) tells the program to include all columns from the EMPLOYEE table. In general, the commands that are used to manipulate the database are part of the **data manipulation language (DML)**. This specific language, provided with the DBMS, allows managers and other database users to access and modify the data, to make queries, and to generate reports. Again, the application programs go through schemas and the DBMS before getting to the data stored on a device such as a disk.

After a database has been set up and loaded with data, it can produce desired reports, documents, and other outputs. See Figure 5.17. These outputs usually appear in screen displays or on hard copy printouts. The output-control features of a database program allow a user to select the records and fields that will appear in a report. Formatting controls and organization options (such as report headings) help users customize reports and create flexible, convenient, and powerful information-handling tools.

data manipulation language (DML): A specific language, provided with a DBMS, which allows users to access and modify the data, to make queries, and to generate reports.

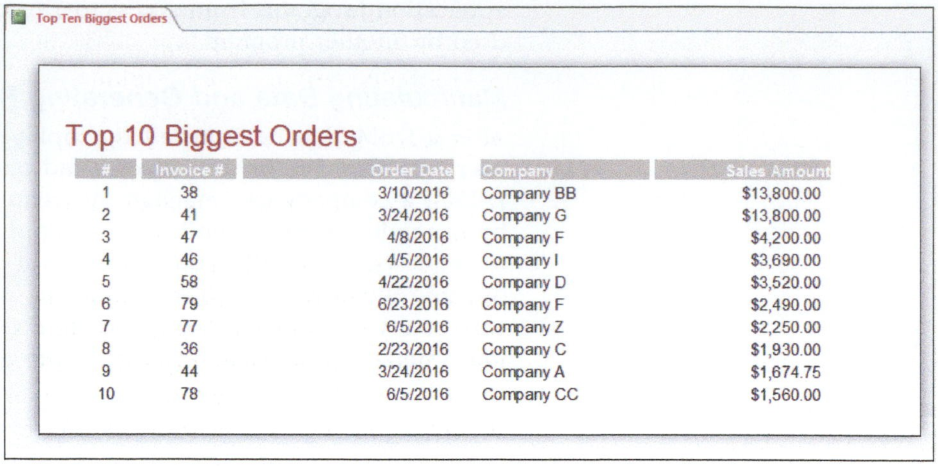

Top Ten Biggest Orders

Top 10 Biggest Orders

#	Invoice #	Order Date	Company	Sales Amount
1	38	3/10/2016	Company BB	$13,800.00
2	41	3/24/2016	Company G	$13,800.00
3	47	4/8/2016	Company F	$4,200.00
4	46	4/5/2016	Company I	$3,690.00
5	58	4/22/2016	Company D	$3,520.00
6	79	6/23/2016	Company F	$2,490.00
7	77	6/5/2016	Company Z	$2,250.00
8	36	2/23/2016	Company C	$1,930.00
9	44	3/24/2016	Company A	$1,674.75
10	78	6/5/2016	Company CC	$1,560.00

Microsoft product screenshots used with permission from Microsoft Corporation

FIGURE 5.17

Database output

A database application offers sophisticated formatting and organization options to produce the right information in the right format.

A DBMS can produce a wide variety of documents, reports, and other output that can help organizations make decisions and achieve their goals. Often, organizations have standard reports that are run on a regular basis. The most common reports select and organize data to present summary information about some aspect of company operations. For example, accounting reports often summarize financial data such as current and past due accounts. Many companies base their routine operating decisions on regular status reports that show the progress of specific orders toward completion and delivery.

Database Administration

database administrators (DBAs): Skilled and trained IS professionals who hold discussions with business users to define their data needs; apply database programming languages to craft a set of databases to meet those needs; test and evaluate databases; implement changes to improve the performance of databases; and assure that data is secure from unauthorized access.

Database administrators (DBAs) are skilled and trained IS professionals who hold discussions with business users to define their data needs; apply database programming languages to craft a set of databases to meet those needs; test and evaluate databases; implement changes to improve their performance; and assure that data is secure from unauthorized access. Database systems require a skilled database administrator (DBA), who must have a clear understanding of the fundamental business of the organization, be proficient in the use of selected database management systems, and stay abreast of emerging technologies and new design approaches. The role of the DBA is to plan, design, create, operate, secure, monitor, and maintain databases. Typically, a DBA has a degree in computer science or management information systems and some on-the-job training with a particular database product or more extensive experience with a range of database products. See Figure 5.18.

Clerkenwell_Images/istockphoto.com

FIGURE 5.18

Database administrator

The role of the database administrator (DBA) is to plan, design, create, operate, secure, monitor, and maintain databases.

The DBA works with users to decide the content of the database—to determine exactly what entities are of interest and what attributes are to be recorded about those entities. Thus, not only is it important that a DBA understand the business of an organization, but personnel outside of IS must also have some idea of what the DBA does and why this function is important. The DBA can play a crucial role in the development of effective information systems to benefit the organization, employees, and managers.

The DBA also works with programmers as they build applications to ensure that their programs comply with database management system standards and conventions. After the database has been built and is operating, the DBA monitors operations logs for security violations. Database performance is also monitored to ensure that the system's response time meets users' needs and that it operates efficiently. If there is a problem, the DBA attempts to correct it before it becomes serious.

An important responsibility of a DBA is to protect the database from attack or other forms of failure. DBAs use security software, preventive measures, and redundant systems to keep data safe and accessible. In spite of the best efforts of DBAs, database security breaches are all too common. For example, customer records of more than 83 million customers of JPMorgan Chase were stolen between June 2014 and August 2014. This represents the largest theft of consumer data from a U.S. financial institution in history.[11]

data administrator: An individual responsible for defining and implementing consistent principles for a variety of data issues.

Some organizations have also created a position called the **data administrator**, an individual responsible for defining and implementing consistent principles for a variety of data issues, including setting data standards and data definitions that apply across all the databases in an organization. For example, the data administrator would ensure that a term such as "customer" is defined and treated consistently in all corporate databases. The data administrator also works with business managers to identify who should have read or update access to certain databases and to selected attributes within those databases. This information is then communicated to the database administrator for implementation. The data administrator can be a high-level position reporting to top-level managers.

Popular Database Management Systems

Many popular database management systems address a wide range of individual, workgroup, and enterprise needs as shown in Table 5.2. The complete

TABLE 5.2 Popular database management systems

Open-Source Relational DBMS	Relational DBMS for Individuals and Workgroups	Relational DBMS for Workgroups and Enterprise
MySQL	Microsoft Access	Oracle
PostgreSQL	IBM Lotus Approach	IBM DB2
MariaDB	Google Base	Sybase Adaptive Server
SQL Lite	OpenOffice Base	Teradata
CouchDB		Microsoft SQL Server
		Progress OpenEdge

DBMS market encompasses software used by people ranging from nontechnical individuals to highly trained, professional programmers and runs on all types of computers from tablets to supercomputers. The entire market generates billions of dollars per year in revenue for companies such as IBM, Oracle, and Microsoft.

Selecting a DBMS begins by analyzing the information needs of the organization. Important characteristics of databases include the size of the database, the number of concurrent users, database performance, the ability of the DBMS to be integrated with other systems, the features of the DBMS, the vendor considerations, and the cost of the database management system.

CouchDB by Couchbase is an open-source database system used by Zynga, the developer of the popular Internet game FarmVille, to process 250 million visitors a month.

database as a service (DaaS):
An arrangement where the database is stored on a service provider's servers and accessed by the service subscriber over a network, typically the Internet, with the database administration handled by the service provider.

With **database as a service (DaaS)**, the database is stored on a service provider's servers and accessed by the service subscriber over the Internet, with the database administration handled by the service provider. More than a dozen companies are now offering DaaS services, including Amazon, Database.com, Google, Heroku, IBM, Intuit, Microsoft, MyOwnDB, Oracle, and Trackvia. Amazon Relational Database Service (Amazon RDS) is a DaaS that enables organizations to set up and operate their choice of a MySQL, Microsoft SQL, Oracle, or PostgreSQL relational database in the cloud. The service automatically backs up the database and stores those backups based on a user-defined retention period.

TinyCo is a mobile gaming firm whose games Tiny Monsters, Tiny Village, and Tiny Zoo Friends can be found at the Amazon, Google Play, and iTunes app stores.[12] The company employs Amazon Web Services (AWS) to enable it to support the rapid growth in the number of its users without having to devote constant time and effort to organize and configure its information systems infrastructure. This arrangement has allowed the company to focus its resources on developing and marketing its new games. TinyCo application data is stored in the Amazon Relational Database Service (Amazon RDS) for MySQL.[13]

Using Databases with Other Software

Database management systems are often used with other software and to interact with users over the Internet. A DBMS can act as a front-end application or a back-end application. A front-end application is one that people interact with directly. Marketing researchers often use a database as a front end to a statistical analysis program. The researchers enter the results of market questionnaires or surveys into a database. The data is then transferred to a statistical analysis program to perform analysis, such as determining the potential for a new product or the effectiveness of an advertising campaign. A back-end application interacts with other programs or applications; it only indirectly interacts with people or users. When people request information from a Web site, the site can interact with a database (the back end) that supplies the desired information. For example, you can connect to a university Web site to find out whether the university's library has a book you want to read. The site then interacts with a database that contains a catalog of library books and articles to determine whether the book you want is available. See Figure 5.19.

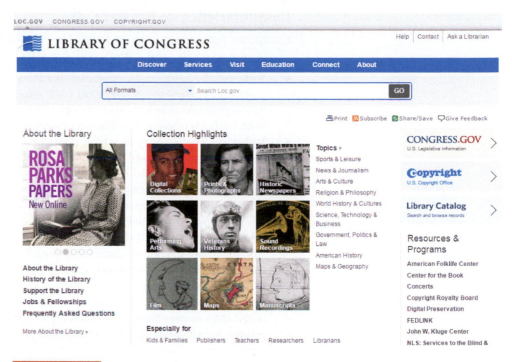

FIGURE **5.19**
Library of Congress Web site
The Library of Congress (LOC) provides a back-end application that allows Web access to its databases, which include references to books and digital media in the LOC collection.

Source: www.loc.gov

Critical Thinking Exercise

Database as a Service

You are the database administrator for the customer database of a medium-sized manufacturing firm. The database runs on an Oracle database management system installed on a server owned and managed by your firm's small IT organization. Recently you have been receiving a number of complaints from users of the database about extremely slow response time to their queries and report requests. Management has asked you to prepare a set of proposed solutions.

Review Questions
1. What advantages might be gained from moving to a database as a service environment?
2. Can you think of any possible disadvantages to this approach?

Critical Thinking Questions
1. What additional questions need to be answered before you can decide if the database as a service approach is right for your firm?
2. How might such a move affect you and your role?

Big Data

Big data is the term used to describe data collections that are so enormous (terabytes or more) and complex (from sensor data to social media data) that traditional data management software, hardware, and analysis processes are incapable of dealing with them.

Characteristics of Big Data

Computer technology analyst Doug Laney associated the three characteristics of volume, velocity, and variety with big data[14]:

- **Volume.** In 2014, it was estimated that the volume of data that exists in the digital universe was 4.4 zettabytes (one zettabyte equals one trillion gigabytes). The digital universe is expected to grow to an amazing 44 zettabytes by 2020, with perhaps one-third of that data being of value to organizations.[15]
- **Velocity.** The velocity at which data is currently coming at us exceeds 5 trillion bits per second.[16] This rate is accelerating rapidly, and the volume of digital data is expected to double every two years between now and 2020.[17]
- **Variety.** Data today comes in a variety of formats. Some of the data is what computer scientists call structured data—its format is known in advance, and it fits nicely into traditional databases. For example, the data generated by the well-defined business transactions that are used to update many corporate databases containing customer, product, inventory, financial, and employee data is generally structured data. However, most of the data that an organization must deal with is unstructured data, meaning that it is not organized in any predefined manner.[18] Unstructured data comes from sources such as word-processing documents, social media, email, photos, surveillance video, and phone messages.

Sources of Big Data

Organizations collect and use data from a variety of sources, including business applications, social media, sensors and controllers that are part of the manufacturing process, systems that manage the physical environment in factories and offices, media sources (including audio and video broadcasts), machine logs that record events and customer call data, public sources (such as government Web sites), and archives of historical records of transactions and communications. See Figure 5.20. Much of this collected data is unstructured and does not fit neatly into traditional relational database management

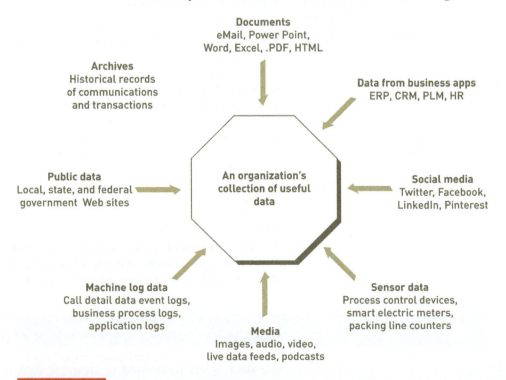

FIGURE **5.20**

Sources of an organization's useful data
An organization has many sources of useful data.

TABLE 5.3 Portals that provide access to free sources of useful big data

Data Source	Description	URL
Amazon Web Services (AWS) public data sets	Portal to a huge repository of public data, including climate data, the million song data set, and data from the 1000 Genomes project.	*http://aws.amazon.com/datasets*
Bureau of Labor Statistics (BLS)	Provides access to data on inflation and prices, wages and benefits, employment, spending and time use, productivity, and workplace injuries	*www.bls.gov*
CIA World Factbook	Portal to information on the economy, government, history, infrastructure, military, and population of 267 countries	*https://cia.gov/library/publications /the-world-factbook*
Data.gov	Portal providing access to over 186,000 government data sets, related to topics such as agriculture, education, health, and public safety	*http://data.gov*
Facebook Graph	Provides a means to query Facebook profile data not classified as private	*https://developers.facebook.com/docs /graph-api*
FBI Uniform Crime Reports	Portal to data on Crime in the United States, Law Enforcement Officers Killed and Assaulted, and Hate Crime Statistics	*https://www.fbi.gov/about-us/cjis/ucr /ucr/*
Justia Federal District Court Opinions and Orders database	A free searchable database of full-text opinions and orders from civil cases heard in U.S. Federal District Courts	*http://law.justia.com/cases/federal /district-courts/*
Gapminder	Portal to data from the World Health Organization and World Bank on economic, medical, and social issues	*www.gapminder.org/data*
Google Finance	Portal to 40 years of stock market data	*http://google.com/finance*
Healthdata.gov	Portal to 125 years of U.S. healthcare data, including national healthcare expenditures, claim-level Medicare data, and data related to healthcare quality, epidemiology, and population, among many other topics	*www.healthdata.gov*
National Centers for Environmental Information	Portal for accessing a variety of climate and weather data sets	*www.ncdc.noaa.gov/data-access /quick-links#loc-clim*
New York Times	Portal that provides users with access to *NYT* articles, book and movie reviews, data on political campaign contributions, and other material	*http://developer.nytimes.com/docs*
Social Institutions and Gender Index	Provides access to country profiles and data that measures the degree of cross-country discrimination against women in social institutions	*http://genderindex.org*
U.S. Census Bureau	Portal to a huge variety of government statistics and data relating to the U.S. economy and its population	*www.census.gov/data.html*

systems. Table 5.3 provides a starter list of some of the many Web portals that provide access to free sources of useful big data sets.

Big Data Uses

Here are just a few examples of how organizations are employing big data to improve their day-to-day operations, planning, and decision making:

• Retail organizations monitor social networks such as Facebook, Google, LinkedIn, Twitter, and Yahoo to engage brand advocates, identify brand adversaries (and attempt to reverse their negative opinions), and even enable passionate customers to sell their products.

- Advertising and marketing agencies track comments on social media to understand consumers' responsiveness to ads, campaigns, and promotions.
- Hospitals analyze medical data and patient records to try to identify patients likely to need readmission within a few months of discharge, with the goal of engaging with those patients in the hope of preventing another expensive hospital stay.
- Consumer product companies monitor social networks to gain insight into customer behavior, likes and dislikes, and product perception to identify necessary changes to their products, services, and advertising.
- Financial services organizations use data from customer interactions to identify customers who are likely to be attracted to increasingly targeted and sophisticated offers.
- Manufacturers analyze minute vibration data from their equipment, which changes slightly as it wears down, to predict the optimal time to perform maintenance or replace the equipment to avoid expensive repairs or potentially catastrophic failure.

Challenges of Big Data

Individuals, organizations, and society in general must find a way to deal with this ever-growing data tsunami to escape the risks of information overload. The challenge is manifold, with a variety of questions that must be answered, including how to choose what subset of data to store, where and how to store the data, how to find those nuggets of data that are relevant to the decision making at hand, how to derive value from the relevant data, and how to identify which data needs to be protected from unauthorized access. With so much data available, business users can have a hard time finding the information they need to make decisions, and they may not trust the validity of the data they can access.

Trying to deal with all this data from so many different sources, much of it from outside the organization, can also increase the risk that the organization fails to comply with government regulations or internal controls (see Table 5.4). If measures to ensure compliance are not defined and followed, compliance issues can arise. Violation of these regulations can lead not only to government investigations but also to dramatic drops in stock prices, as when computer chipmaker Marvell Technologies alarmed

TABLE 5.4 Partial list of rules, regulations, and standards with which U.S. information system organizations must comply

Rule, Regulation, or Standard	Intent
Bank Secrecy Act	Detects and prevents money laundering by requiring financial institutions to report certain transactions to government agencies and to withhold from clients that such reports were filed about them
Basel II Accord	Creates international standards that strengthen global capital and liquidity rules, with the goal of promoting a more resilient banking sector worldwide
California Senate Bill 1386	Protects against identity theft by imposing disclosure requirements for businesses and government agencies that experience security breaches that might put the personal information of California residents at risk; the first of many state laws aimed at protecting consumers from identity theft
European Union Data Protection Directive	Protects the privacy of European Union citizens' personal information by placing limitations on sending such data outside of the European Union to areas that are deemed to have less than adequate standards for data security
Foreign Account Tax Compliance Act	Identifies U.S. taxpayers who hold financial assets in non-U.S. financial institutions and offshore accounts, to ensure that they do not avoid their U.S. tax obligations

TABLE 5.4 Partial list of rules, regulations, and standards with which U.S. information system organizations must comply (*continued*)

Rule, Regulation, or Standard	Intent
Foreign Corrupt Practices Act	Prevents certain classes of persons and entities from making payments to foreign government officials in an attempt to obtain or retain business
Gramm-Leach-Bliley Act	Protects the privacy and security of individually identifiable financial information collected and processed by financial institutions
Health Insurance Portability and Accountability Act (HIPAA)	Safeguards protected health information (PHI) and electronic PHI (ePHI) data gathered in the healthcare process and standardizes certain electronic transactions within the healthcare industry
Payment Card Industry (PCI) Data Security Standard	Protects cardholder data and ensures that merchants and service providers maintain strict information security standards
Personal Information Protection and Electronic Documents Act (Canada)	Governs the collection, use, and disclosure of personally identifiable information in the course of commercial transactions; created in response to European Union data protection directives
Sarbanes-Oxley Act	Protects the interests of investors and consumers by requiring that the annual reports of public companies include an evaluation of the effectiveness of internal control over financial reporting; requires that the company's CEO and CFO attest to and report on this assessment
USA PATRIOT Act	This wide-ranging act has many facets; one portion of the Act relating to information system compliance is called the Financial Anti-Terrorism Act and is designed to combat the financing of terrorism through money laundering and other financial crimes

investors by announcing that it had found problems with the way it booked revenue, resulting in a 16 percent drop in its stock price in just one day.[19]

Optimists believe that we can conquer these challenges and that more data will lead to more accurate analyses and better decision making, which in turn will result in deliberate actions that improve matters.

Not everyone, however, is happy with big data applications. Some people have privacy concerns about the fact that corporations are harvesting huge amounts of personal data that can be shared with other organizations. With all this data, organizations can develop extensive profiles of people without their knowledge or consent. Big data also introduces security concerns. Are organizations able to keep big data secure from competitors and malicious hackers? Some experts believe companies that collect and store big data could be open to liability suits from individuals and organizations. Even with these potential disadvantages, many companies are rushing into big data due to the lure of a potential treasure trove of information and new applications.

Data Management

Data management is an integrated set of functions that defines the processes by which data is obtained, certified fit for use, stored, secured, and processed in such a way as to ensure that the accessibility, reliability, and timeliness of the data meet the needs of the data users within an organization. The Data Management Association (DAMA) International is a nonprofit, vendor-independent, international association whose members promote the understanding, development, and practice of managing data as an essential enterprise asset. This organization has identified 10 major functions of data management, as shown in Figure 5.21. **Data governance** is the core component of data management; it defines the roles, responsibilities, and processes for ensuring that data can be trusted and used by the entire organization, with people identified and in place who are responsible for fixing and preventing issues with data.

data management: An integrated set of functions that defines the processes by which data is obtained, certified fit for use, stored, secured, and processed in such a way as to ensure that the accessibility, reliability, and timeliness of the data meet the needs of the data users within an organization.

data governance: The core component of data management; it defines the roles, responsibilities, and processes for ensuring that data can be trusted and used by the entire organization, with people identified and in place who are responsible for fixing and preventing issues with data.

FIGURE 5.21

Data management

The Data Management Association (DAMA) International has identified 10 basic functions associated with data management.

Source: "Body of Knowledge," DAMA International, *https://www.dama.org/content /body-knowledge*. Copyright DAMA International.

data steward: An individual responsible for the management of critical data elements, including identifying and acquiring new data sources; creating and maintaining consistent reference data and master data definitions; and analyzing data for quality and reconciling data issues.

The need for data management is driven by a variety of factors, including the need to meet external regulations designed to manage risk associated with financial misstatement, the need to avoid the inadvertent release of sensitive data, or the need to ensure that high data quality is available for key decisions. Haphazard or incomplete business processes and controls simply will not meet these requirements. Formal management processes are needed to govern data.

Effective data governance requires business leadership and active participation—it cannot be an effort that is led by the information system organization. The use of a cross-functional team is recommended because data and information systems are used by many different departments. No one individual has a complete view of the organization's data needs. Employment of a cross-functional team is particularly important for ensuring that compliance needs are met. The data governance team should be a cross-functional, multilevel data governance team, consisting of executives, project managers, line-of-business managers, and data stewards. The **data steward** is an individual responsible for the management of critical data elements, including identifying and acquiring new data sources; creating and maintaining consistent reference data and master data definitions; and analyzing data for quality and reconciling data issues. Data users consult with a data steward when they need to know what data to use to answer a business question, or to confirm the accuracy, completeness, or soundness of data within a business context.

The data governance team defines the owners of the data assets in the enterprise. The team also develops a policy that specifies who is accountable for various portions or aspects of the data, including its accuracy, accessibility, consistency, completeness, updating, and archiving. The team defines processes for how the data is to be stored, archived, backed up, and protected from cyberattacks, inadvertent destruction or disclosure, or theft. It also develops standards and procedures that define who is authorized to update, access, and use the data. The team also puts in place a set of controls and audit procedures to ensure ongoing compliance with organizational data policies and government regulations.

data lifecycle management (DLM): A policy-based approach to managing the flow of an enterprise's data, from its initial acquisition or creation and storage to the time when it becomes outdated and is deleted.

Data lifecycle management (DLM) is a policy-based approach to managing the flow of an enterprise's data, from its initial acquisition or creation and storage to the time when it becomes outdated and is deleted. See Figure 5.22. Several vendors offer software products to support DLM such as IBM Information Lifecycle Governance suite of software products.

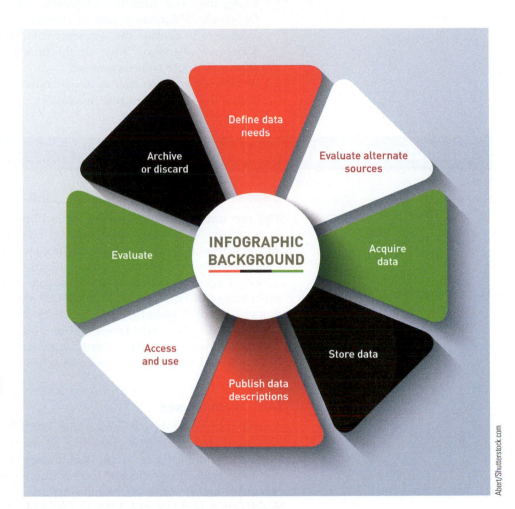

FIGURE 5.22
The big data life cycle
A policy-based approach to managing the flow of an enterprise's data, from its initial acquisition or creation and storage to the time when it becomes outdated and is deleted.

Critical Thinking Exercise

Walgreens Data Assimilation

As of this writing, Walgreens is making moves to acquire Rite Aide in a move that would combine the nation's second- and third-largest drugstore chains by market share, behind only fierce rival CVS Health. If this acquisition is approved, Rite Aide customer data will need to be assimilated into Walgreens' information systems. For pharmacy customers, this includes sensitive information, such as personal data, details of medications prescribed, health insurance identification codes, and doctors used. Walgreens will need this data to provide smooth and uninterrupted service to the old Rite Aide customers. In addition, Walgreen has in place a system that automatically checks each new medication prescribed against other medications the customer is taking to ensure there will be no adverse drug interactions. The data must be captured in such a way that ensures its accuracy and completeness.

Review Questions

1. Identify specific federal regulations that apply to the use and management of Walgreens and Rite Aide data.
2. Would it make sense for Walgreen to appoint a data governance team to oversee the Rite Aide data assimilation process? What might the responsibilities of such a team be?

Critical Thinking Questions

1. Do you think that Walgreens should attempt to automate the process of assimilating Rite Aide customer, insurance, and medication data into its systems? Or, should Walgreens design an efficient manual process for former Rite Aide customers to provide the necessary data prior to or on their initial visit to a Walgreens pharmacy? What are the pros and cons of each approach? Which approach would you recommend?
2. Identify several potential negative consequences resulting from poor execution of the data assimilation process.

Technologies Used to Process Big Data

Data Warehouses, Data Marts, and Data Lakes

The raw data necessary to make sound business decisions is typically stored in a variety of locations and formats. This data is initially captured, stored, and managed by transaction-processing systems that are designed to support the day-to-day operations of an organization. For decades, organizations have collected operational, sales, and financial data with their online transaction processing (OLTP) systems. These OLTP systems put data into databases very quickly, reliably, and efficiently, but they do not support the types of big data analysis that today's businesses and organizations require. Through the use of data warehouses and data marts, organizations are now able to access the data gathered via OLTP system and use it more effectively to support decision making.

Data Warehouses

A data warehouse is a database that holds business information from many sources in the enterprise, covering all aspects of the company's processes, products, and customers. Data warehouses allow managers to "drill down" to get greater detail or "roll up" to generate aggregate or summary reports. The primary purpose is to relate information in innovative ways and help managers and executives make better decisions. A data warehouse stores historical data that has been extracted from operational systems and external data sources. See Figure 5.23.

Companies use data warehouses in a variety of ways, as shown in the following examples:

- Walmart operates separate data warehouses for Walmart and Sam's Club and allows suppliers access to almost any data they could possibly need to determine which of their products are selling, how fast, and even whether they should redesign their packaging to fit more product on store shelves.[20]
- UPS manages a 16-petabyte data warehouse containing data on some 16.3 million packages it ships per day for 8.8 million customers, who make an average of 39.5 million tracking requests per day.[21]
- Orscheln (a billion dollar retailer that sells farm- and home-related products through its some 150 stores spread across the Midwest)

implemented an Oracle data warehouse that is used by merchants, buyers, planners, and store managers to perform analysis on inventory management, sales performance, pricing and promotions effectiveness, vendor compliance, and loss prevention.[22]

- General Electric uses a data warehouse to hold data from sensors on the performance of the blades on jet engines it manufactures.[23]

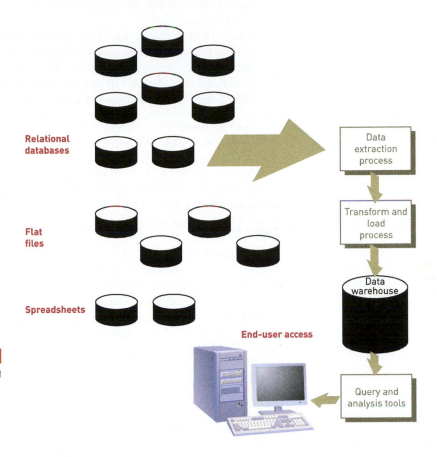

Elements of a data warehouse
A data warehouse can help managers and executives relate information in innovative ways to make better decisions.

Because data warehouses are used for decision making, maintaining a high quality of data is vital so that organizations avoid wrong conclusions. For instance, duplicated or missing information will produce incorrect or misleading statistics ("garbage in, garbage out"). Due to the wide range of possible data inconsistencies and the sheer data volume, data quality is considered one of the biggest issues in data warehousing.

Data warehouses are continuously refreshed with huge amounts of data from a variety of sources so the probability that some of the sources contain "dirty data" is high. The ETL (extract, transform, load) process takes data from a variety of sources, edits and transforms it into the format used in the data warehouse, and then loads this data into the warehouse, as shown in Figure 5.23. This process is essential in ensuring the quality of the data in the data warehouse.

- **Extract.** Source data for the data warehouse comes from many sources and may be represented in a variety of formats. The goal of this process is to extract the source data from all the various sources and convert it into a single format suitable for processing. During the extract step, data that fails to meet expected patterns or values may be rejected from further processing (e.g., blank or nonnumeric data in net sales field or a product code outside the defined range of valid codes).

- **Transform.** During this stage of the ETL process, a series of rules or algorithms are applied to the extracted data to derive the data that will be stored in the data warehouse. A common type of transformation is to convert a customer's street address, city, state, and zip code to an organization-assigned sales district or government census tract. Also, data is often aggregated to reduce the processing time required to create anticipated reports. For example, total sales may be accumulated by store or sales district.

- **Load.** During this stage of the ETL process, the extracted and transformed data is loaded into the data warehouse. As the data is being loaded into the data warehouse, new indices are created and the data is checked against the constraints defined in the database schema to ensure its quality. As a result, the data load stage for a large data warehouse can take days.

A large number of software tools are available to support these ETL tasks, including Ab Initio, IBM InfoSphereDatastage, Oracle Data Integrator, and the SAP Data Integrator. Several open-source ETL tools are also available, including Apatar, Clover ETL, Pentaho, and Talend. Unfortunately, much of the ETL work must be done by low-level proprietary programs that are difficult to write and maintain.

Data Marts

data mart: A subset of a data warehouse that is used by small- and medium-sized businesses and departments within large companies to support decision making.

A **data mart** is a subset of a data warehouse. Data marts bring the data warehouse concept—online analysis of sales, inventory, and other vital business data that have been gathered from transaction processing systems—to small- and medium-sized businesses and to departments within larger companies. Rather than store all enterprise data in one monolithic database, data marts contain a subset of the data for a single aspect of a company's business—for example, finance, inventory, or personnel.

Data Lakes

data lake (enterprise data hub): A "store everything" approach to big data that saves all the data in its raw and unaltered form.

A traditional data warehouse is created by extracting (and discarding some data in the process), transforming (modifying), and loading incoming data for predetermined and specific analyses and applications. This process can be lengthy and computer intensive, taking days to complete. A **data lake** (also called an **enterprise data hub**) takes a "store everything" approach to big data, saving all the data in its raw and unaltered form. The raw data residing in a data lake is available when users decide just how they want to use the data to glean new insights. Only when the data is accessed for a specific analysis is it extracted from the data lake, classified, organized, edited, or transformed. Thus a data lake serves as the definitive source of data in its original, unaltered form. Its contents can include business transactions, clickstream data, sensor data, server logs, social media, videos, and more.

NoSQL Databases

NoSQL database: A way to store and retrieve data that is modeled using some means other than the simple two-dimensional tabular relations used in relational databases.

A **NoSQL database** provides a means to store and retrieve data that is modeled using some means other than the simple two-dimensional tabular relations used in relational databases. Such databases are being used to deal with the variety of data found in big data and Web applications. A major advantage of NoSQL databases is the ability to spread data over multiple servers so that each server contains only a subset of the total data. This so-called horizontal scaling capability enables hundreds or even thousands of servers to operate on the data, providing faster response times for queries and updates. Most relational database management systems have problems with such horizontal scaling and instead require large, powerful, and expensive proprietary servers and large storage systems.

Another advantage of NoSQL databases is that they do not require a predefined schema; data entities can have attributes edited or assigned to them at any time. If a new entity or attribute is discovered, it can be added to the database dynamically, extending what is already modeled in the database.

Most NoSQL databases do not conform to true ACID properties when processing transactions. Instead they provide for "eventual consistency" in which database changes are propagated to all nodes eventually (typically within milliseconds), so it is possible that user queries for data might not return the most current data.

The choice of a relational database management system versus a NoSQL solution depends on the problem that needs to be addressed. Often, the data structures used by NoSQL databases are more flexible than relational database tables and, in many cases, they can provide improved access speed and redundancy.

The four main categories of NoSQL databases and offerings for each category are shown in Table 5.5 and summarized below. Note that some NoSQL database products can meet the needs of more than one category.

- Key–value NoSQL databases are similar to SQL databases, but have only two columns ("key" and "value"), with more complex information sometimes stored within the "value" columns.
- Document NoSQL databases are used to store, retrieve, and manage document-oriented information, such as social media posts and multimedia, also known as semi-structured data.
- Graph NoSQL databases are used to understand the relationships among events, people, transactions, locations, and sensor readings and are well-suited for analyzing interconnections such as when extracting data from social media.
- Column NoSQL databases store data in columns, rather than in rows, and are able to deliver fast response times for large volumes of data.

TABLE 5.5 Popular NoSQL database products, by category

Key–Value	Document	Graph	Column
HyperDEX	Lotus Notes	Allegro	Accumulo
Couchbase Server	Couchbase Server	Neo4J	Cassandra
Oracle NoSQL Database	Oracle NoSQL Database	InfiniteGraph	Druid
OrientDB	OrientDB	OrientDB	Vertica
	MongoDB	Virtuoso	HBase

Criteo is a digital-advertising organization serving up ads to over one billion unique Internet users around the world every month. The firm automates the recommendation of ads and the selection of products from advertiser catalogs up to 30 billion times each day. A recommendation can require a calculation involving some 100 variables, and it must be completed quickly—within 100 milliseconds or less. Criteo has deployed a Couchbase Server NoSQL database across 1,000 servers grouped into 24 clusters, providing access to a total of 107 terabytes of database storage to meet these demanding processing requirements.[24]

The National Security Agency (NSA), through its controversial PRISM program, uses NoSQL technology to analyze email messages, phone conversations, video chats, and social media interactions gleaned from the servers of major service providers, including Apple, Facebook, Google, Microsoft, Skype, Yahoo, and YouTube. The Accumulo NoSQL database enables its users to assign each piece of data a security tag that defines how people can access that data and who can access that data. This feature makes it possible for NSA agents to interrogate certain details while blocking access to personally identifiable information.[25]

Amazon DynamoDB is a NoSQL database that supports both document and key–value store models. MLB Advanced Media (MLBAM) uses DynamoDB to power its revolutionary Player Tracking System, which reveals detailed information about the nuances and athleticism of the game. Fans, broadcasters, and teams are finding this new data entertaining and useful. The system takes in data from ballparks across North America and provides enough computing power to support real-time analytics and produce results in seconds.[26]

Hadoop

Hadoop: An open-source software framework including several software modules that provide a means for storing and processing extremely large data sets.

Hadoop Distributed File System (HDFS): A system used for data storage that divides the data into subsets and distributes the subsets onto different servers for processing.

Hadoop is an open-source software framework that includes several software modules that provide a means for storing and processing extremely large data sets, as shown in Figure 5.24. Hadoop has two primary components: a data processing component (a Java-based system called MapReduce, which is discussed in the next section) and a distributed file system (**Hadoop Distributed File System, HDFS**) for data storage. Hadoop divides data into subsets and distributes the subsets onto different servers for processing. A Hadoop cluster may consist of thousands of servers. In a Hadoop cluster, a subset of the data within the HDFS and the MapReduce system are housed on every server in the cluster. This places the data processing software on the same servers where the data is stored, thus speeding up data retrieval. This approach creates a highly redundant computing environment that allows the application to keep running even if individual servers fail.

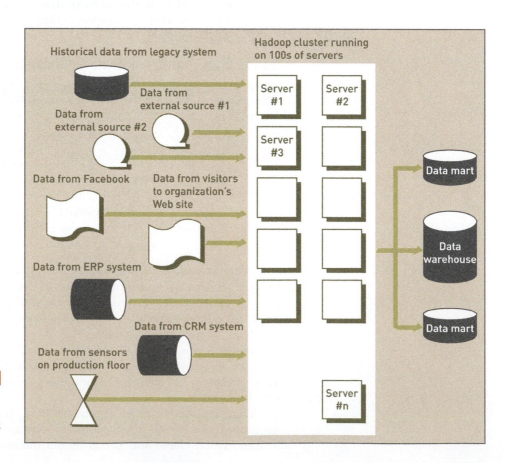

FIGURE 5.24

Hadoop environment

Hadoop can be used as a staging area for data to be loaded into a data warehouse or data mart.

MapReduce program: A composite program that consists of a Map procedure that performs filtering and sorting and a Reduce method that performs a summary operation.

A **MapReduce program** is composed of a Map procedure that performs filtering and sorting (such as sorting customer orders by product ID into queues, with one queue for each product ID) and a Reduce method that performs a summary operation (such as counting the number of orders in each queue, thus determining product ID frequencies). MapReduce employs a JobTracker that resides on the Hadoop master server as well as TaskTrackers that sit on each server within the Hadoop cluster of servers. The JobTracker divides the computing job up into well-defined tasks and moves those tasks out to the individual TaskTrackers on the servers in the Hadoop cluster where the needed data resides. These servers operate in parallel to complete the necessary computing. Once their work is complete, the resulting subset of data is reduced back to the central node of the Hadoop cluster.

For years, Yahoo! used Hadoop to better personalize the ads and articles that its visitors see. Now Hadoop is used by many popular Web sites and services (such as eBay, Etsy, Twitter, and Yelp). Verizon Wireless uses big data to perform customer churn analysis to get a better sense of when a customer becomes dissatisfied. Hadoop allows Verizon to include more detailed data about each customer, including clickstream data, chats, and even social media searches, to predict when a customer might switch to a new carrier.

Hadoop has a limitation in that it can only perform batch processing; it cannot process real-time streaming data such as stock prices as they flow into the various stock exchanges. However, Apache Storm and Apache Spark are often integrated with Hadoop to provide real-time data processing. Apache Storm is a free and open source distributed real-time computation system. Storm makes it easy to reliably process unbounded streams of data. Apache Spark is a framework for performing general data analytics in a distributed computing cluster environment like Hadoop. It provides in memory computations for increased speed of data processing. Both Storm and Spark run on top of an existing Hadoop cluster and access data in a Hadoop data store (HDFS).

Medscape MedPulse is a medical news app for iPhone and iPad users that enables healthcare professionals to stay up-to-date on the latest medical news and expert perspectives. The app uses Apache Storm to include an automatic Twitter feed (about 500 million tweets per day are tweeted on Twitter) to help users stay informed about important medical trends being shared in real time by physicians and other leading medical commentators.[27,28]

In-Memory Databases

in-memory database (IMDB): A database management system that stores the entire database in random access memory (RAM).

An **in-memory database (IMDB)** is a database management system that stores the entire database in random access memory (RAM). This approach provides access to data at rates much faster than storing data on some form of secondary storage (e.g., a hard drive or flash drive) as is done with traditional database management systems. IMDBs enable the analysis of big data and other challenging data-processing applications, and they have become feasible because of the increase in RAM capacities and a corresponding decrease in RAM costs. In-memory databases perform best on multiple multicore CPUs that can process parallel requests to the data, further speeding access to and processing of large amounts of data.[29] Furthermore, the advent of 64-bit processors enabled the direct addressing of larger amounts of main memory. Some of the leading providers of IMDBs are shown in Table 5.6.

KDDI Corporation is a Japanese telecommunications company that provides mobile cellular services for some 40 million customers. The company consolidated 40 existing servers into a single Oracle SuperCluster running the Oracle Times Ten in-memory database to make its authentication system that manages subscriber and connectivity data run faster and more efficiently. This move reduced its data center footprint by 83 percent and power consumption by 70 percent while improving the overall performance and

TABLE 5.6 IMDB providers

Database Software Manufacturer	Product Name	Major Customers
Altibase	HDB	E*Trade, China Telecom
Oracle	Times Ten	Lockheed Martin, Verizon Wireless
SAP	High-Performance Analytic Appliance (HANA)	eBay, Colgate
Software AG	Terracotta Big Memory	AdJuggler

availability of the system. As a result, system costs were reduced and customer service improved.[30]

Critical Thinking Exercise

Telefonica Brasil

Telefonica Brasil is one of the largest telecommunications companies in Brazil, and it provides landline and mobile services under the brand name Vivo for millions of consumers. The company is considering using big data to perform customer churn analysis in order to anticipate when a customer is unhappy and likely to drop its service for that of a competitor.

Review Questions

1. What sources of data might Telefonica Brasil use to perform customer churn analysis?
2. What database technology options might the firm elect to use?

Critical Thinking Questions

1. Why is it unlikely that a traditional SQL database would be able to meet the firm's needs?
2. In addition to a database management system, what other information system technology and resources are likely needed for this type of project?

Summary

Principle:

The database approach to data management has become broadly accepted.

Data is one of the most valuable resources that a firm possesses. It is organized into a hierarchy that builds from the smallest element to the largest. The smallest element is the bit, a binary digit. A byte (a character such as a letter or numeric digit) is made up of eight bits. A group of characters, such as a name or number, is called a field (an object). A collection of related fields is a record; a collection of related records is called a file. The database, at the top of the hierarchy, is an integrated collection of records and files.

An entity is a generalized class of objects (such as a person, place, or thing) for which data is collected, stored, and maintained. An attribute is a characteristic of an entity. Specific values of attributes—called data items—can be found in the fields of the record describing an entity. A data key is a field within a record that is used to identify the record. A primary key uniquely identifies a record, while a secondary key is a field in a record that does not uniquely identify the record.

Principle:

Data modelling is a key aspect of organizing data and information.

When building a database, an organization must consider content, access, logical structure, physical organization, archiving, and security of the database. One of the tools that database designers use to show the logical structure and relationships among data is a data model. A data model is a map or diagram of entities and their relationships. Enterprise data modeling involves analyzing the data and information needs of an entire organization and provides a roadmap for building database and information systems by creating a single definition and format for data that can ensure compatibility and the ability to exchange and integrate data among systems. Entity-relationship (ER) diagrams can be used to show the relationships among entities in the organization.

The relational database model places data in two-dimensional tables. Tables can be linked by common data elements, which are used to access data when the database is queried. Each row in a relational database table represents a record, and each column represents an attribute (or field). The allowable values for each attribute are called the attribute's domain. Basic data manipulations include selecting, projecting, joining, and linking. The relational model is easier to control, more flexible, and more intuitive than other database models because it organizes data in tables.

Data cleansing is the process of detecting and then correcting or deleting incomplete, incorrect, inaccurate, or irrelevant records that reside in the database. The goal of data cleansing is to improve the quality of the data used in decision making.

Principle:

A well-designed and well-managed database is an extremely valuable tool in supporting decision making.

A database management system (DBMS) is a group of programs used as an interface between a database and its users and between a database and other application programs. When an application program requests data from the database, it follows a logical access path. The actual retrieval of the data follows a physical access path. Records can be considered in the same way: A logical record is what the record contains; a physical record is where the record is stored on storage devices. Schemas are used to describe the entire database, its record types, and its relationships to the DBMS. Schemas are entered into the computer via a data definition language, which describes the data and relationships in a specific database. Another tool used in database management is the data dictionary, which contains detailed descriptions of all data in the database.

A DBMS provides four basic functions: offering user views, creating and modifying the database, storing and retrieving data, and manipulating data and generating reports. After a DBMS has been installed, the database can be accessed, modified, and queried via a data manipulation language. A type of specialized data manipulation language is the query language, the most common being Structured Query Language (SQL). SQL is used in several popular database packages today and can be installed in PCs and mainframes.

A database administrator (DBA) plans, designs, creates, operates, secures, monitors, and maintains databases. A data administrator is a person position responsible for defining and implementing consistent principles for a variety of data issues, including setting data standards and data definitions that apply across all the databases in an organization.

Selecting a DBMS begins by analyzing the information needs of the organization. Important characteristics of databases include the size of the database, the number of concurrent users, the performance of the database, the ability of the DBMS to be integrated with other systems, the features of the DBMS, the vendor considerations, and the cost of the database management system.

In database as a service (DaaS) arrangement, the database is stored on a service provider's servers and accessed by the subscriber over a network, typically the Internet. In DaaS, database administration is provided by the service provider.

Principle:

We have entered an era where organizations are grappling with a tremendous growth in the amount of data available and struggling how to manage and make use of it.

"Big data" is the term used to describe data collections that are so enormous and complex that traditional data management software, hardware, and analysis processes are incapable of dealing with them.

There are many challenges associated with big data, including how to choose what subset of data to store, where and how to store the data, how to find those nuggets of data that are relevant to the decision making at hand, how to derive value from the relevant data, and how to identify which data needs to be protected from unauthorized access.

Data management is an integrated set of 10 functions that defines the processes by which data is obtained, certified fit for use, stored, secured, and processed in such a way as to ensure that the accessibility, reliability, and timeliness of the data meet the needs of the data users within an organization. Data governance is the core component of data management; it defines the roles, responsibilities, and processes for ensuring that data can be trusted and used by the entire organization with people identified and in place who are responsible for fixing and preventing issues with data.

Principle:

A number of available tools and technologies allow organizations to take advantage of the opportunities offered by big data.

Traditional online transaction processing (OLTP) systems put data into databases very quickly, reliably, and efficiently, but they do not support the types of data analysis that today's businesses and organizations require. To address this need, organizations are building data warehouses specifically designed to support management decision making.

An extract, transform, load process takes data from a variety of sources, edits and transforms it into the format to be used in the data warehouse, and then loads the data into the warehouse.

Data marts are subdivisions of data warehouses and are commonly devoted to specific purposes or functional business areas.

A data lake (also called an enterprise data hub) takes a "store everything" approach to big data, saving all the data in its raw and unaltered form.

A NoSQL database provides a means to store and retrieve data that is modelled using some means other than the simple two-dimensional tabular relations used in relational databases. There are four types of NoSQL databases—key-value, document, graph, and column.

Hadoop is an open-source software framework that includes several software modules that provide a means for storing and processing extremely large data sets. Hadoop has two primary components—a data processing component (MapReduce) and a distributed file system (Hadoop Distributed File System or HDFS) for data storage. Hadoop divides data into subsets and distributes the subsets onto different servers for processing. A Hadoop cluster may consist of thousands of servers. A subset of the data within the HDFS and the MapReduce system are housed on every server in the cluster.

An in-memory database (IMDB) is a database management system that stores the entire database in random access memory to improve storage and retrieval speed.

Key Terms

ACID properties	database management system (DBMS)
attribute	domain
bit	enterprise data model
character	entity
concurrency control	entity-relationship (ER) diagram
data administrator	field
data cleansing (data cleaning or data scrubbing)	file
data definition language (DDL)	Hadoop
data dictionary	Hadoop Distributed File System (HDFS)
data governance	hierarchy of data
data item	in-memory database (IMDB)
data lake (enterprise data hub)	joining
data lifecycle management (DLM)	linking
data management	MapReduce program
data manipulation language (DML)	NoSQL database
data mart	primary key
data model	projecting
data steward	record
database	relational database model
database administrators (DBAs)	schema
database approach to data management	selecting
database as a service (DaaS)	SQL

Chapter 5: Self-Assessment Test

The database approach to data management has become broadly accepted.

1. A field or set of fields that uniquely identifies a record in a database is called a(n) _____.
   a. attribute
   b. data item
   c. record
   d. primary key

2. The key concept of the database approach to data management is that _____.
   a. all records in the database are stored in a two-dimensional table
   b. multiple information systems share access to a pool of related data
   c. only authorized users can access the data
   d. a database administrator "owns" the data

Data modeling is a key aspect of organizing data and information.

3. A(n) _____ provides an organizational-level roadmap for building databases and information systems by creating a single definition and format for data.

   a. database
   b. enterprise data model
   c. entity relationship diagram
   d. database management system

4. The _____ model is a simple but highly useful way to organize data into collections of two-dimensional tables called relations.

5. The ability to combine two or more tables through common data attributes to form a new table with only the unique data attributes is called _____.

6. SQL databases conform to ACID properties, which include atomicity, consistency, isolation, and _____.

A well-designed and well-managed database is an extremely valuable tool in supporting decision making.

7. The process of detecting and then correcting or deleting incomplete, incorrect, inaccurate, or irrelevant records that reside in a database is called _____.

8. Because the DBMS is responsible for providing access to a database, one of the first steps in installing and using a relational database involves "telling" the DBMS the logical and physical structure of the data and relationships among the data in the database. This description of an entire database is called a(n) _____.

9. A(n) _____ is an individual responsible for the management of critical data elements, including identifying and acquiring new data sources; creating and maintaining consistent reference data and master data definitions; and analyzing data for quality and reconciling data issues.

10. Data administrators are skilled and trained IS professionals who hold discussions with users to define their data needs; apply database programming languages to craft a set of databases to meet those needs; and assure that data is secure from unauthorized access. True or False?

11. With _____, the database is stored on a service provider's servers and accessed by the service subscriber over the Internet, with the database administration handled by the service provider.

We have entered an era where organizations are grappling with a tremendous growth in the amount of data available and struggling to understand how to manage and make use of it.

12. Three characteristics associated with big data include volume, velocity, and _____.

13. The Data Management Association has defined 10 major functions of data management, with the core component being _____.
    a. data quality management
    b. data security management
    c. data governance
    d. data architecture management

A number of available tools and technologies allow organizations to take advantage of the opportunities offered by big data.

14. A(n) _____ database provides a means to store and retrieve data that is modeled using some means other than simple two-dimensional relations used in relational databases.

15. Hadoop has two primary components—a data processing component and a distributed file system called _____.
    a. MapReduce and HDFS
    b. TaskTracker and JobTracker
    c. Key-value and graph
    d. SQL and NoSQL

16. An _____ is a database management system that stores the entire database in random access memory to provide fast access.

Chapter 5: Self-Assessment Test Answers

1. d
2. b
3. b
4. relational database
5. linking
6. durability
7. data cleansing, data cleaning, or data scrubbing
8. schema
9. data steward
10. False
11. database as a service (DaaS)
12. variety
13. c
14. NoSQL
15. a
16. in-memory database

Review Questions

1. How would you define the term "database"? How would you define the term "database management system"?

2. In the hierarchy of data, what is the difference between a data attribute and a data item? What is the domain of an attribute?

3. What is meant by the database approach to data management?

4. What is meant by data archiving? Why is this an important consideration when operating a database?

5. What is an entity-relationship diagram, and what is its purpose?

6. Identify four basic data manipulations performed on a relational database using SQL.

7. What is data scrubbing?

8. What is database as a service (DaaS)? What are the advantages and disadvantages of using the DaaS approach?

9. What is Hadoop? What are its primary components, and what does each do?

10. What is a schema, and how is it used?

11. What is concurrency control? Why is it important?

12. What is in-memory database processing, and what advantages does it provide?

13. What is the difference between projecting and joining?
14. What is big data? Identify three characteristics associated with big data.
15. What is a data warehouse, and how is it different from a traditional database used to support OLTP?
16. What is a data lake, and how is it different from a data warehouse?
17. How does an in-memory database provide fast access to data?

Discussion Questions

1. What concerns might be raised by performing data cleansing on a large set of raw data before it is used for analysis? How might these concerns be addressed?
2. Outline some specific steps an organization might take to perform data cleansing to ensure the accuracy and completeness of its customer database before adding this data to a data warehouse. How would you decide when the data is accurate enough?
3. SQL databases conform to ACID properties. Briefly describe the ACID properties, and state the purpose of each. How does conformance to ACID properties affect the performance of SQL databases?
4. Describe how a NoSQL database differs from a relational database. Identify and briefly discuss the four types of NoSQL databases.
5. Review Table 5.4, which provides a list of rules, regulations, and standards with which U.S. information systems organizations must comply. Which of these standards do you think has the most impact on safeguarding the security of personal information? Which of these standards have minimal impact on you personally?
6. Identify and briefly describe the steps in the ETL process. What is the goal of the ETL process?
7. Consider three organizations that have databases that likely store information about you—the Federal Internal Revenue Service, your state's Bureau of Motor Vehicles, and Equifax, the consumer reporting agency. Go to the home page of each of these organizations, and find answers to the following questions. How is the data in each database captured? Is it possible for you to request a printout of the contents of your data record from each database? Is it possible for you to correct errors you find in your data record? What data privacy concerns do you have concerning how these databases are managed?
8. Identity theft, where people steal personal information, continues to be a problem for consumers and businesses. Assume that you are the database administrator for a corporation with a large database that is accessible from the Web. What steps would you implement to prevent people from stealing personal information from the corporate database?
9. Read the article "Why 'Big Data' Is a Big Deal" by Jonathan Shaw in the March-April 2014 Harvard Magazine. What does Shaw think is the revolution in big data? Which of the many big data applications that he mentions do you find to be the most interesting? Why?

Problem-Solving Exercises

1. Develop a simple data model for a student database that includes student contact data, student demographic data, student grades data, and student financial data. Determine the data attributes that should be present in each table, and identify the primary key for each table. Develop a complete ER diagram that shows how these tables are related to one another.
2. A company that provides a movie-streaming subscription service uses a relational database to store information on movies to answer customer questions. Each entry in the database contains the following items: Movie ID (the primary key), movie title, year made, movie type, MPAA rating, starring actor #1, starring actor #2, starring actor #3, and director. Movie types are action, comedy, family, drama, horror, science fiction, and western. MPAA ratings are G, PG, PG-13, R, NC-17, and NR (not rated). Using a graphics program, develop an entity-relationship diagram for a database application for this database.
3. Use a database management system to build a data-entry screen to enter this data. Build a small database with at least a dozen entries.
4. To improve service to their customers, the employees of the movie-streaming company have proposed several changes that are being considered for the database in the previous exercise. From this list, choose two database modifications, and then modify the data-entry screen to capture

and store this new information. The proposed changes are as follows:

a. Add the date that the movie was first released to the theaters.

b. Add the executive producer's name.

c. Add a customer rating of one, two, three, four, or five stars, based on the number of rentals.

d. Add the number of Academy Award nominations.

Team Activities

1. Imagine that you and your team have been hired to develop an improved process for evaluating which students should be accepted to your college and, of those, which should be awarded academic scholarships. What data besides college entrance scores and high school transcripts might you consider using to make these determinations? Where might you get this data? Develop an ER diagram showing the various tables of data that might be used.

2. You and your team have been selected to represent the student body in defining the user requirements for a new student database for your school. What actions would you take to ensure that the student reporting needs and data privacy concerns of the students are fully identified? What

other resources might you enlist to help you in defining these requirements?

3. As a team of three or four classmates, interview managers from three different organizations that have implemented a customer database. What data entities and data attributes are contained in each database? What database management system did each company select to implement its database, and why? How does each organization access its database to perform analysis? Have the managers and their staff received training in any query or reporting tools? What do they like about their databases, and what could be improved? Weighing the information obtained, identify which company has implemented the best customer database.

Web Exercises

1. Do research to find out more about the controversial NSA PRISM program. What is the source of data for this program? What is the purpose of the program? Are you a supporter of the PRISM program? Why or why not?

2. Do research to find an example of an organization struggling to deal with the rapid growth of

the big data it needs for decision making. What are the primary issues it is facing? What is the organization doing to get a good grip on data management and data governance?

3. Do research to find three different estimates of the rate at which the amount of data in our digital universe is growing. Discuss why these estimates differ.

Career Exercises

1. Describe the role of a database administrator. What skills, training, and experiences are necessary to fulfill this role? How does this differ from the role of a data administrator? What about the

role of a data steward? Is any one of these roles of interest to you? Why or why not?

2. How could you use big data to do a better job at work? Give some specific examples of how you might use big data to gain valuable new insights.

Case Studies

Case One

WholeWorldBand: Digital Recording Studio
WholeWorldBand is a collaborative online music and video platform that enables anyone to collaborate with others to create music videos. The service was founded by Kevin Godley, a musician and music video director, and is accessible via a Web-based app available on the iPhone and iPad and on Windows and MacOS computers. Anyone can

contribute to WholeWorldBand using just the camera and microphone in their computer or mobile device. The service enables users—whatever their level of musical ability—to record and perform with music legends and friends. Using WholeWorldBand, you can start a video-recording session that others may join, create your own personal video mix with up to six performers, and then share the results with your friends and fans via Facebook, Twitter, or YouTube. Users can also pay to collaborate with other musicians who have posted their own content. Collaborating on a project might mean providing new audio or video components or remixing existing ones.

WholeWorldBand uses a sophisticated digital rights management system to ensure that artists earn revenue for the work they contribute—if your work gets used, you get paid. WholeWorldBand provides users the opportunity to perform and record with popular artists. A number of major recording artists have already uploaded tracks including The Edge (U2), Ronnie Wood (Rolling Stones), Taylor Hawkins (Foo Fighters), Stewart Copeland (The Police), Liam Ó Maonlaí (Hot House Flowers), Michael Bublé, Phil Manzanera (Roxy Music), Dave Stewart (Eurythmics), and Danny O'Reilly (The Coronas).

The platform generates revenue from registered users who purchase subscriptions (or sessions) and from royalties paid by third parties in situations where users have shared and distributed content using the app or the Web site. Each session artist is entitled to receive a share of the revenue generated when other registered users purchase sessions for the purpose of creating contributions and/or mixes in relation to their original track. Keeping track of contributing artists, royalty payments, and the necessary revenue splits among artists, third parties, and WholeWorldBand can become quite detailed and tedious.

Critical Thinking Questions:

1. Identify some of the challenges associated with building an information system infrastructure to support this new service. Would cloud computing be an appropriate solution to address these challenges? Why or why not?
2. Would WholeWorldBand be likely to employ SQL, NoSQL, or a mix of both kinds of databases? Explain your answer.
3. Go to the WholeWorldBand Web site at *www.whole worldband.com/about*, and find its Terms of Use. Summarize the measures outlined to protect the unauthorized use of copyrighted material. Do you think these measures are adequate? Why or why not?

SOURCES: "WholeWorldBand" YouTube video, 0:33, *www. youtube.com/user/WholeWorldBand*, accessed October 7, 2015; "EnterpriseDB'sPostgres Plus Cloud Database Strikes a Chord with WholeWorldBand," EntrepriseDB, *www .enterprisedb.com/success-stories/enterprisedb-s-postgres-plus-cloud-database-strikes-chord-wholeworldband*, accessed October 7, 2015; John, "WholeWorldBand Wins "Buma Music Meets Tech" Award at EurosonicNoorsderslag in Holland," *Irish Tech News*, January 18, 2014, *http://irishtechnews.net /ITN3/wholeworldband-wins-buma-music-meets-tech-award -at-eurosonic-noorsderslag-in-holland*; "WholeWorldBand Terms of Use," WholeWorldBand, *www.wholeworldband .com/about*, accessed October 7, 2015.

Case Two

Mercy's Big Data Project Aims to Boost Operations
Making the most of the data it collects is a challenge for any organization, and those in the healthcare industry are no exception. Based in St. Louis, Missouri, Mercy health system includes 46 acute care and specialty hospitals, with more

than 700 outpatient facilities and physician practices in Arkansas, Kansas, Missouri, and Oklahoma. With more than 40,000 employees, including over 2,000 physicians, Mercy's vision is to deliver a "transformative health experience" through a new model of care. With such ambitious goals, Mercy has a compelling interest in harnessing the power of the data it collects. To do so, the health system needed to overhaul is data-management infrastructure and move into the world of big data.

To make that move, Mercy partnered with software provider Hortonworks to create the Mercy Data Library, a Hadoop-based data lake that contains batch data as well as real-time data (stored in HBase, a distributed nonrelational database structure) from sources such as the Mercy's ERP and electronic health record (EHR) systems. According to Paul Boal, director of data engineering and analytics at Mercy, "The blending of base batch data and real-time updates happens on demand when a query is run against the system." Mercy's new Hadoop environment, which contains information on more than 8 million patients, holds over 40 terabytes of data housed on 41 servers spread out over four clusters.

Outside of improving patient care, a primary motive for the move to Hadoop was to improve Mercy's administrative efficiency, particularly in the areas of medical documentation and claims generation. Ensuring that physicians, nurses, and lab staff complete the necessary documentation for a patient prior to discharge improves the chances that the hospital will generate an accurate and complete claim-reimbursement request. Prior to its Hadoop implementation, the health system had already initiated an automatic-documentation-review process. Now, Mercy plans to make use of real-time data along with the power of Hadoop to further improve upon this process. For instance, documentation specialists can generate reports that help them follow up with physicians regarding missing documentation during each morning's clinical rounds. The hospital expects the new system will generate more than $1 million annually in new revenue based on claims that accurately reflect hospital patients' diagnoses and treatment.

Mercy is also focusing the power of its new technology on areas directly related to clinical care. "What we're building out is a real-time clinical applications platform, so we're looking for other opportunities to turn that into decision support," says Boal. One such project involves leveraging the Hadoop environment to make better use of data generated by the electronic monitors in the intensive care units (ICUs) across the health system. Mercy now gathers 900 times more detailed data from its ICUs than it did before its implementation of Hadoop. The previous database system was only capable of pulling vital sign information for Mercy's most critically ill patients every 15 minutes; the new system can do it once every second. The goal is to use the real-time data for better analysis, such as refining the health system's predictive models on the early-warning signs of life-threatening medical problems in the ICU setting.

Like all healthcare providers, Mercy is required to maintain an audit trail for its EHR system. The audit trail keeps track of everyone who accesses any piece of patient information via the EHR. In addition to satisfying this regulatory requirement, Mercy expects Hadoop will help it put that audit trail data to a new use—analyzing staff behavior patterns and developing a better understanding of how processes actually get done. And in another Hadoop-related project, lab staff are now able to quickly search through terabytes worth of lab notes that were previously inaccessible.

Critical Thinking Questions

1. One of the advantages of a Hadoop implementation is that it provides a high level of computing redundancy. Why is that particularly important in a healthcare setting?

2. Explain how the three characteristics of big data (volume, velocity, and variety) apply to the data being collected by healthcare providers such as Mercy.

3. How might Mercy benefit from an enterprise data model? Does Mercy's move into big data make it more or less important that it have a clearly developed model that states the organizations' data needs and priorities?

SOURCES: "Transforming the Health of Our Communities," Mercy, *www.mercy.net/about/transforming-the-health-of-our-communities*, accessed December 16, 2015; "Towards a Healthcare Data Lake: Hadoop at Mercy," Hortonworks, *http://hortonworks.com/customers*, accessed December 16, 2015; Wilson, Linda, "Mercy's Big Data Project Aims to Boost Operations," *Information Management*, October 7, 2015, *www.information-management.com/news/big-data-analytics/mercy-health-big-data-project-aims-to-boost-operations-10027562-1.html*; Perna, Gabriel, "Moving Data Down I-44 and Making it Actionable," *Healthcare Informatics*, May 13, 2015, *www.healthcare-informatics.com/article/moving-data-down-i-44-and-making-it-actionable*; Henschen, Doug, "Hadoop's Growing Enterprise Presence Demonstrated by Three Innovative Use Cases," *ZDNet*, September 10, 2015, *www.zdnet.com/article/hadoop-growing-enterprise-presence-demonstrated-by-three-innovative-use-cases*; "Handling Electronic Health Records (EHR) Access Logs with Hadoop," StampedeCon, *http://stampedecon.com/sessions/handling-access-logs-with-hadoop*, accessed December 17, 2015.

Notes

1. Zettel, Jonathan, "Offshore Leaks Database Allows Public to Search Offshore Tax Haven Info," *CTV News*, June 15, 2013, *www.ctvnews.ca/business/offshore-leaks-database-allows-public-to-search-offshore-tax-haven-info-1.1327088*.

2. "FAQ on Lost/Stolen Devices," *CTIA Wireless Association*, *www.ctia.org/your-wireless-life/consumer-tips/how-to-deter-smartphone-thefts-and-protect-your-data/faq-on-lost-stolen-devices*, accessed September 4, 2015.

3. "Overview of the GTD," Global Terrorism Database, *www.start.umd.edu/gtd/about*, accessed September 4, 2015.

4. Hibbard, Katharine, "New Resource Available in Recovering Stolen Property," *Leads Online*, August 14, 2015, *www.leadsonline.com/main/news/2015-news-archive/new-resource-available-in-recovering-stolen-property.php*.

5. "I-Nexus Selects AppDynamics to Drive Continuous Performance Improvement,"AppDynamics, *www.appdynamics.com/case-study/inexus*, accessed September 6, 2015.

6. "IBM Healthcare Provider Data Model," IBM, *www-03.ibm.com/software/products/en/healthcare-provider-data-model*, accessed September 6, 2015.

7. "Complete Data Integration from Legacy Systems and Epic, In Half the Time,"Perficient, *www.perficient.com/About/Case-Studies/2014/UNC-Health-Care-System-Completes-Data-Integration-from-Legacy-Systems-and-Epic-In-Half-the-Time*, accessed September 6, 2015.

8. "Banco Popular," Trillium Software, *www.trilliumsoftware.com/uploadedFiles/Banco_CS_2010_screen.pdf*, accessed September 7, 2015.

9. Proffitt, Brian, "FoundationDB's NoSQL Breakthrough Challenges Relational Database Dominance," *Read Write*, March 8, 2013, *http://readwrite.com/2013/03/08/foundationdbs-nosql-breakthrough-challenges-relational-database-dominance#awesm=~oncfIkqw3jiMQJ*.

10. Golden, Matt, "New DOE Effort to Standardize the Energy Efficiency Data Dictionary," *EDF Blogs*, August 8, 2013, *http://blogs.edf.org/energyexchange/2013/08/08/new-doe-effort-to-standardize-the-energy-efficiency-data-dictionary*.

11. "Three Charged for Largest-Ever Bank Data Breach," *CBS News*, November 10, 2015, *www.cbsnews.com/news/three-charged-for-jpmorgan-data-breach-the-largest-ever*.

12. "About TinyCo,"TinyCo, *www.tinyco.com/about-us*, accessed September 8, 2015.

13. "AWS Case Study: TinyCo," Amazon Web Services, *http://aws.amazon.com/solutions/case-studies/tinyco*, accessed September 8, 2015.

14. Laney, Doug, "3D Data Management: Controlling Data Volume, Velocity, and Variety," META Group, February 6, 2001, *http://blogs.gartner.com/doug-laney/files/2012/01/ad949-3D-Data-Management-Controlling-Data-Volume-Velocity-and-Variety.pdf*.

15. Turner, Vernon, David Reinsel, John F. Gantz, and Stephen Minton, "The Digital Universe of Opportunities: Rich Data and the Increasing Value of the Internet of Things," EMC^2, April 2014, *www.emc.com/collateral/analyst-reports/idc-digital-universe-2014.pdf*.

16. "Seminars about Long-Term Thinking," The Long Now Foundation, *http://longnow.org/seminars/02013/mar/19/no-time-there-digital-universe-and-why-things-appear-be-speeding*, accessed November 8, 2013.

17. Rosenbaum, Steven, "Is It Possible to Analyze Digital Data If It's Growing Exponentially?" *Fast Company*, January 13, 2013, *www.fastcompany.com/3005128/it-possible-analyze-digital-data-if-its-growing-exponentially*.

18. Ibid.

19. Krantz, Matt, "Lack of Accuracy Can Wreak Havoc on Stock Market," *USA Today-The Enquirer*, September 12, 2015, p. 6B.

20. Harris, Derrick, "Why Apple, eBay, and Walmart Have Some of the Biggest Data Warehouses You've Ever Seen," GIGAOM, March 27, 2013, *https://gigaom.com*

/2013/03/27/why-apple-ebay-and-walmart-have-some -of-the-biggest-data-warehouses-youve-ever-seen/.

21. Davenport, Thomas H. and Jill Dyché, "Big Data in Big Companies," International Institute for Analytics, *www .sas.com/reg/gen/corp/2266746*, accessed April 1, 2015.

22. "Yormari Customer Success Stories: Orscheln Farm & Home,"Yomari, *www.yomari.com/clients/orscheln-farm -home-case-study.php*, accessed November 12, 2015.

23. Davenport, Thomas H. and Jill Dyché, "Big Data in Big Companies," International Institute for Analytics, *www. sas.com/reg/gen/corp/2266746*, accessed April 1, 2015.

24. "Customer Story:Criteo Boosts Performance, Scale of Digital Ad Platform with Couchbase Server,"Couchbase, *www.couchbase.com/case-studies/criteo.html*, accessed September 19, 2015.

25. Henschen, Doug, "Defending NSA Prism's Big Data Tools," *InformationWeek*, June 11, 2013, *www.informa tionweek.com/big-data/big-data-analytics/defending -nsa-prisms-big-data-tools/d/d-id/1110318?*.

26. "AWS Case Study: MLB Advanced Media," Amazon Web Services, *aws.amazon.com/solutions/case-studies /major-league-baseball-mlbam*, accessed November 12, 2015.

27. Dvorkin, Eugene, "Scalable Big Data Stream Processing with Storm and Groovy," November 4, 2014, *www.slide share.net/SpringCentral/storm-twtterwebmd*.

28. "Press Release: WebMD Medscape," Newswire, April 24, 2014, *www.multivu.com/mnr/7040259-meds cape-launches-new-medpulse-app-for-iphone-and -ipad*.

29. Brocke, Jan vom, "In-Memory Database Business Value," *Business Innovation*, July 25, 2013. *www.business2com munity.com/business-innovation/in-memory-database -business-value-0564636*.

30. "Oracle Press Release:KDDI Selects Oracle SuperCluster to Strengthen Authentication System for Mobile Core Net- work and Support Rapid Data Growth," Oracle, January 22, 2014, *www.oracle.com/us/corporate/press/2111600*.

CHAPTER 6

Networks and Cloud Computing

Did You Know?

- Auto insurers are testing usage-based insurance programs in which premiums are based on data gathered from a device installed in the insured auto. Instead of setting the premium based on traditional factors such as the driver's age and gender, it is based on miles driven per year, where and when they drive, and how safely they drive. The goal is to charge a premium that is commensurate with the risk associated with auto owner's driving habits.

- Sensors embedded in General Electric (GE) aircraft engines collect some 5,000 individual data points per second. This data is analyzed while the aircraft is in flight to adjust the way the aircraft performs, thereby reducing fuel consumption. The data is also used to plan predictive maintenance on the engines based on engine component wear and tear. In 2013, this technology helped GE earn $1 billion in incremental income by delivering performance improvements, less downtime, and more flying miles.

- It is estimated that in just one year, mobile operators lost $23 billion in revenue as teens shifted away from texting over cellular networks in favor of communicating with their friends over the Internet using instant messaging apps.[1]

Principles

- A network has many fundamental components, which—when carefully selected and effectively integrated—enable people to meet personal and organizational objectives.

- Together, the Internet and the World Wide Web provide a highly effective infrastructure for delivering and accessing information and services.

- Organizations are using the Internet of Things (IoT) to capture and analyze streams of sensor data to detect patterns and anomalies—not after the fact, but while they are occurring—in order to have a considerable impact on the event outcome.

- Cloud computing provides access to state-of-the-art technology at a fraction of the cost of ownership and without the lengthy delays that can occur when an organization tries to acquire its own resources.

Learning Objectives

- Identify and briefly describe three network topologies and four different network types, including the uses and limitations of each.

- Identify and briefly discuss several types of both guided and wireless communications.

- Identify several network hardware devices and define their functions.

- Briefly describe how the Internet and the Web work, including various methods for connecting to the Internet.

- Outline the process and tools used in developing Web content and applications.

- List and briefly describe several Internet and Web applications.

- Explain how intranets and extranets use Internet technologies, and describe how the two differ.

- Define what is meant by the Internet of Things (IoT), and explain how it works.

- Identify and briefly discuss several practical applications of the Internet of Things (IoT).

- Categorize and summarize several potential issues and barriers associated with the expansion of the Internet of Things (IoT).

- Discuss how cloud computing can increase the speed and reduce the costs of new product and service launches.

- Summarize three common problems organizations encounter in moving to the cloud.

- Discuss the pros and cons of private and hybrid cloud computing compared to public cloud computing.

Why Learn about Networks and Cloud Computing?

Today's decision makers need to access data wherever it resides. They must be able to establish fast, reliable connections to exchange messages, upload and download data and software, route business transactions to processors, connect to databases and network services, and send output to wherever it is needed. Regardless of your chosen major or future career field, you will make use of the communications capabilities provided by networks, including the Internet, intranets, and extranets. This is especially true for those whose role is connected to the supply chain and who rely heavily on networks to support cooperation and communication among workers in inbound logistics, warehouse and storage, production, finished product storage, outbound logistics, and, most importantly, with customers, suppliers, and shippers. Many supply chain organizations make use of the Internet to purchase raw materials, parts, and supplies at competitive prices. All members of the supply chain must work together effectively to increase the value perceived by the customer, so partners must communicate well. Other employees in human resources, finance, research and development, marketing, manufacturing, and sales positions must also use communications technology to communicate with people inside and outside the organization. To be a successful member of any organization, you must be able to take advantage of the capabilities that these technologies offer you. This chapter begins by discussing the importance of effective communications.

As you read this chapter, consider the following:

- How are organizations using networks to support their business strategies and achieve organizational objectives?
- What benefits do search engines, social networks, and other Internet services provide to make organizations successful?

In today's high-speed global business world, organizations need always-on, always-connected computing for traveling employees and for network connections to their key business partners and customers. Forward-thinking organizations strive to increase revenue, reduce time to market, and enable collaboration with their suppliers, customers, and business partners by using networks. Here are just a few examples of organizations using networks to move ahead:

- Many retail organizations are launching their own mobile payment system, with the hopes of reducing payments to financial services organizations while also increasing customer loyalty. Some of these new systems include Android Pay, Apple Pay, Chase Pay, PayPal, Paydiant, Samsung Pay, Urban Airship, and Walmart Pay.[2]

- Networks make it possible for you to access a wealth of educational material and earn certifications or an online degree. A wide range of courses are available online from such leading educational institutions as Cornell, Carnegie Mellon, Harvard, MIT, and Yale. Many educational organizations such as Coursera, ed2Go, and Kahn Academy offer continuing education, certification programs, and professional development courses. Hundreds of schools such as DeVry, Kaplan University, University of Phoenix, and Strayer University enable students to earn online degrees.

- Levi Stadium, home of the San Francisco 49ers, is deploying new wireless technology to make it easier for fans to use a special stadium navigation app on their smartphones and other devices. With the app, fans can watch instant replays and order food directly from their mobile devices.[3]

- Telemedicine provides remote access to a physician via a network (typically via a phone or videoconference) to address a healthcare issue. Its use has become well established in rural areas for specialty consultations and even many primary care practices like pediatrics. There are currently about 200 telemedicine networks, with 3,500 service sites in the United States alone.[4]

Advances in network technology allow us to communicate in real time with customers, clients, business partners, and coworkers almost anywhere in the world. Networks also reduce the amount of time required to transmit information necessary for driving and concluding business transactions.

Network Fundamentals

computer network: The communications media, devices, and software connecting two or more computer systems or devices.

communications medium: Any material substance that carries an electronic signal to support communications between a sending and a receiving device.

A **computer network** consists of communications media, devices, and software connecting two or more computer systems or devices. **Communications media** are any material substance that carries an electronic signal to support communications between a sending and a receiving device. The computers and devices on the networks are also sometimes called network nodes. Organizations can use networks to share hardware, programs, and databases and to transmit and receive information, allowing for improved organizational effectiveness and efficiency. Networks enable geographically separated workgroups to share documents and opinions, which fosters teamwork, innovative ideas, and new business strategies. Effective use of networks can help a company grow into an agile, powerful, and creative organization, giving it a long-term competitive advantage.

Network Topology

network topology: The shape or structure of a network, including the arrangement of the communication links and hardware devices on the network.

star network: A network in which all network devices connect to one another through a single central device called the hub node.

bus network: A network in which all network devices are connected to a common backbone that serves as a shared communications medium.

Network topology is the shape or structure of a network, including the arrangement of the communication links and hardware devices on the network. The transmission rates, distances between devices, signal types, and physical interconnection may differ between networks, but they may all have the same topology. The three most common network topologies in use today are the star, bus, and mesh.

In a **star network**, all network devices connect to one another through a single central device called the hub node. See Figure 6.1. Many home networks employ the star topology. A failure in any link of the star network will isolate only the device connected to that link. However, should the hub fail, all devices on the entire network will be unable to communicate.

In a **bus network**, all network devices are connected to a common backbone that serves as a shared communications medium. See Figure 6.2. To communicate with any other device on the network, a device sends a broadcast message onto the communications medium. All devices on the network can "see" the message, but only the intended recipient actually accepts and processes the message.

FIGURE 6.1

Star network

In a star network, all network devices connect to one another through a single central hub node.

Vladru/Shutterstock.com

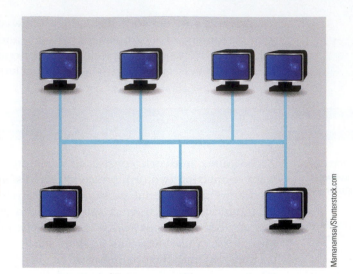

Mamanamsai/Shutterstock.com

FIGURE **6.2**
Bus network

In a bus network, all network devices are connected to a common backbone that serves as a shared communications medium.

mesh network: A network that uses multiple access points to link a series of devices that speak to each other to form a network connection across a large area.

Mesh networks use multiple access points to link a series of devices that speak to each other to form a network connection across a large area. See Figure 6.3. Communications are routed among network nodes by allowing for continuous connections and by bypassing blocked paths by "hopping" from node to node until a connection can be established. Mesh networks are very robust: if one node fails, all the other nodes can still communicate with each other, directly or through one or more intermediate nodes.

Saudi Telecom Company (STC) is the largest communications services provider in the Middle East and North Africa. STC recently deployed a mesh network that ensures network survivability even in the case of multiple outages with restoration of service within 50 milliseconds. The mesh network offers STC customers faster transmission speeds and improved network reliability.[5]

Network Types

A network can be classified as personal area, local area, metropolitan, or wide area network depending on the physical distance between the nodes on the network and the communications and services it provides.

FIGURE **6.3**
Mesh network

Mesh networks use multiple access points to link a series of devices that speak to each other to form a network connection across a large area.

Vladru/Shutterstock.com

Personal Area Networks

personal area network (PAN): A network that supports the interconnection of information technology devices close to one person.

A **personal area network (PAN)** is a wireless network that connects information technology devices close to one person. With a PAN, you can connect a laptop, digital camera, and portable printer without cables. You can download digital image data from the camera to the laptop and then print it on a high-quality printer—all wirelessly. A PAN could also be used to enable data captured by sensors placed on your body to be transmitted to your smartphone as input to applications that can serve as calorie trackers, heart monitors, glucose monitors, and pedometers.

Local Area Networks

local area network (LAN): A network that connects computer systems and devices within a small area, such as an office, home, or several floors in a building.

A network that connects computer systems and devices within a small area, such as an office, home, or several floors in a building is a **local area network (LAN)**. Typically, LANs are wired into office buildings and factories, as shown in Figure 6.4. Although LANs often use unshielded twisted-pair copper wire, other media—including fiber-optic cable—is also popular. Increasingly, LANs use some form of wireless communications. You can build LANs to connect personal computers, laptop computers, or powerful mainframe computers.

A basic type of LAN is a simple peer-to-peer network that a small business might use to share files and hardware devices, such as printers. In a peer-to-peer network, you set up each computer as an independent computer, but you let other computers access specific files on its hard drive or share its printer. These types of networks have no server. Instead, each computer is connected to the next machine. Examples of peer-to-peer networks include ANts, BitTorrent, StealthNet, Tixati, and Windows 10 Homegroup. Performance of the computers on a peer-to-peer network is usually slower because one computer is actually sharing the resources of another computer.

Increasingly, home and small business networks are being set up to connect computers, printers, scanners, and other devices. A person working on one computer on a home network, for example, can use data and programs stored on another computer's hard disk. In addition, several computers on the network can share a single printer.

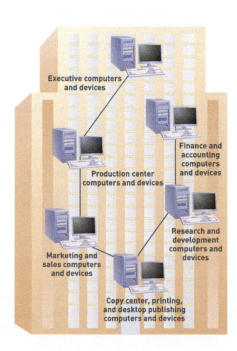

FIGURE 6.4

Typical LAN

All network users within an office building can connect to each other's devices for rapid communication. For instance, a user in research and development could send a document from her computer to be printed at a printer located in the desktop publishing center. Most computer labs employ a LAN to enable the users to share the use of high-speed and/or color printers and plotters as well as to download software applications and save files.

Executive computers and devices

Finance and accounting computers and devices

Production center computers and devices

Research and development computers and devices

Marketing and sales computers and devices

Copy center, printing, and desktop publishing computers and devices

Metropolitan Area Networks

A metropolitan area network (MAN) is a network that connects users and their computers in a geographical area that spans a campus or city. A MAN might redefine the many networks within a city into a single larger network or connect several LANs into a single campus MAN. Often, the MAN is owned either by a consortium of users or by a single network provider who sells the service to users. PIONIER is a Polish national research and education network created to provide high-speed Internet access and to conduct network-based research. The network connects 21 MANs and 5 high-performance computing centers using 6,467 km of fiber optic transmission media.[6]

Wide Area Networks

A wide area network (WAN) is a network that connects large geographic regions. A WAN might be privately owned or rented and includes public (shared-users) networks. When you make a long-distance phone call or access the Internet, you are using a WAN. WANs usually consist of computer equipment owned by the user, together with data communications equipment and network links provided by various carriers and service providers.

WANs often provide communications across national borders, which involves national and international laws regulating the electronic flow of data across international boundaries, often called transborder data flow. Some countries have strict laws limiting the use of networks and databases, making normal business transactions such as payroll processing costly, slow, or extremely difficult.

Client/Server Systems

In client/server architecture, multiple computer platforms are dedicated to special functions, such as database management, printing, communications, and program execution. These platforms are called servers. Each server is accessible by all computers on the network. Servers can be computers of all sizes; they store both application programs and data files and are equipped with operating system software to manage the activities of the network. The server distributes programs and data to the other computers (clients) on the network as they request them. An application server holds the programs and data files for a particular application, such as an inventory database. The client or the server might do the actual data processing.

A client is any computer (often a user's personal computer) that sends messages requesting services from the servers on the network. A client can converse with many servers concurrently. Consider the example of a user at a personal computer who initiates a request to extract data that resides in a database somewhere on the network. A data request server intercepts the request and determines on which database server the data resides. The server then formats the user's request into a message that the database server will understand. When it receives the message, the database server extracts and formats the requested data and sends the results to the client. The database server sends only the data that satisfies a specific query—not the entire file. When the downloaded data is on the user's machine, it can then be analyzed, manipulated, formatted, and displayed by a program that runs on the user's personal computer.

Channel Bandwidth

Network professionals consider the capacity of the communications path or channel when they recommend transmission media for a network. Channel bandwidth refers to the rate at which data is exchanged, usually measured in bits per second (bps)—the broader the bandwidth, the more information can

broadband communications:
High-speed Internet access that is always on and that is faster than traditional dial-up access.

be exchanged at one time. In the context of Internet access, the term **broadband communications** refers to any high-speed Internet access that is always on and that is faster than traditional dial-up access. Most organizations need high bandwidth to accommodate the transaction volume and transmission speed required to carry out their daily functions.

Communications Media

The communications media selected for a network depends on the amount of information to be exchanged, the speed at which data must be exchanged, the level of concern about data privacy, whether the users are stationary or mobile, and a variety of business requirements. Transmission media can be divided into two broad categories guided (also called wired) transmission media, in which communications signals are guided along a solid medium, and wireless, in which the communications signal is broadcast over airwaves as a form of electromagnetic radiation.

Guided Transmission Media Types

There are many different guided transmission media types. Table 6.1 summarizes the guided media types by physical media form. The three most common guided transmission media types are shown in Figure 6.5.

10-Gigabit Ethernet is a standard for transmitting data at the speed of 10 billion bps for limited distances over high-quality twisted-pair wire. The 10-Gigabit Ethernet cable can be used for the high-speed links that connect groups of computers or to move data stored in large databases on large computers to stand-alone storage devices.

Chi-X Japan provides investors with an alternative venue for trading in Tokyo-listed stocks. Its goal is to attract new international investors, in turn,

TABLE 6.1 Guided transmission media types

Media Form	Description	Advantages	Disadvantages
Twisted-pair wire	Twisted pairs of copper wire, shielded or unshielded; used for telephone service	Widely available	Limitations on transmission speed and distance
Coaxial cable	Inner conductor wire surrounded by insulation	Cleaner and faster data transmission than twisted-pair wire	More expensive than twisted-pair wire
Fiber-optic cable	Many extremely thin strands of glass bound together in a sheathing; uses light beams to transmit signals	Diameter of cable is much smaller than coaxial cable; less distortion of signal; capable of high transmission rates	Expensive to purchase and install

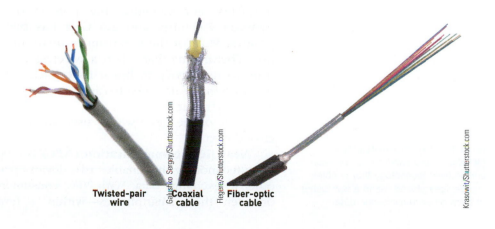

FIGURE 6.5

Types of guided transmission media

Common guided transmission media include twisted-pair wire, coaxial cable, and fiber-optic cable.

Twisted-pair wire   Coaxial cable   Fiber-optic cable

Galushko Sergey/Shutterstock.com
Flegere/Shutterstock.com
Krasowit/Shutterstock.com

increasing overall Japanese market volumes, reducing transaction costs, and improving investment performance.[7] The firm implemented 10 Gbps Ethernet network adapters to upgrade its network and ensure customers minimal transaction processing delays.

Wireless Technologies

Wireless communications coupled with the Internet are revolutionizing how and where we gather and share information, collaborate in teams, listen to music or watch video, and stay in touch with our families and coworkers while on the road. With wireless capability, a coffee shop can become our living room and the bleachers at a ballpark can become our office. The many advantages and freedom provided by wireless communications are causing many organizations to consider moving to an all-wireless environment.

wireless communication: The transfer of information between two or more points that are not connected by an electrical conductor.

Wireless communication is the transfer of information between two or more points that are not connected by an electrical conductor. All wireless communications signals are sent within a range of frequencies of the electromagnetic spectrum that represents the entire range of light that exists from long waves to gamma rays as shown in Figure 6.6.

The propagation of light is similar to waves crossing an ocean. Like any other wave, light has two fundamental properties that describe it. One is its frequency, measured in hertz (Hz), which counts the number of waves that pass by a stationary point in one second. The second fundamental property is wavelength, which is the distance from the peak of one wave to the peak of the next. These two attributes are inversely related so the higher the frequency, the shorter the wavelength.

All wireless communication devices operate in a similar way. A transmitter generates a signal, which contains encoded voice, video, or data at a specific frequency, that is broadcast into the environment by an antenna. This signal spreads out in the environment, with only a very small portion being captured by the antenna of the receiving device, which then decodes the information. Depending on the distance involved, the frequency of the transmitted signal, and other conditions, the received signal can be incredibly weak, perhaps one trillionth of the original signal strength.

The signals used in wireless networks are broadcast in one of three frequency ranges: microwave, radio, and infrared, as shown in Table 6.2.

Because there are so many competing uses for wireless communication, strict rules are necessary to prevent one type of transmission from interfering with the next. And because the spectrum is limited—there are only so many frequency bands—governments must oversee appropriate licensing of this valuable resource to facilitate use in all bands. In the United States, the Federal Communications Commission (FCC) decides which frequencies of the communications spectrum can be used for which purposes. For example, the portion of the electromagnetic spectrum between 700 MHz and 2.6 GHz has been allocated for use by mobile phones. Most of the spectrum in this range has already been allocated for use. This means that when a wireless company wants to add more spectrum to its service to boost its capacity, it may have problems obtaining the necessary licenses because other companies are already using the available frequencies.

Some of the more widely used wireless communications options are discussed next.

near field communication (NFC): A very short-range wireless connectivity technology that enables two devices placed within a few inches of each other to exchange data.

Near field communication (NFC) is a very short-range wireless connectivity technology that enables two devices placed within a few inches of each other to exchange data. With NFC, consumers can swipe their credit cards—or even their smartphones—within a few inches of NFC point-of-sale

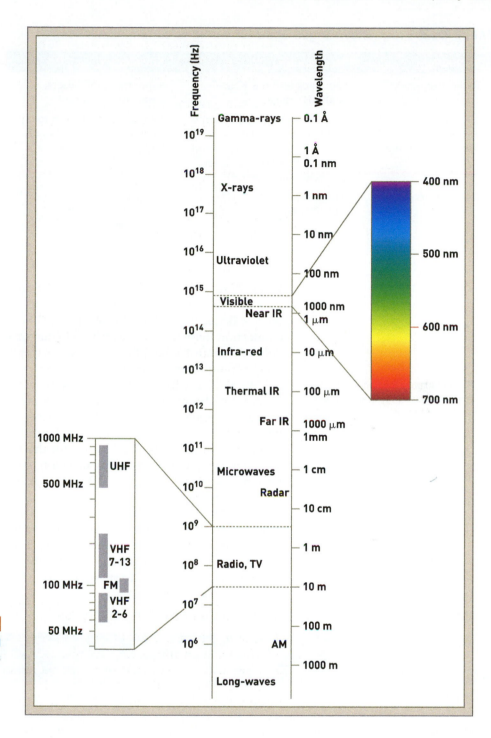

The electromagnetic spectrum
The range of all possible frequencies
of electromagnetic radiation.

Source: *https//upload.wikimedia.org
/wikipedia/commons/2/25/Electro
magnetic-Spectrum.svg*

terminals to pay for purchases. Apple Pay, the mobile payment and digital wallet service that lets users make payments using an iPhone, an iPad, or an Apple Watch–compatible device, uses NFC to communicate between the user's device and the point-of-sale terminal.

Many retailers—including Target, Macys, and Walgreens—already have NFC-based contactless pay terminals in place. Shoppers in these stores can also use their smartphones and NFC to gain access to loyalty programs to earn points, view marketing information, and share content and interact with brands via social media.

Bluetooth is a wireless communications specification that describes how cell phones, computers, printers, and other electronic devices can be interconnected over distances of 10 to 30 feet at a transmission rate of about 2 Mbps.

Bluetooth: A wireless communications specification that describes how cell phones, computers, faxes, printers, and other electronic devices can be interconnected over distances of 10 to 30 feet at a rate of about 2 Mbps.

TABLE 6.2 Frequency ranges used for wireless communications

Technology	Description	Advantages	Disadvantages
Radio frequency range	Operates in the 3 KHz–300 MHz range	Supports mobile users; costs are dropping	Signal is highly susceptible to interception
Microwave—terrestrial and satellite frequency range	High-frequency radio signal (300 MHz–300 GHz) sent through the atmosphere and space (often involves communications satellites)	Avoids cost and effort to lay cable or wires; capable of high-speed transmission	Must have unobstructed line of sight between sender and receiver; signal is highly susceptible to interception
Infrared frequency range	Signals in the 300 GHz–400 THz frequency range	Lets you move, remove, and install devices without expensive wiring	Must have unobstructed line of sight between sender and receiver; transmission is effective only for short distances

Wi-Fi: A medium-range wireless communications technology brand owned by the Wi-Fi Alliance.

Using Bluetooth technology, users of multifunctional devices can synchronize data on their device with information stored in a desktop computer, send or receive faxes, and print. The Bluetooth G-Shock watch enables you to make a connection between your watch and your smartphone. With a G-shock watch, you can control your phone's music player from the watch and the watch's timekeeping functions from your phone.

Wi-Fi is a wireless network brand owned by the Wi-Fi Alliance, which consists of about 300 technology companies, including AT&T, Dell, Microsoft, Nokia, and Qualcomm. The alliance exists to improve the interoperability of wireless local area network products based on the IEEE 802.11 series of communications standards. IEEE stands for the Institute of Electrical and Electronics Engineers, a nonprofit organization and one of the leading standards-setting organizations. Table 6.3 summarizes several variations of the IEEE 802.11 standard.

In a Wi-Fi wireless network, the user's computer, smartphone, or other mobile device has a wireless adapter that translates data into a radio signal and transmits it using an antenna. A wireless access point, which consists of a transmitter with an antenna, receives the signal and decodes it. The access point then sends the information to the Internet over a wired connection.

TABLE 6.3 IEEE 802.11 wireless local area networking standards

Wireless Networking Protocol	Maximum Data Rate per Data Stream	Comments
IEEE 802.11a	54 Mbps	Transmits at 5 GHz, which means it is incompatible with 802.11b and 802.11g
IEEE 802.11b	11 Mbps	First widely accepted wireless network standard and transmits at 2.4 GHz; equipment using this protocol may occasionally suffer from interference from microwave ovens, cordless telephones, and Bluetooth devices
IEEE 802.11g	54 Mbps	Equipment using this protocol transmits at 2.4 GHz and may occasionally suffer from interference from microwave ovens, cordless telephones, and Bluetooth devices
IEEE 802.11n	300 Mbps	Employs multiple input, multiple output (MIMO) technology, which allows multiple data streams to be transmitted over the same channel using the same bandwidth that is used for only a single data stream in 802.11a/b/g
IEEE 802.11ac	400 Mbps–1.3 Gbps	An 802.11 standard that provides higher data transmission speeds and more stable connections; it can transmit at either 2.4 GHz or 5 GHz

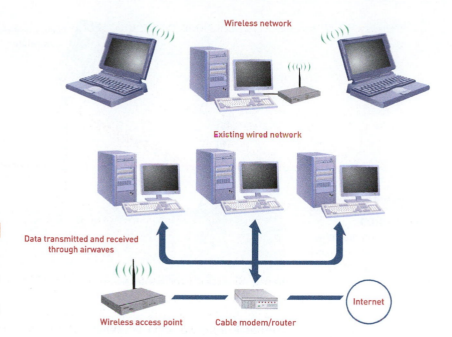

Wireless network

Existing wired network

Data transmitted and received through airwaves

Wireless access point

Cable modem/router

Internet

FIGURE 6.7

Wi-Fi network

In a Wi-Fi network, the user's computer, smartphone, or cell phone has a wireless adapter that translates data into a radio signal and transmits it using an antenna.

See Figure 6.7. When receiving data, the wireless access point takes the information from the Internet, translates it into a radio signal, and sends it to the device's wireless adapter. These devices typically come with built-in wireless transmitters and software to enable them to alert the user to the existence of a Wi-Fi network. The area covered by one or more interconnected wireless access points is called a "hot spot." Wi-Fi has proven so popular that hot spots are popping up in places such as airports, coffee shops, college campuses, libraries, and restaurants. The availability of free Wi-Fi within a hotel's premises has become very popular with business travelers. Meanwhile, hundreds of cities in the United States have implemented municipal Wi-Fi networks for use by meter readers and other municipal workers and to provide Internet access to their citizens and visitors.

Microwave Transmission

Microwave is a high-frequency (300 MHz to 300 GHz) signal sent through the air. Terrestrial (Earth-bound) microwaves are transmitted by line-of-sight devices, so the line of sight between the transmitter and receiver must be unobstructed. Typically, microwave stations are placed in a series—one station receives a signal, amplifies it, and retransmits it to the next microwave transmission tower. Such stations can be located roughly 30 miles apart before the curvature of the Earth makes it impossible for the towers to "see" one another. Because they are line-of-sight transmission devices, microwave dishes are frequently placed in relatively high locations, such as mountains, towers, or tall buildings.

A communications satellite also operates in the microwave frequency range. See Figure 6.8. The satellite receives the signal from the Earth station, amplifies the relatively weak signal, and then rebroadcasts it at a different frequency. The advantage of satellite communications is that satellites can receive and broadcast over large geographic regions. Problems such as the curvature of the Earth, mountains, and other structures that block the line-of-sight microwave transmission make satellites an attractive alternative. Geostationary, low earth orbit, and small mobile satellite stations are the most common forms of satellite communications.

A geostationary satellite orbits the Earth directly over the equator, approximately 22,300 miles above the Earth, so that it appears stationary. The U.S.

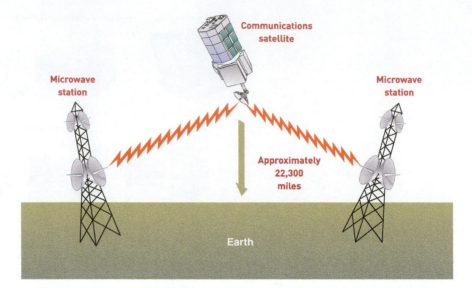

FIGURE **6.8**
Satellite transmission
Communications satellites are relay stations that receive signals from one Earth station and rebroadcast them to another.

National Weather Service relies on the Geostationary Operational Environmental Satellite program for weather imagery and quantitative data to support weather forecasting, severe storm tracking, and meteorological research.

A low earth orbit (LEO) satellite system employs many satellites, each in an orbit at an altitude of less than 1,000 miles. The satellites are spaced so that, from any point on the Earth at any time, at least one satellite is in a line of sight. Iridium Communications provides a global communications network that spans the entire Earth, using 66 satellites in a near-polar orbit at an altitude of 485 miles. Calls are routed among the satellites to create a reliable connection between call participants that cannot be disrupted by natural disasters such as earthquakes, tsunamis, or hurricanes that may knock out ground-based wireless towers and wire- or cable-based networks.[8] Every day, thousands of vessels and tankers traveling the world's seas and oceans use Iridium's network to establish reliable global communications to optimize their daily activities.

4G Wireless Communications

Wireless communications has evolved through four generations of technology and services. The first generation (1G) of wireless communications standards originated in the 1980s and was based on analog communications. The second-generation (2G) networks were fully digital, superseding 1G networks in the early 1990s. With 2G networks, phone conversations were encrypted, mobile phone usage was expanded, and short message services (SMS)—or texting—was introduced. 3G wireless communications supports wireless voice and broadband speed data communications in a mobile environment at speeds of 2 to 4 Mbps. Additional capabilities include mobile video, mobile e-commerce, location-based services, mobile gaming, and the downloading and playing of music.

4G broadband mobile wireless delivers more advanced versions of enhanced multimedia, smooth streaming video, universal access, and portability across all types of devices; eventually 4G will also make possible worldwide roaming. 4G can deliver 3 to 20 times the speed of 3G networks for mobile devices such as smartphones, tablets, and laptops.

Each of the four major U.S. wireless network operators (AT&T, Verizon, Sprint, and T-Mobile) is rapidly expanding its 4G networks based on the Long Term Evolution (LTE) standard. **Long Term Evolution (LTE)** is a standard for wireless communications for mobile phones based on packet switching, which is an entirely different approach from the circuit-switching approach employed

Long Term Evolution (LTE): A standard for wireless communications for mobile phones based on packet switching.

in 3G communications networks. To convert to the LTE standard, carriers must reengineer their voice call networks.

The biggest benefit of LTE is how quickly a mobile device can connect to the Internet and how much data it can download or upload in a given amount of time. LTE makes it reasonable to stream video to your phone, using services such as Amazon Prime Instant Video, Hulu Plus, Netflix, or YouTube. It also speeds up Web browsing, with most pages loading in seconds. LTE enables video calling using services such as Skype or Google Hangouts. LTE's faster speed also makes sharing photos and videos from your phone quick and easy.

5G Wireless Communications

A new mobile communications generation has come on the scene about every 10 years since the first 1G system. 5G is a term used to identify the next major phase of mobile communications standards beyond 4G. No 5G mobile standard has been formally defined yet, but 5G will bring with it higher data transmission rates, lower power consumption, higher connect reliability with fewer dropped calls, increased geographic coverage, and lower infrastructure costs. If 5G networks meet the goal of a 50 times faster data rate than the most advanced Wi-Fi networks today, they will be able to stream a two-hour movie in less than three seconds. Verizon plans to start field trials of 5G technology by late 2016, with some level of commercial deployment to start by 2017—far sooner than the 2020 time frame that many industry observers anticipate for the initial adoption of 5G technology.[9]

Communications Hardware

Networks require various communications hardware devices to operate, including modems, fax modems, multiplexers, private branch exchanges, front-end processors, switches, bridges, routers, and gateways. These devices are summarized in Table 6.4.

Communications Software

network operating system (NOS): Systems software that controls the computer systems and devices on a network and allows them to communicate with each other.

A **network operating system (NOS)** is systems software that controls the computer systems and devices on a network and allows them to communicate

TABLE 6.4 Common communications devices

Device	Function
Modem	Translates data from a digital form (as it is stored in the computer) into an analog signal that can be transmitted over ordinary telephone lines
Fax modem	Combines a fax with a modem; facsimile devices, commonly called fax devices, allow businesses to transmit text, graphs, photographs, and other digital files via standard telephone lines
Multiplexer	Allows several communications signals to be transmitted over a single communications medium at the same time, thus saving expensive long-distance communications costs
PBX (private branch exchange)	Manages both voice and data transfer within a building and to outside lines; PBXs can be used to connect hundreds of internal phone lines to a few outside phone company lines
Front-end processor	Manages communications to and from a computer system serving many people
Switch	Uses the physical device address in each incoming message on the network to determine which output port it should forward the message to reach another device on the same network
Bridge	Connects one LAN to another LAN where both LANs use the same communications protocol
Router	Forwards data packets across two or more distinct networks toward their destinations through a process known as routing; often, an Internet service provider (ISP) installs a router in a subscriber's home that connects the ISP's network to the network within the home
Gateway	Serves as an entrance to another network, such as the Internet

with each other. The NOS performs similar functions for the network as operating system software does for a computer, such as memory and task management and coordination of hardware. When network equipment (such as printers, plotters, and disk drives) is required, the NOS makes sure that these resources are used correctly. Linux (used on workstations), OS X (used on Apple MACs), UNIX (used on servers), and Windows Server (used on workstations and servers) are common network operating systems.

Because companies use networks to communicate with customers, business partners, and employees, network outages or slow performance can mean a loss of business. Network management includes a wide range of technologies and processes that monitor the network and help identify and address problems before they can create a serious impact.

Software tools and utilities are available for managing networks. With **network-management software**, a manager on a networked personal computer can monitor the use of individual computers and shared hardware (such as printers), scan for viruses, and ensure compliance with software licenses. Network-management software also simplifies the process of updating files and programs on computers on the network—a manager can make changes through a communications server instead of having to visit each individual computer. In addition, network-management software protects software from being copied, modified, or downloaded illegally. It can also locate communications errors and potential network problems. Some of the many benefits of network-management software include fewer hours spent on routine tasks (such as installing new software), faster response to problems, and greater overall network control.

Banks use a special form of network-management software to monitor the performance of their automated teller machines (ATMs). Status messages can be sent over the network to a central monitoring location to inform support people about situations such as low cash or receipt paper levels, card reader problems, and printer paper jams. Once a status message is received, a service provider or branch location employee can be dispatched to fix the ATM problem.

Today, most IS organizations use network-management software to ensure that their network remains up and running and that every network component and application is performing acceptably. The software enables IS staff to identify and resolve fault and performance issues before they affect end users. The latest network-management technology even incorporates automatic fixes: The network-management system identifies a problem, notifies the IS manager, and automatically corrects the problem before anyone outside the IS department notices it.

The Covell Group is a small IT consulting group in San Diego that provides server and Web site monitoring for small- and medium-sized companies. The firm uses network-monitoring software to watch sensors and remote probes that track CPU, disk space, and Windows services. Constant monitoring enables the firm to detect if a communications line is down or if there is a power failure overnight so that everything is up and ready by the start of the next work day.[10]

Mobile device management (MDM) software manages and troubleshoots mobile devices remotely, pushing out applications, data, patches, and settings. With the software, a central control group can maintain group policies for security, control system settings, ensure malware protection is in place for mobile devices used across the network, and make it mandatory to use passwords to access the network. In addition to smartphones and tablets, laptops and desktops are sometimes supported using MDM software as mobile device management becomes more about basic device management and less about a specific mobile platform.

network-management software: Software that enables a manager on a networked desktop to monitor the use of individual computers and shared hardware (such as printers), scan for viruses, and ensure compliance with software licenses.

mobile device management (MDM) software: Software that manages and troubleshoots mobile devices remotely, pushing out applications, data, patches, and settings while enforcing group policies for security.

Software-Defined Networking (SDN)

A typical network is comprised of hundreds or thousands of network devices that perform such tasks as routing and switching of data through the network, providing network access and control, and enabling access to a variety of applications and services. In today's current network environment, each network device must be configured individually, usually via manual keyboard input. For a network of any size, this becomes a labor-intensive and error-prone effort, making it difficult to change the network so it can meet the changing needs of the organization. **Software-defined networking (SDN)** is an emerging approach to networking that allows network administrators to manage a network via a controller that does not require physical access to all the network devices. This approach automates tasks such as configuration and policy management and enables the network to dynamically respond to application requirements. As a result, new applications can be made available sooner, the risk of human error (a major contributor to network downtime) is reduced, and overall network support and operations costs are reduced.

Google is implementing Andromeda, the underlying software-defined networking architecture that will enable Google's cloud computing services to scale better, more cheaply and more quickly. With software-defined networking, even though many customers are sharing the same network, they can be configured and managed independently with their own address management, firewalls, and access control lists. Google competitors in cloud services like Microsoft and Amazon also employ software-defined networks.[11]

software-defined networking (SDN): An emerging approach to networking that allows network administrators to have programmable central control of the network via a controller without requiring physical access to all the network devices.

Critical Thinking Exercise

Network-Management Software for a University

The Ohio State University has over 58,000 undergraduate students spread across several major campuses and research centers located around Ohio. Its information system administrators are considering the use of network-management software and are evaluating the use of mobile device management software from various vendors.

Review Questions

1. What features should the administrators look for in choosing its network-management software?
2. What specific benefits would be gained by installing network-management software?

Critical Thinking Questions

1. Should a goal of a mobile device management software implementation be to reduce the number of information systems support staff dedicated to support the university's students, administrators, and faculty? Or should any productivity gains be applied to providing new services and superior support?
2. Identify common issues that students may have with the use of their devices that could be addressed through the use of mobile device management software.

The Internet and World Wide Web

The Internet has grown rapidly (see Figure 6.9) and is truly international in scope, with users on every continent—including Antarctica. Although the United States has high Internet penetration among its population, it does not constitute the majority of people online. As of November 2015, citizens of Asian countries make up about 48 percent, Europeans about 18 percent,

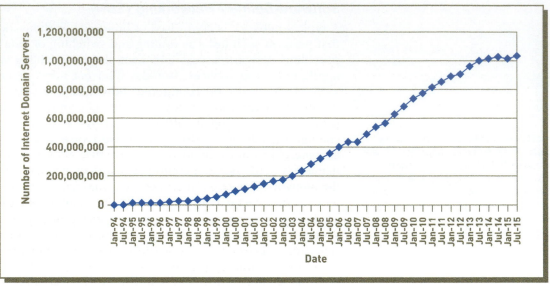

FIGURE **6.9**
Internet growth: Number of Internet hosts
The number of worldwide Internet users is expected to continue growing.
Source: Data from "ISC Domain Survey," *https://www.isc.org/network/survey/.*

Latin America/Caribbean about 10 percent, and North Americans about 9 percent of all Internet users. China is the country with the most Internet users, with 674 million—which is more users than the next two countries combined (India 354 million and United States 280 million).[12] Being connected to the Internet provides global economic opportunity to individuals, businesses, and countries.

The Internet and social media Web sites have emerged as important new channels for learning about world events, protesting the actions of organizations and governments, and urging others to support one's favorite causes or candidates. For example, some believe that Barack Obama's effective use of the Internet and social media provided him with a distinct advantage over his opponents in the presidential elections of 2008 and 2012.[13] In another example, Syrian rebels used the Internet to communicate about events within the country and to provide a useful link to others around the world.[14]

On the other hand, Internet censorship, the control or suppression of the publishing or accessing of information on the Internet, is a growing problem. For example, in May 2015, the Chinese-language version of Wikipedia was blocked in China.[15] The organizations Human Rights Watch and Amnesty International allege that the Saudi Arabian government uses malicious spyware to target activists and it hunts down, silences, and flogs bloggers who criticize the government.[16] In Hungary the government employs fines, licensing, and taxes to coerce critical media, and it directs state advertising to friendly outlets.[17]

The ancestor of the Internet was the ARPANET, a project started by the U.S. Department of Defense (DoD) in 1969. The ARPANET was both an experiment in reliable networking and a means to link DoD and military research contractors, including many universities doing military-funded research. (ARPA stands for the Advanced Research Projects Agency, the branch of the DoD in charge of awarding grant money. The agency is now known as DARPA—the added *D* is for Defense.) The ARPANET was highly successful, and every university in the country wanted to use it. This wildfire growth made it difficult to manage the ARPANET, particularly the rapidly growing number of university sites. So, the ARPANET was broken into two networks: MILNET, which included all military sites, and a new, smaller ARPANET, which included all the nonmilitary sites. The two networks remained connected, however, through use of the **Internet protocol (IP)**, which enables traffic to be routed from one network to another as needed. All the networks connected to the Internet use IP, so they all can exchange messages.

Internet Protocol (IP): A communication standard that enables computers to route communications traffic from one network to another as needed.

How the Internet Works

In the early days of the Internet, the major communications companies around the world agreed to connect their networks so that users on all the networks could share information over the Internet. These large communications companies, called network service providers (NSPs), include Verizon, Sprint, British Telecom, and AT&T. The cables, routers, switching stations, communication towers, and satellites that make up these networks are the hardware over which Internet traffic flows. The combined hardware of these and other NSPs—the fiber-optic cables that span the globe over land and under sea—make up the **Internet backbone**.

Internet backbone: One of the Internet's high-speed, long-distance communications links.

The Internet transmits data from one computer (called a host) to another. See Figure 6.10. If the receiving computer is on a network to which the first computer is directly connected, it can send the message directly. If the receiving and sending computers are not directly connected to the same network, the sending computer relays the message to another computer that can forward it. The message is typically sent through one or more routers to reach its destination. It is not unusual for a message to pass through several routers on its way from one part of the Internet to another.

The various communications networks that are linked to form the Internet work much the same way—they pass data around in chunks called packets, each of which carries the addresses of its sender and receiver along with other technical information. The set of rules used to pass packets from one host to another is the IP protocol. Many other communications protocols are used in connection with IP. The best known is the Transmission Control Protocol (TCP). Many people use "TCP/IP" as an abbreviation for the combination of TCP and IP used by most Internet applications. After a network following these standards links to the Internet's backbone, it becomes part of the worldwide Internet community.

Each computer on the Internet has an assigned address, called its IP address, that identifies it on the Internet. An **IP address** is a 64-bit number that identifies a computer on the Internet. The 64-bit number is typically

IP address: A 64-bit number that identifies a computer on the Internet.

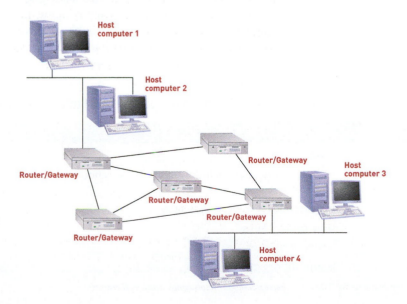

FIGURE **6.10**

Routing messages over the Internet

Data is transmitted from one host computer to another on the Internet.

divided into four bytes and translated to decimal; for example, 69.32.133.79. The Internet is migrating to Internet Protocol version 6 (IPv6), which uses 128-bit addresses to provide for many more devices; however, this change is expected to take years.

Because people prefer to work with words rather than numbers, a system called the Domain Name System (DNS) was created. Domain names such as *www.cengage.com* are mapped to IP addresses such as 69.32.133.79 using the DNS. To make room for more Web addresses, efforts are underway to increase the number of available domain names.

Uniform Resource Locator (URL): A Web address that specifies the exact location of a Web page using letters and words that map to an IP address and a location on the host.

A **Uniform Resource Locator (URL)** is a Web address that specifies the exact location of a Web page using letters and words that map to an IP address and a location on the host. The URL gives those who provide information over the Internet a standard way to designate where Internet resources such as servers and documents are located. Consider the URL for Cengage Learning, *http://www.cengage.com/us/*.

The "http" specifies the access method and tells your software to access a file using the Hypertext Transport Protocol. This is the primary method for interacting with the Internet. In many cases, you don't need to include http:// in a URL because it is the default protocol. The "www" part of the address signifies that the address is associated with the World Wide Web service. The URL *www.cengage.com* is the domain name that identifies the Internet host site. The part of the address following the domain name—/us—specifies an exact location on the host site.

Domain names must adhere to strict rules. They always have at least two parts, with each part separated by a dot (period). For some Internet addresses, the far right part of the domain name is the country code, such as au for Australia, ca for Canada, dk for Denmark, fr for France, de (Deutschland) for Germany, and jp for Japan. Many Internet addresses have a code denoting affiliation categories, such as com for business sites and edu for education sites. Table 6.5 contains a few popular domain affiliation categories. The far left part of the domain name identifies the host network or host provider, which might be the name of a university or business. Other countries use different top-level domain affiliations from the U.S. ones described in the table.

The Internet Corporation for Assigned Names and Numbers (ICANN) is responsible for managing IP addresses and Internet domain names. One of ICANN's primary concerns is to make sure that each domain name represents only one individual or entity—the one that legally registers it. For example, if your teacher wanted to use *www.cengage.com* for a course Web site, he or she would discover that domain name has already been registered by Cengage Learning and is not available. ICANN uses companies called accredited domain name registrars to handle the business of registering domain names.

TABLE 6.5 Number of domains in U.S. top-level domain affiliations—Winter 2015

Affiliation ID	Affiliation	Number of Hosts
Biz	Business sites	2,428,269
Com	All types of entities including nonprofits, schools, and private individuals	123,743,892
Edu	Post-secondary educational sites	7,446
Gov	Government sites	5,503
Net	Networking sites	15,805,152
Org	Nonprofit organization sites	10,984,293

Source: Domain Count Statistics for TLDs, *http//research.domaintools.com/statistics/tld-counts/*.

For example, you can visit *www.namecheap.com*, an accredited registrar, to find out if a particular name has already been registered. If not, you can register the name for around $9 per year. Once you do so, ICANN will not allow anyone else to use that domain name as long as you pay the yearly fee.

Accessing the Internet

You can connect to the Internet in numerous ways. See Figure 6.11. Which access method you choose is determined by the size and capability of your organization or system, your budget, and the services available to you.

Connecting via a LAN Server

This approach is used by businesses and organizations that manage a local area network (LAN). By connecting a server on the LAN to the Internet using a router, all users on the LAN are provided access to the Internet. Business LAN servers are typically connected to the Internet at very fast data rates, sometimes in the hundreds of Mbps.

Connecting via Internet Service Providers

Companies and residences unable to connect directly to the Internet through a LAN server must access the Internet through an Internet service provider. An **Internet service provider (ISP)** is any organization that provides Internet access to people. Thousands of organizations serve as ISPs, ranging from universities that make the Internet available to students and faculty to small Internet businesses to major communications giants such as AT&T and Comcast. To connect to the Internet through an ISP, you must have an account with the service provider (for which you usually pay) along with software (such as a browser) and devices (such as a computer or smartphone) that support a connection via TCP/IP.

Internet service provider (ISP):
Any organization that provides Internet access to people.

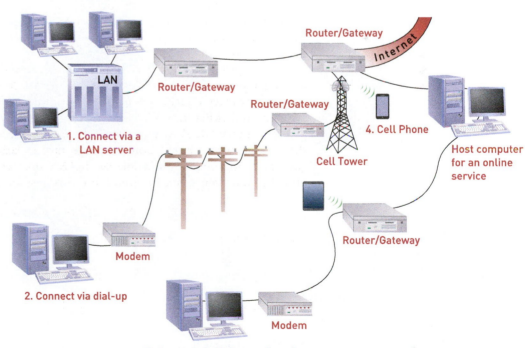

FIGURE 6.11

Several ways to access the Internet

Users can access the Internet in several ways, including using a LAN server, telephone lines, a high-speed service, or a wireless network.

Perhaps the least expensive but also slowest connection provided by ISPs is a dial-up connection. A dial-up Internet connection uses a modem and standard phone line to "dial up" and connect to the ISP server. Dial-up is considered the slowest of connections. A dial-up connection also ties up the phone line so that it is unavailable for voice calls. While dial-up was originally the only way to connect to the Internet from home, it is rapidly becoming replaced by high-speed services.

Several high-speed Internet services are available for home and business. They include cable modem connections from cable television companies, DSL connections from phone companies, and satellite connections from satellite television companies.

Wireless Connection

In addition to connecting to the Internet through wired systems such as phone lines and fiber optic cables, wireless Internet service over cellular and Wi-Fi networks has become common. Thousands of public Wi-Fi services are available in coffee shops, airports, hotels, and elsewhere, where Internet access is provided free, for an hourly rate, or for a monthly subscription fee. Wi-Fi has even made its way into aircraft, allowing business travelers to be productive during air travel by accessing email and corporate networks.

Cell phone carriers also provide Internet access for smartphones, notebooks, and tablets. The 4G mobile phone services rival wired high-speed connections enjoyed at home and work. Sprint, Verizon, AT&T, and other popular carriers are working to bring 4G service to subscribers, beginning in large metropolitan areas as shown in Figure 6.12.

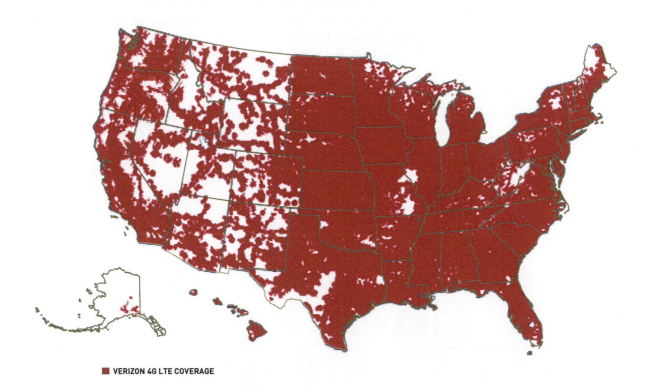

■ **VERIZON 4G LTE COVERAGE**

FIGURE 6.12

Verizon 4G LTE Coverage

While Verizon's 4G LTE coverage is extensive, there are still vast expanses where there is no coverage.

Source: *Verizon 4G LTE Coverage, http://www.bing.com/images/search?q=verizon+4g+coverage+2016&view=detailv2&&id=C8AA6A1F887 C24A96743E0CC64307E5D5E5BF96A&selectedIndex=7&ccid=SAETURq2&simid=6080358624264854141&thid=OIP. M480113511ab6e162480a92e07aeff074o0&ajaxhist=0.*

How the Web Works

The World Wide Web was developed by Tim Berners-Lee at CERN, the European Organization for Nuclear Research in Geneva. He originally conceived of it as an internal document-management system. From this modest beginning, the Web has grown to become a primary source of news and information, an indispensable conduit for commerce, and a popular hub for social interaction, entertainment, and communication.

While the terms Internet and Web are often used interchangeably, technically, the two are different technologies. The Internet is the infrastructure on which the Web exists. The Internet is made up of computers, network hardware such as routers and fiber-optic cables, software, and the TCP/IP protocols. The World Wide Web (Web), on the other hand, consists of server and client software, the hypertext transfer protocol (http), standards, and markup languages that combine to deliver information and services over the Internet.

The Web was designed to make information easy to find and organize. It connects billions of documents, called Web pages, stored on millions of servers around the world. Web pages are connected to each other using **hyperlinks**, specially denoted text or graphics on a Web page, that, when clicked, open a new Web page containing related content. Using hyperlinks, users can jump between Web pages stored on various Web servers—creating the illusion of interacting with one big computer. Because of the vast amount of information available on the Web and the wide variety of media, the Web has become the most popular means of accessing information in the world today.

In short, the Web is a hyperlink-based system that uses the client/server model. It organizes Internet resources throughout the world into a series of linked files, called pages, which are accessed and viewed using Web client software called a **Web browser**. Google Chrome, Mozilla Firefox, Microsoft Edge, Internet Explorer, Apple Safari, and Opera are popular Web browsers. See Figure 6.13. A collection of pages on one particular topic, accessed under one Web domain, is called a Web site. The Web was originally designed to support formatted text and pictures on a page. It has evolved to support many more types of information and communication including user interactivity, animation, and video. Web plug-ins help provide additional features to standard Web sites. Adobe Flash and Real Player are examples of Web plug-ins.

Hypertext Markup Language (HTML) is the standard page description language for Web pages. HTML is defined by the World Wide Web Consortium

hyperlink: Highlighted text or graphics in a Web document that, when clicked, opens a new Web page containing related content.

Web browser: Web client software—such as Chrome, Edge, Firefox, Internet Explorer, and Safari—used to view Web pages.

Hypertext Markup Language (HTML): The standard page description language for Web pages.

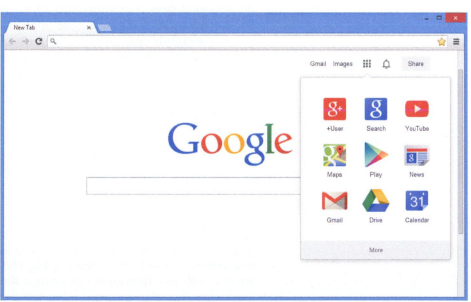

FIGURE **6.13**
Google Chrome
Web browsers such as Google Chrome let you access Internet resources such as email and other online applications.

tag: A code that tells the Web browser how to format text—as a heading, as a list, or as body text—and whether images, sound, and other elements should be inserted.

(referred to as "W3C") and has developed through numerous revisions. It is currently in its fifth revision—HTML5. HTML tells the browser how to display font characteristics, paragraph formatting, page layout, image placement, hyperlinks, and the content of a Web page. HTML uses tags, which are codes that tell the browser how to format the text or graphics as a heading, list, or body text, for example. Web site creators "mark up" a page by placing HTML tags before and after one or more words. For example, to have the browser display a sentence as a heading, you place the <h1> tag at the start of the sentence and an </h1> tag at the end of the sentence. When that page is viewed in a browser, the sentence is displayed as a heading. HTML also provides tags to import objects stored in files—such as photos, graphics, audio, and movies—into a Web page. In short, a Web page is made up of three components: text, tags, and references to files. The text is your Web page content, the tags are codes that mark the way words will be displayed, and the references to files insert photos and media into the Web page at specific locations. All HTML tags are enclosed in a set of angle brackets (< and >), such as <h2>. The closing tag has a forward slash in it, such as </b> for closing bold. Consider the following text and tags.

Extensible Markup Language (XML): The markup language designed to transport and store data on the Web.

Extensible Markup Language (XML) is a markup language for Web documents containing structured information, including words and pictures. XML does not have a predefined tag set. With HTML, for example, the <hl> tag always means a first-level heading. The content and formatting are contained in the same HTML document. XML Web documents contain the content of a Web page. The formatting of the content is contained in a style sheet. A few typical instructions in XML follow:

```
<book>
<chapter>Hardware</chapter>
<topic>Input Devices</topic>
<topic>Processing and Storage Devices</topic>
<topic>Output Devices</topic>
</book>
```

Cascading Style Sheet (CSS): A markup language for defining the visual design of a Web page or group of pages.

A **Cascading Style Sheet (CSS)** is a file or portion of an HTML file that defines the visual appearance of content in a Web page. Using CSS is convenient because you only need to define the technical details of the page's appearance once, rather than in each HTML tag. CSS uses special HTML tags to globally define characteristics for a variety of page elements as well as how those elements are laid out on the Web page. Rather than having to specify a font for each occurrence of an element throughout a document, formatting can be specified once and applied to all occurrences. CSS styles are often defined in a separate file and then can be applied to many pages on a Web site.

For example, the visual appearance of the preceding XML content could be contained in the following style sheet:

```
chapter (font-size 18pt; color blue; font-weight bold; display
block; font-family Arial; margin-top 10pt; margin-left 5pt)
topic (font-size 12pt; color red; font-style italic; display
block; font-family Arial; margin-left 12pt)
```

This style sheet specifies that the chapter title "Hardware" is displayed on the Web page in a large Arial font (18 points). "Hardware" will also appear in bold blue text. The "Input Devices" title will appear in a smaller Arial font (12 points) and italic red text.

XML is extremely useful for organizing Web content and making data easy to find. Many Web sites use CSS to define the design and layout of Web pages, XML to define the content, and HTML to join the design (CSS) with the content (XML). See Figure 6.14. This modular approach to Web design allows Web site developers to change the visual design without affecting the content and to change the content without affecting the visual design.

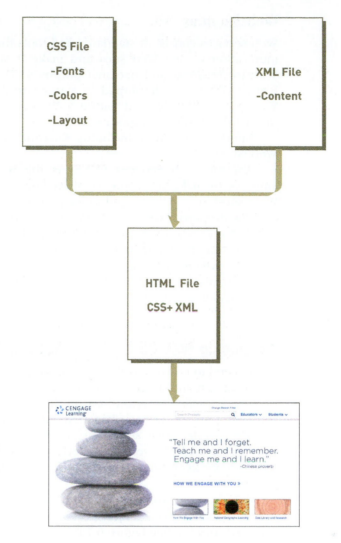

XML, CSS, and HTML

Today's Web sites are created using XML to define content, CSS to define the visual style, and HTML to put it all together.

Web Programming Languages

Many of the services offered on the Web are delivered through the use of programs and scripts. A Web program may be something as simple as a menu that expands when you click it or as complicated as a full-blown spreadsheet application. Web applications may run on a Web server, delivering the results of the processing to the user, or they may run directly on a client, such as a user's PC. These two categories are commonly referred to as server-side and client-side software.

JavaScript is a popular programming language for client-side applications. Using JavaScript, you can create interactive Web pages that respond to user actions. JavaScript can be used to validate data entry in a Web form, to display photos in a slideshow style, to embed simple computer games in a Web page, and to provide a currency conversion calculator. Java is a programming language from Sun Microsystems based on the C++ programming language, which allows small programs, called applets, to be embedded within an HTML document. When the user clicks the appropriate part of an HTML page to retrieve an applet from a Web server, the applet is downloaded onto the client workstation where it begins executing. Unlike other programs, Java software can run on any type of computer. It can be used to develop client-side or server-side applications. Programmers use Java to make Web pages come alive, adding splashy graphics, animation, and real-time updates. ASP.NET, C, C++, Perl, PHP, and Python are among other widely used client-side programming languages.

Web Services

Web services consist of standards and tools that streamline and simplify communication among Web sites and make it simpler to develop and use the Web for business and personal purposes. The key to Web services is XML. Just as HTML was developed as a standard for formatting Web content into Web pages, XML is used within a Web page to describe and transfer data between Web service applications.

Internet companies, including Amazon, eBay, and Google, are now using Web services.

Amazon Web Services (AWS) is the basic infrastructure that Amazon employs to make the contents of its huge online catalog available to other Web sites or software applications. Airbnb is an online marketplace that enables property owners and travelers to interact for the purpose of renting distinctive vacation spaces in more than 34,000 cities in 190 countries. Shortly after Airbnb began operations, it migrated its cloud computing functions to AWS, which distributes incoming traffic to ensure high availability and fast response time. AWS also allows Airbnb to store backups and static files, including 10 TB of user pictures, and to monitor all of its server resources.[18]

Developing Web Content and Applications

If you need to create a Web site, you have lots of options. You can hire someone to design and build it, or you can do it yourself. If you do it yourself, you can use an online service to create the Web pages, use a Web page creation software tool, or use a plain text editor to create the site. The software includes features that allow the developer to work directly with the HTML code or to use auto-generated code. Web development software also helps the designer keep track of all files in a Web site and the hyperlinks that connect them.

Popular tools for creating Web pages and managing Web sites include Adobe Dreamweaver, RapidWeaver (for Mac developers), and Nvu (pronounced n-view). See Figure 6.15.

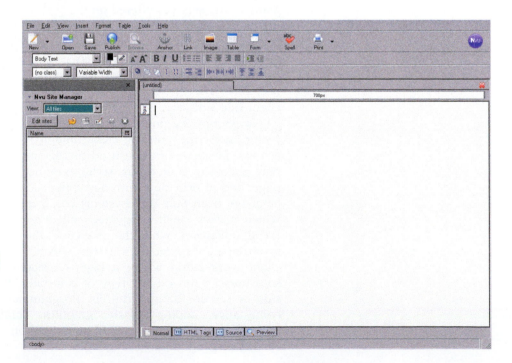

FIGURE 6.15

Creating Web pages

Nvu makes Web design nearly as easy as using a word processor.

Source: Nvu Tutorial: by Tim VanSlyke at *http://faculty.chemeketa.edu/tvanslyk/computerskills/tutorials/nvu_tutorial.pdf.*

Many products make it easy to develop Web content and interconnect Web services. Microsoft, for example, provides a development and Web services platform called .NET, which allows developers to use various programming languages to create and run programs, including those for the Web. The .NET platform also includes a rich library of programming code to help build XML Web applications. Other popular Web development platforms include JavaServer Pages, Microsoft ASP.NET, and Adobe ColdFusion.

After you create Web pages, your next step is to place or publish the content on a Web server. Popular publishing options include using ISPs, free sites, and Web hosting services. Web hosting services provide space on their Web servers for people and businesses that don't have the financial resources, time, or skills to host their own Web sites. A Web host can charge $15 or more per month, depending on services. Some Web hosting sites include domain name registration, Web authoring software, activity reporting, and Web site monitoring. Some ISPs also provide limited storage space, typically 1 to 6 megabytes, as part of their monthly fee. If more disk space is needed, additional fees are charged. Free sites offer limited space for a Web site. In return, free sites often require the user to view advertising or agree to other terms and conditions.

Some Web developers are creating programs and procedures to combine two or more Web applications into a new service, called a mashup—named after the process of mixing two or more hip-hop songs into one song. Map applications such as Google Maps provide tool kits that allow them to be combined with other Web applications. For example, Google Maps can be used with Twitter to display the location where various tweets were posted. Likewise, Google Maps combined with Flickr can overlay photos of specific geographic locations.

Internet and Web Applications

The variety of Internet and Web applications available to individuals and organizations around the world is vast and ever expanding. Using the Internet, entrepreneurs can start online companies and thrive. For example, Aaron Goldstein and Colin Hill met at the University of Pennsylvania's Wharton School. At the time, Hill was battling Hodgkin's lymphoma and undergoing chemotherapy. It was necessary for him to monitor his temperature constantly to avoid infections while his immune system was weakened. Although his temperature would be normal when he fell asleep, Hill often woke up during the night with a high fever and had to be rushed to intensive care. He became exasperated with his inability to track his temperature continuously and frustrated that his doctor couldn't monitor him remotely. So Goldstein and Hill set out to find a solution. After two years and an investment of a few hundred thousand dollars, they developed Fever Smart, a small electronic monitor worn under the armpit that sends temperature readings to a relay device, which forwards the data to Fever Smart's servers and, finally, to a smartphone or other device. Using a smartphone or any Internet-connected device, a Fever Smart user, be it a parent or healthcare provider, can constantly monitor the patient's temperature in real time and even receive alerts when the patient's temperature begins to rise or reaches unsafe levels.[19]

Web 2.0 and the Social Web

Over the years, the Web has evolved from a one-directional resource where users only obtain information to a two-directional resource where users obtain and contribute information. Consider Web sites such as YouTube, Wikipedia, and Facebook as just a few examples. The Web has also grown

Web 2.0: The Web as a computing platform that supports software applications and the sharing of information among users.

in power to support full-blown software applications such as Google Docs and is becoming a computing platform itself. These two major trends in how the Web is used and perceived have created dramatic changes in how people, businesses, and organizations use the Web, creating a paradigm shift to **Web 2.0**.

The original Web—Web 1.0—provided a platform for technology-savvy developers and the businesses and organizations that hired them to publish information for the general public to view. Web sites such as YouTube and Flickr allow users to share video and photos with other people, groups, and the world. Microblogging sites such as Twitter allow people to post thoughts and ideas throughout the day for friends to read. See Figure 6.16.

Social networking Web sites provide Web-based tools for users to share information about themselves and to find, meet, and converse with other members. Instagram is a popular social networking service through which users can share photos and videos—either publicly or with a set group of friends. Another social network, LinkedIn, is designed for professional use to assist its members with creating and maintaining valuable professional connections. Ning provides tools for Web users to create their own social networks dedicated to a topic or interest.

Social networks have become very popular for finding old friends, staying in touch with current friends and family, and making new friends. Besides their personal value, these networks provide a wealth of consumer information and opportunities for businesses as well. Some businesses are including social networking features in their workplaces.

The use of social media in business is called Enterprise 2.0. Enterprise 2.0 applications, such as Salesforce's Chatter, Jive Software's Engage Dialog, and Yammer, enable employees to create business wikis, support social networking, perform blogging, and create social bookmarks to quickly find information. Tyco, a fire protection and security company, recently went through a major restructuring, changing from a conglomerate of holding companies to a united global enterprise with more than 69,000 employees in 50 countries. Throughout its transition, Tyco relied on Yammer rather than email to educate its workforce on the differences between the old Tyco and the new Tyco and to increase employee engagement across the company.[20]

Not everyone is happy with social networking sites, however. Employers might use social networking sites to get personal information about you.

FIGURE **6.16**
Flickr
Flickr allows users to share photos with other people around the world.
Source: *www.flickr.com*

Some people worry that their privacy will be invaded or their personal information used without their knowledge or consent.

News

The Web is a powerful tool for keeping informed about local, state, national, and global news. It has an abundance of special-interest coverage and provides the capacity to deliver deeper analysis of the subject matter. Text and photos are supported by the HTML standard. Video (sometimes called a Webcast) and audio are provided in a browser through plug-in technology and in podcasts.

As traditional news sources migrate to the Web, new sources are emerging from online companies. News Web sites from Google, Yahoo!, Digg, and Newsvine provide popular or interesting stories from a variety of news sources. In a trend some refer to as social journalism or citizen journalism, ordinary citizens are more involved in reporting the news than ever before. Although social journalism provides important news not available elsewhere, its sources may not be as reliable as mainstream media sources. It is also sometimes difficult to discern news from opinion.

Education and Training

Today, institutions and organizations at all levels provide online education and training, which can be accessed via PCs, tablets, and smartphones. Kahn Academy, for example, provides free online training and learning in economics, math, banking and money, biology, chemistry, history, and many other subjects.[21] NPower helps nonprofit organizations, schools, and individuals develop information system skills. The nonprofit organization provides training to hundreds of disadvantaged young adults through a 22-week training program that can result in certification from companies such as Microsoft and Cisco.[22]

High school and college students are using mobile devices to read electronic textbooks instead of carrying heavy printed textbooks to class. And educational support products, such as Blackboard, provide an integrated Web environment that includes virtual chat for class members; a discussion group for posting questions and comments; access to the class syllabus and agenda, student grades, and class announcements; and links to class-related material. Conducting classes over the Web with no physical class meetings is called distance learning.

Job Information

The Web is also an excellent source of job-related information. People looking for their first jobs or seeking information about new job opportunities can find a wealth of information online. Search engines, such as Google or Bing (discussed next), can be a good starting point for searching for specific companies or industries. You can use a directory on Yahoo's home page, for example, to explore industries and careers. Most medium and large companies have Web sites that list open positions, salaries, benefits, and people to contact for further information. The IBM Web site, *www.ibm.com*, has a link to "Careers." When you click this link, you can find information on jobs with IBM around the world. In addition, several sites specialize in helping you find job information and even apply for jobs online, including *www.linkedin.com* (see Figure 6.17), *www.monster.com*, and *www.careerbuilder.com*.

Search Engines and Web Research

search engine: A valuable tool that enables you to find information on the Web by specifying words that are key to a topic of interest, known as keywords.

A **search engine** is a valuable tool that enables you to find information on the Web by specifying words or phrases known as keywords, which are related to a topic of interest. You can also use operators such as AND, OR, and NOT for more precise search results.

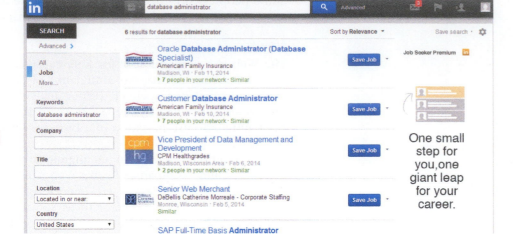

Microsoft product screenshots used with permission from Microsoft Corporation

FIGURE 6.17

LinkedIn jobs listing

LinkedIn and many other Web sites specialize in helping people get information about jobs and apply for jobs online.

Source: LinkedIn

The search engine market is dominated by Google. Other popular search engines include Yahoo! Search, Bing, Ask, Dogpile, and China's Baidu. Google has taken advantage of its market dominance to expand into other Web-based services, most notably email, scheduling, maps, social networking, Web-based applications, and mobile device software. Search engines like Google often have to modify how they display search results, depending on pending litigation from other Internet companies and government scrutiny, such as antitrust investigations.

The Bing search engine has attempted to innovate with its design. Bing refers to itself as a decision engine because it attempts to minimize the amount of information that it returns in its searches that is not useful or pertinent. Bing also includes media—music, videos, and games—in its search results. See Figure 6.18.

Savvy Web site operators know that the search engine results are tools that can draw visitors to certain Web sites. Many businesses invest in **search engine optimization (SEO)**—a process for driving traffic to a Web site by using techniques that improve the site's ranking in search results. Normally, when a user gets a list of results from a Web search, the links listed highest on the first page of search results have a far greater chance of being clicked. SEO professionals, therefore, try to get the Web sites of their businesses to be listed with as many appropriate keywords as possible. They study the algorithms that search engines use, and then they alter the contents of their

search engine optimization (SEO): A process for driving traffic to a Web site by using techniques that improve the site's ranking in search results.

FIGURE 6.18

Microsoft Bing decision engine

Microsoft calls its search engine a decision engine to distinguish it from other search software.

Web pages to improve the page's chance of being ranked number one. SEO professionals use Web analytics software to study detailed statistics about visitors to their sites.

Search engines offer just one option for performing research on the Web. Libraries typically provide access to online catalogs as well as links to public and sometimes private research databases on the Web. Online research databases allow visitors to search for information in thousands of journal, magazine, and newspaper articles. Information database services are valuable because they offer the best in quality and convenience. They conveniently provide full-text articles from reputable sources over the Web. College and public libraries typically subscribe to many databases to support research. One of the most popular private databases is LexisNexis Academic Universe. See Figure 6.19.

Instant Messaging

Instant messaging: The online, real-time communication between two or more people who are connected via the Internet.

Instant messaging is online, real-time communication between two or more people who are connected via the Internet. With instant messaging, participants build contact lists of people they want to chat with. Some applications allow you to see which of your contacts are currently logged on to the Internet and available to chat. If you send messages to one of your contacts, that message appears within the messaging app on a smartphone or other mobile device, or, for those working on PCs, the message opens in a small dialog box on the recipient's computer. Although chat typically involves exchanging text messages with one other person, many messaging apps allow for group chats. And today's instant messaging software supports not only text messages but also the sharing of images, videos, files, and voice communications. Popular instant messaging services include Facebook Messenger, KIK, Instagram, Skype, Snapchat, WhatsApp, and WeChat. It is estimated that mobile operators lost $23 billion in 2012 alone as teens shifted away from texting over cellular networks in favor of communicating with their friends over the Internet using instant messaging apps.[23]

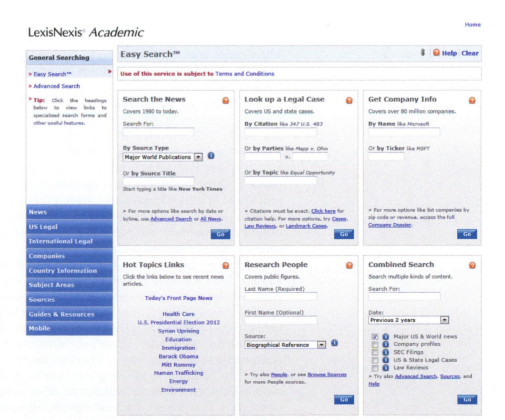

FIGURE 6.19

LexisNexis

At LexisNexis Academic Universe, you can search the news, legal cases, company information, people, or a combination of categories.

Source: *www.lexisnexis.com*

Microblogging, Status Updates, and News Feeds

Referred to as a microblogging service, Twitter is a Web application that allows users to send short text updates (up to 140 characters) from a smartphone or a Web browser to their Twitter followers. While Twitter has been hugely successful for personal use, many businesses are finding value in the service as well. Business people use Twitter to stay in touch with associates by sharing their location and activities throughout the day. Businesses also find Twitter to be a rich source of consumer sentiment that can be tapped to improve marketing, customer relations, and product development. Many businesses have a presence on Twitter, dedicating personnel to communicate with customers by posting announcements and reaching out to individual users. Village Books, an independent bookstore in Bellingham, Washington, uses Twitter to build relationships with its customers and to make them feel part of their community.

The popularity of Twitter has caused social networks, such as Facebook, LinkedIn, and Tumblr, to include Twitter-like news or blog post feeds. Previously referred to as Status Updates, Facebook users share their thoughts and activities with their friends by posting messages to Facebook's News Feed.

Conferencing

Some Internet technologies support real-time online conferencing. Participants dial into a common phone number to share a multiparty phone conversation and, in many cases, live video of the participants. The Internet has made it possible for those involved in teleconferences to share computer desktops. Using services such as WebEx or GoToMeeting, conference participants log on to common software that allows them to broadcast their computer display to the group. This ability is quite useful for presenting with PowerPoint, demonstrating software, training, or collaborating on documents. Participants verbally communicate by phone or PC microphone. Some conferencing software uses Webcams to broadcast video of the presenter and group participants. The Addison Fire Protection District provides professional fire protection and paramedic services to the 35,000 residents of Addison, Illinois. The district uses GoToMeeting to enable its employees to attend training and to support chief-to-chief meetings without requiring personnel to leave their assigned stations.[24]

Telepresence takes videoconferencing to the ultimate level. Telepresence systems, such as those from Cisco and Polycom, use high-resolution video and audio with high-definition displays to make it appear that conference participants are actually sitting around a table. Participants enter a telepresence studio where they sit at a table facing display screens that show other participants in other locations. Cameras and microphones collect high-quality video and audio at all locations and transmit them over high-speed network connections to provide an environment that replicates actual physical presence. Document cameras and computer software are used to share views of computer screens and documents with all participants.

You don't need to be a big business to enjoy the benefits of video conversations. Free software is available to make video chat easy to use for anyone with a computer, a Webcam, and a high-speed Internet connection. Online applications such as Google Voice support video connections between Web users. For spontaneous, random video chat with strangers, you can go to the Chatroulette Web site. Software, such as FaceTime and Skype, provide computer-to-computer video chat so users can speak to each other face-to-face. In addition to offering text, audio, and video chat on computers and mobile devices, Facetime and Skype offer video phone service over Internet-connected TVs. Recent Internet-connected sets from Panasonic and Samsung ship with the Skype software preloaded. You attach a Webcam to your TV to have a video chat from your sofa.

Blogging and Podcasting

Web log (blog): A Web site that people and businesses use to share their observations, experiences, and opinions on a wide range of topics.

A **Web log**, typically called a **blog**, is a Web site that people and businesses use to share their observations, experiences, and opinions on a wide range of topics. The community of blogs and bloggers is often called the blogosphere. A blogger is a person who creates a blog, whereas blogging refers to the process of placing entries on a blog site. A blog is like a journal. When people post information to a blog, it is placed at the top of the blog page. Blogs can include links to external information and an area for comments submitted by visitors. Many organizations launch blogs as a way to communicate with customers and generate new business. Video content can also be placed on the Internet using the same approach as a blog. This is often called a *video log* or *vlog*.

podcast: An audio broadcast you can listen to over the Internet.

A **podcast** is an audio broadcast you can listen to over the Internet. The name podcast originated from Apple's *iPod* combined with the word *broadcast*. A podcast is like an audio blog. Using PCs, recording software, and microphones, you can record podcast programs and place them on the Internet. Apple's iTunes provides free access to tens of thousands of podcasts, which are sorted by topic and searchable by key word. See Figure 6.20. After you find a podcast, you can download it to your PC (Windows or Mac), to an MP3 player such as an iPod, or to any smartphone or tablet. You can also subscribe to podcasts using RSS software included in iTunes and other digital audio software.

Online Media and Entertainment

Like news and information, all forms of media and entertainment have followed their audiences online. Music, movies, television program episodes,

1.
NPR: Science Friday Podcast
by Ira Flatow

Science Friday, as heard on NPR, is a weekly discussion of the latest news in science, technology, health, and the environment hosted by Ira Flatow.

▶ PLAY

2.
TEDTalks Podcast
by Anthony Robbins

Each year, TED hosts some of the world's most fascinating people: Trusted voices and convention-breaking mavericks, icons and geniuses.

▶ PLAY

3. **Entrepreneurial Thought Leaders Podcast**
by Forrest Glick

The DFJ Entrepreneurial Thought Leaders Seminar (ETL) is a weekly seminar series on entrepreneurship, co-sponsored by BASES (a student entrepreneurship group), Stanford Technology Ventures Program, and the Department of Management Science and Engineering.

▶ PLAY

4. **Mixergy Video Podcast**
by Andrew Warner

MIXERGY

Interviews with a mix of successful online businesspeople. Andrew Warner asks them to teach ambitious startups how to build companies that leave a legacy...

▶ PLAY

FIGURE 6.20

Podcasts
iTunes and other sites provide free access to tens of thousands of podcasts.

Source: *www.learnoutloud.com*

5.
Ruby on Rails Podcast
by Scott Barron

The Rails podcast is a super-agile way for you to get the inside scoop on the Rails community.

content streaming: A method for transferring large media files over the Internet so that the data stream of voice and pictures plays more or less continuously as the file is being downloaded.

user-generated videos, e-books, and audio books are all available online to download and purchase or stream.

Content streaming is a method of transferring large media files over the Internet so that the data stream of voice and pictures plays more or less continuously as the file is being downloaded. For example, rather than wait for an entire 5 MB video clip to download before they can play it, users can begin viewing a streamed video as it is being received. Content streaming works best when the transmission of a file can keep up with the playback of the file.

Music The Internet and the Web have made music more accessible than ever, with artists distributing their songs through online radio, subscription services, and download services. Spotify, Pandora, Napster, and Google Play Music are just a few examples of Internet music sites. Rhapsody International has more than 3 million subscribers globally for its premium music services, including Napster, Rhapsody, and its Internet radio service, Rhapsody unRadio.[25] See Figure 6.21. Internet music has even helped sales of classical music by Mozart, Beethoven, and others. Internet companies, including Facebook, are starting to make music, movies, and other digital content available on their Web sites. Facebook, for example, allows online music companies, such as Spotify and Rdio, to post music-related news on its Web site.

Apple's iTunes was one of the first online music services to find success. Microsoft, Amazon, Walmart, and other retailers also sell music online. Downloaded music may include digital rights management (DRM) technology that prevents or limits the user's ability to make copies or to play the music on multiple players.

Podcasts are yet another way to access music on the Web. Many independent artists provide samples of their music through podcasts. Podcast Alley includes podcasts from unsigned artists.

Movies, Video, and Television Television and movies are expanding to the Web in leaps and bounds. Online services such as Amazon Instant Video, Hulu, and Netflix provide television programming from hundreds of providers, including most mainstream television networks. Walmart's acquisition of Vudu has allowed the big discount retailer to successfully get into the Internet movie business. Increasingly, TV networks offer apps for streaming TV content to tablets and other mobile devices. Some TV networks charge viewers to watch episodes of their favorite shows online. The Roku LT Streaming Media Box connects wirelessly to your TV and streams TV shows and movies from

FIGURE 6.21

Rhapsody

Rhapsody provides streaming music by subscription.

Source: *rhapsody.com*

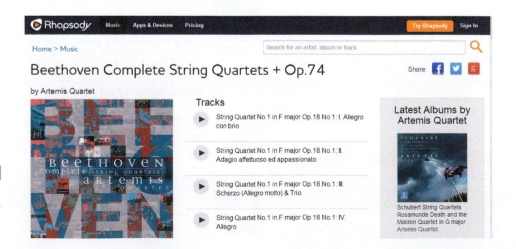

online sources such as Amazon Instant, Crackle, Disney, Hulu, Netflix, Pandora, and Xfinity TV.

Popcorn Time is a free program that uses peer-to-peer networking to download movies and TV programs. However, the software explicitly states that its users may be violating copyright law in their country. And indeed, Voltage Pictures has filed mass lawsuits against people who downloaded *The Hurt Locker* and *Dallas Buyers Club*. While these lawsuits aren't always successful, they do create a risk for users who don't anonymize their activity through a VPN service.[26]

No discussion of Internet video would be complete without mentioning YouTube. YouTube supports the online sharing of user-created videos. YouTube videos tend to be relatively short and cover a wide range of categories from the nonsensical to college lectures. See Figure 6.22. It is estimated that 100 hours of video are uploaded to YouTube every minute and that over 6 billion hours of video are watched each month on YouTube. YouTube reaches more U.S. adults in the 18 to 34 age category than any cable network.[27] Other video-streaming sites include AOL Video, Metacafe, and Vimeo. As more companies create and post videos to Web sites like YouTube, some IS departments are creating a new position—video content manager.

Online Games and Entertainment   Video games have become a huge industry with worldwide annual revenue projected to exceed $100 billion by 2017.[28] Zynga, a fast-growing Internet company, sells virtual animals and other virtual items for games, such as FarmVille. The company, for example, sells a clown pony with colorful clothes for about $5. Zynga has a VIP club for people that spend a lot on virtual items it offers for sale. Some Internet companies also sell food for virtual animals. People can feed and breed virtual animals and sell their offspring. The market for online gaming is very competitive and constantly changing. After Google included online games on its Web site, Facebook updated its online gaming offerings. Many video games are available online. They include single-user, multiuser, and massively multiuser games. The Web offers a multitude of games for all ages, including role-playing games, strategy games, and simulation games.

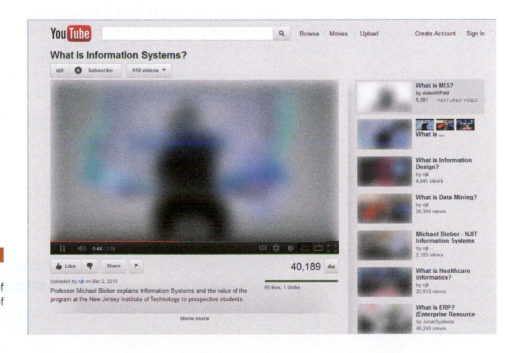

FIGURE 6.22
YouTube EDU
YouTube EDU provides thousands of educational videos from hundreds of universities.
Source: *youtube.com/edu*

Game consoles such as the PlayStation, Wii, and Xbox provide multiplayer options for online gaming over the Internet. Subscribers can play with or against other subscribers in 3D virtual environments. They can even talk to each other using a microphone headset.

Shopping Online

Shopping on the Web can be convenient, easy, and cost effective. You can buy almost anything online, from books and clothing to cars and sports equipment. Groupon, for example, offers discounts at restaurants, spas, auto repair shops, music performances, and almost any other product or service offered in your area or city. Revenues for Groupon exceeded $3.1 billion in 2015.[29]

Other online companies offer different services. Dell and many other computer retailers provide tools that allow shoppers to specify every aspect and component of a computer system to purchase. ResumePlanet.com would be happy to create your professional résumé. AmazonFresh, Instacart, and Peapod are all willing to deliver groceries to your doorstep. Products and services abound online.

Many online shopping options are available to Web users. Online versions of retail stores often provide access to products that may be unavailable in local stores. JCPenney, Target, Walmart, and many others carry only a percentage of their inventory in their retail stores; the other inventory is available online. To add to their other conveniences, many Web sites offer free shipping and pickup for returned items that don't fit or otherwise meet a customer's needs.

Web sites such as *www.mySimon.com*, *www.DealTime.com*, *www.PriceSCAN.com*, *www.PriceGrabber.com*, and *www.NexTag.com* provide product price quotations from numerous online retailers to help you to find the best deal. Apps such as BuyVia, Purchx, RedLaser, and Shop Savvy enable users to compare prices at national and local outlets and lets you set up alerts (including location-based) for products. At a store and unsure if the price on the shelf is the lowest you can find? Use the UPC barcode scanner to get an answer on the spot.

Online clearinghouses, Web auctions, and marketplaces offer a platform for businesses and individuals to sell their products and belongings. Online clearinghouses, such as *www.uBid.com*, provide a method for manufacturers to liquidate stock and for consumers to find a good deal. Outdated or overstocked items are put on the virtual auction block and users bid on the items. The highest bidder when the auction closes gets the merchandise—often for less than 50 percent of the advertised retail price.

The most popular online auction or marketplace is eBay, shown in Figure 6.23. The site provides a public platform for global trading where anyone can buy, sell, or trade practically anything. It offers a wide variety of

FIGURE 6.23

eBay

eBay provides an online marketplace where anyone can buy, sell, or trade practically anything.

Source: *www.ebay.com*

features and services that enable members to buy and sell on the site quickly and conveniently. Buyers have the option to purchase items at a fixed price or in an auction-style format, where the highest bid wins the product.

Auction houses such as eBay accept limited liability for problems that buyers or sellers may experience in their transactions. Transactions that make use of the PayPal service are protected on eBay. Others, however, may be more risky. Participants should be aware that auction fraud is the most prevalent type of fraud on the Internet.

Craigslist is a network of online communities that provides free online classified advertisements. It is a popular online marketplace for purchasing items from local individuals. Many shoppers turn to Craigslist rather than going to the classifieds in the local paper.

Businesses benefit from shopping online as well. Global supply management online services provide methods for businesses to find the best deals on the global market for raw materials and supplies needed to manufacture their products. Electronic exchanges provide an industry-specific Web resource created to deliver a convenient centralized platform for B2B e-commerce among manufacturers, suppliers, and customers.

Travel, Geolocation, and Navigation

The Web has had a profound effect on the travel industry and the way people plan and prepare for trips. From getting assistance with short trips across town to planning long holidays abroad, travelers are turning to the Web to save time and money and to overcome much of the risk involved in visiting unknown places.

Travel Web sites such as Travelocity, Expedia, Kayak, and Priceline help travelers find the best deals on flights, hotels, car rentals, vacation packages, and cruises. Priceline offers a slightly different approach from the other Web sites. It allows shoppers to name a price they're willing to pay for an airline ticket or a hotel room and then works to find an airline or hotel that can meet that price.

Mapping and geolocation tools are among the most popular and successful Web applications. MapQuest, Google Maps, and Bing Maps are examples. See Figure 6.24. By offering free street maps for locations around the world,

FIGURE 6.24

Google Maps

Mapping software, such as Google Maps, provides streetside views of Times Square.

Source: Google

these tools help travelers find their way. Provide your departure location and destination, and these online applications produce a map that displays the fastest route. Using GPS technologies, these tools can detect your current location and provide directions from where you are.

Google Maps also provides extensive location-specific business information, satellite imagery, up-to-the-minute traffic reports, and Street View. The latter is the result of Google employees driving the streets of the world's cities in vehicles with high-tech camera gear, taking 360-degree images. These images are integrated into Google Maps to allow users to get a "street view" of an area that can be manipulated as if the viewer were actually walking down the street looking around. Bing Maps and Google Maps both offer high-resolution aerial photos and street-level 3D photographs.

Geographic information systems (GISs) provide geographic information layered over a map. For example, Google Earth provides options for viewing traffic, weather, local photos and videos, underwater features such as shipwrecks and marine life, local attractions, businesses, and places of interest. Software such as Connect, Find My Friends, Phone Tracker, and Tracker allow you to find your friends on a map—with their permission—and will automatically notify you if a friend is near.

Geo-tagging is technology that allows for tagging information with an associated location. For example, Flickr and other photo software and services allow photos to be tagged with the location they were taken. Once tagged, it becomes easy to search for photos taken, for example, in Florida. Geo-tagging also makes it easy to overlay photos on a map, as Google Maps and Bing Maps have done. Facebook, Instagram, Snapchat, Twitter, and many other social networks have also made it possible for users to geo-tag photos, comments, tweets, and posts.

Geolocation information does pose a risk to privacy and security. Many people prefer that their location remain unknown, at least to strangers and often to acquaintances and even friends. Recently, criminals have made use of location information to determine when people are away from their residences so that they can burglarize without fear of interruption.

Intranets and Extranets

An intranet is an internal corporate network built using Internet and World Wide Web standards and products. Employees of an organization can use an intranet to gain access to corporate information. After getting their feet wet with public Web sites that promote company products and services, corporations are seizing the Web as a swift way to streamline—even transform—their organizations. These private networks use the infrastructure and standards of the Internet and the World Wide Web. Using an intranet offers one considerable advantage: many people are already familiar with Internet technology, so they need little training to make effective use of their corporate intranet.

An intranet is an inexpensive yet powerful alternative to other forms of internal communication, including conventional computer setups. One of an intranet's most obvious virtues is its ability to reduce the need for paper. Because Web browsers run on all types of computers, the same electronic information can be viewed by any employee. That means that all sorts of documents (such as internal phone books, procedure manuals, training manuals, and requisition forms) can be inexpensively converted to electronic form, posted online, and easily updated. An intranet provides employees with an easy and intuitive approach to accessing information that was previously difficult to obtain. For example, it is an ideal solution to providing information to a mobile salesforce that needs access to rapidly changing information.

TABLE **6.6** Summary of Internet, intranet, and extranet users

Type	User	Need User ID and Password?
Internet	Anyone	No
Intranet	Employees	Yes
Extranet	Business partners	Yes

A growing number of companies offer limited network access to selected customers and suppliers. Such networks are referred to as extranets, which connect people who are external to the company. An extranet is a network built using Web technologies that links selected resources of the intranet of a company with its customers, suppliers, or other business partners.

Corporate executives at a well-known global fast food chain wanted to improve their understanding of what was happening at each restaurant location and needed to communicate with franchisees to better serve their customers. The firm implemented an extranet, enabling individual franchisees to fine-tune their location-specific advertising and get it approved quickly by corporate-level staff. In addition, with the extranet, corporate employees now have a much better understanding of customers, both by location and in aggregate, based on information they are receiving from franchisees.[30]

Security and performance concerns are different for an extranet than for a Web site or network-based intranet. User authentication and privacy are critical on an extranet so that information is protected. Obviously, the network must also be reliable and provide quick response to customers and suppliers. Table 6.6 summarizes the differences between users of the Internet, intranets, and extranets.

Secure intranet and extranet access applications usually require the use of a **virtual private network (VPN)**, a secure connection between two points on the Internet. VPNs transfer information by encapsulating traffic in IP packets and sending the packets over the Internet, a practice called tunneling. Most VPNs are built and run by ISPs. Companies that use a VPN from an ISP have essentially outsourced their networks to save money on wide area network equipment and personnel. To limit access to the VPN to just individuals authorized to use it, authorized users may be issued a logon ID and a security token assigned to that logon ID. The security token displays a 10- to 12-digit password that changes every 30 seconds or so. A user must enter their logon ID and the security password valid for that logon ID at that moment in time.

virtual private network (VPN): A secure connection between two points on the Internet; VPNs transfer information by encapsulating traffic in IP packets and sending the packets over the Internet.

Critical Thinking Exercise

Extranet to Support Craft Brewers

There are currently more than 3,000 breweries in the United States, double the number a decade ago. Much of this growth has come from the popularity of craft brewers who, by definition, produce no more than 6 million barrels annually—many produce much less. Within the craft brewing industry, there is a strong trend toward packaging beer in four packs of 16-ounce cans rather than the six packs of 12-ounce cans, bottles, or jugs associated with the major U.S. brewers. One practical reason for cans is that glass bottles typically cost more, which can make a big impact on the bottom line of many small brewers. In addition, craft brewers use 16-ounce cans as a means to set themselves apart from traditional beverage companies, and many have built their identities around the distinct look of their 16-ounce can. However, most craft brewers are too small to afford their own canning lines.

Ball, Crown, and Rexam are major can manufacturers who work with many craft brewers to fill their cans. But these companies recently raised their minimum can order to the industry-standard truckload, which can range from roughly

155,000 to 200,000, depending on the size of the can. Typically the smaller breweries and their distributors need only a few thousand cans at a time. The new minimum can orders translate into a lot of cash up front as well as an increased amount of storage space for breweries. Many small breweries are struggling as a result.

A new type of company, mobile canners, has emerged to address this problem. These firms haul their equipment to breweries, spend less than a day filling and labeling a few thousand cans, and then move on to the next customer. Over the past three years, about two dozen mobile canner companies have started offering mobile canning across the United States.

You are the owner of one of these mobile canners serving craft breweries across the Midwest, a very competitive market. One of your employees has approached you with an idea to set up an extranet that will allow your craft brewery customers to communicate their production schedules to you electronically. Their individual production schedules would be fed into a master schedule that would enable you to see and plan three to six months into the future. This way you could commit the people, equipment, and other resources to ensure that your customers' needs will be met. Running out of cans is catastrophic for the brewers. If you let down a customer who is depending on you, you've lost a customer for life.

Review Questions

1. What advantages does use of an extranet provide versus more conventional methods of communication—over the phone, via fax, etc.?
2. What measures can you take to control access to the master production schedule so that only authorized customers may enter their data?

Critical Thinking Questions

1. What potential start-up issues may be involved in preparing your craft brewery customers to use this new system? How will you overcome these issues?
2. Can you identify any other purposes for the extranet in addition to one-way communication of production schedules? Briefly elaborate.

The Internet of Things

The Internet of Things (IoT) is a network of physical objects or "things" embedded with sensors, processors, software, and network connectivity capability to enable them to exchange data with the manufacturer of the device, device operators, and other connected devices. See Figure 6.25.

Sensors are being installed in a variety of machines and products, ranging from home appliances and parking garages to clothing and grocery products. A sensor is a device that is capable of sensing something about its surroundings such as pressure, temperature, humidity, pH level, motion, vibration, or level of light. The sensor detects an event or changes in quantity and produces a corresponding output, usually an electrical or optical signal. To be truly part of the IoT, these networked devices need IP addresses and a connection to the public Internet. The data is then transmitted over the Internet to an operational historical database containing data from many sensors. The database may be on a data storage device in a local control room, in an enterprise data center in another state, or hundreds of miles away in the cloud. The operational data can be accessed via the Internet and analyzed by users with personal computers or portable devices including smartphones. Updates, alerts, or even automatic adjustments may be sent to the devices on the IoT based on this analysis. According to Don DeLoach, CEO and president of Infobright Inc., "manufacturing has been automated at various levels for many years, but IoT brings automation to a deep, broad level—one where

1. Sensors gather data

2. Data passes over network

3. Data from across the IoT is gathered and stored—often in the cloud

4. Data is combined with other data from other systems

5. Data is analyzed to gain insights into operation of devices on IoT

6. Alerts sent to people, Enterprise systems, or IoT Devices based on these insights

FIGURE 6.25

The Internet of Things

The IoT is a network of physical objects or "things" embedded with sensors, processors, software, and network connectivity capability to enable them to exchange data with the manufacturer of the device, device operators, and other connected devices.

interconnectivity between various elements in manufacturing exists in a way it did not before."[31]

Enlightened organizations apply analytics to these streams of data—even before the data is stored for post event analysis. This enables workers to detect patterns and potential problems as they are occurring and to make appropriate adjustments in the operation of the devices being measured. For example, sensors embedded in General Electric (GE) aircraft engines collect some 5,000 individual data points per second. This data is analyzed while the aircraft is in flight to adjust the way the aircraft performs, thereby reducing fuel consumption. The data is also used to plan predictive maintenance on the engines based on engine component wear and tear. In 2013, this technology helped GE earn $1 billion in incremental income by delivering performance improvements, less downtime, and more flying miles.[32]

Here are additional examples of organizations using sensors and the IoT to monitor and control key operational activities:

- **Asset monitoring**. Food and drug manufacturers can monitor shipping containers for changes in temperatures that could affect product quality and safety using cheap battery-powered sensors and 4G LTE connectivity.
- **Construction**. SK Solutions is using IoT technology to prevent cranes from colliding on a crowded construction site with 37 cranes and 5,000 workers near the world's tallest building in the United Arab Emirates (UAE) city of Dubai. The Internet-connected system collects data from sensors mounted to the cranes and other equipment to detect if construction cranes are swinging too close to each other, and, if so, halts them from moving further.[33]
- **Agriculture**. Farmers are using IoT technology to collect data about water moisture and nitrogen levels to improve yields while conserving water, a precious commodity in many places.
- **Manufacturing**. IoT enabled sensors on plant-floor equipment, such as a conveyor line, can alert plant floor personnel to problems in real time.

The data can also be analyzed to uncover patterns to allow technicians to predict potential failures or redeploy resources in a more optimal fashion.

- **Monitoring parking spaces**. San Francisco uses connected sensors and meters to determine the demand for parking on certain streets, periodically adjusting hourly rates so drivers are more likely to find a space when they arrive. Rates go up on more-crowded blocks and down on less-crowded ones. The city has deployed a low-power wide area network similar to a cellular network but designed for low-power IoT equipment—such as parking meters—to provide a low energy way for devices that are slower and cheaper than the typical LTE cellular network.
- **Predictive Maintenance**. Sensors are used extensively in the utilities industry to capture operational data to achieve 24/7 uptime. Sensor data is carefully analyzed to predict when critical pieces of equipment or power lines are about to fail so that quick, anticipatory corrective action can take place before any failure.
- **Retailing**. Retailers use in-store sensors to detect in-store behavior and optimize the shopping experience in order to increase revenue and market share. Streaming data from sensors is analyzed, along with other information (like inventory, social media chatter, and online-shop user profiles), to send customized and personal offers while the shopper is in the process of making a purchase decision.
- **Traffic monitoring**. The Aegan motorway is the oldest and most important motorway of Greece, connecting the country's largest cities, Athens and Thessaloniki. More than 5,000 devices are deployed along a 200-km (124-mile) stretch of the highway to keep drivers safe and the roadway running efficiently. All these devices must work in a smooth and coordinated fashion to monitor traffic, detect traffic incidents using traffic cameras, warn travelers of road conditions via electronic billboards, and operate toll booths. The devices are connected to a central control system using Cisco's Internet of Everything system to connect data, people, processes, and things.[34]

IoT applications can be classified into one of four types as shown in Table 6.7.

Unfortunately, there can be many issues with simply receiving and recognizing usable sensor data. Sometimes a faulty sensor or bad network connection results in missing data or sensor data lacking time stamps indicating when the reading occurred. As a result, sensor data can be incomplete or contain inconsistent values indicating a potential sensor failure or a drop in a network. Developers of IoT systems must be prepared for and be able to detect faulty sensor data.

TABLE 6.7 Types of IoT applications

Type of IoT Application	Degree of Sensing	Degree of Action
Connect and monitor	Individual devices each gathering a small amount of data	Enables manual monitoring using simple threshold-based exception alerting
Control and react	Individual devices each gathering a small amount of data	Automatic monitoring combined with remote control with trend analysis and reporting
Predict and adapt	External data is used to augment sensor data	Data used to preform predictive analysis and initiate preemptive action
Transform and explore	Sensor and external data used to provide new insights	New business models, products, and services are created

Security is a very major issue with IoT applications. In today's manufacturing environment, the factory network is a closed environment designed to communicate with plant sensors and devices but not typically with the outside world. So a key decision organizations must make when considering implementation of an IoT is as follows: Are the benefits of doing so sufficient to overcome the risk of making detailed company information accessible through the Internet and exposing internal systems to hacking, viruses, and destructive malware? Hackers who gain access to an organization's IoT can steal data, transfer money out of accounts, and shut down Web sites, and they can also wreck physical havoc by tampering with critical infrastructure like air traffic control systems, healthcare devices, power grids, and supervisory control and data acquisition (SCADA) systems. One of the first things developers of IoT application should focus on is building in security from the start. This needs to include ways of updating the system in a secure manner.

Critical Thinking Exercise

Manufacturer Weighs Converting to Internet of Things

You are a member of the plant information systems group for a small manufacturer of all-natural ingredient cosmetics. Your firm promotes itself as adhering to the highest standards of compliance and quality. Manufacturing is rigorously monitored via sensors and computer controls throughout the entire process, and automated temperature controls ensure complete stability in the manufacturing environment. Sensor tracking is performed from the moment that raw materials enter your facility, throughout the manufacturing process, packaging, and on to distribution. The sensors and computer controls were installed when the plant was built in the 1990s and use proprietary communications protocols and are not Internet enabled. Data from these sensors is monitored by a group of three technicians in the computer control room. Twelve workers are required to staff the control room 24/7, including weekends and most holidays.

Your company has just purchased a plant previously owned by one of your competitors in a nearby state. Your group has been asked to look at the feasibility of upgrading the sensors used in both plants to Internet-enabled sensors connected to the Internet of Things. This would make it possible for technicians in one control room to monitor the operation of both plants. Plant staffing could be reduced by 12 workers saving $1.2 million in labor expenses per year. It is estimated that the cost of replacing the existing sensors and converting to the Internet of Things is in the vicinity of $1.5 million.

Review Questions

1. Why is it necessary to replace the existing sensors to implement an IoT network?
2. What additional benefits may arise from converting the plants to the Internet of Things?

Critical Thinking Questions

1. What new risks are raised by placing the new system of sensors on the Internet of Things?
2. What actions could be taken to reduce these risks?

Cloud Computing

cloud computing: A computing environment where software and storage are provided as an Internet service and are accessed with a Web browser.

Cloud computing refers to a computing environment in which software and storage are provided as an Internet service and accessed by users with their Web browser. See Figure 6.26. Google and Yahoo!, for example, store the email of many users, along with calendars, contacts, and to-do lists. Apple

FIGURE 6.26

Cloud computing

Cloud computing uses applications and resources delivered via the Web.

developed its iCloud service to allow people to store their documents, music, photos, apps, and other content on its servers.[35] In addition to its social networking features, Facebook offers users the ability to store personal photos in the cloud—as does Flickr and a dozen other photo sites. Pandora delivers music, and Hulu and YouTube deliver movies via the cloud. Apache OpenOffice, Google Apps, Microsoft Office 365, Zoho, and others provide Web-delivered productivity and information management software. Communications, contacts, photos, documents, music, and media are available to you from any Internet-connected device with cloud computing.

Cloud computing offers many advantages to businesses. With cloud computing, organizations can avoid large, up-front investments in hardware as well as the ongoing investment in the resources that would be required to manage that hardware. Instead, they can provision just the right type and size of information system resources from their cloud computing provider, pay for it on an ongoing basis, and let the service provider handle the system support and maintenance. In most cases, the cloud computing service provider provides access to state-of-the-art technology at a fraction of the cost of owning it and without the lengthy delays that can occur when an organizations tries to acquire its own resources. This can increase the speed and reduce the costs of new product and service launches. For example, Spotify offers its users instant access to over 16 million licensed songs. The company faces an ongoing struggle to keep pace with the rapid release of new music, adding over 20,000 tracks to its catalog each day. Emil Fredriksson, operations director for Spotify, explains why the company employs cloud computing, "Spotify needed a storage solution that could scale very quickly without incurring long lead times for upgrades. This led us to cloud storage." While establishing new storage previously required several months of preparation, it can now be obtained instantly through cloud computing.[36]

Cloud computing can be deployed in several different ways. The methods discussed thus far in this chapter are considered public cloud services. Public cloud computing refers to deployments in which service providers offer their cloud-based services to the general public, whether that is an individual using Google Calendar or a corporation using the Salesforce.com application. In a private cloud deployment, cloud technology is used within the confines of a private network.

Since 1992, The College Network and its partner universities have provided accessible educational programs for individuals seeking degrees or professional certificates, entirely through distance learning. The College Network chose EarthLink to provide a customized private cloud with dedicated servers. Conversion to the private network reduced the capital required for computer hardware and software, increased systems availability and avoided outages, and reallocated its valuable IT resources while EarthLink resources trouble-shoot any systems issues.[37]

Many organizations are turning to cloud computing as an approach to outsource some or all of their IT operations. This section defines cloud computing and its variations and points out some of its advantages as well as some potential issues, including problems associated with cost, scalability, security, and regulatory compliance.

Public Cloud Computing

In a public cloud computing environment, a service provider organization owns and manages the infrastructure (including computing, networking, and storage devices) with cloud user organizations (called tenants) accessing slices of shared hardware resources via the Internet. The service provider can deliver increasing amounts of computing, network, and storage capacity on demand and without requiring any capital investment on the part of the cloud users. Thus, public cloud computing is a great solution for organizations whose computing needs vary greatly depending on changes in demand. Amazon, Cisco Systems, IBM, Microsoft, Rackspace, Verizon Communications Inc., and VMWare are among the largest cloud computing service providers. These firms typically offer a monthly or annual subscription service model; they may also provide training, support, and data integration services.[38]

Public cloud computing can be a faster, cheaper, and more agile approach to building and managing your own IT infrastructure. However, since cloud users are using someone else's data center, potential issues with service levels, loss of control, disaster recovery, and data security should not be overlooked. Data security in particular is a key concern because when using a public cloud computing service, you are relying on someone else to safeguard your data. In addition, your organization's data may reside on the same storage device as another organization's (perhaps even a competitor's) data. All of the potential issues of concern must be investigated fully before entering into a public cloud computing arrangement. Organizations subject to tight regulation and complex regulatory requirements (e.g., financial, healthcare, and public utility organizations) must ensure that their own processes and applications as well as those of the cloud provider are compliant.

A major start-up issue is the effort of getting your organization's data moved to the cloud in the first place. That introduces an issue of vendor lock-in—meaning once an organization's servers and data are hosted with one cloud provider, it is not likely to be willing to go through the time-consuming migration process a second time to move to a different provider in the future. So choose your cloud provider wisely, as it is a business relationship that you and your business will likely need to live with for the foreseeable future.

Cloud computing can be divided into three main types of services (see Figure 6.27)

infrastructure as a service (IaaS): An information systems strategy in which an organization outsources the equipment used to support its data processing operations, including servers, storage devices, and networking components.

- **Infrastructure as a service (IaaS)** is an information systems strategy in which an organization outsources the equipment used to support its data processing operations, including servers, storage devices, and networking components. The service provider owns the equipment and is responsible for housing, running, and maintaining it. The outsourcing organization may pay on a per-use or monthly basis.
- **Software as a service (SaaS)** is a software delivery approach that provides users with access to software remotely as a Web-based service. SaaS pricing is based on a monthly fee per user and typically results in lower

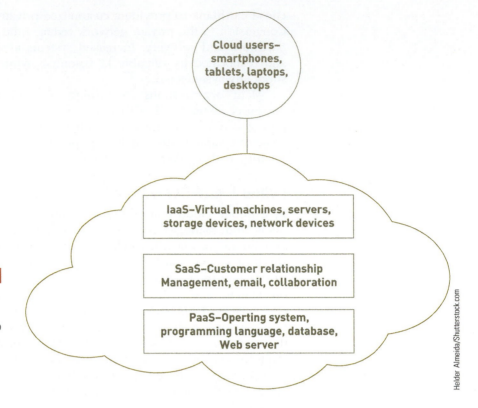

Cloud users–smartphones, tablets, laptops, desktops

IaaS–Virtual machines, servers, storage devices, network devices

SaaS–Customer relationship Management, email, collaboration

PaaS–Operting system, programming language, database, Web server

Helder Almeida/Shutterstock.com

Helder Almeida/Shutterstock.com

FIGURE 6.27

The cloud computing environment

Cloud computing can be divided into three main types of services: infrastructure as a service (IaaS), software as a service (SaaS), and platform as a service (PaaS).

platform as a service (PaaS): An approach that provides users with a computing platform, typically including operating system, programming language execution environment, database services, and Web server.

costs than a licensed application. Another advantage of SaaS is that because the software is hosted remotely, users do not need to purchase and install additional hardware to provide increased capacity. Furthermore, the service provider handles necessary software maintenance and upgrades.

• **Platform as a service (PaaS)** provides users with a computing platform, typically including operating system, programming language execution environment, database services, and a Web server. The user can create an application or service using tools and/or libraries from the provider. The user also controls software deployment and configuration settings. The PaaS provider provides the networks, servers, storage, and other services required to host the consumer's application. PaaS enables application developers to develop, test, and run their software solutions on a cloud platform without the cost and complexity of buying and managing the underlying hardware and software.

Organizations contemplating moving to the cloud are advised to proceed carefully, as almost one in three organizations encounter major challenges during the transition. Frequent problems include complex pricing arrangements and hidden costs that reduce expected cost savings, performance issues that cause wide variations in performance over time, poor user support, and greater than expected downtime.[39]

Condé Nast, publisher of *Vogue*, *The New Yorker*, and *Wired* magazines, among many others, decommissioned its 67,000-square-foot data center and migrated its data and processing capacity to Amazon Web Services (AWS). Over a period of just three months in 2014, the firm migrated 500 servers; 1 petabyte of storage; 100 database servers; 100 switches, routers, and firewalls; and all of its mission-critical applications to AWS. According to Condé Nast, operating costs have been cut by 40 percent and performance has improved by 30 percent to 40 percent since the transition, which created a dynamic environment that can adjust as the company needs it to. The old data center facilities were eventually put on the market and sold.[40]

Private Cloud Computing

private cloud environment: A single tenant cloud.

A **private cloud environment** is a single tenant cloud. Organizations that implement a private cloud often do so because they are concerned that their data will not be secure in a public cloud. Private clouds can be divided into two distinct types. Some organizations build their own on-premise private cloud, and others elect to have a service provider build and manage their private cloud (sometimes called a virtual private cloud). A general rule of thumb is that companies that spend $1 million or more per month on outsourced computing are better off implementing an on-premise private cloud.[41] Many complications must be overcome—and deep technical skills and sophisticated software are needed—to build and manage a successful private cloud. An organization might establish several private clouds with one for finance, another one for product development, and a third for sales, for example. Each private cloud has a defined set of available resources and users, with predefined quotas that limit how much capacity users of that cloud can consume.

Revlon is a global cosmetics, hair color, fragrance, and skin-care company with recent annual sales exceeding $1.9 billion.[42] The firm implemented an on-premises private cloud that includes 531 applications and makes up 97 percent of the company's computing power. The private cloud has helped reduce application deployment time by 70 percent and, as a result of virtualization and consolidation, reduced data center power consumption by 72 percent. In addition, the company achieved a net dollar savings of $70 million over a two-year period.[43]

Hybrid Cloud Computing

hybrid cloud: A cloud computing environment is composed of both private and public clouds integrated through networking.

Many IT industry observers believe that the desire for both agility and security will eventually lead organizations to adopt a hybrid cloud approach.[44] A **hybrid cloud** is composed of both private and public clouds integrated through networking. Organizations typically use the public cloud to run applications with less sensitive security requirements and highly fluctuating capacity needs, but run more critical applications, such as those with significant compliance requirements, on the private portion of their hybrid cloud. So a hospital may run its Web conferencing and email applications on a public cloud while running its applications that access patient records on a private cloud to meet Health Insurance Portability and Accountability Act (HIPAA) and other compliance requirements.

Autonomic Computing

autonomic computing: The ability of IT systems to manage themselves and adapt to changes in the computing environment, business policies, and operating objectives.

An enabling technology for cloud computing is **autonomic computing** or the ability of IT systems to manage themselves and adapt to changes in the computing environment, business policies, and operating objectives. The goal of autonomic computing is to create complex systems that run themselves, while keeping the system's complexity invisible to the end user. Autonomic computing addresses four key functions: self-configuring, self-healing, self-optimizing, and self-protecting.[45] As cloud computing environments become increasingly complex, the number of skilled people required to manage these environments also increases. Software and hardware that implement autonomic computing are needed to reduce the overall cost of operating and managing complex cloud computing environments. While this is an emerging area, software products such as Tivoli from IBM are partially filling the need.

Critical Thinking Exercise

Should Heel Swaps Move to the Cloud?

Heel Swaps is a Chicago-based start-up that sells a stretchable high heel shoe cover that contains a slip resistant out-sole, comes in a variety of sizes, colors and patterns, and slips on in seconds. The product enables you to transform your heels to match different outfits and is sold online at *www.heelswaps.com*.

The firm is just three weeks away from debuting its advertising on the popular Steve Harvey show with some 3 million viewers per episode. Sales and product demand are expected to skyrocket. Unfortunately, management at Heel Swaps has just realized that the firm's Web site does not have the processing capacity to serve the expected increase in shoppers. An IT consulting firm was hired to confirm the need for additional capacity and to make recommendations on how to proceed. Their recommendation is that the current Web site platform be moved to Amazon Web Services (AWS) with elastic load. This service is capable of automatically scaling its request handling capacity to meet the demands of application traffic.

Review Questions

1. What advantages will moving the Web site to the cloud provide for Heel Swaps?
2. What form of cloud computing is best for Heel Swaps—public, private, or hybrid? Why?

Critical Thinking Questions

1. What common start-up problems should the IT consulting firm advise Heel Swaps to avoid?
2. What future changes and developments should be planned for the Heel Swaps Web site as the volume of business grows?

Summary

Principle:

A network has many fundamental components, which—when carefully selected and effectively integrated—enable people to meet personal and organizational objectives.

A computer network consists of communications media, devices, and software connecting two or more computer systems or devices. Communications media are any material substance that carries an electronic signal to support communications between a sending and a receiving device. The computers and devices on the networks are also sometimes called network nodes.

The effective use of networks can help a company grow into an agile, powerful, and creative organization, giving it a long-term competitive advantage. Networks let users share hardware, programs, and databases across the organization. They can transmit and receive information to improve organizational effectiveness and efficiency. They enable geographically separated workgroups to share documents and opinions, which fosters teamwork, innovative ideas, and new business strategies.

Network topology indicates how the communications links and hardware devices of the network are arranged. The three most common network topologies are the star, bus, and mesh.

A network can be classified as personal area, local area, metropolitan, or wide area network depending on the physical distance between nodes on the network and the communications and services it provides.

The electronic flow of data across international and global boundaries is often called transborder data flow.

A client/server system is a network that connects a user's computer (a client) to one or more server computers (servers). A client is often a PC that requests services from the server, shares processing tasks with the server, and displays the results.

Channel bandwidth refers to the rate at which data can be exchanged measured in bits per second.

Communications media can be divided into two broad categories: guided transmission media, in which a communications signal travels along a solid medium, and wireless media, in which the communications signal is sent over airwaves. Guided transmission media include twisted-pair wire cable, coaxial cable, and fiber-optic cable.

Wireless communication is the transfer of information between two or more points that are not connected by an electrical conductor. Wireless communications involves the broadcast of communications in one of three frequency ranges: microwave, radio, and infrared. Wireless communications options include near field communications, Bluetooth, Wi-Fi, and a variety of 3G and 4G communications options.

Networks require various communications hardware devices to operate, including modems, fax modems, multiplexers, private branch exchanges, front-end processors, switches, bridges, routers, and gateways.

Network management includes a wide range of technologies and processes that monitor the network and help identify and address problems before they can create a serious impact.

A network operating system (NOS) controls the computer systems and devices on a network, allowing them to communicate with one another. Network-management software enables a manager to monitor the use of individual computers and shared hardware, scan for viruses, and ensure compliance with software licenses.

Mobile device management (MDM) software manages and troubleshoots mobile devices remotely, pushing out applications, data, patches, and settings.

Software-defined networking (SDN) is an emerging approach to networking that allows network administrators to manage a network via a controller that does not require physical access to all the network devices.

Principle:

Together, the Internet and the World Wide Web provide a highly effective infrastructure for delivering and accessing information and services.

The Internet is truly international in scope, with users on every continent. It is the world's largest computer network. Actually, it is a collection of interconnected networks, all freely exchanging information.

The Internet transmits data from one computer (called a host) to another. The set of conventions used to pass packets from one host to another is known as the Internet Protocol (IP). Many other protocols are used with IP. The best known is the Transmission Control Protocol (TCP). TCP is so widely used that many people refer to the Internet protocol as TCP/IP, the combination of TCP and IP used by most Internet applications.

Each computer on the Internet has an assigned IP address for easy identification. A Uniform Resource Locator (URL) is a Web address that specifies the exact location of a Web page using letters and words that map to an IP address and a location on the host.

People can connect to the Internet backbone in several ways: via a LAN whose server is an Internet host, or via a dial-up connection, high-speed service, or wireless service. An Internet service provider is any company that provides access to the Internet. To connect to the Internet through an ISP, you must have an account with the service provider and software that allows a direct link via TCP/IP.

The Internet and social media Web sites have emerged as important new channels for learning about world events, protesting the actions of organizations and governments, and urging others to support one's favorite causes or candidates. On the other hand, Internet censorship, the control or suppression of the publishing or accessing of information on the Internet, is a growing problem.

The Web was designed to make information easy to find and organize. It connects billions of documents, which are now called Web pages, stored on millions of servers around the world. Web pages are connected to each other using hyperlinks, specially denoted text or graphics on a Web page, that, when clicked, open a new Web page containing related content. The pages are accessed and viewed using Web client software called a Web browser.

Many Web sites use CSS to define the design and layout of Web pages, XML to define the content, and HTML to join the content (XML) with the design (CSS).

Internet companies, including Amazon, eBay, and Google, use Web services to streamline and simplify communication among Web sites.

XML is also used within a Web page to describe and transfer data between Web service applications.

Today's Web development applications allow developers to create Web sites using software that resembles a word processor. The software includes features that allow the developer to work directly with the HTML code or to use auto-generated code.

The use of social media in business is called Enterprise 2.0. Enterprise 2.0 applications, such as Salesforce's Chatter, Jive Software's Engage Dialog, and Yammer, enable employees to create business wikis, support social networking, perform blogging, and create social bookmarks to quickly find information.

Social journalism provides important news not available elsewhere; however, its sources may not be as reliable as mainstream media sources.

Today, schools at all levels provide online education and training. The Web is also an excellent source of job-related information.

A search engine is a valuable tool that enables you to find information on the Web by specifying words or phrases known as keywords, which are related to a topic of interest. Search engine optimization (SEO) is a process for driving traffic to a Web site by using techniques that improve the site's ranking in search results.

Instant messaging is online, real-time communication between two or more people who are connected via the Internet.

Twitter is a Web application that allows users to send short text updates (up to 140 characters) from a smartphone or a Web browser to their Twitter followers.

Internet technologies support real-time online conferencing where participants dial into a common phone number to share a multiparty phone conversation and, in many cases, live video of the participants.

A Web log, typically called a blog, is a Web site that people that people and businesses use to share their observations, experiences, and opinions on a wide range of topics.

A podcast is an audio broadcast you can listen to over the Internet.

Content streaming is a method of transferring large media files over the Internet so that the data stream of voice and pictures plays more or less continuously as the file is being downloaded.

The Internet and the Web have made music more accessible than ever, with artists distributing their songs through online radio, subscription services, and download services.

Television and movies are expanding to the Web in leaps and bounds. Online services such as Amazon Instant Video, Hulu, and Netflix provide television programming from hundreds of providers, including most mainstream television networks.

Video games have become a huge industry with worldwide annual revenue projected to exceed $100 billion by 2017.

You can buy almost anything via the Web, from books and clothing to cars and sports equipment.

Travel Web sites help travelers find the best deals on flights, hotels, car rentals, vacation packages, and cruises. They have profoundly changed the travel industry and the way people plan trips and vacations.

An intranet is an internal corporate network built using Internet and World Wide Web standards and products. Employees of an organization can use an intranet to access corporate information.

A growing number of companies offer limited network access to selected customers and suppliers. Such networks are referred to as extranets, which connect people who are external to the company.

Principle:

Organizations are using the Internet of Things (IoT) to capture and analyze streams of sensor data to detect patterns and anomalies—not after the fact, but while they are occurring—in order to have a considerable impact on the event outcome.

The Internet of Things (IoT) is a network of physical objects or "things" embedded with sensors, processors, software, and network connectivity capability to enable them to exchange data with the manufacturer of the device, device operators, and other connected devices.

There can be many issues with simply receiving and recognizing usable sensor data resulting in missing data or sensor data lacking time stamps indicating when the reading occurred.

One of the first things developers of IoT applications should focus on is building in security from the start.

Principle:

Cloud computing provides access to state-of-the-art technology at a fraction of the cost of ownership and without the lengthy delays that can occur when an organization tries to acquire its own resources.

Cloud computing refers to a computing environment in which software and storage are provided as an Internet service and can be accessed by users with their Web browser. Computing activities are increasingly being delivered over the Internet rather than from installed software on PCs.

Cloud computing offers many advantages to businesses. By outsourcing business information systems to the cloud, a business saves on system design, installation, and maintenance. Employees can also access corporate systems from any Internet-connected computer using a standard Web browser.

Cloud computing can be deployed in several different ways, including public cloud computing, private cloud computing, and hybrid cloud computing.

Public cloud computing refers to deployments in which service providers offer their cloud-based services to the general public, whether that is an individual using Google Calendar or a corporation using the Salesforce.com application. In a private cloud deployment, cloud technology is used within the confines of a private network. Organizations that implement a private cloud often do so because they are concerned that their data will not be secure in a public cloud.

A hybrid cloud is composed of both private and public clouds integrated through networking. Organizations typically use the public cloud to run applications with less sensitive security requirements and highly fluctuating capacity needs, but run more critical applications, such as those with significant compliance requirements, on the private portion of their hybrid cloud.

Autonomic computing is an enabling technology for cloud computing that enables systems to manage themselves and adapt to changes in the computing environment, business policies, and operating objectives.

Cloud computing can be divided into three main types of services: infrastructure as a service (IaaS), software as a service (SaaS), and platform as a service (PaaS).

Organizations contemplating moving to the cloud are advised to proceed carefully, as almost one in three organizations encounter major challenges in their move. Frequent problems include complex pricing arrangements and hidden costs that reduce expected cost savings, performance issues that cause wide variations in performance over time, poor user support, and greater than expected downtime.

Key Terms

autonomic computing

Bluetooth

broadband communications

bus network

Cascading Style Sheet (CSS)

channel bandwidth

client/server architecture

cloud computing

communications medium

computer network

content streaming

Extensible Markup Language (XML)

hybrid cloud

hyperlink

Hypertext Markup Language (HTML)

infrastructure as a service (IaaS)

instant messaging

Internet backbone

Internet Protocol (IP)

Internet service provider (ISP)

IP address

local area network (LAN)

Long Term Evolution (LTE)

mesh network

metropolitan area network (MAN)

mobile device management (MDM) software

near field communication (NFC)

network operating system (NOS)

network topology

network-management software

personal area network (PAN)

platform as a service (PaaS)

podcast

private cloud environment

search engine

search engine optimization (SEO)

software-defined networking (SDN)

star network

tag

Uniform Resource Locator (URL)

virtual private network (VPN)

Web 2.0

Web browser

Web log (blog)

wide area network (WAN)

Wi-Fi

wireless communication

Chapter 6: Self-Assessment Test

A network has many fundamental components—which, when carefully selected and effectively integrated—enable people to meet personal and organizational objectives.

1. Communications media can be divided into two broad categories _____.
   a. infrared and microwave
   b. fiber optic and cable
   c. packet switching and circuit switching
   d. guided and wireless

2. _____ refers to the rate at which data can be exchanged and is measured in bits per second.
   a. Communications frequency
   b. Channel bandwidth
   c. Communications wavelength
   d. Broadband

3. _____ indicates how the communications links and hardware devices of the network are arranged.
   a. Communications protocol
   b. Transmission media

   c. Network topology
   d. None of the above
4. Twisted-pair wire, cable, coaxial cable, and fiber optic cable are all examples of guided communications media. True/False
5. Systems software that controls the computer systems and devices on a network and allows them to communicate with one another is called _____.
   a. network operating system
   b. mobile device management software
   c. network-management software
   d. software-defined networking

Together, the Internet and the World Wide Web provide a highly effective infrastructure for delivering and accessing information and services.

6. The Internet transmits data in packets from one computer to another using a set of communications conventions called the _____.
7. Every computer on the Internet has an assigned IP address for easy identification. True/False
8. A _____ is a Web address that specifies the exact location of a Web page using letters and words that map to an IP address and the location on the host.
   a. Universal Resource Locator
   b. Uniform Reference Locator
   c. Universal Web address
   d. Uniform Resource Locator
9. Many Web sites use CSS to define the design and layout of Web pages, and XML to define the content, and HTML to join the content with the design. True/False
10. The use of social media in business is called _____.
   a. social journalism
   b. blogging
   c. business wikis
   d. Enterprise 2.0

11. A(n) _____ is an internal corporate network built using Internet and World Wide Web standards and products.

Organizations are using the Internet of Things (IoT) to capture and analyze streams of sensor data to detect patterns and anomalies—not after the fact, but while they are occurring—in order to have a considerable impact on the event outcome.

12. There can be many issues with simply receiving and recognizing usable sensor data resulting in sensor data lacking time stamps indicating when the reading occurred or in _____ data.
13. One of the first things developers of IoT applications should focus on is building in _____ from the start.
   a. redundancy and backup
   b. cost controls
   c. security
   d. disaster recovery

Cloud computing provides access to state-of-the-art technology at a fraction of the cost of ownership and without the lengthy delays that can occur when an organization tries to acquire its own resources.

14. Cloud computing is a computing environment in which software and storage are provided as an Internet service and accessed by users with their _____.
   a. Web browser
   b. mobile computing device such as a smartphone or tablet
   c. search engine
   d. Virtual Private Network (VPN)
15. _____ is an enabling technology for cloud computing that enables systems to manage themselves and adapt to changes in the computing environment, business policies, and operating objectives.

Chapter 6: Self-Assessment Test Answers

1. d
2. b
3. c
4. True
5. a
6. Internet protocol or TCP/IP
7. True
8. d
9. True
10. d
11. intranet
12. missing
13. c
14. a
15. Autonomic computing

Review Questions

1. Define the term "computer network."
2. Define the term "network topology," and identify three common network topologies in use today.
3. What is meant by client/server architecture? Describe how this architecture works.
4. Define the term "channel bandwidth." Why is this an important characteristic of a communication channel?
5. Identify the names of the three primary frequency ranges used for wireless communications.
6. What is Bluetooth wireless communication? Give an example of the use of this technology.
7. What advantage does a communications satellite have over a terrestrial microwave system?
8. What role does a network operating system play?
9. What is software-defined networking (SDN), and what advantages does it offer?
10. What is Internet censorship? Identify some countries in which this is a major issue.
11. What comprises the Internet backbone?
12. What is an IP address? What is a Uniform Resource Locator, and how is it used?
13. What is XML, and how is it used?
14. What are CSS, and are how are they used?
15. What are Web services? Give an example of a Web service.
16. What is Enterprise 2.0 and how is it used?
17. What is the Internet of Things (IoT), and how is it used?
18. What is cloud computing? Identify three approaches to deploying cloud computing.
19. What is autonomic computing, and how does it benefit cloud computing?

Discussion Questions

1. Briefly discuss the differences between the star, bus, peer-to-peer, and mesh network topologies.
2. Briefly discuss the differences between a personal area network, a local area network, a metropolitan area network, and a wide area network.
3. Identify and briefly discuss three common guided transmission media types.
4. Describe how near field communications works, and give an example of the use of this technology.
5. Describe how a Wi-Fi network works.
6. Describe how a terrestrial microwave system works.
7. Summarize the differences among 1G, 2G, 3G, and 4G wireless communications systems.
8. Discuss the role of network-management software—including mobile device management software.
9. Provide a brief history of the Internet.
10. Briefly describe how the Internet works.
11. Identify and briefly describe five different ways to access the Internet.
12. Briefly describe how the World Wide Web works.
13. Discuss the role of Hypertext Markup Language and HTML tags.
14. What is search engine optimization, and how is it accomplished?
15. Identify some of the issues and concerns associated with connecting devices to the Internet of Things (IoT).
16. Identify and briefly discuss four problems frequently encountered by organizations moving to the cloud.
17. One of the key issues associated with the development of a Web site is getting people to visit it. If you were developing a Web site, how would you inform others about it and make it interesting enough that they would return and tell others about it?
18. Keep track of the amount of time you spend on social networking sites for one week. Do you think that this is time well spent? Why or why not?
19. Briefly summarize the differences in how the Internet, a company intranet, and an extranet are accessed and used.

Problem-Solving Exercises

1. Develop a spreadsheet to track the amount of time you spend each day on Twitter, Instagram, Facebook, and other social networks. Record your times on each network for a two-week period. How much of this time would you consider informative and worthwhile? How much time is just entertainment?

2. Do research to learn about the Amazon Web Services, Google Compute Engine, and Windows Azure cloud computing services. Write a paragraph summarizing each service. Prepare a spreadsheet to compare the three services based on ease of use, cost, and other key criteria of your choosing.

3. Think of a business that you might like to establish. Use a word processor to define the business in terms of what product(s) or service(s) it provides, where it is located, and its name. Go to *www.godaddy.com*, and find an appropriate domain name for your business that is not yet

taken. Shop around online for the best deal on Web site hosting. Write a paragraph about your experience finding a name, why you chose the name that you did, and how much it would cost you to register the name and host a site.

Team Activities

1. Form a team to identify IoT sensors in high demand in the medical device/pharma/bio-med industry. How are these sensors being used? What companies manufacture them? What do they cost if purchased in large quantities? Write a summary of your team's findings.
2. Plan, set up, and execute a meeting with another team wherein you meet via the use of a Web service such as GoToMeeting or WebEx. What are

some of the problems you encountered in setting up and executing the meeting? How would you evaluate the effectiveness of the meeting? What could have been done to make the meeting more effective?
3. Try using the Chinese search engine Baidu to find information on several politically sensitive topics or people. Write a brief summary of your experience.

Web Exercises

1. Do research on the Web to identify the three to five countries that exercise the greatest amount of Internet censorship on its citizens. Briefly document each country's censorship practices.
2. Net neutrality is the principle that Internet service providers should be required to treat all Internet traffic running over their wired and wireless networks the same—without favoring content from some sources and/or blocking or slowing (also known as throttling) content from others. The debate over net neutrality raises questions about how best to keep the Internet open and impartial

while still offering Internet service providers sufficient incentive to expand their networks to serve more customers and to support new services. Do research to find out the current status of net neutrality in the United States. Write a report summarizing your findings.
3. Do research to identify the top ten social networks in terms of number of worldwide active accounts. Which of these networks appears to be the fastest growing, slowest growing? Can you find a reason for the difference in growth rates? Write a report summarizing what you found.

Career Exercises

1. View the movie *The Social Network* or read the book *The Boy Billionaire*, which offers insights into Mark Zuckerberg, the founder of Facebook. How did Zuckerberg recognize the potential of social networking? How was he able to turn this basic idea into a billion dollar organization? What background, education, and experiences did he have that helped him in this endeavor?
2. Identify a social networking organization that interests you. Do research to identify current job

openings and the qualifications needed to fill open positions at the firm. Do any of these positions appeal to you? Why or why not?
3. Explore LinkedIn, a social media network for professional networking. Use some of its features to find former students of your school or coworkers at your place of employment. What are some of the advantages of using such a Web site? What are some of the potential problems? Would you consider joining LinkedIn? Why or why not?

Case Studies

Case One

Cloud Helps Fight Cancer
Each minute one person in the United States dies from cancer—over half a million deaths per year. Thousands of

scientists and physicians are working around the clock to fight cancer where it starts—in our DNA.

DNA is a molecule present in our cells that carries most of the genetic instructions used in the development, functioning, and reproduction of all known living organisms.

The information in DNA is stored as a code made up of four chemical bases adenine (A), guanine (G), cytosine (C), and thymine (T). Human DNA consists of about 3 billion bases, and more than 99 percent of those bases are the same in all people. The complete set of DNA instructions is called your genome, and it comes packaged into two sets of chromosomes, one set from your mother and one set from your father. Sometimes those instructions are miscoded or misread, which can cause cells to malfunction and grow out of control—resulting in cancer.

Doctors now routinely use patient genetic data along with personal data and health factors to design highly personalized treatments for cancer patients. However, genome sequencing is a highly complex effort—it takes about 100 gigabytes of data to represent just a single human genome. Only a few years ago, it was not even feasible to analyze an entire human genome. The Human Genome Project (HGP) was the international, collaborative research program whose goal was the complete mapping and understanding of all the genes of human beings. The HGP took over 15 years and cost in the neighborhood of $3 billion, but the result was the ability to read the complete genetic blueprint for humans.

It takes a computer with powerful processing power and prodigious amounts of storage capacity to process all the patient data required to sequence their genome. Most researchers simply do not have the in-house computing facilities equal to the challenge. As a result, they turn to cloud computing solutions, such as the Amazon Web Services public cloud system. Thanks to cloud computing and other technical advances, sequencing of a human genome can now be done in about 40 hours at a cost of under $5000.

Researchers at Nationwide Children's Hospital in Columbus, Ohio invented Churchill, a software application that analyzes gene sequences very efficiently. Using cloud computing and this new algorithm, researchers at the hospital are now able to analyze a thousand individual genomes over the period of a week. Not only does this technology enable the hospital to help individual patients, it also helps large-scale research efforts exploring the genetic mutations that cause diseases.

Using the cloud also enables doctors and researchers worldwide to share information and collaborate more easily. The Cancer Genome Atlas (TCGA) is a research program supported by the National Cancer Institute and the National Human Genome Research Institute, whose goal is to identify genomic changes in more than 20 different types of human cancer. TCGA researchers compare the DNA samples of normal tissue with cancer tissue taken from the same patient to identify changes specific to that cancer. The researchers hope to analyze hundreds of samples for each type of cancer from many different patients to better understand what makes one cancer different from another cancer. This is critical because two patients with the same type of cancer can experience very different outcomes and respond very differently to the same treatment. Researchers hope to develop more effective, individualized treatments for each patient by connecting specific genomic changes with specific outcomes.

Critical Thinking Questions:

1. What advantages does cloud computing offer physicians and researchers in their fight against cancer?

2. Estimate the amount of data required to analyze the human genome of 100 patients for each of 20 different types of cancer.

3. Physicians must abide by HIPAA regulations when transmitting data back and forth to the cloud. The penalties for noncompliance are based on the level of negligence and can range from $100 to $50,000 per violation (or per record). Violations can also carry criminal charges, resulting in jail time. What measures can be taken when using cloud computing to ensure that patient confidentiality will not be violated?

SOURCES: Gaudin, Sharon, "How The Cloud Helps Fight Cancer," *Computerworld*, May 20, 2015, *www.computerworld.com/article /2923753/cloud-computing/how-the-cloud-helps-fight-cancer.html*; "Deoxyribonucleic Acid Fact Sheet," *www.genome.gov/25520880*, accessed December 7, 2015; "Cancer Genomics What Does It Mean to You?," The Cancer Genome Atlas, *http//cancergenome.nih.gov/Publish edContent/Files/pdfs/1.1.0_CancerGenomics_TCGA-Genomics-Bro chure-508.pdf*; "TCGA on AWS," *http//aws.amazon.com/public-data-sets/tcga*, accessed December 7, 2015; "An Overview of the Human Genome Project," National Human Genome Research Institute, *www .genome.gov/12011238*, accessed December 10, 2015.

Case Two

Globacom Invests in Its Mobile Network Infrastructure in Africa

Approximately 46 percent of the world's population now has access to the Internet—a key factor in encouraging economic activity and expanding educational opportunities. However, Internet access in Africa continues to trail that of the rest of the world. The continent contains 16 percent of the world's population, but represents only about 9.8 percent of the world's Internet users. Affordability and logistical barriers still prevent the vast majority of Africa's population from accessing the wealth of information and services available online.

Increasingly, however, people in Africa—and around the globe—are breaking down those barriers by using mobile devices to gain access to the Internet. In 2015, there were an estimated 7 billion mobile broadband subscriptions worldwide, and that number is growing by almost 25 percent each year. As the world's dependence on mobile technologies grows, telecommunications companies are increasing their investment in the networks that support those technologies.

Globacom Limited is one of the fastest-growing mobile communications companies in the world, operating mobile networks in Nigeria and several other West African countries under the GLO brand. The company is the second largest mobile network operator in Nigeria, where mobile devices account for over 76 percent of Web traffic (more than double the world average of 33 percent).

In order to provide reliable Internet access to its mobile subscribers, Globacom invests heavily in its network infrastructure. In 2011, the company became the first to lay a high-capacity, fiber-optic submarine cable from the United Kingdom to Nigeria. The large-scale project, which also connects points in Ghana, Senegal, Mauritania, Morocco, Portugal, and Spain, cost the company more than $800 million. The underwater cable system allowed Globacom to expand its network, boost capacity, and increase Internet upload and download speeds. For Globacom's mobile subscribers in Nigeria, the new cable also represented a significant jump in international connectivity—considered to be one of the critical requirements for the development of the Internet in any country.

Globacom also makes use of big data capabilities to improve its network performance and enhance the quality of the customer service it provides its subscribers. The company recently implemented Oracle's Big Data Appliance platform, a hardware and software package that allows the company to analyze both structured and unstructured data related to issues such as terminated networks, event times and durations, event cost, quality of service, and overall network performance. Globacom's IT staff uses the Oracle platform to capture and analyze more than 1 billion call-data records per day—the equivalent of 5 gigabytes of user-traffic information per second. According to Jameel Mohammed, Globacom's group chief operating officer, the Oracle platform "enables us to capture, store, and analyze data that we were unable to access before. We now analyze network events 40 times faster."

With a reduction in average query response time for network events from three minutes to five seconds, Globacom's call center agents are better able to provide subscribers fast and reliable information regarding network performance. The company has significantly increased its "first-call resolution rate," saving the company more than 13 million call center minutes, or the equivalent of 80 full-time customer service employees, annually.

For subscribers, Globacom's investment in its network infrastructure along with its big data initiatives translate into improved network coverage and reliability, better customer service, and, perhaps most importantly, easier and more consistent access to the Internet—including a wide range of modern communications services, such as online banking and payment services, teleconferencing, distance learning, and telemedicine.

Critical Thinking Questions

1. What incentives does a mobile network operator have to make ongoing, expensive investments in its network infrastructure? What have been some of the benefits to Globacom's subscribers of the company's investment in its mobile network?

2. Big data applications and techniques allow network operators to make use of large quantities of network-related data, which was previously discarded due to the time and resources required to effectively analyze the data. What are some data points that you think would be most useful for a communications company to analyze when looking for ways to improve their network performance? What data points related to network activity and performance might be useful from a customer service or marketing standpoint?

3. Do research online to learn about some of the other factors that have impeded Internet access for most of the population in Africa and other parts of the world. What factors besides the level of network infrastructure investment might affect Internet access rates in a given country?

SOURCES: "Ericsson Mobility Report," Ericsson, *www .ericsson.com/res/docs/2016/mobility-report/ericsson -mobility-report-feb-2016-interim.pdf*, accessed February 20, 2016; "ICT Facts & Figures: The World in 2015," International Telecommunication Union, *www.itu.int/en/ITU-D/Statistics /Documents/facts/ICTFactsFigures2015.pdf, May 2015*; "Internet Users in the World by Region, November 2015" Internet World Stats, *www.internetworldstats.com/stats.htm*, accessed February 20, 2016; "Internet Goes Mobile: Country Report Nigeria," Ericsson *www.ericsson.com/res/docs/2015 /consumerlab/ericsson-consumerlab-internet-goes-mobile- nigeria.pdf*, accessed February 21, 2016; "Globacom Saves Over 35,000 Call-Processing Minutes Daily and Improves Data for Decision-Making and Customer Service," Oracle, *www.oracle.com/us/corporate/customers/customersearch /globacom-1-big-data-ss-2207715.html*, accessed February 20, 2016; Banks, Roland, "There Are Now 3 Billion Internet Users Worldwide in 2015," *Mobile Industry Review*, January 26, 2015, *www.mobileindustryreview.com/2015 /01/3- billion-internet-users-2015.html*; "Africa's 50 Richest: #7 Mike Adenuga," *Forbes*, accessed February 21, 2016.

Notes

1. Ignatescu, Adrian, "Most Popular Instant Messaging Apps in 2014-Review & Infographic," *Techchangers* (blog), March 30, 2014, *www.techchangers.com /instant-messaging-apps-review-most-popular-2014 -top10*.

2. Claburn, Thomas, "Walmart Jumps into Crowded Mobile Payment Market," *Information Week*, December 10, 2015, *www.informationweek.com/mobile/mobile-appli cations/walmart-jumps-into-crowded-mobile-payment -market/d/d-id/1323518*.

3. Hamblen, Matt, "Levi's Stadium App Makes Use of Aruba Beacons to Help 49ers Fans Get Around," *Computer- world*, November 4, 2014, *www.computerworld.com /article/2842829/levis-stadium-app-makes-use-of -aruba-beacons-to-help-49ers-fans-get-around.html*.

4. Wohnoutak, Bill, "Childhood Burn Care: A Telemedicine Success Story," *Dermatology Times*, February 18, 2015, *dermatologytimes.modernmedicine.com/dermatology -times/news/telemedicines-role-childhood-burn-care? page=full*.

5. "Saudi Telecom Company Deploys High-Capacity International Mesh Network Powered by Ciena," Investors.com, October 21, 2015, *news.investors .com/newsfeed-business-wire/102115-141851937-saudi -telecom-company-deploys-high-capacity-international -mesh-network-powered-by-ciena.aspx*.

6. "PIONIER-Polish Optical Internet," PIONIER, *http://blog. pionier.net.pl/sc2013/pionier*, accessed January 6, 2014.

7. "About Chi-X Japan," Chi-X Japan, *www.chi-x.jp/ABOUT US.aspx*, accessed February 19, 2016.

8. "Iridium Everywhere," Iridium, *www.iridium.com*, accessed December 11, 2015.
9. Cheng, Roger, "Verizon to Be First to Field-Test Crazy-Fast 5G Wireless," *CNET*, September 8, 2015, *www.cnet.com/news/verizon-to-hold-worlds-first-crazy-fast-5g-wireless-field-tests-next-year*.
10. "PRTG Network Monitor Helps Small, Family-Owned IT Consulting Business Provide World-Class Reliability," Paessler, *www.paessler.com/company/casestudies/covell_group_uses_prtg*, accessed December 16, 2015.
11. Higginbotham, Stacy, "Google Launches Andromeda, a Software Defined Network Underlying Its Cloud," *Gigaom*, April 2, 2014, *https://gigaom.com/2014/04/02/google-launches-andromeda-a-software-defined-network-underlying-its-cloud*.
12. "Internet World Stats," *Internet World Stats, www.internetworldstats.com/stats.htm*, accessed December 13, 2015.
13. Alexandrova, Katerina, "Using New Media Effectively: An Analysis of Barack Obama's Election Campaign Aimed at Young Americans," Thesis, New York 2010, *www.academia.edu/1526998/Using_New_Media_Effectively_an_Analysis_of_Barack_Obamas_Election_Campaign_Aimed_at_Young_Americans*.
14. "Electronic Weapons: Syria Shows the Way," *Strategy-Page*, January 13, 2014, *www.strategypage.com/htmw/htecm/articles/20140113.aspx*.
15. Smith, Charlie, "Jimmy Wales on Censorship in China," *The WorldPost*, September 4, 2015, *www.huffingtonpost.com/charlie-smith/jimmy-wales-on-censorship_b_8087400.html*.
16. Howard, Alexander, "In Saudi Arabia, Embracing New 'Freedom' on Social Media May Come with Serious Risks," *Huffington Post*, May 26, 2015, *www.huffingtonpost.com/2015/05/26/saudi-arabia-social-media_n_7444742.html*.
17. Naím, Moisés and Bennet, Phillip, "The Anti-Information Age," *The Atlantic*, February 16, 2015, *www.theatlantic.com/international/archive/2015/02/government-censorship-21st-century-internet/385528*.
18. "AWS Case Study: Airbnb," Amazon Web Services, *http://aws.amazon.com/solutions/case-studies/airbnb*, accessed December 13, 2015.
19. Schnuer, Jenna, "Meet the Winners of Our Entrepreneur of 2014 Awards," *Entrepreneur*, January 20, 2015, *www.entrepreneur.com/slideshow/240844*.
20. "Transforming Tyco with Yammer," Yammer, *https://about.yammer.com/customers/tyco*, accessed January 13, 2014.
21. "About Khan Academy," Khan Academy, *www.khanacademy.org/about*, accessed December 13, 2015.
22. "About Us," NPower, *www.npower.org/Our-Purpose/Our-Purpose.aspx*, accessed December 13, 2015.
23. Ignatescu, "Most Popular Instant Messaging Apps in 2014."
24. "Addison Fire Saves $5K Yearly Using GoToMeeting with HDFaces Video Conferencing," Citrix, *http://news.citrixonline.com/wp-content/uploads/2013/07/Addison-Fire-District_G2M_ss.pdf*, accessed January 30, 2014.
25. "Rhapsody Music Service Now Has 3 Million Paying Subscribers," *Variety*, July 22, 2015, *http://variety.com/2015/digital/news/rhapsody-music-service-now-has-3-million-paying-subscribers-1201545576*.
26. Newman, Jared, "Popcorn Time Users Sued again, This Time for Streaming 2015's Survivor," *PC World*, September 2, 2015, *www.pcworld.com/article/2979681/software-entertainment/popcorn-time-users-sued-again-this-time-for-streaming-2015s-survivor.html*.
27. "YouTube Statistics," YouTube, *www.youtube.com/yt/press/statistics.html*, accessed January 21, 2014.
28. Takahashi, Dean, "Mobile Gaming Could Drive Entire Video Game Industry to $100 Billion in Revenue by 2017," *Gamesbeat*, January 14, 2014, *http://venturebeat.com/2014/01/14/mobile-gaming-could-drive-entire-game-industry-to-100b-in-revenue-by-2017*.
29. "Groupon Announces Fourth Quarter and Fiscal Year 2015 Results," Groupon, February 11, 2016, *http://investor.groupon.com/releasedetail.cfm?releaseid=954580*.
30. "4 Real-World Stories about the Interactive Intranet," *Jive* (blog), June 18, 2015, *www.jivesoftware.com/blog/real-world-stories-about-interactive-intranet*.
31. Romeo, Jim, et al, "A Practical Guide to the Internet of Things," Tech Target, (c) 2015.
32. Kepes, Ben, "The Internet of Things, Coming Soon to an Airline near You," *Runway Girl Network*, March 14, 2015, *www.runwaygirlnetwork.com/2015/03/14/the-internet-of-things-coming-soon-to-an-airline-near-you*.
33. van Zyl, Gareth, "Internet of Everything Helps Prevent Dubai Crane Collisions," *Web Africa*, June 4, 2014, *www.itwebafrica.com/cloud/516-africa/233009-internet-of-everything-helps-prevent-dubai-crane-collisions*.
34. "Reducing Costs with a Converged Roadway Network," Cisco, *www.cisco.com/c/dam/en/us/solutions/collateral/industry-solutions/Aegean-Motorway-voc-case-study.pdf*, accessed January 4, 2015.
35. "iCloud," Apple, *www.apple.com/icloud*, accessed January 8, 2014.
36. "AWS Case Study: Spotify," Amazon Web Services, *aws.amazon.com/solutions/case-studies/spotify*, accessed December 17, 2015.
37. "The College Network," *www.slideshare.net/EarthLinkBusiness/private-cloud-case-study-the-college-network-earth-link-business*, accessed January 9, 2014.
38. "Cloud Computing Options," *PC Today*, June 2014.
39. Ramel, David, "New Research Shows 'Staggering' Failure Rates for Cloud Projects," *Enterprise Systems*, June 26, 2014, *http://esj.com/articles/2014/06/26/cloud-projects-fail.aspx*.
40. Olavsrud, Thor, "Why a Media Giant Sold Its Data Center and Headed to the Cloud," *CIO*, July 15, 2014, *www.cio.com/article/2453894/data-center/why-a-media-giant-sold-its-data-center-and-headed-to-the-cloud.html*.
41. Ovide, Shira and Boulton, Clint, "Flood of Rivals Could Burst Amazon's Cloud," *The Wall Street Journal*, July 25, 2014, *www.wsj.com/articles/storm-clouds-over-amazon-business-1406328539?mg=id=wsj*.
42. "Revlon Fact Sheet," Revlon, *www.revlon.com/about/fact-sheet*, accessed February 21, 2016.
43. "Revlon, Inc. Moves to the Cloud with Juniper Networks to Increase Global Business Agility," Juniper Networks, *www.juniper.net/assets/us/en/local/pdf/case-studies/3520444-en.pdf*, accessed October 6, 2014.
44. "Cloud Computing Options," *PC Today*, June 2014.
45. "Autonomic Computing," IBM, *www.ibm.com/developerworks/tivoli/autonomic.html*, accessed October 7, 2014.

PART 3

Business Information Systems

Sergey Nivens/Shutterstock.com

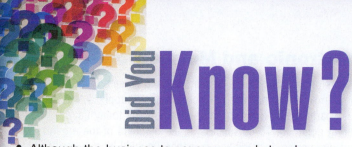

Did You Know?

- Although the business-to-consumer market grabs more of the news headlines, the B2B market is considerably larger and is growing more rapidly. B2B sales within the United States were estimated to be over $780 billion in 2015, twice the size of B2C commerce.

- Target reported that cyberthieves compromised the credit card data and personal information including phone numbers, email and home addresses, credit and debit card numbers, PINS, expiration dates, and magnetic stripe data of as many as 110 million of its customers. Within two days after the Target data breach was announced, a class action lawsuit was filed claiming that Target was negligent in its failure to implement and maintain reasonable security procedures and practices.

Principles

- Electronic and mobile commerce are evolving, providing new ways of conducting business that present both potential benefits and problems.

- E-commerce and m-commerce can be used in many innovative ways to improve the operations of an organization.

- E-commerce and m-commerce offer many advantages yet raise many challenges.

- Organizations must define and execute an effective strategy to be successful in e-commerce and m-commerce.

- E-commerce and m-commerce require the careful planning and integration of a number of technology infrastructure components.

Learning Objectives

- Describe the current status of various forms of e-commerce, including B2B, B2C, C2C, and e-government.

- Outline a multistage purchasing model that describes how e-commerce works.

- Define m-commerce and identify some of its unique challenges.

- Identify several e-commerce and m-commerce applications.

- Identify several advantages associated with the use of e-commerce and m-commerce.

- Identify the many benefits and challenges associated with the continued growth of e-commerce and m-commerce.

- Outline the key components of a successful e-commerce and m-commerce strategy.

- Identify the key components of technology infrastructure that must be in place for e-commerce and m-commerce to work.

- Discuss the key features of the electronic payment systems needed to support e-commerce and m-commerce.

Why Learn about Electronic and Mobile Commerce?

Electronic and mobile commerce have transformed many areas of our lives and careers. One fundamental change has been the manner in which companies interact with their suppliers, customers, government agencies, and other business partners. As a result, most organizations today have set up business on the Internet or are considering doing so. To be successful, all members of the organization need to plan and participate in that effort. As a sales or marketing manager, you will be expected to help define your firm's e-commerce business model. As a customer service employee, you can expect to participate in the development and operation of your firm's Web site. As a human resource or public relations manager, you will likely be asked to provide Web site content for use by potential employees and shareholders. As an analyst in finance, you will need to know how to measure the business impact of your firm's Web operations and how to compare that to competitors' efforts. Clearly, as an employee in today's organization, you must understand what the potential role of e-commerce is, how to capitalize on its many opportunities, and how to avoid its pitfalls. The emergence of m-commerce adds an exciting new dimension to these opportunities and challenges. Many customers, potential employees, and shareholders will be accessing your firm's Web site via smartphones, tablets, and laptops. This chapter begins by providing a brief overview of the dynamic world of e-commerce.

As you read this chapter, consider the following:

- What are the advantages of e-commerce and m-commerce?
- How do innovations in technology and infrastructure affect regions across the globe?

An Introduction to Electronic Commerce

Electronic commerce (e-commerce) is the conducting of business activities (e.g., distribution, buying, selling, marketing, and servicing of products or services) electronically over computer networks. It includes any business transaction executed electronically between companies (business-to-business), companies and consumers (business-to-consumer), consumers and other consumers (consumer-to-consumer), public sector and business (government-to-business), public sector to citizens (government-to-citizen), and public sector to public sector (government-to-government). Business activities that are strong candidates for conversion to e-commerce are ones that are paper based, time consuming, and inconvenient for customers.

Business-to-Business E-Commerce

business-to-business (B2B) e-commerce: A subset of e-commerce in which all the participants are organizations.

Business-to-business (B2B) e-commerce is a subset of e-commerce in which all the participants are organizations. B2B e-commerce is a useful tool for connecting business partners in a virtual supply chain to cut resupply times and reduce costs. Although the business-to-consumer market grabs more of the news headlines, the B2B market is considerably larger and is growing more rapidly. B2B sales within the United States were estimated to be over $780 billion in 2015, twice the size of B2C commerce.[1]

A recent survey by Forrester Research and *Internet Retailer* showed that 30 percent of B2B buyers now make more than half of their purchases online, and that percentage will likely increase to 56 percent by 2017, with much of that growth coming from purchases that are researched or completed through mobile devices.[2] Popular B2C Web sites have helped raise expectations as to how an e-commerce site must operate, and many B2B companies are responding to those heightened expectations by investing heavily in their B2B platforms. Spending on e-commerce technologies by large U.S. manufacturers, wholesalers, and distributors is expected to top $2 billion in 2019.[3]

Moving more customers online is key to B2B commerce success, so in addition to investing in new technologies, B2B companies are focusing on new ways of engaging their customer across multiple channels—both online and offline. Providing customers with a consistent experience regardless of channel was a top priority for 68 percent of B2B organizations who took part in another recent survey commissioned by Accenture Interactive and SAP. The top e-commerce priorities for many B2B buyers include transparent pricing, easily accessible product details, purchase tracking, and personalized recommendations.[4]

Many organizations use both *buy-side e-commerce* to purchase goods and services from their suppliers and *sell-side e-commerce* to sell products to their customers. Buy-side e-commerce activities include identifying and comparing competitive suppliers and products, negotiating and establishing prices and terms, ordering and tracking shipments, and steering organizational buyers to preferred suppliers and products. Sell-side e-commerce activities include enabling the purchase of products online, providing information for customers to evaluate the organization's goods and services, encouraging sales and generating leads from potential customers, providing a portal of information of interest to the customer, and enabling interactions among a community of consumers. Thus, buy-side and sell-side e-commerce activities support the organization's value chain and help the organization provide lower prices, better service, higher quality, or uniqueness of product and service.

Grainger is a B2B distributor of products for facilities maintenance, repair, and operations (a category called MRO) with more than 1.5 million different items offered online. See Figure 7.1. In 2015, the company's online sales exceeded $4 billion or more than 40 percent of the company's total sales.[5] A key part of Grainger's e-commerce success is its suite of mobile apps, which make it possible for customers to access products online and quickly find and order products via a smartphone or other mobile device. Currently, 15 percent of the company's e-commerce traffic comes to its Web site through mobile devices.[6]

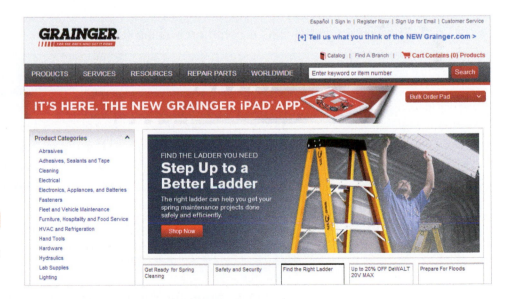

FIGURE 7.1

Grainger e-commerce

Grainger offers more than 1.5 million items online.

Source: grainger.com

Business-to-Consumer E-Commerce

business-to-consumer (B2C) e-commerce: A form of e-commerce in which customers deal directly with an organization and avoid intermediaries.

Business-to-consumer (B2C) e-commerce is a form of e-commerce in which customers deal directly with an organization and avoid intermediaries. Early B2C pioneers competed with the traditional "brick-and-mortar" retailers in an industry, selling their products directly to consumers. For example, in 1995, upstart Amazon.com challenged well-established booksellers Waldenbooks and Barnes & Noble. Amazon did not become profitable until 2003; the firm has grown from selling only books on a U.S.-based Web site to selling a wide variety of products through international Web sites in Canada, China, France, Germany, Japan, and the United Kingdom. A recent Forrester Research Inc. and Internet Retailer survey found that the average B2C order value was $158.[7] As with B2B sales, B2C revenues are increasingly being driven by customers using mobile devices. In Q3 of 2015, smartphones accounted for 14 percent of all B2C revenue—a 98 percent jump from the previous year.[8]

By using B2C e-commerce to sell directly to consumers, producers or providers of consumer products can eliminate the middlemen, or intermediaries, between them and the consumer. In many cases, this squeezes costs and inefficiencies out of the supply chain and can lead to higher profits for businesses and lower prices for consumers. The elimination of intermediate organizations between the producer and the consumer is called disintermediation.

More than just a tool for placing orders, the Internet enables shoppers to compare prices, features, and value, and to check other customers' opinions. Consumers can, for example, easily and quickly compare information about automobiles, cruises, loans, insurance, and home prices to find better values. Internet shoppers can unleash shopping bots or access sites such as eBay Shopping.com, Google Shopping, Shopzilla, PriceGrabber, Yahoo! Shopping, or Excite to browse the Internet and obtain lists of items, prices, and merchants.

Worldwide, B2C e-commerce sales continue to grow rapidly, reaching $1.9 trillion in 2014. The Asia-Pacific region represents the world's largest and fastest-growing B2C market; it accounts for almost 40 percent of total worldwide B2C sales.[9] China's e-commerce sales are now over $670 billion and are growing at a rate of over 40 percent per year. Other top markets with double-digit e-commerce sales growth include: United Kingdom ($99.4 billion), Japan ($89.6 billion), and Germany ($61.8 billion).[10] Table 7.1 shows the estimated B2C e-commerce sales by world region from 2012 to 2017 (estimated).

TABLE 7.1 Forecasted global B2C e-commerce sales (USD billions)

Region	Sales (billions)					
	2012	2013	2014	2015	2016	2017
Asia-Pacific	$301.2	$383.9	$525.2	$681.2	$855.7	$1,052.9
North America	$379.8	$431.0	$482.6	$538.3	$597.9	$660.4
Western Europe	$277.5	$312.0	$347.4	$382.7	$414.2	$445.0
Central and Eastern Europe	$41.5	$49.5	$58.0	$64.4	$68.9	$73.1
Latin America	$37.6	$48.1	$57.7	$64.9	$70.6	$74.6
Middle East and Africa	$20.6	$27.0	$33.8	$39.6	$45.5	$51.4
Worldwide	$1,058.2	$1,251.4	$1,504.6	$1,771.0	$2,052.7	$2,357.4

Source: "Global B2C Ecommerce Sales to Hit $1.5 Trillion This Year Driven by Growth in Emerging Markets," e-Marketer, February 3, 2014, *http://www.emarketer.com/Article/Global-B2C-Ecommerce-Sales-Hit-15-Trillion-This-Year-Driven-by-Growth-Emerging-Markets/1010575#sthash.ZQGggr6U.dpuf.*

One reason for the steady growth in B2C e-commerce is shoppers find that many goods and services are cheaper when purchased online, including stocks, books, newspapers, airline tickets, and hotel rooms.

Another reason for the growth in B2C e-commerce is that online B2C shoppers have the ability to design a personalized product. Nike, Inc., provides a successful example of this approach to personalization. The company's online NIKEiD service enables purchasers to customize a pair of shoes by selecting from different material, features, and fit options—including the level of insole cushioning, sole material, and the fabric color and design of everything from the lining of the shoe to the laces. Nike also recently added a Personalized ID (PiD) service, which allows customers to further individualize their shoes by adding a personal message to their shoes—whether that be a personal mantra, a sports team affiliation, or a personal record. According to Ken Dice, NIKEiD's vice president and general manager, "The new Personalized iD service is exciting because it gives athletes the opportunity to communicate inspiration, support, passion and connection to the world around them in a meaningful and timely way."[11,12]

Yet a third reason for the continued growth of B2C e-commerce is the effective use of social media networks by many companies looking to reach consumers, promote their products, and generate online sales. Vera Bradley is a luggage design company that produces a variety of products, including quilted cotton luggage, handbags, and accessories. The firm has more than 1.6 million Facebook followers and is one of the most followed Internet retailers on Pinterest. Indeed, Vera Bradley has been extremely conscientious in cross-posting items from Facebook, Flickr, and YouTube to Pinterest. When you visit the Vera Bradley Web site, Pinterest and other social buttons appear on the product pages so that shoppers can share their likes with friends. Vera Bradley is an example of a B2C retailer that makes social media channels work together effectively to reach more potential customers.

Facebook, Instagram, Pinterest, and Twitter are just a few social networking sites that are continuing to add "paid social" features designed to help e-commerce companies generate sales by reaching a targeted audience. Pinterest is gradually rolling out "Buyable Pins," starting with large retailers like Macy's and Nordstrom, allowing more of the social network's 100 million active users to purchase products online without ever leaving the site.[13]

Many B2C merchants have also added social commerce or social shopping tools to their own sites. For example, Target's online Awesome Shop features user-generated images of Target products from Instagram. Customers have three options for exploring the online shop: Products, Looks, and Places. When a shopper clicks on an image in the shop, they can get details on the products shown, and with another click, they can initiate a purchase of the item from Target's Web site.[14]

Another important trend is that of consumers researching products online but then purchasing those products at a local brick-and-mortar store. Sales in local stores that are stimulated through online marketing and research are called Web-influenced sales. Such sales are estimated to exceed $1.7 trillion—roughly 40 percent of total retail sales, and in some categories, such as baby/toddler and home furnishing, Web-influenced sales make up more than 55 percent of total sales.[15]

Amazon is the dominant B2C retailer in the United States, as illustrated in Table 7.2, which lists the country's five largest B2C retailers.

TABLE **7.2** Largest business-to-consumer retailers in the United States

Rank	Company	Total Web Sales (Billions of Dollars)
1	Amazon	$71.8
2	Walmart	$13.2
3	Apple	$10.7
4	Macy's	$4.7
5	Home Depot	$4.3

Source: Wahba, Phil, "This Chart Shows Just How Dominant Amazon Is," *Fortune, http://fortune.com/2015/11/06/amazon-retailers-ecommerce.*

As a result of a 1992 Supreme Court ruling that says online retailers don't have to collect sales taxes in states where they lack a physical presence, millions of online shoppers do not pay state or local tax on their online purchases. Consumers who live in states with sales tax are supposed to keep track of their out-of-state purchases and report those "use taxes" on their state income tax returns. However, few tax filers report such purchases. Thus, despite having a legal basis to do so, states find it very difficult to collect sales taxes on Internet purchases. This avoidance of sales tax creates a price advantage for online retailers over brick-and-mortar stores, where sales taxes must be collected. It also results in the loss of about $23 billion in tax revenue that could go to state and local governments to provide services for their citizens. In 2013, and again in 2015, the U.S. Supreme Court declined to get involved in state efforts to force Web retailers such as Overstock and eBay to collect sales tax from customers. The court's failure to act has put pressure on Congress to devise a national solution, as both online and traditional retailers complain about a patchwork of state laws and conflicting lower-court decisions; however, efforts to revise federal Internet sales tax rules have, so far, been unsuccessful. Many states are now devising ways to sidestep the Supreme Court's rulings or initiate new challenges in the courts. Louisiana, Nebraska, and Utah are all considering measures that would expand the definition of "physical presence" to include a company's use of a third-party shipping company to deliver products to customers' homes.[16] In the meantime, several other states are simply moving forward with efforts to collect tax online purchases, and many merchants are already complying. Amazon, for instance, already collects sales tax on purchases in 24 states.[17]

Consumer-to-Consumer E-Commerce

consumer-to-consumer (C2C) e-commerce: A subset of e-commerce that involves electronic transactions between consumers using a third party to facilitate the process.

Consumer-to-consumer (C2C) e-commerce is a subset of e-commerce that involves electronic transactions between consumers using a third party to facilitate the process. eBay is an example of a C2C e-commerce site; customers buy and sell items to each other through the site. Founded in 1995, eBay has become one of the most popular Web sites in the world, with 2015 net revenue of $8.5 billion.[18]

Other popular C2C sites include Bidz.com, Craigslist, eBid, Etsy, Fiverr, Ibidfree, Kijiji, Ubid, and Taobao. The growth of C2C is responsible for a drastic reduction in the use of the classified pages of newspapers to advertise and sell personal items and services, so it has had a negative impact on that industry. On the other hand, C2C has created an opportunity for many people to make a living out of selling items on auction Web sites. According to eBay, the gross merchandise volume for items sold on its site in 2015 was $82 billion.[19]

Companies and individuals engaging in e-commerce must be careful that their sales do not violate the rules of various county, state, or country legal jurisdictions. More than 4,000 Web sites offer guns for sale and over 20,000 gun ads are posted each week on the Web site Armslist alone. Extending background checks to the flourishing world of online gun sales has become a highly controversial issue in the United States. Under current law, the question of when a background check must occur depends on who is selling the gun. Federal regulations require licensed dealers to perform checks, but the legal definition of who must be licensed has not been clear.[20] An Executive Order signed by President Barack Obama on January, 4, 2016, is designed to extend background check requirements to more types of online gun sellers, including more private sellers who had previously been exempted.[21]

Table 7.3 summarizes the key factors that differentiate B2B, B2C, and C2C e-commerce.

TABLE 7.3 Differences among B2B, B2C, and C2C

Factors	B2B	B2C	C2C
Typical value of sale	Thousands or millions of dollars	Tens or hundreds of dollars	Tens of dollars
Length of sales process	Days to months	Days to weeks	Hours to days
Number of decision makers involved	Several people to a dozen or more	One or two	One or two
Uniformity of offer	Typically a uniform product offering	More customized product offering	Single product offering, one of a kind
Complexity of buying process	Extremely complex; much room for negotiation on quantity, quality, options and features, price, payment, and delivery options	Relatively simple; limited negotiation on price, payment, and delivery options	Relatively simple; limited negotiation on payment and delivery options; negotiations focus on price
Motivation for sale	Driven by a business decision or need	Driven by an individual consumer's need or emotion	Driven by an individual consumer's need or emotion

E-Government

e-government: The use of information and communications technology to simplify the sharing of information, speed formerly paper-based processes, and improve the relationship between citizens and government.

E-government is the use of information and communications technology to simplify the sharing of information, speed formerly paper-based processes, and improve the relationship between citizens and government. Government-to-citizen (G2C), government-to-business (G2B), and government-to-government (G2G) are all forms of e-government, each with different applications.

Citizens can use G2C applications to submit their state and federal tax returns online, renew auto licenses, purchase postage, and apply for student loans. Citizens can purchase items from the U.S. government through its GSA Auctions Web site, which offers the general public the opportunity to bid electronically on a wide range of government assets. Healthcare.gov is a healthcare exchange Web site created by and operated under the U.S. federal government as specified in the Patient Protection and Affordable Care Act. It is designed for use by residents in the 36 U.S. states that opted not to create their own state exchanges. By accessing this Web site, users can view healthcare options, determine if they are eligible for healthcare subsidiaries, and enroll in a plan.[22]

G2B applications support the purchase of materials and services from private industry by government procurement offices, enable firms to bid on government contracts, and help businesses identify government contracts on which they may bid. The Web site Business.USA.gov allows businesses to access information about laws and regulations and to download relevant forms needed to comply with federal requirements for their businesses. The *http://reverseauctions.gsa.gov/reverseauctions/reverseauctions/* Web site is a business and auction exchange Web site that helps federal government agencies purchase information system products by using reverse auctions and by aggregating demand for commonly purchased products. FedBizOpps.gov is a Web site where government agencies post procurement notices to provide an easy point of contact for businesses that want to bid on government contracts.

G2G applications support transactions between government entities, such as between the federal government and state or local governments. Government to Government Services Online (GSO) is a suite of Web applications that enables government organizations to report information—such as birth and death data, arrest warrant information, and information about the amount of state aid being received—to the administration of Social Security services. This information can affect the payment of benefits to individuals. Many state governments provide a range of e-government services to various state and local agencies. For example, the state of Oregon's transaction payment engine (TPE) option enables agencies to use an efficient Internet payment solution while adhering to statewide policies and procedures. This service is just one aspect of Oregon's E-Government Program, whose goals are creating a uniform state of Oregon online identity, promoting digital government, and saving Oregon taxpayers money.[23,24]

Critical Thinking Exercise

Building a Successful B2B Web Site

Your company operates a single store outside Atlanta, Georgia, that sells nearly $50 million in maintenance, repair, and operations (MRO) supplies each year. Any product that is used in the manufacturing process, but that isn't incorporated into the product itself, can be classified as MRO including consumables like cleaning supplies used to clean production machinery, supplies that are used to support operations, and office supplies and small equipment like fans and compressors. Your customers are mainly professional buyers who work for one of the many manufacturing companies in the area. They buy items based on annual purchase contracts negotiated with your company's sales reps.

Your company is keenly interesting in building a Web site to enable it to reach customers nationwide. The firm tried entering e-commerce a few years ago but the venture was a failure. The Web site was poorly designed so that customers found it difficult to use and the technology selected proved to be unreliable with the Web site crashing for a few hours every week. A small group of employees is working with an experienced Web designer to design the new Web site.

Review Questions

1. Provide a strong justification for creating a new B2B Web site for your firm.
2. In what ways would this new B2B Web site differ from a typical B2C Web site?

Critical Thinking Questions

1. The Web site design team believes that the firm's Web site should incorporate a design and features similar to some of the best B2C Web sites. What do you think this means? Can you offer some specific design ideas and features that should be included?
2. What are some potential issues the team faces in implementing and operating this Web site?

Introduction to Mobile Commerce

Mobile commerce (m-commerce) relies on the use of mobile devices, such as tablets and smartphones, to place orders and conduct business. Smartphone manufacturers such as Apple, Huawei, Lenovo, LG, Samsung, and Xiaomi are working with communications carriers such as AT&T, Sprint/Nextel, T-Mobile, and Verizon to develop wireless devices, related technology, and services to support m-commerce. The Internet Corporation for Assigned Names and Numbers (ICANN) created a .mobi domain in 2005 to help attract mobile users to the Web. Afilias administers this domain and helps to ensure that the .mobi destinations work quickly, efficiently, and effectively with all mobile devices.

Mobile Commerce in Perspective

Mobile commerce is a rapidly growing segment of e-commerce, with Japan, the United Kingdom, and South Korea leading the world in m-commerce growth.[25] The market for m-commerce in North America is maturing much later than in other countries for several reasons. In North America, responsibility for network infrastructure is fragmented among many providers and consumer payments are usually made by credit card. In most Western European countries, consumers are much more willing to use m-commerce. Japanese consumers are generally enthusiastic about new technology and therefore have been much more likely to use mobile technologies to make purchases.

Worldwide, m-commerce accounted for 35 percent of all retail e-commerce sales in the fourth quarter of 2015. In the United States, the share of e-commerce transactions completed on a mobile device grew 15 percent from the prior year, representing 30 percent of all e-commerce transactions.[26]

The number of mobile Web sites worldwide is growing rapidly because of advances in wireless broadband technologies, the development of new and useful applications, and the availability of less costly but more powerful smartphones. Experts point out that the relative clumsiness of mobile browsers and security concerns still must be overcome to speed the growth of m-commerce.

M-Commerce Web Sites

A number of retailers have established special Web sites for mobile devices users. Table 7.4 provides a list of some of the top-ranked mobile Web sites according to a recent survey of more than 400,000 people by OC&C Strategy Consultants.

TABLE 7.4 Highly rated m-commerce retail Web sites

Rank	Company
1	eBay
2	Amazon
3	Apple
4	Burberry
5	John Lewis
6	Lush

Source: Goldfingle, Gemma, "The Top 10 M-Commerce Sites, according to OC&C's Proposition Index," *RetailWeek*, January 25, 2016, *www.retail-week.com/technology/online-retail/the-top-10-m-commerce-sites-according-to-occs-proposition-index/7004140.fullarticle*.

Consumers often place high value on different criteria, depending on the type of mobile site. In the OC&C survey, eBay and Amazon ranked highly due to their convenience, effective search tools, and transaction speed. The mobile site for natural cosmetics company Lush was rated highly because it created a strong emotional connection with consumers.

Advantages of Electronic and Mobile Commerce

Conversion to an e-commerce or m-commerce system enables organizations to reach new customers, reduce the cost of doing business, speed the flow of goods and information, increase the accuracy of order processing and order fulfillment, and improve the level of customer service.

Reach New Customers

The establishment of an e-commerce Web site enables a firm to reach new customers in new markets. Indeed, this is one of the primary reasons organizations give for establishing a Web site.

Founded in 1978, Shoe Carnival is a chain of more than 400 footwear stores located in 33 states.[27] Shoe Carnival's unique concept involves creating a high-energy atmosphere within each store through features such as a "spinning wheel of savings" and a team member on a microphone interacting with shoppers. According to Ken Zimmerman, vice president of e-commerce, the chain's goal is "to entertain our customers. We create a fun place with music and excitement." Until recently, the Shoe Carnival Web site served only as a source of information for customers; however, the company has now launched a full e-commerce site—which includes social shopping tools such as customer-generated reviews of individual items—that is allowing the company to expand its reach to customers in areas where it does not have physical stores. The company's national advertising campaign is focused on driving more traffic to the company's e-commerce site, and the company's future online efforts will be focused on re-creating its "surprise and delight" concept online to differentiate it from other online shoe stores.[28]

Reduce Costs

By eliminating or reducing time-consuming and labor-intensive steps throughout the order and delivery process, more sales can be completed in the same period and with increased accuracy. With increased speed and accuracy of customer order information, companies can reduce the need for inventory—from raw materials to safety stocks and finished goods—at all the intermediate manufacturing, storage, and transportation points.

BloomNation bills itself as a "trusted community marketplace for people to list, discover, and send unique bouquets handcrafted by local florists across the country."[29] Launched as a response to the rising commissions being charged by the dominant floral wire services, including FTD, 1-800-Flowers, and Teleflora, the BloomNation site offers floral arrangements from over 1,500 florists around the country who take and post their own photos on the site. The florists are able to take advantage of the increased exposure and stability that BloomNation's site offers, without some of the staffing and other costs associated with processing individual customer orders and payments. The florists also pay lower per-order fees—just 10 percent per order rather than 27 percent charged by the large wire services.[30]

Speed the Flow of Goods and Information

When organizations and their customers are connected via e-commerce, the flow of information is accelerated because electronic connections and communications are already established. As a result, information can flow from buyer to seller easily, directly, and rapidly.

Shutterfly, an online provider of photographic products and services to both businesses and consumers, generates $1 billion in sales annually. While the vast majority of Shutterfly's e-commerce revenue comes from B2C transactions, the company also offers B2B marketing products and services through its Web site, where business customers can order customized, four-color marketing materials. The company's e-commerce capabilities, automated workflow, and large-scale production centers allow business customers to quickly customize and place their orders—cutting the project completion time from weeks to days for many clients.[31,32]

Increase Accuracy

By enabling buyers to enter their own product specifications and order information directly, human data-entry error on the part of the supplier is eliminated. And order accuracy is important—no matter what the product is. Domino's, the second-largest pizza chain in the world, was one of the first chain restaurants to offer an e-commerce site where customers could enter and pay for their orders. Half of Domino's sales now comes through its e-commerce site. Using the site's Easy Order feature, customers can enter their orders and address information directly—improving order and delivery accuracy. And for customers who create a "Pizza Profile" online, ordering can be as simple as sending a tweet or a text (customers can initiate an order using just a pizza emoji) or just clicking a button on the Domino's smartphone app.[33]

Improve Customer Service

Increased and more detailed information about delivery dates and current status can increase customer loyalty. In addition, the ability to consistently meet customers' desired delivery dates with high-quality goods and services eliminates any incentive for customers to seek other sources of supply.

Customers come to Sticker Mule's e-commerce site to order customized stickers for a wide range of projects, whether that be to market a business, label products, drive traffic to a Web site, or raise money for a crowdfunding project. When developing its e-commerce site, Sticker Mule placed a high priority on ease of use. Customers using the site can place their orders within a matter of minutes, and then view and approve order proofs online, further reducing the time it takes to complete orders. Sticker Mule's Web infrastructure allows their customer service team to consolidate support inquiries from a variety of channels—including email, Web, and phone—into one place, making it easier and faster for team members to respond to customer queries. And since customer service is a top priority for Sticker Mule, their site also includes a sophisticated help center with more than 200 articles (in multiple languages) that customers can research on their own. The site also allows customers to post reviews, and even includes a Marketplace section where customers can sell their stickers.[34]

Multistage Model for E-Commerce

A successful e-commerce system must address the many stages that consumers experience in the sales life cycle. At the heart of any e-commerce system is the user's ability to search for and identify items for sale; select those items and negotiate prices, terms of payment, and delivery date; send an order to the vendor to purchase the items; pay for the product or service; obtain product delivery; and receive after-sales support. Figure 7.2 shows how e-commerce can support each

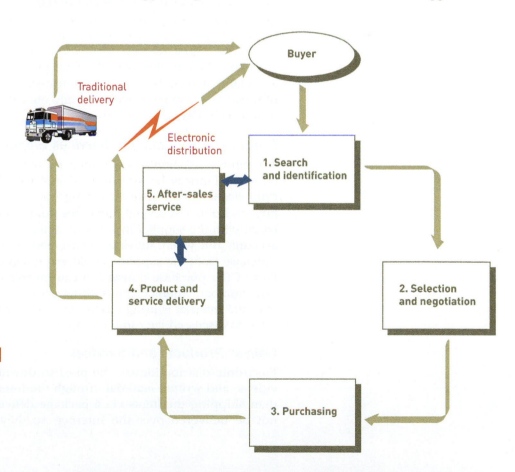

FIGURE 7.2

Multistage model for e-commerce (B2B and B2C)

A successful e-commerce system addresses the stages that consumers experience in the sales life cycle.

of these stages. Product delivery can involve tangible goods delivered in a traditional form (e.g., clothing delivered via a shipping company) or goods and services delivered electronically (e.g., software downloaded over the Internet).

Search and Identification

An employee ordering parts for a storeroom at a manufacturing plant would follow the steps shown in Figure 7.2. Assume the storeroom stocks a wide range of office supplies, spare parts, and maintenance supplies. The employee prepares a list of needed items—for example, fasteners, piping, and plastic tubing. Typically, for each item carried in the storeroom, a corporate buyer has already identified a preferred supplier based on the vendor's price competitiveness, level of service, quality of products, and speed of delivery. The employee then logs on to the Internet and goes to the Web site of the preferred supplier.

From the supplier's home page, the employee can access a product catalog and browse until he or she finds the items that meet the storeroom's specifications. The employee fills out a request-for-quotation form by entering the item codes and quantities needed. When the employee completes the quotation form, the supplier's Web application calculates the total charge of the order with the most current prices and shows the additional cost for various forms of delivery—overnight, within two working days, or the next week. The employee might elect to visit other suppliers' Web home pages and repeat this process to search for additional items or obtain competing prices for the same items.

Select and Negotiate

After price quotations have been received from each supplier, the employee examines them and indicates by clicking the request-for-quotation form which items to order from a given supplier. The employee also specifies the desired delivery date. This data is used as input into the supplier's order-processing transaction-processing system (TPS). In addition to price, an item's quality and the supplier's service and speed of delivery can be important in the selection and negotiation process.

B2B e-commerce systems need to support negotiation between a buyer and the selected seller over the final price, delivery date, delivery costs, and any extra charges. However, these features are not fundamental requirements of most B2C systems, which typically offer their products for sale on a "take-it-or-leave-it" basis.

Purchase Products and Services Electronically

The employee completes the purchase order specifying the final agreed-upon terms and prices by sending a completed electronic form to the supplier. Complications can arise in paying for the products. Typically, a corporate buyer who makes several purchases from a supplier each year has established credit with the supplier in advance, and all purchases are billed to a corporate account. But when individual consumers make their first, and perhaps only, purchase from the supplier, additional safeguards and measures are required. Part of the purchase transaction can involve the customer providing a credit card number. Another approach to paying for goods and services purchased over the Internet is using electronic money, which can be exchanged for hard cash, as discussed later in the chapter.

Deliver Products and Services

Electronic distribution can be used to download software, music, pictures, videos, and written material through the Internet faster and for less expense than shipping the items via a package delivery service. Most products cannot be delivered over the Internet, so they are delivered in a variety of other ways: overnight carrier, regular mail service, truck, or rail. In some cases, the customer might elect to drive to the supplier and pick up the product.

Many manufacturers and retailers have outsourced the physical logistics of delivering merchandise to other companies that take care of the storing, packing, shipping, and tracking of products. To provide this service, DHL, Federal Express, United Parcel Service, and other delivery firms have developed software tools and interfaces that directly link customer ordering, manufacturing, and inventory systems with their own systems of highly automated warehouses, call centers, and worldwide shipping networks. The goal is to make the transfer of all information and inventory, from the manufacturer to the delivery firm to the consumer, fast and simple.

For example, when a customer orders a printer on the Hewlett-Packard (HP) Web site, that order actually goes to FedEx, which stocks all the products that HP sells online at a dedicated e-distribution facility in Memphis, Tennessee, a major FedEx shipping hub. FedEx ships the order, which triggers an email notification to the customer that the printer is on its way and an inventory notice is sent to HP that the FedEx warehouse now has one less printer in stock. See Figure 7.3.

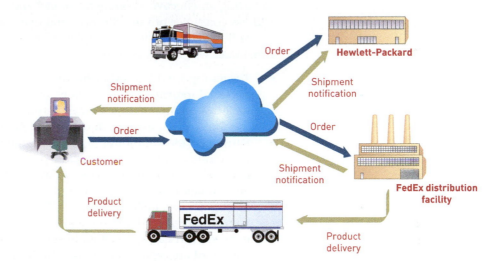

FIGURE 7.3

Product and information flow

When a customer orders an HP printer online, the order goes first to FedEx, which ships the order, triggering an email notification to the customer and an inventory notice to HP.

For product returns, HP enters return information into its own system, which is linked to FedEx's systems. This information signals a FedEx courier to pick up the unwanted item at the customer's house or business. Customers don't need to fill out shipping labels or package the item. Instead, the FedEx courier uses information transmitted over the Internet to a computer in his truck to print a label from a portable printer attached to his belt. FedEx has control of the return, and HP can monitor its progress from start to finish.

After-Sales Service

In addition to the information required to complete an order, comprehensive customer information is also captured from each order and stored in the supplier's customer database. This information can include the customer name, address, telephone numbers, contact person, credit history, and other details. For example, if a customer later contacts the supplier to complain that not all items were received, that some arrived damaged, or even that the product provides unclear instructions, any customer service representative will be able to retrieve the order information from the database. Many companies also provide extensive after-sale information on their Web sites, such as how to maintain a piece of equipment, how to effectively use a product, and how to receive repairs under warranty.

E-Commerce Challenges

A company must overcome many challenges to convert its business processes from the traditional form to e-commerce processes, especially for B2C e-commerce. As a result, not all e-commerce ventures are successful. For example, Borders began an online Web site in the late 1990s, but after three years of operating in the red, the bookseller outsourced its e-commerce operations to Amazon in 2001. Borders reversed course and decided to relaunch its own Borders.com Web site in May 2008, but continued to generate disappointing sales figures. As a result of the substandard results, many top executives were replaced, including the CIO and senior vice president of sales. Finally in early 2011, Borders applied for bankruptcy protection and began closing its stores.[35]

Dealing with Consumer Privacy Concerns

The following are three key challenges to e-commerce: (1) dealing with consumer privacy concerns, (2) overcoming consumers' lack of trust, and (3) overcoming global issues. While two-thirds of U.S. Internet users have purchased an item online and most Internet users say online shopping saves them time, about one-third of all adult Internet users will not buy anything online primarily because they have privacy concerns or lack trust in online merchants. In addition to having an effective e-commerce model and strategy, companies must carefully address consumer privacy concerns and overcome consumers' lack of trust.

Following are a few examples of recent security beaches in which personal data was compromised:

- Target reported that cyberthieves compromised the credit card data and personal information of as many as 110 million customers. That data includes phone numbers, email and home addresses, credit and debit card numbers, PINs, expiration dates, and magnetic stripe information.[36]
- Patreon, a crowdfunding platform that allows users to make ongoing donations to a Web site, artist, or project sustained a security breach that resulted in their entire cache of data—including names, email addresses, and donation records—being published online in 2015.[37,38]
- More than one million CareFirst BlueCross Blue Shield patient records were compromised when hackers accessed a database containing member names, birth dates, email addresses, and subscriber information. Member password encryption prevented the hackers from accessing Social Security numbers, medical claims, and credit card and employment data.[39]
- The personal data of 15 million consumers was stolen when cyberthieves accessed data that mobile provider T-Mobile had shared with Experian for the purpose of conducting credit checks. The stolen data included names, addresses, and birthdates—as well as encrypted Social Security numbers, drivers' license ID numbers, and passport ID numbers, which may also have been compromised.[40]

identity theft: The use of someone's personal identification information without his or her permission, often to commit fraud or other crimes.

In some cases, the compromise of personal data can lead to identity theft. According to the Federal Trade Commission (FTC), "**Identity theft** occurs when someone steals your personal information and uses it without your permission."[41] Often stolen personal identification information (PII), such as your name, Social Security number, or credit card number, is used to commit fraud or other crimes. Thieves may use a consumer's credit card numbers to charge items to that person's accounts, use identification information to apply for a new credit card or a loan in a consumer's name, or use a consumer's name and Social Security number to receive government benefits.

Companies must be prepared to make a substantial investment to safeguard their customers' privacy or run the risk of losing customers and generating potential class action lawsuits should the data be compromised. It is not uncommon for customers to initiate a class action lawsuit for millions of dollars in damages for emotional distress and loss of privacy. In addition to potential damages, companies must frequently pay for customer credit monitoring and identity theft insurance to ensure that their customers' data is secure.

Within two days after the Target data breach was announced, the first lawsuit was filed. The California class action lawsuit claims that Target was negligent in its failure to implement and maintain reasonable security procedures and practices. A second lawsuit claims that Target broke Minnesota law by not alerting customers quickly enough after learning of the security issue. A third lawsuit was filed in California alleging both negligence and invasion of privacy.[42]

In order to address customers' privacy concerns, companies looking to do business online must invest in the latest security technology and employ highly trained security experts to protect their consumers' data. For large companies, that can mean a sizable in-house staff that monitors security issues 24/7. Smaller companies often rely on security services provided by companies such as Symantec, whose Norton Secured Seal is intended to provide customers with the confidence they need to transact e-commerce business.

Akimbo Financial is a financial services company based in San Antonio, Texas. Even though Akimbo is a small player in the financial services industry, it is still obligated to comply with Payment Card Industry (PCI) and other regulations requiring encryption for online transactions and communication. And because Akimbo collects social security numbers and other confidential data, it must assure users that their data is secure. The company employs Symantec's Secure Site with EV (Extended Validation) SSL Certificate to secure its site, and it prominently displays the Norton Secured Seal. The EV certificate presents online visitors with a green bar in their browser address bar, intended to highlight the secure nature of the site. According to Akimbo CEO and founder, Houston Frost, "We have to have the green bar, because it makes people feel warm and fuzzy inside," which is important for a start-up financial services firm looking to build its customer base.[43]

Overcoming Consumers' Lack of Trust

Lack of trust in online sellers is one of the most frequently cited reasons that some consumers give to explain why they are unwilling to purchase online. Can they be sure that the company or person with which they are dealing is legitimate and will send the item(s) they purchase? What if there is a problem with the product or service when it is received: for example, if it does not match the description on the Web site, is the wrong size or wrong color, is damaged during the delivery process, or does not work as advertised?

Online marketers must create specific trust-building strategies for their Web sites by analyzing their customers, products, and services. A perception of trustworthiness can be created by implementing one or more of the following strategies:

- Demonstrate a strong desire to build an ongoing relationship with customers by giving first-time price incentives, offering loyalty programs, or eliciting and sharing customer feedback.
- Demonstrate that the company has been in business for a long time.
- Make it clear that considerable investment has been made in the Web site.
- Provide brand endorsements from well-known experts or well-respected individuals.
- Demonstrate participation in appropriate regulatory programs or industry associations.
- Display Web site accreditation by the Better Business Bureau Online or TRUSTe programs.

Here are some tips to help online shoppers avoid problems:

- Only buy from a well-known Web site you trust—one that advertises on national media, is recommended by a friend, or receives strong ratings in the media.

- Look for a seal of approval from organizations such as the Better Business Bureau Online or TRUSTe. See Figure 7.4.

Courtesy Better Business Bureau and TRUSTe

FIGURE 7.4

Seals of approval

To avoid problems when shopping online, look on the Web site for a seal of approval from organizations such as the Better Business Bureau Online or TRUSTe.

- Review the Web site's privacy policy to be sure that you are comfortable with its conditions before you provide personal information.
- Determine what the Web site policy is for return of products purchased.
- Be wary if you must enter any personal information other than what's required to complete the purchase (name, credit card number, address, and telephone number).
- Do not, under any conditions, ever provide information such as your Social Security number, bank account numbers, or your mother's maiden name.
- When you open the Web page where you enter credit card information or other personal data, make sure that the Web address begins with "https," and check to see if a locked padlock icon appears in the Address bar or status bar, as shown in Figure 7.5.

Microsoft product screenshots used with permission from Microsoft Corporation

FIGURE 7.5

Web site security

Web site that uses "https" in the address and a secure site lock icon.

- Consider using virtual credit cards, which expire after one use, when doing business.
- Before downloading music, change your browser's advanced settings to disable access to all computer areas that contain personal information.

Overcoming Global Issues

E-commerce and m-commerce offer enormous opportunities by allowing manufacturers to buy supplies at a low cost worldwide. They also offer enterprises the chance to sell to a global market right from the start. Moreover, they offer great promise for developing countries, helping them to enter the prosperous global marketplace, which can help to reduce the gap between rich and poor countries. People and companies can get products and services from around the world, instead of around the corner or across town. These opportunities, however, come with numerous obstacles and issues associated with all global systems:

- **Cultural challenges**. Great care must be taken to ensure that a Web site is appealing, easy to use, and inoffensive to potential customers around the world.
- **Language challenges**. Language differences can make it difficult to understand the information and directions posted on a Web site.
- **Time and distance challenges**. Significant time differences make it difficult for some people to be able to speak to customer services representatives or to get technical support during regular waking hours.
- **Infrastructure challenges**. The Web site must support access by customers using a wide variety of hardware and software devices.

- **Currency challenges**. The Web site must be able to state prices and accept payment in a variety of currencies.
- **State, regional, and national law challenges**. The Web site must operate in conformance to a wide variety of laws that cover a variety of issues, including the protection of trademarks and patents, the sale of copyrighted material, the collection and safeguarding of personal or financial data, the payment of sales taxes and fees, and much more.

Critical Thinking Exercise

Extreme Sports Web Site

Extreme sports encompasses certain activities perceived as having a high level of inherent danger such as BMX racing, skate boarding, mountain biking, ice climbing, and base jumping. You've always been a major fan and began selling caps and t-shirts with extreme sport themes, personalities, and inspirational sayings. As a result, over the past two years you have enjoyed traveling to many exotic venues around the world to sell your highly popular products at various events and competitions. You are thinking of starting a Web site to sell your products to extreme sports fans around the globe.

Review Questions

1. What challenges can you expect in trying to set up and run a Web site with global appeal? How might you address these?
2. What information do you need to capture from a customer in order to accurately and completely fill an order?

Critical Thinking Questions

1. What issues might come up in trying to deliver your product to customers in a foreign country?
2. What after sales service issues might arise and how could you handle these?

Electronic and Mobile Commerce Applications

E-commerce and m-commerce are being used in innovative and exciting ways. This section examines a few of the many B2B, B2C, C2C, and m-commerce applications in retail and wholesale, manufacturing, marketing, advertising, bartering, retargeting, price comparison, couponing, investment and finance, and banking. As with any new technology, m-commerce will succeed only if it provides users with real benefits. Companies involved in e-commerce and m-commerce must think through their strategies carefully and ensure that they provide services that truly meet customers' needs.

Wholesale e-Commerce

Wholesale e-commerce spending now represents more than 40 percent of all wholesale sales revenue, according to a 2015 survey.[44] A key sector of wholesale e-commerce is spending on manufacturing, repair, and operations (MRO) goods and services—from simple office supplies to mission-critical equipment, such as the motors, pumps, compressors, and instruments that keep manufacturing facilities running smoothly. MRO purchases often approach 40 percent of a manufacturing company's total revenues, but the purchasing systems within many companies are haphazard, without automated controls. Companies face significant internal costs resulting from outdated and cumbersome MRO management processes. For example, studies show that a high percentage of manufacturing downtime is often caused by not having the right part at the right time in the right place. The result is lost productivity and capacity. E-commerce software for plant operations provides powerful comparative searching capabilities to enable managers to identify functionally equivalent items, helping them spot opportunities to combine purchases for cost savings. Comparing various suppliers, coupled with consolidating more spending with fewer suppliers, leads to decreased costs. In addition, automated workflows are typically based on industry best practices, which can streamline processes.

MSC Industrial Supply is a leading North American distributor of MRO products and services. The company generates $2.8 billion in sales revenue from more than one million products it offers for sale—including 900,000 items that can be purchased through its Web site. In 2015, for the first time, e-commerce sales accounted for more than 50 percent of the company's total sales.[45,46]

Manufacturing

electronic exchange: An electronic forum where manufacturers, suppliers, and competitors buy and sell goods, trade market information, and run back-office operations.

One approach taken by many manufacturers to raise profitability and improve customer service is to move their supply chain operations onto the Internet. Here, they can form an **electronic exchange**, an electronic forum where manufacturers, suppliers, and competitors buy and sell goods, trade market information, and run back-office operations, such as inventory control, as shown in Figure 7.6. This approach speeds up the movement of raw materials and finished products and reduces the amount of inventory that must be maintained. It also leads to a much more competitive marketplace and lower prices.

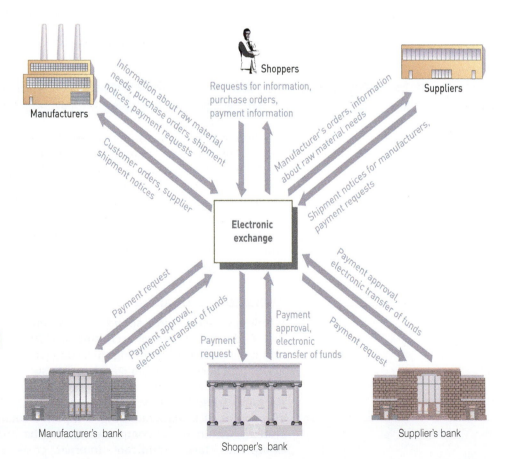

Manufacturers — Information about raw material needs, purchase orders, shipment notices, payment requests

Customer orders, supplier shipment notices

Shoppers — Requests for information, purchase orders, payment information

Suppliers — Manufacturer's orders, information about raw material needs

Shipment notices for manufacturers, payment requests

Electronic exchange

Payment request

Payment approval, electronic transfer of funds

Manufacturer's bank

Payment request

Payment approval, electronic transfer of funds

Shopper's bank

Payment approval, electronic transfer of funds

Payment request

Supplier's bank

FIGURE 7.6

Model of an electronic exchange

An electronic exchange is an electronic forum where manufacturers, suppliers, and competitors buy and sell goods, trade market information, and run back-office operations.

Companies can join one of three types of exchanges based on who operates the exchange. Private exchanges are owned and operated by a single company. The owner uses the exchange to trade exclusively with established business partners. Walmart's Retail Link is such an exchange. Consortium-operated exchanges are run by a group of traditionally competing companies with common procurement needs. For example, Covisint was developed as an exchange to serve the needs of the big three auto makers. Independent exchanges are open to any set of buyers and sellers within a given market. They provide services and a common technology platform to their members and are open, usually for a fee, to any company that wants to use them. For example, Tinypass is a flexible e-commerce platform that enables content publishers to choose from a variety of payment models to sell access to their media. Publishers can offer limited previews to readers before they subscribe, ask for payment to view each video or article, or allow the audience to pay what they believe the content is worth. Content is defined by the publisher and can be any sort of digital media: an article, a movie, a song, a blog post, a PDF, access to a forum, or access to an entire Web site. Tinypass exchange members can use the platform to crowd-fund projects from within their own Web sites, rather than working through third party sites, such as GoFundMe or KickStarter.[47,48]

Several strategic and competitive issues are associated with the use of exchanges. Many companies distrust their corporate rivals and fear they might lose trade secrets through participation in such exchanges. Suppliers worry that online marketplaces will drive down the prices of goods and favor buyers. Suppliers also can spend a great deal of money configuring their systems and work processes to participate in multiple exchanges. For example, more than a dozen new exchanges have appeared in the oil industry, and the printing industry has more than 20 online marketplaces. Until a clear winner emerges in particular industries, suppliers may feel compelled to sign on to several or all of them. Yet another issue is potential government scrutiny of exchange participants: When competitors get together to share information, it raises questions of collusion or antitrust behavior.

Many companies that already use the Internet for their private exchanges have no desire to share their expertise with competitors. At Walmart, the world's largest retail chain, executives turned down several invitations to join exchanges in the retail and consumer goods industries before building its own in-house exchange, Retail Link, which connects the company to 7,000 worldwide suppliers that sell everything from toothpaste to furniture. Through Retail Link, Walmart has created a supplier-managed inventory system where it lets each supplier decide where to put SKUs (stock keeping units) and how to ship through to stores. It empowers suppliers to make these decisions by providing them with inventory and sales data by SKU by hour, by store. This in turn makes Walmart more profitable, because it can hold each supplier accountable to maximize margin, with the lowest inventory possible, to produce the greatest return on investment in inventory.[49]

Marketing

The nature of the Web enables firms to gather more information about customer behavior and preferences as customers and potential customers gather their own information and make their purchase decisions. Analysis of this data is complicated because of the Web's interactivity and because each visitor voluntarily provides or refuses to provide personal data such as name, address, email address, telephone number, and demographic data. Internet advertisers use the data to identify specific markets and target them with tailored advertising messages. This practice, called **market segmentation**, divides the pool of potential customers into subgroups usually defined in terms of demographic characteristics, such as age, gender, marital status, income level, and geographic location.

market segmentation: The identification of specific markets to target them with tailored advertising messages.

In the past, market segmentation has been difficult for B2B marketers because firmographic data (addresses, financials, number of employees, and industry classification code) was difficult to obtain. Now, however, eXelate, a subsidiary of Nielsen, the marketing and media information company, has joined forces with Dun & Bradstreet to provide data as a service solution that customers can use to access a database of more than 250 million business records, including critical company information such as contact names, job titles and seniority levels, locations, addresses, number of employees, annual sales, and Standard Industry Code (SIC) and North America Industry Classification System (NAICS) classification codes. See Figure 7.7. Using this data, analysts can identify, access, and segment their potential B2B audience; estimate potential sales for each business; and rank the business against other prospects and customers.[50]

FIGURE 7.7

Nielsen marketing company

eXelate, a subsidiary of Nielsen, the marketing and media information company, has joined forces with Dun & Bradstreet to provide data as a service solution that customers can use to access a database of more than 250 million business records.

Source: http://info.exelate.com/b2b-audiences_1-sheet

Advertising

Mobile ad networks distribute mobile ads to publishers such as mobile Web sites, application developers, and mobile operators. Mobile ad impressions are generally bought at a cost per thousand (CPM), cost per click (CPC), or cost per action (CPA), in which the advertiser pays only if the customer clicks through and then buys the product or service. The main measures of success are the number of users reached, click through rate (CTR), and the number of actions users take, such as the number of downloads prompted by the ad. Advertisers are keenly interested in this data to measure the effectiveness of their advertising spending, and many organizations are willing to pay extra to purchase the data from a mobile ad network or a third party. Generally, there are three types of mobile ad networks—blind, premium blind, and premium networks—though no clear lines separate them. The characteristics of these mobile advertising networks are summarized in Table 7.5.

TABLE 7.5 Characteristics of three types of mobile advertising networks

Characteristic	Blind Networks	Premium Blind Networks	Premium Networks
Degree to which advertisers can specify where ads are run	An advertiser can specify country and content channel (e.g., news, sports, or entertainment) on which the ad will run but not a specific Web site.	Most advertising is blind, but for an additional charge, the advertiser can buy a specific spot on a Web site of its choice.	Big brand advertisers can secure elite locations on top-tier destinations.
Predominant pricing model and typical rate	CPC (e.g., $0.01 per click)	CPM (e.g., $20 per thousand impressions)	CPM (e.g., $40 per thousand impressions)
Examples	Admoda/Adultmoda AdMob BuzzCity InMobi	Jumptap Madhouse Millennial Media Quattro Wireless	Advertising.com/AOL Hands Microsoft Mobile Advertising Nokia Interactive Advertising Pudding Media YOC Group

InMobi is a mobile advertising provider that reaches 1 billion active users with over 130 billion monthly ad impressions. The company uses a technique it calls "appographic targeting" to help marketers increase the chance of connecting users to the type of media and apps they are most likely to engage with. By analyzing the core functional, design, and interactive attributes of more than 10,000 apps, InMobi has divided its audience of active users into 200 "appographic segments," based on each user's existing and previous application downloads rather than on more traditional metrics, such as demographics or geography. Marketers can use the segments to more accurately target app-install campaigns. For example, a flight-booking app could be promoted to users who engage with apps that offer hotel-booking services or travel-related reviews.[51,52]

Because m-commerce devices usually have a single user, they are ideal for accessing personal information and receiving targeted messages for a particular consumer. Through m-commerce, companies can reach individual consumers to establish one-to-one marketing relationships and communicate whenever it is convenient—in short, anytime and anywhere. See Figure 7.8.

FIGURE 7.8

M-commerce is convenient and personal

Consumers are increasingly using mobile phones to purchase goods and perform other transactions online.

Bartering

During the recent economic downturn, many people and businesses turned to bartering as a means of gaining goods and services. A number of Web sites have been created to support this activity, as shown in Table 7.6. Some businesses are willing to barter to reduce excess inventory, gain new customers, or avoid paying cash for necessary raw materials or services. Cash-strapped customers may find bartering to be an attractive alternative to paying scarce dollars. Generally, bartering transactions have tax-reporting, accounting, and other record-keeping responsibilities associated with them. Indeed, the IRS hosts a Bartering Tax Center Web site that provides details about the tax laws and responsibilities for bartering transactions.

TABLE 7.6 Popular bartering Web sites

Web site	Purpose
Craiglist.org	Includes a section where users can request an item in exchange for services or exchange services for services
Swapagift.com	Enables users to buy, sell, or swap merchant gift cards
Swapstyle.com	Allows users to swap, sell, or buy direct women's accessories, clothes, cosmetics, and shoes
Swaptrees.com	Users trade books, CDs, DVDs, and video games on a one-for-one basis
TradeAway.com	Enables users to exchange a wide variety of new or used items, services, or real estate

Retargeting

An average of 74 percent of all online shopping carts are abandoned, representing more than $4 trillion worth of merchandise in 2013.[53] "Retargeting" is a technique used by advertisers to recapture these shoppers by using targeted and personalized ads to direct shoppers back to a retailer's site. For example, a visitor who viewed the men's clothing portion of a retailer's Web site and then abandoned the Web site would be targeted with banner ads showing various men's clothing items from that retailer. The banner ads might even display the exact items the visitor viewed, such as men's casual slacks. The retargeting could be further enhanced to include comments and recommendations from other consumers who purchased the same items. Retargeting ensures that potential consumers see relevant, targeted ads for products they've already expressed interest in.

Price Comparison

An increasing number of companies provide mobile phone apps that enable shoppers to compare prices and products online. RedLaser enables shoppers to do a quick price comparison by simply scanning the product's bar code. Amazon's Price Check app also lets you search for pricing by taking a picture of a book, DVD, CD, or video game cover. The Barcode Scanner app allows shoppers to scan UPC or Quick Response codes to perform a price comparison and read the latest product reviews.[54,55]

Couponing

During 2015, more than $515 billion in consumer incentives were distributed via 286 billion free-standing insert (FSI) coupons, with an average face value of $1.80 per coupon.[56] Surprisingly, only 0.95 percent of those coupons were redeemed even during tough economic times for many people.[57]

Many businesses now offer a variety of digital coupons—which tend to be redeemed at higher rates than FSI coupons—including printable coupons available on a company's Web site or delivered to customers via email. Shoppers at some retail chains can go to the store's Web site and load digital coupons onto their store loyalty card. Other retailers have programs that allow a person to enter their mobile number and a PIN at checkout to redeem coupons they selected online. Many consumer product good manufacturers and retailers and other businesses now send mobile coupons directly to consumers' smartphones via SMS technology.

More recently, some larger retailers have been experimenting with "proximity marketing," using in-store beacons to deliver coupons to customers who are already in their stores. Beacons, which can be as small as a sticker that is placed on an item or store shelf, uses Bluetooth low-energy (BLE) wireless technology to pinpoint the location of consumers in a store and to deliver mobile coupons directly to a customer's smartphone. A recent study estimates that by 2020 more than 1.5 billion mobile coupons will be delivered using beacon technology.[58,59]

The estimated number of mobile coupon redeemers is expected to increase due to the integration of couponing into social networks, along with an increase in smartphone and tablet users, new mobile apps, and location-based deals.[60] See Figure 7.9.

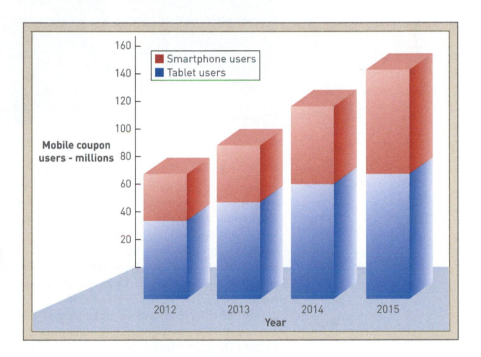

FIGURE 7.9
Growth in U.S. mobile coupon users
The number of mobile coupon redeemers is increasing significantly.

Newer online marketplaces, such as Groupon and LivingSocial offer an updated approach to digital couponing. Discount coupons for consumers are valid only if a predetermined minimum number of people sign up for them. Merchants do not pay any money up front to participate in Groupon of LivingSocial but must pay the companies a fee (up to 50 percent for Groupon) whenever a customer purchase a coupon.

Investment and Finance

The Internet has revolutionized the world of investment and finance. Perhaps the changes have been so significant because this industry had so many built-in inefficiencies and so much opportunity for improvement.

The brokerage business adapted to the Internet faster than any other arm of finance. See Figure 7.10. The allure of online trading that enables investors to do quick, thorough research and then buy shares in any company in a few seconds and at a fraction of the cost of a full-commission firm has brought many investors to the Web. Fidelity offers mobile trading apps for tablets, smartphones, and even Apple Watch. The apps allow investors a secure platform to monitor their portfolios, view real-time stock quotes, track preferred stocks, and execute trades.[61]

FIGURE 7.10

Mobile investment and finance

Investment firms provide mobile trading apps to support clients on the go.

Banking

Online banking customers can check balances of their savings, checking, and loan accounts; transfer money among accounts; and pay bills. These customers enjoy the convenience of not writing checks by hand, of tracking their current balances, and of reducing expenditures on envelopes and stamps. In addition, online banking customers have the satisfaction of knowing that paying bills online is good for the environment because it reduces the amount of paper used, thus saving trees and reducing greenhouse gases.

All of the major banks and many of the smaller banks in the United States enable their customers to pay bills online, and most support bill payment via mobile devices. Banks are eager to gain more customers who pay bills online because such customers tend to stay with the bank longer, have higher cash balances, and use more of the bank's products and services. To encourage the use of this service, many banks have eliminated all fees associated with online bill payment.

Consumers who have enrolled in mobile banking and downloaded the mobile application to their cell phones can check credit card balances before making major purchases to avoid credit rejections. They can also transfer funds from savings to checking accounts to avoid an overdraft.

M-Pesa (M for mobile, Pesa for money in Swahili) with some 20 million users worldwide is considered by many to be the most developed mobile payment system in the world. The service is operated by Safaricom and Vodacom, the largest mobile network operators in Kenya and Tanzania. M-Pesa enables users with a national ID card or passport to deposit, withdraw, and transfer money easily with a mobile device. Its services have expanded from a basic mobile money transfer scheme to include loans and savings products, bill pay, and salary disbursements. In 2013, more than 40 percent of Kenya's GDP flowed through M-Pesa.[62,63]

Online Personalized Shopping

An increasing number of Web sites offer personalized shopping consultations for shoppers interested in upscale, contemporary clothing—dresses, sportswear, denim clothing, handbags, jewelry, shoes, and luxury gifts. Key to the success of companies such as MyTheresa and Net-a-Porter is a philosophy of high customer service and strong, personal client relationships. Net-a-Porter offers same-day delivery in Hong Kong, New York, and London, and a team of personal shoppers stock the virtual carts of women around the globe who are looking for high fashion and luxury items.[64]

Quintessentially Gifts is a luxury gifts and shopping service whose researchers and editorial stylists can find the rarest and most exquisite gifts for the affluent shopper. See Figure 7.11. From a McQueen Luxury Dive Toy's underwater scooter to a Hermes Birkin handbag sans the usual two-year wait, the gift team can get it for you.[65]

FIGURE 7.11

Luxury gifts online

Quintessentially Gifts is an online shopping service that features unusual luxury gifts.

Source: www.quintessentiallygifts.com

Critical Thinking Exercise

Establishing a Consortium

You are a recent business major graduate and a new manager in the supply chain management organization of Marriott International. The organization is looking to reduce the amount of money spent each year on basic supplies such as linens and towels, cleaning supplies, furniture, and appliances. You have been asked to explore the feasibility of establishing an electronic exchange (consortium) of other hotel chains and the suppliers of the items in an attempt to lower total costs.

Review Questions

1. Explain how such an electronic exchange might operate.
2. What are some of the pros and cons of participating in an electronic exchange?

Critical Thinking Questions

1. Identify several strategic and competitive issues that may complicate the formation of such a consortium.
2. Would you recommend that Marriott continue to explore the feasibility of setting up a consortium? Why or why not?

Strategies for Successful E-Commerce and M-Commerce

With all the constraints to e-commerce already discussed in this chapter, it's clear that an effective Web site must be one that is easy to use and accomplishes the goals of the company yet is safe, secure, and affordable to set up and maintain. However, before building a Web site, a company must first define an effective e-commerce model and strategy. The next sections examine several issues for a successful e-commerce site.

Defining an Effective E-Commerce Model and Strategy

The first major challenge is for the company to decide on the effective e-commerce model it wants to use and formulate an effective e-commerce strategy. Although companies can select from a number of approaches, the most successful e-commerce models include three basic components: community, content, and commerce, as shown in Figure 7.12. Discussion forums and other social shopping tools can build a loyal community of people who are interested in and enthusiastic about the company and its products and services. Providing useful, accurate, and timely content, such as industry and economic news and stock quotes, is a sound approach to encourage people to return to your Web site time and again. Commerce involves consumers and businesses paying to purchase physical goods, information, or services that are posted or advertised online.

FIGURE 7.12

Content, commerce, and community

A successful e-commerce model includes three basic components.

Defining the Functions of a Web Site

When building a Web site, you should first decide which tasks the site must accomplish. Most people agree that an effective Web site is one that creates an attractive presence and that meets the needs of its visitors, which might include the following:

- Obtaining general information about the organization
- Obtaining financial information for making an investment decision in the organization
- Learning the organization's position on social issues
- Learning about the products or services that the organization sells
- Buying the products or services that the company offers
- Checking the status of an order

- Getting advice or help on effective use of the products
- Registering a complaint about the organization's products
- Registering a complaint concerning the organization's position on social issues
- Providing a product testimonial or an idea for product improvement or a new product
- Obtaining information about warranties or service and repair policies for products
- Obtaining contact information for a person or department in the organization

After a company determines which objectives its site should accomplish, it can move on planning and developing the site, keeping in mind that the priorities and objectives of customers may change over time. As the number of e-commerce shoppers increases and they become more comfortable—and more selective—making online purchases, a company might need to redefine the basic business model of its site to capture new business opportunities. For example, consider the major travel sites such as Expedia, Travelocity, CheapTickets, Orbitz, and Priceline. These sites used to specialize in one area of travel—inexpensive airline tickets. Now they offer a full range of travel products, including airline tickets, auto rentals, hotel rooms, tours, and last-minute trip packages. Expedia provides in-depth hotel descriptions to help comparison shoppers and even offers 360-degree visual tours and expanded photo displays. It also entices flexible travelers to search for rates, compare airfares, and configure hotel and air prices at the same time. Expedia has also developed numerous hotel partnerships to reduce costs and help secure great values for consumers. Meanwhile, Orbitz has launched a special full-service program for corporate business travelers.

Establishing a Web Site

Companies large and small can establish Web sites. Some companies elect to develop their sites in-house, but this decision requires a Web development staff that is experienced with HTML, Java, and Web design software. Many firms, especially those with few or no experienced Web developers, have decided to outsource the building of their Web sites in order to get their sites up and running faster and cheaper than they could by doing the job themselves. Web development firms can provide organizations with prebuilt templates and Web site builder tools to enable customers to construct their own Web sites. Businesses can custom design a new Web site or redesign an existing Web site. Many of these firms have worked with thousands of customers to help them get their Web sites up and running.

Web site hosting companies such as HostWay and BroadSpire make it possible to set up a Web page and conduct e-commerce within a matter of days, with little up-front cost. However, to allow visitors to pay for merchandise with credit cards, a company needs a merchant account with a bank. If your company doesn't already have one, it must establish one.

storefront broker: A company that acts as an intermediary between your Web site and online merchants who have the products and retail expertise.

Another model for setting up a Web site is the use of a **storefront broker**, a business that serves as an intermediary between your Web site and online merchants who have the actual products and retail expertise. The storefront broker deals with the details of the transactions, including who gets paid for what, and is responsible for bringing together merchants and reseller sites. The storefront broker is similar to a distributor in standard retail operations, but in this case, no product moves—only electronic data flows back and forth. Products are ordered by a customer at your site, orders are processed through a user interface provided by the storefront broker, and the product is shipped by the merchant.

Shopify is a Canadian-based firm that helps retailers create their own online store without all the technical work involved in developing their own

Web site or the huge expense of contracting someone else to build it. Clients can select a stylish e-commerce Web site template, customize it to meet their unique needs, upload product information, and then start taking orders and accepting payments. Thousands of online retailers, including General Electric, CrossFit, Tesla Motors, Red Bull, Foo Fighters, and GitHub built their Web sites using the Shopify platform. To date, more than 240,000 online stores have used Shopify to generate more than $14 billion in sales.[66]

Building Traffic to Your Web Site

The Internet includes hundreds of thousands of e-commerce Web sites. With all those potential competitors, a company must take strong measures to ensure that the customers it wants to attract can find its Web site. The first step is to obtain and register a domain name, which should say something about your business. For instance, stuff4u might seem to be a good catchall, but it doesn't describe the nature of the business—it could be anything. If you want to sell soccer uniforms and equipment, then you'd try to get a domain name such as *www.soccerstuff4u.com*, *www.soccerequipment.com*, or *www.stuff4soccercoaches.com*. The more specific the Web address, the better.

The next step to attracting customers is to make your site search-engine friendly by improving its rankings. Following are several ideas on how to accomplish this goal:

meta tag: An HTML code, not visible on the displayed Web page, that contains keywords representing your site's content, which search engines use to build indexes pointing to your Web site.

- Include meta tags in your site's home page. A **meta tag** is an HTML code, not visible on the displayed Web page, that contains keywords representing your site's content. Search engines use these keywords to build indexes pointing to your Web site. Keywords are critical to attracting customers, so they should be chosen carefully. They should clearly define the scope of the products or services you offer.

- Use Web site traffic data analysis software to turn the data captured in the Web log file into useful information. This data can tell you the URLs from which your site is being accessed, the search engines and keywords that find your site, and other useful information. Using this data can help you identify search engines to which you need to market your Web site, allowing you to submit your Web pages to them for inclusion in the search engine's index.

- Provide quality, keyword-rich content. Be careful not to use too many keywords, as search engines often ban sites that do this. Judiciously place keywords throughout your site, ensuring that the Web content is sensible and easy to read by humans as well as search engines.

- Add new content to the Web site on a regular basis. Again, this makes the site attractive to humans as well as search engines.

- Acquire links to your site from other reputable Web sites that are popular and related to your Web site. Avoid the use of low-quality links, as they can actually hurt your Web site's rating.

The use of the Internet is growing rapidly in markets throughout Europe, Asia, and Latin America. Obviously, companies that want to succeed on the Web cannot ignore this global shift. A company must be aware that consumers outside the United States will access sites with a variety of devices. A Web site's design should reflect that diversity if the company wants to be successful in other markets. In Europe, for example, closed-system iDTVs (integrated digital televisions) are becoming popular for accessing online content, with more than 50 percent of the population now using them. Because such devices have better resolution and more screen space than the PC monitors that many U.S. consumers use to access the Internet, iDTV users expect more ambitious graphics. Successful global firms operate with a portfolio of sites designed for each market, with shared sourcing and infrastructure to support the network of stores and with local marketing and business development teams to take advantage of local opportunities. Service providers continue to emerge to solve the cross-border logistics, payments, and customer service needs of these global retailers.

Maintaining and Improving Your Web Site

Web site operators must constantly monitor the traffic to their sites and the response times experienced by visitors. AMR Research, a Boston-based independent research analysis firm, reports that Internet shoppers expect service to be better than or equal to their in-store experience. Nothing will drive potential customers away faster than experiencing unreasonable delays while trying to view or order products or services. To keep pace with technology and increasing traffic, it might be necessary to modify the software, databases, or hardware on which a Web site runs to ensure acceptable response times.

Retailing giant Walmart recently invested over $2 billion as part of a multiyear project designed to improve its Web site and strengthen its e-commerce infrastructure. Walmart's technology team overhauled the company's e-commerce capabilities from the ground up—with changes to the look of the Web site, the launch of an improved, proprietary site search engine, and upgrades to the underlying transaction software and supporting databases and Web servers. In addition to revamping its Web site to make it easier for customers to shop, Walmart continues to add to the number of items available through its e-commerce site, with a recent focus on expanding its online grocery offerings.[67,68]

Web site operators must also continually be alert to new trends and developments in the area of e-commerce and be prepared to take advantage of new opportunities. For example, recent studies show that customers more frequently visit Web sites they can customize. **Personalization** is the process of tailoring Web pages to specifically target individual consumers. The goal is to meet the customer's needs more effectively, make interactions faster and easier, and consequently, increase customer satisfaction and the likelihood of repeat visits. Building a better understanding of customer preferences can also aid in cross-selling related products and more expensive products. The most basic form of personalization involves using the consumer's name in an email campaign or in a greeting on the Web page. Amazon uses a more advanced form of personalization in which the Web site greets each repeat customer by name and recommends a list of new products based on the customer's previous purchases.

Businesses use two types of personalization techniques to capture data and build customer profiles. Implicit personalization techniques capture data from actual customer Web sessions—primarily based on which pages were viewed and which weren't. Explicit personalization techniques capture user-provided information, such as information from warranties, surveys, user registrations, and contest-entry forms completed online. Data can also be gathered through access to other data sources such as the Bureau of Motor Vehicles, Bureau of Vital Statistics, and marketing affiliates (firms that share marketing data). Marketing firms aggregate this information to build databases containing a huge amount of consumer behavioral data. During each customer interaction, powerful algorithms analyze both types of data in real time to predict the consumer's needs and interests. This analysis makes it possible to deliver new, targeted information before the customer leaves the site. Because personalization depends on gathering and using personal user information, privacy issues are a major concern.

Salesforce Marketing Cloud is a provider of digital marketing automation and analytics software and services that its customers use to personalize email marketing, target mobile messaging campaigns, and make personalized,

personalization: The process of tailoring Web pages to specifically target individual consumers.

predictive recommendations to online customers. Room & Board, a Minnesota-based national furniture chain specializing in modern furniture and home accessories, uses Salesforce to create a digital experience that reflects the ways their customers use the Web as well as one that extends the company's personalized sales approach to its Web site. The Salesforce system, which ties into customers' sales histories as well as years' worth of data about what styles and individual pieces of furniture work well together and what products customers tend to view and purchase in groups, allows the company to make increasingly effective personal recommendations to its online customers. Customers who engage with Room & Board's recommendations place online orders with 40 percent higher average values than those who don't.[69]

The tips and real-world examples presented in this section represent just a few ideas that can help a company set up and maintain an effective e-commerce site. With technology and competition changing constantly, managers should read articles in print and online to keep up to date on ever-evolving issues.

Critical Thinking Exercise

Door-to-Dorm Laundry Service

You have decided to start a door-to-dorm laundry service for the college students at the local university. Students log on to your Web site and provide specific information to create an account including address information needed for pickup and delivery plus credit, charge, or debit card information for payment. At the time of the initial pickup, students are given a large plastic bag that they fill with their laundry. You pick up the laundry and wash, dry, fold, and return it within one week. Once the student has created an account, they can text, email, or logon on to the Web site to request future pickups.

Review Questions

1. Define the basic functions that this Web site must perform in order to meet the basic needs of the laundry service as well as attract and maintain the interests of students. What are some things you might do to entice students to return time and time again to your Web site?
2. What actions can you take to increase traffic and draw students to your Web site?

Critical Thinking Questions

1. Can you identify additional laundry-related services that might be added to your basic wash, dry, and fold offering that would be attractive to students? How could the initial Web site design allow for these potential opportunities?
2. What steps might you take to personalize the Web site so that the students feel welcome each time they visit?

Technology Infrastructure Required to Support E-Commerce and M-Commerce

Now that we've examined some key factors in establishing an effective e-commerce initiative, let's look at some of the technical issues related to e-commerce systems and the technology that makes it possible. Successful implementation of e-business requires significant changes to existing business processes and substantial investment in IS technology. These technology components must be chosen carefully and be integrated to support a large volume of transactions with customers, suppliers, and other business partners worldwide. In surveys, online consumers frequently note that poor Web site performance (e.g., slow response time, inadequate customer support, and lost orders) drives them to abandon some e-commerce sites in favor of those with better, more reliable performance. This section provides a brief overview of the key technology infrastructure components. See Figure 7.13.

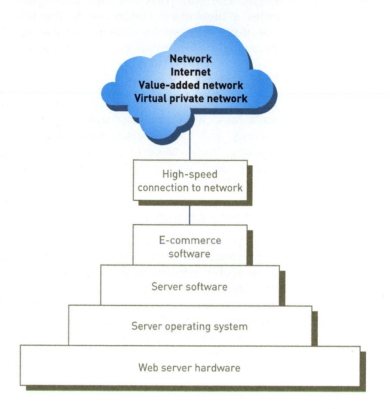

FIGURE **7.13**

Key technology infrastructure components

E-commerce systems require specific kinds of hardware and software to be successful.

Hardware

A Web server hardware platform complete with the appropriate software is a key ingredient to e-commerce infrastructure. The amount of storage capacity and computing power required of the Web server depends primarily on two things: the software that must run on the server and the volume of e-commerce transactions that must be processed. The most successful e-commerce solutions are designed to be highly scalable so that they can be upgraded to meet unexpected user traffic.

Key Web site performance measures include response time, transaction success rate, and system availability. Table 7.7 shows the values for the key measures for five popular online retailers for one week.

TABLE 7.7 Key performance measures for some popular retail Web sites

Site	Response Time (seconds)	Success Rate	Outage Time During One Week
Zappos	0.71	100%	0
Apple Store	0.82	100%	0
Costco	1.02	100%	0
Nike	1.60	100%	0
Best Buy	2.00	100%	0

Source: "Performance Index: Top Retailers," Keynote, February 21, 2016, *www.keynote.com/performance-indexes/retail-us*.

A key decision facing a new e-commerce company is whether to host its own Web site or to let someone else do it. Many companies decide that using a third-party Web service provider is the best way to meet initial e-commerce needs. The third-party company rents space on its computer system and provides a high-speed connection to the Internet, thus minimizing the initial out-of-pocket costs for e-commerce start-up. The third party can also provide personnel trained to operate, troubleshoot, and manage the Web server.

Web Server Software

In addition to the Web server operating system, each e-commerce Web site must have Web server software to perform fundamental services, including security and identification, retrieval and sending of Web pages, Web site tracking, Web site development, and Web page development. The two most widely used Web server software packages are Apache HTTP Server and Microsoft Internet Information Services.

E-Commerce Software

After you have located or built a host server, including the hardware, operating system, and Web server software, you can begin to investigate and install e-commerce software to support five core tasks: catalog management to create and update the product catalog, product configuration to help customers select the necessary components and options, shopping cart facilities to track the items selected for purchase (see Figure 7.14), e-commerce transaction processing, and Web traffic data analysis to provide details to adjust the operations of the Web site.

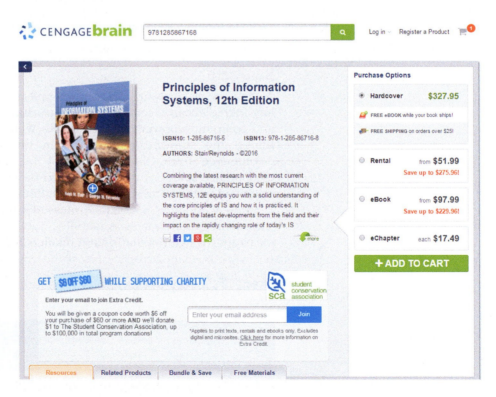

Electronic shopping cart
An electronic shopping cart allows online shoppers to view their selections and add or remove items.

Mobile Commerce Hardware and Software

For m-commerce to work effectively, the interface between the mobile device and its user must improve to the point that it is nearly as easy to purchase an item on a wireless device as it is to purchase it on a PC. In addition, network speeds must continue to improve so that users do not become frustrated.

Security is also a major concern, particularly in two areas: the security of the transmission itself and the trust that the transaction is being made with the intended party. Encryption can provide secure transmission. Digital certificates can ensure that transactions are made between the intended parties.

The mobile devices used for m-commerce have several limitations that complicate their use. Their screens are small, perhaps no more than several square inches, and might be able to display only small portions of a Web site. In addition, entering data on a mobile device can be tedious and error prone. Mobile devices also have less processing power and less bandwidth than desktop or laptop computers, which are usually connected to a high-speed LAN. They also operate on limited-life batteries. For these reasons, Web developers must often rewrite Web applications so that users with mobile devices can access them.

Electronic Payment Systems

Electronic payment systems are a key component of the e-commerce infrastructure. Current e-commerce technology relies on user identification and encryption to safeguard business transactions. Actual payments are made in a variety of ways, including electronic cash, electronic wallets, and smart, credit, charge, and debit cards. Web sites that accept multiple payment types convert more visitors to purchasing customers than merchants who offer only a single payment method.

Authentication technologies are used by many organizations to confirm the identity of a user requesting access to information or assets. A **digital certificate** is an attachment to an email message or data embedded in a Web site that verifies the identity of a sender or Web site. A **certificate authority (CA)** is a trusted third-party organization or company that issues digital certificates. The CA is responsible for guaranteeing that the people or organizations granted these unique certificates are in fact who they claim to be. Digital certificates thus create a trust chain throughout the transaction, verifying both purchaser and supplier identities.

Many organizations that accept credit cards to pay for items purchased via e-commerce have adopted the Payment Card Industry (PCI) security standard. This standard spells out measures and security procedures to safeguard the card issuer, the cardholder, and the merchant. Some of the measures include installing and maintaining a firewall configuration to control access to computers and data, never using software or hardware vendor-supplier defaults for system passwords, and requiring merchants to protect stored data, encrypt transmission of cardholder information across public networks, use and regularly update antivirus software, and restrict access to sensitive data on a need-to-know basis.

Various measures are being implemented to increase the security associated with the use of credit cards at the time of purchase. The Address Verification System is a check built into the payment authorization request that compares the address on file with the card issuer to the billing address provided by the cardholder. The Card Verification Number technique is a check of the additional digits typically printed on the back of the card (or on the front, in the case of American Express cards). Visa has Advanced Authorization, a Visa-patented process that provides an instantaneous rating of that transaction's potential for fraud—using factors such as the value of the transaction, type of merchant, time of day the purchase is being made, and whether the site is one where the card owner has previously shopped. The card issuer can then send an immediate response to the merchant regarding whether to accept or decline the transaction. The technology is applied to every Visa credit and check card purchase today, and has contributed to a two-thirds reduction in system-wide fraud for Visa over the past two decades. Visa has continued to add other features and data inputs to its fraud-detection

digital certificate: An attachment to an email message or data embedded in a Web site that verifies the identity of a sender or Web site.

certificate authority (CA): A trusted third-party organization or company that issues digital certificates.

systems, such as extended cardholder transaction data and even mobile location confirmation.[70]

The Federal Financial Institutions Examination Council has developed a set of guidelines called "Authentication in an Internet Banking Environment," which recommend two-factor authorization. This approach adds another identity check along with the password system. A number of multifactor authentication schemes can be used, such as biometrics, one-time passwords, or hardware tokens that plug into a USB port on the computer and generate a password that matches the ones used by a bank's security system.

The use of biometric technology to secure digital transactions has been slow to develop due to cost and privacy concerns. However, MasterCard recently announced it will begin rolling out its new MasterCard Identity Check service that allows users to take an initial ID photo that will be used to create a digital map of their face, which will be stored on MasterCard's servers. When the user wants to make a payment using their smartphone, the MasterCard app will capture their image, which, along with a user-entered password, will be authenticated before the transaction is approved. MasterCard's system also offers a fingerprint sensor that can be used to verify purchases.[71] Apple's new ApplePay system makes use of the fingerprint sensors on newer iPhones. Consumers paying with ApplePay, which is tied to a credit or debit card, just hold their iPhone close to the contactless reader with their finger on the Touch ID button. [72]

Transport Layer Security

Transport Layer Security (TLS): A communications protocol or system of rules that ensures privacy between communicating applications and their users on the Internet.

All online shoppers fear the theft of credit card numbers and banking information. To help prevent this type of identity theft, the Transport Layer Security communications protocol is used to secure sensitive data. **Transport Layer Security (TLS)** is a communications protocol or system of rules that ensures privacy between communicating applications and their users on the Internet. TLS enables a client (like a Web browser) to initiate a temporary, private conversation with a server (like a shopping site on the Web or an online bank). Before the client and server start communicating, they perform an automated process called a "handshake" where they exchange information about who they are, and which secret codes and algorithms they'll use to encode their messages to each other. Then for the duration of the conversation, all the data that passes between the client and server is encrypted so that even if somebody does listen in, they won't be able to determine what's being communicated. TLS is the successor to the Secure Sockets Layer (SSL).

In addition to TLS handling the encryption part of a secure e-commerce transaction, a digital certificate is assigned to the Web site to provide positive server identification so shoppers can be assured of with whom that are dealing.

Electronic Cash

electronic cash: An amount of money that is computerized, stored, and used as cash for e-commerce transactions.

Electronic cash is an amount of money that is computerized, stored, and used as cash for e-commerce transactions. Typically, consumers must open an account with an electronic cash service provider by providing identification information. When the consumers want to withdraw electronic cash to make a purchase, they access the service provider via the Internet and present proof of identity—a digital certificate issued by a certification authority or a username and password. After verifying a consumer's identity, the system debits the consumer's account and credits the seller's account with the amount of the purchase. ApplePay, PayPal, Square, Stripe, and WePay are leading online payment service providers that facilitate the use of electronic cash.

PayPal enables any person or business with an email address to securely, easily, and quickly send and receive payments online. To send money, you enter the recipient's email address and the amount you want to send. You can pay with a credit card, debit card, or funds from a checking account. The recipient gets an email message that says, "You've Got Cash!" Recipients can then collect their money by clicking a link in the email message that takes them to *www.paypal.com*. To receive the money, the user also must have a credit card or checking account to accept fund transfers. To request money for an auction, invoice a customer, or send a personal bill, you enter the recipient's email address and the amount you are requesting. The recipient gets an email message and instructions on how to pay you using PayPal. Today over 179 million Internet users use PayPal to send money in more than 100 currencies and some 90 percent of eBay purchases go through PayPal.[73]

PayPal is rolling out Beacon, a hardware device for merchants that uses Bluetooth technology to improve the shopper's experience. Consumers must download the PayPal app to their smartphone and opt in to the service to use Beacon for hands-free check-in and payments. Beacon can communicate with compatible point-of-sale systems from Erply, Leaf, Leapset, Micros, NCR, ShopKeep, or Vend. When Beacon consumers walk into a store, Beacon will trigger a vibration or sound to confirm a successful check-in and their photo will appear on the screen of the merchant's point-of-sale system so they can be identified. Payment requires only a verbal confirmation and a receipt is emailed to the consumer. Using Beacon, a drugstore could fill your prescriptions or your name could be added to a wait list for tables at a restaurant simply by walking into the establishment.[74]

The use of smartphones to make purchases and transfer funds between consumers and businesses has become commonplace. The goal is to make the payment process as simple and secure as possible and for it to work on many different phones and through many different mobile network providers—not simple tasks. Fortunately, the intelligence built into the iPhone and other smartphones can make this all possible.

You can use several services (e.g., Phone Transact iMerchant Pro, Square, ROAMPay, and PayWare Mobile) to plug a credit card reader device into the headphone jack on a cell phone to accept credit card payments. Intuit's GoPayment service does not require a credit card reader but provides software that lets you enter the credit card number.

With Xipwire, consumers can text someone with a special code to place a purchase on their monthly phone bill and bypass any credit card system altogether. A free Starbucks mobile app that runs on iPhone and Android smartphones enables customers to order and pay for their java using their smartphones—without ever having to wait in line. App users, whose mobile purchases are tied to a credit card, can even tip their barista digitally.[75]

Credit, Charge, Debit, and Smart Cards

Many online shoppers use credit and charge cards for most of their Internet purchases. A credit card, such as Visa or MasterCard, has a preset spending limit based on the user's credit history, and each month the user can pay all or part of the amount owed. Interest is charged on the unpaid amount. A charge card, such as American Express, carries no preset spending limit, and the entire amount charged to the card is due at the end of the billing period. You can't carry a balance from month to month with a charge card like you can with a credit card. Charge cards require customers to pay in full every month or face a fee. Debit cards look like credit cards, but they operate like cash or a personal check. The debit card is linked directly to your savings or checking account. Each time you use the card, money is automatically taken from your checking or savings account to cover the purchase. Credit, charge, and debit cards currently store limited information about you on a magnetic stripe. This information is read each time the card is swiped to make a purchase. All credit card customers are protected by law from paying more than $50 for fraudulent transactions.

The smart card is a credit card–sized device with an embedded microchip to provide electronic memory and processing capability. Smart cards can be used for a variety of purposes, including storing a user's financial facts, health insurance data, credit card numbers, and network identification codes and passwords. They can also store monetary values for spending.

Smart cards are better protected from misuse than conventional credit, charge, and debit cards because the smart-card information is encrypted. Conventional credit, charge, and debit cards clearly show your account number on the face of the card. The card number, along with a forged signature, is all that a thief needs to purchase items and charge them against your card. A smart card makes credit theft practically impossible because a key to unlock the encrypted information is required, and there is no external number that a thief can identify and no physical signature a thief can forge. Table 7.8 compares various types of payment systems.

TABLE 7.8 Comparison of payment systems

Payment System	Description	Advantages	Disadvantages
Credit card	Carries preset spending limit based on the user's credit history	Each month the user can pay all or part of the amount owed	Unpaid balance accumulates interest charges—often at a high rate of interest
Charge card	Looks like a credit card but carries no preset spending limit	Does not involve lines of credit and does not accumulate interest charges	The entire amount charged to the card is due at the end of the billing period or the user must pay a fee
Debit card	Looks like a credit card or automated teller machine (ATM) card	Operates like cash or a personal check	Money is immediately deducted from user's account balance
Smart card	Is a credit card device with embedded microchip capable of storing facts about cardholder	Better protected from misuse than conventional credit, charge, and debit cards because the smart card information is encrypted	Slowly becoming more widely used in the United States

Here in the United States, credit cards with only magnetic stripes are being replaced by cards with chips that employ the EMV (Europay, Mastercard, Visa) global standard for working with point-of-sale systems. Each time the EMV card is used or inserted into a point-of-sale device for payment, it creates a unique transaction code that can never be reused. Unlike the European version of the card which requires the user to enter a PIN number to complete the transaction, the U.S. card user simply signs the receipt. While such cards are nearly impossible to counterfeit, the account number of these cards is clearly visible and can be used by fraudsters for online purchases.

The United States financial institutions elected to implement the chip-and-sign EMV card rather than chip-and-PIN card. The later card requires the user to enter their personal PIN number for each transaction. While the chip in the EMV cards prevents the use of counterfeit cards, it is expected that card-present fraud in stores will migrate to card-not-present fraud online and that total dollar volume of fraud will actually increase. It is projected that counterfeit card fraud in the U.S. will fall by roughly $1.8 billion between 2015 and 2018 due to EMV chips, however, online card (card-not-present) fraud will rise $3.1 billion. That's a projected net card fraud *gain* of $1.3 billion during the initial post EMV time period—a very poor financial return on the $8 billion issuers and merchants are spending to deploy EMV.[76]

p-card (procurement card or purchasing card): A credit card used to streamline the traditional purchase order and invoice payment processes.

P-Card

A **p-card (procurement card or purchasing card)** is a credit card used to streamline the traditional purchase order and invoice payment processes. The p-card is typically issued to selected employees who must follow company rules and guidelines that may include a single purchase limit, a monthly spending limit, or merchant category code restrictions. Due to an increased risk of unauthorized purchases, each p-card holder's spending activity is reviewed periodically by someone independent of the cardholder to ensure adherence to the guidelines. Spending on p-cards is expected to increase from $245 billion in 2013 to $377 billion in 2018.[77]

Critical Thinking Exercise

Third Party Operation of Web Site

Your firm has been hosting and operating its own Web site for over five years now. However, in the face of negative consumer reviews and poor performance, management is considering having a third-party host and operate the Web site.

Review Questions

1. What parameters might be used to measure the current performance of the Web site?
2. What are the pros and cons of having a third-party host and operate your Web site?

Critical Thinking Questions

1. Management is concerned that the migration to chip-and-sign EMV cards will increase the level of online consumer fraud. Do you have any ideas to combat this increase in fraud?
2. What other potential risks and opportunities lie in the future of B2C e-commerce?

Summary

Principle:

Electronic and mobile commerce are evolving, providing new ways of conducting business that present both potential benefits and problems.

Electronic commerce is the conducting of business activities (e.g., distribution, buying, selling, marketing, and servicing of products or services) electronically over computer networks. Business-to-business (B2B) e-commerce allows manufacturers to buy at a low cost worldwide, and offers enterprises the chance to sell to a global market. Currently, the greatest dollar volume of e-commerce sales falls under the category of B2B e-commerce. Business-to-consumer (B2C) e-commerce enables organizations to sell directly to consumers, eliminating intermediaries. In many cases, this practice squeezes costs and inefficiencies out of the supply chain and can lead to higher profits and lower prices for consumers. Consumer-to-consumer (C2C) e-commerce involves consumers selling directly to other consumers. Online auctions are the chief method by which C2C e-commerce is currently conducted. E-government involves the use of information and communications technology to simplify the sharing of information, speed formerly paper-based processes, and improve the relationship between citizens and government.

Mobile commerce is the use of mobile devices such as tablets and smartphones to facilitate the sale of goods or services—anytime and anywhere. Mobile commerce is a rapidly growing segment of e-commerce, with Japan, the United Kingdom, and South Korea leading the world in m-commerce growth. The market for m-commerce in North America is maturing much later than in other countries for several reasons. Numerous retailers have established special Web sites for users of mobile devices.

Conversion to an e-commerce or m-commerce system enables organizations to reach new customers, reduce the cost of doing business, speed the flow of goods and information, increase the accuracy of order-processing and order fulfillment, and improve the level of customer service.

A successful e-commerce system must address the many stages consumers experience in the sales life cycle. At the heart of any e-commerce system is the ability of the user to search for and identify items for sale; select those items; negotiate prices, terms of payment, and delivery date; send an order to the vendor to purchase the items; pay for the product or service; obtain product delivery; and receive after-sales support.

From the perspective of the provider of goods or services, an effective e-commerce system must be able to support the activities associated with supply chain management and customer relationship management.

A firm faces three key challenges when converting its business processes from the traditional form to e-commerce processes: (1) dealing effectively with consumer privacy concerns, (2) successfully overcoming consumers' lack of trust, and (3) overcoming global issues.

Principle:

E-commerce and m-commerce can be used in many innovative ways to improve the operations of an organization.

Many manufacturers are joining electronic exchanges, where they can work with competitors and suppliers to buy and sell goods, trade market information, and run back-office operations, such as inventory control. They are also using e-commerce to improve the efficiency of the selling process by moving customer queries about product availability and prices online.

The Web allows firms to gather much more information about customer behavior and preferences than they could using other marketing approaches. This new technology has greatly enhanced the practice of market segmentation and has enabled many companies to establish closer relationships with their customers.

The Internet has revolutionized the world of investment and finance, especially online stock trading and online banking. The Internet has also created many options for electronic auctions, where geographically dispersed buyers and sellers can come together.

The numerous m-commerce applications include advertising, bartering, retargeting, price comparison, couponing, investment and finance, and banking.

Principle:

E-commerce and m-commerce offer many advantages yet raise many challenges.

Businesses and people use e-commerce and m-commerce to reduce transaction costs, speed the flow of goods and information, improve the level of customer service, and enable the close coordination of actions among manufacturers, suppliers, and customers.

E-commerce and m-commerce also enable consumers and companies to gain access to worldwide markets. They offer great promise for developing countries, enabling them to enter the prosperous global marketplace and hence helping to reduce the gap between rich and poor countries.

Because e-commerce and m-commerce are global systems, they face cultural, language, time and distance, infrastructure, currency, product and service, and state, regional, and national law challenges.

Principle:

Organizations must define and execute an effective strategy to be successful in e-commerce and m-commerce.

Most people agree that an effective Web site is one that creates an attractive presence and meets the needs of its visitors. E-commerce start-ups must decide whether they will build and operate the Web site themselves or outsource this function. Web site hosting services and storefront brokers provide alternatives to building your own Web site.

To build traffic to your Web site, you should register a domain name that is relevant to your business, make your site search-engine friendly by including a meta tag in your home page, use Web site traffic data analysis software to attract additional customers, and modify your Web site so that it supports global commerce. Web site operators must constantly monitor the traffic and response times associated with their sites and adjust software, databases, and hardware to ensure that visitors have a good experience when they visit.

Web site operators must also continually be alert to new trends and developments in the area of e-commerce and be prepared to take advantage of new opportunities, including personalization—the process of tailoring Web pages to specifically target individual consumers.

Principle:

E-commerce and m-commerce require the careful planning and integration of a number of technology infrastructure components.

A number of infrastructure components must be chosen and integrated to support a large volume of transactions with customers, suppliers, and other business partners worldwide. These components include hardware, Web server software, and e-commerce software.

M-commerce presents additional infrastructure challenges, including improving the ease of use of wireless devices, addressing the security of wireless transactions, and improving network speed. The Wireless Application Protocol (WAP) is a standard set of specifications to enable development of m-commerce software for wireless devices. The development of WAP and its derivatives addresses many m-commerce issues.

Electronic payment systems are a key component of the e-commerce infrastructure. A digital certificate is an attachment to an email message or data embedded in a Web page that verifies the identity of a sender or a Web site. To help prevent the theft of credit card numbers and banking information, the Transport layer Security (TLS) communications protocol is used to secure all sensitive data. Several electronic cash alternatives require the purchaser to open an account with an electronic cash service provider and to present proof of identity whenever payments are to be made. Payments can also be made by credit, charge, debit, smart cards, and p-cards. Retail and banking industries are developing means to enable payments using the cell phone like a credit card.

Key Terms

business-to-business (B2B) e-commerce	identity theft
business-to-consumer (B2C) e-commerce	market segmentation
certificate authority (CA)	meta tag
consumer-to-consumer (C2C) e-commerce	p-card (procurement card or purchasing card)
digital certificate	personalization
e-government	storefront broker
electronic cash	Transport Layer Security (TLS)
electronic exchange	

Chapter 7: Self-Assessment Test

Electronic and mobile commerce are evolving, providing new ways of conducting business that present both potential benefits and problems.

1. _____ e-commerce activities include identifying and comparing competitive suppliers and products, negotiating and establishing prices and terms, ordering and tracking shipments, and steering organizational buyers to preferred suppliers and products.

2. _____ involves conducting business activities (e.g., distribution, buying, selling, marketing, and servicing of products or services) electronically over computer networks.
   a. B2B
   b. C2C
   c. B2C
   d. E-commerce

3. Popular B2C Web sites have helped raise expectations as to how e-commerce must operate, and many B2B companies are responding to those heightened expectations by investing heavily in their B2B platforms. True or False?

4. The largest B2C retailer in the United States is _____.
   a. Amazon
   b. Staples
   c. Apple
   d. Walmart

5. The elimination of intermediate organizations between the producer and the consumer is called _____.

E-commerce and m-commerce can be used in many innovative ways to improve the operations of an organization.

6. B2B is smaller and growing more slowly than B2C. True or False?

7. _____ is *not* a key challenge for e-commerce.
   a. Dealing with consumer privacy concerns
   b. Training customers on how to access and use e-commerce Web sites
   c. Overcoming consumers' lack of trust
   d. Overcoming global issues

8. The Internet Corporation for Assigned Names and Numbers (ICANN) created a domain called _____ to attract mobile users to the Web.

E-commerce and m-commerce offer many advantages yet raise many challenges.

9. The market for m-commerce is North America is maturing much sooner than in other countries. True or False?

10. Key components of a multistage model for e-commerce includes search and identification, selection and negotiation, purchasing, product and service delivery and _____.

11. Which of the following is NOT considered to be a key challenge to e-commerce?
    a. Dealing with consumer privacy concerns
    b. Overcoming consumer's lack of trust
    c. Overcoming global cultural challenges, language, time and distance, infrastructure, and currency challenges
    d. Low user interest in access to global markets and competitive pricing

12. Some businesses are willing to _____ as a means to reduce excess inventory, gain new customers, or avoid paying cash for necessary raw materials or services.

13. The _____ security standard spells out measures and security procedures to safeguard the card issuer, the cardholder, and the merchant.

Organizations must define and execute an effective strategy to be successful in e-commerce and m-commerce.

14. _____ divides the pool of potential customers into subgroups usually defined in terms of demographic characteristics, such as age, gender, marital status, income level, and geographic location.

15. Mobile ad impressions are generally bought at a cost per thousand (CPM), cost per action (CPA), or _____ (CPC).

E-commerce and m-commerce require the careful planning and integration of a number of technology infrastructure components.

16. The amount of storage capacity and computing power required of a Web server depends primarily on _____.
    a. the geographical location of the server and number of different products sold
    b. the software that must run on the server and the volume of e-commerce transactions
    c. the size of the business organization and the location of its customers
    d. the number of potential customers and average dollar value of each transaction

17. Key Web site performance measures include response time, transaction success rate, and system availability. True or False?

Chapter 7: Self-Assessment Test Answers

1. Buy-side
2. d.
3. True
4. a.
5. disintermediation
6. False
7. b.
8. .mobi
9. False
10. after-sales service
11. d.
12. barter
13. Payment Card Industry or PCI
14. Market segmentation
15. cost per click
16. b.
17. True

Review Questions

1. Briefly define the term electronic commerce, and identify six forms of electronic commerce based on the parties involved in the transactions.
2. What is buy-side e-commerce and how does it differ from sell-side e-commerce?
3. What is disintermediation?
4. What region of the world represents the world's largest and fastest B2C market?
5. What are Web-influenced sales and what is a reasonable estimate of total Web-influenced sales?
6. What is the status of background checks on online gun sales?
7. Identify three forms of e-government e-commerce.
8. Why is the market for m-commerce in North America maturing much later than in other regions of the world?
9. Outline specific actions online shoppers can take to ensure that they are dealing with a legitimate and reputable Web site.
10. Identify six global issues associated with e-commerce.
11. What is an electronic exchange? Provide an example.
12. What is market segmentation? What is its purpose?
13. What is the difference between blind, premium blind, and premium networks for mobile advertising?
14. What is meant by retargeting? What percent of all online shopping carts are abandoned?
15. Identify three key Web site performance measures.
16. What is a digital certificate? What is a certificate authority? What is the Payment Card Industry security standard? What is the Transport Security Layer?
17. Why is it necessary to continue to maintain and improve an existing Web site?
18. Identify the key elements of the technology infrastructure required to successfully implement e-commerce within an organization.

Discussion Questions

1. Identify and briefly discuss three reasons for the steady growth in B2C e-commerce.
2. Briefly discuss the status of online retailers collecting sales taxes on online sales.
3. Identify and briefly discuss five advantages of electronic and mobile commerce.
4. Identify and briefly discuss the five stages consumers experience in the sales life cycle that must be supported by a successful e-commerce system.
5. Identify and briefly discuss three key challenges that an organization faces in creating a successful e-commerce operation. What steps can an organization take to overcome these barriers?
6. Briefly discuss three models for selling mobile ad impressions. What are the primary measures for the success of mobile advertising?
7. Discuss how you might go about increasing the amount of traffic to your Web site.
8. What is personalization of Web pages? How might one go about doing this?
9. Briefly describe the differences between a credit, charge, debit and smart card.
10. Identify and briefly describe three m-commerce applications you have used.

11. Discuss the use of e-commerce to control spending on manufacturing, repair, and operations (MRO) of goods and services.

12. Outline the key steps in developing a corporate global e-commerce strategy.

Problem-Solving Exercises

1. Do research to learn more about the American Consumer Satisfaction Index methodology developed by the University of Michigan. Prepare a brief slide presentation about the methodology and how it was used to rate B2C Web sites. Using this information, develop one final slide providing at least five recommendations for someone developing a B2C Web site.

2. Use PowerPoint or some other presentation preparation software to produce a presentation of the key steps that an organization must take in the aftermath of a data breach to calm its customers and restore their faith in the firm.

3. Your washing machine just gave out and must be replaced within the week! Use your Web-enabled smartphone (or borrow a friend's) to perform a price and product comparison to identify the manufacturer and model that best meets your needs and the retailer with the lowest delivered cost. Obtain peer input to validate your choice. Write a brief summary of your experience, and identify the Web sites you found most useful.

Team Activities

1. As a team, develop a set of criteria that you would use to evaluate the effectiveness of a mobile advertising campaign to boost the sales of one of your firm's products. Identify the measures you would use and the data that must be gathered.

2. Imagine that your team has been hired as consultants to a large organization that has just suffered a major public relations setback due to a large-scale data breach that it handled poorly. Identify three things that the organization must do if it wishes to regain consumer confidence.

3. As a team, develop a set of criteria that you would use to evaluate the effectiveness of a mobile advertising campaign to boost the popularity of a candidate for an elected state government position. Identify the measures you would use and the data that must be gathered.

Web Exercises

1. Do research to capture data on the growth of B2C e-commerce and retail sales over the past 10 years. Use the charting capability of your spreadsheet software to plot the growth of B2C e-commerce and retail sales and predict the year that B2C e-commerce will exceed 10 percent of retail sales. Document any assumptions you make.

2. Do research on the Web to find a dozen Web sites that offer mobile coupons. Separate the sites into two groups: those that provide coupons for a single retailer and those that aggregate coupons for multiple retailers. Produce a table that summarizes your results and shows the approximate number of coupons available at each site.

Career Exercises

1. Do research and write a brief report on the impact of mobile advertising on sales and marketing.

2. Do research to identify three top organizations that develop and operate e-commerce Web sites for their clients. Visit their Web sites and identify current job openings. What sort of responsibilities are associated with these positions? What experience and education requirements are needed to fill these positions? Do any of these positions appeal to you? Why or why not?

3. For your chosen career field, describe how you might use or be involved with e-commerce. If you have not chosen a career yet, answer this question for someone in marketing, finance, or human resources.

Case Studies

Case One

Facebook Moves into E-Commerce

On the social networking site Facebook, users create profiles that allow them to connect with friends, organizations, and companies through posts and ads that appear in their personal News Feed as well as through Pages that are designed to help organizations and companies connect with interested users. And with more than 1.4 billion active users, including 900 million who visit the site every day, Facebook represents a huge potential online marketplace.

Over the years, Facebook has experimented with many different features designed to help marketers connect with prospective customers—from banner ads to sponsored links to highly visual engagement ads that allow advertisers to show several clickable images or videos within a single News Feed ad. Although Facebook has incorporated ads for some time, it is now focusing more intently on tools that make it easier for customers to purchase something immediately based on an ad they see—ideally, all while staying within Facebook's site. In particular, the company is concentrating on ways it can streamline mobile purchasing, currently an often slow and cumbersome process. According to Emma Rodgers, Facebook's head of product marketing for commerce, "We're looking to give people an easier way to find products that will be interesting to them on mobile, make shopping easier and help businesses drive sales."

For starters, Facebook is testing a new Shopping tool within the Favorites section that will aggregate a personalized mix of products users are likely to be interested in based on their Facebook likes and connections. In addition, Facebook has begun experimenting with "conversational commerce," a highly personalized form of e-commerce in which consumers and retailers conduct entire transactions within a messaging application—in this case, Facebook's Messenger app.

Facebook has also been rolling out a new mobile ad feature it calls Canvas, which offers marketers a customizable space where they can use video, images, text, and "call-to-action buttons" (such as Book Now, Sign Up, and Shop Now) to engage with consumers. When Facebook users click on a Canvas, they will almost instantaneously see a full-screen ad that lives within Facebook's infrastructure—rather than being redirected to an advertiser's Web site, which may be slow to load and not always optimized for mobile devices. Canvas appeals to marketers looking for a new way to engage customers without losing them as they are being redirected to an outside Web site, and it offers Facebook the chance to keep more of a user's online activity within its site.

Recently, Facebook has been testing a "shop" concept that goes one step further—allowing companies using Shopify's e-commerce platform to build what amounts to a mini e-commerce site within their Page through the use of a Buy button. For now, retailers involved in the test can choose between an option that directs shoppers to their own sites and one that keeps the entire shopping experience—from product discovery to checkout—within Facebook.

A recent study found that 13 percent of all the time spent on mobile apps is spent within Facebook's apps, and according to a Facebook survey, nearly half of its users come to Facebook to actively look for products. Facebook clearly intends to capitalize on these trends with e-commerce and m-commerce initiatives that will likely continue to evolve and expand. And marketers looking for new ways to extend customer engagement to online purchases will certainly be paying attention.

Critical Thinking Questions

1. What are some of the privacy concerns that consumers might have in terms of shopping on a social network such as Facebook, which already has access to so much personal information?

2. Are people likely to use Facebook's current e-commerce offerings the same way they might shop on Amazon?

3. Do research online to find out more about some of the e-commerce initiatives of other social networks, such as Instagram, Pinterest, and Twitter. What features do they offer that differentiate them from Facebook? Do you think any of these sites will ever be a strong competitor to Amazon in terms of total e-commerce sales? If not, what niche could they succeed at?

SOURCES: "Easy and Effective Facebook Ads," Facebook, *www.facebook.com/business/products/ads*, accessed February 29, 2016; "Facebook Pushes Shopping Features in Move to E-Commerce," *Reuters*, October 12, 2015, *http://uk.reuters.com/article/us-facebook-retail-idUKKCN0S61N720151012*; "FB Moves into E-Commerce, Challenges Amazon with New In-App," *Money Control*, October 13, 2015, *www.moneycontrol.com/news/technology/fb-moves-into-e-commerce-challenges-amazonnew-in-app_3559061.html*; Stambor, Zak, "Facebook Makes a Major E-Commerce Move," *Internet Retailer*, October 12, 2015, *www.internetretailer.com/2015/10/09/facebook-makes-major-e-commerce-move*; Mac, Ryan, "Facebook Goes All in On E-Commerce by Bringing Businesses onto Messenger, *Forbes*, March 25, 2015, *www.forbes.com/sites/ryanmac/2015/03/25/facebook-goes-all-in-on-e-commerce-by-bringing-businesses-onto-messenger/#132d7acd4747*; Plummer, Quinten, "Facebook May Launch Risky Messenger Ad Program," *E-Commerce Times*, February 22, 2016, *www.ecommercetimes.com/story/83139.html*; "Introducing Canvas, A Full-Screen Ad Experience Built for Bringing Brands and Products to Life on Mobile," Facebook, February 25, 2016, *www.facebook.com/business/news/introducing-canvas*; Plummer, Quinten, "Facebook Gives Marketers a Blank Canvas," *E-Commerce Times*, February 27, 2016, *www.ecommercetimes.com/story/83165.html*; Kantrowitz, Alex, "Facebook Takes Big Step Forward On Commerce, Builds Shops into Pages," *BuzzFeed*, July 15, 2015, *www.buzzfeed.com/alexkantrowitz/facebook-takes-big-step-forward-on-commerce-builds-shops-int#.kxovdqa3V*; Stambor, Zak, "Facebook Launches Another Buy Button Test," *Internet Retailer*, July 17, 2015, *www.internetretailer.com/2015/07/17/facebook-launches-another-buy-button-test*.

Case Two

MobiKash: Bringing Financial Services to Rural Africa

Full participation in the twenty-first century economy requires access to financial services. However, this access is a luxury for many citizens of African nations. Due to the long distances between bank branches and the lack of rapid, cost-effective transportation to the urban areas in which banks are typically found, fewer than 10 percent of Africans participate in formal banking. Those who do often face time-consuming inefficiencies.

A new company, MobiKash Afrika, hopes to change this by empowering people in Africa with a secure and independent mobile commerce system that is easy to use. In planning its system, MobiKash established several standards:

- The service must be independent of specific mobile telephone operators.
- The service must be independent of specific banks or financial institutions.
- The service must work with all bill issuers.
- The service must not require the use of a smartphone.

MobiKash offers its members five services, all accessible from a mobile phone: loading money into their MobiKash account from any bank account, paying bills, sending money to any other mobile phone user or bank account, managing a bank or MobiKash account, and obtaining or depositing cash. Only the last pair of services requires members to visit a physical location where cash can be handled, but that site doesn't have to be a bank. MobiKash agents in market towns, convenient to rural areas, can handle transactions that require cash. Approximately 3,000 MobiKash agents operate in Kenya. Account holders don't even need to visit a bank to set up their MobiKash accounts: in fact, anyone with a mobile phone to whom a MobiKash user sends money becomes a MobiKash user automatically.

MobiKash charges for some services. Withdrawing cash costs 25 to 75 Kenya shillings (Kshs) (about U.S. $0.30 to $0.90), for withdrawals up to Kshs 10,000 (about U.S. $20), with higher fees for larger withdrawals. Paying bills from a mobile phone incurs a fixed fee of Kshs 25, no matter how large the bill is. The largest fee that MobiKash charges is Kshs 350 (about U.S. $4), for cash withdrawals in excess of Kshs 75,000 (about U.S. $900). This fee schedule is consistent with the financial resources of MobiKash users and the value those users place on each financial service.

The MobiKash system is based on Sybase 365 mCommerce software. Several factors contributed to this choice, including the local presence of Sybase in Africa with experience in similar applications, its understanding of how to integrate with African financial institutions, and the system's ability to work with any mobile telephone. It operates from an existing Sybase data center in Frankfurt, Germany.

MobiKash services expects to expand in east, west, and southern Africa, starting with Zimbabwe. It is working with Masary, an Egyptian e-wallet firm, to cover northern Africa as well. Work is also under way to support intercontinental fund transfers to and from North America, Europe, and the Middle East. As for the future, CEO Duncan Otieno said, "We see MobiKash in the next five years playing with the international or global mobile commerce space in at least 40 countries. The plans for building this network are already in progress."

Critical Thinking Questions

1. Firms can base m-commerce systems on commercially available software, as MobiKash did here. Alternatively, they can write their own software. List three pros and cons of each approach. Do you think MobiKash made the right choice?

2. What challenges does a company like MobiKash face when they try to penetrate different national markets in developing countries? Why might Kenya be a good choice for the launch of m-commerce operations in Africa?

3. Contrast your m-commerce needs with those of a typical rural African. Would you find the MobiKash offering attractive in full, in part (which parts?), or not at all?

SOURCES: Masary, *www.e-masary.com*, accessed March 1, 2012; MobiKash Afrika, "The First Intra-region Mobile Network and Bank Agnostic Mobile Commerce Solution," *Computerworld* case study, *www .eiseverywhere.com/file_uploads/e1bfbec2f385506b3890cbd7e b7e9dd9_MobiKash_Afrika_-_The_First_Intra-region_Mobile_Network_ and_Bank_Agnostic_Mobile_Commerce_Solution.pdf*, accessed March 1, 2012; MobiKash Africa Web site, *www.mobikash.com*, accessed March 1, 2012; "Reaching the Unbanked in a MobiKash World," interview with CEO Duncan Otieno, *MobileWorld, www.mobileworldmag.com /reaching-the-unbanked-in-a-mobikash-world/*, December 28, 2011; Sybase, "MobiKash Africa: Customer Case Study," *www.sybase.com/files /Success_Stories/Mobikash-CS.pdf*, accessed March 1, 2012.

Notes

1. Demery, Paul, "B2B E-Commerce Sales Will Top $1.13 Trillion by 2020," *Internet Retailer*, April 2, 2015, *www .internetretailer.com/2015/04/02/new-report-predicts -1-trillion-market-us-b2b-e-commerce*.

2. Ibid.

3. Davis, Don, "E-commerce Software Spending Will Nearly Double in the U.S. by 2019," February 9, 2015, *www .internetretailer.com/2015/02/09/us-e-commerce-soft ware-spending-nearly-double-2019*.

4. "Mastering Omni-Channel B2B Customer Engagement," Accenture, October 2015, *www.accenture.com/us-en /insight-mastering-omni-channel-b2b-customer-engage ment.aspx*.

5. Tepper, Nona, "E-Commerce Accounts for 41% of Grainger Sales in 2015, B2B E-Commerce World, January 26, 2016, *www.b2becommerceworld.com/2016/01/26 /e-commerce-accounts-41-grainger-sales-2015*.

6. "Our Strengths at Work: 2015 Fact Book," Grainger, *http://phx.corporate-ir.net/External.File?item=UG FyZW50SUQ9Mjc5MDI1fENoaWxk SUQ9LTF8VHlwZT0z&t=1*, accessed February 24, 2016.

7. Linder, Matt, "E-Commerce Revenue for Retailers with Stores and Websites Grows over 36% in Q3," *Internet Retailer*, October 29, 2015, *www.internetretailer.com /2015/10/29/e-commerce-retailers-stores-and-Websites -grows-over-36*.

8. "Press Release: MarketLive's Fall Performance Index Shows Double-Digit Revenue Gains for E-Commerce Retailers; Smartphones & Direct Traffic Are Major Trends," *Market Wired*, October 8, 2015, *www.market*

*wired.com/press-release/marketlives-fall-performance
-index-shows-double-digit-revenue-gains-e-commerce
-2067871.htm.*

9. "Global E-Commerce Turnover Grew by 24.0% to Reach
$ 1,943BN in 2014," Ecommerce Europe, September 17.
2015, *www.ecommerce-europe.eu/news/2015/global
-e-commerce-turnover-grew-by-24.0-to-reach-1943bn
-in-2014.*

10. Linder, Matt, "Global E-Commerce Sales Set to Grow 25%
in 2015, *Internet Retailer, www.internetretailer.com
/2015/07/29/global-e-commerce-set-grow-25-2015.*

11. "Customize Nike Shoes with NIKEiD," Nike, *http://help
-en-us.nike.com/app/answers/detail/article/nikeid-help
/a_id/3393/kw/nikeid/country/us*, accessed February 25,
2016.

12. "Inside New NIKEiD Personalization Program," Nike,
November 9, 2015, *http://news.nike.com/news/pid.*

13. Brousell, Lauren, "Why Pinterest's 'Buy It' Button Is Big
for Online Retailers," *CIO*, June 10, 2015, *www.cio.com
/article/2933381/pinterest/why-pinterests-buy-it-button
-is-big-for-online-retailers.html.*

14. "You'll Love These New Ways Target is Making Mobile
Shopping More Awesome," Target, November 5, 2015,
*https://corporate.target.com/article/2015/11/target
-crush-awesome-shop.*

15. "Deloitte Digital Study: Digitally-Influenced Sales in
Retail Brick-And-Mortar Stores to Reach $2.2 Trillion by
Year-End," Deloitte, May 13, 2015, *www2.deloitte
.com/us/en/pages/about-deloitte/articles/press-releases
/retail-digital-divide.html.*

16. Reisinger, Don, "Your State May Fight for Internet Sales
Tax," *Fortune*, February 24, 2016, *http://fortune.com
/2016/02/24/state-internet-sales-tax.*

17. Steverman, Ben, "This Supreme Court Justice Wants You
to Pay Your Online Sales Tax, *BloombergBusiness*,
March 6, 2015, *www.bloomberg.com/news/articles/2015
-03-06/this-supreme-court-justice-wants-you-to-pay-your
-online-sales-tax.*

18. "eBay Inc. Reports Fourth Quarter and Full Year 2015
Results," eBay, January 27, 2016, *https://investors
.ebayinc.com/releasedetail.cfm?ReleaseID=952024.*

19. Ibid.

20. Luo, Michael, McIntire, Mike, and Palmer, Griff, "Seeking
Gun or Selling One, Web is a Land of Few Rules," *The
New York Times*, April 17, 2013, *www.nytimes.com
/2013/04/17/us/seeking-gun-or-selling-one-Web-is-a
-land-of-few-rules.html?pagewanted=all&_r=0.*

21. Rose, Joel, "Obama Aims to Expand Background Checks
to Online Gun Sales," *NPR*, January 8, 2016, *www.npr
.org/2016/01/06/462114352/obama-aims-to-expand
-background-checks-to-online-gun-sales.*

22. Nussbaum, Alex, "Accenture Wins U.S. Contract for
Obamacare Enrollment," *Bloomberg*, January 12, 2014,
*www.bloomberg.com/news/2014-01-12/accenture-wins
-u-s-contract-for-obamacare-enrollment-Website.html.*

23. "Oregon E-Government Program," State of Oregon,
www.oregon.gov/DAS/ETS/EGOV/pages/ecommerce.aspx,
accessed February 27, 2016.

24. "Making the Internet Work for Oregon," State of Oregon,
*www.oregon.gov/DAS/ETS/EGOV/pages/ev_internet
.aspx#Objectives*, accessed February 27, 2016.

25. "Press Release: It's a Cross-Device World: Criteo's Q4
Mobile Commerce Report Reveals Top Companies Bet Big
on Mobile Consumers," Criteo, February 17, 2016, *www
.prnewswire.com/news-releases/its-a-cross-device-world
-criteos-q4-mobile-commerce-report-reveals-top-compa
nies-bet-big-on-mobile-consumers-300221060.html.*

26. Ibid.

27. "About Shoe Carnival," Shoe Carnival, *www.shoecarni
val.com/aboutshoecarnival, www.shoecarnival.com
/aboutshoecarnival*, accessed February 27, 2016.

28. "Customer Stories: Shoe Carnival," Rackspace, *http://stor
ies.rackspace.com/wp-content/uploads/2015/09/CRP
-Shoe-Carnival-Case-Study-Final.pdf*, accessed February
27, 2016.

29. "About Us," BloomNation, *https://www.bloomnation
.com/about-us*, accessed February 27, 2016.

30. Cowley, Stacy, "Florist-Friendly Marketplaces Help Local
Flower Shops Hang On," *New York Times*, February 10,
2016, *www.nytimes.com/2016/02/11/business/smallbusi
ness/florist-friendly-marketplaces-help-local-flower
-shops-hang-on.html?ref=topics.*

31. Demery, Paul, "Online Photo Service Shutterfly Posts A
16% Increase in Q2 Sales, *Internet Retailer*, August 24,
2015, *www.internetretailer.com/2015/08/24/online
-photo-service-shutterfly-posts-16-increase-q2-sales.*

32. "About Shutterfly," Shutterfly, *http://businesssolutions
.shutterfly.com/Learn*, accessed February 27, 2016.

33. Ryssdal, Kai and Tommy Andres, "Domino's CEO Patrick
Doyle: Tech with a Side of Pizza," Marketplace, September 24, 2015, *www.marketplace.org/2015/09/24/busi
ness/corner-office/dominos-ceo-patrick-doyle-tech-side
-pizza.*

34. "About," Sticker Mule, *www.stickermule.com/about*,
accessed February 29, 2016.

35. Wahba, Phil, "Borders Files for Bankruptcy, to Close
Stores," *The Huffington Post*, February 16, 2011, *www
.huffingtonpost.com/2011/02/16/borders-files-for-bank
ruptcy_n_823889.html.*

36. Leger, Donna Leinwand, "Target Data Breach under
Close Investigative Scrutiny," *USA Today*, January 13,
2014, *www.usatoday.com/story/news/nation/2014/01
/10/target-data-breach-investigations-continue
/4421345/.*

37. "These Companies Lost Your Data in 2015's Biggest
Hacks, Breaches," *ZDNet*, August 14, 2015, *www.zdnet
.com/pictures/biggest-hacks-security-data-breaches-2015.*

38. Goodin, Dan, "Gigabytes of User Data from Hack of
Patreon Donations Site Dumped Online," *Ars Technica*,
October 1, 2015, *http://arstechnica.com/security/2015
/10/gigabytes-of-user-data-from-hack-of-patreon-dona
tions-site-dumped-online.*

39. "The Top 10 Security Breaches of 2015, *Forbes*, December 31, 2015, *www.forbes.com/sites/quora/2015/12/31
/the-top-10-security-breaches-of-2015/4/#58cc002e15e9.*

40. Greenberg, Andy, "Hack Brief: Hackers Steal 15M
T-Mobile Customers' Data from Experian," *Wired*,
October 1, 2015, *www.wired.com/2015/10/hack-brief
-hackers-steal-15m-t-mobile-customers-data-experian.*

41. "What Is Identity Theft," Federal Trade Commission,
*www.consumer.ftc.gov/articles/pdf-0014-identity-theft
.pdf*, accessed February 10, 2014.

42. "Target Debit and Credit Card Breach Lawsuit," *LawyersandSettlements.com, www.lawyersandsettlements.com/lawsuit/data-breach.html#.Uvom26-A1Ms*, accessed February 11, 2014.

43. "Akimbo Financial," Symantec, *www.symantec.com/content/en/us/enterprise/customer_successes/b-akimbo-financial-SuccessStory-en-us.pdf* accessed February 11, 2016.

44. Tepper, Nona, "Wholesalers Call E-Commerce Their Top Sales Channel for 2015," *Internet Retailer*, March 2, 2015, *www.internetretailer.com/2015/03/02/wholesalers-call-e-commerce-their-top-sales-channel-2015*.

45. "About MSC," MSC Industrial Supply Co., *www.mscdirect.com/corporate/about-msc*, accessed February 28, 2016.

46. Tepper, Nona, "E-Commerce Accounts for All the Q2 Sales Growth at MSC Industrial Supply," Internet Retailer, April 27, 2015, *www.internetretailer.com/2015/04/27/e-commerce-builds-sales-growth-msc-industrial-supply*.

47. "Tinypass in Ruby," Tinypass Press Releases, *www.tinypass.com/blog/category/press-releases/*, accessed February 11, 2016.

48. "Crowdfunding…Your Way," Tinypass, *http://publisher.tinypass.com/archives/howto/crowdfund*, accessed February 27, 2016.

49. Petersen, Chris, "Walmart's Secret Sauce: How the Largest Survives and Thrives," *RetailCustomerExperience.com*, March 27, 2013, *www.retailcustomerexperience.com/blog/10111/Walmart-s-secret-sauce-How-the-largest-survives-and-thrives*.

50. "Exelate and Dun & Bradstreet Collaborate to Offer One of the Most Comprehensive B2B Datasets in Digital Media," Nielsen, February 25, 2016, *www.nielsen.com/us/en/press-room/2016/exelate-and-dun-bradstreet-collaborate-to-offer-one-of-the-most-comprehensive-b2b-datasets-in-digital-media.html*.

51. "InMobi Launches Appographic Targeting—An Industry-first, App-Interest-Based Audience Targeting Capability," InMobi, March 5, 2015, *www.inmobi.com/company/press/inmobi-launches-appographic-targeting-an-industry-first-app-interest-based*.

52. Jatain, Visheshwar, "Top 8 Best-Paying Mobile Ad Networks You Should Try," *AdPushup* (blog), May 29, 2015, *www.adpushup.com/blog/top-8-best-paying-mobile-ad-networks-you-should-try*.

53. Smith, Cooper, "Shopping Cart Abandonment: Online Retailers' Biggest Headache Is Actually a Huge Opportunity," *Business Insider*, July 23, 2015, *www.businessinsider.com/heres-how-retailers-can-reduce-shopping-cart-abandonment-and-recoup-billions-of-dollars-in-lost-sales-2015-7*.

54. Steele, Chandra, "The 11 Best Shopping Apps to Compare Prices," *PCMag*, November 23, 2015, *www.pcmag.com/slideshow/story/290959/the-11-best-shopping-apps-to-compare-prices*.

55. "Barcode Scanner," Google Play, *https://play.google.com/store/apps/details?id=com.google.zxing.client.android*, accessed February 28, 2016.

56. Loechner, Jack, "FSI Coupon Incentives Continue to Grow," *MediaPost*, January 21, 2016, *www.mediapost.com/publications/article/266825/fsi-coupon-incentives-continue-to-grow.html*.

57. Dunn, Amy, "Coupon Use Plummets, and Some Wonder Whether It's the End of an Era," *NewsObserver.com*, March 9, 2013, *www.newsobserver.com/2013/03/09/2735590/coupon-use-plummets-and-some-wonder.html#storylink=cpy*.

58. Heller, Laura, "Beacons to Push 1.6 Billion Coupons by 2020," *FierceRetail*, December 10, 2015, *www.fierceretail.com/story/beacons-push-16-billion-coupons-2020/2015-12-10*.

59. Maycotte, H.O., "Beacon Technology: The Where, What, Who, How and Why," *Forbes*, September 1, 2015, *www.forbes.co.m/sites/homaycotte/2015/09/01/beacon-technology-the-what-who-how-why-and-where/#b74a5664fc19*.

60. Donovan, Fred, "Mobile Couponers to Fuel 11% Growth in Digital Coupon Use This Year," *FierceMobileIT*, October 21, 2013, *www.fiercemobileit.Com/Story/Mobile-Couponers-Fuel-11ex-Growth-Digital-Coupon-Use-Year/2013-10-21#Ixzz2teth8gu8*.

61. "Fidelity Mobile Apps," Fidelity, *www.fidelity.com/mobile/overview*, accessed February 28, 2016.

62. Perez, Sarah, "How T-Mobile's New Mobile Banking Service Compares with Simple and Amex Serve," *Tech Crunch*, January 22, 2014, *http://Techcrunch.Com/2014/01/22/How-T-Mobiles-New-Mobile-Banking-Service-Compares-With-Simple-And-Amex-Serve*.

63. Runde, Daniel, "M-Pesa and The Rise of the Global Mobile Money Market," *Forbes*, August 12, 2015, *www.forbes.com/sites/danielrunde/2015/08/12/m-pesa-and-the-rise-of-the-global-mobile-money-market/#7058eca423f5*.

64. Pressler, Jessica, "The World Is Not Enough," *New York*, August 11, 2015, *http://nymag.com/thecut/2015/08/net-a-porter-bigger-better-future.html*.

65. "About Us," Quintessentially Gifts, *www.quintessentiallygifts.com/about-us*, accessed February 14, 2014.

66. "About Us," Shopify, *www.shopify.com/about*, accessed February 27, 2016.

67. Nash, Kim S., "Wal-Mart, Reporting Slower E-Commerce Growth, Makes Plans to Expand Number of Products Available Online," *Wall Street Journal*, February 18, 2016, *http://blogs.wsj.com/cio/2016/02/18/wal-mart-reporting-slower-e-commerce-growth-makes-plans-to-expand-number-of-products-available-online*.

68. Nash, Kim S., "Wal-Mart Revamps E-Commerce Technology as Amazon Applies Pressure," Wall Street Journal, November 25, 2015, *http://blogs.wsj.com/cio/2015/11/25/wal-mart-revamps-e-commerce-technology-as-amazon-applies-pressure*.

69. "Room & Board," Salesforce, *www.salesforce.com/customers/stories/room-and-board.jsp*, accessed February 29, 2016.

70. Nelson, Mark, "Outsmarting Fraudsters with Advanced Analytics," VISA, *https://usa.visa.com/visa-everywhere/security/outsmarting-fraudsters-with-advanced-analytics.html*, accessed February 29, 2016.

71. Pesce, Nicole, "MasterCard Will Launch 'Selfie Pay' Technology This Summer," *Daily News*, February 23, 2016, *www.nydailynews.com/life-style/mastercard-launch-selfie-pay-technology-summer-article-1.2540983*.

72. "Apple Pay," Apple, *www.apple.com/apple-pay*, accessed February 29, 2016.

73. "Who We Are," PayPal, *www.paypal.com/us/Webapps /mpp/about*, accessed February 29, 2016.

74. Rao, Leena, "Paypal Debuts Its Newest Hardware, Beacon, a Bluetooth LE Enabled Device for Hands-Free Check Ins and Payments," *Tech Crunch*, September 9, 2013, *http://Techcrunch.Com/2013/09/09/Paypal -Debuts-Its-Newest-Hardware-Beacon-A-Bluetooth -Le-Enabled-Device-For-Hands-Free-Check-Ins-And -Payments/*.

75. "Get the Starbucks App for iPhone and Android," Starbucks, *www.starbucks.com/coffeehouse/mobile-apps*, accessed February 29, 2016.

76. Wetherington, Lee, "Chip and Quill: How EMV Will Increase Card Fraud in the U.S.," Information Week, November 18, 2014, *www.banktech.com/fraud/chip -and-quill-how-emv-will-increase-card-fraud-in-the-us /a/d-id/1317543*.

77. Morgan, Orson, "Commercial Payments Overview," VISA, October 2014, *www.des.wa.gov/sitecollectiondocuments /contractingpurchasing/pcard/visacmrclpymtoview.pptx*.

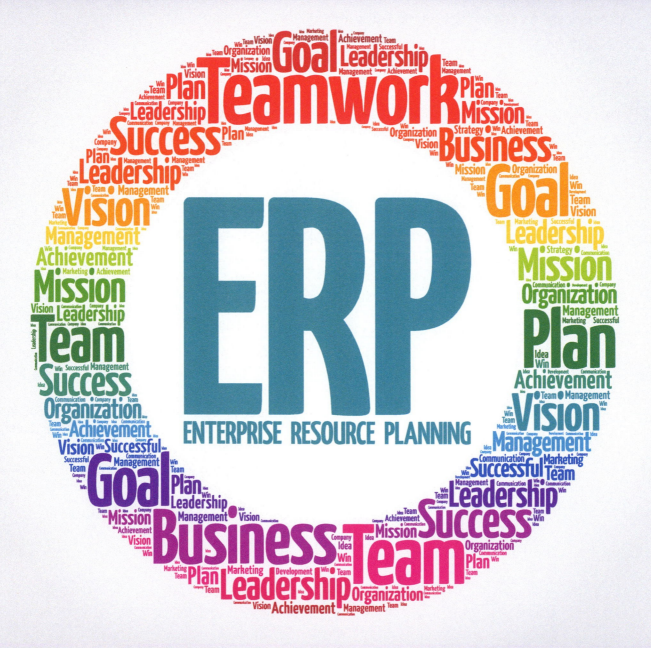

Did You Know?

- Automatic Data Processing (ADP) is a major provider of business outsourcing solutions for payroll administration for 610,000 organizations in more than 125 countries. It uses a batch processing system to prepare the paychecks of one out of six workers in the United States, as well as 12 million other workers around the world.

- The Red Cross uses a cloud-based CRM platform from Salesforce so that volunteers and employees can quickly access the data and services required to get the organization's operations up and running during a disaster. The Red Cross has even integrated social networking tools into its CRM system, providing the organization with new channels to connect with volunteers and donors as well as new tools for delivering disaster-relief updates to the public, soliciting financial and volunteer help, and helping people affected by a disaster communicate with family and friends.

Principles

- An organization must have information systems that support routine, day-to-day activities and that help a company add value to its products and services.

- An organization that implements an enterprise system is creating a highly integrated set of systems, which can lead to many business benefits.

Learning Objectives

- Identify the basic activities and business objectives common to all transaction processing systems.

- Describe the transaction processing systems associated with the order processing, purchasing, and accounting business functions.

- Identify the basic functions performed and the benefits derived from the implementation of an enterprise resource planning system, customer resource management, and product lifecycle management system.

- Describe the hosted software model for enterprise systems and explain why this approach is so appealing to SMEs.

- Identify the challenges that organizations face in planning, building, and operating their enterprise systems.

- Identify tips for avoiding many of the common causes for failed enterprise system implementations.

Why Learn about Enterprise Systems?

Individuals and organizations today are moving from a collection of nonintegrated transaction processing systems to highly integrated enterprise systems that perform routine business processes and maintain records about them. These systems support a wide range of business activities associated with supply chain management, customer relationship management, and product lifecycle management. Although they were initially thought to be cost effective only for very large companies, even small and mid-sized companies are now implementing these systems to reduce costs, speed time to market, and improve service.

In our service-oriented economy, outstanding customer service has become a goal of virtually all companies. To provide good customer service, employees who work directly with customers—whether in sales, customer service, or marketing—require high-quality and timely data to make good decisions. Such workers might use an enterprise system to check the inventory status of ordered items, view the production-planning schedule to tell a customer when an item will be in stock, or enter data to schedule a delivery.

No matter what your role, it is very likely that you will provide input to or use the output from your organization's enterprise systems. Your effective use of these systems will be essential to raise the productivity of your firm, improve customer service, and enable better decision making. Thus, it is important that you understand how these systems work and what their capabilities and limitations are.

As you read this chapter, consider the following:

- What advantages do integrated enterprise systems offer an organization?
- What factors should organizations consider when adopting enterprise systems to support their business processes and plan for the future?

This chapter begins with an overview of the individual transaction processing systems that support the fundamental operations of many organizations. Their processing methods, objectives, and primary activities are covered. Then enterprise systems, collections of integrated information systems that share a common database, are discussed. Enterprise systems ensure that data can be shared across all business functions and all levels of management to support the operational and management decision making needed to run the organization. The basic functions and benefits of these systems as well as the challenges of successfully implementing them are discussed.

Transaction Processing Systems

Many organizations employ transaction processing systems (TPSs), which capture and process the detailed data necessary to update records about the fundamental business operations of the organization. These systems include order entry, inventory control, payroll, accounts payable, accounts receivable, and the general ledger, to name just a few. The input to these systems includes basic business transactions, such as customer orders, purchase orders, receipts, time cards, invoices, and customer payments. The processing activities include data collection, data editing, data correction, data processing, data storage, and document production. The result of processing business transactions is that the organization's records are updated to reflect the status of the operation at the time of the last processed transaction.

A TPS also provides valuable input to management information systems, decision support systems, and knowledge management systems. Indeed, transaction processing systems serve as the foundation for these other systems. See Figure 8.1.

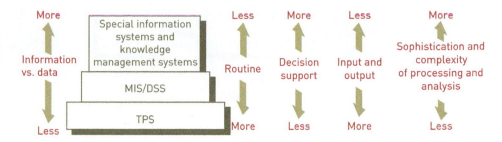

FIGURE **8.1**

TPS, MIS/DSS, and special information systems in perspective

A TPS provides valuable input to MIS, DSS, and KM systems.

Transaction processing systems support routine operations associated with business processes, such as customer ordering and billing, shipping, employee payroll, purchasing, and accounting. TPSs use a large amount of input and output data to update the official records of the company about orders, sales, customers, and so on. TPSs, however, don't provide much support for decision making.

Headquartered in Chicago, Revere Electric Supply is an electrical distributor with a large customer base it serves from eight locations across the Midwest. The company receives orders from its customers through a variety of channels, including email, fax, phone, EDI (electronic data interchange), and the company's e-commerce Web site. Revere's customer service agents often spend 20 to 30 minutes entering an order into the company's ERP system until the company rolled out an order automation system that cut transaction processing time by 95 percent, while also improving order accuracy.[1]

The Helen Ross McNabb Center is a community-based, nonprofit organization that provides behavioral health services to families in eastern Tennessee who are struggling due to the impact of mental illness, addiction, and other challenges.[2] Because the organization is a nonprofit, keeping its operating costs under control is particularly important. The center implemented a Web-based human resources platform with payroll and benefits transaction processing functions that have allowed the organization to add 400 employees without having to increase their human resource staffing levels.[3]

Because TPSs often perform activities related to customer contacts—such as order processing and invoicing—these information systems play a critical role in providing value to the customer. For example, by capturing and tracking the movement of each package, shippers such as FedEx and DHL can provide timely and accurate data on the exact location of a package. Shippers and receivers can access an online database and, by providing the tracking number of a package, find the package's current location. If the package has been delivered, they can see who signed for it (a service that is especially useful in large companies where packages can become "lost" in internal distribution systems and mailrooms). Such a system provides the basis for added value through improved customer service.

Traditional Transaction Processing Methods and Objectives

batch processing system: A form of data processing whereby business transactions are accumulated over a period of time and prepared for processing as a single unit or batch.

With batch processing systems, business transactions are accumulated over a period of time and prepared for processing as a single unit or batch. See Figure 8.2a. Transactions are accumulated for as long as necessary to meet the needs of the users of that system. For example, it might be important to process invoices and customer payments for the accounts receivable system daily. On the other hand, the payroll system might process time cards biweekly to create checks, update employee earnings records, and distribute labor costs. The essential characteristic of a batch processing system is the delay between an event and the eventual processing of the related transaction to update the organization's records. For many applications, batch processing is an appropriate and cost effective approach. Payroll transactions and billing are typically done via batch processing.

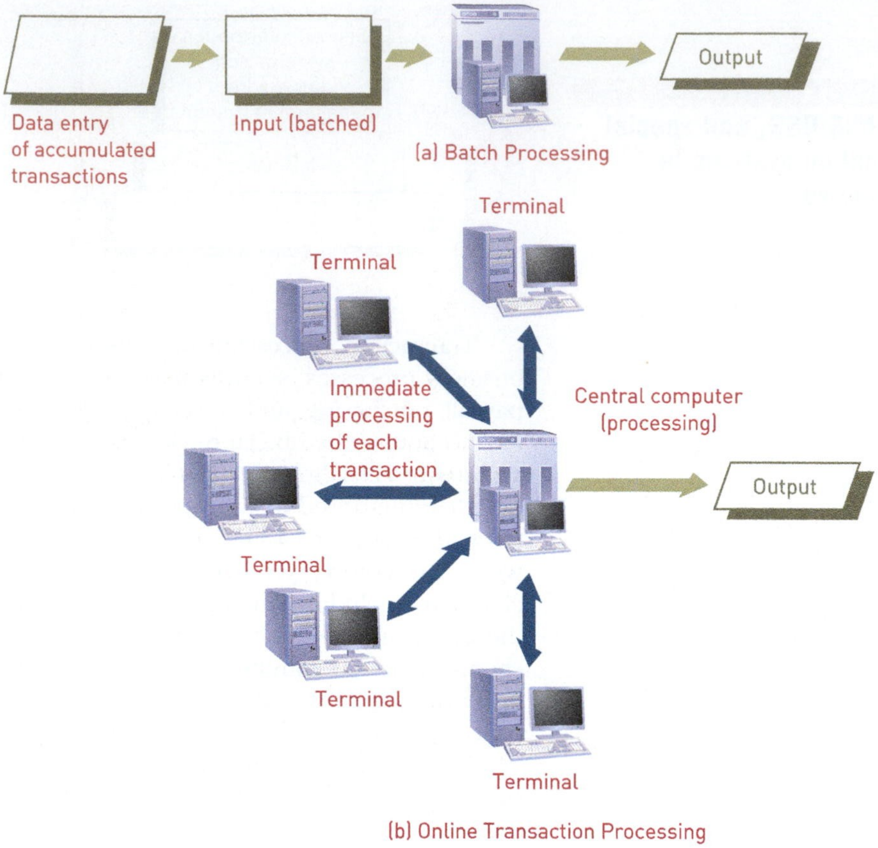

Data entry of accumulated transactions → Input (batched) → (a) Batch Processing → Output

Terminal
Terminal
Immediate processing of each transaction
Central computer (processing)
Terminal
Output
Terminal
Terminal

(b) Online Transaction Processing

FIGURE 8.2

Batch versus online transaction processing

(a) Batch processing inputs and processes data in groups. (b) In online processing, transactions are completed as they occur.

online transaction processing (OLTP): A form of data processing where each transaction is processed immediately without the delay of accumulating transactions into a batch.

Automatic Data Processing (ADP) is a major provider of business outsourcing solutions for payroll administration for 610,000 organizations in more than 125 countries. It uses a batch processing system to prepare the paychecks of one out of six workers in the United States, as well as 12 million other workers around the world.[4]

Sumerian is an IT company that specializes in helping organizations plan and manage their hardware and software infrastructure to avoid processing backlogs and other system capacity issues. The firm recently worked with a large brokerage firm that needed to optimize its global trading platform, which handles over 70 percent of its business transactions. Of particular concern were the brokerage's overnight batch processing activities, which must be completed within a five-hour window to ensure the company's systems are updated by the time the markets open each morning. Using analytics software, Sumerian was able to reduce the brokerage's overnight batch processing time by 15 percent, allowing the firm's systems to handle an increasing volume of trading transactions while staying within the five-hour processing window.[5]

With **online transaction processing (OLTP)**, each transaction is processed immediately without the delay of accumulating transactions into a batch, as shown in Figure 8.2b. Consequently, at any time, the data in an online system reflects the current status. This type of processing is essential for businesses that require access to current data such as airlines, ticket agencies, and stock investment firms. Many companies find that OLTP helps them provide faster, more efficient service—one way to add value to their activities in the eyes of the customer. See Figure 8.3.

FIGURE 8.3

Example of an OLTP system

Hospitality companies such as ResortCom International can use an OLTP system to manage timeshare payments and other financial transactions.

Online payments giant PayPal Holdings, Inc., employs a massive OLTP system to process more than 13 million payments each day through its Braintree, PayPal, Venmo, and Xoom products. The payments between merchants and consumers—as well as between individual users—total more than $280 billion annually.[6]

The specific business needs and goals of the organization define the method of transaction processing best suited for the various applications of the company. Increasingly, the need for current data for decision making is driving many organizations to move from batch processing systems to online transaction processing systems when it is economically feasible. For example, the State of Wisconsin Department of Health Services (DHS) runs the Women, Infants, and Children (WIC) program. WIC's goal is to support and sustain the health and well-being of nutritionally at-risk pregnant, breastfeeding, and postpartum women, as well as their infants and children. DHS employed a batch processing system to manage this program and processed the WIC data in a batch at the end of the day. This practice created a built-in delay in obtaining information needed for decision-making and government-reporting requirements. However, DHS needs up-to-date data to avoid dual participation incidents, such as a client or caregiver receiving more WIC checks than allowed for one month or receiving WIC checks and the Commodity Supplemental Food Program (CSFP) payments at the same time. DHS moved to an online transaction processing system to ensure that all data is now available on a current basis. The system is Web-based and WIC staff needs only a Web browser and secure Internet access to work with the data.[7]

Figure 8.4 shows the traditional flow of key pieces of information from one TPS to another for a typical manufacturing organization. When transactions entered into one system are processed, they create new transactions that flow into another system.

Because of the importance of transaction processing, organizations expect their TPSs to accomplish a number of specific objectives, including the following:

- Capture, process, and update databases of business data required to support routine business activities
- Ensure that the data is processed accurately and completely

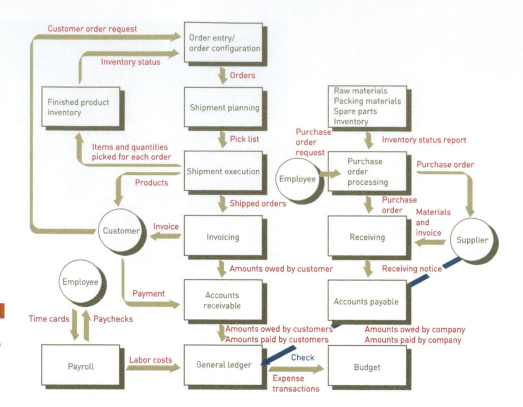

Integration of a firm's TPS

When transactions entered into one system are processed, they create new transactions that flow into another system.

- Avoid processing fraudulent transactions
- Produce timely user responses and reports
- Reduce clerical and other labor requirements
- Help improve customer service
- Achieve competitive advantage

A TPS typically includes the following types of systems:

- **Order processing systems**. Running these systems efficiently and reliably is so critical that the order processing system is sometimes referred to as the lifeblood of the organization. The processing flow begins with the receipt of a customer order. The finished product inventory is checked to see if sufficient inventory is on hand to fill the order. If sufficient inventory is available, the customer shipment is planned to meet the customer's desired receipt date. A product pick list is printed at the warehouse from which the order is to be filled on the day the order is to be shipped. At the warehouse, workers gather the items needed to fill the order and enter the item identifier and quantity for each item to update the finished product inventory. When the order is complete and sent on its way, a customer invoice is created, with a copy included in the customer shipment.

- **Accounting systems**. The accounting systems must track the flow of data related to all the cash flows that affect the organization. As mentioned earlier, the order processing system generates an invoice for customer orders to include with the shipment. This information is also sent to the accounts receivable system to update the customer's account. When the customer pays the invoice, the payment information is also used to update the customer's account. The necessary accounting transactions are sent to the general ledger system, which tracks amounts owed from customers and amounts due to vendors. Similarly, as the purchasing systems generate purchase orders and those items are received, information is sent to the accounts payable system to manage the amounts owed by the company.

Data about amounts owed and paid by customers to the company and from the company to vendors and others are sent to the general ledger system, which records and reports all financial transactions for the company.

- **Purchasing systems**. The traditional transaction processing systems that support the purchasing business function include inventory control, purchase order processing, receiving, and accounts payable. Employees place purchase order requests in response to shortages identified in inventory control reports. Purchase order information flows to the receiving system and accounts payable systems. A record is created upon receipt of the items ordered. When the invoice arrives from the supplier, it is matched to the original order and the receiving report, and a check is generated if all data is complete and consistent.

In the past, organizations knitted together a hodgepodge of systems to accomplish the transaction processing activities shown in Figure 8.4. Some of the systems might have been applications developed using in-house resources, some may have been developed by outside contractors, and others may have been off-the-shelf software packages. Much customization and modification of this diverse software was typically necessary for all the applications to work together efficiently. In some cases, it was necessary to print data from one system and then manually reenter it into other systems. Of course, this increased the amount of effort required and increased the likelihood of processing delays and errors.

The approach taken today by many organizations is to implement an integrated set of transaction processing systems—from a single or limited number of software vendors—that handle most or all of the transaction processing activities shown in Figure 8.4. The data flows automatically from one application to another with no delay or need to reenter data. For example, Lukas Nursery, a fourth-generation family-owned agribusiness in central Florida, recently implemented a suite of software applications that is now integrated into the garden center's POS system. The nursery consolidated its systems (including several manual systems) into an integrated retail business management solution provided by one vendor, allowing it to update its business practices, optimize seasonal inventory, manage a customer loyalty program, and make more informed business decisions through the use of the software's analytics capabilities.[8,9]

Table 8.1 summarizes some of the ways that companies can use transaction processing systems to achieve competitive advantage.

TABLE 8.1 Examples of TPSs yielding significant benefits

Competitive Advantage	Example
Better relationship with suppliers	Internet marketplace to allow the company to purchase products from suppliers at discounted prices
Costs dramatically reduced	Warehouse management system employing RFID technology to reduce labor hours and improve inventory accuracy
Customer loyalty increased	Customer interaction system to monitor and track each customer interaction with the company
Inventory levels reduced	Collaborative planning, forecasting, and replenishing system to ensure the right amount of inventory is in stores
Superior information gathering	Order configuration system to ensure that products ordered will meet customer's objectives
Superior service provided to customers	Tracking systems that customers can access to determine shipping status

Depending on the specific nature and goals of the organization, any of the objectives in Table 8.1 might be more important than others. By meeting these objectives, TPSs can support corporate goals such as reducing costs; increasing productivity, quality, and customer satisfaction; and running more efficient and effective operations.

Transaction Processing Systems for Entrepreneurs and Small and Medium-Sized Enterprises

Many software packages provide integrated transaction processing system solutions for small and medium-sized enterprises (SMEs), wherein SME is a legally independent enterprise with no more than 500 employees. Integrated transaction processing systems for SMEs are typically easy to install and operate and usually have a low total cost of ownership, with an initial cost of a few hundred to a few thousand dollars. Such solutions are highly attractive to firms that have outgrown their current software but cannot afford a complex, high-end integrated system solution. Table 8.2 presents some of the dozens of such software solutions available.

TABLE 8.2 Sample of integrated TPS solutions for SMEs

Vendor	Software	Type of TPS Offered	Target Customers
AccuFund	AccuFund	Financial reporting and accounting	Nonprofit, municipal, and government organizations
OpenPro	OpenPro	Complete ERP solution, including financials, supply chain management, e-commerce, customer relationship management, and retail POS system	Manufacturers, distributors, and retailers
Intuit	QuickBooks	Financial reporting and accounting	Manufacturers, professional services, contractors, nonprofits, and retailers
Sage	Sage 300 Construction and Real Estate	Financial reporting, accounting, and operations	Contractors, real estate developers, and residential builders
Redwing	TurningPoint	Financial reporting and accounting	Professional services, banks, and retailers

Sage is a provider of accounting, ERP, human resources, payroll, asset management, and payment systems software. Its Sage 300 Construction and Real Estate software provides an integrated set of applications specifically designed for customers in the construction, property management, and real estate industries, and its Sage Construction Anywhere application offers cloud-based construction management services that can be incorporated with the Sage 300 software.[10]

Echo Valley Irrigation is a golf course and sports field irrigation design and construction company founded in 1986. For years, Echo Valley utilized a patchwork of processes and technologies to run its business. As the company continued to grow, however, its systems were not keeping up. Eventually, Echo Valley implemented the Sage 300 software package, which provides the company with an accounting platform with a range of automated functions, including a tool that allows project managers to perform a job-specific profit-and-loss analysis when bidding on new projects. The firm also takes advantage of Sage Construction Anywhere, which enables job foremen to track project status, generate reports, and approve payroll through Web-based services.[11]

Transaction Processing Activities

Along with having common characteristics, all TPSs perform a common set of basic data-processing activities. TPSs capture and process data that describes fundamental business transactions. This data is used to update databases and to produce a variety of reports for people both within and outside the enterprise. The business data goes through a **transaction processing cycle** that includes data collection, data editing, data correction, data processing, data storage, and document production. See Figure 8.5.

transaction processing cycle: The process of data collection, data editing, data correction, data processing, data storage, and document production.

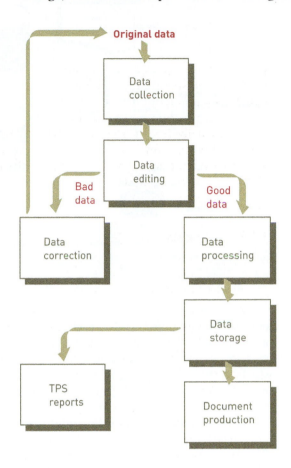

FIGURE 8.5

Transaction processing activities

A transaction processing cycle includes data collection, data editing, data correction, data processing, data storage, and document production.

Data Collection

Capturing and gathering all data necessary to complete the processing of transactions is called **data collection**. In some cases, it can be done manually, such as by collecting handwritten sales orders or inventory update forms. In other cases, data collection is automated via special input devices such as scanners, point-of-sale (POS) devices, and terminals.

Data collection begins with a transaction (e.g., taking a customer order) and results in data that serves as input to the TPS. Data should be captured at its source and recorded accurately in a timely fashion, with minimal manual effort and in an electronic or digital form that can be directly entered into the computer. This approach is called **source data automation**. An example of source data automation is an automated device at a retail store that speeds the checkout process—either UPC codes read by a scanner or RFID signals picked up when the items approach the checkout stand. Using UPC bar codes or RFID tags is quicker and more accurate than having a clerk enter codes manually at the cash register. The product ID for each item is determined automatically, and its price retrieved from the item database. The point-of-sale TPS uses the price data to determine the customer's total. The store's inventory and purchase databases record the number of units of an item purchased, along with the price and the date and time of the purchase. The inventory database generates a management report notifying the store

data collection: Capturing and gathering all data necessary to complete the processing of transactions.

source data automation: Capturing data at its source and recording it accurately in a timely fashion, with minimal manual effort and in an electronic or digital form so that it can be directly entered into the computer.

manager to reorder items that have fallen below the reorder quantity. The detailed purchases database can be used by the store or sold to marketing research firms or manufacturers for detailed sales analysis. See Figure 8.6.

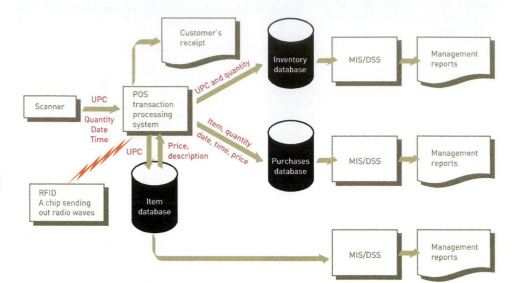

FIGURE 8.6

Point-of-sale transaction processing system

The purchase of items at the checkout stand updates a store's inventory database and its database of purchases.

Many grocery stores combine POS scanners and coupon printers. The systems are programmed so that each time a specific product—for example, a box of cereal—crosses a checkout scanner, an appropriate coupon, perhaps a milk coupon, is printed. Companies can pay to be promoted through the system, which is then programmed to print those companies' coupons if the customer buys a competing brand. These TPSs help grocery stores increase profits by improving their repeat sales and bringing in revenue from other businesses.

Many mobile POS (point of sale) systems operate on iPads, iPhones, and iPod Touch devices. Some mobile POS systems include marketing tools that SMEs can use to thank first-time customers and send automated emails to longtime customers who have not visited recently.

Cloud-based POS systems provide a range of capabilities, including advanced integration with digital loyalty programs, various accounting tools, and the ability to generate gift cards and coupons. An SME can implement such a system for a few thousand dollars compared to more traditional cash register-based POS systems that can cost tens of thousands.[12] The owners of The Creative Wedge, an artisan market that sells cheese and charcuterie along with craft beer and local wine, implemented a truly mobile POS system that allows them to sell product out of their store as well as at various local events, including farmer's markets and festivals.[13]

Data Editing

data editing: Checking data for validity and completeness to detect any problems.

An important step in processing transaction data is to check data for validity and completeness to detect any problems, a task called **data editing**. For example, quantity and cost data must be numeric, and names must be alphabetic; otherwise, the data is not valid. Often, the codes associated with an individual transaction are edited against a database containing valid codes. If any code entered (or scanned) is not present in the database, the transaction is rejected.

Data Correction

It is not enough simply to reject invalid data. The system should also provide error messages that alert those responsible for editing the data. Error messages must specify the problem so proper corrections can be made.

data correction: Reentering data that was not typed or scanned properly.

A **data correction** involves reentering data that was not typed or scanned properly. For example, a scanned UPC code must match a code in a master table of valid UPCs. If the code is misread or does not exist in the table, the checkout clerk is given an instruction to rescan the item or type the information manually.

Data Processing

data processing: Performing calculations and other data transformations related to business transactions.

Another major activity of a TPS is **data processing**, performing calculations and other data transformations related to business transactions. Data processing can include classifying data, sorting data into categories, performing calculations, summarizing results, and storing data in the organization's database for further processing. In a payroll TPS, for example, data processing includes multiplying an employee's hours worked by the hourly pay rate. Overtime pay, federal and state tax withholdings, and deductions are also calculated.

Data Storage

data storage: Updating one or more databases with new transactions.

Data storage involves updating one or more databases with new transactions. After being updated, this data can be further processed by other systems so that it is available for management reporting and decision making. Thus, although transaction databases can be considered a by-product of transaction processing, they can significantly affect nearly all other information systems and decision-making processes within an organization.

Document Production

document production: Generating output records, documents, and reports.

Document production involves generating output records, documents, and reports. These can be hard-copy paper reports or displays on computer screens (sometimes referred to as soft copy). Printed paychecks, for example, are hard-copy documents produced by a payroll TPS, whereas an outstanding balance report for invoices might be an electronic report displayed by an accounts receivable TPS. Often, as shown earlier in Figure 8.6, results from one TPS flow downstream to become input to other systems, which might use the results of an inventory database update to create a stock exception report, a type of management report showing items with inventory levels below the specified reorder point.

In addition to major documents such as checks and invoices, most TPSs provide other useful management information, such as printed or on-screen reports that help managers and employees perform various activities. A report showing current inventory is one example; another might be a document listing items ordered from a supplier to help a receiving clerk check the order for completeness when it arrives. A TPS can also produce reports required by local, state, and federal agencies, such as statements of tax withholding and quarterly income statements.

 **Critical Thinking Exercise**

TPS Needed to Support Small Business

Cal is setting up a small business to prep, cook, and deliver healthy and nutritionally balanced meals to customers in his local area. Cal meets with prospective customers to acquaint them with the program, discuss their eating habits and nutritional needs, and help them select from one of several menus (vegetarian, gluten free, low carb but high protein) that meets their needs. Twice a week Cal and his workers buy food ingredients based on what has been ordered. They then cook three or four days of meals for each customer and seal them in airtight bags for reheating. Deliveries are made twice a week. All the customer has to do is take the bag from the refrigerator and pop it into the microwave for 60 seconds.

Business has really taken off and Cal has had to hire two part-time cooks and two part-time delivery people. Cal has been so busy lining up new customers, shopping, and cooking that he has not had time to carefully track all his expenses. He pays his workers in cash, but realizes he will need to set up a formal payroll system and start deducting for taxes, social security, and Medicaid. Cal also wishes he had some sort of system that could help him better plan the kinds and amounts of ingredients needed based on customer orders. As it is, he usually purchases too much of the various ingredients and ends up giving leftovers away at the free store.

Review Questions

1. What kind of transaction processing systems does Cal need to manage and support the basic functions of his business?
2. Identify six specific tasks that the TPS must perform to meet his needs.

Critical Thinking Questions

1. Should Cal consider developing his own programs using spreadsheet and database software or should he purchase an integrated package to meet his needs?
2. Business is going so well that Cal is thinking of expanding the scope of his business to include catering for weddings, parties, and various business functions. As the scope of his business expands, how might this impact the choice of transaction processing systems?

Enterprise Systems

enterprise system: A system central to the organization that ensures information can be shared with authorized users across all business functions and at all levels of management to support the running and managing of a business.

An **enterprise system** is central to individuals and organizations of all sizes and ensures that information can be shared with authorized users across all business functions and at all levels of management to support the running and managing of a business. Enterprise systems employ a database of key operational and planning data that can be shared by all, eliminating the problems of missing information and inconsistent information caused by multiple transaction processing systems that each support only one business function or one department in an organization. Examples of enterprise systems include enterprise resource planning systems that support supply chain processes, such as order processing, inventory management, and purchasing, and customer relationship management systems that support sales, marketing, and customer service-related processes.

Businesses rely on enterprise systems to perform many of their daily activities in areas such as product supply, distribution, sales, marketing, human resources, manufacturing, accounting, and taxation so that work can be performed quickly without waste or mistakes. Without such systems, recording and processing business transactions would consume huge amounts of an organization's resources. This collection of processed transactions also forms a storehouse of data invaluable to decision making. The ultimate goal of such systems is to satisfy customers and provide significant benefits by reducing costs and improving service.

Enterprise Resource Planning

Enterprise resource planning (ERP) is a set of integrated programs that manage a company's vital business operations for an entire organization, even a complex, multisite, global organization. Recall that a business process is a set of coordinated and related activities that takes one or more types of input and creates an output of value to the customer of that process. The customer might be a traditional external business customer who buys goods or services from the firm. An example of such a process is capturing a sales order, which takes customer input and generates an order. The customer in a business process might also be an internal customer, such as an employee in another department of the firm. For example, the shipment process generates the internal documents workers need in the warehouse and shipping departments to pick, pack, and ship orders. At the core of the ERP system is a database that is shared by all users so that all business functions have access to current and consistent data for operational decision making and planning, as shown in Figure 8.7.

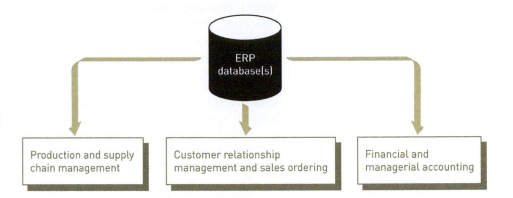

FIGURE **8.7**

Enterprise resource planning system

An ERP integrates business processes and the ERP database.

ERP systems evolved from materials requirement planning (MRP) systems developed in the 1970s. These systems tied together the production planning, inventory control, and purchasing business functions for manufacturing organizations. During the late 1980s and early 1990s, many organizations recognized that their legacy TPSs lacked the integration needed to coordinate activities and share valuable information across all the business functions of the firm. As a result, costs were higher and customer service was poorer than desired. Large organizations, specifically members of the *Fortune* 1000, were the first to take on the challenge of implementing ERP. As they did, they uncovered many advantages as well as some disadvantages, which are summarized in the following sections.

Advantages of ERP

Increased global competition, new needs of executives for control over the total cost and product flow through their enterprises, and ever-more-numerous customer interactions drive the demand for enterprise-wide access to real-time information. ERP offers integrated software from a single vendor to help meet those needs. The primary benefits of implementing ERP include improved access to quality data for operational decision making, elimination of costly, inflexible legacy systems, improvement of work processes, and the opportunity to upgrade and standardize technology infrastructure. ERP vendors have also developed specialized systems that provide effective solutions for specific industries and market segments.

Improved Access to Quality Data for Operational Decision Making

ERP systems operate via an integrated database, using one set of data to support all business functions. For example, the systems can support decisions on optimal sourcing or cost accounting for the entire enterprise or business units. With an ERP system, data is integrated from the start, eliminating the need to gather data from multiple business functions and/or reconcile data from more than one application. The result is an organization that looks seamless, not only to the outside world but also to the decision makers who are deploying resources within the organization. Data is integrated to facilitate operational decision making and allows companies to provide better customer service and support, strengthen customer and supplier relationships, and generate new business opportunities. To ensure that an ERP system contributes to improved decision making, the data used in an ERP system must be of high quality.

Based in New York, Women's World Banking is a global nonprofit focused on providing low-income women access to the financial tools and resources they need to build secure and prosperous lives. The organization works through a network of 40 institutions in 29 countries to create new financial products that must meet the needs of women in each of its markets while also being sustainable for its partner financial institutions.[14] Women's World Banking needs access to detailed transaction information so it can maintain complete transparency into its balances by entity, donor, and grant—even down to the project level. To accomplish this, the organization previously utilized two stand-alone systems that often gave front and back office staff very different views of the organization's key performance metrics, resulting in time-consuming data entry and reconciliation between the two systems. To streamline its operations, Women's World Banking implemented an ERP system that provides it with access to the data it needs to apply for new funding grants, quickly and accurately report on existing grants, and make decisions regarding investments in new business development opportunities. Since its ERP roll-out, the organization has cut 200 hours of accounts payable and grant-reporting time annually, reduced data entry by 14 hours per month, and gained greater visibility into its spending across multiple entities, grants, donors, and projects.[15]

Elimination of Costly, Inflexible Legacy Systems

Adoption of an ERP system enables an organization to eliminate dozens or even hundreds of separate systems and replace them with a single integrated set of applications for the entire enterprise. In many cases, these systems are decades old, the original developers are long gone, and the systems are poorly documented. As a result, the systems are extremely difficult to fix when they break, and adapting them to meet new business needs takes too long. They become an anchor around the organization that keeps it from moving ahead and remaining competitive. An ERP system helps match the capabilities of an organization's information systems to its business needs—even as these needs evolve.

Steinwall Scientific is a Minnesota-based precision thermoplastic injection molder specializing in manufacturing plastic parts using engineering-grade resins. The company, which has been in business for more than 45 years, employs 110 employees and has facilities that encompass more than 100,000 square feet of manufacturing and warehouse space spread across five acres.[16] For many years, most aspects of the company's business were managed using an outdated proprietary system that had been originally programmed by the company's president as a simple inventory management program. In addition to its internally developed system, Steinwall was also using a separate IBM accounting software program. However, the company's two main systems were unable to communicate with each other, creating ongoing data entry errors and significant manufacturing bottlenecks as the company worked to take on new clients. Ultimately, Steinwall made the choice to upgrade its system to a single-database manufacturing ERP system. Over the course of six months, Steinwall gradually moved all of its processing tasks, along with all of its data, to the new system. Among the many benefits that Steinwall has experienced after moving all of its business functions to its new ERP system are improved inventory control, enhanced warehouse management, and a greater efficiency across all its departments.[17]

Improvement of Work Processes

Competition requires companies to structure their business processes to be as effective and customer oriented as possible. To further that goal, ERP vendors do considerable research to define the best business processes. They gather requirements of leading organizations within the same industry and combine

best practices: The most efficient and effective ways to complete a business process.

them with findings from research institutions and consultants. The individual application modules included in the ERP system are then designed to support these **best practices**, the most efficient and effective ways to complete a business process. Thus, implementation of an ERP system ensures work processes will be based on industry best practices. For example, for managing customer payments, the ERP system's finance module can be configured to reflect the most efficient practices of leading companies in an industry. This increased efficiency ensures that everyday business operations follow the optimal chain of activities, with all users supplied the information and tools they need to complete each step.

Prime Meats has been providing high-quality, aged steaks to steakhouses and other restaurants around the country for more than 20 years. Recently, the Atlanta-based company also began offering its USDA Prime and Choice quality steaks directly to consumers through its e-commerce Web site. The company found success with its new business model, but it also found challenges as it existing systems were unable to keep up with the company's growth. To overcome these challenges, Prime Meats implemented an ERP system that offered the company a flexible, fully integrated end-to-end business and accounting software along with prepackaged industry best practice functionality for handling the specific pricing, packaging, and delivery requirements of an online meat business.[18,19]

Opportunity to Upgrade and Standardize Technology Infrastructure

When implementing an ERP system, an organization has an opportunity to upgrade the information technology (such as hardware, operating systems, and databases) that it uses. While centralizing and formalizing these decisions, the organization can eliminate the hodgepodge of multiple hardware platforms, operating systems, and databases it is currently using—most likely from a variety of vendors. Standardizing on fewer technologies and vendors reduces ongoing maintenance and support costs as well as the training load for those who must support the infrastructure.

Whirlpool is the world's leading manufacturer of home appliances, with over 97,000 employees and $20 billion in sales generated from operations in 170 countries.[20] While the company has utilized a collection of ERP systems across its global operations for years, the company recently undertook a complete overhaul of all its ERP infrastructure, with the goal of creating a new operational backbone that will support the company's growth for the next decade. As the company moves forward with its implementation of next-generation SAP ERP software, the company is also updating its ERP infrastructure to a hybrid cloud system hosted by IBM. As part of the project, Whirlpool's IT team is also spending time cleaning up duplicate and inaccurate data, a result of years of cumulative and regionalized ERP system customizations.[21]

Leading ERP Systems

ERP systems are commonly used in manufacturing companies, colleges and universities, professional service organizations, retailers, and healthcare organizations. The business needs for each of these types of organizations varies greatly. In addition, the needs of a large multinational organization are far different from the needs of a small, local organization. Thus, no one ERP software solution from a single vendor is "best" for all organizations. To help simplify comparisons, ERP vendors are classified as Tier I, II, or III according to the type of customers they target.[22]

- Tier I vendors target large multinational firms with multiple geographic locations and annual revenues in excess of $1 billion. Tier I ERP system solutions are highly complex and expensive to implement and support. Implementation across multiple locations can take years. The primary Tier I vendors are Oracle and SAP.

- Tier II vendors target medium-sized firms with annual revenues in the $50 million to $1 billion range operating out of one or more locations. Tier II solutions are much less complex and less expensive to implement and support. There are two dozen or more Tier II vendors, including Oracle, SAP, Microsoft, Infor, Epicor, and Lawson.
- Tier III vendors target smaller firms with annual revenues in the $10 million to $50 million range that typically operate out of a single location. Tier III solutions are comparatively easy and inexpensive to implement and support. There are dozens of Tier III vendors, including Abas, Bluebee Software, Cincom Systems, Compiere, ESP Technologies, Frontier Software, GCS Software, Microsoft, Netsuite, PDS, Plex, and Syspro. Many of the Tier I and Tier II vendors also offer solutions for smaller firms. See Figure 8.8.

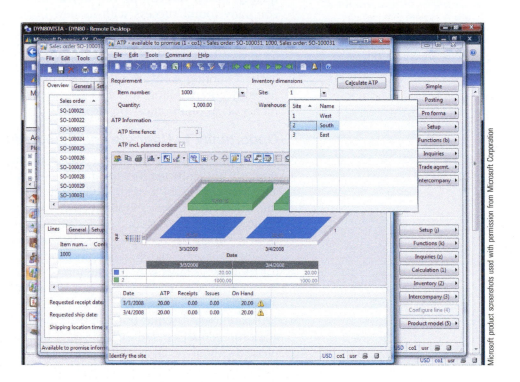

FIGURE 8.8

ERP software

Microsoft Dynamics is an ERP solution that is very popular among small businesses.

Microsoft product screenshots used with permission from Microsoft Corporation

Large organizations were the leaders in adopting ERP systems as only they could afford the associated large hardware and software costs and dedicate sufficient people resources to the implementation and support of these systems. Many large company implementations occurred in the 2000s and involved installing the ERP software on the organizations' large mainframe computers. In many cases, this required upgrading the hardware at a cost of millions of dollars.

Smaller organizations moved to ERP systems about 10 years after larger organizations did. The smaller firms simply could not afford the investment required in hardware, software, and people to implement and support ERP. However, ERP software vendors gradually created new ERP solutions with much lower start-up costs and faster, easier implementations. Some ERP vendors introduced cloud-based solutions, which further reduced the start-up costs by avoiding the need to purchase expensive ERP software and make major hardware upgrades. Instead, with a cloud-based solution, organizations could rent the software and run it on the vendor's hardware. Plex and NetSuite are two of the many cloud-based ERP solutions that enable users to access an ERP application using a Web browser and avoid paying for and maintaining expensive hardware.

As an alternative, many organizations elect to implement open-source ERP systems from vendors such as Compiere. With open-source software, organizations can see and modify the source code to customize it to meet their needs. Such systems are much less costly to acquire and are relatively easy to modify to meet business needs.

Organizations frequently need to customize the vendor's ERP software to integrate other business systems, to add data fields or change field sizes, or to meet regulatory requirements. A wide range of software service organizations can perform the system development and maintenance.

Supply Chain Management

supply chain management (SCM): A system that includes planning, executing, and controlling all activities involved in raw material sourcing and procurement, the conversion of raw materials to finished products, and the warehousing and delivery of finished products to customers.

An organization can use an ERP system within a manufacturing organization to support what is known as **supply chain management (SCM)**, which includes planning, executing, and controlling all activities involved in raw material sourcing and procurement, conversion of raw materials to finished products, and the warehousing and delivery of finished product to customers. The goal of SCM is to decrease costs and improve customer service, while at the same time reducing the overall investment in inventory in the supply chain.

Another way to think about SCM is that it manages materials, information, and finances as they move from supplier to manufacturer to wholesaler to retailer to consumer. The materials flow includes the inbound movement of raw materials from supplier to manufacturer as well as the outbound movement of finished product from manufacturer to wholesaler, retailer, and customer. The information flow involves capturing and transmitting orders and invoices among suppliers, manufacturers, wholesalers, retailers, and customers. The financial flow consists of payment transactions among suppliers, manufacturers, wholesalers, retailers, customers, and their financial institutions.

Newman Technology manufactures exhaust parts and other components for automobiles, motorcycles, and all-terrain vehicles (ATVs). Before switching to a cloud-based SCM system from Plex, the company had been relying on an outdated and inflexible spreadsheet and paper purchase order system that made forecasting, managing, and tracking orders challenging. The updated SCM system has streamlined Newman's supply chain, cutting down on manual procedures (and paper), improving inventory and forecasting accuracy, and freeing up more time for buyers to develop supplier relationships.[23]

The ERP system for a manufacturing organization typically encompasses SCM activities and manages the flow of materials, information, and finances. Manufacturing ERP systems follow a systematic process for developing a production plan that draws on the information available in the ERP system database.

The process starts with *sales forecasting* to develop an estimate of future customer demand. This initial forecast is at a fairly high level, with estimates made by product group rather than by each product item. The sales forecast extends for months into the future; it might be developed using an ERP software module or produced by other means, using specialized software and techniques. Many organizations are moving to a collaborative process with major customers to plan future inventory levels and production rather than relying on an internally generated sales forecast.

The *sales and operations plan* (*S&OP*) takes demand and current inventory levels into account and determines the specific product items that need to be produced as well as when to meet the forecast future demand. Production capacity and any seasonal variability in demand must also be considered.

Demand management refines the production plan by determining the amount of weekly or daily production needed to meet the demand for individual products. The output of the demand management process is the master production schedule, which is a production plan for all finished goods.

Detailed scheduling uses the production plan defined by the demand management process to develop a detailed production schedule that specifies production scheduling details such as which item to produce first and when production should be switched from one item to another. A key decision is how long to make the production runs for each product. Longer production runs reduce the number of machine setups required, thus reducing production costs. Shorter production runs generate less finished product inventory and reduce inventory holding costs.

Materials requirement planning (MRP) determines the amount and timing for placing raw material orders with suppliers. The types and amounts of raw materials required to support the planned production schedule are determined by the existing raw material inventory and the bill of materials (BOM), which serves as a recipe of ingredients needed to make each item. The quantity of raw materials to order also depends on the lead time and lot sizing. *Lead time* is the amount of time it takes from the placement of a purchase order until the raw materials arrive at the production facility. *Lot size* refers to the discrete quantities that the supplier will ship, which can result in purchasing complexities if those amounts don't line up with quantities that are economical for the manufacturer to receive or store. For example, a supplier might ship a certain raw material in units of 80,000-pound rail cars. The producer might need 95,000 pounds of the raw material. A decision must be made to order one or two rail cars of the raw material.

Purchasing uses the information from MRP to place purchase orders for raw materials with qualified suppliers. Typically, purchase orders are released so that raw materials arrive just in time to be used in production and to minimize warehouse and storage costs. Often, producers will allow suppliers to tap into data via an extranet that enables them to determine what raw materials the producer needs, minimizing the effort and lead time to place and fill purchase orders.

Production uses the high-level production schedule to plan the details of running and staffing the production operation. This more detailed schedule takes into account employee, equipment, and raw material availability along with detailed customer demand data.

Sales ordering is the set of activities that must be performed to capture a customer sales order. Essential sales order steps include recording the items to be purchased, setting the sales price, recording the order quantity, determining the total cost of the order including delivery costs, and confirming the customer's available credit. If the item(s) the customer wants to order are out of stock, the sales order process should communicate this fact and suggest other items to substitute for the customer's initial choice. Setting sales prices can be quite complicated and can include quantity discounts, promotions, and incentives. After the total cost of the order is determined, a company must check the customer's available credit to see if this order is within the credit limit. Figure 8.9 shows a sales order entry window in SAP business software.

ERP systems do not work directly with manufacturing machines on the production floor, so they need a way to capture information about what was produced. This data must be passed to the ERP accounting modules to keep an accurate count of finished product inventory. Many companies have computers on the production floor, which are used to track the number of cases of each product item produced, typically by having a worker scan a UPC

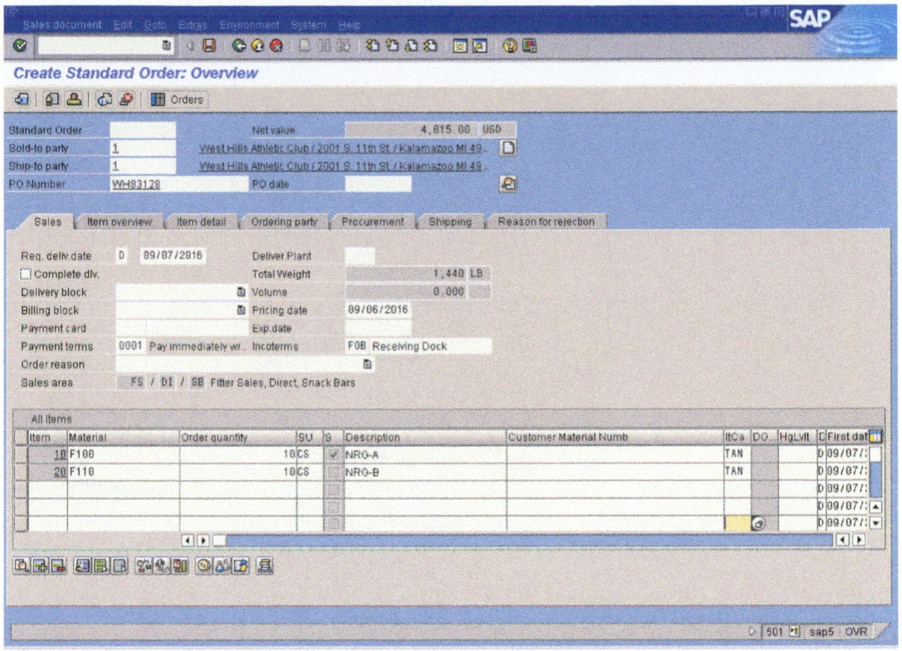

FIGURE 8.9

Sales order entry window

Sales ordering is the set of activities that must be performed to capture a customer sales order.

Source: SAP AG

code on the packing cases used to ship the material. Other approaches for capturing production quantities include using RFID chips and manually entering the data.

Separately, production quality data can be added based on the results of quality tests run on a sample of the product for each batch of product produced. Typically, this data includes the batch identification number, which identifies the production run and the results of various product quality tests.

Retailers as well as manufacturers use demand forecasting to match production to consumer demand and to allocate products to stores. Curry's Art Store, which has been supplying arts and crafts materials and framing services since 1911, has an inventory that includes more than 20,000 SKUs available to customers in its 10 stores and through its e-commerce Web site. Because much of Curry's business is seasonal, with peaks in demand during back-to-school time and near major holidays, it utilizes a complex supply chain management system, which provides it with accurate long-range forecasting tools that help ensure it has the stock it needs to meet demand surges. The system has the tools the company needs to manage a supply chain that includes in-store and online retails sales in addition to bulk orders from large educational institutions, and it also supports Curry's complicated warehousing and distribution needs.[24]

Customer Relationship Management

customer relationship management (CRM) system: A system that helps a company manage all aspects of customer encounters, including marketing, sales, distribution, accounting, and customer service.

A **customer relationship management (CRM) system** helps a company manage all aspects of customer encounters, including marketing, sales, distribution, accounting, and customer service. See Figure 8.10. Think of a CRM system as an address book with a historical record of all the organization's interactions with each customer. The goal of CRM is to understand and anticipate the needs of current and potential customers to increase customer retention and loyalty while optimizing the way that products and services are sold. CRM is used primarily by people in the sales, marketing, distribution, accounting, and service organizations to capture and view data about customers and to improve communications. Businesses implementing CRM systems often report benefits such as improved customer satisfaction, increased customer retention, reduced operating costs, and the ability to meet customer demand.

Means of communication

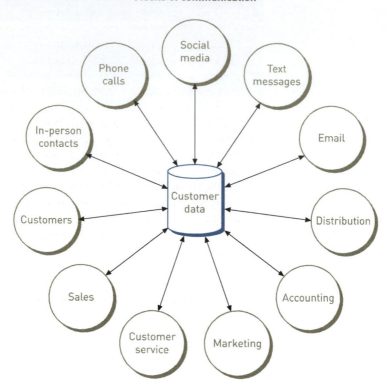

Users and providers of customer data

Customer relationship management system

A CRM system provides a central repository of customer data used by the organization.

CRM software automates and integrates the functions of sales, marketing, and service in an organization. The objective is to capture data about every contact a company has with a customer through every channel and to store it in the CRM system so that the company can truly understand customer actions. CRM software helps an organization build a database about its customers that describes relationships in sufficient detail so that management, salespeople, customer service providers, and even customers can access information to match customer needs with product plans and offerings, remind them of service requirements, and report on the other products the customers have purchased.

Small, medium, and large organizations in a wide variety of industries choose to implement CRM for many reasons, depending on their needs. Consider the following examples:

- Expensify is a financial services firm that provides online expense-management services for customers around the world. The company has grown quickly since it was founded in San Francisco in 2008, and it recently opened a London office to support its expansion into the European market. As a start-up, Expensify's initial attempts at CRM were built around an Excel spreadsheet. Before long, the company shifted to Google Apps' CRM tools, but soon found those could not handle its increasing volume of customer data. Eventually, the company implemented a customizable CRM system that provides all the tools Expensify's sales and customers service teams require—without the need to manage and coordinate workflows in other systems. Expensify's top priorities for a CRM system included automated and customizable lead-prioritization tools, the ability to track all sales communication within one system, and the ability to generate in-depth reports to identify areas of opportunity within a geographic region as well as for individual salespeople.[25]

- TUMI luggage, handbags, and travel accessories are available through a global network of 100 company-owned stores as well as department and specialty stores in over 70 countries. Since it started in 1965, TUMI has placed a priority on offering a wide selection of high-quality business and travel products. Although TUMI's culture is focused on providing world-class service, the company's outdated systems were getting in the way of its relationships with both wholesale and retail customers. For instance, tracking an order or a repair job for a customer typically meant putting a caller on hold and calling the warehouse for an update. To address its customer service issues, TUMI chose to implement a CRM application that was integrated with a comprehensive ERP system designed to help the company improve its inventory tracking, sales forecasting, and financial reporting. Now, TUMI's customer service team is able to quickly provide customers with precise real-time information about order and repair status. And because TUMI tracks individual customer purchases using the CRM software, it is better able to keep up with market trends and respond to customers' changing needs—all of which have helped drive a 20 percent increase in sales since the system was implemented.[26]

- The American Red Cross was founded in 1881 by Clara Barton as a non-profit, humanitarian organization. Today, the organization relies on 35,000 employees and more than 500,000 volunteers to deliver a range of services across the United States, including providing relief to people affected by disasters, supporting members of the military and their families, and collecting, processing, and distributing blood supplies. The Red Cross uses a cloud-based CRM platform from Salesforce to manage its relationships with its large network of financial donors, volunteers, blood donors, and recipients. Because its CRM system is cloud-based, Red Cross volunteers and employees can quickly access the data and services required to get the organization's operations up and running during a disaster. The Red Cross integrated social networking tools into its CRM system, providing the organization with new channels to connect with volunteers and donors as well as new tools for delivering disaster-relief updates to the public, soliciting financial and volunteer help, and helping people affected by a disaster communicate with family and friends.[27,28]

The key features of a CRM system include the following:

- **Contact management**. The ability to track data on individual customers and sales leads and then access that data from any part of the organization. See Figure 8.11, which shows the SAP Contact Manager.
- **Sales management**. The ability to organize data about customers and sales leads and then to prioritize the potential sales opportunities and identify appropriate next steps.
- **Customer support**. The ability to support customer service representatives so that they can quickly, thoroughly, and appropriately address customer requests and resolve customer issues while collecting and storing data about those interactions.
- **Marketing automation**. The ability to capture and analyze all customer interactions, generate appropriate responses, and gather data to create and build effective and efficient marketing campaigns.
- **Analysis**. The ability to analyze customer data to identify ways to increase revenue and decrease costs, identify the firm's "best customers," and determine how to retain and find more of them.

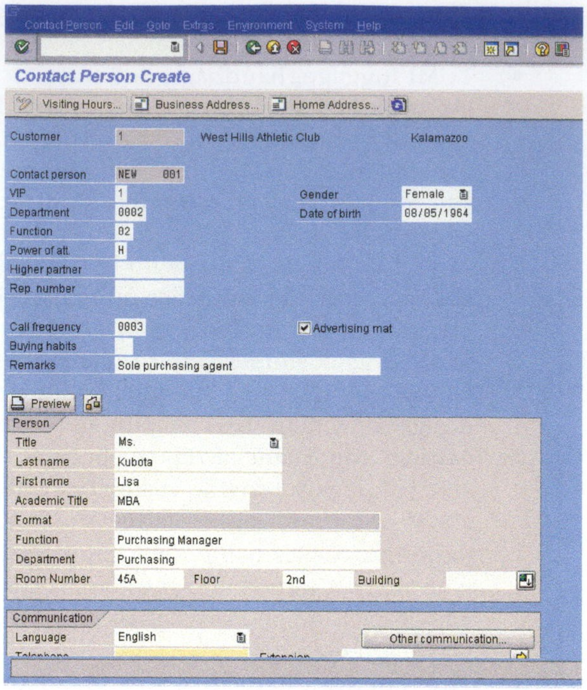

FIGURE **8.11**

SAP Contact Manager

Contact management involves tracking data on individual customers and sales leads and accessing that data from any part of the organization.
Source: SAP AG

- **Social networking**. The ability to create and join sites such as Facebook, where salespeople can make contacts with potential customers.
- **Access by mobile devices**. The ability to access Web-based customer relationship management software by smartphones, tablets, and other mobile devices.
- **Import contact data**. The ability for users to import contact data from various data service providers that can be downloaded for free directly into the CRM application.

The focus of CRM involves much more than installing new software. Moving from a culture of simply selling products to placing the customer first is essential to a successful CRM deployment. Before any software is loaded onto a computer, a company must retrain employees. Who handles customer issues and when must be clearly defined, and computer systems need to be integrated so that all pertinent information is available immediately, whether a customer calls a sales representative or a customer service representative.

Nu Skin Enterprises is a $2 billion direct sales organization that develops and distributes nutritional supplements and personal care products through a network of more than 5,000 independent sales distributors. The company's 250 call center agents are the key point of contact between the company and its customers and distributors; however, rapid turnover of call center staff and three disconnected customer contact tools meant that many customers became quickly frustrated during their interactions with the company. A solution to Nu Skin's customer service challenges came in the form of a CRM system from SAP, which was integrated with the company's existing SAP ERP system to provide agents immediate access to customer sales histories. Nu Skin call center employees now use the system's customer interaction center and order management tools to resolve callers' queries more quickly, and with frustration levels down—for both agents and customers—agents have been able to focus on developing stronger relationship with customers and distributors and increasing sales.[29,30]

Table 8.3 lists a few highly rated CRM systems.[31]

TABLE 8.3 Highly rated CRM systems

Vendor/Product	Select Customers	Pricing Starts At
Infusionsoft CRM	Clean Corp Swim Fitness	$67 per user/month
OnContact CRM 7	Prudential Carfax	$50 per user/month
Oracle Marketing Cloud	Bass Pro Shops Whole Foods	$80 per user/month
Prophet CRM	AT&T Century 21	$24 per user/month
Sage Software CRM	Panasonic Lockheed Martin	$39 per user/month
Salesforce Sales Cloud	Dell Dr. Pepper Snapple	$5 per user/month

Due to the popularity of mobile devices, shoppers can easily compare products and prices on their mobile phones and instantly tweet their experiences with a brand to dozens of friends. Savvy retailers today use their CRM systems to stay on top of what these customers are saying on social networks. For instance, Wells Fargo Bank uses social media to keep track of what its customers are saying and then responds quickly to their issues and questions to improve customer satisfaction.[32]

Most CRM systems can now be accessed via smartphones to gain work with the most current customer information even while on the move. However, in a recent survey, just under 25 percent of salespeople who have a smartphone use it to access their firm's CRM system. Another 10 percent of salespeople worked for a company whose CRM system did not allow mobile access.[33]

Product Lifecycle Management

product lifecycle management (PLM): An enterprise business strategy that creates a common repository of product information and processes to support the collaborative creation, management, dissemination, and use of product and packaging definition information.

Product lifecycle management (PLM) is an enterprise business strategy that creates a common repository of product information and processes to support the collaborative creation, management, dissemination, and use of product and packaging definition information.

product lifecycle management (PLM) software: Software that provides a means for managing the data and processes associated with the various phases of the product life cycle, including sales and marketing, research and development, concept development, product design, prototyping and testing, process design, production and assembly, delivery and product installation, service and support, and product retirement and replacement.

Product lifecycle management (PLM) software provides a means for managing the data and processes associated with the various phases of the product life cycle, including sales and marketing, research and development, concept development, product design, prototyping and testing, manufacturing process design, production and assembly, delivery and product installation, service and support, and product retirement and replacement. See Figure 8.12. As products advance through these stages, product data is generated and distributed to various groups both within and outside the manufacturing firm. This data includes design and process documents, bill of material definitions, product attributes, product formulations, and documents needed for FDA and environmental compliance. PLM software provides support for the key functions of configuration management, document management, engineering change management, release management, and collaboration with suppliers and original equipment manufacturers (OEMs).

computer-aided design (CAD): The use of software to assist in the creation, analysis, and modification of the design of a component or product.

The scope of PLM software may include computer-aided design, computer-aided engineering, and computer-aided manufacturing. **Computer-aided design (CAD)** is the use of software to assist in the creation, analysis, and modification of the design of a component or product. Its use can increase the productivity of the designer, improve the quality of design, and create a database that describes the item. This data can be shared with others or used in

Retire & replace

Sales & marketing

Service & support

Research & development

PLM software supports the product development lifecycle

Concept development

Product delivery & installation

Production & assembly

Product design

Process design

Prototype & test

Scope of PLM software

Using PLM software, organizations can manage the data and processes associated with the various phases of the product life cycle.

computer-aided engineering (CAE): The use of software to analyze the robustness and performance of components and assemblies.

computer-aided manufacturing (CAM): The use of software to control machine tools and related machinery in the manufacture of components and products.

the machining of the part or in other manufacturing operations. **Computer-aided engineering (CAE)** is the use of software to analyze the robustness and performance of components and assemblies. CAE software supports the simulation, validation, and optimization of products and manufacturing tools. CAE is extremely useful to design teams in evaluating and decision making. **Computer-aided manufacturing (CAM)** is the use of software to control machine tools and related machinery in the manufacture of components and products. The model generated in CAD and verified in CAE can be input into CAM software, which then controls the machine tool. See Figure 8.13.

CAD, CAE, and CAM software

In manufacturing, the model generated in CAD and verified in CAE can be entered into CAM software, which then controls the machine tool.

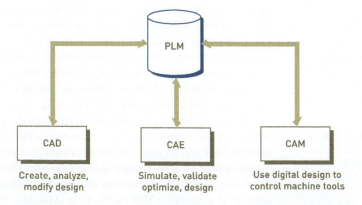

CAD — Create, analyze, modify design

CAE — Simulate, validate optimize, design

CAM — Use digital design to control machine tools

Some organizations elect to implement a single, integrated PLM system that encompasses all the phases of the product life cycle with which it is most concerned. Other organizations choose to implement multiple, separate PLM software components from different vendors over time. This piecemeal approach enables an organization to choose the software that best meets it needs for a particular phase in the product life cycle. It also allows for incremental investment in the PLM strategy. However, it may be difficult to link all the various components together in such a manner that a single comprehensive database of product and process data is created.

Use of an effective PLM system enables global organizations to work as a single team to design, produce, support, and retire products, while capturing best practices and lessons learned along the way.[34] PLM powers innovation and improves productivity by connecting people across global product development and manufacturing organizations with the product and process knowledge they need to succeed. See Figure 8.14.

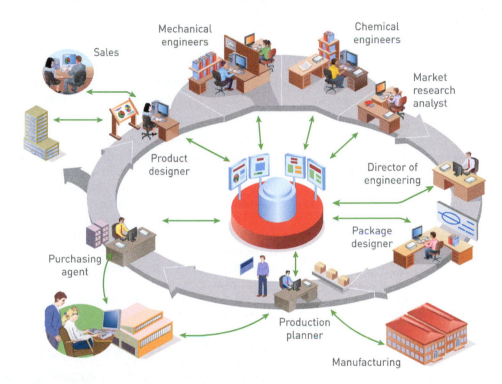

FIGURE **8.14**

PLM business strategy

PLM powers innovation and improves productivity.

PLM software and its data are used by both internal and external users. Internal users include engineering, operations and manufacturing, procurement and sourcing, manufacturing, marketing, quality assurance, customer service, regulatory, and others. External users include the manufacturer's design partners, packaging suppliers, raw material suppliers, and contract manufacturers. These users must collaborate to define, maintain, update, and securely share product information throughout the life cycle of the product. Frequently, these external users are asked to sign nondisclosure agreements to reduce the risk of proprietary information being shared with competitors.

Based in Fort Collins, Colorado, Water Pik develops and sells a variety of personal and oral healthcare products under the Waterpik brand. The company prides itself on innovation and since its founding in 1962, Water Pik has acquired over 500 patents. Over time, the company's approach to managing its product information through traditional directory structures on file systems was resulting in an increasing number of inefficiencies in Water Pik's development and manufacturing processes. To better manage its CAD product data, Water Pik chose to implement SofTech's ProductCenter PLM software. The company now uses the software to manage product information—which is secured through permissions—for three of its four main product lines. Water Pik also uses the software to manage all of its business processes, which are automatically set to expire every two years, triggering a review and update process that helps the company ensure that its procedures are current and compliant with various industry standards.[35,36]

Table 8.4 presents a list of some of the top-rated PLM software products (in alphabetic order) according to a 2013 report by Business-Software.com.[37]

TABLE 8.4 Highly rated PLM software products

Organization	Primary PLM Software Product	Technology Model	Select Customers
Arena	Cloud PLM	Cloud-based solution	SiriusXM, SunLink
Infor	Optiva	On-premise solution	Henkel, Sypris
Integware	Enovia Collaborative PLM	On-premise solution	Cummins, Steelcase
PTC	Windchill	SaaS solution	Medco Equipment, InterComm
SAP	PLM	On-premise solution	Porsche, Anadarko Petroleum
Siemens	Teamcenter	On-premise solution	Procter & Gamble, BAE Systems
SofTech	ProductCenter PLM	SaaS solution	Hayward Tyler Motors, Monarch Hydraulics
Sopheon	Accolade	Cloud-based solution	PepsiCo, ConAgra

discrete manufacturing: The production of distinct items such as autos, airplanes, furniture, or toys that can be decomposed into their basic components.

process manufacturing: The production of products—such as soda, laundry detergent, gasoline, and pharmaceutical drugs—that are the result of a chemical process; these products cannot be easily decomposed into their basic components.

PLM software is created for two broad categories of manufacturing: discrete manufacturing and process manufacturing. **Discrete manufacturing** is the production of distinct items such as autos, airplanes, furniture, or toys that can be decomposed back into their basic components. **Process manufacturing** is the production of products—such as soda, laundry detergent, gasoline, and pharmaceutical drugs—that are the result of a chemical process; these products cannot be easily decomposed back into their basic components. Within these two broad categories, PLM software manufacturers specialize in specific industries such as aircraft manufacturing, consumer goods manufacturing, or drug manufacturing.

Table 8.5 outlines the benefits a business can realize when using a PLM system effectively.

TABLE 8.5 Benefits of a PLM system

Benefit	How Achieved
Reduce time to market	• By connecting design, research and development, procurement, manufacturing, and customer service seamlessly through a flexible collaboration environment • By improving collaboration among the organization and its suppliers, contract manufacturers, and OEMs
Reduce costs	• By reducing prototyping costs through the use of software simulation • By reducing scrap and rework through improved processes • By reducing the number of product components through standardization
Ensure regulatory compliance	• By providing a secure repository, tracking and audit trails, change and document management controls, workflow and communications, and improved security

Industrial Control Associates Inc. (ICA) specializes in providing engineering, design, construction, and start-up support services for programmable logic control (PLC) systems for government agencies and industrial clients in the Southeast and abroad. Its diverse client base includes the Department of

Energy, DuPont Chemical, Procter & Gamble Paper Products, and Tyson Foods. ICA uses Siemens PLM software—which serves as a repository for all of the company's product data—to manage its product design processes, improve the quality of its drawings and bills of materials (BOMs), and increase the accuracy of its machine designs. The software also provides Web-based collaboration tools that make it easy for ICA and its clients to work together throughout the design process, cutting down on redesign work and increasing customers' confidence in ICA's design process. Since implementing the Siemens' software, the company has achieved a 30 percent reduction in the time it takes to complete a job and has cut its remanufacturing rate from 20 percent down to 2 percent.[38,39]

Overcoming Challenges in Implementing Enterprise Systems

Implementing an enterprise system, particularly for a large organization, is extremely challenging and requires tremendous amounts of resources, the best IS and businesspeople, and plenty of management support. In spite of all this, many enterprise system implementations fail, and problems with an enterprise system implementation can require expensive solutions. The following is a sample of major enterprise system implementation project failures:

- The state of Michigan sued HP over a $49 million IT project for the Secretary of State's office that remains incomplete after 10 years. Michigan is asking for more than $11 million in damages, and it is looking to reclaim its attorney's fee as well as the costs involved with rebidding and re-procuring the contract. The state is also asking that HP be required to turn over source code for an online services portal that HP delivered as part of the project.[40]
- H.B. Fuller, a large U.S. industrial adhesives and sealants manufacturer, was awarded $14 million in an arbitration case against consulting agency Accenture in connection with a failed companywide SAP ERP system implementation. Problems with the system became apparent almost as soon as it was implemented, which was behind schedule. In addition to the $60 million in planned capital expenditures, Fuller spent over $8 million in the first two months after the system was launched to address problems related to the implementation.[41]
- The Hawaii Department of Transportation (HDOT) sued Ciber, Inc., alleging the consulting firm engaged in fraud and other misconduct on an ERP software implementation project for the state agency. HDOT accuses Ciber of misrepresenting its capabilities in order to secure the state contract and submitting erroneous invoices and fictitious project change orders. Eventually, Ciber was terminated from the project after a series of missed deadlines and problems with software bugs and missing functionality. HDOT is seeking tens of millions in damages, including more than $8 million in fees it paid to Ciber.[42]

Half of nearly 200 ERP implementations worldwide evaluated by Panorama, an ERP consulting firm, were judged to be failures. Table 8.6 lists and describes the most significant challenges to successful implementation of an enterprise system.[43]

The following list provides tips for avoiding many common causes for failed enterprise system implementations:

- Assign a full-time executive to manage the project.
- Appoint an experienced, independent resource to provide project oversight and to verify and validate system performance.
- Allow sufficient time to transition from the old way of doing things to the new system and new processes.
- Allocate sufficient time and money for training staff; many project managers recommend budgeting 30 to 60 days per employee for training.
- Define metrics to assess project progress and to identify project-related risks.

TABLE **8.6** Challenges to successful enterprise system implementation

Challenge	Description
Cost and disruption of upgrades	Most companies have other systems that must be integrated with the enterprise system, such as financial analysis programs, e-commerce operations, and other applications that communicate with suppliers, customers, distributors, and other business partners. Integration of multiple systems adds time and complexity to an ERP implementation.
Cost and long implementation lead time	The average ERP implementation cost is $5.5 million with an average project duration of just over 14 months.
Difficulty in managing change	Companies often must radically change how they operate to conform to the enterprise work processes. These changes can be so drastic to longtime employees that they depart rather than adapt to the change, leaving the firm short of experienced workers.
Management of software customization	The base enterprise system may need to be modified to meet mandatory business requirements. System customizations can become extremely expensive and further delay implementation.
User frustration with the new system	Effective use of an enterprise system requires changes in work processes and in the details of how work gets done. Many users initially balk at these changes and require extensive training and encouragement.

- Keep the scope of the project well defined and contained to essential business processes.
- Be wary of modifying the enterprise system software to conform to your firm's business practices.

Hosted Software Model for Enterprise Software

Many business application software vendors are pushing the use of the hosted software model. The goal is to help customers acquire, use, and benefit from the new technology while avoiding much of the associated complexity and high start-up costs. Applicor, Intacct, NetSuite, SAP, and Workday are among the software vendors who offer hosted versions of their ERP or CRM software at a cost of $50 to $200 per month per user.

This pay-as-you-go approach is appealing because organizations can experiment with powerful software capabilities without making a major financial investment. Organizations can then dispose of the software without large investments if the software fails to provide value or otherwise misses expectations. Also, using the hosted software model means the business firm does not need to employ a full-time IT person to maintain key business applications. The business firm can expect additional savings from reduced hardware costs and costs associated with maintaining an appropriate computer environment (such as air conditioning, power, and an uninterruptible power supply).

Table 8.7 lists the advantages and disadvantages of hosted software.

LoneStar Heart is a California company that researches and develops restorative therapies and technologies for patients with advanced heart failure. In its early years as a start-up company, LoneStar relied on a paper-based approach to document control that resulted in researchers spending extensive time searching and managing product documentation—taking them away from their critical design and development work. To gain efficiencies in its development processes and free up time for its research and development team, LoneStar eventually decided to implement a cloud-based PLM that would support

TABLE 8.7 Advantages and disadvantages of hosted software model

Advantages	Disadvantages
Decreased total cost of ownership	Potential availability and reliability issues
Faster system start-up	Potential data security issues
Lower implementation risk	Potential problems integrating the hosted products of different vendors
Management of systems outsourced to experts	Savings anticipated from outsourcing may be offset by increased effort to manage vendor

employees in the company's facilities as well as those who work remotely. The PLM system from Omnify Software provides LoneStar with a secure, yet easily accessible centralized product information database and the tools it requires to maintain compliant with the extensive set of FDA regulations governing its work. By using a cloud-based PLM, LoneStar was able to avoid close to $40,000 in server installation and maintenance costs annually.[44,45]

Critical Thinking Exercise

Implementing CRM

iProspect is a global digital performance marketing firm. It works to increase Web site traffic for its clients through services such as search engine optimization, lead generation, Web site analytics, and Web site conversion enhancement. Its clients include such firms as Adidas, American Express, Coca-Cola, Ford Motor Company, General Motors, and Sharp Electronics. The firm needs a formal means of capturing information about its customers and their interactions with the company. It also hopes to implement a CRM system that will capture its best business practices to enable it to build on sales and customer satisfaction successes.

Review Questions

1. What specific tasks must this CRM software perform?
2. What are the potential benefits that iProspect might capture from use of a CRM system?

Critical Thinking Questions

1. The CFO has asked you to lead a team to assess the potential benefits associated with this system. Who would you choose to make up this team (job title and organization)? How could your team attempt to quantify the potential benefits of such a system?
2. What are the pros and cons of choosing a hosted software solution to "test drive" a potential CRM solution?

Summary

Principle:

An organization must have information systems that support routine, day-to-day activities and that help a company add value to its products and services.

Transaction processing systems (TPSs) are at the heart of most information systems in businesses today. A TPS is an organized collection of people, procedures, software, databases, and devices used to capture fundamental data about events that affect the organization (transactions) and that use that data to update the official records of the organization.

The methods of TPSs include batch and online processing. Batch processing involves the collection of transactions into batches, which are entered into the system at regular intervals as a group. Online transaction processing (OLTP) allows transactions to be processed as they occur.

Organizations expect TPSs to accomplish a number of specific objectives, including processing data generated by and about transactions, maintaining a high degree of accuracy and information integrity, compiling accurate and timely reports and documents, increasing labor efficiency, helping provide increased and enhanced service, and building and maintaining customer loyalty. In some situations, an effective TPS can help an organization gain a competitive advantage.

Order processing systems capture and process customer order data—from the receipt of the order through creation of a customer invoice.

Accounting systems track the flow of data related to all the cash flows that affect the organization.

Purchasing systems support the inventory control, purchase order processing, receiving, and accounts payable business functions.

Organizations today, including SMEs, typically implement an integrated set of TPSs from a single or limited number of software vendors to meet their transaction processing needs.

All TPSs perform the following basic activities: data collection, which involves the capture of source data to complete a set of transactions; data editing, which checks for data validity and completeness; data correction, which involves providing feedback regarding a potential problem and enabling users to change the data; data processing, which is the performance of calculations, sorting, categorizing, summarizing, and storing data for further processing; data storage, which involves placing transaction data into one or more databases; and document production, which involves outputting electronic or hard-copy records and reports.

Principle:

An organization that implements an enterprise system is creating a highly integrated set of systems, which can lead to many business benefits.

ERP software supports the efficient operation of business processes by integrating activities throughout a business, including sales, marketing, manufacturing, logistics, accounting, and staffing.

Implementing an ERP system can provide many advantages, including allowing access to data for operational decision making; eliminating costly, inflexible legacy systems; providing improved work processes; and creating the opportunity to upgrade technology infrastructure.

Some of the disadvantages associated with ERP systems are that they are time consuming, difficult, and expensive to implement; they can also be difficult to integrate with other systems.

No one ERP software solution is "best" for all organizations. SAP, Oracle, Infor, and Microsoft are among the leading ERP suppliers.

Although the scope of ERP implementation can vary, most manufacturing organizations use ERP to support the supply chain management (SCM) activities of planning, executing, and controlling all activities involved in raw material sourcing and procurement, conversion of raw materials to finished products, and the warehousing and delivery of finished product to customers.

The production and supply chain management process starts with sales forecasting to develop an estimate of future customer demand. This initial forecast is at a fairly high level, with estimates made by product group rather than by individual product item. The sales and operations plan (S&OP) takes demand and current inventory levels into account and determines the specific product items that need to be produced as well as when to meet the forecast future demand. Demand management refines the production plan by determining the amount of weekly or daily production needed to meet the demand for individual products. Detailed scheduling uses the production plan defined by the demand management process to develop a detailed production schedule that specifies details such as which item to produce first and when production should be switched from one item to another. Materials requirement planning determines the amount and timing for placing raw material orders with suppliers. Purchasing uses the information from materials requirement planning to place purchase orders for raw materials and transmit them to qualified suppliers. Production uses the detailed schedule to plan the logistics of running and staffing the production operation. Sales ordering is the set of activities that must be performed to capture a customer sales order. The individual application modules included in the ERP system are designed to support best practices, the most efficient and effective ways to complete a business process.

Organizations are implementing customer relationship management (CRM) systems to manage all aspects of customer encounters, including marketing, sales, distribution, accounting, and customer service. The goal of CRM is to understand and anticipate the needs of current and potential customers to increase customer retention and loyalty while optimizing the way products and services are sold.

Manufacturing organizations are implementing product lifecycle management (PLM) software to manage the data and processes associated with the various phases of the product life cycle, including sales and marketing, research and development, concept development, product design, prototyping and testing, manufacturing process design, production and assembly, delivery and product installation, service and support, and product retirement and replacement. These systems are used by both internal and external users to enable them to collaborate and capture best practices and lessons learned along the way.

The most significant challenges to successful implementation of an enterprise system include the cost and disruption of upgrades, the cost and long implementation lead time, the difficulty in managing change, the management of software customization, and user frustration with the new system.

Business application software vendors are experimenting with the hosted software model to see if the approach meets customer needs and is likely to generate significant revenue. This approach is especially appealing to SMEs due to the low initial cost, which makes it possible to experiment with powerful software capabilities.

Key Terms

batch processing system

best practices

computer-aided design (CAD)

computer-aided engineering (CAE)

computer-aided manufacturing (CAM)

customer relationship management (CRM) system

data collection

data correction

data editing

data processing

data storage

discrete manufacturing

document production

enterprise system

online transaction processing (OLTP)

process manufacturing

product lifecycle management (PLM)

product lifecycle management (PLM) software

source data automation

supply chain management (SCM)

transaction processing cycle

Chapter 8: Self-Assessment Test

An organization must have information systems that support routine, day-to-day activities and that help a company add value to its products and services.

1. Transaction processing systems (TPSs) capture and process the fundamental data about events that affect the organization called _____ that are used to update the official records of the organization.

2. The essential characteristic of a(n) _____ transaction processing system is that it processes transactions as they occur.

3. Which of the following is *not* one of the basic components of a TPS?
   a. Databases
   b. Networks
   c. Procedures
   d. Analytical models

4. _____ involves providing feedback regarding a potential data problem and enables users to change the data.
   a. Data collection
   b. Data correction
   c. Data editing
   d. Data processing

5. The specific business needs and goals of the organization define the method of transaction processing best suited for the various application of the company. True or False?

6. Which of the following is not an objective of an organization's batch transaction processing system?
   a. Capture, process, and update databases of business data required to support routine business activities
   b. Ensure that data is processed immediately upon occurrence of a business transaction
   c. Avoid processing fraudulent transactions
   d. Produce timely user responses and reports

7. Business data goes through a cycle that includes data collection, data _____, data correction, data processing, data storage, and documentation production.

8. Unfortunately, there are few choices for software packages that provide integrated transaction processing system solutions for small and medium-sized enterprises. True or False?

9. Capturing and gathering all the data necessary to complete the processing of transactions is called _____.

An organization that implements an enterprise system is creating a highly integrated set of systems, which can lead to many business benefits.

10. Small organizations were slow to adopt ERP systems because of the relative complexity and cost of implementing these systems. True or False?

11. The individual application modules included in an ERP system are designed to support _____, the most efficient and effective ways to complete a business process.

12. _____ software helps a customer manage all aspects of customer encounters, including marketing, sales, distribution, accounting, and customer service.

13. The hosted software model for enterprise software helps customers acquire, use, and benefit from new technology while avoiding much of the associated complexity and high start-up costs. True or False?

14. _____ is software used to analyze the robustness and performance of components and assemblies.
   a. PLM
   b. CAD
   c. CAE
   d. CAM

15. Many multinational companies roll out standard IS applications for all to use. However, standard applications often don't account for all the differences among business partners and employees operating in other parts of the world. Which of the following is a frequent modification that is needed for standard software?
   a. Software might need to be designed with local language interfaces to ensure the successful implementation of a new IS.
   b. Customization might be needed to handle date fields correctly.
   c. Users might also have to implement manual processes and overrides to enable systems to function correctly.
   d. All of the above

Chapter 8: Self-Assessment Test Answers

1. transactions
2. online
3. d
4. b
5. True
6. b
7. editing
8. False

9. data collection
10. True
11. best practices
12. Customer relationship management (CRM)
13. True
14. c
15. d

Review Questions

1. Identify and briefly describe six basic transaction processing activities performed by all transaction processing systems.
2. Provide a data processing example for which the use of a batch processing system to handle transactions is appropriate. Provide an example for which the use of online transaction processing is appropriate.
3. What is an enterprise system? Identify and briefly discuss the goals of three types of enterprise systems.
4. What are best practices?
5. Define supply chain management (SCM).
6. What is a Tier I ERP software vendor?
7. What are some of the advantages and disadvantages of the hosted software model?
8. How does materials requirement planning support the purchasing process in an ERP environment? What are some of the issues and complications that arise in materials requirement planning?
9. Identify and briefly describe at least four key business capabilities provided by the use of a CRM system.
10. Identify the basic business processes included within the scope of product lifecycle management.
11. Discuss the difference between discrete and process manufacturing.
12. What is source data automation? What benefits can it be expected to deliver?

Discussion Questions

1. Identify and discuss key benefits that are common to the use of ERP, CRM, and PLM enterprise systems, whether it be for a small, medium, or large organization.
2. Identify and briefly discuss five challenges to the successful implementation of an enterprise system. Provide several tips to overcome these challenges.
3. Assume that you are the owner of a small bicycle sales and repair shop serving hundreds of customers in your area. Identify the kinds of customer information you would like your firm's CRM system to capture. How might this information be used to provide better service or increase revenue? Identify where or how you might capture this data.
4. Why were SMEs slow to adopt ERP software? What changed to make ERP software more attractive for SMEs?
5. Briefly describe the hosted software model for enterprise software and discuss its primary appeal for business organizations.
6. Explain how CAD, CAE, and CAM software can work together to support the product development life cycle.
7. In what ways is the implementation of a CRM system simpler and less risky for an SME than for a large multinational corporation?
8. You are a member of the engineering organization for an aircraft parts manufacturer. The firm is considering the implementation of a PLM system. Make a convincing argument for selecting a system whose scope includes CAD, CAE, and CAM software.
9. What benefits should the suppliers and customers of a firm that has successfully implemented an ERP system expect to see? How might an ERP implementation affect an organization's suppliers?
10. Many organizations are moving to a collaborative process with their major suppliers to get their input on designing and planning future product modification or new products. Explain how a PLM system might enhance such a process. What issues and concerns might a manufacturer have in terms of sharing product data with suppliers?

Problem-Solving Exercises

1. Develop a list of seven key criteria that a non-profit charitable organization should consider in selecting a CRM system. Discuss each criterion and assign a weight representing the relative importance of that criterion, Develop a simple spreadsheet to use in scoring various CRM alternatives in terms of how well they meet those criteria on a scale of 1 to 10. Do research on one CRM package and use your spreadsheet to develop its score.
2. Imagine that you are a new employee in the engineering organization of a large camping equipment and outdoor furniture manufacturing firm. The company is considering implementing a PLM system to better manage the design and manufacture of its products. You have been invited to a meeting to share your thoughts on how such a system might be used and what capabilities are most important. How would you prepare for this meeting? What points would you

make? Develop a presentation containing three to six slides that summarize your thoughts.

3. In a spreadsheet program, enter the ingredients and quantity required to make your favorite homemade cookie. This represents a simple bill of materials (BOM). Add a column to show the cost for each ingredient. Now "explode" the BOM to show the quantity and cost of each ingredient required to make 10,000 cookies.

Team Activities

1. Your team is working with the owner of a small appliance sales and repair shop serving hundreds of customers in your area. How might the owner use a CRM system to capture customer data that could be used to provide better service and increase revenue?

2. With your team members, meet with several business managers at a firm that has implemented an enterprise system. Interview them to document the scope, cost, and schedule for the overall project. Find out why the organization decided it was time to implement the enterprise system. Make a list of what the business managers see as the primary benefits of the implementation. What were the biggest hurdles they had to overcome? Are there any remaining issues that must be resolved before the project can be deemed a success? What are they? With the benefit of 20–20 hindsight, is there anything they would have done differently that could made the project go more smoothly?

3. As a team, do research online to identify three candidate PLM software packages. Based on information presented on each company's Web site, score each alternative using a set of criteria your team agrees upon. Which candidate PLM software does your team select?

Web Exercises

1. Do research online to identify several companies that have implemented an enterprise system in the last few years. Classify the implementation as a success, partial success, or failure. What is your basis for making this classification?

2. Do research online to find several sources that discuss the challenges associated with the implementation of an enterprise system. Is there general agreement among the sources as to what the most significant challenges are? What advice is offered as to the most effective way to overcome these challenges? Develop your own list of the five most significant challenges and five most effective tactics for overcoming these challenges.

3. Using the Web, identify several software services firms that offer consulting services to help organizations implement enterprise systems. Gain an understanding of what sort of services they offer and become familiar with several of their success stories. If you had to choose one of the software services firms to assist your SME organization, which one would you choose and why?

Career Exercises

1. Initially thought to be cost-effective for only very large companies, enterprise systems are now being implemented in SME's to reduce costs, improve service, and increase sales revenue. A firm's finance and accounting personnel play a dual role in the implementation of such a system: (1) they must ensure a good payback on the investment in information systems and (2) they must also ensure that the system meets the needs of the finance and accounting organization. Identify three or four tasks that the finance and accounting people need to perform to ensure that these two goals are met.

2. Enterprise system software vendors need business systems analysts who understand both information systems and business processes. Make a list of six or more specific qualifications needed to be a strong business systems analyst who supports the implementation and conversion to an enterprise system within an SME. Are there additional/different qualifications needed for someone who is doing similar work but for a large multinational organization?

3. Imagine that you are a commercial solar heating salesperson for a manufacturing and installation firm. You make frequent sales calls on potential customers in a three-state area. The purpose of these sales calls is to acquaint the firms with your company's products and get them to consider purchase of your products. Describe the basic functionality you would want in your organization's CRM system for it to help you identify potential new customers and to support you in preparing and making sales presentations.

Case Studies

Case One

Dunkin' Donuts Prepares for Rapid Growth

Dunkin' Donuts has a strong following of customers around the world who rely on the restaurant chain's coffee, donuts, and other baked goods to get their day started. Established in 1950, Dunkin' Donuts still uses the original proprietary coffee blend recipe created by its founder William Rosenburg, but what started as a small donut shop in Quincy, Massachusetts, has grown into a global business generating more than $800 million in revenue in 2015. And as the restaurant chain has grown, its business operations have become increasingly sophisticated.

Today, Dunkin' Donuts franchises are backed up by a complex supply chain managed by National DCP (NDCP)—the exclusive supply chain management cooperative for more than 8,900 Dunkin' Donuts stores in the United States and 51 other countries. Founded as a membership cooperative in 2012 with the merger of five regional food and beverage operating companies, NDCP's mission is to support the daily operations of Dunkin' Donuts franchisees and facilitate their growth and expansion plans. The company employs 1,700 people and maintains seven regional distribution centers along with another 32 logistics hubs.

Recently, NDCP began a massive multiyear project, dubbed "Project Freshstart," to consolidate and upgrade its systems and transform its business processes throughout every area of the company—from accounting to customer service to warehousing and distribution. The goals of the project are to improve customer service, lower costs, and create supply chain efficiencies through inventory- and order-management improvements. According to Darrell Riekena, CIO at NDCP, the company began the process by asking "what capabilities and corresponding systems were needed to drive business process changes using leading-edge technologies, without a lot of customization."

NDCP spent considerable time researching and evaluating implementation consulting partners and technology providers before opting to implement SAP's Business Suite in partnership with Deloitte Consulting. NDCP selected the SAP system as the underlying technology for its business transformation because of SAP's track record and experience with wholesale distribution. SAP's software also offered NDCP the analytics and reporting tools the company felt were critical to supporting their plans for growth. According to Riekena, it was essential for the company to choose a technology platform that was flexible and could serve as the foundation for the company's future expansion. Deloitte was chosen as NDCP's implementation partner because it offered an extensive background in process redesign and a proven project methodology developed through years of experience in the wholesale distribution industry.

One of the first things Deloitte did during the implementation was to work with NDCP executives to define a business case for the project, which was used to establish a set of objectives and success criteria. Then, according to Deloitte Consulting's Jerry Hoberman, they defined the scope of the project to meet those business objectives. Once the scope was set, the project team members worked together to set an aggressive but realistic two-year project plan.

According to Riekena, an important contribution from Deloitte—outside of its technical expertise—was its framework for change management and communication, which helped ensure that NDCP was effectively reaching out to all of its stakeholders throughout the project. "We recognized right off the bat that effective change management was critical for the success of the project," Riekena says. "Leveraging multiple channels to reach all of the stakeholders, we took advantage of Dunkin' Brands training programs, launched a comprehensive communications effort, and promoted face-to-face interactions with franchise store managers and field operations teams whenever possible."

Unlike many companies that undertake a major system upgrade, NDCP was willing to change many of its business processes in order to truly transform its business, but Deloitte and NDCP also placed a priority on working within NDCP's culture—a balanced approach the recently led to the successful deployment of the new SAP system in the first of the company's four regions. As the system is rolled out across the remaining regions, more franchisees will see the benefits of NDCP's careful planning and implementation efforts—from better demand forecasting and inventory management tools to improvements in NDCP's customer service delivered by a centralized staff who will have immediate access to customer histories and will be able to provide real-time updates on order status and issue resolution.

Critical Thinking Questions

1. Because NDCP is a membership cooperative, Dunkin' Donuts franchisees are both owners and customers. What might be some advantages to such an ownership structure in terms of getting the support of all stakeholders for a massive project like the one NDCP undertook? What might be some disadvantages?
2. How important do you think the communication and change management aspects of this project were? Why do you think so many companies underestimate the importance of those facets of an enterprise-level project?
3. What are some of the risks for a company that chooses to make changes to so many parts of its business and underlying technology at once? What are some of the things a company could do to mitigate those risks?

SOURCES: "About Us," Dunkin' Donuts, *news.dunkindonuts.com/about*, accessed March 7, 2016; "Revenue of Dunkin' Brands Worldwide from 2007 to 2015 (in Million U.S. Dollars)," Statista, *'www.statista.com /statistics/291392/annual-revenue-dunkin–brands*, accessed March 10, 2016; "About Us," National DCP, *http://nationaldcp.com/node/893*, accessed March 8, 2016; Murphy, Ken, "Rise and Shine: "Project Freshstart" Energizes Distributor," *SAPinsider*, April 1, 2015, *http:// sapinsider.wispubs.com/Assets/Case-Studies/2015/April/IP-Project-Fresh start-energizes-National-DCP*; "National DCP: Serving Up the Best Customer Service for Dunkin' Donuts Franchisees," SAP video, *http://go .sap.com/assetdetail/2015/11/324168ae-4e7c-0010-82c7-eda71af511fa .html*, accessed March 9, 2016; "Deloitte Global SAP Practice: National DCP (Dunkin' Donuts)," ReqCloud video, accessed March 10, 2016.

Case Two

Kerry Group Is on Your Table

In business, sourcing is the set of activities involved in finding, evaluating, and then engaging suppliers of goods or services. Before a business can start to manage its supply chain, as described in this chapter, it must complete a sourcing process.

Ireland's Kerry Group, a supplier of food ingredients and flavors to the worldwide food industry and of consumer food products to the British Isles, requires a wide range of raw materials from many suppliers. With annual revenue of €5.8 billion (about U.S. $10 billion) in 2013, it needs a lot of those materials. With plants in 24 countries and 40 percent of revenue from outside Europe, it is impossible for the people in one plant to know about all possible suppliers worldwide, but making local sourcing decisions would reduce economies of scale. With the thin profit margins of the food industry, good sourcing decisions are vital to Kerry Group's profitability. Software to manage the sourcing process is one way to help make those decisions.

Kerry Group was already a SAP customer when it chose SAP Sourcing OnDemand, having used SAP ERP systems since 2009. The advantage of obtaining a new system from its existing ERP supplier is assured compatibility with applications the company already uses. "What we needed was an intuitive sourcing system that would be completely integrated with our SAP back-office for an end-to-end procurement process," said Peter Fotios, Kerry Group's director of e-procurement services.

SAP Sourcing OnDemand uses the cloud computing concept. As its OnDemand name suggests, customers do not have to dedicate computing resources to the software. They use SAP resources on demand as their needs require, paying on a per-user, per-month subscription basis. Meanwhile, SAP is responsible for administrative tasks such as data backup and, if necessary, restoration.

Kerry Group implemented SAP Sourcing OnDemand by beginning with a pilot plant. "We rolled it out smoothly in Ireland first, then England and then throughout our global operations in 23 countries," explains Fotios. If any problems appeared in Ireland, the pilot site, Kerry Group could have focused all its problem-solving resources on that location. Fortunately, no major issues arose.

Another thing that Kerry Group did right at implementation time was training. Recognizing that it had competent in-house trainers and competent technical professionals, but few if any who were both, the firm engaged SAP's Irish training partner Olas to assist with that end of the project. Olas brought SAP expertise to the training team, completing the required set of capabilities.

Moving forward, Kerry Group has project plans extending into 2016 for the full roll-out of all its planned SAP ERP capabilities. The smoothness of its Sourcing OnDemand implementation, which took a total of four weeks elapsed time because the software was already running in the cloud when they began, is a good indication that the rest of the project (which is in many ways more complex) will probably go well. If Kerry Group is to carry out its mission statement, which includes being "the world leader in food ingredients and flavors serving the food and beverage industry," the roll-out will have to be smooth.

Critical Thinking Questions

1. Kerry Group is taking a slow and methodical approach to implementing the parts of SAP ERP software. What does the company gain and what does it lose by taking its time in this way?
2. Why should Kerry Group standardize on one ERP package? Wouldn't it be simpler and less expensive to let each plant and sales operation choose its own software, as long as it can report its financial results to headquarters in a standard form?
3. What are the advantages and disadvantages to using a third-party vendor like Olas to deploy a new ERP system? What steps can companies take to overcome the disadvantages of relying on third-party vendors when deploying enterprise-wide systems?

SOURCES: Kerry Group Web site, *www.kerrygroup.com*, accessed April 11, 2014; Staff, "Kerry's SAP Transformation Measures Up to Their L&D Beliefs," Olas, *www.olas.ie*, May 18, 2011; Staff, "Kerry Group Transforms Its Global Procurement Group in Weeks With SAP Sourcing OnDemand Solution," SAP, *www.sap.com/news-reader/index.epx?pressid=18809*, May 1, 2012.

Notes

1. "Revere Electric Supply," Conexiom, *https://conexiom.com/case_studies/revere-electric-supply*, accessed March 4, 2016.
2. "About" Helen Ross McNabb Center, *www.mcnabbcenter.org/content/about*, accessed March 4, 2016.
3. "Helen Ross McNabb Center," DATIS, *www.datis.com/why-datis/customer-success-stories/helen-ross-mcnabb-center-2/*, accessed March 4, 2016.
4. "Who We Are ADP," *www.adp.com/about-us.aspx*, accessed March 4, 2016.
5. "Asset Brokerage Firm Reduces Batch Processing Time by 15%," Sumerian, *www.sumerian.com/resources/customer-stories/15-batch-time-saved*, accessed March 4, 2016.
6. "Form 10-K: Paypal Holdings, Inc," Paypal Holdings, Inc., February 11, 2016, *https://investor.paypal-corp.com/secfiling.cfm?filingID=1633917-16-113&CIK=1633917*.
7. "Ciber Case Study: Wisconsin Department of Health Services—WIC," *www.ciber.com/tasks/render/file/?whitepaper=wisconsin-department-of-health-services-wic-program&fileID=2BEF3900-A42E-F37F-92DD52E2C5F22E4A*, accessed March 3, 2014.
8. "About Us," Lukas Nursery, *www.lukasnursery.com/about.php*, accessed March 6, 2016.
9. "Lukas Nursery Chooses Epicor Eagle N Series to Refresh 100 Year-Old Business," Epicor, January 20, 2016, *www.epicor.com/Press-Room/News-Releases/Lukas-Nursery*

-Chooses-Epicor-Eagle-N-Series-to-Refresh-100-Year-Old
-Business.aspx.

10. "Sage 300 Construction and Real Estate," Sage, *www
.sage.com/us/sage-construction-and-real-estate/sage-300
-construction-and-real-estate*, accessed March 4, 2016.

11. "Echo Valley Irrigation Automates to Save Time and
Monitor Processes," Sage, *www.sage.com/us/sage
-construction-and-real-estate/sage-300-construction
-and-real-estate#*, accessed March 5, 2016.

12. Miles, Stephanie, "7 Cloud-Based POS Systems for SMBs,"
Street Fight, February 4, 2013, *http://streetfightmag.com
/2013/02/04/7-cloud-based-pos-systems-for-smbs/*.

13. "Creative Wedge Slices Up Ways to Improve Inventory,"
NCS Small Business, *http://blog.ncrsilver.com/2014/10
/09/creative-wedge-ways-to-improve-inventory-manage
ment-go-mobile*, accessed March 5, 2015.

14. "About Us," Women's World Banking, *www.womens
worldbanking.org/about-us*, accessed March 8, 2016.

15. "Women's World Banking," Intacct, *http://online.intacct
.com/rs/intacct/images/cs_womensworldbanking.pdf*,
accessed March 8, 2016.

16. "About Steinwall Incorporated," Steinwall, *www.steinwall
.com/pages/AboutUs*, accessed March 7, 2016.

17. "Steinwall Scientific, Inc.," IQMS Manufacturing ERP,
*www.iqms.com/files/case-studies/Steinwall%
20Scientific_ERP_success.pdf*, accessed March 7, 2016.

18. "Beefing Up a Growing Business," SAP, *www.sap.com
/customer-testimonials/retail/prime-meats.html*,
accessed March 8, 2016.

19. Trites, David, "How Prime Meats Cuts Through Business
Complexity," SAP Community Network (blog), July 28,
2015, *http://scn.sap.com/community/business-trends
/blog/2015/07/28/how-prime-meats-cuts-through
-business-complexity*.

20. "Who We Are," Whirlpool, *www.whirlpoolcorp.com/our
-company*, accessed March 8, 2016.

21. Boulton, Clint, "Whirlpool CIO Tackles ERP Overhaul
and IoT-Powered Appliances," February 20, 2016, *www
.cio.com/article/3039093/internet-of-things/whirlpool
-cio-tackles-erp-overhaul-and-iot-powered-appliances
.html*.

22. "Top Ten Enterprise Resource Planning (ERP) Vendors,"
Compare Business Products, *http://resources.idgenter
prise.com/original/AST-0067016_Top_10_ERP_Vendors
.pdf*, accessed March 7, 2014.

23. "Newman Technology," Plex, *www.plex.com/customers
/newman-technology.html*, accessed March 9, 2016.

24. "Curry's Art Store Leaps Forward with TECSYS Total
Supply Chain Management," TECSYS, *www.tecsys.com
/customers/success/TECSYS-Currys-Success-Story.pdf*,
accessed March 8, 2016.

25. "Expensify: Base Helps Expensify Engage with
Customers," Base, *https://getbase.com/customers
/expensify*, accessed March 7, 2016.

26. "The TUMI Difference," TUMI, *www.tumi.com/s/tumi
-difference*, accessed March 9, 2016.

27. "A Brief History of the Red Cross," American Red Cross,
www.redcross.org/about-us/who-we-are/history,
accessed March 9, 2016.

28. "American Red Cross Utilizes Salesforce to Accelerate
Their Mission," Salesforce, *www.salesforce.com/customers
/stories/redcross.jsp*, accessed March 9, 2016.

29. "Investors," Nu Skin Enterprises, *http://ir.nuskin.com
/phoenix.zhtml?c=103888&p=irol-irhome*, accessed
March 7, 2016.

30. "Customer Journey: Nu Skin Enterprises Inc.," SAP,
*www.sap.com/customer-testimonials/consumer/nu-skin
.html*, accessed March 5 2016.

31. "CRM Software Review 2014," *http://crm-software-review
.toptenreviews.com*, accessed March 13, 2014, and "2014
Edition Top 40 CRM Software Report,"
Business-Software.com, accessed March 13, 2014.

32. "Wells Fargo Bank," Salesforce.com Success Story,
www.salesforce.com/customers/stories/wells-fargo.jsp,
accessed March 14, 2014.

33. Chipman, Steve, "2014 Smartphone CRM Access by
Salespeople," *CRM Switch*, February 11, 2014, *www
.crmswitch.com/mobile-crm/2014-crm-smartphone-sales
person-access/*.

34. "What Is PLM Software?" Siemens, *www.plm.automa
tion.siemens.com/en_us/plm/*, accessed March 1, 2014.

35. "About Water Pik, Inc.," Water Pik, Inc., *www.waterpik
.com/about-us*, accessed March 9, 2016.

36. "Water Pik Improves Its Flow with ProductCenter PLM,"
SofTech, *www.softech.com/success/customer-success
/Water_Pik_Improves_Its_Flow_with_ProductCenter
_PLM/28*.

37. 2013 Edition Top 10 Product Lifecycle Management
(PLM) Software Report, Business-Software.com *http://
ptccreo.files.wordpress.com/2013/10/top_10_plm_report
.pdf* accessed March 1, 2014.

38. "Case Study: Industrial Control Associates," Siemens,
*www.plm.automation.siemens.com/en_us/about_us/suc
cess/case_study.cfm?Component=83695&Component
Template=1481*, accessed March 9, 2016.

39. "About Us," Industrial Control Associates, Inc., *www.i-c-a
-inc.com/about.html*, accessed March 9, 2016.

40. Noyes, Katherine, "State Employees Are Stuck Using a
Legacy System from the 1960s; New System from HP
Was Due by 2010," *Computerworld*, September 21, 2015,
*www.computerworld.com/article/2985070/government
-it/michigan-sues-hp-over-49m-project-thats-5-years-late
.html*.

41. Kennedy, Patrick, "H.B. Fuller Wins Case against
Accenture," *Star Tribune*, November 13, 2015, *www
.startribune.com/h-b-fuller-wins-case-against-accenture
/347256802*.

42. "HDOT News Release: HDOT Files Lawsuit against
Ciber, Inc., a Consulting Firm, Alleging Fraud and
Breach of Contract on State Highway Software Upgrade
Project," Office of the Governor of the State of Hawaii,
September 2, 2015, *http://governor.hawaii.gov/news
room/hdot-news-release-hdot-files-lawsuit-against
-ciber-inc-a-consulting-firm-alleging-fraud-and-breach
-of-contract-on-state-highway-software-upgrade-project*.

43. Jutras, Cindy, "2011 ERP Solution Study Highlights,"
Epicor, September 2011.

44. "History," LoneStar Heart, *www.lonestarheartinc.com
/index.php?option=com_content&view=article&id=175&
Itemid=196*, accessed March 10, 2016.

45. "LoneStar Heart: Efficiencies in Product Development
Processes Result in Estimated $80,000 in Savings,"
Omnify Software, *www.omnifysoft.com/customers
/success.aspx?customer=37*, accessed March 10, 2016.

CHAPTER 9

Business Intelligence and Analytics

- MetLife is implementing analytical software to identify medical provider, attorney, and repair shop fraud to aid its special investigations unit (SIU).

- Nearly 20 percent of Medicare patients were readmitted to the hospital within 30 days of their initial discharge, running up an additional $17 billion in healthcare costs. Hospitals are now using BI analytics to identify patients are high risk of readmission—especially now that Medicare has begun reducing payments to hospitals with high readmission rates.

- IBM Watson Analytics services, a cloud-based business analytics tool that offers a variety of tools for uncovering trends hidden in large sets of data, uses baseball statistics on every player in Major League Baseball from AriBall to build predictions of player performance. You can use this service to gain an edge over your fantasy baseball league competitors.

Principles

- Business intelligence (BI) and analytics are used to support improved decision making.

- There are many BI and analytics techniques and tools that can be used in a wide range of problem-solving situations.

Learning Objectives

- Define the terms *business intelligence* (BI) and analytics.

- Provide several real-world examples of BI and analytics being used to improve decision making.

- Identify the key components that must be in place for an organization to get real value from its BI and analytics efforts.

- Identify several BI techniques and discuss how they are used.

- Identify several BI tools.

- Define the term *self-service analytics* and discuss its pros and cons.

Why Learn about Business Intelligence (BI) and Analytics?

We are living in the age of big data, with new data flooding us from all directions at the incomprehensible speed of nearly a zettabyte (1 trillion gigabytes or a 1 followed by 21 zeros) per year. What is most exciting about this data is not its amount, but rather the fact that we are gaining the tools and understanding to do something truly meaningful with it. Organizations are learning to analyze large amounts of data not only to measure past and current performance but also to make predictions about the future. These forecasts will drive anticipatory actions to improve business strategies, strengthen business operations, and enrich decision making—enabling the organization to become more competitive.

A wide range of business users can derive benefits from access to data, but most of them lack deep information systems or data science skills. Business users need easier and faster ways to discover relevant patterns and insights into data to better support their decision making and to make their companies more agile. Companies that have access to the same kind of data as their competitors but can analyze it sooner to take action faster will outpace their peers. Providing BI tools and making business analytics more understandable and accessible to these users should be a key strategy of organizations.

Members of financial services organizations use BI and analytics to better understand their customers to enhance service, create new and more appealing products, and better manage risk. Marketing managers analyze data related to the Web-surfing habits, past purchases, and even social media activity of existing and potential customers to create highly effective marketing programs that generate consumer interest and increased sales. Health care professionals who are able to improve the patient experience will reap the benefits of maximized reimbursements, lower costs, and higher market share, and they will ultimately deliver higher quality care for patients. Physicians use business analytics to analyze data in an attempt to identify factors that lead to readmission of hospital patients. Human resources managers use analytics to evaluate job candidates and choose those most likely to be successful. They also analyze the impact of raises and changes in employee-benefit packages on employee retention and long-term costs.

Regardless of your field of study in school and your future career, using BI and analytics, will likely be a significant component of your job. As you read this chapter, pay attention to how different organizations use business analytics. This chapter starts by introducing basic concepts related to BI and analytics. Later in the chapter, several BI and analytics tools and strategies are discussed.

As you read this chapter, consider the following:

- What is business intelligence (BI) and analytics, and how can they be used to improve the operations and results of an organization?

- What are some business intelligence and analytics techniques and tools, and how can they be used?

This chapter begins with a definition of business intelligence (BI) and business analytics and the components necessary for a successful BI and analytics program. The chapter goes on to describe and provide examples of the use of several BI techniques and tools. It ends with a discussion of some of the issues associated with BI and analytics.

What Are Analytics and Business Intelligence?

Business analytics is the extensive use of data and quantitative analysis to support fact-based decision making within organizations. Business analytics can be used to gain a better understanding of current business performance, reveal new business patterns and relationships, explain why certain results occurred, optimize current operations, and forecast future business results.

business intelligence (BI): A wide range of applications, practices, and technologies for the extraction, transformation, integration, visualization, analysis, interpretation, and presentation of data to support improved decision making.

Business intelligence (BI) includes a wide range of applications, practices, and technologies for the extraction, transformation, integration, visualization, analysis, interpretation, and presentation of data to support improved decision making. The data used in BI is often pulled from multiple sources and may come from sources internal or external to the organization. Many organizations use this data to build large collections of data called data warehouses, data marts, and data lakes, for use in BI applications. Users, including employees, customers, and authorized suppliers and business partners, may access the data and BI applications via the Web or through organizational intranets and extranets—often using mobile devices, such as smartphones and tablets. The goal of business intelligence is to get the most value out of information and present the results of analysis in an easy to understand manner that the layman can understand.

Often the data used in BI and analytics must be gathered from a variety of sources. Helse Vest, a regional health authority in Norway, has 26,500 employees who serve 1 million people in 50 healthcare facilities, including 10 hospitals. Helse Vest implemented a BI system to meet the requirements of a government-sponsored national patient safety program. The system collects, visualizes, and shares medical data used to identify quality measures and reporting requirements across all care teams and regional hospitals. A major challenge for the project was the need for each of the 10 hospitals to combine data from all the facilities within its region for analysis by the program's board and hospital managers. Prior to implementing the new system, it took up to 14 days for employees to produce some reports, making it difficult for hospital staff to assess and act on performance data because it was not current. With the new system, Helse Vest analysts can easily combine data from different sources and create analytical reports in less than one day. Real-time data enables Helse Vest to act on information much more quickly, while the metrics are still valid for the staff, and a quick response to performance data is more likely to lead to significant improvements in patient safety measures.[1]

Benefits Achieved from BI and Analytics

BI and analytics are used to achieve a number of benefits as illustrated by the following examples:

- **Detect fraud.** MetLife implemented analytical software to help its special investigations unit (SIU) identify medical provider, attorney, and repair shop fraud. Although an accident claim may not have enough data to be flagged as suspicious when it is first filed, as more claim data is added, a claim is continually rescored by the software. After the first six months of using the software, the number of claims under investigation by the SIU increased 16 percent.[2]
- **Improve forecasting.** Kroger serves customers in 2,422 supermarkets and 1,950 in-store pharmacies. The company found that by better predicting pharmacy customer demand, it could reduce the number of prescriptions that it was unable to fill because a drug is out of stock. To do so, Kroger developed a sophisticated inventory management system that could provide employees with a visualization of inventory levels, adapt to user feedback, and support "what-if" analysis. Out-of-stock prescriptions have been reduced by 1.5 million per year, with a resulting increase in sales of $80 million per year. In addition, by carrying the right drugs in the right quantities, Kroger was able to reduce its overall inventory costs by $120 million per year.[3]
- **Increase Sales.** DaimlerChrysler and many other auto manufacturers set their suggested retail and wholesale prices for the year, then adjust pricing through seasonal incentives based on the impact of supply and demand. DaimlerChrysler implemented a price-elasticity model to

optimize the company's pricing decisions. The system enables managers to evaluate many potential incentives for each combination of vehicle model (e.g., Jeep Grand Cherokee), acquisition method (cash, finance, or lease), and incentive program (cash back, promotional APR, and a combination of cash back and promotional APR). The firm estimates that use of the system has generated additional annual sales of $500 million.[4]

- **Optimize operations.** Chevron is one of the world's leading integrated energy companies. Its refineries work with crude oil that is used to make a wide range of oil products, including gasoline, jet fuel, diesel fuel, lubricants, and specialty products such as additives. With market prices of crude oil and its various products constantly changing, determining which products to refine at a given time is quite complex. Chevron uses an analytical system called Petro to aid analysts in advising the refineries and oil traders on the mix of products to produce, buy, and sell in order to maximize profit.[5]

- **Reduce costs.** Coca-Cola Enterprises is the world's largest bottler and distributor of Coca Cola products. Its delivery fleet of 54,000 trucks is second in size to only to the U.S. Postal Service. Using analytics software, the firm implemented a vehicle-routing optimization system that resulted in savings of $45 million a year from reduced gas consumption and reduction in the number of drivers required.[6]

The Role of a Data Scientist

Data scientists are individuals who combine strong business acumen, a deep understanding of analytics, and a healthy appreciation of the limitations of their data, tools, and techniques to deliver real improvements in decision making. Data scientists do not simply collect and report on data; they view a situation from many angles, determine what data and tools can help further an understanding of the situation, and then apply the appropriate data and tools. They often work in a team setting with business managers and specialists from the business area being studied, market research and financial analysts, data stewards, information system resources, and experts highly knowledgeable about the company's competitors, markets, products, and services. The goal of the data scientist is to uncover valuable insights that will influence organizational decisions and help the organization to achieve competitive advantage.

Data scientists are highly inquisitive, continually asking questions, performing "what-if" analyses, and challenging assumptions and existing processes. Successful data scientists have an ability to communicate their findings to organizational leaders so convincingly that they are able to strongly influence how an organization approaches a business opportunity.

The educational requirements for being a data scientist are quite rigorous—requiring a mastery of statistics, math, and computer programming. Most data scientist positions require an advanced degree, such as a master's degree or a doctorate. Some organizations accept data scientists with undergraduate degrees in an analytical concentration, such as computer science, math and statistics, management information systems, economics, and engineering. Colorado Technical University, Syracuse University, and Villanova University are among the many schools that offer online master degree programs related to BI and analytics.

Many schools also offer career-focused courses, degrees, and certificates in analytical-related disciplines such as database management, predictive analytics, BI, big data analysis, and data mining. Such courses provide a great way for current business and information systems professionals to learn data scientist skills. Most data scientists have computer programming skills and are familiar with languages and tools used to process big data, such as Hadoop, Hive, SQL, Python, R, and Java.

The job outlook for data scientists is extremely bright. The McKinsey Global Institute (the business and economics research arm of the management consulting firm McKinsey & Co.) predicts that by 2018 the United States may face a shortage of 140,000 to 190,000 data scientists.[7] The recruitment agency Glassdoor pegs the average salary for a data scientist at $118,709, and highly talented, educated, and experienced data scientists can earn well over $250,000 per year.

Components Required for Effective BI and Analytics

A number of components must be in place for an organization to get real value from its BI and analytics efforts. First and foremost is the existence of a solid data management program, including data governance. Recall that data management is an integrated set of functions that defines the processes by which data is obtained, certified fit for use, stored, secured, and processed in such a way as to ensure that the accessibility, reliability, and timeliness of the data meet the needs of the data users within an organization. Data governance is the core component of data management; it defines the roles, responsibilities, and processes for ensuring that data can be trusted and used by the entire organization, with people identified and in place who are responsible for fixing and preventing issues with data.

Another key component that an organization needs is creative data scientists—people who understand the business as well as the business analytics technology, while also recognizing the limitations of their data, tools, and techniques. A data scientist puts all of this together to deliver real improvements in decision making with an organization.

Finally, to ensure the success of a BI and analytics program, the management team within an organization must have a strong commitment to data-driven decision making. Organizations that can put the necessary components in place can act quickly to make superior decisions in uncertain and changing environments to gain a strong competitive advantage.

Critical Thinking Exercise

Argosy Gaming

Argosy Gaming Company is the owner and operator of six riverboat gambling casinos and hotels in the United States. Argosy has developed a centralized enterprise data warehouse to capture the data generated at each property. As part of this effort, Argosy selected an extract-transform-load (ETL) tool to gather and integrate the data from six different operational databases to create its data warehouse. The plan is to use the data to help Argosy management make quicker, well-informed decisions based on patrons' behaviors, purchases, and preferences. Argosy hopes to pack more entertainment value into each patron's visit by better understanding their gambling preferences and favorite services. The data will also be used to develop targeted direct mail campaigns, customize offers for specific customer segments, and adapt programs for individual casinos.[8]

Review Questions

1. What are the key components that Argosy must put into place to create an environment for a successful BI and analytics program?
2. What complications can arise from gathering data from six different operational databases covering six riverboat gambling casinos and hotels?

Critical Thinking Questions

1. The Argosy BI and analytics program is aimed at boosting revenue not at reducing costs. Why do you think this is so?
2. What specific actions must Argosy take to have a successful program that will boost revenue and offset some of the increases in costs?

Business Intelligence and Analytics Tools

This section introduces and provides examples of many BI and analytics tools, including spreadsheets, reporting and querying tools, data visualization tools, online analytical processing (OLAP), drill-down analysis, linear regression, data mining, and dashboards. It will also cover the strategy of self-service analytics, presenting its pros and cons.

Spreadsheets

Business managers often import data into a spreadsheet program, such as Excel, which then can be used to perform operations on the data based on formulas created by the end user. Spreadsheets are also used to create reports and graphs based on that data. End users can employ tools such as the Excel Scenario Manager to perform "what-if" analysis to evaluate various alternatives. The Excel Solver Add-in can be used to find the optimal solution to a problem with multiple constraints (e.g., determine a production plan that will maximize profit subject to certain limitations on raw materials).

North Tees and Hartlepool National Health Services Trust provides healthcare services and screenings to a population of 400,000 people in the United Kingdom. Professor Philip Dean, head of the Department of Pharmacy and Quality Control Laboratory Services, wanted a way to better understand the clinical use of drugs, the efficacy of treatment, and the associated costs. Dean worked with resources from Ascribe, a BI software and consulting firm, to pilot the use of Microsoft Power BI for Office 365, part of the Microsoft Office 365 cloud-based business productivity suite that works through familiar Excel spreadsheet software (see Figure 9.1). Ascribe developers took an extract of North Tees's data and imported it into a Power BI model. They then incorporated other data sets of interest to Dean and his colleagues, such as publicly available data on the activity of general practitioners, weather data, and

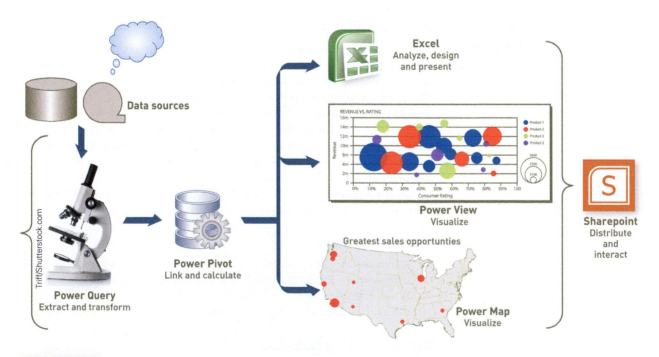

FIGURE 9.1

Components of Microsoft Power BI for Office 365

Microsoft Power BI has been used to better understand the clinical use of drugs, the efficacy of treatment, and the associated costs.

Source: Access Analytics, Power BI for Business, Power Analytics, *http://www.accessanalytic.com.au/Power-BI.html.*

treatment data. With all of this new data integrated in the Power BI model, Dean was able to create graphs of his findings, visualize data on regional maps, and even zoom in and around the data to gain various levels of insight. According to Dean, the ability to link disparate data sets for an integrated analysis was "one of the 'wow' things" that impressed him most in his use of BI tools. Incorporating additional, external data sets into his analyses complemented and helped explain trends, as well as provided useful benchmarks. Use of the weather data helped identify the impact of inclement weather on the frequency of respiratory disease. The treatment data helped Dean and his team to understand which drugs were being prescribed and how prescription patterns varied by locality.[9]

Reporting and Querying Tools

Most organizations have invested in some reporting tools to help their employees get the data they need to solve a problem or identify an opportunity. Reporting and querying tools can present that data in an easy-to-understand fashion—via formatted data, graphs, and charts. Many of the reporting and querying tools enable end users to make their own data requests and format the results without the need for additional help from the IT organization.

FFF Enterprises is a supplier of critical-care biopharmaceuticals, plasma products, and vaccines. Its 46,000 customers include over 80 percent of U.S. hospitals.[10] The company employs the QlikView query and reporting tool to provide employees with real-time access to data that affects its business and the timely delivery of safe, effective products and services. For example, the company is the largest flu vaccine distributor in the United States, and accurately tracking its vaccine shipments is critical to avoiding shortages. As part of those efforts, FFF Enterprises uses QlikView to track and monitor the volume and value of all product transactions, such as the receipt, internal movement, and distribution of products.[11]

Data Visualization Tools

Data visualization: The presentation of data in a pictorial or graphical format.

Data visualization is the presentation of data in a pictorial or graphical format. The human brain works such that most people are better able to see significant trends, patterns, and relationships in data that is presented in a graphical format rather than in tabular reports and spreadsheets. As a result, decision makers welcome data visualization software that presents analytical results visually. In addition, representing data in visual form is a recognized technique to bring immediate impact to dull and boring numbers. A wide array of tools and techniques are available for creating visual representations that can immediately reveal otherwise difficult-to-perceive patterns or relationships in the underlying data.

Many companies now troll Facebook, Google Plus+, LinkedIn, Pinterest, Tumblr, Twitter, and other social media feeds to monitor any mention of their company or product. Data visualization tools can take that raw data and immediately provide a rich visual that reveals precisely who is talking about the product and what they are saying. Techniques as simple and intuitive as a word cloud can provide a surprisingly effective visual summary of conversations, reviews, and user feedback about a new product. A **word cloud** is a visual depiction of a set of words that have been grouped together because of the frequency of their occurrence. Word clouds are generated from analyses of text documents or a Web page. Using the text from these sources, a simple count is carried out on the number of times a word or phrase appears. Words or phrases that have been mentioned more often than other words or phrases are shown in a larger font size and/or a darker color, as shown in Figure 9.2. ABCya, Image Chef, TagCloud, ToCloud, and ToCloud, Tagul, and Wordle are examples of word cloud generator software.

word cloud: A visual depiction of a set of words that have been grouped together because of the frequency of their occurrence.

mindscanner/Shutterstock.com

Word cloud
This Word cloud shows the topics covered in this chapter.

conversion funnel: A graphical representation that summarizes the steps a consumer takes in making the decision to buy your product and become a customer.

A **conversion funnel** is a graphical representation that summarizes the steps a consumer takes in making the decision to buy your product and become a customer. It provides a visual representation of the conversion data between each step and enables decision makers to see what steps are causing customers confusion or trouble. Figure 9.3 shows a conversion funnel for an online sales organization. It shows where visitors to a Web site are dropping off the successful sales path.

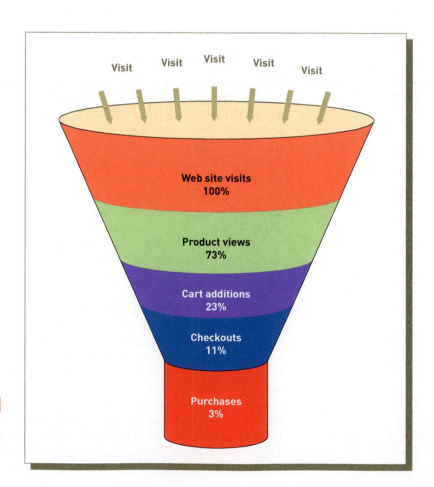

The conversion funnel
The conversion funnel shows the key steps in converting a consumer to a buyer.

Technologia is a business training firm that has trained over 70,000 clients in dozens of technical topics, such as project management, SQL, and Microsoft Windows. One Technologia course can cost $1,000 or more, so most potential customers do careful detailed research and make multiple visits to the company's Web site before enrolling in a course. Technologia used Multi-Channel Funnels from Google Analytics to determine what factors had the most impact in influencing students to enroll. For the first time, Technologia learned that nearly 18 percent of its sales paths included paid advertising—much higher than previously thought. As a result, it raised its online ad budget by nearly 100 percent, and online conversions shot up 120 percent.[12]

Dozens of data visualization software products are available for creating various charts, graphs, infographics, and data maps (see Figure 9.4). Some of the more commonly products include Google Charts, iCharts, Infogram, Modest Maps, SAS Visual Statistics, and Tableau. These tools make it easy to visually explore data on the fly, spot patterns, and quickly gain insights.

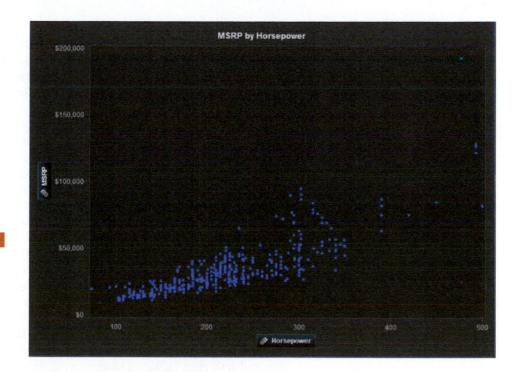

FIGURE **9.4**

Data visualization

This scatter diagram shows the relationship between MSRP and horsepower.

Source: "Data Visualization," SAS, *http://www.sas.com/en_us/insights/big-data/data-visualization.html#m=lightbox5*, accessed April 19, 2016.

online analytical processing (OLAP): A method to analyze multidimensional data from many different perspectives, enabling users to identify issues and opportunities as well as perform trend analysis.

data cube: A collection of data that contains numeric facts called measures, which are categorized by dimensions, such as time and geography.

Online Analytical Processing

Online analytical processing (OLAP) is a method to analyze multidimensional data from many different perspectives. It enables users to identify issues and opportunities as well as perform trend analysis. Databases built to support OLAP processing consist of **data cubes** that contain numeric facts called measures, which are categorized by dimensions, such as time and geography. A simple example would be a data cube that contains the unit sales of a specific product as a measure. This value would be displayed along the metric dimension axis shown in Figure 9.5. The time dimension might be a specific day (e.g., September 30, 2018), whereas the geography dimension might define a specific store (e.g., Krogers in the Cincinnati, Ohio community of Hyde Park).

The key to the quick responsiveness of OLAP processing is the preaggregation of detailed data into useful data summaries in anticipation of questions that might be raised. For example, data cubes can be built to summarize unit sales of a specific item on a specific day for a specific store. In addition, the detailed store-level data may be summarized to create data cubes that show

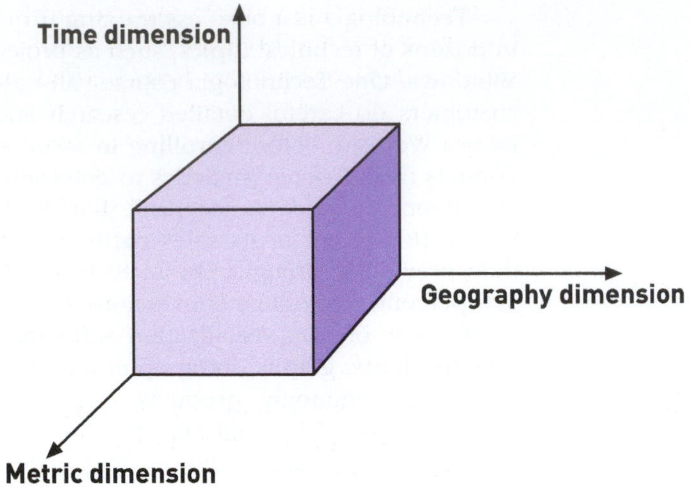

FIGURE 9.5

A data cube

The data cube contains numeric facts that are categorized by dimensions, such as time and geography.

unit sales for a specific item, on a specific day for all stores within each major market (e.g., Boston, New York, Phoenix), for all stores within the United States, or for all stores within North America. In a similar fashion, data cubes can be built in anticipation of queries seeking information on unit sales on a given day, week, month, or fiscal quarter.

It is important to note that if the data within a data cube has been summarized at a given level, for example, unit sales by day by store, it is not possible to use that data cube to answer questions at a more detailed level, such as what were the unit sales of this item by hour on a given day.

Data cubes need not be restricted to just three dimensions. Indeed, most OLAP systems can build data cubes with many more dimensions. In the business world, data cubes are often constructed with many dimensions, but users typically look at just three at a time. For example, a consumer packaged goods manufacturer might build a multidimensional data cube with information about unit sales, shelf space, unit price, promotion price, and level of newspaper advertising—all for a specific product, on a specific date, in a specific store.

In the retail industry, OLAP is used to help firms to predict better customer demand and maximize sales. Starbucks employs some 149,000 workers in 10,000 retail stores in the United States. The firm built a data warehouse to hold 70 terabytes of point-of-sale and customer loyalty data. This data is compressed into data cubes of summarized data to enable users to perform OLAP analysis of store-level sales and operational data.[13]

Drill-Down Analysis

The small things in plans and schemes that don't go as expected can frequently cause serious problems later on—the devil is in the details. Drill-down analysis is a powerful tool that enables decision makers to gain insight into the details of business data to better understand why something happened.

drill-down analysis: The interactive examination of high-level summary data in increasing detail to gain insight into certain elements—sort of like slowly peeling off the layers of an onion.

Drill-down analysis involves the interactive examination of high-level summary data in increasing detail to gain insight into certain elements—sort of like slowly peeling off the layers of an onion. For example, in reviewing the worldwide sales for the past quarter, the vice president of sales might want to drill down to view the sales for each country. Further drilling could be done to view the sales for a specific country (say Germany) for the last quarter. A third level of drill-down analysis could be done to see the sales for a specific country for a specific month of the quarter (e.g., Germany for the month of September). A fourth level of analysis could be accomplished by drilling down to sales by product line for a particular country by month (e.g., each product line sold in Germany for the month of September).

Brisbane is a city on the east coast of Australia that is subject to frequent creek flash flooding from the many streams in the area. One year, particularly heavy rainfall caused many houses to be flooded, brought down power lines, closed roads, and put the city into a state of emergency. Following this disaster, the city installed telemetry gauges across Brisbane to obtain real-time measurements of rainfall and water levels. The data is captured and displayed on color-coded maps, which enable staff to quickly spot areas of concern. They can also perform a drill-down analysis to see increasing levels of detail within any critical area. The system enables staff to provide more advanced warnings to the population of impending flooding and take action to close roads or clean up debris.[14]

Linear Regression

linear regression: A mathematical procedure to predict the value of a dependent variable based on a single independent variable and the linear relationship between the two.

Simple **linear regression** is a mathematical technique for predicting the value of a dependent variable based on a single independent variable and the linear relationship between the two. Linear regression consists of finding the best-fitting straight line through a set of observations of the dependent and independent variables. By far, the most commonly used measure for the best-fitting line is the line that minimizes the sum of the squared errors of prediction. This best-fitting line is called the regression line (see Figure 9.6). Linear regression does not mean that one variable causes the other; it simply says that when one value goes up, the other variable also increases or decreases proportionally.

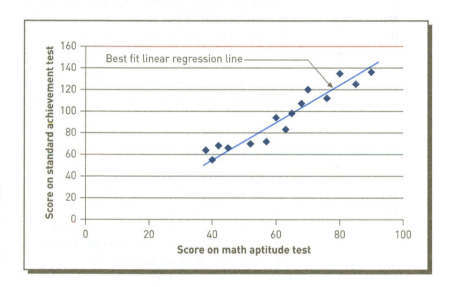

FIGURE 9.6

Simple linear regression

This graph shows a linear regression that predicts students' final exam scores based on their math aptitude test score.

The regression line can be written as $Y = a + bX + \varepsilon$.
In this equation, the following are true:

- X is the value of the independent variable that is observed
- Y is the value of the dependent variable that is being predicted
- a is the value of Y when X is zero, or the Y intercept
- b is the slope of the regression line
- ε is the error in predicting the value of Y, given a value of X

The following key assumptions must be satisfied when using linear regression on a set of data:

- A linear relationship between the independent (X) and dependent (Y) variables must exist.
- Errors in the prediction of the value of Y are distributed in a manner that approaches the normal distribution curve.
- Errors in the prediction of the value of Y are all independent of one another.

A number of advanced statistical tests can be used to examine whether or not these assumptions are true for a given set of data and the resulting linear regression equation. For example, the coefficient of determination, denoted r^2 (and pronounced r squared) is a number that indicates how well data fit a statistical model—sometimes simply a line or a curve. An r^2 of 1 indicates that the regression line perfectly fits the data, whereas an r^2 of 0 indicates that the line does not fit the data at all. An r^2 of 0.92 means that 92 percent of the total variation in Y can be explained by the linear relationship between X and Y as described by the regression equation. The other 8 percent of total variation in Y remains unexplained. A data scientist would always perform several tests to determine the validity of a linear regression to understand how well the model matches to actual data.

Data Mining

data mining: A BI analytics tool used to explore large amounts of data for hidden patterns to predict future trends and behaviors for use in decision making.

Data mining is a BI analytics tool used to explore large amounts of data for hidden patterns to predict future trends and behaviors for use in decision making. Used appropriately, data mining tools enable organizations to make predictions about what will happen so that managers can be proactive in capitalizing on opportunities and avoiding potential problems.

Among the three most commonly used data mining techniques are association analysis (a specialized set of algorithms sorts through data and forms statistical rules about relationships among the items), neural computing (historical data is examined for patterns that are then used to make predictions), and case-based reasoning (historical if-then-else cases are used to recognize patterns).

Cross-Industry Process for Data Mining (CRISP-DM): A six-phase structured approach for the planning and execution of a data mining project.

The **Cross-Industry Process for Data Mining (CRISP-DM)** is a six-phase structured approach for the planning and execution of a data mining project (see Figure 9.7). It is a robust and well-proven methodology, and although it was first conceived in 1999, it remains the most widely used methodology for data mining projects.[15] The goals for each step of the process are summarized in Table 9.1.

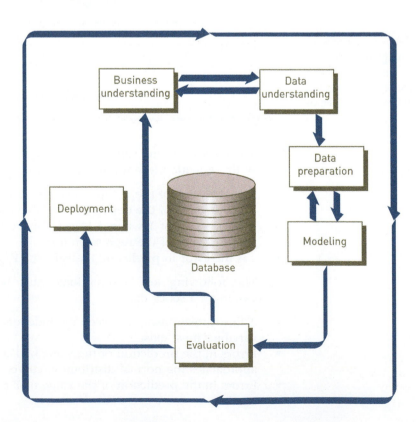

FIGURE 9.7

The Cross-Industry Process for Data Mining (CRISP-DM)

CRISP-DM provides a structured approach for planning and executing a data mining project.

Source: Piatetsky, Gregory, "CRISP-DM, Still the Top Methodology for Analytics, Data Mining, or Data Science Projects," KDNuggets, October 28, 2014, *www.kdnuggets .com/2014/10/crisp-dm-top-methodology -analytics-data-mining-data-science-pro jects.html.*

TABLE 9.1 Goals for each phase of CRISP-DM

Phase	Goal
Business understanding	• Clarify the business goals for the data mining project, convert the goals into a predictive analysis problem, and design a project plan to accomplish these objectives.
Data understanding	• Gather data to be used (may involve multiple sources), become familiar with the data, and identify any data quality problems (lack of data, missing data, data needs adjustment, etc.) that must be addressed.
Data preparation	• Select a subset of data to be used, clean data to address quality issues, and transform data into form suitable for analysis.
Modeling	• Apply selected modeling techniques.
Evaluation	• Assess if the model achieves business goals.
Deployment	• Deploy the model into the organization's decision-making process.

Source: Leaper, Nicole, "A Visual Guide to CRISP-DM Methodology," *https://exde.files.wordpress.com/2009/03/crisp_visualguide.pdf*, accessed January 20, 2016.

Here are a few examples showing how data mining can be used:

- Based on past responses to promotional mailings, identify those consumers most likely to take advantage of future mailings.
- Examine retail sales data to identify seemingly unrelated products that are frequently purchased together.
- Monitor credit card transactions to identify likely fraudulent requests for authorization.
- Use hotel booking data to adjust room rates so as to maximize revenue.
- Analyze demographic data and behavior data about potential customers to identify those who would be the most profitable customers to recruit.
- Study demographic data and the characteristics of an organization's most valuable employees to help focus future recruiting efforts.
- Recognize how changes in an individual's DNA sequence affect the risk of developing common diseases such as Alzheimer's or cancer.

The average production cost of a Hollywood movie in 2007 was $106 million, with an additional $36 million spent on marketing of the film. With that kind of money being spent, potential investors need to have a good sense of what films will earn a profit and which ones won't. Researchers from the University of Iowa took data from two online sources (the Internet Movie Database and Box Office Mojo) to build a database of over 14,000 films and 4,000 actors and directors from films released between 2000 and 2010. They calculated return on investment for each film to get an estimate of its profitability. The researchers then used a data mining algorithm to discover patterns that predict movie profitability. Using the algorithm, the researchers discovered that the factor most strongly correlated with a film's profitability is the average gross revenue made by the director's previous films—directors who have generated more revenue in the past are correlated with greater profitability in future. Somewhat surprisingly, while big stars boost box office receipts, they don't guarantee a profit, because they cost a lot to hire in the first place and they are often involved in higher budget films that require more revenue to generate a profit.[16]

Dashboards

key performance indicator (KPI): A metric that tracks progress in executing chosen strategies to attain organizational objectives and goals and consists of a direction, measure, target, and time frame.

Measures are metrics that track progress in executing chosen strategies to attain organizational objectives and goals. These metrics are also called **key performance indicators (KPIs)** and consist of a direction, measure, target, and time frame. To enable comparisons over different time periods, it is also important to define the KPIs and to use the same definition from year to year. Over time, some existing KPIs may be dropped and new ones added as the organization changes its objectives and goals. Obviously, just as different organizations have different goals, various organizations will have different KPIs. The following are examples of well-defined KPIs:

- **For a university.** Increase (direction) the five-year graduation rate for incoming freshman (measure) to at least 80 percent (target) starting with the graduating class of 2022 (time frame).
- **For a customer service department.** Increase (direction) the number of customer phone calls answered within the first four rings (measure) to at least 90 percent (target) within the next three months (time frame).
- **For an HR organization.** Reduce (direction) the number of voluntary resignations and terminations for performance (measure) to 6 percent or less (target) for the 2018 fiscal year and subsequent years (time frame).

dashboard: A presentation of a set of KPIs about the state of a process at a specific point in time.

A **dashboard** presents a set of KPIs about the state of a process at a specific point in time. Dashboards provide rapid access to information, in an easy-to-interpret and concise manner, which helps organizations run more effectively and efficiently.

Options for displaying results in a dashboard can include maps, gauges, bar charts, trend lines, scatter diagrams, and other representations, as shown in Figures 9.8 and Figure 9.9. Often items are color coded (e.g., red = problem; yellow = warning; and green = OK) so that users can see at a glance where attention is needed. Many dashboards are designed in such a manner that users can click on a section of the chart displaying data in one format and drill down into the data to gain insight into more specific areas. For example, Figure 9.9 represents the results of drilling down on the sales region of Figure 9.8.

Dashboards provide users at every level of the organization the information they need to make improved decisions. Operational dashboards can be designed to draw data in real time from various sources, including corporate databases and spreadsheets, so decision makers can make use of up-to-the-minute data.

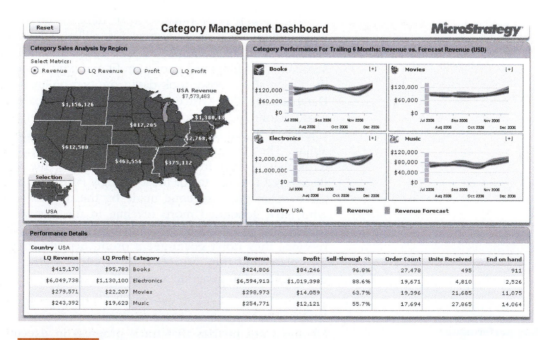

FIGURE 9.8

Category management dashboard for total U.S. region

This dashboard summarizes a number of sales measures.

Source: *www.microstrategy.com/us/analytics/technology.*

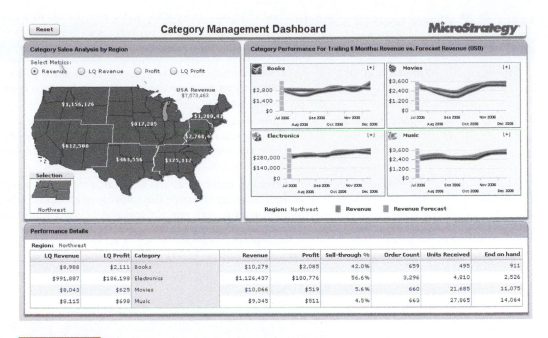

FIGURE **9.9**
Category management dashboard for Northwest region
This dashboard summarizes a number of revenue measures.
Source: *www.microstrategy.com/us/analytics/technology.*

Widely used BI software comes from many different vendors, including Hewlett Packard, IBM, Information Builders, Microsoft, Oracle, and SAP, as shown in Table 9.2. Vendors such as JasperSoft and Pentaho also provide open-source BI software, which is appealing to some organizations.

Self-Service Analytics

self-service analytics: Training, techniques, and processes that empower end users to work independently to access data from approved sources to perform their own analyses using an endorsed set of tools.

Self-service analytics includes training, techniques, and processes that empower end users to work independently to access data from approved sources to perform their own analyses using an endorsed set of tools. In the past, such data analysis could only be performed by data scientists. Self-service analytics encourages nontechnical end users to make decisions based on facts and analyses rather than intuition. Using a self-service analytics application, end users can gather insights, analyze trends, uncover opportunities and issues, and accelerate decision making by rapidly creating reports, charts, dashboards, and documents from any combination of enterprise information assets. Self-service analytics eliminates decision-making delays that can arise if all requests for data analyses must be made through a limited number of data scientists and/or information system resources. It also frees up these resources to do higher-level analytics work. Ideally, self-service analytics will lead to faster and better decision making.

An organization can take several actions to ensure an effective self-service analytics program. First, to mitigate the risks associated with self-service analytics, data managers should work with business units to determine key metrics, an agreed-upon vocabulary, processes for creating and publishing reports, the privileges required to access confidential data, and how to define and implement security and privacy policies. The information systems organization should help users understand what data is available and recommended for business analytics. One approach to accomplishing this is to provide a data dictionary for use by end users. Training, on both the data and on the use of self-service applications, is critical for getting end workers up to speed

TABLE 9.2 Widely used BI software

Vendor	Product	Description
HP	Autonomy IDOL[17]	Enables organizations to process unstructured as well as structured data; the software can examine the intricate relationships between data to answer the crucial question "Why has this happened?"
IBM	Cognos Business Intelligence[18]	Turns data into past, present, and future views of an organization's operations and performance so decision makers can identify opportunities and minimize risks; snapshots of business performance are provided in reports and independently assembled dashboards.
Information Builders	WebFOCUS[19]	Produces dashboards and scorecards to display a high-level view of critical indicators and metrics; the software enables users to analyze and manipulate information, with minimal training. It also supports dynamic report distribution, with real-time alerts, and fully automates the scheduling and delivery of vital information.
Microsoft	Power BI for Office 365[20]	Allows users to model and analyze data and query large data sets with powerful natural-language queries; it also allows users to easily visualize data in Excel.
Oracle	Business Intelligence[21]	Offers a collection of enterprise BI technology and applications; tools including an integrated array of query, reporting, analysis, mobile analytics, data integration and management, desktop integration, and financial performance management applications; operational BI applications; and data warehousing.
Oracle	Hyperion[22]	Provides software modules to enable financial management; modules include those for budgeting, planning, and forecasting; financial reporting; database management; financial consolidation; treasury management; and analytics.
SAS	Enterprise BI Server[23]	Provides software modules to support query and analysis, perform OLAP processing, and create customizable dashboards; the software integrates with Microsoft Office.
SAP	Business Objects[24]	Offers a suite of applications that enable users to design and generate reports, create interactive dashboards that contain charts and graphs for visualizing data, and create ad hoc queries and analysis of data; also allows users to search through BI data sources.

on how they can use the information in the BI system. Finally, data privacy and security measures should be in place to ensure that the use of the data meets legal, compliance, and regulatory requirements.

A well-managed self-service analytics program allows technology professionals to retain ultimate data control and governance while limiting information systems staff involvement in routine tasks. Modern data management requires a true balancing act between enabling self-service analysis and protecting sensitive business information, as shown in Figure 9.10.

Table 9.3 presents the pros and cons associated with self-service BI and analytics.

For self-service analytics tools to be effective, they must be intuitive and easy to use. Business users simply don't have the time to learn how to work with complex tools or sophisticated interfaces. A self-service analytics application will only be embraced by end users if it allows them to easily access their own customized information, without extensive training. Microstrategy, Power BI, Qlik, SAS Analytics, Tableau, and TIBCO Software are just a few examples of the dozens of software options available for self-service analytics.

Expert Storybooks, a cloud-based, self-service analytics service from IBM's Watson Analytics line, provides data analysis models that offer connections to a range of data sources, along with secure connections to corporate data. Expert Storybooks are tools for creating sophisticated data visualizations to help users find relevant facts and discover patterns and relationships to make predictive decisions. There are several Expert Storybooks available, including

FIGURE **9.10**

Importance of data management

Modern data management requires a true balancing act between enabling self-service analysis and protecting sensitive business information.

Self-service analytics

Protecting sensitive business information

TABLE 9.3 Pros and cons associated with self-service BI and analytics

Pros	Cons
Gets valuable data into the hands of the people who need it the most—end users.	If not well managed, it can create the risk of erroneous analysis and reporting, leading to potentially damaging decisions within an organization.
Encourages nontechnical end users to make decisions based on facts and analyses rather than intuition.	Different analyses can yield inconsistent conclusions, resulting in wasted time trying to explain the differences. Self-service analytics can also result in proliferating "data islands," with duplications of time and money spent on analyses.
Accelerates and improves decision making.	Can lead to over spending on unapproved data sources and business analytics tools.
Business people can access and use the data they need for decision making, without having to go to technology experts each time they have a new question, thus filling the gap caused by a shortage of trained data scientists.	Can exacerbate problems by removing the checks and balances on data preparation and use. Without strong data governance, organizations can end up with lots of silos of information, bad analysis, and extra costs.

one that uses baseball statistics from AriBall to build predictions of player performance, enabling users to gain an edge over their fantasy baseball competitors. A variety of other Storybooks help end users incorporate weather data into revenue analysis; analyze social data to measure reputational risk; analyze marketing campaign data; identify and analyze trends in customer profitability; analyze market trends for investment strategy; and examine relationships among pay, performance, and credit risk.[25]

Critical Thinking Exercise

Fire Department Turns to BI Analytics

New York City has nearly 1 million buildings, and each year, more than 3,000 of them experience a major fire. The Fire Department of the City of New York (FDNY) is adding BI analytics to its arsenal of firefighting equipment. It has created a database of over 60 different factors (e.g., building location, age of the building, whether it has electrical issues, the number and location of sprinklers) in an attempt to determine which buildings are more likely to have a fire than others. The values of these parameters for each building are fed into a BI analytics system that assigns each of the city's 330,000 inspectable buildings a risk score. (FDNY doesn't inspect single and two-family homes.) Fire inspectors then use these risk scores to prioritize which buildings to visit on their weekly inspections.[26]

Review Questions

1. What kinds of BI analytics tools and techniques is the FDNY likely to use in sifting through all this data and determining a building's risk score?
2. Identify three other parameters that ought to be taken into consideration when setting priorities for building inspections.

Critical Thinking Questions

1. While making investments in BI analytics seems like a good idea, FDNY is strongly challenged in measuring its success. Officials may be able to cite statistics showing a reduction in the number of fires, but demonstrating that BI analytics tools were the reason behind that decrease may be difficult because it involves proving a negative—that something didn't happen because of its efforts. Go to the FDNY citywide statistics Web site at *www.nyc.gov/html/fdny/html/stats/citywide.shtml*. Use those statistics and a data visualization tool of your choice to see if you can discern any change in the number of fires since the BI analytics system was installed in 2014.
2. Can you identify other approaches that would be effective in demonstrating the value of BI analytics in reducing the impact of fires in New York City?

Summary

Principle:

The goal of business intelligence (BI) and analytics is to support improved decision making.

Business intelligence (BI) includes a wide range of applications, practices, and technologies for the extraction, transformation, integration, visualization, analysis, and presentation of data to support improved decision making.

Business analytics is the extensive use of data and quantitative analysis to support fact-based decision making within organizations.

A data scientist is an individual who combines strong business acumen, a deep understanding of analytics, and a healthy appreciation of the limitations of their data, tools, and techniques to deliver real improvements in decision making. The educational requirements for a data scientist are quite rigorous, and the job outlook for this profession is extremely good.

A number of components must be in place for an organization to get real value from its BI and analytics efforts: a solid data management program (including a strong data governance element), creative data scientists, and a strong organizational commitment to data-driven decision making.

Principle:

There are many BI and analytics techniques and tools that can be used in a wide range of problem-solving situations.

Spreadsheets, reporting and querying tools, data visualization, online analytical processing (OLAP), drill-down analysis, linear regression, data mining, and dashboards are examples of commonly used BI tools.

Business managers and end users often turn to spreadsheets to create useful reports and graphs, as well as to employ "what-if" analyses and find the optimal solution to a problem with multiple constraints.

Reporting and querying tools can present data in an easy-to-understand fashion—via formatted data, graphs, and charts. Many of the reporting and querying tools enable end users to make their own data requests and format the results without the need for additional help from the IT organization.

Data visualization is the presentation of data in a pictorial or graphical format. A wide array of tools and techniques are available for creating visual representations that can immediately reveal otherwise difficult-to-perceive patterns or relationships in the underlying data.

Online analytical processing (OLAP) is a method to analyze multidimensional data (data cubes) from many different perspectives. Databases built to support OLAP processing consist of data cubes that contain numeric facts called measures, which are categorized by dimensions, such as time and geography.

Drill-down analysis involves the interactive examination of high-level summary data in increasing detail to gain insight into certain elements.

Simple linear regression is a mathematical procedure technique for predicting the value of a dependent variable based on a single independent variable and the linear relationship between the two.

Data mining is a BI analytics tools used to explore large amounts of data for hidden patterns to predict future trends and behaviors for use in decision making. The Cross-Industry Process for Data Mining (CRISP-DM) is a six-phase structured approach used for the planning and execution of a data mining project.

A dashboard presents a set of KPIs about the state of a process at a specific point in time. Dashboards provide rapid access to information, in an easy-to-interpret and concise manner, which helps organizations run more effectively and efficiently.

Self-service analytics includes training, techniques, and processes that empower end users to work independently to access data from approved sources to perform their own analyses using an endorsed set of tools. Self-service analytics empowers end users to work independently. A number of measures must be in place to ensure an effective self-serve analytics program and to reduce the risk of invalid analyses leading to poor decisions.

Key Terms

business intelligence (BI)	drill-down analysis
conversion funnel	key performance indicator (KPI)
Cross-Industry Process for Data Mining (CRISP-DM)	linear regression
dashboard	online analytical processing (OLAP)
data cube	self-service analytics
data mining	word cloud
data visualization	

Chapter 9: Self-Assessment Test

The goal of business intelligence (BI) is to support improved decision making.

1. Which of the following statements is not true?
   a. The data used in BI is often pulled from multiple sources—both internal and external to the organization.
   b. Users may access the data and BI applications via the Web or through organizational intranets and extranets—often using mobile devices, such as smartphones and tablets.
   c. The data used in BI applications can come from data warehouses, data marts, and data lakes.

d. BI is strictly the realm of data scientists; end users and business managers should be discouraged from using these tools and techniques.

2. An individual who combines strong business acumen, a deep understanding of analytics, and healthy appreciation of their data, tools, and techniques to deliver real improvements in decision making is called a _____.
   a. data steward
   b. database administrator
   c. data scientist
   d. database manager

3. Which of the following is not an essential component for a highly effective BI program?
   a. Creative data scientists
   b. Strong data management program
   c. Strong management commitment to data-driven decision making
   d. The most current and powerful BI and analytics tools and software

4. Most data scientists have computer programming skills and are familiar with languages and tools used to process big data, such as:
   a. Hadoop, Hive, R
   b. Python, R, and Assembly
   c. Visual Basic, Java, and Cobol
   d. PL/1, Hadoop, PHP

Principle: There are many business intelligence (BI) and analytics techniques and tools that can be used in a wide range of problem-solving situations.

5. _____ is a BI analytics tool that involves the interactive examination of high-level summary data in increasing detail to gain insight.
   a. OLAP
   b. Drill-down analysis
   c. Linear regression
   d. Dashboard

6. A(n) _____ is a measure that tracks progress in executing chosen strategies to attain organizational objectives and goals.

7. Self-service analytics encourages nontechnical end users to make decisions based on facts and analyses rather than intuition. True or False?

8. _____ is a BI analytics tool used to explore large amounts of data for hidden patterns to predict future trends and behaviors for use in decision making.
   a. Linear regression
   b. Data mining
   c. OLAP
   d. Data visualization

9. A(n) _____ is a graphical representation that summarizes the steps a consumer takes in making the decision to buy your product and become a customer.

Chapter 9: Self-Assessment Test Answers

1. d
2. c
3. d
4. a
5. b

6. key performance indicator (KPI)
7. True
8. b
9. conversion funnel

Review Questions

1. Provide a definition of business intelligence (BI).
2. Provide a definition of business analytics.
3. Identify and briefly discuss several benefits that can be gained through the use of BI and analytics.
4. Describe the role of a data scientist. What education and training are required of data scientists?
5. What is online analytical processing (OLAP), and how is it used?
6. What is a data cube? Define three data dimensions of a data cube that might be used to analyze sales by product line.
7. What is drill-down analysis and how is it used?

8. What is linear regression? Identify two variables that have a strong linear relationship.
9. What is r^2, and how is it used to evaluate how well data fits a linear regression model?
10. What is data mining? Identify three commonly used data mining techniques.
11. What are key performance indicators (KPIs)? Identify three KPIs that might be used in a doctor's or dentist's office to measure the patient office visit experience.
12. What is meant by self-service analytics? Identify some of the pros and cons of self-service analytics.

Discussion Questions

1. Identify and briefly discuss the components that must be in place for an organization to gain real value from its BI and analytics efforts.

2. How would you define BI? Identify and briefly discuss a real-world application of BI that you recently experienced.

3. Imagine that you are the sales manager of a large luxury auto dealer. What sort of data would be useful to you in order to contact potential new car customers and invite them to visit your dealership? Where might you get such data? What sort of BI tools might you need to make sense of this data?

4. You answer your door to find a political activist who asks you to sign a petition to place a proposition on the ballot that, if approved, would ban the use of data mining that includes any data about the citizens of your state. What would you do?

5. What is the difference between OLAP analysis and drill-down analysis? Provide an example of the effective use of each technique.

6. Identify at least four well-defined KPIs that could be used by the general manager at a large, full-service health club to track the current state of operations, including availability of trainers; status of workout equipment; condition of indoor and outdoor swimming pools; use of the spa and salon; utilization of the basketball, handball, and tennis courts; and condition of the showers and locker rooms. Sketch what a dashboard displaying those KPIs might look like.

7. Your nonprofit organization wishes to increase the efficiency of its fundraising efforts. What sort of data might be useful to achieve this goal? How might BI tools be used to analyze this data?

8. Describe the CRISP-DM model, and explain how it can be used to plan and execute a data mining effort.

9. Must you be a trained statistician to draw valid conclusions from the use of BI tools? Why or why not?

Problem-Solving Exercises

1. You are the sales manager of a software firm that provides BI software for reporting, query, and business data analysis via OLAP and data mining. Write a few paragraphs and create a 3-5 slide presentation that your sales reps can use when calling on potential customers to help them understand the business benefits of BI.

2. Go to the NASA Goddard Institute for Space Studies Web site at *http://data.giss.nasa.gov/gistemp* and read about the temperature data sets available. Next, use the NASA Global land-sea temperature data set for the period 1880 to present at *http://data.giss.nasa.gov/gistemp/tabledata_v3/GLB.Ts+dSST.txt* and create a linear regression of annual mean temperature in degrees Fahrenheit versus year. Be sure to adjust the table values based on the notes that accompany this table.

3. Use the Help function of Excel to learn more about the Excel Scenario Manager and the Excel Solver Add-in.

Team Activities

1. A large customer call center for a multinational retailer has been in operation for several months, but has continually failed to meet both customers' and senior management's expectations. Your team has been called in to develop a dashboard to help monitor and improve the operations of the call center. What KPIs would you track? Sketch a sample dashboard for this application.

2. Your team has decided to enter a Fantasy Baseball League. Use IBM's Watson analytics Storybooks to select the best team in the league.

3. Your team has been hired to reapply the NYCFD BI analytics system to the NYCPD in order to prioritize areas of the city for patrol. Describe what data you might need for such an analysis. What BI analytics techniques would you use to become familiar with the data and develop an algorithm for ranking the various area for patrol?

Web Exercises

1. Do research to learn more about the Goddard Institute of Space Science Surface Temperature Analysis (GISTEMP) temperature measurements used by many scientists to assert that global warming is occurring. One source of such information can be found at *http://data.giss.nasa.gov /gistemp/FAQ.html*. Read carefully the sections that explain why adjusted rather than raw data is used. Briefly summarize the kinds of adjustments made to temperature measurements and discuss how this affects your confidence in the data.

2. Do research on the Web to find business analytics applications that can run on a smartphone.

Prepare a brief paragraph summarizing the features and potential applications of three applications of most interest to you.

3. Do research on the Web to identify examples of a social network allowing a large national retailer to mine its data to learn more about the social network members and to develop targeted direct mailings and emails promoting its products. What are the pros and cons of sharing such data? How do social network members feel when they learn that their data is being shared? In your opinion, under what conditions is this a legitimate use of social network member data?

Career Exercises

1. Do research on CareerBuilder, Indeed, LinkedIn, or SimplyHired to identify what you think is an attractive job opening available for a data scientist. What does this role entail, and what responsibilities must the data scientist perform? What sort of education and experience is required for this position? Is the role of a data scientist of any interest to you? Why or why not?

2. What kinds of decisions are critical for success in a career that interests you? How might you use BI

or analytics to help improve your decision making? Can you identify and specific techniques or tools that you might use?

3. Copy and paste the text describing a job opportunity in which you are interested into an online word cloud generator. What insights do you gain from the resulting word cloud? How might the results lead you to customize your resume to respond to this job posting?

Case Studies

Case One

Analytics Used to Predict Patients Likely to Be Readmitted

Unplanned hospital readmissions are a serious matter for patients and a quality and cost issue for the healthcare system of every country. For example, in the United States, during 2011, nearly 19 percent of Medicare patients were readmitted to the hospital within 30 days of their initial discharge, running up an additional $26 billion in healthcare costs. Hospitals are seeking more effective ways to identify patients at high risk of readmission—especially now that Medicare has begun reducing payments to hospitals with high readmission rates.

Identifying patients at high risk for readmission is important so that hospitals can take a range of preventative measures, including heightened patient education along with medication reconciliation on the day of discharge, increased home services to ensure patient effective at home convalescence, follow-up appointments scheduled for soon after discharge, and follow-up phone calls to ensure an additional level of protection.

Several studies have attempted to identify the key factors that indicate a high risk for unplanned hospital readmission. One study was based on the analysis of the Belgian Hospital Discharge Dataset. This data set contains

patient demographics, data about the hospital stay (date and type of admission and discharge, referral data, admitting department, and destination after discharge), and clinical data (primary and secondary diagnoses). Since 1990, Belgium has required the collection of this data for all inpatients in all acute hospitals. The data is managed by a commission that controls the content and format of patient registration, the data collecting procedures, and the completeness, validity, and reliability of the collected data. In addition, the quality of the data is audited by the Belgium Ministry of Public Health in two ways. First, a software program checks the data for missing, illogical, and outlier values. Second, by regular hospital visits, a random selection of patient records is reviewed to ensure that data were recoded correctly.

Key factors for hospital readmission based on analysis of the Belgian Hospital Discharge Dataset included: (1) chronic cardiovascular disease, (2) patients with chronic pulmonary disease, (3) patients who experienced multiple emergency room visits over the past six months, (4) patients discharged on a Friday, and (5) patients who had a prolonged length of hospital stay. The study also found that patients with short hospital stays were not at high risk for readmission. The research highlighted the need for healthcare providers to work with caregivers and primary care physicians to coordinate a smoother transition from hospital to home, especially for patients discharged on Friday, to reduce unplanned readmissions.

The mission of Penn Medicine Center for Evidence-based Practice (CEP) is to support healthcare quality and safety at the University of Pennsylvania Health System (UPHS) through the practice of evidence-based medicine. Established in 2006, Penn Medicine's CEP is staffed by a hospital director, three research analysts, six physician and nurse liaisons, a health economist, a biostatistician, administrator, and librarians. A study conducted by a team at the CEP examined two years of UPHS discharge data and found that a single variable—prior admission to the hospital two or more times within a span of one year—was the best predictor of being readmitted in the future. This marker was added to UPHS's EHR, and patient results were tracked for the next year. During that time, patients who triggered the readmission alert were subsequently readmitted 31 percent of the time. When an alert was not triggered, patients were readmitted only 11 percent of the time.

A group of physicians conducted yet a third study using data from a 966-bed, teaching hospital during a five-month period in 2011. Their objective was to determine the association between a composite measure of patient condition at discharge, the Rothman Index (RI), and unplanned readmission within 30 days of discharge. Software employing the Rothman Index tracks the overall state of health of patients by continuously gathering 26 key pieces of data, including vital signs (temperature, blood pressure, heart, blood oxygen saturation, and respiratory rate), nursing assessments, cardiac rhythms, and lab test results from a patient's EHR to calculate the Rothman Index, a number between 1 and 100. A patient's Rothman Index is updated continuously throughout the day. A high score indicates a relatively healthy patient, whereas a low score indicates the patient warrants close monitoring or immediate assistance. A physician or nurse can quickly grasp the condition of the patient based on both current score and the trend in the score. The software also draws a graph of the patient's Rothman Index over time that can be displayed in the patient's room, on a central nursing station screen, or on a care provider's mobile device. The software can even send mobile phone alerts to doctors and nurses when a patient's condition warrants attention.

The Rothman Index study included clinical data from the hospital's EHR system as well as from a patient activity database for all adult discharges. There was a total of 12,844 such cases. The researchers excluded encounters that were readmissions within 30 days of a previous discharge (2,574), patients who were admitted for observation only (501), patients with length of stay less than 48 hours (3,243), and patients who died during the hospital stay (189)—yielding a sample of 6,337 eligible inpatient discharges. From this sample, 535 additional patients were eliminated due to missing clinical data, for a sample of 5,802 patients, or 92 percent of all eligible inpatient discharges. Sixteen percent of the sample patients had an unplanned readmission within 30 days of discharge. The risk of readmission for a patient in the highest risk category (Rothman Index lower than 70) was more than 1 in 5 while the risk of readmission for patients in the lowest risk category was about 1 in 10.

Critical Thinking Questions

1. Three different analytic studies by three experienced and highly respected groups of researchers yielded three similar but somewhat different results. Do you believe that the results of these studies are consistent? Why or why not?

2. Do you think the findings of these studies can be applied broadly to all hospitals and medical centers across the United States and around the world? Why or why not?

3. A hospital specializing in the care of patients with various forms of heart disease is attempting to determine the cause of readmission of its patients. Should it rely of the results of general studies such as those described here or should it gather its own data, perform an analysis and draw its own conclusions? Support your recommendation.

SOURCES: Shinkman, Ron, "Readmissions Lead to $41.3B in Additional Hospital Costs," *FierceHealthFinance*, April 20, 2014, *www.fiercehealthfinance.com/story/readmissions-lead-413b-additional-hospital-costs/2014-04-20*; Kern, Christine, "5 Risk Factors for Unplanned Readmissions Identified," *Health IT Outcomes*, September 8, 2015, *www.healthitoutcomes.com/doc/risk-factors-for-unplanned-readmissions-identified-0001*; van den Heede, Koen; Sermeus, Walter; Diya, Luwis; Lesaffre, Emmanuel; and Vleugels, Arthur, "Adverse Outcomes in Belgian Acute Hospitals: Retrospective Analysis of the National Hospital Discharge Dataset," *International Journal for Quality in Health Care*, vol. 18, no. 3, 2006, pp. 211–219, Advance Access Publication: 23 March 2006, *http://intqhc.oxfordjournals.org/content/intqhc/18/3/211.full.pdf*; "Center for Evidence-Based Practice," *Penn Medicine*, *www.uphs.upenn.edu/cep/*, accessed January 12, 2015; " 'Rothman Index' May Help to Lower Repeat Hospitalization Risk," *Medical Press*, August 15, 2013, *http://medicalxpress.com/news/2013-08-rothman-index-hospitalization.html*. Bradley, Elizabeth, PhD; Yakusheva, Olga, PhD; Horwitz, Leora, MD; Sipsma, Heather, PhD; and Fletcher, Jason, PhD, "Identifying Patients at Increased Risk for Unplanned Readmission," US National Library of Medicine National Institutes of Health, September 1, 2014, *http://www.ncbi.nlm.nih.gov/pmc/articles/PMC3771868/*.

Case Two

Sunny Delight Improves Profitability with a Self-Service BI Solution

When implementing a self-service analytics program, information systems staff and end users across an organization often must be willing to give up some control and autonomy in exchange for a cohesive data management strategy. Companies that effectively implement self-service analytics, however, usually find those trade-offs are outweighed by the competitive advantages gained for the organization as a whole.

For Sunny Delight Beverages, a Cincinnati-based producer of juice-based drinks, the payoff from using self-service analytics software has been significant. The company, which generates more than $550 million in annual revenue through sales of its SunnyD, Fruit$_2$0, and VeryFine brands, estimates that its newly implemented, self-service analytics program has resulted in a $195,000 annual reduction in staffing costs and a $2 million annual increase in profits.

Getting to these results, however, has not been easy for Sunny Delight. Like many companies, it had developed a patchwork of departmental business analytics applications over the years. Sunny Delight's infrastructure was particularly complex as the company has been bought and sold multiple times since it was founded in 1963. At one point, Sunny Delight's 480 employees were working with eight different legacy BI applications, resulting in some departments spending up to a week each month producing data that was often not in agreement with the data generated by other departments. Reconciling and rolling up the data was time consuming and left little time for in-depth analysis, much less strategy development and execution.

The data silos also meant that Sunny Delight had no real visibility into its business, which lead to revenue unpredictably, higher-than-necessary inventory levels, and lower margins. The company's sales efforts were hampered because the sales team did not have a true understanding of the effectiveness and profitability of specific sales promotions. For example, the sales department was unable to correlate the impact of a promotional discount with order volume—a key metric for judging the effectiveness of a promotional program. The company was also unable to tie shipping costs directly to specific promotions, which was significant since the timing of many promotions required shipping products to stores on weekends, when shipping and warehouse labor costs were higher.

When the company made the decision to revamp its analytics efforts, the company's CIO and CFO pulled together a cross-functional team of managers from sales, marketing, logistics, warehousing, and accounting who were responsible for developing a comprehensive picture of the required BI functionality—which ranged from simple, canned reports to complex, ad hoc data analysis tools. Working to understand each department's needs built credibility for the project team and helped them choose the solution that would be most effective across the company, which they did after evaluating 17 different options.

The team selected Birst, a cloud-based, self-service BI solution that offers an end to data silos with what it refers to as "local execution with global governance." Because the project team understood that a centrally managed data source was critical to ensuring consistent user-generated data and analysis across the company, they also opted to implement a data warehouse at the same time Birst was rolled out to employees.

According to John Gordos, Sunny Delight's associate director of application development, Birst provides Sunny Delight with a single, networked source of data, which employees at all levels can access quickly and easily, regardless of where they work. Birst's data governance features mean that Sunny Delight's IS team maintains final control over all data, while the user-friendly interface, which is the same whether users are accessing data on a PC, laptop, or smartphone, makes it easy for nontechnical users to access and customize the system's departmental dashboards.

With the data from the new system, Sunny Delight was able to create a more efficient production schedule that allowed it to cut back on production, decrease inventory levels, and reduce plant overtime costs by 90 percent—all without impacting order fulfillment. And with a clearer picture of overall costs, the sales and distribution teams worked together to revise shipping schedules, resulting in a 7 percent drop in the transportation costs tied to promotions.

According to Gordos, "Birst helps [Sunny Delight] employees to think fast because they no longer have to worry about building and aggregating the data. They just get the data, and then they think about it—instead of accumulating it."

Critical Thinking Questions

1. Is it surprising to you that a relatively small company like Sunny Delight could end up with so many different analytics tools? How might the fact that Sunny Delight has changed ownership multiple times have impacted the number and variety of BI tools being used?

2. What are some of the trade-offs of a move to an enterprise-level analytics solution for individual end users who might have grown accustomed to working with their own customized solutions for generating data?

3. According to a recent report by Gartner, most business users will have access to some sort of self-service BI tool within the next few years; however, Gartner estimates that less than 10 percent of companies will have sufficient data governance practices in place to prevent data inconsistencies across the organization. Why do you think so many companies continue to invest in new analytics tools without implementing governance programs that ensure data consistency?

SOURCES: "Sunny Delight Beverages Co," Sunny Delight Beverages, Co., ww2.sunnyd.com/company/overview.shtml, accessed March 16, 2016; Boulton, Clint, "How Sunny Delight Juices up Sales with Cloud-Based Analytics," CIO, September 14, 2015, www.cio.com/article/2983624 /business-analytics/how-sunny-delight-juices-up-sales-with-cloud-based -analytics.html; "Birst Customer Testimonial: John Gordos - Associate Director, Application Development," YouTube video, posted by BirstBI, August 14, 2014, www.youtube.com/watch?v=d3AjCIzWO5Y; "SunnyD Case Study," Birst, February 1, 2016, www.google.com/url?sa=t&rct =j&q=&esrc=s&source=Web&cd=4&cad=rja&uact=8&ved=0ahUKEwi nieHr78XLAhXFwj4KHa-5CzMQFggtMAM&url=https%3A%2F%2Fwww .birst.com%2Fwp-content%2Fuploads%2F2016%2F02%2FBirst _CaseStudy_SunnyD_NetworkedBI.pdf&usg=AFQjCNFwbr-mGBWeu5zU mu_k40JAPOO_Mw&bvm=bv.116954456,d.amc; "Birst Sunny D Testi- monial," YouTube video, posted by BirstBI, October 9, 2015, www .youtube.com/watch?v=tEuHH4IGHLU; Roberts, Shawn, "How Analytics Saved Sunny Delight $1M," CIO Insight, October 14, 2015, www .cioinsight.com/it-strategy/big-data/how-analytics-saved-sunny-delight -1m.html; "Networked BI," Birst, www.birst.com/product, accessed March 16, 2016.

Notes

1. "Helse Vest," Microsoft, February 6, 2014, https://custo mers.microsoft.com/Pages/CustomerStory.aspx? recid=2223.

2. "MetLife Auto & Home Puts Brakes on Fraud with CSC's Fraud Evaluator," CSC, www.csc.com/p_and_c_genera l_insurance/success_stories/45406-metlife_auto_and_ho

me_puts_brakes_on_fraud_with_csc_s_fraud_evaluator, accessed January 8, 2016.

3. "Getting Started with Analytics: Kroger Uses Simulation Optimization to Improve Pharmacy Inventory Management," INFORMS, *www.informs.org/Sites/Getting -Started-With-Analytics/Analytics-Success-Stories/Case -Studies/Kroger*, accessed January 8, 2016.

4. "Getting Started with Analytics: DaimlerChrysler: Using a Decision Support System for Promotional Pricing at the Major Auto Manufacturer, INFORMS, *www.informs.org /Sites/Getting-Started-With-Analytics/Analytics-Success -Stories/Case-Studies/DaimlerChrysler*, accessed January 8, 2016.

5. "Getting Started with Analytics: Optimizing Chevron's Refineries," INFORMS, *https://www.informs.org/Sites /Getting-Started-With-Analytics/Analytics-Success-Stories /Case-Studies/Chevron*, accessed January 8, 2016.

6. "Getting Started with Analytics: Coca-Cola Enterprises: Optimizing Product Delivery of 42 Billon Soft Drinks a Year," INFORMS, *www.informs.org/Sites/Getting -Started-With-Analytics/Analytics-Success-Stories/Case -Studies/Coca-Cola-Enterprises*, accessed January 8, 2016.

7. Violino, Bob, "The Hottest Jobs in IT: Training Tomorrow's Data Scientists," *Forbes*, June 26, 2014, *www.for bes.com/sites/emc/2014/06/26/the-hottest-jobs-in-it-train ing-tomorrows-data-scientists/#131733cd4b63*.

8. "Argosy Hits the Jackpot with OpenText and Teradata," Open Text, *http://connectivity.opentext.com/resource -centre/success-stories/Success_Story_Argosy_Hits_the _Jackpot_with_OTIC_and_Teradata.pdf.pdf*, accessed January 19, 2015.

9. "UK Hospital Sees Cloud-Based BI Service as a Tool to Boost Clinical Outcomes and Efficiency," Microsoft, *http://blogs.msdn.com/b/powerbi/archive/2014/04/16 /uk-hospital-sees-cloud-based-bi-service-as-a-tool-to -boost-clinical-outcomes-and-efficiency.aspx*, accessed February 8, 2015.

10. "Who We Are," FFF Enterprises, *www.fffenterprises.com /company/who-we-are.html*, accessed January 20, 2014.

11. "At FFF Enterprises Collaboration Is Key to Success with QlikView," Qlik, *www.qlik.com/us/explore/customers /customer-listing/f/fff-enterprises*, accessed January 20, 2015.

12. "Adviso and Technologia Use the Power of Multi-Channel Funnels to Discover the True Paths to Conversion," Google Analytics, *https://static.googleusercontent .com/media/www.google.com/en/us/analytics/customers /pdfs/technologia.pdf*, accessed January 25, 2016.

13. "Starbucks Coffee Company Delivers Daily, Actionable Information to Store Managers, Improves Business Insight with High Performance Data Warehouse," Oracle, *www.oracle.com/us/corporate/customers/customer search/starbucks-coffee-co-1-exadata-ss-1907993.html*, accessed January 20, 2014.

14. Misson, Chris, "AQUARIUS WebPortal—a Flash Flooding Emergency Management Success Story," Hydrology Corner Blog, October 21, 2014, *http://aquaticinformatics .com/blog/aquarius-webportal-flash-flooding-emergency -management*.

15. Piatetsky, Gregory, "CRISP-DM, Still the Top Methodology for Analytics, Data Mining, or Data Science Projects," *KDNuggets*, October 28, 2014, *www.kdnuggets.com /2014/10/crisp-dm-top-methodology-analytics-data-min ing-data-science-projects.html*.

16. "Data Mining Reveals the Surprising Factors behind Successful Movies," *MIT Technology Review*, June 22, 2015, *www.technologyreview.com/view/538701/data -mining-reveals-the-surprising-factors-behind-successful -movies*.

17. McNulty, Eileen, "HP Rolls Out BI and Analytics Software Bundle," *dataconomy*, June 10, 2014, *http://datac onomy.com/hp-rolls-bi-analytics-software-bundle*.

18. "Cognos Business Intelligence: Coming Soon to the Cloud," IBM, *www-03.ibm.com/software/products/en /business-intelligence*, accessed January 19, 2015.

19. "Business Intelligence for Everyone," Information Builders, *www.informationbuilders.com/products/webfo cus*, accessed January 19, 2015.

20. Lardinois, Frederic, "Microsoft's Power BI for Office 365 Comes out of Preview, Simplifies Data Analysis and Visualizations," *Tech Crunch*, February 10, 2014, *http:// techcrunch.com/2014/02/10/microsofts-power-bi-for -office-365-comes-out-of-preview-simplifies-data-analy sis-and-visualizations*.

21. "Oracle Business Intelligence," Oracle, *www.oracle.com /technetwork/middleware/index-084205.html*, accessed January 19, 2015.

22. Rouse, Margaret, "Oracle Hyperion," *TechTarget*, *http:// searchfinancialapplications.techtarget.com/definition /Oracle-Hyperion*, accessed January 19, 2015.

23. "SAS Enterprise BI Server," SAS, *www.sas.com/en_us /software/business-intelligence/enterprise-bi-server.html*, accessed January 30, 2015.

24. Rouse, Margaret, "SAP Business Objects BI," *TechTarget*, *http://searchsap.techtarget.com/definition/SAP-Busines sObjects-BI*, accessed January 19, 2015.

25. Ferranti, Marc, "IBM's Watson Analytics Offers New Data Discovery Tools for Everyday Business Users," *PC World*, October 13, 2015, *www.pcworld.com/article /2992124/ibms-watson-analytics-offers-new-data-discov ery-tools-for-everyday-business-users.html*.

26. Dwoskin, Elizabeth, "How New York's Fire Department Uses Data Mining," *Digits*, January 24, 2014, *http://blogs .wsj.com/digits/2014/01/24/how-new-yorks-fire-depart ment-uses-data-mining*.

Did You Know?

- Watson, a supercomputer developed by IBM with artificial intelligence capabilities, was able to soundly defeat two prior champions of the popular TV game show, *Jeopardy!* Now a cloud-based Watson system is being used by doctors to develop treatment options for a wide range of diseases.

- Some experts have predicted that every home will have a robot of some sort by 2025. One area of particular interest is the use of robots as companions and caregivers for people who are sick, elderly, or physically challenged.

▶ Principles

- Knowledge management allows organizations to share knowledge and experience among its workers.

- Artificial intelligence systems form a broad and diverse set of systems that can replicate human decision making for certain types of well-defined problems.

- Multimedia and virtual reality systems can reshape the interface between people and information technology by offering new ways to communicate information, visualize processes, and express ideas creatively.

- Specialized systems can help organizations and individuals achieve their goals.

▶ Learning Objectives

- Discuss the relationships between data, information, and knowledge.

- Identify the benefits associated with a sound knowledge management program.

- List some of the tools and techniques used in knowledge management.

- Define the term "artificial intelligence" and state the objective of developing artificial intelligence systems.

- List the characteristics of intelligent behavior and compare the performance of natural and artificial intelligence systems for each of these characteristics.

- Identify the major components of the artificial intelligence field and provide one example of each type of system.

- Discuss the use of multimedia in a business setting.

- Define the terms "virtual reality" and "augmented reality" and provide three examples of these applications.

- Discuss examples of specialized systems for organizational and individual use.

Why Learn about Knowledge Management and Specialized Information Systems?

Knowledge management and specialized information systems are used in almost every industry. As a manager, you might use a knowledge management system to obtain advice on how to approach a problem that others in your organization have already encountered. As an executive at an automotive company, you might oversee robots that attach windshields to cars or paint body panels. As a stock trader, you might use a special system called a neural network to uncover patterns to make investment decisions. As a new car sales manager you might incorporate virtual reality into a company Web site to show potential customers the features of your various models. As a member of the military, you might use computer simulation as a training tool to prepare you for combat. As an employee of a petroleum company, you might use an expert system to determine where to drill for oil and gas. This chapter provides many additional examples of these types of specialized information systems. Learning about these systems will help you discover new ways to use information systems in your day-to-day work.

As you read this chapter, consider the following:

- What are the many uses of information systems designed to collect knowledge and provide expertise?
- Can specialized information systems and devices provide expertise superior to that which can be obtained through human effort?

This chapter identifies the challenges associated with knowledge management, provides guidance to overcome these challenges, presents best practices for selling and implementing a successful knowledge management project, and outlines various technologies that support knowledge management. We begin with a definition of knowledge management and identify several knowledge management applications and their associated benefits.

What Is Knowledge Management?

knowledge management (KM): A range of practices concerned with increasing awareness, fostering learning, speeding collaboration and innovation, and exchanging insights.

explicit knowledge: Knowledge that is documented, stored, and codified—such as standard procedures, product formulas, customer contact lists, market research results, and patents.

tacit knowledge: The know-how that someone has developed as a result of personal experience; it involves intangible factors such as beliefs, perspective, and a value system.

Knowledge management (KM) comprises a range of practices concerned with increasing awareness, fostering learning, speeding collaboration and innovation, and exchanging insights. Knowledge management is used by organizations to enable individuals, teams, and entire organizations to collectively and systematically create, share, and apply knowledge in order to achieve their objectives. Globalization, the expansion of the services sector, and the emergence of new information technologies have caused many organizations to establish KM programs in their IT or human resource management departments. The goal is to improve the creation, retention, sharing, and reuse of knowledge. As already discussed, a knowledge management system is an organized collection of people, procedures, software, databases, and devices that creates, captures, refines, stores, manages, and disseminates knowledge, as shown in Figure 10.1.

An organization's knowledge assets often are classified as either explicit or tacit (see Table 10.1). **Explicit knowledge** is knowledge that is documented, stored, and codified—such as standard procedures, product formulas, customer contact lists, market research results, and patents. **Tacit knowledge** is the know-how that someone has developed as a result of personal experience; it involves intangible factors such as beliefs, perspective, and a value system. Examples include how to ride a bike, the decision-making process used by an experienced coach to make adjustments when her team is down at halftime of a big game, a physician's technique for diagnosing a rare illness and prescribing a course of treatment, and an engineer's approach to cutting

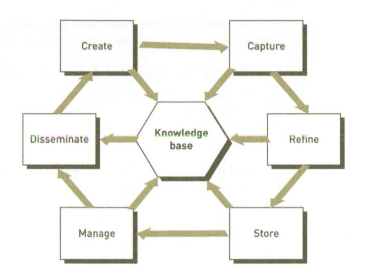

FIGURE 10.1

Knowledge management processes

Knowledge management comprises a number of practices.

Source: From Reynolds, Information Technology for Managers, 2E. © 2016 Cengage Learning.

TABLE 10.1 Explicit and tacit knowledge

Asset Type	Description	Examples
Explicit knowledge	Knowledge that is documented, stored, and codified	Customer lists, product data, price lists, a database for telemarketing and direct mail, patents, best practices, standard procedures, and market research results
Tacit knowledge	Personal knowledge is not documented but embedded in individual experience	Expertise and skills unique to individual employees, such as how to close a sale or troubleshoot a complex piece of equipment

costs for a project that is over budget. This knowledge cannot be documented easily; yet, tacit knowledge is key to high performance and competitive advantage because it's difficult for others to copy.

Much of the tacit knowledge that people carry with them is extremely useful but cannot be shared with others easily. This means that new employees might spend weeks, months, or even years learning things on their own that more experienced coworkers might have been able to convey to them. In some cases, these nuggets of valuable knowledge are lost forever when experienced employees retire, and others never learn them.

A major goal of knowledge management is to somehow capture and document the valuable work-related tacit knowledge of others and to turn it into explicit knowledge that can be shared with others. This is much easier said than done, however. Over time, experts develop their own processes for their areas of expertise. Their processes become second nature and are so internalized that they are sometimes unable to write down step-by-step instructions to document the processes.

Two processes are frequently used to capture tacit knowledge—shadowing and joint problem solving. **Shadowing** involves a novice observing an expert executing her job to learn how she performs. This technique is often used in the medical field to help young interns learn from experienced physicians. With **joint problem solving**, the novice and the expert work side by side to solve a problem so that the expert's approach is slowly revealed to the observant novice. Thus a plumber trainee will work with a master plumber to learn the trade.

shadowing: A process used to capture tacit knowledge that involves a novice observing an expert executing her job to learn how she performs.

joint problem solving: A process used to capture tacit knowledge where the novice and the expert work side by side to solve a problem so that the expert's approach is slowly revealed to the observant novice.

The next section discusses how KM is used in organizations and illustrates how these applications lead to real business benefits.

Knowledge Management Applications and Associated Benefits

Organizations employ KM to foster innovation, leverage the expertise of people across the organization, and capture the expertise of key individuals before they retire. Examples of knowledge management efforts that led to these results and their associated benefits are discussed in the following sections.

Foster Innovation by Encouraging the Free Flow of Ideas

Organizations must continuously innovate to evolve, grow, and prosper. Organizations that fail to innovate will soon fall behind their competition. Many organizations implement knowledge management projects to foster innovation by encouraging the free flow of ideas among employees, contractors, suppliers, and other business partners. Such collaboration can lead to the discovery of a wealth of new opportunities, which, after evaluation and testing, may lead to an increase in revenue, a decrease in costs, or the creation of new products and services.

TMW Systems, a provider of logistics operations and fleet management systems, has experienced rapid growth over the past several years. The company now has more than 700 employees in its Cleveland headquarters and in satellite offices across North America.[1] As the company grew, it became more difficult to ensure that all employees had access to the most current knowledge available within the company because most information was shared via email or shared network drives. To ensure that its base of institutional knowledge was being preserved and to encourage collaboration and innovation across all of its offices, TMW implemented a knowledge management system with a strong social learning feature, which places an emphasis on decentralized information sharing. The system, which is part of an intentional cultural shift at TMW toward a more open and collaborative working environment, allows employees to easily share new ideas, expertise, and best practices with other employees no matter where they are based.[2]

Leverage the Expertise of People across the Organization

It is critical that an organization enables its employees to share and build on one another's experience and expertise. In this manner, new employees or employees moving into new positions are able to get up to speed more quickly. Workers can share thoughts and experiences about what works well and what does not, thus preventing new employees from repeating some of the mistakes of others. Employees facing new (to them) challenges can get help from coworkers in other parts of the organization whom they have never even met to avoid a costly and time-consuming "reinvention of the wheel." All of this enables employees to deliver valuable results more quickly, improve their productivity, and get products and new ideas to market faster.

White & Case, an international law firm headquartered in New York City, represents well-known organizations around the world through its offices in more than 20 countries in Africa, Asia, Europe, Latin America, the Middle East, and North America. The firm's employees have diverse backgrounds and speak more than 60 different languages.[3] One strength of the firm is that the lawyers truly operate as a team by constantly sharing know-how, experience, and market and client information. Thus, a client anywhere in the world receives the full benefit of White & Case's global knowledge. The firm's knowledge management system pulls relevant information from the firm's document management, CRM, case management, and billing and financial management systems as well as from lawyers' work histories to create a context for all this information. The system enables lawyers to find all relevant knowledge within the firm about a case or subject, often within a matter of minutes. As a result of its ability to leverage its global knowledge, White & Case has been able to win new business, such as that of a major manufacturing company that approached the firm's New York office to find out if it had expertise in privatizing an Eastern European company. Using the enterprise search software, an attorney in New York quickly determined that the company had experience in this area and that the best lawyer for the job was working out of the firm's Germany office.[4]

Capture the Expertise of Key Individuals before They Retire

In the United States, 3 to 4 million employees will retire each year for the next 20 years or so. Add to that a 5 to 7 percent employee turnover as workers move to different companies, and it is clear that organizations are facing a tremendous challenge in trying to avoid the loss of valuable experience and expertise. Many organizations are using knowledge management to capture this valuable expertise before it simply walks out the door and is lost forever. The permanent loss of expertise related to the core operations of an organization can result in a significant loss of productivity and a decrease in the quality of service over time.

The state of New Hampshire has developed a knowledge management and transfer model to prevent critical knowledge loss as state employees retire. The process begins by identifying what critical tasks the individual performs and assessing whether others can perform these tasks. To do this, the employee is asked to answer questions such as the following:

- If you left your position today, what wouldn't get done because no one else knows how to do it?
- How important is this work? What is the impact of it not getting done?
- If this work is important, what resources exist to help others learn this task?
- If this work is important, how should we plan to address this knowledge gap? Who will learn this? How and when?

Following this discussion, the employee and his manager define appropriate methods to transfer any critical knowledge. This could include transferring the knowledge to others, creating job aids, providing on-the-job training for a replacement, and so on.[5]

Best Practices for Selling and Implementing a KM Project

Establishing a successful KM program is challenging, but most of the challenges involved have nothing to do with the technologies or vendors employed. Instead they are challenges associated with human nature and the manner in which people are accustomed to working together. A set of best practices for selling and implementing a KM project are summarized in Figure 10.2 and are discussed in the following sections.

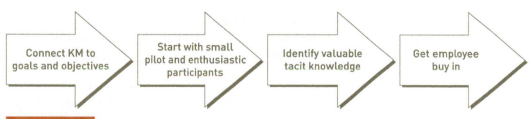

FIGURE 10.2

Steps in selling and implementing a knowledge management project

The key challenges have to do with human nature and how people work together.

Source: From Reynolds, Information Technology for Managers, 2E. © 2016 Cengage Learning.

Connect the KM Effort to Organizational Goals and Objectives

When starting a KM effort, just as with any other project, you must clearly define how that effort will support specific organizational goals and objectives, such as increasing revenue, reducing costs, improving customer service, or speeding up the time to bring a product to market. Doing so will help you sell the project to others and elicit their support and enthusiasm; it will also help you determine if the project is worthwhile before the organization commits resources to it. Although many people may intuitively believe that sharing knowledge and best practices is a worthy idea, there must be an underlying business reason to do so. The fundamental business case for implementing knowledge management must be clearly defined.

Start with a Small Pilot Involving Enthusiasts

Containing the scope of a project to impact only a small part of the organization and a few employees is definitely less risky than trying to take on a project very large in scope. With a small-scale project, you have more control over the outcome, and if the outcome is not successful, the organization will not be seriously impacted. Indeed, failure on a small scale can be considered a learning experience on which to build future KM efforts. In addition, obtaining the resources (people, dollars, etc.) for a series of small, successful projects is typically much easier than getting large amounts of resources for a major organization-wide project.

Furthermore, defining a pilot project to address the business needs of a group of people who are somewhat informed about KM and are enthusiastic about its potential can greatly improve the odds of success. Targeting such a group of users reduces the problem of trying to overcome skepticism and unwillingness to change, which have doomed many a project. Also, such a group of users, once the pilot has demonstrated some degree of success, can serve as strong advocates who communicate the positive business benefits of KM to others.

Identify Valuable Tacit Knowledge

Not all tacit knowledge is equally valuable, and priorities must be set in terms of what knowledge to go after. The intent of a KM program is to identify, capture, and disseminate knowledge gems from a sea of information. Within the scope of the initial pilot project, an organization should identify and prioritize the tacit knowledge it wants to include in its KM system.

As Toyota Financial Services (TFS) was preparing to move its North American headquarters from California to Texas, the company implemented a cloud-based knowledge management system, with the goal of ensuring that the important tacit knowledge of its employees was not lost during the transition. In the two-year lead-up to the move, TFS employees were encouraged to use the platform to post questions and share expertise, allowing the company to develop a repository of curated subject matter expertise that the company will use to train new employees in Texas.[6]

Get Employees to Buy In

Managers must create a work culture that places a high value on tacit knowledge and that strongly encourages people to share it. In a highly competitive work environment, it can be especially difficult to get workers to surrender their knowledge and experience as these traits make the employees more valuable as individual contributors. For example, it would be extremely difficult to get a highly successful mutual fund manager to share her stock-picking technique with other fund managers. Such sharing of information would tend to put all fund managers on a similar level of performance and would also tend to level the amount of their annual compensation.

Some organizations believe that the most powerful incentive for experts to share their knowledge is to receive public recognition from senior managers and their peers. For example, some organizations provide recognition by mentioning the accomplishments of contributors in a company email or newsletter, or during a meeting. Other companies identify knowledge sharing as a key expectation for all employees and even build this expectation into the employees' formal job performance reviews. Many organizations provide incentives in a combination of ways—linking KM directly to job performance, creating a work environment where sharing knowledge seems like a safe and natural thing to do, and recognizing people who contribute.

Technologies That Support KM

We are living in a period of unprecedented change where the amount of available knowledge is expanding rapidly. As a result, there is an increasing need for knowledge to be quality filtered and distributed to people in a more specific task relevant and timely manner. Technology is needed to acquire, produce, store, distribute, integrate, and manage this knowledge. Organizations interested in piloting KM should be aware of the wide range of technologies that can support KM efforts. These include communities of practice, organizational network analysis, a variety of Web 2.0 technologies, business rules management systems, and enterprise search tools. These technologies are discussed in the following sections.

Communities of Practice

community of practice (CoP): A group whose members share a common set of goals and interests and regularly engage in sharing and learning as they strive to meet those goals.

A community of practice (CoP) is a group whose members share a common set of goals and interests and regularly engage in sharing and learning as they strive to meet those goals. A community of practice develops around topics that are important to its members. Over time, a CoP typically develops resources such as models, tools, documents, processes, and terminology that represent the accumulated knowledge of the community. It is not uncommon for a CoP to include members from many different organizations. CoP has become associated with knowledge management because participation in a CoP is one means of developing new knowledge, stimulating innovation, or sharing existing tacit knowledge within an organization.

The origins and structures of CoPs vary widely. Some may start up and organize of their own accord; in other cases, there may be some sort of organizational stimulus that leads to their creation. Members of an informal CoP typically meet with little advanced planning or formality to discuss problems of interest, share ideas, and provide advice and counsel to one another. Members of a more formal CoP meet on a regularly scheduled basis with a planned agenda and identified speakers.

The General Services Administration (GSA) was established in 1949 to streamline the administrative work of the federal government.[7] The GSA's Office of Citizen Services and Innovative Technologies supports eight different communities of practice that focus on topics such as crowdsourcing, citizen science, and mobile government.[8] Recently, the agency founded an interagency CoP focused on improving the delivery of government services. The Customer Experience Community of Practice (CX-COP), which has close to 600 members from more than 140 federal, state, and local U.S. government offices and agencies, provides government customer experience professionals a hub where they can gather—both online and in person—to ask questions, share best practices, and collaborate.[9,10]

Organizational Network Analysis

organizational network analysis (ONA): A technique used for documenting and measuring flows of information among individuals, workgroups, organizations, computers, Web sites, and other information sources.

Organizational network analysis (ONA) is a technique used for documenting and measuring flows of information among individuals, workgroups, organizations, computers, Web sites, and other information sources (see Figure 10.3). Each node in the diagram represents a knowledge source; each link represents a flow of information between two nodes. Many software tools support organizational network analysis, including Cytoscape, Gephi, GraphChi, NetDraw, NetMiner, NetworkX, and UCINET.

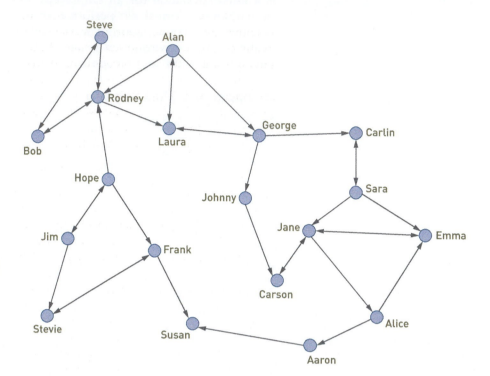

Organizational network analysis

Each node in the diagram represents a knowledge source; each link represents a flow of information between two nodes.

metadata: Data that describes other data.

In analyzing social media communications from sources such as text, video, and chat as well as "likes" and "shares," many experts agree that the most significant data isn't the content itself, but rather the metadata that connects various pieces of content to form a complete picture. **Metadata** is data that describes other data. For instance, metadata about social media use could relate to properties of the message (e.g., whether the message is comical, sarcastic, genuine, or phony) and of the author (e.g., sex, age, interests, political viewpoint, ideological beliefs, and degree of influence on the audience). The metadata enables analysts to make judgments about how to interpret and value the content of the message. Without the important metadata, it is not possible to know the value of the communications and how to take effective action.[11]

ONA has many knowledge management applications, ranging from mapping knowledge flows and identifying knowledge gaps within organizations to helping establish collaborative networks. ONA provides a clear picture of how geographically dispersed employees and organizational units collaborate (or don't collaborate). Organizations frequently employ ONA as part of a larger organizational network analysis to identify subject experts and then set up mechanisms (e.g., communities of practice) to facilitate the passing of knowledge from those experts to colleagues. Software programs that track email and other kinds of electronic communications may be used to identify in-house experts.

Westwood Professional Services, Inc., a Minnesota-based engineering and survey firm, recently conducted an organizational network analysis of one of its business units, which had been experiencing extensive change due to rapid growth. Through the analysis, the company was able to determine which employees within the business unit were connecting most frequently and the extent to which members of different subteams were collaborating.

The company used the results of the analysis to develop targeted team-building initiatives and reevaluate its organizational structures to ensure they continued to support information sharing and creative problem solving—both high priorities for the company.[12]

Web 2.0 Technologies

"Web 2.0" is a term describing changes in technology and Web site design to enhance information sharing, collaboration, and functionality on the Web. Major corporations have integrated Web 2.0 technologies such as blogs, forums, podcasts, RSS newsfeeds, and wikis to support knowledge management to improve collaboration, encourage knowledge sharing, and build a corporate memory. For example, many organizations are using Web 2.0 technologies such as podcasts and wikis to capture the knowledge of longtime employees, provide answers to cover frequently asked questions, and save time and effort in training new hires.

Business Rules Management Systems

Change is occurring all the time and at a faster and faster pace—changes in economic conditions, new government and industry rules and regulations, new competitors, product improvements, new pricing and promotion strategies, and on and on. Organizations must be able to react to these changes quickly to remain competitive. The decision logic of the operational systems that support the organization—systems such as order processing, pricing, inventory control, and customer relationship management (CRM)—must continually be modified to reflect these business changes. Decision logic, also called business rules, includes policies, requirements, and conditional statements that govern how the systems work.

The traditional method of modifying the decision logic of information systems involves heavy interaction between business users and IT analysts working together over a period of weeks, or even months, to define new systems requirements and then to design, implement, and test the new decision logic. Unfortunately, this approach to handling system changes is often too slow, and in some cases, results in incorrect system changes.

business rule management system (BRMS): Software used to define, execute, monitor, and maintain the decision logic that is used by the operational systems and processes that run the organization.

A **business rule management system (BRMS)** is software used to define, execute, monitor, and maintain the decision logic that is used by the operational systems and processes that run the organization. A BRMS enables business users to define, deploy, monitor, and maintain organizational policies and the decisions flowing from those policies—such as claim approvals, credit approvals, cross-sell offer selection, and eligibility determinations—without requiring involvement from IT resources. This process avoids a potential bottleneck and lengthy delays in implementing changes and improves the accuracy of the changes.

BRMS components include a business rule engine that determines which rules need to be executed and in what order. Other BRMS components include an enterprise rules repository for storing all rules, software to manage the various versions of rules as they are modified, and additional software for reporting and multiplatform deployment. Thus, a BRMS can become a repository of important knowledge and decision-making processes that includes the learnings and experiences of experts in the field. The creation and maintenance of a BRMS can become an important part of an organization's knowledge management program.

BRMS is increasingly used to manage the changes in decision logic in applications that support credit applications, underwriting, complex order processing, and difficult scheduling. The use of BRMS leads to faster and more accurate implementation of necessary changes to organizations' policies and procedures. Table 10.2 lists several business rule management software vendors and their products.

TABLE 10.2 Business rule management software

Software Manufacturer	Product
Appian Corporation	Business Process Management (BPM) Software Suite
Bosch Software Innovations	inubit BPM
CA Aion	Business Rules Expert
IBM	Operational Decision Manager
Open Source	Process Maker BPM
Oracle	Business Rules
Pegasystems	Pega Business Rules Platform
Progress	Corticon

HanseMerkur Krankenversicherung is a German health insurance company. The firm developed a BRMS to replace the time-consuming manual processes required to confirm insurance coverage with an automatic reconciliation of the information extracted from invoices (contract type, service submitted, insured party, billing amount, etc.). Automation of this and many of its other billing processes enabled HanseMerkur to maintain its level of service with no increase in staff even though the number of customers tripled from 366,000 to 1.2 million over the course of six years.[13]

Adobe is a digital marketing and digital media solutions provider whose products include Adobe Creative Cloud, a cloud-based subscription service; Adobe Digital Publishing Suite, which enables users to create, distribute, and optimize content for tablets; Adobe Photoshop for working with digital images; and Adobe Acrobat, which supports communication and collaboration on documents and other content both inside and outside an organization.[14] Maintaining the rules needed for effective and efficient territory assignment and sales-lead distribution was a significant challenge for Adobe given its size, number of customers, personnel turnover, and the geographic distribution of its sales force and product lines. To enable the company to react quickly to changes within its sales organization, Adobe implemented a BRMS system that includes tools that allow for the routine shifting of assignments due to personnel changes as well as more complex annual go-to-market territory changes.[15]

DBS (formerly known as the Development Bank of Singapore) is a leading financial services group in Asia and a leading consumer bank in Singapore and Hong Kong. The bank has a growing presence across Asia, and it serves more than 4 million customers, including 1 million retail customers through 250 branches.[16] Assessing the risk and creditworthiness of individuals and businesses is a critical activity for DBS. However, until recently, this was an error-prone, labor-intensive process built around the completion of a questionnaire during an interview between a relationship manager and an applicant. During the interview, applicants could provide any answer they chose as the process was not linked directly to any data. To revamp its inadequate credit reporting system, DBS implemented a BRMS that relies on verifiable customer and credit data rather than on unsubstantiated information supplied by the applicant. The BRMS supports eight different scoring models, each with hundreds of rules and hundreds of factors that go into a score. The rules are derived from a combination of regulatory sources, such as the Monetary Authority of Singapore, and statistical analysis performed by the bank's credit portfolio analytics department. DBS has greatly improved its credit model with a resulting reduction in risk. As a result, the amount of financial reserves required to cover unanticipated losses has been reduced. The BRMS also allows the bank to quickly adapt the rules and factors inherent in its credit reporting process to respond to new opportunities and changing business conditions.[17]

Enterprise Search Software

enterprise search: The application of search technology to find information within an organization.

enterprise search software: Software that matches a user's query to many sources of information in an attempt to identify the most important content and the most reliable and relevant source.

Enterprise search is the application of search technology to find information within an organization. **Enterprise search software** matches a user's query to many sources of information in an attempt to identify the most important content and the most reliable and relevant source.

Enterprise search software indexes documents from a variety of sources—such as corporate databases, departmental files, email, corporate wikis, and document repositories. When a search is executed, the software uses the index to present a list of relevance-ranked documents from these various sources. The software must be capable of implementing access controls so users are restricted to viewing only documents to which they have been granted access. Enterprise search software may also allow employees to move selected information to a new storage repository and apply controls to ensure that the files cannot be changed or deleted. Table 10.3 lists a number of enterprise search products.[18]

TABLE 10.3 Enterprise search solutions

Software Manufacturer	Software Product
Attivio	Active Intelligence Engine
BA Insight	Knowledge Integration Platform
Coveo	Enterprise Search & Relevance
Dassault Systemes	Exalead CloudView
Google	Google Search Appliance
HP	HP Autonomy
Mark Logic Corporation	Mark Logic

Members of IT and human resources organizations may use enterprise search software to enforce corporate guidelines on the storage of confidential data on laptops that leave the office, and governance officials may use it to ensure that all guidelines for the storage of information are being followed.

Founded in the 1890s as a printing press manufacturer, Harris Corporation now generates $1 billion in annual revenue through the sale of communication services and systems to clients in a wide range of industries, including avionics, defense, energy, government, health care, and transportation.[19] Harris employs more than 15,000 people across 125 countries, including 3,000 engineers in the Government Communications Systems Division (GCSD). The engineers in this division work in 12 different offices and need a more effective way to access existing information assets in a variety of repositories—all while maintaining very high levels of security. GCSD implemented a unified enterprise search platform that allows engineers to search various company databases, file shares, SharePoint sites, and the company intranet using one search engine. Access permissions are granted through the system on a "need-to-know" basis. The search engine indexes document files as well as videos, which the company uses extensively to record meetings and training sessions. The software has cut down on the time engineers spend looking for relevant information; enabled faster, incremental innovation that is built on knowledge accrued through previous projects; and increased collaboration among employees in different offices.[20]

Enterprise search software can also be used to support Web site visitor searches. It is critical that such software returns meaningful results to ensure that visitors get search results that meet their needs, thus increasing the rate at which Web site visitors convert to paying customers and are encouraged to spend more time at your site.

Electronic discovery is another important application of enterprise search software. **Electronic discovery (e-discovery)** refers to any process in which electronic data is sought, located, secured, and searched with the intent of using it as evidence in a civil or criminal legal case. The Federal Rules of Civil Procedure governs the processes and requirements of parties in federal civil suits and sets the rules regarding e-discovery. These rules compel civil litigants to both preserve and produce electronic documents and data related to a case, such as email, voice mail, texts, graphics, photographs, contents of databases, spreadsheets, Web pages, and so on. "We can't find it" is no longer an acceptable excuse for not producing information relevant to a lawsuit.

Effective e-discovery software solutions preserve and destroy data based on approved organizational policies through processes that cannot be altered by unauthorized users. To be useful, this software must also allow users to locate all of the information pertinent to a lawsuit quickly, with a minimum amount of manual effort. Furthermore, the solution must work for all data types across dissimilar data sources and systems and operate at a reasonable cost. The legal departments of many organizations are collaborating with their IT organization and technology vendors to identify and implement a solution that meets these e-discovery requirements.

A recent development in the area of e-discovery is the use of "predictive coding," which involves the use of computer algorithms rather than a full manual review to determine the relevance of electronic documents in a lawsuit. The algorithms are developed by having attorneys and other people knowledgeable about the case documents review a subset of documents; the results of that review are used to "teach" the software what to search for.[21] Ideally, predictive coding would greatly reduce the costs and time required to complete e-discovery in large-scale litigations. In practice, however, this process can be another area of contention in a lawsuit. In *Rio Tinto v. Vale, S.A. et al.*, a much-watched case in which predictive coding was used, the parties to the lawsuit spent months arguing over the protocols being used to develop the coding algorithms.[22]

electronic discovery (e-discovery): Any process in which electronic data is sought, located, secured, and searched with the intent of using it as evidence in a civil or criminal legal case.

 **Critical Thinking Exercise**

KM Experiment

You are a talent scout for a professional sports team. Over the years, the players you have recommended have had outstanding performance records for your team. Indeed, although you are only in your late thirties, you are frequently cited as one of the top talent recruiters in the league.

You have read and reread the study guide on knowledge management your general manager provided you two weeks ago. In addition to some basic definitions and discussion of KM, it includes several examples of successful applications of KM to the selection of top recruits for academic and athletic scholarships. Now you are sitting in your hotel room staring at the email from the general manager. He wants you to become the subject of a KM experiment for the team. The goal is to train the other three talent scouts for the team in your approach.

Review Questions

1. Do you think that shadowing or joint problem solving would be a more effective way to share your tacit knowledge with the other scouts? Why?
2. Would the formation of a community of practice be an effective method for sharing tacit knowledge among all the scouts? How might such a CoP operate?

Critical Thinking Questions

1. For years, you have competed against the other scouts to sign the most productive new talent. How do you feel about being asked to share your insights and expertise with the other scouts?
2. What sort of bonus or incentive could management offer to make you strongly motivated to participate in this experiment and make it a success?

Overview of Artificial Intelligence

artificial intelligence: The ability to mimic or duplicate the functions of the human brain.

At a Dartmouth College conference in 1956, John McCarthy proposed the use of the term **artificial intelligence (AI)** to describe computers with the ability to mimic or duplicate the functions of the human brain. A paper was presented at the conference proposing a study of AI based on the conjecture that "every aspect of learning or any other feature of intelligence can in principle be so precisely described that a machine can be made to simulate it."[23] Many AI pioneers attended this first conference; a few predicted that computers would be as "smart" as people by the 1960s. The prediction has not yet been realized, but many applications of artificial intelligence can be seen today, and research continues.

Watson is the first commercially available cognitive computing capability, a computer capable of processing information like a human. As such, Watson represents a new era in computing. The system, delivered through the cloud, analyzes large volumes of data, understands complex questions posed in natural language, and proposes evidence-based answers. Watson continuously learns, gaining in value and knowledge over time, from previous interactions. Watson learns in three ways: by being taught by its users, by learning from prior interactions, and by being presented with new information.[24] An early version of Watson was able to soundly defeat prior champions of the popular TV game show, *Jeopardy!* The artificial intelligence computer can process human speech, search its vast databases for possible responses, and reply in a human voice. See Figure 10.4.

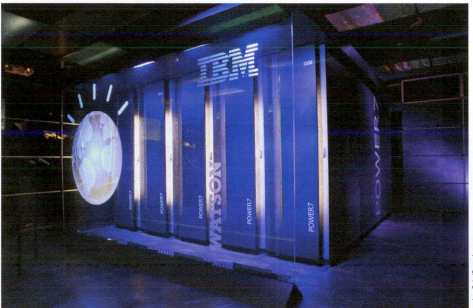

FIGURE 10.4

IBM Watson

IBM Watson is being used to develop treatment options for cancer patients based on the DNA of their disease

Carolyn Cole/Getty Images

Now a cloud-based Watson system is being used by doctors to develop treatment options for a wide range of diseases, including glioblastoma, an aggressive brain cancer that kills over 13,000 people in the United States each year. Watson will correlate data from the DNA associated with each glioblastoma patient's disease to the latest findings from medical journals, new studies, medical images, and clinical records to develop a highly personalized treatment regimen. The goal is for Watson to increase the number of patients who can benefit from care options uniquely tailored to their disease's DNA. Watson will continually learn and improve as it deals with each new patient scenario and new medical research becomes available.

Artificial Intelligence in Perspective

Computers were originally designed to perform simple mathematical operations, using fixed programmed rules and eventually operating at millions of computations per second. When it comes to performing mathematical operations quickly and accurately, computers beat humans' hands down. However, computers still have trouble recognizing patterns, adapting to new situations, and drawing conclusions when not provided complete information—all activities that humans can perform quite well. Artificial intelligence systems tackle these sorts of problems. **Artificial intelligence systems** include the people, procedures, hardware, software, data, and knowledge needed to develop computer systems and machines that can simulate human intelligence processes, including learning (the acquisition of information and rules for using the information), reasoning (using rules to reach conclusions), and self-correction (using the outcome from one scenario to improve its performance on future scenarios).

AI is a complex and interdisciplinary field that involves several specialties, including biology, computer science, linguistics, mathematics, neuroscience, philosophy, and psychology. The study of AI systems causes one to ponder philosophical issues such as the nature of the human mind and the ethics of creating objects gifted with human-like intelligence. Today, artificial intelligence systems are used in many industries and applications. Researchers, scientists, and experts on how human beings think are often involved in developing these systems.

Nature of Intelligence

From its earliest stages, the emphasis of much AI research has been on developing machines with the ability to "learn" from experiences and apply knowledge acquired from those experiences; to handle complex situations; to solve problems when important information is missing; to determine what is important and to react quickly and correctly to a new situation; to understand visual images, process and manipulate symbols, and be creative and imaginative; and to use heuristics—all of which together is considered **intelligent behavior**.

The Turing Test, designed by Alan Turing, a British mathematician, attempts to determine whether a computer can successfully impersonate a human. Human judges are connected to the computer and to another human via an instant messaging system and the only information flowing between the contestants is text. The judges pose questions on any topic from the arts to zoology, even questions about personal history and social relationships. To pass the test, the computer must communicate via this medium so competently that the judges cannot tell the difference between the computer's responses and the human's responses.[25] No computer has yet passed the Turing Test, although many computer scientists believe it may happen in the next few years.[26] The Loebner Prize is an annual competition in artificial intelligence that awards prizes to the computer system designed to simulate an intelligent conversation

artificial intelligence system: The people, procedures, hardware, software, data, and knowledge needed to develop computer systems and machines that can simulate human intelligence processes, including learning (the acquisition of information and rules for using the information), reasoning (using rules to reach conclusions), and self-correction (using the outcome from one scenario to improve its performance on future scenarios).

intelligent behavior: The ability to learn from experiences and apply knowledge acquired from those experiences; to handle complex situations; to solve problems when important information is missing; to determine what is important and to react quickly and correctly to a new situation; to understand visual images, process and manipulate symbols, and be creative and imaginative; and to use heuristics.

that is considered by the judges to be the most humanlike. Although no one has yet won the $100,000 top prize for passing the Turing Test, each year a prize of $4,000 and a bronze medal is awarded for the computer that is considered by the judges to be the most humanlike.[27]

Some of the specific characteristics of intelligent behavior include the ability to do the following:

- **Learn from experience and apply the knowledge acquired from experience**. Learning from past situations and events is a key component of intelligent behavior and is a natural ability of humans, who learn by trial and error. This ability, however, must be carefully programmed into a computer system. Today, researchers are developing systems that can "learn" from experience. The 20 Questions (20Q) Web site, *www.20q.net* (see Figure 10.5), is an example of a system that learns.[28] The Web site is an artificial intelligence game that learns as people play.

FIGURE 10.5

The 20Q Web site

20Q is a game where users play the popular game, 20 Questions, against an artificial intelligence foe.

Source: *www.20q.net*

- **Handle complex situations**. In a business setting, top-level managers and executives must handle a complex market, challenging competitors, intricate government regulations, and a demanding workforce. Even human experts make mistakes in dealing with these matters. Very careful planning and elaborate computer programming are necessary to develop systems that can handle complex situations.
- **Solve problems when important information is missing**. An integral part of decision making is dealing with uncertainty. Often, decisions must be made with little or inaccurate information because obtaining complete information is too costly or impossible. Today, AI systems can make important calculations, comparisons, and decisions even when information is missing.
- **Determine what is important**. Knowing what is truly important is the mark of a good decision maker. Developing programs and approaches to allow computer systems and machines to identify important information is not a simple task.
- **React quickly and correctly to a new situation**. A small child, for example, can look over an edge and know not to venture too close. The child reacts quickly and correctly to a new situation. On the other hand, without complex programming, computers do not have this ability.

- **Understand visual images**. Interpreting visual images can be extremely difficult, even for sophisticated computers. Moving through a room of chairs, tables, and other objects can be trivial for people but extremely complex for machines, robots, and computers. Such machines require an extension of understanding visual images, called a **perceptive system**. Having a perceptive system allows a machine to approximate the way a person sees, hears, and feels objects.

- **Process and manipulate symbols**. People see, manipulate, and process symbols every day. Visual images provide a constant stream of information to our brains. By contrast, computers have difficulty handling symbolic processing and reasoning. Although computers excel at numerical calculations, they aren't as good at dealing with symbols and three-dimensional objects. Recent developments in machine-vision hardware and software, however, allow some computers to process and manipulate certain symbols.

- **Be creative and imaginative**. Throughout history, some people have turned difficult situations into advantages by being creative and imaginative. For instance, when defective mints with holes in the middle arrived at a candy factory, an enterprising entrepreneur decided to market these new mints as LifeSavers instead of returning them to the manufacturer. Ice cream cones were invented at the St. Louis World's Fair when an imaginative store owner decided to wrap ice cream with a waffle from his grill for portability. Developing new products and services from an existing (perhaps negative) situation is a human characteristic. While software has been developed to enable a computer to write short stories, few computers can be imaginative or creative in this way.

- **Use heuristics**. For some decisions, people use heuristics (rules of thumb arising from experience) or even guesses. Some computer systems obtain good solutions to complex problems (e.g., scheduling the flight crews for a large airline) based on heuristics rather than trying to search for an optimal solution, which might be technically difficult or too time consuming.

perceptive system: A system that approximates the way a person sees, hears, and feels objects.

Brain-Computer Interface

Developing a link between the human brain and the computer is another exciting aspect of artificial intelligence research. The idea behind a brain-computer interface (BCI) is to directly connect the human brain to a computer so that human thought can control the activities of the computer. One potential use of BCI technology would be to give people without the ability to speak or move (a condition called locked-in syndrome) the capability to communicate, control a computer, and move artificial limbs. Honda Motors has developed a BCI system that allows a person to complete certain operations, such as bending a leg, with 90 percent accuracy. See Figure 10.6. The new system uses a special helmet that can measure and transmit brain activity to a computer.

AI is a broad field that includes several specialty areas, such as expert systems, robotics, vision systems, natural language processing, learning systems, and neural networks. See Figure 10.7. Many of these areas are related; advances in one can occur simultaneously with or result in advances in others.

Expert Systems

An **expert system** consists of hardware and software that stores knowledge and makes inferences, enabling a novice to perform at the level of an expert. Like human experts, computerized expert systems use heuristics, or rules of thumb, to arrive at conclusions or make suggestions. Since expert systems can be difficult, expensive, and time consuming to develop, they should be developed when there is a high potential payoff or when they have the potential to significantly reduce downside risk and the organization wants to capture and preserve irreplaceable human expertise.

expert system: A system that consists of hardware and software that stores knowledge and makes inferences, enabling a novice to perform at the level of an expert.

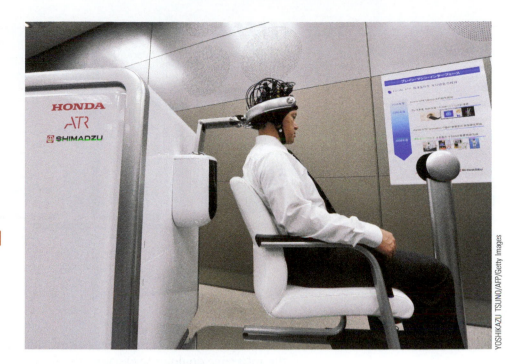

FIGURE **10.6**

Brain-machine interface

Honda Motors has developed a
brain-machine interface that measures electrical current and blood
flow change in the brain and uses
the data to control ASIMO, the
Honda robot.

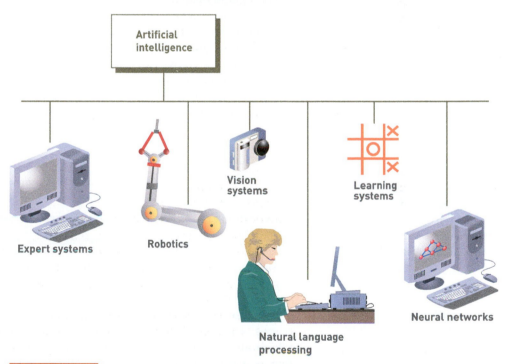

FIGURE **10.7**

Conceptual model of artificial intelligence

AI is a broad field that includes several specialty areas.

Components of Expert Systems

An expert system is made up of a collection of integrated and related components, including a knowledge base, an inference engine, an explanation facility, a knowledge base acquisition facility, and a user interface. A diagram of a
typical expert system is shown in Figure 10.8.

As shown in the figure, the user interacts with the user interface, which
interacts with the inference engine. The inference engine interacts with the

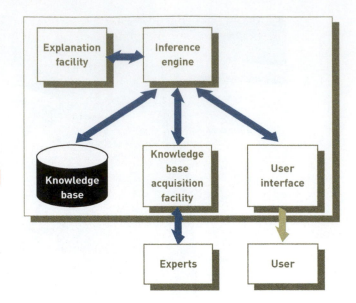

FIGURE **10.8**

Components of an expert system

An expert system includes a knowledge base, an inference engine, an explanation facility, a knowledge base acquisition facility, and a user interface.

other expert system components to provide expertise. This figure also shows the inference engine coordinating the flow of knowledge to other components of the expert system.

Knowledge Base   The knowledge base stores all relevant information, data, rules, cases, and relationships that the expert system uses. As shown in Figure 10.9, a knowledge base is a natural extension of a database and an information and decision support system. A knowledge base must be developed for each unique expert system supplication. Rules and cases are frequently used to create a knowledge base.

FIGURE **10.9**

Relationships between data, information, and knowledge

A knowledge base stores all relevant information, data, rules, cases, and relationships that an expert system uses.

| Database raw facts | → | Information and decision support information | → | Knowledge base patterns and relationships |

Increasing understanding

rule: A conditional statement that links conditions to actions or outcomes.

IF-THEN statement: A rule that suggests certain conclusions.

A **rule** is a conditional statement that links conditions to actions or outcomes. In many instances, these rules are stored as **IF-THEN statements**, which are rules that suggest certain conclusions. The FICO Blaze Advisor system is a rules-based platform that allows business users to develop and test rule-based decision applications used by clients for benefits eligibility determination, insurance underwriting, regulatory compliance monitoring, and personal and commercial lending—among other uses.[29]

A case-based system can also be used to develop a solution to a current problem or situation. In such a system, each case typically contains a description of the problem, plus a solution and/or the outcome. The case-based solution process involves (1) finding cases stored in the knowledge base that are similar to the problem or situation at hand, (2) reusing the case in an attempt to solve the problem at hand, (3) revising the proposed solution if necessary, and (4) retaining the new solution as part of a new case. A washing machine repairman who fixes a washer recalling another washer that presented similar symptoms is using case-based reasoning, so is the lawyer who advocates a particular outcome in a trial based on legal precedents.

inference engine: Part of the expert system that seeks information and relationships from the knowledge base and provides answers, predictions, and suggestions similar to the way a human expert would.

Inference Engine The main purpose of an **inference engine** is to seek information and relationships from the knowledge base and to provide answers, predictions, and suggestions similar to the way a human expert would. In other words, the inference engine is the component that delivers the expert advice. Consider the expert system that forecasts future sales for a product. One approach is to start with a fact such as "The demand for the product last month was 20,000 units." The expert system searches for rules that contain a reference to product demand. For example, "IF product demand is over 15,000 units, THEN check the demand for competing products." As a result of this process, the expert system might use information on the demand for competitive products. Next, after searching additional rules, the expert system might use information on personal income or national inflation rates. This process continues until the expert system can reach a conclusion using the data supplied by the user and the rules that apply in the knowledge base.

explanation facility: Component of an expert system that allows a user or decision maker to understand how the expert system arrived at certain conclusions or results.

Explanation Facility An important part of an expert system is the **explanation facility**, which allows a user or decision maker to understand how the expert system arrived at certain conclusions or results. A medical expert system, for example, might reach the conclusion that a patient has a defective heart valve given certain symptoms and the results of tests on the patient. The explanation facility allows a doctor to find out the logic or rationale of the diagnosis made by the expert system. The expert system, using the explanation facility, can indicate all the facts and rules that were used in reaching the conclusion, which the doctors can look at to determine whether the expert system is processing the data and information correctly and logically.

Knowledge Acquisition Facility A challenging aspect of developing a useful expert system is the creation and updating of the knowledge base. In the past, when more traditional programming languages were used, developing a knowledge base was tedious and time consuming. Each fact, relationship, and rule had to be programmed—usually by an experienced programmer.

knowledge acquisition facility: Part of the expert system that provides a convenient and efficient means of capturing and storing all the components of the knowledge base.

Today, specialized software allows users and decision makers to create and modify their own knowledge bases through the knowledge acquisition facility, using user-friendly menus. The purpose of the **knowledge acquisition facility** is to provide a convenient and efficient means of capturing and storing all components of the knowledge base. The knowledge acquisition facility acts as an interface between experts and the knowledge base.

User Interface The main purpose of the user interface is to make an expert system easier for users and decision makers to develop and use. At one time, skilled computer personnel created and operated most expert systems; today, simplified user interfaces permit decision makers to develop and use their own expert systems.

Participants in Developing and Using Expert Systems

knowledge user: The person or group who uses and benefits from the expert system.

knowledge engineer: A person who has training or experience in the design, development, implementation, and maintenance of an expert system.

knowledge user: The person or group who uses and benefits from the expert system.

Typically, several people are involved in developing and using an expert system. The **domain expert** is the person or group with the expertise or knowledge the expert system is trying to capture (domain). In most cases, the domain expert is a group of human experts. A **knowledge engineer** is a person who has training or experience in the design, development, implementation, and maintenance of an expert system, including training or experience with expert system shells. Knowledge engineers can help transfer the knowledge from the expert system to the knowledge user. The **knowledge user** is the person or group who uses and benefits from the expert system. Knowledge users do not need any previous training in computers or expert systems.

Expert System Shells and Products

An expert system shell is a suite of software that allows construction of a knowledge base and interaction with this knowledge base through the use of an inference engine. Expert system shells are available for both personal computers and mainframe systems, with some shells being inexpensive, costing less than $500. In addition, off-the-shelf expert system shells are complete and ready to run. The user enters the appropriate data or parameters, and the expert system provides output to the problem or situation.

Robotics

robotics: A branch of engineering that involves the development and manufacture of mechanical or computer devices that can perform tasks requiring a high degree of precision or that are tedious or hazardous for humans.

Robotics is a branch of engineering that involves development and manufacture of mechanical or computer devices that can perform tasks that require a high degree of precision or are tedious or hazardous for human beings, such as painting cars or making make precision welds. Karel Capek introduced the word "robot" in his 1921 play, *R.U.R.* (an abbreviation of Rostrum's Universal Robots). The play was about an island factory that produced artificial people called "robots" who are consigned to do drudgery work and eventually rebel and overthrow their creators, causing the extinction of human beings.[30] Organizations today do indeed use robots to perform dull, dirty, and/or dangerous jobs. They are often used to lift and move heavy pallets in warehouses, perform welding operations, and provide a way to view radioactively contaminated areas of power plants inaccessible by people.

However, the use of robots has expanded and is likely to continue to grow. Robots are increasingly being used in surgical procedures ranging from prostrate removal to open-heart surgery. See Figure 10.10. Robots can provide doctors with enhanced precision, improved dexterity, and better visualization. In 2014, the U.S. Navy's Bluefin 21 robotic submarine made several trips below the Indian Ocean's surface to scan the seabed for any trace of the missing Malaysia Airlines Flight 370. iRobot (*www.irobot.com*) is a company that builds a variety of robots, including the Roomba for vacuuming floors, the

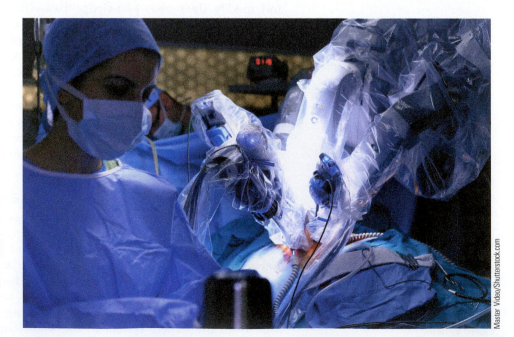

FIGURE 10.10
Robotic surgery
The arms of the Da Vinci robot assist in a kidney transplant. A surgeon controls the robot remotely from a corner of the operating room.

Looj for cleaning gutters, and the PackBot, an unmanned vehicle used to assist and protect soldiers.[31]

Some robots, such as the ER series by Intelitek, can be used for training or entertainment.[32] Wonder Workshop created robots Dash and Dot to help young children (ages 5+) to learn programming concepts and creative problem solving.[33]

Some people fear that robots will increasingly take jobs from human employees. For example, the use of autonomous vehicles may place millions of truck drivers, chauffeurs, and cab drivers out of work. Some experts have predicted that every home will have a robot of some sort by 2025. One area of particular interest is the use of robots as companions and caregivers for people who are sick, elderly, or physically challenged.[34,35]

Vision Systems

vision system: The hardware and software that permit computers to capture, store, and manipulate visual images.

Another area of AI involves **vision systems**, which include hardware and software that permit computers to capture, store, and process visual images. 3D machine-vision systems are used to increase the accuracy and speed of industrial inspections of parts. Automated fruit-picking machines use a unique vacuum gripper combined with a vision system to pick fruit. Facebook is developing an AI vision system called DeepFace, which creates 3D models of the faces in photos. The technology represents a vast improvement over current facial recognition software. DeepFace can correctly tell if two photos show the same person with 97.25 percent accuracy. This nearly matches humans, who are correct 97.53 percent of the time. The technology, which uses more than 120 million parameters, can also recognize people whose faces are not showing with 83 percent accuracy, using features such as body shape, posture, hairstyle, and clothing. [36,37]

Natural Language Processing

natural language processing: An aspect of artificial intelligence that involves technology that allows computers to understand, analyze, manipulate, and/or generate "natural" languages, such as English.

Natural language processing is an aspect of artificial intelligence that involves technology that allows computers to understand, analyze, manipulate, and/or generate "natural" languages, such as English. Many companies provide natural language processing help over the phone. When you call a help phone number, you are typically given a menu of options and asked to speak your responses. Many people, however, become easily frustrated talking to a machine instead of a human. The Naturally Speaking application from Dragon Systems uses continuous voice recognition, or natural speech, that allows the user to speak to the computer at a normal pace without pausing between words. The spoken words are transcribed immediately onto the computer screen. See Figure 10.11.

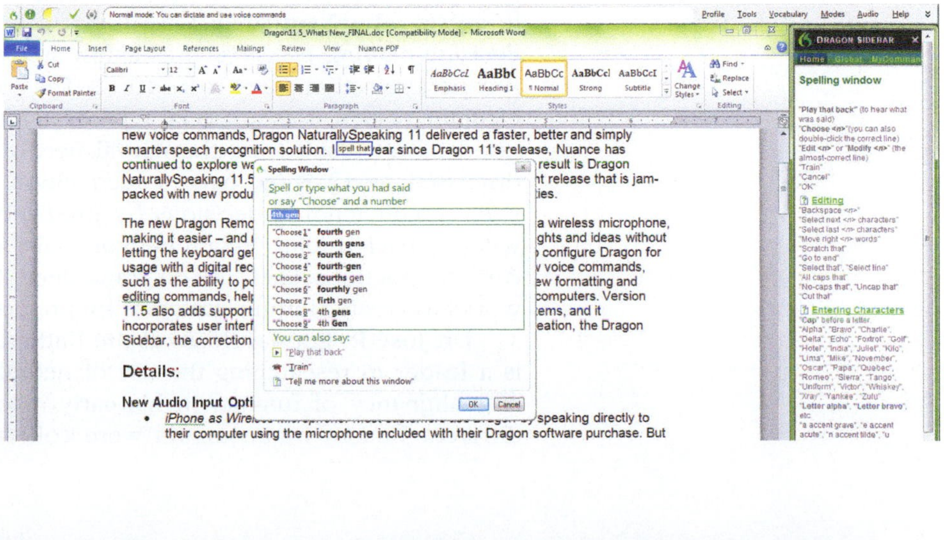

FIGURE 10.11

Voice recognition software

With the NaturallySpeaking application from Dragon Systems, computer users can speak and have their words transcribed into text for input to software such as Microsoft Word.

Source: Nuance Communications.

After converting sounds into words, natural language-processing systems react to the words or commands by performing a variety of tasks. Brokerage services are a perfect fit for voice recognition and natural language-processing technology to replace the existing "press 1 to buy or sell a stock" touchpad telephone menu system. Using voice recognition to convert recordings into text is also possible. Some companies claim that voice recognition and natural language-processing software is so good that customers forget they are talking to a computer and start discussing the weather or sports scores.

Learning Systems

learning system: A combination of software and hardware that allows a computer to change how it functions or how it reacts to situations based on feedback it receives.

Another aspect of AI deals with learning systems, a combination of software and hardware that allows a computer to change how it functions or how it reacts to situations based on feedback it receives. For example, some computerized games have learning abilities. If the computer does not win a game, it remembers not to make the same moves under the same conditions again. Some learning systems utilize reinforcement learning, which involves the use of sequential decisions—with learning taking place between each decision. Reinforcement learning often involves sophisticated computer programming and optimization techniques. The computer makes a decision, analyzes the results, and then makes a better decision based on the analysis. The process, often called dynamic programming, is repeated until it is impossible to make improvements in the decision.

Learning systems software requires feedback on the results of actions or decisions. At a minimum, the feedback needs to indicate whether the results are desirable (winning a game) or undesirable (losing a game). The feedback is then used to alter what the system will do in the future.

After Google combined natural language processing with learning systems in its Android smartphone operating system, it reduced word-recognition errors by 25 percent.[38] With this new technology, the voice assistant is also able to ask questions to clarify what a user is searching for.

Neural Networks

neural network: A computer system that can recognize and act on patterns or trends that it detects in large sets of data.

An increasingly important aspect of AI involves neural networks, also called neural nets. A neural network is a computer system that can recognize and act on patterns or trends that it detects in large sets of data. A neural network employs massively parallel processors in an architecture that is based on the human brain's own meshlike structure. As a result, neural networks can process many pieces of data at the same time and learn to recognize patterns.

AI Trilogy, available from the Ward Systems Group (*www.wardsystems.com*), is a neural network software program that can run on a standard PC. The software package's NeuroShell Predictor component can be used to make predictions, such as agricultural production estimates and call volume forecasts. The NeuroShell Classifier can be used to aid in classification and decision-making tasks, such as alarm system malfunction diagnosis and sales prospect selection. See Figure 10.12. The software package also contains GeneHunter, which uses a special type of algorithm called a genetic algorithm to get the best result from the neural network system. (Genetic algorithms are discussed next.) Some pattern recognition software uses neural networks to make credit lending decisions by predicting the likelihood a new borrower will pay back a loan. Neural networks are also used to identify bank or credit card transactions likely to be fraudulent. Large call centers use neural networks to create staffing strategies by predicting call volumes.

Dr. José R. Iglesias-Rozas at the Katharinenhospital in Stuttgart, Germany, is a leader in researching the use of neural networks to diagnose the degree of malignancy of tumors. In his early research, microscopic sections of 786 different human brain tumors were collected. A neural network tool called

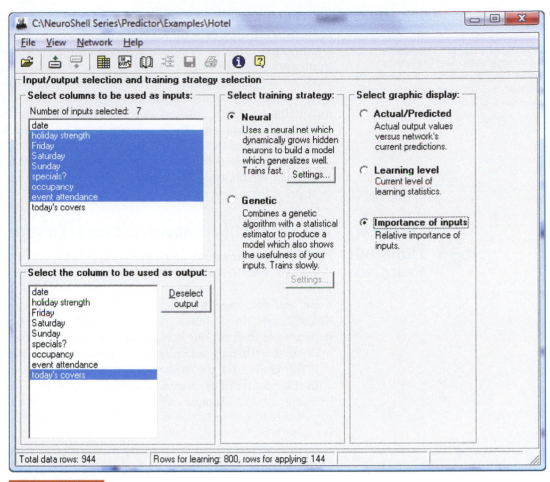

FIGURE 10.12
Neural network software
NeuroShell Predictor uses recognized forecasting methods to look for future trends in data.
Source: Ward Systems Group, Inc.

NeuralTools was then used to predict the degree of malignancy based on the presence of 10 histological characteristics. The neural network accurately predicted over 95 percent of the sample cases. Dr. Iglesias-Rozas plans to expand his research to analyze over 30 years of data from more than 8,000 patients with brain tumors.[39]

Other Artificial Intelligence Applications

genetic algorithm: An approach to solving problems based on the theory of evolution; uses the concept of survival of the fittest as a problem-solving strategy.

Other artificial intelligence applications include **genetic algorithms**, which solve problems based on the theory of evolution—using the concept of survival of the fittest as a problem-solving strategy. The genetic algorithm uses a fitness function that quantitatively evaluates a set of initial candidate solutions. The highest-scoring candidate solutions are allowed to "reproduce," with random changes introduced to create new candidate solutions. These digital offspring are subjected to a second round of fitness evaluation. Again, the most promising candidate solutions are selected and used to create a new generation with random changes. The process repeats for hundreds or even thousands of rounds. The expectation is that the average fitness of the population will increase each round and that eventually very good solutions to the problem will be discovered.

Genetic algorithms have been used to solve large, complex scheduling problems, such as scheduling airline crews to meet flight requirements while minimizing total costs and staying within federal guidelines on maximum crew flight hours and required hours of rest. Genetic algorithms have also

intelligent agent: Programs and a knowledge base used to perform a specific task for a person, a process, or another program; also called an intelligent robot or bot.

been used to design mirrors that funnel sunlight to a solar collection and radio antenna that pick up signals from space.

Another artificial intelligence application, **intelligent agent** (also called an intelligent robot or bot), consists of programs and a knowledge base used to perform a specific task for a person, a process, or another program. Like a sports agent who searches for the best endorsement deals for a top athlete, an intelligent agent is often used to search for the best price, schedule, or solution to a problem. The programs used by an intelligent agent can search large amounts of data as the knowledge base refines the search or accommodates user preferences. Often used to search the vast resources of the Internet, intelligent agents can help people find information on any topic, such as the best price for a new camera or used car.

 **Critical Thinking Exercise**

IBM Watson Offers Advice to Cancer Patients

IBM and the American Cancer Society (ACS) are working in partnership to develop a Watson-based advisor to support cancer patients. They will create this robust resource by drawing upon massive sources of data from both organizations, and then train Watson to use the data to understand and anticipate individuals' needs. In addition, the advisor will learn about the patient and that patient's planned treatment regimen, allowing it to offer personalized advice that matches the patient's individual characteristics, preferences, and treatment plan.[40]

The goal is for the Watson-based advisor to anticipate the needs of people with different types of cancers, at different stages of disease, and at various points in treatment. For example, a person with lung cancer experiencing unusual levels of pain could ask what might be causing pain. The advisor would be designed to respond with information on symptoms and self-management options associated with that persons' current and future phases of treatment, based on the experiences of people with similar characteristics.

Review Questions

1. How might visual systems and natural language processing be incorporated into the Watson cancer adviser system?
2. What other major branches of artificial intelligence are employed in the Watson cancer patient adviser?

Critical Thinking Questions

1. One of the challenges of a cognitive computing capability such as the Watson cancer adviser is keeping the information that Watson draws on as current as possible. Over time, new approaches, courses of treatment, medicines, and ideas will be discovered that are improvement over the old way of doing things. How might the Watson cancer adviser be kept as current as possible?
2. Cancer patients frequently suffer from depression. Do you think it is possible for Watson to recognize symptoms of depression and provide encouragement and advice to the patient? How might this be accomplished?

Multimedia and Virtual Reality

The use of multimedia and virtual reality has helped many companies achieve a competitive advantage and increase profits. The approach and technology used in multimedia is often the foundation of virtual reality systems, discussed later in this section. While these specialized information systems are not used by all organizations, they can play a key role for many. We begin with a discussion of multimedia.

Overview of Multimedia

Multimedia is content that uses more than one form of communication—such as text, graphics, video, animation, audio, and other media. Multimedia tools can be used to help an organization achieve its goals through the production of compelling brochures, presentations, reports, and documents. Many companies use multimedia approaches to develop animations and video games to help advertise products and services. For example, insurance company Geico uses an animated gecko in some of its TV ads. Animation software, such as Blender, GoAnimate, and Powtoon, offer tools for individuals and businesses looking to develop these types of animations. Although not all organizations use the full capabilities of multimedia, most use text and graphics capabilities.

Text and Graphics

Most organizations use text and graphics to develop reports, financial statements, advertising pieces, and other documents for internal and external use. Internally, organizations use text and graphics to communicate policies, guidelines, procedures, and much more to employees. Externally, they use text and graphics to communicate to suppliers, customers, federal and state governmental agencies, and a variety of other stakeholders. Different sizes, fonts, and colors can be used to create different effects with text. Graphics such as photographs, illustrations, drawings, a variety of charts, and other still images can be used to create interest and illustrate a message. Some popular digital image formats include EPS (Encapsulated PostScript), GIF (Graphic Interchange Format), JPEG (Joint Photographic Experts Group format), PNG (Portable Network Graphics), TIFF (Tagged Image File Format), and Raw image files.

While standard word-processing programs are an inexpensive and simple way to develop documents and reports that require text and graphics, most organizations use specialized software. Adobe Illustrator, for example, can be used to create typography and vector graphics, such as illustrations and logos. Other graphics programs include CorelDraw by Corel Corporation and Serif DrawPlus. Software products such as Adobe InDesign can be used for page design, layout, and publishing of digital and print manuals, brochures, and reports. Adobe Photoshop is a sophisticated and popular software package that can be used to edit photographs and other visual images. Once created, these documents and reports can be saved in an Adobe PDF file, which can be used for printing or for digital delivery. Other photo-editing software includes Apple's iPhoto, Corel PaintShop Pro, and Pixelmator—among many others.

Microsoft PowerPoint can be used to develop presentations with sound and animation that can be displayed on a large viewing screen. Prezi and Swipe are both Web-based presentation software alternatives to PowerPoint.

Many graphics programs can also create 3D images. Once used primarily in movies, 3D technology can be employed by companies to design products, such as motorcycles, jet engines, and bridges. Autodesk, for example, makes exciting 3D software that companies can use to design everything from flat fruit-packing machines for Sunkist to large skyscrapers and other buildings for architectural firms.[41] The technology used to produce 3D movies is also available with some TV programs. Nintendo developed the Nintendo 3DS, one of the first portable gaming devices that displays images in 3D.

Audio

Audio, which includes music, human voices, recorded sounds, and a variety of computer-generated sounds, can be stored in a variety of file formats, including AAC (Advanced Audio Coding), AIFF (Audio Interchange File Format), ALAC (Apple Lossless Audio Codec), FLAC (Free Lossless Audio Codec), MIDI (Musical Instrument Digital Interface), MP3 (Motion Picture Experts

Group Audio Layer 3), and WAV (wave format). The term "streaming audio" refers to audio files that are played while they are being downloaded from the Internet.

Input to audio software includes audio recording devices, microphones, imported music or sound from CDs or audio files, MIDI instruments that can create music and sounds directly, and other audio sources. Once stored, audio files can be edited and augmented using audio software, such as Apple Quick-Time, Microsoft Sound Recorder, Adobe Audition, and SourceForge Audacity. See Figure 10.13. Once edited, audio files can also be used to enhance presentations, create music, broadcast satellite radio signals, develop audio books, record podcasts, add realism to movies, and enrich video and animation.

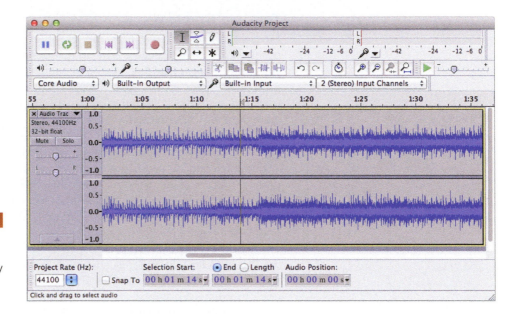

Audio-editing software
Audacity provides tools for editing and producing audio files in a variety of formats.
Source: Audacity.

Video and Animation

The moving images of video and animation are typically created by rapidly displaying one still image after another. Video and animation can be stored in a variety of file formats, including AVI (Audio Video Interleave), FLV/FV4 (Flash Video), MOV (QuickTime format) files, MPEG (Motion Picture Experts Group format), QTFF (QuickTime File Format), and WMV (Windows Media Video). When video files are played while they are being downloaded from the Internet, it's called streaming video. For example, Amazon Prime, Hulu, and Netflix are just three of the many sites through which users can stream movies and TV programs. On the Internet, Java applets (small downloadable programs) and animated GIF files can be used to animate or create "moving" images.

A number of video and animation software products can be used to create and edit video and animation files. Many video and animation programs can create realistic 3D moving images. James Cameron's movie *Avatar* used sophisticated computers and 3D imaging to create one of the most profitable movies in history. Adobe's Premiere and After Effects and Apple's Final Cut Pro can be used to edit video images taken from cameras and other sources. Final Cut Pro, for example, has been used to edit and produce full-length motion pictures shown in movie theaters. Adobe Flash and LiveMotion can be used to add motion and animation to Web pages.

Video and animation have many business uses. Companies that develop computer-based or Internet training materials often use video and audio software. An information kiosk at an airport or shopping mall can use animation to help customers check in for a flight or get information.

Visual effects involve the integration of live-action footage and generated imagery to create settings that look completely lifelike, but would be dangerous or extremely expensive to capture on film. RenderMan is Pixar's technical specification for a standard communications interface between 3D computer graphics programs and rendering programs. (Rendering is the final step in the animation process and provides the final appearance to the animation with visual effects such as shading, texture mapping, shadows, reflections, and motion blurs.) RenderMan software is used widely to create outstanding graphics for feature films and broadcast television. Indeed, it was used on every Visual Effects Academy Award Winner for 15 straight years.[42]

File Conversion and Compression

Most multimedia applications are created, edited, and distributed in a digital file format, such as the ones discussed earlier. Older inputs to these applications, however, can be in an analog format—from old home movies, magnetic tapes, vinyl records, or similar sources. In addition, some older digital formats are no longer popular or used. In order to edit and process analog and older digital formats using current multimedia software, the content must be converted into a newer digital format. Files can be converted using software or specialized hardware. Some of the multimedia software, such as Adobe Premiere, Adobe Audition, and others, have this analog-to-digital conversion capability. Standalone software and specialized hardware can also be used. Grass Valley, for example, is a hardware device that can be used to convert analog video to digital video or digital video to analog video. With this device, you can convert old VHS tapes to digital video files or digital video files to an analog format.

Because multimedia files can be large, it's sometimes necessary to compress files to make them easier to download from the Internet or send as email attachments. Many of the multimedia software programs discussed earlier can be used to compress multimedia files. In addition, standalone file conversion programs, such as PNGGauntlet, ScriptPNG, WinZip, and Wondershare Video Converter Ultimate, can be used to compress many file formats.

Designing a Multimedia Application

Designing multimedia applications requires careful thought and a systematic approach. Multimedia applications can be printed in brochures, placed into corporate reports, uploaded to the Internet, or displayed on large screens for viewing. Because these applications are typically more expensive than preparing documents and files in a word-processing program, it is important to spend time designing the best possible multimedia application. Designing a multimedia application requires that the end use of the document or file be carefully considered. For example, some text styles and fonts are designed for Internet display. Because different computers and Web browsers display information differently, it is a good idea to select styles, fonts, and presentations based on computers and browsers that are likely to display the multimedia application. Because large files can take much longer to load into a Web page, smaller files are usually preferred for Web-based multimedia applications.

Overview of Virtual Reality

The term "virtual reality" was initially coined in 1989 by Jaron Lanier, founder of VPL Research. Originally, the term referred to immersive virtual reality in which the user becomes fully immersed in an artificial, 3D world that is completely generated by a computer. Through immersion, the user can gain a deeper understanding of the virtual world's behavior and functionality.

A **virtual reality system** enables one or more users to move and react in a computer-simulated environment. Virtual reality simulations require special interface devices that transmit the sights, sounds, and sensations of the

virtual reality system: A system that enables one or more users to move and react in a computer-simulated environment.

simulated world to the user. These devices can also record and send the speech and movements of the participants to the simulation program, enabling users to sense and manipulate virtual objects much as they would real objects. This natural style of interaction gives the participants the feeling that they are immersed in the simulated world. For example, an auto manufacturer can use virtual reality to simulate and design automobiles and production lines in factories.

In justifying Facebook's $2 billion acquisition of virtual reality company Oculus VR, Mark Zuckerberg said that "while mobile is the key platform for today, virtual reality will be one of the major platforms for tomorrow. Imagine enjoying a courtside seat at a game, studying in a classroom of students and teachers all over the world or consulting with a doctor face-to-face, just by putting on goggles in your home."[43] In late 2015, Oculus VR released one of the first social virtual reality applications—an app that allows users of the Samsung Gear VR headset to go to a virtual movie theater (in the form of a selected avatar), watch a movie, and chat with other people who are also in the theater.[44]

Interface Devices

To see in a virtual world, the user often wears a head-mounted display (HMD) with screens directed at each eye. The HMD also contains a position tracker to monitor the location of the user's head and the direction in which the user is looking. Employing this information, a computer generates images of the virtual world—a slightly different view for each eye—to match the direction in which the user is looking and displays these images on the HMD. In addition to Oculus VR (Oculus Rift) and Samsung (Gear VR), other big players in the emerging virtual reality interface industry include Google (Cardboard), HTC (Vive), Microsoft (Hololens), and Sony (PlayStation VR).

The Electronic Visualization Laboratory (EVL) at the University of Illinois at Chicago introduced a room constructed of large screens on three walls and a floor on which the graphics are projected. The CAVE (Cave Automatic Virtual Environment), as the room is called, provides the illusion of immersion by projecting stereo images on the walls and floor of a room-sized cube (*www.evl.uic.edu*). Several people wearing lightweight stereo glasses can enter and walk freely inside the CAVE. A head-tracking system continuously adjusts the stereo projection to the current position of the leading viewer. The most recent version of the CAVE is called CAVE2 and features realistic high-resolution graphics that respond to user interactions. See Figure 10.14.

FIGURE **10.14**

Large-scale virtual reality environment

The CAVE2 virtual reality system has 72 stereoscopic LCD panels encircling the viewer 320 degrees and creates a 3D environment that can simulate the bridge of the Starship U.S.S. Enterprise, a flyover of the planet Mars, or a journey through the blood vessels of the brain.

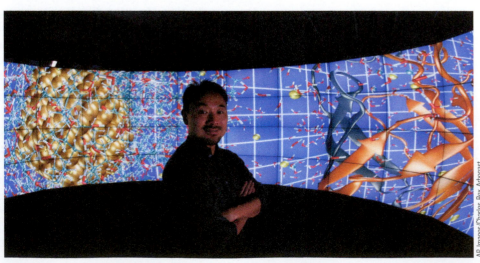

In a virtual world, users hear sounds through earphones, and information reported by the position tracker is used to update audio signals. When a sound source in virtual space is not directly in front of or behind the user, the computer transmits sounds to arrive at one ear a little earlier or later than at the other and to be a little louder or softer and slightly different in pitch.

The haptic interface, which relays the sense of touch and other physical sensations in the virtual world, is the least developed and perhaps the most challenging virtual reality component to create. One virtual reality company has developed a haptic interface device that can be placed on a person's fingertips to give an accurate feel for game players, surgeons, and others. With the use of a glove and position tracker, the computer locates the user's hand and measures finger movements. The user can reach into the virtual world and handle objects; still, it is difficult to generate the sensations of a person tapping a hard surface, picking up an object, or running a finger across a textured surface. Touch sensations also have to be synchronized with the sights and sounds users experience. Today, some virtual reality developers are even trying to incorporate taste and smell into virtual reality applications.

Forms of Virtual Reality

Aside from immersive virtual reality, virtual reality can also refer to applications that are not fully immersive, such as mouse-controlled navigation through a 3D environment on a graphics monitor, stereo viewing from the monitor via stereo glasses, and stereo projection systems. Augmented reality, a newer form of virtual reality, has the ability to superimpose digital data over real photos or images. Augmented reality is being used in a variety of settings. Some luxury car manufacturers, for example, display dashboard information, such as speed and remaining fuel, on windshields. The technology is also used in some military aircraft and is often called heads-up display. The use of lines (typically yellow and blue) that are superimposed onto a football field during broadcasted games to indicate the first down marker and the line of scrimmage is another example of augmented reality. GPS maps can be combined with real pictures of stores and streets to help you locate your position or find your way to a new destination. Using augmented reality, you could point a smartphone camera at a historic landmark, such as a castle, museum, or other building, and have information about the landmark appear on your screen, including a brief description of the landmark, admission price, and hours of operation. Although still in its early phases of implementation, augmented reality has the potential to become an important feature of tomorrow's smartphones and similar mobile devices.

Virtual Reality Applications

Thousands of applications of virtual reality are available, with more being developed as the cost of hardware and software declines and as people's imaginations are opened to the potential of virtual reality. Virtual reality applications are being used in medicine, education and training, business, and entertainment, among other fields.

Medicine

Virtual reality has been successful in treating children with autism by helping them pick up on social cues, refine their motor skills, and acquire real-life skills, such as looking both ways before crossing the street. Some children with autism interact well with technology because of its predictability, controllability, and incredible patience. Virtual reality has also been used to help train medical students with simulations for many forms of surgery from brain surgery to delivery of a baby.[45]

Education and Training

Virtual environments are used in education to bring new resources into the classroom. Thousands of administrators, faculty, researchers, staff, and students are members of the Immersive Education Initiative (IEI), a nonprofit international partnership of colleges, companies, research institutes, and universities working together to define and develop open standards, best practices, platforms, and communities of support for virtual reality and game-based learning and training systems. The IEI sponsors immersive education summits as well as clubs and camps for children, college students, and corporate professionals.

Google's Expeditions Pioneer Program is a pilot immersive education initiative that brings virtual reality kits into the classroom so that students can take part in expeditions that help them learn about locations around world. Using cheap cardboard headsets, Android phones, and a teacher-operated tablet, Google Expeditions lets students experience 360-degree views of outer space, the White House, caves in Slovakia, Buckingham Palace, Antarctica, the Amazon rainforest, the Great Barrier Reef, and 100 other locations.[46,47]

Virtual technology is also being used to train members of the military. To help with aircraft maintenance, a virtual reality system has been developed to simulate an aircraft and give a user a sense of touch, while computer graphics provide a sense of sight and sound. The user sees, touches, and manipulates the various parts of the virtual aircraft during training. Also, the Pentagon is using a virtual reality training lab to prepare for a military crisis. The virtual reality system simulates various war scenarios.

Business and Commerce

Virtual reality is being used in business for many purposes—to provide virtual tours of plants and buildings, enable 360-degree viewing of a product or machine, and train employees. For example, Ford uses virtual reality technology to refine its auto designs. Designers and engineers are able to scrutinize the interior and exterior of a car design. Because the virtual reality technology is tied directly into Ford's Autodesk computer aided design (CAD) system, workers can even inspect a particular component to see exactly how it is designed.[48]

Several teams within the National Football League (NFL) have begun using virtual reality applications to train players. The teams are able to load all of their offensive and defensive plays into the system, which uses a 360-degree high-definition capture of each position on the football field. Players training with the system are able to study the plays from a first-person perspective, rewinding plays as necessary. While the player is training, coaches can see what the player is seeing and doing, providing ongoing feedback. The VR systems are an enhancement to the previous off-field training programs that focused on players learning plays by reading large playbooks and watching DVDs of games.[49,50]

Swedish furniture chain IKEA recently launched a virtual reality app that allows users to experiment with different kitchen design features, such as cabinet configurations, countertop materials, and drawer pulls. The app is intended to help consumers make design choices and visualize space in three dimensions by allowing them to quickly make changes and view their customized kitchens from different perspectives. The company is using this pilot program to explore the possibilities of virtual reality technology in terms of connecting with and empowering its customers.[51]

Microsoft is developing its Oculus virtual reality headset for enterprise workers to interact with office productivity software.[52] With this headset and associated software, users can see Microsoft Excel PivotTables that actually pivot in 3D, send weekly status reports that appear in a fully immersive environment, and generate PowerPoint presentations that support full positional head tracking and provide a 3D stereo sound sensation for the listener. Virtual reality headsets such as those by Oculus Rift can be used to walk through the simulated environment.

Critical Thinking Exercise

Launching Google Expeditions

You have been asked to help a local elementary school explore the feasibility of implementing the Google Expeditions Pioneer Program. This program enables students to experience over 100 locations around the world using virtual reality.

Review Questions

1. Do research to find out how the school can sign up for this program and what hardware and software is required.
2. What training is necessary for teachers to lead this program?

Critical Thinking Questions

1. Prepare a recommendation for the school outlining the steps and resources necessary to take advantage of this program.
2. What potential barriers to implementing this program could arise? How might these be overcome?

Other Specialized Systems

In addition to artificial intelligence, expert systems, and virtual reality, other interesting specialized systems continue to be developed, including assistive technology systems, game theory, and informatics.

Assistive Technology Systems

assistive technology system:
An assistive, adaptive, or rehabilitative device designed to help people with disabilities perform tasks that they were formerly unable to accomplish or had great difficulty accomplishing.

Assistive technology systems includes a wide range of assistive, adaptive, and rehabilitative devices to help people with disabilities perform tasks that they were formerly unable to accomplish or had great difficulty accomplishing.

Many assistive technology products are designed to enhance the human-computer interface. Electronic pointing devices are available that enable users to control the pointer on the screen without the use of hands, using ultrasound, infrared beams, eye movements, and even nerve signals and brain waves. Sip-and-puff systems are activated by inhaling or exhaling. Braille embossers can translate text into embossed Braille output. Screen readers can be used to speak everything displayed on the computer screen, including text, graphics, control buttons, and menus. Speech recognition software enables users to give commands and enter data using their voices rather than a mouse or keyboard. Text-to-speech synthesizers can "speak" all data entered to the computer to allow users who are visually impaired or who have learning difficulties to hear what they are typing.[53] Stephen Hawking is an English theoretical physicist and cosmologist considered by many to be the most intelligent man alive today. Hawking is almost entirely paralyzed and uses assistive technology systems to communicate his thoughts and to interact with computers. See Figure 10.15.

Personal assistive listening devices help people understand speech in difficult situations. They separate the speech that a person wants to hear from background noise by improving what is known as the "speech to noise ratio." A personal assistive learning device typically has at least three components: a microphone, a transmission technology, and a device for receiving the signal and bringing the sound to the ear.[54]

The World in HDR/Shutterstock.com

FIGURE 10.15

Stephen Hawking

Stephen Hawking employs a number of assistive technology systems to support his activities.

Personal emergency response systems use electronic sensors connected to an alarm system to help maintain security, independence, and peace of mind for anyone who is living alone, at risk for falls, or recuperating from an illness or surgery. These systems include fall detectors, heart monitors, and unlit gas sensors. When an alert is triggered, a message is sent to a caregiver or contact center who can respond appropriately.

Game Theory

game theory: A mathematical theory for developing strategies that maximize gains and minimize losses while adhering to a given set of rules and constraints.

Game theory is a mathematical theory for developing strategies that maximize gains and minimize losses while adhering to a given set of rules and constraints. Game theory is frequently applied to solve various decision-making problems in which two or more participants are faced with choices of action, by which each may gain or lose, depending on what others choose to do or not to do. Thus, the final outcome of a game is determined jointly by the strategies chosen by all participants. Such decisions involve a degree of uncertainty because no participant knows for sure what course of action the other participants will take. In zero-sum games, the fortunes of the players are inversely related so that one participant's gain is the other participant's loss. In non-zero-sum games, it is wise for the participants to cooperate so that the action taken by one participant may benefit both participants. Two-person zero-sum games are used by military strategists. Many-person non-zero-sum games are used in many business decision-making settings. Game theory Explorer and Gambit are collections of software tools for building, analyzing, and exploring game models.[55]

In the TV game show *Jeopardy!*, contestants typically select a single category and progressively move down from the top question (easiest and lowest dollar value) to the bottom (hardest and highest dollar value). This provides the contestants and viewers with an easy-to-understand escalation of difficulty. Recently, however, one player used a much different strategy, employing the fundamentals of game theory. The player sought out the Daily Double questions, which are usually hidden in one of the three highest-paying and most difficult questions in the categories. Thus rather than selecting a single category and increasing the degree of difficulty, he began with the two most difficult questions in the category. Once the two most difficult questions were taken off the board in one category, he skipped to another category in search of the Daily Doubles. This strategy proved highly successful.[56]

The U.S. Coast Guard employs a game theory system called PROTECT (Port Resiliency for Operational/Tactical Enforcement to Combat Terrorism) to randomize patrols while still achieving a very high level of security that provides maximum deterrence. There are insufficient resources to provide full security coverage around the clock at all high-value potential targets in the 361 shipping ports in the United States. This means that enemies can observe patrol and monitor activities and take actions in an attempt to avoid patrols. PROTECT generates patrol and monitoring schedules that take into account the importance of different targets at each port and the enemy's likely surveillance and anticipated reaction to those patrols.[57]

Informatics

informatics: The combination of information technology with traditional disciplines, such as medicine or science, while considering the impact on individuals, organizations, and society.

Informatics is the combination of information technology with traditional disciplines, such as medicine or science, while considering the impact on individuals, organizations, and society. Informatics places a strong emphasis on the interaction between humans and technology—with the goal of engineering information systems that provide users with the best possible user experience. Indeed, informatics represents the intersection of people, information, and technology. See Figure 10.16. The field of informatics has great breadth and encompasses many individual specializations such as biomedical, health, nursing, medical, and pharmacy informatics. Those who study informatics learn how to build new computing tools and applications. They gain an understanding of how people interact with information technology and how information technology shapes our relationships, our organizations, and our world.

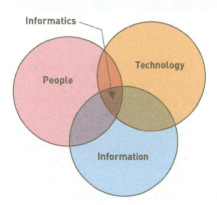

FIGURE 10.16

Informatics

Informatics represents the intersection of people, information, and technology.

Biomedical informatics (or bioinformatics) develops, studies, and applies theories, methods, and processes for the generation, storage, retrieval, use, and sharing of biomedical data, information, and knowledge. Bioinformatics has been used to help map the human genome and conduct research on biological organisms. Using sophisticated databases and artificial intelligence, bioinformatics helps unlock the secrets of the human genome, with the objective of preventing diseases and saving lives. Many universities have courses on bioinformatics and offer bioinformatics certification.

Healthcare informatics is the science of how to use data, information, and technology to improve human health and the delivery of healthcare services. Healthcare informatics applies principles of computer and information science to the advancement of patient care, life sciences research, health professional education, and public health. Journals, such as *Healthcare Informatics*, report current research on applying computer systems and technology to increase efficiency, reduce medical errors, and improve health care.

Boston Medical Center (BMC) has implemented a healthcare informatics program to develop and measure several key operational metrics to improve efficiency in its operating room procedures. The system is being used to optimize surgical schedules, wait times, postsurgical unit availability, and patient-discharge processes. By optimizing the use of its operating rooms, the hospital is able to ensure that surgeons are fully utilizing their assigned operating room time, and—even more important for patient care—reduce the time it takes for a patient to have surgery after diagnosis.[58]

Critical Thinking Exercise

Allina Health Employs Healthcare Informatics

Allina Health is a not-for-profit healthcare system that owns or operates 14 hospitals and over 90 clinics throughout Minnesota and western Wisconsin. The organization created an enterprise-wide data warehouse of clinical, financial, operational, patient satisfaction, and other data. The data is used to calculate and track various healthcare measures that measure performance and can identify opportunities for improvement.

Review Questions

1. What sort of training and experience is needed by the individuals who built and operate this system? What about by the individuals who use this system?
2. Identify several sources from which the data for this system may be obtained.

Critical Thinking Questions

1. Provide several examples of key patient healthcare measures that are tracked by this system.
2. Provide an example or two of how this system might be used to identify an opportunity for improvement in the treatment of patients.

Summary

Principle:

Knowledge management allows organizations to share knowledge and experience among its workers.

Knowledge management is a range of practices concerned with increasing awareness, fostering learning, speeding collaboration and innovation, and exchanging insights. A knowledge management system is an organized collection of people, procedures, software, databases, and devices used to create, capture, store, share, and use the organization's knowledge and experience.

Explicit knowledge is objective and can be measured and documented in reports, papers, and rules. Tacit knowledge is hard to measure and document and is typically not objective or formalized.

A major goal of knowledge management is to somehow capture and document the valuable work-related tacit knowledge of others and to turn it into explicit knowledge that can be shared with others.

Two processes are frequently used to capture tacit knowledge—shadowing and joint problem solving. Shadowing involves a novice observing an expert executing her job to learn how she performs. This technique often is used in the medical field to help young interns learn from experienced physicians. With joint problem solving, the novice and the expert work side by side to solve a problem so that the expert's approach is slowly revealed to the observant novice.

Organizations employ KM to foster innovation, leverage the expertise of people across the organization, and capture the expertise of key individuals before they retire.

Some organizations and professions use communities of practice (CoP), which are groups of people with common interests who come together to create, store, and share knowledge on a specific topic.

Obtaining, storing, sharing, and using knowledge is the key to any knowledge management system, which often leads to additional knowledge creation, storage, sharing, and usage. Many tools and techniques can be used to create, store, and use knowledge. These tools and techniques are available from IBM, Microsoft, and other companies and organizations.

Establishing a successful KM program is challenging, but most of the challenges involved have nothing to do with the technologies or vendors employed. Instead they are challenges associated with human nature and the manner in which people are accustomed to working together. Best practices for selling and implementing a KM project include connecting KM to goals and objectives, starting with a small pilot and enthusiastic participants, identifying tacit knowledge, and getting employee buy in.

Organizations interested in piloting KM should be aware of the wide range of technologies that can support KM efforts. These include communities of practice, organizational network analysis, a variety of Web 2.0 technologies, business rules management systems, and enterprise search tools.

Principle:

Artificial intelligence systems form a broad and diverse set of systems that can replicate human decision making for certain types of well-defined problems.

The term artificial intelligence (AI) is used to describe computers with the ability to mimic or duplicate the functions of the human brain. The objective of building AI systems is not to replace human decision making but to replicate it for certain types of well-defined problems.

Artificial intelligence systems include the people, procedures, hardware, software, data, and knowledge needed to develop computer systems and machines that can simulate human intelligence processes, including learning (the acquisition of information and rules for using the information), reasoning (using rules to reach conclusions), and self-correction (using the outcome from one scenario to improve its performance on future scenarios).

Intelligent behavior encompasses several characteristics, including the abilities to learn from experience and apply this knowledge to new experiences, handle complex situations and solve problems for which pieces of information might be missing, determine relevant information in a given situation, think in a logical and rational manner and give a quick and correct response, and understand visual images and process symbols. Computers are better than people at transferring information, making a series of calculations rapidly and accurately, and making complex calculations, but human beings are better than computers at all other attributes of intelligence.

Artificial intelligence is a broad field that includes several key components, such as expert systems, robotics, vision systems, natural language processing, learning systems, and neural networks.

An expert system consists of hardware and software that stores knowledge and makes inferences, enabling a novice to perform at the level of an expert. An expert system is made up of a collection of integrated and related components, including a knowledge base, an inference engine, an explanation facility, a knowledge acquisition facility, and a user interface.

Robotics is a branch of engineering that involves development and manufacture of mechanical or computer devices that can perform tasks that require a high degree of precision or are tedious or hazardous for human beings, such as painting cars or making make precision welds.

Vision systems include hardware and software that permit computers to capture, store, and manipulate images and pictures (e.g., face-recognition software).

Natural language processing allows the computer to understand and react to statements and commands made in a "natural" language, such as English.

Learning systems use a combination of software and hardware to allow a computer to change how it functions or reacts to situations based on feedback it receives (e.g., a computerized chess game).

A neural network is a computer system that can recognize and act on patterns or trends that it detects in large sets of data.

A genetic algorithm is an approach to solving problems based on the theory of evolution and the concept of survival of the fittest. Intelligent agents consist of programs and a knowledge base used to perform a specific task for a person, a process, or another program.

Principle:

Multimedia and virtual reality systems can reshape the interface between people and information technology by offering new ways to communicate information, visualize processes, and express ideas creatively.

Multimedia is content that uses more than one form of communication—such as text, graphics, video, animation, audio, and other media that can be used to help an organization efficiently and effectively achieve its goals. Multimedia tools can be used to help an organization achieve its goals through the production of compelling brochures, presentations, reports, and documents. Although not all organizations use the full capabilities of multimedia, most use text and graphics capabilities. Presentation software such as Microsoft PowerPoint, Prezi, and Swipe can be used to develop presentations with sound and animation that can be displayed on a large screen. Other applications of multimedia include audio, video, and animation. File compression and conversion are often needed in multimedia applications to import or export analog files and to reduce file size when storing multimedia files and sending them to others. Designing a multimedia application requires careful thought to get the best results and achieve corporate goals.

A virtual reality system enables one or more users to move and react in a computer-simulated environment. Virtual reality simulations require special interface devices that transmit the sights, sounds, and sensations of the simulated world to the user. These devices can also record and send the speech and movements of the participants to the simulation program. Thus, users can sense and manipulate virtual objects much as they would real objects. This natural style of interaction gives the participants the feeling that they are immersed in the simulated world.

Virtual reality can also refer to applications that are not fully immersive, such as mouse-controlled navigation through a three-dimensional environment on a graphics monitor, stereo viewing from the monitor via stereo glasses, and stereo projection systems. Some virtual reality applications allow views of real environments with superimposed virtual objects. Augmented reality, a newer form of virtual reality, can superimpose digital data over real photos or images. Virtual reality applications are found in medicine, education and training, real estate and tourism, and entertainment.

Principle:

Specialized systems can help organizations and individuals achieve their goals.

A number of specialized systems have recently appeared to assist organizations and individuals in new and exciting ways. Assistive technology systems include a wide range of assistive, adaptive, and rehabilitative devices to help people with disabilities perform tasks that they were formerly unable to accomplish or had great difficulty accomplishing. Game theory is a mathematical theory that helps to develop strategies for maximizing gains and minimizing losses while adhering to a given set of rules and constraints. Informatics is the combination of information technology with traditional disciplines such as medicine or science, while considering the impact on individuals, organizations, and society. It represents the intersection of people, information, and technology.

Key Terms

artificial intelligence	joint problem solving
artificial intelligence system	knowledge acquisition facility
assistive technology system	knowledge engineer
business rule management system (BRMS)	knowledge management (KM)
community of practice (CoP)	knowledge user
domain expert	learning systems
electronic discovery (e-discovery)	metadata
enterprise search	multimedia
enterprise search software	natural language processing
expert system	neural network
explanation facility	perceptive system
explicit knowledge	robotics
game theory	rule
genetic algorithm	shadowing
IF-THEN statement	organizational network analysis (ONA)
inference engine	tacit knowledge
informatics	virtual reality system
intelligent agent	vision system
intelligent behavior	

Chapter 10: Self-Assessment Test

Knowledge management allows organizations to share knowledge and experience among its workers.

1. _____ knowledge is knowledge that is documented, stored, and codified.
2. Tacit knowledge is extremely useful and can be easily shared with others. True or False?
3. Which of the following is not a benefit associated with knowledge management?
   a. It helps leverage the expertise of people across the organization.
   b. It helps capture the expertise of key individuals before they retire.
   c. It helps contain the specialized knowledge of experts to a few people on a need-to-know basis.
   d. It fosters innovation by encouraging the free flow of ideas.

4. The initial step in selling and implementing a knowledge management project is _____.
   a. get employee buy in
   b. identify valuable tacit knowledge
   c. start with a small pilot project and enthusiastic participants
   d. connect knowledge management to goals and objectives

Artificial intelligence systems form a broad and diverse set of systems that can replicate human decision making for certain types of well-defined problems.

5. The use of _____ enables humans and computers to find a good solution, although not optimal, to a complex problem.
   a. perceptive systems
   b. heuristics
   c. visual systems
   d. robotics

6. The _____ component of an expert system seeks information and relationships to provide answers, predictions, and suggestions similar to the way a human expert would.
   a. knowledge base
   b. explanation facility
   c. inference engine
   d. user interface

7. Robots are increasingly being used in surgical procedures including open-heart surgery. True or False?

8. Facebook's AI vision system called DeepFace can correctly tell if two photos show the same person with _____ accuracy.
   a. less than 50 percent
   b. between 50 percent and 75 percent
   c. between 75 percent and 95 percent
   d. over 95 percent

9. _____ is a type of artificial system that enables a computer to change how it functions or reacts to situations based on feedback it receives.
   a. Neural network
   b. Voice recognition system
   c. Learning system
   d. Vision system

10. _____ is a computer system that can recognize and act on patterns or trends that it detects in large sets of data.
    a. Neural network
    b. Voice recognition system
    c. Learning system
    d. Vision system

11. _____ algorithms solve problems using the concept of survival of the fittest as a problem-solving strategy.

Multimedia and virtual reality systems can reshape the interface between people and information technology by offering new ways to communicate information, visualize processes, and express ideas creatively.

12. _____ are some of the file formats that can be used to store graphic images.
    a. MP3, WAV, and MIDI
    b. AVI, MPEG, and MOV
    c. DOC and DOCX
    d. EPS, GIF, JPEG, PNG, TIFF, and Raw

13. When video files are played while they are being downloaded from the Internet, it is called _____ video.

14. _____ software is used widely to create outstanding graphics for feature films and has been used on every Visual Effects Academy Award for over 15 years.
    a. Apple's Final Cut Pro
    b. Adobe Audition
    c. Prezi
    d. Pixar's RenderMan

15. _____ acquired the virtual reality company Oculus VR.
    a. Apple
    b. Microsoft
    c. Facebook
    d. Google

Specialized systems can help organizations and individuals achieve their goals.

16. _____ systems include a wide range of devices that help people with disabilities to perform tasks that they were formerly unable to accomplish or had great difficulty accomplishing.

17. _____ involves the use of information systems to develop competitive strategies for people, organizations, or even countries.

Chapter 10: Self-Assessment Test Answers

1. Explicit
2. False
3. c
4. d
5. b
6. c
7. True
8. d
9. c
10. a
11. Genetic
12. d
13. streaming
14. d
15. c
16. Assistive technology
17. Game theory

Review Questions

1. Identify and briefly discuss the six processes that comprise knowledge management.

2. Briefly explain the difference between explicit and tacit knowledge. Give an example of each.

3. Identify and briefly describe two processes frequently used to capture explicit knowledge.
4. Name four key steps in selling and implementing a knowledge management project.
5. What is a community of practice (CoP)? Give an example of a CoP. What are some of the advantages of participating in a CoP?
6. What is organizational network analysis? How is it used?
7. What is enterprise search software and how is it used?
8. How would you define artificial intelligence?
9. Identify several specific characteristics of intelligent behavior.
10. Identify six major branches of artificial intelligence.
11. What are the fundamental components of an expert system and what function does each perform?
12. Give several examples of robots being used in the real world. What advantages do robots provide?

13. What is DeepFace and how is it used?
14. What is natural language processing?
15. What is a learning system? Give an example of a learning system.
16. What is a neural network? Give an example of a neural network.
17. What is a genetic algorithm? Give an example of the use of a genetic algorithm.
18. Identify and briefly describe five forms of media that can be used to help an organization achieve its goals. Identify at least two software programs that are used to work with each of these media types.
19. What is the difference between file conversion and file compression?
20. What is a virtual reality system? Identify three areas of virtual reality application.
21. What is an assistive technology system?
22. What is game theory? Identify two applications of game theory.
23. What is informatics?

Discussion Questions

1. You are an entry-level manager for the customer service desk of a telecommunications firm that provides telephone, Internet access, and cable TV services. A knowledge management system would be useful to capture, store, and retrieve much of the explicit and tacit knowledge needed to provide excellent service. An expert system would prove valuable in helping customer service reps to handle common, reoccurring problems. The organization only has the time and resources to develop one of these two systems. What factors must you consider in making the choice of which system to develop?
2. We are capable of building computers that exhibit human-level intelligence. Are there certain areas of application where we should push to accelerate the building of such computers? Why these application areas? Are there certain areas of application we should avoid? Why these application areas?
3. Many of us use heuristics each day in completing ordinary activities—such as planning our meals, executing our workout routine, or determining what route to drive to school or work. Imagine that you are developing a set of heuristics for deciding which social invitations to accept. What rules or heuristics would you include?
4. How could you use a community of practice to help you in your work or studies? How would you go about identifying who to invite to join the CoP?
5. A bank is considering implementing a business rules management system for assessing the risk and creditworthiness of individuals as part of the loan approval process. What might be the benefits of such a system? What are some of the factors that must be weighed in this decision? What potential legal or ethical issues might arise in the use of such a system?
6. Describe a situation in which the use of an expert system would be highly practical as well as very beneficial.
7. What are some of the routine day-to-day household tasks that robots are able to accomplish today? What additional tasks might they be able to do in the near future? Are there certain limitations that restrict the kind of household chores robots can do?
8. Describe how a combination expert system and natural language processing could be used to provide student counseling for registering for classes. How successful do you think such a system would be? Explain.
9. Discuss the similarities and differences between learning systems and neural systems. Give an example of how each technology might be used.
10. What is the differences and similarities between a database and a knowledge base?
11. Describe how game theory might be used in a business setting.
12. Describe how augmented reality can be used in a classroom. How could it be used in a work setting?
13. Describe how assistive living systems might benefit the residents of a nursing home.

Problem-Solving Exercises

1. You are investigating the use of automated robots to replace some of the tasks performed by waiters and waitresses in your neighborhood restaurant. The robots are capable of clearing tables and delivering food to customers. Customer interactions to order food would continue to be done by humans. You estimate that you could reduce your staff from 15 workers making $15/hour to around 7 workers. In addition, you are sure that use of the robots would attract additional customers perhaps increasing sales by $100,000/year. The robots cost $75,000 each and you figure you will need two or three depending on how fast business increases. Perform an analysis to determine if hiring robots and letting humans go makes good economic sense.

2. Shoot a brief video of you and some friends. Download the video to a computer in your school's computer lab that has video editing software. Use this software to experiment making edits to the video. Write a brief report summarizing your experience learning and using this software.

3. Capture a large text file and use a data compression program to reduce the size of the file and email it to a friend. Verify that your friend is able to open and decompress the file. Repeat this exercise with a large video file.

Team Activities

1. You and your team are challenged to visit the local entertainment centers in search of the most realistic virtual reality game that requires a player to wear a head-mounted display. What makes this game so realistic? Is there any way it could be improved? Talk to the manager and try to identify the hardware and software employed. Summarize your findings in a brief report.

2. Work with your team to design an expert system to predict how many years it will take a typical student to graduate from your college or university. Some factors to consider include the major the student selects, the student's SAT score, the number of courses taken each semester, and the number of parties or social activities the student attends each month. Identify six other factors that should be considered. Develop six IF-THEN rules or cases to be used in the expert system.

3. Have your team members explore the use of assistive technology systems by recent combat veterans. Write a short paper summarizing your findings and the advantages and disadvantages of these type systems.

Web Exercises

1. NelNet is one of the nation's largest student loan servicing companies. The U.S. Department of Education contracts with companies like NelNet to provide servicing options for their student loans including:

   • Take in and apply payments to student loans
   • Administer the transfer of student loans
   • Process student loan programs, such as forgiveness, forbearance, and deferment
   • Report to credit agencies past due payments
   • Seek repayment from defaulted loans

   NelNet chose to deploy a knowledge management system called OpenText Process Suite. Go online and investigate the features and capabilities of this suite of software products. What functions does OpenText provide that can augment and assist customer relationship management (CRM) systems? Research and briefly document students' recent experience with NelNet.

2. Do research to identify instances in which robots have taken jobs away from human employees. Do you believe that the increasing use of robots should be encouraged? Why or why not? Write a one-page summary of your findings and opinions.

3. Use the Internet to identify several applications of neural networks. Write a brief summary of these applications.

Career Exercises

1. Identify several career fields that are likely to be negatively impacted by artificial intelligence applications. Can you identify any career fields that might be positively impacted?

2. Do research to explore career opportunities in healthcare informatics. What sort of training and experience is necessary for such a career? What sort of role does this prepare one to fulfill? What is the forecast for the number of job openings and starting salaries? Does this career field interest you?

3. Imagine that you are forming a community of practice to deal with the issues associated with transitioning to a new career. Identify people from your experience who you would like to include as members. Why factors did you consider when you selected these people? Identify three key topics you would like the community to address.

Case Studies

Case One

The NASA Knowledge Map

At 11:38 a.m. on January 28, 1986, the space shuttle orbiter Challenger launched from Cape Canaveral, Florida. Less than a second later, gray smoke streamed out from a hot flare burning in the rocket motor. The flare ignited liquid hydrogen and nitrogen inside the fuel tank, which exploded 73 seconds after liftoff. The Challenger was torn apart, and all seven astronauts were killed.

In the days and weeks following the disaster, it became clear that two O-ring seals within the rocket booster had failed. Engineers working for the space agency had warned of just such a failure. In particular, they had expressed concerns that the O-ring seals could fail when outside temperatures dropped below 53 degrees Fahrenheit. On the morning of January 28, the temperature was 36 degrees. The launch pad was covered with solid ice.

In response to the Challenger disaster, NASA established the Program and Project Initiative whose purpose was to improve individual competency for NASA employees—and to prevent another catastrophe. The Challenger, however, was followed by the failure of three expensive Mars missions. The software system used for the Mars Climate Orbiter mission erred when one part of the software used pound-force units to calculate thrust, whereas another part used the newton metric unit. Less than a month later, the Mars Polar Lander crashed into the surface of the planet at too high velocity—triggering the failure of a concurrent mission, the Mars Deep Space 2 probes. A review of the Deep Space 2 mission revealed that NASA engineers had decided to skip a complete system impact test in order to meet the project's tight deadline. In the wake of these failures, NASA sought to improve communication and collaboration among teams. Yet in 2003, a large piece of insulation foam broke off from the Columbia space shuttle during launch, creating a hole in its wing, ultimately causing a catastrophic breach of the shuttle during reentry; again, all seven astronauts on board were killed.

These terrible losses brought about a fundamental change in NASA's approach to knowledge management. In 1976, NASA had created the Office of the Chief Engineer (OCE), which was initially staffed by only one employee whose job was to offer advice and expertise on NASA's administration. In response to the Challenger disaster, NASA established the Academy of Project/Program and Engineering Leadership (APPEL) as a resource for developing NASA's technical staff. In 2004, the agency moved APPEL to the OCE in order to promote talent development through the analysis

of lessons learned and through knowledge capture—the codification of knowledge. The purpose was to improve not only individual but also team performance and to overcome the disconnect between the different engineering and decision-making teams across the huge organization. The overarching goal was to create an organization that learns from its mistakes. APPEL emphasized not only technical training curriculum but also the sharing of practitioner experience, storytelling, and reflective activities. In 2012, NASA furthered this initiative and established the role of chief knowledge officer whose mission is to capture implicit and explicit knowledge. Today, the agency has an extensive knowledge management system called NASA Knowledge Map, which is a tool that helps employees navigate the enormous collection of knowledge within NASA. The map encompasses six major categories: (1) Case Studies and Publications, (2) Face-to-Face Knowledge Services, (3) Online Tools, (4) Knowledge Networks, (5) Lessons Learned and Knowledge Processes, and (6) Search/Tag/Taxonomy Tools.

Fifteen organizations within NASA contribute to Case Studies and Publications. The Goddard Space Flight Center, for example, publishes studies that range from analysis of the Challenger disaster to an analysis of a protest submitted by a NASA contractor who lost a follow-up contract. The latter case may not seem critical, but in one such case, the Office of Inspector General had to launch a formal investigation that cost NASA time, money, and energy. This case study was then integrated into the APPEL curriculum with the goal of avoiding the mistakes that led to the protest. The Johnson Space Center issues oral history transcripts, as well as newsletters, case studies, and reports. The Jet Propulsion Laboratory publishes conference papers and a Flight Anatomy wiki that tracks prelaunch and in-flight anomalies.

Face-to-Face Knowledge Services comprise programs that are conducted in person at many locations, including, for example, workshops presented by the NASA Engineering and Safety Center. Within the Online Tools category are video libraries, portals, document repositories, and synchronous and asynchronous collaboration and sharing sites. Some of these tools are quite sophisticated. For example, Human Exploration and Operations (HEO) deploys a GroupSystems Think Tank decision support tool to improve group decision making. The Knowledge Networks category includes information about formal and informal communities of practice, mass collaborative activities, and methods for locating and accessing experts, and group workspaces for projects such as static code analysis.

Twenty organizations within NASA contribute data to the Lessons Learned and Knowledge Processes databases, which capture and store knowledge, lessons learned, and best practices. These include, for example, HEO's knowledge-based risks library with topics covering project management, design and development, systems engineering, and integration and testing. HEO also sponsors lessons-learned workshops and forums on topics such as solar array deployment, shuttle transition and retirement, system safety, and risk management.

Finally, the system's Search/Tag/Taxonomy Tools allow individuals to access organization-specific sites as well as the abundance of materials offered through the five other KM programs. This final category within the KM system may be the most important, as NASA's own inspector general issued a report indicating that the tremendous wealth of KM resources is still significantly underutilized. For instance, NASA managers rarely consult the Lessons Learned Information System (LLIS) despite NASA requirements that they do so. The Glenn Research Center received $470,000 over two years to support LLIS activities, but contributed only five reports to the system during that time. Moreover, the inspector general concluded that inconsistent policy direction, disparate KM project development, and insufficient coordination marginalize the system.

NASA is clearly at the bleeding edge of large-scale KM system development, creating the tools of the future. APPEL and other NASA teams are able to make use of some amazing tools that are being developed within the agency. It may be, however, that NASA's KM system suffers from the same disjointed development and communication barriers that led to the space shuttle disasters and the failures of the Mars missions. Yet, it is vital that NASA learn to make use of its state-of-the-art KM system as the success of every NASA mission requires that thousands of employees are able to make the most of NASA's vast collection of knowledge.

Critical Thinking Questions

1. How is the KM system at NASA different from other KM systems that you have studied within the chapter? How is it similar?
2. What steps can NASA take to make sure that the KM system is better utilized by individuals and teams?
3. What can NASA do to ensure that individuals and teams can find what they need within the mountain of data residing within the KM system?
4. Is NASA's KM system, as it exists now, a good way to combat the type of failures the agency has experienced in the past? If not, how could the KM system be changed to support mission success?
5. Are there other measures that NASA should take in addition to or in conjunction with the development of its KM system?

SOURCES: Oberg, James, "7 Myths about the Challenger Shuttle Disaster," *NBC News*, January 25, 2011, *www.nbcnews.com/id /11103097/ns/technology_and_science-space/t/myths-about-challenger -shuttle-disaster/#.U2AsyIFdUrU*; Atkinson, Joe, "Engineer Who Opposed Challenger Launch Offers Personal Look at Tragedy," *NASA Researcher News*, October 5, 2012, *www.nasa.gov/centers/langley/news/researcher news/rn_Colloquium1012.html*; "Challenger Disaster," History Channel, *www.history.com/topics/challenger-disaster*, accessed April 29, 2014; "Failure as a Design Criteria," Plymouth University, *www.tech.plym.ac .uk/sme/interactive_resources/tutorials/failurecases/hs1.html*, accessed April 29, 2014; Lipowicz, Alice, "Is NASA's Knowledge Management Program Obsolete?," GCN Technology, Tools and Tactics for Public Sector IT, March 19, 2012, *http://gcn.com/Articles/2012/03/15/NASA -knowledge-management-IG.aspx*; Luttrell, Anne, "NASA's PMO: Building and Sustaining a Learning Organization," Project Management Institute, *www.pmi.org/Learning/articles/nasa.aspx*, accessed February 9, 2015; Hoffman, Edward J. and Boyle, Jon, "Tapping Agency Culture to Advance Knowledge Services at NASA," ATD, September 15, 2013, *www.td.org /Publications/Magazines/The-Public-Manager/Archives/2013/Fall/Tap ping-Agency-Culture-to-Advance-Knowledge-Services-at-NASA*; "Knowledge Map," NASA, *http://km.nasa.gov/knowledge-map/*, accessed February 9, 2015.

Case Two

Doctor on Demand Enables Physicians to Make House Calls

In addition to cost, provider availability and travel time are barriers for many Americans seeking access to healthcare services. In fact, a recent study of 4,000 patients determined that, on average, patients spend 38 minutes on travel time to and from outpatient appointments. Improving patient's access to care continues to be a priority for healthcare providers and government agencies across the United States, and an increasing number of companies have begun offering telemedicine services, such as video-based doctors' appointments, as a potential solution.

Founded in 2013, Doctor on Demand, offers the possibility of increasing access to health care through video visits with doctors who can diagnose and treat a range of noncritical symptoms for patients who are unable or unwilling to visit a clinic. Using the Doctor on Demand services, patients can connect with one of more than 1,400 licensed physicians through the company's Web site using a Chrome, Firefox, or Safari browser or via an Android or iOS app. In addition to video conferences, the Doctor on Demand app allows patients to upload high-resolution images so that doctors can better assess certain conditions.

The top conditions treated by the service are cold and flu symptoms, sore throats, urinary tract infections, skin rashes, diarrhea and vomiting, eye issues, sports injuries, and travel-related illnesses. The site also offers video visits with board-certified lactation consultants for women who are breastfeeding. In addition, patients who need psychological or psychiatric services can consult with mental health professionals via the service.

According to Adam Jackson, CEO of Doctor on Demand, the most frequent users of the company's services are working mothers, who often have questions about their children's health but aren't always able (or willing) to take time off to get every question answered. According to Jackson, 92 percent of video consultations require no in-person follow-up.

Although Doctor on Demand suggests that patients have access to Wi-Fi to ensure the highest quality appointment, the company promises a smooth experience as long as patients have a 4G or LTE connection. Patients who have connection problems can also switch to audio only to complete a visit, if necessary. The Doctor on Demand network runs on a cloud-based platform run by Amazon Web Services. Due to the nature of the communication, the company had to go through several steps to ensure that all of its infrastructure was compliant with HIPAA (Health Insurance Portability and Accountability Act) requirements.

Most experts predict a shift to telemedicine, including video doctors' visits, will continue. In fact, a report by analytics company IHS Technology predicts that video consultations will increase from 2 million in 2015 to 5.4 million by 2020. For some patients, however, technology limitations will continue to impede their ability to access health care through telemedicine services. A grainy connection or one that cuts out in the middle of an appointment is unlikely to result in a high quality of care. Other hurdles that will also need to be overcome include patient's privacy concerns, patients' uncertainty about when a video appointment is appropriate in terms of symptoms, and patients' lack of trust that a virtual provider can accurately diagnose and treat them. That concern was reinforced by a recent study published in the *JAMA Internal Medicine* that found significant variations in the quality of care provided by different companies offering virtual visits for the diagnosis and treatment of common acute illnesses.

Critical Thinking Questions

1. Would you consider using Doctor on Demand or a similar service to access treatment for a minor health-care issue? If not, which aspects of the service are most concerning to you (privacy, quality of care, security or other technology issues, etc.)?
2. Do more research online about Doctor on Demand and two of its competitors (such as Amwell, MDLive, and Teladoc). What information does each company provide on its Web site that is designed to ease patients' concerns about privacy, quality, and technology-

related issues? Which company does the best job of convincing you that their service is safe and secure?

3. In the study on patient travel time, researchers found that minority patients and those who were unemployed faced longer travel times when visiting a doctor. Rural Americans also often have more difficulty accessing health care. Is a video-based telemedicine app likely to improve access for those populations? How might this technology be used in a way that would be more likely to improve healthcare access for those populations?

SOURCES: Doyle, Kathryn, "Study: How Long You Wait to See a Doctor Is Linked to Race, Employment," *Huffington Post*, October 6, 2015, *www.huffingtonpost.com/entry/study-how-long-you-wait-to-see-a-doctor-is-linked-to-race-employment_us_5613b0cbe4b0baa355ad2621*; "Troubleshooting," Doctor on Demand, *https://doctorondemand.zendesk.com/hc/en-us/sections/200218868-Troubleshooting*, accessed April 9, 2016; "Our Mission," Doctor on Demand, *www.doctorondemand.com/our-mission*, April 8, 2016; Lapowsky, Issie, "Video Is about to Become the Way We All Visit the Doctor," *Wired*, *www.wired.com/2015/04/united-healthcare-telemedicine*; Van Thoen, Lindsay, "Healthcare IT is Failing (And It Needs AWS)," *Logicworks* (blog), July 20, 2015, *www.logicworks.net/blog/2015/07/healthcare-cloud-saas-aws*; Japsen, Bruce, "Doctors' Virtual Consults with Patients to Double by 2020," *Forbes*, August 9, 2015, *www.forbes.com/sites/brucejapsen/2015/08/09/as-telehealth-booms-doctor-video-consults-to-double-by-2020/#639cbc4e5d66*; "Press Release: "39% of Tech-Savvy Consumers Have Not Heard of Telemedicine: HealthMine Survey," HealthMine, March 27, 2016, *www.prnewswire.com/news-releases/39-of-tech-savvy-consumers-have-not-heard-of-telemedicine-healthmine-survey-300241737.html#continue-jump*; Schoenfield, Adam J., et al., "Variation in Quality of Urgent Health Care Provided during Commercial Virtual Visits," *JAMA Internal Medicine*, April 4, 2016, *http://archinte.jamanetwork.com/article.aspx?articleid=2511324*.

Notes

1. "About TMW," TMW, *www.tmwsystems.com/about-tmw*, accessed March 22, 2016.
2. "TMW Deploys Bloomfire for Social Learning," *Bloomfire* (blog), April 16, 2015, *https://bloomfire.com/blog/tmw-deploys-bloomfire-for-social-learning*.
3. "About the Firm," White & Case, *www.whitecase.com/about/*, accessed February 5, 2015.
4. Britt, Phil, "Creating a More Knowledgeable, Nimble Organization," *KM World*, January 30, 2015, *www.kmworld.com/Articles/Editorial/Features/Creating-a-more-knowledgeable-nimble-organization-101536.aspx*.
5. "Knowledge Management & Transfer Model {Techniques and Forms}," Division of Personnel, Department of Administrative Service, State of New Hampshire, *www.admin.state.nh.us/hr/documents/Workforce_Development/Knowledge%20Management%20&%20Transfer%20Model.doc*, accessed February 26, 2015.
6. "Kaleo Software Secures $7 Million to Accelerate Innovation and Growth," Kaleo, October 15, 2015, *www.kaleosoftware.com/press/seriesa*.
7. "This is GSA," U.S. General Services Administration (GSA), *www.gsa.gov/thisisgsa/#/welcome*, accessed April 2, 2016.
8. "Communities," DigitalGov, *www.digitalgov.gov/communities*, accessed April 3, 2016.
9. "GSA Leads Customer Service Community of Practice," *FedScoop*, October 7, 2015, *http://fedscoop.com/gsa-leads-customer-experience-community-of-practice*.
10. "Customer Experience Community," U.S. General Services Administration (GSA), *www.digitalgov.gov/communities/customer-experience-community*, accessed April 2, 2015.
11. Grimes, Seth, "Metadata, Connection, and the Big Data Story," Breakthrough Analysis, April 26, 2014, *http://breakthroughanalysis.com/2014/04/26/metadata-connection-and-the-big-data-story/*.
12. "Using Organizational Network Analysis to Build a Better Business," Society for Human Resource Management," May 2015, *www.shrm.org/publications/hrmagazine/editorialcontent/2015/0515/pages/05115-organizational-network-analysis.aspx*.
13. "HanseMerkur Automates Its Service Billing Processes Using inubit," Bosch Financial Software, *www.bosch-si.com/media/en/finance_7/documents_2/brochures_1/success_stories/insurance_3/hansemerkur.pdf*, accessed February 7, 2015.
14. "Adobe Fast Facts," Adobe, *www.images.adobe.com/content/dam/acom/en/fast-facts/pdfs/fast-facts.pdf*, accessed April 6, 2016.

15. "Adobe," Progress, *www.progress.com/customers/adobe*, accessed February 7, 2015.

16. "About Us," DBS, *www.dbs.com/about-us/default.page*, accessed January 29, 2016.

17. "DBS," Progress, *www.progress.com/customers/dbs*, accessed January 29, 2016.

18. Andrews, Whit and Koehler-Kruener, Hanns, "Magic Quadrant for Enterprise Search," Gartner, August 19, 2015, *www.gartner.com/doc/reprints?id=1 -2LH0EF0&ct=150820&st=sg*.

19. "Company Information," Harris Corporation," *http://har ris.com/about*, accessed April 6, 2017.

20. "Harris Corporation Increases Productivity with Coveo," Coveo, *www.coveo.com/~/media/Files/CaseStudies/Har ris_Corporation_Increases_Productivity_with_Coveo _for_Advanced_Enterprise_Search.ashx*, accessed April 6, 2016.

21. Deutchman, Leonard, "2015 in Review: What Happened, Is Happening and Will Happen," *Legal Intelligencer*, January 5, 2016, *www.thelegalintelligencer.com/latest -news/id=1202746177129/2015-in-Review-What-Hap pened-Is-Happening-aibnd-Will-Happen?mcode =1395262324557&curindex=918&slreturn=2016 0307160543*.

22. Krause, Jason, "The Battle of Rio Tinto–Predictive Cod-ing Hits Snags in Marquee Case," *Association of Certified E-Discovery Specialists* (blog), July 24, 2015, *www.aceds .org/the-battle-of-rio-tinto-predictive-coding-hits-snags -in-marquee-case*.

23. McCarthy, J., Minsky, M.L., Rochester, N., and Shannon, C.E., "A Proposal for the Dartmouth Summer Research Project on Artificial Intelligence," August 31, 1955, *www-formal.stanford.edu/jmc/history/dartmouth/dart mouth.html*.

24. "What is Watson," *http://www.ibm.com/smarterplanet /us/en/ibmwatson/what-is-watson.html*, accessed April 26, 2016.

25. "By 2029 No Computer—or 'Machine Intelligence'—Will Have Passed the Turing Test," Long Bets, *http://longbets .org/1/*, accessed May 2, 2014.

26. "The Aspen Institute: Google's Eric Schmidt with Walter Isaacson on 'The New Digital Age,'" YouTube video, 1:09, July 24, 2013, *www.youtube.com/watch? v=3Ox4EMFMy48*.

27. Gee, Sue, "Mitsuku Wins Loebner Prize 2013," I-Programmer, September 15, 2013, *www.i-programmer .info/news/105-artificial-intelligence/6382-mitsuku-wins -loebner-prize-2013.html*.

28. 20Q Web site, *www.20q.net*, accessed May 2, 2014.

29. "FICO® Blaze Advisor® Decision Rules Management System," FICO, *www.fico.com/en/products/fico-blaze -advisor-decision-rules-management-system#overview*, accessed April 7, 2016.

30. Capek, Karel, "Beyond the Robots," Legacy.com, *www .legacy.com/news/legends-and-legacies/karel-capek –beyond-the-robots/302/#sthash.RQyp1B1R*, accessed May 3, 2014.

31. The Web site for iRobot Web page, *www.irobot.com*, accessed April 8, 2016.

32. "REC (Robotics Engineering Curriculum)," Intelitek, *www.intelitek.com/engineering/rec_curriculum*, accessed April 8, 2016.

33. "Meet Dash and Dot," Wonder Workshop, *www.make wonder.com*, accessed April 8, 2016

34. Martin, Alexander, "SoftBank, Alibaba Team Up on Robot," *The Wall Street Journal*, June 18, 2015, *www.wsj .com/articles/pepper-softbanks-emotional-robot-goes -global-1434618111*.

35. Smith, Aaron and Janna Anderson, "Predictions for the State of AI and Robotics in 2025," PewResearchCenter, August 6, 2014, *www.pewinternet.org/2014/08/06/pre dictions-for-the-state-of-ai-and-robotics-in-2025*.

36. "Facebook's New Face Recognition Knows You from the Side," CNN Money, April 4, 2014, *http://money.cnn.com /2014/04/04/technology/innovation/facebook-facial-rec ognition/*.

37. Elgan, Mike, "Is Facial Recognition a Threat on Facebook and Google," June 29, 2015, *www.computerworld.com /article/2941415/data-privacy/is-facial-recognition-a -threat-on-facebook-and-google.html*.

38. D'Orazio, Dante, "Google Now and Speech Recognition Get Big Updates in Android 4.4 Kitkat," *The Verge*, October 31, 2013, *www.theverge.com/2013/10/31 /5051458/android-kit-kat-bring-big-updates-to-google -now-and-speech-recognition*.

39. "Neural Tools Used for Tumor Diagnosis," Palisade Case Studies, *www.palisade.com/cases/katherinenhospital .asp?caseNav=byIndustry*, accessed May 3, 2014.

40. Taft, Darryl, "IBM Partners with American Cancer Society on Watson Cancer Advisor," eWeek, April 12, 2016, *http:// www.eweek.com/database/ibm-partners-with-american -cancer-society-on-watson-cancer-advisor.html*.

41. "KEITV Customer Success Stories—Sunkist Growers," *http://ketiv.com/company/customer-success-stories/sunk ist*, accessed May 6, 2014.

42. Seymour, Mike, "Pixar's RenderMan Turns 25 (Exclu-sive)," *fx Guide*, July 25, 2013, *www.fxguide.com/fea tured/pixars-renderman-turns-25*.

43. King, Leo, "Facebook, Oculus, and Businesses' Thirst for Virtual Reality," *Forbes*, March 30, 2014, *www.forbes .com/sites/leoking/2014/03/30/facebook-oculus-and-busi nesses-thirst-for-virtual-reality*.

44. Elgan, Mike, "Why Virtual Reality Is the Next Social Net-work," *Computerworld*, November 2, 2015, *www.compu terworld.com/article/2999819/social-media/why-virtual -reality-is-the-next-social-network.html?phint=newt% 3Dcomputerworld_thisweek&phint=idg_eid% 3D144dfe65577ba4663c4cefdadfff5932#tk. CTWNLE_nlt_thisweek_2015-11-02*.

45. Casti, Taylor, "6 Ways Virtual Reality Is Already Chang-ing the World (No Facebook Required)," *Huffington Post*, March 28, 2014, *www.huffingtonpost.com/2014 /03/28/virtual-reality-uses-medicine-autism-ptsd-burn -amputee-victims_n_5045111.html*.

46. Lardinois, Frederic, "Google Expands Its VR Program for Students to More U.S. Schools," TechCrunch, November 9, 2015, *http://techcrunch.com/2015/11/09/google -expands-its-vr-program-for-students-to-more-u-s-schools*.

47. "Introducing the Expeditions Pioneer Program," Google, *www.google.com/edu/expeditions*, accessed April 8, 2016.

48. King, Leo, "Ford, Where Virtual Reality Is Already Manufacturing Reality," *Forbes*, May 3, 2014, *www .forbes.com/sites/leoking/2014/05/03/ford-where-virtual -reality-is-already-manufacturing-reality*.

49. Gaudiosi, John, "Here's Why NFL Teams Are Training in Virtual Reality," *Fortune*, August 10, 2015, *http://fortune.com/2015/08/10/strivr-virtual-reality-nfl*.

50. "The Story," STRIVR, *www.strivrlabs.com/about*, accessed April 9, 2016.

51. "IKEA Launches Pilot Virtual Reality (VR) Kitchen Experience for HTC Vive on Steam," IKEA, April 4, 2016, *www.ikea.com/us/en/about_ikea/newsitem/040516_Virtual-Reality*.

52. Hart, Brian, "Microsoft Targets Enterprise Virtual Reality with Business Oriented VR Headset," Road to VR, April 1, 2014, *www.roadtovr.com/microsoft-enterprise-virtual-reality-business-vr-headset/*.

53. "Microsoft Accessibility—Types of Assistive Technology Products," *www.microsoft.com/enable/at/types.aspx*, accessed May 12, 2014.

54. "Assistive Listening Systems and Devices," *http://nad.org/issues/technology/assistive-listening/systems-and-devices*, accessed May 12, 2014.

55. Savani, Rahul and von Stengel, Bernhard, "Game Theory Explorer—Software for the Applied Game Theorist," March 16, 2014, *www.maths.lse.ac.uk/Personal/stengel/TEXTE/largeongte.pdf*.

56. Levenson, Eric, "Jeopardy's New Game-Theory Devotee Is One to Keep an Eye on," *The Wire*, Jan 31, 2014, *www.thewire.com/entertainment/2014/01/jeopardys-newest-star-proves-optimal-strategy-really-unfriendly/357609*.

57. "Port Resilience Operational / Tactical Enforcement to Combat Terrorism (PROTECT) Model for the United States Coast Guard," *http://teamcore.usc.edu/projects/coastguard/*, accessed May 13, 2014.

58. Leventhal, Rajiv, "At Boston Medical Center, Using Analytics to Improve OR Efficiencies," *Healthcare Informatics*," March 24, 2016, *www.healthcare-informatics.com/article/boston-medical-center-using-analytics-improve-or-efficiencies*.

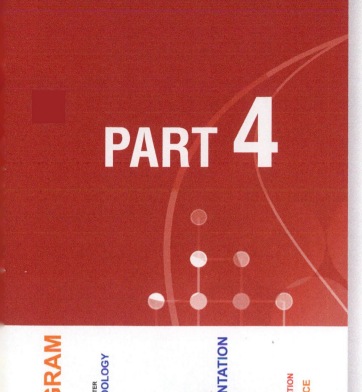

PART 4

master_art/Shutterstock.com

Planning, Acquiring, and Building Systems

Strategic Planning and Project Management

Did You Know?

- Over 2,000 years ago, the ancient Greek philosopher and scientist Aristotle identified the essence of good project management when he said: "First, have a definite, clear practical ideal: a goal or an objective. Second, have the necessary means to achieve your ends: wisdom, money, materials, and methods. Third, adjust all your means to that end."

- A 2015 study of 50,000 projects from around the world, ranging from small system enhancements to massive systems reengineering implementations, found that roughly 71 percent of all information system projects fail or face major challenges such as lateness, budget overruns, and lack of required features.

Principles

- Organizations that are more advanced in their planning processes develop multiple-year strategic plans.

- The strategic planning process for the IS organization and the factors that influence it depend on how the organization is perceived by the rest of the organization.

- Organizations must always make a clear connection among business objectives, goals, and projects. In addition, projects must be consistent with business strategies.

Learning Objectives

- State the benefits of creating a strategic plan.

- Identify and briefly describe the phases of a goals-based strategic planning process.

- Explain what SWOT analysis is and how it is used.

- Identify and briefly describe the components of a strategic plan.

- State the purpose of the IS strategic plan.

- Identify four drivers that set information system organizational strategy and determine information system investments.

- Identify three ways the IS organization can be perceived by the rest of the organization and discuss how that influences the IS strategy.

- Discuss why project management is considered to be a core competency for many organizations.

- Identify and briefly discuss the five highly interrelated parameters that define a project.

- Identify and briefly discuss the nine knowledge areas associated with the science of project management.

Why Learn about Strategic Planning and Project Management?

Ever since the dawn of the computer age, business and IS executives have been working to improve the alignment between business and IS as a top business priority. In this context, alignment means that the IS organization and its resources are focused on efforts that support the key objectives defined in the strategic plan of the business. This implies that IS and business managers have a shared vision of where the organization is headed and agree on its key strategies. This shared vision will guide the IS organization in hiring the right people with the correct skills and competencies, choosing the right technologies and vendors to explore and develop, installing the right systems, and focusing on projects that will best help the organization meet its mission. Projects are the way that much of an organization's work gets done. No matter what the industry and no matter whether the organization is a for-profit company or a nonprofit organization—large or small, multinational or local—good strategic planning coupled with good project management are positive forces that enable an organization to get results from its efforts. Knowing the basics of strategic planning and project management will make you an extremely valuable resource within any organization.

As you read this chapter, consider the following:

- What is an effective strategic planning process, who needs to participate in it, and what are the deliverables of such a process?
- What is project management, and what are the key elements of an effective project management process?

This chapter defines strategic planning and outlines an effective process for accomplishing this critical activity. It also clarifies the importance of project management and outlines a proven process for successful project management. Organizations today need people who can develop strategic plans and lead projects.

Strategic Planning

strategic planning: A process that helps managers identify desired outcomes and formulate feasible plans to achieve their objectives by using available resources and capabilities.

Strategic planning is a process that helps managers identify desired outcomes and formulate feasible plans to achieve their objectives by using available resources and capabilities. The strategic plan must take into account that the organization and everything around it is changing: consumers' likes and dislikes change; old competitors leave and new ones enter the marketplace; the costs and availability of raw materials and labor fluctuate, as does the fundamental economic environment (interest rates, growth in gross domestic product, inflation rates); and the degree of industry and government regulation changes.

The following is a set of frequently cited benefits of strategic planning:

- Provides a framework and a clearly defined direction to guide decision making at all levels throughout the organization
- Ensures the most effective use is made of the organization's resources by focusing those resources on agreed-on key priorities
- Enables the organization to be proactive and take advantage of opportunities and trends, rather than passively reacting to them
- Enables all organizational units to participate and work together toward accomplishing a common set of goals

- Provides a set of measures for judging organizational and personnel performance
- Improves communication among management and the board of directors, shareholders, and other interested parties

In some organizations with immature planning processes, strategic planning is an annual process timed to yield results used to prepare the annual expense budget and capital forecast. The process is focused inward, concentrating on the individual needs of various departments. Organizations that are more advanced in their planning processes develop multiple-year plans based on a situational analysis, competitive assessments, consideration of factors external to the organization, and an evaluation of strategic options.

The CEO of an organization must make long-term decisions about where the organization is headed and how it will operate and has ultimate responsibility for strategic planning. Subordinates, lower-level managers, and consultants typically gather useful information, perform much of the underlying analysis, and provide valuable input. But the CEO must thoroughly understand the analysis and be heavily involved in setting high-level business objectives and defining strategies. The CEO also must be seen as a champion and supporter of the chosen strategies; otherwise, the rest of the organization is unlikely to "buy into" those strategies and take the necessary actions to make it all happen.

There are a variety of strategic planning approaches, including issues based, organic, and goals based. **Issues-based strategic planning** begins by identifying and analyzing key issues that face the organization, setting strategies to address those issues, and identifying projects and initiatives that are consistent with those strategies. **Organic strategic planning** defines the organization's vision and values and then identifies projects and initiatives to achieve the vision while adhering to the values.

Goals-based strategic planning is a multiphase strategic planning process that begins by performing a situation analysis to identify an organization's strengths, weaknesses, opportunities, and threats. Next, management sets direction for the organization by defining its mission, vision, values, objectives, and goals. The results of the situation analysis and direction-setting phases are used to define strategies to enable the organization to fulfill its mission. Initiatives, programs, and projects are then identified and executed to enable the organization to meet the objectives and goals. These ongoing efforts are evaluated to ensure that they remain on track toward achieving the goals of the organization. The major phases in goals-based strategic planning are (1) analyze situation, (2) set direction, (3) define strategies, and (4) deploy plan (see Figure 11.1).

Analyze Situation

All levels and business units of an organization must be involved in assessing its strengths and weaknesses. Preparing a historical perspective that summarizes

issues-based strategic planning: A strategic planning process that begins by identifying and analyzing key issues that face the organization, setting strategies to address those issues, and identifying projects and initiatives that are consistent with those strategies.

organic strategic planning: A strategic planning process that defines the organization's vision and values and then identifies projects and initiatives to achieve the vision while adhering to the values.

goals-based strategic planning: A multiphase strategic planning process that begins by performing a situation analysis to identify an organization's strengths, weaknesses, opportunities, and threats.

FIGURE **11.1**

The goals-based strategic planning process

Goals-based strategic planning is a multiphase process for strategic planning.

Where are we now?	Where do we want to go?	How will we get there?	How do we engage others?
Analyze situation	Set direction	Define strategies	Deploy plan
Strengths Weaknesses Opportunities Threats	Mission Vision Values Objectives Goals	Strategies	Corporate and business unit: • Plans • Initiatives • Programs • Projects

the company's development is an excellent way to begin this strategic planning step. Next, a multitude of data is gathered about internal processes and operations, including survey data from customers and suppliers and other objective assessments of the organization. The collected data is analyzed to identify and assess how well the firm is meeting current objectives and goals, and how well its current strategies are working. This process identifies many of the strengths and weaknesses of the firm.

Strategic planning requires careful study of the external environment surrounding the organization and assessing where the organization fits within it. This analysis begins with an examination of the industry in which the organization competes: What is the size of the market? How fast is it growing or shrinking? What are the significant industry trends?

Next, the organization must collect and analyze facts about its key customers, competitors, and suppliers. The goal is twofold: capture a clear picture of the strategically important issues that the organization must address in the future and reveal the firm's competitive position against its rivals. During this step, the organization must get input from customers, suppliers, and industry experts—all of whom will likely be able to provide more objective viewpoints than employees. Members of the organization should be prepared to hear things they do not like, but that may offer tremendous opportunities for improvement. It is critical that unmet customer needs are identified to form the basis for future growth.

Michael Porter's Five Forces Model: A model that identifies the fundamental factors that determine the level of competition and long-term profitability of an industry.

The most frequently used model for assessing the nature of industry competition is **Michael Porter's Five Forces Model**, which identifies the fundamental factors that determine the level of competition and long-term profitability of an industry (see Figure 11.2).

The fundamental factors that determine the level of competition and long-term profitability of an industry are the following:

1. The threat of new competitors will raise the level of competition. Entry barriers determine the relative threat of new competitors. These barriers include the capital required to enter the industry and the cost to customers to switch to a competitor.

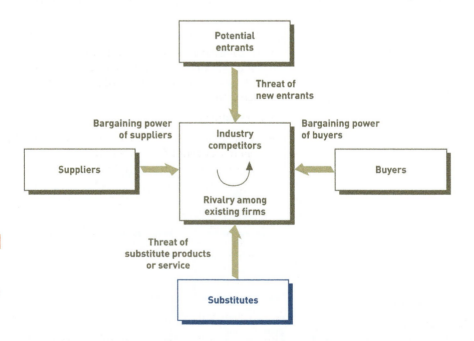

Michael Porter's Five Forces Model
This model can be used to determine the level of competition and long-term profitability of an industry.

2. The threat of substitute products can lower the profitability of industry competitors. The willingness of buyers to switch products and the relative cost and performance of substitutes are key factors in this threat.

3. The bargaining power of buyers determines prices and long-term profitability. This bargaining power is stronger when there are relatively few buyers but many sellers in the industry, or when the products offered are all essentially the same.

4. The bargaining power of suppliers can significantly affect the industry's profitability. Suppliers have strong bargaining power in industries that have many buyers and only a few dominant suppliers and in industries that do not represent a key customer group for suppliers.

5. The degree of rivalry between competitors is high in industries with many equally sized competitors or little differentiation between products.

Many organizations also perform a competitive financial analysis to determine how their revenue, costs, profits, cash flow, and other key financial parameters match up against those of their competitors. Most of the information needed to prepare such comparisons is readily available from competitors' annual reports.

Strengths, Weaknesses, Opportunities, Threats (SWOT) matrix: A simple way to illustrate what a company is doing well, where it can improve, what opportunities are available, and what environmental factors threaten the future of the organization.

The analysis of an organization's internal assessment and study of its external environment is summarized into a **Strengths, Weaknesses, Opportunities, Threats (SWOT) matrix**, as shown in Table 11.1, which provides a SWOT matrix for Starbucks.[1] The SWOT matrix is a simple way to illustrate what the company is doing well, where it can improve, what opportunities are available, and what environmental factors threaten the future of the organization. Typically, the internal assessment identifies most of the strengths and weaknesses, while the analysis of the external environment uncovers most of the opportunities and threats. The technique is based on the assumption that an effective strategy derives from maximizing a firm's strengths and opportunities and minimizing its weaknesses and threats.

TABLE 11.1 SWOT analysis for Starbucks

Strengths	Weaknesses
• Strong revenue and profit growth • Rapid increase in global store count • Strong comparable store sales growth	• Uneven international growth • Investing lots of money on expansion

Opportunities	Threats
• Rising incomes in China should fuel higher demand for "premium" Western products such as Starbucks • Top premium coffee brand in the K-Cup category, presenting a growth opportunity • Experimenting with various concept stores, including tea bars and wine bars	• Unstable price of coffee beans • Rising competition (e.g., Dunkin' Donuts and Tim Hortons)

Set Direction

The direction-setting phase of strategic planning involves defining the mission, vision, values, objectives, and goals of the organization. Determining these will enable the organization to identify the proper strategies and projects, as shown in Figure 11.3.

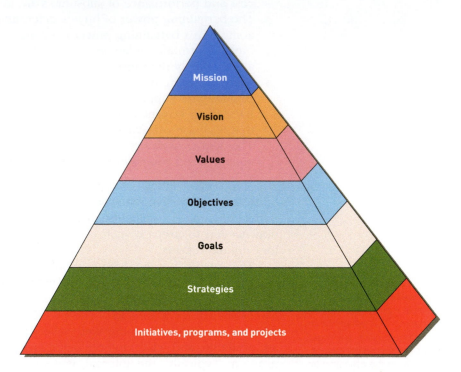

The strategic planning pyramid
The strategic planning pyramid is a top-down approach to identify initiatives, program, and projects.

vision/mission statement: A statement that communicates an organization's overarching aspirations to guide it through changing objectives, goals, and strategies.

mission statement: A statement that concisely defines an organization's fundamental purpose for existing.

vision: A concise statement of what an organization intends to achieve in the future.

core value: A widely accepted principle that guides how people behave and make decisions in the organization.

objective: A statement of a compelling business need that an organization must meet to achieve its vision and mission.

Vision and Mission

Senior management must create a **vision/mission statement** that communicates an organization's overarching aspirations to guide it through changing objectives, goals, and strategies. The organization's vision/mission statement forms a foundation for making decisions and taking action. The most effective vision/mission statements inspire and require employees to stretch to reach the organization's goals. These statements seldom change once they are formulated. An effective statement consists of three components: a mission statement, a vision of a desirable future, and a set of core values.

The **mission statement** concisely defines the organization's fundamental purpose for existing. It usually is stated in a challenging manner to inspire employees, customers, and shareholders.

The organization's **vision** is a concise statement of what the organization intends to achieve in the future. The following are the earmarks of a good vision:

- It motivates and inspires.
- It is easy to communicate, simple to understand, and memorable.
- It is challenging and yet achievable and moves the organization toward greatness.

A **core value** is a widely accepted principle that guides how people behave and make decisions in the organization.

Table 11.2 provides the mission, vision, and values of Google.[2,3]

Objectives

The terms "objective" and "goal" are frequently used interchangeably. For this discussion, we distinguish between the two—defining **objective** as a statement of a compelling business need that an organization must meet to achieve its vision and mission.

Each week, Walmart serves close to 260 million customers in its stores and through its Web sites globally. Recent annual revenue for the company

TABLE 11.2 Google's mission, vision, and values

Mission

To organize the world's information and make it universally accessible and useful.

Vision

To provide access to the world's information in one click.

Values

1) We want to work with great people.

2) Technology innovation is our lifeblood.

3) Working at Google is fun.

4) Be actively involved; you are Google.

5) Don't take success for granted.

6) Do the right thing; don't be evil.

7) Earn customer and user loyalty and respect every day.

8) Sustainable long-term growth and profitability are key to our success.

9) Google cares about and supports the communities where we work and live.

10) We aspire to improve and change the world.

exceeded $485 billion. The organization has defined its mission, vision, values, and objectives, as shown in Table 11.3.[4]

TABLE 11.3 Walmart's mission, vision, and values

Mission: We save people money so they can live better.

Vision: If we work together, we'll lower the cost of living for everyone … we'll give the world an opportunity to see what it's like to save and have a better life.

Core Values:

- **Open door policy.** Managers' doors are open to employees at all levels.
- **Sundown rule.** Answer employee, customer, and supplier questions on the same day the questions are received.
- **Grass roots process.** Capture suggestions and ideas from the sales floor and front lines.
- **Three basic beliefs & values.** Respect for the individual; service to our customers; and striving for excellence.
- **Ten-foot rule.** Make eye contact, greet, and offer help to customers who come within 10 feet.
- **Servant leadership.** Leaders are in service to their team.

Objectives:

- Give the consumer greater value for each product category.
- Optimize the products in each of stores by reducing the number of products and number of suppliers.
- Improve the customer's in-store experience and become more efficient in and out of each store.

Goals

goal: A specific result that must be achieved to reach an objective.

A **goal** is a specific result that must be achieved to reach an objective. In fact, several goals may be associated with a single objective. The objective states what must be accomplished, and the associated goals specify how to determine whether the objective is being met.

Goals track progress in meeting an organization's objectives. They help managers determine if a specific objective is being achieved. Results, determined by how well the goals are met, provide a feedback loop. Depending on the difference between the actual and desired results, adjustments may be needed in the objectives, goals, and strategies as well as with the actual projects being worked on.

Some organizations encourage their managers to set Big Hairy Audacious Goals (BHAGs) that require a breakthrough in the organization's products or services to achieve. Such a goal "may be daunting and perhaps risky, but the challenge of it grabs people in the gut and gets their juices flowing and creates tremendous forward momentum."[5]

In April 2012, Facebook purchased the two-year-old photo-sharing service Instagram for $1 billion, a move that many industry analysts viewed as imprudent investment at the time.[6] However, since then, Instagram usage has grown rapidly with both personal and business users. Achieving the goal of successfully integrating Instagram with Facebook expanded the company's mobile offerings while removing a rival for users' attention.[7]

The use of so-called SMART goals has long been advocated by management consultants.[8] The principal advantages of SMART goals are that they are easy to understand, are easily tracked, and contribute real value to the organization. The SMART acronym stands for:

- **Specific.** Specific goals have a much greater chance of being understood and accomplished than vague goals. Specific goals use action verbs and specify who, what, when, where, and why.
- **Measurable.** Goals that are measurable include numeric or descriptive measures that define criteria such as quantity, quality, and cost so that progress toward meeting the goal can be determined.
- **Achievable.** Goals should be ambitious yet realistic and attainable. Goals that are either completely out of reach or below standard performance are worthless and demotivating.
- **Relevant.** Goals should strongly contribute to the mission of the department, else why expend the effort?
- **Time constrained.** A time limit should be set to reach the goal to help define the priority to assign to meeting the goal.

An example of a SMART goal for a customer service organization of a large retail store might be: Reduce customer complaints about mispriced merchandise from 9 per day to less than 3 per day by June 30.

Define Strategies

strategy: A plan that describes how an organization will achieve its vision, mission, objectives, and goals.

A **strategy** describes how an organization will achieve its vision, mission, objectives, and goals. Selecting a specific strategy focuses and coordinates an organization's resources and activities from the top down to accomplish its mission. Indeed, creating a set of strategies that will garner committed supporters across the organization—all aligned on the mission and vision—is key to organizational success.

Common themes in setting strategies include "increase revenue," "attract and retain new customers," "increase customer loyalty," and "reduce the time required to deliver new products to market." In choosing from alternative strategies, managers should consider the long-term impact of each strategy on revenue and profit, the degree of risk involved, the amount and types of resources that will be required, and the potential competitive reaction. In setting strategies, managers draw on the results of the SWOT analysis and consider the following questions:

- How can we best capitalize on our strengths and use them to their full potential?

- How do we reduce or eliminate the negative impact of our weaknesses?
- Which opportunities represent the best opportunities for our organization?
- How can we exploit these opportunities?
- Will our strengths enable us to make the most of this opportunity?
- Will our weaknesses undermine our ability to capitalize on this opportunity?
- How can we defend against threats to achieve our vision/mission, objectives, and goals?
- Can we turn this threat into an opportunity?

Amazon has made a strategic decision to explore the possible use of delivery drones to gain a real competitive advantage over competitors who rely on less efficient ground transportation. Because a large percentage of Amazon packages weigh less than 5 pounds, drones could make the ideal rapid-delivery vehicles. Amazon has detailed plans for this service, however, the company cannot announce if or when the program will start until regulators set out the rules regarding the commercial use of drones. Such a strategy has the potential to attract new customers and increase revenue.[9]

Deploy Plan

The strategic plan defines objectives for an organization, establishes SMART goals, and sets strategies on how to reach those goals. These objectives, goals, and strategies are then communicated to the organization's business units and functional units so that everyone is "on the same page." The managers of the various organizational units can then develop more detailed plans for initiatives, programs, and projects that align with the firm's objectives, goals, and strategies. Alignment ensures that the efforts will draw on the strengths of the organization, capitalize on new opportunities, fix organizational weaknesses, and minimize the impact of potential threats.

The extent of strategic planning done at lower levels within the organization depends on the amount of autonomy granted those units as well as the leadership style and capabilities of the managers in charge of each unit. For these reasons, the amount of effort, the process used, and the level of creativity that goes into the creation of a business unit strategic plan can vary greatly across an organization.

Alstom Transport, which develops and markets railway systems, equipment, and services, won a contract to supply Virgin Trains' West Coast Mainline operations in the United Kingdom.[10] Alstom supplied Virgin Trains 52 of its high-speed (125 mph) Pendolino trains. However, the train was initially too unreliable—too many trains were shut down on any given day due to maintenance issues.[11] Only 38 of the 52 trains were available on a given day; however, 46 trains were needed to meet service-level goals. The situation was affecting Alstom's relationship with Virgin Trains, and, if not improved, would likely affect contract renewal. Alstom Transport executives met and set key objectives to improve the relationship with Virgin Trains:

- Meet availability goals and improve reliability.
- Do not increase costs.
- Provide greater value to the customer.

Alstom leaders then employed a "catch-ball" process to deploy these objectives to other workers at the firm. The management team "threw" the goals back and forth with the entire management chain, including senior management, operations leaders, and depot and production management. By means of this process, Alstom identified over 15 potential improvement projects to support the goals, leading to an increased train availability rate—72 percent to 90 percent—while headcount and costs were kept flat. Alstom won renewal of a service maintenance contract with Virgin Trains three years earlier than expected because of its improved service.[12]

Critical Thinking Exercise

Strategic Planning at Johns Hopkins Medicine

Johns Hopkins Medicine, with headquarters in Baltimore, Maryland, is a $7.7 billion global healthcare organization that operates 6 academic and community hospitals, along with 4 suburban healthcare and surgery centers, and 39 primary and specialty care outpatient sites. The organization strives to create a culture in which diversity, inclusion, civility, collegiality, and professionalism are championed through actions, incentives, and accountability. Johns Hopkins Medicine's mission, vision, core values, and objectives are presented in Table 11.4.[13]

TABLE 11.4 Johns Hopkins Medicine mission, vision, values, and objectives

Mission: To improve the health of the community and the world by setting the standard of excellence in medical education, research, and clinical care.

Vision: Johns Hopkins Medicine pushes the boundaries of discovery, transforms health care, advances medical education, and creates hope for humanity. Together we will deliver the promise of medicine.

Core Values:

- Excellence and discovery
- Leadership and integrity
- Diversity and inclusion
- Respect and collegiality

Objectives:

- Attract, engage, develop, and retain the world's best people.
- Become the exemplar for biomedical research by advancing and integrating discovery, innovation, translation, and dissemination.
- Be the national leader in the safety science, teaching, and provision of patient- and family-centered care.
- Lead the world in the education and training of physicians and biomedical scientists.
- Become the model for an academically based, integrated healthcare delivery and financing system.
- Create sustainable financial success and implement continuous performance improvement.

You are a member of a three-person team within the finance organization that is working under the direction of the CFO to define a set of strategies that will support Johns Hopkins Medicine's financial objectives and goals.

Review Questions

The CFO has asked each member of the team to express his or her thoughts on two topics:

1. Should any resources from outside the finance organization be recruited to help identify and evaluate alternative strategies? Why or why not?
2. How should potential strategies for the finance organization be evaluated?

Critical Thinking Questions

1. Develop two hypothetical objectives specific to the finance organization that are consistent with Johns Hopkins Medicine's overall vision, mission, and objectives.
2. For each objective develop one SMART goal.

Setting the Information System Organizational Strategy

The strategic plan of the information system (IS) organization must identify those technologies, vendors, competencies, people, systems, and projects in which the organization will invest to support the corporate and business unit objectives, goals, and strategies. The IS strategic plan is strongly influenced by new technology innovations (e.g., increasingly more powerful mobile devices, advanced printers that can generate three-dimensional objects from a digital file, access to shared computer resources over the Internet, advanced software that can analyze large amounts of structured and unstructured data) and innovative thinking by others both inside and outside the organization (see Figure 11.4).

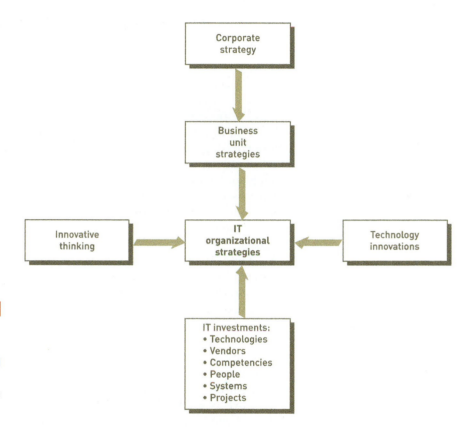

Drivers that set IS organizational strategy and determine information system investments

Planners must consider many factors in setting IS organizational strategy.

The strategic planning process for the IS organization and the factors that influence it depend on how the organization is perceived by the rest of the organization. An IS organization can be viewed as a cost center/service provider, a business partner/business peer, or as a game changer (see Table 11.5).

In a recent survey of more than 700 CIOs, 38 percent said that their IS organization is viewed as a cost center/service provider that is expected to reduce IS costs and improve IS services.[14] The strategic planning process for such an organization is typically directed inward and focused on determining how to do what it is currently doing but cheaper, faster, and better.

The IS organization of the state of Delaware is viewed as a cost center/ service provider. One of the organization's primary strategic initiatives is to consolidate IS resources and to eliminate redundant functions and resources within the various state agencies. The goal is to deliver significant improvements in customer service and to reduce costs.[15]

The majority of CIOs surveyed, about 52 percent, said that their IS organization is viewed as a business partner/business peer that is expected to control IS costs and expand IS services in support of business initiatives.[16] The

TABLE 11.5 The IS strategic planning spectrum

	Cost Center/Service Provider	Business Partner/ Business Peer	Game Changer
Strategic planning focus	Inward looking	Business focused	Outward looking
IS goals	Reduce IS costs; improve IS services	Control IS costs; expand IS services	Make IS investments to deliver new products and services
Strategy	React to strategic plans of business units	Execute IS projects to support plans of business	Use IS to achieve competitive advantage
Typical projects	Eliminate redundant or ineffective IS services	Implement corporate database and/or enterprise systems	Provide new ways for customers to interact with organization

strategic planning process of these organizations is based on understanding the collective business plans for the next year and determining what those mean for the IS organization in terms of new technologies, vendors, competencies, people, systems, and projects.

The IS organization for the city of Seattle operates under the constraint of a decreasing budget but is continually striving to expand its services and capitalize on the latest technology developments. It employs newer technologies, such as mobile computing, to improve the interaction of city government with its constituents and to support city services on the move. The organization also seeks opportunities to access shared computer resources through cloud-based applications to gain advantages and efficiencies where it makes sense.[17]

Only 10 percent of surveyed CIOs stated that their IS organization is viewed by fellow employees as a game-changing organization that is asked to lead product innovation efforts and open new markets.[18] Their strategic planning process is outwardly focused and involves meeting with customers, suppliers, and leading IS consultants and vendors to answer questions like "What do we want to be?" and "How can we create competitive advantage?"[19] In such organizations, IS is not only a means for implementing business-defined objectives but also a catalyst for achieving new business objectives unreachable without IS.

GAF is a $3 billion privately held manufacturer of commercial and residential roofing. GAF's IS employees regularly collaborate with external customers to learn from them and to help educate potential customers about why they should do business with GAF.[20] Using these collaboration sessions to gain a better understanding of its customers' needs, GAF developed a mobile app that allows a contractor to take a photo of a prospect's house and then use that photo to allow the prospect to preview different GAF shingle styles and colors on an actual image of their home. The app was a game changer for the organization as it helps GAF contractors demonstrate the beauty of GAF shingles and eliminates one of the biggest barriers to closing the sale—answering the question, "How will it look on my house?"[21]

No matter how an IS organization is perceived, the odds of achieving good alignment between the IS strategic plan and the rest of the business are vastly increased if IS workers have experience in the business and can talk to business managers in business terms rather than technology terms. IS staff must be able to recognize and understand business needs and develop effective solutions. The CIO especially must be able to communicate well and should be accessible to other corporate executives. However, the entire burden of achieving alignment between the business and IS cannot be placed solely on the IS organization.

Identifying IS Projects and Initiatives

In mature planning organizations, IS workers are constantly picking up ideas for potential projects through their interactions with various business managers and from observing other IS organizations and competitors. They also keep abreast of new IS developments and consider how innovations and new technologies might be applied in their firm. As members of the IS organization review and consider the corporate objectives, goals, and strategies, they can generate many ideas for IS projects that support corporate objectives and goals. They also recognize the need for IS projects that help other corporate units fulfill their business objectives. Often, experienced IS managers are assigned to serve as liaisons with the business units in order to gain a deeper understanding of each business unit and its needs. The IS managers are then able to help identify and define IS projects needed to meet those needs.

Most organizations find it useful to classify various potential projects by type. One such classification system is shown in Table 11.6.

TABLE 11.6 Project classification example

Project Type	Definition	Risk Factors Associated with Project Type
Breakthrough	Creates a competitive advantage that enables the organization to earn a greater than normal return on investment than its competitors	High cost; very high risk of failure and potential business disruption
Growth	Generates substantial new revenue or profits for the firm	High cost; high risk of failure and potential business disruption
Innovation	Explores the use of technology (or a new technology) in a new way	Risk can be managed by setting cost limits, establishing an end date, and defining criteria for success
Enhancement	Upgrades an existing system to provide new capabilities that meet new business needs	Risk that scope of upgrade may expand, making it difficult to control cost and schedule
Maintenance	Implements changes to an existing system to enable operation in a different technology environment (e.g., underlying changes in hardware, operating systems, or database management systems)	Risk that major rework may be required to make system work in a new technology environment; potential for system performance degradation
Mandatory	Needed to meet requirements of a legal entity or regulatory agency	Risk that mandated completion date is missed; may be difficult to define tangible benefits; costs can be skyrocketed

Prioritizing IS Projects and Initiatives

Typically, an organization identifies more IS-related projects and initiatives than it has the people and resources to staff. An iterative process of setting priorities and determining the resulting budget, staffing, and timing is needed to define which projects will be initiated and when they will be executed. Many organizations create an IS investment board of business unit executives to review potential projects and evaluate them from several different perspectives:

1. First and foremost, each viable project must relate to a specific organizational goal. These relationships make it clear that executing each project will help meet important organizational objectives (see Figure 11.5).
2. Can the organization measure the business value of the initiative? Will there be tangible benefits, or are the benefits intangible? **Tangible benefits** can be measured directly and assigned a monetary value. For example, the number of staff before and after the completion of an initiative

tangible benefit: A benefit that can be measured directly and assigned a monetary value.

Organizational objective

Organizational goal

Potential IT-related project

FIGURE **11.5**

Projects must be related to goals and objectives

Objectives define goals that in turn identify projects consistent with those objectives and goals.

intangible benefit: A benefit that cannot directly be measured and cannot easily be quantified in monetary terms.

can be measured, and the monetary value is the decrease in staffing costs, such as salary, benefits, and overhead. **Intangible benefits** cannot directly be measured and cannot easily be quantified in monetary terms. For example, an increase in customer satisfaction due to an initiative is important but is difficult to measure and cannot easily be converted into a monetary value.

3. What kinds of costs (hardware, software, personnel, consultants, etc.) are associated with the project, and what is the likely total cost of the effort over multiple years? Consider not just the initial development cost but the total cost of ownership, including operating costs, support costs, and maintenance fees.

4. Preliminary costs and benefits are weighed to see if the project has an attractive rate of return. Unfortunately, costs and benefits may not be well understood at an early phase of the project, and many worthwhile projects do not have benefits that are easy to quantify.

5. Risk is another factor to consider. Managers must consider the likelihood that the project will fail to deliver the expected benefits; the actual cost will be significantly more than expected; the technology will become obsolete before the project is completed; the technology is too "cutting edge" and will not deliver what is promised; or the business situation will change so that the proposed project is no longer necessary.

6. Some projects enable other projects. For example, a new customer database may be required before the order-processing application can be upgraded. Therefore, some sequencing of projects must be considered.

7. Is the organization capable of taking on this project? Does the IS organization have the skills and expertise to execute the project successfully? Is the organization willing and able to make the required changes to receive their full value?

Critical Thinking Exercise

Business Liaison Role

You have been employed as a systems analyst in the information systems organization of a medium-sized consumer goods manufacturer for three years. You are quite surprised when your manager offers you a one-year special assignment as a manager supervising workers and operations in the large distribution center used to store your company's finished products and prepare them for shipment to retail stores around the country. Your manager explains that the company wishes to groom you to become the business liaison with the distribution organization and wants you to become familiar with the entire order-fulfillment process. Based on its recent growth, the company is planning to open at least two new distribution centers in different regions of the country over the next two to three years. Management has chosen you to be a key player in leading a future project to design and implement the information systems and automated equipment to support these new centers.

Review Questions

1. What is the role of a business liaison person, and what skills and knowledge do they need?
2. How would you classify the project to outfit the organization's new distribution center?

Critical Thinking Questions

1. For you, personally, what are the pros and cons of accepting this position?
2. Would you take this assignment? Why or why not?

Project Management

A project is a temporary endeavor undertaken to create a unique product, service, or result. Each project attempts to achieve specific business objectives and is subject to certain constraints, such as total cost and completion date. Organizations must always make clear connections among business objectives, goals, and projects; also, projects must be consistent with business strategies. For example, an organization may have a business objective to improve customer service by offering a consistently high level of service that exceeds customers' expectations. Initiating a project to reduce costs in the customer service area by eliminating all but essential services would be inconsistent with this business objective.

At any point in time, an organization may have dozens or even hundreds of active projects, aimed at accomplishing a wide range of results. Projects are different from operational activities, which are repetitive activities performed over and over again. Projects are not repetitive; they come to a definite end once the project objectives are met or the project is cancelled. Projects come in all sizes and levels of complexity, as you can see from the following examples:

- A senior executive led a project to integrate two organizations following a corporate merger.
- A consumer goods company executed a project to launch a new product.
- An operations manager led a project to outsource part of a firm's operations to a contract manufacturer.
- A hospital executed a project to load an app on physicians' smartphones that would enable them to access patient data.
- A computer software manufacturer completed a project to improve the scheduling of help desk technicians and reduce the time on hold for callers to its telephone support services.
- A staff assistant led a project to plan the annual sales meeting.
- A manager completed a project to enter her departmental budget into a preformatted spreadsheet template.

Unfortunately, IS-related projects are not always successful. The Standish Group has been tracking the success rate of IS projects for over 20 years, and although the success rate has improved over time due to improved methods, training, and tools, roughly 71 percent of all IS projects fail or face major challenges such as lateness, budget overruns, and lack of required features.[22]

core competency: Something that a firm can do well and that provides customer benefits, is hard for competitors to imitate, and can be leveraged widely to many products and markets.

Researchers Hamel and Prahalad defined the term **core competency** to mean something that a firm can do well and that provides customer benefits, is hard for competitors to imitate, and can be leveraged widely to many products and markets.[23] Today, many organizations recognize project management as one of their core competencies and see their ability to manage projects better as a way to achieve an edge over competitors and deliver greater value to shareholders and customers. As a result, those organizations spend considerable effort identifying potential project managers and then training and developing them. For many managers, their ability to manage projects effectively is a key to their success within an organization.

Project Variables

Five highly interrelated parameters define a project—scope, cost, time, quality, and user expectations. If any one of these parameters changes for a project, there must be a corresponding change in one or more of the other parameters. A brief discussion of these parameters follows.

Scope

project scope: A definition of which tasks are included and which tasks are not included in a project.

Project scope is a definition of which tasks are included and which tasks are not included in a project. Project scope is a key determinant of the other project factors and must carefully be defined to ensure that a project meets its essential objectives. In general, the larger the scope of the project, the more difficult it is to meet cost, schedule, quality, and stakeholder expectations.

For example, the California Case Management System was a major IS project intended to automate court operations for the state of California with a common system across the state that would replace 70 different legacy systems. At the start of the project, planners expected the system to cost $260 million; however, court administrators terminated the project after spending $500 million on the effort. Today, it is estimated that the project would have cost nearly $2 billion if it had run to completion. While a variety of factors contributed to this waste of resources, one primary cause was inadequate control of the project scope, with some 102 changes in requirements and scope approved over the life of the project.[24]

Cost

The cost of a project includes all the capital, expenses, and internal cross-charges associated with the project's buildings, operation, maintenance, and support. Capital is money spent to purchase assets that appear on the organization's balance sheet and are depreciated over the life of the asset. Capital items typically have a useful life of at least several years. A building, office equipment, computer hardware, and network equipment are examples of capital assets. Computer software also can be classified as a capital item if it costs more than $1,000 per unit, has a useful life exceeding one year, and is not used for research and development.

Expense items are nondepreciable items that are consumed shortly after they are purchased. Typical expenses associated with an IS-related project include the use of outside labor or consultants, travel, and training. Software that does not meet the criteria to be classified as a capital item is classified as an expense item.

sponsoring business unit: The business unit most affected by the project and the one whose budget will cover the project costs.

Many organizations use a system of internal cross-charges to account for the cost of employees assigned to a project. For example, the fully loaded cost (salary, benefits, and overhead) of a manager might be set at $120,000 per year. The sponsoring organization's budget is cross-charged this amount for each manager who works full time on the project. (The **sponsoring business unit** is the business unit most affected by the project and the one whose budget will cover the project costs.) So, if a manager works at a 75 percent level of effort on a project for five months, the cross-charge is $120,000 × 0.75 × 5/12 = $37,500. The rationale behind cross-charging is to enable sound economic decisions about whether employees should be assigned to project work or to operational activities. If employees are assigned to a project, cross-charging helps organizations determine which project makes the most economic sense.

Organizations have different processes and mechanisms for budgeting and controlling each of the three types of costs: capital, expense, and internal cross-charge. Money from the budget for one type of cost cannot be used to pay for an item associated with another type of cost. Thus, a project with a large amount of capital remaining in its budget cannot use the available dollars to pay for an expense item even if the expense budget is overspent.

Table 11.7 summarizes and classifies various types of common costs associated with an IS-related project.

TABLE 11.7 Typical IS-related project costs

	Development Costs		
	Capital	Internal Cross-Charge	Expense
Employee-related expenses			
• Employees' effort		X	
• Travel-related expenses			X
• Training-related expenses			X
Contractor and consultant charges			X
IS-related capital and expenses			
• Software licenses (software purchases that qualify as a capital expense)	X		
• Software licenses (software that does not qualify as a capital expense)			X
• Computing hardware devices	X		
• Network hardware devices	X		
• Data capture/data entry equipment	X		
Total development costs	X	X	X

Time

The timing of a project is frequently a critical constraint. For example, in most organizations, projects that involve finance and accounting must be scheduled to avoid any conflict with operations associated with the closing of end-of-quarter books. Often, projects must be completed by a certain date to meet an important business goal or a government mandate.

CGI, a Canadian consulting, systems integration, outsourcing, and solutions company, was awarded a $36 million contract in December 2012 to build the Vermont Health Connect state health exchange.[25] Work on the project quickly fell behind schedule—with CGI failing to meet more than half of Vermont's 21 performance deadlines—so the state and CGI entered into an amended $84 million contract in August 2013 to complete the project.[26] The Vermont Health Connect site launched in October 2013 as required to meet American Affordable Care Act mandates, but with serious deficiencies. Users were unable to edit their information, and the site did not work for small businesses. Despite calls to dump CGI after the flawed launch, state officials decided to continue working with CGI to complete the site. In April 2014, the state and CGI signed off on yet another agreement that set a new schedule for delivering missing functionality and included financial penalties for missed deadlines.[27] When CGI failed to meet a May deadline for enabling users to edit their information, the state extended the deadline again—without assessing any penalties.[28] CGI failed to meet the revised deadline, and in August 2014, the state fired CGI and announced it would transition the remaining work to a new contractor. In the end, Vermont paid CGI $66.7 million for completed work on the $84 million contract.[29,30] CGI was replaced by Optum, a healthcare technology company based in Minnesota that is owned by United Health Group, the nation's largest health insurer.[31]

Quality

quality: The degree to which a project meets the needs of its users.

The **quality** of a project can be defined as the degree to which the project meets the needs of its users. The quality of a project that delivers an IS-related system may be defined in terms of the system's functionality, features, system outputs, performance, reliability, and maintainability.

Failure to meet users' functionality and performance needs detracted from the initial introduction of the iPhone 6. Apple sold an astounding 10 million of the iPhone 6 and iPhone 6 Plus models in the first few days they were available. Unfortunately, the new iPhones had both hardware and software problems that caused the devices to fail to meet users' functionality and performance expectations. Apple's new mobile operating system iOS 8 for the devices came without promised apps that used a health and fitness feature called HealthKit. In addition, it turned out that the iPhone 6 Plus was too pliable, with some users complaining that the phone bent when sitting in their pockets for extended periods. Then, when Apple released an iOS 8 update aimed at fixing the HealthKit problem, some users complained the update had caused their iPhones to lose the ability to make phone calls.[32]

User Expectations

As a project begins, stakeholders will form expectations—or will already have expectations—about how the project will be conducted and how it will affect them. For example, based on previous project experience, the end users of a new IS system may expect that they will have no involvement with the system until it is time for them to be trained. However, the project manager may follow a more progressive development process that requires users to help define system requirements, evaluate system options, try out system prototypes, develop user documentation, and define and conduct the user acceptance test.

As another example, end users may expect to participate in weekly project status meetings to hear progress reports firsthand. However, the project manager may not have considered involving them in the status meetings or may not even be planning weekly meetings.

Both examples illustrate the huge differences in expectations that can exist between stakeholders and project members. It is critical to a project's success to identify expectations of key stakeholders and team members; any differences must be resolved to avoid future problems and misunderstandings.

The five project parameters—scope, cost, time, quality, and user expectations—are all closely interrelated, as shown in Figure 11.6. For example, if the time allowed to complete the project is decreased, it may require an increase in project costs, a reduction in project quality and scope, and a change of expectations among the project stakeholders, as shown in Figure 11.7.

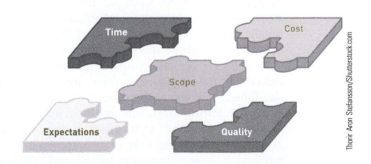

FIGURE 11.6

The five parameters that define a project

The five parameters that define a project are all highly interrelated.

Andrey_Popov/Shutterstock.com

Revised project definition
A change in any one of the project variables (cost, time, scope, or expectations) can impact the other variables.

project stakeholders: The people involved in the project or those affected by its outcome.

project management: The application of knowledge, skills, and techniques to project activities to meet project requirements.

What Is Project Management?

Project management is the application of knowledge, skills, and techniques to project activities to meet project requirements. Project managers must deliver a solution that meets specific scope, cost, time, and quality goals while managing the expectations of the **project stakeholders**—the people involved in the project or those affected by its outcome.

The essence of artistic activity is that it involves high levels of creativity and freedom to do whatever the artist feels. Scientific activity, on the other hand, involves following defined routines and exacting adherence to laws. Under these definitions, part of project management can be considered an art, because project managers must apply intuitive skills that vary from project to project and even from team member to team member. The "art" of project management also involves salesmanship and psychology in convincing others of the need to change and that this project is right to do.

Project management is also part science because it uses time-proven, repeatable processes and techniques to achieve project goals. Thus, one challenge to successful project management is recognizing when to act as an artist and rely on one's own instinct and when to act as a scientist and apply fundamental project management principles and practices. The following section covers the nine areas associated with the science of project management.

Project Management Knowledge Areas

According to the Project Management Institute (PMI), project managers must coordinate nine areas of expertise: scope, time, cost, quality, human resources, communications, risk, procurement, and integration as shown in Figure 11.8.

Scope Management

scope management: A set of activities that include defining the work that must be done as part of a project and then controlling the work to stay within the agreed-upon scope.

Scope management includes defining the work that must be done as part of the project and then controlling the work to stay within the agreed-upon scope. Key activities include initiation, scope planning, scope definition, scope verification, and scope change control.

functional decomposition: A frequently used technique to define the scope of an information system by identifying the business processes it will affect.

Functional decomposition is a frequently used technique to define the scope of an information system by identifying the business processes it will affect. Figure 11.9 shows an example of a functional decomposition chart for a stock management system. A process is usually initiated in response to a

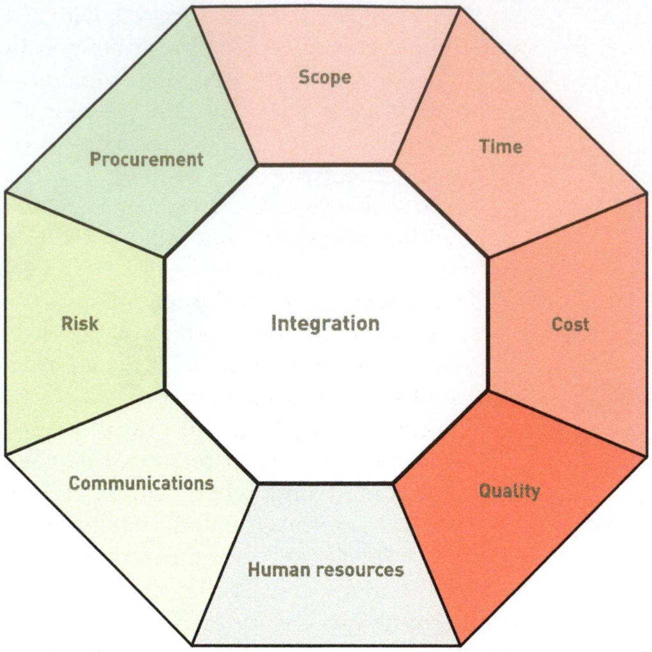

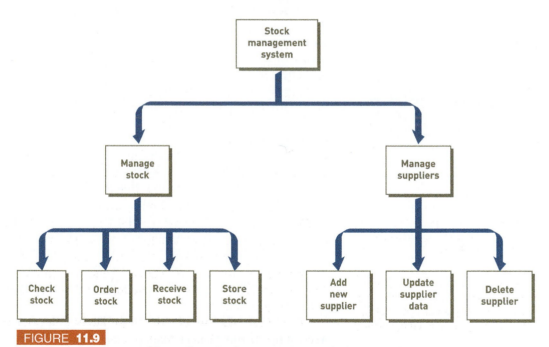

FIGURE **11.8**

The nine project management knowledge areas

There are nine areas associated with the science of project management.

FIGURE **11.9**

Functional decomposition of a stock management system project

Functional decomposition is used to define the scope of the system.

specific event and requires input, which it processes to create output. Often a process generates feedback that is used to monitor and refine the process.

To create the functional decomposition chart, begin with the name of the system and then identify the highest-level processes to be performed. Each process should be given a two-word "verb-subject" name that clearly defines the process. Next, break those high-level processes down into lower-level subprocesses. Typically, two or three levels of decomposition are sufficient to define the scope of the system.

To avoid problems associated with a change in project scope, a formal scope change process should be defined before the project begins. The project manager and key business managers should decide whether they will allow scope changes at any time during the project, only in the early stages of the project, or not at all. The trade-off is that the more flexibility you allow for scope changes, the more likely the project will meet user needs for features and performance. However, the project will be more difficult to complete within changing time and budget constraints as it is harder to hit a moving target.

The change process should capture a clear definition of the change that is being requested, who is requesting it, and why. If the project team has decided not to allow any scope changes during the project, then each new requested scope change is filed with other requested changes. Once the original project is complete, the entire set of requested scope changes can be reviewed and the project team can decide which, if any, of the changes will be implemented and when. Often, it is cheaper to initiate one project to implement numerous related changes rather than start several independent projects. A follow-on project can then be considered to implement the recommended changes. The scope, cost, schedule, and benefits of the project must be determined to ensure that it is well defined and worth doing.

If the project team has decided to allow scope changes during the project, then time and effort must be allowed to assess how the scope change will affect the interrelated project variables of cost, schedule, quality, and expectations. This impact on the project must be weighed against the benefits of implementing the scope change, and the team must decide whether to implement the scope change. Of course, there may be alternatives for implementing a particular scope change, and the pros and cons must be weighed for each. The time required just to research scope changes can add considerable cost and time to the original project. Each scope change should be approved formally or rejected by the project manager and key stakeholders.

Time Management

Time management includes defining an achievable completion date that is acceptable to the project stakeholders, developing a workable project schedule, and ensuring the timely completion of the project. Successful project time management requires identifying specific tasks that project team members and/or other resources must complete; sequencing these tasks, taking into account any task dependencies or hard deadlines; estimating the amount of resources required to complete each task, including people, material, and equipment; estimating the elapsed time to complete each task; analyzing all this data to create a project schedule; and controlling and managing changes to the project schedule.

The bigger the project, the more likely that poor planning will lead to significant problems. Well-managed projects use effective planning tools and techniques, including schedules, milestones, and deadlines. A **project schedule** identifies the project activities that must be completed, the expected start and end dates, and what resources are assigned to each task. A project schedule is needed to complete a project by a defined deadline, avoid rework, and ensure that people know what to do and when to do it. A **project milestone** is a critical date for completing a major part of the project, such as program design, coding, testing, and release (for a programming project). The **project deadline** is the date the entire project should be completed and operational—when the organization can expect to begin to reap the benefits of the project.

In a systems development project, each activity is assigned an earliest start time and an earliest finish time. Each activity is also allocated **slack time**, which is the amount of time an activity can be delayed without delaying the entire project. The **critical path** of a project consists of all activities that, if

time management: A set of activities that includes defining an achievable completion date that is acceptable to the project stakeholders, developing a workable project schedule, and ensuring the timely completion of the project.

project schedule: A plan that identifies the project activities that must be completed, the expected start and end dates, and what resources are assigned to each task.

project milestone: A critical date for completing a major part of the project, such as program design, coding, testing, and release (for a programming project).

project deadline: The date the entire project should be completed and operational—when the organization can expect to begin to reap the benefits of the project.

slack time: The amount of time an activity can be delayed without delaying the entire project.

critical path: All project activities that, if delayed, would delay the entire project.

delayed, would delay the entire project. These activities have zero slack time. Any problems with critical path activities will cause problems for the entire project. To ensure that critical path activities are completed on time, project managers use certain approaches and tools such as Microsoft Project to help compute these critical project attributes.

Although the steps of systems development seem straightforward, larger projects can become complex, requiring hundreds or thousands of separate activities. For these systems development efforts, formal project management methods and tools are essential. **Program Evaluation and Review Technique (PERT)** is a formal approach for estimating project duration based on three time estimates for an activity: the most optimistic time where everything goes right (T_O), the most likely time (T_M) given normal problems and opportunities, and the most pessimistic case where everything goes wrong (T_P). A formula can then be applied to determine the expected time to complete a task (T_E), as shown below:

$$T_E = (T_O + 4T_M + T_P)/6$$

The standard deviation of time required for the task is $(T_P - T_O)/6$ and is an indication of the degree of uncertainty in time required to accomplish the task. The smaller the standard deviation, the less variability in estimates of the time required to complete the task.

Some project managers insist on three time estimates for each task of the project. Others develop three time estimates only for those tasks about which they are most uncertain.

A **Gantt chart** is a graphical tool used for planning, monitoring, and coordinating projects; it is essentially a grid that lists activities and deadlines. Each time a task is completed, a marker such as a darkened line is placed in the proper grid cell to indicate the completion of a task.

The development of a work breakdown structure is a critical activity needed for effective time management. A **work breakdown structure (WBS)** is an outline of the work to be done to complete the project. You start by breaking the project into various stages or groups of activities that need to be performed. Then, you identify the tasks associated with each project stage. A task typically requires a week or less to complete and produces a specific deliverable—tangible output like a flowchart or end-user training plan. Then the tasks within each stage are sequenced. Finally, any **predecessor tasks** are identified—these are tasks that must be completed before a later task can begin. For example, the testing of a unit of program code cannot begin until the program has been coded, compiled, and debugged. Next, you must determine how long each task in the WBS will take.

Thus, building a WBS allows you to look at a project in great detail to get a complete picture of all the work that must be performed. Development of a WBS is another approach to defining the scope of a project—work not included in the WBS is outside the scope of the project.

Table 11.8 shows a sample WBS for a project whose goal is to establish a wireless network in a warehouse and install RFID scanning equipment on forklift trucks for the tracking of inventory. The three phases of the project in Table 11.8 are "Define warehouse network," "Configure forklift trucks," and "Test warehouse network." Figure 11.10 shows the associated schedule in the form of a Gantt chart, with each bar in the chart indicating the start and end dates of each major activity (heavy black lines) and task (lighter lines).

Cost Management

Cost management includes developing and managing the project budget. This area involves resource planning, cost estimating, cost budgeting, and cost control. As previously discussed, a separate budget must be established

Program Evaluation and Review Technique (PERT): A formal method for estimating the duration of a project using three time estimates for an activity: shortest possible time, most likely time, and longest possible time; working with those estimates, a formula is used to determine a single PERT time estimate.

Gantt chart: A graphical tool used for planning, monitoring, and coordinating projects; it is essentially a grid that lists activities and deadlines.

work breakdown structure (WBS): An outline of the work to be done to complete the project.

predecessor task: A task that must be completed before a later task can begin.

cost management: A set of activities that include the development and management of the project budget.

TABLE 11.8 Work breakdown structure

Task		Duration (in days)	Start Date	End Date	Predecessor Tasks
1	**Implement warehouse network**	28	5/06/16	6/14/16	
2	**Define warehouse network**	25	5/06/16	6/09/16	
3	Conduct survey	3	5/06/16	5/10/16	
4	Order RF equipment	14	5/11/16	5/30/16	3
5	Install RF equipment	6	5/31/16	6/07/16	4
6	Test RF equipment	2	6/06/16	6/08/16	5
7	**Configure forklift trucks**	19	5/06/16	6/01/16	
8	Order RFID scanners for trucks	12	5/06/16	5/23/16	
9	Install RFID scanners on trucks	5	5/24/16	5/30/16	8
10	Test RFID scanners	2	5/31/16	6/01/16	9
53	**Test warehouse network**	28	5/06/16	6/14/16	
12	Develop test plan	2	5/06/16	5/09/16	
13	Conduct test	3	6/10/16	6/14/16	6, 10, 12

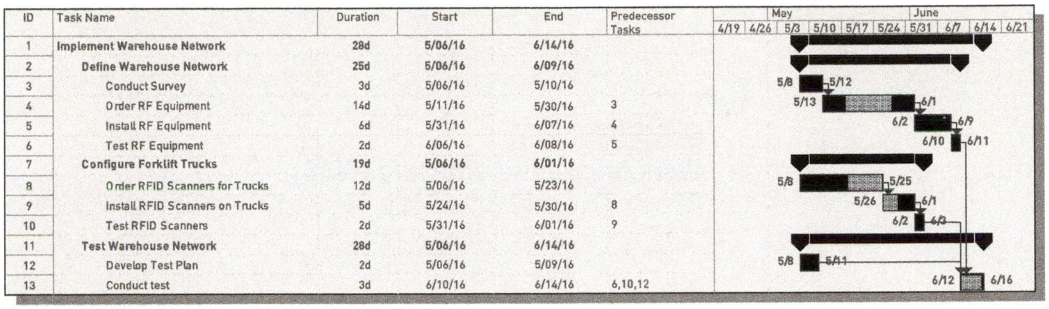

FIGURE 11.10
Gantt chart
A Gantt chart depicts the start and finish dates for project tasks.

for each of the three types of costs—capital, expense, and internal cross-charge—and money in one budget cannot be spent to pay for another type of cost.

One approach to cost estimating uses the WBS to estimate all costs (capital, expense, and cross-charge) associated with the completion of each task. This approach can require a fair amount of detail work, such as determining the hourly rate of each resource assigned to the task and multiplying by the hours the resource will work on the task, estimating the cost per unit for supplies and multiplying that by the number of units required, and so on. If possible, the people who will complete the tasks should be allowed to estimate the time duration and associated costs. This approach helps them to better understand the tasks they are expected to complete, gives them some degree of control in defining how the work will be done, and obtains their "buy-in" to the project schedule and budget. You can develop a project duration based on the sequence in which the tasks must be performed and the duration of each task. You can also sum the cost of each task to develop an estimate of the total project budget. This entire process is outlined in Figure 11.11, and the resulting budget is depicted in Table 11.9.

As an example, suppose that a company plans to implement a new software package for its accounts payable process. The company must spend

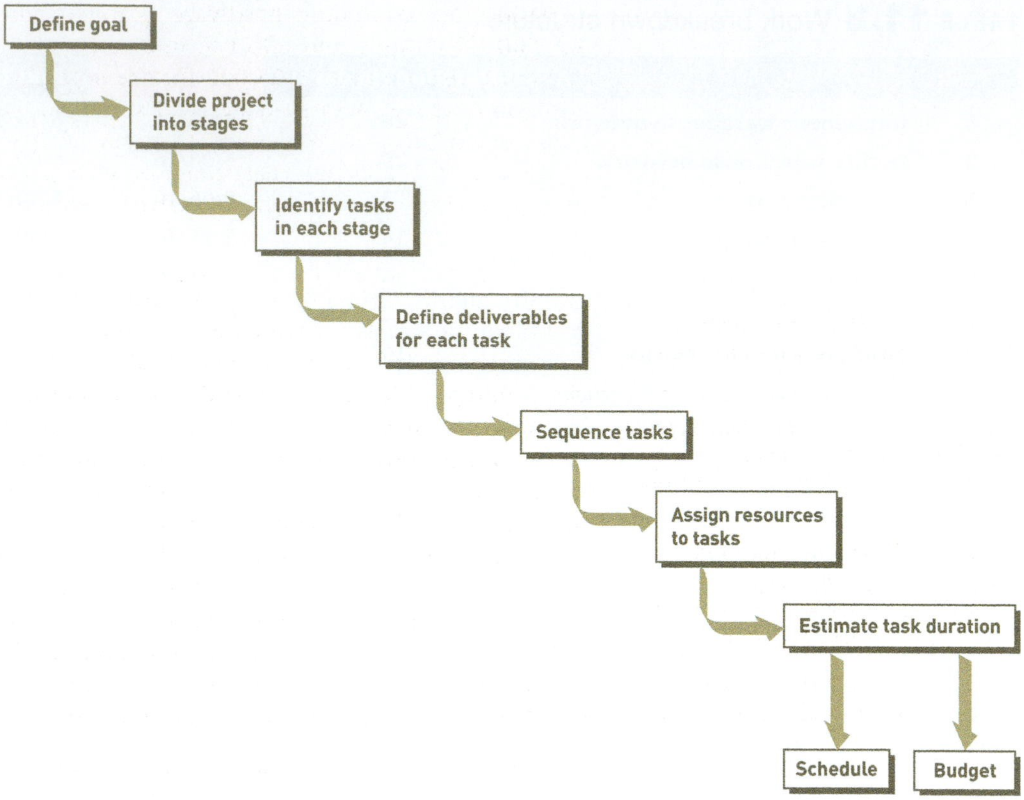

FIGURE **11.11**
Work breakdown structure (WBS)
Development of a WBS leads to definition of a project schedule and budget.

TABLE **11.9** Project budget

Task		Capital	Expense	Cross-Charges
1	**Implement warehouse network**			
2	**Define warehouse network**			
3	Conduct survey		$2,400	
4	Order RF equipment	$9,000		
5	Install RF equipment		$7,800	
6	Test RF equipment			$960
7	**Configure forklift trucks**			
8	Order RFID scanners for trucks	$12,500		
9	Install RFID scanners on trucks			$2,400
10	Test RFID scanners			$1,200
11	**Test warehouse network**			$960
12	Develop test plan			
13	Conduct test			$1,440
TOTAL costs		**$21,500**	**$10,200**	**$6,960**

$150,000 on computer hardware (capital) and pay the software vendor $20,000 for its time and effort to implement the software (expense). The vendor must also be paid $125,000 for the software package license (capital). In addition, one business manager will spend six months leading the implementation effort full time. Six months' worth of the fully loaded cost of the manager (say, $120,000 per year) must be charged to the cross-charge budget of the accounting organization. The cross-charge is a total of $60,000.

Quality Management

quality management: A set of activities designed to ensure that a project will meet the needs for which it was undertaken.

quality planning: The determination of which quality standards are relevant to the project and determining how they will be met.

quality assurance: The evaluation of the progress of the project on an ongoing basis to ensure that it meets the identified quality standards.

quality control: The checking of project results to ensure that they meet identified quality standards.

Quality management is a set of activities designed to ensure that a project will meet the needs for which it was undertaken. This process involves quality planning, quality assurance, and quality control. **Quality planning** involves determining which quality standards are relevant to the project and determining how they will be met. **Quality assurance** involves evaluating the progress of the project on an ongoing basis to ensure that it meets the identified quality standards. **Quality control** involves checking project results to ensure that they meet identified quality standards.

In many IS-related systems development projects, the source of the majority of defects uncovered in system testing can be traced back to an error in specifying requirements. Thus, most organizations put a heavy emphasis on accurately capturing and documenting system requirements and carefully managing changes in user requirements over the course of the project. A useful checklist for assessing the validity of system requirements includes the following questions:[33]

- Does the requirement describe something actually needed by the customer?
- Is the requirement correctly defined?
- Is the requirement consistent with other requirements?
- Is the requirement defined completely?
- Is the requirement verifiable (testable)?
- Is the requirement traceable back to a user need?

Hewlett Packard's Quality Center, Jama from Jama Software, and Innoslate from Systems and Proposal Engineering Company are three examples of requirements management software.

Human Resource Management

human resource management: Activities designed to make the most effective use of the people involved with a project.

forming-storming-norming-performing-adjourning model: A model that describes how teams develop and evolve.

Human resource management are activities designed to make the most effective use of the people involved with a project. Human resources management includes organizational planning, staff acquisition, and team development. The project manager must be able to build a project team staffed with people with the right mix of skills and experience and then train, develop, coach, and motivate them to perform effectively on the project.

All members of a project team may be assigned, or the project manager may have the luxury of selecting all or some team members. Ideally, team members are selected based on their skills in the technology needed for the project, their understanding of the business area affected by the project, their expertise in a specific area of the project, and their ability to work well on a team. Often, compromises must be made. For example, the best available subject matter expert may not work well with others, which becomes an additional challenge for the project manager.

Experienced project managers have learned that forming an effective team to accomplish a difficult goal is a challenge in itself. It takes considerable effort and a willingness to change on the part of all team members in order for a team to reach high levels of performance. A useful model to describe how teams develop and evolve is the **forming-storming-norming-performing-adjourning model**, which was first proposed by Bruce Tuckman (see Figure 11.12).[34]

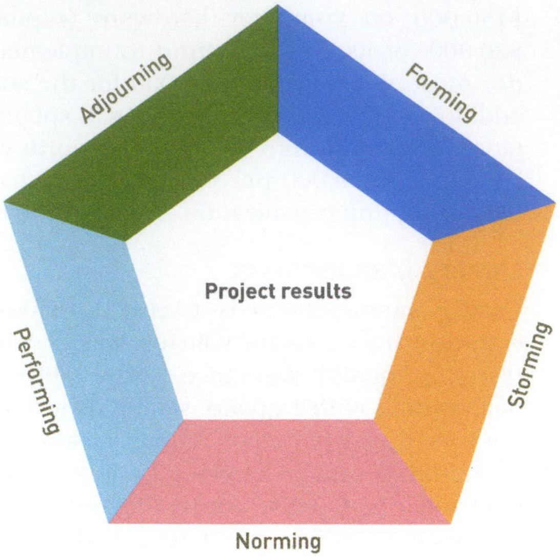

FIGURE **11.12**
Tuckman's forming-storming-norming-performing-adjourning model
Forming an effective team is a challenge in itself.

During the forming stage, the team meets to learn about the project, agrees on basic goals, and begins to work on project tasks. Team members are on their best behavior and try to be pleasant to one another while avoiding any conflict or disagreement. Team members work independently of one another and focus on their role or tasks without understanding what others are attempting to do. In the formation stage, the team's project manager tends to be highly directive and tells members what needs to be done. If the team remains in this stage, it is unlikely to perform well, and it will never develop breakthrough solutions to problems or effectively solve a conflicting set of priorities and constraints.

The team has moved into the storming stage when it recognizes that differences of opinion exist among team members and allows these ideas to compete for consideration. Team members will raise such important questions as "What problems are we *really* supposed to solve?" "How can we work well together?" "What sort of project leadership will we accept?" The team might argue and struggle, so it can be an unpleasant time for everyone. An inexperienced project manager, not recognizing what is happening, may give up, feeling that the team will never work together effectively. The project manager and team members must be tolerant of one another as they explore their differences. The project manager may need to continue to be highly directive.

If the team survives the storming stage, it may enter the norming stage. During this stage, individual team members give up their preconceived judgments and opinions. Members who felt a need to take control of the team give up this impulse. Team members adjust their behavior and begin to trust one another. The team may decide to document a set of team rules or norms to guide how they will work together. Teamwork actually begins. The project manager can be less directive and can expect team members to take more responsibility for decision making.

Some teams advance beyond the norming stage into the performing stage. At this point, the team is performing at a high level. Team members are competent, highly motivated, and knowledgeable about all aspects of the project. They have become interdependent on one another and have developed an effective decision-making process that does not require the project manager. Dissent is expected, and the team has developed an effective process to ensure that everyone's ideas and opinions are heard. Work is done quickly and with high quality. Problems that once seemed unsolvable now have "obvious" solutions. The team's effectiveness is much more than the sum of the individual members' contributions. The project manager encourages participative decision making, with the team members making most of the decisions.

Adjourning, the final stage in the model, involves the dissolution of the team. Ideally, this occurs when the project has been completed successfully and all team members can move on to new projects or assignments with a positive sense of accomplishment. From an organizational perspective, it is important that team members be recognized and rewarded for their contributions.

No matter what stage a team is operating in, it commonly will revert to less advanced stages in the model when confronted with major changes in the work to be done, a change in project leadership, or substantial changes in the team's makeup. The project manager and business managers must recognize and consider this important dynamic when contemplating project changes.

Another key aspect of human resource management is getting the project team and the sponsoring business unit to take *equal* responsibility for making the project a success. The project team members must realize that on their own they cannot possibly make the project a success. They must ensure that the business managers and end users become deeply involved in the project and take an active role. The project team must actively involve the end users, provide information for them to make wise choices, and insist on their participation in major decisions. The business unit must remain engaged in the project, challenge recommendations, ask questions, and weigh options. It cannot simply sit back and "let the project happen to them." Key users need to be identified as part of the project team with responsibility for developing and reviewing deliverables. Indeed, some organizations require that the project manager comes from the sponsoring business unit. Other organizations assign co-project managers to IS-related projects—one from the IS organization and one from the business unit.

In addition to the development team, each project should have a **project steering team**—made up of senior managers representing the business and IS organizations—to provide guidance and support to the project. The number of members on the steering team should be limited (three to five) to simplify the decision-making process and ease the effort to schedule a quorum of these busy executives. The project manager and select members of the development team should meet with the steering team on an as-needed basis, typically at the end of each project phase or every few months. The three key members of the steering team include: (1) the **project champion** who is a well-respected manager with a passion to see the project succeed and who removes barriers to the success of the project, (2) the **project sponsor** who is a senior manager from the business unit most affected by the project and who ensures the project will indeed meet the needs of his or her organization, and (3) the IS manager who ensures proper IS staffing for the project and ensures the project uses approved technology and vendors. These roles are further explained in Figure 11.13 and outlined in Table 11.10.

Many projects also draw on key resources who are not assigned to the project team but who provide valuable input and advice. A **subject matter expert** is someone who provides knowledge and expertise in a particular aspect important to the project. For example, an accounting system project may seek advice from a member of the internal auditing group in defining the mandatory control features of a new system. A **technical resource** is essentially a subject matter expert in an IS topic of value to the project. For example, the accounting system project may seek advice from a database management system guru (either inside or outside the company) to minimize the response time for certain key business transactions.

project steering team: A group of senior managers representing the business and IS organizations that provide guidance and support to a project.

project champion: A well-respected manager with a passion to see a project succeed and who removes barriers to the success of the project.

project sponsor: A senior manager from the business unit most affected by a project and who ensures the project will indeed meet the needs of his or her organization.

subject matter expert: Someone who provides knowledge and expertise in a particular aspect important to the project.

technical resource: A subject matter expert in an IS topic of value to the project.

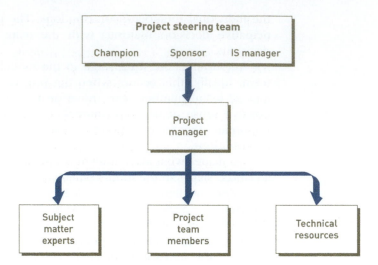

Project organization
A project steering team is critical to the success of any project.

TABLE **11.10** Responsibilities of the project steering team

Project Champion	Project Sponsor	IS Manager
Well-respected senior manager with a passion to see the project succeed	Senior manager of business unit most affected by the project	Well-respected IS manager
Assures that project goals and objectives are aligned with organizational goals and objectives	Ensures that the business unit's expectations and needs are clearly communicated and understood	Ensures the project is staffed with appropriate IS staff
Convinces other senior managers of the project's merits in order to gain their approval to fund and staff it	Ensures that the project solution is truly workable and consistent with business and end-user requirements	Ensures technology and vendors suggested for inclusion in the project are consistent with IS strategy
Acts as a vocal and visible champion for the project to gain the support of others	Works to overcome resistance to change and prepare the organization to embrace the new system and way of doing things	
Identifies and removes barriers to project success	Identifies workers from the business unit to be assigned on a full- or part-time basis to project	
Resolves any issues outside the control of the project manager		
Provides advice and counsel to the project team		
Keeps informed of major project activities and developments		
Has final approval of all requests for changes in project scope, budget, and schedule		
Signs off on approvals to proceed to each succeeding project phase		

Communications Management

communications management: The generation, collection, dissemination, and storage of project information in a timely and effective manner.

Communications management involves the generation, collection, dissemination, and storage of project information in a timely and effective manner. It includes communications planning, information distribution, performance reporting, and managing communications to meet the needs of project shareholders. The key stakeholders include the project steering team, the team itself, end users, and others who may be affected by the project (potentially customers or suppliers).

In preparing a communications plan, the project manager should recognize that the various stakeholders have different information needs in the project. A useful tool for identifying and documenting these needs is the stakeholder analysis matrix, shown in Table 11.11. This matrix identifies the interests of the stakeholders, their information needs, and important facts for managing communications with the champion, sponsor, project team members, and key end users associated with the project. The project manager should include his or her manager in this analysis. Based on analysis of this data, the preferred form and frequency of communication is identified for each stakeholder.

TABLE 11.11 Sample stakeholder analysis matrix

Key Stakeholders	Ray Boaz	Klem Kiddlehopper	John Smith	Forklift Drivers
Organization	Project champion and VP of supply chain	Project sponsor and warehouse manager	Experienced forklift driver	15 different drivers
Useful facts	• Very persuasive • Trusted by CEO	• Risk taker, very aggressive • Will push this through, no matter what	• Has driven forklift truck for five years • Well respected by peers	• Not highly motivated to make project a success
Level of interest	High	High	Medium	Low
Level of influence	High	Medium	High	Low
Suggestions on managing relationship	• Demands respect, somewhat formal • Speak in business terms, never get technical; no surprises!	• Poor listener, forgets details • Put it in writing	• Must keep John enthusiastic about project	• Don't ignore • Attend occasional shift changeover meeting
Information needs	• ROI, budget, and schedule	• Schedule and potential operational conflicts	• Schedule, especially timing of training • Safety and productivity issues	• Schedule, especially timing of training • Safety issues
Information medium, format, and timing	• Biweekly face-to-face meeting	• Newsletter • Biweekly face-to-face	• Newsletter • Catch-as-catch can	• Brief updates at weekly department meeting

If the project team is unable to recruit either a project champion or sponsor, the problem may be that management does not see clearly that the benefits of the project outweigh its costs, or that the project appears to run counter to organizational goals and strategies. A potential project without either a champion or a sponsor is highly unlikely to get the needed resources, and for good reason. No project should be started without both a champion and a sponsor.

Risk Management

"Things will go wrong, and at the worst possible time," according to a variation of Murphy's Law, a popular adage. **Project risk** is an uncertain event or condition that, if it occurs, has a positive or a negative effect on a project objective. Known risks are risks that can be identified and analyzed. For example, in creating a new IS-related system that includes the acquisition of new computing

project risk: An uncertain event or condition that, if it occurs, has a positive or a negative effect on a project objective.

and/or networking hardware, a known risk might be that the hardware will take longer than expected to arrive at the installation site. If the hardware is delayed by several weeks, it could have a negative effect on the project completion date. Countermeasures can be defined to avoid some known risks entirely, and contingency plans can be developed to address unavoidable known risks if they occur. Of course, some risks simply cannot be anticipated.

A hallmark of experienced project managers is that they follow a deliberate and systematic process of **risk management** to identify, analyze, and manage project risks. Having identified potential risks, they can make plans to avoid them entirely. When an unavoidable risk occurs and becomes an issue, the project team has already defined an alternative course of action to minimize the impact on the project. They waste no time executing the backup plan. Unknown risks cannot be managed directly; however, an experienced project manager will build some contingency into the project budget and schedule to allow for their occurrence.

While inexperienced project managers realize that things may go wrong, they often fail to identify and address known risks and do not build in contingencies for unknown risks. Thus, they are often unsure of what to do, at least temporarily, when a project setback occurs. In their haste to react to a risk, they may not implement the best course of action.

The project manager needs to lead a rigorous effort to identify all risks associated with the project. The project team, business managers, and end users should participate in the effort. These resources can include seasoned project managers and members of the organization's risk management department. After each risk is identified and defined, as shown in Table 11.12, the group should attempt to classify the risk by the probability that it will occur and the impact on the project if the risk does occur. Both the probability and the impact can be classified as high, medium, or low, as shown in the example in Table 11.13.

risk management: A deliberate and systematic process designed to identify, analyze, and manage project risks.

TABLE 11.12 Identification of project risks

Risk	Example
R1	The required new servers arrive at the installation site more than two weeks late.
R2	Business pressures make key end users unavailable to develop the user acceptance test by the date it is needed.
R3	Business pressures make end users unavailable during the time scheduled for training.
R4	One or more end-user computers have insufficient memory or CPU capacity to run the new software efficiently (or at all).
R*n*	....

TABLE 11.13 Example of an assessment of project risks

		Impact on Project		
		Low	Medium	High
	High	R10		R2, R3
Probability risk occurs	Medium	R5, R6	R*n*	R1
	Low	R8, R11	R7, R9	R4

Dark = High risk/high impact; risk management plan is needed
Lightest = Medium or high risk and impact; risk management plan recommended
Lighter = Low or medium risk and impact; risk management plan not needed

The project team then needs to consider which risks need to be addressed in the risk management plan. Generally, the team can ignore risks with a low probability of occurrence and low potential impact. Risks with a high probability of occurrence and a high potential impact need to have a risk owner assigned. The **risk owner** is responsible for developing a risk management strategy and monitoring the project to determine if the risk is about to occur or has occurred. One strategy is to take steps to avoid the risk altogether, while another is to develop a backup plan. The risk management plan can be documented as shown in Table 11.14.

risk owner: The individual responsible for developing a risk management strategy and monitoring the project to determine if the risk is about to occur or has occurred.

TABLE 11.14 Risk management plan

Risk	Description	Risk Owner	Risk Strategy	Current Status
R2	Business pressures make key end users unavailable to develop the user acceptance test by the deadline.	Jon Andersen, manager of end users in the business area	Try to avoid this problem by starting development of the user acceptance test three weeks earlier than originally planned. Monitor progress carefully.	Key users have been identified and have started developing the test.
R3	Business pressures make end users unavailable during the time scheduled for training.	Jon Andersen, manager of end users in the business area	Try to avoid this problem by hiring and training four temporary workers to fill in for end users as they participate in training.	Three of four temporary workers have been hired. Their training is scheduled to begin next week.
R1	The required new servers arrive at the installation site more than two weeks late.	Alice Fields, team member responsible for hardware acquisition	Set a firm delivery deadline with the vendor, with a substantial dollar penalty for each day that the equipment is late.	The contract with the penalty clause has been signed by the vendor, who agrees to provide a shipment status update each Tuesday and Friday.

One of the biggest risks associated with a project is that considerable time, energy, and resources might be consumed with little value to show in return. To avoid this potential risk, an organization must ensure that a strong rationale exists for completing a project. The project must have a direct link to an organizational strategy and goal, as shown in Figure 11.14. In this example, assume that an organization has been losing sales because of customer dissatisfaction. It has set an objective of improving customer service, with a goal of increasing the retention rate of existing customers. The organization has defined one of its key strategies as improving customer service to world-class levels. A project that is consistent with this strategy and that can deliver results to achieve this goal is clearly aligned with the organization's objectives.

- **Objective.** Improve customer service.
- **Goal.** Reduce customer turnover from 25 percent per year to 10 percent by June 2017 by responding to 95 percent of customers' inquiries within 90 seconds, with less than 5 percent callbacks about the same problem.
- **Strategy.** Improve customer service to world-class levels.
- **Project.** Implement a state-of-the-art customer call center with "24/7" availability and a well-trained staff.

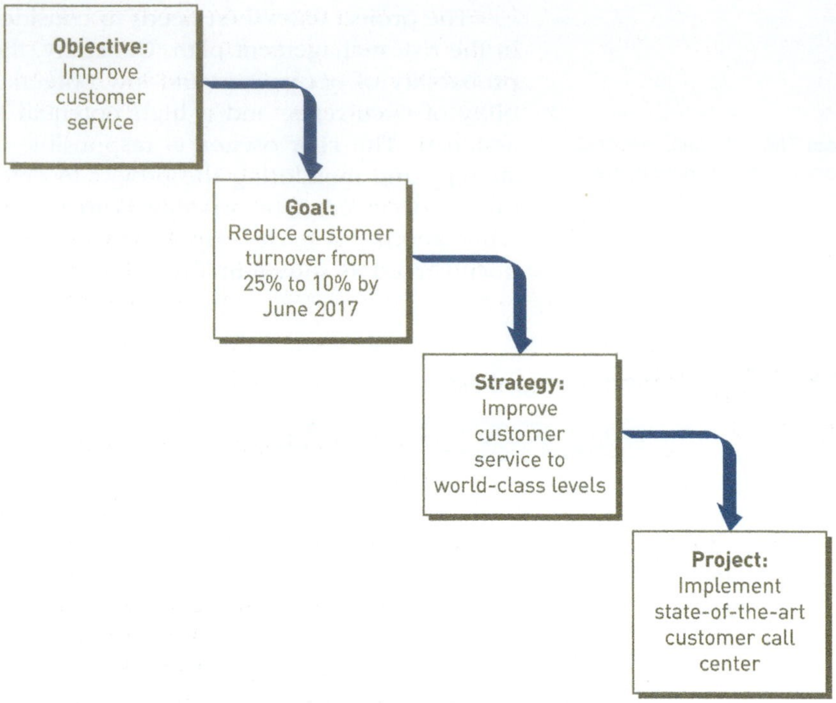

FIGURE **11.14**

Projects must be well linked to an organizational goal and strategy

Objectives, goals, strategy, and projects should be aligned.

Risk management software—such as Risk Management from Intelex, Full Monte from Barbecana, and @Risk from Intaver Institute—integrates with project scheduling software and can reflect the potential impact of various risks on the project schedule and cost. Use of such software can lead to more realistic estimates for project milestones and budgets.

Procurement Management

procurement management: A set of activities related to the acquisition of goods and/or services for the project from sources outside the performing organization.

Procurement management are activities related to the acquisition of goods and/or services for a project from sources outside the performing organization. Procurement management is divided into the following processes:

- **Plan purchase and acquisition.** This process determines what is needed and when.
- **Plan contracting.** This process documents requirements for products and services and identifies potential providers.
- **Request seller responses.** This process obtains bids, information, proposals, or quotations from potential providers.
- **Select seller.** During this process, offers are reviewed, the preferred provider is identified, and negotiations are started.
- **Contract administration.** This process manages all aspects of the contract and the relationship between the buyer and the provider. The process includes tracking and documenting the provider's performance, managing contract changes, and taking any necessary corrective actions.
- **Contract closure.** This process completes and settles the terms of any contracts, including resolving any open items.

make-or-buy decision: The act of comparing the pros and cons of in-house production versus outsourcing of a given product or service.

The make-or-buy decision is a key decision made during the plan purchase and acquisition process. The **make-or-buy decision** involves comparing the pros and cons of in-house production versus outsourcing of a given product or service. In addition to cost, two key factors to consider in this decision are (1) "Do we have a sufficient number of employees with the skills and experience required to deliver the product or service at an acceptable level of quality and within the required deadlines?" and (2) "Are we willing to invest the management time, energy, and money required to identify, recruit, train, develop, and manage people with the skills to do this kind of work?"

A contract is a legally binding agreement that defines the terms and conditions of the buyer-provider relationship, including who is authorized to do what, who holds what responsibilities, costs and terms of payment, remedies in case of breach of contract, and the process for revising the contract. Contract types fall into three main categories:

fixed-price contract: A contract in which the buyer and provider agree to a total fixed price for a well-defined product or service.

- **Fixed-price contract**. With this type of contract, the buyer and provider agree to a total fixed price for a well-defined product or service. For example, the purchase of a large number of laptop computers with specified capabilities and features frequently involves a fixed-price contract.

cost-reimbursable contract: A contract that requires the buyer to pay the provider an amount that covers the provider's actual costs plus an additional amount or percentage for profit.

- **Cost-reimbursable contract**. This type of contract requires the buyer to pay the provider an amount that covers the provider's actual costs plus an additional amount or percentage for profit. Three common types of cost-reimbursable contracts exist. In a cost-plus-fee or cost-plus-percentage of cost contract, the provider is reimbursed for all allowable costs and receives a percentage of the costs as a fee. In a cost-plus-fixed-fee contract, the provider is reimbursed for all allowable costs and receives a fixed fee. In a cost-plus-incentive-fee contract, the provider is reimbursed for all allowable costs. In addition, a predetermined fee is paid if the provider achieves specified performance objectives—for example, the provider's hardware must be received, installed, and operational by a specific date. In such contracts, buyers run the risk of paying more for the work but are rewarded by having their objectives met or exceeded. Providers run the risk of reduced profits if they fail to deliver, but can be rewarded for superior performance.

time and material contract: A contract that requires the buyer to pay the provider for both the time and materials required to complete the contract.

- **Time and material contract**. Under this type of contract, the buyer pays the provider for both the time and materials required to complete the contract. The contract includes an agreed-upon hourly rate and unit price for the various materials to be used. The exact number of hours and precise quantity of each material are not known, however. Thus, the true value of the contract is not defined when the contract is approved. If not managed carefully, time and material contracts actually can motivate suppliers to extend projects to maximize their fees.

Poor procurement management can result in serious project problems and even a project's outright cancellation.

Project Integration Management

Project integration management is perhaps the most important knowledge area because it requires the assimilation of all eight other project management knowledge areas. **Project integration management** requires the coordination of all appropriate people, resources, plans, and efforts to complete a project successfully. Project integration management comprises seven project management processes:

project integration management: The coordination of all appropriate people, resources, plans, and efforts to complete a project successfully.

1. Developing the project charter that formally recognizes the existence of the project, outlines the project objectives and how they will be met, lists key assumptions, and identifies major roles and responsibilities.

2. Developing a preliminary project scope statement to define and gain consensus about the work to be done; over the life of the project, the scope statement will become fuller and more detailed.

3. Developing the project management plan that describes the overall scope, schedule, and budget for the project; this plan coordinates all subsequent project planning efforts and is used in the execution and control of the project.

4. Directing and managing project execution by following the project management plan.

5. Monitoring and controlling the project work to meet the project's performance objectives; this process requires regularly measuring effort and expenditures against the project tasks, recognizing when significant deviations occur from the schedule or budget, and taking corrective action to regain alignment with the plan.

6. Performing integrated change control by managing changes over the course of the project that can affect its scope, schedule, and/or cost.

7. Closing the project successfully by gaining stakeholder and customer acceptance of the final product, closing all budgets and purchase orders after confirming that final disbursements have been made, and capturing knowledge from the project that may prove useful for future projects.

As an example of a firm that excels in project integration management, consider Atos, an international IS services company that employs over 80,000 workers in more than 52 countries, with 2015 annual revenue of €10.7 billion (U.S. $12.2 billion). The firm successfully delivered the information technology systems that enabled the smooth running of the Sochi 2014 Olympic Games in Russia. Atos had the primary responsibility for project integration, consulting, systems integration, operations management, information security, and software applications development for the games. Through its experience with previous Olympics (Atos has been the worldwide IS partner for the Olympic Games, both winter and summer, since Salt Lake City in 2002), Atos has developed an effective project management process. The firm spent over four years configuring, testing, and retesting some 10,000 pieces of equipment deployed to 30 different venues. Atos coordinated the work of hundreds of subcontractors to deliver a reliable IS infrastructure and IS services in support of one of the world's widely viewed sporting events. The Sochi project was coordinated so that custom software, thousands of workstations and laptops, tens of thousands of phones, hundreds of servers, and multiple operations centers and data centers all operated together effectively and efficiently.[35]

Critical Thinking Exercise

Reluctant Project Sponsor

You are on the phone with the project sponsor of a $2 million project you are managing. She informs you that she accepted the role reluctantly, and now, one month into this eight-month project, she is considering withdrawing as project sponsor. She does not see the need for this role and is extremely busy with her other responsibilities.

Review Questions

1. What is the role of the project sponsor?
2. What might be the impact on the project if you attempt to proceed without a sponsor? Is it likely that some project tasks would need to be done over if a new sponsor is appointed?

Critical Thinking Questions

1. If you are unable to persuade the sponsor to remain on the project, should you enlist the help of the project champion? How might you do this in such a way that you do not appear weak and ineffective and avoid creating hard feelings with the current sponsor?

2. After speaking to the project champion, you and she both agree that the current sponsor should be replaced with someone new. What characteristics, traits, and experiences would you look for in a new sponsor?

Summary

Principle:

Organizations that are more advanced in their planning processes develop multiple-year strategic plans.

Strategic planning is a process that helps managers identify desired outcomes and formulate feasible plans to achieve their objectives using available resources and capabilities.

Goal-based strategic planning is divided into four phases: analyze situation, set direction, define strategies, and deploy plan.

The analyze situation phase involves looking internally to identify the organization's strengths and weaknesses and looking externally to determine its opportunities and threats.

An analysis of an organization's internal assessment and study of its external environment are frequently summarized into a Strengths, Weaknesses, Opportunities, Threats (SWOT) matrix.

The set direction phase involves defining the mission, vision, values, objectives, and goals of the organization.

SMART goals are specific, measurable, achievable, relevant, and time constrained.

The define strategies phase involves describing how an organization will achieve its mission, vision, objectives, and goals.

Deploy plan includes communicating the organization's mission, vision, values, objectives, goals, and strategies so that everyone can help define the actions required to meet organizational goals.

Principle:

The strategic planning process for the IS organization and the factors that influence it depend on how the organization is perceived by the rest of the organization.

IS strategic planning is influenced by the corporate and business unit strategic plans as well as technology innovations and innovative thinking.

The IS strategy will set direction for the technologies, vendors, competencies, people, systems, and projects.

Principle:

Organizations must always make a clear connection among business objectives, goals, and projects. In addition, projects must be consistent with business strategies.

A project is a temporary endeavor undertaken to create a unique product, service, or result.

Roughly 71 percent of all IS projects are challenged, fail, or face major changes such as lateness, budget overruns, and lack of required features.

Today, many organizations have recognized project management as one of their core competencies.

Five highly interrelated parameters define a project—scope, cost, time, quality, and user expectations. If any one of these project parameters is changed, there must be a corresponding change in one or more of the other parameters.

Project scope is the definition of which work is included and which work is not included in a project.

The cost of a project includes all the capital, expenses, and internal cross-charges associated with the project's buildings, operation, maintenance, and support.

The timing of a project is frequently a critical constraint.

Quality of a project can be defined as the degree to which the project meets the needs of its users.

Project management is the application of knowledge, skills, and techniques to project activities to meet project requirements. Project managers must attempt to deliver a solution that meets specific scope, cost, time, and quality goals while managing the expectations of the project stakeholders—the people involved in the project or those affected by its outcome.

According to the Project Management Institute (PMI), project managers must coordinate nine areas of expertise: scope, time, cost, quality, human resources, communications, risk, procurement, and integration.

Scope management includes defining the work that must be done as part of the project and then controlling the work to stay within the agreed-upon scope.

Functional decomposition is a frequently used technique to define the scope of an information system by identifying the business processes it will affect.

A process is a set of logically related tasks performed to achieve a defined outcome.

Time management includes defining an achievable completion date? that is acceptable to the project stakeholders, developing a workable project schedule, and ensuring the timely completion of the project.

Cost management includes developing and managing the project budget.

Quality management is a set of activities designed to ensure that the project will meet the needs for which it was undertaken.

Human resource management activities are designed to make the most effective use of the people involved in the project.

The forming-storming-norming-performing-adjourning model describes how teams form, evolve, and dissolve.

Each project should have a project steering team—made up of senior managers representing the business and IS organizations—to provide guidance and support to the project. Three key members of the steering team are the project champion, project sponsor, and IS manager.

Communications management involves the generation, collection, dissemination, and storage of project information in a timely and effective manner.

Risk management is a process that attempts to identify, analyze, and manage project risks. Experienced project managers follow a deliberate and systematic process of risk management to avoid risks or minimize their negative impact on a project.

Procurement management is a set of activities related to the acquisition of goods and/or services for the project from sources outside the organization.

Project integration management is a critical knowledge area of project? management that involves chartering, scoping, planning, executing, monitoring and controlling, change control, and project closing.

Key Terms

communications management	project risk
core competency	project schedule
core value	project scope
cost management	project sponsor
cost-reimbursable contract	project stakeholder
critical path	project steering team
fixed-price contract	quality
forming-storming-norming-performing-adjourning model	quality assurance
	quality control
functional decomposition	quality management
Gantt chart	quality planning
goal	risk management
goals-based strategic planning	risk owner
human resource management	scope management
intangible benefit	slack time
issues-based strategic planning	sponsoring business unit
make-or-buy decision	strategic planning
Michael Porter's Five Forces Model	strategy
mission statement	Strengths, Weaknesses, Opportunities, Threats (SWOT) matrix
objective	
organic strategic planning	subject matter expert
predecessor task	tangible benefit
procurement management	technical resource
Program Evaluation and Review Technique (PERT)	time and material contract
project champion	time management
project deadline	vision
project integration management	vision/mission statement
project management	work breakdown structure (WBS)
project milestone	

Chapter 11: Self-Assessment Test

Organizations that are more advanced in their planning processes develop multiple-year strategic plans.

1. Goal-based strategic planning is divided into four phases: _____, set direction, define strategies, and deploy plan.
2. Analysis of the internal assessment and external environment are frequently summarized into a _____ matrix.

3. _____ includes communicating the organization's mission, vision, values, objectives, goals, and strategies so that everyone can help define the actions required to meet organizational goals.
   a. Analyze situation
   b. Define strategies
   c. Set direction
   d. Deploy plan

4. Which of the following is an example of a SMART goal?
   a. Achieve 100 percent customer satisfaction within the next year.
   b. Improve customer service by 50 percent.
   c. Reduce customer complaints about mispriced merchandise from 12 per day to less than 3 per day by June 30.
   d. The customer is always right.

The strategic planning process for the IS organization and the factors that influence it depend on how the organization is perceived by the rest of the organization.

5. IS strategic planning is influenced by the corporate and _____ strategic plans as well as technology innovations and innovative thinking.
6. An IS organization can be viewed as either a cost center/service provider, a business partner/business peer, or as a game changer.
   True or False?
7. A clear example of a tangible benefit is
   _____.
   a. the increase in employee morale from implementing a self-service employee benefits software package
   b. the reduction in headcount in the accounting organization resulting from improvements in the payroll processing system
   c. the increase in customer satisfaction from modifications to the organization's Web site
   d. the value of improved decision making resulting from self-service analytics tools

Organizations must always make a clear connection among business objectives, goals, and projects. In addition, projects must be consistent with business strategies.

8. _____ of all IS projects are challenged or failed.
   a. Less than 25 percent
   b. Nearly half
   c. About 71 percent
   d. Over 80 percent
9. A _____ is a temporary endeavor undertaken to create a unique product, service, or result.
10. Five highly interrelated parameters define a project—scope, cost, time, _____, and user expectations.
11. According to the Project Management Institute (PMI), project managers must coordinate _____ areas of expertise.
    a. three
    b. five
    c. seven
    d. nine
12. The _____ model describes how teams form, evolve, and dissolve.

Chapter 11: Self-Assessment Test Answers

1. analyze situation
2. Strengths, Weaknesses, Opportunities, Threats (SWOT)
3. d
4. c.
5. business unit
6. True
7. b
8. c
9. project
10. quality
11. d
12. forming-storming-norming-performing-adjourning

Review Questions

1. State three benefits that an organization can achieve through strategic planning.
2. Briefly describe issues-based strategic planning, organic strategic planning, and goals-based strategic planning.
3. Outline the four phases of goals-based strategic planning.
4. State the fundamental factors that determine the level of competition and long-term profitability of an industry, and draw a sketch of Michael Porter's Five Forces Model.
5. What is included in a SWOT matrix, and how is one used?
6. What does an organization's vision/mission statement communicate?
7. What does the acronym SMART goal stand for? What is a BHAG?
8. How does a strategy differ from an objective?

9. Define the term "project."
10. What is a core competency? Project scope? Project stakeholder?
11. Identify the five highly interrelated parameters that define a project. What happens if one of these parameters is changed?
12. Identify and briefly describe the nine areas of expertise that a project manager must coordinate.
13. Explain how PERT and Gantt are used to develop and/or communicate the schedule of a project.
14. What is the difference between quality planning, quality assurance, and quality control?

15. Briefly describe the stages that a project team experiences over the course of a successful project.
16. What is a stakeholder analysis matrix and how is it used?
17. What is the purpose of risk management? Briefly outline a recommended risk management process.
18. Identify and briefly describe three types of contracts frequently used in the procurement of goods and services.

Discussion Questions

1. To what degree do you think an organization's strategic plan is influenced by the vision, personality, and leadership capabilities of the CEO? Do research to identify an example of a strategic plan developed by a CEO you consider to be a strong, charismatic leader. Briefly summarize the notable aspects of this plan.
2. Identify an event that would trigger a need to redefine the organization's vision/mission statement.
3. What would it imply if, while performing a SWOT analysis, an organization could not identify any opportunities? What if it could not identify any threats?
4. How would you distinguish between an organizational weakness and a threat to the organization? How would you distinguish between a strength and an opportunity?
5. Brainstorm an approach you might use to gather data to identify the strengths and weaknesses of a competing organization. Identify resources, specific tools, or techniques you might apply to gain useful insights.
6. Would you recommend that an organization set BHAGs? Why or why not? Identify an example of a BHAG from a real organization. Was that BHAG achieved?
7. Distinguish between the role of the project champion and the role of the project sponsor. Is one more important to the success of a project than the other?

8. Describe three specific actions that the ideal project sponsor would take to ensure the success of a project.
9. Is there a difference between project time management and personal time management? Can someone be "good" at one but not the other? Explain your answer.
10. Discuss the team dynamics for a highly effective (or ineffective) team of which you were a member. Can you explain why the team performed so well (or poorly) using the forming-storming-norming-performing-adjourning model?
11. What sort of behaviors would indicate that the business organization is not fully engaged in a project and instead is simply replying on the project team to make the project a success? What is the danger with this attitude?
12. Identify some of the challenges of performing project integration management on a project in which team members are distributed globally and cannot physically meet in one location. How might these challenges be overcome?
13. Imagine that you are hiring a firm to complete a large but undetermined amount of project work for your firm. Which form of contract would you prefer and why?
14. How would you respond to a project team member who feels that risk management is a waste of time because the future cannot be predicted? Instead, this person prefers to react to problems as they occur.

Problem-Solving Exercises

1. Complete this table. Which tasks have the highest degree of uncertainty in terms of the time required to complete them?
2. Many free and open source project management software programs are available online,

including: Asana, BaseCamp, Bitrix24, GanttProject, MeisterTask, Trello, and Zoho. Choose one of these programs or use a spreadsheet or another project management program with which you are familiar. Create a Gantt chart using the

Task	T_O	T_M	T_P	T	Standard Deviation	Predecessor Task
1	3 days	7 days	14 days	_____	_____	0
2	16 days	21 days	43 days	_____	_____	1
3	6 days	8 days	15 days	_____	_____	2
4	9 days	11 days	19 days	_____	_____	2
5	18 days	21 days	38 days	_____	_____	2, 3
6	13 days	18 days	30 days	_____	_____	5
7	12 days	17 days	27 days	_____	_____	6
8	7 days	9 days	13 days	_____	_____	6, 7

values from this table. How long will it take to complete a project consisting of these tasks? Identify the critical path for this project.

3. Evaluate any three of the many free and open source project management software programs.

Create a spreadsheet that displays the pros, cons, and special features of each of the three programs.

Team Activities

1. Choose a company that interests your team and do research to document its strategic plan. Include a SWOT analysis and a statement of the organization's vision, mission, objectives, goals, and strategies. Identify and briefly describe two IS-related projects that would be consistent with this plan.

2. Imagine that your team is serving as a facilitator for a strategic planning session for a new, small organization that was spun off from a much larger organization just six months ago. The CEO and four senior managers involved in the session seem drained at the close of the first day of a two-day off-site meeting. As the leadership team discusses their results, your team is struck by how conservative and uninspiring their objectives and goals are. Brainstorm ideas on what your team can do to help stimulate these managers to think more creatively and broadly.

3. Your team has been hired as consultants to work with a large city to implement a program to

place hundreds of high-tech digital cameras in strategic locations to aid in reducing crime and speeding help to victims. The cameras are state-of-the-art with infrared capability for night vision, high resolution, and rapid zoom in and out capability. Your city will be the first in the United States to deploy them. The manufacturer is a relatively newcomer to the digital camera industry. The program has not yet been fully funded nor has it been announced to the residents of the city. The city management and top level officers within the police department are fully behind the program, however, lower level officers and cops on the street have mixed support. Your team has been asked to perform a risk assessment for this project. You are to identify various risks that could occur; assign them a high, medium, or low level of risk, and assess the potential impact (high, medium, or low) on the project if that risk should occur.

Web Exercises

1. Steve Jobs was a strong, charismatic leader who cofounded Apple and is accredited with much of the success of the company. Some believe that Tim Cook, who became CEO in 2011, embraces a more collaborative leadership style. Do research to compare and contrast the leadership style of the two CEOs. (You may wish to view the 2013

movie *Jobs*, which portrays the story of Steve Jobs' ascension from college dropout to Apple CEO.) Which CEO—Jobs or Cook—do you think developed and executed the most effective strategic plan? What evidence can you find to support your opinion?

2. Do research online to identify what experts think are the keys to project success. You will find many different ideas and suggestions. Consolidate these ideas to create a top five list.

3. Do research on the Web to learn the history of the PERT technique and identify some of the early projects that used this technique.

Career Exercises

1. Visit the Project Management Institute (PMI) Web site at *www.pmi.org*. Do research to learn more about the value that employers place on project management certification. What are the certifications offered by PMI that you may be qualified to take? Do you think that PMI certification would enhance your career opportunities? Why or why not?
2. Can you state the vision and mission of your organization? Has it documented its core values?

Can you identify any key objectives and strategies?
3. Talk with your manager and others at work about the need for good project management in your organization. Do the people you spoke with see project management as a core competency? Do they feel that there is a shortage of good project managers?

Case Studies

Case One

UConn's University Information Technology Services (UITS) Develops a Five-Year Strategic Plan

The University of Connecticut was founded in 1881 under the name Storrs Agricultural School. As the name implies, the school was originally focused solely on agricultural studies. In 1893, the school became part of the national land-grant college program, which provided land and funding to one college in each state whose focus was on teaching practical skills in agriculture, engineering, military arts, and science.

Over the years, the school's name changed three more times—finally becoming the University of Connecticut in 1939—while its programs expanded into areas such as social work, law, and nursing. Today, UConn, as the school is commonly called, has more than 18,000 undergraduate students at its main campus in Storrs, Connecticut, as well as 4,500 students who take classes at five smaller campuses across the state. Another 8,200 UConn students are pursuing graduate-level degrees in dentistry, education, law, medicine, and pharmacy, among others.

The 200 employees who work for the University Information Technology Services (UITS) division at UConn are responsible for deploying, managing, and maintaining IT systems and services—including classroom applications, data management, desktop and software support, email, file services, high-performance computing, mobile applications, and Web services as well as the university's entire data network and telecommunications infrastructure.

The primary mission of UITS is "to facilitate, coordinate, or implement information technologies that effectively enable the institutional missions of research, teaching, learning, and outreach." In an effort to ensure that it is fulfilling its mission, UITS recently undertook

an intensive strategic planning process, the end result of which was a five-year strategic plan that defines the role UITS will play in fulfilling the university's larger mission.

From the start, UITS utilized a collaborative approach to its strategic planning process, which began with conversations with key stakeholders, including students, alumni, faculty, staff, and administrators. The information gathered during these meetings helped UITS staff assess the current state of IT services across the university. The planning process then extended for several more months, with participation by various college deans and directors, members of the president's cabinet, and representatives from the IT Partners program, which includes three advisory committees, made up of faculty, administrators, and IT staff, respectively. At that point, UITS released a draft version of the plan and then spent more time gathering feedback from its various constituencies.

The final version of the strategic plan identifies five high-level objectives (referred to as goals in the plan) that establish how UITS will support UConn's institutional mission and the changing IT needs of the university community:

- Goal 1: Pursue IT solutions that empower members of our community to successfully, productively, and securely engage in all of their institutional roles as individuals.
- Goal 2: Pursue IT solutions under the guidance of our academic partners that facilitate effective research, enrich teaching and learning, and enhance institutional competitiveness for extramural funding.
- Goal 3: Pursue IT solutions in concert with functional partners that support the business of the university and increase operational effectiveness.
- Goal 4: Pursue IT solutions that assist technical partners at all UConn campuses to successfully

provide for the specific needs of their respective communities.

- Goal 5: Pursue IT solutions that can best be provided centrally and deliver them securely, efficiently, and robustly at scale.

These goals now guide UITS staff in their efforts to identify, develop, and implement specific initiatives intended to support its mission. For example, some of the UITS initiatives that fall under Goal 1 of the strategic plan relate to the delivery of mobile device services and collaboration tools that members of the university community can use no matter whether they are on or off campus. In addition, UITS has placed a priority on developing high-performance computing capabilities and instructional technologies in support of Goal 2. Initiatives connected to Goal 3 include one intended to enhance the paperless document-management tools available to the various administrative and academic departments.

According to UConn's CIO and Vice Provost for Information Technology, Michael Mundrane, who led the strategic planning process, "Our primary goal for the plan itself was to produce a marketing document that would explain to the organization and to our community where we were going and why." And as Mundrane explains in the plan document, "The challenge was never to generate a laundry list of technologies but was always to identify the smallest practical number of key choices that would have the greatest impact on the success of the university."

From Mundrane's perspective, a strategic plan offers guidance to help an IT organization ensure that "the important" is not squeezed out by "the urgent." As he puts it, "By focusing on the big picture, you can ensure that your goals are accomplished and that it is easier to find the resources needed to tackle unexpected challenges or to pursue unique and innovative opportunities that appear throughout the year."

Critical Thinking Questions

1. How well do the five high-level goals in the UITS strategic plan support the IT organization's stated mission? How well do the goals address the needs of the various constituencies within the university?

2. UITS's commitment to collaboration did not end when the UITS strategic plan was finalized. Michael Mundrane considers the plan to be a dynamic document and has pledged to actively solicit feedback from the university community every two years to reassess the plan and its relevance to the changing needs of the university. Do you think such a strong commitment to collaborative strategic planning is more or less important at a public institution, such as the University of Connecticut, versus a private company? Is it more or less difficult to implement?

3. Do you agree with Michael Mundrane's statement that a strategic plan should be treated as a marketing document? Go to the UITS Strategic Plan Web site (*http://itstrategy.uconn.edu*), and click the link to view the strategic plan. What do you think of the final document? Is it effective as both a strategic plan and a marketing document?

SOURCES: "History," University of Connecticut, *http://uconn.edu/about-us/history*, accessed April 18, 2016; "Transcript of Morrill Act (1862)," Our Documents Initiative, *www.ourdocuments.gov/doc.php?flash= true&doc=33&page=transcript*, accessed April 17, 2016; "2016 Fact Sheet," University of Connecticut, *http://uconn.edu/factsheet/latest.pdf*, accessed April 17, 2016; "University Information Technology Services," University of Connecticut, *http://uits.uconn.edu/services*, accessed April 18, 2016; "About UITS," University of Connecticut, *http://uits.uconn.edu/about-uits*, accessed April 17, 2016; "UITS Strategic Plan: Annual Review and Progress Report," University of Connecticut University Information Technology Services, October 2015, *http://itstrategy.uconn.edu/wp-content/uploads/sites/850/2015/10/strategic-plan-progress-report_2015.pdf*; "IT Strategic Plan: 2014–18," University of Connecticut University Information Technology Services, accessed April 16, 2016, *http://itstrategy.uconn.edu/wp-content/uploads/sites/850/2015/08/UITS-strategic-plan_2015-8-24.pdf*; Mundrane, Michael R., "Why a Strategic IT Plan Is a CIO's Best Asset," *The Enterprisers Project*," March 22, 2016, *https://enterprisersproject.com/article/2016/3/why-strategic-it-plan-cios-best-asset*; "IT Strategic Plan: 2014–18," University of Connecticut University Information Technology Services, accessed April 16, 2016, *http://itstrategy.uconn.edu/wp-content/uploads/sites/850/2015/08/UITS-strategic-plan_2015-8-24.pdf*.

Case Two

Webcor: Building Buy-In in the Brick-and-Mortar Business

Founded in 1971, Webcor Builders is one of the largest construction companies in California and one of the largest green construction companies in the United States. Committed to innovative practices, Webcor has gained considerable attention due to its award-winning work, including interior construction, historic restoration, and seismic renovation. As Webcor expanded from multifamily residences to commercial offices, interiors, retail, public works, parking structures, and federal, education, and healthcare facilities, the company opened offices first in San Francisco, and then in San Diego, Los Angeles, and Alameda. Its merger with the large Japanese construction firm Obayashi positioned the company to reach customers along the Pacific Rim, with a new office in Honolulu.

Along with developing innovations in building materials and methods, Webcor has leveraged cutting-edge information technologies—in an industry that is often slow to consider, accept, and adopt IS advances. As early as 1984, Webcor integrated the Apple desktop into its work process. In 2011, Webcor made a significant commitment to virtual design and construction in its public sector building projects. Adopting Vico Software's 5D Virtual Construction application allowed Webcor to estimate costs, schedule projects, and manage projects with increased efficiency. With this software, Webcor can take its customers through a series of what-if scenarios that enable them to make key design decisions. Frank Haase, Director of Virtual Building at

Webcor, explains, "We have amassed a knowledge base of real data—from past projects and from our subcontractors—that when combined with the integrated 5D approach gives us an unprecedented planning and management capability on all projects. The precise information derived from this approach, both in preconstruction planning and in ongoing construction operations, helps us to resolve issues early and to make prompt fact-based decisions." Using the software, Webcor can also predict the scheduling and cost impact of changes that occur throughout building design and construction.

The big question many observers asked was, "How did Webcor Building manage to persuade its workforce to adopt the new technologies?" The decision to adopt the system involved fairly high risks, given the potential resistance of its end users. Vince Sarrubi, Webcor CIO, explained the complexity of the challenge, "Blue collar industries tend to focus on completing tasks, meeting deadlines, and doing what they know how to do best to minimize time loss. New technologies mean changes to physical work practices, which could mean missing a deadline. These workers live in the physical world and have been manually practicing their art for years. There's a mentality of 'head down and nose to the grindstone gets the work done' and 'if it ain't broke, don't fix it.'"

So, how did Webcor achieve this success? First, Sarrubi is not alone in leading the call for innovative IS utilization within the company. Webcor cites innovation as one of its strengths, and its top management has been firmly committed to technological innovation. Company CEO Andy Ball spearheaded the virtual construction project. He insists, "Change is never easy, and it has an emotional toll and it has a financial toll. Initially, it has a reduction in productivity in order to have a significant gain in productivity. So all of these things sort of work against change, but if you don't embrace it and you don't move forward, you're just going to move backward and fall off the back because it occurs every day." The management of Webcor understands the risks and advantage of innovation and is fully invested in seeing it through.

With the firm backing of the top management team, Sarrubi has used two tactics to persuade his blue-collar workforce to adopt technological innovation. First, Sarrubi searches for and hires what he calls technology "cheerleaders," young college graduates who are more collaborative and who have embraced technology from their early years as a means of producing higher quality work in less time. According to Sarrubi, "Once older workers see a 'greenhorn'—a new construction worker—using technology to manage a job, the older, senior superintendents begin to see the benefits of the technology and start to hop on the wagon." This strategy successfully persuaded older employees to adopt Box, a cloud-based storage platform for the company's

architectural drawings and financial documents. Cloud technology has facilitated low-cost collaboration and electronic document management for both Webcor and its subcontractors. Workers can use the Box application and an iPad to access drawings and 3D models, report problems, submit inspections, and notify all stakeholders of issues or changes.

Sarrubi recalls how Webcor adopted Box technology: "Our enterprise adoption of Box grew out of a trial at one job site and just took off, caught fire, adoption-wise…. All of a sudden, what started as a small group test project grew into almost one hundred Box users within a few weeks. The match that lit the Box fuse was word-of-mouth employee testimonials within the company."

In addition to his cheerleader approach, Sarrubi also makes sure that working with the new technology is "as easy as using Amazon." Cost, scalability, and return-on-investment are important factors the company considers when making IS decisions, but end-user preference is also a big factor in what technologies the company adopts. When deciding between different technology solutions, Sarrubi tells Webcor's top management to "slip on the user's boots and walk a mile." That he feels will lead to the best IS choice.

Critical Thinking Questions

1. List the key ideas IS managers can reapply from Webcor Builders to improve the successful adoption of new technologies within their own organization.
2. What additional strategies can you identify to encourage the adoption of new technology?
3. Imagine that you are a disgruntled employee and that you wish to sabotage the implementation of a new technology project at Webcor, without drawing too much attention to yourself. What might you do?

SOURCES: "Built Through Trust," Webcor Builders, *www.webcor.com*, accessed October 5, 2014; "Webcor Builders Standardizes on Vico Office for Virtual Construction," Vico Software, June 9, 2011, *www.vicosoft ware.com/0/webcor-builders-standardizes-on-vico-office-for-virtual-con struction/tabid/250240/Default.aspx*; Florentine, Sharon, "Construction Company CIO Builds a Better Business with the Cloud," *CIO*, August 1, 2014, *www.cio.com/article/2459507/leadership-management/construc tion-company-cio-builds-a-better-business-with-the-cloud.html*; "Press Release: Webcor Builders Named as 2014 Contractor of the Year," *Market Watch*, August 6, 2014, *www.marketwatch.com/story/webcor-builders-named-as-2014-contractor-of-the-year-2014-08-06*; Geron, Tomio, "Webcor Moves Construction Industry to the Cloud," *Forbes*, August 21, 2013, *www.forbes.com/sites/tomiogeron/2013/08/21/webcor-moves-construction-industry-to-the-cloud*; Green, Laura, "Andy Ball Leads Webcor Builders into a New Age of Construction," *Smart Business*, September 1, 2011, *www.sbnonline.com/article/andy-ball-leads-webcor-builders-into-a-new-age-of-construction*.

Notes

1. Sun, Leo, "SWOT Analysis of Starbucks Corporation (SBUX)," *Motley Fool*, June 19, 2015, *www.fool.com /investing/general/2015/06/19/swot-analysis-of-star bucks-corporation-sbux.aspx*.

2. Thompson, Andrew, "Google's Vision Statement & Mission Statement," *Panmore Institute* (blog), September 20, 2015, *http://panmore.com/google-vision-statement -mission-statement*.

3. Gaddam, Ajit, "List of Google Core Values," Ask Student, *www.askstudent.com/google/list-of-google-core-values/*, accessed January 31, 2016.

4. Farfan, Barbara, "Wal-Mart Stores' Mission Statement— People, Saving Money, Living a Better Life," November 20, 2015, *About.com*, *http://retailindustry.about.com/od /retailbestpractices/ig/Company-Mission-Statements /Wal-Mart-Mission-Statement.htm*.

5. Collins, James and Porras, Jerry, *Built to Last: Successful Habits of Visionary Companies*, New York: Harper Collins Publishers, 1994, 1997, p. 9.

6. Raice, Shayndi and Ante, Spencer E., "Insta-Rich: $1 Billion for Instagram," *The Wall Street Journal*, April 10, 2012, *http://online.wsj.com/news/articles/SB1000142405 2702303815404577333840377381670*.

7. Kuittinen, Tero, "On Oculus Rift and Facebook's Grand Acquisitions," *BGR*, March 26, 2014, *http://bgr.com /2014/03/26/facebook-oculus-rift-acquisition-analysis*.

8. Doran, George T., Miller, Arthur, and Cunningham, James, "There's a S.M.A.R.T. Way to Write Management's Goals and Objectives," *Management Review*, vol. 70, no. 11, pp. 35–36, 1981.

9. Utermohlen, Karl, "Amazon Drone Delivery: Details Finally Revealed!," *Investor Place* (blog), January 19, 2016, *http://investorplace.com/2016/01/amazon-drone -delivery-amzn-stock/#.VrJo0432b4g*.

10. "About Us," Alstom Transport, *www.alstom.com/micro sites/transport/about-us*, accessed February 3, 2016.

11. "Our Trains," Virgin Trains, *www.virgintrains.co.uk /trains*, accessed February 3, 2016.

12. "'Unreasonable Ambition' Puts Alstom on the Fast Track for Growth," *OpEx Review*, December 2012, Issue 5, *www.tbmcg.com/misc_assets/newsletter/opex_1212_cover _story.pdf*.

13. "About Johns Hopkins Medicine," Johns Hopkins Medicine, *www.hopkinsmedicine.org/about/*, accessed February 2, 2015.

14. Nash, Kim S., "State of the CIO 2014: The Great Schism," *CIO*, January 1, 2014, *www.cio.com/article/2380234 /cio-roletate-of-the-cio-2014-the-great-schism/cio-role /state-of-the-cio-2014-the-great-schism.html*.

15. "Statewide Information Technology 2012–2014 Strategic Plan," Delaware Department of Technology and Information, *http://dti.delaware.gov/pdfs/strategicplan/Dela ware-Statewide-IT-Strategic-Plan.pdf*, September 2012.

16. Nash, "The Great Schism."

17. "City of Seattle Enterprise Information Technology Strategic Plan 2012–2014," City of Seattle, *www.seattle.gov /Documents/Departments/InformationTechnology/RFP /SOHIPRFPAppendixCEnterpriseITStrategic Plan20122014.pdf*, accessed September 16, 2014.

18. Nash, "The Great Schism."

19. May, Thornton, "A Strategy for Strategy: Figuring Out How to Figure Out What IT Should Do Next," *Computerworld*, September 2, 2014, *www.computerworld.com /article/2600346/it-management/a-strategy-for-strategy -figuring-out-how-to-figure-out-what-it-should-do-next .html*.

20. Nash, "The Great Schism."

21. "GAF Creates First Ever Virtual Home Remodeler App with 'Instantaneous' Roof Mapping Feature," GAF, *www.gaf.com/About_GAF/Press_Room/Press_Releases /65077248*, accessed September 3, 2014.

22. Hastie, Shane and Wojewoda, Stéphane, "Standish Group 2015 Chaos Report—Q&A with Jennifer Lynch," *InfoQ* (blog), October 24, 2015, *www.infoq.com/articles /standish-chaos-2015*.

23. Hamel, Gary and Prahalad, C.K., "The Core Competence of the Corporation," *Harvard Business Review*, vol. 68, no. 3, pp. 79–93, May–June 1990.

24. Krigsman, Michael, "California Abandons $2 Billion Court Management System," *ZDNet*, April 2, 2012, *www .zdnet.com/blog/projectfailures/california-abandons -2-billion-court-management-system/15363*.

25. Brino, Anthony, "CGI to Build Vermont's HIX," *Government Health IT*, December 20, 2012, *www.govhealthit .com/news/vermont-sign-hix-it-contract-cgi*.

26. Stein, Andrew, "Builder of State's Health Care Exchange Misses Key Deadlines," *VTDigger.org* (blog), September 27, 2013, *http://vtdigger.org/2013/09/27/builder-states -health-care-exchange-misses-key-deadliness*.

27. Goswami, Neal P., "State, CGI Sign Amended Contract with New Timetable and Penalties," *Vermont Press Bureau*, April 3, 2014, *www.vermontpressbureau.com /2014/04/03/state-cgi-sign-amended-contract-with-new -timeline-and-penalties*.

28. True, Morgan, "CGI Misses Vermont Health Connect Deadline Again," *VermontBiz*, May 21, 2014, *www.ver montbiz.com/news/may/cgi-misses-vermont-health-con nect-deadline-again*.

29. Remsen, Nancy, "Health Site Contractor Misses Deadline, Again," Burlington Free Press, June 10, 2014, *www.bur lingtonfreepress.com/story/news/local/2014/06/06 /health-site-contractor-misses-deadline/10090537*.

30. Parker, Bruce, "Vermont Fires Creator of Its 'Unacceptable,' Glitchy ObamaCare Site," *Fox News*, August 5, 2014, *www.foxnews.com/politics/2014/08/05/vermont -fires-creator-its-unacceptable-glitchy-obamacare-site*.

31. Browning, Lynnley, "Thanks for Nothing: Obamacare Website Bunglers Fired," *Newsweek*, August 6, 2014, *www.newsweek.com/thanks-nothing-obamacare -website-bunglers-fired-263205*.

32. Fitzpatrick, Alex, "Apple Has an iPhone Headache, But It Won't Last Long," *Time*, September 24, 2014, *http://time .com/3426561/apple-iphone-6-plus-ios-8-problems*.

33. Brown, James, "6 Things to Remember When Projects Spiral Out of Control," SAP Community Network, September 27, 2013, *http://scn.sap.com/community /it-management/blog/2013/09/27/6-things-to-remember -when-projects-spiral-out-of-control*.

34. Tuckman, Bruce, "Developmental Sequence in Small Groups," *Psychological Bulletin*, Volume 63, pages 384–389, 1965.

35. "Lead Integrator Atos Successfully Completes Delivery of World's Biggest IT Sports Contract for Sochi 2014 Games," Atos, February 24, 2014, *http://webcache.goo gleusercontent.com/search?q=cache:IcukDP1ZdWYJ: http://atos.net/en-us/home/we-are/news/press-release /2014/pr-2014_02_24_02.html*.

- Amazon is contemplating entering into competition with FedEx and UPS to deliver products directly to its customers by creating a global delivery network, with the goal of dramatically cutting costs and speeding delivery. Amazon is facing a major development effort to build the information systems to support this plan.

- The waterfall approach to system development allows for a high degree of management control. It is for this reason that this 50-year-old approach is frequently followed when an organization contracts with another to build its information system, even though the agile software development is often faster and can lead to higher quality results.

Principles

- Organizations can obtain software using one of two basic approaches: buy or build.

- A system under development following the waterfall approach moves from one phase to the next, with a management review at the end of each phase.

- Agile development is an iterative system development process that develops a system in "sprint" increments lasting from two weeks to two months.

- When buying off-the-shelf software, the effort required to modify the software package as well as existing software so that they work well together must be taken into account as a major factor in selecting the final vendor and software.

Learning Objectives

- Identify the pros and cons associated with both buying and building software.

- Identify the advantages and disadvantages of the waterfall approach to system development.

- Identify and state the goal of each of the six phases of the waterfall approach.

- Identify and briefly describe the primary tools and techniques used during system development.

- Define five types of feasibility that must be assessed.

- Identify the purpose and participants involved in various types of testing from unit testing to user acceptance testing.

- Identify three approaches for system cutover.

- Describe the agile development process.

- Identify the advantages and disadvantages of the agile system development approach.

- Describe the role of the scrum master and product owner in the scrum framework.

- Discuss extreme programming (XP) and DevOps.

- Outline a process for evaluation and selection of a software package.

- Identify the key factors to be considered in selecting a software package.

Why Learn about System Acquisition and Development?

Throughout this book, you have seen many examples of the use of information systems to support organizations and people in a variety of careers. But where does an organization start when looking to acquire or develop these systems? And how can you work with IS personnel, such as system analysts and computer programmers, to get the information systems that you need to succeed on the job or in your own business? This chapter provides the answers to these questions along with specific examples of how new or modified systems are initiated, analyzed, designed, constructed, tested, and implemented in a number of industries. We start with a discussion of the forces that lead an organization to acquire new software and then move on to an overview of the two basic approaches to acquiring software.

As you read this chapter, consider the following:

- What options exist for organizations to acquire or develop an information system?
- What role should end users and other stakeholders play in the acquisition or development of a new system?

Buy versus Build

Organizations continue to spend considerable time and resources developing and acquiring software to support a wide range of applications, including business intelligence and analytics; e-commerce, enterprise level functions, and mobile apps. Opportunities and problems that frequently trigger the initiation of an information system project include the following:

- Organizations may pursue opportunities to use information systems to support a key organization strategy or to seize a significant, and ideally long-term, competitive advantage. Amazon is evaluating just such a move—it is contemplating entering into competition with FedEx and UPS to deliver products directly to its customers. Such an aggressive supply chain move would create a global delivery network controlling the flow of goods from factories around the world to customer doorsteps in Boston, Los Angeles, or anywhere—cutting costs and speeding delivery. Major changes in information systems and business processes at Amazon will be necessary to support this plan.[1]
- Pressure to increase profitability and improve operational efficiencies often drives organizations to implement new approaches and technology. NBTY, Inc., a manufacturer of vitamins and nutritional supplements, has been conducting a multiyear business transformation focused on achieving operational efficiency and productivity gains to meet challenging financial targets mandated by NBTY's parent Carlyle Group. The company implemented custom software to enable architects, construction workers, and contractors to quickly share information and cut the time required to remodel a Vitamin World store in half. NBTY is reapplying lessons learned from that experience to automate business processes and boost operational efficiencies for its Puritan's Pride and Holland & Barrett brands.[2]
- The availability of new technology can create an opportunity to offer new services or attract new customers. Walgreens was an early adopter of mobile technology and developed a mobile app that enables customers to print photos, order prescription refills, and earn points toward future purchases. Walgreens went beyond these basics by allowing more than 240 third-party software providers to integrate with the company's mobile application through APIs. Now customers can manage their medication

schedules from their Apple Watches and earn and redeem points using Apple Pay.[3]

Organizations can obtain software using one of two basic approaches: buy or build. Buying off-the-shelf software is less risky and leads to quicker deployment; however, maintenance and support costs may become expensive with this approach, and the software may not be an exact match to the needs and work processes of the organization. Building custom software can provide a better match to the current work processes and provide a potential competitive advantage; however, software development can be extremely costly, and it can take months or even years to develop custom software. The advantages and disadvantages of these two approaches are summarized in Table 12.1.

TABLE 12.1 The pros and cons of buying versus building software

Strategy	Pros	Cons
Buy	A software solution can be acquired and deployed relatively quickly. An organization can "test drive" software before acquiring it.	Unmodified, the software may not be a good match to an organization's needs. Maintenance and support costs can become excessive.
Build	Customized software is more likely to be a good match to an organization's needs. A custom application provides the potential to achieve competitive advantage.	The cost to build a system can be quite high compared to the cost of purchasing off-the-shelf software. Customized software can take months or even years to deploy.

Buying existing software developed by a software manufacturer enables an organization to test drive and evaluate it before making a major commitment to purchase it and install it. Once purchased, the existing software can be installed with minimal disruption (ideally) so that user needs can be quickly met and the organization can begin reaping the benefits from the information system. Software buyers do not actually own the software, nor can they access it to make changes or improvements; they are simply licensed to use the software on a computer. With no access to the underlying source code, user organizations must pay maintenance and support costs to the manufacturer or to a third party authorized to fix bugs or add new functionality. For some organizations, these costs can become excessive. As a result, many organizations are turning to open source software with access to the source code permitted so that it can be studied, changed, and improved by the organization's own software professionals—with no maintenance charges. Indeed, the amount and quality of support for open source software is dependent on whether or not there are people, resources, and interest among the organizations using the software to develop updates and fix bugs.

The set of activities involved in building information systems to meet users' needs is called system development. System development projects can range from small to very large and are conducted in fields as diverse as nuclear science research and video game development. If an organization elects to build a system, it can use its own employees (perhaps augmented with contractors) to develop the system, or it can hire an outside company to manage and/or perform all of the system development work. The latter approach allows an organization to focus on what it does best, by delegating software development to companies that have world-class development capabilities. This can be important since the system development efforts for even relatively small projects can require months, with large projects requiring years of effort. Unfortunately, in spite of everyone's best efforts, a significant number of large system development projects are likely to fail.

Organizations can use several different approaches when developing their own software. Two of those—the waterfall and agile software development processes—are discussed in the next section, followed by a discussion of a process to follow when purchasing off-the-shelf software.

Waterfall System Development Process

waterfall system development process: A sequential, multistage system development process in which work on the next stage cannot begin until the results of the current stage are reviewed and approved or modified as necessary.

The **waterfall system development process** is a sequential, multistage system development process in which work on the next stage cannot begin until the results of the current stage are reviewed and approved or modified as necessary. It is referred to as a waterfall process because progress is seen as flowing steadily downward (like a waterfall) through the various phases of development. The phases of the waterfall system development process can vary from one company to the next, but many organizations use an approach with six phases: investigation, analysis, design, construction, integration and testing, and implementation. Once the system is built, organizations complete the additional steps of operation, maintenance, and disposition. See Figure 12.1.

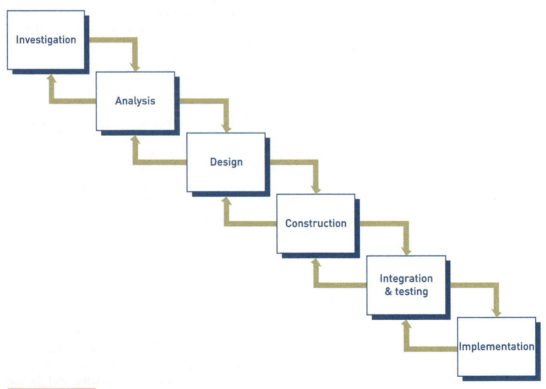

FIGURE **12.1**
Waterfall system development process
Progress flows steadily downward (like a waterfall) through the various phases of development.

As shown in Figure 12.1, a system under development moves from one phase of the waterfall process to the next. At the end of each phase, a review is conducted to ensure that all tasks and deliverables associated with that phase were produced and that they are of good quality. In addition, at the end of each phase, the overall project scope, costs, schedule, and benefits associated with the project are reviewed to ensure that the project is on track and worth completing. As a result, the waterfall approach allows for a high degree of management control. It is for this reason that this approach is frequently followed when an organization contracts with another to build its information system. However, a major problem with this approach is that users do not interact with the solution until the integration and testing phase when the system is nearly complete. This can lead to a mismatch between system capabilities, users' expectations, and organizational needs. Table 12.2 lists additional advantages and disadvantages of the waterfall system development process.

TABLE 12.2 Advantages and disadvantages of waterfall system development process

Advantages	Disadvantages
Formal review at the end of each phase allows maximum management control.	Users get a system that meets the needs as understood by the developers; however, this might not be what the users really needed.
This approach requires creation of considerable system documentation so that system requirements can be traced back to stated business needs.	Often, user needs go unstated or are miscommunicated or misunderstood.
Approach produces many intermediate products that can be reviewed to measure progress toward developing the system.	Users can't easily review intermediate products and evaluate whether a particular product (e.g., a data-flow diagram) will lead to a system that meets their business requirements.

The Energy Information Administration (EIA) serves as an advisor to the U.S. Department of Energy and is responsible for collecting energy data, conducting analysis, and making forecasts about future energy inventories, demand, and prices. Since 2011, EIA has spent close to $20 million on its IT Transformation Project, a major system development effort designed to enhance efficiencies within the agency. However, the program has been mired in poor project management and has failed to produce any significant results or benefits.[4] This project obviously would have benefitted from a higher degree of management control.

System Investigation

system investigation: The initial phase in the development of a new or modified business information system whose purpose is to gain a clear understanding of the specifics of the problem to solve or the opportunity to address.

System investigation is the initial phase in the development of a new or modified business information system whose purpose is to gain a clear understanding of the specifics of the problem to solve or the opportunity to address. What is the scope of the problem? Who is affected and how? How often does this occur? After gaining a good understanding of the problem, the next question is, "Is the problem worth addressing?" Given that organizations have limited resources—people and money—this question deserves careful attention. What are the potential costs, both the one-time initial costs and recurring costs? What risks are associated with the project? If successful, what benefits, both tangible and intangible, will the system provide? The steps of the investigation phase are outlined next and discussed on the following pages:

1. Review system investigation request.
2. Identify and recruit team leader and team members.
3. Develop budget and schedule for investigation.
4. Perform investigation.

5. Perform preliminary feasibility analysis.
6. Prepare draft of investigation report.
7. Review results of investigation with steering team.

Review System Investigation Request

Because system development requests can require considerable time and effort to investigate, many organizations have adopted a formal procedure for initiating a system investigation. Ideally, a system investigation request is completed by members of the organization that will be most affected by the new or modified system. This request typically includes the following information:

- A preliminary statement of the problem or opportunity to be addressed (this will be refined during the course of the investigation)
- A brief discussion of how this effort aligns with previously defined company and organization objectives, goals, and strategies
- Identification of the general areas of the business and business processes to be included in the scope of the study (e.g., the handling of customer discounts in the order-processing system)

The information in the system request helps senior management rationalize and prioritize the activities of the IS department and decide which investigation projects should be staffed. Based on the overall IS plan, the organization's needs and goals, and the estimated value and priority of the proposed projects, managers make decisions regarding which system investigation requests will be approved.

Identify and Recruit Team Leader and Team Members

After managers grant approval to initiate a system investigation, the next step is to identify and recruit a person who will lead the investigation phase, followed by the other members of the investigation team. The members of the investigation team are responsible for gathering and analyzing data, preparing an investigation phase report, and presenting the results to the project steering team. The system investigation team can be quite diverse, often with members located around the world. Business knowledge of the areas under study, communication, and collaboration are keys to successful investigation teams. Members of the development team may change as a project moves through the various development phases, depending on the knowledge, experience, and skills required during each phase.

Develop Budget and Schedule for Investigation

After the team has been formed, its members work together to develop a list of specific objectives and activities that must be accomplished during the system investigation phase along with a schedule for completing the work. The team establishes major milestones to help monitor progress and determine whether problems or delays occur in performing system investigation. The group also prepares a budget to complete the investigation including any travel required and funds necessary to cover the use of any outside resources or consultants.

Perform Investigation

The major tasks to perform during investigation include refining the initial problem definition and scope described in the system investigation request, identifying the high-level business requirements the system must meet, and identifying any issues or risks associated with the project.

joint application development (JAD): A structured meeting process that can accelerate and improve the efficiency and effectiveness of the investigation, analysis, and design phases of a system development project.

Joint Application Development Joint application development (JAD) is a structured meeting process that can accelerate and improve the efficiency and effectiveness of not only the investigation phase but also the analysis and design phases of a system development project. JAD involves carefully planned and designed meetings in which users, stakeholders, and IS professionals work together to analyze existing systems, define problems, identify solution requirements, and propose and evaluate possible solutions including costs and benefits. See Figure 12.2. The JAD process has proven to be extremely effective and efficient at accomplishing these tasks. In addition, the highly participative nature of the sessions goes a long way to helping ensure stakeholders and users buy into the results. With today's technology, such as group decision support systems and video conferencing, it is possible to conduct effective live JAD sessions with people located in many different places without the need for expensive travel.

FIGURE 12.2

JAD session

JAD can accelerate and improve the efficiency and effectiveness of the investigation, analysis, and design phases of a system development project.

The success or failure of a JAD session depends on how well the JAD facilitator plans and manages the session. It is not unusual for the facilitator to spend three hours planning and preparing for the JAD session for each hour the JAD session lasts. In addition, the participants of a JAD session must be carefully chosen to include users of the system as well as people from other organizations who will likely be affected by, provide input for, or receive output from the system. Ideally, people from the operational level as well as the executive level will attend. Table 12.3 identifies the JAD session participants as well as their role and qualifications.

The consulting firm Liquid Mercury Solutions uses JAD in working with its clients on a routine basis to define and develop information system solutions.[5]

Functional Decomposition   Functional decomposition is a technique that involves breaking down a complex problem or system into smaller parts that are more manageable and easier to understand. It is frequently used during the investigation phase to define the business processes included within the scope of the system. Recall that a process is a set of logically related tasks performed to achieve a defined outcome. A process is usually initiated in response to a specific event and requires input that it processes to create output. Often, feedback is generated that is used to monitor and refine the process.

To create the functional decomposition chart (see Figure 12.3), begin with the name of the system and then identify the highest-level processes to be performed. Each process should have a two word "verb-subject" name that clearly

TABLE 12.3 JAD participants and their role

Role	Responsibilities	Qualifications
Facilitator	• Determines JAD session objectives • Plans JAD session to meet objectives • Leads JAD session • Encourages everyone to participate	• Excellent meeting facilitator • Unbiased and does not take sides
Decision makers	• Resolve conflicts • Avoid gridlock	• Stakeholders selected by project sponsor to make decisions • Have the authority and willingness to make decisions
Users	• Describe business as it is and as it should be • Provide business expertise • Define problems, identify potential benefits, analyze existing system, define requirements of a new system, and propose and evaluate possible solutions	• Represent all major areas affected • Expert in their area of the business
System developers	• Observe carefully • Offer technical opinion on cost or feasibility, if requested • Gain deep understanding of customers' needs and desires	• Member of system development team
Scribe	• Participate in discussion to clarify points and capture them accurately • Document key points, issues, next steps, and decisions throughout the JAD session • Publish results of JAD session and solicit feedback	• Excellent listening skills • Experience in using software engineering tools to document requirements and create system models

defines the process. Next, break those high-level processes down into lower-level subprocesses. For the system investigation phase, two or three levels of decomposition are usually sufficient to define the scope of the system.

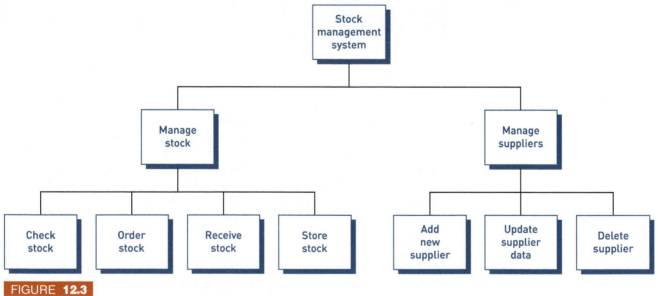

FIGURE 12.3

Functional decomposition chart

Functional decomposition is used to define the scope of the system.

Perform Preliminary Feasibility Analysis

feasibility analysis: An assessment of the technical, economic, legal, operational, and schedule feasibility of a project.

The technical, economic, legal, operational, and schedule feasibility are assessed during the **feasibility analysis**, which is only a preliminary analysis that will be repeated with more accuracy during the analysis and design phases, when more details about the system and its requirements are known.

technical feasibility: The process of determining whether a project is feasible within the current limits of available technology.

economic feasibility: The process of determining whether the project makes financial sense and whether predicted benefits offset the cost and time needed to obtain them.

legal feasibility: The process of determining whether laws or regulations may prevent or limit a system development project.

operational feasibility: The process of determining how a system will be accepted by people and how well it will meet various system performance expectations.

schedule feasibility: The process of determining whether the project can be completed within a desired time frame.

Technical feasibility examines whether a project is feasible within the current limits of available technology. Determining the technical feasibility is critical when new technology is first being considered for use within an organization, prior to its widespread use. A number of companies are currently participating in a technical feasibility study to determine if advanced positioning signals transmitted from a GPS satellite can be used to control a self-steering robotic tractor to within an accuracy of 5 centimeters. Such accuracy is needed to ensure that the self-steering robotic tractor tires can be guided to run between rows of planted rice without causing damage to the crop.[6]

Economic feasibility determines whether the expected benefits associated with the project outweigh the expected costs sufficiently to make the project financially attractive. Cost and benefit estimates should be made for multiple years to allow for calculation of the internal rate of return or net present value of the project. It is important to recognize that at this early stage of the development process, the cost and benefit amounts are rough estimates and subject to change should the project continue. So, while the mathematics involved may make it appear that the results are precise, in actuality, the result is no more accurate than cash flow estimates, which are often no more than refined guesses. Table 12.4 lists some of the typical costs and benefits that need to be considered.

Organizations must guard against spending more than is appropriate as the success or failure of a system development effort will, at least to some degree, be measured against meeting the project budget. The U.K. Ministry of Defence wasted millions of pounds on a planned £1.3 billion (approximately $2.2 billion) information system designed to enable the army to recruit online. A key benefit to be derived from the project was to increase recruitment levels above historic levels; however, this goal has not been achieved.[7]

Legal feasibility is the process of determining whether laws or regulations may prevent or limit a system development project. Legal feasibility involves an analysis of existing and future laws to determine the likelihood of legal action against the system development project and the possible consequences of such action. For example, nearly every country in Europe and many in Latin America, Asia, and Africa have implemented data protection laws that prohibit the disclosure or misuse of information held on private individuals. These laws make it possible for the human resources departments of multinational companies to share personal employee data across country borders only in limited circumstances.

Operational feasibility is the process of determining how a system will be accepted by people and how well it will meet various system performance expectations. Assessing the operational feasibility of a project includes taking into consideration people issues, such as overcoming employee resistance to change, gaining managerial support for the system, providing sufficient motivation and training, and rationalizing any conflicts with organizational norms and policies. In other words, if the system is developed, will it be used? Operational feasibility also takes into account the need to meet certain system performance requirements (e.g., response time for frequent online transactions, number of concurrent users it must support, reliability, and ease of use) that are considered important to system users and stakeholders.

Schedule feasibility is the process of determining whether a project can be completed within a desired time frame. This process involves balancing the time and resource requirements of the project with other projects. For example, many projects that involve delivering a new financial information system have a desired start-up date at the beginning of the organization's fiscal year. Unfortunately, it is not always possible to meet this date, and so a compromise must be made—deliver part of the system at the start of the fiscal year or wait another year to deliver the full system.

TABLE 12.4 Cost/benefit table

Costs	Year 1	Year 2	Year ...	Year N
Costs to analyze, design, construct, integrate and test, and implement system				
Employees				
Vendor				
Software customization				
Travel				
Hardware costs				
Software tools costs				
Other costs				
Initial costs to establish system				
Software license fees				
New hardware costs				
Cost to upgrade existing hardware				
Cost to upgrade network				
User training				
Purchase of any necessary data				
Cost to migrate existing data to new system				
Other costs				
Ongoing operations costs				
Software lease or rental fees				
Hardware lease or rental fees				
Network usage fees				
System operations and support staff				
User training				
Increased electric and other utilities				
Costs associated with disaster recovery				
Other costs				
Tangible benefits (can be quantified in dollars)				
Reduction in current costs				
Reduction in current staff				
Reduction in inventory levels				
Reduction in computer hardware costs				
Reduction in software costs				
Other reduced costs				
Increase in revenue				
Increase in sales from reaching new customers				
Increase in sales from charging more				
Acceleration in cash flow				
Other increases in revenue				
Intangible benefits (difficult to quantify in dollars)				
Improved customer service				
Improved employee morale				

Prepare Draft of Investigation Report

system investigation report: A summary of the results of the system investigation, with a recommendation of a course of action.

The system investigation ends with production of a **system investigation report** that summarizes the results of the system investigation and recommends a course of action: continue on to system analysis, modify the project in some manner and perhaps repeat the system investigation, or drop the project altogether. See Figure 12.4. A typical table of contents for a system investigation report is shown in Figure 12.5.

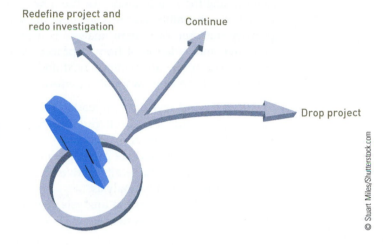

Redefine project and redo investigation

Continue

Drop project

© Stuart Miles/Shutterstock.com

FIGURE 12.4

System investigation recommendation

The system investigation report summarizes the results of the system investigation and recommends a course of action.

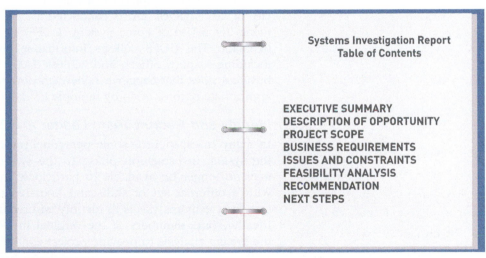

Systems Investigation Report
Table of Contents

EXECUTIVE SUMMARY
DESCRIPTION OF OPPORTUNITY
PROJECT SCOPE
BUSINESS REQUIREMENTS
ISSUES AND CONSTRAINTS
FEASIBILITY ANALYSIS
RECOMMENDATION
NEXT STEPS

FIGURE 12.5

Table of contents for a system investigation report

A typical system investigation report begins with an executive summary and ends with a list of next steps.

Review Results of Investigation with Steering Team

The system investigation report is reviewed with the steering team to gain their input and counsel. Typically, the written report is shared in advance and then the project manager and selected members of the team meet with the steering team to present their recommendations.

After the project review, the steering team might agree with the recommendations of the system development team or it might suggest a change in project focus to concentrate more directly on meeting a specific company objective. Another alternative is that everyone might decide that the project is not feasible and thus cancel the effort. This input is used to finalize the system investigation report.

System Analysis

system analysis: The phase of system development that focuses on gathering data on the existing system, determining the requirements for the new system, considering alternatives within identified constraints, and investigating the feasibility of alternative solutions.

After a project has completed the investigation phase and been approved for further study, the next step is to answer the question, "What must the information system do to solve the problem or capitalize on the opportunity?" The overall emphasis of the system analysis is on gathering data on the existing system, determining the requirements for the new system, considering alternatives within identified constraints, and investigating the feasibility of alternative solutions. The primary outcome of system analysis is a prioritized list of system requirements and a recommendation of how to proceed with the project. The steps in the system analysis phase are outlined next and discussed in the following pages. Note that many of the steps were also performed during system investigation:

1. Identify and recruit team leader and team members.
2. Develop budget and schedule for system analysis activities.
3. Study existing system.
4. Develop prioritized set of requirements.
5. Identify and evaluate alternative solutions.
6. Perform feasibility analysis.
7. Prepare draft of system analysis report.
8. Review results of system analysis with steering team.

The Los Angeles Police Department (LAPD) is comprised of over 9,000 officers and serves 3.9 million residents spread across the 485 square miles of the city of Los Angeles. LAPD conducted a system analysis to define the requirements for a Use of Force System (UOFS) to monitor officer performance and behavior. The UOFS collects information about each use of force incident including suspect, officer, and witness data. The application applies a series of business rules that trigger a review and investigation into the use of force by appropriate parties, often by multiple levels of LAPD management.[8]

Identify and Recruit Team Leader and Team Members

In many cases, there is some personnel turnover when a project moves from the system investigation phase to the system analysis phase. Some players may no longer be available to participate in the project, and new members with a different set of skills and knowledge may be required. So, the first step in system analysis is to identify and recruit the team leader and members. Ideally, some members of the original investigation team will participate in the system analysis to provide project continuity.

Develop Budget and Schedule for System Analysis Activities

After the participants in the system analysis phase are determined, the team develops a list of specific objectives and activities required to complete the system analysis. The team also establishes a schedule—complete with major milestones to track project progress. The group also prepares a budget of the resources required to complete the system analysis, including any required travel expenses as well as funds to cover the use of outside resources.

Study Existing System

The purpose of studying the existing system is to identify its strengths and weaknesses and examine current inputs, outputs, processes, security and controls, and system performance. While analysis of the existing system is important to understanding the current situation, the study team must recognize that after a point of diminishing returns, further study of the existing system will fail to yield additional useful information.

Many useful sources of information about the existing system are available, as shown in Figure 12.6. JAD sessions, direct observation with one or more members of the analysis team directly observing the existing system in action, and surveys are often used to uncover pertinent information from the various sources.

Internal Sources	External Sources
Users, stakeholders, and managers	Customers
Organization charts	Suppliers
Forms and documents	Stockholders
Procedure manuals and policies	Government agencies
Financial reports	Competitors
IS manuals	Outside groups
Other measures of business process	Journals, etc.
	Consultants

FIGURE 12.6

Internal and external sources of data for system analysis

JAD sessions, direct observation, and surveys are often used to uncover data from the various sources.

Develop Prioritized Set of Requirements

The purpose of this step is to determine user, stakeholder, and organizational needs for the new or modified system. A set of requirements must be determined for system processes (including inputs, processing, outputs, and feedback), databases, security and controls, and system performance. See Figure 12.7. As requirements are identified, an attempt is made to prioritize each one by using the following categories:

- **Critical.** Almost all users agree that the system is simply not acceptable unless it performs this function or provides this capability. Lack of this feature or capability would cause users to call a halt to the project.
- **Medium priority.** While highly desirable, most users agree that although their work will be somewhat impaired, the system will still be effective without this feature or capability. Some users may argue strongly for this feature or capability but, in the end, would want the project to continue even without this capability.
- **Low priority.** Most users agree that their ability to use the system to accomplish their work will only be minimally impaired by lack of this feature or capability, although it would be "nice to have." Almost no user argues strongly for this feature or capability.

Identifying, confirming, and prioritizing system requirements is perhaps the single most critical step in the entire waterfall system development process because failure to identify a requirement or an incorrect definition of a requirement may not be discovered until much later in the project, causing much rework, additional costs, and delay in the system effort.

The use of JAD sessions with a cross section of users and stakeholders in the project is an effective way to define system requirements. A technique often used in a JAD session is to ask managers and decision makers to list only the factors that are critical to the success of their areas of the organization.

© rentiia/Shutterstock.com

FIGURE **12.7**
Defining system requirements
System requirements must be checked for consistency so that they all fit together.

A critical success factor (CSF) for a production manager might be adequate raw materials from suppliers, while a CSF for a sales representative could be a list of customers currently buying a certain type of product. Starting from these CSFs, the processes, databases, security and control, and performance requirements associated with each CSF can be identified.

Processes The functional decomposition performed during the investigation phase identifies the majority of the processes to be included within the scope of a new system. Now, the processes must be further defined so that they will be practical, efficient, economical, accurate, and timely to avoid project delays. In addition, the individuals or organizations responsible for completing each step in the process must be identified.

A process requires input that it uses to create output. Often, feedback is generated. The questions that need to be answered during system analysis are: what data entities are required, where will this data come from, what methods will be used to collect and enter the data, who is responsible for data input, and what edits should be performed on the input data to ensure that it is accurate and complete? Another important consideration is the creation of an audit trail that records the source of each data item, when it entered the system, and who entered it. The audit trail may also need to capture when the data is accessed or changed and by whom.

Because the success of a new system is highly dependent upon the acceptability of its output, the identification of common system outputs—such as printed reports, screens, and files—is critical to developing a complete set of system requirements.

data-flow diagram (DFD): A diagram used during both the analysis and design phases to document the processes of the current system or to provide a model of a proposed new system.

Data-Flow Diagram A **data-flow diagram (DFD)** is a diagram used during both the analysis and design phases to document the processes of the current system or to provide a model of a proposed new system. A DFD shows not only the various processes within the system but also where the data needed for each process comes from, where the output of each process will be sent, and what data will be stored and where. The DFD does not provide any information about the process timing (e.g., whether the various processes happen in sequence or are parallel).

DFDs are easy to develop and are easily understood by nontechnical people. Data-flow diagrams use four primary symbols:

- The data-flow line includes arrows that show the direction of data movement.

- The process symbol identifies the function being performed (e.g., check status, issue status message).
- The entity symbol shows either the source or destination of the data (e.g., customer, warehouse).
- A data store symbol reveals a storage location for data (e.g., pending orders, accounts receivable).

Figure 12.8 shows a level 1 DFD. Each of the processes shown in this diagram could be documented in more detail to show the subprocesses and create a level 2 DFD. Frequently, level 3 DFD diagrams are created and used in the analysis and design phases.

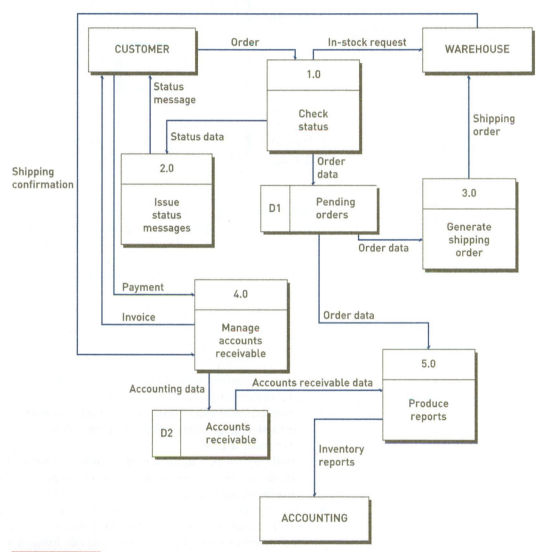

FIGURE **12.8**
Data-flow diagram
A data-flow diagram documents the processes of the current system or provides a model of a proposed new system.

Databases Data modeling is the process of defining the databases that a system will draw data from as well as any new databases that it will create. The use of entity-relationship (ER) diagrams is one technique that is frequently used for this critical step. An ER diagram is used to show logical relationships among data entities, such as in Figure 12.9. An ER diagram (or any other modeling tool) cannot by itself fully describe a business problem or solution because it lacks descriptions of the related activities. It is, however, a good place to start because it describes entity types and attributes about which data might need to be collected for processing.

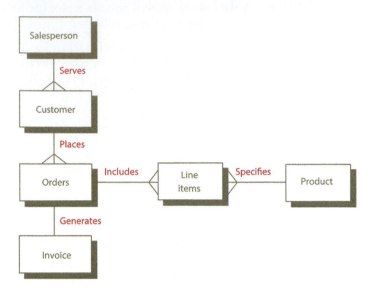

Entity-relationship (ER) diagram for a customer order database
Development of ER diagrams helps ensure that the logical structure of application programs is consistent with the data relationships in the database.

Security and Control   Security and control considerations need to be an integral part of the entire system development process. Unfortunately, they are often treated as an afterthought, after system requirements have been defined and system design is well underway. This approach usually leads to problems that become security vulnerabilities, which can cause major security breaches resulting in significant legal and system modification expenses. A more effective and less costly approach is to define security and control requirements when other system requirements are being identified. The following list provides examples of areas for which security and control requirements might need to be defined:[9]

- Access controls, including controls to authenticate and permit access only to authorized individuals
- Encryption of electronic customer information, including while in transit or in storage on networks or systems to which unauthorized individuals may have access
- Dual control procedures, segregation of duties, and employee background checks for employees with responsibilities for or access to customer, employee, or organization-sensitive information
- Monitoring systems and procedures to detect actual and attempted attacks on or intrusions into information systems
- Measures to protect against destruction, loss, or damage of customer, employee, or organization-sensitive data due to potential environmental hazards, such as fire and water damage, technological failures, or disasters such as hurricanes and terrorism
- Business resumption procedures to get the system up and running with no major business disruption and with no loss of data in the event of a disaster (e.g., fire, hurricane, terrorism)

People with a special interest in security and control include the organization's internal auditors and members of senior management. They should provide input and advice during the system analysis and design phases.

System security and control requirements need to be defined in the context of the organization's existing policies, standards, and guidelines. See

Figure 12.10. For example, the Gramm–Leach–Bliley Act requires companies legally defined as financial institutions to ensure the security and confidentiality of customer information. Thus, financial institutions have established policies, standards, and guidelines to which any new information system must adhere.

Context for new system security and control requirements
New system security and control requirements must be developed within the organization's existing policies, standards, and guidelines.

System Performance   How well a system performs can be measured through its performance requirements. Failure to meet these system performance requirements results in unproductive workers, dissatisfied customers, and missed opportunities to deliver outstanding business results. System performance is usually determined by factors such as the following:

- **Timeliness of output.** Is the system generating output in time to meet organizational goals and operational objectives? Since GEICO began advertising that you can save 15 percent on auto insurance in just 15 minutes, speed has become a key factor for many consumers in selecting an insurance company. Nationwide now touts its online tool as the fastest path to a quick car insurance quote, and The General insurance company boasts, "Give us two minutes and we'll give you an auto insurance quote."
- **Ease of use.** Developing applications that managers and employees can easily learn and use is essential to ensure that people will work with the applications productively.
- **Scalability.** A scalable information system can handle business growth and increased business volume without a noticeable degradation in performance.
- **System response time.** The average response time for frequent online transactions is a key factor in determining worker productivity and customer service.
- **Availability.** Availability measures the hours per month the system is scheduled to be available for use. Systems typically must be unavailable a few hours a week to allow for software upgrades and maintenance.
- **Reliability.** Reliability measures the hours the system is actually available for use divided by the hours the system is scheduled to be available and is expressed as a percentage. Worker productivity decreases and customer dissatisfaction increases as system reliability decreases.

Identify and Evaluate Alternative Solutions

The analysis team must think creatively and consider several system solution options. By looking at the problem in new or different ways, questioning current assumptions and the way things are done today, and removing current constraints and barriers, the team is free to identify highly creative and effective information system solutions. Such critical analysis requires unbiased and careful questioning of whether system elements are related in the most effective ways, considering new or different relationships among system elements, and possibly introducing new elements into the system. Critical analysis also involves challenging users about their needs and determining which are truly critical requirements rather than "nice to have" features.

Pareto principle (80–20 rule): An observation that for many events, roughly 80 percent of the effects come from 20 percent of the causes.

The **Pareto principle** (also known as the **80–20 rule**) is a rule of thumb used in business that helps people focus on the vital 20 percent that generate 80 percent of the results. This principle means that 80 percent of the desired system benefits can be achieved by implementing 20 percent of the system requirements. An 80–20 option will have a low cost and quick completion schedule relative to other potential options. However, this option may not be an ideal solution and may not even be acceptable to the users, stakeholders, and the steering team who may be expecting more. Additional candidate solutions can be defined that implement all or most of the critical priority system requirements and team-selected subsets of the medium and low-priority requirements. Table 12.5 illustrates some of the many potential candidates the analysis team may want to evaluate.

TABLE 12.5 Additional candidates for system analysis

Scope of System	Build System	Customize Software Package
Build system that meets all critical requirements, but no medium or low-priority requirements	Option #1	
Modify package so that it meets all critical requirements, but no medium or low-priority requirements		Option #2
Build system that meets 20 percent of all requirements that will provide 80 percent of the system benefits	Option #3	
Modify package so that it meets 20 percent of all requirements that will provide 80 percent of the system benefits		Option #4
Implement software package as is, with no customization to enable it to meet unique requirements		Option #5

Perform Feasibility Analysis

At this stage in the system development process, the project team has identified several promising solutions based on implementing all or most of the critical requirements and various subsets of the medium and low-priority requirements. The feasibility analysis conducted during the investigation phase is repeated for each of the candidate solutions the team wants to consider. At this stage, the analysis can be more in-depth because more is known about the system and its requirements as well as the costs and benefits of the various options.

Prepare Draft of System Analysis Report

System analysis concludes with a formal system analysis report summarizing the findings of this phase of the project. The table of contents for a typical system analysis report is shown in Figure 12.11. This report is a more complete and detailed version of the system investigation report. At this phase of the project, the costs and benefits of the project should be fairly accurate, certainly more accurate than at the end of the investigation phase.

Review Results of System Analysis with Steering Team

The system analysis report is presented to the project steering team with a recommendation to stop, revise, or go forward with the system development project. Following the steering team meeting, the project team incorporates

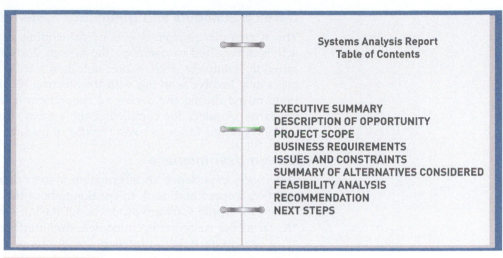

**Systems Analysis Report
Table of Contents**

EXECUTIVE SUMMARY
DESCRIPTION OF OPPORTUNITY
PROJECT SCOPE
BUSINESS REQUIREMENTS
ISSUES AND CONSTRAINTS
SUMMARY OF ALTERNATIVES CONSIDERED
FEASIBILITY ANALYSIS
RECOMMENDATION
NEXT STEPS

FIGURE **12.11**

Typical table of contents for a report on an existing system
The system analysis report is a more complete and detailed version of the system investigation report.

the recommendations and suggested changes into the final report. It is not unusual for changes to the project scope, budget, benefits, or schedule to be requested based on the findings from the analysis phase. However, the project sponsor and the steering team must request and formally approve of any changes.

System Design

The purpose of system design phase is to answer the question, "How will the information system solve this problem?" The primary result of the system design phase is a technical design that details system outputs, inputs, controls, and user interfaces; specifies hardware, software, databases, telecommunications, personnel, and procedures; and shows how these components are interrelated. In other words, **system design** creates a complete set of technical specifications that can be used to construct the information system. The steps in the system design phase are outlined next and discussed in the following pages. Again, note that many of the steps were performed in the investigation and system analysis phase but are now repeated with more current and complete information.

system design: The stage of system development that answers the question, "How will the information system solve a problem?"

1. Identify and recruit team leader and team members.
2. Develop schedule and budget for system design activities.
3. Design user interface.
4. Design system security and controls.
5. Design disaster recovery plan.
6. Design database.
7. Perform feasibility analysis.
8. Prepare draft of system design report.
9. Review results of system design with steering team.

Identify and Recruit Team Leader and Team Members

Because some personnel turnover is likely when moving from the system analysis phase to the system design phase, the first step in system design is to identify and recruit the team leader and members. Ideally, some members of the system analysis team will participate in the system design to ensure project continuity.

Develop Schedule and Budget for System Design Activities

The system design team begins by developing a list of specific objectives and activities required to complete the system design phase. It also establishes a schedule complete with major milestones to track project progress. Some tasks may involve working with the steering team to resolve issues and questions raised during the review of the system analysis phase. The group also prepares a budget for completing the system design, including any required travel costs and funds to cover the use of outside resources.

Design User Interface

How users experience an information system determines whether the system will be accepted and used. In speaking about the importance of user interface design for Apple software products, Jef Raskin, an interface expert, once said, "As far as the customer is concerned, the interface is the product."[10]

User interface design integrates concepts and methods from computer science, graphics design, and psychology to build interfaces that are accessible, easy to use, and efficient. Over the years, various authors have identified user interface design principles, including those listed in Table 12.6.[11,12]

TABLE 12.6 Principles of good user interface design

Principle	How to Apply
Strive for consistency	Consistent sequences of actions should be required in similar situations; identical terminology should be used in prompts, menus, and help screens; and consistent commands should be employed throughout.
Offer informative feedback	For every user action, there should be some system feedback. For frequent and minor actions, the response can be modest, while for infrequent and major actions, the response should be more substantial.
Offer simple error handling	As much as possible, design the system so the user cannot make a serious error. If an error is made, the system should be able to detect the error and offer simple, comprehensible instructions for handling the error.
One primary action per screen	Every screen should support a single action of real value to the user.
Provide progressive disclosure	Show only what is necessary on each screen. If the user is making a choice, show enough information to allow the user to choose and then display details on a subsequent screen.
Strive for aesthetic integrity	The graphic design elements used in an interface should be simple and clean, pleasant to look at, and easy to understand.

User interface design must consider a number of components. Most systems provide a sign-on procedure that requires identification numbers, passwords, and other safeguards to improve security and prevent unauthorized use. With a menu-driven system, users select what they want to do from a list of alternatives. Most people can easily operate these types of systems. In addition, many designers incorporate a help feature into the system or program. When users want to know more about a program or software feature or what type of response is expected, they can activate the help feature. Systems often use lookup tables to simplify and shorten data entry. For example, if you are entering a sales order for a company, you can type its abbreviation, such as ABCO. The program searches the customer table, and looks up the information you need to complete the sales order for the company abbreviated as ABCO.

Using screen painter software, an analyst can efficiently design the features, layout, and format of the user interface screens. See Figure 12.12. Several screens can be linked together to simulate how the user can move from screen to screen to accomplish tasks. Conducting an interactive screen design session with a few users at a time is an effective process for defining the system user interface.

FIGURE 12.12

User interface design

Analysts can develop screen mock-ups and simulate how the user moves from screen to screen.

Design System Security and Controls

The system analysis phase identified areas where system security and controls need to be defined. During the design phase, designers must develop specific system security and controls for all aspects of the information system, including hardware, software, database systems, telecommunications, and Internet operations, as shown in Table 12.7. Security considerations involve error prevention, detection, and correction; disaster planning and recovery; and systems controls. The goal is to ensure secure systems without burdening users with too many identification numbers and passwords for different applications.

After the controls are developed, they should be documented in standards manuals that indicate how to implement the controls. The controls should then be implemented and frequently reviewed. It is common practice to measure how often control techniques are used and to take action if the controls have not been implemented. Organizations often have compliance departments to make sure the IS department is adhering to its systems controls along with all local, state, and federal laws and regulations.

Design Disaster Recovery Plan

disaster recovery plan: A documented process to recover an organization's business information system assets including hardware, software, data, networks, and facilities in the event of a disaster.

A **disaster recovery plan** is a documented process to recover an organization's business information system assets including hardware, software, data, networks, and facilities in the event of a disaster. It is a component of the organization's overall business continuity plan, which also includes an occupant emergency plan, a continuity of operations plan, and an incident management plan. A disaster recovery plan focuses on technology recovery and identifies the people or the teams responsible to take action in the event of a disaster, what exactly these people will do when a disaster strikes, and the information system resources required to support critical business processes.

Disasters can be natural or manmade, as shown in Table 12.8. In performing disaster recovery planning, organizations should think in terms of not being able to gain access to their normal place of business for an extended period of time, possibly up to several months.

TABLE **12.7** Using system controls to enhance security

Controls	Description
Input controls	Maintain input integrity and security; their purpose is to reduce errors while protecting the computer system against improper or fraudulent input. Input controls range from using standardized input forms to eliminating data-entry errors and using tight password and identification controls.
Processing controls	Deal with all aspects of processing and storage; the use of passwords and user authentication controls, backup copies of data, and storage rooms that have tight security systems are examples of processing and storage controls.
Output controls	Ensure that output is handled correctly; in many cases, output generated from the computer system is recorded in a file that indicates the reports and documents that were generated, the time they were generated, and their final destinations.
Database controls	Deal with ensuring an efficient and effective database system; these controls include the use of user authentication controls and passwords, without which a user is denied access to certain data and information. Many of these controls are provided by database management systems.
Telecommunications controls	Provide accurate and reliable data and information transfer among systems; network controls include firewalls and encryption to ensure correct communication while eliminating the potential for fraud and crime.
Personnel controls	Ensure that only authorized personnel have access to certain systems to help prevent computer-related mistakes and crime; personnel controls can involve the use of user authentication controls and passwords that allow only certain people access to particular data and information. ID badges and other security devices (such as smart cards) can prevent unauthorized people from entering strategic areas in the information systems facility.

TABLE **12.8** Various disasters can disrupt business operations

Intentional Man-Made Disasters	Accidental Man-Made Disasters	Natural Disasters
Sabotage	Auto accident knocks down power lines to a data center	Flood
Terrorism	Backhoe digs up a telecommunications line	Tsunami
Civil unrest	Operator error	Hurricane/cyclone
	Fire	Earthquake
		Volcanic eruption

As part of defining the business continuity plan, organizations conduct a business impact analysis to identify critical business processes and the resources that support them. The recovery time for an information system resource should match the recovery time objective for the most critical business processes that depend on that resource. Some business processes are more pivotal to continued operations and goal attainment than others. These processes are called **mission-critical processes**. An order-processing system, for example, is usually considered mission-critical. Without it, the sales organization cannot continue its daily activities, which generate the cash flow needed to keep the business operating.

For some companies, personnel backup can be critical. Without the right number of trained employees, the business process can't function. For information system hardware, hot and cold sites can be used as backups. A duplicate, operational hardware system that is ready for use (or immediate access to one through a specialized vendor) is an example of a **hot site**. If the primary computer has problems, the hot site can be used immediately as a backup. However, the hot site must be situated so that it will not be affected by the same disaster. Another approach is to use a **cold site**, which is a computer environment that includes rooms, electrical service, network links, data

mission-critical process: A process that plays a pivotal role in an organization's continued operations and goal attainment.

hot site: A duplicate, operational hardware system that is ready for use (or immediate access to one through a specialized vendor).

cold site: A computer environment that includes rooms, electrical service, telecommunications links, data storage devices, and the like.

storage devices, and similar equipment. If a primary computer has a problem, backup computer hardware is brought into the cold site, and the complete system is made operational.

Cloud computing has added another dimension to disaster recovery planning. If your organization is hit by a disaster, information systems that are running on the cloud are likely to be operational and accessible by workers from anywhere they can access the Internet. Data is also stored safely and securely at the site of the cloud-computing service provider, which could be hundreds of miles from the organization. On the other hand, if the cloud service provider is hit by a disaster, it may cause a serious business disruption for your organization even if it is otherwise unaffected by a distant disaster. Thus, part of the evaluation of a cloud service provider must include analysis of the provider's disaster recovery plans.

Files and databases can be protected by making a copy of all files and databases changed during the last few days or the last week, a technique called incremental backup. This approach to backup uses an image log, which is a separate file that contains only changes to applications or data. Whenever an application is run, an image log is created that contains all changes made to all files. If a problem occurs with a database, an old database with the last full backup of the data, along with the image log, can be used to re-create the current database.

Organizations can also hire outside companies to help them perform disaster planning and recovery. EMC, for example, offers data backup in its RecoverPoint product.[13] For individuals and some applications, backup copies of important files can be placed on the Internet. Failover is another approach to backup. When a server, network, or database fails or is no longer functioning, failover automatically switches applications and other programs to a redundant or replicated server, network, or database to prevent an interruption of service. SteelEye's LifeKeeper and Application Continuous Availability by NeverFail are examples of failover software.[14,15] Failover is especially important for applications that must be operational at all times.

Design Database

The database provides a user view of data and makes it possible to add and modify data, store and retrieve data, manipulate the data, and generate reports. One of the steps in designing a database involves "telling" the database management system (DBMS) the logical and physical structure of the data and the relationships among the data for each user. Recall that this description is called a schema, and it is entered into the DBMS using a data definition language. A data definition language (DDL) is a collection of instructions and commands that define and describe data and relationships in a specific database.

Another important step in designing the database is to establish a data dictionary, a detailed description of all data used in the database. A data dictionary is valuable in maintaining an efficient database that stores reliable information with no redundancy, and it makes it easy to modify the database when necessary. Data dictionaries also help computer and system programmers who require a detailed description of data elements stored in a database to create the code to access the data. Adhering to the standards defined in the data dictionary also makes it easy to share data among various organizations without the need for extensive data scrubbing and translation.

Perform Feasibility Analysis

As a result of the work done during the design phase, the project team has a much better understanding of what it will take to build the system, how it will operate, and what benefits it can deliver. It is appropriate to reassess the technical, economic, legal, operational, and schedule feasibility based on these new learnings.

Prepare Draft of System Design Report

System design concludes with a formal system design report summarizing the findings of this phase of the project. Any changes from the system analysis findings are highlighted and explained. The table of contents for a typical system design report is shown in Figure 12.13. This report is a more complete and detailed version of the system investigation report.

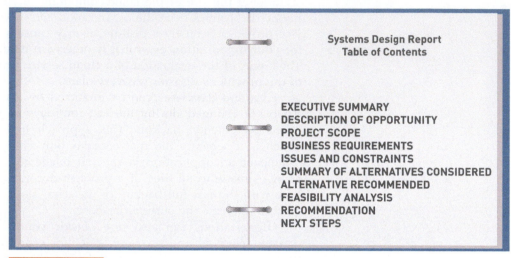

FIGURE **12.13**

Typical table of contents for a system design report
The system design report is a more complete and detailed version of the system investigation report.

Review Results of System Design with Steering Team

The system design report is presented to the project steering team with a recommendation to stop, revise, or go forward with the system development project. The steering team carefully reviews the recommendations because if the project is to proceed, considerable human and financial resources will be committed and legally binding vendor contracts will be signed. Following the steering team meeting, the project team incorporates the recommendations and changes suggested into the final report.

At the end of the design phase, organizations employing the waterfall system development process freeze the scope and the user and business requirements. Any potential changes that are identified or suggested after this point must go through a formal scope change process. This process requires the organization to assess how the proposed changes affect the project feasibility, cost, and schedule. It may be necessary to rerun cost/benefit analyses to ensure that the project is still financially viable. Next, the proposed changes are presented to the project steering team along with their associated costs and schedule impact. The steering team must approve the changes before the project team can begin work to incorporate them into the current design. Frequently, the steering team disapproves changes to ensure that the project is completed without exceeding the current budget and schedule. If the steering team approves the changes, however, the project team might need to repeat portions of the system analysis and design phases to incorporate the changes.

Construction

The system construction phase follows the completion of the system design phase when the project steering team approves of proceeding with the

system construction: The phase of system development that converts the system design into an operational system by acquiring and installing hardware and software, coding and testing software programs, creating and loading data into databases, and performing initial program testing.

project. **System construction** converts the system design into an operational system by coding and testing software programs, creating and loading data into databases, and performing initial program testing. These steps are outlined next and are discussed in the following sections:

1. Code software components.
2. Create and load data.
3. Perform unit testing.

Code Software Components

Software code must be written according to defined design specifications so that the system meets user and business needs and operates in the manner the user expects. Most software development organizations use a variety of software tools to generate program source code that conforms to those specifications. The following list includes a sampling of these types of software tools:

- Some template-driven code generators can create source code automatically. CodeSmith Generator is an example of a template-driven code generator that automates the creation of common application source code for several languages (e.g., C#, Java, VB, PHP, ASP.NET, and SQL). The templates are designed to create typical types of business programs. Developers using CodeSmith Generator can modify a template or create a customized template to generate necessary code.[16]
- Screen painter programs are used to design new data-entry screens for software applications. This easy-to-use software allows developers to create screens by "painting" them and then use "dialog boxes" to define the characteristics of the data that goes in each field.
- Menu-creation software allows users to develop and format menus with features such as color palettes, graphics characters, automatically generated boxes, headings, and system variables.
- Report generator software captures an image of a desired report and generates the code to produce that report based on the database and database schema you are using. In many cases, users can design and code reports with this software.

The Arizona court system, which includes the State Supreme Court, 15 Superior Courts, 85 Municipal, and 76 Limited Jurisdiction courts, decided to use software code generators to code components for a recent systems overhaul. All the courts must coordinate scheduling of court dates, keep track of state-issued citations, and track adults and juveniles on probation. Over time, the Arizona courts developed a number of systems using various programming languages, making it difficult to modify programs to keep up with changes in the law. The court system is now rewriting many of its applications and standardizing on the Microsoft ASP.NET architecture. The courts are using a software code generator called Visible Developer to generate 85 to 90 percent of the code.[17]

technical documentation: Written details used by computer operators to execute the program and by analysts and programmers to solve problems or modify the program.

user documentation: Written descriptions developed for people who use a program; in easy-to-understand language, it shows how the program can and should be used to meet the needs of its various users.

An organization also needs useful software documentation to accompany the software code. **Technical documentation** includes written details that computer operators follow to execute the program and that analysts and programmers use to solve problems or modify the program. Technical documentation explains the purpose of every major piece of computer code. It also identifies and describes key variables.

User documentation is developed for the people who use the system. In easy-to-understand language, this type of documentation shows how the program can and should be used to perform user tasks. Linx Software produces LinxCRM, a customer relationship management system. The company implemented special software to help it create high-quality user documentation including annotated screen shots from the system. Linx also created a video to help train users.[18]

Create and Load Data

This step of the construction phase involves making sure that all files and databases are populated and ready to be used with the new information system. Data for the initial loading of a new database may come from several sources—the old files or database of the system being replaced, from files of other systems used in the organization, or from data sources purchased from an outside organization. In any case, it may be necessary to write at least one new program to read the old data from these sources, reformat the data into a format compatible with the database design of the new system, and then merge these data sources together. Another program may be needed to edit the merged data for accuracy and completeness and to add new entities, attributes, and/or relationships. For example, if an organization is installing a new customer relationship management program, a program might need to read the old customer contact data and convert it to a format that the new system can use. However, if the old customer contact data does not contain the same data, such as a separate "bill to" and "ship to" address for existing customers, this data may need to be added manually. The "bill to" address may be used to calculate to which of the organization's sales regions the customer belongs for sales reporting and accounting purposes. For many projects, considerable time and effort is expended in creating and loading a new database. See Figure 12.14.

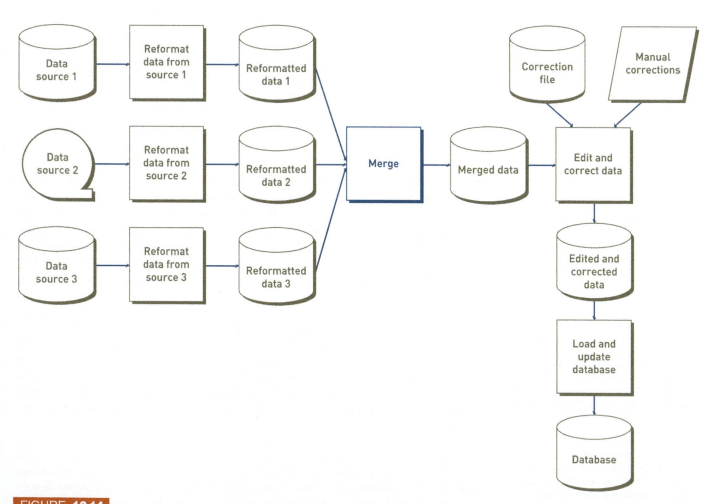

FIGURE **12.14**

Database preparation tasks

Creating and loading a new database can take considerable resources.

Perform Unit Testing

With the programs written and the database available, it is now possible for the developers to do initial testing of code components. This process is called **unit testing**, which involves testing individual components of code (subroutines, modules, and programs) to verify that each unit performs as designed. Unit testing is accomplished by developing test data that ideally will force an individual component to execute all of its various functions and user features. In addition, each program is tested with abnormal input to determine how it will handle erroneous input. As testers find problems, they modify the programs to work correctly. A good set of unit tests can be saved and rerun each time any code is changed to quickly detect any new defects.

unit testing: Testing of individual components of code (subroutines, modules, and programs) to verify that each unit performs as designed.

Integration and Testing

Several types of testing must be conducted before a new or modified information system is ready to be put into production. These tests are outlined next and discussed in the following sections:

1. Integration testing
2. System testing
3. Volume testing
4. User acceptance testing

Integration Testing

Integration testing involves linking individual components together and testing them as a group to uncover any defects in the interface between one component and another (e.g., component 1 fails to pass a key parameter to component 2). Even if unit testing is successful, developers cannot assume that individual components can be combined into a working system. Unfortunately, one component that functions incorrectly can affect another component and, if these problems go undetected, they can cause serious trouble later.

integration testing: Testing that involves linking all of the individual components together and testing them as a group to uncover any defects in the interfaces between individual components.

System Testing

System testing involves testing the complete, integrated system (hardware, software, databases, people, and procedures) to validate that the information system meets all specified requirements. System testing is often done by independent testers who were not involved in developing program code. They attempt to make the system fail. They frequently employ testing called black box testing because it requires no specific knowledge of the application's code and internal logic. In other words, the system tester is aware of what the software is supposed to do but is not aware of how it does it.

System testing: Testing the complete, integrated system (hardware, software, databases, people, and procedures) to validate that the information system meets all specified requirements.

Volume Testing

Volume testing involves evaluating the performance of the information system under varying yet realistic work volume and operating conditions (e.g., database size, number of concurrent users, number of transactions, and number of queries). The goals of volume testing are to determine the work load at which systems performance begins to degrade and to identify and eliminate any issues that prevent the system from reaching its required system-level performance.

volume testing: Testing to evaluate the performance of the information system under varying yet realistic work volume and operating conditions to determine the work load at which system performance begins to degrade and to identify and eliminate any issues that prevent the system from reaching its required service-level performance.

User Acceptance Testing

During **user acceptance testing (UAT)**, trained users test the information system to verify that it can complete required tasks in a real-world operating environment and perform according to the system design specifications. UAT is also known as beta testing, application testing, and end-user testing. Unlike system testing, which ensures that the system itself works, UAT determines whether the system meets its intended business needs.

user acceptance testing (UAT): Testing performed by trained system users to verify that the system can complete required tasks in a real-world operating environment and perform according to the system design specifications.

UAT is a critical activity that must be completed successfully before newly developed software can be rolled out to the market. In the case of implementing a software package or software developed by an outside organization, the customer performs user acceptance testing before accepting transfer of ownership. UAT involves the following steps:

1. The UAT test team is selected from the set of likely users.
2. The UAT test team is trained using the currently available training material.
3. The overall UAT strategy and schedule is defined.
4. The UAT team designs test cases to exercise the functions and features of the information system.
5. The test cases are documented in a clear and simple step-by-step manner to make the tests easy to execute.
6. The UAT team executes the defined test cases and documents the results of each test.
7. The software development team reviews the test results and makes any required changes to the code so it meets the design specifications.
8. The UAT team retests the information system until all defects have been fixed or it is agreed that certain defects will not be fixed.
9. The UAT team indicates its acceptance or nonacceptance of the information system. If accepted, the information system is ready to be fully implemented.
10. The UAT team provides feedback on the user training material so it can be updated and improved.

Prior to releasing a new software package or a major revision of an existing package, commercial software development organizations conduct alpha and beta testing. Alpha testing is a limited internal acceptance test where employees of the software development organization and a limited number of other "friendlies" use the software and provide feedback. After fixing problems uncovered in alpha testing, the developer makes a beta test version of the software available to potential users outside the organization. For example, Microsoft might make a free beta test version of software available on the Internet to increase the amount of feedback.

user acceptance document: A formal agreement that the organization signs stating that a phase of the installation or the complete system is approved.

Most software manufacturers and third-party software developers have a **user acceptance document**—a formal agreement the end user organization signs stating that a phase of the installation or the complete system is approved. This is a legal document that usually removes or reduces the IS vendor's liability for problems that occur after the user acceptance document has been signed. Because this document is so important, many companies get legal assistance before they sign it. Stakeholders can also be involved in acceptance testing to make sure that their benefits are indeed realized.

Table 12.9 summarizes five types of testing: unit testing, integration testing, system testing, volume testing, and user acceptance testing.

Implementation

A number of steps are involved in system implementation. These are outlined next and discussed in the following sections.

1. User preparation
2. Site preparation
3. Installation
4. Cutover

User Preparation

user preparation: The process of readying managers, decision makers, employees, other users, and stakeholders to accept and use the new system.

User preparation is the process of readying managers, decision makers, employees, system users, and stakeholders to accept and use the new system.

TABLE 12.9 Tests conducted on an information system

Form of Test	What Is Tested	Purpose of Test	Who Does It
Unit	Test individual units of the system.	Verify that each unit performs as designed.	Software developers
Integration	Test all of the individual units of the information system linked together.	Uncover any defects between individual components of the information system.	Software developers or independent software testers, using black box testing measures
System	Test the complete, integrated system (hardware, software, databases, people, and procedures).	Validate that the information system meets all specified requirements.	Independent test team, separate from the software development team
Volume	Evaluate the performance of the information system under realistic and varying work volume and operating conditions.	Determine the work load at which system performance begins to degrade and identify and eliminate any issues that prevent the system from performing at the required service level.	System development team and members of the operations organization
User acceptance	Test the complete, integrated system (hardware, software, databases, people, and procedures).	Verify the information system can complete required tasks in a real-world operating environment and do this according to the system design specifications.	Trained users of the system

Ideally, user preparation begins in the early stages of system investigation and continues through implementation.

The major challenges to successful implementation of an information system are often more behavioral than technical. Successfully introducing an information system into an organization requires a mix of organizational change skills and technical skills. Strong, effective leadership is required to overcome the behavioral resistance to change and achieve a smooth and successful system introduction.

The dynamics of how change is implemented can be viewed in terms of the Lewin and Schein three-stage model for change: (1) ceasing old habits and creating a climate that is receptive to change; (2) learning new work methods, behaviors, and systems; and (3) reinforcing changes to make the new process second nature, accepted, and part of the job.

Leavitt's Diamond is a change model that proposes that every organizational system is made up of people, tasks, structure, and technology—any change in one of these elements will necessitate a change in the other three elements. Thus, to successfully implement a new information system, appropriate changes must be made to the people, structure, and tasks affected by the new system. People must be convinced to take a positive attitude to the change and be willing to exhibit new behaviors consistent with the change. Management might need to modify the reward system to recognize those who exhibit the desired new behaviors. Training in any required new skills is also necessary.

The technology acceptance model (TAM) specifies the factors that can lead to better attitudes about the use of a new information system, along with its higher acceptance and usage. Perceived usefulness and perceived ease of use strongly influence whether someone will use an information system. Management can improve that perception by demonstrating that others have used the system effectively and by providing user training and support.

The diffusion of innovation theory cautions that adoption of any innovation does not happen all at once for all members of the targeted population;

rather, it is a drawn-out process, with some people quicker to adopt the innovation than others. Rogers' diffusion of innovation theory defined five categories of adopters, each with different attitudes toward innovation. When promoting an innovation to a target population, first understand the characteristics of the target population that will help or hinder adoption of the innovation and then apply the appropriate strategy. This theory can be useful in planning the roll-out of a new information system.

Because user training is so important, some companies employ a variety of training approaches including in-house, software, video, Internet, among others. The material used to train the UAT team can serve as a starting point, with changes based on feedback from the test team.

The eventual success of any system depends not only on how users work with it, but how well the IS personnel within the organization can operate and support it. The IS personnel should also attend training sessions similar to those for the users, although their sessions can provide more technical details. Effective training will help IS personnel use the new system to perform their jobs and support other users in the organization. IBM and many other companies use online and simulated training programs to cut training costs and improve effectiveness.

Site Preparation

site preparation: Preparation of the location of a new system.

A location for the hardware associated with the new system needs to be prepared, a process called **site preparation**. For a small system, site preparation can be as simple as rearranging the furniture in an office to make room for a computer. The computer and associated hardware in a larger system might require special wiring, air conditioning, or construction. A special floor, for example, might have to be built and cables placed under it to connect the various computer components, and a new security system might be needed to protect the equipment. The project team needs to consider the amount of site preparation that may be necessary and build sufficient lead time into the schedule to allow for it.

Today, most organizations place a priority on developing IS sites that are energy efficient and secure. One company, for example, installed special security kiosks that let company visitors log on and request a meeting with a company employee. The employee can see the visitor on his or her computer screen and accept or reject the visitor. If the visitor is accepted, the kiosk prints a visitor pass, which allows the person access to the building.

M&T Bank is the largest deposit holder in western New York, with headquarters in Buffalo. The bank invested around $60 million in data centers over a three-year period to meet current business needs and strengthen its backup systems in case of disasters.[19]

Installation

installation: The process of physically placing the computer equipment on the site and making it operational.

Installation is the process of physically placing the computer equipment on the site and making it operational. Although normally the manufacturer is responsible for installing computer equipment, someone from the organization (usually the IS manager) should oversee the process, making sure that all equipment specified in the contract is installed at the proper location. After the system is installed, the manufacturer performs several tests to ensure that the equipment is operating as it should.

Cutover

cutover: The process of switching from an old information system to a replacement system.

Cutover is the process of switching from an old information system to a replacement system. Cutover is critical to the success of the organization; if not done properly, the results can be disastrous.

Hershey's, the largest chocolate manufacturer in North America, provides a classic example of a failed system cutover. The company planned to upgrade a mix of legacy information systems into an integrated environment of the latest software from leading vendors, including SAP for ERP functionality, Manugistics for supply chain management, and Siebel for customer relationship management. The cutover was targeted for July, one of the company's busiest months, when it was shipping orders for Halloween and Christmas. Unfortunately, Hershey's was not well prepared, and the cutover was a fiasco. As a result, Hershey was unable to process over $100 million worth of orders. The resulting operational paralysis led to nearly a 20 percent drop in quarterly profits and an 8 percent decline in share price.

Organizations can follow one of several cutover strategies. See Figure 12.15. **Direct conversion** (also called plunge or direct cutover) involves stopping the old system and starting the new system on a given date. Direct conversion is a high-risk approach because of the potential for problems and errors when the old system is shut off and the new system is turned on at the same instant.

direct conversion: A cutover strategy that involves stopping the old system and starting the new system on a given date; also called plunge or direct cutover.

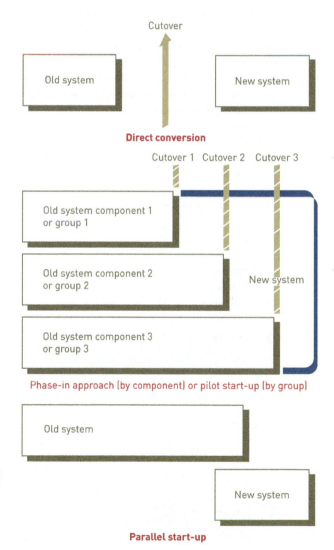

Direct conversion

Phase-in approach (by component) or pilot start-up (by group)

Parallel start-up

FIGURE 12.15
System cutover strategies
Cutover can be through direct conversion, phase-in approach, pilot start-up, or parallel start-up.

Shell is one of the largest corporations in the world, with recent annual revenues exceeding $265 billion.[20] One of Shell's major business units is called Downstream, an organization that converts crude oil into a range of refined products, which are moved and marketed around the world for domestic, industrial, and transport use.[21] The 37,000 workers in 36 countries in the Downstream business rely on SAP-based software to complete their work, making it a mission-critical application. A few years ago, Shell decided to upgrade to a new version of the Downstream software to access new functions and support services. The planning and work involved in completing the world's largest SAP upgrade culminated in a direct cutover 18 months after that project started. Shell had many tasks to accomplish before the cutover, including updating several databases, installing new application servers, replacing hardware, and expanding storage capacity by 30 percent. Despite its huge complexity and the high risk associated with such a major cutover, the upgrade was a success.[22]

phase-in approach: A cutover strategy that involves slowly replacing components of the old system with those of the new one; this process is repeated for each application until the new system is running every application and performing as expected; also called a piecemeal approach.

Many organizations follow a **phase-in approach**, where components of the new system are slowly phased in while components of the old one are slowly phased out. When everyone is confident that all components of the new system are performing as expected, the old system is completely phased out. This gradual replacement is repeated for each component until the new system has fully replaced the old system. In some cases, the phase-in approach, also called a piecemeal approach, can take several months.

pilot start-up: A cutover strategy that involves running the complete new system for one group of users rather than for all users.

Pilot start-up involves running the complete new system for one group of users rather than for all users. For example, a manufacturing company with many retail outlets throughout the country could use the pilot start-up approach and install a new inventory control system at one of its retail outlets. When the system runs without problems at the pilot location, the new inventory control system can then be implemented at other outlets, one by one.

parallel start-up: A cutover strategy that involves running both the old and new systems for a period of time and closely comparing the output of the new system with the output of the old system; any differences are reconciled. When users are comfortable that the new system is working correctly, the old system is eliminated.

Parallel start-up involves running both the old and new systems for a period of time. The performance and output of the new system are compared closely with the performance and output of the old system, and any differences are reconciled. When users are comfortable that the new system is working correctly, the old system is eliminated.

System Operation and Maintenance

The steps involved in system operation and maintenance are outlined next and discussed in the following sections.

1. Operation
2. Maintenance
3. Disposal

Operation

system operation: Involves the use of a new or modified system under all kinds of operating conditions.

System operation involves the use of a new or modified system under all kinds of operating conditions. Getting the most out of a new or modified system during its operation is the most important aspect of system operations for many organizations. To provide adequate user support, many companies establish a formal help desk for their employees and customers. A help desk consists of computer systems, manuals, people with technical expertise, and other resources needed to solve problems and give accurate answers to questions. End users, who experience problems accessing or using an information system, can access the help desk's Web site or request support via a call or text to the help desk.

monitoring: The process of measuring system performance by tracking the number of errors encountered, the amount of memory required, the amount of processing or CPU time needed, and other performance indicators.

Monitoring is the process of measuring system performance by tracking the number of errors encountered, the amount of memory required, the amount of processing or CPU time needed, and other performance indicators. If a particular system is not performing as expected, it should be modified or a new system should be developed or acquired.

System performance products can measure all components of an information system, including hardware, software, database, and network systems. Microsoft Visual Studio, for example, has features that allow system developers to monitor and review how applications are running and performing, enabling developers to make changes if needed. IBM Tivoli OMEGAMON XE is a suite of performance monitors designed for the analysis of IBM mainframe operating systems—such as z/OS and z/VM—and various subsystems, such as CICS, DB2, and IMS. Precise Software Solutions has system performance products that provide around-the-clock performance monitoring for ERP systems, Oracle database applications, and other programs.[23] HP also offers a software tool called Business Technology Optimization (BTO) to help companies analyze the performance of their computer systems, diagnose potential problems, and take corrective action if needed. When properly used, system performance products can quickly and efficiently locate actual or potential problems.

Allscripts is a $2.6 billion publicly traded company that provides practice management, electronic healthcare records, and financial software to hundreds of physician practices, hospitals, and other healthcare organizations. Its customers typically have between 7 and 20 servers running Allscripts applications at all times, and keeping the software running without interruption is a major challenge. To solve this problem, Allscripts has its customers install eG performance monitoring software from Citrix to monitor the network, operating system, and applications on its servers. This enables Allscripts to quickly identify and fix system and software problems before they affect users.[24]

System review is the process of analyzing a system to make sure it is operating as intended. System review often compares the performance and benefits of the system as it was designed with the actual performance and benefits of the system in operation.

U.S. citizens were alarmed and dismayed when an audit of 731 Veterans Affairs (VA) hospitals and clinics found that some 57,000 veterans nationwide in need of medical care experienced wait times of 90 days or longer for their first medical appointments. An additional 64,000 veterans were not even on the VA electronic waiting list for doctor appointments that they had requested. Shockingly, 13 percent of VA employees interviewed said they were told to falsify records so that wait times would appear shorter.[25] In a separate audit of its information systems, the VA inspector reported that the agency had continuing problems protecting its mission-critical systems. The audit found that although the VA had made progress developing security policies and procedures, it still suffered from "significant deficiencies related to access controls, configuration management controls, continuous monitoring controls, and service continuity practices designed to protect mission-critical systems."[26] It is not clear to what degree these system shortcomings contributed to the incorrect reporting of wait times.

Internal employees, external consultants, or both can perform a system review. An organization's billing application, for example, might be reviewed for errors, inefficiencies, and opportunities to reduce operating costs. In addition, the billing application might be reviewed if corporations merge, if one or more new managers require different information or reports, or if federal laws on bill collecting and privacy change. This is an event-driven approach to system review.

Maintenance

System maintenance is a stage of system development that involves changing and enhancing the system to make it more useful in achieving user and organizational goals. Reasons for program maintenance include the following:

- Poor system performance, such as slow response time for frequent transactions
- Changes in business processes
- Changes in the needs of system stakeholders, users, and managers
- Bugs or errors in the program
- Technical and hardware problems

---

system review: The process of analyzing a system to make sure it is operating as intended.

system maintenance: A stage of system development that involves changing and enhancing the system to make it more useful in achieving user and organizational goals.

- Corporate mergers and acquisitions
- Changes in government regulations
- Changes in the operating system or hardware on which the application runs

Organizations can perform system maintenance in-house, or they can hire outside companies to perform maintenance for them. Many companies that use information systems from Oracle or SAP, for example, hire those companies to maintain their systems. System maintenance is important for individuals, groups, and organizations. Individuals looking to system-maintenance services, for example, can use the Internet, computer vendors, and independent maintenance companies, including YourTechOnline.com (*www.yourtechonline.com*), Geek Squad (*www.geeksquad.com*), and PC Pinpoint (*www.pcpinpoint.com*). Organizations often have personnel dedicated to system maintenance. Software maintenance for purchased software can cost 20 percent or more of the purchase price annually.

The maintenance process can be especially difficult for older software. A legacy system is an old system, which might have cost millions of dollars to develop, patch, and modify over the years. The maintenance costs for legacy systems can become quite expensive, and, at some point, it becomes more cost effective to switch to new programs and applications than to repair and maintain the legacy system.

Royal Bank of Scotland (RBS) and National Westminster Bank (NatWest) are two of the United Kingdom's largest and most established banks. However, some customers of these banks have experienced problems using ATMs or debit cards due to problems with legacy banking systems. Some of the banks' systems are over 30 years old and were originally designed to handle simple branch banking. Over the years, the banks have had to make changes to support ATMs, online banking, and mobile banking as well as changes to accommodate new regulatory requirements. Many of these changes were implemented by different development teams using different programming languages running on different computers and operating systems, making it impossible for one person or team to fully comprehend the entire system.[27] The two banks recently announced that they will be spending £1 billion (approximately $1.7 billion USD) to improve their personal and small business banking services to make it easier for customers on the move.[28]

Four generally accepted categories signify the amount of change involved in maintenance. A **slipstream upgrade** is a minor system upgrade—typically a code adjustment or minor bug fix. Many companies don't announce to users that a slipstream upgrade has been made; however, because a slipstream upgrade usually requires recompiling all the code, it can create entirely new bugs. This maintenance practice explains why the same computers sometimes work differently with what is supposedly the same software. A **patch** is a minor change to correct a problem or make a small enhancement. The fix is usually patched into an existing program; that is, the programming code representing the system enhancement is usually added to the existing code. Many patches come from off-the-shelf software vendors. Although slipstream upgrades and patches are minor changes, they can cause users and support personnel big problems if the programs do not run as before. A new **release** is a significant program change that often requires changes in the documentation of the software. Finally, a new **version** is a major program change, typically encompassing many new features. Figure 12.16 shows the relative amount of change and effort required to test and implement these four categories of system maintenance.

Because of the amount of effort that can be spent on maintenance, many organizations require a request for maintenance form to be completed and approved before authorizing the modification of an information system. This

slipstream upgrade: A minor system upgrade-typically a code adjustment or minor bug fix; it usually requires recompiling all the code, and in so doing, it can create entirely new bugs.

patch: A minor system change to correct a problem or make a small enhancement; it is usually an addition to an existing program.

release: A significant program change that often requires changes in the documentation of the software.

version: A major program change, typically encompassing many new features.

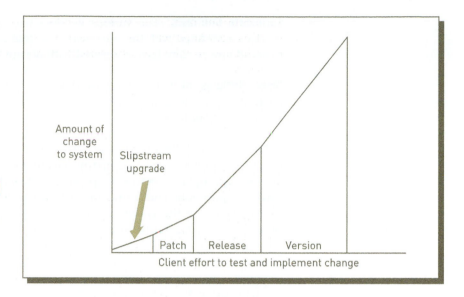

System-maintenance efforts

This chart shows the relative amount of change and effort associated to test and implement slipstream upgrades, patches, releases, and versions.

form is usually signed by a business manager who documents the need for the change and identifies the priority of the change relative to other work that has been requested. The IS group reviews the form and identifies the programs that need to be changed, determines the programmer to assign to the project, estimates the expected completion date, and develops a technical description of the change. A cost/benefit analysis might be required if the change requires substantial resources. The completed change request is then reviewed and prioritized relative to the other change requests that have been made.

Disposal

At some point, an existing information system may become obsolete, uneconomical to operate and/or maintain, or unrepairable. Information systems typically evolve to this stage in the life cycle because the system can no longer be modified to keep up with changing user and business requirements, outdated technology causes the system to run slowly or unreliably, or key vendors are no longer able or willing to continue to provide necessary service or support.

system disposal: A stage of system development that involves those activities that ensure the orderly dissolution of the system, including disposing of all equipment in an environmentally friendly manner, closing out contracts, and safely migrating information from the system to another system or archiving it in accordance with applicable records management policies.

System disposal is a stage of system development that involves those activities that ensure the orderly dissolution of the system, including disposing of all equipment in an environmentally friendly manner, closing out contracts, and safely migrating information from the system to another system or archiving it in accordance with applicable records management policies. The steps involved in system disposal are outlined and discussed in the following sections.

1. Communicate intent.
2. Terminate contracts.
3. Make backups of data.
4. Delete sensitive data.
5. Dispose of hardware.

Communicate Intent   A memo communicating the intent to terminate the information system should be distributed to all key stakeholders, months in advance of the actual shutdown. This ensures that everyone is aware of the shutdown and allows time for them to convert to the new system or process replacing the terminated system. For example, the Microsoft Windows XP operating system was released in 2001. Microsoft announced in September 2007 that it would end support of this popular operating system in April 2014. Despite the end-of-life announcement, an estimated 25 percent of consumers and businesses including 75 percent of ATMs in the United States had not converted to a replacement operating system by early 2014.[29]

Terminate Contracts The various vendors who provide hardware, software, or services associated with the information system must be notified well in advance to avoid any penalty fees associated with abrupt termination of a contract.

Make Backups of Data Prior to deleting files associated with the system, backup copies of data must be made according to the organization's records-management policies.

Delete Sensitive Data Extreme care must be taken to remove customer, employee, financial, and company-sensitive data from all computer hardware and storage devices before disposing of it. Otherwise, an organization's discarded equipment could become a treasure trove to competitors or identity thieves. When a file is deleted, the bits and pieces of the file physically stay on a computer hard drive until they are overwritten, and they can be retrieved with a data recovery program. To remove data from a hard drive permanently, the hard drive needs to be wiped clean. The program used should overwrite or wipe the hard drive several times. An alternative is to remove the hard drive and physically destroy it.

Dispose of Hardware After backing up and then removing data from drives, members of the project team can dispose of obsolete or damaged computer hardware. Governments, environmental agencies, and leading hardware manufacturers are attempting to reduce hazardous materials in electronic products; however, some hardware components still contain materials that are toxic to the environment. Responsible disposal techniques should be used regardless of whether the hardware is sold, given away, or discarded. Many computer hardware manufacturers including Dell and HP have developed programs to assist their customers in disposing of old equipment.

Now that we have discussed the waterfall system development process, we turn our attention to discussion of the agile system development process.

 **Critical Thinking Exercise**

User Acceptance Testing for New Accounting System

You are a member of the finance and accounting organization of a midsized sporting goods retailer. You are knowledgeable of all facets of your firm's current accounting systems and have been working in accounts receivable for the past three years. The firm is implementing a new cloud-based accounting system to handle general ledger, accounts payable, accounts receivable, and payroll tasks. You have been selected to plan and lead the user acceptance testing for the accounts receivable portion of the system. This will be a full-time activity for you over the next two-to-three months, and during that time, other employees will fill in to take care of most of your day-to-day responsibilities.

Review Questions

1. Outline the tasks that must be accomplished to successfully complete user acceptance testing.
2. Your normal work activities and responsibilities have not allowed you time to become familiar with this project and the new system and its capabilities. What actions would you take to get caught up quickly?

Critical Thinking Questions

1. How would you go about selecting and recruiting end users to participate in the user acceptance testing? How would you determine how many end users are needed for testing?
2. What do you think might be the biggest barriers to completion of the user acceptance testing in a timely manner?

Agile Development

agile development: An iterative system development process that develops the system in "sprint" increments lasting from two weeks to two months.

scrum: An agile development framework that emphasizes a team-based approach in order to keep the development effort focused and moving quickly.

scrum master: The person who coordinates all the scrum activities of a team.

product owner: A person who represents the project stakeholders and is responsible for communicating and aligning project priorities between the stakeholders and development team.

Agile development is an iterative system development process that develops the system in "sprint" increments lasting from two weeks to two months. Unlike the waterfall system development process, agile development accepts the fact that system requirements are evolving and cannot be fully understood or defined at the start of the project. Agile development concentrates instead on maximizing the team's ability to deliver quickly and respond to emerging requirements—hence the name agile. In an agile development project, the team stops and reevaluates the system every two weeks to two months, giving it ample opportunity to identify and implement new or changed system requirements.[30]

Scrum is an agile development framework that uses a team-based approach in order to keep the development effort focused and moving quickly. Scrum emphasizes individuals and interactions over processes and tools, working software over comprehensive documentation, customer collaboration over contract negotiation, and responding to change over following a plan.[31]

A **scrum master** is the person who coordinates all scrum activities, and a scrum team consists of a dozen or fewer people who perform all system development activities from investigation to testing so there is less personnel turnover than on the typical waterfall system development project. The scrum master does not fill the role of a traditional project manager and has no people management responsibilities. Instead, the primary responsibility of the scrum master is to anticipate and remove barriers to the project team producing its deliverables and meeting the project schedule.[32]

The **product owner** is a person who represents the project stakeholders and is responsible for communicating and aligning project priorities between the stakeholders and development team. The product owner holds the product vision; he or she is responsible for describing what should be built and why—but now how.[33]

Using the scrum method, the product owner works with the stakeholders and team to create a prioritized list of project requirements called a product backlog. Next, a sprint planning session is held, during which the team selects the highest priority requirements from the top of the product backlog to create the sprint backlog; they then decide how to implement those requirements. The team sets a certain amount of time—typically two to eight weeks—to complete its work. During the sprint, each day at the same time, the team meets briefly (15 minutes at most) to share information necessary for coordination. At this meeting, team members describe what they completed the previous day and identify any obstacles that stand in their way of completing the day's activities. The sprint is complete when the team presents a working system that incorporates the new requirements and that can be used and evaluated. During the sprint review meeting, the team shares what it learned from the current sprint iteration so that knowledge can be applied in the next sprint iteration. See Figure 12.17. Along the way, the scrum master keeps the team focused on its goals.[34]

Agile development requires cooperation and frequent face-to-face meetings with all participants, including system developers and users, as they modify, refine, and test the system's capabilities and how it meets users' needs. Organizations are using agile development to a greater extent today to improve the results of system development, including global projects requiring IS resources distributed in many locations. Agile is often better suited for developing smaller information systems than larger ones. During an agile project, the level of participation of stakeholders and users is much higher than in other approaches. Table 12.10 lists advantages and disadvantages of agile development.[35]

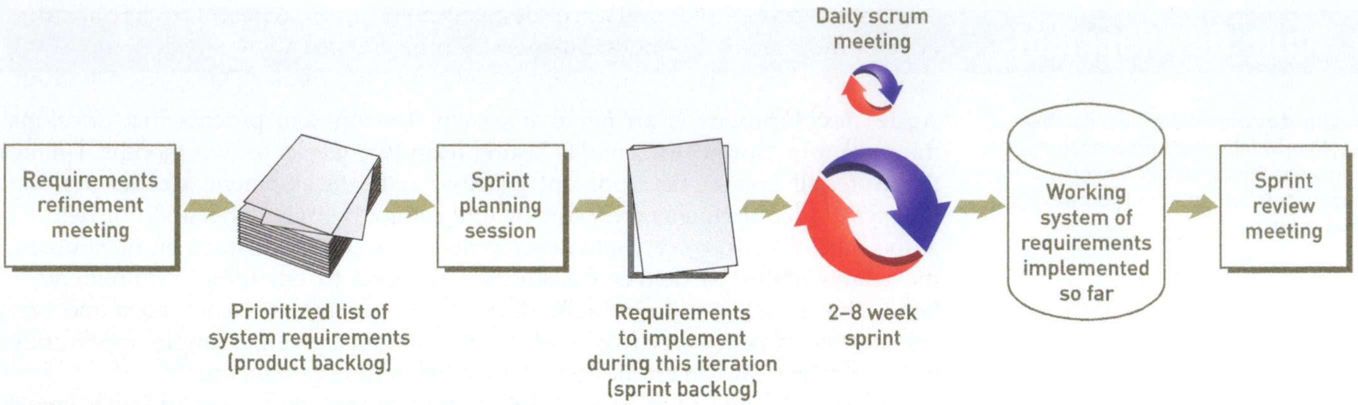

FIGURE **12.17**

The Scrum agile software development process
The Scrum agile approach develops a system in sprint increments lasting from two weeks to two months.

TABLE 12.10 Advantages and disadvantages of agile development

Advantages	Disadvantages
For appropriate projects, this approach puts an application into production sooner than any other approach.	It is an intense process that can burn out system developers and other project participants.
Documentation is produced as a by-product of completing project tasks.	This approach requires system analysts and users to be skilled in agile system development tools and agile techniques.
Agile forces teamwork and lots of interaction between users and stakeholders.	Agile requires a larger percentage of stakeholders' and users' time than other approaches.

extreme programming (XP): A form of agile software development that promotes incremental development of a system using short development cycles to improve productivity and to accommodate new customer requirements.

Extreme programming (XP) is a form of agile software development that promotes incremental development of a system using short development cycles to improve productivity and to accommodate new customer requirements. Other essentials of extreme programming include programming in pairs, performing extensive code review, unit testing of all code, putting off the programming of system features until they are actually needed, use of a flat project management structure, simplicity and clarity in code, expecting changes in system requirements as the project progresses and the desired solution is better understood, and frequent communication with the customer and among programmers. These qualities make extreme programming compatible with agile software development.[36]

DevOps: The practice of blending the tasks performed by the development and IT operations groups to enable faster and more reliable software releases.

DevOps is the practice of blending the tasks performed by the development staff (who are typically responsible for design, coding, and testing) and the IT operations groups (who typically handle operational deployment tasks, such as server provisioning and job scheduling) to enable faster and more reliable software releases.[37] This approach is key to successful agile development environments where organizations go live with new software releases every two to four weeks. And in many organizations, DevOps is being used as part of a continuous deployment strategy, in which releases are launched daily—and in some cases, multiple times a day. Many industry experts view DevOps as an outgrowth of the agile development movement, with an extension of agile development principles to include systems and operations rather than just code.

Under traditional software development approaches, the application development team gathers business requirements, writes code, and tests programs in an isolated development environment. The code is then released to the IT operations group to deploy in the real-world operational environment of end users. This involves gluing together all the components of an application, including databases, messaging infrastructure, external services, the passing and receiving of data to/from other systems, and third-party dependencies.

DevOps principles reshape all the move-into-production activities so that they become automated, collaborative, continuous, incremental, iterative, and self-service. Responsive teams adopt DevOps practices of self-service configuration, automated provisioning (using predefined procedures that are carried out electronically without requiring human intervention), continuous build, continuous integration, continuous delivery, automated release management, and incremental testing, as shown in Figure 12.18.

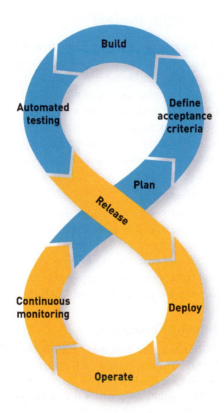

FIGURE 12.18

DevOps is part of a continuous deployment strategy in which releases can be launched daily

DevOps blends tasks performed by development staff and IT operations groups.

Source: Chris Haddad, "Overcome DevOps Adoption Barriers to Accelerate Software Delivery," Tech Well Insights, May 8, 2015, *www.techwell.com/techwell-insights/2015 /05/overcome-devops-adoption-barriers-accelerate-software-delivery.*

Although DevOps can mean slightly different things depending on how it is deployed at different companies, at its core, DevOps places a priority on collaboration, with operations staff and development engineers participating together, over the entire systems life cycle—from design and development through testing and implementation.[38]

Starwood Hotels and Resorts Worldwide used the DevOps approach with good success on a $150 million project aimed at redoing the company's central reservation system. As Starwood has continued to implement DevOps, it has found the process has led to a more complete description of user requirements, a 66 percent reduction in time to deploy systems, and 20 percent fewer errors in production.[39]

Table 12.11 compares the key features of the agile and waterfall system development processes.

TABLE 12.11 Comparison of approaches to system development

Characteristic	Software Development Approach	
	Agile	**Waterfall**
Description	An iterative process that develops the system in sprint increments lasting 2–8 weeks; each increment focuses on implementing the highest priority requirements that can be completed in the allotted time	A sequential multistage process where work on the next stage cannot begin until the results of the previous stage are reviewed and approved or modified as necessary
Basic assumption	System requirements cannot be fully defined at start of project	All critical system requirements must be fully defined before any coding begins
How requirements and design are defined	Users interacting with system analysts and working software	Users interacting with system analysts and system documentation and/or models
Associated processes	Scrum	Structured system analysis and design

Critical Thinking Exercise

Firm's First Agile Project

You were hired into a new company that was impressed with your two years of experience as a scrum master on a variety of information systems projects. Your new firm has a large in-house information system development staff that is trained and experienced in the use of the waterfall software development process. You have been assigned responsibility as a scrum master for a key project that will be the firm's first agile project. You have also been asked to train the project manager, team, and newly appointed product owner in the agile process and their associated roles and responsibilities.

Review Questions

1. As part of the team's initial project kickoff meeting, you have been asked to briefly summarize the differences between the waterfall and agile software development process. What would you say?
2. Following your discussion, one of the team members asks, "so why are we changing to a new software development process? We are all comfortable with the way we do things now." What do you say?

Critical Thinking Questions

1. There is likely to be some confusion over the role of project manager, scrum master, and product owner. What can you do to avoid this potential problem?
2. What other potential problems can you anticipate as the team moves forward with its first agile project? What can be done to avoid these potential issues?

Buying Off-the-Shelf Software

Today, most organizations purchase or rent the software they need rather than make it—simply because it costs too much and takes too long to build a quality information system. Organizations elect to build proprietary systems only when its information system requirements are unique. This may be because of the nature of the business or because the organization is attempting to build an information system that will provide it with a strategic competitive advantage.

A software application can vary from an unmodified, commercial off-the-shelf (COTS) software package at one extreme to a custom, written-from-scratch program at the other extreme. Between those two extremes is a range of options based on the degree of customization. A comparison of the two extreme approaches is shown in Table 12.12. One question that must be answered during system analysis phase is: which solution approach is best for this particular system? This decision is often called the make-or-buy decision.

TABLE 12.12 Comparison of developed and off-the-shelf software

Factor	Develop (Make)	Off-the-Shelf (Buy)
Cost	The cost to build the system can be difficult to estimate accurately and is frequently higher than off-the-shelf	The full cost to implement an off-the-shelf solution is also difficult to estimate accurately but is likely to be less than a custom software solution
Needs	Custom software is more likely to satisfy your needs	Might not get exactly what you need
Process improvement	Tend to automate existing business processes even if they are poor	Adoption of a package may simplify or streamline a poor existing business process
Quality	Quality can vary depending on the programming team	Can assess the quality before buying
Speed	Can take years to develop	Can acquire it right now
Staffing and support	Requires in-house skilled resources to build and support a custom-built solution	Requires paying the vendor for support
Competitive advantage	Can develop a competitive advantage with good software	Other organizations can have the same software and same advantage

Package Evaluation Phase

As with system development, purchasing off-the-shelf software requires that an organization go through several steps to ensure that it purchases the software that best meets its needs and then implements it effectively. These steps are part of the package evaluation phase of a project that comes after the system analysis phase as shown in Figure 12.19. At this point in the project, the scope of the system and critical business and user requirements should be known. There should be a rough budget and schedule as well.

Package Evaluation Phase

1. Identify potential solutions.
2. Select top contenders.
3. Research top contenders.
4. Perform final evaluation of leading solutions.
5. Make selection.
6. Finalize contract.

Identify Potential Solutions

request for information (RFI):
A document that outlines an organization's hardware or software needs and requests vendors to provide information about if and how they can meet those needs and the time and resources required.

The project team should make a preliminary assessment of the software marketplace to determine whether existing packages can meet the organization's needs. The primary tool for doing this is the **request for information (RFI)**, a document that outlines an organization's needs and requests vendors to respond with information about if and how they can meet those needs and the time and resources required. See Figure 12.20. The RFI outlines the scope of the desired system and preliminary system requirements based on the results so far of the system analysis. Importantly, the RFI should ask each vendor to identify two or three customers who may be contacted as references. The RFI is typically sent to several vendors who are thought to be capable of providing the desired software.

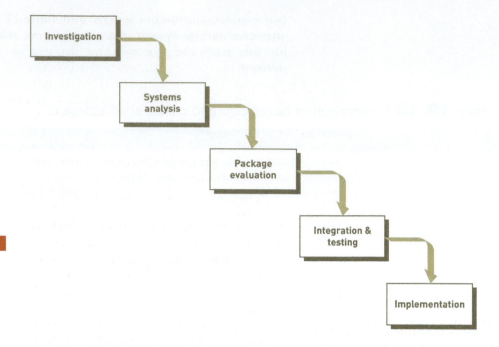

FIGURE **12.19**

Software package implementation process

Software package implementation eliminates several of the phases of the waterfall approach.

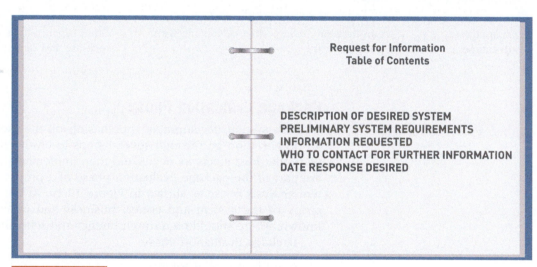

FIGURE **12.20**

Recommended table of contents for a request for information

The RFI outlines the desired system and its requirements, identifying key pieces of data that the software vendor must include in the proposal.

Select Top Contenders

The project team will review the information provided by the vendors in response to the RFI and narrow their choice down to the most promising alternatives for further evaluation. This may require a visit to a vendor's place of business to meet key managers and observe a demo of the vendor's system. This selection is made on the basis on how well the vendor's software appears to meet the organization's needs, preliminary cost and timing estimates, information gleaned from references, and how easy the vendor has been to work with so far.

Research Top Contenders

A final evaluation begins with a detailed investigation of the contenders' proposals as well as in-depth discussions with two or three customers of each contender to learn about their experience with the vendor and the software.

An organization must carefully evaluate each vendor's software package to see how well it supports the business processes that are within the scope of the project. Looking at each business process, the organization should determine if the package supports the process fully and exactly as it needs to be performed. If not, must the software be modified to meet the organization's requirements, or must the organization modify its business process? If an organization decides it must modify the software to meet its business requirements, it must then determine who will do the necessary modifications, how long will they take, and how much will they cost.

Often purchased software must integrate with other existing software (e.g., a new accounts payable and accounts receivable software package must integrate with the firm's existing general ledger system). The amount of effort required to modify the new software and existing software so that they work well together must be determined and taken into account as a major factor in selecting the final vendor and software.

For major software purchases, the contenders should be asked to make a final presentation and to fully demonstrate their solution using a **performance evaluation test** conducted in a computing environment (e.g., computing hardware, operating system software, database management system) and with a workload (e.g., number of concurrent users, database size, and number of transactions) that matches the intended operating conditions. Such a test can help measure system performance attributes such as ease of use and response time.

performance evaluation test: A comparison of vendor options conducted in a computing environment (e.g., computing hardware, operating system software, database management system) and with a workload (e.g., number of concurrent users, database size, and number of transactions) that matches its intended operating conditions.

Make Selection

Selecting the best software package solution involves weighing the following factors:

- How well the vendor's solution matches the needs of the users and business
- The amount of effort required to integrate the new software with existing software
- Results of the performance evaluation test
- Relative costs (including any software modifications) and benefits
- The technical, economic, legal, operational, and schedule feasibility
- Input from legal and purchasing resources on the legal and financial viability of the contender
- Feedback from customers on how well the software performs as well as on the quality of the support provided by the vendor

Finalize Contract

Once a selection is made, a contract with the vendor must be negotiated and finalized. Although the vendor may insist that everyone signs a standard contract, every contract should be thoroughly reviewed by experienced members of an organization's legal and purchasing departments. Recognize that the standard contract is written from the vendor's perspective and protects its interests, not yours. Request a copy of the vendor's standard contract at the start of the software package evaluation process and allow at least two months for review and negotiation of a final contract.

Organizations that use the cloud-computing or software-as-a-service approach need to take special precautions in signing contracts with the service provider. The contract should clarify how the provider ensures data privacy, handles discovery if there is a lawsuit, resolves service-level problems, and manages disaster recovery; it should also detail where the cloud-computing servers and computers are located. Organizations should confirm this information in discussions with other customers of the service provider and by a visit to the service provider's facilities.

A contract covering the modification of a software package should have provisions for monitoring system modification quality and progress, ownership and property rights of the new or modified system, contingency provisions in case something doesn't work as expected, and dispute resolution if something goes wrong. Customizing the package actually changes the package into custom-made software, resulting in the potential loss of support from the original vendor. This might necessitate third-party support, which should be factored into the contract negotiations.

Integration and Testing

Several types of testing must be conducted before a software package is ready to be put into production. This is particularly true if the software package has been modified to meet the needs of the organization or the software package must integrate with existing information systems (e.g., a new accounts payable system must integrate with the organization's existing general ledger system). The following types of tests, already discussed earlier in the chapter, need to be completed.

1. Integration testing
2. System testing
3. Volume testing
4. User acceptance testing

Implementation

The organization cannot just count on the vendor to execute the implementation of the package—full and active participation by the project's stakeholders and end users is essential to success. Key implementation tasks include:

- Use data-flow diagrams to map current business processes and requirements to the software, and identify any gaps that must be filled by changing current processes or by modifying the software.
- Install the software and configure all of its capabilities and options to meet the project requirements.
- Customize any aspects of the solution needed for the organization.
- Integrate existing software with the new software.
- Train end users.
- Test the software to ensure that it meets all processes and requirements.
- Convert historical data from the old software so that it can be used by the new software.
- Roll out the new software to users in a live work environment.
- Provide for ongoing end-user support and training.

Critical Thinking Exercise

Hospital Switches Electronic Health Record Software

Midwest Regional Hospital (fictional) is a 500-bed general medical and surgical facility with 25,000 admissions and 7,500 annual inpatient and 17,500 outpatient surgeries annually. Its emergency room has 52,000 visits each year. It is a nonprofit hospital that treats both adult and child patients. Over 1,200 nurses, technicians, doctors, and physicians practice at the hospital.

An electronic health record (EHR) is an electronic version of a patient's medical history that is maintained by the provider over time and may include all of the key administrative clinical data relevant to that person's care, including demographics, progress notes, problems, medications, vital signs, past medical history, immunizations, laboratory data, and radiology reports. The EHR automates access to this information, and the more sophisticated versions of EHR software can also produce an online "digital chart" that displays up-to-date patient information in real time, complete with decision support tools for physicians and nurses. One of the key features of an EHR is that health information can be created and managed by authorized providers in a digital format capable of being shared with other providers across more than one healthcare organization, including laboratories, specialists, medical imaging facilities, pharmacies, emergency facilities, and school and workplace clinics.

Midwest Hospital was an early pioneer in the adoption of EHR software, implementing the technology in 2004. Unfortunately, the vendor that Midwest selected has not been able to keep up with evolving regulatory requirements and the changing needs of its healthcare clients. Its software is fast becoming obsolete, and it is rumored that the firm will soon eliminate support of its software. You have been hired as a consultant to lead a project to replace the original software with software from one of the current leading EHR software providers—Allscripts, Cerner Corporation, or Epic Systems Corporation.

Review Questions

1. Is there a need to conduct a preliminary software package evaluation? Why or why not?
2. What tasks would you attempt to complete in your first two weeks as a project leader?

Critical Thinking Questions

1. The hospital administrators have made it clear to you that the software vendor must be chosen and the software installed as soon as possible. What measures do you feel comfortable taking to accelerate the process without raising the risk of choosing the wrong software or having a rough system start-up?
2. A safety-critical system is one whose failure or misuse may cause human injury or death. Given that an EHR system can be considered to be such a system, which tasks associated with software implementation deserve special attention?

Summary

Principle:

Organizations can obtain software using one of two basic approaches: buy or build.

Buying off-the-shelf software is less risky and leads to quicker deployment; however, maintenance and support costs may become expensive with this approach, and the software may not be an exact match to the needs and work processes of the organization.

Building custom software can provide a better match to the current work processes of the organization and provide a potential competitive advantage; however, the cost can become extremely high, and it can take months or even years to develop the software.

Principle:

A system under development following the waterfall approach moves from one phase to the next, with a management review at the end of each phase.

The set of activities involved in building information systems to meet users' needs is called system development.

The waterfall system development process cycle is a sequential, multistage system development process in which work on the next stage cannot begin until the results of the current stage are reviewed and approved or modified as necessary. It is referred to as a waterfall process because progress is seen as flowing steadily downward (like a waterfall) through the various phases of development.

The phases of the waterfall system development process can vary from one company to the next, but many organizations use an approach with six phases: investigation, analysis, design, construction, integration and testing, and implementation. Once the system is built, organizations complete the additional steps of operation and maintenance and disposition.

At the end of each phase, a review is conducted to ensure that all tasks and deliverables associated with that phase were produced and that they are of good quality. In addition, at the end of each phase, the overall project scope, costs, schedule, and benefits associated with the project are reviewed to ensure that the project is on track and worth completing. As a result, the waterfall system development process allows for a high degree of management control.

System investigation is the key initial phase in the development of a new or modified business information system. The purpose of this phase is to gain a clear understanding of the specifics of the problem to solve or the opportunity to address.

Joint application development (JAD) is a structured meeting process that can accelerate and improve the efficiency and effectiveness of not only the investigation phase but also the analysis and design phases of a system development project.

Functional decomposition is a technique used primarily during the investigation phase to define the business processes included within the scope of the system.

The technical, economic, legal, operational, and schedule feasibility are assessed during the feasibility analysis.

After a project has completed the investigation phase and been approved for further study, the next step is system analysis, which answers the question, "What must the information system do to solve the problem or capitalize on the opportunity?"

The overall emphasis of analysis is gathering data on the existing system, determining the requirements for the new system, considering alternatives within identified constraints, and investigating the feasibility of alternative solutions.

Identifying, confirming, and prioritizing system requirements is perhaps the single most critical step in the entire waterfall system development process because failure to identify a requirement or an incorrect definition of a requirement may not be discovered until much later in the project, causing much rework, additional costs, and delay in the systems effort.

A data-flow diagram (DFD) is a diagram used during both the analysis and design phases to document the processes of the current system or to provide a model of a proposed new system. A DFD shows not only the various processes within the system but also where the data needed for each process comes from, where the output of each process will be sent, and what data will be stored and where.

The purpose of system design phase is to answer the question, "How will the information system solve this problem?" The primary result of the system design phase is a technical design that details system outputs, inputs, controls, and user interfaces; specifies hardware, software, databases, telecommunications, personnel, and procedures; and shows how these components are interrelated. In other words, system design creates a complete set of technical specifications that can be used to construct the information system.

During the design phase, designers must develop specific system security and controls for all aspects of the information system, including hardware, software, database systems, telecommunications, and Internet operations.

System construction converts the system design into an operational system by coding and testing software programs, creating and loading data into databases, and performing initial program testing.

Several types of testing must be conducted before a new or modified information system is ready to be put into production, including unit testing, integration testing, system testing, volume testing, and user acceptance testing.

System implementation includes the following activities: user preparation, site preparation, installation, and cutover.

System operation involves using the new or modified system under all kinds of operating conditions. Getting the most out of a new or modified system during its operation is the most important aspect of system operations for many organizations.

System maintenance involves changing and enhancing the system to make it more useful in achieving user and organizational goals. There are many reasons why system maintenance is required.

System disposal involves those activities that ensure the orderly dissolution of the system, including disposing of all equipment in an environmentally friendly manner, closing out contracts, and safely migrating information from the system to another system or archiving it in accordance with applicable records management policies.

Principle:

Agile development is an iterative system development process that develops a system in "sprint" increments lasting from two weeks to two months.

Unlike the waterfall system development process, agile development accepts the fact that system requirements are evolving and cannot be fully understood or defined at the start of the project. Agile development concentrates instead on maximizing the team's ability to deliver quickly and respond to emerging requirements—hence the name agile.

Scrum is an agile development framework that uses a team-based approach in order to keep the development effort focused and moving quickly. Scrum emphasizes individuals and interactions over processes and tools, working software over comprehensive documentation, customer collaboration over contract negotiation, and responding to change over following a plan.

A scrum master is the person who coordinates all scrum activities, and a scrum team consists of a dozen or fewer people who perform all system development activities from investigation to testing.

The product owner is a person who represents the project stakeholders and is responsible for communicating and aligning project priorities between the stakeholders and development team. The product owner holds the product vision; he or she is responsible for describing what should be built and why—but now how.

Extreme programming (XP) is another agile software development approach that promotes incremental development of a system using short development cycles to improve productivity and to accommodate new customer requirements.

DevOps is the practice of blending the tasks performed by the development and IT operations groups to enable faster and more reliable software releases. This approach is key to successful agile development.

Principle:

When buying off-the-shelf software, the effort required to modify the software package as well as existing software so that they work well together must be taken into account as a major factor in selecting the final vendor and software.

Today, most organizations purchase or rent the software they need rather than build it—simply because it costs too much or takes too long to build a quality information system.

The analysis team should make a preliminary assessment of the software marketplace to determine whether existing packages can meet the organization's needs. The primary tool for doing this is the request for information (RFI), a document that outlines an organization's hardware or software needs and requests vendors to respond with information about if and how they can meet those needs and the time and resources required.

A preliminary evaluation of software packages and vendors began during system analysis when the two or three strongest contenders were identified. The final evaluation begins with a detailed investigation of the contenders' proposals as well as discussions with two or three customers of each vendor.

Key Terms

agile development	request for information (RFI)
cold site	schedule feasibility
cutover	scrum
data-flow diagram (DFD)	scrum master
DevOps	site preparation
direct conversion	slipstream upgrade
disaster recovery plan	system analysis
economic feasibility	system construction
extreme programming (XP)	system disposal
feasibility analysis	system testing
hot site	system design
installation	system investigation
integration testing	system investigation report
joint application development (JAD)	system maintenance
legal feasibility	system operation
mission-critical processes	system review
monitoring	technical documentation
operational feasibility	technical feasibility
parallel start-up	unit testing
Pareto principle (80–20 rule)	user acceptance document
patch	user acceptance testing (UAT)
performance evaluation test	user documentation
phase-in approach	user preparation
pilot start-up	version
product owner	volume testing
release	waterfall system development process

Chapter 12: Self-Assessment Test

Organizations can obtain software using one of two basic approaches: buy or build.

1. _____ software is less risky and leads to quicker deployment; however, maintenance and support costs may become expensive.
   a. Custom
   b. Enterprise
   c. Off-the-shelf
   d. Personal productivity

2. _____ software can provide a better match to the current work processes of the organization and may provide a potential competitive advantage; however, software development can be extremely costly, and it can take months or even years to complete.
   a. Custom
   b. Enterprise
   c. Off-the-shelf
   d. Personal productivity

A system under development following the waterfall approach moves from one phase to the next, with a management review at the end of each phase.

3. Many organizations use a waterfall approach with six phases, including investigation, analysis, design, _____, integration and testing, and implementation.

4. The waterfall approach allows for a high degree of management control, but it does not allow for user interaction with the system until the integration and testing phase, when the system is nearly complete. True or False?

5. The purpose of the system investigation phase is to _____.
   a. define what the information system must do to solve the problem or capitalize on the opportunity
   b. gain a clear understanding of the specifics of the problem to solve or the opportunity to address
   c. gather data on the existing system and determine the requirements for the new system
   d. identify, confirm, and prioritize system requirements

6. _____ is a diagram used to document the processes of the current system or to provide a model of a proposed new system.

7. The overall emphasis of the _____ phase is on gathering data on the existing system,

determining the requirements of the new system, considering alternatives within identified constraints, and investigating the feasibility of alternative solutions.
   a. investigation
   b. analysis
   c. design
   d. construction

8. The primary tool for assessing the software marketplace to determine whether existing packages can meet the organization's needs is the _____.
   a. system investigation report
   b. request for quotation
   c. RFI
   d. system design report

9. The _____ phase converts the system design into an operational system by coding and testing software programs, creating and loading data into databases, and performing initial program testing.
   a. system analysis
   b. system construction
   c. system implementation
   d. system testing and integration

Agile development is an iterative system development process that develops a system in "sprint" increments lasting from two weeks to two months.

10. _____ is an agile development framework that uses a team-based approach in order to keep the development effort focused and moving quickly.

11. In the scrum framework, the _____ is a person who represents the project stakeholders and is responsible for communicating and aligning project priorities between stakeholders and the development team.
    a. project manager
    b. scrum master
    c. product owner
    d. project sponsor

12. _____ is the practice of blending the tasks performed by the development and IT operations groups to enable faster and more reliable software releases.
    a. Scrum
    b. Extreme programming
    c. JAD
    d. DevOps

When buying off-the-shelf software, the effort required to modify the software package as well as existing software so that they work well together must be taken into account as a major factor in selecting the final vendor and software.

13. A preliminary evaluation of software packages and vendors begins during the _____

phase when the two or three strongest contenders are identified.
a. system investigation
b. system design
c. system analysis
d. feasibility analysis

Chapter 12: Self-Assessment Test Answers

1. c
2. a
3. construction
4. True
5. b
6. Data-flow diagram
7. b
8. c
9. b
10. Scrum
11. c
12. d
13. c

Review Questions

1. What are primary characteristics of the waterfall system development process? What is the rationale for using the term "waterfall" to describe it?
2. Identify and state the purpose of each of the six phases of the waterfall system development process.
3. Why do many organizations have a formal process for requesting a system investigation?
4. What are the four different kinds of feasibility that must be assessed? Why is the feasibility of a system reviewed during the investigation, analysis, and design phases?
5. What is the difference between tangible and intangible benefits? Identify five tangible benefits that are frequently associated with an information system.
6. What are the key elements of a system investigation report?
7. What is the purpose of studying the existing system during the analysis phase?
8. Identify several areas for which system security and control requirements need to be defined.
9. Identify and briefly describe six system performance factors.
10. What is a business continuity plan? What is a disaster recovery plan?
11. Identify and briefly describe four types of testing that are conducted during the integration and testing phase.
12. Define the terms slipstream upgrade, patch, release, and version as they relate to system maintenance.
13. What is the difference between the roles and responsibilities of a scrum master and product owner?
14. What is extreme programming (XP)? What is its goal?
15. An organization has selected and is now implementing a software package. Identify three key factors that will determine the cost and time required for implementation.

Discussion Questions

1. Provide two examples of opportunities or problems that are likely to trigger the need for an information system project.
2. Thoroughly discuss the pros and cons of buying versus building software.
3. What are the advantages and disadvantages of following the waterfall system development process?
4. Outline the steps necessary to conduct an effective joint application development (JAD) session. Who should participate in such a session? What is the role of the JAD facilitator?
5. Once a project has successfully made it through the system investigation phase, should it ever be cancelled? Why or why not?

6. You have been assigned to write a newspaper report on a major information system project failure run by your school's information system organization. Where would you start, and who would you speak with?

7. Why is it important for business managers to have a basic understanding of the system development process?

8. Define the Pareto principle, and discuss how it applies to prioritizing system requirements.

9. Identify and describe how three different change models that can be applied to improve the probability of successful system implementation.

10. Describe and discuss the pros and cons of three different system cutover strategies.

11. What is the fundamental difference in approach between waterfall and agile system development?

12. How does DevOps support the agile system development process?

13. Identify and briefly discuss four key tasks associated with the successful implementation of a software package.

Problem-Solving Exercises

1. You are acquiring a new information system for The Fitness Center, a company with three fitness centers in your metropolitan area, with a total of 1,200 members and 20 to 30 full and part-time employees in each location. Through previous research efforts, the director of marketing has determined that your clientele is interested in a state-of-the-art software system to track all their fitness and health-related activities. Each piece of equipment in the gym will be modified to allow entry of the member's ID number, recording the date, time of day, weight used, and number of reps or workout length. Members and fitness consultants want to be able to log in to the system from any computer or mobile device and see displays of various reports (calories burned, muscle groups worked, blood pressure, distance run, steps taken, etc.) for a user-specified time period. Use word-processing software to identify at least six high-priority requirements for such a system. Use a spreadsheet or project management program to identify and schedule the tasks that must be performed in order to choose the best software package and implement it.

2. The preliminary investigation of a software project has been completed. Two different project teams have estimated the costs associated with the development and maintenance of a new system. One team based their estimates on the assumption that the waterfall system development process would be used for the project; the other team plans to follow the agile approach. A third option is to purchase off-the-shelf software that provides nearly all the benefits of a custom-built solution. Review the estimates below, and choose the best approach for the project: waterfall development, agile development, or off-the-shelf software implementation. Provide a solid rational for your choice. Identify any assumptions you must make in reaching your decision.

	Waterfall	Agile	Off-the-Shelf Software
Total effort months to complete the system	45	38	6
Cost per effort month	$10k	$10k	$10k
Cost of software package			$350k
Elapsed time until a partial working version is available (months)	Not applicable	2	Not applicable
Elapsed time until all currently envisioned features are available (months)	8	5	3
Annual savings generated by the complete system	$180k	$180k	$160k

3. A new sales ordering system needs a relational database that contains a customer table, a product inventory table, and an order table. Use a word-processing, graphics, or spreadsheet program to draw an entity-relationship diagram showing the relationships among these entities. Next, design each of these tables showing the keys and attributes to be included in each table. Include five sample records for each table.

Team Activities

1. Your team has been hired to define the scope and feasibility of a project to create a database of job openings and descriptions for the companies visiting your campus each term. Students would be able to log on to the system and request an appointment with each company's recruiter. Recruiters would be granted access to each student's summary transcript (courses taken, but no grades shown) and resume. Describe the tasks your team would perform to complete the system investigation phase. Who else needs to be involved in the system investigation? Develop a data-flow diagram that defines the scope of this system.

2. Your team has been selected to monitor the disposal of your school's 10-year-old student-registration system. Develop a list of the activities that need to be completed to complete this task. Which activities are of most concern?

3. You and your team have been hired to perform a system investigation for a fast food restaurant that wants to implement new tools and processes to improve its customer service. Currently, the restaurant has a poor reputation for not correctly filling customers' orders and for taking too long to do it. Perform a functional decomposition to define the scope and basic requirements of such a system. Brainstorm some ideas to improve the situation, and choose one to pursue based on its technical, economic, legal, operational, and schedule feasibility.

Web Exercises

1. Do research on the Web to identify application development tools that support the rapid development of high-quality apps for both iPhone and Android-based smartphones. Develop a spreadsheet that summarizes the features and pros and cons of three of these tools.

2. Do research to identify the three leading electronic health record (EHR) systems. Go on social media and find comments from the users of these systems. If you were leading a project team to select an EHR system for a large hospital, which one would you choose? Why?

3. Do research to determine the current level of adoption of DevOps around the globe. Which organizations seem to be leaders in DevOps? What initiatives are these companies taking that makes them leaders?

Career Exercises

1. A new advertising and promotion-planning system is being developed for a major manufacturer of consumer products. Management is seeking candidates to serve as the product owner on this key $2 million, nine-month project. Identify some characteristics and desired experience that the ideal candidate would possess.

2. Perform research to learn what is required to have a successful career as a software developer for smartphones. What sort of education and experience is needed? What personal characteristics would be helpful in such a career? How would one get started in such a career, and what are starting salaries?

3. Identify an information system frequently employed by people in a career field you are interested in. Discuss how you might be involved as a user in the development or acquisition of such a system for your future company. Identify three things that you could do as a project participant that would greatly improve the likelihood of a successful project. Now, identify three things that you could do (or fail to do) that could greatly diminish the probability of success of such a project.

Case Studies

Case One

Etsy Uses DevOps for Rapid Deployment

Looking for a unique gift—such as a personalized, hand-stamped fishing lure or maybe a vintage gold hairpin or even a crocheted hat for your cat? If so, you might want to join the 24 million active buyers who turn to the Web site Etsy as their source for handmade and vintage products—ranging from art and photography to clothing and jewelry to home décor and furniture.

Etsy was founded in 2005 in an apartment in Brooklyn, New York, by a small group of people who saw a need for an online exchange where crafters and artists could sell their handmade and vintage goods along with art and craft supplies. The company, which views itself as a global community of creative entrepreneurs, shoppers, manufacturers, and suppliers, now has more than 800 employees and a peer-to-peer e-commerce site that generated close to $2.4 billion in sales in 2015. Currently, the site has over 35 million items available for sale from 1.6 million active sellers around the world.

Early on, Etsy placed a high priority on developing a sophisticated technology platform to support its business, with an engineering culture centered around a philosophy that the company has dubbed "Code as Craft" (the company even operates an engineering blog under that name). However, as with many startups, the development of Etsy's internal structures was not always carefully planned. As a result, siloes and other barriers to collaboration gradually developed across the company, affecting its ability to keep its software development efforts on the cutting edge.

Despite those challenges, the company grew rapidly, and as early as 2008, the company was deploying new releases to its site twice a week—a pace matched by few other companies at the time. However, each of those deployments typically took over four hours to complete, and according to Michael Rembetsy, vice president of technical operations at Etsy, "Deploys were very painful. We had a traditional mindset: developers write the code and ops deploys it." That divide often resulted in faulty releases that shut down the site for prolonged periods, causing real concern for the users around the world who relied on the site to make a living.

When Chad Dickerson, who had spent years as CTO at Yahoo!, joined Etsy as its new CTO, he quickly brought in a new technical management team, which pushed the company to adopt a more agile approach to software development in order to roll out improvements and updates with greater ease and fewer disruptions. According to Jon Cowie, an operations engineer at Etsy, "Bringing that group in is what first planted the seed of DevOps and the move to a continuous rate of delivery, and it's all really grown from there. As the company has grown, this idea that the closer developers and operations work together and understand each other's problems, the more the company can achieve, has really taken hold."

Like many companies, Etsy was attracted to DevOps as a way to create a more responsive software development process—one that allows for continuous integration and deployment. However, adopting DevOps practices has also encouraged a more collaborative approach to development—a shift that has been both challenging and rewarding for the company. Notes Cowie, "The hardest part is getting the business culture right…. You may have to deal with stakeholders at different levels who may not like this idea of relinquishing some power or giving people access to systems they previously haven't had."

One of the big rewards for Etsy is that its developers are now able to push code to a production server up to 60 times a day. Often, the first release is to a limited audience of employees or a small, randomly selected group of users. With testing and feedback, the code can then be pushed to the entire Etsy community. According to Rembetsy, "We started to understand that if developers felt the responsibility for deploying code to the site they would also, by nature, take responsibility for if the site was up or down, take into consideration performance, and gain an understanding of the stress and fear of a deploy."

As Rembetsy notes, "Mistakes happen, we find them, fix them, and move on. The important thing is to learn something from the process, and never make the mistake again in the future."

Critical Thinking Questions

1. It is perhaps not surprising that Etsy was an early adopter of DevOps. It is a relatively small company, with a start-up culture, and its move to DevOps was championed by company leaders. Do you think deploying DevOps practices would be more difficult in a larger, more established organization? How might a company begin to make the cultural changes needed to move to the more collaborative, rapid-deployment approach that DevOps offers?

2. At Etsy, new developers are expected to begin pushing code to production on day one. That expectation is one way Etsy encourages it employees to embrace change—and a certain degree of risk—instead of fearing it. Would you feel comfortable working as a business manager in a company that gives individual developers so much freedom and responsibility? What would be some of the advantages to a business manager of such a culture? What might be some of the disadvantages?

3. What would be some of the criteria you would use to measure the success of a shift to DevOps practices within a company?

SOURCES: "About Etsy," Etsy, *www.etsy.com/about/?ref=ftr*, April 28, 2016; Dix, John, "How Etsy Makes DevOps Work," *Network World*, February 19, 2015, *www.networkworld.com/article/2886672/software /how-etsy-makes-devops-work.html*; Donnelly, Caroline, "Case Study: What the Enterprise Can Learn from Etsy's DevOps Strategy," *ComputerWeekly*, June 9, 2015, *www.computerweekly.com/news/4500247782 /Case-study-What-the-enterprise-can-learn-from-Etsys-DevOps-strategy*; Heusser, Matthew, "Continuous Deployment Done in Unique Fashion at Etsy.com," *CIO*, March 12, 2012, *www.cio.com/article/2397663/devel oper/continuous-deployment-done-in-unique-fashion-at-etsy-com.html*; "What Is DevOps," The Agile Admin, *https://theagileadmin.com/what-is -devops*, accessed April 27, 2016.

Case Two

British Telecom Spreading Agile Development across the Globe

In 2005, British Telecom (BT) took a big risk: the company dropped its use of the waterfall system development process and embraced agile development. Previously, BT had outsourced the gathering of system requirements to a third company, which would typically take three to nine months to meet with customers and stakeholders and create a requirements list. Next, the project would move back to BT where programmers often struggled to interpret the requirements and then develop and test the system within 18 months—although some projects needed more time. In late 2005, however, BT took only 90 days to roll out a new Web-based system for monitoring phone traffic. The new system allowed traffic managers to change switches and other physical devices more quickly in order to handle shifts in load along BT's telecommunications network. The success of this initial project reverberated throughout the IT world, as BT became the first telecommunications giant to adopt agile development—sometimes developing products in three 30-day iterative cycles.

The new system development approach had other advantages, too: programmers and customers communicated closely and teams from different locations around the world, initially the United Kingdom and India, worked together to develop the system. To overcome customer doubts, BT invited them to development "hot houses" to see how the agile development process worked. Many customers became such ardent believers that they adopted the agile approach themselves. In 2010, BT used its new system development process to create the 21st Century Next Generation Access Network process, which enjoyed an 80 percent return on its initial investment within its first year. Today, BT deploys agile development to service its customers across the globe.

In 2014, for example, BT applied the agile approach to deploy telepresence solutions for the international energy and chemical producer Sasol, a company with over 34,000 employees based in 37 countries. To oversee its operations and interact with clients, senior Sasol managers based in South Africa were traveling millions of miles each year, which was not good for the managers, the company's budget, or the planet. As an alternative, BT installed telepresence suites across South Africa and in Houston, London, Calgary, and Hamburg. Sasol achieved a 100 percent usage rate at each of these suites, and BT secured a five-year contract to provide continued support.

BT had one major concern about agile development: previously, the company had conducted 16 or 17 types of tests before deploying a new system. Many feared that a shorter life cycle meant compromising on quality assurance. However, BT now continues testing with customers after system setup and finds that testing the product with customer involvement has significant advantages.

"The main advantage I see is that you spend more time working on the right [system] features by talking to customers all the time and working on it," says Kerry Buckley, a software developer who worked on the initial phone-traffic monitoring system. Moreover, software engineers working at BT are excited about working on customer-facing live applications. As one engineer notes, "All your work matters and will be released to the public." Agile development at BT has taken system developers out of their isolated bubble, inspiring them, and proving to the IT world that agile development can work.

Critical Thinking Questions

1. Are there certain personal characteristics one should look for in candidates who will participate in or lead agile system projects? If so, what are they, and why are they important?
2. How might the establishment of telepresence suites support the use of the agile system development process? What do you think are some of the capabilities of such suites?
3. How might extreme programming and DevOps provide further improvements in the BT system development process?

SOURCES: Hoffman, Thomas, "BT: A Case Study in Agile Programming," *InfoWorld*, March 11, 2008, *www.infoworld.com/d/developer-world /bt-case-study-in-agile-programming-112?page=0,0*; Grant, Ian, "BT Switches to Agile Techniques to Create New Products," *ComputerWeekly*, January 29, 2010, *www.computerweekly.com/news/1280091969 /BT-switches-to-agile-techniques-to-create-new-products*; "About Sasol: Overview," Sasol, *www.sasol.com/about-sasol/company-profile/over view*; accessed July 8, 2014; "Turning a Far-Flung Organisation into a Single Community," BT, July 9, 2014, *http://letstalk.globalservices.bt .com/en*; "Software Engineer, IVR at BT (British Telecom)," The JobCrowd, April 23, 2014, *www.thejobcrowd.com/employer/bt-british -telecom/reviews/software-engineer-ivr-at-bt-british-telecom*.

Notes

1. Schuman, Evan, "What Amazon Is Doing with Its Supply Chain Could Devastate the Competition," *Computerworld*, February 12, 2016, *www.computerworld.com/article/3032656/retail-it/amazons-supply-chain-move-could-prove-devastating.html*

2. Boulton, Clint, "Custom Software Drives Vitamin World Stores Remodeling," *CIO*, Feb 12, 2016, *www.cio.com/article/3033084/software/custom-software-drives-vitamin-world-stores-remodeling.html*.

3. Boulton, Clint, "Walgreens CIO Starts with the Customer and Works Backward," *CIO*, February 9, 2016, *www.cio.com/article/3031054/vertical-industries/walgreens-cio-starts-with-the-customer-and-works-backward.html*.

4. Boyd, Aaron, "Energy IT Project Failing due to Mismanagement, Poor Planning," *Federal Times*, November 24, 2015, *www.federaltimes.com/story/government/it/management/2015/11/24/eia-it-transformation/76307870/*.

5. "Joint Application Development," Liquid Mercury Solutions, *http://liquidmercurysolutions.com/whatwedo/spdev/Pages/Joint-Application-Development.aspx*, accessed February 21, 2016.

6. "Utilizing a Self-Steering Robotic Tractor in the Developmental Phases of Rice," Hitachi, *www.hitachi.com.au/documents/news/150114-Utilizing-a-Self-steering-Robotic-Tractor-in-the-Developmental-Phases-of-Rice.pdf*, accessed February 21, 2016.

7. "Ministry of Defence 'Wasted Millions on Failed Computer System'," *Guardian*, January 13, 2014, *www.theguardian.com/uk-news/2014/jan/14/ministry-of-defence-failed-computer-system*.

8. "LAPD Best Policing Practices through Early Intervention," Sierra-Cedar, *www.sierra-cedar.com/wp-content/uploads/sites/12/2015/07/CSS-LAPD.pdf*, accessed February 22, 2016.

9. "Interagency Guidelines Establishing Information Security Standards," Board of Governors of the Federal Reserve System, *www.federalreserve.gov/bankinforeg/interagencyguidelines.htm*, accessed June 9, 2014.

10. Ward, Brian, "The Importance of Good Interface Design," *heehaw.digital* (blog), February 27, 2013, *http://blog.heehaw.co.uk/2013/02/the-importance-of-good-interface-design*.

11. Shneiderman, Ben and Plaisant, Catherine, Designing the User Interface: Strategies for Effective Human-Computer Interaction, 5.ed, 2009, Pearson: New York.

12. Porter, Joshua, "Principles of User Interface Design," *Bokardo* (blog), *http://bokardo.com/principles-of-user-interface-design/*, accessed July 3, 2014.

13. "RecoverPoint," EMC, *www.emc.com/storage/recover point/recoverpoint.htm*, accessed June 16, 2014.

14. "SteelEye LifeKeeper," SteelEye Technology, Inc., *www.ha-cc.org/high_availability/components/application_availability/cluster/high_availability_cluster/steeleye_lifekeeper*, accessed June 16, 2014.

15. "NeverFail Application Continuous Availability," VirtualizationAdmin.com, *www.virtualizationadmin.com/software/High-Availability/Neverfail-for-VMware-VirtualCenter-.html*, accessed June 16, 2014.

16. "CodeSmith Generator," CodeSmith, *www.codesmithtools.com/product/generator*, accessed July 1, 2014.

17. "The Arizona Supreme Court Creates the Ultimate Outsource and Insource Simultaneously," *Visible*, *www.visible.com/News/arizona.htm*, accessed July 2, 2014.

18. Dr. Explain Web site, *www.drexplain.com/what-do-users-say*, accessed July 14, 2014.

19. Kline, Allissa, "M&T to Invest $20M, Upgrade Data Center," *Buffalo Business First*, March 10, 2014, *www.bizjournals.com/buffalo/news/2014/03/10/m-t-to-invest-20m-in-data-center-upgrade.html*.

20. "Selected Financial Data," Shell, *http://reports.shell.com/annual-report/2015/strategic-report/selected-financial-data.php*, accessed April 26, 2016.

21. "Shell Businesses in the U.S.," Shell, *www.shell.us/aboutshell/shell-businesses.html*, accessed July 8, 2014.

22. "A Record-Breaking Feat," T-Systems, February 2013, *www.t-systems.com/umn/global-collaboration-from-a-private-cloud-shell-pulls-off-the-largest-sap-upgrade-in-history-/1125808_2/blobBinary/Best-Practice_02-2013_Shell_EN.pdf?ts_layoutId=1100966*.

23. "Precise Application Performance Platform," Precise, *www.precise.com*, accessed July 14, 2014.

24. "Allscripts," eG Innovations, *www.eginnovations.com/news/Allscripts_Case_study_letter_12914.pdf*, accessed July 14, 2014.

25. Wagner, Dennis, "VA Scandal Audit: 120,000 Veterans Experience Long Waits for Care," *Azcentral*, June 9, 2014, *www.azcentral.com/story/news/arizona/investigations/2014/06/09/va-scandal-audit-veterans-delayed-care/10234881*.

26. Brewin, Bob, "VA Failed to Protect Critical Computer Systems, Audit Finds," *Nextgov* (blog), May 29, 2014, *www.nextgov.com/defense/whats-brewin/2014/05/va-failed-protect-critical-computer-systems-audit-finds/85429*.

27. Osborne, Hilary, "Why Do Bank IT Systems Keep Failing?" *Guardian*, January 27, 2014, *www.theguardian.com/money/2014/jan/27/bank-it-systems-keep-failing-lloyds-rbs-natwest*.

28. "More than £1BN Committed to Improve Banking Services," RBS, June 27, 2014, *www.rbs.com/news/2014/06/more-than-p1bn-committed-to-improve-banking-services.html*.

29. "End of Windows XP Support Will Be Trouble for Businesses and Consumers," *CBS Evening News*, April 8, 2014, *www.cbsnews.com/videos/end-of-windows-xp-support-will-be-trouble-for-businesses-consumers/*.

30. "What Is Agile?" Agile Methodology, *http://agilemethodology.org*, accessed August 3, 2014.

31. "Core Scrum: What is Scrum?," ScrumAlliance, *www .scrumalliance.org/scrum/media/ScrumAllianceMedia /Files%20and%20PDFs/Learn%20About%20Scrum /Core-Scrum.pdf*, accessed April 26, 2016.

32. "Learn About Scrum?" Scrum Alliance, *www.scrumalliance .org/why-scrum*, accessed April 26, 2016.

33. "Core Scrum: What is Scrum?," ScrumAlliance.

34. "Scrum Methodology," My PM Expert, *http://scrummethod ology.com/*, accessed August 3, 2014. *www.my-project -management-expert.com/the-advantages-and-disadvan tages-of-agile-software-development.html*, accessed August 3, 2014.

35. De Sousa, Susan, "The Advantages and Disadvantages of Agile Development," My PM Expert, *www.my-project -management-expert.com/the-advantages-and -disadvantages-of-agile-software-development.html*, accessed August 3, 2014.

36. "The Rules of Extreme Programming," Extreme Pro-gramming, *www.extremeprogramming.org/rules.html*, accessed August 3, 2014.

37. Greene, Daniel, "What Is DevOps," *TechCrunch*, May 1, 2015, *http://techcrunch.com/2015/05/15/what-is-devops*.

38. Barker, Colin, "What Is DevOps and Why Does It Mat-ter?," ZDNet, *www.zdnet.com/article/what-is-devops -and-why-does-it-matter*.

39. Gates, Robert, "Hotel Hits the Gas Pedal with Souped Up DevOps Model," *TechTarget*, March 7, 2016, *http:// searchdatacenter.techtarget.com/news/4500278116 /Hotel-hits-the-gas-pedal-with-souped-up-DevOps-model*.

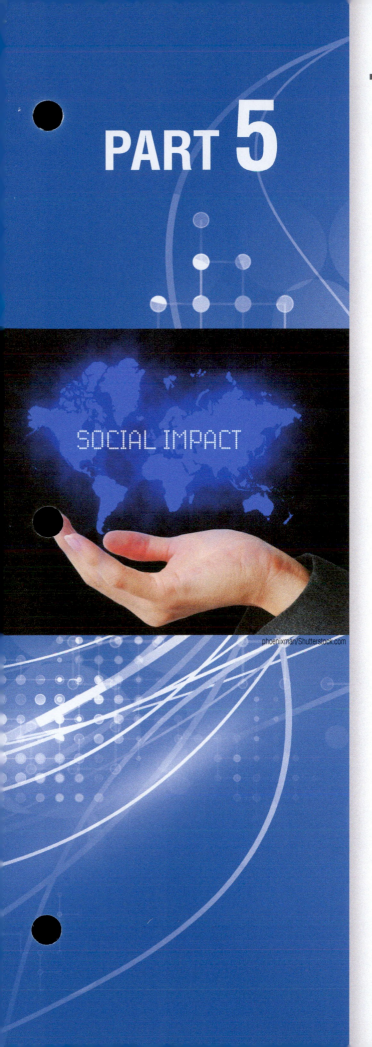

PART 5

Information Systems in Business and Society

Chapter 13
Cybercrime and Information System Security

Chapter 14
Ethical, Legal, and Social Issues of Information Systems

SOCIAL IMPACT

phoenixman/Shutterstock.com

- A zero-day attack is one that takes place before the security community and/or software developers become aware of and fix a security vulnerability. While one would hope that the discoverer of a zero-day vulnerability would immediately inform the original software manufacturer so that a fix can be created for the problem, in some cases, this knowledge is sold on the black market to cyberterrorists, governments, or large organizations that may then use it to launch their own cyberattacks. For example, information about one zero-day vulnerability in Apple's iOS reportedly sold for $500,000. Packages of zero-day exploits have been sold to U.S. government contractors for $2.5 million a year.

- The volume of global phishing attacks is alarming. It is estimated that about 156 million phishing emails are sent each day, with 16 million of those successfully evading email filters. Of those, roughly 50 percent (or 8 million) are opened, and 800,000 recipients per day click on malicious URL links contained in the emails.

Principles

- Computer crime is a serious and rapidly growing area of concern requiring management attention.

- Organizations must take strong measures to ensure secure, private, and reliable computing experiences for their employees, customers, and business partners.

Learning Objectives

- Explain why computer incidents are so prevalent.

- Identify and briefly describe the types of computer exploits and their impact.

- Describe the earmarks of a strong security program.

- Identify specific measures used to prevent computer crime.

- Outline actions that must be taken in the event of a successful security intrusion.

Why Learn about Cybercrime and Information System Security?

The security of data and information systems used in business is of utmost importance. Confidential business data and private customer and employee information must be safeguarded, and systems must be protected against malicious acts of theft or disruption. Although the need for security is obvious, it must often be balanced against other business needs. Business managers, IS professionals, and IS users all face a number of complex trade-offs regarding IS security, such as the following: How much effort and money should be spent to safeguard against computer crime? (In other words, how safe is safe enough?) What should be done if recommended computer security safeguards make conducting business more difficult for customers and employees, resulting in lost sales and increased costs? If a firm is a victim of a computer crime, should it pursue prosecution of the criminals at all costs, maintain a low profile to avoid the negative publicity, inform affected customers, or take some other action?

As you read this chapter, consider the following:

- What key trade-offs and ethical issues are associated with the safeguarding of data and information systems?
- What are the key elements of a multilayer process for managing security vulnerabilities based on the concept of reasonable assurance?

The Threat Landscape

The number of cybercrimes being committed against individuals, organizations, and governments continues to increase, and the destructive impact of these crimes is also intensifying. The brands, reputation, and earnings of many organizations around the world have been negatively impacted by such crimes. As a result, organizations are putting in place a range of countermeasures to combat cybercrime. For instance, the worldwide financial services industry spent $27.4 billion on IT security and fraud prevention in 2015.[1] And a recent survey of more than 10,000 IT professionals around the world revealed the following:[2]

- 58 percent of global companies have an overall security strategy.
- 54 percent have a CISO (chief information security officer) in charge of security.
- 53 percent have employee security-awareness and training programs.
- 52 percent have security standards for third parties.
- 49 percent conduct threat assessments.
- 48 percent actively monitor and analyze security intelligence.

In spite of all these countermeasures, however, the number of computer security incidents surged from 2014 to 2015 in the following industries: public sector organizations; entertainment, media and communications; technology and telecommunications companies; pharmaceuticals and life sciences; and power and utilities organizations.[3]

Why Computer Incidents Are So Prevalent

Increasing computing complexity, higher computer user expectations, expanding and changing systems, an increase in the prevalence of bring your own device (BYOD) policies, a growing reliance on software with known vulnerabilities, and the increasing sophistication of those who would do harm have caused a dramatic increase in the number, variety, and severity of security incidents are increasing dramatically.

Increasing Complexity Increases Vulnerability

The computing environment has become enormously complex. Cloud computing, networks, computers, mobile devices, virtualization, operating systems applications, Web sites, switches, routers, and gateways are interconnected and driven by hundreds of millions of lines of code. This environment continues to increase in complexity every day. The number of possible entry points to a network expands continually as more devices are added, increasing the possibility of security breaches.

Higher Computer User Expectations

Today, time means money, and the faster computer users can solve a problem, the sooner they can be productive. As a result, computer help desks are under intense pressure to respond very quickly to users' questions. Under duress, help desk personnel sometimes forget to verify users' identities or to check whether they are authorized to perform a requested action. In addition, even though most have been warned against doing so, some computer users share their login ID and password with other coworkers who have forgotten their own passwords. This can enable workers to gain access to information systems and data for which they are not authorized.

Expanding and Changing Systems Introduce New Risks

Business has moved from an era of stand-alone computers, in which critical data was stored on an isolated mainframe computer in a locked room, to an era in which personal computers and mobile devices connect to networks with millions of other computers, all capable of sharing information. Businesses have moved quickly into e-commerce, mobile computing, collaborative work groups, global business, and interorganizational information systems. Information technology has become ubiquitous and is a necessary tool for organizations to achieve their goals. However, it is increasingly difficult for IT organizations to keep up with the pace of technological change, successfully perform an ongoing assessment of new security risks, and implement approaches for dealing with them.

Increased Prevalence of Bring Your Own Device Policies

bring your own device (BYOD): A business policy that permits, and in some cases encourages, employees to use their own mobile devices (smartphones, tablets, or laptops) to access company computing resources and applications, including email, corporate databases, the corporate intranet, and the Internet.

Bring your own device (BYOD) is a business policy that permits, and in some cases encourages, employees to use their own mobile devices (smartphones, tablets, or laptops) to access company computing resources and applications, including email, corporate databases, the corporate intranet, and the Internet. Proponents of BYOD say it improves employee productivity by allowing workers to use devices with which they are already familiar—while also helping to create an image of a company as a flexible and progressive employer. Most companies have found they cannot entirely prevent employees from using their own devices to perform work functions. However, this practice raises many potential security issues as it is highly likely that such devices are also used for nonwork activity (browsing Web sites, blogging, shopping, visiting social networks, etc.) that exposes them to malware much more frequently than a device used strictly for business purposes. That malware may then be spread throughout the company. In addition, BYOD makes it extremely difficult for IT organizations to adequately safeguard additional portable devices with various operating systems and a myriad of applications.

Growing Reliance on Commercial Software with Known Vulnerabilities

exploit: An attack on an information system that takes advantage of a particular system vulnerability.

In computing, an **exploit** is an attack on an information system that takes advantage of a particular system vulnerability. Often this attack is due to poor system design or implementation. Once the vulnerability is discovered, software developers create and issue a "fix," or patch, to eliminate the problem. Users of the system or application are responsible for obtaining and installing the patch, which they can usually download from the Web. (These fixes are in addition to other maintenance and project work that software developers perform.)

Any delay in installing a patch exposes the user to a potential security breach. The need to install a fix to prevent a hacker from taking advantage of a known system vulnerability can create a time-management dilemma for system support personnel trying to balance a busy work schedule. Should they install a patch that, if left uninstalled, could lead to a security breach, or should they complete assigned project work so that the anticipated project savings and benefits from the project can begin to accrue on schedule? According to Secunia, a provider of vulnerability intelligence and management tools, the number of new software vulnerabilities identified in 2014 jumped 18 percent from the previous year to 15,435—an average of 42 per day—as shown in Table 13.1.[4,5]

TABLE 13.1 Total number of new software vulnerabilities identified annually

Year	Number of Software Vulnerabilities Identified
2007	7,540
2008	8,369
2009	7,716
2010	9,747
2011	9,307
2012	9,875
2013	13,075
2014	15,435

zero-day attack: An attack that takes place before the security community and/or software developers become aware of and fix a security vulnerability.

Clearly, it can be difficult to keep up with all the required patches to fix these vulnerabilities. Of special concern is a **zero-day attack**, which is an attack that takes place before the security community and/or software developers become aware of and fix a security vulnerability. While one would hope that the discoverer of a zero-day vulnerability would immediately inform the original software manufacturer so that a fix can be created for the problem, in some cases, this knowledge is sold on the black market to cyberterrorists, governments, or large organizations that may then use it to launch their own cyberattacks. For example, information about one zero-day vulnerability in Apple's iOS reportedly sold for $500,000.[6] On the other hand, the U.S. government has also chosen to keep information about vulnerabilities secret in cases in which government security experts have determined that the hole has "a clear national security or law enforcement" use. Packages of zero-day exploits have been sold to U.S. government contractors for $2.5 million a year.[7]

A serious zero-day vulnerability was discovered in Apple's OS X El Capitan operating system, enabling hackers to circumvent the company's System Integrity Protection (SIP), which is designed to prevent malicious code from modifying protected files and stealing sensitive data. The infection is difficult to detect, and even if users do discover it, it is impossible for them to remove the infection, since SIP would work against them, preventing users from reaching or altering the malware-laced system file. Apple patched the vulnerability in updates for El Capitan 10.11.4 and iOS 9.3 that were released on March 21, 2016.[8]

U.S. companies increasingly rely on commercial software with known vulnerabilities. Even when vulnerabilities are exposed, many corporate IT organizations prefer to use already installed software as is rather than implement security fixes that will either make the software harder to use or eliminate "nice-to-have" features that will help sell the software to end users.

Increasing Sophistication of Those Who Would Do Harm

Previously, the stereotype of a computer troublemaker was that of an introverted "geek" working on his own and motivated by the desire to gain some degree of notoriety. This individual was armed with specialized, but limited, knowledge of computers and networks and used rudimentary tools, perhaps downloaded from the Internet, to execute his exploits. While such individuals still exist, it is not this stereotyped individual who is the biggest threat to IT security. Today's computer menace is much better organized and may be part of an organized group (e.g., Anonymous, Chaos Computer Club, Lizard Squad, TeslaTeam) that has an agenda and targets specific organizations and Web sites. Some of these groups have ample resources, including money and sophisticated tools to support their efforts. Today's computer attacker has greater depth of knowledge and expertise in getting around computer and network security safeguards. Table 13.2 summarizes the types of perpetrators of computer mischief, crime, and damage.

TABLE 13.2 Classifying perpetrators of computer crime

Type of Perpetrator	Description
Black hat hacker	Someone who violates computer or Internet security maliciously or for illegal personal gain (in contrast to a white hat hacker who is someone who has been hired by an organization to test the security of its information systems)
Cracker	An individual who causes problems, steals data, and corrupts systems
Malicious insider	An employee or contractor who attempts to gain financially and/or disrupt a company's information systems and business operations
Industrial spy	An individual who captures trade secrets and attempts to gain an unfair competitive advantage
Cybercriminal	Someone who attacks a computer system or network for financial gain
Hacktivist	An individual who hacks computers or Web sites in an attempt to promote a political ideology
Cyberterrorist	Someone who attempts to destroy the infrastructure components of governments, financial institutions, and other corporations, utilities, and emergency response units

Types of Exploits

There are numerous types of computer attacks, with new varieties being invented all the time. This section discusses some of the more common attacks, including ransomware, viruses, worms, Trojan horses, blended threat, spam, distributed denial-of-service, rootkits, advanced persistent threat, phishing, spear-phishing, smishing and vishing, identity theft, cyberespionage, and cyberterrorism.

While we usually think of such exploits being aimed at computers, smartphones continue to become more computer capable. Increasingly, smartphone users store an array of personal identity information on their devices, including credit card numbers and bank account numbers. Smartphones are used to surf the Web and transact business electronically. The more people use their smartphones for these purposes, the more attractive these devices become as targets for cyberthieves. One form of smartphone malware runs up charges on users' accounts by automatically sending messages to numbers that charge fees upon receipt of a message.

Ransomware

ransomware: Malware that stops you from using your computer or accessing your data until you meet certain demands such as paying a ransom or sending photos to the attacker.

Ransomware is malware that stops you from using your computer or accessing your data until you meet certain demands such as paying a ransom or sending photos to the attacker. Computers become infected when users open an email attachment containing the malware or are lured to a compromised Web site by a deceptive email or pop-up window. Ransomware can also be spread through removable USB drives or Yahoo Messenger, with the payload disguised as an image.

Hollywood Presbyterian Medical Center was forced to shut down its computer network after hackers encrypted some of its data in February, 2016. Initially, the hospital refused to pay the ransom, and hospital employees were forced to resort to paper, pencil, phones, and fax machines to carry out many of their tasks, including accessing patient data. The hospital sought help from the FBI, the Los Angeles Police Department, and cybersecurity consultants, but it was never able to access to the data. After a week, the hospital paid the ransom of $12,000. By February 15, access to the data was fully restored and there was no evidence that any patient or employee data had been accessed.[9]

Viruses

virus: A piece of programming code, usually disguised as something else, that causes a computer to behave in an unexpected and usually undesirable manner.

Computer virus has become an umbrella term for many types of malicious code. Technically, a **virus** is a piece of programming code, usually disguised as something else, that causes a computer to behave in an unexpected and usually undesirable manner. For example, the virus may be programmed to display a certain message on the computer's display screen, delete or modify a certain document, or reformat the hard drive. Almost all viruses are attached to a file, so that only when the infected file is opened, the virus executes. A virus is spread to other machines when a computer user shares an infected file or sends an email with a virus-infected attachment. In other words, viruses spread by the action of the "infected" computer user.

Macro viruses have become a common and easily created form of virus. Attackers use an application macro language (such as Visual Basic or VBScript) to create programs that infect documents and templates. After an infected document is opened, the virus is executed and infects the user's application templates. Macros can insert unwanted words, numbers, or phrases into documents or alter command functions. After a macro virus infects a user's application, it can embed itself in all future documents created with the application. The "WM97/Resume.A" virus is a Word macro virus spread via an email message with the subject line "Resume - Janet Simons." If the email recipient clicks on the attachment, the virus deletes all data in the user's computer or mobile device.

Worms

worm: A harmful program that resides in the active memory of the computer and duplicates itself.

Unlike a computer virus, which requires users to spread infected files to other users, a **worm** is a harmful program that resides in the active memory of the computer and duplicates itself. Worms differ from viruses in that they can propagate without human intervention, often sending copies of themselves to other computers by email. A worm is capable of replicating itself on your computer so that it can potentially send out thousands of copies of itself to everyone in your email address book, for example.

The negative impact of a worm attack on an organization's computers can be considerable—lost data and programs, lost productivity due to workers being unable to use their computers, additional lost productivity as workers attempt to recover data and programs, and lots of effort for IT workers to clean up the mess and restore everything to as close to normal as possible. The cost to repair the damage done by each of the Code Red, SirCam, and Melissa worms was estimated to exceed $1 billion, with that of the Conficker, Storm, and ILOVEYOU worms totaling well over $5 billion.[10,11]

Trojan Horses

Trojan horse: A seemingly harmless program in which malicious code is hidden.

A **Trojan horse** is a seemingly harmless program in which malicious code is hidden. A victim on the receiving end of a Trojan horse is usually tricked into opening it because it appears to be useful software from a legitimate source, such as an update for software the user currently has installed on his or her computer. The program's harmful payload might be designed to enable the hacker to destroy hard drives, corrupt files, control the computer remotely, launch attacks against other computers, steal passwords or spy on users by recording keystrokes and transmitting them to a server operated by a third party. A Trojan horse often creates a "backdoor" on a computer that enables an attacker to gain future access to the system and compromise confidential or private information.

A Trojan horse can be delivered via an email attachment, downloaded to a user's computers when he or she visits a Web site, or contracted via a removable media device, such as a DVD or USB memory stick. Once an unsuspecting user executes the program that hosts the Trojan horse, the malicious payload is automatically launched as well—with no telltale signs. Common host programs include screen savers, greeting card systems, and games.

Department of Homeland Security (DHS) officials say they have evidence that harmful Trojan horse malware has been planted in the software that runs much of the U.S. critical infrastructure, including oil and gas pipelines, power transmission grids, water distribution and filtration systems, and even nuclear power generation plants. DHS believes that the malware was planted by the Russians as early as 2011 as a deterrent to a U.S. cyberattack on Russia. The Trojan horse would allow nonauthorized users to control or shut down key components of U.S. infrastructure remotely from their computer or mobile device.[12]

logic bomb: A form of Trojan horse malware that executes when it is triggered by a specific event.

Another type of Trojan horse is a **logic bomb**, which executes when it is triggered by a specific event. For example, logic bombs can be triggered by a change in a particular file, by typing a specific series of keystrokes, or at a specific time or date. Malware attacks employing logic bombs compromised some 32,000 Windows, Unix, and Linux systems at half a dozen South Korean organizations, including three major television broadcasters and two large banks. A component of the attack was "wiper" malware triggered by a logic bomb set to begin overwriting a computer's master boot record at a preset time and day.[13]

Blended Threat

blended threat: A sophisticated threat that combines the features of a virus, worm, Trojan horse, and other malicious code into a single payload.

A **blended threat** is a sophisticated threat that combines the features of a virus, worm, Trojan horse, and other malicious code into a single payload. A blended threat attack might use server and Internet vulnerabilities to initiate and then transmit and spread an attack on an organization's computing devices, using multiple modes to transport itself, including email, IRC (Internet Relay Chat), and file-sharing networks. Rather than launching a narrowly focused attack on specific EXE files, a blended threat might attack multiple EXE files, HTML files, and registry keys simultaneously.

Spam

spam: The use of email systems to send unsolicited email to large numbers of people.

Email **spam** is the use of email systems to send unsolicited email to large numbers of people. Most spam is a form of low-cost commercial advertising, sometimes for questionable products such as pornography, phony get-rich-quick schemes, and worthless stock. Spam is also an extremely inexpensive method of marketing used by many legitimate organizations. For example, a company might send email to a broad cross section of potential customers to announce the release of a new product in an attempt to increase initial sales. However, spam is also used to deliver harmful worms and other malware.

The cost of creating an email campaign for a product or service is several hundred to a few thousand dollars, compared to tens of thousands of dollars for direct-mail campaigns. In addition, email campaigns might take only a couple of weeks (or less) to develop, compared with three months or more for direct-mail campaigns, and the turnaround time for feedback averages 48 hours for email as opposed to weeks for direct mail. However, the benefits of spam to companies may be largely offset by the public's generally negative reaction to receiving unsolicited ads.

Spam forces unwanted and often objectionable material into email boxes, detracts from the ability of recipients to communicate effectively due to full mailboxes and relevant emails being hidden among many unsolicited messages, and costs Internet users and service providers millions of dollars annually. It takes users time to scan and delete spam email, a cost that can add up if they pay for Internet connection charges on an hourly basis (such as at an Internet café). It also costs money for Internet service providers (ISPs) and online services to transmit spam, which is reflected in the rates charged to all subscribers.

There is an even more sinister side to spam—often it is used to entice unsuspecting recipients to take actions that will result in malware being downloaded to their computer. Symantec, a provider of security, storage, and systems management solutions, began noticing multiple instances of short-duration, high-volume spam attacks targeting millions of users. The messages instructed recipients to click on a link to a URL, which, if done, resulted in the Trojan "Infostealer.Dyranges (Dyre)" being downloaded to their computer. This Trojan is known to steal financial information.[14]

The **Controlling the Assault of Non-Solicited Pornography and Marketing (CAN-SPAM) Act** states that it is legal to spam, provided the messages meet a few basic requirements—spammers cannot disguise their identity by using a false return address, the email must include a label specifying that it is an ad or a solicitation, and the email must include a way for recipients to indicate that they do not want future mass mailings. Despite CAN-SPAM and other measures, the percentage of spam in email messages averaged 57 percent in one week in January, 2015, according to Trustwave, an organization that helps businesses protect data and reduce security risk.[15]

Many companies—including Google, Microsoft, and Yahoo!—offer free email services. Spammers often seek to use email accounts from such major, free, and reputable Web-based email service providers, as their spam can be sent at no charge and is less likely to be blocked. Spammers can defeat the registration process of the free email services by launching a coordinated bot attack that can sign up for thousands of email accounts. These accounts are then used by the spammers to send thousands of untraceable email messages for free.

A partial solution to this problem is the use of CAPTCHA to ensure that only humans obtain free accounts. **CAPTCHA (Completely Automated Public Turing Test to Tell Computers and Humans Apart)** software generates and grades tests that humans can pass and all but the most sophisticated computer programs cannot. For example, humans can read the distorted text in Figure 13.1, but simple computer programs cannot.

Controlling the Assault of Non-Solicited Pornography and Marketing (CAN-SPAM) Act: An act that states that it is legal to spam, provided the messages meet a few basic requirements.

CAPTCHA (Completely Automated Public Turing Test to Tell Computers and Humans Apart): Software that generates and grades tests that humans can pass all but the most sophisticated computer programs cannot.

FIGURE 13.1

Example of CAPTCHA
CAPTCHA is used to distinguish humans from automated bots.

Distributed Denial-of-Service Attacks

A **distributed denial-of-service (DDoS) attack** is one in which a malicious hacker takes over computers via the Internet and causes them to flood a target site with demands for data and other small tasks. A distributed denial-of-service attack does not involve infiltration of the targeted system. Instead, it keeps the target so busy responding to a stream of automated requests that legitimate users cannot get in—the Internet equivalent of dialing a telephone number repeatedly so that all other callers hear a busy signal (see Figure 13.2). The targeted machine essentially holds the line open while waiting for a reply that never comes; eventually, the requests exhaust all resources of the target.

distributed denial-of-service (DDoS) attack: An attack in which a malicious hacker takes over computers via the Internet and causes them to flood a target site with demands for data and other small tasks.

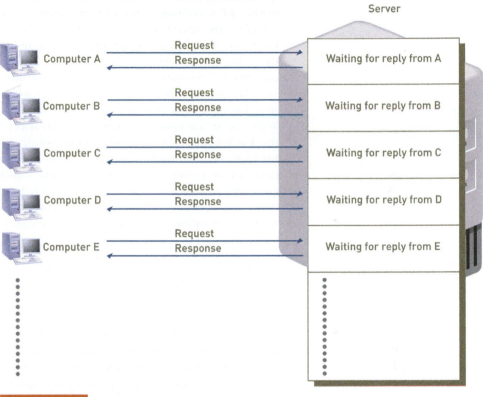

FIGURE 13.2

Distributed denial-of-service attack

A DDoS attack floods a target site with demands for data and other small tasks.

The software to initiate a denial-of-service attack is simple to use, and many DDoS tools are readily available at a variety of hacker sites. In a DDoS attack, a tiny program is downloaded surreptitiously from the attacker's computer to dozens, hundreds, or even thousands of computers all over the world. The term **botnet** is used to describe a large group of such computers, which are controlled from one or more remote locations by hackers, without the knowledge or consent of their owners. The collective processing capacity of some botnets exceeds that of the world's most powerful supercomputers. Based on a command by the attacker or at a preset time, the botnet computers (called **zombies**) go into action, each sending a simple request for access to the target site again and again—dozens of times per second. The target computers become so overwhelmed by requests for service that legitimate users are unable to get through to the target computer.

botnet: A term used to describe a large group of computers, that are controlled from one or more remote locations by hackers, without the knowledge or consent of their owners.

zombie: A computer that has been taken over by a hacker to be used as part of a botnet.

Software company Arbor Networks follows DDoS attacks closely and believes that such attacks are getting more sophisticated and are targeting an increasing number of organizations. The company estimates that over 200 of the reported attacks in 2015 generated 100 gigabits per second (Gbps) of traffic, with the largest attack generating traffic at a rate of 500 Gbps—enough to disrupt the entire network of an Internet service provider.[16]

Botnets are also frequently used to distribute spam and malicious code. The Grum botnet was first detected in 2008 and operated until 2012 when it was brought down by cybercrime fighters. Grum infected several hundred thousand computers around the world. It generated prodigious amounts of spam advertising cheap pharmaceutical products. At its peak, Grum is estimated to have been responsible for 35 percent of the world's spam.[17]

Rootkit

rootkit: A set of programs that enables its user to gain administrator-level access to a computer without the end user's consent or knowledge.

A **rootkit** is a set of programs that enables its user to gain administrator-level access to a computer without the end user's consent or knowledge. Once installed, the attacker can gain full control of the system and even obscure the presence of the rootkit from legitimate system administrators. Attackers can use the rootkit to execute files, access logs, monitor user activity, and change the computer's configuration. Rootkits are one part of a type of blended threat that consists of a dropper, a loader, and a rootkit. The dropper code gets the rootkit installation started and can be activated by clicking on a link to a malicious Web site in an email or opening an infected PDF file. The dropper launches the loader program and then deletes itself. The loader loads the rootkit into memory; at that point, the computer has been compromised. Rootkits are designed so cleverly that it is difficult even to discover if they are installed on a computer. The fundamental problem with trying to detect a rootkit is that the operating system currently running cannot be trusted to provide valid test results. The following are some symptoms of rootkit infections:

- The computer locks up or fails to respond to input from the keyboard or mouse.
- The screen saver changes without any action on the part of the user.
- The taskbar disappears.
- Network activities function extremely slowly.

When it is determined that a computer has been infected with a rootkit, there is little to do but reformat the disk; reinstall the operating system and all applications; and reconfigure the user's settings, such as mapped drives. This can take hours, and the user may be left with a basic working machine, but all locally held data and settings may be lost.

The "2012 rootkit virus" is a nasty piece of malware that deletes information from a computer and makes it impossible to run some applications, such as Microsoft Word. The longer the rootkit is present, the more damage it causes. The virus asks users to install what appears to be a legitimate update to their antivirus software or some other application. By the time the user sees the prompt to install the software, it is too late, the computer has already been infected by the rootkit.[18]

Advanced Persistent Threat

advanced persistent threat (APT): A network attack in which an intruder gains access to a network and stays there—undetected—with the intention of stealing data over a long period of time.

An **advanced persistent threat (APT)** is a network attack in which an intruder gains access to a network and stays there—undetected—with the intention of stealing data over a long period of time. Attackers in an APT must continuously rewrite code and employ sophisticated evasion techniques to avoid discovery. APT attacks target organizations with high-value information, such as banks and financial institutions, government agencies, and insurance companies with the goal of stealing data rather than disrupting services.[19] An APT attack advances through the following five phases:

1. Reconnaissance—The intruder begins by conducting reconnaissance on the network to gain useful information about the target (security software

installed, computing resources connected to the network, number of users).

2. Incursion—The attacker next gains incursion to the network at a low level to avoid setting off any alarms or suspicion. Some form of spear-fishing may be employed in this phase. Once incursion to the target has been gained, the attacker establishes a back door, or a means of accessing a computer program that bypasses security mechanisms.

3. Discovery—The intruder now begins a discovery process to gather valid user credentials (especially administrative ones) and move laterally across the network, installing more back doors. These back doors enable the attacker to install bogus utilities for distributing malware that remains hidden in plain sight.

4. Capture—The attacker is now ready to access unprotected or compromised systems and capture information over a long period of time.

5. Export—Captured data is then exported back to the attacker's home base for analysis and/or used to commit fraud and other crimes.[20]

Although APT attacks are difficult to identify, the theft of data can never be completely invisible. Detecting anomalies in outbound data is perhaps the best way for an administrator to discover that the network has been the target of an APT attack.

The hacker group Carbanak is thought to have stolen over $1 billion from banks in China, Russia, the Ukraine, and the United States. The group's modus operandi includes use of an APT that initially hooks its victims using spear-fishing emails imitating legitimate banking communications. The gang performs a reconnaissance phase to gather data about system administrators and uses this information to navigate through various bank systems, including ATMs, financial accounts, and money processing services. Once access to these systems is gained, the hackers steal money by transferring funds to accounts in China and the United States. They have even programmed ATM machines to dispense money at specific times for collection by money mules.[21]

Phishing

phishing: The act of fraudulently using email to try to get the recipient to reveal personal data.

Phishing is the act of fraudulently using email to try to get the recipient to reveal personal data. In a phishing scam, con artists send legitimate-looking emails urging the recipient to take action to avoid a negative consequence or to receive a reward. The requested action may involve clicking on a link to a Web site or opening an email attachment. These emails, such as the one shown in Figure 13.3, lead consumers to counterfeit Web sites designed to trick them into divulging personal data or to download malware onto their computers.

The volume of global phishing attacks is alarming. It is estimated that about 156 million phishing emails are sent each day, with 16 million of those successfully evading email filters. Of those, roughly 50 percent (or 8 million) are opened, and 800,000 recipients per day click on malicious URL links contained in the emails.[22]

Savvy users often become suspicious and refuse to enter data into the fake Web sites; however, sometimes just accessing the Web site can trigger an automatic and unnoticeable download of malicious software to a computer. Indeed, the percentage of malicious URLs in unsolicited emails surged to an average of 10 per cent in 2014.[23] As one might guess, financial institutions such as Bank of America, Citibank, Chase, MasterCard, Visa, and Wells Fargo are among the Web sites that phishers spoof most frequently.

The University of Connecticut was recently hit by two phishing attacks over a period on five weeks. The first phishing attack appeared to come from Support—University Information Technology Services. The subject line was "email quota," and the message informed recipients that their email quota

FIGURE **13.3**
Example of phishing email
Phishing attacks attempt to get the recipient to reveal personal data.

had been exceeded and asked them to click on a link to revalidate their email account.[24] The second phishing attack had the subject line "UCONN.EDU ACCOUNT LOCK WARNING." The message indicated that the recipient's email account was being used to send bulk email by spammers, and it asked recipients to click on a link to change their password.[25] Victims who clicked on either link were asked to enter their user logon id and password, and if they did so, they provided the necessary information to compromise their email account.

spear-phishing: A variation of phishing in which the phisher sends fraudulent emails to a certain organization's employees.

    Spear-phishing is a variation of phishing in which the phisher sends fraudulent emails to a certain organization's employees. It is known as spear-phishing because the attack is much more precise and narrow, like the tip of a spear. The phony emails are designed to look like they came from high-level executives within the organization. Employees are directed to a fake Web site and then asked to enter personal information, such as name, Social Security number, and network passwords. Botnets have become the primary means for distributing phishing scams.

    In early 2016, more than three dozen large and small organizations were victimized by spear-phishing attacks that were designed to obtain data from employee tax records. Many of these attacks spoofed the email address of the CEO, CFO, or someone else of authority within the organization, prompting many employees to comply with the request.[26]

Smishing and Vishing

smishing: Another variation of phishing that involves the use of Short Message Service (SMS) texting.

    Smishing is another variation of phishing that involves the use of texting. In a smishing scam, people receive a legitimate-looking text message telling them to call a specific phone number or log on to a Web site. This is often done under the guise that there is a problem with their bank account or credit card that requires immediate attention. However, the phone number or Web site is phony and is used to trick unsuspecting victims into providing personal information such as a bank account number, personal identification number, or credit card number, which can then be used to steal money from victims' bank accounts, charge purchases on their credit cards, or open new accounts. In some cases, if victims log on to a Web site, malicious software is downloaded onto their smartphones, providing criminals with access to information stored on the phones. The number of smishing scams typically increases around the holidays as more people use their smartphones to make online purchases.

vishing: Similar to smishing except that the victims receive a voice mail message telling them to call a phone number or access a Web site.

Vishing is similar to smishing except that the victims receive a voice mail message telling them to call a phone number or access a Web site. One recent vishing campaign captured the payment card information of an estimated 250 Americans per day. In the attack, users were sent a message that their ATM card had been deactivated. The users were prompted to call a phone number to reactivate the card by entering their card number and their PIN—data that, of course, is recorded and then used by the criminals to withdraw money from the accounts.[27]

Financial institutions, credit card companies, and other organizations whose customers may be targeted by criminals in this manner should be on the alert for phishing, smishing, and vishing scams. They must be prepared to act quickly and decisively, without alarming their customers if such a scam is detected. Recommended action steps for institutions and organizations include the following:

- Companies should educate their customers about the dangers of phishing, smishing, and vishing through letters, recorded messages for those calling into the company's call center, and articles on the company's Web site.
- Call center service employees should be trained to detect customer complaints that indicate a scam is being perpetrated. They should attempt to capture key pieces of information, such as the callback number the customer was directed to use, details of the phone message or text message, and the type of information requested.
- Customers should be notified immediately if a scam occurs. This can be done via a recorded message for customers phoning the call center, working with local media to place a news article in papers serving the area of the attack, placing a banner on the institution's Web page, and even displaying posters in bank drive-through and lobby areas.
- If it is determined that the calls are originating from within the United States, companies should report the scam to the Federal Bureau of Investigation (FBI).
- Institutions can also try to notify the telecommunications carrier for the particular numbers to request that they shut down the phone numbers victims are requested to call.[28]

Identity Theft

identity theft: The theft of personal information, which is then used without the owner's permission, often to commit fraud or other crimes.

Identity theft is the theft of personal information, which is then used without the owner's permission. Often, stolen personal identification information, such as a person's name, Social Security number, or credit card number, is used to commit fraud or other crimes. Thieves may use a consumer's credit card number to charge items to that person's account, use identification information to apply for a new credit card or a loan in a consumer's name, or use a consumer's name and Social Security number to receive government benefits. Thieves also often sell personal identification information on the black market.[29]

data breach: The unintended release of sensitive data or the access of sensitive data by unauthorized individuals.

A **data breach** is the unintended release of sensitive data or the access of sensitive data by unauthorized individuals, often resulting in identify theft. Table 13.3 lists the five largest U.S. data breaches, all of which involved personal identification information.[30]

Some 37 million customer records of Ashley Madison (a Web site for married people seeking other married people with whom to have affairs) were

TABLE 13.3 Five largest data breaches in the United States

Organization	Year	Number of Records Compromised	Data Stolen
Heartland Payment Systems	2008	130 million	Credit and debit card data
Target	2013	110 million	Credit and debit card data
Sony Online Entertainment Systems	2011	102 million	Login credentials, names, addresses, phone numbers, email addresses
Anthem	2015	80 million	Names, addresses, dates of birth, Social Security numbers, health insurance ID numbers
National Archives and Records Administration	2008	76 million	Names and contact information, Social Security numbers

compromised in an attack in 2015. Names and addresses were posted publicly, resulting in several lawsuits against the company for failing to safeguard the personal information of the plaintiffs.[31]

To reduce the potential for online credit card fraud, most e-commerce Web sites use some form of encryption technology to protect information as it comes in from the consumer. Some sites also verify the address submitted online against the one the issuing bank has on file, although the merchant may inadvertently throw out legitimate orders as a result—for example, a consumer might place a legitimate order but request shipment to a different address because it is a gift. Another security technique is to ask for a card verification value (CVV), the three-digit number above the signature panel on the back of a credit card. This technique makes it impossible to make purchases with a credit card number stolen online. An additional security option is transaction-risk scoring software, which keeps track of a customer's historical shopping patterns and notes deviations from the norm. For example, say that you have never been to a casino and your credit card information is being used at Caesar's Palace at 2 am. The transaction-risk score would go up dramatically, so much so that the transaction would likely be declined.

Cyberespionage

cyberespionage: The deployment of malware that secretly steals data in the computer systems of organizations, such as government agencies, military contractors, political organizations, and manufacturing firms.

Cyberespionage involves the deployment of malware that secretly steals data in the computer systems of organizations, such as government agencies, military contractors, political organizations, and manufacturing firms. The type of data most frequently targeted includes data that can provide an unfair competitive advantage to the perpetrator. This data is typically not public knowledge and may even be protected via patent, copyright, or trade secret. High-value data includes the following:

- Sales, marketing, and new product development plans, schedules, and budgets
- Details about product designs and innovative processes
- Employee personal information
- Customer and client data
- Sensitive information about partners and partner agreements

Tensions have long simmered between the China and the United States over alleged cyberattacks. United States experts claim cyberespionage has helped China to accelerate the research and development process and cut years off the time for that country to acquire new technology in a variety of industries. Alleged targets have included aluminum and steel producers, a company that designs nuclear power plants, a solar panel manufacturer, and an aircraft manufacturer. Meanwhile, China's Foreign Ministry portrays the

United States as a hypocrite that engages in cyberespionage by conducting cybertheft, wiretapping, and surveillance activities against Chinese government departments, companies, and universities. After years of discussion and behind the scenes efforts, President Obama and Chinese President Xi announced in 2015 that the two nations had agreed to initial norms of cyber-activities with the two nations pledging each will avoid conducting cybertheft of intellectual property for commercial gain. It remains to be seen how much of an impact this agreement will have.[32,33]

Cyberterrorism

cyberterrorism: The intimidation of government or civilian population by using information technology to disable critical national infrastructure (e.g., energy, transportation, financial, law enforcement, emergency response) to achieve political, religious, or ideological goals.

Cyberterrorism is the intimidation of government or civilian population by using information technology to disable critical national infrastructure (e.g., energy, transportation, financial, law enforcement, emergency response) to achieve political, religious, or ideological goals. Cyberterrorism is an increasing concern for countries and organizations around the globe. Indeed in a statement released by the White House in early 2015, President Obama said, "Cyberthreats pose one the gravest national security dangers that the United States faces."[34]

Department of Homeland Security (DHS): A large federal agency with more than 240,000 employees and a budget of almost $65 billion whose goal is to provide for a "safer, more secure America, which is resilient against terrorism and other potential threats."

The **Department of Homeland Security (DHS)** is a large federal agency with more than 240,000 employees and a budget of almost $65 billion whose goal is to provide for a "safer, more secure America, which is resilient against terrorism and other potential threats." The agency was formed in 2002 when 22 different federal departments and agencies were combined into a unified, integrated cabinet agency.[35] The agency's Office of Cybersecurity and Communications resides within the National Protection and Programs Directorate and is responsible for enhancing the security, resilience, and reliability of U.S. cyber and communications infrastructure. It works to prevent or minimize disruptions to critical information infrastructure in order to protect the public, the economy, and government services.[36] The Department of Homeland Security Web site (*www.dhs.gov*) provides a link that enables users to report cyber incidents. Incident reports go to the US-CERT Incident Reporting System, which assists analysts at the **U.S. Computer Emergency Readiness Team (US-CERT)** (a partnership between the Department of Homeland Security and the public and private sectors) in providing timely handling of security incidents as well as in conducting improved analysis of such incidents.[37] Established in 2003 to protect the nation's Internet infrastructure against cyberattacks, US-CERT serves as a clearinghouse for information on new viruses, worms, and other computer security topics.

U.S. Computer Emergency Readiness Team (US-CERT): A partnership between the Department of Homeland Security and the public and private sectors; established to provide timely handling of security incidents as well as conducting improved analysis of such incidents.

Cyberterrorists try on a daily basis to gain unauthorized access to a number of important and sensitive sites, such as the computers at the British, French, Israeli, and U.S. foreign intelligence agencies; North American Aerospace Defense Command (NORAD); and numerous government ministries and private companies around the world. In particular, companies in the oil and gas industry are seen as high-value targets. Some cyberterrorists are interested in taking control over the flow of oil and natural gas in computer-controlled refineries and the movement of oil through pipelines. This could result in devastating consequences—with oil and gas being cut off from freezing populations in the dead of winter or skyrocketing prices at the gasoline pumps.

In late 2015, Cyberterrorists attacked the two electric utility companies in western Ukraine, causing a three-hour power outage affecting some 80,000 customers. Not only did the hackers cut the power, they also froze the data displayed on the screens of plant operators so they could not view the changing plant conditions; thus, fooling the operators into believing power was still flowing. To prolong the outage, the attackers also launched a telephone denial-of-service attack against the utility's call center to prevent customers from reporting the outage—the center's phone system was flooded with bogus calls to prevent legitimate callers from getting through. Once operators became aware of the outage, the attackers activated KillDisk malware that rendered infected servers and systems unusable. The operators' machines were completely destroyed by the malware.[38]

Federal Laws for Prosecuting Computer Attacks

Over the years, several laws have been enacted to help prosecute those responsible for computer-related crime; these are summarized in Table 13.4. For example, Section 814 of the USA Patriot Act defines cyberterrorism as any hacking attempts designed to gain unauthorized access to a protected computer, which, if successful, would cause a person an aggregate loss greater than $5,000; adversely affect someone's medical examination, diagnosis, or treatment; cause a person to be injured; cause a threat to public health or safety; or cause damage to a governmental computer that is used as a tool to administer justice, national defense, or national security.[39] Those convicted of cyberterrorism are subject to a prison term of 5 to 20 years. (The $5,000 threshold is quite easy to exceed, and, as a result, many young people who have been involved in what they consider to be minor computer pranks have found themselves meeting the criteria to be tried as cyberterrorists.)

TABLE 13.4 Federal laws that address computer crime

Federal Law	Subject Area
Computer Fraud and Abuse Act (U.S. Code Title 18, Section 1030)	Addresses fraud and related activities in association with computers, including the following: • Accessing a computer without authorization or exceeding authorized access • Transmitting a program, code, or command that causes harm to a computer • Trafficking of computer passwords • Threatening to cause damage to a protected computer
Fraud and Related Activity in Connection with Access Devices Statute (U.S. Code Title 18, Section 1029)	Covers false claims regarding unauthorized use of credit cards
Identity Theft and Assumption Deterrence Act (U.S. Code Title 18, Section 1028)	Makes identity theft a federal crime, with penalties of up to 15 years' of imprisonment and a maximum fine of $250,000
Stored Wire and Electronic Communications and Transactional Records Access Statutes (U.S. Code Title 18, Chapter 121)	Focuses on unlawful access to stored communications to obtain, alter, or prevent authorized access to a wire or electronic communication while it is in electronic storage
USA Patriot Act	Defines cyberterrorism and associated penalties

Critical Thinking Exercise

Hiring a Black Hat Hacker

You are a member of the Human Resources Department of a software manufacturer that has several products and annual revenue in excess of $500 million. You're on the phone with the manager of software development who has made a request to hire a notorious black hat hacker to probe your company's software products in an attempt to identify any vulnerabilities. The reasoning is that if anyone can find a vulnerability in your software, she can. This will give your firm a head start on developing patches to fix the problems before anyone can exploit them. You feel uneasy about hiring people with criminal records and connections to unsavory members of the hacker/cracker community and are unsure if you should approve the hire.

Review Questions

1. What is the difference between a black hat hacker and a white hat hacker?
2. What potential harm could this hacker do to your software products?

Critical Thinking Questions

1. Provide three good reasons to hire this individual. Provide three good reasons not to hire this individual.
2. How would you respond to this request? Why?

Now that we have discussed various types of computer exploits, the people who perpetrate these exploits, and the laws under which they can be prosecuted, we will discuss how organizations can take steps to implement a trustworthy computing environment to defend against such attacks.

Implementing Secure, Private, Reliable Computing

Organizations worldwide are increasingly demanding methods of computing that deliver secure, private, and reliable computing experiences based on sound business practices. Software and hardware manufacturers, consultants, and system designers and developers all understand that this is a priority for their customers.

A strong security program begins by assessing threats to the organization's computers and network, identifying actions that address the most serious vulnerabilities, and educating end users about the risks involved and the actions they must take to prevent a security incident. An organization's IS security group must lead the effort to prevent security breaches by implementing security policies and procedures, as well as effectively employing available hardware and software tools. However, no security system is perfect, so systems and procedures must be monitored to detect a possible intrusion. If an intrusion occurs, there must be a clear reaction plan that addresses notification, evidence protection, activity log maintenance, containment, eradication, and recovery.

Risk Assessment

risk assessment: The process of assessing security-related risks to an organization's computers and networks from both internal and external threats.

Risk assessment is the process of assessing security-related risks to an organization's computers and networks from both internal and external threats. Such threats can prevent an organization from meeting its key business objectives. The goal of risk assessment is to identify which investments of time and resources will best protect the organization from its most likely and serious threats. In the context of an IS risk assessment, an asset is any hardware, software, information system, network, or database that is used by the organization to achieve its business objectives. A loss event is any occurrence that has a negative impact on an asset, such as a computer contracting a virus or a Web site undergoing a distributed denial-of-service attack. The steps in a general security risk assessment process are as follows:

- **Step 1**. Identify the set of IS assets about which the organization is most concerned. Priority is typically given to those assets that support the organization's mission and the meeting of its primary business goals.
- **Step 2**. Identify the loss events or the risks or threats that could occur, such as a distributed denial-of-service attack or insider fraud.
- **Step 3**. Assess the frequency of events or the likelihood of each potential threat; some threats, such as insider fraud, are more likely to occur than others.

- **Step 4**. Determine the impact of each threat occurring. Would the threat have a minor impact on the organization, or could it keep the organization from carrying out its mission for a lengthy period of time?
- **Step 5**. Determine how each threat can be mitigated so that it becomes much less likely to occur or, if it does occur, has less of an impact on the organization. For example, installing virus protection on all computers makes it much less likely for a computer to contract a virus. Due to time and resource limitations, most organizations choose to focus on just those threats that have a high (relative to all other threats) probability of occurrence and a high (relative to all other threats) impact. In other words, first address those threats that are likely to occur and that would have a high negative impact on the organization.
- **Step 6**. Assess the feasibility of implementing the mitigation options.
- **Step 7**. Perform a cost-benefit analysis to ensure that your efforts will be cost effective.

   No amount of resources can guarantee a perfect security system, so organizations must balance the risk of a security breach with the cost of preventing one. The concept of **reasonable assurance** in connection with IS security recognizes that managers must use their judgment to ensure that the cost of control does not exceed the system's benefits or the risks involved.

- **Step 8**. Make the decision on whether or not to implement a particular countermeasure. If you decide against implementing a particular countermeasure, you need to reassess if the threat is truly serious and, if so, identify a less costly countermeasure.

The general security risk assessment process—and the results of that process—will vary by organization. Table 13.5 illustrates a risk assessment for a hypothetical organization.

reasonable assurance: The IS security concept that recognizes that managers must use their judgment to ensure that the cost of control does not exceed the system's benefits or the risks involved.

TABLE 13.5 Risk assessment for a hypothetical company

Adverse Event	Business Objective Threatened	Threat (Estimated Frequency of Event)	Vulnerability (Likelihood of Success of This Threat)	Estimated Cost of a Successful Attack	Risk = Threat × Vulnerability × Estimated Cost	Relative Priority to Be Fixed
Distributed denial-of-service attack	24/7 operation of a retail Web site	3 per year	25%	$500,000	$375,000	1
Email attachment with harmful worm	Rapid and reliable communications among employees and suppliers	1,000 per year	0.05%	$200,000	$100,000	2
Harmful virus	Employees' use of personal productivity software	2,000 per year	0.04%	$50,000	$40,000	3
Invoice and payment fraud	Reliable cash flow	1 per year	10%	$200,000	$20,000	4

A completed risk assessment identifies the most dangerous threats to a company and helps focus security efforts on the areas of highest payoff.

Establishing a Security Policy

A security policy defines an organization's security requirements, as well as the controls and sanctions needed to meet those requirements. A good security policy delineates responsibilities and the behavior expected of members of the organization. A security policy outlines *what* needs to be done but not *how* to do it. The details of *how* to accomplish the goals of the policy are typically provided in separate documents and procedure guidelines.

The SANS (SysAdmin, Audit, Network, Security) Institute's Web site (*www.sans.org*) offers a number of security-related policy templates that can help an organization to quickly develop effective security policies. The templates and other security policy information, which can be found at *www. sans.org/security-resources/policies*, and provide guidelines for creating various policies, including acceptable use policy, email policy, password protection policy, remote access policy, and software installation policy.

Whenever possible, automated system rules should mirror an organization's written policies. Automated system rules can often be put into practice using the configuration options in a software program. For example, if a written policy states that passwords must be changed every 30 days, then all systems should be configured to enforce this policy automatically. However, users will often attempt to circumvent security policies or simply ignore them altogether.

Many times system administrators believe that the default username and passwords for specific network devices are generally not known. This is not true, in fact, there are Web sites that provide the default username and password combinations for many vendors' products. Default usernames and passwords should always be changed.

A growing area of concern for security experts is the use of wireless devices to access corporate email; store confidential data; and run critical applications, such as inventory management and sales force automation. Mobile devices such as smartphones can be susceptible to viruses and worms. However, the primary security threat for mobile devices continues to be loss or theft of the device. Wary companies have begun to include special security requirements for mobile devices as part of their security policies. In some cases, users of laptops and mobile devices must use a virtual private network (a method employing encryption to provide secure access to a remote computer over the Internet) to gain access to their corporate network.

Educating Employees and Contract Workers

Creating and enhancing user awareness of security policies is an ongoing security priority for companies. Employees and contract workers must be educated about the importance of security so that they will be motivated to understand and follow security policies. This can often be accomplished by discussing recent security incidents that affected the organization. Users must understand that they are a key part of the security system and that they have certain responsibilities. For example, users must help protect an organization's information systems and data by doing the following:

- Guarding their passwords to protect against unauthorized access to their accounts
- Prohibiting others from using their passwords
- Applying strict access controls (file and directory permissions) to protect data from disclosure or destruction
- Reporting all unusual activity to the organization's IT security group
- Taking care to ensure that portable computing and data storage devices are protected (hundreds of thousands of laptops are lost or stolen per year)

Table 13.6 provides a simple self-assessment security test that employees and contractors alike should be asked to complete.

TABLE 13.6 Self-assessment security test

Security Assessment Question
Do you have the most current version of your operating system installed?
Do you have the most current version of firewall, antivirus, and malware software installed?
Do you install updates to all your software when you receive notice that a new update is available?
Do you use different, strong passwords for each of your accounts and applications—a minimum of 10 characters with a mix of capital and lower case letters, numbers, and special characters?
Are you familiar with and do you follow your organization's policies in regard to accessing corporate Web sites and applications from your home or remote locations (typically involves use of VPN)?
Have you set the encryption method to WPA2 and changed the default name and password on your home wireless router?
When using a free, public wireless network, do you avoid checking your email or accessing Web sites requiring a username and password?
Do you refrain from clicking on a URL in an email from someone you do not know?
Do you back up critical files to a separate device at least once a week?
Are you familiar with and do you follow your organization's policies in regard to storing personal or confidential data on your device?
Does your device have a security passcode that must be entered before it accepts further input?
Have you installed Locate My Device or similar software in case your device is lost or stolen?
Do you make sure not to leave your device unattended in a public place where it can be easily stolen?
Have you reviewed and do you understand the privacy settings that control who can see or read what you do on Facebook and other social media sites?

Prevention

No organization can ever be completely secure from attack. The key is to implement a layered security solution to make computer break-ins so difficult that an attacker eventually gives up. In a layered solution, if an attacker breaks through one layer of security, another layer must then be overcome. These layers of protective measures are explained in more detail in the following sections.

Implementing a Corporate Firewall

firewall: A system of software, hardware, or a combination of both that stands guard between an organization's internal network and the Internet and limits network access based on the organization's access policy.

Installation of a corporate firewall is the most common security precaution taken by businesses. A **firewall** is a system of software, hardware, or a combination of both that stands guard between an organization's internal network and the Internet and limits network access based on the organization's access policy.

Any Internet traffic that is not explicitly permitted into the internal network is denied entry through a firewall. Similarly, most firewalls can be configured so that internal network users can be blocked from gaining access to certain Web sites based on content such as sex and violence. Most firewalls can also be configured to block instant messaging, access to newsgroups, and other Internet activities.

Software vendors Agnitum, Check Point, Comodo, Kaspersky, and Total Defense provide some of the top-rated firewall software used to protect personal computers. Their software provide antivirus, firewall, antispam, parental control, and phishing protection capabilities and sell for $30 to $80 per single user license.

next-generation firewall (NGFW): A hardware- or software-based network security system that is able to detect and block sophisticated attacks by filtering network traffic dependent on the packet contents.

A **next-generation firewall (NGFW)** is a hardware- or software-based network security system that is able to detect and block sophisticated attacks by filtering network traffic dependent on the packet contents. Compared to first- and second-generation firewalls, a NGFW goes deeper to inspect the payload of packets and match sequences of bytes for harmful activities, such as known vulnerabilities, exploit attacks, viruses, and malware.

Utilizing a Security Dashboard

Many organizations use security dashboard software to provide a comprehensive display of all vital data related to an organization's security defenses, including threats, exposures, policy compliance, and incident alerts. The purpose of a security dashboard is to reduce the effort required to monitor and identify threats in time to take action. Data that appears in a security dashboard can come from a variety of sources, including security audits, firewalls, applications, servers, and other hardware and software devices. Figure 13.4 is a screenshot from ISACA showing an example of a security dashboard.

No	Operation-level Scorecard: KPI Control/KPI	Target	Actual	Status	Remarks
1	Number of violations of segregation of duties	0	3		
2	Number of users who do not comply with password standards	Max. 2	7		
3	Percentage of suspected and actual violations	Max. 5	7		
4	Pecentage of critical assets covered by internal/external penetration tests	Min. 95	98		
5	Number of computers with patches behind agreed-upon SLA	Max. 2	1		
6	Number of outdated policies, procedures, standards and guidelines	Max. 4	5		
7	Number of internal audits scheduled	Min. 2	2		
8	Number of penetration tests not performed as required for the quarter	Max. 1	0		
9	Percentage of agents/employees trained on information security policies and procedures as part of induction	100	90		
10	Number of corrective/preventive actions taken based on analysis of logs	Min. 5	10		
11	Percentage of changes carried out as per change control procedure	100	90		

Note: Target and actual amounts are hypothetical figures for the purpose of this example. Categorization into green, amber and red is done on a predefined basis.

FIGURE 13.4
Security dashboard
A security dashboard provides a comprehensive display of all vital data related to an organization's security defenses.
Source: ISACA

Algoma Central Corporation is a leading Canadian shipping company, owning and operating the largest Canadian flag fleet of dry-bulk carriers and product tankers operating on the Great Lakes—St. Lawrence Seaway system. The firm recently implemented a security dashboard from Avaap, Inc., to improve access to security information and alleviate the complexity of managing security data for its shipping operations.[40]

Installing Antivirus Software on Personal Computers

antivirus software: Software that scans a computer's memory, disk drives, and USB ports regularly for viruses.

virus signature: A sequence of bytes that indicates the presence of a specific virus.

Antivirus software should be installed on each user's personal computer to scan a computer's memory and disk drives regularly for viruses. Antivirus software scans for a specific sequence of bytes, known as a **virus signature**, that indicates the presence of a specific virus. If it finds a virus, the antivirus software informs the user, and it may clean, delete, or quarantine any files, directories, or disks affected by the malicious code. Good antivirus software checks vital system files when the system is booted up, monitors the system continuously for virus-like activity, scans disks, scans memory when a program is run, checks programs when they are downloaded, and scans email attachments before they are opened. Two of the most widely used antivirus software products are Norton AntiVirus from Symantec and Personal Firewall from McAfee.

According to US-CERT, most of the virus and worm attacks use already known malware programs. Thus, it is crucial that antivirus software be continually updated with the latest virus signatures. In most corporations, the network administrator is responsible for monitoring network security Web sites frequently and downloading updated antivirus software as needed. Many antivirus vendors recommend—and provide for—automatic and frequent updates. Unfortunately, antivirus software is not able to identify and block all viruses.

Implementing Safeguards against Attacks by Malicious Insiders

User accounts that remain active after employees leave a company are another potential security risk. To reduce the threat of attack by malicious insiders, IS staff must promptly delete the computer accounts, login IDs, and passwords of departing employees and contractors.

Organizations also need to define employee roles carefully and separate key responsibilities properly, so that a single person is not responsible for accomplishing a task that has high security implications. For example, it would not make sense to allow an employee to initiate as well as approve purchase orders. That would allow an employee to input large invoices on behalf of a dishonest vendor, approve the invoices for payment, and then disappear from the company to split the money with that vendor. In addition to separating duties, many organizations frequently rotate people in sensitive positions to prevent potential insider crimes.

Another important safeguard is to create roles and user accounts so that users have the authority to perform their responsibilities and nothing more. For example, members of the Finance Department should have different authorizations from members of the Human Resources Department. An accountant should not be able to review the pay and attendance records of an employee, and a member of the Human Resources Department should not know how much was spent to modernize a piece of equipment. Even within one department, not all members should be given the same capabilities. Within the Finance Department, for example, some users may be able to approve invoices for payment, but others may only be able to enter them. An effective system administrator will identify the similarities among users and create profiles associated with these groups.

Addressing the Most Critical Internet Security Threats

The overwhelming majority of successful computer attacks take advantage of well-known vulnerabilities. Computer attackers know that many organizations are slow to fix problems, which makes scanning the Internet for vulnerable systems an effective attack strategy. The rampant and destructive spread of worms, such as Blaster, Slammer, and Code Red, was made possible by the exploitation of known but unpatched vulnerabilities. US-CERT regularly updates a summary of the most frequent, high-impact vulnerabilities being reported to them. You can read this summary at *www.us-cert.gov/current*. The actions required to address these issues include installing a known patch to the software and keeping applications and operating systems up-to-date. Those responsible for computer security must make it a priority to prevent attacks using these vulnerabilities.

Conducting Periodic IT Security Audits

security audit: A careful and thorough analysis that evaluates whether an organization has a well-considered security policy in place and if it is being followed.

Another important prevention tool is a **security audit** that evaluates whether an organization has a well-considered security policy in place and if it is being followed. For example, if a policy says that all users must change their passwords every 30 days, the audit must check how well that policy is being implemented. The audit should also review who has access to particular systems and data and what level of authority each user has. It is not unusual for an audit to reveal that too many people have access to critical data and that many people have capabilities beyond those needed to perform their jobs. One result of a good audit is a list of items that needs to be addressed in order to ensure that the security policy is being met.

A thorough security audit should also test system safeguards to ensure that they are operating as intended. Such tests might include trying the default system passwords that are active when software is first received from the vendor. The goal of such a test is to ensure that all such known passwords have been changed.

Some organizations will also perform a penetration test of their defenses. This entails assigning individuals to try to break through the measures and identify vulnerabilities that still need to be addressed. The individuals used for this test are knowledgeable and are likely to take unique approaches in testing the security measures.

Detection

intrusion detection system (IDS): Software and/or hardware that monitors system and network resources and activities and notifies network security personnel when it detects network traffic that attempts to circumvent the security measures of a networked computer environment.

Even when preventive measures are implemented, no organization is completely secure from a determined attack. Thus, organizations should implement detection systems to catch intruders in the act. Organizations often employ an intrusion detection system to minimize the impact of intruders.

An **intrusion detection system (IDS)** is software and/or hardware that monitors system and network resources and activities and notifies network security personnel when it detects network traffic that attempts to circumvent the security measures of a networked computer environment (see Figure 13.5). Such activities usually signal an attempt to breach the integrity of the system or to limit the availability of network resources.

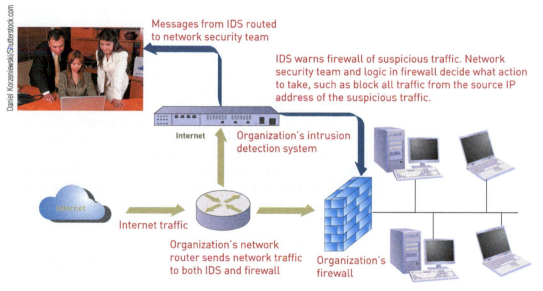

Messages from IDS routed to network security team

IDS warns firewall of suspicious traffic. Network security team and logic in firewall decide what action to take, such as block all traffic from the source IP address of the suspicious traffic.

Internet

Organization's intrusion detection system

Internet traffic

Organization's network router sends network traffic to both IDS and firewall

Organization's firewall

Organization's internal network

Daniel Korzeniewski/Shutterstock.com

FIGURE 13.5
Intrusion detection system
An IDS notifies network security personnel when it detects network traffic that attempts to circumvent the security measures of a networked computer environment.

Knowledge-based approaches and behavior-based approaches are two fundamentally different approaches to intrusion detection. Knowledge-based intrusion detection systems contain information about specific attacks and system vulnerabilities and watch for attempts to exploit these vulnerabilities, such as repeated failed login attempts or recurring attempts to download a program to a server. When such an attempt is detected, an alarm is triggered.

A behavior-based intrusion detection system models normal behavior of a system and its users from reference information collected by various means. The intrusion detection system compares current activity to this model and generates an alarm if it finds a deviation. Examples include unusual traffic at odd hours or a user in the Human Resources Department who accesses an accounting program that she has never before used.

Response

An organization should be prepared for the worst—a successful attack that defeats all or some of a system's defenses and damages data and information systems. A response plan should be developed well in advance of any incident and be approved by both the organization's legal department and senior management. A well-developed response plan helps keep an incident under technical and emotional control.

In a security incident, the primary goal must be to regain control and limit damage, not to attempt to monitor or catch an intruder. Sometimes system administrators take the discovery of an intruder as a personal challenge and lose valuable time that should be used to restore data and information systems to normal.

Incident Notification

A key element of any response plan is to define who to notify and who not to notify in the event of a computer security incident. Questions to cover include the following: Within the company, who needs to be notified, and what information does each person need to have? Under what conditions should the company contact major customers and suppliers? How does the company inform them of a disruption in business without unnecessarily alarming them? When should local authorities or the FBI be contacted?

Most security experts recommend against giving out specific information about a compromise in public forums, such as news reports, conferences, professional meetings, and online discussion groups. All parties working on the problem must be kept informed and up-to-date without using systems connected to the compromised system. The intruder may be monitoring these systems and emails to learn what is known about the security breach.

A critical ethical decision that must be made is what to tell customers and others whose personal data may have been compromised by a computer incident. Many organizations are tempted to conceal such information for fear of bad publicity and loss of customers. Because such inaction is perceived by many to be unethical and harmful, a number of state and federal laws have been passed to force organizations to reveal when customer data has been breached.

Protection of Evidence and Activity Logs

An organization should document all details of a security incident as it works to resolve the incident. Documentation captures valuable evidence for a future prosecution and provides data to help during the incident eradication and follow-up phases. It is especially important to capture all system events, the specific actions taken (what, when, and who), and all external conversations (what, when, and who) in a logbook. Because this may become court evidence, an organization should establish a set of document-handling procedures using the legal department as a resource.

Incident Containment

Often, it is necessary to act quickly to contain an attack and to keep a bad situation from becoming even worse. The incident response plan should clearly define the process for deciding if an attack is dangerous enough to warrant shutting down or disconnecting critical systems from the network. How such decisions are made, how fast they are made, and who makes them are all elements of an effective response plan.

Eradication

Before the IT security group begins the eradication effort, it must collect and log all possible criminal evidence from the system and then verify that all necessary backups are current, complete, and free of any malware. Creating a forensic disk image of each compromised system on write-only media both for later study and as evidence can be very useful. After virus eradication, a new backup must be created. Throughout this process, a log should be kept of all actions taken. This will prove helpful during the incident follow-up phase and ensure that the problem does not recur. It is imperative to back up critical applications and data regularly. Many organizations, however, have implemented inadequate backup processes and found that they could not fully restore original data after a security incident. All backups should be created with enough frequency to enable a full and quick restoration of data if an attack destroys the original, and this process must be tested to confirm that it works.

Incident Follow-Up

Of course, an essential part of follow-up is to determine how the organization's security was compromised so that it does not happen again. Often the fix is as simple as getting a software patch from a product vendor. However, it is important to look deeper than the immediate fix to discover why the incident occurred. If a simple software fix could have prevented the incident, then why wasn't the fix installed before the incident occurred?

A review should be conducted after an incident to determine exactly what happened and to evaluate how the organization responded. One approach is to write a formal incident report that includes a detailed chronology of events and the impact of the incident. This report should identify any mistakes so that they are not repeated in the future. The experience from this incident should be used to update and revise the security incident response plan. The key elements of a formal incident report should include the following:

- IP address and name of host computer(s) involved
- The data and time when the incident was discovered
- The length of the incident
- How the incident was discovered
- The method used to gain access to the host computer
- A detailed discussion of vulnerabilities that were exploited
- A determination of whether or not the host was compromised as a result of the attack
- The nature of the data stored on the computer (customer, employee, financial, etc.)
- A determination of whether the accessed data is considered personal, private, or confidential
- The number of hours the system was down
- The overall impact on the business
- An estimate of total monetary damage from the incident
- A detailed chronology of all events associated with the incident

Creating a detailed chronology of all events will also document the incident for possible later prosecution. To this end, it is critical to develop an estimate of the monetary damage. Potential costs include loss of revenue, loss in productivity, and the salaries of people working to address the incident, along with the cost to replace data, software, and hardware.

Another important issue is the amount of effort that should be put into capturing the perpetrator. If a Web site was simply defaced, it is easy to fix or restore the site's HTML (Hypertext Markup Language—the code that describes to your browser how a Web page should look). However, what if the intruders inflicted more serious damage, such as erasing proprietary program source code or the contents of key corporate databases? What if they stole company trade secrets? Expert crackers can conceal their identity, and tracking them down can take a long time as well as a tremendous amount of corporate resources.

The potential for negative publicity must also be considered. Discussing security attacks through public trials and the associated publicity has not only enormous potential costs in public relations but real monetary costs as well. For example, a bank or a brokerage firm might lose customers who learn of an attack and think their money or records aren't secure. Even if a company decides that the negative publicity risk is worth it and goes after the perpetrator, documents containing proprietary information that must be provided to the court could cause even greater security threats in the future. On the other hand, an organization must consider whether it has an ethical or a legal duty to inform customers or clients of a cyberattack that may have put their personal data or financial resources at risk.

Using a Managed Security Service Provider (MSSP)

managed security service provider (MSSP): A company that monitors, manages, and maintains computer and network security for other organizations.

Keeping up with computer criminals—and with new laws and regulations—can be daunting for organizations. Criminal hackers are constantly poking and prodding, trying to breach the security defenses of organizations. Also, laws such as HIPAA, Sarbanes-Oxley, and the USA Patriot Act require businesses to prove that they are securing their data. For most small and midsized organizations, the level of in-house network security expertise needed to protect their business operations can be too costly to acquire and maintain. As a result, many organizations outsource their network security operations to a **managed security service provider (MSSP)**, which is a company that monitors, manages, and maintains computer and network security for other organizations. MSSPs include such companies as AT&T, Computer Sciences Corporation, Dell SecureWorks, IBM, Symantec, and Verizon. MSSPs provide a valuable service for IS departments drowning in reams of alerts and false alarms coming from virtual private networks (VPNs); antivirus, firewall, and intrusion detection systems; and other security-monitoring systems. In addition, some MSSPs provide vulnerability scanning and Web blocking and filtering capabilities.

Computer Forensics

computer forensics: A discipline that combines elements of law and computer science to identify, collect, examine, and preserve data from computer systems, networks, and storage devices in a manner that preserves the integrity of the data gathered so that it is admissible as evidence in a court of law.

Computer forensics is a discipline that combines elements of law and computer science to identify, collect, examine, and preserve data from computer systems, networks, and storage devices in a manner that preserves the integrity of the data gathered so that it is admissible as evidence in a court of law. A computer forensics investigation may be opened in response to a criminal investigation or civil litigation. It may also be launched for a variety of other reasons, for example, to retrace steps taken when data has been lost, assess damage following a computer incident, investigate the unauthorized disclosure of personal or corporate confidential data, or to confirm or evaluate the impact of industrial espionage.

Computer forensics investigators work as a team to investigate an incident and conduct the forensic analysis by using various methodologies and tools to ensure the computer network system is secure in an organization. For example, accounting, tax, and advisory company Grant Thornton International has a number of IS labs around the world that employ numerous forensic experts who examine digital evidence for use in legal cases. Grant Thornton employs forensic software called Summation (a Web-based legal document, electronic data, and transcript review platform that supports litigation teams) and Forensic Toolkit (used to scan a hard drive to find a variety of information, including deleted emails and text strings, to crack encryption). The software from AccessData provides a combination of mobile forensics, computer forensics, and functions for encoding and reviewing multilingual documents.[41]

Proper handling of a computer forensics investigation is the key to fighting computer crime successfully in a court of law. In addition, extensive training and certification increases the stature of a computer forensics investigator in a court of law. Numerous certifications relate to computer forensics, including the CCE (Certified Computer Examiner), CISSP (Certified Information Systems Security Professional), CSFA (CyberSecurity Forensic Analyst), and GCFA (Global Information Assurance Certification Certified Forensics Analyst). The EnCE Certified Examiner program certifies professionals who have mastered computer investigation methods as well as the use of Guidance Software's EnCase computer forensic software. Numerous universities (both online and traditional) offer degrees specializing in computer forensics. Such degree programs should include training in accounting, particularly auditing, as this is very useful in the investigation of cases involving fraud.

Table 13.7 provides a list of questions that should be asked when an organization is evaluating its readiness for a security incident.

TABLE 13.7 Questions to be considered when evaluating an organization's readiness for a security incident

Question
Has a risk assessment been performed to identify investments in time and resources that can protect the organization from its most likely and most serious threats?
Have senior management and employees involved in implementing security measures been educated about the concept of reasonable assurance?
Has a security policy been formulated and broadly shared throughout the organization?
Have automated systems policies been implemented that mirror written policies?
Does the security policy address the following: • Email with executable file attachments? • Wireless networks and devices? • Use of smartphones deployed as part of corporate rollouts as well as those purchased by end users?
Is there an effective security education program for employees and contract workers?
Has a layered security solution been implemented to prevent break-ins?
Has a firewall been installed?
Is antivirus software installed on all personal computers?
Is the antivirus software frequently updated?
Have precautions been taken to limit the impact of malicious insiders?
Are the accounts, passwords, and login IDs of former employees promptly deleted?
Are employee responsibilities adequately defined and separated?
Are individual roles defined so that users have authority to perform their responsibilities and nothing more?
Is it a requirement to review at least quarterly the most critical Internet security threats and implement safeguards against them?
Has it been verified that backup processes for critical software and databases work correctly?
Has an intrusion detection system been implemented to catch intruders in the act—both in the network and on critical computers on the network?

TABLE 13.7 Questions to be considered when evaluating an organization's readiness for a security incident (*Continued*)

Question
Are periodic IT security audits conducted?
Has a comprehensive incident response plan been developed?
Has the security plan been reviewed and approved by legal and senior management?
Does the plan address all of the following areas:

• Incident notification?
    • Protection of evidence and activity logs?
    • Incident containment?
    • Eradication?
    • Incident follow-up?

Critical Thinking Exercise

Spear-Phishing Attack!

It appears that someone is using your firm's corporate directory—which includes job titles and email addresses—to contact senior managers and directors via email. The email requests that the recipient click on a URL, which leads to a Web site that looks as if it were designed by your Human Resources organization. Once at this phony Web site, the employees are asked to confirm the bank and account number to be used for electronic deposit of their annual bonus check.

Review Questions

1. How is this attack different from an ordinary phishing attack?
2. Craft a communications that might be sent out to employees to thwart this attack.

Critical Thinking Questions

1. Should this communications come from Human Resources, the corporate information systems security organization, or some other entity?
2. What actions can be taken to lessen the potential impact of future such attacks?

Summary

Principle:

Computer crime is a serious and rapidly growing area of concern requiring management attention.

The number of cybercrimes being committed against individuals, organizations, and governments continues to increase, and the destructive impact of these crimes is also intensifying.

The security of data and information systems used in business is of the utmost importance, but it must be balanced against other business needs.

Increasing computing complexity, higher computer user expectations, expanding and changing systems, an increase in the prevalence of bring your own device (BYOD) policies, a growing reliance on software with known vulnerabilities, and the increasing sophistication of those who would do harm have caused a dramatic increase in the number, variety, and severity of security incidents.

Many different types of people launch computer attacks, including the hacker, cracker, malicious insider, industrial spy, cybercriminal, hacktivist, and cyberterrorist. Each type has a different motivation.

Ransomware, viruses, worms, Trojan horses, logic bombs, blended threats, spam, distributed denial-of-service attacks, rootkits, advanced persistent threats, phishing, spear-phishing, smishing, vishing, identity theft, cyberespionage, and cyberterrorism are among the most common computer exploits.

The Department of Homeland Security (DHS) has the responsibility to provide for a "safer, more secure America, which is resilient against terrorism and other potential threats." The agency's Office of Cybersecurity and Communications is responsible for enhancing the security, resilience, and reliability of U.S. cyber and communications infrastructure.

The U.S. Computer Emergency Readiness Team (US-CERT) is a partnership between DHS and the public and private sectors that was established to protect the nation's Internet infrastructure against cyberattacks by serving as a clearinghouse for information on new viruses, worms, and other computer security topics.

Over the years, several laws have been enacted to prosecute those responsible for computer-related crime, including the Computer Fraud and Abuse Act, the Fraud and Related Activity in Connection with Access Devices Statute, the Identity Theft and Assumption Deterrence Act, the Stored Wire and Electronic Communications and Transactional Records Access Statutes, and the USA Patriot Act.

Principle:

Organizations must take strong measures to ensure secure, private, and reliable computing experiences for their employees, customers, and business partners.

A strong security program begins by assessing threats to the organization's computers and network, identifying actions that address the most serious vulnerabilities, and educating users about the risks involved and the actions they must take to prevent a security incident.

The IS security group must lead the effort to implement security policies and procedures, as well as effectively employing available hardware and software tools to help prevent security breaches.

Risk assessment is the process of assessing security-related risks to an organization's computers and networks from both internal and external threats.

The concept of reasonable assurance in connection with IS security recognizes that managers must use their judgment to ensure that the cost of control does not exceed the system's benefits or the risks involved.

No organization can ever be completely secure from attack. The key to prevention of a computer security incident is to implement a layered security solution to make computer break-ins so difficult that an attacker eventually gives up. Protective measures include implementing a corporate firewall, installing an intrusion detection system, utilizing a security dashboard, installing antivirus software on personal computers, implementing safeguards against attacks by malicious insiders, addressing the most critical security threats, and conducting periodic IT security audits.

No security system is perfect, so systems and procedures must be monitored to detect a possible intrusion.

If an intrusion occurs, there must be a clear reaction plan that addresses notification, evidence protection, activity log maintenance, containment, eradication, and follow-up.

Special measures must be taken to implement safeguards against attacks by malicious insiders and to defend against cyberterrorism.

Organizations must implement fixes against well-known vulnerabilities and conduct periodic IT security audits.

Many organizations outsource their network security operations to a managed security service provider (MSSP), which is a company that monitors, manages, and maintains computer and network security for other organizations.

Organizations must be knowledgeable of and have access to trained experts in computer forensics to identify, collect, examine, and preserve data from computer systems, networks, and storage devices in a manner that preserves the integrity of the data gathered so that it is admissible as evidence in a court of law.

Key Terms

advanced persistent threat (APT)

antivirus software

blended threat

botnet

bring your own device (BYOD)

CAPTCHA (Completely Automated Public Turing Test to Tell Computers and Humans Apart)

computer forensics

Controlling the Assault of Non-Solicited Pornography and Marketing (CAN-SPAM) Act

cyberespionage

cyberterrorism

data breach

Department of Homeland Security (DHS)

distributed denial-of-service (DDoS) attack

exploit

firewall

identity theft

intrusion detection system (IDS)

logic bomb

managed security service provider (MSSP)

next-generation firewall (NGFW)

phishing

ransomware

reasonable assurance

risk assessment

rootkit

security audit

security policy

smishing

spam

spear-phishing

Trojan horse

U.S. Computer Emergency Readiness Team (US-CERT)

virus

virus signature

vishing

worm

zero-day attack

zombie

Chapter 13: Self-Assessment Test

Computer crime is a serious and rapidly growing area of concern requiring management attention.

1. The number, variety, and severity of computer security incidents is slowly on the decline. True or False?

2. _____ is a business policy that permits, and in some cases encourages, employees to use their own mobile devices to access company computing resources and applications.

3. A(n) _____ is an attack on an information system that takes advantage of a particular system vulnerability.
   a. virus
   b. worm
   c. Trojan horse
   d. exploit

4. U.S. organizations increasingly rely on commercial software with known vulnerabilities. True or False?

5. A _____ is someone who attacks a computer system or network for financial gain.
   a. hacker
   b. cracker
   c. malicious insider
   d. cybercriminal
6. A _____ is a form of malware that fools its victims into thinking that it is useful software from a legitimate source.
   a. virus
   b. worm
   c. Trojan horse
   d. ransomware
7. A _____ is a set of programs that enables a user to gain administrative access to the computer without the end user's consent or knowledge.
   a. zombie
   b. rootkit
   c. botnet
   d. blended threat
8. _____ is an exploit in which victims receive a voice mail message telling them to call a phone number or access a Web site.
9. _____ involves the deployment of malware that secretly steals data in the computer systems of organizations.
   a. Cyberterrorism
   b. Cyberespionage
   c. Data breach
   d. Smishing

Organizations must take strong measures to ensure secure, private, and reliable computing experiences for their employees, customers, and business partners.

10. _____ is the process of assessing security-related risks to an organization's computers and networks from both internal and external threats.
11. The concept of _____ recognizes that managers must use their judgment to ensure that the cost of control does not exceed the system's benefits or the risks involved.
    a. risk assessment
    b. reasonable assurance
    c. security policy
    d. security versus privacy
12. A(n) _____ stands guard between an organization's internal network and the Internet and it limits network access based on the organization's access policy.
    a. router
    b. worm hole
    c. intrusion detection system
    d. firewall
13. A(n) _____ instruction detection system contains information about specific attacks and system vulnerabilities and watches for attempts to exploit these vulnerabilities.
14. _____ is a discipline that combines elements of law and computer science to identify, collect, examine, and preserve data from computer system, networks, and storage devices in a manner that preserves the integrity of data gathered so that it is admissible as evidence in a court of law.

Chapter 13: Self-Assessment Test Answers

1. False
2. bring your own device (BYOD)
3. d
4. True
5. d
6. c
7. b
8. Vishing
9. b
10. Risk assessment
11. b
12. d
13. knowledge-based
14. Computer forensics

Review Questions

1. Provide six reasons why computer incidents are so prevalent.
2. What is BYOD? What security issues does it raise?
3. Discuss the importance of installing computer patches and fixes.
4. What is a zero-day attack?
5. What is the difference between a black hat hacker and a cracker?
6. What is the difference between a virus, worm, a Trojan horse, and a blended threat?
7. What is the CAN-SPAM Act? What is CAPTCHA?
8. Explain how a distributed denial-of-service attack works.
9. Is a rootkit a blended threat? Explain.
10. What is the difference between phishing, smishing, and vishing?
11. What is the role of the US-CERT organization?

12. Outline the steps necessary to conduct an effective computer security risk assessment.
13. What is meant by reasonable assurance? Give a hypothetical example of a security measure that fails the reasonable assurance test.
14. What is the intent of a security policy? What are some of the earmarks of a good security policy?
15. What is meant by a layered security solution? Identify several layers of protective measures commonly employed in many organizations.
16. What is a managed security service provider (MSSP)? What sort of services does such an organization provide?

Discussion Questions

1. A successful distributed denial-of-service attack requires the downloading of software that turns unprotected computers into zombies under the control of the malicious hacker. Should the owners of the zombie computers be fined or otherwise punished as a means of encouraging people to better safeguard their computers? Why or why not?
2. Document a real-world example of a legitimate organization using spam in an effective and nonintrusive manner to promote a product or service.
3. Some IT security personnel believe that their organizations should employ former computer criminals who now claim to be white hat hackers to identify weaknesses in their organizations' security defenses. Do you agree? Why or why not?
4. You are a computer security trainer for your firm's 200 employees and contract workers. What are the key topics you would cover in your initial one-hour basic training program on security for non-IT personnel? What sort of additional security-related training might be appropriate once people have the basics covered?
5. Hundreds of a bank's customers have called the customer service call center to complain that they are receiving text messages on their phone telling them to log on to a Web site and enter personal information to resolve an issue with their account. What action should the bank take?
6. How would you distinguish between a hacktivist and a cyberterrorist? Should the use of hacktivists by a country against enemy organizations be considered an act of war? Why or why not? How about the use of cyberterrorists?
7. What is the difference between a risk assessment and an IT security audit?

Problem-Solving Exercises

1. Identify three commonly used antivirus software packages. Develop a spreadsheet that compares the cost and fundamental features of each package. Which antivirus solution would you choose and why?
2. Draft a legitimate-looking phishing email that would strongly tempt its recipients to click on a link to a Web site or open an email attachment.
3. Use the data breach statistics found at *http://www .idtheftcenter.org/images/breach/2005to2015mul tiyear.pdf* to develop a bar chart showing the number of data breaches year-by-year by entity (business, educational, government/ military, medical/health, and banking/credit/financial) from 2005 to 2015. In which entity is the number of data breaches increasing fastest? What other conclusions can you draw from your graph?

Team Activities

1. You and your team have been hired to assess the computer security of a small retailer. Where would you begin your assessment? What would you look for?
2. Your team is assigned responsibility to identify an appropriate MSSP provider for a small, rural hospital. What criteria will you use to select an appropriate provider? Do research online to identify three MSSP providers. Use the criteria to rate each of the three and choose the one that would be best for the hospital.
3. Imagine that your team must obtain the email logon and password to as many email accounts as possible. Brainstorm ideas that might enable you to obtain these credentials.

Web Exercises

1. Do research on the effectiveness of the Controlling the Assault of Non-Solicited Pornography and Marketing (CAN-SPAM) Act. Would you recommend any changes to this act? If so, what changes would you like to see implemented and why?
2. Do research to gain an understanding of why policies regarding BYOD are necessary for organizations that must abide by HIPAA regulations. Do you believe that employees of a large healthcare provider should be able to bring their own device to work? Why or why not?
3. Do research to find out more about DEF CON, one of the world's largest hacker conventions, held annually in Las Vegas, Nevada. Who attends this conference, and what sort of topics are covered? Is there value in IS security professionals attending this conference? Why or why not?

Career Exercises

1. Do research to determine typical starting salaries for someone with a four-year degree in computer forensics. What is the future demand for individuals trained in computer forensics? Do further research to find three universities that offer four-year degrees specializing in computer forensics. Compare the three programs, and choose the best one. Why did you choose this university?
2. You are one of the top students in your university's computer science program of 100 students, and you have agreed to meet with a recruiter from the Department of Homeland Security. Over dinner, he talks to you about the increasing threat of cyberterrorist attacks launched on the United States by foreign countries and the need to counter those attacks. The agency has a strong need for people that can both develop and defend against zero-day exploits that could be used to plant malware in the software used by the government and military computers. At the end of the dinner, the recruiter turns to you and asks: "Would such a role be of interest to you?" How do you respond?
3. Do research to learn more about the role of an information system security auditor. What is the role of an auditor, what sort of tasks does one perform, and what skills and training are necessary?

Case Studies

Case One

Fairplay Turns to a Managed Security Service Provider

Fairplay Finer Foods is an independent grocery retailer that operates in the greater Chicago area. From its beginning, Fairplay's mission has been to provide quality foods at an affordable price along with exceptional customer service. Starting with a single store in 1975, Fairplay has since grown to seven locations. The opening of each new store led to increased sales and attracted new customers; however, expansion also raised new information system needs as well as information security risks.

Due to its size, it was not practical for Fairplay to create and run its own information systems organization, so it contracted with KCS Computer Technology, Inc., to provide these services along with the necessary computer hardware and systems. One of KCS's key accomplishments for Fairplay was to implement and manage a corporate network that the grocery chain uses to run applications and communicate across all of its stores.

Another important area of focus for KCS involved helping Fairplay manage issues related to the Payment Card Industry Data Security Standard (PCI DSS). Retailers accepting credit cards and other forms of electronic payment are required to comply with the PCI DSS. The PCI DSS standard ensures that businesses follow best practices for protecting their customers' payment card information. A strong desire to ensure compliance with the PCI DSS standard and concern over potential network security issues led Fairplay and KCS to seek out a managed security service provider (MSSP).

After a thorough investigation, Fairplay and KCS selected ControlScan, an MSSP headquartered in Atlanta, based on its simple pricing model, stable of certified security experts, advanced technology, and solid reputation. As part of its contract with Fairplay, ControlScan agreed to serve as an extension of KCS, delivering cloud-based security technologies and related security support services, including:

- Installing, configuring, and monitoring a system of next-generation firewalls
- Investigating, responding to, and reporting on security-related events
- Providing network usage reports for insights into company resource utilization
- Upgrading the network on an ongoing basis by implementing the latest security enhancements
- Providing expertise to reduce network complexity and contain network-related costs

ControlScan's initial action was to install next-generation firewall appliances to protect each of Fairplay's locations. This work was completed overnight in a single night to minimize business disruption. ControlScan then conducted a thorough PCI gap analysis to compare current Fairplay security controls with those required by the PCI DSS. ControlScan developed a detailed set of recommendations and options for eliminating the gaps; thus, giving Fairplay management a roadmap to achieve full PCI DSS compliance. Finally, ControlScan did a full review of all of Fairplay's existing information systems and security policies, working with the chain's IS staff to tweak and customize policies where necessary.

Critical Thinking Questions

1. What advantages does use of an MSSP offer a small retailer like Fairplay? Can you think of any potential drawbacks of this approach? Is there a danger in placing too much trust in the use of an MSSP? Explain?

2. Data breaches at major retailers, such as Neiman Marcus, Target, and others, in recent years have shown that compliance with the Payment Card Industry Data Security Standard (PCI DSS) is no guarantee against an intrusion (see Vijayan, Jaikumar, "After Target, Neiman Marcus Breaches, Does PCI Compliance Mean Anything?," *ComputerWorld*, January 24, 2014). If you were a member of Fairplay's management team, what additional actions would you take to ensure your customer's credit card data is not stolen?

3. Do research on the Web to gain insight into the evolution of the PCI DSS standard. What major changes were made in moving from PCI 2.0 to PCI 3.0? What changes are being suggested for future versions of the PCI standard?

SOURCES: "About Fairplay," Fairplay, *www.fairplayfoods.com/about*, accessed April 12, 2016; "KCS Computer Technology," KCS Computer Technology, Inc., *www.kcstech.com*, accessed March 12, 2016; "Fairplay Finer Foods Secures Chain Stores with ControlScan Managed Security Services," ControlScan, *www.controlscan.com/fairplay-finer-foods -secures-chain-stores-with-controlscan-managed-security-services*, accessed April 12, 2016; "PCI Facts," PCI Compliance Guide, *www .pcicomplianceguide.org/pci-faqs-2/#1*, April 12, 2016.

Case Two

Sony's Response to North Korea's Cyberattack

On November 24, 2014, employees of Sony Pictures Entertainment booted up their computers to find an image of a skull along with a message from a group calling itself the Guardians of Peace. The message read: "We've already warned you and this is just the beginning. We've obtained all your internal data including your secrets and top secrets [which will be released] if you don't obey us."

As Sony would eventually discover, the hackers had stolen reams of sensitive data, including the Social Security numbers of 47,000 current and former employees, system passwords, salary lists, contracts, and even copies of some Sony employees' passports. The hackers accessed hundreds of Outlook mailboxes as well as Sony IT audit documents. They also stole media files and placed pirated copies of five of Sony's movies on illegal file-sharing servers. Sony was forced to completely shut down its information systems in an attempt to stem the data breach. Ultimately, Sony would determine that the damage done by the hackers was far more extensive than it first believed. Not only had data been stolen, but 75 percent of the company's servers had been destroyed and several internal data centers had been wiped clean.

Contacted within hours of the event, the FBI soon identified the culprit. In June, several months before the hack, North Korea's Ministry of Foreign Affairs had declared that it would take "a decisive and merciless countermeasure" if the U.S. government did not prevent the planned release of Sony's motion picture *The Interview*, which features two reporters who venture to North Korea to interview and assassinate the country's dictator, Kim Jong-un. In the film, the main character, initially won over by the dictator's apparent kindness, discovers that the tyrant is lying about the country's prosperity and freedoms. The plot, along with the movie's unflattering portrayal of the dictator as ruthless and childish, had caught the attention of the North Korean government.

The U.S. government disclosed that it had proof that the North Koreans had made good on their threat. The U.S. National Security Agency (NSA) had reportedly penetrated the North Korean cyberwarfare unit four years prior to the attack and had been monitoring its capabilities since then. After Sony alerted the FBI of the attack, the NSA was able to trace the attack back to North Korea, using a digital fingerprint the hackers had left in the malware. Several weeks after the attack, FBI Director James Comey, revealed in a speech that the Sony hackers had been sloppy. "We could see that the IP [Internet protocol] addresses that were being used to post and to send the emails were coming from IPs that were exclusively used by the North Koreans."

The hackers warned Sony not to release *The Interview*, and then on December 16, the group issued a message threatening large terrorist attacks on theaters that showed the film. The National Organization of Theatre Owners contacted the Department of Homeland Security for information and advice. The FBI and NSA released a bulletin explaining that they had no credible information about a plan to attack theaters, but they could neither confirm nor deny whether the hackers had the ability to launch such an attack. Shortly after the bulletin was released, the four largest U.S. theater chains withdrew their requests to show the movie—Carmike Cinemas first, followed by Regal Entertainment, AMC Entertainment, and Cinemark. Within hours, Sony announced that it had canceled the film's release. White House officials, Hollywood personalities, and the media were aghast. Comedian Jimmy Kimmel tweeted that the decision by the major theater chains to refuse to screen *The Interview* was "an un-American act of cowardice that validates terrorist actions and sets a terrifying precedent."

On December 19, President Obama addressed the issue publicly: "Sony is a corporation. It suffered significant damage. There were threats against its employees. I'm sympathetic to the concerns that they faced. Having said all that, yes, I think they made a mistake." Obama explained, "We cannot have a society in which some dictator in some place can start imposing censorship in the United States." The president's remarks highlighted the seriousness of the incident to the American public, many of whom came to view the incident as an attack on the freedom of expression.

In response to Obama's comments, Sony officials released a statement later the same day: "Let us be clear—the only decision that we have made with respect to release of the film was not to release it on Christmas Day in theaters, after the theater owners declined to show it.... After that decision, we immediately began actively surveying alternatives to enable us to release the movie on a different platform. It is still our hope that anyone who wants to see this movie will get the opportunity to do so."

In fact, on Christmas Day, the planned release day in the theater, *The Interview* became available through video-on-demand outlets such as Amazon.com, and within less than a month, the movie had brought in over $40 million in revenue. Approximately 6 million viewers had rented or purchased the movie in this way. Several hundred movie theaters that opted to screen the movie generated another $6 million. Over the next two months, Sony also released the movie on Netflix, on DVD and Blu-Ray, and in theaters in other countries.

Meanwhile, Sony has worked to recover from the damage done to the company itself by the hack. Sony Pictures' parent company, which is based in Japan, asked regulators there for an extension to file its third-quarter financial results. It also fired executive Amy Pascal whose leaked emails contained derogatory remarks about Hollywood producers and the U.S. president's movie preferences. The company also provided one year of free credit protection services to current and former employees.

In February 2015, President Obama held the first-ever White House summit on cybersecurity issues in Silicon Valley. The summit was billed as an attempt to deal with the increasing vulnerability of U.S. companies to cyberattacks—including those backed by foreign governments. However, the chief executives of Microsoft, Google, Facebook, and Yahoo all refused to attend the summit. Those companies have long advocated for the government to stop its practice of collecting and using private data to track terrorist and criminal activities and have worked to find better ways to encrypt the data of their customers. However, U.S. security agencies have continually pressured the IT giants to keep the data as unencrypted as possible to facilitate the government's law enforcement work. Ultimately, both the government and private businesses will need to find a way to work together to meet two contradictory needs—the country's need to make itself less vulnerable to cyberattacks while at the same time protecting itself from potential real-world violence.

Critical Thinking Questions

1. Do you think that Sony's response to the attack was appropriate? Why or why not?
2. What might Sony and the U.S. government done differently to discourage future such attacks on other U.S. organizations?
3. Are there measures that organizations and the U.S. government can take together to prevent both real-world terrorist violence and cyberattacks?

SOURCES: Barrett, Devlin and Danny Yadron, "Sony, U.S. Agencies Fumbled After Cyberattack," *Wall Street Journal*, February 22, 2015, *www.wsj.com/articles/sony-u-s-agencies-fumbled-after-cyberattack-1424641424*; Mitchell, Andrea, "Sony Hack: N. Korean Intel Gleaned by NSA during Incursion," *NBC News*, January 18, 2015, *www.nbcnews.com/storyline/sony-hack/sony-hack-n-korean-intel-gleaned-nsa-during-incursion-n288761*; Schatz, Amy, "Obama Acknowledges Strains with SiliconValley," *SFGate*, February 14, 2015, *http://blog.sfgate.com/techchron/2015/02/14/obama-acknowledges-strains-with-silicon-valley/*; Dwyer, Devin and Mary Bruce, "Sony Hacking: President Obama Says Company Made ?Mistake' in Canceling 'The Interview,'" *ABC News*, December 19, 2014, *http://abcnews.go.com/Politics/obama-sony-made-mistake-canceling-film-release/story?id=27720800*; Pallotta, Frank, "Sony's 'The Interview' Coming to Netflix," *CNN Money*, January 20, 2015, *http://money.cnn.com/2015/01/20/media/the-interview-makes-40-million/*; Pepitone, Julianne, "Sony Hack: 'Critical' Systems Won't Be Back Online until February," *NBC News*, January 23, 2015, *www.nbcnews.com/storyline/sony-hack/sony-hack-critical-systems-wont-be-back-online-until-february-n292126*; Cieply, Michael and Brooks Barnes, "Sony Cyberattack, First a Nuisance, Swiftly Grew into a Firestorm," *New York Times*, December 30, 2014, *www.nytimes.com/2014/12/31/business/media/sony-attack-first-a-nuisance-swiftly-grew-into-a-firestorm-.html*; "The Interview: A Guide to the Cyber Attack on Hollywood," *BBC*, December 29, 2014, *www.bbc.com/news/entertainment-arts-30512032*; Whittaker, Zack, "FBI Says North Korea Is 'Responsible' for Sony Hack, as White House Mulls Response," *ZDNet*, December 19, 2014, *www.zdnet.com/article/us-government-officially-blames-north-korea-for-sony-hack/*; Osborne, Charlie, "Sony Pictures Corporate Files Stolen and Released in Cyberattack," *ZDNet*, November 28, 2014, *www.zdnet.com/article/sony-pictures-corporate-files-stolen-and-released-in-cyberattack*; Osborne, Charlie, "Sony Hack Exposed Social Security Numbers of Hollywood Celebrities," *ZDNet*, December 5, 2015, *www.zdnet.com/article/sony-hack-exposed-social-security-numbers-of-hollywood-celebrities/*; Sanger, David E. and Nicole Perlroth, "Obama Heads to Tech Security Talks amid Tensions," *New York Times*, February 12, 2015, *www.nytimes.com/2015/02/13/business/obama-heads-to-security-talks-amid-tensions.html*; Whitney, Lance, "Sony Seeks to Delay Filing Earnings in Wake of Cyberattack," *CNET*, January 23, 2015, *www.cnet.com/news/sony-asks-to-delay-filing-earnings-due-to-cyberattack*.

Notes

1. "Big Data and Predictive Analytics: On the Cybersecurity Frontline," International Data Corporation, February 2015.
2. "The Global State of Information Security Survey 2016," PwC, *www.pwc.com/gx/en/issues/cyber-security/information-security-survey/industry.html*, accessed April 16, 2016.
3. "The Global State of Information Security Survey 2016," PwC, *www.pwc.com/gx/en/issues/cyber-security/information-security-survey/industry.html*, accessed April 16, 2016.
4. "Secunia Vulnerability Review—The Highlights," Secunia, *http://secunia.com/vulnerability-review/vulnerability_update_all.html*, accessed February 14, 2015.
5. "Flexera Software Vulnerability Review 2016," Flexera, March 16, 2016, *http://learn.flexerasoftware.com/SVM-WP-Vulnerability-Review-2016*.
6. Perlroth, Nicole and Sanger, David E., "Nations Buying as Hackers Sell Flaws in Computer Code." July 13, 2013, *New York Times*, *www.nytimes.com/2013/07/14/world*

/europe/nations-buying-as-hackers-sell-computer-flaws.
html?_r=0.

7. Markert, Jennifer, "How Zero-Day Exploits Are Bought
    and Sold in a Murky, Unregulated Market," Curious-
    matic, February 23, 2015, *https://curiousmatic.com/zero
    -day-exploits*.

8. Khandelwal, Swati, "MAC OS X Zero-Day Exploit Can
    Bypass Apple's Latest Protection Feature," *Hacker News*,
    March 24, 2016, *http://thehackernews.com/2016/03
    /system-integrity-protection.html*.

9. Ashford, Warick, "US Hospital Pays •12,000 to Ransom-
    ware Attackers," *Computer Weekly*, February 18, 2016,
    *www.computerweekly.com/news/4500273343/US-hospi
    tal-pays-12000-to-ransomware-attackers*.

10. Danchev, Dancho, "Cornficker's Estimated Economic
    Cost? $9.1 Billion," *ZDNet*, April 23, 2009, *www.zdnet.
    com/blog/security/confickers-estimated-economic-cost
    -9-1-billion/3207*.

11. Aksoy, Pelin Aksoy and Denardis, Laura, *Information
    Technology in Theory* (Boston: Cengage Learning,
    ©2007), pp. 299–301.

12. Cloherty, Jack and Thomas, Pierre, "'Trojan Horse' Bug
    Lurking in Vital US Computers since 2011," *ABC News*,
    November 6, 2014, *http://abcnews.go.com/US/trojan
    -horse-bug-lurking-vital-us-computers-2011/story?
    id=26737476*.

13. Schwartz, Matthew, J., "How South Korean Bank Mal-
    ware Spread," *InformationWeek*, March 25, 2013, *www
    .darkreading.com/attacks-and-breaches/how-south-
    korean-bank-malware-spread/d/d-id/1109239?*.

14. Johnston, Nick, "Short, Sharp Spam Attacks Aiming to
    Spread Dyre Financial Malware," Symantec, January 28,
    2015, *www.symantec.com/connect/blogs/short-sharp
    -spam-attacks-aiming-spread-dyre-financial-malware*.

15. "Spam Statistics for the Week Ending January 18, 2015,"
    Trustwave, *www3.trustwave.com/support/labs/spam
    _statistics.asp*.

16. Baraniuk, Chris, "DDoS: Website-Crippling Cyber-
    Attacks to Rise in 2016," *BBC News*, January 27, 2016,
    www.bbc.com/news/technology-35376327.

17. Cowly, Stacy, "Grum Takedown: '50 Percent of World-
    wide Spam Is Gone'," *CNN Money*, July 19, 2012, *http://
    money.cnn.com/2012/07/19/technology/grum-spam-bot
    net/index.htm*.

18. Kalunian, Kim, "2012 Rootkit Computer Virus 'Worst in
    Years'," *Warwick Beacon*, December 20, 2011, *www.
    warwickonline.com/stories/2012-rootkit-computer-virus
    -worst-in-years,65964*.

19. Rouse, Margaret, "Advanced Persistent Threat," *Tech-
    Target*, *http://searchsecurity.techtarget.com/definition
    /advanced-persistent-threat-APT*, accessed February 17,
    2015.

20. "Advanced Persistent Threats: How They Work,"
    Symantec, *www.symantec.com/theme.jsp?themeid=apt-
    infographic-1*, accessed February 17, 2015.

21. "International Hacking Ring Steal up to $1 Billion from
    Banks," *Economic Times*, February 16, 2015, *http://eco
    nomictimes.indiatimes.com/articleshow/46256846.cms?
    utm_source=contentofinterest&utm_medium=text&utm
    _campaign=cppst*.

22. "Fraud Alert: New Phishing Tactics—and How They
    Impact Your Business," Thawte, *https://community

.thawte.com/system/files/download-attachments/Phish
ing%20WP_D2.pdf*, accessed March 11, 2015.

23. Raywood, Dan, "Anthem Breach Victims Hit with Yet
    another Phishing Scam," *Security News*, February 16,
    2015, *www.itproportal.com/2015/02/16/anthem-breach
    -victims-hit-yet-another-phishing-scam*.

24. "3/2/2016 Phishing Attack," UITS Help Center, March 2,
    2016, *http://helpcenter.uconn.edu/2016/03/15/322016
    -phishing-attack*.

25. "4/7/2016 Phishing Attack," Information Security Office,
    University of Connecticut, April 7, 2016, *http://security
    .uconn.edu/2016/04/07/472016-phishing-attack*.

26. Ragan, Steve, "Phishing Attacks Targeting W-2 Data Hit
    41 Organizations in Q1 2016," *CSO*, March 24, 2016,
    *www.csoonline.com/article/3048263/security/phishing
    -attacks-targeting-w-2-data-hit-41-organizations-in-q1
    -2016.html*.

27. Brook, Chris, "Vishing Attacks Are Targeting Dozens of
    Banks," *Threat Post*, April 29, 2014, *https://threatpost
    .com/vishing-attacks-targeting-dozens-of-banks/105774*.

28. McGlasson, Linda, "How to Respond to Vishing Attacks:
    Bank, State Associations Share Tips for Incident
    Response Plan," BankInfoSecurity.com, April 26,
    2010, *www.bankinfosecurity.com/p_print.php?t=a
    &id=2457*.

29. Greene, Tim, "Anthem Hack: Personal Data Stolen Sells
    for 10× Price of Stolen Credit Card Numbers," *Network
    World*, February 6, 2015, *www.networkworld.com/arti
    cle/2880366/security0/anthem-hack-personal-data-sto
    len-sells-for-10x-price-of-stolen-credit-card-numbers.
    html*.

30. Palermo, Elizabeth, "10 Worst Data Breaches of All
    Time," Tom's Guide, February 6, 2015, *www.tomsguide.
    com/us/biggest-data-breaches,news-19083.html*.

31. Greene, Tim, "The Biggest Data Breaches of 2015," *Net-
    work World*, December 2, 2015, *www.networkworld.
    com/article/3011103/security/biggest-data-breaches-of
    -2015.html*.

32. Kan, Michael, "China Counters US Claims with Own
    Charges of Cyber-Espionage," *PC World*, May 19, 2014,
    *www.pcworld.com/article/2157080/china-counters-us-
    claims-with-own-charges-of-cyberespionage.html*.

33. Yan, Sophia, "Chinese Man Admits to Cyber Spying on
    Boeing and Other U.S. Firms," *CNN Money*, March 24,
    2016, *http://money.cnn.com/2016/03/24/technology
    /china-cyber-espionage-military/index.html*.

34. Pellerin, Cheryl, "White House Announces Voluntary
    Cybersecurity Framework," U.S. Department of Defense,
    February 13, 2015, *http://archive.defense.gov/news/news
    article.aspx?id=121660*.

35. "About DHS," Department of Homeland Security, *www.
    dhs.gov/about-dhs*, accessed April 7, 2016.

36. "Office of Cybersecurity and Communications," Depart-
    ment of Homeland Security, *http://www.dhs.gov/office
    -cybersecurity-and-communications*, accessed April 7,
    2016.

37. "About DHS," Department of Homeland Security, *www
    .dhs.gov/about-dhs*, accessed April 8, 2016.

38. Zetter, Kim, "Everything We Know about Ukraine's
    Power Plant Hack," *Wired*, January 20, 2016, *http://www
    .wired.com/2016/01/everything-we-know-about-ukraines
    -power-plant-hack*.

39. H. R. 3162, 107th Cong. (2001), *www.gpo.gov/fdsys/pkg /BILLS-107hr3162enr/pdf/BILLS-107hr3162enr.pdf*, accessed April 8, 2016.

40. "AVAAP Case Studies: Algoma Central Corporation," AVAAP, *www.avaap.com/case-studies*, accessed April 12, 2016.

41. "Case Study: Grant Thornton, Global Accounting, Tax And Advisory Company Puts Its Trust in AccessData for Computer Forensics and E-Discovery Solutions," Access-Data, *http://accessdata.com/resources/digital-forensics /case-study-grant-thornton-global-accounting-tax -and-advisory-company-puts-i*, accessed April 9, 2016.

CHAPTER 14

Ethical, Legal, and Social Issues of Information Systems

SOCIAL IMPACT

Did You Know?

- The Government Accounting Office (GAO) conducted a check of the three federal departments with the largest IS budgets—the Defense Department, Department of Homeland Security, and Department of Health and Human Services. It uncovered a total of $321 million spent in the six-year period from 2008 to 2013 on projects that duplicated other efforts within those same agencies.

- A study conducted by researchers at the University of Nevada estimated that wasting time online (or "cyberloafing," as it is sometime called) costs U.S. businesses more than $85 billion annually.

- Over the course of 12 years, a problem with the software used by the Washington State Department of Corrections to calculate prison sentences caused the early release of 3,200 inmates—approximately 3 percent of all inmates released during that time period.

- The city of Houston was forced to switch providers for its online wellness program after many city employees balked at providing private information to a company whose authorization form indicated that it might pass the data to other third-party vendors and that the data might be subject to "re-disclosure," could be posted in areas reviewable by the public, and might no longer protected by privacy law.

Principles

- Policies and procedures must be established to avoid waste and mistakes associated with computer usage.

- The use of technology requires balancing the needs of those who use the information that is collected against the rights of those whose information is being used.

- Jobs, equipment, and working conditions must be designed to avoid negative health effects from computers.

- Practitioners in many professions subscribe to a code of ethics that states the principles and core values that are essential to their work.

Learning Objectives

- Describe some examples of waste and mistakes in an IS environment, their causes, and possible solutions.

- Identify policies and procedures useful in eliminating waste and mistakes.

- Discuss the principles and limits of an individual's right to privacy.

- Discuss the tradeoffs between security and privacy.

- List the important negative effects of computers on the work environment.

- Identify specific actions that must be taken to ensure the health and safety of employees.

- Outline a process for including ethical considerations in decision making.

- Define the intent and key elements of an effective code of ethics.

Why Learn about the Personal and Social Impact of Information Systems?

Both opportunities and threats surround a wide range of nontechnical issues associated with the use of information systems and the Internet. The issues span the full spectrum—from preventing computer waste and mistakes and avoiding violations of privacy to complying with laws on collecting data about customers and monitoring employees. If you become a member of the human resources, information systems, or legal department within an organization, you will likely be challenged with leading your organization in dealing with these and other issues covered in this chapter. Also, as a user of information systems and the Internet, it is in your own self-interest to become well versed on these issues. Developing a better understanding of the topics covered in this chapter will help you to manage in an ethical manner and avoid technology-related problems.

As you read this chapter, consider the following:

- How can the use of technology affect you and your organization?
- How can you include ethical factors in your decision making process?

Earlier chapters detailed the significant benefits of computer-based information systems in business, including increased profits, superior goods and services, and higher quality of work life. Computers have become such valuable tools that most businesspeople today have difficulty imagining how they would accomplish their work without them. Yet, the information age has also brought the potential for cybercrime as well as the following potential problems for workers, companies, and society in general:

- Computer waste and mistakes
- Trade-offs between privacy and security
- Work environment problems
- Ethical issues

This chapter discusses these important social and ethical issues, which underlie the design, building, and use of computer-based information systems. No business organization, and hence, no information system, operates in a vacuum. All IS professionals, business managers, and users have a responsibility to see that the potential consequences of IS use are fully considered. Even entrepreneurs, especially those who use computers and the Internet, must be aware of the potential personal and social impact of computers. We'll begin with a discussion of preventing computer waste and mistakes.

Computer Waste and Mistakes

Computer-related waste and mistakes are major causes of computer problems, contributing to unnecessarily high costs and lost profits. Examples of computer-related waste include organizations operating unintegrated information systems, acquiring redundant systems, and wasting information system resources. Computer-related mistakes refer to errors, failures, and other computer problems that make computer output incorrect or not useful; most of these are caused by human error. This section explores the damage that can be done as a result of computer waste and mistakes.

Computer Waste

Some organizations continue to operate their businesses using unintegrated information systems, which makes it difficult for decisions makers to collaborate and share information. This practice leads to missed opportunities, increased costs, and lost sales. For example, most local health departments use a combination of state-provided and locally implemented information systems for patient data collection, management, and reporting. In a recent study of the use of such information systems, many public health workers reported system inefficiencies, difficulties in generating reports, and limited data accessibility, necessitating the need for system workarounds. In addition, the use of a "shadow system" to maintain a duplicate—and more easily accessible—set of information is common.[1] Such inefficient systems add to the growth in healthcare costs.

Many organizations unknowingly waste money to acquire systems in different organizational units that perform nearly the same functions. Implementation of such duplicate systems unnecessarily increases hardware and software costs. The U.S. government spends billions of dollars on information systems each year, with almost $90 billion spent in fiscal year 2015 alone.[2] Some of this spending goes toward providing information systems that provide similar functions across the various branches and agencies of the government. The Government Accounting Office (GAO) conducted a check of the three federal departments with the largest IS budgets—the Defense Department, Department of Homeland Security, and Department of Health and Human Services. It uncovered a total of $321 million spent in the six-year period from 2008 to 2013 on projects that duplicated other efforts within those same agencies.[3] In 2015, the GAO released a follow-up report urging government agencies to increase the use of strategic sourcing contracts as one way to cut down on duplicative IS spending. Strategic sourcing is the structured and collaborative process of analyzing an organization's spending patterns to better leverage its purchasing power, eliminate contract duplication, reduce costs, and improve overall performance.[4]

A less dramatic, yet still relevant, example of waste is the amount of company time, money, and IS resources that some employees misuse through texting, sending personal email, playing computer games, surfing the Web, shopping online, and checking for updates on Instagram or Facebook. In fact, in a recent survey of more than 2,100 human resource professionals, cell phones/texting (52 percent) and the Internet (44 percent) were listed as the biggest productivity killers in the workplace.[5] A study conducted by researchers at the University of Nevada estimated that wasting time online (or "cyberloafing," as it is sometime called) costs U.S. businesses more than $85 billion annually.[6]

As a result, many companies are exploring new tools to help improve workers' productivity, such as using an open space layout instead of cubicles, banning personal calls/cell phones, monitoring emails and Internet usage, and blocking certain Internet sites entirely.[7] A team of researchers from the University of Arizona has developed software that is designed to reduce cyberloafing by dividing the Internet into sites that employees can always visit, sometimes visit, and never visit (the software completely blocks certain Web sites, such as pornography sites and video-streaming sites that use up too much company bandwidth). The software includes on-screen reminders that alert employees when they are visiting sites that are likely not work-related, and after a total of 90 minutes spent browsing leisure sites in any given day, an employee loses access to those sites unless they get approval from their manager.[8]

Computer-Related Mistakes

Despite many people's distrust of them, computers rarely make mistakes. If users do not follow proper procedures, however, even the most sophisticated hardware cannot produce meaningful output. Mistakes can be caused by unclear expectations coupled with inadequate training and a lack of feedback.

A programmer might also develop a program that contains errors, or a data-entry clerk might enter the wrong data. Unless errors are caught early and corrected, the speed of computers can intensify mistakes.

Some of the most common computer-related mistakes include the following:

- Data-entry or data-capture errors
- Programming errors
- Errors in handling files, including formatting a disk by mistake, copying an old file over a newer one, and deleting a file by mistake
- Mishandling of computer output
- Inadequate planning for and control of equipment malfunctions
- Inadequate planning for and control of environmental difficulties (e.g., electrical and humidity problems)
- Inadequate planning for hardware and software upgrades
- Installing computing capacity inadequate for the level of activity
- Failure to provide access to the most current information either by not adding new Web links or not deleting old links

As information technology becomes faster, more complex, and more powerful, organizations and computer users face increased risks of experiencing the results of computer-related mistakes. Consider these recent examples of computer-related mistakes:

- In late 2015, the Treasury Inspector General for Tax Administration (TIGTA) released an audit showing that due to a programming error, the IRS issued over $27 million in refunds on more than 13,000 tax returns that had initially been flagged as potentially fraudulent for the 2013 tax year. The computer glitch overrode the fraud warning flags, causing the returns to be processed rather than set aside for review. The inspector general's report warned that if the programming error was not fixed, it could allow the IRS to issue more than $135 million in potentially erroneous refunds over the next five years.[9]
- Over the course of 12 years, a problem with the software used by the Washington State Department of Corrections to calculate prison sentences caused the early release of 3,200 inmates—approximately 3 percent of all inmates released during that time period. The problem first came to light when the family of a crime victim was notified of the impending release of the inmate involved in the crime. After doing its own calculations, the family contacted the Department of Corrections, pointing out that the inmate was being released earlier than had been ordered by the court; however, the department delayed fixing the software for another three years. During that time, two inmates who were mistakenly released early were each charged with killing someone in separate incidents.[10]
- The New York Stock Exchange (NYSE) was forced to cancel all open orders and suspend trading for almost four hours in July 2015 due to "technical issues" tied to the phased roll-out of a new software release to one trading unit. According to the exchange, which handles approximately 10 percent of all stock trading worldwide, the update caused communications problems between the new software and the exchange's gateways, which are the access points used by traders and other exchanges to connect with the NYSE—ultimately requiring the temporary shutdown of all trading operations.[11,12]
- In April 2016, an error with its payment processing software caused American Honda Finance Corporation (AHFC) to double-charge many customers for their monthly vehicle payments, resulting in some customers also being hit with overdraft fees from their banks. Because of the number of customers affected, AHFC's customer service team became overwhelmed, and customer hold times exceeded 20 to 30 minutes. AHFC

issued refunds to most customers within two to three days, but the company's reputation took a hit as many affected consumers took to social media to criticize the company's handling of the software glitch.[13,14]

Preventing Computer-Related Waste and Mistakes

To remain profitable in a competitive environment, organizations must use their resources wisely. To employ IS resources efficiently and effectively, employees and managers alike should strive to minimize waste and mistakes. This effort involves establishing, implementing, monitoring, and reviewing effective policies and procedures.

Establishing Policies and Procedures

The first step in preventing computer-related waste and mistakes is to establish policies and procedures regarding efficient acquisition, use, and disposal of systems and devices. Computers permeate organizations today, and it is critical for organizations to ensure that systems are used to their full potential. As a result, most companies have implemented stringent policies on the acquisition of computer systems and equipment, including requiring a formal justification statement before computer equipment is purchased, defining standard computing platforms (operating system, type of computer chip, minimum amount of RAM, etc.), and mandating the use of preferred vendors for all acquisitions. Most organizations have also established strong policies to prevent employees from wasting time using computers inappropriately at work.

Training programs for individuals and work groups as well as manuals and documents covering the use and maintenance of information systems can also help prevent computer waste and mistakes. The Error Prevention Institute offers online training on preventing human errors that explains the underlying reasons that humans make mistakes and how these mistakes can be prevented.[15] Additional preventive measures include the requirement that all new applications be approved through an established process before they are rolled out in order to ensure cost effectiveness and compatibility with other systems and hardware. Some organizations also require that documentation and descriptions of certain applications, including all cell formulas for spreadsheets and a description of all data elements and relationships in a database system, be filed or submitted to a central office. Such standardization can ease access and use for all personnel. Examples of other useful policies to minimize waste and mistakes include the following:

- Changes to critical tables, HTML, and URLs should be tightly controlled, with all changes documented and authorized by responsible owners.
- A user manual should be available covering operating procedures and documenting the management and control of the application.
- Each system report should indicate its general content in its title and specify the time period covered.
- The system should have controls to prevent invalid and unreasonable data entry.
- Controls should exist to ensure that data input, HTML, and URLs are valid, applicable, and posted in the right time frame.
- Users should implement proper procedures to ensure correct input data.

After companies plan and develop policies and procedures, they must consider how best to implement them.

Implementing Policies and Procedures

The process of implementing policies and procedures to minimize waste and mistakes varies by organization. Most companies develop such policies and procedures with advice from the firm's internal auditing group or its external auditing firm. The policies often focus on the implementation of source data automation, the use of data editing to ensure data accuracy and completeness, and the assignment of clear responsibility for data accuracy within each information system.

Training and communication are the keys to the successful acceptance and implementation of policies and procedures. Because more and more people use computers in their daily work, they must understand how to use them. See Figure 14.1. Many users are not properly trained in using applications, and their mistakes can be very costly. Others do not have a good understanding of the policies and procedures they are expected to follow as part of their job due to inadequate training. Importantly, employees should be educated on the rationale behind the IS policies and procedures they are expected to follow, including how the policies and procedures tie into the organization's overall strategy.[16]

Godluz/Shutterstock.com

FIGURE 14.1

Computer training

Training helps to ensure acceptance and implementation of policies and procedures.

Monitoring Policies and Procedures

To ensure that users throughout an organization are following established procedures, routine practices must be monitored and corrective action must be taken when necessary. By understanding what is happening in day-to-day activities, organizations can make adjustments or develop new procedures. Many organizations perform audits to measure actual results against established goals, such as percentage of end-user reports produced on time, percentage of data-input errors detected, and number of input transactions entered per eight-hour shift. Audits can also be used to track the amount of time employees spend on non-work-related Web sites and to determine if specific system policies and procedures are being followed consistently.

An audit at the U.S. Department of Veterans Affairs found that while the agency has recently made improvements in its efforts to develop and distribute policies and procedures related to its information security and risk management programs, it continues to struggle with the implementation of such policies and procedures. For example, by monitoring the permissions settings related to system ID management and access controls, the auditors found multiple instances of "unnecessary system privileges, excessive and unauthorized user accounts, accounts without formal access authorizations, and active accounts for terminated personnel." The auditors' report included recommendations that all VA locations implement periodic access reviews, enable audit logs, and enforce password policies on all operating systems, databases, applications, and network devices.[17]

Reviewing Policies and Procedures

The final step in preventing computer-related waste and mistakes is to review existing policies and procedures to determine whether they are adequate. During the review, people should ask the following questions:

* Do current policies cover existing practices adequately? Were any problems or opportunities uncovered during monitoring?
* Does the organization plan any new activities in the future? If so, does it need new policies or procedures addressing who will handle them and what must be done?
* Are contingencies and disasters covered?

This review and planning allows companies to take a proactive approach to problem solving, which can enhance a company's performance by increasing such as by increasing productivity and improving customer service. During such a review, companies can take into account upcoming changes in information systems that could have a profound effect on many business activities.

The results of failing to review and plan changes in policies and procedures can lead to disastrous consequences. For example, an internal review at Boston-based State Street Corporation revealed that the financial services giant had been overcharging its customers for a variety of administrative services for more than 18 years—to the tune of $200 million. Although State Street had assured its clients, who are primarily large institutions, such as pension funds and mutual funds, that it was only passing along actual costs, it was in fact significantly overcharging those customers for postage and for services such as printing and sending secure emails (State Street allegedly charged $5 per email message, even though the actual cost was only 25 cents). When the company announced its findings, it did not reveal the cause of the systemic overcharging, indicate how it had been detected, nor explain why earlier policy and systems reviews did not highlight the problem—key questions as the Massachusetts Securities Division has since found evidence that State Street employees were questioning the charges as far back as 2004. The company is now faced with reimbursing its clients—with interest—as well as with responding to a civil complaint filed by the Massachusetts's Secretary of State, which could result in a censure and administrative fines.[18,19]

Information systems professionals and users need to be aware of the misuse of resources throughout an organization. Preventing errors and mistakes is one way to do so.

Critical Thinking Exercise

Cutting Down on Cyberloafing

You are a member of the Human Resources organization of a small tech training development company with some 50 full and part-time workers. A casual check of how workers spend their time indicates that there is a large amount of time spent sending and receiving personal texts and emails, shopping online, and checking of social media Web sites. Especially alarming is the casual viewing of "soft porn" which could open the firm to an expensive lawsuit if an employee sees a coworker viewing porn at work and complains that the company has created a hostile work environment. While the company has made it clear that it can monitor workers' use of information system resources, no guidelines have been set that clearly indicate acceptable and unacceptable use of information system resources.

Review Questions

1. What is the harm in nonproductive use of information system resources, isn't everybody doing it?
2. What are the keys to successful acceptance and implementation of new policies and procedures to reduce cyberloafing?

Critical Thinking Questions

1. Do you think that it would help to involve a small group of employees in defining appropriate use guidelines or should this be done strictly by members of the Human Resources organization (you and one other person)? Why do you feel this way?
2. Should some sort of penalty be defined for violation of the guidelines or will this simply come across as "too heavy handed" and cause a worker rebellion?

Privacy Issues

Privacy is an important social issue related to the use of information systems. In 1890, U.S. Supreme Court Justice Louis Brandeis stated that the "right to be left alone" is one of the most "comprehensive of rights and the most valued by civilized man." Basically, the issue of privacy deals with this right to be left alone or to be withdrawn from public view. In terms of information systems, issues of privacy relate to the collection and use or misuse of data. Data is constantly being collected and stored on each of us. This data is often distributed over easily accessed networks and without our knowledge or consent. Concerns of privacy regarding this data raise difficult questions, including "Who owns this information and knowledge?" If a public or private organization spends time and resources to obtain data on you, does the organization own the data, and should it be allowed to use the data in any way it desires? To some extent, laws and regulations answer these questions for federal agencies, but many questions remain unanswered for private organizations. Today, many businesses rely on collected personal data to enhance their sales and marketing efforts, and for some organizations, buying and selling personal data is their business. In addition, businesses are sometimes required to respond to requests from law enforcement agencies for information about its employees, customers, and suppliers. Indeed, some phone and Internet companies have employees whose full-time role it is to deal with information requests from local, state, and federal law enforcement agencies. These and other aspects of privacy create opportunities and challenges for organizations and individuals.

Privacy and the Federal Government

Over the last several decades, Congress has approved, and the federal government has implemented, many laws addressing personal privacy—some of which have been challenged in court cases that have made their way all the way up to the Supreme Court. Some of these laws are renewed periodically, and others have been revised and updated via new legislative action. Some of the most important federal laws relating to privacy are summarized in Table 14.1.

A number of recent revelations—many of which came as a result of the public release of a vast collection of previously classified documents by former NSA contractor, Edward Snowden—regarding previously clandestine federal government data-collection programs have raised concerns and debate between those who favor data collection as a means to increased security and those who view such programs as a violation of rights guaranteed by the

TABLE 14.1 Key federal privacy laws and their provisions

Law	Provisions
Fair Credit Reporting Act of 1970 (FCRA)	Regulates operations of credit-reporting bureaus, including how they collect, store, and use credit information
Family Education Privacy Act of 1974	Restricts the collection and use of data by federally funded educational institutions, including specifications for the type of data collected, access by parents and students to the data, and limitations on disclosure
Tax Reform Act of 1976	Restricts collection and use of certain information by the Internal Revenue Service
Right to Financial Privacy Act of 1978	Restricts government access to certain records held by financial institutions
Foreign Intelligence Surveillance Act of 1978	Defines procedures to request judicial authorization for electronic surveillance of persons engaged in espionage or international terrorism against the United States on behalf of a foreign power
Electronic Communications Privacy Act of 1986	Defines provisions for the access, use, disclosure, interception, and privacy protections of electronic communications
Computer Matching and Privacy Act of 1988	Regulates cross-references between federal agencies' computer files (e.g., to verify eligibility for federal programs)
Cable Act of 1992	Regulates companies and organizations that provide wireless communications services, including cellular phones
Gramm-Leach-Bliley Act of 1999	Requires all financial institutions to protect and secure customers' nonpublic data from unauthorized access or use
USA Patriot Act of 2001	Requires Internet service providers and telephone companies to turn over customer information, including numbers called, without a court order, if the FBI claims that the records are relevant to a terrorism investigation; Section 215 allowed for the bulk collection of domestic telecommunications metadata (phone numbers, time stamps, call duration, etc.); some provisions of this act were extended by President Barack Obama in 2011, and some provisions (most significantly, the Section 215 provisions allowing for the bulk collection of metadata) briefly expired in June 2015 before being restored in somewhat modified form under the USA Freedom Act
E-Government Act of 2002	Requires federal agencies to post machine-readable privacy policies on their Web sites and to perform privacy impact assessments on all new collections of data of 10 or more people
Fair and Accurate Credit Transactions Act of 2003	Combats the growing crime of identity theft by allowing consumers to get free credit reports from each of the three major consumer credit-reporting agencies every 12 months and to place alerts on their credit histories under certain circumstances
Foreign Intelligence Surveillance Act (FISA) Amendments Act of 2008	Renews the U.S. government's authority to monitor electronic communications of foreigners abroad and authorizes foreign surveillance programs by the NSA, such as PRISM and some earlier data-collection activities
USA Freedom Act (2015)	Imposes limitations on the bulk collection of the telecommunications metadata of U.S. citizens; prohibits large-scale indiscriminate data collection (such as all records from an entire zip code); requires the NSA to obtain permission from the Foreign Intelligence Surveillance Court (FISC) to access the metadata records, which are now held by telecommunication companies rather than by the government; restored in a modified form some other provisions of the USA Patriot Act that lapsed in June 2015, including authorization for roving wiretaps and for tracking so-called lone-wolf terrorists; and allows challenges of national security letter gag orders

Constitution and Bill of Rights.[20] The following examples highlight details of just some of the known federal data-collection programs:

- The NSA began the collection of metadata (the phone numbers of the parties involved in the call, call duration, call location, time and data of the call, and other data) from millions of telephone calls soon after the September 11, 2001, attacks on the United States. The data enables the

NSA to create a network of associations for every caller. A provision known as Section 215 of the Patriot Act provided the legal justification needed for many proponents of data gathering. That the data was being used to help the government "connect the dots" between overseas terrorists and coconspirators within the United States offered additional justification for many. However, in June 2015, the NSA's authority to collect bulk data under Section 215 expired.[21] Under the USA Freedom Act, which was passed within days of the expiration of that authority, the NSA must request permission from the Foreign Intelligence Surveillance Court (FISC) before obtaining records—which are now held by the telecommunications companies rather than by the NSA—pertaining to a specific phone number.[22,23,24] On December 31, 2015, the FISC issued its first order approving a request from the NSA for access to "the ongoing daily production of detailed call records relating to an authorized international terrorism investigation."[25,26] See Figure 14.2.

AP Images/Rick Bowmer

FIGURE **14.2**
The NSA's Utah Data Center

This data center, code-named Bumblehive, is billed by the NSA as the first Intelligence Community Comprehensive National Cybersecurity Initiative (IC CNCI) data center designed to support the intelligence community's efforts to monitor, strengthen, and protect the nation. The data center was designed to handle the vast increases in digital data that have accompanied the rise of the global network and the NSA data-collection programs.

- PRISM is a tool used by the NSA and the FBI to collect private electronic data belonging to users of major Internet services such as AOL, Apple, Facebook, Google, Microsoft, Skype, Yahoo!, YouTube, and others. PRISM enables the NSA to access the servers of these organizations to collect material, including search history, the content of email messages, videos, photos, file transfers, and live chats. Unlike the collection of telephone call records, this surveillance includes the content of communications and not just the metadata. With PRISM, the NSA can obtain targeted communications without having to request them from the service providers and without having to obtain individual court orders. Under the program, the NSA is also allowed to share the data with other U.S. intelligence agencies for the purposes of a domestic criminal investigation—not just a national security investigation.[27,28]

- Another NSA program called MYSTIC has been used to intercept and record all telephone conversations in certain countries, including Afghanistan, the Bahamas, Mexico, Kenya, and the Philippines.[29,30] Because there is no practical way to exclude them, the conversations include those of Americans who make calls to or from the targeted countries. [31] In 2014, public revelations about MYSTIC resulted in the government of Afghanistan shutting down the program in that country.[32]

- In February 2016, the administration of Barack Obama revealed that it was on the verge of allowing the NSA to provide analysts at other U.S. intelligence agencies direct access to raw data from the NSA's surveillance programs, without first applying any privacy protections to the data. Prior to the rule change, which had been in the works since President George W. Bush was in office, the NSA filtered the surveillance data, evaluating and passing along only the portions of email or phone calls it deemed pertinent to other U.S. intelligence agencies—masking names and any irrelevant information about innocent American citizens before releasing the data.[33]

In addition to data-collection activities that are designed to capture a broad range of potentially useful data, the federal government uses other techniques to obtain data in relation to specific cases and individual targets; some of these activities have raised privacy concerns for some Americans. In a highly publicized case involving the cell phone of one of the alleged perpetrators of a mass shooting in San Bernardino, California, in December 2015, the FBI used a variety of techniques to access the data on the phone—including attempting to legally compel the phone's manufacturer, Apple, to develop a new version of its OS that would allow the FBI to use a "brute-force" attack on the phone to break through its password.[34] This case is covered in greater detail in a Case Study at the end of this chapter.

Privacy at Work

The right to privacy at work is also an important issue. Employers are using technology and corporate policies to manage worker productivity and protect the use of IS resources. Employers are mostly concerned about inappropriate Web surfing, with over half of employers monitoring the Web activity of their employees. Organizations also monitor employees' email, with more than half retaining and reviewing messages. Statistics such as these have raised employee privacy concerns. In many cases, workers claim their right to privacy trumps their companies' rights to monitor employee use of IS resources. However, most employers today have a policy that explicitly eliminates any expectation of privacy when an employee uses any company-owned computer, server, or email system. The **Fourth Amendment** protects individuals against unreasonable searches and seizures and requires that warrants be issued only upon probable cause and specifying the place to be searched and the persons or things to be seized. However, the courts have ruled that, without a reasonable expectation of privacy, there is no Fourth Amendment protection for the employee.

A California appeals court ruled in *Holmes v Petrovich Development Company* that emails sent by an employee to her attorney on the employer's computer were not "confidential communications between a client and lawyer." An Ohio federal district court in *Moore v University Hospital Cleveland Medical Center* ruled that an employee could be terminated for showing coworkers sexually explicit photos on his employer's computer. The court stated that the employee could have no expectation of privacy when accessing a hospital computer situated in the middle of a hospital floor within easy view of both patients and staff.[35]

The proliferation of health and wellness programs at many U.S. companies has prompted some privacy advocates to call for updated regulations regarding the use of data collected in connection with such programs. For instance, some programs require employees to provide health and medical details to a third-party provider in return for lower insurance premiums. And not all programs clearly state what data is protected, what data will be shared third parties, and what data will be shared with the employer (and whether that information will include individually identifiable data). Privacy advocates note that workplace wellness programs offered separately from an employer's

Fourth Amendment: This amendment to the U.S. constitution protects individuals against unreasonable searches and seizures and requires that warrants be issued only upon probable cause and specifying the place to be searched and the persons or things to be seized.

group health insurance plan are not covered under HIPAA and, so, are not bound by the same privacy constraints.[36]

The city of Houston was forced to switch providers for its online wellness program after many city employees balked at providing private information to a company whose authorization form indicated that it might pass the data to other third-party vendors and that the data might be subject to "re-disclosure," could be posted in areas reviewable by the public, and might no longer be protected by privacy law.[37]

New questions regarding employee data privacy have also arisen as more employers are encouraging—or requiring—the use of wearable technology that monitors not only employees' health but also their locations. As more companies make use of such technology, experts are encouraging them to develop and distribute policies that outline the job-related rationale for collecting such data as well as the limits on its use.[38,39]

The European Union (EU) has developed strict regulations to enforce data privacy standards across all members of the organization. Under these regulations, personal data can only be gathered legally under strict conditions and only for reasonable purposes. Furthermore, persons or organizations that collect and manage individuals' personal information must protect it from misuse and must respect certain rights of the data owners, which are guaranteed by EU law. These regulations, which were strengthened by the passage of the General Data Protection Regulation in 2016, affect virtually any company doing business in Europe.[40]

The Safe Harbor Framework is an agreement that had been in place since 2000 between the United States and the European Union (EU), allowing the transfer of personal data from the EU to the United States, despite the more limited scope of U.S. data privacy protections. However, in late 2015, the European Court of Justice found that the Safe Harbor Framework did not adequately protect the personal data of citizens residing in EU countries—a decision based, in part, on concerns over the data-collection programs of the NSA.[41,42] In early 2016, EU and U.S. negotiators agreed on a revised framework, termed "Privacy Shield" that would allow transborder data transfer to continue based on written guarantees, which must be renewed annually, that U.S. intelligence agencies would not have unlimited access to such data.[43] The next step for that agreement, which still faces opposition in Europe, is adoption by the European Commission, the executive body of the EU—an action that is not guaranteed after an EU data advisory group issued an opinion in April 2016 critical of the agreement.[44]

Privacy and Email

The use of email also raises some interesting issues about privacy. Sending an email message is like having an open conversation in a large room—many people can listen to your messages, especially if they are not encrypted. In addition, federal law permits employers to monitor email sent and received by employees. Another important aspect that should be considered when using email is that even email messages that have been erased from hard disks can be retrieved; in some cases, such emails must be retrieved as part of the discovery process in a lawsuit because the laws of discovery demand that companies produce all relevant business documents. On the other hand, the use of email among public officials might violate "open meeting" laws. These laws, which apply to many local, state, and federal agencies, prevent public officials from meeting in private about matters that affect the state or local area.

In Freeman, Massachusetts, the Board of Selectman, which serves as the executive branch of the city government, was hit with a $1,000 penalty by the state's attorney general's office in connection with a string of email messages between members of the board and the city administrator about the employment status of a city employee. Massachusetts' Open Meeting Law limits the content of email to items such as scheduling information or the distribution of a meeting agenda or other documents that are to be discussed at a public meeting. The law prohibits the expression of any opinions by public officials via email, as that constitutes an improper deliberation outside of a public meeting. Some of the emails in question contained opinions about the board's impending decision to place the employee on administrative leave. The Freeman board also violated the law by attempting to use a third party, city administrator, to relay messages.[45,46]

Privacy and Instant Messaging

Using texting and instant messaging (IM) apps to send and receive messages, files, and images introduces the same privacy issues associated with email. As with email, federal law permits employers to monitor instant messages sent and received by employees. Employers' major concern involves text and IMs sent by employees over their employer's IM network or using employer-provided phones. To protect your privacy and your employer's property, do not send personal or private messages at work.

Even outside of work, users of texting and instant messaging apps should be aware of the potential privacy issues associated with such technology. The following are some tips to keep in mind:

- Select a texting or instant messaging app that receives high security ratings, and consider using a service that encrypts texts.
- Disable text previews (which include the name of the sender and a portion of the incoming message) that appear in a pop-up window on the lock screen by default.
- Do not open files or click links in messages from people you do not know.
- Never send sensitive personal data such as credit card numbers, bank account numbers, or passwords via text or IM.
- Choose a nonrevealing, nongender-specific, unprovocative IM screen name (Sweet Sixteen, 2hot4u, UCLAMBA, all fail this test).
- Don't send messages you would be embarrassed to have your family members, colleagues, or friends read.

Privacy issues have come into play in some recent cases involving sexting—or the sending of sexually explicit texts and/or photos. Some older teenagers who have engaged in consensual sexting have found that those texts are not considered private if the sexting involves someone who is still a minor. Currently, only 20 states have sexting laws with provisions that provide for leniency for adolescents in cases where the sexting was consensual. Statutes in many states can result in teenagers who are prosecuted in cases involving underage texting being charged with possessing child pornography, resulting in a mandatory, lifetime sex offender designation.[47]

Privacy and Personal Sensing Devices

RFID tags, essentially microchips with antenna, are embedded in many of the products we buy, from medicine containers, clothing, and library books to computer printers, car keys, and tires. RFID tags generate radio transmissions that, if appropriate measures are not taken, can lead to potential privacy concerns. Once these tags are associated with the individual who purchased the item, someone can potentially track individuals by the unique identifier associated with the RFID chip.

A handful of states have reacted to the potential for abuse of RFID tags by passing legislation prohibiting the implantation of RFID chips under people's skin without their approval. Still, advocates for RFID chip implantation argue their potential value in tracking children or criminals and their value in carrying an individual's medical records.

Mobile crowd sensing (MCS) is a means of acquiring data (i.e., location, noise level, traffic conditions, and pollution levels) through sensor-enhanced mobile devices and then sharing this data with individuals, healthcare providers, utility firms, and local, state, and federal government agencies for decision making. While such data can be potentially useful in a variety of fields, the technology carries with it some privacy risks if people are unaware (or forget) that their personal mobile data is being shared.

Privacy and the Internet

Some people approach the Internet with the assumption that there is no privacy online and that people who choose to use the Internet do so at their own risk. Others believe that companies with Web sites should have strict privacy procedures and be held accountable for privacy invasion. Regardless of your view, the potential for privacy invasion on the Internet is huge. People and organizations looking to invade your privacy could be anyone from criminal hackers to marketing companies to corporate bosses. Your personal and professional information can be seized on the Internet without your knowledge or consent. Email is a prime target, as discussed previously. When you visit a Web site on the Internet, information about you and your computer can be captured. If this information is combined with other personal information, companies can find out what you read, where you shop, what products you buy, and what your interests are.

Most people who buy products on the Web say it's very important for a site to have a policy explaining how personal information is used, and that the policy statement must make people feel comfortable and be extremely clear about what information is collected and what will and will not be done with it. However, many Web sites still do not prominently display their privacy policy or implement practices completely consistent with that policy. Ultimately, the issue of most concern to many Internet users is what do content providers want to do with the personal information they gather online? If a site requests that you provide your name and address, you have every right to know why and what will be done with it. If you buy something and provide a shipping address, will it be sold to other retailers? Will your email address be sold on a list of active Internet shoppers? Consumers have the right to be taken off any mailing list, whether it is for traditional mail or email.

Children's Online Privacy Protection Act (COPPA): An act, directed at Web sites catering to children, that requires site owners to post comprehensive privacy policies and to obtain parental consent before they collect any personal information from children under 13 years of age.

The **Children's Online Privacy Protection Act (COPPA)** was passed by Congress in October 1998. This act, directed at Web sites catering to children, requires site owners to post comprehensive privacy policies and to obtain parental consent before they collect any personal information from children under 13 years of age. Web site operators who violate the rule could be liable for civil penalties of up to $11,000 per violation. Web sites and creators of apps directed at children are also prohibited by COPPA from using "persistent identifiers," which are pieces of data tied to a particular user or device, to serve advertising to children. In December 2015, the Federal Trade Commission settled cases with two different companies who were accused of allowing third-party advertisers to collect personal information (in the form of persistent identifiers) from children who used their apps. The FTC issued a total of $360,000 in fines in connection with these two cases.[48]

Popular social media apps and sites such as Facebook, Twitter, LinkedIn, Pinterest, Google Plus, Tumblr, and Instagram—all of which have over 100 million unique monthly visitors—allow users to easily create a user profile that provides personal details, photos, and even videos that can be viewed by other visitors.[49] Some of the sites have age restrictions or require that a parent register his or her preteen by providing a credit card to validate the parent's identity. Others simply require users to verify that they are over the site's age limit—a restriction that is easily overcome. Once on social media, children and teens often provide information about where they live, go to school, their favorite music, and their interests in hopes of meeting new friends. Unfortunately, they can also meet ill-intentioned strangers at these sites. There have been documented encounters involving adults masquerading as teens attempting to meet young people for illicit purposes. Experts advise parents to discuss the potential dangers of social media with their children, check their children's profiles, and monitor their social media activities.

Privacy concerns related to the use of social media are not limited to minors. The privacy rights of adults are also often at risk because of their social media habits. Facebook, in particular, holds a startling amount of information about its more than 1 billion users.[50] In addition to the information they provide when setting up an account, many Facebook users are not discrete and reveal such information as their health conditions and treatments; where they will be on a certain day (helpful to potential burglars); personal details of members of their family; their sexual, racial, religious, and political affiliations and preferences; and other personal information about their friends and family. Facebook receives a notice every time you visit a Web site with a "Like" button whether or not you click the "Like" button, log on to Facebook, or are a Facebook user. Users and observers have raised concerns about how Facebook treats this sometimes very personal information. For example, if law enforcement officials filed a subpoena for your Facebook information, they could obtain all these details as well as records of your postings, photos you have uploaded, photos in which you have been tagged, and a list of all your Facebook friends. Many privacy advocates have raised concerns about the ways in which Facebook provides this information to third parties for marketing or other purposes.

Privacy and Internet Libel Concerns

Libel involves publishing an intentionally false written statement that is damaging to a person's or organization's reputation. Examples of Internet libel include an ex-husband posting lies about his former wife on a blog, a disgruntled former employee posting lies about a company on a message board, and a jilted girlfriend posting false statements to her former boyfriend's Facebook account. In Brooklyn, New York, residents of two co-op apartment buildings have become entangled in defamation lawsuits that grew out of online comments criticizing co-op board members and building management.[51] A Hong Kong court even ruled that a local billionaire can sue Google for libel over its autocomplete search results, which suggest that he is connected to organized crime. The tycoon filed the lawsuit after Google refused to remove autocomplete suggestions, such as "triad" (in China, this is another name for an organized crime gang), which appear with searches on his name. The billionaire maintains that his reputation has been "gravely injured" and wants recompense.[52]

Individuals can post information on the Internet using anonymous email accounts or screen names. This anonymity makes it more difficult, but not impossible, to identify the libeler. The offended party can file what is known as a John Doe lawsuit and use the subpoena power it grants to force the ISP to provide whatever information it has about the anonymous poster, including IP address, name, and street address. (Under Section 230 of the Communications Decency Act, ISPs are not usually held accountable for the bad behavior of their subscribers.)

Brian Burke, the current general manager (GM) and president of the National Hockey League's (NHL) Calgary Flames, and former GM of several other NHL teams filed a lawsuit in the Supreme Court of British Columbia against 18 individuals who allegedly made defamatory statements regarding Burke on various Internet message boards and blogs.[53]

Privacy and Fairness in Information Use

Selling information to other companies can be so lucrative that many companies store and sell the data they collect on customers, employees, and others. When is this information storage and use fair and reasonable to the people whose data is stored and sold? Do people have a right to know about data stored about them and to decide what data is stored and used? As shown in Table 14.2, these questions can be broken down into four issues that should be addressed: knowledge, control, notice, and consent.

TABLE 14.2 The right to know and the ability to decide federal privacy laws and regulations

Fairness Issues	Database Storage	Database Usage
The right to know	Knowledge	Notice
The ability to decide	Control	Consent

Knowledge. Should people know what data is stored about them? In some cases, people are informed that information about them is stored in a corporate database. In others, they are unaware that their personal information is being stored.

Control. Should people be able to correct errors in corporate database systems? This ability is possible with most organizations, although it can be difficult in some cases.

Notice. Should an organization that uses personal data for a purpose other than the original designated purpose be required to notify individuals in advance? Most companies don't do this.

Consent. If information on people is to be used for other purposes, should these people be asked to give their consent before data on them is used? Many companies do not give people the ability to decide if such information will be sold or used for other purposes.

Privacy and Filtering and Classifying Internet Content

filtering software: Software used to help protect personal data and screen objectionable Internet content.

To help parents control what their children see on the Internet, some companies provide **filtering software** to help screen Internet content. Many of these screening programs also prevent children from sending personal information over email, in chat groups, or through instant messaging apps. These programs stop children from broadcasting their name, address, phone number, or other personal information over the Internet. The 2016 top-rated Internet filtering software for both Windows and Mac systems is presented in Table 14.3.[54,55]

TABLE 14.3 Top-rated Internet filtering software

Windows Systems	Mac Systems
NetNanny ($28.99)	Net Nanny ($28.99)
SpyAgent ($69.95)	Safe Eyes ($49.95)
Qustodio ($44.95)	Spector Pro ($99.95)

Organizations also implement filtering software to prevent employees from visiting Web sites not related to work, particularly those involving gambling and those containing pornographic or other offensive material. Before an organization implements Web site blocking, it should educate employees about the company's Internet policies and why they exist. To increase compliance, it is best if the organization's Internet users, management, and IS organization work together to define the policy to be implemented. The policy should be clear about the repercussions to employees who attempt to circumvent the blocking measures.

The U.S. Congress has made several attempts to limit children's exposure to online pornography, including the Communications Decency Act (enacted 1996) and the Child Online Protection Act (enacted 1998). Within two years of being enacted, the U.S. Supreme Court found that both these acts violated the First Amendment (freedom of speech) and ruled them to be unconstitutional. The Children's Internet Protection Act (CIPA) was signed into law in 2000 and later upheld by the Supreme Court in 2003. Under CIPA, schools and libraries subject to CIPA do not receive the discounts offered by the E-Rate program (provides funding to help pay for the cost of Internet connections) unless they certify that they have certain Internet safety measures in place to block or filter "visual depictions that are obscene, child pornography, or are harmful to minors." (The E-Rate program provides many schools and libraries support to purchase Internet access and computers.)

Corporate Privacy Policies

Even though privacy laws for private organizations are not very restrictive, most organizations are sensitive to privacy issues and fairness. They realize that invasions of privacy can damage their reputation, turn away customers, and dramatically reduce revenues and profits. Consider a major international credit card company. If the company sold confidential financial information on millions of customers to other companies, the results could be disastrous. In a matter of days, the firm's business and revenues could be reduced dramatically. Therefore, most organizations maintain privacy policies, even though they are not required by law to do so. Some companies even have a privacy bill of rights that specifies how the privacy of employees, clients, and customers will be protected. Corporate privacy policies should address a customer's knowledge, control, notice, and consent over the storage and use of information. They can also cover who has access to private data and when it can be used.

The United States does not have a specific federal regulation requiring implementation of privacy policies except in specific circumstances, such as:

- Health Insurance Portability and Accountability Act (HIPAA) privacy rules require notice in writing of the privacy practices of health care services.
- Children's Online Privacy Protection Act (COPPA) requires Web sites that collect information about children under the age of 13 to post a privacy policy and adhere to certain information-sharing restrictions.
- Gramm–Leach–Bliley Act requires financial institutions to provide "clear, conspicuous, and accurate statements" of their information-sharing practices.

The Federal Trade Commission (FTC) enforces federal consumer protection laws (e.g., Federal Trade Commission Act, Telemarketing Sale Rule, Identity Theft Act, and Fair Credit Reporting Act) that prevent fraud, deception, and unfair business practices. This gives it the power to enforce the terms of privacy policies as promises made to consumers. So it cases where an organization does not follow the terms of its privacy policy, consumers may file lawsuits which can result in settlements or judgments. However, such lawsuits are often not an option, due to arbitration clauses in the privacy policies or other terms of service agreements.

The BBB Code of Business Practices (BBB Accreditation Standards) requires that BBB-accredited businesses have some sort of privacy notice on their Web site. See Figure 14.3. BBB recommends that an organization's privacy notice include the following elements:[56]

Privacy Notice

This privacy notice discloses the privacy practices for [Web site address]. This privacy notice applies solely to information collected by this web site. It will notify you of the following:

1. What personally identifiable information is collected from you through the web site, how it is used and with whom it may be shared.
2. What choices are available to you regarding the use of your data.
3. The security procedures in place to protect the misuse of your information.
4. How you can correct any inaccuracies in the information.

Information Collection, Use, and Sharing

We are the sole owners of the information collected on this site. We only have access to/collect information that you voluntarily give us via email or other direct contact from you. We will not sell or rent this information to anyone.

We will use your information to respond to you, regarding the reason you contacted us. We will not share your information with any third party outside of our organization, other than as necessary to fulfill your request, e.g. to ship an order.

Unless you ask us not to, we may contact you via email in the future to tell you about specials, new products or services, or changes to this privacy policy.

Your Access to and Control Over Information

You may opt out of any future contacts from us at any time. You can do the following at any time by contacting us via the email address or phone number given on our Web site:

- See what data we have about you, if any.
- Change/correct any data we have about you.
- Have us delete any data we have about you.
- Express any concern you have about our use of your data.

Security

We take precautions to protect your information. When you submit sensitive information via the Web site, your information is protected both online and offline.

Wherever we collect sensitive information (such as credit card data), that information is encrypted and transmitted to us in a secure way. You can verify this by looking for a closed lock icon at the bottom of your web browser, or looking for "https" at the beginning of the address of the web page.

While we use encryption to protect sensitive information transmitted online, we also protect your information offline. Only employees who need the information to perform a specific job (for example, billing or customer service) are granted access to personally identifiable information. The computers/servers in which we store personally identifiable information are kept in a secure environment.

If you feel that we are not abiding by this privacy policy, you should contact us immediately via telephone at XXX YYY-ZZZZ or via email.

FIGURE **14.3**

Sample privacy notice

The BBB provides this sample privacy notice as a guide to businesses to post on their Web sites.

Source: The Better Business Bureau

- **Policy.** What personal information is being collected on the site
- **Choice.** What options the customer has about how/whether his or her data is collected and used
- **Access.** How a customer can see what data has been collected and change/correct it if necessary
- **Security.** State how any data that is collected is stored/protected
- **Redress.** What a customer can do if the privacy policy is not met
- **Updates.** How policy changes will be communicated

Multinational companies face an extremely difficult challenge in implementing data collection and dissemination processes and policies because of the multitude of differing country or regional statutes. For example, Australia requires companies to destroy customer data (including backup files) or make it anonymous after it's no longer needed. As discussed earlier in the chapter, firms that transfer customer and personnel data out of Europe must comply with European privacy laws that allow customers and employees to access data about themselves and determine how that information can be used.

Links to some sample corporate privacy policies are provided in Table 14.4.

TABLE 14.4 Links to sample corporate privacy policies

Company	URL
Intel	*www.intel.com/content/www/us/en/privacy/intel-privacy-notice.html*
Starwood Hotels & Resorts	*www.starwoodhotels.com/corporate/privacy_policy.html*
TransUnion	*www.transunion.com/corporate/privacyPolicy.page*
United Parcel Service	*www.ups.com/content/corp/privacy_policy.html*
Visa	*http://usa.visa.com/legal/privacy-policy/index.jsp*
Walt Disney Company	*https://disneyprivacycenter.com/*

A good database design practice is to assign a single unique identifier to each customer so each has a single record describing all relationships with the company across all its business units. That way, the organization can apply customer privacy preferences consistently throughout all databases. Failure to do so can expose the organization to legal risks—in addition to upsetting customers who opted out of some collection practices. The 1999 Gramm–Leach–Bliley Financial Services Modernization Act requires all financial service institutions to communicate their data privacy rules and honor customer preferences.

Individual Efforts to Protect Privacy

Although numerous state and federal laws deal with privacy, the laws do not completely protect individual privacy. In addition, not all companies have privacy policies. As a result, many people are taking steps to increase their own privacy protection. Some of the steps that you can take to protect personal privacy include the following:

- **Find out what is stored about you in existing databases**. Call the major credit bureaus to get a copy of your credit report. You are entitled to a free credit report every 12 months from each of the three major consumer reporting agencies (Equifax, Experian, and TransUnion). You can also obtain a free report if you have been denied credit in the last 60 days. Note that the only Web site authorized by federal law to provide the free credit reports is AnnualCreditReport.com. Other Web sites claim to offer free credit reports but actually charge consumers, sometimes on an ongoing basis, for access to their credit report.[57] The major companies are Equifax (*www.equifax.com*), TransUnion (*www.transunion.com*), and Experian (*www.experian.com*). You can also submit a Freedom of Information Act request to a federal agency that you suspect might have information stored on you.

- **Be careful when you share information about yourself**. Don't share information unless it is absolutely necessary. Every time you give information about yourself through an 800, 888, or 900 call, your privacy is at risk. Be vigilant in insisting that your doctor, bank, or financial institution not share information about you with others without your written consent.

- **Be proactive in protecting your privacy**. You can get an unlisted phone number and ask the phone company to block caller ID systems from reading your phone number. If you change your address, don't fill out a change-of-address form with the U.S. Postal Service; you can notify the people and companies that you want to have your new address. Destroy copies of your charge card bills and shred monthly statements before disposing of them in the garbage. Be careful about sending personal email messages over a corporate email system. You can also cut down on the junk mail and telemarketing calls you receive by visiting the Direct Marketing Association Web site (*www.thedma.org*). Go to the site and look under Consumer Help-Remove Name from Lists.

- **Take extra care when purchasing anything from a Web site.** Make sure that you safeguard your credit card numbers, passwords, and personal information. Do not do business with a site unless you know that it handles credit card information securely. (Look for a seal of approval from organizations such as the Better Business Bureau Online or TRUSTe. When you open the Web page where you enter credit card information or other personal data, make sure that the Web address begins with *https* and check to see if a locked padlock icon appears in the Address bar or status bar.) Do not provide personal information without reviewing the site's data privacy policy. Many credit card companies will issue single-use credit card numbers on request. Charges appear on your usual bill, but the number is destroyed after a single use, eliminating the risk of stolen credit card numbers.

Critical Thinking Exercise

Seeking Greater Customer Acceptance

Your organization has been in business over 10 years selling consumer home products over the Internet. A year ago, the firm gained much negative publicity when it was uncovered that the personal data it gathered was being sold, unknown to its customers, to third parties. The result was over a 15 percent drop in sales. At this time, the firm has no privacy policy and is debating whether to create such a policy, and if so, what terms it should include.

Review Questions

1. What is the purpose and intent of a privacy policy?
2. What are the key elements that need to be included in an effective privacy policy?

Critical Thinking Questions

1. What obligations and potential issues are raised by creating a privacy policy?
2. What measures should be taken to avoid potential litigation over any new privacy policy?

Work Environment

The use of computer-based information systems has changed the makeup of the workforce. Jobs that require IS literacy have increased, and many less-skilled positions have been eliminated. Corporate programs, such as those focused on reengineering and continuous improvement, bring with them the concern that, as business processes are restructured and information systems are integrated within them, the people involved in these processes will be removed. Even the simplest tasks have been aided by computers, making customer checkout faster, streamlining order processing, and allowing people with disabilities to participate more actively in the workforce. As computers and other IS components drop in cost and become easier to use, more workers will benefit from the increased productivity and efficiency provided by computers. Yet, despite these increases in productivity and efficiency, the use of information systems can raise other concerns.

Health Concerns

Organizations can increase employee productivity by paying attention to the health concerns in today's work environment. For some people, working with computers can cause occupational stress. Anxieties about job insecurity, loss of control, incompetence, and demotion are just a few of the fears workers might experience. In some cases, the stress can become so severe that workers avoid taking training to learn how to use new computer systems and equipment. Monitoring employee stress can alert companies to potential problems. Training and counseling can often help the employee and deter problems. Although they can cause negative health consequences, information systems can also be used to provide a wealth of information on health topics through the Internet and other sources.

Heavy computer use can affect one's physical health as well. A job that requires sitting at a desk and using a computer for many hours a day qualifies as a sedentary job. Such work can double the risk of seated immobility thromboembolism (SIT), the formation of blood clots in the legs or lungs. People leading a sedentary lifestyle are also likely to experience an undesirable weight gain, which can lead to increased fatigue and greater risk of type 2 diabetes, heart problems, and other serious ailments.

Repetitive strain injury (RSI) is an injury or disorder of the muscles, nerves, tendons, ligaments, or joints caused by repetitive motion. RSI is a very common job-related injury. Tendonitis is inflammation of a tendon due to repetitive motion on that tendon. Carpal tunnel syndrome (CTS) is an inflammation of the nerve that connects the forearm to the palm of the wrist. CTS involves wrist pain, a feeling of tingling and numbness, and difficulty grasping and holding objects.

Avoiding Health and Environmental Problems

Two primary causes of computer-related health problems are a poorly designed work environment and failure to take regular breaks to stretch the muscles and rest the eyes. Computer screens can be hard to read because of glare and poor contrast. Desks and chairs can also be uncomfortable. Keyboards and computer screens might be fixed in an awkward position or difficult to move. The hazardous activities associated with these unfavorable conditions are collectively referred to as *work stressors*. Although these problems might not be of major concern to casual users of computer systems, continued stressors such as repetitive motion, awkward posture, and eye strain can cause more serious and long-term injuries. If nothing else, these problems can severely limit productivity and performance.

ergonomics: The science of designing machines, products, and systems to maximize the safety, comfort, and efficiency of the people who use them.

The science of designing machines, products, and systems to maximize the safety, comfort, and efficiency of the people who use them, called **ergonomics**, has suggested some approaches to reducing these health problems. Ergonomic experts carefully study the slope of the keyboard, the positioning and design of display screens, and the placement and design of computer tables and chairs. Flexibility is a major component of ergonomics and an important consideration in the design of computer devices. People come in many sizes, have differing preferences, and require different positioning of equipment for best results. Some people, for example, want to place the keyboard in their laps; others prefer it on a solid table. Because of these individual differences, computer designers are attempting to develop systems that provide a great deal of flexibility. See Figure 14.4.

FIGURE **14.4**
Ergonomics
Developing certain ergonomically correct habits can reduce the risk of adverse health effects when using a computer.

It is never too soon to stop unhealthy computer work habits. Prolonged computer use under poor working conditions can lead to carpal tunnel syndrome, bursitis, headaches, and permanent eye damage. Strain and poor office conditions should not be left unchecked. Unfortunately, at times, we are all distracted by pressing issues such as the organization's need to raise productivity, improve quality, meet deadlines, and cut costs. We become complacent and fail to pay attention to the importance of healthy working conditions. Table 14.5 lists some common remedies for heavy computer users.

TABLE 14.5 Avoiding common discomforts associated with heavy use of computers

Common Discomforts Associated with Heavy Use of Computers	Preventative Action
Red, dry, itchy eyes	Change your focus away from the screen every 20 or 30 minutes by looking into the distance and focusing on an object for 20 to 30 seconds.
	Make a conscious effort to blink more often.
	Consider the use of artificial tears.
	Use an LCD screen, which provides a better viewing experience for your eyes by eliminating most screen flicker while still being bright without harsh incandescence.
Neck and shoulder pain	Use proper posture when working at the computer.
	Stand up, stretch, and walk around for a few minutes every hour.
	Shrug and rotate your shoulders occasionally.
Pain, numbness, or tingling sensation in hands	Use proper posture when working at the computer.
	Do not rest your elbows on hard surfaces.
	Place a wrist rest between your computer keyboard and the edge of your desk.
	Take an occasional break and spread fingers apart while keeping your wrists straight.Taken an occasional break with your arms resting at your sides and gently shake your hands.

Source: Pekker, Michael, "Long Hours at Computer: Health Risks and Prevention Tips," *http://webfreebies4u.blogspot.com/2011/01/long-hours-at-computer-health-risks-and.html*, January 4, 2011.

The following is a useful checklist to help you determine if you are properly seated at a correctly positioned keyboard:[58]

- Your elbows are near your body in an open angle to allow circulation to the lower arms and hands.

- Your arms are nearly perpendicular to the floor.
- Your wrists are nearly straight.
- The height of the surface holding your keyboard and mouse is 1 or 2 inches above your thighs.
- The keyboard is centered in front of your body.
- The monitor is about one arm's length (20 to 26 inches) away.
- The top of your monitor is at eye level.
- Your chair has a backrest that supports the curve of your lower (lumbar) back.

Critical Thinking Exercise

Demanding Role of the Care Manager

You are a member of a healthcare company that offers a variety of services designed to provide an integrated approach to lifelong well-being. One of the most effective programs is the case management program where members are assigned a care manager who supports them by phone. The care manager is an experienced RN whose goal is to anticipate the member's needs and problems, encourage preventive care, and prevent costly interventions. Services frequently include:

- Facilitating conference calls between the member, the physician, and the care manager as needed to clarify treatment plans, medication regimens, or other urgent issues
- Monitoring medication adherence
- Assessing the member's daily living activities and cognitive, behavioral, and social abilities
- Assessing the member's risk for falls and providing fall-prevention education
- Connecting members and their families with professionals who can help them address medical, legal, housing, insurance and financial issues facing older adults
- Arranging access to transportation
- Assisting members in obtaining home health and durable medical equipment
- Referring members to meal-delivery programs and advance directive preparation services

The role of care manager is a demanding one and, in your company, requires that the worker be on the phone and in front of a computer 100 percent of their work day talking with members, other health professionals, and logging key pieces of information into the computer. The care manager does have the benefits of being able to work at home with flexible work hours—as long as the care manager interacts with 15 members a day between 8 am and 8 pm. Care givers must provide their own computer and office equipment but all Internet connection and phone bills are paid by the company. The turnover rate for care managers is extremely high with few lasting more than 9 months. Many of the care managers cite stress and health issues as reasons for quitting.

Review Questions

1. What sort of health issues would you expect are common among care managers?
2. What immediate measures might be taken to relieve the stress and health issues from which the care managers suffer?

Critical Thinking Questions

1. Management is considering fundamental changes to the role of the care managers, their goals, compensation, and their work environment? Should the care managers be involved in such discussions? What suggestions would you make?
2. Can you identify other jobs that have similar working conditions and issues?

Ethical Issues in Information Systems

Ethical issues deal with what is generally considered right or wrong. People are continually faced with ethical issues in a wide range of settings, and the use of information systems brings with it some new and challenging ethical considerations for end users and for society as a whole. Ethical information system users define acceptable practices more strictly than just refraining from committing crimes; they also consider the effects of their IS activities, including Internet usage, on other people and organizations.

IS professionals are often faced with their own unique set of ethical challenges in their work developing, implementing, and maintaining information systems. As a result, some IS professional organizations have developed codes of ethics to guide people working in IS professions. The next few sections provide an overview of ethics and ethical decision making before moving on to a discussion of code of ethics, including a review of a sample code of ethics.

What Is Ethics?

As previously defined, ethics is a set of beliefs about right and wrong behavior. Ethical behavior conforms to generally accepted social norms—many of which are almost universally accepted. Doing what is ethical can be difficult in certain situations. For example, although nearly everyone would agree that lying and cheating are unethical, some people might consider it acceptable to tell a lie to protect someone's feelings or to keep a friend from getting into trouble.

morals: One's personal beliefs about right and wrong.

Morals are one's personal beliefs about right and wrong, whereas the term "ethics" describes standards or codes of behavior expected of an individual by a group (nation, organization, and profession) to which an individual belongs. For example, the ethics of the law profession demand that defense attorneys defend an accused client to the best of their ability, even if they know that the client is guilty of the most heinous and morally objectionable crime one could imagine.

law: A system of rules that tells us what we can and cannot do.

Law is a system of rules that tells us what we can and cannot do. Laws are enforced by a set of institutions (the police, courts, law-making bodies). Legal acts are acts that conform to the law. Moral acts conform to what an individual believes to be the right thing to do. Laws can proclaim an act as legal, although some people may consider the act immoral—for example, abortion.

Including Ethical Considerations in Decision Making

We are all faced with difficult decisions in our work and in our personal life, and most of us have developed a decision-making process that we execute almost automatically, without thinking about the steps we go through. For many of us, the process generally follows these steps: (1) gather information, (2) develop a problem statement, (3) consult those involved as well as other appropriate resources, (4) identify options, (5) weigh options, (6) choose an option, (7) implement a solution, and (8) review results (see Figure 14.5).

Often the decision on what course of action to take in a given situation is further complicated because it involves significant value conflicts among the various stakeholders as to what is the fairest option to pursue. Such a decision represents an ethical dilemma, and all parties involved can benefit when ethical considerations are introduced into the decision-making process by answering the questions outlined in Table 14.6. There are many factors to be considered, and reaching a good, ethical decision can be difficult, as illustrated in Figure 14.6.

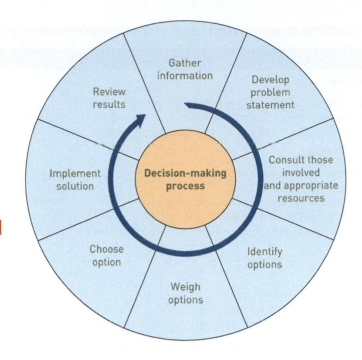

FIGURE **14.5**

Steps involved in the decision-making process

Most of us have developed a decision-making process that we execute almost automatically, without thinking about the steps we go through.

TABLE 14.6 Key questions to ask at each step in the decision-making process

Questions to Consider
Step 1: Gather information
• Have you spoken to everyone directly involved and gathered all the facts necessary to define the problem?
• Have you avoided assuming facts, motivations, or actions for which there is no evidence?
Step 2: Develop a problem statement
• Do you know the answers to the following questions:
• What do people observe that causes them to think there is a problem?
• Who is directly affected by the problem?
• Is anyone else affected?
• How often does the problem occur?
• What is the impact of the problem?
• How serious is the problem?
• What are the ethical issues involved?
• When is a solution needed?
• Have you shared the problem statement with the stakeholders, and do they concur?
Step 3: Consult those involved as well as other appropriate resources
• Have you discussed this issue with your manager?
• Have you sought input from human resources, legal, or other appropriate subject matter experts?
Step 4: Identify options
• Have you identified the success criteria for a "good solution"?
• Have the stakeholders had an opportunity to offer solutions?
Step 5: Weigh options
• How does each alternative fit with your organization's code of ethics, policies, regulations, and organizational norms?
• Is each alternative legal and consistent with industry standards?
• Does each alternative have possible unintended consequences? If so, how will you deal with those?

TABLE 14.6 Key questions to ask at each step in the decision-making process *(continued)*

Questions to Consider
Step 6: Choose an option
• Have you considered how choice of this option might appear to others?
• Would you be comfortable explaining your decision and describing your decision-making process to others?
• Is your decision grounded in a basic sense of fairness to all affected parties?
Step 7: Implement a solution
• Have you provided to all stakeholders answers to the following questions:
• Why are we doing this?
• What is wrong with the current way we do things?
• What are the benefits of the new way for you?
• Do you have a clear transition plan that explains to people how they will move from the old way of doing things to the new way?
Step 8: Review results
• Were the success criteria fully met?
• Were there any unintended consequences?
• Is there a need for further refinements?

Personal beliefs, values, and morals?

Industry and corporate standards?

Laws and regulations?

Organizational code of ethics?

Personal goals?

Organizational norms and reward system?

Code of professional conduct?

Deamles for Sale/Shutterstoc.com

FIGURE 14.6

There are many factors to weigh in decision making

code of ethics: A code that states the principles and core values that are essential to a set of people and that, therefore, govern these people's behavior.

Codes of Ethics

Laws do not provide a complete guide to ethical behavior. Just because an activity is defined as legal does not mean that it is ethical (see Figure 14.7). As a result, practitioners in many professions subscribe to a **code of ethics** that states the principles and core values that are essential to their work and, therefore, govern their behavior. The code can become a reference point for weighing what is legal and what is ethical. For example, doctors adhere to varying versions of the 2,000-year-old Hippocratic Oath, which medical schools offer as an affirmation to their graduating classes.

Some IS professionals believe that their field offers many opportunities for unethical behavior. They also believe that unethical behavior can be reduced by top-level managers developing, discussing, and enforcing codes of ethics. Various IS-related organizations and associations promote ethically responsible use of information systems and have developed useful codes of ethics. Founded in 1947, the Association for Computing Machinery (ACM) is

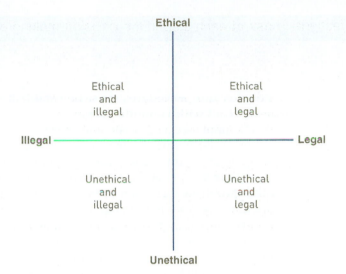

FIGURE 14.7

Legal versus ethical

Just because an activity is defined as legal does not mean that it is ethical.

the oldest computing society and boasts more than 100,000 members in more than 100 countries.[59] The ACM has a code of ethics and professional conduct that includes eight general moral imperatives that can be used to help guide the actions of IS professionals. These guidelines can also be used for those who employ or hire IS professionals to monitor and guide their work. These imperatives are outlined in the following list:[60] As an ACM member I will

1. contribute to society and human well-being.
2. avoid harm to others.
3. be honest and trustworthy.
4. be fair and take action not to discriminate.
5. honor property rights including copyrights and patents.
6. give proper credit for intellectual property.
7. respect the privacy of others.
8. honor confidentiality.

The mishandling of the social issues discussed in this chapter—including waste and mistakes, crime, privacy, health, and ethics—can devastate an organization. The prevention of these problems and recovery from them are important aspects of managing information and information systems as critical corporate assets. More organizations are recognizing that people are the most important component of a computer-based information system and that long-term competitive advantage can be found in a well-trained, motivated, and knowledgeable workforce that adheres to a set of principles and core values that help guide that workforce's actions.

Critical Thinking Exercise

Code of Ethics

You have been asked to lead an effort to develop a code of ethics for a student professional organization in your career field.

Review Questions

1. What is a code of ethics and what is its intent?
2. What are some of the key elements in almost every code of ethics?

Critical Thinking Questions

1. Are there some unique issues that need to be addressed for people entering your career?
2. What sort of process and who would you involve in establishing a code of ethics for this professional organization?

Summary

Principle:

Policies and procedures must be established to avoid waste and mistakes associated with computer usage.

Computer-related waste and mistakes are major causes of computer problems, contributing to unnecessarily high costs and lost profits. Computer waste is the inappropriate use of computer technology and resources in both the public and private sectors. Computer mistakes relate to errors, failures, and other problems that result in output that is incorrect and without value. Waste often results from poor integration of IS components, leading to duplication of efforts and overcapacity. Inefficient procedures also waste IS resources, as do thoughtless disposal of useful resources and misuse of computer time and resources for personal use. Inappropriate processing instructions, inaccurate data entry, mishandling of IS output, and poor systems design all cause computer mistakes.

Preventing waste and mistakes involves establishing, implementing, monitoring, and reviewing effective policies and procedures. Companies should develop manuals and training programs to avoid waste and mistakes. Training programs for individuals and work groups as well as manuals and documents covering the use and maintenance of computer systems can also help prevent computer waste and mistakes. Training and communication are also the keys to the successful acceptance and implementation of policies and procedures implementation. To ensure that users throughout an organization are following established procedures, routine practices must be monitored and corrective action taken when necessary. The final step in preventing computer-related waste and mistakes is to review existing policies and procedures to determine whether they are adequate.

Principle:

The use of technology requires balancing the needs of those who use the information that is collected against the rights of those whose information is being used.

Privacy is an important social issue related to the use of information systems. Balancing the right to privacy versus the need for additional monitoring to protect against terrorism and cyberattacks is an especially challenging problem.

Privacy issues are a concern with email, instant messaging, and personal sensing devices.

The federal government has implemented many laws addressing personal privacy; however, data-collection programs have raised concerns and debate between those who favor data collection as a means to increased security and those who view such programs as a violation of their rights.

Employers use technology and corporate policies to manage worker productivity and protect the use of IS resources. This activity includes monitoring of employees' Web surfing, email, and instant messaging. Most employers today have a policy that explicitly eliminates any expectation of privacy when an employee uses any company-owned computer, server, or email system.

The proliferation of health and wellness programs at many U.S. companies has prompted some privacy advocates to call for updated regulations regarding the use of data collected in connection with such programs. New questions regarding employee data privacy have also arisen as more employers are encouraging—or requiring—the use of wearable technology that monitors not only employees' health but also their locations.

Some people approach the Internet with the assumption that there is no privacy online and that people who choose to use the Internet do so at their own risk. Others believe that companies with Web sites should have strict privacy procedures and be held accountable for privacy invasion. Regardless of your view, the potential for privacy invasion on the Internet is huge.

Selling information to other companies can be so lucrative that many companies store and sell the data they collect on customers, employees, and others. Fairness in information use for privacy rights emphasizes knowledge, control, notice, and consent for people profiled in databases. People should know about the data that is stored about them and be able to correct errors in corporate database systems. If information on people is to be used for other purposes, individuals should be asked to give their consent beforehand. Each person has the right to know and to decide.

To help parents control what their children see on the Internet, some companies provide filtering software to help screen Internet content.

A business should develop a clear and thorough policy about privacy rights for customers, including database access. That policy should also address the rights of employees, including electronic monitoring systems and email.

Principle:

Jobs, equipment, and working conditions must be designed to avoid negative health effects from computers.

Jobs that involve heavy use of computers contribute to a sedentary lifestyle, which increases the risk of health problems.

The study of designing and positioning computer equipment, called "ergonomics," has suggested some approaches to reducing these health problems. Ergonomic design principles help to reduce harmful effects and increase the efficiency of an information system. RSI (repetitive strain injury) prevention includes keeping good posture, not ignoring pain or problems, performing stretching and strengthening exercises, and seeking proper treatment.

Principle:

Practitioners in many professions subscribe to a code of ethics that states the principles and core values that are essential to their work.

Ethical issues deal with what is generally considered right or wrong. Ethics is a set of beliefs about right and wrong behavior.

Ethical computer users define acceptable practices more strictly than just refraining from committing crimes; they also consider the effects of their IS activities, including Internet usage, on other people and organizations.

Often the decision on what course of action to take in a given situation is further complicated because it involves significant value conflicts among the various stakeholders as to what is the fairest option to pursue. Such a decision represents an ethical dilemma, and all parties involved can benefit when ethical considerations are introduced into the decision-making process.

Laws do not provide a complete guide to ethical behavior. Just because an activity is defined as legal does not mean that it is ethical. As a result, practitioners in many professions subscribe to a code of ethics that states the principles and core values that are essential to the members of a profession or organization. The Association for Computing Machinery developed guidelines and a code of ethics. Many IS professionals join computer-related associations and agree to abide by detailed ethical codes.

Key Terms

Children's Online Privacy Protection Act (COPPA)

code of ethics

ergonomics

filtering software

Fourth Amendment

law

morals

Chapter 14: Self-Assessment Test

Policies and procedures must be established to avoid waste and mistakes associated with computer usage.

1. Wasting time online costs U.S. businesses more than _____ annually.
   a. $385 billion
   b. $285 billion
   c. $185 million
   d. $85 billion
2. Which of the following is not a common computer-related mistake?
   a. Programming errors
   b. Shopping online while at work
   c. Data-entry or data-capture errors
   d. Errors in handling files
3. The Government Accounting Office uncovered a total of $321 million spent in the six-year period 2008 to 2013 on projects that duplicated other efforts within the Defense Department, Department of Homeland Security, and the Department of Health and Human Services. True or False?
4. Preventing waste and mistakes involves establishing, implementing, monitoring, and _____ policies and procedures.
5. Few companies have found it necessary to limit employee access to non-work-related Web sites. True or False?

The use of technology requires balancing the needs of those who use the information that is collected against the rights of those whose information is being used.

6. The United States has implemented few laws addressing personal privacy. True or False?
7. The _____ imposes limitations on the bulk collection of the telecommunications metadata of U.S. citizens; prohibits large-scale indiscriminate data collection (such as all records from an entire zip code); and requires the NSA to obtain permission from the Foreign Intelligence Surveillance Court (FISC) to access the metadata records, which are now held by telecommunication companies rather than by the government.

8. _____ is a tool used by the NSA and FBI to access the servers of major Internet services such as Facebook, Google, YouTube, and others to collect the content of emails, video, photos, file transfers, and live chats.
9. In 2015, the European Court of Justice found that the Safe Harbor Framework (an agreement that had been in place since 2000 between the United States and the European Union (EU), allowing the transfer of personal data from the EU to the United States) did not adequately protect the personal data of citizens residing in EU countries. True or False?
10. The Children's Online Privacy Protection Act (COPPA) was passed by Congress in October 1998. This act, directed at Web sites catering to children, requires site owners to post comprehensive privacy policies and to obtain parental consent before they collect any personal information from children under _____ years of age.
    a. 10
    b. 13
    c. 18
    d. 21

Jobs, equipment, and working conditions must be designed to avoid negative health effects from computers.

11. Heavy computer use can negatively affect one's physical health. True or False?
12. Two primary causes of computer-related health problems are a poorly designed _____ and failure to take regular breaks to stretch the muscles and rest the eyes.
13. The study of designing and positioning computer equipment is called _____.

Practitioners in many professions subscribe to a code of ethics that states the principles and core values that are essential to their work.

14. Morals are one's personal beliefs about right and wrong, whereas the term _____ describes standards or codes of behavior expected of an individual by a group (nation, organization, and profession) to which an individual belongs.

15. Just because an activity is defined as legal does not mean that it is ethical. True or False?
16. Founded in 1977, the Association for Computing Machinery (ACM) is the oldest computing society and boasts more than 200,000 members in more than 120 countries. True or False?

Chapter 14: Self-Assessment Test Answers

1. d
2. b
3. True
4. reviewing
5. False
6. False
7. USA Freedom Act (2015)
8. PRISM
9. True
10. b
11. True
12. work environment
13. ergonomics
14. ethics
15. True
16. False

Review Questions

1. What issues and problems are raised by the use of unintegrated information systems?
2. What is ergonomics? How can it be applied to office workers?
3. Provide a few examples of actions organizations are taking to help eliminate workers' nonproductive computer-related activity.
4. What is the First Amendment? What is the Fourth Amendment? What rights do they guarantee?
5. What is meant by "reasonable expectation of privacy"? How does this impact the application of the Fourth Amendment?
6. What is the purpose of the Safe Harbor Framework and Privacy Shield?
7. What is sexting? What issues can arise from sexting?
8. What is mobile crowd sensing? How might it be used?
9. Provide a brief summary of the various attempts by Congress to limit children's exposure to online pornography,
10. In collecting telephone call data, what is metadata? How might it be used?
11. What changes did the USA Freedom Act make in the collection and viewing of telephone call data?
12. What is a code of ethics? Give an example.

Discussion Questions

1. Identify recent examples of information system snafus causing disruptions. Do research to identify the root cause of the problem.
2. Identify and briefly discuss the most common examples you observe of coworkers wasting time in nonproductive use of information system resources. Do you believe your organization should take action to limit or end to these practices? What actions could be taken?
3. Do you feel that the measures in place to protect your personal data you provide to health care organizations are sufficient? Why or why not? What would you like to see changed?
4. How do you feel about the data you provide your bank being shared with other financial institutions who can use that data to tailor special offers and promotions for you to refinance your home, obtain an auto loan, buy additional insurance, and so forth? Should such sharing of data be prohibited or does it sometimes provide a useful service?
5. What are your feelings about the PRISM tool used the FBI and NSA to collect private electronic data belonging to users of major Internet services without having to request this data from the service providers and without having to obtain individual court orders?
6. Imagine that you are starting a dating Web site to help match compatible couples. What sort of personal data might you need to gather? What measures would need to be taken to protect this sensitive data? What key statements would potential users likely want to see in the privacy statement of this Web site?
7. Your 13-year-old nephew shows you a half-dozen or so innocent photos of himself and a brief biography, including address and cell phone number that he plans to post on a social network

for teens. What advice might you offer him about posting personal information and photos?

8. Identify and briefly discuss a difficult decision you had to make that had some ethical considerations. How do you feel about your decision-making process in reaching a decision in this case? With 20–20 hindsight, is there anything you would have done differently?

9. Do you think that there is a difference between acting ethically and acting legally? Explain.

10. Should employers be able to monitor the email, text, and phone calls of employees? Is there any degree of "monitoring" that you find acceptable/unacceptable?

Problem-Solving Exercises

1. Do research to identify the latest findings on the negative effects of sitting for long hours working at a computer. Find recommendations on how to arrange your desk and computer to avoid health problems. Prepare a brief presentation that summarizes your findings and identifies what can be done to offset these negative effects.

2. Organizational network analysis is a method for studying communication among individuals. Read the article: Making the Invisible Visible: SNA of the NSA by Joseph A.E. Shaheen at *https://www.josephshaheen.com/nsa-sna-xkeyscore/370*. The NSA uses the techniques described there to analyze communications among individuals. Use graphics software to create an organizational network analysis that depicts your email and text communications for a week. If someone were to

study this network analysis, what conclusions might they draw about you?

3. Create an algorithm that rates how well individuals protect their privacy based on the data they reveal in their user profile and postings to social networks. The algorithm should generate a score of 0 for anyone who is completely oblivious of the need to protect their privacy and identity and 100 for someone who does an excellent job at this. Factors to consider include how discrete they are in revealing personal information such as sexual orientation, health conditions, addictions, income data, and personal details about friends. Now test your algorithm using data from two of your contacts. Based on the results, adjust the algorithm as you see fit. Now test the revised algorithm with two other contacts. Summarize your findings from this exercise.

Team Activities

1. Your team has been asked to develop your school's first student code of ethics. How might you approach this task? Who might you try to involve? What might be some key tenants of such a code of ethics?

2. Imagine that your team has been hired to conduct a review of the information system policies and procedures employed in the student registration department at your school or university. Develop a list of at least 10 specific questions that your

team would use to assess the effectiveness of these policies and procedures in reducing mistakes, waste, and costs.

3. Have each member of your team access six different Web sites and summarize their findings in terms of the existence of data privacy policy statements. Did each site have such a policy? Was it easy to find? Did it seem complete and easy to understand? Does it adequately cover any concerns you might have as a visitor to that site?

Web Exercises

1. Do research on Edward Snowden the U.S. computer professional, former Central Intelligence Agency employee, and former contractor for the United States government who copied and leaked classified information from the National Security Agency in 2013 without prior authorization. Do you consider him to be a traitor, patriot, or something else? Why?

2. Do research to determine the current status of the Privacy Shield as a framework for governing transborder data flow. Write a brief report summarizing your findings.

3. Request a current copy of your free credit report through the AnnualCreditReport.com Web site. Review the report carefully for any inaccuracies. Follow the necessary steps to remove these inaccuracies.

Career Exercises

1. You have been offered an entry-level management position with a military aircraft manufacturer. Due to national security concerns, the organization has very strong policies against the personal use of computers and smartphones while you are at ework. They have also made it clear that all forms of employee communications are closely monitored to avoid the intentional or unintentional leak of classified material. How might these policies affect your decision to accept a position with this firm?

2. You have been approached by the NSA to work in an information systems group that will use high-powered computers and advanced analytic techniques to study phone call metadata and other data that has been obtained through Foreign Intelligence Surveillance Court (FISC) orders in an attempt to identify terrorists and stop impending terrorist acts. Obviously, you will not be able to talk to anyone about your work; however, your total compensation will be more than 10 percent greater than any position for which you have applied. Would you accept this position? Why or why not?

3. Do research to find any professional organization or code of ethics associated with your current or desired future career. What might be the benefits of joining such a professional organization? How might a code of ethics help guide you in career-related decision making?

Case Studies

Case One

FBI Orders Apple to Unlock iPhone

On December 2, 2015, Syed Rizwan Farook and Tashfeen Malik burst into a holiday gathering of county employees at the Inland Regional Center in San Bernardino, California, and began shooting—ultimately killing 14 people and wounding another 21. In the hours after the attack, the couple became involved in a shootout with police, and both were killed.

With their deaths, the investigation into the deadliest terrorist attack in the United States since September 11, 2001, entered a new phase, as hundreds of FBI agents in California and around the world began investigating the attackers' online and offline activities in the hours, weeks, and months leading up to the shootings. In addition to the stockpile of weapons and homemade pipe bombs found in the home of Farook and Malik, investigators found multiple electronic devices. While attempts had been made by the couple to delete data and damage some of the devices, FBI Director James Comey reported two weeks after the attack that investigators had found private messages between the two that showed their "joint commitment to jihad and to martyrdom." In addition, Malik posted a note on Facebook shortly after the shootings, pledging the couple's allegiance to the leader of ISIS, a terrorist network also known as the Islamic State.

In order to further investigate possible connections to extremist groups, the FBI attempted to access the data on an iPhone used by Farook. The phone, which belonged to Farook's employer, the San Bernardino County Health Department, was locked by a passcode, and neither the county nor the FBI were able to unlock the phone. The iOS software installed on Apple's phones allows only 10 unsuccessful passcode attempts before it wipes the phone's memory clean. This security feature prevented the FBI from attempting a "brute-force" attack, which is essentially a trial-and-error method in which all possible passcodes are tried systematically until the correct one is uncovered.

In the weeks following the shootings, Apple representatives cooperated with the FBI's investigation, providing some older data backups from the phone as well as suggesting possible methods the agency could use to access the data on the phone itself. The company balked, however, when the FBI demanded that the company develop new software that would disable the functionality that wipes the phone's memory when too many wrong passcodes are entered in a row. The FBI also wanted Apple to eliminate the built-in delay between passcode attempts, which, by Apple's estimates, meant that a brute-force attack on a phone with a six-digit passcode could take more than five years to complete.

The FBI's demand that Apple develop new software that would allow it to unlock the phone in this case is an extension of an ongoing debate about whether tech companies should be compelled to build a "backdoor" into their software that would allow the government to access data even when secure encryption has been used to protect it. Without it, some law enforcement experts warn, the United States could be faced with the prospect of what has been dubbed the "Going Dark" problem, which some experts fear would lead to the inability of law enforcement to access electronic data even with a warrant. That concern was heightened for some when Apple announced in 2014 that it had altered its software so that it was no longer "technically feasible for us to respond to government warrants for the extraction of data from devices" running iOS 8 or later versions of that software.

On February 16, 2016, a U.S. magistrate in California ordered Apple to assist the government by creating a custom version of iOS that would run only on the iPhone in question and that would provide the functionality demanded by the FBI. In its motion requesting the order, the Department of Justice cited the All Writs Act, a law signed by President George Washington, which, among other things, gives federal judges the power to issue court orders compelling people to do things within the limits of the law and which has frequently been used as the basis for court orders compelling telecommunications companies to install and operate call-tracking devices. In its filing, the DOJ alleged that Apple "deliberately raised technological barriers that now stand between a lawful warrant and an iPhone containing evidence related to the terrorist mass murder of 14 Americans."

Apple challenged the judge's order, arguing that it would set dangerous legal precedent. The company also issued a statement on its Web site that said, in part, "The implications of the government's demands are chilling. If the government can use the All Writs Act to make it easier to unlock your iPhone, it would have the power to reach into anyone's device to capture their data. The government could extend this breach of privacy and demand that Apple build surveillance software to intercept your messages, access your health records or financial data, track your location, or even access your phone's microphone or camera without your knowledge." According to Apple, "Opposing this order is not something we take lightly. We feel we must speak up in the face of what we see as an overreach by the U.S. government."

The case took another turn before the scheduled court hearing on the issue in March 2016, when the Justice Department announced that it had successfully accessed the contents of the phone using a tool provided the government by an unnamed third party. After its announcement, the Justice Department withdrew its motion to compel Apple to develop the requested software; however, according to a Justice Department spokeswoman, "It remains a priority for the government to ensure that law enforcement can obtain crucial digital information to protect national security and public safety, either with cooperation from relevant parties, or through the court system when cooperation fails."

Critical Thinking Questions

1. Why did Apple object to the court order in this case? What was the government's rationale for compelling Apply to comply with the order?
2. Do you think Americans should be willing to surrender some of their privacy for increased security by allowing backdoors that enable law enforcement access to smartphones and other devices after a search warrant has been issued? Why or why not?
3. The FBI and Apple are involved in similar disputes in other cases, including one in New York involving an alleged drug conspiracy. Shortly before the government dropped its legal action against Apple in the San Bernardino case, the judge in the New York case ruled against the government, rejecting the argument that the All Writs Act gave prosecutors the authority to compel Apple to bypass the lock on the seized phone. Do your opinions about the issues involved in the San Bernardino case change when they arise in connection with a case that does not have national security implications? Why or why not?

SOURCES: Almasy, Steve, "FBI Asks for Help Filling in San Bernardino Terrorist Attack Timeline," *CNN*, January 5, 2016, *www.cnn.com/2016 /01/05/us/san-bernardino-terrorist-attack*; Nelson, Joe, "Investigation into San Bernardino Mass Shooting Will Be 'Expansive and Expensive'," *San Bernardino County Sun*, *www.sbsun.com/general-news/20151220 /investigation-into-san-bernardino-mass-shooting-will-be-expansive -and-expensive*; Medina, Jennifer, Richard Perez-Pena, Michael S. Schmidt, and Laurie Goldstein, "San Bernardino Suspects Left Trail of Clues, but No Clear Motive," *New York Times*, December 3, 2015, *www .nytimes.com/2015/12/04/us/san-bernardino-shooting.html?_r=0*; Goldman, Adam and Mark Berman, "FBI: San Bernardino Attackers Didn't Show Public Support for Jihad On Social Media," *Washington Post*, December 16, 2015, *www.washingtonpost.com/news/post-nation/wp /2015/12/16/fbi-san-bernardino-attackers-didnt-show-public-support -for-jihad-on-social-media*; Green, Chloe, "Brute Force Attacks: How You Can Stop Hackers Breaking Your Door In," *Information Age*, May 11, 2016, *www.information-age.com/technology/security/123461414/brute -force-attacks-how-you-can-stop-hackers-breaking-your-door*; "Operational Technology: Going Dark Issue," Federal Bureau of Investigation, *www.fbi.gov/about-us/otd/going-dark-issue*, accessed May 9, 2016; Panzarino, Matthew, "No, Apple Has Not Unlocked 70 iPhones for Law Enforcement," *TechCrunch*, February 18, 2016, *http://techcrunch.com /2016/02/18/no-apple-has-not-unlocked-70-iphones-for-law-enforce ment*; Palazzolo, Joe and Devlin Barrett, "Roots of Apple-FBI Standoff Reach Back to 2008 Case," *Wall Street Journal*, *www.wsj.com/articles /roots-of-apple-fbi-standoff-reach-back-to-2008-case-1460052008? mg=id-wsj*; Timberg, Craig, "Apple Will No Longer Unlock Most iPhones, iPads for Police, Even with Search Warrants," *Washington Post*, September 18, 2014, *www.washingtonpost.com/business/technology /2014/09/17/2612af58-3ed2-11e4-b03f-de718edeb92f_story.html*; Lewis, Danny, "What the All Writs Act of 1789 Has to Do with the iPhone," *Smithsonian*, February 24, 2016, *www.smithsonianmag.com /smart-news/what-all-writs-act-1789-has-do-iphone-180958188/?no-ist*; Hollister, Sean and Connie Guglielmo, "How an iPhone Became the FBI's Public Enemy No. 1 (FAQ)," *CNET*, February 25, 2016, *www.cnet.com /news/apple-versus-the-fbi-why-the-lowest-priced-iphone-has-the-us-in- a-tizzy-faq*; "A Message to Our Customers," Apple, February 16, 2016, *www.apple.com/customer-letter*; Barrett, Devlin, "FBI Paid More than $1 Million to Hack San Bernardino iPhone," *Wall Street Journal*, April 21, 2016, *www.wsj.com/articles/comey-fbi-paid-more-than-1-million-to -hack-san-bernardino-iphone-1461266641*; Zetter, Kim, "Apple's FBI Battle Is Complicated. Here's What's Really Going On," *Wired*, February 18, 2016, *www.wired.com/2016/02/apples-fbi-battle-is-complicated -heres-whats-really-going-on*; Barrett, Devlin, "Judge Sides with Apple in N.Y. Drug Case Involving Locked Phone," *Wall Street Journal*, March 1, 2016, *www.wsj.com/articles/judge-sides-with-apple-in-drug-case-invol ving-locked-phone-1456785910*.

Case Two

Protecting Health Care Privacy

The U.S. Health Insurance Portability and Accountability Act (HIPAA) addresses (among other things) the privacy of health information. Title 2 of the act regulates the use and disclosure of protected health information (PHI), such as billing services, by healthcare providers, insurance carriers, employers, and business associates.

Email is often the best way for a hospital to communicate with off-site specialists and insurance carriers about a patient. Unfortunately, standard email is insecure. It allows eavesdropping, later retrieval of messages from unprotected backups, message modification before it is received, potential invasion of the sender's privacy by providing access to information about the identity and location of the sending computer, and more. Since healthcare provider email often includes PHI, healthcare facilities must be sure their email systems meet HIPAA privacy and security requirements.

Children's National Medical Center (CNMC) of Washington, D.C., "The Nation's Children's Hospital," is especially aware of privacy concerns because its patients are children. CNMC did what many organizations do when faced with a specialized problem: rather than try to become specialists or hire specialists for whom the hospital has no long-term full-time need, it turned to a specialist firm.

CNMC chose Proofpoint of Sunnyvale, California, for its security as a service (SaaS) email privacy protection service. Matt Johnston, senior security analyst at CNMC, says that children are "the highest target for identity theft. A small kid's record is worth its weight in gold on the black market. It's not the doctor's job to protect that information. It's *my* job."

Johnston explains that he likes several things about the Proofpoint service:

- "I don't have to worry about backups." Proofpoint handles those.
- "I don't have to worry about if a server goes down. [If it was a CNMC server, I would have to] get my staff ramped up and bring up another server. Proofpoint does that for us. It's one less headache."
- "We had a product in-house before. It required several servers which took a full FTE [full-time employee] just to manage this product. It took out too much time."
- "Spam has been on the rise. Since Proofpoint came in, we've seen a dramatic decrease in spam. It takes care of itself. The end user is given a digest daily."
- Email can be encrypted or not, according to rules that the end user need not be personally concerned with.
- "Their tech support has been great."

Proofpoint is not the only company that provides healthcare providers with email security services. LuxSci of Cambridge, Massachusetts, also offers HIPAA-compliant email hosting services, as do several other firms. They all provide the same basic features: user authentication, transmission security (encryption), logging, and audit. Software that runs on the provider's computers can also deliver media control and backup. Software that runs on a user organization's server necessarily relies on that organization to manage storage; for example, deleting messages from the server after four weeks as HIPAA requires.

As people become more aware of the privacy risks associated with standard email, the use of more secure solutions such as these will undoubtedly become more common in the future.

Critical Thinking Questions

1. What requirement does HIPAA institute to safeguard patient privacy?
2. Universities use email to communicate private information. For example, an instructor might send you an email explaining what you must do to raise your grade. The regulations about protecting that information under the Family Educational Rights and Privacy Act (FERPA) are not as strict as those under HIPAA. Do you think they should be as strict as HIPAA's requirements? Why or why not?
3. How does Proofpoint safeguard patient privacy? Could Proofpoint do the same for university and corporate emails? Why or why not?

SOURCES: Children's National Medical Center Web site, *www.childrensnational.org*, accessed August 28, 2014; LuxSci Web site, *www.luxsci.com*, accessed August 28, 2014; Proofpoint Web site, *www.proofpoint.com*, accessed August 28, 2014; Staff, "HIPAA Email Security Case Study: Children's National Medical Center," Proofpoint, *www.youtube.com/watch?v=RVaBaNvwkQE*, accessed August 7, 2014.

Notes

1. Vest, Joshua R., Issel, L. Michele, and Lee, Sean, "Experience of Using Information Systems in Public Health Practice: Findings from a Qualitative Study," February 5, 2014, *www.ncbi.nlm.nih.gov/pmc/articles/PMC3959909/*.
2. Thibodeau, Patrick, "Government Wants to Increase IT Spending 1.3% in Proposed Budget," *Computerworld*, February 9, 2016, *www.computerworld.com/article/3031664/it-management/government-wants-to-increase-it-spending-13-in-proposed-budget.html*.
3. Gallagher, Sean, "De-Dupe Time: GAO Finds $321 Million in Redundant Government IT Spending," *Ars Technica*, September 17, 2013, *http://arstechnica.com/information-technology/2013/09/de-dupe-time-gao-finds-321-million-in-redundant-government-it-spending*.
4. "Federal Strategic Sourcing Initiative (FSSI)," General Services Administration, accessed May 6, 2016, *www.gsa.gov/portal/content/105156*.
5. "New CareerBuilder Survey Reveals the Most Common and Strangest Productivity Killers at Work," CareerBuilder, June 11, 2015, *www.careerbuilder.com/share/aboutus/pressreleasesdetail.aspx?sd=6%2F11%2F2015&id=pr898&ed=12%2F31%2F2015*.
6. Zakrzewski, Cat, "The Key to Getting Workers to Stop Wasting Time Online," *Wall Street Journal*, March 13, 2016, *www.wsj.com/articles/the-key-to-getting-workers-to-stop-wasting-time-online-1457921545?mg=id-wsj*.
7. "New CareerBuilder Survey," CareerBuilder.
8. Zakrzewski, "Stop Wasting Time Online."
9. Rein, Lisa," Watchdog: IRS Sent Out $46M in Tax Refunds Flagged as Potentially Fraudulent," *Chicago Tribune*, December 23, 2015, *www.chicagotribune.com/news/nationworld/ct-irs-tax-refunds-flagged-fraudulent-20151223-story.html*.
10. Kaste, Martin, "2 Prisoners Mistakenly Released Early Now Charged in Killings," *NPR*, January 1, 2016, *www.npr.org/2016/01/01/461700642/computer-glitch-leads-to-mistaken-early-release-of-prisoners-in-washington*.
11. Lorenzetti, Laura, "NYSE Explains Why It Went Down Wednesday," *Fortune*, July 9, 2015, *http://fortune.com/2015/07/09/nyse-explains-why-it-went-down-wednesday*.
12. Gandel, Stephen, "This Is Why the NYSE Shut Down Today," *Fortune*, July 8, 2015, *http://fortune.com/2015/07/08/nyse-halt*.
13. Golson, Jordan, "Honda Accidentally Charges Many Customers Twice for Single Car Payment," *Verge*, April 6, 2016, *www.theverge.com/2016/4/6/11380448/honda-car-payment-overcharge-double-price-error-mistake*.
14. Lutz, Hannah, "Honda 'Working Feverishly' to Fix Customer Billing Glitch," *Automotive News*, April 6, 2016,

www.autonews.com/article/20160406/OEM/160409849
/honda-working-feverishly-to-fix-customer-billing-glitch.

15. "Corporate E-Learning," Error Prevention Training Institute, *smartpeopledumbthings.com/e-learning
/corporate-training/*, accessed July 21, 2014.

16. McCormick, Jonathan, "How to Manage IT in a Growing
Business: Implementing IT Policies," *NetworkWorld*,
April 11, 2016, *www.networkworld.com/article
/3054601/careers/how-to-manage-it-in-a-growing
-business-implementing-it-policies.html*.

17. Kanowitz, Stephanie, "VA's Information Security Still
Lacking, Audit Shows," *FierceGovernmentIT*, March 17,
2016, *www.fiercegovernmentit.com/story/vas-information
-security-still-lacking-audit-shows/2016-03-17*.

18. Healy, Beth, "State Street Overbilled Customers $200M
over 18 Years," *Boston Globe*, December 17, 2015, *www
.bostonglobe.com/business/2015/12/17/state-street-says
-overbilled-customers-million-over-years/eiHpkMswIB9
glkZO9z06VO/story.html*.

19. Healy, Beth, "State Street Hit by Galvin for Overbilling
Clients," *Boston Globe*, April 20, 1016, *www.bostonglobe
.com/business/2016/04/20/state-street-hit-galvin-for
-overbilling-clients/8j3n0XMwUOLddJQcijtMRK/story.html*.

20. "Edward Snowden, Whistle-Blower," *New York Times*,
January 1, 2014, *www.nytimes.com/2014/01/02/opinion
/edward-snowden-whistle-blower.html*.

21. Diamond, Jeremy, "Thought Bulk Data Collection Was
Gone? Think Again," *CNN*, June 2, 2015, *www.cnn.com
/2015/06/02/politics/bulk-data-collection-coming-back
-usa-freedom-act*.

22. Kelly, Erin, "Senate Approves USA Freedom Act," *USA
Today*, June 2, 2015, *www.usatoday.com/story/news
/politics/2015/06/02/patriot-act-usa-freedom-act-senate
-vote/28345747*.

23. Rampton, Rebecca, "Obama to Propose Ending NSA
Bulk Collection of Phone Records: Official," *Reuters*,
March 24, 2014, *www.reuters.com/article/2014/03/25
/us-usa-security-obama-nsa-idUSBREA2O03O20140325*.

24. Walker, Laura, "NSA to Destroy Data Collected from
Mass Phone Surveillance," *Newsweek*, July 27, 2015,
*www.newsweek.com/nsa-destroy-data-collected-mass
-phone-surveillance-357500*.

25. Sutton, James, "NSA Obtains Permission to Collect
Metadata under New Law," *The Hill Talk*, April 24, 2016,
http://thebilltalk.com/2016/04/24/17121.

26. Hosenball, Mark, "Secret U.S. Court Issues First Order
for Phone Data under New Law," *Reuters*, April 19, 2016,
*www.reuters.com/article/usa-surveillance-court-
idUSL2N17M26C*.

27. "NSA Prism Program Taps into User Data of Apple, Google and Others," *Guardian*, June 6, 2013, *www.theguar
dian.com/world/2013/jun/06/us-tech-giants-nsa-data*.

28. Nakashima, Ellen, "Public Advocate: FBI's Use of PRISM
Surveillance Data Is Unconstitutional," *Washington Post*,
April 20, 2016, *www.washingtonpost.com/world
/national-security/public-advocate-fbis-use-of-prism
-surveillance-data-is-unconstitutional/2016/04/20
/0282ed52-0693-11e6-b283-e79d81c63c1b_story.html*.

29. "NSA Reportedly Recording All Phone Calls in a Foreign
Country," *Associated Press*, March 19, 2014, *www
.foxnews.com/politics/2014/03/19/nsa-reportedly-recording
-all-phone-calls-in-foreign-country/*.

30. Makarechi, Kia, "Julian Assange Goes Where Glenn
Greenwald Wouldn't," *Vanity Fair*, May 19, 2014, *www
.vanityfair.com/online/daily/2014/05/julian-assange
-glenn-greenwald-nsa-afghanistan*.

31. "NSA Recording All Phone Calls," *Associated Press*.

32. Nakashima, Ellen, "Top Spy Bemoans Loss of Key
Information-Gathering Program," *Washington Post*,
September 9, 2015, *www.washingtonpost.com/world
/national-security/top-spy-bemoans-loss-of-key-intelli
gence-program/2015/09/09/a214bda4-5717-11e5
-abe9-27d53f250b11_story.html*.

33. Savage, Charlie, "Obama Administration Set to Expand
Sharing of Data That N.S.A. Intercepts," *New York Times*,
*www.nytimes.com/2016/02/26/us/politics/obama
-administration-set-to-expand-sharing-of-data-that
-nsa-intercepts.html*.

34. Grossman, Lev, "Inside Apple CEO Tim Cook's Fight
with the FBI," *Time*, March 17, 2016, *http://time.com
/4262480/tim-cook-apple-fbi-2*.

35. Miller, Ron, "Employees Have No Reasonable Expectation to Privacy for Material Viewed or Stored on
Employer-Owned Computers or Servers," Wolters
Kluwer, November 24, 2011, *www.employmentlawdaily
.com/index.php/2011/11/24/employees-have-no-reason
able-expectation-to-privacy-for-materials-viewed-or
-stored-on-employer-owned-computers-or-servers*, access
August 28, 2014.

36. Hancock, Jay and Julie Appleby, "7 Questions to Ask
Your Employer about Wellness Privacy," Kaiser Health
News, September 30, 2015, *http://khn.org/news
/7-questions-to-ask-your-employer-about-wellness-privacy*.

37. Hancock. Jay, "Workplace Wellness Programs Put
Employee Privacy at Risk," *CNN*, October 2, 2015, *www
.cnn.com/2015/09/28/health/workplace-wellness-privacy
-risk-exclusive*.

38. Haggin, Patience, "As Wearables in Workplace Spread,
So Do Legal Concerns," *Wall Street Journal*, March 13,
2016, *www.wsj.com/articles/as-wearables-in-workplace
-spread-so-do-legal-concerns-1457921550*.

39. Thiel, Scott, "Wearables at Work: Data Privacy and
Employment Law Implications," DLA Piper, April 22,
2016, *www.dlapiper.com/en/us/insights/publications
/2016/04/wearables-at-work*.

40. "Protection of Personal Data," European Commission,
http://ec.europa.eu/justice/data-protection, accessed
August 17, 2014.

41. Meltzer, Joshua, "Examining the EU Safe Harbor Decision and Impacts for Transatlantic Data Flows," The
Brookings Institute, November 3, 2015, *www.brookings.
edu/research/testimony/2015/11/03-eu-safe-harbor
-decision-transatlantic-data-flows-meltzer*.

42. Cline, Jay, "Five Predictions for the EU-U.S. Safe Harbor
Showdown," *Computerworld*, October 27, 2015, *www
.computerworld.com/article/2997882/data-privacy/five
-predictions-for-the-eu-u-s-safe-harbor-showdown
.html*.

43. Scott, Mark, "U.S. and Europe in 'Safe Harbor' Data Deal,
but Legal Fight May Await," *New York Times*, *www.
nytimes.com/2016/02/03/technology/us-europe-safe
-harbor-data-deal.html*.

44. Gibbs, Samuel, "Data Regulators Reject EU-US Privacy
Shield Safe Harbour Deal," *Guardian*, April 14, 2016,

www.theguardian.com/technology/2016/apr/14/data
-regulators-reject-eu-us-privacy-shield-safe-harbour-deal.

45. Urbon, Steve, "Freetown Selectmen Hit with $1,000 Civil Penalty in Open Meeting Law Violation," *SouthCoast Today*, March 10, 2016, *www.southcoasttoday.com /article/20160310/NEWS/160319911*.

46. "The Commonwealth of Massachusetts Open Meeting Law, G.L. c. 30A, §§ 18-25," Commonwealth of Massachusetts, *www.mass.gov/ago/docs/government/oml /open-meeting-law-gl-c-30a-18-25.pdf*, accessed May 9, 2016.

47. Botelho, Greg and Michael Martinez, "DA: No Charges against Colorado Students in Sexting Scandal," *CNN*, December 9, 2015, *www.cnn.com/2015/12/09/us /colorado-sexting-scandal-canon-city*.

48. "Two App Developers Settle FTC Charges They Violated Children's Online Privacy Protection Act," Federal Trade Commission, December 17, 2015, *www.ftc.gov/news -events/press-releases/2015/12/two-app-developers-settle -ftc-charges-they-violated-childrens*.

49. "Top 15 Most Popular Social Networking Sites," Ebizma, May 2016," *http://www.ebizmba.com/articles/social -networking-websites*.

50. "Number of Monthly Active Facebook Users Worldwide as of 1st Quarter 2016 (in Millions)," Statista, *http://www .statista.com/statistics/264810/number-of-monthly -active-facebook-users-worldwide*, accessed May 9, 2016.

51. Kaysen, Ronda, "When Neighbors Tangle Online," *New York Times*, November 6, 2016, *www.nytimes.com/2015 /11/08/realestate/when-neighbors-tangle-online.html?_r=0*.

52. Worstall, Tim, "Now Google Autocomplete Could Be Found Guilty of Libel in Hong Kong," *Forbes*, August 6, 2014, *www.forbes.com/sites/timworstall/2014/08/06 /now-google-autocomplete-could-be-found-guilty-of -libel-in-hong-kong*.

53. Matthew, Lee, "Defamation, Celebrities, and the Internet," *Harvard Journal on Sports and Entertainment Law*, April 17, 2014, *http://harvardjsel.com/2014/04 /defamation-internet/*.

54. "2016 Best Internet Filter Software Reviews," TopTenReviews, *http://internet-filter-review.toptenreviews.com*, accessed May 9, 2016.

55. "2016 Best Mac Internet Filter Software Reviews," *http://internet-filter-review.toptenreviews.com/mac -internet-filter-software*, accessed May 10, 2016.

56. "BBB Sample Privacy Policy," *www.bbb.org/dallas /for-businesses/bbb-sample-privacy-policy1*, accessed August 14, 2014.

57. "Can I Review My Credit Report?," Consumer Financial Protection Bureau, *www.consumerfinance.gov/askcfpb /5/can-i-review-my-credit-report.html*, accessed May 8, 2016.

58. "How to Sit at a Computer," American Academy of Orthopedic Surgeons, *http://orthoinfo.aaos.org/topic .cfm?topic=a00261*, accessed May 10, 2016.

59. "What Is ACM?" www.acm.org/about, accessed August 14, 2014.

60. "ACM Code of Ethics and Professional Conduct," *www .acm.org/about/code-of-ethics*, accessed August 14, 2014.

Glossary

A

ACID properties Properties (atomicity, consistency, isolation, durability) that guarantee relational database transactions are processed reliably and ensure the integrity of data in the database.

advanced persistent threat (APT) A network attack in which an intruder gains access to a network and stays there—undetected—with the intention of stealing data over a long period of time.

agile development An iterative system development process that develops the system in "sprint" increments lasting from two weeks to two months.

antivirus software Software that scans a computer's memory, disk drives, and USB ports regularly for viruses.

application programming interface (API) A set of programming instructions and standards that enables one software program to access and use the services of another software program.

application software Programs that help users solve particular computing problems.

artificial intelligence The ability to mimic or duplicate the functions of the human brain.

artificial intelligence system The people, procedures, hardware, software, data, and knowledge needed to develop computer systems and machines that can simulate human intelligence processes, including learning (the acquisition of information and rules for using the information), reasoning (using rules to reach conclusions), and self-correction (using the outcome from one scenario to improve its performance on future scenarios).

assistive technology system An assistive, adaptive, or rehabilitative device designed to help people with disabilities perform tasks that they were formerly unable to accomplish or had great difficulty accomplishing.

attribute A characteristic of an entity.

autonomic computing The ability of IT systems to manage themselves and adapt to changes in the computing environment, business policies, and operating objectives.

B

batch processing system A form of data processing whereby business transactions are accumulated over a period of time and prepared for processing as a single unit or batch.

best practices The most efficient and effective ways to complete a business process.

big data A term used to describe data collections that are so enormous (think petabytes or larger) and complex (from sensor data to social media data) that traditional data management software, hardware, and analysis processes are incapable of dealing with them.

bioprinting The use of 3D printers to build human parts and organs from actual human cells.

bit A binary digit (i.e., 0 or 1) that represents a circuit that is either on or off.

blade server A server that houses many individual computer motherboards that include one or more processors, computer memory, computer storage, and computer network connections.

blended threat A sophisticated threat that combines the features of a virus, worm, Trojan horse, and other malicious code into a single payload.

Bluetooth A wireless communications specification that describes how cell phones, computers, faxes, printers, and other electronic devices can be interconnected over distances of 10 to 30 feet at a rate of about 2 Mbps.

botnet A term used to describe a large group of computers, which are controlled from one or more remote locations by hackers, without the knowledge or consent of their owners.

bring your own device (BYOD) A business policy that permits, and in some cases encourages, employees to use their own mobile devices (smartphones, tablets, or laptops) to access company computing resources and applications, including email, corporate databases, the corporate intranet, and the Internet.

broadband communications High-speed Internet access that is always on and that is faster than traditional dial-up access.

bus A set of electronic circuits used to route data and instructions to and from the various components of a computer.

bus network A network in which all network devices are connected to a common backbone that serves as a shared communications medium.

business analytics The extensive use of data and quantitative analysis to support fact-based decision making within organizations.

business intelligence (BI) A wide range of applications, practices, and technologies for the extraction, transformation, integration, visualization, analysis, interpretation, and presentation of data to support improved decision making.

business rule management system (BRMS) Software used to define, execute, monitor, and maintain the decision logic that is used by the operational systems and processes that run the organization.

business-to-business (B2B) e-commerce A subset of e-commerce in which all the participants are organizations.

business-to-consumer (B2C) e-commerce A form of e-commerce in which customers deal directly with an organization and avoid intermediaries.

byte (B) Eight bits that together represent a single character of data.

C

CAPTCHA (Completely Automated Public Turing Test to Tell Computers and Humans Apart) Software that generates and grades tests that humans can pass all but the most sophisticated computer programs cannot.

cache memory A type of high-speed memory that a processor can access more rapidly than main memory.

Cascading Style Sheet (CSS) A markup language for defining the visual design of a Web page or group of pages.

central processing unit (CPU) The part of a computer that sequences and executes instructions.

certificate authority (CA) A trusted third-party organization or company that issues digital certificates.

certification A process for testing skills and knowledge; successful completion of a certification exam results in a statement by the certifying authority that confirms an individual is capable of performing particular tasks.

change management model A description of the phases an individual or organization goes through in making a change and principles for successful implementation of change.

channel bandwidth The rate at which data is exchanged, usually measured in bits per second (bps).

character A basic building block of most information, consisting of uppercase letters, lowercase letters, numeric digits, or special symbols.

Children's Online Privacy Protection Act (COPPA) An act directed at websites catering to children, requires site owners to post comprehensive privacy policies and to obtain parental consent before they collect any personal information from children under 13 years of age.

client/server architecture An approach to computing wherein multiple computer platforms are dedicated to special functions, such as database management, printing, communications, and program execution.

clock speed A series of electronic pulses produced at a predetermined rate that affects machine cycle time.

cloud computing A computing environment where software and storage are provided as an Internet service and are accessed with a Web browser.

code of ethics A code that states the principles and core values that are essential to a set of people and that, therefore, govern these people's behavior.

cold site A computer environment that includes rooms, electrical service, telecommunications links, data storage devices, and the like.

command-based user interface A user interface that requires you to give text commands to the computer to perform basic activities.

communications management The generation, collection, dissemination, and storage of project information in a timely and effective manner.

communications medium Any material substance that carries an electronic signal to support communications between a sending and a receiving device.

community of practice (CoP) A group whose members share a common set of goals and interests and regularly engage in sharing and learning as they strive to meet those goals.

compact disc read-only memory (CD-ROM) A common form of optical disc on which data cannot be modified once it has been recorded.

compiler A special software program that converts the programmer's source code into the machine-language instructions, which consist of binary digits.

computer forensics A discipline that combines elements of law and computer science to identify, collect, examine, and preserve data from computer systems, networks, and storage devices in a manner that preserves the integrity of the data gathered so that it is admissible as evidence in a court of law.

computer graphics card A component of a computer that takes binary data from the CPU and translates it into an image you see on your display device.

computer network The communications media, devices, and software connecting two or more computer systems or devices.

computer-aided design (CAD) The use of software to assist in the creation, analysis, and modification of the design of a component or product.

computer-aided engineering (CAE) The use of software to analyze the robustness and performance of components and assemblies.

computer-aided manufacturing (CAM) The use of software to control machine tools and related machinery in the manufacture of components and products.

computer-based information system (CBIS) A single set of hardware, software, databases, networks, people, and procedures that are configured to collect, manipulate, store, and process data into information.

concurrency control A method of dealing with a situation in which two or more users or applications need to access the same record at the same time.

consumerization of IT The trend of consumer technology practices influencing the way business software is designed and delivered.

consumer-to-consumer (C2C) e-commerce A subset of e-commerce that involves electronic transactions between consumers using a third party to facilitate the process.

contactless payment card A card with an embedded chip that only needs to be held close to a terminal to transfer its data; no PIN number needs to be entered.

container A way for software developers and hardware managers to package applications and software components into a well-defined, compact envelope that can be used to more easily manage it, including moving it across various hosts.

content streaming A method for transferring large media files over the Internet so that the data stream of voice and pictures plays more or less continuously as the file is being downloaded.

continuous improvement Constantly seeking ways to improve business processes and add value to products and services.

Controlling the Assault of Non-Solicited Pornography and Marketing (CAN-SPAM) Act An act that states that it is legal to spam, provided the messages meet a few basic requirements.

conversion funnel A graphical representation that summarizes the steps a consumer takes in making the decision to buy your product and become a customer.

coprocessor The part of the computer that speeds processing by executing specific types of instructions while the CPU works on another processing activity.

core competency Something that a firm can do well and that provides customer benefits, is hard for competitors to imitate, and can be leveraged widely to many products and markets.

core value A widely accepted principle that guides how people behave and make decisions in the organization.

cost management A set of activities that include the development and management of the project budget.

cost-reimbursable contract A contract that requires the buyer to pay the provider an amount that covers the provider's actual costs plus an additional amount or percentage for profit.

critical path All project activities that, if delayed, would delay the entire project.

Cross-Industry Process for Data Mining (CRISP-DM) A six-phase structured approach for the planning and execution of a data mining project.

culture A set of major understandings and assumptions shared by a group, such as within an ethnic group or a country.

customer relationship management (CRM) system A system that helps a company manage all aspects of customer encounters, including marketing, sales, distribution, accounting, and customer service.

cutover The process of switching from an old information system to a replacement system.

cybercriminal A computer hacker who is motivated by the potential for monetary gain; cybercriminals hack into computer systems to steal, often by transferring money from one account to another or by stealing and reselling credit card numbers, personal identities, and financial account information.

cyberespionage The deployment of malware that secretly steals data in the computer systems of organizations, such as government agencies, military contractors, political organizations, and manufacturing firms.

cyberterrorism The intimidation of a government or a civilian population by using information technology to disable critical national infrastructure (e.g., energy, transportation, financial, law enforcement, emergency response) to achieve political, religious, or ideological goals.

D

dashboard A presentation of a set of KPIs about the state of a process at a specific point in time.

data Raw facts such as an employee number or total hours worked in a week.

data administrator An individual responsible for defining and implementing consistent principles for a variety of data issues.

data breach The unintended release of sensitive data or the access of sensitive data by unauthorized individuals.

data center A climate-and-access-controlled building or a set of buildings that houses the computer hardware that delivers an organization's data and information services.

Data cleansing (data cleaning/data scrubbing) The process of detecting and then correcting or deleting incomplete, incorrect, inaccurate, or irrelevant records that reside in a database.

data collection Capturing and gathering all data necessary to complete the processing of transactions.

data correction Reentering data that was not typed or scanned properly.

data cube A collection of data that contains numeric facts called measures, which are categorized by dimensions, such as time and geography.

data definition language (DDL) A collection of instructions and commands used to define and describe data and relationships in a specific database.

data dictionary A detailed description of all the data used in the database.

data editing Checking data for validity and completeness to detect any problems.

data entry Converting human-readable data into a machine-readable form.

data-flow diagram (DFD) A diagram used during both the analysis and design phases to document the processes of the current system or to provide a model of a proposed new system.

data governance The core component of data management; it defines the roles, responsibilities, and processes for ensuring that data can be trusted and used by the entire organization, with people identified and in place who are responsible for fixing and preventing issues with data.

data input Transferring machine-readable data into the system.

data item The specific value of an attribute.

data lake (enterprise data hub) A "store everything" approach to big data that saves all the data in its raw and unaltered form.

data lifecycle management (DLM) A policy-based approach to managing the flow of an enterprise's data, from its initial acquisition or creation and storage to the time when it becomes outdated and is deleted.

data management An integrated set of functions that defines the processes by which data is obtained, certified fit for use, stored, secured, and processed in such a way as to ensure that the accessibility, reliability, and timeliness of the data meet the needs of the data users within an organization.

data manipulation language (DML) A specific language, provided with a DBMS, which allows users to access and modify the data, to make queries, and to generate reports.

data mart A subset of a data warehouse that is used by small- and medium-sized businesses and departments within large companies to support decision making.

data mining A BI analytics tool used to explore large amounts of data for hidden patterns to predict future trends and behaviors for use in decision making.

data model A diagram of data entities and their relationships.

data processing Performing calculations and other data transformations related to business transactions.

data scientist A person who understands the business and the business analytics technology, while also recognizing the limitations of their data, tools, and techniques; a data scientist puts all of this together to deliver real improvements in decision making within an organization.

data steward An individual responsible for the management of critical data elements, including identifying and acquiring new data sources; creating and maintaining consistent reference data and master data definitions; and analyzing data for quality and reconciling data issues.

data storage Updating one or more databases with new transactions.

data visualization The presentation of data in a pictorial or graphical format.

data warehouse A database that stores large amounts of historical data in a form that readily supports analysis and management decision making.

database A well-designed, organized, and carefully managed collection of data.

database administrators (DBAs) Skilled and trained IS professionals who hold discussions with business users to define their data needs; apply database programming languages to craft a set of databases to meet those needs; test and evaluate databases; implement changes to improve the performance of databases; and assure that data is secure from unauthorized access.

database approach to data management An approach to data management where multiple information systems share a pool of related data.

database as a service (DaaS) An arrangement where the database is stored on a service provider's servers and accessed by the service subscriber over a network, typically the Internet, with the database administration handled by the service provider.

database management system (DBMS) A group of programs used to access and manage a database as well as provide an interface between the database and its users and other application programs.

Department of Homeland Security (DHS) A large federal agency with more than 240,000 employees and a budget of almost $65 billion whose goal is to provide for a "safer, more secure America, which is resilient against terrorism and other potential threats."

desktop computer A nonportable computer that fits on a desktop and provides sufficient computing power, memory, and storage for most business computing tasks.

DevOps The practice of blending the tasks performed by the development and IT operations groups to enable faster and more reliable software releases.

diffusion of innovation theory A theory developed by E.M. Rogers to explain how a new idea or product gains acceptance and diffuses (or spreads) through a specific population or subset of an organization.

digital audio player A device that can store, organize, and play digital music files.

digital certificate An attachment to an email message or data embedded in a Web site that verifies the identity of a sender or Web site.

digital divide The gulf between those who do and those who don't have access to modern information and communications technology such as smartphones, personal computers, and the Internet.

digital video disc (DVD) A form of optical disc storage that looks like a CD but that can store more data and access it more quickly.

direct conversion A cutover strategy that involves stopping the old system and starting the new system on a given date; also called plunge or direct cutover.

disaster recovery plan A documented process to recover an organization's business information system assets including hardware, software, data, networks, and facilities in the event of a disaster.

discrete manufacturing The production of distinct items such as autos, airplanes, furniture, or toys that can be decomposed into their basic components.

distributed denial-of-service (DDoS) attack An attack in which a malicious hacker takes over computers via the Internet and causes them to flood a target site with demands for data and other small tasks.

document production Generating output records, documents, and reports.

domain The range of allowable values for a data attribute.

domain expert The person or group with the expertise or knowledge the expert system is trying to capture (domain).

downsizing Reducing the number of employees to cut costs.

drill-down analysis The interactive examination of high-level summary data in increasing detail to gain insight into certain elements—sort of like slowly peeling off the layers of an onion.

driving forces The beliefs, expectations, and cultural norms that tend to encourage a change and give it momentum.

e-book The digital media equivalent of a conventional printed book.

e-commerce Involves the exchange of money for goods and services over electronic networks and encompasses many of an organization's outward facing processes—such as sales, marketing, order taking, delivery, procurement of goods and services, and customer service—that touch customers, suppliers, and other business partners.

E

economic feasibility The process of determining whether the project makes financial sense and whether predicted benefits offset the cost and time needed to obtain them.

e-government The use of information and communications technology to simplify the sharing of information, speed formerly paper-based processes, and improve the relationship between citizens and government.

electronic business (e-business) The use of information systems and networks to perform business-related tasks and functions beyond those performed for e-commerce.

electronic cash An amount of money that is computerized, stored, and used as cash for e-commerce transactions.

electronic discovery (e-discovery) Any process in which electronic data is sought, located, secured, and searched with the intent of using it as evidence in a civil or criminal legal case.

electronic exchange An electronic forum where manufacturers, suppliers, and competitors buy and sell goods, trade market information, and run back-office operations.

Electronic Product Environmental Assessment Tool (EPEAT) A system that enables purchasers to evaluate, compare, and select electronic products based on a set of environmental criteria.

embedded system A computer system (including some sort of processor) that is implanted in and dedicated to the control of another device.

enterprise application integration (EAI) The systematic tying together of disparate applications so that they can communicate.

enterprise data model A data model that provides a roadmap for building database and information systems by creating a single definition and format for data that can ensure data compatibility and the ability to exchange and integrate data among systems.

enterprise IS An information system that an organization uses to define structured interactions among its own employees and/ or with external customers, suppliers, government agencies, and other business partners.

enterprise resource planning (ERP) system A system that supports an organization's routine business processes, maintains records about those processes, and provides extensive reporting and data analysis capabilities.

enterprise search The application of search technology to find information within an organization.

enterprise search software Software that matches a user's query to many sources of information in an attempt to identify the most important content and the most reliable and relevant source.

enterprise sphere of influence The sphere of influence that serves the needs of an organization in its interactions with its environment.

enterprise system A system central to the organization that ensures information can be shared with authorized users across all business functions and at all levels of management to support the running and managing of a business.

entity A person, place, or thing for which data is collected, stored, and maintained.

ergonomics The science of designing machines, products, and systems to maximize the safety, comfort, and efficiency of the people who use them.

entity-relationship (ER) diagram A data model that uses basic graphical symbols to show the organization of and relationships between data.

ethics A set of beliefs about right and wrong behavior. Ethical behavior conforms to generally accepted social norms—many of which are almost universally accepted.

expert system A system that consists of hardware and software that stores knowledge and makes inferences, enabling a novice to perform at the level of an expert.

explanation facility Component of an expert system that allows a user or decision maker to understand how the expert system arrived at certain conclusions or results.

explicit knowledge Knowledge that is documented, stored, and codified—such as standard procedures, product formulas, customer contact lists, market research results, and patents.

exploit An attack on an information system that takes advantage of a particular system vulnerability.

Extensible Markup Language (XML) The markup language designed to transport and store data on the Web.

extract-transform-load (ETL) The process by which raw data is extracted from various sources, transformed into a format to support the analysis to be performed, and loaded into the data warehouse.

extranet A network based on Web technologies that allows selected outsiders, such as business partners and customers, to access authorized resources of a company's intranet.

extreme programming (XP) A form of agile software development that promotes incremental development of a system using short development cycles to improve productivity and to accommodate new customer requirements.

F

feasibility analysis An assessment of the technical, economic, legal, operational, and schedule feasibility of a project.

field Typically a name, a number, or a combination of characters that describes an aspect of a business object or activity.

file A collection of related records.

firewall A system of software, hardware, or a combination of both that stands guard between an organization's internal network and the Internet and limits network access based on the organization's access policy.

fixed-price contract A contract in which the buyer and provider agree to a total fixed price for a well-defined product or service.

filtering software Software used to help protect personal data and screen objectionable Internet content.

force field analysis An approach to identifying both the driving (positive) and restraining (negative) forces that influence whether change can occur.

forming-storming-norming-performing-adjourning model A model that describes how teams develop and evolve.

Fourth Amendment This amendment to the U.S. constitution protects individuals against unreasonable searches and seizures and requires that warrants be issued only upon probable cause and specifying the place to be searched and the persons or things to be seized.

functional decomposition A frequently used technique to define the scope of an information system by identifying the business processes it will affect.

G

game theory A mathematical theory for developing strategies that maximize gains and minimize losses while adhering to a given set of rules and constraints.

Gantt chart A graphical tool used for planning, monitoring, and coordinating projects; it is essentially a grid that lists activities and deadlines.

genetic algorithm An approach to solving problems based on the theory of evolution; uses the concept of survival of the fittest as a problem-solving strategy.

gigahertz (GHz) A unit of frequency that is equal to one billion cycles per second; a measure of clock speed.

goal A specific result that must be achieved to reach an objective.

goals-based strategic planning A multi-phase strategic planning process that begins by performing a situation analysis to identify an organization's strengths, weaknesses, opportunities, and threats.

graphical user interface (GUI) An interface that displays pictures (icons) and menus that people use to send commands to the computer system.

graphics processing unit (GPU) A powerful processing chip that renders images on the screen display.

green computing A program concerned with the efficient and environmentally responsible design, manufacture, operation, and disposal of IS-related products.

grid computing The use of a collection of computers, often owned by multiple individuals or organizations, that work in a coordinated manner to solve a common problem.

group IS An information system that improves communications and support collaboration among members of a workgroup.

H

Hadoop An open-source software framework including several software modules that provide a means for storing and processing extremely large data sets.

Hadoop Distributed File System (HDFS) A system used for data storage that divides the data into subsets and distributes the subsets onto different servers for processing.

hard disk drive (HDD) A direct access storage device used to store and retrieve data from rapidly rotating disks coated with magnetic material.

hardware independence The ability of a software program to run on any platform,

without concern for the specific underlying hardware.

hot site A duplicate, operational hardware system that is ready for use (or immediate access to one through a specialized vendor).

hierarchy of data Bits, characters, fields, records, files, and databases.

human resource management Activities designed to make the most effective use of the people involved with a project.

hybrid cloud A cloud computing environment is composed of both private and public clouds integrated through networking.

hyperlink Highlighted text or graphics in a Web document that, when clicked, opens a new Web page containing related content.

Hypertext Markup Language (HTML) The standard page description language for Web pages.

I

identity theft The theft of personal information, which is then used without the owner's permission, often to commit fraud or other crimes.

IF-THEN statement A rule that suggests certain conclusions

inference engine Part of the expert system that seeks information and relationships from the knowledge base and provides answers, predictions, and suggestions similar to the way a human expert would.

informatics The combination of information technology with traditional disciplines, such as medicine or science, while considering the impact on individuals, organizations, and society.

information A collection of data organized and processed so that it has additional value beyond the value of the individual facts.

information silo An isolated information system not easily capable of exchanging information with other information systems.

information system (IS) A set of interrelated components that collect, process, store, and disseminate data and information; an information system provides a feedback mechanism to monitor and control its operation to make sure it continues to meet its goals and objectives.

infrastructure as a service (IaaS) An information systems strategy in which an organization outsources the equipment used to support its data processing operations, including servers, storage devices, and networking components.

in-memory database (IMDB) A database management system that stores the entire database in random access memory (RAM).

innovation The application of new ideas to the products, processes, and activities of a firm, leading to increased value.

input/output device A computer component that provides data and instructions to the computer and receives results from it.

installation The process of physically placing the computer equipment on the site and making it operational.

instant messaging The online, real-time communication between two or more people who are connected via the Internet.

instruction set architecture (ISA) A basic set of commands (opcodes) that the processor can execute.

intangible benefit A benefit that cannot directly be measured and cannot easily be quantified in monetary terms.

integrated circuit (IC) A set of electronic circuits on one small piece of semiconductor material, normally silicon.

integration testing Testing that involves linking all of the individual components together and testing them as a group to uncover any defects in the interfaces between individual components.

intelligent agent Programs and a knowledge base used to perform a specific task for a person, a process, or another program; also called an intelligent robot or bot.

intelligent behavior The ability to learn from experiences and apply knowledge acquired from those experiences; to handle complex situations; to solve problems when important information is missing; to determine what is important and to react quickly and correctly to a new situation; to understand visual images, process and manipulate symbols, and be creative and imaginative; and to use heuristics.

Internet backbone One of the Internet's high-speed, long-distance communications links.

Internet censorship The control or suppression of the publishing or accessing of information on the Internet.

Internet of Everything A network that encompasses not only machine-to-machine but also people-to-people and people-to-machine connections.

Internet of Things (IoT) A network of physical objects or "things" embedded with sensors, processors, software, and network connectivity capability to enable them to exchange data with the manufacturer of the device, device operators, and other connected devices.

Internet Protocol (IP) A communication standard that enables computers to route communications traffic from one network to another as needed.

Internet service provider (ISP) Any organization that provides Internet access to people.

Internet The world's largest computer network, consisting of thousands of interconnected networks, all freely exchanging information.

intranet A network that enables communication, collaboration, search functions, and information sharing between the members of an organization's team using a Web browser.

intrusion detection system (IDS) Software and/or hardware that monitors system and network resources and activities and notifies network security personnel when it detects network traffic that attempts to circumvent the security measures of a networked computer environment.

IP address A 64-bit number that identifies a computer on the Internet.

issues-based strategic planning A strategic planning process that begins by identifying and analyzing key issues that face the organization, setting strategies to address those issues, and identifying projects and initiatives that are consistent with those strategies.

J

joining Manipulating data to combine two or more tables.

joint application development (JAD) A structured meeting process that can accelerate and improve the efficiency and effectiveness of the investigation, analysis, and design phases of a system development project.

joint problem solving A process used to capture tacit knowledge where the novice and the expert work side by side to solve a problem so that the expert's approach is slowly revealed to the observant novice.

K

kernel The heart of the operating system that controls the most critical processes of the OS.

key performance indicator (KPI) A metric that tracks progress in executing chosen strategies to attain organizational objectives and goals and consists of a direction, measure, target, and time frame.

knowledge The awareness and understanding of a set of information and the ways that information can be made useful to support a specific task or reach a decision.

knowledge acquisition facility Part of the expert system that provides a convenient and efficient means of capturing and storing all the components of the knowledge base.

knowledge engineer A person who has training or experience in the design, development, implementation, and maintenance of an expert system.

knowledge management (KM) A range of practices concerned with increasing awareness, fostering learning, speeding

collaboration and innovation, and exchanging insights.

knowledge management system (KMS) An organized collection of people, procedures, software, databases, and devices that stores and retrieves knowledge, improves collaboration, locates knowledge sources, captures and uses knowledge, or in some other way enhances the knowledge management process.

knowledge user The person or group who uses and benefits from the expert system.

L

laptop A personal computer designed for use by mobile users, being small and light enough to sit comfortably on a user's lap.

law A system of rules that tells us what we can and cannot do.

legal feasibility The process of determining whether laws or regulations may prevent or limit a system development project.

learning system A combination of software and hardware that allows a computer to change how it functions or how it reacts to situations based on feedback it receives.

Leavitt's diamond An organizational change model that proposes that every organizational system is made up of four main components—people, tasks, structure, and technology—that all interact; any change in one of these elements will necessitate a change in the other three elements.

Lewin's change model A three stage approach for implementing change that involves unfreezing, moving, and refreezing.

linear regression A mathematical procedure to predict the value of a dependent variable based on a single independent variable and the linear relationship between the two.

linking The ability to combine two or more tables through common data attributes to form a new table with only the unique data attributes.

local area network (LAN) A network that connects computer systems and devices within a small area, such as an office, home, or several floors in a building.

logic bomb A form of Trojan horse malware that executes when it is triggered by a specific event.

Long Term Evolution (LTE) A standard for wireless communications for mobile phones based on packet switching.

M

magnetic stripe card A type of card that stores a limited amount of data by modifying the magnetism of tiny iron-based particles contained in a band on the card.

magnetic tape A type of sequential secondary storage medium, now used primarily

for storing backups of critical organizational data in the event of a disaster.

main memory The component of a computer that provides the CPU with a working storage area for program instructions and data.

mainframe computer A large, powerful computer often shared by hundreds of concurrent users connected to the machine over a network.

make-or-buy decision The act of comparing the pros and cons of in-house production versus outsourcing of a given product or service.

managed security service provider (MSSP) A company that monitors, manages, and maintains computer and network security for other organizations.

management information system An organized collection of people, procedures, software, databases, and devices that provides routine information to managers and decision makers.

MapReduce program A composite program that consists of a Map procedure that performs filtering and sorting and a Reduce method that performs a summary operation.

market segmentation The identification of specific markets to target them with tailored advertising messages.

massively parallel processing system A system that speeds processing by linking hundreds or thousands of processors to operate at the same time, or in parallel, with each processor having its own bus, memory, disks, copy of the operating system, and applications.

memory A component of the computer that provides the processor with a working storage area to hold program instructions and data.

mesh network A network that uses multiple access points to link a series of devices that communicate with each other to form a network connection across a large area.

meta tag An HTML code, not visible on the displayed Web page, that contains keywords representing your site's content, which search engines use to build indexes pointing to your Web site.

metadata Data that describes other data.

metropolitan area network (MAN) A network that connects users and their computers in a geographical area that spans a campus or city.

Michael Porter's Five Forces Model A model that identifies the fundamental factors that determine the level of competition and long-term profitability of an industry.

middleware Software that allows various systems to communicate and exchange data.

mission statement A statement that concisely defines an organization's fundamental purpose for existing.

mission-critical process A process that plays a pivotal role in an organization's continued operations and goal attainment.

mobile commerce (m-commerce) The buying and selling of goods and/or services using a mobile device, such as a tablet, smartphone, or other portable device.

mobile device management (MDM) software Software that manages and troubleshoots mobile devices remotely, pushing out applications, data, patches, and settings while enforcing group policies for security.

monitoring The process of measuring system performance by tracking the number of errors encountered, the amount of memory required, the amount of processing or CPU time needed, and other performance indicators.

morals One's personal beliefs about right and wrong.

MP3 A standard format for compressing a sound sequence into a small file.

multicore processor A microprocessor that has two or more independent processing units, called cores, which are capable of sequencing and executing instructions.

multimedia Content that uses more than one form of communication—such as text, graphics, video, animation, audio, and other media.

multiprocessing The simultaneous execution of two or more instructions at the same time.

N

natural language processing An aspect of artificial intelligence that involves technology that allows computers to understand, analyze, manipulate, and/or generate "natural" languages, such as English.

near field communication (NFC) A very short-range wireless connectivity technology that enables two devices placed within a few inches of each other to exchange data.

net neutrality The principle that Internet service providers (ISPs) should be required to treat all Internet traffic running over their wired and wireless broadband networks the same—without favoring content from some sources and/or blocking or slowing (also known as throttling) content from others.

nettop A very small, inexpensive desktop computer typically used for Internet access, email, accessing Web-based applications, document processing, and audio/video playback.

network A group or system of connected computers and equipment—in a room, building, campus, city, across the country, or around the world—that enables electronic communication.

network operating system (NOS) Systems software that controls the computer systems and devices on a network and allows them to communicate with each other.

network topology The shape or structure of a network, including the arrangement of the communication links and hardware devices on the network.

network-attached storage (NAS) A hard disk drive storage device that is set up with its own network address and provides file-based storage services to other devices on the network.

network-management software Software that enables a manager on a networked desktop to monitor the use of individual computers and shared hardware (such as printers), scan for viruses, and ensure compliance with software licenses.

neural network A computer system that can recognize and act on patterns or trends that it detects in large sets of data.

next-generation firewall (NGFW) A hardware- or software-based network security system that is able to detect and block sophisticated attacks by filtering network traffic dependent on the packet contents.

NoSQL database A way to store and retrieve data that is modeled using some means other than the simple two dimensional tabular relations used in relational databases.

O

objective A statement of a compelling business need that an organization must meet to achieve its vision and mission.

offshore outsourcing (offshoring) An outsourcing arrangement where the organization providing the service is located in a country different from the firm obtaining the services.

off-the-shelf software Software produced by software vendors to address needs that are common across businesses, organizations, or individuals.

online analytical processing (OLAP) A method to analyze multidimensional data from many different perspectives, enabling users to identify issues and opportunities as well as perform trend analysis.

online transaction processing (OLTP) A form of data processing where each transaction is processed immediately without the delay of accumulating transactions into a batch.

open source software Software that is distributed for free, with access permitted to the source code so that it can be studied, changed, and improved by software professionals at the various user organizations—with no maintenance charges.

operating system (OS) A set of computer programs that controls the computer hardware and acts as an interface to application software.

operational feasibility The process of determining how a system will be accepted by people and how well it will meet various system performance expectations.

optical storage device A form of data storage that uses lasers to read and write data.

organic strategic planning A strategic planning process that defines the organization's vision and values and then identifies projects and initiatives to achieve the vision while adhering to the values.

organization A group of people that is structured and managed to meet its mission or set of group goals.

organizational change How forprofit and nonprofit organizations plan for, implement, and handle change.

organizational complement A key component that must be in place to ensure successful implementation and use of an information system.

organizational culture The major understandings and assumptions for a business, corporation, or other organization.

organizational learning The adaptations and adjustments made within an organization based on experience and ideas over time.

organizational network analysis (ONA) A technique used for documenting and measuring flows of information among individuals, workgroups, organizations, computers, Web sites, and other information sources.

outsourcing A long-term business arrangement in which a company contracts for services with an outside organization that has expertise in providing a specific function.

P

parallel computing The simultaneous execution of the same task on multiple processors to obtain results faster.

parallel start-up A cutover strategy that involves running both the old and new systems for a period of time and closely comparing the output of the new system with the output of the old system; any differences are reconciled. When users are comfortable that the new system is working correctly, the old system is eliminated.

Pareto principle (80–20 rule) An observation that for many events, roughly 80 percent of the effects come from 20 percent of the causes.

patch A minor system change to correct a problem or make a small enhancement; it is usually an addition to an existing program.

p-card (procurement card or purchasing card) A credit card used to streamline the traditional purchase order and invoice payment processes.

perceptive system A system that approximates the way a person sees, hears, and feels objects.

performance evaluation test A comparison of vendor options conducted in a computing environment (e.g., computing hardware, operating system software, database management system) and with a workload (e.g., number of concurrent users, database size, and number of transactions) that matches its intended operating conditions.

personal area network (PAN) A network that supports the interconnection of information technology devices close to one person.

personal IS An information system that improves the productivity of individual users in performing stand-alone tasks.

personal productivity software Software that enables users to improve their personal effectiveness, increasing the amount of work and quality of work they can do.

personal sphere of influence The sphere of influence that serves the needs of an individual user.

personalization The process of tailoring Web pages to specifically target individual consumers.

pilot start-up A cutover strategy that involves running the complete new system for one group of users rather than for all users.

phase-in approach A cutover strategy that involves slowly replacing components of the old system with those of the new one; this process is repeated for each application until the new system is running every application and performing as expected; also called a piecemeal approach.

phishing The act of fraudulently using email to try to get the recipient to reveal personal data.

platform as a service (PaaS) An approach that provides users with a computing platform, typically including operating system, programming language execution environment, database services, and Web server.

podcast An audio broadcast you can listen to over the Internet.

point-of-sale (POS) device A device used to enter data into a computer system.

policy-based storage management The automation of storage using previously defined policies.

portable computer A computer small enough to carry easily.

predecessor task A task that must be completed before a later task can begin.

primary key A field or set of fields that uniquely identifies the record.

private cloud environment A single tenant cloud.

procedure A set of steps that need to be followed to achieve a specific end result, such as enter a customer order, pay a supplier invoice, or request a current inventory report.

process A set of logically related tasks performed to achieve a defined outcome.

process manufacturing The production of products—such as soda, laundry detergent, gasoline, and pharmaceutical drugs—that are the result of a chemical process; these products cannot be easily decomposed into their basic components.

processor family A set of processors from the same manufacturer that have similar features and capabilities.

procurement management A set of activities related to the acquisition of goods and/or services for the project from sources outside the performing organization.

product lifecycle management (PLM) An enterprise business strategy that creates a common repository of product information and processes to support the collaborative creation, management, dissemination, and use of product and packaging definition information.

product lifecycle management (PLM) software Software that provides a means for managing the data and processes associated with the various phases of the product life cycle, including sales and marketing, research and development, concept development, product design, prototyping and testing, process design, production and assembly, delivery and product installation, service and support, and product retirement and replacement.

product owner A person who represents the project stakeholders and is responsible for communicating and aligning project priorities between the stakeholders and development team.

Program Evaluation and Review Technique (PERT) A formal method for estimating the duration of a project using three time estimates for an activity: shortest possible time, most likely time, and longest possible time; working with those estimates, a formula is used to determine a single PERT time estimate.

programming languages Sets of keywords, commands, symbols, and rules for constructing statements by which humans can communicate instructions to a computer.

project A temporary endeavor undertaken to create a unique product, service, or result.

project champion A well respected manager with a passion to see a project succeed and who removes barriers to the success of the project.

project deadline The date the entire project should be completed and operational—when the organization can expect to begin to reap the benefits of the project.

project integration management The coordination of all appropriate people, resources, plans, and efforts to complete a project successfully.

project management The application of knowledge, skills, and techniques to project activities to meet project requirements.

project milestone A critical date for completing a major part of the project, such as program design, coding, testing, and release (for a programming project).

project risk An uncertain event or condition that, if it occurs, has a positive or a negative effect on a project objective.

project schedule A plan that identifies the project activities that must be completed, the expected start and end dates, and what resources are assigned to each task.

project scope A definition of which tasks are included and which tasks are not included in a project.

project sponsor A senior manager from the business unit most affected by a project and who ensures the project will indeed meet the needs of his or her organization.

project stakeholders The people involved in the project or those affected by its outcome.

project steering team A group of senior managers representing the business and IS organizations that provide guidance and support to a project.

projecting Manipulating data to eliminate columns in a table.

proprietary software One-of-a-kind software designed for a specific application and owned by the company, organization, or person that uses it.

public cloud computing A means of providing computing services wherein a service provider organization owns and manages the hardware, software, networking, and storage devices, with cloud user organizations (called tenants) accessing slices of shared resources via the Internet.

Q

quality The degree to which a project meets the needs of its users.

quality assurance The evaluation of the progress of the project on an ongoing basis to ensure that it meets the identified quality standards.

quality control The checking of project results to ensure that they meet identified quality standards.

quality management A set of activities designed to ensure that a project will meet the needs for which it was undertaken.

quality planning The determination of which quality standards are relevant to the project and determining how they will be met.

R

radio frequency identification (RFID) A technology that employs a microchip with an antenna to broadcast its unique identifier and location to receivers.

random access memory (RAM) A form of memory in which instructions or data can be temporarily stored.

ransomware Malware that stops you from using your computer or accessing your data until you meet certain demands such as paying a ransom or sending photos to the attacker.

read-only memory (ROM) A nonvolatile form of memory.

reasonable assurance The IS security concept that recognizes that managers must use their judgment to ensure that the cost of control does not exceed the system's benefits or the risks involved.

record A collection of data fields all related to one object, activity, or individual.

redundant array of independent/inexpensive disks (RAID) A method of storing data that generates extra bits of data from existing data, allowing the system to create a "reconstruction map" so that if a hard drive fails, the system can rebuild lost data.

reengineering (process redesign/business process reengineering, BPR) The radical redesign of business processes, organizational structures, information systems, and values of the organization to achieve a breakthrough in business results.

relational database model A simple but highly useful way to organize data into collections of two-dimensional tables called relations.

release A significant program change that often requires changes in the documentation of the software.

request for information (RFI) A document that outlines an organization's hardware or software needs and requests vendors to provide information about if and how they can meet those needs and the time and resources required.

restraining forces Forces that make it difficult to accept a change or to work to implement a change.

rich Internet application (RIA) A Web-delivered application combines hardware resources of the Web server and the PC to deliver valuable software services through a Web browser interface.

risk assessment The process of assessing security-related risks to an organization's computers and networks from both internal and external threats.

risk management A deliberate and systematic process designed to identify, analyze, and manage project risks.

risk owner The individual responsible for developing a risk management strategy and monitoring the project to determine if the risk is about to occur or has occurred.

robotics A branch of engineering that involves the development and manufacture of mechanical or computer devices that can perform tasks requiring a high degree of precision or that are tedious or hazardous for humans.

rootkit A set of programs that enables its user to gain administrator level access to a computer without the end user's consent or knowledge.

rule A conditional statement that links conditions to actions or outcomes.

S

scalability The ability to increase the processing capability of a computer system so that it can handle more users, more data, or more transactions in a given period.

schedule feasibility The process of determining whether the project can be completed within a desired time frame.

schema A description that defines the logical and physical structure of the database by identifying the tables, the fields in each table, and the relationships between fields and tables.

scope management A set of activities that include defining the work that must be done as part of a project and then controlling the work to stay within the agreed-upon scope.

scrum An agile development framework that emphasizes a team based approach in order to keep the development effort focused and moving quickly.

scrum master The person who coordinates all the scrum activities of a team.

search engine A valuable tool that enables you to find information on the Web by specifying words that are key to a topic of interest, known as keywords.

search engine optimization (SEO) A process for driving traffic to a Web site by using techniques that improve the site's ranking in search results.

secondary storage A device that stores large amounts of data, instructions, and information more permanently than allowed with main memory.

security audit A careful and thorough analysis that evaluates whether an organization has a well-considered security policy in place and if it is being followed.

security policy A statement that defines an organization's security requirements, as well as the controls and sanctions needed to meet those requirements.

selecting Manipulating data to eliminate rows according to certain criteria.

self-service analytics Training, techniques, and processes that empower end users to work independently to access data from approved sources to perform their own analyses using an endorsed set of tools.

semiconductor fabrication plant A factory where integrated circuits are manufactured; also called a fab or a foundry.

server A computer employed by many users to perform a specific task, such as running network or Internet applications.

server farm A facility that houses a large number of servers in the same room, where access to the machines can be controlled and authorized support personnel can more easily manage and maintain the servers.

service-oriented architecture (SOA) A software design approach based on the use of discrete pieces of software (modules) to provide specific functions as services to other applications.

shadow IT The information systems and solutions built and deployed by departments other than the information systems department. In many cases, the information systems department may not even be aware of these efforts.

shadowing A process used to capture tacit knowledge that involves a novice observing an expert executing her job to learn how she performs.

single-user license A software license that permits you to install the software on one or more computers, used by one person.

site preparation Preparation of the location of a new system.

slack time The amount of time an activity can be delayed without delaying the entire project.

slipstream upgrade A minor system upgrade-typically a code adjustment or minor bug fix; it usually requires recompiling all the code, and in so doing, it can create entirely new bugs.

smart card A credit card embedded with a computer chip that contains key consumer and account data; smart card users must either enter their PIN (chip-and-PIN) or sign (chip-and-sign) for each transaction to be approved.

smishing Another variation of phishing that involves the use of Short Message Service (SMS) texting.

soft side of implementing change The work designed to help employees embrace a new information system and way of working.

software The computer programs that govern the operation of a particular computing device, be it desktop, laptop, tablet, smartphone, or some other device.

Software as a Service (SaaS) A service that allows businesses to subscribe to Web-delivered application software.

software suite A collection of programs packaged together and sold in a bundle.

software-defined networking (SDN) An emerging approach to networking that allows network administrators to have programmable central control of the network via a controller without requiring physical access to all the network devices.

solid state storage device (SSD) A storage device that stores data in memory chips rather than on hard disk drives or optical media.

source data automation Capturing data at its source and recording it accurately in a timely fashion, with minimal manual effort and in an electronic or digital form so that it can be directly entered into the computer thus ensuring accuracy and timeliness.

spam The use of email systems to send unsolicited email to large numbers of people.

spear-phishing A variation of phishing in which the phisher sends fraudulent emails to a certain organization's employees.

speech-recognition technology Input devices that recognize human speech.

sphere of influence The scope of the problems and opportunities that the software addresses.

sponsoring business unit The business unit most affected by the project and the one whose budget will cover the project costs.

SQL A special-purpose programming language for accessing and manipulating data stored in a relational database.

star network A network in which all network devices connect to one another through a single central device called the hub node.

storage area network (SAN) A high-speed, special-purpose network that integrates different types of data storage devices (e.g., hard disk drives, magnetic tape, solid state secondary storage devices) into a single storage system and connects that to computing resources across an entire organization.

storage as a service A data storage model where a data storage service provider rents space to individuals and organizations.

storefront broker A company that acts as an intermediary between your Web site and online merchants who have the products and retail expertise.

strategic planning A process that helps managers identify desired outcomes and formulate feasible plans to achieve their objectives by using available resources and capabilities.

strategy A plan that describes how an organization will achieve its vision, mission, objectives, and goals.

Strengths, Weaknesses, Opportunities, Threats (SWOT) matrix A simple way to illustrate what a company is doing well, where it can improve, what opportunities are available, and what environmental factors threaten the future of the organization.

subject matter expert Someone who provides knowledge and expertise in a particular aspect important to the project.

supercomputers The most powerful computer systems with the fastest processing speeds.

supply chain A key value chain whose primary activities include inbound logistics, operations, outbound logistics, marketing and sales, and service.

supply chain management (SCM) A system that includes planning, executing, and controlling all activities involved in raw material sourcing and procurement, the conversion of raw materials to finished products, and the warehousing and delivery of finished products to customers.

syntax A set of rules associated with a programming language.

system acquisition The process used to obtain the information system resources needed to provide the services necessary to meet a specific set of needs.

system analysis The phase of system development that focuses on gathering data on the existing system, determining the requirements for the new system, considering alternatives within identified constraints, and investigating the feasibility of alternative solutions.

system construction The phase of system development that converts the system design into an operational system by acquiring and installing hardware and software, coding and testing software programs, creating and loading data into databases, and performing initial program testing.

system design The stage of system development that answers the question, "How will the information system solve a problem?"

system development The activity of building information systems to meet users' needs.

system disposal A stage of system development that involves those activities that ensure the orderly dissolution of the system, including disposing of all equipment in an environmentally friendly manner, closing out contracts, and safely migrating information from the system to another system or archiving it in accordance with applicable records management policies.

system investigation The initial phase in the development of a new or modified business information system whose purpose is to gain a clear understanding of the specifics of the problem to solve or the opportunity to address.

system investigation report A summary of the results of the system investigation, with a recommendation of a course of action.

system maintenance A stage of system development that involves changing and enhancing the system to make it more useful in achieving user and organizational goals.

system operation Involves the use of a new or modified system under all kinds of operating conditions.

system review The process of analyzing a system to make sure it is operating as intended.

system software Software that includes operating systems, utilities, and middleware that coordinate the activities and functions of the hardware and other programs throughout the computer system.

system testing Testing the complete, integrated system (hardware, software, databases, people, and procedures) to validate that the information system meets all specified requirements.

T

tablet A portable, lightweight computer with no keyboard that allows you to roam the office, home, or factory floor carrying the device like a clipboard.

tacit knowledge The know-how that someone has developed as a result of personal experience; it involves intangible factors such as beliefs, perspective, and a value system.

tag A code that tells the Web browser how to format text—as a heading, as a list, or as body text—and whether images, sound, and other elements should be inserted.

tangible benefit A benefit that can be measured directly and assigned a monetary value.

technical documentation Written details used by computer operators to execute the program and by analysts and programmers to solve problems or modify the program.

technical feasibility The process of determining whether a project is feasible within the current limits of available technology.

technical resource A subject matter expert in an IS topic of value to the project.

technology acceptance model (TAM) A model that specifies the factors that can lead to better attitudes about an information system, along with higher acceptance and usage of it.

technology infrastructure All the hardware, software, databases, networks, people, and procedures that are configured to collect, manipulate, store, and process data into information.

thin client A low-cost, centrally managed computer with no internal or external attached drives for data storage.

time and material contract A contract that requires the buyer to pay the provider for both the time and materials required to complete the contract.

time management A set of activities that includes defining an achievable completion date that is acceptable to the project stakeholders, developing a workable project schedule, and ensuring the timely completion of the project.

transaction Any business-related exchange such as a payment to an employee, a sale to a customer, or a payment to a supplier.

transaction processing cycle The process of data collection, data editing, data correction, data processing, data storage, and document production.

transaction processing system (TPS) An organized collection of people, procedures, software, databases, and devices used to process and record business transactions.

Transport Layer Security (TLS) A communications protocol or system of rules that ensures privacy between communicating applications and their users on the Internet.

Trojan horse A seemingly harmless program in which malicious code is hidden.

U

Uniform Resource Locator (URL) A Web address that specifies the exact location of a Web page using letters and words that map to an IP address and a location on the host.

unit testing Testing of individual components of code (subroutines, modules, and programs) to verify that each unit performs as designed.

U.S. Computer Emergency Readiness Team (US-CERT) A partnership between the Department of Homeland Security and the public and private sectors; established to provide timely handling of security incidents as well as conducting improved analysis of such incidents.

user acceptance document A formal agreement that the organization signs stating that a phase of the installation or the complete system is approved.

user acceptance testing (UAT) Testing performed by trained system users to verify that the system can complete required tasks in a real-world operating environment and perform according to the system design specifications.

user documentation Written descriptions developed for people who use a program; in easy-to-understand language, it shows how the program can and should be used to meet the needs of its various users.

user interface The element of the operating system that allows people to access and interact with the computer system.

user preparation The process of readying managers, decision makers, employees, other users, and stakeholders to accept and use the new system.

utility program A program that helps to perform maintenance or correct problems with a computer system.

V

value chain A series (chain) of activities that an organization performs to transform inputs into outputs in such a way that the value of the input is increased.

version A major program change, typically encompassing many new features.

virtual private network (VPN) A secure connection between two points on the Internet; VPNs transfer information by encapsulating traffic in IP packets and sending the packets over the Internet.

virtual reality system A system that enables one or more users to move and react in a computer-simulated environment.

virtual server A method of logically dividing the resources of a single physical server to create multiple logical servers, each acting as its own dedicated machine.

virtual tape A storage device for less frequently needed data. With virtual tape systems, data appears to be stored entirely on tape cartridges, although some parts of it might actually be located on faster hard disks.

virtual team A group of individuals whose members are distributed geographically, but who collaborate and complete work through the use of information systems.

virus A piece of programming code, usually disguised as something else, that causes a computer to behave in an unexpected and usually undesirable manner.

virus signature A sequence of bytes that indicates the presence of a specific virus.

vishing Similar to smishing except that the victims receive a voice mail message telling them to call a phone number or access a Web site.

vision A concise statement of what an organization intends to achieve in the future.

vision system The hardware and software that permit computers to capture, store, and manipulate visual images.

vision/mission statement A statement that communicates an organization's overarching aspirations to guide it through changing objectives, goals, and strategies.

volume testing Testing to evaluate the performance of the information system under varying yet realistic work volume and operating conditions to determine the work load at which systems performance begins to degrade and to identify and eliminate any issues that prevent the system from reaching its required service-level performance.

W

waterfall systems development process A sequential, multistage systems development process in which work on the next stage cannot begin until the results of the current stage are reviewed and approved or modified as necessary.

wearable computer An electronic device capable of storing and processing data that is incorporated into a person's clothing or personal accessories.

Web 2.0 The Web as a computing platform that supports software applications and the sharing of information among users.

Web browser Web client software—such as Chrome, Edge, Firefox, Internet Explorer, and Safari—used to view Web pages.

Web log (blog) A Web site that people and businesses use to share their observations, experiences, and opinions on a wide range of topics.

wide area network (WAN) A network that connects large geographic regions.

Wi-Fi A medium-range wireless communications technology brand owned by the Wi-Fi Alliance.

wireless communication The transfer of information between two or more points that are not connected by an electrical conductor.

word cloud A visual depiction of a set of words that have been grouped together because of the frequency of their occurrence.

work breakdown structure (WBS) An outline of the work to be done to complete the project.

workgroup Two or more people who work together to achieve a common goal.

workgroup application software Software that supports teamwork, whether team members are in the same location or dispersed around the world.

workgroup sphere of influence The sphere of influence that helps workgroup members attain their common goals.

workstation A more powerful personal computer used for mathematical computing, computer-assisted design, and other high-end processing but still small enough to fit on a desktop.

World Wide Web (WWW) A network of links on the Internet to files containing text, graphics, video, and sound.

worm A harmful program that resides in the active memory of the computer and duplicates itself.

zero-day attack An attack that takes place before the security community and/or software developers become aware of and fix a security vulnerability.

Z

zombie A computer that has been taken over by a hacker to be used as part of a botnet.

Subject Index

Note: A boldface page number indicates a key term and the location of its definition in the text.

Company Index